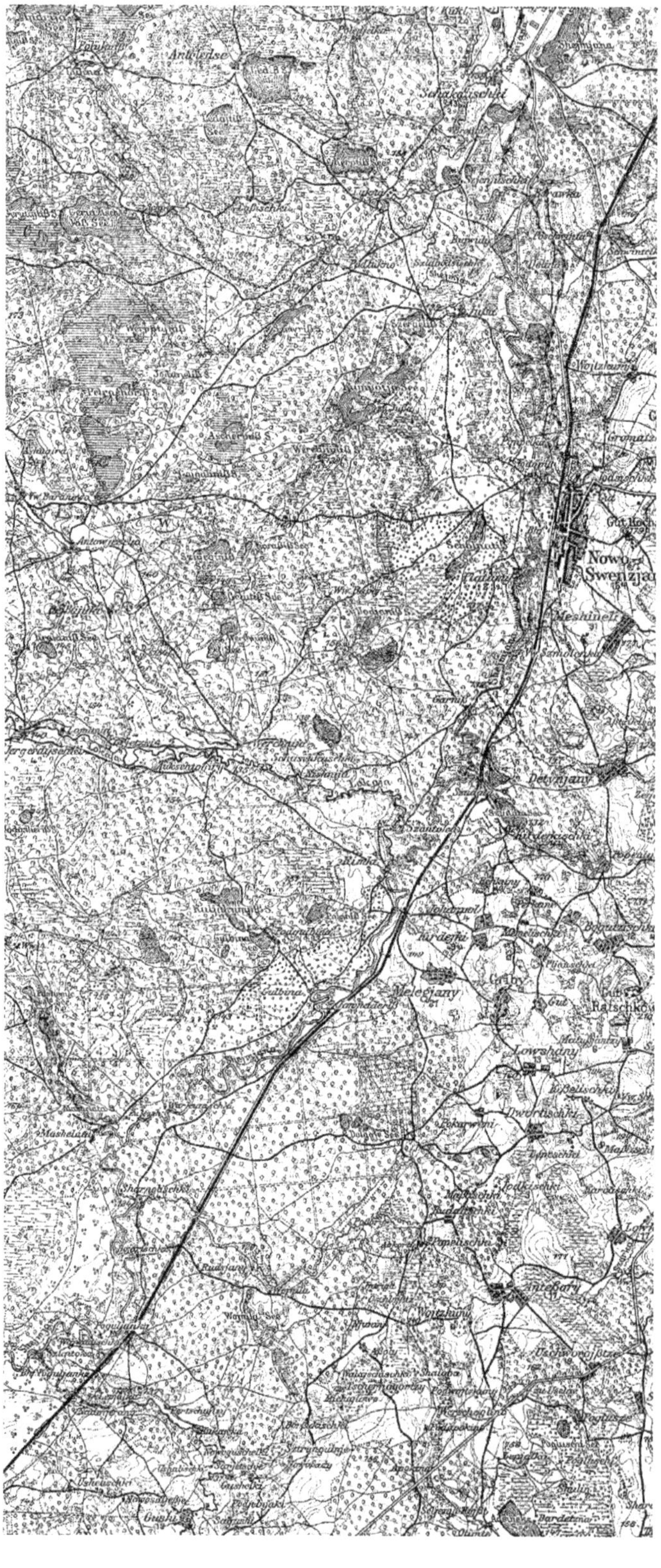

1917 Map of Sventzian Region, from *Karte des westlichen Russlands.*
Public domain. Source: Topographic Maps of Eastern Europe, easteurope-topo.org, held by Geography and Map Division, Library of Congress.

Poschemen
Nowo Swenzjany
SWENZJANY
Gut Zirkischki
Sztrunojtzy
Lyntupy
Retschany
Szwentzjanka
Gut Andrenjewo
Gut Schwinto
Mesharu
Sybalischki
Borowa
Szredniaki
Kuklinzy
Schenka

Memorial Book of the Sventzian Region (Švenčionys, Lithuania)

Part II - Shoah

Translation of
Sefer zikaron le-esrim ve-shalosh kehilot she-nehrevu be-ezor Svintsian

Memorial Book of Twenty-Three Destroyed Communities in the Sventzian Region

Original Yizkor Book Edited by: Shimon Kantz
Published by the Former Residents of Sventzian in Israel
Published in Tel Aviv, 1965

Published by JewishGen

An Affiliate of the Museum of Jewish Heritage—A Living Memorial to the Holocaust
New York

Memorial Book of the Sventzian Region – Part II - Shoah
(Švenčionys, Lithuania)
Translation of: *Sefer zikaron le-esrim ve-shalosh kehilot she-nehrevu be-ezor Svintsian*
Memorial Book of Twenty - Three Destroyed Jewish Communities in the Svintzian Region

First Printing: July 2020, Tamuz 5780

Editor of the original Yizkor Book: Shimon Kantz
Translation Project Coordinator: Anita Frishman Gabbay
Translators: Anita Frishman Gabbay Jerrold Landau, Janie Respitz, Meir Razy
Layout: Donni Magid
Cover Design: Nina Schwartz, Impulse Graphics
Name Indexing: Jonathan Wind

Published by JewishGen, Inc.
An Affiliate of the Museum of Jewish Heritage
A Living Memorial to the Holocaust
36 Battery Place, New York, NY 10280

JewishGen, Inc. is not responsible for inaccuracies or omissions in the original work and makes no representations regarding the accuracy of this translation. Digital images of the original book's contents can be seen online at the New York Public Library website.

The mission of the JewishGen organization is to produce a translation of the original work, and we cannot verify the accuracy of statements or alter facts cited.

Printed in the United States of America by Lightning Source, Inc.

Library of Congress Control Number (LCCN): 2020940078
ISBN: 978-1-939561-92-3 (hard cover: 1076 pages, alk. paper)

Cover Credits:

Front Cover:

Ruins of Svencionys Synagogue, circa 1943. Courtesy of Vilna Gaon Museum of Jewish History, Vilnius, Lithuania, www.jmuseum.lt/en/

Birthday party for Chane Swirski, 1937. Photo by Yaakov Levin, courtesy of Debby Ozinsky Myers and Avner Holtzman. Only four of the 16 people in this photo survived to liberation in 1945.

Background: Synagogue, circa 1915. Postcard, public domain.

Back Cover:

Katz family visits matzevot (monuments) for their parents, Rivka Beila and Yehuda Isser Katz, 1934. Courtesy of Naomi Stone nee Ozinsky. In the center is Yitzhak Katz, flanked by (left to right) his wife Chana, sister Tzivia Gilinsky, sister-in-law Frida Katz, and sister Rachel Katzelnik. The bottoms of the tombstones say that they were endowed "by their children in America."

Yulian Geizericker, 1941. Courtesy of Karina Yasinova.

Cousins Frida Geizericker and Basia Borovik, unknown girl in center, 21 February 1946. Courtesy of Karina Yasinova.

JewishGen and the Yizkor Books in Print Project

This book has been published by the **Yizkor Books in Print Project**, as part of the **Yizkor Book Project** of JewishGen, Inc.

JewishGen, Inc. is a non-profit organization founded in 1987 as a resource for Jewish genealogy. Its website [www.jewishgen.org] serves as an international clearinghouse and resource center to assist individuals who are researching the history of their Jewish families and the places where they lived. JewishGen provides databases, facilitates discussion groups, and coordinates projects relating to Jewish genealogy and the history of the Jewish people. In 2003, JewishGen became an affiliate of the **Museum of Jewish Heritage—A Living Memorial to the Holocaust** in New York.

The **JewishGen Yizkor Book Project** was organized to make more widely known the existence of Yizkor (Memorial) Books written by survivors and former residents of various Jewish communities throughout the world. Later, volunteers connected to the different destroyed communities began cooperating to have these books translated from the original language—usually Hebrew or Yiddish—into English, thus enabling a wider audience to have access to the valuable information contained within them. As each chapter of these books was translated, it was posted on the JewishGen website and made available to the general public.

The **Yizkor Books in Print Project** began in 2011 as an initiative to print and publish Yizkor Books that had been fully translated, so that hard copies would be available for purchase by the descendants of these communities and also by scholars, universities, synagogues, libraries, and museums.

These Yizkor books have been produced almost entirely through the volunteer effort of researchers from around the world, assisted by donations from private individuals. The books are printed and sold at near cost, so as to make them as affordable as possible. Our goal is to make this important genre of Jewish literature and history available in English in book form, so that people can have the personal histories of their ancestral towns on their bookshelves for themselves and for their children and grandchildren.

A list of all published translated Yizkor Books in the project with prices and ordering information can be found at:
http://www.jewishgen.org/Yizkor/ybip.html

Binny Lewis, Yizkor Book Project Manager
Joel Alpert, Yizkor-Book-in-Print Project Coordinator

JewishGen
Yizkor Book Project

This book is presented by the
Yizkor-Books-In-Print Project
Project Coordinator: Joel Alpert

Part of the Yizkor Books Project of JewishGen. Inc.
Project Manager: Binny Lewis

These books have been produced solely through efforts of volunteers from around the world. The books are printed using the Print-on-Demand technology and sold at near cost, to make them as affordable as possible.

Our goal is to make this intimate history of the destroyed Jewish shtetls of Eastern Europe available in book form in English, so that people can experience the near-personal histories of their ancestral town on their bookshelves and those of their children and grandchildren.

All donations to the Yizkor Books Project, which translated the books, are sincerely appreciated.

Please send donations to:

Yizkor Book Project
JewishGen, Inc.
36 Battery Place
New York, NY, 10280

JewishGen, Inc. is an affiliate of the
Museum of Jewish Heritage
A Living Memorial to the Holocaust

Foreword for the Translation

In memory of my grandmother Raitza Gilinski Yavnovitch, my grandfather Shlomo Yavnovitch, my aunt Baila Yavnovitch Chodosh and her husband Yosef (father Leib), children Chaja and Yitzhak, David Yavnovitch and Bunia(Basia) Kudevitzki, children Leibel and Baruch, Sholem, Itsko, Michal and Matla(Chodesh), Josef and Rachel(Gantovnik), aunts, uncles, nieces, nephews, friends and neighbours and the entire region who perished in the Holocaust.

First, I undertook the translation of the Kobylnik Yiskor Book, which came after many years of geneological research for my roots; my family that perished in the Holocaust with the help, inspiration and dedication of the late Meir Swirsky, of Haifa, Israel.
It was a labour of love and also pain, my mother, Rasza(Rachel) who survived [see Kobylnik to Bergen Belsen] was not the person she had been prior to the war and therefore I needed to know how she lived and what kind of family she came from. We [second and third generation] will never know the meaning of "loss"! Those destroyed communities were our foundation- for a love of Israel and a love of Zion: compassion, learning, brotherhood and Tzedaka were instilled in their souls from birth...use these Yiskor Books with pride and know the people you came from!
These Yiskor Books were written when we children in the Diaspora could not read Yiddish or Hebrew; we will now benefit from the English translations. You will find some stories contradicted or repeated, but the people that wrote them were not trained authors, but read this book and others. Find out how your grandparents lived and how they died. Read about their town and especially about their destruction and the Holocaust. With anti-Semitism rearing its ugly head again, let us remember and never forget these Holy martyrs!

In Memory of all our families and friends from Kobylnik: Swirsky, Yavnovitch, Gilinski, Rubenstein, Hadash[Chodosh], Gantovnick, Kudevitski, Krivitski, Todres, Gordon, Narodski, Menkes, Shapiro, Horowitz and others

....and this is how I discovered Sventzian. My fascination with the Kobylnik Yiskor Book led me on an incredible journey, I became the project coordinator of the Svenzian, 23 communities Yiskor

Book. I discovered nearby shtetls, some in Lithuania, some in Belarus. I realized we were all connected.

This is a Book of Remembrance and a Memorial Candle for the lives that were lost; for the dear souls that were cut down, for whole families that perished, for babies that were slain, for infants who were torn to pieces, for traditions and values that were uprooted; for temples that were burnt-and for tiny communities that were erased from under God's heavens. The blood of our beloved ones cry out from the earth and demand remembrance forever. A book to immortalize the lives, actions and death of simple as well as outstanding people; of those that contributed to the aggrandizing of these shtetls' spirit and name among our people throughout the world; and of all those that perished in strange deaths, invented by the Satanic enemy; in the period of the most tragic Holocaust in the history of our people-which shakes every chord of heart and soul. As long as earth stands it will not cease telling the storied of these terrible deeds. We will revere the memory of these unfortunates as long as their descendants live.

Although our tragedy is too large to bear, and is inconsolable; although our eyes shed tears over our huge and cruel loss, these are but one drop in the general suffering and mourning of our nation. When we now immortalize our pure and beloved martyrs, we are but adding our tears to a sea of blood and tears; a sea of loss, sorrow, orphan hood and destruction, that cries from the depths-REVENGE! NEVER FORGET!

Anita Frishman Gabbay, June 2020

Notes to the Reader:

We apologize ahead of time for the poor quality of images in the book. Often these images had been scanned from the original Yizkor books which were of poor quality to begin with, being copies of old photographs. Each transfer results in loss of quality. We have done the best we could, given the original material and the resources and technology at hand. Even though images often appear of higher quality on computer screens, that does not transfer to high quality images in print. A reader can view the original scans on the web sites listed below.

Within the text the reader will note "{34}" standing ahead of a paragraph. This indicates that the material translated below was on page 34 of the original book. However, when a paragraph was split between two pages in the original book, the marker is placed in this book after the end of the paragraph for ease of reading.

Also please note that all references within the text of the book to page numbers, refer to the page numbers of the original Yizkor Book.

The original book can be seen online at the New York Public Library site:

https://digitalcollections.nypl.org/items/d500c660-6a13-0133-b734-00505686a51c

or at the Yiddish Book Center web site:

https://www.yiddishbookcenter.org/search/collection?search_api_views_fulltext=svintzian&Submit+search=&restrict=

In order to obtain a list of all Shoah victims from Svintzian, the reader should access the Yad Vashem web site listed below; one can also search for specific family names using family name option. These lists are continually updated by Yad Vashem, so it is worthwhile to periodically search these lists.

There is much valuable information available on this web site, including the Pages of Testimony, etc.
http://yvng.yadvashem.org

A list of this book and all books available in the Yizkor-Book-In-Print Project along with prices is available at:
http://www.jewishgen.org/Yizkor/ybip.html

Geopolitical Information:

The information below is for the town of Sventzian (Yiddish) in the Sventzian Region in present day Lithuania.

The town is located at 55°09' N 26°10' E, 47 miles NE of Vilnius

Period	Town	District	Province	Country
Before WWI (c. 1900):	Shventsian	Sventsyany	Vilna	Russian Empire
Between the wars	Święciany	Święciany	Wilno	Poland
After WWII (c. 1950):	Švenčionys			Soviet Union
Today (c. 2000):	Švenčionys			Lithuania

Alternate names for the town: Švenčionys [Lith], Sventzion [Yid], Święciany [Pol], Shventsian [Rus], Śvianciany [Bel], Schwintzen [Ger], Švenčoņi [Latv], Svencionyz, Shvintzion, Shvyentsiani, Shvyetsiani, Sventsian, Sventsiany, Swenziany, Svintzian

Nearby Jewish Communities:

- Švenčionėliai 7 miles W
- Ceikiniai 9 miles NNE
- Lyntupy, Belarus 9 miles SE
- Kaltanėnai 10 miles NW
- Mielagėnai 13 miles NE
- Linkmenys 13 miles NW
- Ignalina 14 miles N
- Stajetiškė 14 miles E
- Naujasis Daugėliškis 16 miles NNE
- Adutiškis 17 miles E
- Pabradė 18 miles SW
- Joniškis 21 miles WSW
- Svir, Belarus 23 miles SSE
- Mikhalishki, Belarus 23 miles S
- Kamelishki, Belarus 24 miles SSW
- Inturkė 24 miles W
- Tauragnai 25 miles NW
- Vidzy, Belarus 25 miles NE
- Narach, Belarus 25 miles SE
- Pastavy, Belarus 26 miles E
- Bystrytsa, Belarus 27 miles SSW
- Dukštas 27 miles NNE
- Rimše 28 miles NNE
- Dubingiai 29 miles WSW
- Vornyany, Belarus 29 miles S
- Kozyany, Belarus 29 miles ENE
- Salakas 30 miles N
- Molėtai 30 miles W

Jewish Population: 3,272 (in 1897), 2,750 (in 1925)

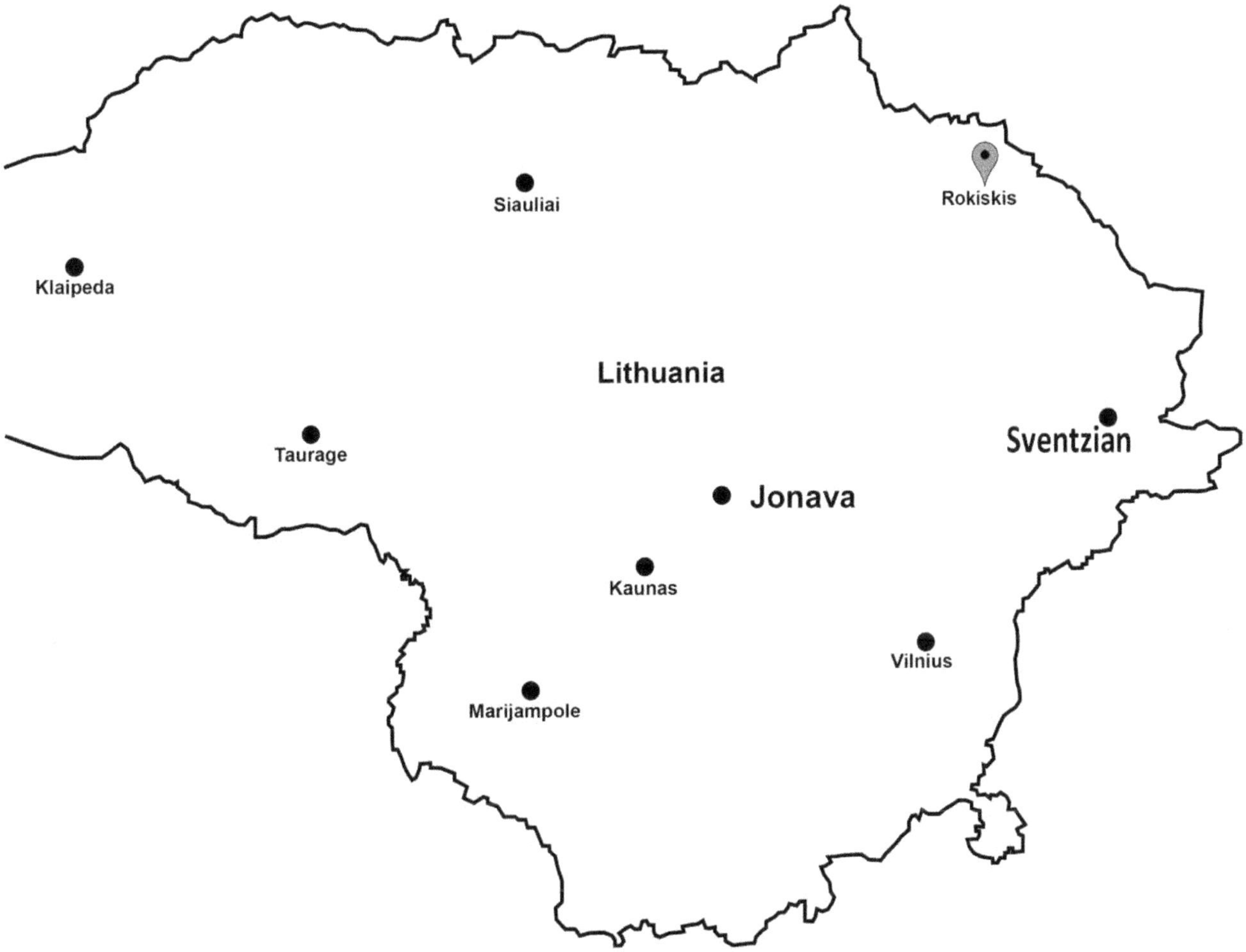

Map of Lithuania with Sventzian

Hebrew Title Page of Original Hebrew Book

ספר זכרון

לעשרים ושלוש קהילות שנחרבו

באזור שוינציאן

העורך: שמעון קאנץ

הוצא לאור ע"י ארגון יוצאי אזור שוינציאן בישראל

תל־אביב תשכ"ה 1965

Translation of the Title Page of the Original Hebrew Book

Memorial Book

To the Twenty-Three Destroyed Jewish Communities In the Svintzian Region

Editor: Shimon Kantz

Published by the Former Residents of the Sventzian Region in Israel

Tel Aviv 1965 5725

Table of Contents

Part 2 - Shoah

Sventzian Region Memorial Book

Part 2 – Shoah

Book Committee

Shimon Bushkanyetz **Moshe Michelson**

Shakhne Akhyasaf **Avraham Krill**

Sender Kowarsky **Eliezer Levin**

Editor: Shimon Kantz

Cover and illustrations:
Alexander Bogen

Assistant Editor:
Heshl Gurvitz

Administration:
Yisroel Gurvitz, Esq.
Dr. Khanokh Drutz

Sventzian Region

YIZKOR BOOK IN MEMORY OF

TWENTY-THREE JEWISH COMMUNITIES

***Editor:* Shimon Kantz**

Published by "Irgun Yotz'e Aizor Sventzian b'Israel," Tel Aviv, 1965

[Col. 925]

The Holocaust

Poligon– the mass grave of more than 8,000 Jews from the Sventzian region

[Col. 927-928]

Upon the Ruins

Chaim Grade

Translated by Janie Respitz

The Ruins were plowed in my face,
The flame remains in my bones,
And like the water boils over red – hot iron,
The pain boils on my body...and I begin to stride
Over scrap, like a watchman on the prison
In the city, the disruption after the enemy's storm.
I see those returning from wandering,
He stirs the ashes from Latvia with spread hands,
And looks for a green sprout of life in the ruins,
As if someone wants to find the ruins of a golden temple –
But the Ghetto is deserted like a cemetery,
And with laughter the wind chases the dust in his mouth.
And his heart cries: oh, who drove me back,
From my home and people – only silence remains?
Everyone is dead – where are the graves?

I hear his silent cry: who can guarantee,
The one who survived can outlive his catastrophe?
Until a new generation is encircled in song,
Until the graves will be aligned in his breast.

And in the emptiness the noise still hangs
From those who no one pitied.
The voices quiver reflections of flames,
Which have been extinguished...as on deserted seas
Old masses from a ship swaying,
And the drowned are whispering in the abyss.
And you touch a small prayer house – opening her wound,
And her stories make you wonder
How she once lived warm, quietly and happily,
And now she is boarded up, rigid and empty.

[Col. 929-940]

In the Abyss of the Horrific Extermination

Asher Bitushunsky

Translated by Janie Respitz

Sunday the 22nd of June 1941 the youth of New – Svencionys played a football match against the youth from Utian[1](Utena). That evening when the train arrived from Vilna, we learned that that morning the larger cities in Poland were bombed and the German – Soviet war had begun.

Monday morning the New – Svencionys train station was bombed where the train from Zegalia to Vilna stood. Besides this, the town was also bombed and people began to build trenches.

The Lithuanian – Soviet military (Lithuanian soldiers and Soviet officers) that were in the camp at Poligon, marched through the town toward Vilna.

The same day we were informed, that the Lithuanian soldiers rebelled, killed their Soviet commanders and ran away to the forest.

All the Soviet officials left town immediately. With them, all the Jewish recruits like Yitzkhak Gurdus, Heshl Sheyn, Nakhman Khagan, Shneour, Dovid and Efraim Guterman, Khasriel Itzikson,Hirshl Bikson, Aharon Boyershteyn, Sholem Karpas and others.

Tuesday morning, the Lithuanians began to organize and attack the retreating Soviet divisions. They also attacked Jews they met on the way. We learned that at Kakhanovka, the Lithuanians killed Motke Wolfson, the son of Yitzkhak the fisherman. They brought him back to town and buried him in the cemetery.

Wednesday morning the first German tanks drove into town. The Lithuanians were still in charge. The Jews were afraid to go out on the street. We knew that on the road, not far from the Christian cemetery, lay the body of Maliuske Guterman, who was killed by Lithuanian bandits. Her body lay there for a few days as we were unable to go out and bring her back for a Jewish burial.

A few days later the official power in town was given to the Lithuanian partisans. The commander was Kurpis from Boyvid, who had been a Lithuanian officer during Smetana's time. The headquarters was on Vilna Street, in a building which in Soviet times housed the NKVD...

Tuesday June 30th, All the Jews you worked in the Soviet cooperatives were arrested. This was a revenge act for the arrest and sentencing of a Lithuanian girl by the Soviets who had worked in one of the cooperatives.

The girl worked in a cooperative on Vilna Street where the manager was Dovid Kimkhi, Khaim Gordon's son - in - law. Others working there were Lyuba Fingerhoyt, Itke Rudnitsky, Sheynke Katz, and a few Lithuanian girls. One of them was caught stealing and was sentenced to a year in jail.

When the Lithuanian partisans took over control of the town, the brother of that girl who was a partisan compiled a list of all the Jews who worked at the cooperative. They were all arrested and shot.

Among the first victims were: Gershon Gurvitch, Hirshl Levishteyn, Hadasah Katz, Layale and Bluma Fingerhoyt, Moishe Zak, Sheyna Katz, Ite Rudnitsky, Yosef Gildin, Zilber,Mendl the blacksmith's borther–in–law and others. Altogether, 18 people.

Dr. Kapeliovitch, who during Soviet times was head of the train hospital, hid at Kazyutke Dach. The Partisans knew. They brought him to the courtyard of their headquarters and shot him there.

A while later the German S.S took over control. The police force remained pure Lithuanian.

They hung notices throughout the town stating that before they kill on German they would kill 100 Jews. They also captured Jews on the street and dragged them to work.

The S.S closed all the prayer houses and forbid Jews to gather in large groups. They called upon Rabbi Kimkhi and made him supply lists of Jewish workers.

The Rabbi assembled a committee to help him with this task. The members of this committee were: Yakov Shvartz, Yisroel Portnoy, Eliyahu Feygel, Berl Guterman, Moishe Gurvitch, Henekh Gurvich, and Yehoshua Katz. The committee worked on specific lists and presented them to the military commanders. They then stopped grabbing Jews off the street.

A few days later, around 5:00 in the morning chaos suddenly broke out in town: the Lithuanian police went around with a list and arrested the parents of all the children who were in the "Komsomol". When they didn't find the listed people at home, they arrested their relatives and neighbours. 43 people were arrested.

Among those arrested were: Yisroel Portnoy, Yakov Shvartz, Motl Gurvich, Eliyahu Feygel, Yitzkhak Milner, Aharon Bank, Nosn Kimkhi, Shmuel Gavenda, Gershon Shutan, Eliyusha Katz, Ben–Zion Fufisky, Yakov Kliatchko, Moishke Abelevitch, Yosl Lipnholtz, Motl Telent, Moishke Wolfson, Feyvke Khayt, the two ritual slaughterers and others. They led them all 3 kilometres from town on the road to Kaltinyan[2] in rows and shot them with machine guns.

The Hasidic slaughterer began to run. They shot him and left him there. Feyvke Khayt was the second to try to run. They shot at him as well but missed. He ran to the forest and hid. At night, he returned to town and hid in the potato fields. Only a few people in town knew Feyvke was saved. Christians came and reported that all 43 had been shot. Thy also brought 100 Jews from Svencionys to the same spot and shot them.

Darkness ruled the Jewish homes. No one knew what to do. Meanwhile, again they asked the Rabbi for lists of workers. No one wanted to sit on that committee.

With great difficulty the rabbi founded a committee that would meet in the small study house in the large prayer house.

The committee had two functions: prepare lists of workers and collect contributions that were demanded from the Jewish population.

This committee continued to operate until the founding of the Ghetto.

Ghetto

Meanwhile, a civilian authority was established in town and Kurpis the leader of the Lithuanian partisans was chosen as mayor. He immediately announced, in the name of the German authority, a ghetto for Jews will be made in New– Svencionys[3]. According to his plan, the ghetto was to be on the synagogue street, – in the two study houses and in the surrounding houses.

At the request of the committee, I went to Kurpis, who I knew well from before the war, and asked if the Ghetto could be on Katilnya Street, which was inhabited only by Jews.

He agreed and the Ghetto went from Ris' house until Fufusik's.

All the Jews had to immediately leave their homes and enter the boundaries of the Ghetto. Only the rabbi remained in his previous place – in the small prayer house next to the house of study.

The Ghetto was not fenced in or guarded. Yet, we were not permitted to leave and walk freely through the town.

Only on market days were Jews permitted to leave the ghetto for two hours in order to buy necessities.

All week we bought products in the special ghetto store which was in Mendl Levin's house.

We lived in the ghetto in perpetual fear. The peasants from the area told us that in the other Lithuanian towns, all the Jews were killed.

We knew about the destruction of Lingmian[4] Jews that took place four days after the outbreak of the war, because my brother Hirsh lived in Lingmian. The day the war broke out he was with us but returned home. He took my younger brother Shimshon with him. We thought that since Lingmian was far from the train station, it would be quieter. Four days later we received the news that all the Jews of Lingmian were killed. They were shot and buried in one grave.

This news left a horrible impression on our town. We were downtrodden and feeling helpless. Apathy ruled. We did not have the strength or will to save ourselves. The majority of the Jews were elderly, women and children – families who were very close and did not want to be separated. We thought our town might be spared.

One day we learned from Kurpis, the Germans decided to remove the Jews from Svencionys and bring them to Poligon where there was a labour camp. Kurpis also informed us this would be carried out by the Svencionys commander.

Liquidation of the Ghetto

Knowing of the exodus that the Jews of Svencionys faced, our committee immediately decided to send Khatzkl Levinshteyn to Svencionys to meet with the committee and try to put an end to this decree.

The Jews of Svecionys actually succeeded in convincing the authorities to allow a group of Jews to remain, 40 families, especially artisans, – the so called useful Jews. We also tried to convince the mayor of New Svencionys to allow the "useful" Jews to remain. At first he promised, but later did not keep his promise.

Early Friday, on the eve of Shabbat Tshuva, the commander of the train station came to the Ghetto and chose 20 youths to be sent to Salduchishak to load boards onto the sawmill for the small train.

I was part of that group. At night, when we returned, we found the Ghetto surrounded by Lithuanian police.

The mood in the Ghetto was like Yom Kippur. Everyone felt the sad hour had arrived. Here and there people were making plans how to escape and be saved. The majority were in despair and helpless. It was the eve of a Holy day: no one slept that night. The next morning at 6 the chased all the Jews out of their homes, lined them up in rows and sent them to Poligon.

One Jew remained in town, Yitzkhal Leyzer Katz the tailor. He had to finish sewing a suit for the Police commander. That evening they brought him to Poligon as well.

Poligon

When we arrive in the camp everyone was reviewed. They took away all our documents, valuables and money.

When they were done they separated the men and the women and sent them to wooden barracks that had no windows, were broken down and filthy. It was horribly overcrowded. There was no place to sit and no room to turn around.

The New – Svencionys Jews were the first to arrive. A little later they brought groups of Jews from other towns: Heydutsishok[5],Stayatsishok[6], Doygelishak[7], Meligan[8] and Sveretz.[9]

Every town occupied another barrack. The Lithuanian police spied and guarded strictly to make sure no one escaped.

The next day they had us choose two of the elders in the barrack who every day had to provide a list of Jews in the barrack and report if someone was sick or escaped.

The two eldest in our barrack were Berl Guterman and me. We divided everyone into groups and sent them to work. The women worked picking potatoes; the men worked on the trains and a variety of other jobs in the town. The Jewish homes were locked, the Ghetto was guarded to make sure we wouldn't "God forbid" remove anything that had been left behind.

A few days later, they opened the Jewish homes, removed the furniture and other important items and auctioned them off to the Christian population.

Life in Poligon was very difficult: overcrowded and filthy, and worst of all – great hunger.

The mayor of New– Svencionys asked us to send him a few bakers to bake bread for the camp.

Among the bakers were: Shmuel, Zerakh and Leyb Broyda, Yosef Elperin, Kalikshteyn, Nosn Broyda and me. We gathered in the home of Shmuel Broyda and baked bread.

We left our barrack early in the morning and returned late at night. Of course we always returned with bread for the others in our barrack.

Approximately 50 Jews remained in Svencionys Ghetto – artisans and their families. They were considered a "useful" element and they were permitted to bring various foods. They were also able to take out friends and relatives from Poligon on the pretext that they were necessary workers. A few people from New – Svencionys were also saved this way: Berl Guterman, Feyvke Khayt, Leybke Troytse and others.

For five days we went to town to bake bread. One day when we returned we encountered this scene in Poligon:

All the Jews were lined up in rows, in front of the barracks. They were surrounded by soldiers with machine guns. In the middle stood a few tall S.S. men and Lithuanian officers. The head German spoke: "The regional commissar decided to free all the Jews from the camp, if they are willing to pay a tax – either in money, gold or valuables".

The crowd breathed a collective sigh of relief: this means they will let us live. If yes, to hell with the money. They immediately chose special collectors who sat in the entrances to the barracks and all the Jews, willingly, began to bring their possessions. Everyone gave all they had brought from home.

When they gave the Germans all the collected money, they returned the Jews to the barracks and enclosed them like cattle.

The following day, Tuesday the first day of Sukkot, our baking group returned to town to bake bread. Around 8:00 in the morning I went out to hear what was happening in town.

Coincidently, I bumped into the young Giru who was studying medicine at the university in Vilna. He told me:

Asherke, why are you wandering around? Did you know the authorities gave an order that all the Christians in the area must come at 5:00 in the evening to dig graves. Everyone has to bring a shovel and dig graves for the Jews that are imprisoned in Poligon.

I returned to the bakery and told them what I had just heard. Yosef Elperin and Kalikshteyn were already gone. We decided to hide. We left Kaltinya Street and snuck over to the Synagogue Street. We threw ourselves into the nettle bushes that grew tall in Yakov Shvartz's garden.

From there we saw, from a distance how all the Christians were arriving with shovels in their hands and gathering in front of the court house. When it was dark, we left our hiding spot and left town.

First we went to Klushtshan, where the Broyda's had a grandfather. On the way, Shmuel Broyda remained with a Christian friend, but in the morning joined us in Klushtshan.

He brought us horrifying news. All the Jews of Poligon had been shot.

We decided to send a Christian friend to New – Svencionys to find out the details of the fate of the Jews in Poligon.

The Christian returned and reported how on Wednesday, the second day of Sukkot, the Lithuanian police removed all the men from the barracks, divided them into groups of 25 and killed them. Thursday, the first day of Khol Hamoed Sukkot, in the same fashion, killed all the women and children. All those shot were thrown into one large grave which the town's Christians and farmers from the surrounding area had been digging since Tuesday.

We realized that all we heard and saw Tuesday was true. The Lithuanian and German animals killed all who were close and dear to us.

My Wanderings

This horrible and terrifying news hit us like a thunder bolt. We walked around confused not knowing what to do.

Few days passed and we decided to move on, in the direction of White Russia. First we headed toeard Vidz[10], where my sister Soreh Hinde from Ignalina was.

On the way we stopped in Mikhalishok where I found people from New - Svencionys: Yosef Zak, Leyb Ring, Rafael Shutan and Isser Katcherginsky with their families.

From Mikhalishok we continued to Svir where we found Basia Gurvitch and her son Khaiml, Berl Guterman and his wife plus the Izikovitch and Svirsky families.

From Svir I left for Postav where I stayed with the old Tsepelevitch who was a member of the Jewish committee. He provided me with a wagon and I left for Kazian(Kaziany)[11].

On the road I saw the police taking away the dental technician Sloimeh Hirsh Ridnitsky and his wife. I later learned they were shot not far from Postav.

I spent the night in Kazian and the next morning left for Vidz. I decided to remain in Vidz and tried to bring back my sister and her family.

A short time later the Vidz Ghetto was liquidated and all the Jews were brought to Svencionys Ghetto. 100 talented Jewish workers remained in Vidz, led by Lipman Levin. I succeeded to stay with them.

We then made a huge effort to contact Partisans and go out to the forest.

One day a farmer came to us with a note from a Partisan which said we should all come to the forest and bring Dr. Ginsburg with us. The farmer was captured and they found the list with our names. They immediately arrested four of us and shot the farmer in front of our eyes.

I needed to tear myself from German hands and escape. For two days I hid in the fields around town, then returned to Vidz, found Dr. Ginsburg and together with him joined the Partisans in the forest.

There began a new chapter in my life.

In the Forest with the Partisans

This is how we arrived in the forest outside Kazian, where there was a Partisan detachment. They numbered around 300, commanded by the former Soviet commander Faniemakhov. There were also many Jewish youth, boys and girls from the surrounding towns.

As soon as we arrived Dr. Ginsburg went straight to headquarters and I joined the general Partisan group.

A few days later there was a big blockade. A part of our detachment was destroyed, and a part broke away and headed east. Only a few remained in place, including some Jewish boys and girls and a few Russians, in total, 29 people.

Although our group was small, we decided to carry on with our independent Partisan work. We began with a few diversion actions, and soon, the whole area feared us.

Our group remained in the Kazan area all winter. Around Pesach, the other part of our detachment which escaped during the blockade returned. We united with them and were no longer alone. Soon after, other detachments joined us and we formed a brigade. Faniemakhov was chosen as our brigadier.

The first task of our brigade was to destroy German garrisons around Kazian.

We attacked two towns where the Germans were situated, burnt all the houses and killed almost everyone.

In the forest, I met Rivka Esterovitch, the woman I would later marry.

Together with her, I joined a group that went to a forest near Glubak. I was chosen by the brigadier to command this group and I was ordered to carry out various attacks.

I felt complete in this position and led my group to Vidz, Postav and Svencionys.

One day I learned the Red Army had parachuted Dovid Guterman not far from us. However, the Germans captured him, and his end was horrific: they poked out his eyes, tortured him, cutting off his sexual organs. Then they tied him to a tree and shot him.

After Liberation

When the Red Army liberated our area, my wife and I left for New - Svencionys. A terrifying scene unfolded before our eyes: most of the town had been burned, in Poligon they showed us the mass grave where we found the bones of 8000 Jews, residents of all the towns from the former Svencionys district.

A short time later, other Jews began to return. Those who arrived were: Yosef Zak with his wife and children, Khaya and Nisn Las, Yitzkhak Gurvitch, Leyvik Zak, Velvl Sakhar, Yosef Kavarsky, Leyzr Gordon, Dovid Kimkhi, Hirsh Bikson and others.

A little later, returning from Russia were: Moyshke Tzinman, Aharon and Ruvke Boyershteyn, Zalman Gurdus, Khaim Rabinovitch, the sons of Sholem Karpas, Yakov Abelevitch, Avrom Gubesky and others.

My first task was to take revenge on the murderers who participated in the extermination of the Jews. I approached the NKVD and based on my information, the arrested Kurpis, the former commander of the Lithuanian police, the Lithuanian Matyukas and a few other Christians.

I then went a group from the NKVD to Lingmian, and there they arrested all the bandits who help exterminate the Jews of Lingmian. Some of the Christians were sentenced to many years in jail and others were sent deep into Russia.

I could not find my place amidst the destruction of our town. It was impossible to begin a new life on the graves of our former home.

We hung around a short while and decided to leave the town where every stone reminded us of spilled Jewish blood.

Our wandering resumed. We left for central Poland, from there to Germany, and after many hardships, we finally left for Eretz Yisrael.

Translator's notes:

Utian is Utena, Lithuania

Kaltinian, Kaltinyan is Kaltinenai, Lithuania

Ligmian is Linkmenys, Lithuania

Hoduciszki is Adustiskis, Lithuania

Stoyatzishok, or Shtayatsisitok(y) is Stajetiske in Lithuania

Daugielishki is Naujasis(Nowe) Dauguliskis, Lithuania

Meligan is Mielagenai, Lithuania

Lintup(y) is Lyntupy, Belarus

New(Novo) Svencionys is Svencioneliai, Lithuania

Podbrodz(y) is Paabrade, Lithuania

Vidz or Vidzy, Belarus

[Col. 941]

Desolate Days and Nights

Efraim Vaynfers

Translated by Janie Respitz

I was born in the town of Yanishok, 25 km from New–Svencionys. My father was a blacksmith. He worked very hard to provide for his family of six. I finished the Folk – Shul and wanted to continue my studies.

In 1939 the Soviets came and I went to work. I worked in Ignalina. When the German – Soviet war broke out I ran away to New–Svencionys where my uncle Yisroel Portnoy lived.

A short while later a Jewish committee was formed headed by Rabbi Kimkhi. My uncle was also a member of the committee. The main function of the committee was to provide workers for the Germans. Because I was not registered in New–Svencionys I was not sent to work.

One morning at 6:00 I heard screaming. My uncle went out to see what was happening. He never returned home.

When the Lithuanian police saw him, they arrested him on the spot. They took 43 men, including my uncle.

From the house we saw how they took them away through Kaltinya Street, toward Poligon. We never saw them again. People were saying they were sent to work. The same day I learned the sad truth, all 43 were shot. A Lithuanian farmer friend happened to be passing by the hill where they were murdered. They stopped him, and he saw everything.

[Col. 942]

He told us my uncle had to bury the others. Then they made him dig a grave, shot him and threw him in.

I did not tell anyone the truth, as I did not want my aunt to know. Portnoy was not just my uncle. He was an uncle to all the Jews in New–Svencionys.

Many Jews in town called him lovingly: Uncle.

If someone needed a loan, they came to Yisroel Portnoy; if a poor Jew had to marry off a daughter and did not have the means, Portnoy would help.

My uncle never refused anyone. He helped everyone as much as possible. He would mainly give money from his own pocket. If the amount request was to too large, he would not be embarrassed to go to this one and that one, explain the importance of the situation and ask them to help out. No one let him leave empty handed. Everyone knew if the Uncle asked, they had to give.

My uncle had an open door and an open hand. His house was a sort of help – society for young and old and all the poor people.

Not only the Jews loved him; the Christians also valued and respected him.

It is not surprising that his cruel and bestial death was looked upon as a thunder on a clear day: if the Gentiles could ill–treat uncle Portnoy as they did, the world must be coming to an end. There is no hope for anyone. And the end came quickly.

[Col. 943]

One time, on a Friday I went to work in Salduchishok, loading planks of wood. In the evening when we were done loading all the wagons, we returned to town. To our surprise, we found the Ghetto surrounded by Lithuanian police. Saturday morning, they told us all to come out of our houses and bring only a light bag. They were taking us away.

I began to imagine where they were taking us and why. I took my aunt Sorele and walked along the railroad tracks. They saw us right away. The caught me and brought me back to town. They let my aunt go. Soon after, I ran away again, through the Shul Street out of town.

I met a farmer I knew from Yanishok and he told me the truth. They were not taking people to work. They were taking them to Poligon where they would be killed. The farmer warned me not to walk around, but to hide and wait a couple of days.

I returned to town and told everything to Hirshl Rotshteyn. We gathered 12 people including my aunt, locked the front door with a key so they would think no one was there and through a back door went down to the cellar.

Lying in the cellar we heard them remove everyone from their homes and lead them through Kaltinya Street. We saw how they led Rabinovitch and the rabbi with their hands up in the air through the street. We even heard Lithuanians arguing about a robbery of flour and a cow they stole from the Jews.

We lay in the cellar until midnight. We had decided to sneak out of town. This was not easy. When we realized the Lithuanian patrol was far from our house, we all quietly, snuck out and walked toward the Shul Street. The Lithuanians detected something and began to shoot. We hid for a while and continued walking out of town toward Rudzan.

[Col. 944]

Our escape was not easy. In our group were 4 children, 2 elderly women and Yerakhmiel who was lame who had twisted hands and feet. We had to carry him.

We walked almost all night, until we arrived in Rudzan, where Hirsh knew a farmer.

That Christian received us well. He hid us and warned us to stay put until he could find us a better hiding place.

When we calmed down we asked him to go to New–Svencionys and find out what happened.

He returned and reported they took all the Jews to Poligon. He warned us to stay put until things calmed down.

At night he came to us and said he was afraid to hide us. He took us to a forest, 3 kilometres from the village, led us into a shed where we remained. He came every day to bring us food and news from the town.

First he told us they were taking the Jews from Poligon to work, took large bribes and with a promise they would be freed. But a day before Sukkot, he brought us horrifying news: he heard there was an order from the Germans and Lithuanians, all the farmers in the area should come in the morning with shovels to dig graves for the Jews in Poligon.

We thought we were going mad. We had no idea what to do. The first day of Khol Hamoed Sukkot, we heard the shooting from Poligon. It lasted all day.

[Col. 945]

In the evening, when it was quiet, the farmer came and told us the truth. They shot all the Jews in Poligon. No one could be saved. We met a Christian who was in Poligon during the execution. He recounted how they murdered. He told us that they did not shoot the children, but threw them into the graves alive.

[Col. 946]

We saw the Christian was carrying a bag of things that were bloodied. He said all the farmers were doing this: they were taking the clothes and shoes from those Jews murdered in Poligon. He explained before they were shot, they were forced to undress, naked.

Our limbs froze. We could not move.

Two days later, with great difficulty, we arrived in Vidz. We left there and went into hiding until liberation.

[Col. 945]

The Cruel Slaughter

Levi Zak

Translated by Janie Respitz

On that Sunday in June, when the German – Soviet war broke out I was in Ponavezh (Panevezys). Tuesday morning, two days later, I returned to New–Svencionys.

The Germans had already bombed the town. The Soviet army immediately withdrew; the civil authority evacuated and escaped to Russia along with a few Jewish families.

There was no official authority in town. The Lithuanian partisans took advantage of this situation. These were Lithuanian soldiers who ran away from the Red Army, former Lithuanian police plus Lithuanian hooligans and bandits. They organized a type of headquarters, created a jail and began to rule the town.

Firstly, they arrested all the former Soviet officials who were suspected of being communists.

[Col. 946]

Among the first arrested were – Hirshl Levinshteyn, Gershon Gurvitch, Lialeh Gurvitch and his daughter Bluma, Dovid and Lyuba Fingerhoyt, Yosef Lipman and Moishe Zak, Nosn Shutan, Yosef Gildin, Hadassah Katz and the author of these lines.(Levi Zak)

Until today I do not know why they freed me, my brothers Yosef and Lipman Zak and Nosn Shutan. The rest were brought to a hill behind Vilna Street, and shot.

The German army arrived in town the second Wednesday. The civil authority remained in Lithuanian hands.

The Germans immediately gave an order that all Jews had to wear a yellow patch; they were forbidden to walk on the sidewalks and were forbidden to be in the streets in the evening.

Besides this, they established a Jewish council which had to provide workers every day and help carry out orders that were placed on the Jewish population.

[Col. 947]

A large meeting was held in the Prayer house, and the members of the Jewish council were chosen. Peopled were asked if they would agree to join. The Jewish council was comprised of; Moishe Gurvitch, Henekh Gurvitch, Yisroel Portnoy, Khatzkl Levinshteyn, Berl Guterman and Yashike Katz.

Every day the council had to put forth workers for the Germans and the Lithuanians.

One day many S.S. and Lithuanian police came to town and removed many Jews from their homes on the pretext their children had been members of the Commosol (Communist youth group). They took 43 men to the outskirts of town to a bridge about 5 kilometres from New–Svencionys and shot them all.

The Christians told us they were all buried by Yisroel Portnoy. Then they shot him and threw him into the same grave.

The horrific annihilation of these 43 men shook the whole town. We now had an idea what the Germans and their Lithuanian collaborators were capable of doing. We now understood what fate awaited the rest of the Jews.

We soon learned they were going to build a Ghetto for the Jews of New–Svencionys. At first they wanted to put the Ghetto near the Shul court yard. But he Lithuanian commandant insisted on Kaltinya Street where many Jews lived.

All of our belongings, furniture and the rest of our things had to be removed from our homes. In the Ghetto, a few families lived in one room. It was crowded, but we could deal with it.

It was not a locked Ghetto and we were able to come and go. On market days, we were even permitted to shop.

The Ghetto existed only for 2 months. Friday, Erev Shabbat Tshuva, they surrounded the Ghetto on all sides and no one was allowed to leave. A Christian friend from a nearby village, Yan Borovsky came to me and told me they were going to murder all the Jews.

[Col. 948]

He knew this from a good source. He suggested I come to his place to hide.

Friday night, I snuck out of the Ghetto and went to his village. The same night, Yosef Zak and his family, Rafael Shutan, Yakov Bak, Nekhama Tzinman and her son also left the Ghetto.

I hid in Borovsky's attic for 2 days. He told me they had taken all the Jews to Poligon and will shoot them there.

Borovsky was afraid to hide me in his attic and suggested I go to another Christian, Karavatsky in a village called Pokumshe. I listened to him and when I got there I found my brother Yosef and his family, Yakov Bak and Rafael Shutan.

We stayed there for a few days, then, we all left together toward Svir, which was in White Russia, where Jews were not yet being persecuted. On the way we hid in Mikhalishok.

A little later we were joined by Asher Bitushunsky, Zerakh and Leyb Broida. They succeeded in escaping from Poligon.

We did not stay in Mikhalishok very long and continued on our way. We wandered for days until we met a Christian who agreed to hide us.

We stayed with this Christian until liberation. Kravatsky would come often and bring us food. We learned from this Christian how our dear ones were murdered in Poligon.

They took them in groups from the barracks, separated the men and the women, and made everyone strip naked. They took each group to a large grave and shot them with machine guns.

The Lithuanian police did not check if they were actually dead or just wounded. They threw everyone in the mass grave.

When they finished with the first group, they brought a second and third and this continued for two days.

[Col. 949]

Many were thrown into the grave alive.

The children were not shot. They were smashed into trees. There was one policeman who enjoyed tearing off their little feet. Without exception, all the children were buried alive. After the peasants covered the grave, they continued to hear cries and see the ground move for hours.

[Col. 950]

There were Christians who fainted doing this work, not able to bear the horrible executions.

The Lithuanians and Germans sang with joy.

When the Red Army freed New–Svencionys, it was learned that amongst the worst murderers were those peasants from the village of Mezhanel who partook in the horrific slaughter. After they covered the grave, they took the clothes and shoes of the slaughtered victims.

[Col. 949]

This is How it Happened

Yitzkhak Gurvitch

Translated by Janie Respitz

1.

This was the first day of Hitler's attack on Soviet–Russia.

In “Poligon”, which was in New–Svencionys there was a Soviet officer's school, with a majority of Lithuanians. At 6:00 in the evening they all marched, led by a military orchestra, through the Streets of New–Svencionys toward Vilna.

At night when they reached the fields of Podbrodz, the future Lithuanian officers deserted. The following morning they organized partisan divisions against the Soviet powers. In New–Svencionys they were led by Kurpis, from the village Boyviz, with the support of the young priest Uzialo from the village Gramatskes, 2 kilometres from town. They immediately began their extermination of the Jews. Together with many other Jews, I was arrested as a collaborator with the Soviets. Miraculously I was freed by a Lithuanian.

The 27 Jews, among them were: Gershon Gurvitch, Gershon Zak, Moishe Elye, Lialieh Gurvitch, Bayle Khatzkelevitch, Zakharia's 2 daughters, Ite Rudnitsky, Hirsh Levinshteyn and others were killed in the forest on the way to Vilna.

[Col. 950]

Not only Jews were killed, they were also against the Poles. They used the same methods and the dead Poles lay among the dead Jews in the same graves.

2.

A few days later the German entered. The German commander called upon Rabbi Kimkhi ,announced many edicts against the Jews and ordered him to carry out his commands.

The Rabbi called a meeting to choose a Jewish council which was comprised of: Rabbi Eliyahu Kimkhi, Henekh Gurvitch, Moishe Gurvitch, Yisroel Portnoy, Yeshua Katz, and Borukh Abelevitch.

One morning the Lithuanian partisans descended on the Jewish homes to take men and women to work. They brought them all to the court house on Vilna Street. The Lithuanian commander freed the women. They took a group of 43 men on trucks, accompanied by armed, drunken Lithuanians, and took them to work in the Baranov forest. Included in this group were: Motl Gurvitch, Yisroel Portnoy, Nokhem Troytse, Mendl Tzinman, Yankl Klatshko, Note Kimkhi, Shmuel Broide, Shmuel Gavenda, Feiveh Khayt, Bank, Itzkhak Miller and others. In the forest they made them dig graves, and then killed them all. The only one to escape was Feiveh Khayt. (Chait)

[Col. 951]

3.

Suddenly, they took all the Jews out of their homes and put them on Kaltinya Street where they built the Ghetto. The Jewish council, led by Rabbi Kimkhi, who lived in a small room in the new prayer house, began to distribute workplaces and collect bribes. They endeared themselves to the "greased" Lithuanians to learn what was going on and to try to repeal the edicts.

When I heard there were preparations for extermination, I decided to leave the Ghetto. Not willing to listen to my brother Moishe, who was a member of the Jewish council, that they had a promise from the "greased" ones, I left New–Svencionys and went to Vidz in White Russia, where I had lived until the First World War with my parents.

I arrived in Vidz the first day of Rosh Hashana. I reported in and was considered a citizen of Vidz. I told my family, my mother, my sister and brother and their families, to come to Vidz. Only my mother, my sister Beyle and her son Sholem, and Moishe's daughter came.

Later, my brother Moishe, his wife Esther, their 2 sons and his brother-in-law Shloime Elperin tried to come. Behind Daugelishok they were noticed by shepherds and were handed over to the Lithuanian bandits. The captured family was killed near Daugelishok.

In Vidz I worked for a Christian who supplied the Germans with hay. This is how I supported the surviving members of my family in Vidz.

In 1943 they took all the Jews from Vidz to the Svencionys Ghetto. By then I was working for Shapiro in a fishing net factory, and maintained contact with my Christian friends in New-Svencionys, in particular the Gratulevichs, who informed me they were already sending people from Svencionys to Vilna and Kovno. I escaped from the Ghetto and began to wander from place to place, from Christian to Christian.

[Col. 952]

When I heard my mother and the remaining ones were in Vilna, I headed there. Getting off the train I met a group of Jewish workers and together with them, I entered the Ghetto. I found my mother, sister and 2 children naked, barefoot and hungry.

After two weeks in Vilna I realized I would die there so I left for New-Svencionys, knowing that my Christians friends would support my family in the Vilna Ghetto.

I remained in the area of New-Svencionys, hiding in the forests, swamps and bath houses. I hid at Vinik the drunkard's, Skirshinis', Mishun's and Drushtzian's. I was denounced a few times and had to run away. Hungry, barefoot and naked, I was hunted like an animal: I thought of ending my life more than once.

4.

June 1944 I heard Soviet artillery shooting. I lay in a trench in an open field and thought that any moment now, I will be free. But the shooting became louder and drew closer. Will I survive the fire? Suddenly it became quiet. It all seemed unbelievable. The Germans were gone and I was free.

Upon entering New-Svencionys I saw the burning houses were still smoldering. Everything was destroyed. Most of what was the Jewish centre, the Train Street, Kaltinya Street, Svencionys Street, Vilna Street and the Shul Street had disappeared.

I knew that Yosef Zak and his family and his brother Moishe were in Pakumshe. I went to them. We were very overwhelmed. The first Jews I found from our town. Levi Zak and I settled in a room, later Hirsh Bikson, Dovid Kimkhi and Khaya Las with her husband and child arrived, Tzipe Bikson. I met a Jewish captain who helped us to get back on our feet. He said to me: "Give me the names of all the bandits and I'll settle with them". That's exactly what we did.

One day I met the Lithuanian bandit who denounced Hirsh Levinshteyn. I told the Soviet authorities about him, and he was arrested. The following morning I received an order to come to

[Col. 953]

the General–Secretary of the party, who tried to get me to repeal the charges I had laid. It turned out the bandit was a member of the Communist party, recommended by the General–Secretary. I refused to drop the charges. A while later I received an order to come to the NKVD. Not knowing why they asked me to come, I notified my friend Gratulevitch what to do for me, if necessary.

At the NKVD they accused me of collaborating with the enemy of the Soviet Union. I explain that I was helping to exterminate the enemies. I, a Jew who had suffered so much would collaborate with the murderers? They arrested me and threw me in a cellar. I informed my friends and they did everything they could to free me. They continued to investigate me. I told them the demands of the General–Secretary. How he wanted me to drop my charges against the Lithuanian bandit. They finally believed me and let me go.

[Col. 954]

5.

One day an inquiry commission arrived that needed to ascertain the slaughter of the Jews and some Poles. The commission was made up of doctors, journalists and legal officials. I went with them to the graves that were on the road to Vilna, and to the large mass grave in the forest near Zemyane.

We did not have to dig for long. After digging one metre we saw the strewn corpses, without any order, mothers and children. They photographed everything and asked me how the Lithuanians participated in the murder. They asked me to sign, and this is how it ended.

It should not have ended like this!

The mass murder should not be forgotten. Remember!

[Col. 953]

Upon the Ruins

Taybe Kagan

Translated by Janie Respitz

Two days after the war broke out I posed the question: Where can I escape to? I answered my own question: to Russia.

Right after I left our town the question bothered me: If I escape, why all alone? It was already too late. There was no turning back.

The question troubled me throughout my wandering through the steppes of Kazakhstan all the way to Siberia. The feeling of remorse stayed with me during the 5 years and did not let me rest.

As soon as the war ended I decided to return home. Once again I had to endure wandering and difficulties until I finally arrived in New–Svencionys.

I got off the train and encountered a horrifying scene: the streets were empty; the houses – burned. Everywhere I turned I saw only smoking walls.

[Col. 954]

Of all the houses that remained was the train station and Heshl Gordon's outside wall.

I walked through the town and could not recognize where the streets had been.

I began to search for someone who may have been saved. Maybe I will meet someone.

No one remained and I did not want to ask the Christians. It was not worth it. The large grave behind Zhemyane gave witness to what had transpired.

I realized I could not live here among the ruins. I decided to continue wandering, if only to escape the terrifying ghosts from the ruins and the graves.

I continued to drag myself from city to city, from country to country, until, with great difficulty I reached our old, historic home – the Land of Israel.

[Col. 955]

How I Was Saved from the Valley of Tears and Anxiety

Esther Feyge Furman Khayt (Chait)

Translated by Janie Respitz

At that I time worked as a cashier in the “Zagot–Skot” (a cooperative that bought cattle). When the Soviets left our town, there were approximately 8000 Rubles in my cash.

The head bookkeeper was Kazlovski, a Lithuanian from Kovno, who later became known as a communist leader who was connected to the underground Lithuanian communist organization in Vilna. He was captured by the Gestapo and betrayed the leader of the United Partisan Organization (P.P.O) in the Vilna Ghetto, Yitzkhak Vittenberg.

He ordered me to give him all the remaining money in the cash. He lived in the village Vikun not far from our town. I went to him and brought all the money.

Meanwhile, there were on going battles between the Soviet Army and the Lithuanian partisans. I could not return safely to town and decided to remain in that village.

I hid in the home of a Lithuanian acquaintance – Pukiyenas, the brother of the priest who was the leader of the Lithuanian partisan headquarters.

His wife would bring me all the news from town. I learned from her how Motke Wolfson had been shot on the road; not far from Mohilnik lay the corpse of the murdered Malyuske Guterman; and the partisans killed Hirshke Broyda.

I stayed with them for one week. Pukiyenas wife was very religious. She tried to convince me to convert and stay with them. I thanked her for her kindness, and when the roads became a bit safer, I returned home.

[Col. 956]

I barely crossed the threshold into our house when the Lithuanian partisans arrived and forced us to leave. They took us to the fields not far from the church and kept us there all day. When it began to rain heavily, the Polish priest came and allowed us to go inside his barn. This is where we spent the night.

Among us was Ben–Zion Avtchinsky, who had a strange, comic face. The Lithuanian guards did not like him. They took him aside, and shot him.

At daybreak, we escaped from the barn and returned to town.

The mood was somber. We were afraid to go out on the street. I noticed how the known criminal Sushchik was leading my teacher Rufeytz's sister down Kaltinya Street. Not long after we heard that he killed her near the Sprunzske bath.

These were only individual victims. A few days later the Lithuanian murderers killed 43 people. The “Action” was carried out with a pre–made plan. They prepared a list of all the Jews whose children had been members of the Comsomol. They arrested everyone. If they they could not find someone from the list, they grabbed a relative or a neighbour to reach the desired 43.

The same day, they took them all outside town and shot them.

A short while later they built the Ghetto which only lasted a short time.

[Col. 957]

Meanwhile, the Lithuanian police were preparing barracks in Poligon, where they would send all the Jews from the region.

For the time being, our friend Kozlovsky moved into the Ghetto. He lived with in the house of Mordkhe Yose the ritual slaughterer. He came to us and suggested that me and my sister Roshke move in with him.

It was Thursday evening, when me and my sister Roshke left the Ghetto to go live with him. The very next morning, Friday, the Lithuanian partisans surrounded the Ghetto and no one could leave. We lay hidden in a dark corridor and were not noticed. Kozlovsky didn't even tell his children.

Early Saturday morning, the Shabbes before Yom Kippur, all the Jews were taken from the Ghetto and brought to Poligon.

Tuesday, the first day of Sukkot, Yurevitch, who worked at the electricity station, came to Kozlovsky and reported how they mobilized all the peasants from the entire area. They all had to come at night with shovels to dig graves for the Jews in Poligon.

Wednesday morning, the shooting in Poligon began. It could be heard the whole day.

All the gentiles ran to see this great wonder. It was said the Christians were celebrating, shouting and singing.

We thought we would go mad from pain and fear. Kazlovsky's wife would come in and try to cheer us up and comfort us.

By evening the shooting stopped.

[Col. 958]

We heard the voices and song of the Lithuanian bandits who were returning from the horrific executions. They gathered in the market place to celebrate their great “victory”.

On Thursday, the shooting in Poligon continued. The executions ended during the day. Once again they mobilized the peasants to cover the grave.

Over 2 days, the Lithuanians murdered almost 8000 Jews in Poligon. They took most of the belongings of the dead. We saw how even the town's Christians took clothing and shoes.

We both believed our hearts would collapse before we would go mad.

Being able to withstand this is a sign that a person is stronger than iron and steel.

Friday morning, Bogdan the medic came to the Kozlovsky's. Through the wall we clearly heard him say:

"Good that we finally got rid of the Jews. They were planning a Communist takeover of the world. Now we have sent them to the next world. There they can bully whomever they want. Ha, ha"...

This was not only the opinion of Bogdan the medic; the majority of the Christian population felt this way.

Morally, they are all responsible for the spilled blood. Here and there you can find individuals who were not carried away in this tide, but they were few, – individual people of good character who must not be forgotten and remembered with gratitude.

[Col. 959]

The Path to Pain

Kayle Ayzikovitch

Translated by Janie Respitz

We lived in Pupisk's house on Kaltinya Sreet where the Ghetto would later be built. Since that house was situated outside the Ghetto, we moved to a Christian building, behind Khaya Elperin.

Living with us were Feyge Gurvitch, Henekh Gurvitch with his wife and children and Basia Gurvich and her son Khaim. Her husband Motl Gurvitch was murdered in the "Operation of the 43".

We quickly decided that we must leave the town as soon as possible. We contacted our family in Svir and asked them to send a wagon. They sent it right away and first took my husband and children. I remained in New–Svencionys with a few things. Friday morning, Erev Shabbes Tshuva, my husband returned from Svir with a wagon to take me there. We packed our belongings and wanted to leave for Svir, but we realized the Ghetto was surrounded on all sides and it would be extremely difficult to leave.

When we saw the Lithuanian police go inside to Matovkas, we quickly escaped through the small Shul Street, and we succeeded in leaving town.

We arrived in Lintup, where my brother Rafael Svirsky had a turpentine factory. He employed 40 Jews from Lintup.

My brother immediately took care of my husband and my brother Yitzkhak, and put them to work as useful Jews.

Later Basia Gurvitch also managed to come to us. Henekh Gurvitch did not want to leave his parents, and at the last minute abandoned his plan to join us.

[Col. 960]

The calm days in Lintup did not last long. The Germans were planning to liquidate the Ghetto. We then moved to Svir.

The Svir Ghetto also did not last long either. The Jews of Svir were sent in two transports to Kovno and Vilna.

The transport to Kovno went straight to Ponar where everyone was killed. The Vilna transport made it to Vilna.

We were in the Vilna Ghetto until our expulsion to Estonia. Basia Gurvitch and her son were also with us. My Family was on the first transport went to Narva, Estonia .Basia and her son were to go on the second.

We had to work very hard in the camp in Estonia. Khaiml was just a boy of 12. As he was tall and well built, they thought he was older. He went to work together with all the men.

The work was hard and they hardly gave us any food. Hunger was great and soon disease began to spread – especially typhus.

Khaiml contracted typhus and died. His mother Basia was killed in Shtuthoff.

My children and I survived all the misery of the camp and had the good fortune to live until liberation. My husband died while walking on our way. He became weak and could not continue. He asked the children to deliver his last greetings to me.

[Col. 961]

The Cry of Blood Shall Not Be Silenced

Arie Popiski

Translated by Meir Razy

Years and years have passed. Sometimes it seems as if it happened only yesterday. Days and nights, months and years, all passed as if it were a dream, a nightmare.

In today's dull, daily life, in the presence of perpetual little quarrels it is impossible to remember, consciously or not, and to think about that most somber day of our lives. Monday, the fourth day of Sukkot, October 1941, the day when the German-Lithuanian murderers killed and slaughtered indiscriminately all our beloved and dear ones, without any fear of punishment or fear of God. Fathers, mothers, brothers and sisters, infants and children, young and old, cruel death was inflicted on these devoted Jews who had remained faithful to their Jewish heritage until their last breath! They understood everything humane; they were sages of Torah and tradition, they were noble people, righteous people and simple people, with warm hearts. Alas, the killing left almost no survivors or descendants to remember them while reciting the words of the Yizkor or the Kaddish prayers, and to shed a tear in memory of the great, the terrible, the unimaginable destruction. They were annihilated through no fault of their own – just for being Jews.

We called the fields across the river Zemiana - "the New Polygon". "Polygon" - the name is well remembered by the inhabitants of the province. The former public officials also knew what had taken place there during the First World War.

Wooden barracks in a windy, open field, whose windows and doors were removed or their openings were sealed with wooden boards, where every wind and winter cold blew-in and froze both the body and soul.

Furnaces and heating materials were rare and limited. A high, double wire fence surrounded the whole camp and kept everyone locked in. Sentries, armed from head to toe, stood on guard to prevent anyone from escaping this "pleasure". A slow death. Hunger, distress, and cold were the destiny of these miserable prisoners. The prisoners were condemned, body and spirit, to absolute destruction. In short – a relentless, cruel death.

"The Master Race" of Goethe, Schiller, and Kant turned into the scholars of "how to enslave and destroy peoples". For this end they instituted a systematic reign of terror, in perpetuity, in organization, in action, with lies and with deceit! In partnership with their "quiet" Lithuanian collaborators, they hatched a comprehensive and final destructive system against all the Jews of the Sventzian region for the sole purpose of destroying them.

This unforgivable murder, fueled by such blind and ignorant hatred, was aimed at cutting down a fruitful branch of the Jewish people; the people of Torah and knowledge, honesty and justice, wisdom and morality.

[Col. 962]

We must not forget! We must tell and re-tell, again and again, to the generations that will follow us, what the Amalekites, the cursed nation, have done to us in our generation.

For the children of our country (=Israel), the children of freedom, it is impossible for them to grasp the enormity of the disaster, the quantity and the quality of what was taken from us. More than once they asked and wondered: "How could it have happened?" "Eight thousand people were led like lambs to the slaughter?" "No one revolted?" "No one reacted against a handful of murderous guards?" "What about the Jewish partisans? They showed their heroism against the enemy. Few against many! Did they not know what was going on?" Comprehensive and strenuous education is needed in order to convince them and instill in their minds all the factors and motives that existed at that time in the psyche and environment of the Jews. The methods used by the "Master Race" must be remembered! "Remember what Amalek did to you!" (The Bible, Deuteronomy, Ch 25, 17). We must remember what they did to our fathers, our mothers, our relatives, and to each of us and to all of our future generations.

It is impossible to cure a wound that refuses to heal, both in the heart and in the soul. Not while watching the pretense of the Germans of today! "We did not know what was going on." "It was not our hands that shed the blood". "This is the first time we hear about this cruelty!"

Lies and falsehood!

You are the accomplices to murder! Knowingly and unknowingly!

The murders of eight thousands, twenty, fifty, hundreds of thousands.

The millions you gathered into the ghettos, wherever your regime occupied and your boots goose-stepped down in our streets! "Kristallnacht" happened in your German cities. Under your noses! Did you not see and know? And you did not see the deportation of all the Jews of Berlin and of Germany, of Austria and of the Netherlands, the Jews of France and many more. Did not you notice or see?

Yes! Everything was done with knowledge, preparation and approval! As you have always been accustomed to "organize" your business! And now you want to declare that your hands are clean? And the loot they sent you home from the East! Where was it taken from? Did you care about those who were robbed and looted? Have you asked yourselves, in your heart, in your souls, whom you have made miserable? Have you inquired of your conscience who was the real victim, who had to pay so dearly?

And those freight trains, fully loaded cargo trains carrying human beings, extracted from all the countries of Europe, passing through your country on their way "to work"! Did you not see? Did you not care? This was done for the sake of victory for the Third Reich! This was done for your prosperity. This was done for your happiness. How could you profess such ignorance? Did your "pure and clear conscience" really allow such a thing and you to remain, forever, silent about it? And your well-known excuse that you acted according to the "orders" from above, not your fault! The German "push" has always been: "Expansion to the East ". Who was the first victim of the "expansion"? Was it not the Jew? This is your Teutonic nature!

"His hand will be against every man, and every man's hand against him." (The Bible, Genesis Ch 16, 12).

[Col. 963]

"Tell it not in Gath, proclaim it not in the streets of Ashkelon" (The Bible, Second Samuel Ch 1, 20) that you have no guilt! You destroyed the unprepared, the ones who could not resist, the weak - the Jew. So you knew of, prepared and carried out your "mission" - murder! Fearing no punishment, either by a court or by G-d's judgement. Not only did you murder - you robbed, you stole, raped, usurped their property and enjoyed yourselves.

There was a belief among the local Jews that their Lithuanian neighbor was peaceful and modest, simple and kind. That he was as innocent as a child who could not even count to two. Will he be dragged along with the wild incitement, the wave of abandonment and participated in the catastrophe about to overwhelm the local Jews? Was he like his other "brothers in religion" - the Poles and the Ukrainians? The Jews could not imagine such a thing. The Jews remembered how the best of their sons bravely fought for the liberation of Lithuania from the burden of Russian servitude (since the partition of Poland in 1793 and after the uprising in 1863). And how Lithuanian independence was achieved in 1919-1920.

With all their heart, the best of the Jews tried to help give freedom and liberty to the Lithuanians. When Lithuania rejoiced - so did the Jews there. For a while, the Jews felt as if they were in their own home, a part of that country. They established an extensive network of independent schools, recognized and supported by the government. All wholesale trade was usually directed by the Jews. The first independent government even included a Jewish minister. I remember how the Lithuanians entered our town after the agreement; everyone breathed a sigh of relief, recalling how good the Lithuanians were to the Jews.

This "ideal situation" held for no more than nineteen years and then the feeling changed to a bitter one. "Out of the sweetness came forth strong" (a play on words by reversing: "Out of the strong came forth sweetness" The Bible, Judges Ch 14, 14).

The Jews became accustomed to think, over almost 700 years, that their neighbors were gracious, peaceful and polite. So they helped them with good deeds and good advice, as was the custom with good neighbors. The Jew forgot the past. In his preoccupation with daily existence and the education of his children he set aside the knowledge that in the Lithuanian home, the baby absorbed the venom of hatred against the Jew, even with his mother's milk. The baby in his cradle heard a lullaby about "the Jew" - the devil. If you will not fall asleep - the Jew will come and take you away. In school, in church, on the street - every conversation between friends ended, of course, with a story about "the Jew".

The priest in the church incited against all the Jews, who had crucified the most exalted, "the Son of God," Jesus! The Jews were insulted, defamed, scorned for their wealth and for their happiness. This was accepted as a self-evident truth in their simple, uneducated, illiterate heads.

[Col. 964]

They said: "The priest always speaks the truth, the priest always says what is "correct". Even the most civilized and intelligent Lithuanian publicly expressed this popular statement, without being even slightly discomforted.

The hatred grew on fruitful soil, fertilized with a spate of hatred and envy for generations, nurtured from the times of the Middle Ages by various highly-positioned hooligans, during the Reformation, during the "Black Reaction" of Russia in the last century and the beginning of this century. It never diminished, even after the liberation of Lithuania from Russian enslavement, the liberation that was the result of the struggle by the best sons of Lithuania, including the Jews.

There were quite a few cases of blood libel, incitement and murder of Jews here and there. Thus the murderous Nazi doctrine, the "Crystal-Nacht doctrine", found such an attentive ear. This doctrine was expressed in the style of the despicable Nazi song "Horst Wessel": "while Jewish blood runs from our knife, do not stand by".

Forty local Lithuanian murderers, thirsty for the Jewish blood of those who had grown up with them in the same town and even the same street, led eight thousand starving, despairing Jews, without any resistance, like lambs to the slaughter. They led them to the sandy hill at the New Polygon, across the Zemiana River.

Jewish youth had flocked to the same hill, to a river that washed over its banks, to sunbathe in the sand during the “idyllic good times”. They enjoyed nature, talked, joked and swam in the river. They discussed and argued, each with their own views, over the brilliant future in the land of their forefathers. A time of peace among all people, a true future of freedom and radiance, understanding among all human beings, as prophesied by the prophet Isaiah: “And the wolf shall dwell with the lamb”.

The thread of life for all those who dreamed and hoped for a better, more sublime tomorrow, full of purity and splendor, freedom and redemption was brutally cut short on this very hill, on that fourth day of Sukkot.

The cruel collaborators, Asmodeus the king of the demons and the Christian inhabitants of the town, rejoiced at their “glorious victory” by actually participating or supporting the murders in their hearts. They eliminated the last of the handful of Jews from the villages surrounding Sventzian.

Eight thousands souls from the holy Jewish communities were wiped out from under the sky, between sunrise and sunset. The abominable murder, the “mission” in their language, was carried out with no sign of shame or remorse, in the full light of day.

With laugher and triumphant faces they publicly said: “It is finally finished ... Once and for all ... There will not be one Jew left in the world ... From now on we rule the future.” Not a single respectable resident raised a voice in protest, neither Providence nor the priesthood ... over these abominable and murderous acts. Pure lives were thrown into the abyss, forever.

[Col. 965]

Babies and young children cried their hearts out. Their screams did not reach the Creator of the world, they were not heard in heaven. As if thick layers of steel separated Him from the children of Israel and prevented Him from hearing them, He heard them not.

The cries remained embedded in the cold, frozen air. The birds, the crows, rose high above even the tops of the trees and tried to pass the cries on to the Heavens and beyond! Like a “cry in the desert”, lost in time.

The sound of the firing machine guns silenced the entire life of holy communities! The large grave, half a kilometer long, was covered by their Christian neighbors. Some of the people buried there were wounded but still alive.

The sons of the Huns, the Teutonic tribes, the successors of Goethe, Schiller, and Kant and the grandchildren of Genghis Khan, who once sowed death and destruction when they conquered Europe, erupted with pleasure on having the “opportunity” to show their “heroism” and to recall “past times.” The wild, foolish hatred of past generations bore their fruit.

This is so painful for us.

The world must remember this dreadful disgrace forever. Remember and not forget!

[Col. 966]

We must tell and recite, again and again, to our children and to future generations and to the children of all the nations of the world, what the contemporary Amalekites did to us! The Nazi-German people and all other peoples who took an active part in the annihilation, as well as the other unenlightened people who did not lift a finger in order to save or even protest against the annihilation! A few tried to intercede directly or indirectly, but most just sat by "with a clear conscience" until there was no one to save.

Today it is we who are being annihilated - tomorrow it may be you. Today, terrible evil has smitten me but tomorrow it may hurt you as well if you will not stand up to and help eradicate this evil which exists.

Remember what the Amalekites did to the whole nation, to our loved ones, our disciples, the wise men of Torah and tradition.

They died as martyrs, sanctifying the name of G-d. They died because they were Jews.

Shema Israel!!

The blood of our martyrs in Europe cries out here in my homeland. I will remember what the Amalekite has done ... fire in my heart, fire forever.

[Col. 967]

How Shall I Dip My Pen in Blood...

Arie Popiski

Translated by Dena Man

My pen, how can I dip thee in blood,
My words, how can they be illuminated when all I see is an ocean of
blood,
And in the middle of this fire,
There is no sound, no word, no dialect to describe
The sea of humanity who choked on their own blood.
I hear babies playing, I hear their groaning,
I will watch over them in their final resting place. I will remember them with great sorrow.

I will look around me, spring is coming, a new leaf, a new bud blooming,
The treetops, bright, covered in dew,
The tree has new leaves, refreshed and green,
But I can only remember?
I sit amongst red sunsets that echo your pain.

My pen, how can I dip thee in this sacred blood, the Holy blood
That has been spilled,
I am forced to dip my pen in blood, so your memory is sharp and not forgotten,
The flow of your blood has no melody, there is no dialect it can use
To forgive or to shock,
Blood has its own language, a sound of sadness
The orphans are "screaming" from the earth,
Sounds that will never be silenced.

[Col. 969]

Ignalina

(Ignalina, Lithuania)

55°21'/26°10'

[Col. 973-974]

Jewish Shetlach[1]

Chaim Grade

Translated by Janie Respitz

The sky was a prayer shawl woven from your prayers
But your moans drastically tore the fabric of your quiet melodies;
You lived with a reflection of untold dreams,
Like the shine of daylight in a dark well.
The thresholds of your houses block the abyss;
You sold herring to the peasants...but the ten commandments from Sinai
Lit up your shops.

Jewish towns from Poland and Lithuania, you lit up my heart and memory,

Just like the Bible shines on the places in the holy land,
My childhood crosses my home river barefoot – and it became my Jordan...

Therefore there is a ruined Western Wall – my every wall.
Scribes would calmly write Mezzuzot on parchment
With goose feathers and gall ink,
And we would knock on the doors – a solution, they should not chase us from the land.
There was a humming in our melody – the autumn wind.
We were twisted in the fields like a golden chain,
And as a result crucifixes on the road were wrapped in a circle dance;
We sowed tress for our grandchildren
As if the land was our own –
But the neighbours all agreed, we should take the wood from our prayer house
To repair the bridge on the river,
And pave the way with our tombstones.

Translator's footnote:

Towns

Grandfather's town

by Avraham Krill

Translated by Meir Razy

Ignalina was a town like all other towns in Lithuania and Poland. It was founded at the end of the 19th century when the railroad line between Warsaw and St Petersburg was laid in the area.

As soon as the railway station was built, dozens of Jewish families who had previously lived in various villages in the area, began to flock to the town. Slowly, the Jewish community grew to 120 people, including 8 large families. The social composition was already an example of a classic Jewish town.

One of the first families was that of Shalom Leib Gordon, who later managed to control the wholesale trade of the town.

A unique character was Rabbi Aharon Chayat, who received a weekly salary for agreeing to be the first person to be buried in the new cemetery.

In addition, he was paid when he was included as the tenth person in a Minyan, or when he agreed to do the "Aliya to the Torah" in the "Tochecha" week (= the weekly Torah reading that includes many curses, Deuteronomy chapters 26-29).

The geography of the place affected the business and livelihoods of the Jewish population. The area was mountainous, surrounded by mountains and lakes on all sides. Some families lived only on fishing. They leased fishing rights to the lakes from the landowners and then sold the fish in Vilna or in the nearby towns.

One family made a living from cattle trading. The animals were led by foot to Vilna, although the distance was more than 100 kilometers. After the end of the Sabbath they would leave the town and arrive in Vilna on Tuesday morning. The cattle were corralled in the Horowitz family's yard on Antakoli Street.

The cattle merchant from Ignalina was known all over the area and farmers from all the surrounding villages came to trade with him during market days.

During the busy season, between Hanukkah and Passover, most of the inhabitants of the town were engaged in the cattle business, some directly and some indirectly. Some were agents or cattle walkers, some were guards and some worked in the slaughterhouse. The most famous of them was Fibke, the skinner.

A loyal servant to the group of cattle dealers was the slaughterer Rabbi Hanna Bin z"l, one of the sons of Abraham Katz of Doglishuk[Daugelishak].

Rabbi Hanna was busy in the slaughterhouse until noon and then he would go to the synagogue to teach Torah.

[Col. 975]

He also influenced the rest of the slaughterhouse workers and many of them became educated. Rabbi Hanna was always proud of his entourage. Rabbi Hanna would also walk to Rimchetzna near Duksht[Dukstas] to slaughter cattle and chickens for Shabbat.

Some families owned lime and brick incinerators. The division of labor was this: they burned lime and bricks during the summer and in winter they produced turpentine and grease ointment from pine resin. Some famous forest merchants came from these families and they sold railroad ties and pillars for bridges.

These traders were led by Berl Soloveitchik and Shalom Leib Gordon.

The Jewish community in Ignalina had a unique social character. The leadership role was in the hands of ordinary Jews, not necessarily the rich ones. Public affairs were handled by those who were seated around the synagogue's stage, not the wealthy men who had their seats "on the stage's east side".

The local market played a central role in the town's economic life. Market days took place every Thursday and many merchants as well as different types of businesses actually survived only from the revenues of this day. Craftsmen, such as shoemakers, diggers, and blacksmiths, received most of their orders on market days. Tailors were hired by the peasants for a whole week and they were paid not with money but with various produce.

It is worth mentioning one very interesting character from the market days - Pesia the baker. She was selling large variety pita bread: with onion or poppy seeds, with holes or smooth. She used to bring her products to the market early in the morning.

Vendors of cold drinks, such as apple juice or lemonade, would gather around her on hot summer days.

The peasants would go to the various inns to sip liquor in the afternoon. The result was that there were dozens of drunks in the town by market closing time. The clowns would call them "Elka's Gentiles" after the woman who sold resinous wine. Since it was forbidden, she used to keep the liquor in the tea samovar.

In time, this market became one of the largest markets in the province. The town was next to a train station and merchants came from far away and sometimes, sometimes even as far as Warsaw.

Large commercial buildings and various partnerships were established in the town. The most famous were two merchants, Korb and Israelowitz, who supplied agriculture and construction equipment and supplies just as business was done in the big cities.

The training drills of the firefighters, which usually took place during the summer months, played an important role in the social life of the town. These exercises also brought some excitement to the town: the bright brass helmets of the firemen, the glittering buttons, the big water tanks pulled by the horses and the sound of the trumpets energized the town for a few hours shaking it out of the doldrums that usually covered it. In addition, the Firehouse Hall served as a cultural and entertainment center for the town residents.

After the First World War, the Zionist movement began to develop. Yehuda Halperin, a beloved and intelligent man, a true Zionist and an enthusiast, arrived at that time and began assembling the nucleus of the first Zionist group in the town around him.

[Col. 977]

He gave public Torah lessons every evening and conducted Hebrew and Jewish history classes. In addition he even organized Gemara classes.

A public school was established in Ignalina after the war, where the language of instruction was Yiddish. An excellent Public Library of 1,500 books was built next door. It had a Reading Room that was open to the public every evening with various daily newspapers and magazines in Yiddish, Hebrew and Polish.

A very successful dramatic group operated next to the school. It performed plays from Yiddish literature and its income was dedicated to supporting the school and Library.

Little by little, youth organizations, especially Zionist ones were founded. They educated the town's residents about the pioneering spirit of national fulfillment in our ancient Homeland.

Many of the trainees immigrated to Israel and are living a life of labor and hard work here.

An independent training commune, recognized by the “Hechalutz” Center in Poland, was created near the town. It is interesting to note that despite the fact that all the teachers and cultural institutions were subject to a more “Yiddish” influence, most of the youth were educated by the Zionist movement and the “Hechalutz” in Hebrew.

After the end of the First World War and with the help of the YEKAPO, a Credit Fund was created in Ignalina. This fund played an important role in the economic life of the town. Among its founders were Mordechai Cessler and Gavenda of the Great Synagogue and Rabbi Hillel Krill of the Hasidic shtibl.

The Accounting Manager of the fund was Rabbi Aharon Chayat. This position provided him with an additional income above the salary he received from the synagogue and from the concession he held for selling yeast.

The entire public would go to the bathhouse every Friday and the on eve of the Holidays. There was real democracy in the bathhouse, and there was no difference between Yaakov Shlomo the wagon driver and the rich man Bromberg, the only owner of a two-story house in town.

The bathhouse was not only for bathing, but it was a place to discuss public issues and to argue about political problems.

In the summer, however, people did not go to the bathhouse but flocked to the lake shore instead. Vacationers from big cities used to come to town during the hot summer months. They rented apartments in the woods and enjoy their vacation near the lakes.

This was how life in Ignalina, private, public, and cultural life proceeded until the great oppressor destroyed and annihilated everything.

God will Avenge the blood of all the innocent victims who died for the Sanctification of God's name during the great and terrible Holocaust in the years 1941-1943.

[Col. 980]

The Origin and Development of the Town

Yerakhmiel Korb

Translated by Janie Respitz

In 1862, in a forest that belonged to the nobleman Kaminsky about 4 kilometres from the towns of Gavikan and Paliush, a train station was built called Ignalina. The station was on the railroad line that connected (St.) Peterburg and Warsaw, at the intersection of

Vilna – Dvinsk, and was not far the towns of Old and New Daugelishak. The first Jew to settle in Ignalina was Zvi Gordon. He leased a piece of land from Kaminsky and built a house and a store. He began dealing in lumber. He brought salt in special wagons and would sell it to the shopkeepers in the surrounding towns. In order that the wagons did return empty, he would buy various wheats, seeds and flax from the peasants and would export to the larger cities, even out of the country. A few Jewish workers and employees worked for Gordon. At his request they settled in Ignalina and this is how a Jewish community began near the train station.

The first Jewish settlers were: Mikhl Postavski, Bitshunsky, Moishe Peretz Guterman and Nekhemiah Brumberg.

The last one was actually the manager of all of Gordon's businesses and left a large impression on the small community. A bit later, other Jewish families from surrounding villages began to arrive. Among those who settled were, Nekhemiah, the father of Moishe – Yose Soloveychik from Zabartze who began to work as a butcher. Eliezer Kraytzer, who laid stones for the railway.

The blacksmith Henekh Reichel from Vidishok. Yehuda Kril from Budri, who would bring mortar. Mikhl – Yerakhmiel, the tailor from Tzeikin; Shloimeh Ikhiltsik, who bought up the bark from a leather factory in Dvinsk and Abba – Yitzkhak Gurvitch.

Meanwhile, Nekhemiah Brumberg bought a small piece of land from the nobleman on the other side of the railroad in Zalesia. He built a house and a store. He was followed by other Jews including Moishe –Yose Soloveychik and Berl Gilinsky and a community was established on the other side of the tracks.

[Col. 981]

The town grew day by day. Businesses were opened as well as handicraft workshops and warehouses. Quickly, Gordon, the wealthy man, bought another house and organized the first Minyan. (Quorum of ten Jews needed for prayer). He also built a wash house. It did not take long until the small community decided to bring a Rabbi and officially establish a new Jewish community.

The first Rabbi in Ignalina was Moishe Aaron Chait, a young man from Kurland, who had studied in the Lid Yeshiva and received his ordination from Rabbi Yakov Yitzkhak Raynes of blessed memory.

Rabbi Moishe Aaron Chait was the son–in–law of Rabinovitch, the owner of the tobacco factory in Svencionys.

The old nobleman Kaminsky died. His huge fortune went to his son Vincenti who served in the Pope's Guard in Rome.

He immediately returned from Italy to take over his father's businesses. The young nobleman was a playboy who enjoyed whisky and cards.

In order to have a lot of cash, he sold some properties and rented out other places. Thanks to this, Ignalina began to spread in all directions. Tens of houses and stores were built.

By 1903 there were more than 30 Jewish families in Ignalina, around 200 people.

In 1905, it was decided that every Thursday a market would take place in town. This is how Ignalina became a business centre.

Peasants and peddlers would come to the market from all the surrounding towns.

Ignalina soon became a town like all others.

[Col. 982]

The market brought in great revenue, and the Jewish population became well established.

The town continued to grow and no doubt would have developed further had not the First World War suddenly broken out. This immediately stopped the growth of the newly founded Ignalina.

The Economy

During the First World War the first line of the front was not far from Ignalina. Whoever had the opportunity, left town. The Germans took whatever they could from our town. They sent wood, wheat, fruit and other life sustaining goods to Germany.

There was great poverty and many families suffered from hunger.

No one in those years remembered how the town once was. When the Germans left and the town was occupied by the Red Army, the situation did not improve.

Only when the Polish authority arrived and created a border between Poland and Lithuania, the people of Ignalina caught their breath, and life began to develop again.

The Paliush Lake was on the border. The Jews of Gavikan and Paliush made a good living from it, but they did not want to live so close to the border, so they moved to Ignalina.

This is what the marketplace looked like on every day of the week. It looked different on Thursdays when the fair took place. Merchants would come from the surrounding area, set up stalls with various goods and loud noises would fill the air. The colours of the various fabrics, wool products, peasant ribbons, kerchiefs, clothing and rugs sparkled. Hanging on poles were boots and sandals, caps and hats, pelts and jackets that Jewish artisans brought from their poor workshops, together with the red hot colour of the peasant's beads that shone a light on the pearls of the modest kerchiefs, wigs and necks of the Jewish women.

The Marketplace

The new residents of the town, the Gilinskys and Eynhorns brought their fish and lumber businesses. The situation began to improve. There were always Polish military in Ignalina and Jewish merchants supplied them with meat. It provided all the butchers with work.

Soon the butchers in Ignalina were supplying meat to other military camps. The town became a meat business centre. A few years later they were transporting meat to Vilna and Warsaw. Those involved were: Hillel Kril, Yose Gendl, Aaron Soleveychik, Ruven Cohen, Dovid Ritveh, and Yosl Eynhorn. This was a cooperative subsidized by an organization (YEKOPO) in Vilna.

[Col. 983]

Ignalina also became the centre of smuggling with Lithuania. They would send manufactured goods and industrial products, and from there bring sugar, pepper, saccharine. These items were much cheaper in Lithuania than in Poland.

The Muskin brothers had a big wheat business. Yisroel Noyekh Aron dealt in skins and leather.

[Col. 984]

Yose Rapaport, Tevye Solomiak, Ruven Kuritsky and other Jewish merchants dealt in fruits and berries that were sent to Vina, Warsaw, Lodz and Katovitz.

The lumber industry held an important place in Ignalina. The families involve were: Gilinsky, Korb, and Berl Soloveychik.

Jewish Folk – Shul 1922

Seated in the middle: **The Board of Directors – Khaim Gilinsky, Nekhemiah Brumberg, the teacher, Bere Gilinsky, Dovid Eynhorn**
From right: ____, _____, _____, **Shaul Kuritsky,** ___, ____, ____, **Velvl Kril, Moishe Korb, Avrom Soloveychik,** ____, ____, **Shmuel Dubinsky, Ruven Brumberg, Dovid Postavsky,** ____, **Yisroel Gilinsky, Khaninya Bitshunsky,** ___, ___, **Nosn Shapiro, Rivke Gilinsky, Rokhl Eynhorn,** ___, ___, **Binyomin Aron,** ____, **Moishe Eynhorn,** ____, ____, ____, ___, **Yitzkhok Gilinsky,** ___, ___, ___, ___, ___, **Rivke Dubinsky,** ___, **Etke Gilinsky,** ___, ___, ___, **Rayzl Gilinsky,** ____, ___, ____, **Feyge Elperin, Beyle Soloveychik,** ___, ___, ____

These seven "good years" did not last long. In Poland in general, and particularly on the estates, a difficult crisis broke out and Jews were caught in the middle. The Jews in the towns suffered greatly from the expulsion – politics of the Polish government. It was not only the merchants who suffered, but the artisans as well.

This ruined the economic situation of Ignalina. According to the records of the Vilna YEKOPO from 1928, there were 250 families living in Ignalina, including 150 Jewish ones.

The Jews were involved in business, storekeeping and handiwork. 47% worked in stores and small business and 23% were artisans.

[Col. 985]

The Christian cooperative brought down the Jewish businesses. Because they received cheaper credit from both the banks and the government, it was easy for them to compete with the Jews. Besides this, the cooperative was also supported by the township. The cooperative also had a lending and saving treasury.

In the town there were two Christian stores and all the Christians shopped mainly there.

The surrounding villages also had small cooperatives so it was not necessary for the peasants to come to town to shop on market days. We have to keep in mind that the surrounding area was very poor. The terrain was sandy and covered with forests. There were also many lakes.

This goes to say that the village peasant was very poor and his buying power was minimal. Even the dealings with wheat, seeds and superphosphates were in the hands of the Christian cooperative.

The expulsion process also harmed the Jewish artisans. The Jewish shoemakers, tailors and blacksmiths suffered from the competition of the Christian workers.

The only branch where the situation was not bad was in the meat business.

The lumber business that had always been in Jewish hands was slowly being taken over by the government, resulting in many Jews losing their jobs.

[Col. 986]

All the above mentioned reasons impoverished the Jewish community. Many lived off aid they received from relatives in America.

Social and Cultural Institutions

Before the war, the Jewish children studied in Heders like everywhere else. In 1910 a Jewish Folk – Shul was founded, which had a modern and traditional teacher. The founder of the school was Shloime Krytzer with the help of Heshl Gurvitch from New–Svencionys.

In 1922 the school officially joined TSYSHO. By 1925, 52 children attended the Jewish school. Since the Tsysho was anti–Zionist, the Zionists in Ignalina opened a Tarbut school in 1928 which quickly developed. The town had 2 Jewish elementary schools. The graduates of both schools would go on to study in Vilna in the local seminaries and high schools.

A branch of HeChalutz (Zionist youth group)

Lying down: **Moishe Korb, Zev Kril, Moishe Soloveychik**
Kneeling: **Eleh Soloveychik, Dobe Katz, Rivke Sharfman, Frume Krimilisky, Khane Elperin**
Standing: **Feyge Elperin, Khane Gilinsky, Khanokh, Rokhl, Rayze Gilinsky**

Ignalina had a fine Jewish intellect. There were useful cultural organizations, including a Jewish public library which had a collection of Yiddish and Hebrew books.

The leadership of the youth looked for ways to raise the cultural level in town.

To reach this goal they founded a horn orchestra, which had a great reputation in the region.

[Col. 987]

The sports club and fire fighters also helped to enrich the social life in town. Both "Hechalutz" and "Shomer Ha Tzair" were founded as well.

Finally, we must mention two economic institutions which helped ease the life of the Jews in Ignalina between the two World Wars. They were: The Jewish People's Bank, and the Interest Free Loan Society.

[Col. 988]

The Jewish population had to work very hard to earn a living, teach their children and carry out certain cultural activities.

The departure of Khane Elperin Shnayder

Eliezer Shapiro, Basia Gilinsky, Avrom Aron, Feyge Elperin, Rayze Gilinsky, Khasye Rapaport, Hene Elperin, Nekhe Gordon, Feyge Dubinsky, Tevye Tzinman, Rivke Sharpman, Rokhl Eynhorn, Esther Gilinsky, Leah Rapaport, Rivke Bank, Shloime Kuritsky, Khaya Soreh Rabinovitch, Khave Lukner, Shayne Shnayderovitch, Rokhl Rapaport

Jewish People's Bank of Ignalina (Written in Polish and Yiddish)

Seated: **Shayne Shnayderovitch, Dovid Ritvo, Hillel Kril, Khone Ruven Liberman**
Standing: **Motl Tsesler, Berl Gilinsky, Ruven Kagan, _____, Tevye Solomiak, Lipke Tsesler**

Gathering of HaShomer HaTzair
New–Svencionys, Podbrodz, Ignalina – 1928

[Col. 989]

People, Streets and Organizations

Yitzkhak Viduchinsky and Ruven Muller

Translated by Janie Respitz

Ruven Muller

Yitzkhak Viduchinsky

Similar to many other towns in Lithuania, Ignalina had 14 streets and only half of one street was paved with cobblestones. This went from the train station until Yisroel–Noyekh Aron. Half of the other streets also had the privilege of having wooden sidewalks.

A large fire bell hung on a pole. The houses were small and built from wood. The only house with a fence belonged to Nekhemiah Brumberg.

There was no electric lighting in town. Small gas lamps hung from ceilings and stood on dressers. The large house of prayer had an extra bright oil lamp which was used for Chanukah and other celebrations.

Many poor people lived in our town. If someone would bring a chicken to the ritual slaughterer mid– week, everyone would ask: “who is sick?”.

In town there were various artisans, peddlers, teamsters and also merchants. The youth, facing great poverty, but with courage and stubbornness, looked for a way to improve their tomorrows.

The economic situation was difficult, often hopeless, but the youth did not give up. They carried on with cultural activities and filled their hearts with faith and confidence.

[Col. 990]

Ignalina did not have a rich history. There was not even a church. The land belonged to the nobleman Kaminsky, who had a son Ignatz and a daughter Galina. The new town was named for both of them: Igna–Lina.

Ignalina was blessed with a picturesque landscape, surrounded by a chain of lakes, beautiful pine forests, and short hills. The road to the town's lake was lined with a row of tall, thick trees. Many families from Polish cities would come for the summer. In the surrounding pine forests, Polish scouts from Krakow and Warsaw would set up camp. During the Second World War, when Ignalina belonged to the Lithuanian–Soviet Republic, people from Leningrad would come for the summer months.

The Main Street. The Big Misnagdish Synagogue

[Col. 991]

There are fourteen lakes within 4 kilometres of Ignalina, making it a fishing centre. Some Jews were involved in the fishing industry. The Jews that leased the lakes were: Shmuel Yosef Gilinsky from Paliush, Leyzer Gavenda from Meran, Shloime Gavenda, Berl Gavenda, Shloime Gilinsky from Gavikan, Zalmen Yidl Soloveychik, Uria Katz, Meir Yosef Glaz, Yoel Gilinsky, Khaim Shneiderovitch and others.

The Jewish fishermen would spend days and nights on the lakes catching fish, that would be sent by train to Vilna.

Forest– Merchants

In the winter, various types of wood were brought from the forest to the trains by horse drawn sleighs. They were brought to the sawmill then exported throughout the land and to other countries as well. Those who worked in this field were: Berl Soloveychik, Yisroel Soloveychik, Yitzkhak Soloveychik,Herzl Gurvitch, Shmuel Gilinsky, Yerakhmiel Korb, Meir Gilinsky, Dovid Soloveychik and others.

Meat–Merchants

Business of meat and chickens was run by Hillel Kril, Eynhorn and others who sent the meat to various larger cities in Poland.

[Col. 992]

Wheat–Merchants

The Mushkin brothers, Vinyunsky, Moishe–Yitzkhak and Nekhemiah Brumberg transported a variety of grains to the mills including flax which was sent to textile factories.

The Market

Market day in Ignalina was Thursday. On this day all the shopkeepers, blacksmiths, shoemakers and tailors awaited merchants and shopkeepers from the surrounding towns and did business with a variety of goods, produce, cows and horses, goats and chickens.

When the sun began to set, the noise quietened and everyone did his calculations from the day. The peasants harnessed their horses, the shopkeepers counted their profit, businessmen looked at their bargains and butchers inspected the cows and calves they bought. Everyone was pleased market day was over.

Sometimes it happened, the peasants would begin drinking and noise and fights would ensue. The Jewish boys would stand and watch them taste their own medicine.

[Col. 993]

Cultural and Educational Work

The first general Jewish Folk–Shul was founded in the early 1920s in a small room in the home of Avrom Rutshteyn. The founders were: Bere Gilinsky, Nekhemiah Brumberg, Yosef Eynhorn, and Khaim Gilinsky. The teachers were: Shloime Kraytzer, Levinson and Vengrov. At the same time the beadle for the prayer house, Chaim Sneiderovitch, taught the boys bible studies.

The Jewish Folk–Shul 1930

At the same time a library was founded and a drama club was organized. The participants were: Herzl Gurvitch, Dovid Soloveychik, Dobe Kraytzer, Dvoyre Soloveychik, Shteyn, Dobe Katz, and Gershon Kideshman. When the Tarbut School was later founded by the cultural organizers Yerkhmiel Korb, Leybe–Khaim Elperin, Milkhiker and others, a second drama club was founded. The leaders were Moishe Soloveychik, Elke Gilinsky, Rivke Sharfman, Rivke Gilinsky, Sholem Gilinsky, Yosef Gilinsky, Rokhl Eynhorn and others.

[Col. 994]

The Board of the Jewish Folk–Shul

Seated: **Gershon Kideshman, Soreh Soloveychik, Dvoyre Soloveychik, ____, Mikhle Vaynshteyn, ____, Dovid Soloveychik, Freda Gurvitch, Avrom Vaynshteyn, Pola Viduchinsky, Bayle Katz, Yudl Viduchinsky, Khasye Vaynshteyn, Zalman Katz, Sholem Gilinsky**

Political Organizations

The first political organization founded in our town was "HeChalutz" (the Pioneer). The founders of HeChalutz were:

Avrom Kril, Tevey Rapaport, Sholem Gilinsky.

Tarbut School

Lying down: **Shloime Hamer, ____Perlmuter, Etl Rayn, Dogim,___Itzikson, Gavenda, Asne Dubinsky, Dovid Aron, Leyb Korb, Dovid Gavenda, ____, Libke___, Tsivia Gdud, Monke Gurvitch, Biteh Litovitch, Khasriel Rayn, Taybe Rapaport, ____,____, Mikhal Perlmuter, Zvi Gilinsky, Rivke Milkhiker, ___,___,___, Rokhl Itzikson, ____Landa, Reyzl Gavenda, Khaya ____, Pesia Aron, Leyble Itzikson, Tevye Brumberg, Yisroel Ilitovitch, Etl Itzikson, Zise Shapiro, Berl Gilinsky, Mordkhai Gurvitch, Dovid Rayn, Eliyahu ____, Ruven Rayn, ___, Yitzkhak Postavsky, Avrom Opeskin, Zvi Khaim Postavsky, Sholem Aron**

Standing: **Simkha Dubinsky, Henekh____, Rivke Sharfman, Rokhl Eynhorn, Elke Soloveychik, Khana Gilinsky, Frume Krimilsky, Moishe Soloveychik, Khana Leah Elperin, Moishe Korb, Rokhl Kril, Eliyau Gdud, Fayge Elperin, Vanyunsky, teacher, Y. Kaplan, Miriam Golub, ___, Rayze Gilinsky, Mikhal Sharfman, Velvl Kril, Bayle Soloveychik, Etl Gilinsky, Yente Krimilisky, Esther Kril, Rivke Gilinsky**

In the middle: **Yiroel Korb, Ruven Aron, Yitzkhok____, Dovid Shayderovitch, Shprintze Korb, Ite Elperin, Sonia Milkhiker, Hertz____, Shmuel Shapir**

[Col. 995]

Pioneers in the land 1925
Zaman Bernshteyn, Yitzkhok Shutan, Avrom Kril, Motl Vilkomirsky

"HeChalutz" built an agricultural training camp on the shores of the Green Lake.

Besides Hechalutz, there was also the revisionist Organization in Ignalina. Its founder was Dr. Yosef Rubinshteyn. Those active were: Aron Gilinsky, Ruven Muler, Eliyah Korb. The last one went to the Land of Israel and enlisted with L'Chai. He was arrested, exiled and suffered greatly at the hands of the British.

There was also an illegal Communist party, where there was vivacious activity. For their Communist activity Gavenda was sent into exile to Kartuz Bereze and Ruven Brumberg was sent to prison.

[Col. 996]

The Football (Soccer) Team

The team was comprised of: Yoyne Gavenda, Sholem Gilinsky, Khaim and Feyve Gilinsky, Shmerke Kuritsky, Aron Gilinsky, Yakov Dogim and others.

The People's Bank

The People's Bank was part of Vilna Central. The following were involved: Tsesler, the chairman was Hillel Kril. The bank allowed the poor Jewish people to stand on their own two feet.

A football team in the First World War

Pioneers in the Land 1926
Yosef Kuritsky, Yisroel Tsarnatsky, Avrom Kril, Yitzkhok Ligumsky, Yehuda Perevaznik

[Col. 997]

Volunteer Fire Department

The volunteer Fire Department in town was comprised mainly of Jews. The firefighters formed a horn orchestra that played for all the Jewish organizations no matter which political movement. The orchestra also played for Jewish weddings and Christian gatherings. Heading up all of that activity stood Abba Katz.

[Col. 998]

The Fire Department

Seated: **Sholem Leyb Gordon, Yerakhmiel Korb, Meir Muler, – Captain Ber Gilinsky, Abbe Gilinsky, Abba Katz, Eliyah Gdud, Yudl Vidutshinsky, Gershon Segal, Dovid Soloveychik**

"HeChalutz"

Lying down: **Dobe____, Rayzl Gilinsky,___,**
Seated: **Moishe Korb, Frume Krimilisky, Elke Soloveychik, Yisroel Korb,____Postavsky, ____, Khane Gilinsky, Berl Hamer**
Standing: **Esther Kril, Miriam Golub, the teacher Rokhl Eynhorn, Shaul Okun, teacher___, Feyge Elperin**
Standing in the back: **Etl Gilinsky, Velvl Kril, ___, Moishe Soloveychik, Velvl Gilinsky, Yose Leybshteyn, Yente Krimilisky**

[Col. 999]

The Religious Life

When the town was founded there was a Misnagdish (Rabbinic) prayer house and a Hasidic prayer group. When Jews arrived in Ignalina from Gavikan and Paliush they brought their brought their two small synagogues with them. That is how Ignalina gained four places of worship. The Rabbi was Moishe Aron Chait who was ordained by Rabbi Raynes. The Rabbi was in fact quite liberal and understood the youth.

For a long time, the ritual slaughterer in town was Reb Khone Katz. He was a quiet, calm Jew, very good natured, ignoring the harassment by the authorities in Ignalina, and in the last years before the war, displayed a strong drive for life. We saw the first graduates from the Vilna High School, the Tarbut High School, and Oks High School. Students came from Vilna University.

[Col. 1000]

In the summer, great literary figures would come to Ignalina like Avrom Sutzkever, Shmerke Kacherginsky and others. They would stay at the Jewish pension near the first lake. Members of the Vilbig choir would enrich the cultural activity in town. The festive letters received from the Ignalina pioneers in the Land of Israel awoke and uplifted the spirits of the people. All these budding hopes were destroyed by dark, black powers. 600 Jewish souls from Ignalina, Paliush and Gavikan were annihilated.

Pioneers from Svenciony and Ignalina

Lying down: **Ruven Muler, Etl Gilinsky, Shifra Layfer, Pine Shulhoyfer**
Standing: **Moishe Korb**
Kneeling: **Rokhl Eynhorn,Berl Gavisser, Frume Krimilisky, Khana Leah Elperin, Eliezer Shapiro, Velvel Zaydl, Khana Gilinsky, Rayzl Gilinsky, Lale Yovitch, ___, Khasia Rapapport, Kaplan the teacher, Leyb Zesiantik, Velvl Sharfman, Sholem Kuritsky, Moishe Eynhorn,Gurvich, ___, Dovid Postavsky, Velvl Kril**
On the side: **Dvoyre Soloveychik, Moishe Ginzburg, Itzik Gilinsky, ___, Elke Bikson, ___, ___, Moishe Soloveychik, Dovid Shapiro**

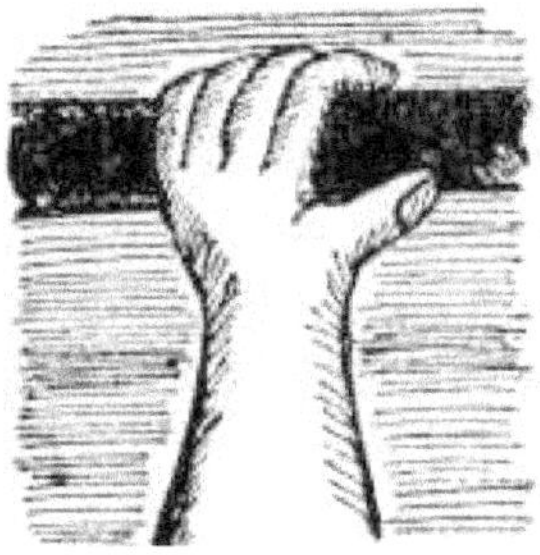

[Col. 1001]

Beautiful People from My Town of Ignalina

by Dvoyre Leyzerovitch – Kraytzer

Translated by Janie Respitz

I left my beloved town the 20th of March, 1935. That day is well etched in my memory. My sisters and friends accompanied me to the train. They were jealous that I was going out into the big world. My parents were worried about me. Everyone wished me well. The train arrived and I had to board quickly. Before I knew it the whistle blew...Adieu to my beautiful home. For a long while I looked out the window at my dear ones. Only as the last dots of Ignalina disappeared from view, I sat down. I arrived in Eretz Yisrael and quickly settled in. I slowly adapted to the new life and new surroundings. However, I could never forget Ignalina. Until today it is clear in my memory. I see the beautiful pine trees, the high mountains and the beautiful lakes. Above all I remember the green lake, where we would spend our Saturdays, until late at night.

[Col. 1003]

Kheyders and Schools

I remember my childhood years in Kheyder. There were two in our town: One run by Shmuel the teacher, who taught the boys. His wife Mirl – Leah was also sort of a teacher, and she would teach the girls. The second Kheyder was more modern. The teacher was Reb Shloimeh Yitzkhak. I had the privilege to go to the "modern" school. Reb Shloimeh

Yitzkhak was a strict Jew. He had a black beard and always wore a long black coat. His house was on the outskirts of town, near the lake.

We had to be in Kheyder all day. We returned home late evening. Christian boys would throw rocks at us on our walk home. They would also call out in hatred: Zhid! (Dirty Jew).

Learning in Kheyder was a hardship. Our teacher would curse, shout at us and even beat us. He would argue with his wife and take his anger out on us.

A few years later two Folk – Shules were founded in Ignalina: One – where instruction was in Yiddish, and was affiliated with TSISHO, the Central Yiddish School Organization. The second had instruction in Hebrew and was affiliated with “Tarbut”.

The organizer and head of the Yiddish school was my brother, Shloimeh Kraytzer. The school was housed in the women's section of the Shul and had great financial difficulties.

In order to exist they organized a drama club. The proceeds from all the performances would go to the school. The first production was Sholem Aleichem's drama: “Scattered and Dispersed”. The lead actors were: Dovid Soloveichik, Vidutshinsky, Eleke Eynhorn, Gershon Kadishman, Herzl Gurvitz, and my brother Shloimeh Kraytzer.

Shloime Kraytzer
The organizer and leader of the
Yiddish school and drama club

Ha Shomer Ha Tzair
Standing: **Tzinman, ____, Hinda Dogim, Rivka Milkhiker, Pesia Oron, Shprintze Korb, ____,Ritvo, Khaya Shneyderovitch, Taybe Rappaport, Khaya Khatkelevich**

When Yehuda Halperin, a passionate Zionist came to town he had a great influence and convinced the well off to start a “Tarbut” school.

The leader of the Tarbut School was Yerakhmiel Karb. The Zionist youth supported the school and held lotteries and events to help with financial support.

A stubborn battle persisted between the Yiddishists and the Zionists that continued up until the outbreak of the Second World War.

[Col. 1004]

Respected Members of the Community and Communal Activists

One of the finest people in Ignalina was the wealthy man Reb Sholem Leyb Gordon. All of his children studied in Vilna and would only come home for holidays and summer vacation.

After the First World War Sholem Leyb's business failed and he endured difficult times. Besides this, his wife passed away, his children remained in Russia and he had a difficult old age.

Another very different upstanding man in Ignalina was my father Reb Eliezer Kraytzer, may he rest in peace.

He had a long beautiful beard. One day he was attacked by hooligans who cut off half his beard.

He was a proud Jew and a great scholar, honest and just. Everyone would borrow money from him. If someone did not pay he back in time, my mother would intervene and my father would extend the terms of payment. There were times when a Jew would receive a second loan before he paid back the first.

My father worked with stones. He would buy fields from the peasants and remove the stones. Therefore he had a lot of labourers working for him.

[Col. 1005]

The stones were delivered by train and my father travelled often to St. Petersburg. He had many business contacts there that treated him with great respect and honour.

My Father's Passover Seder

I have very fond memories of how my father led the Passover Seder.

A few weeks before Passover things began to change in town. First of all, nature was changing all around. The sun was stronger melting the snow and the frozen lakes.

Cupboards and kitchen utensils were bring removed from the Jewish homes. People hung out their clothes. Everything was being shined, scrubbed and cleaned. There was a great hullabaloo from Khaya Taybe's Matzah bakery. My mother, may she rest in peace, would cook a feast for all the workers in the Matzah bakery.

First, they baked for the wealthy families and were well paid. During the last week they would bake, without pay, for the poor.

[Col. 1006]

During those days, all the youth of the town would gather in the Matzah bakery. The boys would knead the dough, the girls would roll it out. During the last days they would bake egg cookies.

The day before Passover there was a joyous mood in town. All the shined dishes were back on the shelves. All the houses were sparkling clean.

They finished Koshering all the utensils in Khaya– Taybe's ritual bath. Everyone returned home with their silver spoons, forks, knives and cups.

Early in the morning we ate dairy rolls and then quickly threw away the last things that were not Kosher for Passover (Hametz). Every corner was sparkling. My father would bring down a basket from the attic with all the Passover dishes. Everything had a special charm.

My mother would put on her flowered apron and begin to cook the special Seder meal.

"HeChalutz"
Moshe Korb, Feyge Elperin, Eliezer Shapiro,
Khaya Soreh Rabinovitch, ____, Dobeh Katz

At lunchtime, we had a tradition of eating a prune Tsimes (stew). We were not yet allowed to eat matzah.

In the evening the men went to the synagogue. My mother would put on a black silk suit with a gold chain around her neck. We thought she was a real queen.

All the children wore new clothes and shoes.

The Divine presence was felt in every corner of the house. The Seder table was set with a white tablecloth. Two candles flickered from the shiny candlesticks. The greens were placed on a decorated plate.

When the men returned from synagogue they happily wished everyone a good holiday and we quickly sat down to begin the Seder.

My father was overjoyed. He read the Haggadah with a special, excited melody. When others would go out for a walk late that night, they would hear how Reb Eliezer Krytzer was still leading his Seder. Only around midnight could one hear the melody of Khad Gadya (the last song), from our house.

[Col. 1007]

Rabbi Reb Moshe Aron Khayt, may he rest in peace.

Rabbi Khayt, the Rabbi of Ignalina was a tall Jew with a long beard and a great scholar. He was an enlightened man, not a fanatic. The very religious said he was worldly.

Our Rabbi read a newspaper every day and the youth of the town liked him very much.

His wife was a beautiful woman who ran a business from home. She sold yeast. In those days, almost everyone baked their own Challah for the Sabbath. This was their main source of income.

Reb Yisroel – Noyekh Aran, may he rest in peace.

Reb Yisroel Noyekh was a broad shouldered Jew, who was a butcher. He came from a small town called Rimshan near Duksht. He married Golda, the daughter of Reb Shimon Ikhiltsik. Not long after their marriage, the First World War broke out and he was mobilized into the Tsar's army. He was later taken prisoner and returned home after the revolution. He then began to deal in cattle and became a well –known merchant in the region.

He had no education and would do all his accounting in his head. It was said he did calculations much better than a bookkeeper and never made a mistake. Saturday night after the Sabbath he would leave home and travel to all the markets and fairs in the area. He would return home Thursday evenings exhausted.

In his few free days he was involved in community affairs: It must be remembered he played a captive role in the founding of the Tarbut school.

He had five sons and one daughter. In the last years he bought land outside of town and built a house. Finally he reached a time in his life to rest on his land, but these good, quiet days did not last long.

The outbreak of the war changed the economic situation and restrained his energy.

[Col. 1008]

When Hitler's beasts arrived, he fell into great despair. He did not have the patience, like the other Jews to experience the suffering of the Ghetto.

Reb Yisroel Noyekh decided he would not leave his estate alive. When he realized there was no way out and lost all hope in a miracle, he took his own life. He hung himself from a tree not far from his home. May his memory be a blessing!

Reb Abba Yitzkhak Gurvitch

Like many others in Ignalina who came from surrounding villages, Reb Abba Yitzkhak came from Labentzeh, where his parents, Reb Yisroel and Henia worked the land. At the end of the village, a house stood which stood out from the other homes in the village on the Sabbath. Candles glowed, the garden was decorated with yellow sand and the animals rested in the barn.

On Saturday, Reb Yisroel would walk with his children to a nearby community to pray. His older children were sent to study in larger towns. Reb Abba – Yitzkhak was sent to study in Vidz and there married his wife Asnah. When Ignalina was built they decided to settle there. He dealt with lumber, mushrooms and berries. He was of middle size, with thick eyebrows, worried eyes, and a long, grey beard. He wore a black Hasidic hat and a long jacket and walked with quiet steps. He spoke quietly and chose his words carefully. He was a passionate Lubavitch Chasid and well learned. The room where he would learn was decorated with a picture of Baal Ha Tanai.

When the bell in his spice shop would ring, indicating there was a customer he did not want to leave his studies and would send his wife Asnah to deal with the customer.

He went to pray with his fellow Hasidim three times a day. He died in 1927. May his memory be a blessing.

[Col. 1009]

Mendl Soloveichik

Reb Mendl Soloveichik was a handsome Jew with a partly shaved small beard. He was a smart man, proud and very strict. At first he dealt in bark and wood and lived in a small house. Later, he lived in a nice house in the marketplace and opened a restaurant.

All the peasants from the region would come to him to eat and drink. His restaurant was always full.

He had 5 sons and 4 daughters. His wife Slaveh was always working and exhausted. She did everything alone. She baked bread, cooked fish, fried various foods and never left the kitchen.

His sons were real heroes. The youngest was called Noyekh Fandreh, after a main character in a book by Zalman Shneour.

The young beautiful Slaveh suddenly fell ill. She suffered for three years and in the prime of her life she died leaving Mendl with 9 small children.

The tragedy is hard to describe. The entire town was deeply saddened by her death. Everyone, old and young went to her funeral.

In her eulogy, her death was compared to a sinking ship carrying many people, suddenly hit by a storm and everyone drowned.

Reb Mordekhai Tsesler

He was a tall, thin Jew who wore glasses. He would always wear a brown suit. He came from Lida and married Soreh, the daughter of Shloimeh.

He was an enlightened man. People called him: The learned Jew. (in Russian).

They had a textile business. His wife would mainly stay in their shop while he worked at the bank and the free loan society. On market days and at fairs, he would come and help her.

[Col. 1010]

On the High Holidays he would read from the Torah in synagogue. He knew everyone's name including their father's and grandfather's.

He had great problems from his work in the banks and the loan society. When someone did not pay back their loan on time, he had to go collect. This would often end in cursing and shouting. Those who owed money did not want to understand that he was just doing his job and it was not his fault they could not pay their debts.

He worked 12 hour days and was always tired.

Once a year he would receive furlough and he treasured this. Even when things in town were crazy, he never passed up his vacation. “Don't bother me, I'm on leave” – he would always say.

Yosef Avigdor the Coachman

He was a short Jew with a thin blond beard. Winter and summer he wore big boots, and a hooded cape tied with a rope. He lived in a small house near the lake. His wife Feyge was well educated. She could pray by heart and would read psalms to the other women.

Yosef Avigdor would wait all day at the train station for the stagecoach. When it would arrive with a wagon filled with flour or corn, he was very happy.

Besides this work at the train, he was the regular wagon driver for Reb Nekhemia Brumberg.

Every evening he would go to the synagogue and recite psalms. He had his own melodies and would repeat them many times.

With tears and pain, we now remember our dear town, which no longer exists, where many honest, hardworking Jews lived. The German executioners and the Lithuanian bandits destroyed our Ignalina, and murdered our entire Jewish community.

May God take revenge on their blood!!!

[Col. 1011]

The Courageous Self-Defense

by Heshl Gurewitz

Translated by Anita Frishman Gabbay

The shtetl of Ignalina was built on the left side of the terminal and the railroad station, which ran from Dukst to Dvinsk. Over time, most of the Jewish folk came to live in this area. Here all the stores were opened and the market day took place every Thursday. On the right hand side of the railroad, several Jewish families also lived until the first world war: Moishe-Yose the butcher with his extended family, Nechme Brumberg and Bere Gilinski.

From the family of Moishe Yose Soleveitchik , through his writing, gave us accounts of those good and proud Jews whose lives were filled with hardships and who endured such adversities to befall these unfortunate Jews.

Being still a child, I always loved to visit Ignalina, because many relatives on my fathers side lived there. Often I would visit my uncle, R' Abba Yitzhak Gurewitz, who was a ...and Hassidic Jew. Also I was a very good guest, I behaved myself when I visited the families of Moishe Yose and Mendl Solevechik. I was very honest and when confrontations occurred, I would be called upon to the shtetl of Ignalina by the young Jewish friends.

One Thursday during market day, I saw the son of Moishe Yose and some of his Jewish friends, confronted by some crazy hooligans. From this time forward, it was known not to antagonize the Jewish youth of Ignalina. All the peasants of Ignalina now knew that we were no push overs.

Onetime a policeman wanted to arrest one of these friends, and it was stopped. The policeman was shamed by this: a Jewish youth beat him up.

[Col. 1012]

One time a policeman came to my uncle Abba Yitzhak Gurewitz, in the marketplace, to control that he didn't sell any liquor. Instead, he found a few packages of tobacco, which we were not allowed to have at home, only in the shop. He didn't know what do, so he sat at the table prepared to make a report. Zelman, my uncle's son, protested and didn't allow him to file his report. So the policeman immediately called for some help and to remove Zelman from the house(arrest). When I saw this I immediately ran out and yelled for help, and from these loud calls for help, immediately my group of young Jewish friends arrived in order to help free Yose Moishe's son. The policeman was told that if he didn't leave here at once, that all his bones would be broken. It didn't take long for him to decide, and he left my uncle's place immediately. The others also left.

Another time when I was visiting, my uncle Moishe Yose bought a cow from a peasant and paid for it, when the peasant suddenly changed his mind. A great quarrel enfolded. Schlomo, the son of Moishe Yose, suddenly appeared (like out of the earth) and gave the peasant a few whacks, and the peasant, bloody, fell to the ground.

This indicates that the Jewish youth of Ignalina were never intimidated (walked with their heads bent over). No deed was left unattended, all the Jews looked after one another in this town. We were always ready and able, just and eager. All the hooligans (Christians) in Ignalina knew that they would be dealt with.

All these antics were already known during the Czarist regime, that Jewish blood and Jewish belongings could not be taken and that they would defend themselves from hooligans and bandits.

This was a warning from our Jewish brethren and Jewish town!

[Col. 1013]

The Rabbi of Ignalina Moshe – Aharon Khayt

by Dr. Yosef Even – Odem (Rubinstein)

Translated by Janie Respitz

The Rabbi of Ignalina, Rabbi Moshe – Aharon Khayt was a person of stately appearance, with a snowy – white patriarchal beard. Hi speech was well thought out, like our sages. He was a true scholar. Sometimes, after a late night visit to a patient, I would see the

Rabbi swaying over his Gemorah through the window. I would go in to discuss Torah or secular subjects...incidentally, the Rabbi knew the Rabbi's I had studied with in my father's house (privately, not in a Yeshiva) – all three were heads of Yeshivas in Vilna. They would come to our home every evening to teach me and my brother for two hours.

The Rabbi from Ignalina knew Rabbi Reb Menakhem Mendl Kozlovsky from his youth, my first head of Yeshiva (from Rebbe Mayle's Yeshiva in Vilna). I remember the joke he would often tell: "Children, Chew cheese!" This was a play on words from tractates of the Talmud. I would have "chewed cheese" for a long time with Rabbi Kozlovsky had he not suddenly launched an Agudah – political sermon in the synagogue, without my father's knowledge, against the San Remo tragedy of 1920, where the "Zionist" Balfour Declaration was confirmed...(This was the same week the Rebbetzin Esther Rubinstein held her impressive "San Remo Speech" in front of 5,000 people in Vilna's Circus – Amphitheatre)

[Col. 1014]

...In conclusion, after such an Agudah "Putch" our studying with the unlucky Rabbi, Reb Menakhem Mendl, could no longer continue.

All evening I told the Rabbi of Ignalina piquant details about the head of our Yeshiva, the Shnipisher Rabbi, who was known in Vilna as the genius, Rabbi Meir Shnipisher (Rabbi Meir Basin), who was quite a pious wonder. He was a clever philosopher who read Emmanuel Kant in German and even understood! And what would permit him to leave Kol Nidre, the fumes from the memorial candle, which he could not tolerate...my father responded to him, "Kol Nidre is really nothing", only a custom, not law, but here the Shnipisher Rabbi did not want to separate himself from the community, that could not comprehend his "violation of Kol Nidre"...Reb Meir Shnipisher would explain simply in Hebrew: You children (already grown students...) should speak correctly, with proper grammar, with correct vowels. I will however say it as I always have until my death...and in science (medicine or chemistry or mathematics), he would add: what do you say? Not so correct? Did our sages not know, but you now know better!

[Col. 1015]

After the death of Rabbi Meir Basin, his successor, Rabbi Moshe Karelitch attacked his "students" very aggressively and without compromise: How do you know all this? From your secular books? From your university? Now listen to what I have to say to you! But there was nothing to hear. After all his "complicated calculations", for example, in the Talmud Bava Batra, the "seller of the house" would always be lacking a piece of land which my brother would always find (having already graduated in mathematics and chemistry before he graduated from medicine...). Until one day, also Rabbi Moshe Karelitch received an immediate "eviction" from my father's house. He exploded when he learned of the opening of the Hebrew University in Jerusalem, he spit with great bitterness and said: "Luckily the Zionists steal money from the Jewish Agency, if not, they would destroy the entire Land of Israel!". Understandably, such a "declaration" did not fit the political stand of Rabbi Rubinstein who was chairman of the Jewish Agency in Poland and a member of the Board of Trustees of the Hebrew Univeristy. Rabbi Karelitch had to "resign" as Talmud teacher of his two students...

[Col. 1016]

How could I have never imagined that the Prime Minister from my State of Israel would go to the brother of my fanatic Rabbi, the leader of Agudah, the great visionary?!

I found a document from one of my long answers from the Rabbi of Ignalina, (typed), written in a pseudo biblical affected style, with half quotations. Here is an excerpt, with all its mistakes:

Translated by Meir Razy

"Peace and blessings upon you, dear and supreme Rabbi and respected wife, peace from Zion to all her lovers[1], who rejoice in her happiness, and to all her mourners. I have seen Tel-Aviv (being) built, built magnificently, may there be peace within its walls and security over her[2], and I saw 'the Glory of the Carmel' in its splendor, its multitudes and its tumult, and I saw Jerusalem again and I mourned her, as she is still in shame and disgrace. Her walls are breached – but shall a nation be born all at once, for as soon as Zion travailed, she brought forth her children[3]. Our sages, in another generation, prophesized truly that the salvation of Israel commences slowly and in small steps, and the more it progresses the bigger and faster it becomes.[4]"

Rabi Yehuda Halevi (1075-1141): On the Sea, Poem #7

Psalms 122,7: May there be peace within your walls and security within your citadels.

Isaiah 66 8: Who hath heard such a thing? who hath seen such things? Shall the earth be made to be brought forth in one day? or shall a nation be born all at once? for as soon as Zion travailed, she brought forth her children.

Talmud Yerushalmi, Berachot, Chapter 1

[Col. 1015]

The Poetess of the “Lakes of Ignalina”

by Esther Rabinovitch

Translated by Janie Respitz

In three separate language domains I continued with my Hebrew writings with great enthusiasm. After a day of work in my medical practice, I devoted my evenings to Hebrew.

Firstly, I work on philology and etymology, comparing Hebrew to other Semitic languages (above all Arabic). Right from the start I was delighted to find hundreds of words of pearl and language diamonds the famous Orientalists had not noticed or recognized. I realized my discoveries would be useful in furthering and widening our very long neglected Hebrew language.

Secondly, I worked, in Ignalina on new plan to reform Hebrew writing, which I spent much time thinking about on long winter nights.

[Col. 1016]

Thirdly, I began to write Hebrew poetry...

From the time I began writing poetry, I wrote quickly, with a good grasp of the language. The first person to recognize my work was the well know Hebrew teacher and poet from Vilna, Dovid Levin, may he rest in peace. He published a few of my children's poems. Another supporter of poetic talent was Herman Shtruk, the world renowned artist.

From 1917 until 1932, over a period of 15 years, I slowly collected a volume of poems, which doubled in size in 1933 in Ignalina, until 1935 in Menakhemiah. By 1936, in Tel Aviv, I already had two volumes – together with a third volume from and unfamiliar poet colleague from Ignalina, Esther Rabinovitch, may she rest in peace.

Before I left Poland, and before she “left” this world, she gave me her volume of

[Col. 1017]

Hebrew poems with the hope I would publish them in Eretz Yisrael. I felt freed from this burden (or her last will) the moment I burned my own poems.

Everything depends on luck, especially a book of songs from a Hebrew poet. Who now even remembers the well – known Russian poet Gretta Yelisaveta Zhirkova – “Eli Sheva” – who was forgotten in her lifetime and died lonely near our Kinneret in Tiberius...Who does not know the luck of “Rachel”, whose name rings out due to the heartfelt melody of her poem “My Kinneret”...the unknown poet “Esther”, from my small town of Ignalina, did not have luck. Had she not met the “good doctor” (who could not help her) but a good composer instead, she may be remembered as the famous "Esther" from the "Lakes of Ignalina" (a sort of Kinneret). Esther Rabinovitch was remarkable, similar to Rachel Blaushteyn. They both died of Tuberculosis, they both began as translators, Rachel from Hebrew to Russian, and Esther – from Russian and German to Hebrew. (I can attest to the fact that her translations were truly masterful, like from the German poet Ludwig Uhland), and both tubercular poets struggled with their original poetry and despair.

The end of my "poetic career" is due to Herman Shtruk:

He once invited me to visit him in Haifa. Arriving at his beautiful villa, I thought it over and decide not to appear before this great artist and old friend...until today I don't know the reason why, – not just because of my "Zionist Congress German"...because my German was not so good, even though in Vilna I spoke a perfectly correct German with Herman Shtruk, the language in which the religious, traditional leader of Mizrachi, after 15 years in Israel, still spoke and wrote.

[Col. 1018]

Returning to Tel Aviv from Haifa by train, in a creative, poetic mood, I un – comprehensively, and quickly, wrote a very comprehensive long and "poetic poem"...in a true biblical style, in an enthusiastic language, allegorically playful and philologically blooming. (Filled with wonders of the language)...my attempt at improvisation pleased me. Upon returning to my hotel, I sat by the open window, near the noisy sea, rewrote the poem, declamatory, like an orator. This was my stormy "Open Letter".

During my first two years in Israel. I became accustomed to the editor they always sent me to, the well- known Yehuda Karni, may he rest in peace, and I know why...(I met him at his best friend's house, Alter Droyanov, may he rest in peace) when I paid him a "Contra – visit" in Tel Aviv, after his "visit" to my father in Vilna, a year earlier, when I arranged for him a grandiose reception with 200 invited guests from the Jerusalem of Lithuania.

[Col. 1018]

An open letter to Zion

by Shulamit Beit–Halachmit, at the women prison

Translated by Anita Frishman Gabbay

Zion, why won't you ask to the farewell of your prisoners
The prisoners who let you shine
The victims who are prisoners behind your gates
Zion. Won't you redeem your writers and teachers
The mother's soul is right, many of my sons have empty hearts

What can I do with my sons as I can't fulfil them?
Is it therefore you observe and judge them and their mothers?
And if you are silent and tearless, will you still call her mother
Mother of Zion, if you won't rise high and let your voice be heard
Then they will fear, and you won't be seen from your place
The voice of the bereaved who lost their sons will hide in their homes
There will be orphans and we will call you and rip upon you

[Col. 1019]

How I Parted From
My Small Town of Ignalina

Dr. Yosef Even – Odem

Translated by Janie Respitz

Today I will tell you about the large goodbye evening, organized in my honour by the Christian intelligentsia in Ignalina.

When the Christians learned I was planning to leave for Palestine, they decide to organize a "goodbye ball" for me. I learned this from the priest Grizhas, as I travelled home with him after a visit to his sick sister. On the long journey, the priest told me all the praise said about me among the Poles, who were upset I was leaving Ignalina. My Christian friends had already decided to mark my departure with a large dinner, but there were many doubts...the priest coughed lightly and stammered: our food is not Kosher, and we know who you are...you are the son of an important Rabbi, the chief Rabbi of Vilna. Perhaps it is not appropriate...even if you are a smart doctor...

In order to keep the peace (as we are instructed by Reb Yehuda Hanasi in the Mishna) I immediately told the priest that the question of Kosher and non – Kosher has nothing to do with being smart, and it is not, God forbid and anti – Aryan question, which I would explain to him...and then, in order to gain time to think of my answer for his Christian supper, I told the priest about my father's "friendship" with the priest Palkovsky, the rector of Vilna University, who would visit my father at home, and sometimes visit the Hebrew girls' school, which was named for my mother. This is how I introduced the priest to the Esther Rubinstein Hebrew School in Vilna, the light of our culture, past and future.

I would like to take the opportunity of the rector – priest Polkovsky's visit to the school to tell how my father built the school across from the big church "Holy Jan", and a few meters from the main university building, and "Napoleon's Palace", the residence of the Governor of Vilna: the interesting thing about the address of the girl's Hebrew School was that it was on the intersection of the Holy Yan Street and the Gaon (Genius) of Vilna Street.

[Col. 1020]

In the centre of town, at the Catholic Church and University Street, hundreds of Sorelakh and Rivkelakh (little Jewish girls) would meet, as they streamed out of the Hebrew school together with hundreds of Polish students from the university, at the same time in the afternoon, in front of open and hidden anti – Semites among the Polish students, professors and priests.

I told Father Grizhas (a friend of the Jews) how my father would meet with rector Palkovsky when he would leave the university. My father would often take him for a longer visit in the school, showing him how the girls, big and small, speak, write, play and sing, free and lively, in the "dead language", Hebrew...Unbelievable! Impossible! The priest – professor Palkovsky was astounded. Hebrew – that is the most difficult of all the three holy languages from antiquity (more difficult than Latin and Greek), of which he hardly remembers anything from what Catholic priests had to learn. He only remembered the conjugation of the verb to slaughter. Father Grizhas laughed as remembered also having to conjugate the same word. Here I added another example of a verb...a priest is called a Galakh in Hebrew because the root of the word comes from the verb to shave. Listen Father Grizhas, my friend: and I conjugated to shave for him in Hebrew.

[Col. 1021]

We both laughed heartily, and he whipped the horse –

Then the priest remembered my going away party. At first I decided not to accept this honour from my Christian friends. Who knows how they will behave and this would leave me with bad memories of my Jewish town Ignalina? But suddenly I changed my mind. Yes, good, Father Grizhas, I accept the invitation from my Christian friends. They don't have to worry about me. Let them eat all sorts of pork. Let them prepare for me a variety of fruits and vegetables.

The "ball" was really very beautiful, prepared from the heart, sponsored by the nobleman Marian Poniatovsky. We ate a lot, and drank a fair bit too. There was singing and dancing and understandably there were speeches, long and short, humorous and serious. Father Grizhas spoke as did the police commander Krasovsky, the director of the school Kamarovitch, and Captain Zavadsky, the military doctor. Also Major Rudmansky and others. The main thing, at the end – "me too" understandably! I had prepared a speech for the "banquet ball".

I began with Ignalina, then right to Palestine, to our "promised land", recently promised by Lord Balfour, and the age old promise from God to Abraham...then I jokingly jumped from "the land of milk and honey" to tasty "pork", to the Torah and the laws of Kashrut. All of my Christians friend looked bewildered and surprised...But yes! God alone made the Jews abandon the tasty pork in the Garden of Eden. Why is this animal called

Khazir? (Hebrew word for pig, which has the same root as the verb to return), so they will return to Eretz Yisrael and eat pure pork! Now every Jew can eat pork. But “unfortunately”, the Jew must ask, what can I do if God forbids it! The command of Moses, our great law giver was an historic necessity, to differentiate the People of Israel from all the idol worshipping nations.

[Col. 1022]

And then, the horrible Roman Empire that persecuted us (as you Christian later did), was later referred to by Jews as “Pigs”, which meant: blood thirsty, unfeeling, dirty, crass animal!

And here I told the tragic–comic “non–Kosher episode” about Rabbi Meir, who I presented as a “well–known Rabbi and a Jewish Revolutionary patriot”, who the Romans recognized in the street and wanted to arrest him! Rabbi Meir calmly walked into a non–Kosher restaurant where he licked his fingers from Roman foods...No, that is not Rabbi Meir said the Roman gendarmes, Rabbi Meir would have sooner gone to the claws of the Roman “Pigs” than eat pork!...But it really was Rabbi Meir, who tricked the Roman police: He put one finger in the pork and licked another...All my listeners burst out laughing. The priest and the police commander laughed harder than everyone.

This is how I ended my speech. Jews cannot make peace with a hateful ugly pig, under any circumstances, in this world, even if his meat is very tasty, if God promises, in the next world, in heaven, together with the Leviathan and the wild boar...so my Christian friends, for you, the pig does not disturb your religion or national feelings, I wish you a good appetite at my beautiful goodbye evening, where you honoured me!

My half serious, half joking speech was received with long applause. They continued to tell my pork speech in Ignalina for many years. It particularly stirred the sensitive Christian pharmacist who was very proud of the pig's afterlife, as I had explained was God's promise....This is what I was told, years later by the head of the Ignalina Jewish community Yerakhmiel Korb, when he visited me in Herzliyah, when he arrived in Israel after surviving the Nazi – hell.

[Col. 1023]

The Tragedy of Yerakhmiel Korb and His Heroic Son Eliyah

in an Open Letter to J. Macdonald

Translated by Janie Respitz

After Yerakhmiel Korb arrived in Eretz Yisrael, his entire correspondence with his son Eliyahu was brought to my attention. Through my mediation, the S.A.D had to mention my name, and I recounted the big miracle that I experienced. I remained free for the long two years (1945 – 1947). I could have easily sat (in jail) "for nothing" just like Eliyahu Korb "sat and sat" without any chronological system and without any court judgement.

With bloody tears, already in his anticipated and expected Eretz Yisrael...Yerakhmiel Korb wrote to me: Dear Dr. Rubinstein, you shared with me there was a letter from Eliyahu – I spoke to your people, and they draw from me ...blood. I don't know if I will live to see my Eliyahu, I don't know..."Yerakhmiel Korb did live to see Eliyahu, but unfortunately his joy was short and tragic. He died embittered after a long and difficult heart disease.

The year was 1946, the time of the English – American commission that was sent to Eretz Yisrael, to decide her fate, and the future of the hundred thousand survivors of Hitler's victims from all of Europe. I found it absolutely necessary to direct this "open letter" to the influential Zionist – English newspaper "The Palestine Post", to the important member of the commission, James Macdonald. I had the official stenogram published on an official United Nations page, a strong warning against Hitler's Swastika moves against the Jewish people – that James Macdonald heard at a special meeting of the High Commission for refugees, when he himself was High Commissioner, for refugees at the United Nations.

[Col. 1024]

The impressive speech was given by my father, Senator Rabbi Rubinstein – November 2, 1935, in London, coincidentally on the day and in the same city the English Foreign Minister, Lord Balfour delivered his famous Balfour Declaration concerning the Jewish national homeland in Eretz Yisrael. At the time, my father wrote me a long letter, and sent me the official stenograph of his speech.

James Macdonald expressed his recognition of my father's activities for the German – Jewish refugee problem, at a press conference in Warsaw, which I enclosed in my letter to Gershon Agronsky in order to persuade him that the mention of my Father's speech in London could really make a big impression on James Macdonald (who would later become the first American Ambassador to the State of Israel). I asked in my "open letter" to the former High Commissioner of Refugees if he does not admit, that the High Commissioner of the United Nations, at that big meeting chaired by Lord Cecil ten years earlier (1935) had made a terrible mistake, when he did not call upon Senator Rubinstein's rescue appeal, to open the doors of our national land "at least for German Jewry", who were totally destroyed.

At this opportunity, in my "open letter" I included some impressive, shocking lines about Yerakhmiel Korb (not only "demonstrative", but really wanting to help the former head of our Jewish community of Ignalina), with the request to allow the old, unfortunate invalid to enter the Land, a victim of Hitler, whose son, who is interned in Sudan, asked me to help save...

[Col. 1025]

In the Struggle for Liberty

by Eliyahu Korev[1]

Translated by Meir Razy

Eliyahu Korev in the camp in Kenya

Dr. Yoseph Rubinstein arrived from Vilna to serve the community as a physician. The Revisionist Party was created in our town under his influence. The list of the party activists included Aharon and Hersch Gilinski, Gershon Katz, Yoseph and Yerachmiel Leibstein, Shmuel Shapira, Yoseph Isaac, Israel and Eliyahu Korev Reuven Muller and his sister Mina.

In 1938 I received a message from the Beitar (=Brith Yosef Trumpeldor youth movement) Governing body that I was allowed to immigrate illegally to Eretz Israel. I, of course, agreed immediately. Our transport group included about nine hundred people and our road took us through Romania.

Our ship wandered over the Black Sea for three weeks[2] before it had hit an underwater boulder and started to take in water. It took four hours for the help to arrive. I was one of the last people to leave the ship that sunk shortly after.

The ship that picked us up had already wandered on the sea for two months. Several people died of hunger due to lack of food and the little stock was quickly diminishing. The conditions were catastrophic! We arrived at the shore of Netanya where we let the people who had spent the longest time on board to get off first.

[Col. 1026]

When the ship returned the next morning to Netanya it was "welcomed" by British bullets. Later we were disembarked on the beach of Kfar Vitkin.[3]

I joined the Beitar troops in Netanya, Hadera, Rosh–Pina and Yesod HaMa–ala. I worked planting tobacco at Yesod HaMa–ala, but the hard work made me sick and the doctor forbad me from more work. I was released from the Beitar troop.

I went to Petach Tikva to see Abraham Krill, who received me very graciously. Afterwards, I met Shneur Korev who was a manager in the orchards of Nes–Ziona and I started working in the orchards there.

When the war started I dedicated myself to LEHI (=Lohamei Herut Israel, "The Fighters for the Freedom of Israel") and after some activities they nominated me to be responsible for the weapon storage depots we had in many places in the country.

I was arrested in Netanya on October 31, 1943. I was charged at the court in Petach Tikva and was found innocent. The invading British Storm–troopers were not satisfied and brought me to the court in Yaffo. After some investigation they moved me to the jail in Jerusalem.

Manifesto: How they tortured him

This is a detailed story of Eliyahu Korev, since he was arrested until his release when the State of Israel was declared in 1948, in the following concentration camps: Latrun,

Eritrea, Sudan and Kenya (according to the book “The Fighters for Liberty of Israel's” volume 1).

For the Public

How the young Hebrew Eliyahu Korev was tortured by the invading British Storm–troopers and their Law Keepers.

Young Eliyahu Korev had already been held by the British police for four months and twenty days when, on March twenty–first of this year, he was taken from jail in Jerusalem at 10:30AM. The troopers first took him to a house next to the jail and from there – out of the city (we assume: to Beit Lechem or to the Police Academy on the road to Beit Lechem). The torturers had waited for him there and around 11:30 they started. These are the details:

They started with strong slaps to his cheeks. Each slap was followed by banging his head against the wall. They then stripped him naked and poured water all over his naked body. They started beating him with a leather–covered steel stick. They beat him all over his body until he fainted.

[Col. 1027]

Prisoners of Zion in a camp in Kenya. They were exiled there by the British Mandate Government on Eretz–Israel

He regained consciousness after they poured water on him and then they continued beating his head with that stick until he fainted again. They revived him with water and immediately continued with a new type of torture: they placed a wooden board on his lower left back and started hitting it with large pliers, intending to damage his kidneys.

The board broke after a few dozen hits. The troopers replaced board with a thick plank of wood and continued hitting it until the tortured man fainted again. They revived him and started a new type of torture: they hit his genitals with the steel stick. He fainted several times, and each time they revived him and continued the torture. They lifted his body several times by pulling him by his genitals, and this sadistic behavior was not enough for them. The criminals found a new method to abuse their victim.

Hitting a person's larynx with a flat hand will immediately cause him to faint. Each time they poured water on him and eventually he laid in a puddle of water. They rested for fifteen minutes and started a new type of torture: two troopers stood on his hands, two – on his legs and the fifth one pulled him by his testicles until he fainted. This time they revived him by pulling his ears. They continued torturing him until sunset. The tortured man was close to insanity. His body was bloated, covered with black marks, he vomited blood and blood came even out of his anus. He felt pain in all his internal and external organs and had problems breathing.

[Col. 1028]

The following day, March 22, they came back. This time they tortured him "only" for two hours, but now they added a new torture: whipping his buttocks and the bottom of his feet with the steel stick. The body of the young man showed no resistance. On the third day of torture, March 23, the troopers came again but they tortured him somewhat less. They "waterboarded" him by forcing his head into a bucket of water until he started choking and getting water into his lungs. They then pulled him out of the water and let him cough the water out. When they decided he coughed enough – they repeated the treatment of drowning him and reviving him by pouring water and pulling his ears. By the time they left him he looked like a lifeless heap of bones. He fell down where he was and laid on the floor unconscious until the night.

At night they took him somewhere for "recovery" and continue torturing him in the car.

In the new location (we assume – Ramle) they hit him a few times and left him to "recover" half naked on a mattress. He had to relieve himself where he was because he was not able to go to a bathroom. He could not eat because of the internal injuries and pain. A medical doctor checked him and gave him an injection. He did not eat anything for seven days. He was kept under guard, without seeing the light of day, suffering pain, hungry and half naked for four weeks until, on April 22, he was brought back to the Jerusalem jail. On May 2 the young man was transferred to the detention camp in Latrun.

Let the public see and judge if there is any difference between the Teutonic Nazi animal and the "democratic" British animal!

Lohamei Herut Yisrael,
"The Fighters for the Freedom of Israel"

Manifesto

The statement of the First Minister of the Government of Palestine (Eretz Israel) during his meeting with the chief editors of the newspapers, that the British police do not use torture to extort confessions from prisoners **is a lie**. The facts of the torture of the young man Eliyahu Korev that we had published in our manifesto to the public **are true in all their details**.

Let it be clear to the rulers who use lies to cover the bloody frenzy of the animals working for the secret police (CID) that cruel torture will not break the spirit of the Hebrew fighters. Those who are responsible for the methods of torture and their executioners **will pay** for their deeds.

The Underground in Zion, Tamuz (=May) 1944
The Fighters for the Freedom of Israel

Translator's footnotes

In Hebrew he is called "Korev" but in the necrology the family name is translated as "Korb". I assume that he changed his name when he arrived at Eretz Israel, maybe even earlier.

Ports all over the world refused ships that carried Jews who had escaped Europe and had no entry Visas, forcing them to wander.

Meir Razy, the translator's home–village

[Col. 1029]

From the Shtetl Ignalina to the Science Prize in Israel

by Pesach Yifar

Translated by Meir Razy

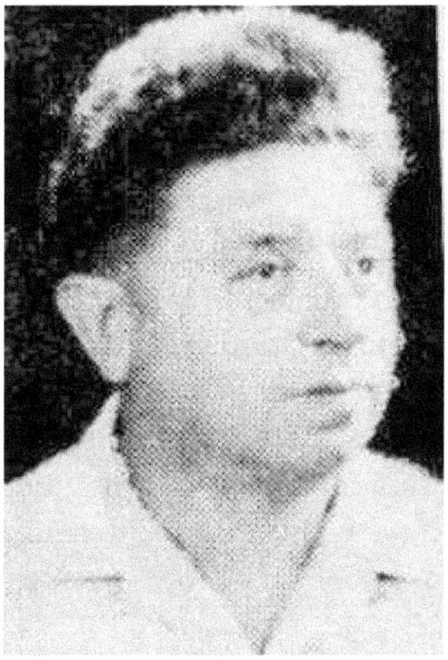

The city council of Herztliya in its meeting on January 28, 1962 decided unanimously to bestow Doctor Yoseph Even–Odem the first and the largest Literature and Science prize, in the sum of 1,000 Israeli Pounds. A public reception will take place at the "Acadia Hotel", with hundreds of attendees from the city of Herztliya and leading Israeli writers and linguists, members of the medical establishment and professors from the medical school of the Hebrew university in Jerusalem.

The prize is given to mark 25 years of dedicated, excellent work of Doctor Yoseph Even–Odem as the City Medical Officer and the manager of city's clinic since Herztliya became a city. This Literature and Science prize is given to mark his excellent linguistic skills and his great success as a researcher and innovator of the Hebrew language and the scientific–medical language in particular. Doctor Yoseph Even–Odem published about ten books over many years covering thousands of pages of Hebrew terms. He did this at his own expense of tens of thousands of Israeli Pounds, money he saved from his salary as an employee. The Mayor of Herztliya lists the reasons for granting him this big prize:

From Ingnalina to a Scientific Prize in Israel

Here are the summaries of two reviews published in the daily newspaper "Davar" in 1954 and 1955 by Dr. David Arie Friedman Z"L, the veteran editor of the "Medicine" publication. Dr. Friedman was a famous writer, a literature and art critic and a member of the City of Tel–Aviv selection committee for the Bialik Prize. These are his reviews of Doctor Yoseph Even–Odem's work:

“Doctor Yoseph Even–Odem's life–work of collecting useful terms in his ten volumes of his book series shows knowledge, understanding, depth and momentum. Beyond his knowledge of the medical subject he showed broad understanding in Arabic, Syrian, Aramaic and Hebrew of different eras. This made him, a single person, the equivalent of a Language Committee. He is very knowledgeable and the reader should enjoy the sharp knowledge of the intellectual author.”

A year later, regarding the continued publication of Doctor Even–Odem books, Dr. Friedman added the following:

“The readers of his books are amazed that this monumental work of the physician from Herztliya did not create any echo in our printed media, neither in the general newspapers nor in the literary or linguistics publications, although these books are, and I am not exaggerating, a treasure trove of cultural and linguistic discoveries, coming from a scientist who is well–versed in the mental processes of the creation of the cultural treasures of our nation. His outstanding grasp of linguistics and his detective skills led Doctor Even–Odem in searching for the original terms in the historical books of the Jewish nation. Each term in these books promotes pondering, vitality and wisdom.

[Col. 1031]

The publication of these books is, without a doubt, a significant event in our literature terminology. Not a single dictionary, as comprehensive and thorough, was published since the time of Ben Yehuda. A whole generation, maybe even generations, will study this encyclopedia and will be encouraged to create even more.”

The city council of Herztliya decided to take all of these praises and blessings that Doctor Even–Odem had received and to convert them from nice statements of principles to something more materialistic and to grant him a prize of 1,000 Rocks (=a biblical coin, actually in the context – Israeli Pounds) in order to support his research and to increase the prestige of our laureate. I used the two words, “Rock” and “prestige”, on purpose as they exemplify the scientific research and the innovations of our winner, two words out of the thousands that he investigated and even created. Dr. Even–Odem is a man of prestige and the man of the rock.

I want to emphasize the fact that the Hebrew Academy and the Government of Israel had already approved and accepted and signed the decision that our national currency would be called “Sela”. This is a historical and personal achievement of our laureate who, by the way, once told me that he had spent more than a thousand “Selas” on pushing the “Sela” into the heads and the hearts of the nation. (Translator's comment: The Pound was eventually replaced by the “Shekel”, another Biblical denomination. “Sela” has never been adopted). I want to add that the adoption of the new–old coin “Agora”, in use for the last two years, is also the initiative of Dr. Even–Odem, and he fought long and hard to make it accepted.

[Col. 1030]

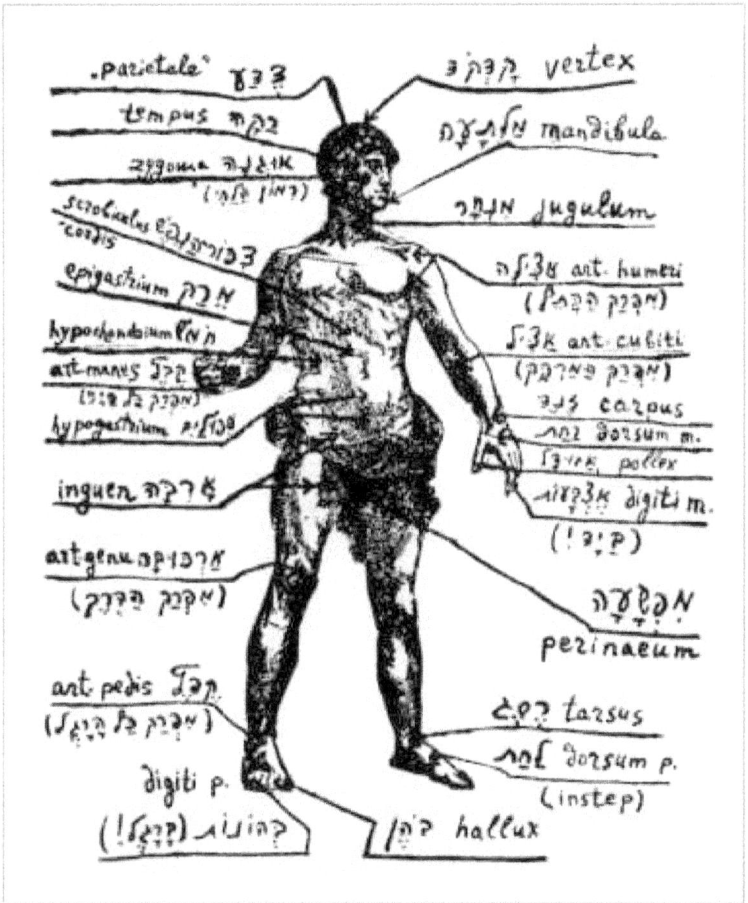

Hebrew Terms Dr. Even–Odem Created for Human Organs

.

And last and very dear is the word "yokra" (=prestige) that was missing from the Hebrew language and that Dr. Even–Odem introduce through the Hebrew Academy, last spring, I think.

About that time I saw a letter on the desk of Doctor Even–Odem, signed by the President of the Hebrew Academy, Professor Tur–Sinai, announcing that the Academy adopted the word "Yokra" for "prestige" based on the proposal by Dr. Even–Odem.

The chairman of the ceremony, the poet Nachman Rapp, describes the laureate Doctor Yoseph Even–Odem: "You gained glory, respect and admiration not only for your enthusiasm but also for innovation and your productive linguistic work. In each domain of your work and your social life you proved that you are a person of the highest quality. Your memory does not lose anything, you revive the past for the present and for the future, but more than anything else – you have a pure heart and great dedication for which we love you."

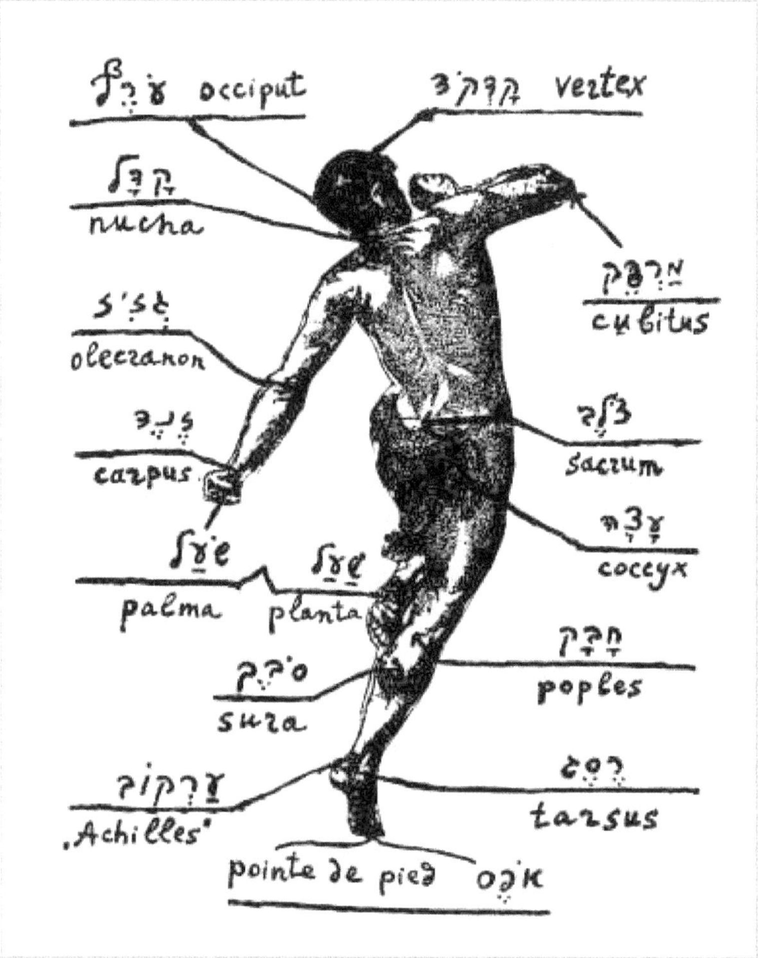

Doctor Yoseph Even–Odem: "copying from or capitulating to other languages is unacceptable"

[Col. 1033]

Immortal Was the Man Even–Odem

From the eulogy the poet Nachman Rapp gave at the grave of Doctor Yoseph Even–Odem Z"L

Translated by Meir Razy

The city of Herztliya is shocked, mourning the departure of the dear dedicated physician, the fighter for the Hebrew language. The city lost one of its magnificent citizens whose life story was an example of self–sacrifice and endless dedication for the individual and for society.

The unique physician, who did not feel tired during the day or rested during the night, stood on guard, tending to his patients' needs. He served as a physician in the municipal clinic for over twenty five years and his medical wisdom saved many lives and recovered many souls. Who among the residents of Herztliya was not treated by the physician Even–Odem? He walked among us as a legend and the splendor of the legend will be kept in our hearts forever.

He was admired always and everywhere, but misunderstood at times. His road in life was not always paved with flowers. There were hands that planted thorns in front of him. Like a prophet in the desert, calling people to follow the light, his voice was raised against the various modern "Greeks" (Translator's note: reference to those who wanted for follow the Greek culture during the time of the Maccabean), those who denied the Jewish culture and its resurrection. He fought a bitter war against the deniers and their supporters, a holy war that only real scholars who were fighting for heaven's sake could sustain. This is why he quoted, in the introduction to his dictionary, the following phrase from his grandfather, the Rabbi of Shaki, Rabbi Chaim Yirmiyahu Flansberg: "With bitterness archers attacked him; They shot at him with hostility." [Bible, Genesis, 49, 23]. The word "bitterness" means hatred that comes out of envy, and it is true that the envy of his opponents was not "the zeal of Pinchas" but they desired his reward [Bible, Numbers, 25, 10–12].

His linguistic research and innovations placed Even–Odem like an eagle soaring above the smaller birds that were not capable of climbing high. In his prolific imagination he could see the magnificent Hebrew language ruling over the nation. There were those who did not have the skills to look up and follow the call of this unique eagle. They remained stubbornly conservative and did not follow his leadership. But the call to liberate the Hebrew language from the subjugation of foreign languages was heard, penetrated the souls and even reached the deniers.

The city of Herztliya was proud to show its respect and praise to the Knight of the Hebrew Thinking, Yoseph Even–Odem, while he was alive. The city council granted him a special large literature prize with the intention of encouraging the important linguist, this lover of the Hebrew language. The city committed itself to supporting him in his on–going war for the Hebrew language.

[Col. 1034]

The man was taken from us. Even–Odem crossed the skies of our city during his short life of plentiful deeds and disappeared in the dark horizon. He left us but his light will stay with us forever. He left his writings, research and innovations, and immortalized himself in the hearts of the nation and in our hearts. The city of Herztliya and its council will find ways to properly remember his lifetime contributions.

Immortal was Even–Odem and his memory will remain in our hearts until the end of time.

[Col. 1035]

The Extinquished Star

by Nachman Rapp

Translated by Anita Frishman Gabbay

Edited by Rhoda Miller

Doctor Yosef Even–Oden was born in the morning and died in the morning. He was born in a time when Jewish life was very fragile in Europe and there was yearning for a better future. Seven years later the great World War broke out and Jewish life would be ripped apart. His father, Rabbi Yitzhak, the well–known Vilna Rabbi and Senator, an activist of Jewish rights in Poland, Russia and Lithuania, was caught in the center stage fighting against anti–Semitism that hit Jews "in the head" without warning. How, otherwise, could a young man like Yosef be brought up if not in the spirit of national identity and with its struggle for existence.

But the young student, Yosef Rubinstein, was influenced from two opposite directions, from his grandfather, the Rabbi of Shoki, who instilled a deep and philosophical understanding that came from generations of what was and what lies ahead, and from his father, the Rabbi and Senator, the vital and dynamic energy which leaves us unsettled (torn), new ideas need to materialize and obstacles need to be overcome. Torn between these two ideals, the young student from the Vilna University was a generation before his time.

The unlucky people of Europe started to heal their wounds after the First World War. Jewish life began to flourish again, a new Jewish identity was born. The Yiddish–Hebrew culture wars and language wars were renewed. In theory, it seemed healed! Enough angry blood was spilled and the time for renewal was practical. But it was still very far away to think of Zionism and Eretz Israel. The remnants of Jewish life was scattered in four corners of the world. This is when the young Yosef Rubinstein came out with his first speech in which the Hebrew language should be adopted as the practical language for all.

Thirty years later, that is, in today's calendar, the Hebrew Academia, problems aside, started making progress in the that direction and the young Rubinstein showed that his directives were ahead of its time!

The Hebrew language will be embraced forever.

[Col. 1036]

He changed his generation with the Hebrew language through his persistence. He continued his struggles alone against the Rabbis and was punished for his antagonisms. After many years like this, the fruit of his labour produced a language that the people would be proud of. It seemed even the Gaon of the Jerusalem of Lita would be proud of his linguistic undertakings and would release him from the accusations made against him.

Now, before his death, the Academia of the Hebrew language would come to appreciate the wonderful–rich Hebrew language that became so important that Dr. Yosef Even–Odem Rubinstein encouraged his encyclopedia and other books which he wrote, through his own initiative, even includes the medical and biological terminologies in the Hebrew language. In a period of twenty years, together with his other works, he produced a dictionary for world academia that was never done in our entire generation. And this he managed to do in his lifetime while still attending to his patients in the daytime in his clinic in Herzliah.

Beautiful letters expressing gratitude were sent by his students in honour of this excellent work and devoted doctor. The president of the Hebrew Academy, Professor Tur–Sinai, expressed gratitude for his dedication and excellence for developing the Hebrew language in medical texts. The State of Israel thanked and approved the national currency called “Sela” to replace the old currency the “Shekel” which was a historical and personal achievement by our laureate. But it still was not easy. The man was still left struggling for his Hebrew language.

A great love for the Hebrew language began to flourish with hopes to rebuild a rich legacy out of ruins; this is the gift he brought to the masses. It must be the Holy Duty of the Regime!

Dr. Even–Odem died prematurely, but let us not forget the legacy he left us. It must become our inheritance from here on.

[Col. 1037]

The Economic Situation in Ignalina from the Yekapo Registry, 1931

As transcribed by Moishe Shalit

Translated by Anita Frishman Gabbay

There were barely 250 families in Ignalina, 150 Jewish ones. The main Jewish industry was shopkeeping, small trade merchants, and artisans. The shopkeepers and merchants made up 47 percent, the tailoring and artisans, 23 percent.

As there were too many shops, their economic situation was poor. The Christian cooperatives added another layer of competition. The cooperatives got large loans and cheap credit from the Polish Bank "Rolni" and in this manner undercut the profits of the Jewish shops. The bank was also a loan and savings banks which benefited the local population. The cooperatives brought wagons full of cheap and much desired goods and this was great competition. The peasants from the region call this :"our store". Anti – Semitism towards the Jews, added another layer to our poor economic situation, the Christians were encouraged to shop in non – Jewish shops. Posters were pasted showing Jews sucking their blood (Christian) and eating their last piece of bread.

No wonder the Christians stopped shopping in our stores. After awhile, 2 more Christian stores opened, the Jewish shops could no longer compete. The Jews suffered, credit was difficult to get. The Folks Bank did not readily give loans to the Jews.

The market took place every Thursday. Merchants come from all the surrounding shtetls and the competition was great. They brought a lot of cheaper merchandise. Also the cooperatives brought wagons loaded with plentiful and cheap merchandise. No wonder there was poverty for the Jews of this region.

The landscape is full of fields and lakes. The best and most productive part belonged to Lithuania. The peasants were also poor. The last years were not easy, in the springtime many were forced to buy even their bread, a necessity to survive.

The result was catastrophic for the Jews in the region, as well as for others.

One small trade that existed here was fishing, raisings hens and geese, but this now was transferred into Christian hands.

[Col. 1038]

The Jewish shoemakers were without work and couldn't provide a living for their families. Just the Jewish blacksmiths were in a better situation. Here in Ignalina, there were 5 Jewish families who began a fishing industry in the nearby lakes. This provided them with a very good income.

When their contracts ended, the Polish regime issued new orders. No Jew can lease these lakes exclusively, and because of this, the economy suffered again.

Also in the forests, the wood trade was now ordered by the Polish regime to be transferred to their own overseers, and they took control and shipped the wood by train.

New edits are issued daily and the economic situation for the Jews was in a steady decline. New taxes and bribes were now increasing. 4 bakeries closed and the other businesses were suffering. The butcher shops were next. Great poverty was created.

A hep – committee was founded. More than 15 families needed help immediately. Many were ashamed to ask for help. The only thing left was for the young people to leave the shtetlach. Everyone's' eyes were focused to go to Eretz Israel and their wish to get there as soon as possible.

This was our economic situation in our shtetl (Ignalina).

[Col. 1039]

Tzeikin

(Ceikiniai, Lithuania) 55°16'/26°16'

My Destroyed Home

By Menucha Feigel Israelewitz

Translation by Anita Frishman Gabbay

Twelve kilometers from Ignalina was a large hamlet with a church. 70 years ago the first Jew, Feige Lapidot, arrived here. Around Tzeikin there were some wealthy villages: Navasani, Fitzul, Zablotzhiski, Shulkiski, Stanun, and others. From the small towns the

Jews arrived in Tzeikin, like Yitzhak Rein, Leiba Chaia Gilinski, Moishe Rein, Moishe Zikinski, Yeruchmiel Zikinski, Gordon(who had a mill), Zelig Gilinski, Gavenda, and others. Feigl Lapidot had a large business(store), others sold fruit, cattle and soda, while others had their own land and worked in agriculture.

All the Jews from Tzeikin and surrounding shtetls got together for Shabbos and holidays in a room in some Jew's house to pray. The children were sent to Ignalina to study.

When the Germans arrived, all the Jewish folk from Tzeikin were brought to the Ignalina Ghetto and were later slaughtered in Poligon.

In order to talk about one person in particular, Yeruchmiel Zikinski,who was a committed partisan, fought valiantly in the Lithuanian-Soviet Partisaner Organization, he was eventually shot defending his people. The ones who survived: Zelig Gilinski with his wife Chasia and Breina Gavenda, who survived and are now in America. Our little shtetl of Tzeikin was small in population and with little means(wealth). Few survived, now scattered throughout the world. Here in Israel, I remain one of the few close to this Yiskor Book, and those Jews who survived from the Sventzian district have dedicated a Maztevah (memorial) to their slaughtered loved-ones.

[Col. 1040]

Truly, we would need more time to tell the stories about the lives and destruction of our nearest and dearest fellow Jews. It would be necessary to have eyewitness accounts what happened to the few Tzeikaner Jews, documents and material that brought about their destruction. This should not be forgotten. We lack the strength, but we thank everyone for helping to remember those precious lives, for including us in this Book, for remembering our little shtetl that is included in the larger district of Sventzian. Their memory should live on.

Rabbi Chaim Alihu Feigl, Zelig Gilinski, Hana Feigl, Sima Feigl, Minucha Feigl

[Col. 1041]

Gavikan

(Gaveikėnai, Lithuania)

55°21'/26°07'

By Leizer Levitan

Translation by Anita Frishman Gabbay

The Fishermen

Near to the lake, not far from the shtetl of Paliush, there was a little hamlet Gavikan, where about 20 families lived and made their living from fishing. The lakes were leased by Schmuel Yose(Gilinski) from Paliush and Leizer Gavenda from Meran. Day and night the fishermen were busy on the lakes and they would transport the fish from village to village to barter and exchange their produce for other products and goods, and often to other middlemen.

The plentiful fish would also be sent to larger cities.

The Jews of Gavikan had a synagogue and Shabbos and holidays they came to pray with their fellow Jews in nearby shtetls. The Pauliusher Shochet (slaughterer), R' Haim Rafael, also came to Gavikan.

The young folk from Gavikan, having a difficult time to make a living, immigrated to a larger world. Today, they can be found in America, where they still remember with fondness and hold dearly in their hearts the memories of their little hamlet Gavikan, the kind and gentle nature of their fellow Jews, who never were envious of anyone, who worked so diligently and quietly: who met their undeserved death in such a painful and agonizing manner.

[Col. 1042]

After the first World War, the small hamlet of Gavikan was "swallowed up" (incorporated) into the nearby town of Ignalina, the Jewish families were absorbed amongst the Jews of Ignalina. The synagogue would not allow that Gavikan be forgotten, thus the name, The Gavikaner Synagogue.

The families that I remember from Gavikan were: Leizer Sneiderovitch, Abraham Yosef Glas, Abraham Yitzhak Rutshtein, Velvel Levitan, Shlomo Gilinski, Chaim Gilinski, Avraham Yitzhak Gilinski, Yosef Rappaport, Leizer Yitzhak Katz, Bina Katz, Motl Sneiderovitch, Zlata Sneiderovitch, Sheina Gavenda, Meir Katz, Uri Katz, and others. The Gavikener, who lived in Ignalina, together with other Jews from the Sventzian district, met their end, perpetrated by the Lithuanian and Germans, in the mass grave of Poligon.

Yose Glaz the Gavinkener

[Col. 1043]

Paliush
The Jews on the Other Side of Lushi

(Palūšė, Lithuania)

55°20'/26°06'

Shmuel Gilinsky

Translated by Janie Respitz

Lake Lushi (Lake Lūšiai) is 15 kilometres long and 4 kilometres wide. It is connected through a small river to Lake Dringis (Lake Dringykštis).

On the other side of the lake there is another small river that connects lush to Lake Zhemiane (Lake Žeimenys) , which leads to Zhemanie (Žeimena) River which runs through the towns of Kaltinian (Kaltanėnai) and New-Svencionys (Švenčionėliai), until Podbrodz (Pabradė) where it flows into the Vilieh River.

An intensive lumber transport was carried out through these lakes and rivers and employed a lot of people. All winter, the lumber was brought from the forests to the shores, and in summer they were loaded on to barges and boats and brought to towns and villages.

Around Paliush, the sandy shores were lined with pine trees that grew on high hills. Nearby, there were large forests.

The settlement Palushi, got its name because in Lithuanian, Pa means – on the other side. Pa – Lushi, on the other side of Lake Lushi (Lake Lūšiai). They helped build the new Church that was very holy to the surrounding population. Prayers were held there every day. Religious Lithuanians came from the surrounding villages and tried to settle as close as possible to the church.

[Col. 1044]

Jews from the surrounding area also came to this town , where they helped develop the fishing industry, became middle-men in buying and selling lumber and opened inns, restaurants and various stores. Jewish artisans also settled in Paliush and earned a living providing services to farmers and workers.

The first group of Jews built a Prayer House. Every Shabbes and holiday, not only would the town Jews come to pray, but the Jewish farmers from the surrounding villages.

In 1861, when planning the railway from Warsaw to St. Petersburg, which had to run through Vilna (Vilnius), Niementshin (Nemenčinė), Svenciony (Švenčionys) and Paliu (Paliūniai), the Jews from Paliush and other nearby towns tried to avoid having the train line run through their villages. They had influence as (in the end) the train station was built four kilometres away in Ignalina.

Time showed that the Jews from Paliush made a mistake. The train station played an important role in the local economy and Ignalina began to grow and Jews from Paliush Palush moved there. In time, Paliush became smaller.

However, Jews of Paliush loved, worked and did business here. Among the wealthiest Jewish families was Shmuel-Yose (Shmuel-Yosef) Gilinsky and his children: Zalman, Boruch, Dovid, Motl, Yakov and Bertha (Basia). This family was successful in lumber and fishing.

[Col. 1045]

Near Paliush there was a village called Meiran (Meironys). Lazar Gavenda lived there. Together with Shmuel Yose (Gilinsky) he leased the lakes. He was connected to our town. He prayed in our House of Prayer, had good friends and was counted among the wealthiest men in town. His son Berl (Later known as Barney Gavenda) emigrated to America (Peoria, Illinois), became a great philanthropist and brought a lot of honour to our town.

Moishe Gilinsky, Khone Garber, Avrom Gilinsky, Lipe Gilinsky, Itze Yose Gilinsky, Khlayne Hirsh Gavende (Chlono Hirsh Gavenda) from Shakarva (Šakarva), Fyeve(Feive/Feivel) Gilinsky, Zalman Gilinsky and many others were admirable in there good deeds and character, with heart and soul. Many of their children emigrated to America, Canada, Brazil and Argentina. Until today you can find Gilinskys and Gavendas in these places. They were from Paliush, Meiran (Meironys), Gavik.[1] The families that did not emigrate, merged with the town of Ignalina.

[Col. 1046]

The last Mohicans of the lakes, rivers and lumber merchants took their prayer houses and Torah scrolls and continued to build a Jewish future until the wild Hitlerism (Nazism) arrived and obliterated all the towns and villages that stood near the Zhemiane River (Žeimena River), New-Svencionys (Švenčionėliai), and buried everyone in the mass grave in Poligon.

Children! Grandchildren of the town of Paliush and surrounding communities do not forget the mass grave in Poligon!

Translator's footnote

Gavik (Gavikan), outside of Paliush, a small town (hamlet) of about 20 families

[Col. 1047]

Holocaust – In the Valley of Lamentation and Pain

Yerachmiel Kariv (Korb)[1]

Translated by Anita Frishman Gabbay

Edited by Rhoda Miller

The Germans warned Poland at the beginning of the outbreak of the Second World War, after capturing Czechoslovakia, through Hitler's speeches on the radio, Poland will become the corridor that they needed to invade the rest of Europe. This is what everyone was waiting to hear... the outbreak of the war. First the Germans bombarded several large towns in Poland, and we were glued to our radio sets in bewilderment of what was yet to come for our Jewish people. We learned that the Germans were advancing quickly, occupying Polish towns and other strategic places. We wondered how the German army advanced so quickly and was able to enlist the Polish Army in only a few days?

Two weeks passed, September 17, 1939, the Red Army entered the war and occupied the Ukraine and the eastern section of Poland. Also, the Sventzian region was now occupied by the Red Army.

[Col. 1047]

When the first Russian tanks arrived in Ignalina, the Jewish youth rejoiced openly with them, praised them and were happy to see them as their liberators. Several days passed and on market day the Russians were buying our products at fair market prices. They bought everything, even outdated articles and paid well. Outdated shoes! All products: knives, forks, string, belts and especially watches (goods in Russia now, were almost a rarity during those years after the Revolution).

In a matter of a few days, all the watches were sold. They even bought the old watches that we inherited from our grandmothers and men's watches from the days of Sobieski and other things.

The Soviet Army did not remain long.

[Col. 1048]

Quickly the Lithuanian region was taken over by the Lithuanians. Four kilometers from Ignalina stretched the border through Daugelishak to Old – Sventzian. The Jewish folk had a little bit of a reprieve, they were happy for the time being. What happened later as a result of Polish anti–Semitism, the German occupation and the Soviet dictatorship, is for later discussions.

The Lithuanians brought into our shtetl many products that they sold at very low prices.

[Col. 1049]

This didn't last long. The Red Army returned and the Soviet style regime was established in Lithuania. From Minsk, a Soviet administrator arrived and the transportation of stones from Ignalina back to the Soviet Union began. The wealthier families, like Brumberg, Korb, Ostrinski, Kuritski, and others were involved in the transportation of these stones. They worked very hard and as long as they were able to remain in their own homes and maintain a healthy environment, they were happy. Everyone knew that the situation could be worse. Every person of means worried not to be arrested or deported into [deep] Russia [Siberia]. We lived in this atmosphere for about six months, no one could imagine that the destruction of our shtetl and the massacre of our Jewish people was so close.

[Col. 1049]

Hitler Attacks the Soviets

Until today, I do not know why I woke up on the morning of June 22, 1941 and opened my radio. It was exactly six in the morning, I was fiddling around with the stations and I suddenly stopped at Berlin! A loud and scratchy voice appeared, I immediately recognized it as Hitler's. A sudden shudder went through my body. He spoke about Russia and in the end he declared poetically "the last word I transfer to my military". I understood immediately that this was a declaration of war against Russia.

I remained paralyzed next to the radio and didn't know what to do! I decided to find some other stations and hear different opinions about this event...

I started with the Moscow station and listened. They announced to the Soviet folk that Hitler attacked the Soviets, without warning. They announced, "all is not as it seems." The Russian Army will decimate Hitler's Regime!

I ran into the streets to share this information with whomever I found; some heard the London radio reports that Germany had amassed over two million soldiers on the Soviet border. "What will the outcome be?"

We all had the same opinion: a dark cloud was approaching our Jewish people and they will pay dearly!

I opened the radio again, Kibart and Virbalen are now in German hands!

[Col. 1050]

Kovno and Vilna were heavily bombarded. The Germans were now in Vilna and many were wounded and dead.

My son Israel came and told me "the Germans had heavy artillery and tanks and by some miracle he had survived the bombardment."

Many friends gathered in our house. They all wanted news about Vilna. We turned on the radio: Filvishok and Suwalki were occupied. The Berlin station read out an appeal to the Lithuanians: "Join the Germans and we will free you from the Bolsheviks and the Jews."

We didn't know what to do. Some said to run away. The main question, "Where to?" A few days later we heard that the Jews of Vilna and Kovno were being shot. A great panic developed in our shtetl. When the Russian Army left, the Lithuanian youth empowered themselves. A known Lithuanian policeman attacked Chaim Rimarin and Josef Glaz in the street for no reason. We were told that all the Lithuanian folk were arming themselves. These "Lithuanian partisans" did as they pleased. A whole week passed like this and Wednesday July 1st, we saw the first German motorized–vehicles [last–autos=armoured vehicle] arriving.

Friday, July 3rd. they caught Jews and rounded them up and sent them to work outside of the town.

They had to lay boards across the sandy ground and understandably, they were made to suffer greatly.

Shabbos morning all the Jews were rounded up for work and the Germans made sure that each Jew did his own lifting. Whoever couldn't manage received a harsh beating.

Monday, July 6, all the Lithuanians hung national banners and now bragged to the Jews and proclaiming the Regime was pure Lithuanian.

[Col. 1051]

Placards were posted in all the streets that Jews were not allowed on the sidewalks, that it is forbidden to leave town, and every Jewish house must have a sign "JEW" posted. Every Jew has to wear a Yellow Jewish Star.

The First Tragedy

Thursday, July 9, 26 Jews were arrested. Amongst them was my son Israel. On Friday I went to the police to inquire what will happen to him. On the way I met a Lithuanian policeman that I knew and told him my story. I begged him to help me free my child. He listened and ensured me that in a few hours Israel would come home.

Immediately I returned to announce the good news, meanwhile we were lighting the candles for the Sabbat. The Shabbat came and no one appeared. We feared that the policeman had misled us.

Suddenly my wife started screaming: "Israelka is coming!" He entered the house still alive!

Saturday morning we learned that all the arrested were not released. First we thought they were sent to work, no one knew where. A few days later we found out all the 26 arrested "Communists" were shot.

This was the first great tragedy in Ignalina. Everyone knew me well and we knew that there were no Communists in the group, this was just the beginning of what was to come next!

Soon a rumor was circulating that the Jews of Lingmian and Kaltinian were next to be slaughtered. At first we didn't believe that this will materialize. We sent a Christian to find out the truth for us. He returned and confirmed that this was true.

Meanwhile, Dovid Soleveitchik came to us, our Jewish representative of Lingmian, to tell us that the German commander wanted to talk to the Jews. They wanted the Rabbi and myself to go to them. I went to the Rabbi but he was sick in bed.

[Col. 1052]

I took Abba Katz and left to see the commander. We barely arrived at the headquarters when we were confronted by two soldiers, "are we the two representatives of the Jews?"

Without knowing the outcome of our reply we acknowledged that we were the representatives.

The two soldiers had a good laugh and they went into the storage room and brought us two large brooms. They ordered us into a room and told us the commander wanted us to clean.

We took the brooms and started to clean. The rooms were extremely dirty and we worked the entire day. In the evening the soldiers arrived and asked us if we had a Talmud?

"Why do you need a Talmud?"

"We need toilet paper in the bathroom," they laughed, "there is no better paper than from your Talmud."

Late at night, tired and broken–hearted, we returned home. All the neighbours anxiously waited at our home for our return to hear the news. They wanted to know why the commander "invited" us to see him. We told them the "good" news and from then on the Jews of Ignalina no longer had any great expectations [they feared for the worst, during WW1, the Germans were more civil towards the Jews]. The Germans arrived to inflict their wrath upon the Jewish nation. In the meantime, news of the condition of the Vilna Jews reached us.

They (the Jews) were told lies that they were going to work, truthfully, they were being sent to their slaughter and shot [at Ponar].

Another time a Lithuanian neighbour who was in the military said all the Jews were taken from Ponevezh, to a forest outside Zarazai and then shot. He believes no one survived.

Peasants Bring the First Bad News

Several days later, on a Friday, Erev Shabbos Nokhmu [Shabbos after Tishe Be'Av], Yerachmiel Leibstain came to me and said some unknown girls were asking for me.

[Col. 1053]

It a short while five girls arrived in our shtetl, one of whom that I knew, a teacher from Salok. They brought a letter with them from a friend of mine from Podbrodz identifying themselves, please help these girls return to their homes. Two of them were from Salok, Hirsch Brava's daughters, [I knew their father], one was a teacher in the Jewish Vilna Gymnasia, another a student in the public school. The other three, were from Zarasai County [Novo–Aleksandrovsk][2], one was a bookkeeper at Shopn's brewery, the other two were students at the Vilna University. They fled from a transport from Vilna, and he begs me to bring them to Salok. [another account= they were captured entering Moledechno and were relieved of their belongings and sent back to Vilna. They arrived on foot as train travel was dangerous, 50 kilometers, looking for help].

I made the arrangements. My daughter noticed the wagon with the girls had returned that same evening. The Christian driver told me when he arrived in Akhres, eight kilometers from Salok, a peasant friend of his told him in secret that the Jews in Salok were being murdered. So he quickly turned around and came back to me.

The five girls stayed with us. I paid the driver for two trips, 1000 rubles, and I asked him to keep this confidential. That is what happened.

One blow after another descended upon us. We heard about the destruction in Lingmian and Kaltinian, then Salok and then another shtetl. Also the Jews of Dukstas were murdered, news brought to me by a Christian friend Kugner, who lived near Dukst.

When I saw him I asked his advice, “What is happening in Dukst?” He didn't answer but I noticed how he started to cry and begged me.

I didn't let him leave. “Tell me, what happened? Why are you so frightened? What happened there?”

“It is not good, Mr. Korb, not good at all! Run away! Run away before it's too late!”

In one hour all the Jews from Tarangini, Zarasai, Dukst were brought to the forest. The men and the women were divided into two sides. They were ordered to undress and then pushed naked into the pits, which was prepared in advance by the local Christians.

The screaming of the woman and children are still resonating in his ears. The carnage that took place will never be forgotten! This upset and frightened him. No one was able to escape because they were surrounded by the military on all sides. They were shot with machine guns and were then thrown into the pits. They didn't care if they were dead or just wounded, all were thrown in. The Lithuanian police told the Christian helpers not to describe what they witnessed, or they too will pay with their lives.

[Col. 1054]

But he couldn't hold back. He came especially to Ignalina to warn me. The Christian Kugner...

“Run away before it's too late!”

I answered him, “Easy to say! Where should I run? Where will it be better?”

He gave me advise to run in the direction of White Russia. “It is much better there!

They [the Germans] are advancing with mobilized tanks, you should know what to expect. This is death for you. Do not believe others if they tell you otherwise, be careful of lies!”

I said goodbye to this honest peasant and asked him not to forget us. In the name of all the Jews of the town I thanked him for his pure heart and friendship and he left.

I wandered through our house thinking what we should do; I felt that Death as so close.

I called for my nephew Josef Gavenda and told him the sad news. Our answer was to find places to hide. Just to run was not the solution. We have to find Christians who were willing to hide us, one by one, or an entire family. Our sole purpose was to avoid death with strength and determination.

A Threat for Death and Destruction

I came home and told my wife Mirl and my children about the news. We are confronted with the beginning of our extermination and must find a way to save ourselves.

[Col. 1055]

It is imperative we leave immediately. We need to carry with us our money and documents and leave one at a time.

September 10, the Germans organized trucks in our shtetl. Don't get into these trucks. We have to run away. I ran to Zastzianik Vachivki, two kilometers from Ignalina (where Leibe Chaim Elperin lived). I left alone as not to alert our Lithuanian neighbours and told my family that we should all meet there. I left with an empty crate and told the neighbours I was going to fetch potatoes from a nearby village. When I arrived at Elperin's house, I told them what was happening. We decided to send a Christian, whose son was a partisan, to make inquiries and see exactly the predicament we were in.

In the meantime I hid in the nearby forest. I thought it over, I will go to Budkevitch, the good- hearted Lithuanian who I bestowed many favors. He will hide me. When Elperin came to the forest I requested him to deliver a letter to my wife where to find me. The letter was sent with his Christian friend Albina.

In the darkness I left the forest for Budkevitch. I begged him to save our lives. He only wanted to hide me, not my entire family. This was his "great debt" that he was willing to repay. Later, with some luck, I managed to bring my son Leibele to hide with me. He arranged for us to sleep in the attic in the hay. We overnighted in the attic. The next morning my older son Israelka came and told us that the shtetl is quiet and the entire story of the trucks had been fabricated.

[Col. 1056]

No one wanted to believe the story. Yerachmiel Korb created this unnecessary panic.[3]

I was convinced to return to Ignalina and several quiet days passed. Four days before Rosh Hashana my Christian friend informed me again the trucks were arriving. They had been delayed, not rerouted.

Again I prepared to leave the shtetl. My wife Mirl went to Tzherniavsky, my daughter with Moishele and Israelka had to go to their uncle in Danilovitch, and Leibele and I will return to the Lithuanian Budkevitch.

Four days I remained like this and I grew restless. I wanted to be among my Jewish people during Rosh Hashana and pray with them.

For Rosh Hashana I returned home. The folk were angry with me that I created another panic.

They wanted to turn me over to the Lithuanian police and get rid of me and my erratic behaviour.

I met with them and asked, “Don't you know that all the Jews from Dukst, Solak and Zarasai were murdered for no reason?” They looked at me with anger in their eyes and shouted, “this is a lie! Falsehoods! They are alive and working in Rakishok!”

[Col. 1056]

“And do you know the fate of the Jews of Utena?

“Nothing! They are alive and well, living in their shtetl!”

Everyone was agitated and angry. There was a large gathering of wealthy Jews, only one sided with me.

“I will give a Christian 100 rubles to go to Utena and bring back the truth!”

[Col. 1057]

We all agreed. The Christian left. The second day of Rosh Hashana the Christian returned, “There are no more Jews in Utena!”

“So,” I asked, “what do you have to say now?”

Cursing the Lithuanian, they answered, “he stole our money, he didn't even go to Utena”.

The Jews of Ignalina were divided, some for, some against.

For Shabbos Tshuva he [Christian friend] told me again, that I should save myself. All the Jews of Sventzian and the region are being deported. The Goyim knew what was happening.

They [the Jews] again mistrusted my information. They went to the Vojt to inquire why the Germans needed so many trucks. The major, pretends not to know the answers, fabricated a story that workers were needed in Kretinga, and the workers will be transported there from the Sventzian region.

[Col. 1057]

This calmed the “believers” and they remained in the shtetl. But I decided to escape wherever I could. Thirty–one people decided to escape to the shtetlech of White Russia.

My Wanderings...

I remember everything. It was a Thursday, September 25, 1941, the Christian woman Shvilfa from Kucariski came to me, very frightened saying she couldn't repay the 100 rubles she owed me.

“Mila” I answered her, “I don't need it today.”

"But they are deporting everyone from Ignalina today, who knows where I will be able find you?"

"How do you know this, that we will be transported?"

"I was at the voijt of Daugelishok, he shared his secret with me and asked me not to tell anyone."

I thanked her for the information and said goodbye. When she left the neighbours ran into my home to share my information. I told them the truth.

[Col. 1058]

They began cursing [curse=a black year on the Gentile woman] the Christian and not believing the Christian lies, I disagreed with them.

"No, I believe her."

These wagons will transport you to your deaths.

My instinct told me this was our final hour. I arranged for my son, as soon as it was dark outside, to join me and bring all our possessions to Budkevitch. Mirl and the children will go to Tzerniavski.

Israel worked at the train and I left to tell him the arrangements.

On the way, I went to Leibstein, the blacksmith, where I met a Christian friend and had to explain where I was going with the crate. I was going to fetch potatoes and actually took the opportunity to dig some up.

I saw Israel at the train station, winked at him to meet me where I would reveal our plan. Do not go on those trucks. Run away immediately after your work ends.

I left for Elperin's in Zastshianik and waited until dark. Then I left for my safe house. It was dark outside, I lay in the hay but was restless and couldn't fall asleep.

In the morning Budkevitch's wife came to me and I asked her to send a letter to my wife, where she will be met in Ignalina by our housekeeper. The housekeeper will then deliver the letter.

[Col. 1058]

The letter requested that necessities, such as oil and food, be given to this woman. I waited impatiently the entire day for her return. I was anxious. Finally, Mrs Budkevitch returned with challahs and fish. I went to sleep in the hay satisfied.

[Col. 1059]

I barely fell asleep, it was still dark outside when the dog started to bark. I heard light footsteps. Someone was coming, the sound was getting closer. “Who can that be?” Suddenly the door opened and I heard, “Father,” and recognized Leibele's voice. I ran to him and kissed him.

“What news my child?”

“Not good, there is a huge panic in town, the officials were preparing the trucks for transport. I [Leibele] waited until dark, arrived at Elperin's house, and from there remained in the forest until dark. No one recognized me in the town of Bitsun and then I escaped to you.” He climbed into the haystack and I noticed him trembling from fear and cold. I took off my coat and wrapped him tightly. Neither of us could fall asleep.

Mrs. Budkevitch came to us in the morning with a warm breakfast.

I gave her another letter to bring to my wife. I had buried a few thousand rubles in our house which needs to be found. She left with the letter.

Eleven in the morning we heard shooting. Our hearts started to race. We were trembling. We heard German voices and Lithuanian bandits and pleading from our fellow Jews. With great unrest we anxiously awaited for the wife [Budkevitch] to bring us some news.

She arrived at night and came to us. We saw the shock in her eyes. She was so disorientated she didn't know how to begin.

In the end her words hit us like a hammer over our heads. All the Jews from Ignalina were deported and my wife Mirl and the children were among them.

[Col. 1060]

She left and our crying and wailing was endless. They will surely be killed. The day dragged, Leibele was cold so I wrapped him and he fell asleep. I couldn't sleep the entire night. The sun came up and it was a little warmer outside. Suddenly the door opened and we see, Mirl.

She came in with Mrs. Budkevitch. We jumped from the haystack and kissed her. We couldn't believe our eyes!

“How did you escape? I was told you were on the transport with all the Jews?”

Mirl was frightened, her eyes were full of tears. Finally she told us everything, how she managed in the last few days.

September 27, all the Jews of Ignalina were ordered to leave their homes and depart for the direction of New– Sventzian. Most went by foot, the old and sick, the children were put into the trucks.

Mirl and her sister Chaia were in the trucks. A few kilometers from town the trucks stopped. What were they waiting for? She noticed they were close to Ratdzizka's house. She ran out of the truck to the house.

She heard her sister screaming, “where are you going?”

Through a crack she saw everyone continuing. She caught a glimpse of Lilianke and Shprinze walking with a group of four.

When it got dark outside she saw Yadviga Ratdzizka leaving her home and she called out to her, begging for mercy. Yadviga told her the Germans searched her home looking for Mirl, opening every room and cupboard.

It appears that the wife Levin with her two daughters were hidden in her attic.

[Col. 1061]

Yadviga fed us all. We took advantage of the dark of night and left town.

I left to Zerviavka. I couldn't stay because I was recognized by a Lithuanian. I returned.

Again we heard shooting. Mrs. Budkevitch came with news that Jews not far from us were caught, Feigl and Brumberg with their son. They were shot. We understood that we could no longer remain here and had to change our plans. The problem, where should we go?

Perhaps to Danilovitch, but Mr. Budkevitch advised us to go to Vidz.

We said our goodbyes and departed again for our dangerous and perilous journey.

Death Approaches

We walk, 100 meters apart, if one of us gets caught the others might have a chance to escape. We meet some scouts in the fields whose job was to lead people to Vidz. It was 35 kilometers by foot. We must listen for every sound and footstep. Not far from Viltande we heard two persons on a motorcycle so we crept quietly into the woods and lay between the trees. They drove by and didn't see us. We then continued on our journey.

“The town Pakritze is on the way, are we near the shtetl of Old–Daugelishok?” We do not want to go through this town, so we detour through the muddy fields filled with swamps. We didn't have a choice.

Barely one kilometer later, we heard a Rover driving towards us, there is nowhere to hide, no woods in sight, just fields all around us. We don't want this to be our end so we flee deeper into the fields.

[Col. 1062]

I ran a few hundred meters, Mirl and Leibel were ahead. This Lithuanian managed to catch up with me. He did me a favour and dragged me back to Daugelishak. It was by chance that I knew him. “Yavitz,” I say, “what benefit do you get if they shoot me? I have a lot of money. Take the money and let me go.” I gave him my wallet with more than 3000 rubles.

He released me an advised me to bypass the road. I managed to reach a small forest and waited for Mirl and Leibele.

I wait and wait but no one arrives. Perhaps they were caught and brought back to Daugelishak. I must continue, as the one who remains alive can later take revenge on these murderous beasts. I leave with a heavy heart. I see in a distance another Rover coming towards me. I throw myself into a ditch and hold my breath.

A miracle happens, the Rover passes me and doesn't notice me. Now I vow not to use the main roads, to continue my trek through the fields.

[Col. 1062]

Half–Naked Through the Fields

On the way, near the town of Michaleva, a Lithuanian partisan saw me and forced me to stop. He started to search me. I told him one hour earlier I was robbed and they took all my money. He wanted to take me back to Daugelishak. I offer him my fine coat and a few pair of pants–“take it all and let me go”. I leave with the shirt on my back and half–naked I drag myself through the muddy fields. I barely have any strength, it is cold, but I must keep going. It might warm me up. When I reached the Zabelener forest I hear someone calling out in Lithuanian.

“Who is here?”

I take several steps and quietly hide in the nearby lake. When all is quiet, I come out. Again a miracle! I survived!

[Col. 1063]

When I came out of the water my foot was sore. The blood in my left foot pooled together, swollen, I dragged myself to the side of the road and sat down to rest.

About an hour later, after I crossed the Disner river, I arrived at the town of Grivali at Shidlovski's house (a Polish friend of mine). I had my first good meal and even managed to smoke a cigarette. I rested and told him about my troubles. “I left with my wife and son and now I am alone.”

“You know,” says his wife, “an hour ago a woman and her son passed through our village and inquired if we had seen anyone passing through. Was this your wife and son?”

“How were they dressed?”

“Without a coat, without a headscarf and even without shoes.”

I thanked her and believed they were mine.

Shidlovski harnessed his horse and wagon and took me immediately to Vidz.

This was Monday, September 29. When I arrived at my friend's home in Vidz, only an experienced writer can describe the emotions I felt when I opened the door and saw my wife Mirl sitting at the table, my Leibele, my in–laws and my entire family. We rejoiced at that very instant of seeing one another, we kissed and we cried!

They all thought the Lithuanian bandits had killed me! We all recounted our ordeals, how we made it to Vidz. Here I learned about the fate of the Jews of Sventzian.

[Col. 1064]

They were packed like sardines into barracks in Poligon, several craftsmen, or "useful" Jews were taken to the Sventzian ghetto, but the majority were slaughtered.

As our son Israel was a good engineer, we hoped that he was among the "necessary" Jews.

In the meantime we needed to integrate ourselves into the Vidz ghetto. The Judenrat was not so eager and they wanted money. I told them the truth. I came naked, without any money in my pockets. It didn't help.

Several day later the Shochet came and gave me 50 rubles. I began to cry, how did my life become so unravelled? That I am receiving charity?

The Sochet understood my circumstances and said:

" I want to help my fellow Jews, I feel fortunate to have a job and I want to help those in need."

He calmed me down and I took the money. It upset me when I thought about the thousands I gave to that Lithuanian bandit.

Nevertheless I was overjoyed that the three of us were alive, saved from the brink of death.

They Amputate My Left Leg

After some rest in Vidz, I began to feel pain in my left foot. I was advised to take warm foot baths, but it didn't help. The pain grew worse.

My cousin Michal Levin came on October 16, from Opsa, and presented me the option to return to Opsa with him. The well–known Sejm–deputy Adamovitch lives there and when he heard I was in such a bad condition in Vidz, he wanted me to come to him in Opsa to help me.

I said my goodbyes to my family and friends and left with my cousin by foot.

I barely walked two kilometers when my left foot could no longer continue.

With great difficulty my cousin found a driver and we made it to Opsa.

[Col. 1065]

The Judenrat of Opsa integrated me into the ghetto. The pain grew worse.

My cousin called the doctor, but the medicine didn't help. Then the feldsher [licensed barber–surgeon] came and he advised “blood–letting”. To be in such a life threating situation in an unknown place was frightening. I needed an operation.

The Judenrat of Opsa arranged a carriage and I was sent to the Braslav hospital for the operation.

In the meantime I received a letter that my Moishel arrived in Vidz and will come to visit me. I decided to wait. When he arrived I became more motivated and we left for Braslav together.

My friend Adamovitch accompanied us, introduced me to his doctor–friend and between them arranged for my operation.

His diagnosis was different from the feldsher, he told me the foot needed to be amputated above the knee.

The problem is where to get the narcotics? Adamovitch tried to help. I couldn't walk, sleep, stand, lie down or rest: the pain grew intolerable. My Leibele knew of the Christian doctor, formerly from Ignalina, who was now in Vidz, Kuchniev.

We were always on good terms with him, so Leibele went to him. He gave him the narcotics but requested 2000 rubles.

Leibele didn't flinch, he promised him the money Leibele ran 40 kilometers from Vidz to Braslav to bring me the narcotics. December 3, they amputated my foot.

[Col. 1066]

In several days, I awoke from the narcotics and I was in a room full of Christians, if only Hitler could see this!

A nurse was changing my bandage and I thought, Jews with two feet were being murdered, is it of any consequence that a Jew with one foot will be allowed to live? Is this operation for nothing?

Nevertheless, I still wanted to live. December 8, my good friend, Adamovitch arrived.

Trembling, he said to me, he had spoken with the mayor of Braslav and nothing will happen to the Jews in Braslav.

And I answered:

I don't believe anyone. He [Hitler] told the world that all the Jews will be murdered. How can I believe him?

Adamovitch left and I remained another twelve days in the hospital. My son Moishe came and took me back to Opsa. I was still weak and continued to look for a solution to save myself. I still had the will to live, even with one foot. Mirl greeted me with tears. She thought only my toes would be amputated: she never thought I would be left with one foot.

"Don't cry, my beloved! it could be worse! God gave us some more time. Our main worry now is to find a Christian to hide us."

[Col. 1067]

The Road to Sventzian

Together with my cousin we decided, the four of us, to go to Adamovitch. His connections will be helpful for us to find hiding places.

We left late Friday night and arrived early in the morning.

He received us in a friendly manner but with uncertainty in his tone of voice. He had Christian workers and that put us in danger.

My children and wife had to return to Opsa and I was to remain at his home.

In a few days we will find another solution. This is how it went.

I remained eight days and Adamovitch himself took care of me. He fed me and I regained some strength. He even took out the night pot.

I was then able to stand, with the help of two sticks under my arms. His wife advised me all was quiet in Opsa and I can return.

December 27, Adamovitch brought me to Opsa and told me to hide Mirl and the children. It would be more difficult to hide a cripple.

I begged him to return me to Budkevitch's attic.

He is a good friend and will not refuse to help an invalid. But it is sixty–five kilometers, a carriage will cost a lot of money and I don't have any.

Adamovitch thought and said: "Good, I myself will bring you there. I remember all the favors you did for me and I want to repay you."

Mirl and I discussed the plan, our separation will be longer than we thought. My plan was to go to Budkevitch and it would be easier for Adamovitch to help her and the children. I alone will go to Budkevitch. Even though all the bandits were Lithuanians, it would be easier to find a friend amongst them [in Lithuania].

[Col. 1068]

December 30 was freezing, the snow was falling. Leibele was anxious and left to see Adamovitch to arrange a sled for me. This was arranged for Wednesday six o'clock in the morning. Adamovitch will come for me. I must wait for him in the last house of the shtetl, at Voliak the teacher. My children brought me to Voliak by sled. Mirl and the children came the next morning.

My wife and children arrived the next morning. Adamovitch arrived. I departed from my dearest with many tears and great heartache and I left Opsa.

In the sled the severe frost entered my bones. I encountered many carriages on the road and it seemed everyone was looking at me, begrudging me because I was a Jew.

I kept my head down and didn't pay attention. My main concern was not to freeze.

I think of walking, then I remember I have only one foot.

The driver tells me we are close to Vidz, and I hope to rest somewhere.

We arrived at 11 o'clock and the driver asks if I want to go to a Jew.

I went to Dr. Kushnitz who had provided the narcotics. I can rest here quietly and need him to change the bandage and give me his prognosis.

The driver brought me into a room, and the doctor excused himself as he still had patients to see.

An hour later he came in to see me, asked about the operation and my way of life, and what brings me here in such a cold weather.

[Col. 1069]

I told him I was going to Budkevitch, near Ignalina, to hide.

He discouraged me, the Lithuanians are like wild beasts, not one Jew will remain alive there.

I told him I had very good Christian friends there and after enjoying a good meal, a warm place and some rest, I continued on my journey.

We passed Podishne and Katchergishki and was close to the border. I think my plan is crazy, I am going to a place where there are no more Jews. Nevertheless, I feel my plan is the right one, no one except a good friend will hide an invalid, and these friends were in Ignalina. I need to take the risk and continue my journey.

I know each village and each house, I see the cursed mud that I blame for my amputation. I pass through Michaleva, where the Lithuanian bandit left me naked.

Suddenly the driver makes a wrong turn and we arrive in Daugelishok, the shtetl that I so feared.

When we left Daugelishok I thanked God that I survived this terrible road.

Night came. Not a soul was seen. The landscape was empty. We arrived at a forest and the sled drove quickly and I was certain all would go well.

Suddenly...

Approaching us was a sled with three people!

“Halt! Police!”

Where are you coming from?

“From Opsa.”

I didn't know that it was forbidden to ride from one poviat to another.

Who knew, who could have told us?

[Col. 1070]

You must turn around and come with us.

We have no choice, the driver turns around and follows.

On the way a policeman asked me in Lithuanian:

“Who are you?”

“An invalid, don't you see, here are my crutches.” He looked and asked:

“So, you still have a long way to go?”

“No,” I answered, “less than four kilometers.”

“If so, go there, sleep, and the following morning turn back. If we meet you again we will arrest you.”

The Lithuanian police whipped their horses and they disappeared.

We both felt we were saved from death.

We got off the main road, took the sides roads passing Pakerze and Veliada and we were getting closer to Budkevitch. I was in need of rest and a good meal but when we approached the house, it was lit and looked like Budkevitch had guests.

The dog started to howl and only Budkevitch came outside and approached the sled.

I started to kiss him, and immediately noticed his coldness.

I begin to beg him to have pity on an invalid and allow me stay in the attic.

He warns me that at his daughter's [house], her–in–laws are there, and he is frightened.

His plan was that I should go to the forest.

“What shall I do there? Where shall I go?”

I had remorse that I put Adamovitch's life in danger and he accompanied me all this way.

I ask him to drive me to Danietz's house and put me close to his door. He agrees but he doesn't want to be seen.

[Col. 1071]

We arrived at Danitz, Adamovitch removed me from the sled and placed me in front of the door. We kissed, parted ways and he wished me good luck.

When the sled disappeared, with difficulty I made it to the door and knocked.

Soon someone answered: “who is there?”

“Your friend, Korb.”

He opened the light and helped me in. He was alone.

His first question: “where did you lose your foot?”

I told him the story and my situation, he brought me milk, bread and butter.

I ate and began to make my request.

I told him about Budkevich and our long friendship, the in–laws and his refusal to hide me, and asked if I could remain several days in order to make another plan.

He thought it over, you will stay with me. But not in my house, but if I put you in the shed, you will freeze to death.

I ask him If I can stay in the cellar, if his potatoes aren't frozen, then nothing will happen to me. He agreed.

He gave me his bed, saying, my first night should be a warm one. I should get a good rest and tomorrow he will take me to the cellar.

He woke me when it was still dark outside, “get up, I don't want anyone seeing me carrying you out of the house.”

[Col. 1072]

Half an hour later I was settled in the cellar and Danietz locked up.

I smoked a cigarette and in the light of the smoke I saw my new dwelling.

Besides the potatoes, there were beats and bread. My first duty in the cellar was to write a letter to Mirl and the children.

Eight o'clock, Danietz brought me hot tea and bread, butter and cheese. Such a delight. I hadn't eaten such a breakfast in a long while.

Now, how was I going to pass the time without going crazy? What can I do? in the dark, I can't read or write. I need a plan. I decided to record the wanderings from Ignalina to Vidz, to Opsa and to Braslav and then again to Opsa. To have a memoire of where I was in these days of wandering. This will help me pass the time if I am going to survive.

In the cellar I had an unfortunate war with the mice.

They were the size of cats. They crept over my head and had to scare them away with my crutches. They weren't scared of me and came back.

They are the owners of the cellar and they wonder what I am doing in their territory?

[Col. 1073]

I start to think that they are right. It is their home and rightfully so, I am their guest and I want to throw them out! I am doing to them what Hitler is doing to the Jews! It is not right!

The mouse theory helps me pass the day! But when they crawl on my head, I use my crutches.

After the mice, the humidity and dampness bothered me. The wetness clung to the stones of the cellar and my coughing started. It was bothersome and I had to make sure no one heard me. In addition, I feared blindness from the dark black cellar. Oh! An invalid and also a blind one!

On the third day I asked my boss to bring Rekst to me to deliver a letter to my wife in Opsa.

Rekst came and agreed to deliver the letter.

Twelve days pass, my coughing grows worse. Where should I go?

One day Danietz arrived sad and disorientated. I instinctively felt bad news coming my way.

The mayor discovered my stay in the village and I must leave immediately.

Don't be frightened! I ordered a wagon to bring you to Vidz.

“No, no, not to Vidz, my dear friend.”

“It means death for me, as I just came from there.”

"God, so where do you want the wagon to take you? Do you have other Christian friends in this region?"

"Bring me to Maxim. Or to Martinav."

The wagon came and when it was dark they took me out of the cellar and put me into the sled.

[Col. 1074]

On the way the driver told me he didn't want Martinov to know who was driving me.

No one will know, drop me at the gate of the house.

When we arrived, he helped me off the sled and with my crutches, when he drove off I approached the house.

I knocked: "who is there?"

"It is I, Yerachmiel."

He opened the door wondering why I came to him.

"The police are here every day," he said. "Besides, I am scared for my own son. He is working with the Lithuanian partisans and he can be a threat to you."

I propose that he bring me to Maxim. He doesn't have a horse. I have no choice so he carries me on his back.

Like a sack of corn, I had no other choice, he shlepped me across the fields to Maxim.

He also didn't want Maxim to know. Again I was dropped off, and I made my way. Maxim was overjoyed to see me alive.

He thought no one from Ignalina remained alive. I asked him to hide me, and after some thought, he proposed to put me on the oven.

"Good!" He helped me up. I was frozen and still unwell from the cellar, so in that moment I was happy with my new home. I soon fell asleep.

[Col. 1075]

I awoke and heard his wife quarreling about me. Why is he is putting his life in danger for a Jew. She will not allow this!

She warmed the oven and I became so hot I couldn't stand it! What shall I do?

I ask Maxim to go to Ignalina to bring my former maid to discuss another hideout.

She arrived in the evening, bringing sugar and jam, and when I saw her I started to cry.

"Sosia—find me a place to hide."

No Christian will hide a healthy Jew, let alone an invalid.

“And what about Zak? I am almost naked.”

Maybe you can find a jacket, a fur or some other things?

The next morning I received a fur, new pants, a vavel and some other small things.

All's well, but I still have no hiding place. Perhaps Maxim can bring me to his attic?

You will freeze, it is winter.

It doesn't matter, I'll manage. He brought me to the attic.

It was cold. Often he brought me hot tea and soup. I couldn't tolerate the cold any longer, and he came to fetch me from the attic. I was fed up. Maxim didn't have any other place for me.

[Col. 1076]

Sosia had told me that Brumberg and Viduchinsky are living in the Sventzian ghetto, so I decided to write them a letter. What will be will be, at least I will be together with my fellow Jews.

Maxim's wife left with the letter and returned with the answer–come to us.

I offered my fur, pants and others things to Maxim to take me to Sventzian, but his wife didn't want him to risk his life. But he didn't listen.

The next morning the horse and sled were prepared and we were set to go. The wife ran into the street and started yelling, Maxim do not go!

I want to calm her and promise her all kinds of things, nothing helped. She insisted and held onto the horse's reins so we couldn't move.

He tried to reassure her, “this will be your death, she screams!”

Maxim waits, jumps into the sled, whips the horse and off we go, leaving his wife screaming in the street.

In six or seven kilometers along the road, Maxim suddenly turns to me and says–Yerachmiel, where did you hide your fortune?

I'll tell you, I reassure him. Probably Maxim was helping me as he knew me previously as the “rich person.” Meanwhile he didn't realize he was lost and not on the main road. I noticed our erratic up and down hill, not seeing my familiar telephone poles.

“Maxim”—I say—“find your way and then I will confide in you when I buried my fortune. Perhaps you can find it?”

[Col. 1077]

Eventually he found his way, and I told where and how to find my money.

He can keep everything, the only condition, he must bring me bread and other products in Sventzian.

I felt that revealing my secret, a new energy flowed through him. He got off the sled, wrapped me warmly and asked if I was comfortable.

The cold worsened but we eventually saw Sventzian.

I was frightened that it shouldn't get light outside, in broad daylight I couldn't ride into the shtetl. I asked Maxim to increase his speed, and as quick as lightening we crossed the fields and I saw the first house.

I saw the mill, then the market square, I remembered every corner, every house. I looked everywhere, perhaps I will recognize someone.

Suddenly I notice Brumberg walking, looking at the sled and he recognizes me. He turns around and goes into a small street. I direct Maxim to follow him, Brumberg giving me a wink.

Maxim stopped at the house where Moishe Yitzhak Brumberg lived. He helped me down and with difficulty I entered the house.

Brumberg told me where I was, this was the Sventzian ghetto and Viduchinsky lives here.

I said goodbye to Maxim, asking him not to forget me and to tell the other Christians where to find me and bring me food.

Maxim turned around and left. I remained with my friends Brumberg and Viduchinsky.

[Col. 1078]

This date is forever etched in my memory, January 18, 1942.

In the Sventzian Ghetto

Frozen, with tears and heartache I arrived at Brumberg and Vidutchinsky, we hugged and kissed like long– lost beloved brothers.

Everyone in the house was crying: my circumstance and my appearance affected them.

We sat around for hours telling them my story.

From me they got firsthand information of the Jews of Vidz, Opsa and Braslav.

They had their own accounts to tell.

Vidutchinsky, they [the Germans] left behind because he was the pharmacist, Brumberg was taken to Poligon from Sept 26–Oct 6 with all the Jews. No one believed that a mass murder would take place, they suffered from lack of space and hunger. He worked digging potatoes in the fields with Israelka.

My son–as he told me—believed as engineer–mechanic that he would be freed and could take Sprintze with him.

On the second day they chose some men and told them they were needed for work, but shooting was heard, we were assured these were only sick and elderly.

Knowing that young people were being murdered, we abandoned all hope, the barracks were guarded by Lithuanian policemen.

No one stood up! The hairdresser managed to say, "Bandits, you will be.

He didn't finish these last few words, he received a bullet. Rabbi Ushphal went to his grave wrapped in a Tallit. Brumberg managed to leave as foreman of the boots [footwear].

[Col. 1079]

These were the "useful" Jews who were allowed to remain in the ghetto. They believed I could remain with them unharmed. I will not die from hunger.

The peasants brought us bread and potatoes and we bartered for clothing and shoes.

In the meantime, Motel Heshel Buskanyetz came to take me to Brumberg's house. He gave me a small room and a bed and I fell asleep, I was with "my Jews."

The next morning Rochel Kroz arrived, or as they called her in the ghetto, Rochel the Zarazaier. She wanted to repay me for my previous goodwill, and she tended to my needs.

She was well acquainted with the head of the police in the ghetto, she was the "macherke" in the ghetto (able to move freely).

She worked as a translator of Lithuanian to German.

She told him about me, that I was her step–father and he [the commander of the ghetto] should pay me a visit. She left me tobacco, bread and salami and actually arranged for my wife and children to join me. As she promised, the head gendarme came to Brumberg and asked about the Jew from Braslav. Brumberg got frightened, but showed him my room. He came into the room to verify who I was. He pulled out a pack of cigarettes and shook my hand–

"You will remain alive"...

Rochke came to me the next morning, I thanked her for her friendship and asked her to help me blend into the ghetto, I didn't want to be that obvious.

They employed me as a glazier, brought me a work–card, and I was pleased that I now became a “useful Jew”, like the others, in the Sventzian ghetto.

I had friends and relatives visiting me, I didn't notice how the time was passing by.

[Col. 1080]

And when there were no visitors, my plan was to write about the events that I experienced. I had a feeling that these notes would be of great historical importance after the war.

Meanwhile Rochel's help dried up, her superior was transferred to Eisishok, and her livelihood dwindled, barely receiving enough to sustain herself.

There were days of hunger, but I don't want to tell anyone the details.

March 5, 1942, was a great day. I received a letter from Mirl saying she and the children were well, not to worry and all was quiet in her zone.

Reading the letter, I think, perhaps they should all come here. They already “cleaned out”, and the useful Jews remained. Perhaps it was one of the safer ghettos [Sventzian].

At that moment Brumberg's wife comes into my room and tell me the “Gestapo” came last night and told the gendarmes the Jews need to be deported. But the gendarmes got them drunk and they left without enforcing the edict. I realized we were not as secure here as well. I didn't have a choice but to remain.

I dreamt of only one thing; after the war, whoever survives, will tell the world about the German and Lithuanian atrocities.

I stay in my room and write. From time to time friends pass by to tell me of the new decrees. Here they murdered the Jews and there they were deported and we don't know where.

Besides the three ghettos of Vilna, Kovno and Shavel, officially, the only Jews left are in the Sventzian ghetto.

All of Lithuania is “Judenrein” (cleansed of Jews) and the Yiddish “kibbutz” (community) doesn't exist any longer.

There is still a ghetto in White Russia, in Gluboke. We found out that most were murdered there as well, especially if they didn't have protectia.

[Col. 1081]

This gives us some hope: we are useful, we are working hard and for free, but for us, the main thing is we are still alive.

One time I heard a terrible story: young people from Svir were told they were being sent to work, they arrived in Big- Vileyka and together with other Jews, put in the Beit Hamidrash and were burnt alive.

It sent shivers through everyone. Everyone is thinking about death. The Jewish population decreases day by day. The Sventzianer Jews are still full of hope and believe their "stars" will burn forever.

I begin to have my doubts but don't want to damage their illusion.

Mirl Comes to Sventzian

May 3, 1942, I received a German newspaper. With a printed speech by Hitler, the Jews will no longer spread their vermin...

I told my friends:" I don't know if all of Hitler's plans will succeed, but his plan is to eradicate all the Jews."

Nevertheless, I started to inquire how to bring Mirl and the children to Sventzian. If we are to die, let it be altogether!

How can I bring her here. All my Christian friends live far and I don't know how to get in touch with them. Hunger sets in and I don't have help from anyone. People were not good. They already suffered (went through hell) and perhaps with all they endured, they were so embittered. Like iron, that lay in the fire too long, they are now worthless.

Just a small percentage of the Jews were hopeful. The others lost faith. I longed for the Jews of Opsa and Braslav.

One time I received a letter from my niece Rivka Gilinski, who was in the Vilna ghetto, telling me that conditions were not better there.

A week before Passover I received news that the Jews of Opsa and region were deported.

[Col. 1082]

The Jews of Braslav were rounded up and sent to Vidz. What will happen to them? Mirl was also in Vidz and wants to come to Sventzian.

The children remained at Adamovitch in hiding. Mirl has no money, what can she do?

Five days pass. Its Erev Pesach and friends are sitting in my room. The door opens and in walks Mirl.

We kiss and cry bitter tears. She tells me that the children are safe and cared for as if they were Adamovitch's own children. It seems that she was lucky. In Vidz she met a peasant who was an old friend, he was going to Sventian and took her along. We are happy that we are both together again. But where shall we get food to eat? Before I needed to find food for one person, now we are two.

God is good and exactly the same day we received a package of food stuffs from Radtzinski.

This is a good sign and I calmed myself.

Mirl, however, is not in the "count" of the ghetto. At this time new edicts were passed in the ghetto. They are always looking for someone. One time after such a role call Mirl hid at Rochele's. She was very frightened.

Our lives in the Sventian ghetto become more difficult day by day. We trembled from fear.

End of May the Gebit–Commisar Wolf arrived in the ghetto, he was responsible for the slaughter of the Jews in the Vilna province. We were told that he is particularly interested in killing the old, the sick and children. I feel that my situation is almost hopeless. Surely he will not let an invalid survive. I must run away again. But where? Who will hide an invalid?

Adding to all my problems, I received a letter from Moishele, that he is in Opsa and he is hiding with Leibele in cellars and attics. Every night another attic, he is working in a milk factory and has enough milk but no bread.

[Col. 1083]

In order to get piece of bread he sold his boots. He is asking if there is way to bring Leibele to us? Then it will be easier on him.

We read the letter and cried. It seems that both sons are in the same predicament as us, and I was still thinking, that their lives were more secure.

Rochele advises us that a Christian friend of hers has a motorcycle and will bring him the following week.

Our lives were not secure in the Sventian ghetto, everyone was in disarray and in hiding. Many of the Jewish workers didn't come home at night to sleep.

All from our house ran away. Only Mirl and myself remained Everyone is looking for a hiding place.

We feel regrets about Leibele's situation, why are we bringing him here? Perhaps he will arrive and no longer find us here.

Several days later the ghetto became quiet again. It seems that Wolf came here only to order the ghetto be surrounded by barbed wire so no one could enter or leave.

The Judenrat must be careful that only the Jews who were on the list be allowed to remain.

We don't know what to do with Leibele, he may arrive and the ghetto will be locked, what will he do then?

July 31,1942, 11a.m, Leibele arrived. Twelve noon the ghetto was locked. He arrived in a car. He gave the chauffeur some cheese that he got from the milk factory.

He is unknown here and Brumburg was scared to have him in his house. He goes to sleep at Rochele's.

In the meantime a new edict came out, the Judenrat needs to bring young workers right away to the village of Stanislavav. We are told that if he [Leibele] goes to work tomorrow they will include him in the count.

Leibele says goodbye to us, takes a piece of bread and departs with the others.

[Col. 1084]

Sunday Leibele returns home and brings us potatoes that he carried on his back. He told us that the person in charge was a good friend of mine and when he saw him he welcomed him politely. He gave him easier work and helped him out of many difficult situations. One time he even brought him a piece of bread with fat in the field. Leibele came to us every Sunday and brought us something to eat, this was a great help.

We also received a letter from Moishele that he is in Podbrodz, and he is working at a sawmill.

Police Commander from the Vilna Ghetto-Gens- His Speech for the Jews of Svenzian

Times in the ghetto became unsettled. There was talk that we were all going to be sent to Vidz. Others said that the Jews of Vidz were going to be sent to Sventian, no one knew exactly what was going on. A short while later the commander from the Vilna ghetto Herr Gens came to the ghetto. Before the war he was an officer in the Lithuanian army.

We welcomed him with a big parade, he held a speech and was amazed at the beauty of the nature. He said that if we allow rotten trees to grow, new young roots will not be able to flourish.

The young people applauded...the old people trembled. I immediately understood that there is no place for me here. Again the same question arose, where to go?

The ghetto is surrounded by barbed wire, not far away I see the mud and a pit filled with water. From both sides I see the Lithuanian police. How can an invalid like myself leave the ghetto?

Meanwhile we were informed that the Jews from Vidz were coming here. How are we all going to manage? There are about 400 Jews here already.

[Col. 1085]

Now another 300 Jews will be arriving.

They arrived in Sventian and were packed into the school. A few hundred were put into the synagogue. The remainder were placed in different homes. Fifteen souls lived in one room. The lack of space and filth became frightening.

The ghetto had only one bathroom and one source of water. I saw this was not a place to live. Sickness will arrive. When I was told that the glazier Yitzhak Bak was going to replace windows in Daugelishok, I asked him to take me with him as his helper and I will thereby make a stop in Ignalina.

Rochele prepared my tools right away, but I needed a pass which was not easy to obtain. Several days passed and I didn't receive the "pass."

I became angry with Brumberg and decide to run away to Stanislavav where my Leibele worked. Perhaps the foreman will take pity and hide me.

Brumberg is not certain if I can manage the ten kilometers on my crutches to Stanislavav. I assure him that I will go step by step, I will rest on the way until I arrive there.

At night a pit was dug out under the wires, Brumberg lifted the wires, I said goodbye to everyone, and managed to crawl to the other side. I lay still for a while until I noticed the policeman was occupied and carrying on with a shiksa. [Gentile woman] I got up and started to crawl in the direction of the mud. I discussed with Mirl that when I crossed the mud it was her turn to crawl under and follow me. I will wait for her. All my friends could not believe that a man with only one foot still had the desire to run away. And again I had another important date to remember... Wednesday October 26, 1942.

[Col. 1086]

On One Foot– from the Sventzian Ghetto

With difficulty I dragged myself to the pit but I could not cross on my crutches. I threw the crutches over the pit, I put one foot into the water and with my hands I crawled until I reached the other side. I rested a while. I took my crutches and wanted to go through the mud but it was not so easy. My crutches sank in the mud and I did not have the strength to pull them out.

I decided to crawl across the swamp on my stomach and to drag my crutches with me. Finally I managed to cross the mud.

Shortly after Mirl arrived. Even she wondered how I managed with one foot to cross the pit and go through such thick mud.

I continued step by step very slowly, I thought the road would be easier but it was a mistake. The road was a sandy one and my crutches sank into the deep sand and it was difficult to pull them out.

Mirl did not believe that I would reach Stanislavav, every 50 feet I needed to stop to rest. It was a warm day and the sweat poured down.

We see a policeman coming in our direction, we left the road immediately for the field. He passed and did not notice us. We continued on the road again. I started to count the telephone poles, until now we only passed 13 poles. According to my calculations we need to pass at least a hundred poles, how will I survive this? The strength is leaving my body.

A wagon is passing with a Lithuanian peasant sitting alone. I ask her: "Can I ride with you?" She looks at me, does not answer and whips the horse to continue further.

We are dragging ourselves, step by step. We rest again every so often. Suddenly we hear another wagon, we wait until it approaches us, sitting in the wagon is a stranger. I beg him to take me several kilometers.

[Col. 1087]

He stops, thinks, and answers me in Russian.

"Sit down" I roll myself into the wagon and ask if he can take my wife with us, how can she go alone? He agrees.

On the way I realize who this peasant is, he is a good friend, I tell him who I am and he starts to tremble. It bothers him to see me in a such a bad situation.

Not far from the hamlet Svinta he dropped us off.

We thanked him and went through the gate. There were many Jewish workers here, they fed us and they showed us our accommodations for the night. The next morning the overseer arrived and when he saw me he said " who are you?"

"I am a glazier. I'm going to Stanislavav to repair windows. "

"If you are a glazier I have work for you, come with me" He takes me to his home and shows me the work to be done. I need to take out the shutters and put in the windows. I begin my work but I have no strength in my hands and I break a window. He tells me to stop working and to go eat. From the other workers I discover he is a Jew and lives /works for the Tatar.

A second night we spent in Svinta, we woke up early and decided to continue our journey to Stanislavav.

We took small side streets travelling slowly step by step, several hours passed when we reached a small stream. Over the water there were several small round stones and a man with two legs would have difficulty making this journey.

But this didn't frighten me, I got down on my stomach and crawled over the bridge. We arrived in a village hungry and dead tired.

[Col. 1088]

We knew that in this village there were known Lithuanian bandits but we didn't have a choice, we passed two houses and went into the third one. Here we begged them for a place to rest. Barely ten minutes passed and three Lithuanian partisans came into the house, I didn't lose my cool and asked them for a cigarette. One gives me a cigarette and asks me where I'm going.

I tell them the old story, I'm a glazier and I'm going to Stanislavav to glaze windows. The partisans didn't bother us any longer and left.

I notice how the Christian finished eating and says to me "Panie: I know you. My husband used to work for you in the forest." "Oy, gutenu!" "What happened to you? Perhaps you would like to eat something?"

We had a hearty meal and then continued on our journey. After a few paces I felt my foot could no longer continue, only on my hands...

The skin under my arms peeled off from my crutches, and it hurt badly. I barely made twenty steps with great difficulty, and had to remain on the spot. I rested and I continued another twenty steps, this is how we dragged ourselves for several hours. From time to time I made a greater effort in order to arrive quicker to my son Leibele in Stanislavav.

When I arrived at the work camp I couldn't speak to anyone. I travelled for fourteen hours on one foot on such a difficult road, the workers didn't want to believe me. I told them I didn't go with one foot but with both hands...

I lay down on the hard ground and wanted to sleep, the ache in my hands didn't allow me to fall asleep. My armpits were sore.

In the morning the foreman came in and welcomed me in a friendly manner, we cried.

"Ra[m]balski, you have to save me, otherwise my days are numbered. Keep me here a few days, until I receive a "pass" to travel to Ignalina".

[Col. 1089]

He felt sorry for me, heated a bath for me and we both washed ourselves. Then he brought me tobacco leaves to smoke, the food was plentiful.

Slowly the ache under my arm went away, I slowly regained my strength and started to plan ahead.

I asked Rambalski to go to Sventian to give an important letter to Rochele. In the letter I asked her to prepare my "pass" for Ignalina.

She answered me that the document had been signed, the delay is due to the unavailability of the glass. Rambalski goes almost everyday to Svenztian and brings back the same news. I write to Rochele again "tell the engineer, that I hid a lot of glass in Ignalina. When I will be there I will give him half the glass."

I also needed to write in the "pass" that they should provide me with a wagon, I can't go with the train, because I will have to pass through Sventzian and I cannot be seen in Svenztian.

Rambalski brings the answer to me late at night. Rochele wrote that my plan with the hidden glass is a perfect plan. I will surely get the "pass" for you in the next few days.

Shabbos Nov 21, 1942 I received my "pass" from the Sventzian Judenrat and within three days I need to be in Ignalina to glaze the windows of the school.

Several words in German were written in the pass... "the glazier Korb Yerachmiel, needs to drive to Ignalina to glaze the windows of the synagogue. He will be taken with a wagon and will arrive on the 21st of November." Signed by the engineer and the head of police.

I read the pass and couldn't believe how well she organized everything, especially that it was written to provide a wagon and not to be sent by train. I went straight away to Rambalski and gave him the news.

[Col. 1090]

I have to leave right away and I need him to arrange for a wagon. He promised me the next day but the next day was Sunday and a Christian worker will not want to bring me.

"That is actually good, my son Leibele will go with me, you just have to give him the right papers." He agreed. Sunday morning the wagon was harnessed and Leibele was ready to head out. As it rained last night, there was a frost in the morning, the road was very slippery. The horse slid and fell down.

Rambalski ordered another horse be prepared, an old and lazy one that cannot run fast. Finally we arrived in Stanislavav. Leibele held onto the reigns so the horses will not run and slip. I had a lot of time to think during the journey, I took pity on my shtetl which I helped build and lived in. How can I now look into these empty Jewish homes?

I know that I will not suffer any hunger here but my welcome will not be same. We passed Tzeiken, the Jewish homes are without windows and doors. We continue further and see the Christians going to church, now we are in Ignalina. I recognize every tree and every house.

My eyes begin to tear, I beg Leibele not to drive by our house, I cannot bare to see my misfortune. Night arrives, its dark outside and again I see my dear town Ignalina, its Sunday November 22, 1942.

Return to Ignalina

When we arrived in our shtetl Ignalina my heart burst and we started to cry. How difficult it was to see our dear old home so destroyed.

[Col. 1091]

I have to be careful to whom I go, I have very good friends here, both Lithuanian and Polish, I weigh my options; my Polish neighbors will receive me well but they also fear the Lithuanians. Better to find a good Lithuanian, it will be safer with him.

I tell Leibele to go back to the mayor as he became an important "bandit", and all the Jewish property is at his home. In front of me he will pretend to be good and pious. Besides this I need to brown–nose because of the "pass". Leibele listened to me and brought me to the mayor, when he saw me he started to kiss me and was happy that I was still alive. I felt something odd, from his kiss and from the smell of his brandy. At first I asked him to find a place for the horse and for Leibele to spend the night. He was very friendly and immediately found a place. Then he brought me into his home which struck me immediately with its familiar belongings [stolen property], everybody was eager to find out how I was saved and how I managed during this difficult period. I told them that I was sent as a glazier to repair the windows of the school. Leibele has to return tomorrow morning and my wife Mirl is in the work camp. In the morning the peasants brought the wagon which they filled with produce, potatoes, bread, meat and even sugar. Leibele left. I alone left to meet the Voijt, who was an honest and good Lithuanian. We found out later that he hid three Jews.

I told him my situation and he proposed to give me a room in his house. Nevertheless I knew that the room he offered would not be suitable and I thanked him for his good intensions. He called Svenztian and told the engineer that I had arrived.

[Col. 1092]

He [the engineer] also needed a glazier and will keep me here. The engineer told him to procure glass from Kovno and he agreed I stay in Ignalina.

In the meantime I was recognized by Boyshi, a former employee and he invited me after lunch. I left with him and noticed he was living in a Jewish house with new furniture.

He put some brandy on the table and a full bowl of cotelets, (meat patties). He drank the whole time and I ate a little [without appetite]. He told me he bought the furniture on liquidation when the Jewish people sold their merchandise.

He had watches on both hands. On the wall hung a clock and on the ceiling a chandelier. It was clear to me where everything came from. Besides, he was very interested if I had hidden my fortune. Word by word he spoke, with intensity and with much emphasis, that the Rabbi's bed is there in his home, this was a big deal for him to sleep in the Rabbi's bed.

I thought that I would fall down and faint, I imagined the Rabbi saying his prayers in this bed and now, instead, here sleeps a drunk...

Darkness descended upon me when I went into his bathroom, there I found hanging on a nail a religious book which served as toilet paper.

I couldn't delay any longer as Boyshi came to the bathroom to see if I was okay.

I came out with tears in my eyes and said to myself: “who by sword, who by starving, who by plague, and who by stoning” [biblical text]....

If there is a God why did he forsake us? He gave the Rabbi's bed to a drunk who hangs a religious book in his bathroom....

On the way from Boyshi I encountered Greize, he lived on the right side of the blacksmith's house and also inherited a house with all its furnishings.

From there I left to find Sosia, our former trustworthy servant, she helped us several times but she was afraid of her husband who was a gangster and enemy of [the people] of Israel.

[Col. 1093]

His brother was one of the first murderers, I didn't stop long and left for the synagogue where the Jewish work camp was now located.

I was greeted with terror, the windows were boarded up, in the women's section many sick people were kept, they were starving to death.

I left and gathered from the peasants some milk, bread and meat and delivered it to the sick ones. From the synagogue I left to see Marzinken, who was living in Kagan's house, across from the minian. He was a former foreman of the animals in the shtetl.

I rested there and ate, however I noticed that Kagan's furniture stood as before, nothing was rearranged, only the boss/ owner was new.

I looked at the windows and saw Kagans old curtains still hanging. The bedroom was open and the beds were covered with white covers. Next to the bed, instead of a divan, was a white cover from a Sefer Torah. He also was dressed in Kagan's holiday clothes and you can tell immediately a tailor did not make this garment for him [Marzinken]...

“How can my heart sustain all of this?” They sat on the Torah covers as if on a sofa!

I left Kagan's house depressed and returned to the Voijt. He brought me to the second floor and showed me a separate room where I should stay.

Officially it means that I am working for him and he needs me to paint the windows. When the Lithuanians will hear about this arrangement they will become angry, but he told me I should disregard it and not worry.

He tells me a secret that he is hiding three Jews... Ritva, with his wife and daughter.

We barely ended our conversation when the soltise came to the house and asked me if I had seen Tczernitch. " He was your best friend, come with me, I will take you to him".

[Col. 1094]

He [Tzcernitch] was glad that I was accompanied by the soltice, otherwise he would be afraid to speak with me. When the solstice left Tczernitch told me a secret, the Lithuanians were not pleased to see me wandering through the shtetl, it was a bad omen and could end badly for me. He claimed that I need to be careful so I returned to Grinevitch.

He tells me the same secret, they [the Lithuanians] are going to kill me, be very vigilant. I don't know what to do. From one side I believe that Tczernitch and Grinevitch are doing me a favor by telling me the truth but from the other side I'm afraid to go into the Jewish labour camp in the Synagogue because, according to the doctor, there is an outbreak of Typhus.

What shall I do? Where shall I go?

After much deliberation I decided to go to the synagogue. These were Jews mostly from Smorgon, Oshmiane and Vidz. I was told the camp director was not a bad person, but he has no provisions, they go from village to village begging for a piece of bread.

Basically, they [the inmates] are more scared of the epidemic than hunger. If the Germans discover the area is infected with Typhus they will surely kill everyone.

We discuss what to do, we decide to write a letter to the Sventzian ghetto and request them to trade the sick with healthy workers.

Several days later we managed to send away the sick to Sventzian and healthy workers arrived in their place.

In the mean time I encountered Andreievski and convinced him to hide Mirl. Leibel will come to me in the labour camp.

December 23, 1942, Leibel used his free time to bring wooden shoes from the camp to Sventzian and then returned to Ignalina to the labour camp.

He was exhausted and the German Camp–director didn't want to take him for work–detail, no matter what.

[Col. 1095]

I gave him a gift, a pair of warm gloves, and he counted him as a 17– year old and took him into the work camp. Leibel was happy to be back in Ignalina, even though it would be hard work.

Andreievitch[4] came several days later, bringing a letter from Mirl, telling me how she made her way and how she is.

I calm down and returned to Tczernitch for further news. I found a newspaper at his home and read what was happening on the front. I remember exactly, January 5, 1943, Meskin and Zolan were in a heated conversation at Tczernitch's.

As I was leaving Tczernitch told me a secret, the Jews of Ignalina will be murdered and I must escape and find another hiding place.

I returned to the synagogue and shared this information with the Jews, they didn't believe me. The chief promised them work until March and they felt secure.

Leibele was the only one that believed me. I needed to find a place for him, not too far away, so he could escape at the very last minute.

My plan was that Leibel will go to Andreievski, Mirl and I to Denishoki and Moishe to a Christian near Dukst. The main thing was not to delay.

In the meantime I received a letter from my daughter in–law in the Vilna ghetto, there is no room here and we have to go to a "dacha"... [dacha=country home=Ponar]

I understood the meaning, and we needed to leave Ignalina immediately: but how? I didn't want anyone to see us!

February 10, 1943, Radtzinski was with me and arranged for a sled to come, he will bring me in the evening to his place. However when we arrived he couldn't stop at this place.

[Col. 1096]

February 15, several days later, Simkun invited me for a meal and I accepted. On the way I was stopped by two Lithuanians who requested I accompany them to repair windows.

I quickly understood and told them I was presently very busy and I will contact them later.

Meanwhile Leibele arrived and told me he encountered Yelilovski and said to him.

"Hand in your father, we already prepared a grave for him! "I told Leibele about the two Lithuanians and now was the moment to disappear! The only one that can save me is Radtzinski.

Leibel must go to him and explain my life is in great danger. The best way for Leibel to leave the work camp was to ask the female doctor, my friend, to request a “pass” for him to leave.

That is exactly what happened and Leibel was freed from work for several days by the head of the work camp.

February 16, Leibel left to Radtzinski. I spent the day worrying, perhaps he changed [attitude towards the Jews] like the others?

Leibel returned with a happy face. Radtzinski and Zilen will come the next day, Thursday, to take me away.

I discuss with Leibel that if he is told that he will be resettled, it means “death”, and to run away to Andreievski.

Besides, when they come searching for me, tell them I had to leave to repair windows.

[Col. 1097]

The next morning Leibel went to the designated spot, not only was Radzinski and Zilen there, but also Zilen's son, and we all agreed to meet at the Tatar's house in the evening.

Fleeing My Shtetl

I said my goodbyes with all the Jews, told them not to trust anyone. They must find ways to escape when they come for them.

I told Tczernitch my plans and asked him to bring me supplies whenever he can. Leibel is still in a bad situation. I kissed him and left for the Tatar's house.

A cold wind was blowing and a light snow falling. I was careful not to fall.

Finally I arrived and entered, as I was sitting by the window I saw Ratdzinki's horse. The Tatar fed me and was friendly. I enjoyed my meal. He started speaking, but I couldn't concentrate. “How was I to escape from here? Perhaps the two Lithuanians will arrive?

Meanwhile, night arrived, the wind died down and it was quiet outside.

I noticed Radzinski and Zilen preparing the two sleds and horses, I said goodbye to the Tatar and departed. I made sure no one saw me and slid in the sled with Zolin's son.

[Col. 1098]

Several minutes we were outside the shtetl.

Several kilometers on, near the railroad, there were Lithuanians. We were in danger as no one was permitted to be out at night. I was scared.

I saw that Zilen's son was also frightened, but we continued on, Radtzinki following.

We leave one calamity behind but another one arises. We must pass though the hamlet of Kilatraki, where the civil servant is an anti–Semite, a murderer, a Jew hater for many years.

I tell the driver about him and ask him to ride through as fast as he can and tighten the reins to make the horses run quicker.

Every minute is an hour. Every snap of a branch makes me tremble. Every creak of a door means an enemy.

When we passed this murderous village I catch my breathe. It was time for a cigarette.

Meanwhile Radtzinski caught up and asked the young son to change places.

I said–" thank God I left Ignalina and arrived here safely, now I must find a good place to hide."

We all agreed. At Radtzinski's there were always unknown workers.

[Col. 1099]

At Zilan's lived a relative, who is "crazy" [demented] and we can't trust him. The bathhouse will be very cold.

We decide to go to Danishukev, where Mirl is hiding and we will be together.

The wife assures me that we will be safe. They are very poor but she will feed us.

She even gave me her bed and she slept in the kitchen. Mirl and I couldn't sleep, I was so upset. I told her how I escaped and how they wanted to murder me.

She told me about the honest and pious Christian, Yelivzheta, and constantly cries with her [commiserate together, each crying over their own problems]. There is such poverty in their house, they themselves have nothing to eat. All she possessed was a cow.

When I sent Mirl the 100 rubles she gave it to Yelivzheta who went to buy straw and hay for the cow.

Yelivzheta was very religious, she always crossed herself. She didn't like the Lithuanians, calling them bandits.

She was also in Poligon and with her own eyes witnessed the murder of the Jews of the Sventzian ghetto. She said these gruesome events will haunt her, she can never forget what she witnessed. Wild animals don't treat people like this, like these German and Lithuanian murders! She will do whatever she can to help the surviving Jews. Yelivzheta says the Day of Judgement will arrive one day for these bandits, God will take revenge on them.

[Col. 1100]

I feel better with these words and believe the best place is to hide at her place. I am hopeful. We are fortunate to come across this type of Christian, good and pious. If we can receive help [food] we can survive until the liberation.

Our New Hiding Place

Yelivzheta Ivanovitch grew up in Tambov with rich parents. She studied in her youth and wanted to become a feldsher (barber–surgeon). She met a supervisor, Danishok, of an estate and got married. Several years later he met a shiksa and ran away with her. She never saw him again.

On this same estate, a Jew Siderovitch cut wood, and she became a tutor to his children. When the Germans arrived, they sent him with all the Jews to Poligon. Everything was stolen from the house except for two iron beds, a table and a long bench. The picture by Boris Abramovitch is hidden until today, under her watchful eye.

She told us many times how she went to Poligon to bring him [Siderovitch] food. The last time she went she witnessed the slaughter of the Jews, for weeks she had tremors throughout her body from that horrific sight.

She remained in that house, where the noblewoman of the estate also came to stay, sick and impoverished. She is called Ana Fietrovna. All was confiscated and the two remained together, poor.

Yelivzheta tells us with tears in her eyes how she swore upon Boris' picture that she will save as many Jews as possible from death. She is very satisfied that we are hiding in her place and she will help us.

The next morning I looked around the house, this was not what I expected.

[Col. 1101]

It was not suited for a hiding place. There were large windows on all sides, it stood on the road not far from the railroad station. In the backyard stood a small structure made of thin boards and a torn roof, on the other side stood a warehouse and under the house was a cellar.

Yelivzheta. convinced me it would be worse in the warehouse, as people came there searching for food.

Mirl assured me no one came to the house. She quelled my fears.

Our main worry is where to find food.

Radtzinski had promised me food, several days past and nothing arrived. Yelivzheta agreed to take a letter to him.

Several days later, at night, I heard a knock on the door. We hid in the second room and Yelivzheta answered the door and screamed: "Pan (Mr.) Radtzinski !"

Even the other two Christians were amazed. He brought us food, a sack of potatoes and a loaf of bread and promised to return in a few days with more products, bread, fat and meat.

We said goodbye and the women immediately began to prepare a meal: to cook a pot with the potatoes.

They were happy and understood they needed to thank us.

Radtzinski came with flour, meat and butter.

The Christian women were so happy they proposed to bring Leibele to us.

[Col. 1102]

I thought this would be unsafe for the three of us.

I asked Yelivzheta to go to Ignalina to bring news about me and to see whether Leibele has found a solution. When she returned she brought a letter with some peas and white flour.

Leibele wrote he was given new work and it seems that it would take awhile to complete.

The word in Ignalina is that I was killed, they even showed where.

This calmed us and also the Christians, who became more amicable towards us.

Fourteen days passed quietly. Then two guests arrived: Mrs Krekinova and her daughter.

When they arrived I and Mirl crept under the bed listening to their voices.

Mrs. Krekinova recounted how they killed Yerachmiel, Yelivzheta listened and asked: who is this Yerachmiel? I don't think I know him?

Mrs. Krekinova looked at Yelivzheta strangely: you did not know Korb? Such an unlucky man? They shot him in the forest and didn't even bury him.

When the guests left, Yelivzheta came with a smile and said: "did you hear our conversation?"

I acknowledged that I heard everything, we were all overjoyed that everyone thought I was dead.

March 10, Yelivzheta. returned to Ignalina and returned to tell us Leibele is now in Sventzian.

[Col. 1103]

All the workers were transferred to Sventzian.

The next week, Yelivzheta returned to Ignalina and I asked her to meet Tczernitch, tell him the truth about me and to help Leibel. Also I needed some small stones [could be parts] and benzene for my lighter, I didn't want to loose contact with him.

Great Fear

March 24, 19, Thursday, Yelivzheta went back to Ignalina. When she returned, no letter. She was sad and told us that Tczernitch didn't know where the Jews from the synagogue were taken. Also the Jews from Dukst were deported. I was besides myself, I didn't know if Moishe had escaped.

March 26, the former maid of Ana Fietrovna, Yavze, came to the house late at night. She wanted to spend the night and wouldn't take no for an answer.

I felt a heavy weight! Where shall we hide?

I immediately slid through the window and went into the stable. I had to sleep in the dirt and endure the cold. I was afraid to close my eyes in order not to freeze to death.

From that day forward I pledged not to find myself in such a situation. I was lucky this time, however, if someone came in the daytime, I needed to have a plan. I didn't want to remain in the house in the daytime.

I sat in the stable during the day and at night went into the house. I lay in the hay.

[Col. 1104]

Every evening Mirl waited and asked if I wasn't too cold in the stable.

April 8, Radtzinski came with news from my two children. He met them both in Sventzian and Moishe asked him for some money.

Again Yelivzheta left to see Tczernitch and returned to tell me that the Jews were told they were going to Vilna, instead they were sent to Ponar and killed. He told her to make sure she was careful. She became very frightened. I asked her to fix the roof of the outhouse [barn] in case I needed another place to hide. The question, we couldn't wait for warmer weather? How can we survive?

Another few days passed, daytime in the attic, back in the house at night. Suddenly, late one evening there was a knock on the door.

Yelivzheta asks who is there, we hear in Yiddish, pleading to open the door.

This was Tuvia Solomyak and Leizer Levitan, who escaped from Sventzian. They escaped together with my two sons and were hiding at the peasant Pioter's, who knew me and decided to hide them. They breathed new life into us, they were both safe.

Solomyak and Levitan told me my hideout wasn't safe. We hid in the attic during the day and at night they left for another Christian. We were alone again.

Yelivzheta didn't speak to me. If she needed to tell me something, she came to the stable and spoke to the cow so I would "understand the situation."

April 22, Mirl had a difficult day. Ana Fietrovna got sick, and her former maid, Yavze came to care for her. Mirl spent the entire day under the bed.

[Col. 1105]

At night she snuck out and joined me in the attic.

Lying under the bed, Mirl heard Ana and Yavze speaking and Yavze showed that she was a true anti–Semite, that Hitler was right killing all the Jews.

Even Ana suggested that Yelivzheta should not hide us. Where can we go? We will contact some other Christian and try to find another place. She must be patient and give us a few weeks to find another safe place.

To calm him, I send her to Radtzinski with a letter, to give her a wagon with hay and straw for the cow. She returned with her wagon and again she was pleased with us.

Seeing the house [outhouse] full of straw, we decided to transfer there. At night a storm broke out and the house was blown over. All the neighbours came running to see the disaster, this was my sign from God, that he wanted to save us. We were happy that we didn't stay there.

A few days later, Radtzinski arrived laden with butter, tobacco and cigarettes. He began to repair the house and Yelivzheta was very pleased.

He also brought me newspapers and I had something to read. He also gave us good news from the front. The Germans were suffering many defeats. Hearing this news, Yelivzheta became more hopeful and happier. She seemed in a better mood. After all, she is also a human, and wants to live. The burden to hide Jews, she understood it consequences.

May 27, I heard a voice: "Father," we got up and saw Leibele. He went up into the attic, and told us, the peasant, wants money and they don't have any. Besides this, they have another misery.

[Col. 1106]

Both him and Moishe have scabies [or crabs] and don't want to tell the peasant, they need to buy some salve to ease the itchiness.

We tell Yelivzheta the story and ask her to bring a letter to Tczernitch in Ignalina.

She returned with the ointment and with five dollars from Rekst.

Leibel left in the evening.

First we regretted this, then we realized that our hideout was not so secure.

Several days later Radtzinski came with newspapers where we read the British defeated the Germans in Africa.

My hopes are returning. The war will soon be over and we will be saved.

Oy, how can I survive to the end of the war?

Beginning June, early in the morning I heard an explosion. The Partisans blew up the railroad–line near our village.

Yelivzheta became frightened again. It is not far from here and perhaps they will come to search our home.

That's exactly what happened. In the evening we heard soldiers entering the house and speaking with the Christian. They asked her to open the stable. They looked in and left after ten minutes.

We barely catch our breath when it all starts again. Death was at the door and we saved ourselves again.

I looked at Mirl, white as a ghost, her eyes filled with fear.

I try to convince her we should be happy that this ended as it did.

We continue and wait for better news from the front. It is several months that we didn't change our clothes nor washed, we were infested with lice which bit us constantly.

[Col. 1107]

Another problem arose: Yelivzheta brought Baranovski and his son to rebuilt the [ware]house and fix the stable. This lasted three days, we were not allowed to cough. Baranovski's son was searching for the ladder and Mirl quietly gave it to him. The shaigetz [Gentile lad] didn't notice, but Yelivzheta was not convinced and made a signal with her hand.

When Yelivzheta brought the milk to the dairy farm, she met Baranovski's daughter–in–law, who quietly called her aside,"tell me, who are you hiding in the attic?"

"No one, how can you think like this?"

"Don't tell me stories, my nephew saw you winking at someone in the attic.

She lied for us, but this did not bring us any peace.

We decided to leave and find a new place.

Where shall we go?

The Departure from Yelivzheta

The only Christian who is our good friend and doesn't live far away was Zulan. He will be frightened because he has children, but if we arrive unannounced, he cannot refuse us.

I don't know the way and Yelivzheta doesn't want to take us.

I tell her to go ahead, make signs on the way and we will follow the route until we arrive there.

She agreed. She left and every twenty meters she placed branches on the right side. When we left the forest, she said we will reach a marker and then a field of corn. Crossing the field you will notice a house with a white chimney, this is the house of Zulan.

[Col. 1108]

In the morning we said goodbye to Yelivzheta and left. I told Mirl, I will go first and she will catch up with and we will meet at the forest.

I turned around and didn't see Mirl. I continued looking all around. The skies clouded over and a heavy rain started. I couldn't turn back. I reached the forest, but I was puzzled why Mirl hadn't followed.

After several hours I left the forest, look at the corn field and think something happened to Mirl. I continue through the fields, it is difficult as it is muddy and my crutches are giving me a hard time. I finally reach the first house, but I notice that I went in the wrong direction. This is not the house with the white chimney. I must go back.

I am wet and its swampy, I am soaked through and through. But I don't have another choice. I drag myself through the corn fields. A miracle that it stopped raining! The sun started to shine and I warmed my body. I found a dry spot, rolled a cigarette and rested. I wanted to get up but I didn't have the strength. I needed to rest awhile longer.

Probably I fell asleep. When I woke up I noticed a horse tied to a tree.

Who brought the horse and did he notice me?

[Col. 1109]

I stood up, it was already dark and I looked around. There was the house with the white chimney.

I crossed the corn field and other cultivated fields when I see a stretch of water. I have to cross it, I throw my crutches across to the other side and put my healthy foot into the water. I stretch out my hands holding onto a branch until I reach the other side.

I have no more strength but I continue till I see Zulan's house and bath and recognize it. I creep into the bath house and fall on the stone floor. I am glad I finally have a roof over my head.

I think how I am going to approach Zulan and suddenly two faces look into the bath house.

With delight I hear Leibel's voice saying to Mirl: “Mother, father is here.”

Thank God! We found each other again. They want to hear what happened, why it took so long for me to get here. I was overcome with fatigue and weakness and couldn't speak.

Leibele brings me cold water from a nearby well to freshen up. I drink and regain a little strength. I told them I got lost and had to return through the cornfield.

Mirl did as I instructed, but left in another direction.

She was afraid to go through the forest alone and returned to Yelivzheta. This turned out a good thing as Leibel came looking for her. They ate and left together following the markers. When they reached the cornfields the markers were erased by the rain.

Leibel tells us about his problems. The peasant was demanding more money and material goods, he made their lives miserable. What should they do?

[Col. 1110]

I note this important date: Monday, June 28, 1943.

Alone in the Forest

Tuesday morning I hear something, and by the sound of his cough I recognize it to be Zule. He came in and we kissed and started crying. I told him about our situation and asked that he allow us to remain in his bath house for a few weeks.

He said we would love to help save us but feared for his children. He left and brought us food.

There was an attic and we all crept into it. Zule brought us some straw. Next to Yelivzheta's attic, this was a “Gan Eden” (paradise). We discussed that if Leibel couldn't stay at Adreievitch, Leibel should come here and Moishe should go to another Christian, whom I had earlier spoken about.

Leibel spent the night and said goodbye the next morning to join Moishe.

Saturday evening we heated the bath and for the first time in five months we bathed, changed our clothing and finally got rid of the lice.

Sunday Radtzinski arrived with various products. We were especially happy to receive a newspaper where we read about the British attacks on the Germans.

Everyone was happy and hopeful. Zule's wife visited us in the upstairs attic of the bath to make conversation.

Mirl, in the evening, often left for a walk in the garden to breath some fresh air. The days dragged and we believed we could stay here until the end of the war. Everyone was so friendly and warm.

One time the wife's brother arrived, they passed the bath house and we heard, him telling her how I was killed in a forest, not far from Ignalina. He sighed and said, what a pity on him!

[Col. 1111]

When he left, she came to me and had a good laugh. We climbed down and couldn't imagine another dark cloud descending upon us.

August 23, Zule came to us in the attic. He told us in the neighbouring village of Vishnun, the partisans torched the train station and the Germans were sending search–parties in all directions. Probably they will search the bath house.

Darkness descended again in front of our eyes. We need to wander and find another place to hide.

Zule advised us to go into the potato fields and spend the night. We listened and spent the night on the damp earth between the potatoes.

His wife brought us a cooked meal and we were refreshed.

We lay in the field when suddenly I felt something biting me under my shirt, I pulled off my shirt and threw off the water–worm [water–snake] from my body.

You see, Mirl, even the water–worms are eating us alive!

Zule came at night and when he saw us curled together in the swamp, his heart began to ache and he started to cry. When he calmed down he asked us about our plans. The region was unsafe.

I asked him to bring us to Neverofski. I am sure he will hide me. Mirl will return to Yelivzheta. The main thing, don't forget her and bring her food.

Zule will go to Radtzinski and to request means to travel, several hours later he returned and said that both of them will bring me to Neverofski. No one must know who is involved.

[Col. 1112]

I gave him my word that I would not speak to anyone regarding this matter.

I said goodbye to Mirl and left for the house where the wagon was meeting me.

They put me in the wagon and covered me with straw. They left only a crack for air. I was told not to cough or make a sound as we will be driving through some terrible villages.

On the way I hear Radtzinski greeting an acquaintance. I wanted to cough but hold it in. We finally arrived. I was uncovered and I saw we arrived in the middle of a forest. Radtzinski showed me the way to Neverofski's house. I said goodbye and they told me to wait until dark to continue.

They turned around and off they went. I found myself alone in the forest. Another chapter in my wandering began: the date, September 5, 1943.

Six Months in a Pig Pen

I was in the forest and looked around. All the trees were familiar, some with the markings of our firm, the forest belonged to Lavrinovitch, which bordered on Neverovski's house. It was a beautiful sunny day. I waited until dark, then I made my way to Neverofski's attic and bath house. I decide to sleep in the bath house and the next morning present myself to the boss.

[Col. 1113]

I approached the bath house, opened the door and lit my cigarette–lighter. In the corner I saw a vat with a cover and clearly can see that Neverofski is making illegal liquor. If he has a partner he will arrive and discover me. I go to the warehouse and am ready to fall asleep in the straw when I hear a commotion.

It was Neverofski's son, who had a fight with a neighbour, and he thought I [the neighbour] was coming to beat him up. I calmed him down and told him who I was, the old boss soon appeared and when he saw me he gave me a hearty welcome. He told his son not to worry. I was a good friend.

He invited me into his house and fed me. Then he proposed I sleep in the attic of the bath house.

In the morning he brought me breakfast and when I finished he told me his wife was afraid to hide a Jew and I must leave.

I offered him bribes and eventually I softened him. He let me stay, brought me food and newspapers. But I noticed he wasn't pleased.

September 8, I received a newspaper. I learned the British captured Sicily and Italy capitulated.

I used this information to calm my boss and his wife.

"You see, Hitler lost Italy and he is sustaining heavy losses in Russia. It shows that the war will end soon."

Thirteen days later, September 19, he came to me frightened out of his mind: "Yerachmiel, you must leave immediately, go into the forest and I will come and explain to you what happened."

[Col. 1114]

I did as he advised and I impatiently waited for him in the forest.

He told me a story, a relative got drunk and fired a shot. The police will come to investigate and I will be caught in the middle. I later found out this was a lie, to get rid of me. At that moment I believed him and asked him to take me to his cousin Karol.

He agreed like the others, no one should know who brought me.

When it got dark he took me to his cousin, he carried me on his back for three kilometers as he saw the distance was difficult for me. He brought me to a bath house, and left. I spent the night and in the morning when they came to take the animals to the fields I should present myself to Karol or his wife.

Karol's mother arrived in the morning to take the animals from the stable. I called out to her and when she saw me she got scared. I calmed her and asked her to take pity on me and to allow me to remain. After the War I will repay them.

She left and returned with some food. Then she told me the difficulties if I remain here, the old Neverofski has become senile, and could turn me in.

Karol came in the evening and told me what his mother told me and they were scared to hide me. He told me to go to the forest and he will bring me food.

I had no choice. I left for the forest. I saw that this was not for me. Where shall I go? To Zakarofski or to Kasimer? I remained in the forest the entire day, at night I returned to the bath house.

[Col. 1115]

The nights were already cold. What was I to do?

October 8, I decide to return to Neverofski. I arrive, but the bath is boarded up, the warehouse is locked. I knock on the door, there is no answer. I sit on the porch and cry. Through the window the old Neverofski calls out,"if you don't leave, I'm calling the police".

With a heavy heart I crawl down from the porch and leave for the forest.

I remember this is the night of Yom Kippur. I sit down and cry. Where shall I go? What shall I do? I am alone, on one foot, a cripple, without money, weak and tired? Thrown out and chased like a homeless dog.

I decide to continue on the road. Perhaps some kind Christian will help me. I wander not knowing where I'm going.

It was morning, I hear a hen crowing. I go in that direction [of the hen crowing] knowing I will find farmhouse. I leave the forest and arrive at a poor hut. I recognize this hut belonging to a Pole, an old friend, Bikofski. I approach the door and the dog begins to bark. "Who's there?"

"Open up, it's a friend!"

He approached the door and asked again, "Who are you?"

"Yerachmiel, it is Yerachmiel Korb from Ignalina."

"Yerachmiel? How is that possible? How did you get here? Everyone mourned you, they thought you were murdered."

He let me in and lit a lamp, and looked at me in an odd manner as if I arose from the dead.

[Col. 1116]

"Tell me, how did you save yourself?"

In short I told my story and asked him to have pity on me and find a place for me to hide. I wanted to live.

He thought for a moment, then brought me into the storage–barn and put me in the hay,"Lie down here in the meanwhile, rest. I will bring you food and a warm glass of tea. Later we shall discuss the hideout." I lay down and as I was so tired I fell asleep.

I awoke in broad daylight, Bukofski's wife brought me food. I barely looked around to see my new "palace". Breakfast was delicious. I thanked her from the bottom of my heart and told her the end was near and I will never forget their kind deeds.

The woman left and I surveyed my surroundings, the storage room had half a roof, the other half uncovered. The door led to a pig pen. Directly across was their poor hut. I always knew he was poor, but not this poor. His entire "wealth" was one room, with a feeding house, which was also his workplace filled with pig–pens.

Bukofski brought me lunch, a warm soup, beans and meat, I couldn't believe my eyes.

Such a stroke of good luck! I had a good feeling, that my boss is poor, but a good human being. He will not throw me out. But the question, can I manage here?

At night I wrapped myself with the hay, but I was still cold. What will I do in the winter? In a great storm? I don't want to think about it. I have no other choice. Perhaps the war will be over by then.

[Col. 1117]

This is how the days passed. Bukofski invited me into his home for the evening meals.

My Human Dignity is Lost

October 18, 1943. Bukovski went to Yelivzheta and Tczernitch, gave Mirl news of my whereabouts. He returned with a letter and news of the children. They were still at Andreievitch [Andreiofski, alternative name=error]. A worker arrived several days later to fix the other half of the roof. He made a place in the feeding house for me, between the pens. It was dark and I couldn't read. Perhaps it was better. I overheard them speaking in the house and didn't feel in the mood. I stayed from October 28 until November 2.

I am lying in the hay, it's about ten o'clock in the morning, the door opens and I hear German. Good morning.

I was out of breath. I bury myself deeper, then hear a second voice in German.

What are they doing here? What are they looking for?

I knew Bukofski left and his wife doesn't understand German. From their speech and carrying on I knew they were looking for schnaps. Someone told them that they were making liquor here.

I hear them cursing her and looking in all the corners, suddenly one soldier sees the pens, and calls his comrade: “come here!” A shiver went through me. Here is my death. The soldier begins to throw down the pens, I don't wait another minute.

[Col. 1118]

I jump out of my bed, throw myself against a pen and scream on top of my lungs:

“You see that we have nothing to eat. From where shall we get you schnaps?”

They thought I was her husband. The poverty of the place lingered in every corner. The soldier that pulled down the pens, turned to the door and said to the other one: “come out! Just another poor, wretched soul.”

Butkovski returned at night and he heard about the miracle we encountered.

You have a great God! From that day I took better care and hid in the storage room.

A month passed. November 29, Bukovski said he needs to go to his sister and can deliver a letter to Mirl.

He returned that evening with a letter from Mirl. Rekst sent her 100 rubles. I have nothing to worry. The children are in the same place. The letter gave me hope and the will to survive.

The cold December arrived. It was not comfortable to remain here, I will freeze. I try to go into the stall. It is warmer there, but the terrible smell is unbearable. There were five pigs, two sheep, two cows, and a young horse. The bad odour came from every direction.

I returned to the [ware]house to catch some fresh air, it didn't smell here but it was cold.

I decide that in the daytime I will remain in the [ware]house and at night I will sleep with the pigs and animals.

Slowly I got used to the smell and made myself a separate corner. Another month passed this way.

December 24, Bukovski brought me news that Mirl and Yelevzheta were taken through a village, where to he doesn't know.

I become nervous and can't swallow my soup. It means, I lost Mirl. If they shoot Yelevzheta, Bukofski will be scared and this means the children aren't safe, nor the other Jews that are hidden in other Christian homes.

[Col. 1119]

I feel my head spinning and all my bones are shivering. How, I being the sick one, how did I manage to survive from such filth and such conditions without getting sick?

My clothes were so wet, they were dripping! The cold grew worse and at night I warmed myself with dry dirt in order not to freeze.

My hope was, if the pigs don't freeze, I will not freeze.

In the day I returned to the warehouse, where I cleaned the "gift" of lice, which attacked me, biting and attacking me like sharp knives.

Unfortunately, there was no bath here and Bukofski went to wash at the brother–in–law's house. In the evening I washed only my face and hands.

This is how I passed January 1944. February 2, I received word from Bukofski that my two children, Leibel and Moishe, were seen passing through the village Kanaish. I wanted to know where they were going. The only one is Tczernitch who can tell me, so I asked Bukofski to deliver a letter.

He said at the first opportunity he would go to Ignalina and so he did.

February 16, 1944 he returned with a letter and 500 rubles, he doesn't know why the children left and where to. I gave Bukofski the 500 rubles. He didn't seem the same, his mannerism changed towards me. I now felt that my food was not free.

February 26, another few days pass. Another incident occurs. A small girl enters the storehouse, I am not expecting anyone, and when she sees me she yells in fright: “Yaki strachni! Yaki strachni!”

Bukofski's wife didn't get anxious and ran to her:

[Col. 1120]

“This is not a man, this is an animal!”

The answer worried me, perhaps she will not believe it. Who will she tell? The incident passed, she actually thought that I was some strange animal. I didn't have a mirror, I thought how I odd I must look from the dirt and fear?

March 2, 1944, I felt a pain in my heart. But no doctor is available to treat me. Bukofski's wife boiled some green grass for me and I drank it. I became worse. I asked for a glass of warm tea. It made me feel better.

I still was living among the pens. March passed, then April arrived, it was still cold.

Bukofski has to clear the filth from the stable and I need to go back to the storage room. The hay is almost all gone and I don't have anywhere to lie down.

If I tell anyone I spent the winter amongst the pigs and animals, no one would believe me.

A man must be a strong creation if he can endure this.

Shabbos, April 29, Bukofski fixed the storage place and brought some straw for my new bed.

After six months I left the stable and returned to the storage area and could breathe some fresh air.

The Red Army is Approaching

April 30, 1944, Sunday, it is snowing and a bitter wind is blowing. Bukofski's wife brings me food and I ask for news from the front.

Suddenly we hear explosions from a distance. I jump from joy! The front is getting closer.

[Col. 1121]

The Red Army is chasing the Germans out of Russia. Our liberation is close.

I listen to the bombardments and tell the Christian it [the explosions] seems to be coming from Polotsk. I take out a map that I cut out from an old newspaper and make a calculation that the Russians are about 200 kilometers from us.

The heavy thunder continues the entire day. I ask Bukofski to check the news on someone's radio, where we stand [our situation]. He left to his father–in–law's, the Russians are advancing very quickly and in about 4 weeks time they will arrive here.

The main thing, 4 or 8 weeks was not the issue, I couldn't live like this another winter. I will no longer have the strength.

I kept looking at the map, making calculations. Now, what are the Christians thinking? We will be able to talk differently to them knowing Hitler will be defeated!

I think about the children. I don't know where they are and they don't know where I am. Perhaps they are not too far, eighteen days pass.

May 18, Bukofski comes to me and tells me a young boy is asking about me. I go into the hut, light my cigarette, and there is Moishele. We kissed and cried.

“How did you find me? Where is Leibele?”

“Leibel is close by, I will bring him here.”

“Wait until dark,” so he came inside the storage room, he told me how he left Andreievitch to Budkevich's and why he had to leave again.

[Col. 1122]

Leibel didn't have any shoes and a goya [Gentile woman] gave him a pair of volikes [boots]. As he passed through swamps he lost the volikes and walked fifteen kilometers barefoot. With difficulty they arrived at Kasimir Neverofski, he fed them but they couldn't remain. They left to Regnis, but couldn't remain there as well.

They finally arrived at Trimkun, and he hid them in the storage room. I gave him praise and hope. The war will soon come to an end.

Moishe left and I waited impatiently for Leibele to arrive. Late at night I heard footsteps, they arrived. Leibele looked terrible. He complained he was suffering from stomach problems.

I told them this is on account of not eating cooked food or clean food.

They tell me they went begging in the villages and the peasants thought they were partisans.

Arriving at Neverofski, he told them I had been there and he was “sorry” that I left. I was happy with my guests but warned them to be careful when they come to visit me. “They can still catch us! Come only when its dark.”

I thought to myself. Who can I trust? Only myself!

Daytime the shooting continued. The front was getting closer.

The children come again. Leibel seems lonely.

[Col. 1123]

I want to hug him, but he says to keep my distance. Moishe also hears his words.

I told them no one in the family is sick. He must have a cold. He needs to drink hot tea with honey and it will pass. Don't lose your willpower and stay strong!

I tell them about my suffering during the First World War and how I remained alive.

June 25, Budkevitch, overjoyed, arrived to tell me the good news. The Russian army is in Vidz.

The children arrived and I told them the good news. Leibele said he drank several glasses of sweet tea and he feels better.

You see, you told yourself you had an illness. When we are free, you will eat and get better.

June 30, Budkevitch told me to come out of my hideout, the Germans were running away. They are leaving their supplies. The Red Army is in Moledechno and Postav.

My heart beats from joy! They are forty kilometers from us. Liberation can come at any minute!

July 6, Budkevich arrived to tell me that the military had arrived in Daugelishok. Everyone is frightened. Are these German or Russian? It is a few kilometers from Zastianik.

The children arrived, confirming the Russians had arrived. Leibele spoke with them.

He said it was a miracle, they came just at the right time.

[Col. 1125]

Trimkund's father–in–law started screaming: “shame on you, you fed and hid Jews!

If the Jews survive, this will not be good for us!”

They were fighting and we ran away.

The next morning I heard airplanes flying overhead. They were bombarding the region. These were German pilots.

Budkevitch came running to tell us to leave the storage room. The Germans are fleeing, I no longer need to hide from them.

Our main concern now was how to survive the bombardment. We have no alternative.

Shabbos, July 8, Zastianek was bombed. They flew over our heads, the bombs fell close to us.

On the Ruins of Ignalina

Early in the morning I heard whistling and a loud thunder and pieces of dirt, lice and wood were flying all over me.

Budkevitch ran in and helped clean the dirt off me and said: "you are very lucky! A bomb landed close by and dug a huge crater." I was overwhelmed and couldn't speak. After several hours I came to my senses.

I want to find my children and quickly leave for Ignalina. It is twelve kilometers from Zastianke to Ignalina. I am waiting, I need a wagon. Perhaps the Red Army will take us.

I wait and wait. Butkevitch runs in.

[Col. 1125]

He tells me that my children are riding with the Red Army.

If so, I need not worry.

I will meet up with them in Ignalina. I decide to go to his father–in–law, one kilometer from Zastianke, who has a horse. Even my right foot was sore, but the urgency willed me to continue. I asked him to bring me to Rimchene, 5 kilometers from Ignalina. I will find a wagon there.

I was lucky, when I arrived at the first house and I entered, it was full of Russian soldiers. They all sprung to their feet when I told them who I was and how I survived.

From there I left to an old peasant friend in the middle of the village, who welcomed me and fed me.

I spent Sunday evening at his place. The next morning, Monday, I left for the carriage station, nearby the Vidziski estate where I knew the priest.

He was happy to see me and I told him all I lived through. He went into the street with me and stopped a motorized vehicle and requested they bring me to Ignalina. As I went inside, I heard a voice screaming in Yiddish—"is that you, Yerachmiel?"

Ritva and Solomyak were sitting there, riding home. We arrived home, all choked up, and then went to my house.

[Col. 1126]

It was an empty and desolate home. No pots, no furniture, empty in every corner. We didn't know where to begin. The Christians were worried we will take our revenge on them.

I think, of course we should take our revenge, but there is no one left. Me? the few left over skeletons that were barely alive, barely skin and bones?

We all sat on the ground, and couldn't speak a word.

No words...no tears, to lament for our nearest and dearest that were murdered in such bestial ways.

How do we lament our destruction...it is impossible! It is very difficult to put into words, to describe what we felt in those darkest hours.

The best writer would not be able to describe these events. We sat quietly and deliberated until I fought with all my strength to say these few words:

Dear friends, what we need to do now, is to tear kriah [rendering the garments when in mourning]and sit shiva [mourning].

We will not only cry for the all the towns that were destroyed, but also for the millions of Jews that were so heinously murdered, cut down by these human–beasts, those wild sadists...

That day, when the first Jews returned to Ignalina, was July 14, 1944.

Actually, this is the historical date of the French revolution.

Translator's notes:

Yerachmiel ben Abraham Moshe Korb was born in Salok and lived in Ignalina since the First World War.

Zarasai apskrite [county]=Novo–Alexandrovsk district.

Additional accounts of Korb [Kariv] are in the Rokiskis Yiskor book, some accounts may vary.

The name Adamovitch and Andreievitch could be the same person.

Page intentionally left blank

[Col. 1127]

Chased by the Horrible Events

Eliezer Levitan

Translated by Anita Frishman Gabbay

As soon as the Germans occupied Ignalina, they immediately sent the Jews to different workplaces. They were sent to work in Gupa, but they mainly worked on the railroad, others worked repairing roads outside the shtetl, to chop wood and to bring it from the forests.

I alone worked in unloading rocks, which the Russians, who were here earlier, prepared to bring to Russia. One time they brought us 26 arrested Communists, which they found hidden amongst the folk of our shtetl. None of them had any idea why they were labelled Communist. They worked with us a whole day and at night they were taken away. Together with them, without warning, they took me with them. The police threw us in a cellar and locked us up. My mother found out about this and ran to the police and pleaded with them for my release. This was 11:00 at night, an hour later, about 12, they released the other prisoners and took them to a nearby forest and shot them.

This was the first big Aktion(massacre) in Ignalina. A short while later, they enclosed us in a separate Ghetto. Then I started working laying rail road tracks, which led in the direction of Vilna. My workplace was about 20 kilometers from our shtetl. Every evening we had to walk home. It is understood that we arrived home in the Ghetto very late in the evening.

Friday, Erev Shabbos, when we arrived late from work, the Ghetto was surrounded on all sides by policemen. We felt that there was a great panic in the Ghetto, it was already quite late and no one was asleep.

[Col. 1128]

We immediately learned the events to follow will bring only chaos. Christians came and told us from a good source, that all the Jews were to be transported the following morning to Poligon. People ran from house to house and still no one had a plan to bring forth. One person said we should run away, another said that nothing could or would happen, we were panicking for nothing. Most of us were paralyzed and were resigned to go to Poligon. Probably, one said, this is our destiny.

Knowing about this Idea, I immediately decided to escape from the Ghetto and was determined not to go to Poligon. I made a plan with several friends and we decided to go to Postov, where brother in law Feive(Feivel) lived with his family..

In the middle of the night we quietly left the Ghetto. We took side roads out of the shtetl in the direction of Meligan.

It was extremely dark and none of us knew the exact direction. We knocked on the door of a peasant and begged him to show us the road.

Luckily, he was a friendly person and showed us and directed us to the right road. We left him and again we only took side roads, when suddenly we heard someone chasing us. We wanted to run, but it was already too late. A group of Lithuanian bandits encircled us with revolvers in their hands and brought us to a nearby village and there they locked us up in a stall. In the morning, they threw us out of the stall, and brought us to Meligan. There they held us in a cellar.

It was then Shabbos, and the Jews from Meligan were praying in the synagogue. About 10 in the morning, the door from the cellar opened, and Jews from the shtetl were thrown into the cellar with us, still dressed in Tefillim on their heads.

[Col. 1129]

It seemed they were brought directly from the synagogue. A few hours later they threw us out into the street, several wagons stood there. The bandits told us to get into these wagons, and we noticed that they were taking us in the direction of New Sventzian. When we looked around, we saw that there were about 100 wagons all going in the same direction. This was an organized transport and amongst us we knew Jews from Haydutishok and Shayatishok. They brought us to the Baronover woods and forced everyone into the military barracks of Poligon.At once, I noticed that the Jews from Ignalina were already there, and I wanted to join them. But they didn't let me.

Everyone spread themselves out on the floors. I spent a restless night. I had an intuition, that to remain in Poligon means Death. I promised myself to do everything possible and escape from here. I planned this with several friends and we did not wait another evening. We escaped through the window. We all ran in the direction of the forest. The police shot at us. I ran like a wild animal and succeeded in reaching the forest. It was very dark that night, but I noticed no one was behind me. I was left alone in the forest, not knowing where to go or what to do. I came to a stream and walking along the banks, not knowing where I found the strength to continue. Suddenly I came to a bridge and not far away I saw a peasant farm. How can I approach this farm and knock on the door? An elderly Christian woman came out and told me that the little shtetl, Kaltinian, is close by.

I decide right away to go to Kaltinian and then in the direction of Ignalina. Meanwhile, it got light outside and I had to get off the road, to hide in a ditch under a large tree.

I heard everything very clearly from the passersby on the road: it was a Sunday and the Christian peasants were going to church, walking or riding. I heard their conversations: they all spoke about the Jews. One said: all the Jews that were brought to Poligon will be put to death. A second peasant said: It is well deserved! All the Jews deserve to die! All these years they sucked our blood, live in fine homes, eat and drink, and now they must pay for this!

[Col. 1130]

I lay in the ditch until it got dark again, I crawled out of this confined space and started to wander. I walk, but I do not know where to go. My vow was to go as far away from Poligon, from this Death! I continue on, and suddenly I see a house of an old Christian acquaintance of mine. I knocked on the door and identified myself. They wouldn't let me enter the house. I tell them that I haven't eaten for days, but it doesn't help. They don't want to give me even a little water.

It's very difficult. This is unexplainable. I go further, hungry and thirsty. I am thinking to myself, if I continue a little further to the town of Bizun, my old friend, Michal Kapusta lives there. I wander in the direction of this small town, hoping he remained unchanged(personality). He would certainly take pity on me and give me something to eat and perhaps allow me to rest for several days at his home.

Opening the door, Kapusta was very frightened, but he allowed me to enter his house. He opened up to me about his secret: he was hiding Dina Levine and her 2 daughters. He also allowed me to hide with them. For several days I stayed hidden together with the Levines.

One day Kapusta came from Ignalina and told us that the Jews that were hidden and then captured, were shot together with those Christians who hid them. Kapusta was too scared to let us stay with him longer. We had no alternative, and we had to leave his home. The Levines decided to go to their Christian acquaintance in Drisvietz, and I decided to go to Petrova, to Mudin(en).

[Col. 1131]

Mudin welcomed me in a very friendly manner, and led me to the stable. I spent the night and in the morning he came to see me in order to tell me that the Levines were caught the previous night, were brought to Daugelishak and were shot right away. That was very lucky for me, that I didn't go with them. At Mudin's I remained 5 days. On the sixth day he came to me, just like Kapusta, and begged me to leave. He was very frightened to hide me. I didn't have any choice, so I continued again. I remained in the stable until dark, then started walking. This time I promised myself to go to Vidz. In Vidz I was told that all the Jews in Poligon were murdered. In Vidz I remained for 4 days only, and then left for Kazian, where I met my cousin Tuvia Solomyak. From there I left for Postov. There was a Ghetto in Postov, for useful Jews. They smuggled me into the Ghetto and made me a Postover(gave me an identity card). Several months later, Tuvia Solomyak also arrived in Postov, and here we met again. Meanwhile, for Postov, those same dreadful days were soon to come. We learned that the Jews from Yodi and Miar were also murdered and the entire region was living in fear and panic. We felt that these were our last days of living, our end was near.

One day there was an alarm. We were told that the entire Ghetto of Postov was encircled with policemen, so Solomyak and I immediately realized the end is near, so we quickly left Postov and went back to Kazian. Meanwhile, Solomyak reminded himself that not far from Kazian he knew a friendly German, and despite the odds, he decided to look for him.

The German saved us and put us up in his barn and every day he brought us food. We stayed here about a month, in the barn and in the forest. Very often we noticed that peasants came to the forest to chop wood and this frightened us. We didn't want to be seen. We thanked the German for his friendship and kindness and decided to turn back to Vidz, where Jews were still working at different jobs.

[Col. 1132]

Actually, this is how it was. Arriving in Vidz, they caught us and immediately sent us to work in a camp in Podbrodz. There we worked in a sawmill.

From Podbrodze they sent us to Dukst, but we didn't remain there very long. An order came, that all the Jews should be sent to the Sventzian Ghetto, from where we would be sent either to the Vilna(Ghetto) or the Kovno(Kaunus Ghetto).

Arriving in Sventzian, we found the Ghetto in such a terrible condition. No one knew what to do. We had 2 solutions: one for Vilna, one for Kovno. No one knew if the conditions would be better. I had a feeling, that we should not go to either place. We have to flee!

I arrived at the conclusion, together with Solomyak and the brothers Moishe and Leibl Korb, to leave the Sventzian Ghetto and return to Ignalina Ghetto and hide there amongst our Christian friends.

We departed, the 4 of us and we arrived back at Kapusta. This was April 23, 1943. The roads were muddy, our boots were torn and we were trodding through the muddy waters. At last we arrived at Kapusta. He was not so happy to see us, but we stayed in his shed for one day only. The next morning we said our farewells. The Korb brothers left by themselves, Solomyak and myself decided to go back to my friend, Mudin in Petrova.

Mudin didn't open the door for us this time, he was very scared and therefore we had to continue our journey. We felt so abandoned and in despair.

We decided to go back to Sventzian, and to join the others and go either to Vilna or Kovno.

We passed several small towns and we didn't hide from anyone. On the way back, we met peasants on the roads who looked at us like we were idiots. How dare the Jews walk in broad daylight without fear??

From Sventzian they brought us to the Vilna Ghetto. I was fortunate to have work the entire time until liberation, in these conditions, I survived and was spared from death.

[Col. 1133]

Human Animals and Human Angels

Shmuel Gilinsky

Translated by Janie Respitz

The sea of suffering and death began the 22nd of June, 1941. The Nazis entered Ignalina the second week after the outbreak of the German – Soviet war.

We heard about this a few days before, so all the Jews ran to the surrounding villages. The Jews understood that they should not be present at the moment of their arrival.

Together with my wife Liza [Daughter of Zalman Gilinsky & Chava/Chasia] and our small son Asherl (Asher), I escaped to a Christian acquaintance, Matsulis in Zabartzi village, 5 kilometres from our town. He received us very nicely. After a few days with him we learned the Nazis had arrived in Ignalina.

The First Days Under the German Regime

The German army marched through Ignalina toward Polotzk and Minsk. Marching away to the front, they left behind approximately 100 S.S and gendarmes, to keep order behind the front lines.

They immediately began to organize the Lithuanian youth and issue the first orders against the Jewish population.

The first decree was a warning to all Christians. If they were caught hiding Jews, they will be shot together with the Jews.

My Christian was very friendly and did not ask us to leave our hiding place.

However, we knew all the Jews were returning from the villages and we decided to return to town. Upon our return we were told a Lithuanian commander was in charge in Ignalina with the help of tens of Germans and Lithuanian police.

[Col. 1134]

Their first task was to capture former communists. In July they rounded up 30 men, 28 Jews and 2 Christians. They were brought to the outskirts of town, to a bridge at Lake Ilgish, and shot.

A few days later they killed Baranchuk, the father of the well know Vilna lawyer whose family lived in Ignalina

During the first few weeks we went to work every day on the train tracks. We took the reserve tracks, and every 10 kilometres made a side track so the Germans could travel quicker without any obstacles.

Many Jews from our town worked the land. Some served various managers, Lithuanian and German.

The first time we felt German sadism, was when Dovid Ritva seriously wounded his hand and foot while lifting a steel spike. He asked the German supervisor permission to see a doctor. My brother Yisroel had also injured a finger. The German told them to tear a piece of material from their undershirts and bandage their wounds. After work they went to the town mayor, Tivnelis and requested a requisition to see a doctor. He too said Jews were not permitted to see a doctor. This was now the attitude of a rich farmer who had for years, lived very well with the Jews.

In the end, they found a Polish doctor who bandaged their wounds. He pleaded with them not to tell anyone.

[Col. 1135]

The second edict against was Jews was that every Jew had to wear a yellow patch in front and a star of David on his back.

My wife Liza fainted while sewing on the patch. I tried to cheer her up and comfort her, but tears ran from her eyes as well.

We saw, in the yellow patch, a bitter warning for our future fate.

The Ghetto

Two months later, our Christian neighbours told us a Ghetto will be made in Ignalina, just like in all the other towns throughout Lithuania.

Some Christians actually told the truth, that would keep the Jews in the Ghetto for a short time only and eventually shoot everyone.

I happened to meet the Mayor of Svencionys, Har [This could be a name] Blazis, with whom I was very well acquainted. He whispered to me that the Ghetto will be on Gavinken Street, bordered between some small houses.

For us, this was not such a bad idea. On that street stood my father Avrom's house as well as my uncle's, Yerachmiel Korb. [Yerachmiel was the brother of the author's (Shmuel Gilinsky's) mother, Chana (Korb) Gilinsky]

Meanwhile, the farmers from the villages came and asked us for our belongings. They told us we would not be permitted to take them with us to the Ghetto. A few of them told us they would bring us vital supplies once we were in the Ghetto.

Merely a day after I met Blazis, the order was carried out and all the Jews were commanded to move into the Ghetto.

The order came at 10:00 at night, when Jews were not permitted to leave their homes. It was even forbidden to look out the window.

We put our little boy to bed, but we did not sleep all night. At 3:00 a.m I looked out the window through a crack. At the end of our street I saw a very familiar policeman.

I quietly called to him. He told me at 6:00 all the Jews will be brought to the Ghetto on Gavinken Street. He then told me to hide all our jewelry and gold. He told me if they find it, they will shoot us on the spot.

[Col. 1139]

I took off my gold watch, gave it to him and asked if at the check, he himself could come to me.

This is what happened. Around 12:00 they led us to the Ghetto. We took a sack of belongings and a bit of food, and moved into my father's house.

It was very crowded in the Ghetto. 1200 people were confined to a small street. People slept in stalls, attics and cellars. There was a great shortage of food.

The first thing was to establish a Judenrat [Jewish Council] which was responsible for sending Jews to work.

We had to go wash and clean the train station. Some people worked on the farms and in the yards. We were happy they were letting us live and not taking us from the Ghetto as they were doing in other Lithuanian towns.

The Lithuanian police would come into the Ghetto daily and exploit from us as much as possible

One day, a Lithuanian from Shabalishok came to our Rabbi and demanded jewelry and gold. By this time, Rabbi (Chait) had nothing left. He took off his and his wife's wedding rings and gave them to him.

The Lithuanian did not believe he did not have more to give him, and beat him and left him unconscious.

This was a wealthy Lithuanian farmer who was always considered to be a friend to the Jews.

After three weeks in the Ghetto, there was no news. By the fourth week, a Polish friend, Reksht arrived and told us a meeting took place in Svencionys with all the mayors of the region, as well as the German regional commissar, Bek. A decision was made to liquidate all the Ghettos and send the Jews to the barracks in Poligon, near New-Svencionys (Švenčionėliai).

Bek instructed the mayors to leave behind only the useful Jews, Jewish professionals and specialists who could come in handy.

[Col. 1137]

All the mayors refused to carry out this privilege. Only the mayor of Svencionys accepted. Bazis even insisted that the useful Jews remain with their families. This is how around 60 Jewish families from Svencionys were saved.

It was the week of Erev Yom Kippur. We noticed that many wagons from Ignalina were being sent to Svencionys. After my conversation with Reksht I met my friend the policeman. He told me to escape to his brother-in-law in Vishnuni and hide there for a few days until the situation becomes clearer.

I went home and told everyone the situation is grave, and we have to escape to the villages.

They did not believe my panic. I asked my uncle, brothers and sisters to run away with me. They refused.

I took my wife Liza and our little boy Asherl (Asher), said goodbye to everyone, and as soon as it became dark, around 7:00 in the evening, we ran away to Vishnuni, to the policeman's brother-in-law.

I Escaped from the Ghetto

Before I left my father's house, I once again warned everyone that Poligon meant death and they should run away, anywhere they could. They all said they would wait and see what will happen.

At 10:00 that night we arrived at our Christian acquaintance. They immediately gave is a place in the barn on a pile of hay. Around 2:00 in the morning, my brother Yisroel arrived with his whole family and my brother Berl. They recounted that at 11:00 that night, the Lithuanian policeman came and told them to escape. He simply asked that they don't make noise in the Ghetto.

Thanks to him, over 100 Jews were saved from the Ghetto. My brother ran around and told as many people as he possibly could.

[Col. 1138]

I was later confirmed, my fear was justified! 12:00 that night the entire Ignalina Ghetto was surrounded with no way of escaping. The next morning they took everyone to Poligon, where they interred thousands of Jews from the Svencionys region.

Leyzer Levitan escaped from Poligon and told us they had wagons for the sick, elderly women and children. Everyone else had to walk.

That night, Asher Gilinsky's wife gave birth to twins. She also went in a wagon. A Christian neighbour saw her and brought her a pillow to put under her head. The magistrate from the town of Tianelis saw this, forbid it and took the pillow away from under her head.

A second incident happened to Yitzkhak Dubinsky's two year old child. Burmistch Tivnelis threw him into the wagon and cracked his head open. The Christians who witnessed it scolded him for being such a bandit.

“You also have children” they told him. “How are you not ashamed to do this to such a small child?”

This scolding did not help at all. The bandits did whatever they wanted. A horrible thing happened to our neighbour Milchkik the Schochet, the ritual slaughter's daughter. A 45 year old Lithuanian raped her on the road in front of parent's eyes.

They kept them in Poligon for 12 days, and on the twelfth day, took them to a mass grave and shot them. Many were buried alive.

Before going to the grave, the Rabbi from New-Svencionys gave a sermon. He appealed to all to die with pride as a martyr.

A few hid and ran away that night.

It is hard to describe how we in Vishnun survived hearing this news. Everyone now knew the policeman told us the truth.

[Col. 1139]

Vidz [Now: Vidzy, Belarus]

We could not remain in Vishnun for long. The Christian was afraid of his nephews who were collaborating with the Nazis. He asked us to look for another hiding place.

Our friend the policeman from Ignalina came himself and took us to the forest 12 kilometres from that village. Between that forest and other forests were a few kilometres of open fields. We hadn't gone halfway when we noticed we were being chased by one man on a horse and a second in a rover.

They were Lithuanians we knew. They stood us beside a tree and wanted to shoot us. I asked them for pity. It did not help. Luckily, two Christians friends suddenly appeared and said: “Let them go. Don't you see these are the Gilinskys. They are good people. You don't have to shoot them!

The hearts of the bandits softened and they let us go.

Only a great writer could describe what we experienced in those two hours. Our lives were counted in minutes.

It was a very hot day. We had nothing to eat. The children were extremely thirsty. It was pitiful to watch them suffer.

We remained in the same place until evening. When it was totally dark my brother asked me to check if the road to White Russia (Belarus) was open. If yes, we will take the children and go there.

I left. On the road I met a Christian friend who was surprised to see that I was free. He asked if the partisans who met us earlier freed us.

I made up a story that I was on my way to a village to look for bread and lost my family. I told him I didn't know what happened to them.

I waited for him to leave and returned to my family in the forest.

[Col. 1140]

When my brother heard the story he said the partisans [not all Partisans were good] must still be looking for us. They think we have money and were still planning to capture us. He suggested we do not move from this place. They will assume we left and will go looking for us.

We did not budge until 11:00 that night. Then we began walking toward Vidz. It was a very dark night. We walked into mud. Since we were all so thirsty, we filled our caps and drank the muddy water.

We rested for a while and then continued our walk all night. When it got light, we approached Vidz which belonged to White Russian territory.

We decided not to enter the town until we were sure what was going on. We had to learn if there were any Jews left in Vidz.

We entered a small forest nearby and sat under a tree to rest. My brother Yisroel said a Jewish friend of his, Katcherginsky, lives in one of the first houses in Vidz. He will go there and see what's happening in his house.

My brother left, found the house, knocked on the door. An unfamiliar Christian farmer opened the door. My brother returned and sadly told us that no Jews were left in Vidz.

We were very sad. We had suffered for so long, and now we had to head back.

We lay there not knowing what to do. Where should we go? To Whom? Why should we continue to suffer?

My brother began to rethink what transpired and began doubting his orientation. Perhaps he knocked on a stranger's door? Maybe he misunderstood the farmer? Is it possible he did not recognize the correct house?

After he rested he decided to return to the town and ask at a second house.

[Col. 1141]

He knocked on the door of the second house. First no one answered. He knocked again and someone came to the window. It was Dovid Ritva from Ignalina. He opened the door. He recognized him immediately through a crack in the window and happily told him the Jews in Vidz are all still living in their own homes.

Yisroel quickly ran back to us in the forest. Weak, hungry, thirsty and barely alive we entered Katcherginsky's house. The children drank some water. It was sheer pleasure.

We lay down but could not fall asleep. At 11:00 at night we heard someone gently knocking at the door. The gentle knock made us think it could be Jews. We opened the door and there stood my father Avrom, my brother Meir, my sister-in-law and their three children.

It appeared their journey had been a lot easier than ours. They were also captured on the road, but only a bit of money was taken from them. Their lives had not been endangered.

We were all happy that so far, we were saved from the bandits. The only ones missing from our family were our sister Alte, her husband Yosef Gavenda and their two children.

The next morning we received new good guests from Ignalina. It was my uncle Yerachmiel Korb, his wife Mirl (Nee Szrolowicz/Srulowitz) and their son Leybl.

Yerachmiel entered the house in silence. He lost his speech from fear, as if it had been taken away.

He had been very active in Jewish causes in town and had a lot of Christian friends. They stripped him on the road down to his underwear searching for money. He overcame many obstacles on the way, but thank God, we all arrived in peace in Vidz.

Within a few days, our Ignalina family in Vidz grew. Berl Gilinsky arrived with his family: Elke Gilinsky and her family; Esther Kril and her family; Dovid Soloveichik and his family; Shayke Dubinsky, Shloimeh Kuritsky, Gitl Gilinsky, Avrom Srolovitch (brother of Mirl, married to Yerachmiel Korb) and his wife; Mirl Brodsky, Leipzig the blacksmith's two sons, Shloimen Ring's wife and two daughters, Leybe Khaim Elpern with his family.

[Col. 1142]

The last to arrive was Gavenda (Yosef Gavenda) the brother-in-law with his family. Quite a large number of Ignalina Jews arrived in Vidz.

The first few days we were all very happy that we had survived. Yet we soon realized that also Vidz was not a safe haven.

We had only been there a few days when we received an order that all the Jews must move to a Ghetto. Since we were all not registered in Vidz, they could not take us into the Ghetto. The Jewish authority explained that in order to register, we would have to bribe the commander with a lot of money. We all had only the shirts on our backs. None of us had a lot of money. What were we all to do?

Our brother-in-law had twenty thousand rubles which he gave them. They said it was too little. They demanded gold and other valuables.

We held a meeting and decided to leave Vidz. We chose a Sunday when the farmers went home, and we left town.

The question remained, where to? We decided to divide into groups and each group would go to a different town. One group went to Apse, another went to Postav – the others went to Yadi and Miori.

Our family was divided in two groups: My older brother went in the direction of Miori and I went, with my other two brothers and our families to Yadi.

Yadi

After walking all night we arrived in Yadi. It was a small town with about 150 people. By the time we got there the Jewish population had increased by 20. Later, Jewish refugees arrived from Lithuania and Estonia bringing the Jewish population close to 300.

[Col. 1143]

Almost all the Jewish residents were farmers. When we arrived they were all still at their regular jobs and living in their own homes. The Jews of Yadi were the exact opposite from the Jews of Vidz. They received us warmly, gave us food and organized places for us to sleep.

We knew the town administratively belonged to the same regional commissary of Gluboke. The chairman of the Jewish council was Lederman, who ran all the towns in White Russia (Belarus).

At this time, the situation of the Jews in Yadi was not bad. We lived there for a few weeks.

Meanwhile, we heard from our family in Miori [Miyory, Belarus] that all was quiet and there was no Ghetto as of yet. We decided to go and join them.

It turned out to be the right thing to do. Not long after we left there was an horrific massacre in Yadi. The reason given, a Jew was caught slaughtering a cow.

Very few were rescued from this massacre. Finsav's daughter ran away with her sister's two children to a farmer friend in a nearby village. He did not think for long, tied them all up and brought them to the mass grave. Christians who witnessed her shooting said in a split second, her black curly hair turned snowy white.

The massacre in the town of Yadi was the first Action in all of White Russia. We felt very fortunate that we left there in time. My family and I headed toward Vidz, the rest went to Miori.

Miori

Everyone in Miori was living in his own home. It was not a big town, but it had a match factory, a sawmill and a large place for wood. We quickly found work. There was no food. They received 30 grams of bread a day, and were happy to be alive.

[Col. 1144]

After two months of living quietly the order came to build a Ghetto for the Jews. They brought Jews from Estonia surrounding towns amounting to about 2 thousand Jews in the Ghetto.

The head of the Braslav community, Mindl, succeeded in convincing the German gendarme to enlarge the Ghetto. Because there were many workshops in the Ghetto and the German were interested in their regular work, they agreed to ease the living conditions.

Often, farmers would come to Miori and bring potatoes, vegetables and other goods.

Whoever did not work in the workshops, worked chopping wood. Since my brothers and brother-in-law were specialists in lumber, they worked in the forest.

We became friendly with the Christians in the area. They would often bring us potatoes, bread, and sometimes a piece of butter for the children. It is true we lived in constant fear, but we lived.

One day they brought forty Gypsies to Miori. The German gendarmes confined them to a prison. The Jews of the Ghetto were ordered to dig graves. Early in the morning they brought the Gypsies to the grave and wanted to shoot them. The Gypsies asked if they could recite a special prayer before being killed.

This was permitted. They used the opportunity to discuss and decide to shout a Hurrah! And run away to the forest. Such a thing did not occur to the Germans and they did not guard carefully.

Almost all the Gypsy men managed to escape. The Gendarmes managed to capture a few children and women and shot them on the spot.

The Jews spent the next two days in great fear, fearful the Germans would take out their anger on them.

Another incident occurred when the Germans found a torn cable from a telephone post. They began to bother the Jews, thinking they were responsible. Mindl, the head of the Jewish council went to the commander and told him it was a false accusation. Jews would never do this. They had to bribe the Gendarmes. They asked for gold, valuables, leather coats and steel boots. Every Jew gave what he had. The deadline was too short and the Jewish council did not succeed in collecting all the demanded goods.

[Col. 1145]

The Christians in the villages told us they were asked to dig graves in the fields. Great despair befell the Jews. Everyone was sure the angel of death had arrived. There was a call for a communal fast in the Ghetto. Everyone wept and cried.

In the last minute, a miracle occurred. The commandant accepted the gifts from the Jewish council and called back the soldiers. They were saved from a sure death.

The situation in Miori Ghetto continued to worsen .Many refugees arrived. It became overcrowded. There was talk about liquidating the Ghetto.

One morning at 5:30 as we were getting ready to go to work, we were ordered to immediately gather in the town square.

They separated the men and women. They also separated the children and then confined us in groups in the warehouses.

We decided we would not, under any conditions go to the town square. My heart told me it would be catastrophic. We hid behind the houses and watched what was happening in town. As there was nowhere to hide, my brother went into a toilet. He told his wife, child and her brother to join him, but they were caught by the police and brought to the warehouse along with everyone else.

He was alone in the toilet and regretted not going together with the rest.

When darkness fell, he climbed out of the hole. I barely made it to a stall and lay down behind the wall.

[Col. 1146]

In the darkness I noticed two shadows along the wall. It appeared to be two Jews from the Ghetto.

From behind the wall, he saw three trucks filled with S.S. They were taking all the jews from the warehouses and leading them to the graves outside of town.

Running away was difficult. Miori was surrounded by a lake and a deep river on one side; on the other side were the S.S. and the graves.

A while later we heard screams and shooting. We saw people running from the graves and being shot. Very few managed to escape. The majority were killed on the horrible evening. My family as well. This was June 2, 1942.

Yisroel and two others lay behind the stall until 11:00. They could come out earlier as the police were going from house to house searching for anyone hiding. Of course they stole whatever they could. At one point the police stood a couple of metres from the stall, but he didn't notice them.

When all was quiet and they no longer heard footsteps of the patrol, they emerged from behind the wall and began to walk toward the large grave. There was no other way to go.

We ran to the big forest 3 kilometres from town. There we found a few who managed to escape. Not many were saved from the slaughter.

There in the forest He drew His conclusions. Precisely here, in White Russia, I had to lose my whole family. They were saved from Poligon, they escaped numerous bandits – and suddenly – such a huge fire in one day. I jotted down in my memory; on June 2, 1942 I lost my whole family in the fields of Miori:

My wife Liza and our dear son Asherl (Asher), may they rest in peace;

My brother Meir and his family, may they rest in peace;

My brother Berl, may he rest in peace; My brother Yisroel and his family, may they rest in peace;

[Col. 1147]

My brother-in-law Yosef Gavenda and his family, may they rest in peace;

My brother-in-law Shloime Galperin and his family, may they rest in peace;

and many, many friends and acquaintances.

The night between the 2nd and 3rd I was left totally alone.

Deep in my heart I had only one desire, one thought: Revenge! Revenge! Where is God of vengeance who will take revenge for so much innocent spilled blood?

Return to Vidz

Three of us remained in the forest. We lay an entire day without food or drink. In the evening we decided there was no point remaining in the forest. As soon as it became dark we began to walk from forest to forest. Perhaps someone would pity us.

On our way, we came across a lonely house. I went over by myself and knocked on the door.

A Christian looked through the window and asked what I wanted. I answered with one word: - Bread!

The Christian went away and returned with a small piece of bread. I did not take it. I explained there were 40 partisans who were all very hungry. I need a lot more.

The Christian called out and I saw 2 young boys come to the window. I did not lose it, and I whistled. They believed there were tens of partisans in the forest.

The Christian was frightened and gave me a large loaf of bread with a piece of cheese. I thanked him politely and returned to my friends in the forest. For the first time in 2 days we put something in our mouths. We were so confused and upset we didn't realize how hungry we were.

We ate well, and even had some food left over for later. After a short break we continued walking. We went from forest to forest. By day we lay down, at night we walked.

[Col. 1148]

One day, we met a Christian who told us there were Jews living in Gluboke and Vidz. I decided to go to Vidz. Perhaps I would find some friends.

We walked for three days through forests and fields. We hid during the day and walked all night. Three days later, in the middle of the night we arrived in Vidz. I quietly passed through the wires of the Ghetto and entered. The Ghetto was as silent as a cemetery. I thought there were already no longer any Jews there.

We went into the bathhouse to rest for a while. At 5:00 am when it was already a bit light I saw someone from a distance. I could not tell if it was a Jew or a Christian. I decided not to go out. I waited. A while later, I saw a woman and I knew she was Jewish.

I approached her and asked if it is still quiet in Vidz. She replied that they lived in fear and no one knows what tomorrow will bring.

I left her and began to look for friends. Coincidently I met the Starabin family who I knew from before the war. They took us to their home and we stayed there temporarily.

Meanwhile, there were about 300 escapees like me in Vidz. Once again the Jewish council did not want to register us. They gave us no food and asked us to leave town. Our complaints that we had nowhere to go did not help. They did not soften.

Understandably, none of us left. We slept in the attics and went from house to house begging for a piece of bread.

We decided to organize and fight together. I was elected leader of all the refugees, and Khanan Epshteyn from Svir was my deputy.

When the Jewish council demanded we go to work, I responded in the name of all the refugees, we will work on the condition they register us.

[Col. 1149]

In the end they gave in and we gave them 50 workers. They were sent off to a camp and we never heard from them again. We did not know what to think.

Finally, we received news they were all alive and life there was better than in the Ghetto. Now the rest of the refugees were volunteering to go to work.

The Jewish council was happy to get rid of us. They gave us a few sacks of bread and a few blankets and we left the Ghetto.

In Podbrodz Labour Camp

The Gendarmes from Vidz took us to Duksht, where we spent the night in a jail. From there they took us by train through Ignalina, Svneciony Svencionys until Podbrodz (Pabradė)

They took us to a work camp with over 200 men. We all had to work in a sawmill that belonged to the known nobleman Tishkevitch.

The camp was surrounded with barbed wire and we were guarded by Lithuanian police. The chief of the camp was a German captain named Saltz.

On the second day I began to work carrying wooden boards. We were a group of five men. A Lithuanian officer sat in a booth and guarded us.

We had to carry the boards from one place to another. At first we were carrying three boards at a time. When we realized there weren't that many, we took less.

The Lithuanian policeman noticed and began to beat us over the head with a board. The first victims were Leyzer Levitan and Shayke Dubinsky. Then he came to Salamiak and me. He hit me so hard I became totally blue. I was sure he was going to kill me. In that last moment I began to talk to him in Lithuanian and asked him for some pity.

[Col. 1150]

When he heard how well I spoke Lithuanian, he softened and asked where I was from. I told him who I was and he stopped beating me and promised to give me better work.

Then I met a Christian acquaintance who knew I was a specialist in the lumber trade. He immediately made me a woodsman.

The boards were being sent by train to carpenter shops and had to be properly sorted. Since there were no professionals, many wagons left filled with defective goods, rubbish. They were looking for a specialist like me.

From that day on my situation greatly improved. The manager was very good to me. He even gave me 2 packs of cigarettes. Even the Lithuanian police treated me well.

I worked in that camp for three months. Then they sent me to another camp near Duksht. [Dukštas, Lithuania]

In the Duksht Camp

In Duksht they brought us to a big house with many windows and long rooms. There were no ovens. The windows were without panes. We had to sleep on wooden boards and I realized it would be much worse here than in Podbrodz

The camp commander was a good person. We had problems with our Jewish supervisor. He believed if he would flatter, he would be better off.

Soon we learned that a Jewish girl from Dinaburg became very friendly with the Chief. We told her what was going on, and thanks to her the Jewish supervisor was sent back to Svencionys Ghetto.

In Duksht I worked with Moishe Korb [likely the son of his uncle Yerahmiel Korb] Levitan and Salamiak. We had to work in 2 divisions: one – by day and the second – at night. They gave us very little to eat. It was cold and we were barefoot. We worked under the open sky at it was cold.

[Col. 1152]

Besides that, we suffered from lice. For months we could not bathe or change our underwear. Everyone had large abscesses and lesions. There was no medication. In short: we lived in worse conditions than the dogs.

One day, ten Jewish workers escaped from a camp wanting to form a Partisan unit. They were captured. Driving through Duksht they recognized one of our friends from our group and greeted him.

That's all we needed. They made us identify the guy they greeted. The chose three men, me, Salamiak and Dubinsky and told us if we don't bring forth the friend, we will be shot. They made us stand with our backs to the wall and the Major said it is worth our while to give him up. Then Shayke announced: I will give him up but he is at work at the sawmill.

The Major told us to return to the camp and went with Dubinsky to the sawmill. The commander Captain Saltz was there.

The friend was Mulke from Braslav. The Major wanted to take him right away but Captain Saltz refused. He told the Major he was a great worker and he needed him.

This is how he was saved from death. We were also freed.

After that incident we worked another few months in Duksht. Then the order came to liquidate the camp. I learned about it in the morning when I wanted to go to work at the sawmill. On my way I met a friendly Gendarme who whispered in my ear: "Don't go there. They will take you today to Svencionys Ghetto where things will not be good for you".

I returned to the house and told all my friends. My suggestion was we escape to the forest. They did not want to listen. I decided to escape alone.

[Col. 1152]

I Escape from Duksht Camp

I left the camp and walked through the fields. My plan was to walk towards Ignalina, find a Christian acquaintance and hide. I had to pass a large lake and I felt walking on the shore was too dangerous. I could run into a patrol. Crossing the lake would also be difficult as the ice was already beginning to melt.

Since I was a good swimmer, I decided to take the risk and cross the frozen lake. I took a pole and tapped the ice. It broke. I began to crawl on my knees. 30 metres from shore I was in the water and swam across.

I went into a farmer's house, where I asked permission to dry my things. Luckily, I found a nice family. They allowed me to take off my wet clothes and even brought me something to eat. I then went to the forest about 5 kilometres from the lake. I remained there until it dark, then continued on my way.

I walked all night. In the morning I found a lonely house. It was light. I climbed into the attic and went to sleep. I slept all day and at night resumed my walking. I had nothing to eat or drink.

The next morning I came across the house of a farmer I knew. I wanted to eat and decided to go to him. He fed me and received me very warmly. I stayed there all day, and when night fell, I continued further.

My plan was to find a Christian friend and hide there until the end of the war.

After much suffering I arrived at his place. As I entered the yard, the dog started to bark. The farmer came out and recognized me right away. He was very happy to see me alive. He took me straight to the barn and showed me a place in the attic where I could hide.

[Col. 1153]

In the morning, his elderly mother brought me food and comforted me, knowing I had lost my entire family. I was there 3 days and they treated me very well. I was happy that I found a place to hide with familiar people.

On the fourth day, the Christian came and told me the Germans were coming to inspect his animals and wheat. He was worried they would find me.

This was really bad. Now I had to leave and find another place. I had no choice. At night, I crept out of the attic and headed off toward a village called Dudi, to another Christian friend who was a manager of a dairy.

I arrived at his place in the evening, and through the window I saw he had guests. I quietly entered the barn and lay down on some straw without his knowledge.

I stayed there all night and no one in the house knew I was there. In the morning when the farmer went to his yard to get water, I called to him. He brought me into his house and gave me food. He then went to the barn, dug a hole in the straw and prepared a place for me to hide.

This was the first time in a year that I washed. He worried about me and told me what was going on the front.

One day, in the afternoon, as I was lying and buried in straw, the children came to play in the barn. A nine year old boy climbed onto the pile of straw and suddenly began to shout: Oy, what kind of horrible person is lying in the straw.

The farmer was at home, came running, and chased them from the barn. "You don't know that Lunis the lunatic lies here?". The children knew there was a lunatic in the neighbouring village, and believed him. That's how I escaped from that problem.

The farmer warned the children that they should never go into the barn alone. The lunatic can kill them. They never came into the barn again.

[Col. 1154]

I spent the next three months with this Christian friend. I would lay there all day, and at night I would get up and move around.

One day, the farmer suggested I go out at night to the meadow and feed the horses. One night German patrols passed, but they did not ask me anything.

Many weeks passed until one day he came and told me there was an order that all the youth from all the villages were being sent to Germany to work. Those who do not go will be severely punished.

Since many of these young guys will go into hiding, he feared, on the search for the patrols will find me. He suggested I go into the forest and when things quieten down, I should return.

I had no choice. I took my shoes in hand and began my wandering through forests and fields. Finally I arrived in a village called Remshentsi, where my former servant- girl lived.

I knew her parents were good Christians and I assumed I would be able to stay with them.

I found the house, knocked on the door and they opened right away. The servant-girl and her parents were very happy I had been saved from death. They gave me food and took me to a barn where I could hide. There I washed, shaved and ate well. They took care of me as if I was their own brother.

After being there for ten days, 100 Germans came to the village looking for young boys to send to work. The entire village ran to the fields. I ran as well and hid in the corn.

When the gendarmes left, everyone returned home. I could not as it was still light outside and I did not want the other farmers to see me. I remained in the corn until evening.

[Col. 1155]

I returned to my spot and stayed a few more days. Then they decided to take me to a large forest. The famer harnessed his horses, filled a wagon with hay, and he and his daughter took me.

On the road, beside the train, there were patrols. The girl got sown from the wagon, spoke to them and we were permitted to travel on.

When we arrived in the forest, I climbed out from under the hay. I said goodbye to them. I remained in the forest and they returned home.

I lay in the forest until evening. Then I remembered a Christian who lived near this forest who had always been a friend. He owed us money. I decided to go to him.

I barely walked 20 metres when I saw a wolf. I lit a match but he did not get scared and remained standing there. I lit one match after another but nothing helped.

For 25 minutes neither of us budged. The wold looked at me, and I looked at him. Finally, he was the first to move on. I took a deep breath and walked deeper into the forest. At dawn I arrived at my friend's house.

I entered the house and asked for something to drink. A young Christian girl brought me water. As I was drinking I suddenly heard a voice from behind the stove: “Shmulke, is that you? Where are you coming from?” This was his elderly mother who recognized me.

She told the children they should take good care of me. They gave me food and brought me to a barn where I could get some rest. I knew my friend, her husband, had died. She herself was very sick and could not get out of bed.

[Col. 1156]

I remained with them for over 4 weeks. One day one of their neighbours told a story how a Dr. Levin from Vilna jumped from a train and was hiding in a village called Budri, near

Ignaline. Someone turned him in. The police took him and the Christian who was hiding him.

I later learned that Dr. Levin had been shot. The end of the story is, my Christians were afraid and I had to leave.

Once again I was alone deep in the forest, not knowing to where or to whom. Being very hungry, I knocked on a door and asked for a piece of bread.

The area was very familiar. I immediately oriented myself and realized where I was. Not far lived the father of the policeman that helped me escape from Ignalina.

I decided not to go to the partisans, but to go to the father of the policeman.

When the Christian saw me he crossed himself and shouted: "Jesus – Mary, you are alive!"

He immediately brought me into his house and did not know what to do for me. His daughter brought me clean underwear, and for the first time in a few years, I changed my underwear. I bathed and became a new man.

This was on a Friday. Sunday, his son who was the police commander in New-Svencionys arrived. When his father brought him to the barn to see me, he began to tremble. I was worried that over the past three years, he had changed.

My fear was unfounded. He was my friend as before. He kissed me and told me how the German army is experiencing great defeats on all fronts. The Germans were retreating and apparently the war will soon be over. He deeply regretted that he had to work for the Germans, but he did not harm the Jews. On the contrary, whenever he could, he helped save Jews.

One day, after the liquidation of the Svencionys Ghetto, he met Elke Gilinsky. He gave him a revolver, which helped him reach the partisans in the forest.

[Col. 1157]

I later learned, all that he told me was true. In those days, it was hard to grasp that were such policemen in the world. This Christian simply had a golden character. This was indeed rare, and I looked at him as an angel from heaven.

My Return to Ignalina Region

Before he left, the police commander asked me not to stay at his father's house. Because of his being a policeman, many Germans come by, and he was afraid they would find me there.

When he left, it was decided they would bring me to another Christian. The same night, they took me in a boat on the river, to a small village about 8 kilometres from them. I knew this Christian as well. A few years earlier, he hid my brother-in-law Yosef Gavenda and his family.

This Christian's name was Marion Bazis. He received me well but refused to hide me. His reason was, he had a mean labourer, who would not protect me. He advised me to take the boat to a small island in the river. There I would find small wooden huts, and nobody goes there. He would bring me food every day.

That's what happened. I went to the island. Bazis came every day and brought me food. I would lie still all day, and I night I would walk around. I spent three weeks there, undisturbed.

After three weeks, Bazis came to bring me food. He told me there are police searches in the area for partisans, and he was worried they may come to the island.

Once again I had to resume my wandering. At night I sailed back to the village and from there, back to the forest.

I wandered until I arrived in the town where I was born, Paliush (Palūšė) There were no Jews there. I went to a neighbour who had served the priest in the local church.

[Col. 1158]

He took me to the priest's barn. It was too cold there to sleep. All the gates were open and the wind blew into every corner. My teeth were chattering.

One night, I was so cold I thought I would freeze to death. Realizing I had nothing to lose I knocked on a door not knowing who lived there.

I did well. It was the house of the organist from the church, a good friend of mine. I had gone to school with his wife and we were good friends.

When they saw how cold I was they gave me tea with raspberry juice. I was delighted.

My joy was short lived. They told me they had no place to hide me. Everyone passed their house to go to church and I will be seen.

When it was light I left their home. I went to the priest's garden and sat under an apple tree to try and decide what to do.

A strong wind blew in my face and snow began to fall. I decide to be a God's mercy. I arrived at a Christian cemetery. I sat down beside a grave, took out the food they gave me and began to eat. I then decided to go to the bell ringer. He worked for us in the forest and was a good person. What did I have to lose? He would certainly not turn me in.

I went to him. When I knocked in the window, he himself asked what I wanted.

When I told him who I was I immediately told his wife that I was standing outside.

[Col. 1159]

Obviously, they were very surprised. I noticed through the window they both crossed themselves. When they opened the door I saw how happy they were that I was alive. I quickly recounted my experiences and asked for a place to sleep. They prepared a place for me on top the oven and I slept until 4:00 that afternoon.

When I awoke, I put on my torn coat and wanted to say goodbye. His wife came to me and really begged for mercy:

"Where do you want to go? The weather is terrible. We will not let you go. Don't be afraid. No one will notice that you are here."

So I took off my coat and climbed back up to my spot above the oven. I spent over 3 months with them.

During this time I had to withstand difficult days. For weeks I lay in a ditch of manure in their barn. They placed a pig on top of me. They did this because the Germans were searching everywhere for partisans.

It the searches subsided I moved to the attic of the barn and the bell ringer's wife brought me food.

It is important to remember that the priest at the church in Paliush was a great friend to the Jews. The bell ringer's wife was a devout Christian and in confession told the priest they were hiding a Jew. He told her they should hide me as long as they can. He said it was a great deed and God would help them.

She returned very happy and told me the whole story.

[Col. 1160]

From that day on, the priest would send me newspapers. I thought that Christians like them belonged to the righteous people of the world.

Even after those searches I experienced a few difficult days. One fine morning, 500 Ukrainians and Germans came to town. When heard about it, I wanted to run away. I took food, said goodbye to the good people and was prepared to leave.

When I opened the door I noticed a rider was heading straight toward us, into the house. I immediately climbed back on top of the oven. Four more joined him in our house.

I lay on that spot as if in a fever. I told myself, this was going to be my end. If they searched the house, they would surely find me. That is exactly what occurred. But as if a miracle happened, they thought I was a Pole who was hiding from deportation. Together with other Christians, they sent me to Germany and then to Stutthoff [Stutthof Concentration Camp]

[Col. 1161]

One of the "Righteous Gentiles"

Eliezer Solomyak

Translated by Anita Frishman Gabbay

I will remember my rescuer, the Christian, Heronium Tarazevitch and his family. His wife Bronia, their daughter Irka, their son Miatek, and Heronium's sister Mania from Polvark Macklova on the way to Dukst. Heronium took upon himself to help me and my cousin Tuvia.

This Christian family brought us food and also helped others who worked in the Dukst labour camp by bringing them provisions. His daughter Irka, one day, routinely bringing us food, encountered German soldiers on their way to Polvark. She thought they saw her with the food and G–d forbid they should discover the hidden Jews and would begin their search in her home, she went into shock. She had a nervous breakdown! This illness stayed with her even after the war. When the Germans began to send the Christian folk to Germany for work, Tarazevitch didn't hide his sister. If he hid her, he was afraid the Germans would come to search his home and would find us. She worked in Germany for two and a half years, and came home physically unwell.

One time when Tatazevitch came to find us, we told him: we will feel very guilty, if G–d forbid, someone will discover our hiding place and you will loose your life as a consequence.

So he answered us: Do not worry, Brother, what will become of you will become of us. Life and Death is the same for everyone.

After Liberation, the Soviet forces sent Tarazevitch to Siberia for 10 years, on the charges that he harboured spies. This was his payback for his kindness and humanity.

[Col. 1162]

When he was freed, the family left for Poland. His daughter Irka remained an invalid because of her nervous breakdown. His sister Mania, as a result of those terrible conditions in Germany, destroyed her physically and shortly after the war she died.

I don't forget my rescuers and do everything to thank them for their humane deeds and personal risks they took for us. I pay back this debt, I owe my life to this family Tarazevitch.

Here is an excerpt from a letter from this selfless and honest Christian: He writes to the Ignaliner landsleit (bretheren) in Israel:

Dear Ignaliner Jews in Israel.

I send you my heartfelt and best wishes for the New Year and want to share the sadness that still exists in our town and the neighbouring towns.

The unforgivable spilling of Jewish blood still lives in the veins of our folk, who are living in the Jewish homes and who robbed the good and honorable Jews. These are signs of a great sin! We expelled G–d from our hearts and our homes and the Almighty went along with this...and even your daily bread...whoever knew what was happening, whoever was a devout Christian, would not allow themselves to become the Devil, to align themselves with Hitler and his willing executioners, wouldn't rob and would never benefit from the downtrodden and afflicted humanity(Jews). Those, who for a piece of clothing or a bottle of whiskey were ready to take a human life brought about upon themselves only misery. In their homes hang G–d's punishment. They brought upon themselves sickness and misfortune, poverty and hunger. They got what they deserved for their sins and for their inhumane deeds. The children of those Godless people are following in their parents footsteps: hooliganism, laziness and violence, and they are bringing this all over the towns of the region. I feel sad in my heart when I look at them, do we expect more from them than from their parents?

[Col. 1163]

My dear friend, very few good people are here in this world. We will always remember you and we plead with you not to put yourselves in an unfortunate position in order to send us these packages and money. It is not necessary. We are healthy and working and earn enough for food and clothing.

[Col. 1164]

We enjoy receiving your good wishes and we wish that you will build a new and better existence for yourselves. You should all know the happiness it gives me to know that people of different backgrounds can live together.

With my heartfelt best wishes and a great thank you for your gifts.

H.B. Tarazevitch

Heronium and Bronislava Tarazevitch

At the Holy Mass Grave

Fania Fisher

Translated by Anita Frishman Gabbay

Our Yiskor Book

This Yiskor Book is a Memorial for my husband, for my children, for my whole family, for all the Jewish people that perished. We should never forget them.

My Yarzheit [1]

The fifth of April
A frightful day
How great was my misfortune
How deep is my sorrow
How deep is my grief
How envious I am of all those mothers who were slaughtered
Together with their children
And I, have to suffer in this world
My poem may not be praise worthy
But it is full of pain and sorrow

There is nothing left of my children, nothing to hold
Not even a grave.

In Hiding

Be still, my child, my prince
Your cry will not help
Be strong, my child
Let another night pass
Do not cry.
The night will soon end
The morning might be better
This child
I hold so dearly to my heart
His face is so pale
His eyes like candles, dimming
The night passed
The morning came
The mother is distraught
The child is in her warm embrace
And it no longer needs any bread.

[Col. 1164]

My Heir

I had a son, talented, intelligent and fine
I hoped, he would be my heir
In his upbringing, a proud and fine Jew
I hoped
To live to see his Bar Mitzvah
Who is going to share in this grief and sorrow.

The Mass Grave of Poligon

Upon entering the Forests of Poligon
Between pathways, fields and trees
Where birds built their nest
There lies a long and broad grave
Covered with earth
Where a larger mound arose
The hill is not made of earth and stone

But of human remains and corpses
Silent! Heads lowered
With heavy hearts, with every limb numb
We stand in front of our Holy Brothers Grave
This is a grave for thousands of our dearest
Of our fathers, mothers, brothers, sisters and children
Our tears are like floods
Hearts are ripped apart by pain and suffering
We stand in front of this Holy Grave
We promise never to forget you
As long as we are alive, we will continue our tears, our longing,
As long as our hearts go on beating
Our pain will never go away
Their memory will glow
Like the stars in the sky
We will never forget you
And your memory shall never be erased!

Translator's footnote

Yearly remembrance

[Col. 1164]

Daugelishak–The History of the Shtetl

(Naujasis Daugeliškis, Lithuania)

55°22' 26°18'

David Tzinman

Translation by Anita Frishman Gabbay

Daugelishak was a very small shtetl in Vilna county, near the shtetls of Ignalina, New–Svenztian, Dukst and Vidz. It was in 2 parts: Old and New. In 1770 the first Jews arrived in the old part, thus Old Daugelishak. It was surrounded by beautiful thick forests. The new part, was built around 1900. In the New Daugelishak many small streams were found, which emptied into larger lakes, like the Disna.

[Col. 1165]

Three small bridges tied the shtetl with the surrounding region. When you arrived at the shtetl you found yourself in front of a tall hill, upon which they were beautiful houses. These belonged to the wealthy folk, who made a living in forestry.

On the left hand side, on the other side of the road, you could see the mill. This mill provided a living for many in the shtetl. A kilometer from the town was the blacksmith's shop, of Faivish the Schmidt (as he was called), who greeted everyone entering the shtetl. A horseshoe hung on his smithy, thus his signature.

On top of the hill the Jewish quarter started with the main street that led to Dukst. On the left side stood the Church surrounded by cement walls, which also housed the priest.

The main street of the shtetl was Gaminava Street, which stretched for about 300 meters and ended by the bridge. At the end of the main street you arrived at the main shtetl.

[Col. 1166]

At the end of the main street were the Folk–schul, the police station, the fire station, and the mill of my friend, Zelner. In the middle of the main street was a large public garden, where young people congregated in the evenings and holidays. On the right of the main street, a narrow street led to the Synagogue. At the edge of town the railroad went to Dukst, passing Vidz and Braslav.

On the other side of the shtetl was the smithy of Mendel the Schmidt. One could see the sparks flying, and you knew right away the hard labour of the old shtetl folk; thy worked long hours, sweat pouring down, in order to earn enough for a piece of bread!

Of the total population, there were about 175 Jews. Most of the Christians worked the land, the Polish were the bureaucrats and in the police–ranks.

[Col. 1167]

A gathering of Jews in Daugelishak with representatives from Vilna.

The Jews, like in the other shtetls, were small tradesmen and shopkeepers. Every Jew had a small plot of land next to his house. He planted potatoes and vegetables. Every Jew had a cow or a goat which provided them with their own milk for the children.

Life was difficult, especially for the Jewish women, who had their household duties, as well as looking after the garden and the fields. Some helped in the shops. She did the shopping in the market and if one owned a store, she was responsible for providing goods for that shop. Life for the young people was also very difficult. There was little work and prospects for the future were dim; so many left for larger cities or distant lands, like Canada, Argentina, South Africa and Eretz Israel. The entitled position of our town was held by the pharmacist, he also served as a doctor (or Feldsher–barber surgeon). He filled the prescriptions, made out the receipts, (looked after the pharmacy) as well as healed the sick.

[Col. 1168]

The pharmacist didn't heal only the body, he healed the spirit and the soul of the patient! One can say he was the only intellectual in the shtetl, who read his newspaper every day and infused our Jewish lives with his knowledge. His house was a meeting place for all: the Mayor, the Secretary of the council, the police commander, the priest and other notable persons. In 1930, a Jewish doctor arrived and stayed several years.

Very important work was performed by the fire brigade–comprised mainly of Jews. Zev Kuritzki was in charge for many years. His commander was Gershon Deutch. It was a delight to see the firefighters in a parade.

Firefighters

Sitting: right to left: **Secretary of the city, Zev Kuritzki, Inspector, Mayor, Gershon Deutsch**

Standing 1st row: **Avrahmke, Moiske, Moshe Isor, Avka Faivish, Almer, Yacov, Shaul**

Standing 2nd row: **Chaimke, Velvke, Hirshke, Abraham Yitzhak, Berke, Chaim Yoske, Melech, Motke**

They were dressed up in special uniforms with shiny buttons, caps on their heads and axes in their hands. They proudly marched through the main street of the shtetl. When a fire broke out, they all left their work and ran immediately to the fire station.

The first one was always Alter the tailor, dragging his ladder. Faivish, the blacksmith, ran with his axe and bucket of water. Abraham and Shmuel Ushpal tore down the burning roof and Moshe Isor Gordon sprayed water through a rubber hose, Yankel Tzinman and Chaim Feigel pumped the water. When the fire was extinguished, they went home in a happy mood and bragged to their friends. This bragging was heard for the entire week and how the Jewish lads were so capable.

[Col. 1169]

Shtetl life was focused around the synagogue. It was not only used for prayer 3 times a day, but also as a meeting place for social and political meetings. The synagogue was the cultural backbone of the shtetl.

In later years, the young people acquired a reading hall, where newspapers or books were available. It was also used for gatherings and lecturs, drama plays, etc.

There was also a library with Yiddish and Hebrew books.

Well known was the drama club and the mandolin orchestra.

Arieh Keshel was the director of the drama club.

Intresting, many Christians participated in the orchestra.

Ha'Halutz Ignalina–Daugelishak

Moishe Korb, Rochel Einhorn, Tuvia Tzinman, Ester Gilinski, Leizer Shapiro, ——, Shloime Kuritzki, Teme Kisberg

[Col. 1170]

Mandolin Orchestra

We have to mention, “Ha'Halutz” separately from the other Zionist organizations that were led by Shloime Rudnitski and Getzel Kesel.

The shtetl had a city council and other Jewish representation. The Jews who were representatives were Asher Ushpal and Eliahu Kuritzki, as well as Yerachmiel Korb from Ignalina.

Every Monday was market day. With this New–Daugelishak started to develop. Slowly the Jews came to the new part of town. Barely 10 Jewish families remained in Old–Daugelishak. One of the families was Rabbi Moshe Isak lipshitz, an old timer.

In September 1939, when the polish military left our region, both towns were neglected. It was far from the other shtetls and a railroad, so they were isolated. The Jews were left under the control of the priest. So, eventually they took matters in their own hands, and established their own city council.

The Jews paid dearly for this, Franik the mail carrier, organized his Christian bandits and a pogrom took place and they captured 2 Jewish lads, led them to the edge of town and shot them. These were Shlomo Geitzen and Abka Zilber. Shlomo was killed immediately and Abka was badly wounded. The Jews immediately felt their insecure future amongst their Christian neighbours!

Watchmen from our group were posted day and night, to avoid robberies of our shops, the burning of our homes, if need be, to shoot the Christian hooligan!

[Col. 1171]

The Jews endured these threats for days until the Red Army came into the shtetl. We felt a little freedom, a sigh of relief, in the meantime our daily lives resumed.

The new border of Daugelishak changed, it was very close to the border between Lithuania and White–Russia.

These were new beginnings for our shopkeepers, but they were slowly pushed out and the cooperatives slowly took over, although many Jews worked in them.

Two years later, when Hitler broke his pact with the Soviet Regime, the Red Army departed our shtetl and Hitler's army and Lithuanian bandits replaced them.

Together with the Soviets, the following left: Israelka Abelevitch, Hirske Berman, Rivka Berman, Blumka Ushpal, Chaim Berl Tzinman, Raitza Lipshitz, Tzirke Gordon, Bielke Rein, Chaim Rafaelka and the 15 year old Abraham Yitzhak Ushpal.

The older Jews couldn't run away. We took everything of value. The old Jews were angry at us.

Until this day, I remember that misfortunate day: I said goodbye to my parents, begging them to join me! They told me with tears in their eyes, —how can we survive this journey? Where shall we go?

I said my goodbyes, cried bitterly and left, never to see them again. I later found out that the Lithuanians took control of the shtetl, and it was certainly Kasimierz Ziber who was in control.

[Col. 1172]

We heard that he took all the parents of the children who fled with the Soviets, led them to the woods, and shot them, not far from Ignalina.

Amongst them were: Yosel Abelevitch, Hirshel the glass blower, Zalman, Yankel and Alter the tailors, Faivka the blacksmith, and Shaul Lifman Ushpal.

The remaining Jews were locked up in a tiny ghetto. This didn't last very long, like in all the shtetels of the Sventzian district, they were all murdered in Poligon. The shtetl was burned and today we find fields of greens and potatoes.

Not a trace of Daugelishak remains. But we must remember that there once was a shtetl there, and these wonderful young men and women made their mark in the Red Army or as partisans in the forests.

Hirshke Ushpal received for his bravery the highest medal from the Red Army. He alone blocked a German division from approaching the Soviet base.

Hirshel Alters died in the battle in Ariel, in 1942. Israelke Abelevitch died in the battle of Smolensk in 1943. Fighting with the partisans, the following died: Chaim Rafal, Tzira Gordon, Beila Rein.

With honor we shall remember, the young Jewish Daugelisher who fought to avenge the spilled blood of their Jewish brothers!

The memory of all our best and dearest, will forever remain etched in our hearts!

[Col. 1173]

Old Daugelishak

(Senasis Daugėliškis, Lithuania)

55°21'/26°16'

by A. Krill

Translated by Meir Razy

On the main road, from the south to the north, between the well-established community of Alt[Old]-Sventzian and the young community of Vidz on the border with White Russia, lay a tiny town with a population that did not exceed even three dozen families. The town was founded by three dozen families spread out on both sides of the road. It happened during the influx of Jews from Prussia to the east, semi-German Jews, who headed toward Lithuania and Russia. At that time, one family separated itself from the flow and settled on some flat land along a kilometer-long stretch. The road was outside the forest area, between the mountain ridge known as the Red Mountain and Faringy spring, whose waters flowed into the only lake in the region. They were mostly skilled workers. Jewish tailors and craftsmen from large cities such as Vilna, Brisk or Grodno, who were being persecuted by the local residents.

Another reason they stayed on the road: when they learned about the decrees and the expulsion of the Jews from Russia in 1742, they began searching for all sorts of ways to settle wherever possible. The closing of the port of Riga in 1743 terrified them and the flow of eastward traffic ceased. Sometimes single families would settle in a village, or sometimes 2 or 3 families would establish themselves in a town.

There were no organized villages at that time. Rather, peasants would work the land using primitive methods. Servants on the estates of large landowners needed craftsmen to help maintain their farms and for their domestic needs. Crafts, such as tailoring, shoemaking, furriers, blacksmiths and tinsmiths were in demand

Until the beginning of the Russian rule of Lithuania and Poland in 1795, they earned their living by cooking and selling wine in addition to their traditional crafts. They earned most of their living during the winter months, dealing mainly with pig hair and processing the skin and leather.

The Ordinance of the Tsarina Katrina the Second became the Law in 1795 and required all those who did not engage in agriculture to register under an urban status.

In order to qualify to stay in their place of residence, each of the Jews of the town of Alt-Daugelishak (and those who were scattered in villages) purchased 10 dunams of land (a dunam =1,000 square meters) and declared themselves (with the addition of a "side tax") as land "laborers".

[Col. 1174]

Although they worked the land in partnership with their out-of-town peasant neighbors, they themselves also cultivated a small area near their homes, about 2-3 dunams, and grew mainly three crops: potatoes, beans and poppy seeds.

Hundreds of Jewish families were scattered in dozens of villages and local land-owners' estates over many kilometers. They were called "settlers" and their spiritual center was in Alt-Daugelishak.

Alt-Daugelishak served as a spiritual center for more than 200 years, until the Nazi oppressor utterly destroyed it. They all gathered together from the area between Sventzian in the south, Vidz in the north, Gavikan in the east and Farigge[?Paliush] in the west for the High Holydays. Whole Jewish families arrived at Alt-Daugelishak which had a magnificent Beit Midrash and a Yeshiva with many students. Additional prayer halls were set up during the High Holydays in the homes of Moshe-Yaakov Katz, the blacksmith, and Moshe Yitzchak Krill. The prayer leaders would replace each other during the services but these visiting Jews not only stood on their feet from "Kol Nidrei" (=the Yom Kippur opening prayer) until "Neila" (=the Yom Kippur closing prayer) but also put hard peas in their boots or shoes in order to "torture" themselves on the day of Fasting and Atonement.

The town renovated the Beit Midrash in the eighteenth century, replacing the straw roof with a one made of wood. They built a bathhouse and a Mikveh with a copper water heater. The town had a Shochet and a Mohel, and later on even two Shochatim. Their livelihood was limited. They taught 3-4 days a week. During the rest of the week, while visiting other Jewish communities, they also taught Torah separately to the children of the families scattered among the villages.

For decades, the residents of Alt-Daugelishak dispersed on Sunday mornings, going to all the surrounding villages and landowners as craftsmen. And they were not just mere craftsmen. They also provided midwife or paramedical services wherever needed. They offered cupping therapy or mustard dressings that either shortened the length of the disease or the length of the patient's life.

Rabbi Aharon Shochat, a Cohen and a teacher of purity of the body as well as the preservation of cleanliness was also an expert in pharmaceuticals. He was already producing "Dermentol" cream by removing pollen from the cones of pines, collecting them in glass jars and using it to stop any bleeding during circumcision ceremonies or in any other serious cases.

[Col. 1175]

His dignified appearance was just as we imagined Aharon, the High Priest, brother of Moses.

The second slaughterer, Rabbi Noach, was not as multi-talented, and mainly taught Torah to the Jewish children in the town and its surroundings. In addition, he provided the service of writing letters and addressing envelops as he was familiar with the Russian script and language. He never received money for his work but bartered, especially for food.

The first industry in the area was established in Alt-Daugelishak. Rabbi Hillel Katz installed a knitting machine in his home and the peasants of the area brought the raw wool to be combed during the shearing season. The machine, which had 12 heads, was brought from Germany and was operated by hand, day and night. As with the flour mill, the peasants waited patiently in line in order to have their wool combed.

In the early 1900s, and especially during the Japanese-Russian War, immigration out of Europe began. The first immigrants went to South Africa.

Pure and loyal Jews, the guardians of the Jewish spirit, scattered to all corners of the globe. A few stayed, like the families of Rabbi Avraham Katz. His son, Rabbi Leib Katz, immigrated to England.

The Sharpman family settled in the city of Leeds, England, where they continued as tailors. Their children and grandchildren became lawyers. Among them was the famous lawyer Sam Sherman of Labor party in Leeds. Rabbi Leib Katz was a long-time rabbi in the Leeds community, and after his death the position was transferred to his only son Rabbi Shimon Wolf Katz.

[Col. 1176]

Only a few arrived in Eretz Israel in the 1930s as most of them immigrated to South Africa.

There was one rich family in Alt-Daugelishak, the family of Moshe Isaac Lifshitz and his two sons Yerachmiel and Koppel. They engaged in wholesale trade and the leasing of forest for timber trading.

The owner of a single grocery shop, Lea Postawski, Lea the Kremerke[shopkeeper] was her Yiddish name. she used to order wrapped candy in boxes especially for us, when we would come from Vilna to grandmother for our summer vacation. She was also an expert in making and marketing Gin. As a result she had good contacts with the local Russian authorities.

Among the first settlers in Ignalina were the Jews of Alt-Daugelishak. The town of Ignalina was founded during the construction of the railroad between Vilna and Dvinsk in 1862, as a commercial center between Novo-Sventzian and Dukstas. The office and supply depot was built in Ignalina in the area between the green lake and the large swamp.

The first Melamdim, Jewish teachers, came from Daugelishak. The first slaughterer, son of Avraham Katz, arrived from Daugelishak and served as a Shochet for the rest of his life.

And this story was confirmed by many people:

Everyone was busy and happy when they laid the railroad tracks. Some even started to learn to read and write Russian at the age of 30 and 40. However, when the first train arrived, about ten families escaped out of fear of this machine, a moving carriage with no horses or harnesses. Among the first of the escapees was my dear grandfather, Rabbi Leib Krill, as he himself told me. Even though he already knew how to sign his name in Russian, he had never believed that it was possible to stop this monster that was actually rolling on the tracks.

He stayed in Rumshanze for two years until he became accustomed to the train, and then with Moshe Yoseph Soloveitchik returned to Ignalina.

[Col. 1177]

Old Daugelishak

(Senasis Daugėliškis, Lithuania)

Reicha Krill

Translated by Anita Frishman Gabbay

On a piece of land, Old–Daugelishak was a very tiny shtetelah on the road between Braslav and Vilna. 3 kilometers away was the new shtetl– New–Daugelishak.

These 2 shtetls were linked by lush fields and it was pleasant to go for walks from one shtetl to another.

In the last years, very few Jews remained in the Old part, not more than 10 families. They were mainly involved in small trade and craftmanship.

The economic situation for the remaining Jews was difficult. The Jewish worker (tailor or shoemaker) had to rely on the impoverished peasant folk, that were so poor themselves they couldn't even afford a new piece of clothing or pair of shoes. There was also an anti–Semitic agitation in the region, that the peasants should not give the Jews an opportunity to make money from them.

All the Jews from old– Daugelishak, barely made a living. They were forced to endure many hardships and could barely make ends meet. These were poor and honest Jews. One of them was Moishe Sharfstein , the tailor, but in this town he was known as Moishe the “Big One”. His wife was called Yehudit, an over– worked Jewish woman. Their children left for different parts of the world, life was very difficult for them. Their youngest daughter married and lived in New –Daugelishak.

[Col. 1178]

Moishe and Yehudit were left alone, like we used to say, Gone, bye, bye! until they were faced with death and destruction by Hitler's mighty forces!

Moishe the “Tall One”, was another Jewish neighbour of ours. On the other side of us, another Jewish tailor lived, Meir Sharfstein, a very interesting person. Always with a smile, always happy.

When he worked, as he had such a pleasant voice, I would come just to listen to his singing and his songs.

A little further away from us was the house of Motl Postavski, who lived with his sister Taiba. Both of them were deaf ‘like the wall’ and spoke between themselves, but with us only with a wink.

Next to them there lived a shop keeper, Rabbi Yakov Shlomo. His wife was a sickly woman and she always lay in a dark room. With great difficulty she managed the household chores.

On the way to Sventzian lived the widow Sprintza with her daughter Pesia. Spritza had more children but in those days, they were all scattered. She was left alone with Pesiala, who was a sick girl and Sprintza had little "nachos"[1] from her.

On another street, which led to Ignalina, lived Moishe Yakov with his family. He spent many years in Estonia. How he used to tell us, he was so home sick, that he vowed to return home to Daugelishak.

Later his sons left him and immigrated to distant lands, only Meir stayed with his father.

[Col. 1179]

They had a workshop where the hammering continued from early morning till late at night, where sparks were flying in all directions: this was a testament to the hard and difficult labour of a blacksmith.

Yitzhak Postavski, the cabinetmaker, had a beautiful house in our shtetl. His children did not stay at home and only came for the holidays.

Hillel Katz was a tailor, but he looked like a Rabbi.

The shochet also had his own house. An entire day he would sit and read the 'Gemara'. His wife Sheina Rochel was always sick. He had a difficult life, barely made a living, and depended on support from America.

[Col. 1180]

This is a brief description of almost all the inhabitants of Old–Daugelishak. For many years they lived in harmony with their Lithuanian peasants. All spoke good Lithuanian and we were all friends.

For years we bartered together and entertained each other. They were invited to our simchas.

Nobody foresaw, that our friends and neighbours would turn against us, become robbers, murders and wild sadists.

As soon as Hitler's forces arrived, our friendly Lithuanians were transformed and life for us was never the same. In every attack, robbery, murder, they took an active role. They became Hilter's willing and able executioners.

The small Jewish Old–Daugelishak community was erased from the earth.

Remember and never forget our beloved brothers and sisters!

Translator's footnote

Good fortune

[Col. 1179]

New–Daugelishak

(Naujasis Daugėliškis, Lithuania)

55°22'/26°18'

Zev Kuritzki

Translated by Anita Frishman Gabbay

New–Daugelishak, a small hamlet of about 40–50 Jewish families, belonged to the Sventzian district. The closest Jewish town was Ignalina, which had a railroad and also had a larger Jewish community. Therefore, the first Jewish inhabitants were very closely connected with Ignalina. There were large markets in Ignalina where Jews from Daugelishak would go to buy and sell their wares. The second connection was the railroad, which went to Vilna. Amongst the Jews were Some wealthy folk who owned their own homes, and enterprises of all sorts. As they were merchants, they travelled all over to different markets (which took place in each shtetl on different days) and traded with whatever they had in order to make a money. This is how the merchants established themselves with the surrounding towns, like Ignalina, Vidz, Dukst, and Svencionys. Part of the folk made a living from other trades, like tailors, shoemakers and other professions.

[Col. 1180]

A group of Young People

Seated: left to right: **Sara Raitza Gaitzen, Devorah Kuritski, Zev Kuritski, Fruma Kuritski**
Standing: **Raicha Krill, Abba Levin, Sara Feigl, Abba Silber, Mera Leah Levin, Shlomo Gaitzen**

[Col. 1181]

For the dozens of smaller hamlets around our town, the only financial institution that the small town was able to maintain, was a Gemilut–Hesed (free loans for the needy), which was managed by Zev Kuritzki, Asher Usphal, and Abraham Eliahu Kuritzki. The Gemilut–Hesed Bank(or society) helped those in need to survive. The most important cultural institution was the library and was founded by B. Kuritzki, now living in Argentina.

Daugelishak had a very well–organized fire fighting team, which was comprised of Jewish youth. It provided a livelihood for them, as well as, being so organized, they provided us with protection against those Christian hooligans when necessary.

These were:

Zev Kaplan

Zelig Levin, the Shamash from the Schul

Moishe Eliahu Reznik, the Shochet

Leib Yitzhak Levin

Yechitiel Usphal

Asher Usphal

[Col. 1182]

Yerachmiel Lifshitz

Yerachmiel Lipshitz, an outstanding director of "YEKAPO" during the first World War

Yekutiel Upsphal, during the Czarist regime was the representative and official who handed out documents (passes) for the Jewish folk of Volosk (province).

In Old–Daugulishok lived: Moishe Issak Lipshitz with his extended family, a Holy Man, he had a shop: Lipe Elia Gurewitz, who dealt with poultry and wood, A. Shaper, who later left for America, the neighbour Aharon and Moishe Sharfstein.

Reb Moishe Issak Lipshitz

[Col. 1183]

Old and New in Our Home

Bluma Ushpal–Vidotchinski and Raisel Lifshitz–Pliner

Translated by Janie Respitz

Raisel Lifshitz–Pliner

Bluma Ushpal–Vidotchinski

Not one, but two, Daugelishoks existed on the way from Svencionys to Vidz. One was called Old, because truthfully it was old because of its age. The second, New–Daugelishak was built thanks to the new church, and thanks to the Volost(gemina) that belonged administratively to the larger town of Ignalina. The land on which these small towns were located belonged to the princely Radziwill family.

From Old–Daugalishok, the Jews were slowly disappearing. Very few families remained. Their children immigrated wherever they could, America, Africa, Argentina and Brazil.

In New Daugalishok existed a small Jewish community of well known families until the second World War, Lipshitz, Ushpal, Gaitzen, Kuritzki and others.

Yechutiel Ushphal, during the Czarist period, was the Jewish representative who was the go between the city official. Yechutiel Lifshitz was the mayor in the time of the first World War and the representative of "YEKAPO"(relief society) for Daugelishok.

Even during the most difficult times, the youth of Daugalishok didn't give up, they had a "Halutz" club, a drama club, a library, a string orchestra, and a fire– fighting brigade.

[Col. 1184]

At the outbreak of the second world war, when our Lithuanian neighbours started to terrorize us and killed a friend, the young people of Daugelishak organized themselves and counter attacked. They would not allow these hooligans to continue in this manner.

A large segment of the youth escaped when the Germans arrived and because of this, the Lithuanian murders killed 18 Jews. Those who escaped enlisted in the Soviet Army, amongst them were: Ber Tzinman, Israel Abelevitch, Hirsh Berman, Hirsh Ushpal, Abraham Yitzhak Ushpal, Meir Kessel and Rafael Kagan.

Some also fell during the Partisan campaigns and fought valiantly: Moishe Gordon and Abraham Usphal. A. Ushphal got a medal: "Help from the Red–Farband"

From Russia those that returned: Bluma Ushpal, Rochel Ushpal, Tzira Gordon, Rebecca Berman, Raizel Lifshitz.

The Daugelisher Jews, together with all the Jews from the Sventzian Region, had the same fate. In the mass grave of Poligon, Old and New Daugelishakers have their final resting place.

Let us never forget these martyred people of Daugelishok.

[Col. 1185]

Rabbi Eliyahu and His Son Dr. Hirsh–Leib Gordon

by David Tidhar

Translated by Meir Razy

Dr. Hirsh–Leib Gordon was the son of Rabbi Eliahu Gordon and Malka Katznelenboygn. He was born in Daugelishak in 1896, grew up in Daugelishak, Vidz and Komai, studied in the Slobodka, Lida, and Volozhin yeshivas starting at the age of nine and completed his rabbinical education in 1914. That year he emigrated to Palestine where, at first, he worked as a laborer in the orchards of Petah Tikva.

Rabbi Eliahu Gordon 96–1892

Being a Russian citizen, he was deported to Egypt by the Ottoman rulers at the outbreak of the first World War (1914). In Egypt he met with Joseph Trumpeldor and Ze'ev Jabotinsky who were creating the Jewish Legion and he joined that Legion. He participated in the Legion's military activities in the Dardanelles (the Gallipoli Campaign) in Turkey. After the unit was dispersed Hirsh moved to Italy, and then, in August 1915, he moved to the U.S.A, where he engaged in educational work and later – journalism. He studied Languages, Bible, and Archeology at Yale University.

When the American Jewish Legion was created in 1918, he travelled to Eretz Israel and joined the 39th Battalion under the command of Colonel Eliezer Margolin and participated in the conquest of Palestine, from Turkey, under General Allenby. At the end of the war he returned to the United States and devoted himself to his studies. He received four master's degrees in international law, Education, Psychology, and Art History.

[Col. 1186]

He continued his studies and earned six Ph.D. degrees. In the U.S. he earned degrees in Languages, Egyptology and Hebrew Literature. He then travelled to Europe where he continued his studies and received a Doctorate in Classical Archeology, a Doctorate in Natural Sciences and an MD, specializing in Neuroscience and Psychiatry.

Dr. Hirsh Leib Gordon, son of rabbi Eliahu

At the outbreak of the Second World War he was appointed Major in the American Army and was later promoted to Commander in the Navy. He was transferred to the Pentagon where he was an adviser in the field of Neurological diseases. Later he became the head of the Neurological Department in the Florida's Veterans Hospital. He is currently a professor of Psychiatry in the New York Medical School, a professor of Socio–Psychiatry at Yeshiva University, a lecturer in Psychiatry at the Alfred Adler Institute. As well, he is a Fellow of the Academy of Medicine, as well as a Fellow of the Academy of Sciences of the American Medical Association and the American Psychiatric Society.

[Col. 1187]

He is a member of the Appeal Committee at the Military Recruiting Office and President of the Hebrew Medical Association of America. In addition, he is active in the field of Hebrew education. He managed Hebrew schools in America and educated many teachers at the teacher seminary.

He is very active in the literary field. Starting as a boy, as a student at the Lida Yeshiva (1909), he published his first article in the newspaper ZMAN (=Time). His first work in Yiddish was "A Pencil Story" in the Yiddish newspaper "Der Yid" in Odessa. He regularly participated in the ZMAN, HATZFIRA, Moment, Das Leben, Der Freund and Shacharit publications.

Since coming to America in 1915, he has published thousands of articles in various newspapers: Der Tag, Tageblatt, Forward, Zukunft, Yid–Folk, Yid–Kammer, Kondas, and more.

[Col. 1188]

For 25 years he published a weekly Book Review section every Sunday in the "Morgan Journal". He wrote a medical column in the weekly "Der Amerikaner" and edited the monthly health journal "Gezund".

In 1929 he published a book "Dramas" and was one of the four founders of the weekly "HaDoar" (=the Post Office) in Hebrew in which, to this day, he has been participating regularly. He frequently wrote in the English–Jewish press, edited the section for the study of Hebrew medicine, edited the collection known as "Pages of Medicine" and is a regular participant in the "Hebrew Doctor".

Dr. Gordon participates in journals about Art, Law and Medicine. His English books are: "The Basilikai and the Stoic in the Talmudic Literature", "Psychological Concepts in the Bible", "The Talmud and the Zohar", "Diplomatic Contracts in Ancient Shinar", "Yoseph Karo", a research about Yoseph Karo's life. This book received many accolades in the world of literature. He is also the author of "Health Care according to Maimonides" and "The New Chemical Therapy for Mental Illness".

He is married to Tamar Leibowitz.

[Col. 1187]

The Economic Situation of Daugelishok

According to the "Pinchas of Vilna" Yekapo 1931, transmitted by M.Shalit

Translated by Anita Frishman Gabbay

Daugelishak was comprised of 350 souls, half of them Jews. The economy was basically in ruins. The Jews are very poor and they had fight to earn a piece of bread. The businesses failed–although they provided a meager living, the taxes were high.

The merchants are unemployed. Most get involved with shtetl–trade, which entails mostly the fish business. This provides a minimal livelihood. They had to walk 15 kilometers and then they brought home 4–5 kilos of fish.

In this manner the Jews are able to save themselves from starvation.

Everyone wants to immigrate. They go to Argentina, South Africa, and other places where they can "push themselves in."

Three months ago we organized a needed market day, every Monday. Very few peasants come, as they are accustomed to the markets of the larger surrounding shtetls.

No animals–trade or horse–trade come to our market. The community is a poor one, the bath, made out of lime is not such a success. The shtetl is therefore in economic ruins. The peasant doesn't have many possessions, therefore cannot make any purchases. The shopkeepers and artisans therefore suffer.

Even the Christian cooperative here barely makes a living.

Due to these cooperatives, all the bakeries and butcher shops close. It is not worth their while to get a permit and pay taxes.

There is no Inn or restaurant in the shtetl, therefore, it is no wonder that the economic situation is bad.

The end is rather a sad one. The inhabitants are rattled by this and each one wants to run away. The big question, is: "where".

[Page 1189]

Kaltinian

(Kaltanenai, Lithuania)

55°16' 26°00'

My Shtetl on the River Zhemiane

Yosef Tabakhowitz (Argentina)

Translated by Anita Frishman Gabbay

Edited by Rhoda Miller

Kaltinian, the home of my birth, it is so difficult for me to talk about you! To cry for you! How can I make peace with the memory, that you, the once beautiful garden, became a trampled ugly place at the hands of the German and Lithuanian murderers, your flowers together with its Jews were torn from its roots!

My dear shtetelah, I gather my strength to write about you and I can still remember you, that is the way you will remain etched in my memory.

Kaltinian was ten kilometers from the train station, which tied Warsaw to Peterburg (Leningrad) at New–Sventzian. The shtetl also had an indirect line with New Sventzian, through its small train, which ran from Ponevesh (Panevezys) to Gluboke. The shtetl was surrounded by thick forests, a lake and a river.

The lake started about two kilometers from the shtetl, passed by Kaltinian and joined other lakes that stretched throughout Lithuania. One of the lakes ran into a river which was called Zhemiane, the same name as the lake. It meandered around the shtetl in the direction of New Sventzian.

The history of the shtetl is not well known to me. Just what the older Jews of the shtetl passed down.

[Col. 1190]

"Is the start of the shtetl a result of the 1863 Polish revolt [emancipation of slaves] against Czarist Russia?" The land, where the shtetl is now located and some nearby terrain, belonged to Polish noblemen and after the Polish defeat it was given to the Russian General, [Pan–Eckx]* (or the Greater Russia annexation], who subdued the rebellion.

This resulted in Jews receiving parcels of land in order to build houses. After the general's death, the stately home and land was given to his daughter, who married a Russian Coronel (Poltvnyk, Russian colonel or governor), Mordvinov, who became the governor/ boss of the shtetl.

The small pieces of land went from father to children who married and started families. This is how the shtetl grew, until it became a Jewish one, consisting of about 30 families.

As you entered the shtetl stood the house of my uncle Natan Tabakhovitch. He had about four Desiaten of land and was a partner in the Barovker Mill. On the left side of him lived the pristav (police commissioner in Czarist Russia). Going to the lake was a garden of vegetables belonging to Hene–Munia Katz, the widow. Further along the small little street, which we called "kol" (sound), lived Itche the teacher. He was also in charge of the bathhouse. After the bathhouse stretched several fields. In this corner only the Christians lived.

[Col. 1191]

Across the market square was the stately–Shul, on one side of the school lived Ben–Zion Volavitch, who had a butcher shop and some interests in the forestry trade. After him lived several Christian families and then Leib Miluntchik with his father– in– law Shmuel Gavenda.

Leib Miluntchik was involved with Voskes, transporting wood to the river. His father in–law fabricated tar and was also in the carpentry business. Next to Chloine Gavenda, or as we called him, Chloine the deaf one, was a fisherman. After these two homes were the Monopole, next to which was the firefighter's Pozarne (firehouse), where Yacov the blacksmith lived.

After the Pozarne was the house of Yitzhak Rudnitzki, who was a wood merchant and across the street towards the river was the wealthy home of Chana Rudnitzki. Closer to the river, Abraham–Yitzhak Guterman lived, who also worked in forestry with his in– law Elia Karapatkin.

Close to the synagogue lived: Abraham Yitzhak Katz, the Potchter[name of his trade], Faive–Yitzhak Popiski, Shloime–Yosef Katz, Hirsh Kremer, and his in– law Gerhon Rudnitzki. They all were wood merchants.

The son of Hirsh Kremer, Elihu (Eloishe)Kremer, later became an important wood merchant in Vilna. He died in Israel. The son of Gershon Rudnitzki, Elihu (Eloishe) Rudnitzki, was a renowned attorney and community leader in Vilna (also died in Israel).

With Gershon Rudnitzki's house the town came to an end; which stretched to the river and the bridge. Across the road from Gershon Rudnitzki and Hirsh Kremer was the church and the house of the priest. After this house was our house. My father made a living in forestry until the First World War, and before with the trade in pelts (fur).

[Col. 1192]

Under one roof with us lived our uncle Mordechai Garshein. He was a glazier and also owned a factory. After us lived: our uncle Yitzhak–Faive Volavitch, who was a butcher and a merchant, Yitzhak–Yacov Rudnitzki, a fisherman, who also baked beigel and was also the Shamash at the synagogue, Dovid Portnoy, a tailor, Yehoushe Rufeitz, who was also in the forestry trade, and Mordechai Mavish, or as he was called, Motel the Rav, also in the forest trade.

Motel Mavish, called Motel the Rav

The mother in– law lived with Mordechai Rudnitzki, or Motel the Elder. He was also in the forest trade. After Motel the Rav lived the Rabbi of the shtetl, Rabbi Yehoushe Barg, who held the position until the German invasion, and Yacov Henech the blacksmith who later left for America.

This is where the Jewish shtetl ended. We should also mention the Jews that left the shtetl, like Mordechai Kovalski, who left for Sventzian, and the brother Zolia and Berl Guterman, who later lived in New–Sventzian.

Life for the Jews in Kaltinian until the First World War was very prosperous. There were barely any poor people. There were those who were in wood export, others bought mushrooms and berries for Eloishe Kremer, who exported them to Germany and a part remained for the local trade.

Kaltinian in those years was also affected by the beginning of social and national changes in the world. Young people began to organize themselves with their involvement in cultural activities and began to connect with the other Jewish youth from the neighbouring shtetls, and banded together to build a unified center for its Jewish people (life).

[Col. 1193]

A Yiddish library was founded in those days, there were no Hebrew books in this library.

Gershon Rudnitzki bought them and created a Hebrew library. When Gershon Rudnitzki left the shtetl he gave the books to the shtetl and both libraries merged.

A Yiddish Shul was founded. When the Soviets occupied Kaltinian, it was closed and there no longer existed a Yiddish school in the shtetl.

The shtetl didn't have a doctor. The feldsher [barber doctor] from Lingmian came, Noger, or the doctors Heifetz and Arlov from Sventzian.

The shtetl didn't have a pharmacy. There was a small pharmacy with the bare essentials for first aid, or a so–called temporary clinic.

The Zionist clubs were very interwoven in the shtetl. After the First World War, the Halutz was founded and most of the young people started to prepare themselves for Aliyah to Eretz Israel.

I was fortunate to be amongst the first group who made Aliyah from Kaltinian, later I had to go back to Kaltinian. I returned in 1926 and found Kaltinian in a situation of "prosperity".

[Col. 1194]

In England the great coal strike broke out and Poland began to export large amounts of wood to them. This revived the wood trade in Kaltinian and Jews made a very good living.

My father bought land in partnership with Velvel Popiski (of New–Sventzian) from the Governor Mardvinov. Other Jews bought land from him and this was a period of a great economic opportunity.

The good times did not last long. Barely two years past and hardships began. All of Poland suffered through an economic crisis in the years 1928/1929, which impacted the Jewish people particularly. The Jewish youth looked for ways to leave Poland, wherever they might be allowed entry.

The shtetl Kaltinian, understandably, had no other way. Shimon Mavish left for France and after my release from the military I also left for Argentina, Ischer Miluntchik left for Argentina.

Kibbutz Hakhshara [preparation] in Gershon Rudnitzki's forest Halutzim from Kaltinian and other shtetelach of the Sventzian region

[Col. 1195]

The Jewish youth who remained in the shtetl didn't have any way of knowing. Everyone felt the dark nightmare approaching, but no one could even comprehend such dark days would descend. A wild beast would arrive, murder and obliterate the shtetl of Kaltinian.

No one had the foresight that a total annihilation was arriving!

[Col. 1196]

Kaltinian, our dear and beloved shtetl!

We will always remember you. You will forever be etched in our memory!

All our nearest and dearest, that were so brutally murdered, Kiddush Hashem [sanctify the Lord], we will never forget you. Their memories will forever remain in our hearts forever!

[Col. 1195]

The Home of My Dreams

Neche Tabakhowitz–Bakaltchuk z"l

Translated by Anita Frishman Gabbay

Edited by Rhoda Miller

My ravaged and abandoned shtetl, Kaltinian, how many fond memories and ties do I have with you? Is it true that our home no longer exists? Is it true that our nearest and dearest met their tragic deaths in such horrendous circumstances?!

Here, here, as if it were yesterday, I still can see them all, all sitting together in their homes or on their porches, sitting quietly during our beautiful summer evenings when the acacia trees were in bloom. My eyes, until today, are filled with tears when I remember the songs that drifted through the air, when we were young carefree people boating on the silvery Zemiane that emptied into the larger lake.

The joyful songs floated together with the rhythm of the waves, whispering through the stillness of a "blanket of lonely trees." Branches were strewn across the edge of the stream and lake. The nature remains untouched with her beauty, sober but awesome! However my lovely dear shtetl is no longer, it lays now in ruins, not one Jew remains, not one trace of a Jewish soul!

My lost–destroyed home, where we grew up together with the trees and the flowers is now empty and meaningless. The faces of the Kaltinianer Jews are wandering in front of my eyes, I can hear singing from Yankel the blacksmith, passing our house on his way to the Synagogue. Now, I see our uncle Natan coming into our house, to drink a glass of tea and catch up on a little conversation.

[Col. 1196]

My dear and outgoing friends are no longer, Chaia–Leia whose laughter and melodious voice filled the streets; the philosophical Shipra; my sister– in– law Beila–Gita the Rebbetzin; Rivka my aunt Meres(could be Rivka, that belonged to my aunt Meres), who was a singer and a dreamer.

How carefree were those days, when we went to the fields to pick berries and mushrooms! We roamed the fields through and through! Not distracted by anything! Then we left with full baskets to our homes.

We used to walk leisurely on the edge of the river and forge new paths. We looked at the boats floating quietly on the water. We watched the fishermen, with the deaf Chloine at the head, throwing their nets into the water and dragging them out, singing, and throwing their catch on the banks.

The river Zemiane

My heartache is so great and my pain is so deep when I remember each detail! Now I remind myself of my house, Which was near to the train that ran from Lingmian to New–Sventzian and Vilna. Alongside the tracks flowed the river Zemiane.

[Col. 1198]

In our shtetl there was a brick Synagogue, which my father, Yacov–Moishe Tabakhovitch z"l built. Yitzik the Chazan was the public emissary of the shtetl for many years. Later Elchanan Yatzkevitch came to pray here, who served as the shochet and superintendent.

[Col. 1197]

The Rabbi of the shtetl as Rabbi Yeschayu Barg. A club was founded by Ida Katz in Kaltinian: there was a large library with Yiddish and Hebrew books, a drama club directed by Mirta Katz.

Life in the shtetl was quiet and tranquil. But the Second World War arrives, the German animals invade our region, the Lithuanian neighbours become the masters of the shtetl.

The drama club

Sitting: right to left: **Beila Gita Mavish, Grisha Kovalski, Chaia Leia Tabakhovitch**
Standing: right to left: **Shloimekeh Rudnitzki, Raizel Rudnitzki(Katz), Meir Rudnitzki, Berl Tabakhovitch, Berl Tabakhovitch (Natan's)**

The persecution towards the Jews begin. My father, Yacov–Moishe, with my brother Berl, die on the third day of the outbreak of the war. They are shot not far from our house. I grab my two young ones and run to New Sventzian. From there we begin again our long and difficult wanderings until we can reach a safer place.

All the Jews of Kaltinian were murdered–either in Gupa, the torture camps of Poligon, or on the roads during their flight.

Kaltinian was destroyed, now JUDENREIN! (free of Jews)

The firefighters group in Kaltinian

[Col. 1199]

Between the Two Wars

Yitzhak Kavalski[1]

Translated by Rena Borow

It's only 27 years that I've been away from my little shtetl Kaltinian and still I can see before my eyes as if it were today. I'm still inspired by the beautiful nature, the forest and fields and the beautiful surroundings. For hundreds of years a few dozen Jewish families lived there who were very friendly with their Lithuanian neighbors. It seemed as if just the trees were rooted in the ground, that's how rooted the Jewish population was and no storm would be able to uproot them. Unfortunately, we all were bitterly wrong. The

Hitlerish animals erased them from the earth and there's no trace of them. That horrific Holocaust was aided by many of their Lithuanian neighbors with whom we had lived well so many generations.

In the history of the Jewish settlement of Kaltinian several important eras need to be signified.

The era before the First World War, when we lived there quietly and securely. Each had his own land, made his own living. Everyone lived his quiet life. Two families, Kramer and Rudnitzky, dealt with the exploitation of the forest (cut down trees) and traded in wood. The Jewish store owners and craftsmen made their living in a large part from the same forest trade and the work that was involved with it.

The First World War turned everything over in the whole region as it was occupied by the Germans. Part of the Jewish population escaped to Russia and the ones that were left suffered of hunger. The situation changed when the Germans took over, the forest around the shtetl in order to ship the wood to Germany. The work was done by the two Jewish wood traders Kramer and Rudnitzky. They were the ones who hired the Jews from the town and the surrounding Jewish shtetlach. They mostly got paid by barter from the Germans for their work and that kind of exchange saved much of the Jewish population from hunger.

At that time there was the Ponivetcher Rabbi, Rabbi Kahanaman, who did everything he could and was very helpful in helping the Jews from the surrounding shtetlach also.

After the war when the Russian army took control the situation again got very very difficult in the surrounding area, but in the little town in Kaltinian things were a little better. The reason was that the Jews here owned little bits of land and they were able to grow vegetables and potatoes and have bread.

When the Poles took over the region and it was taken away from Lithuania, the town was practically on the border. A few of the families, especially the more well to do ones left the town and went to Vilna and the larger surrounding town of Svencionys and New-Svencionys.

The situation in Kaltinian became hopeless. The youth had instinctively felt the oncoming storm and the pioneer organizations, the Zionist organizations, the Halutz organizations began to prepare the youth for Aliyah to Israel and now many are in Israel.

A gathering of young people before the departure of Yitzhak Kavalski to Eretz Israel

Kneeling: **Rivka Korapatkin, Beila Guterman**
Sitting: **Golda, Yitzhak, Eida Kavalski**
Standing: **Gita Kurapatkin, Moishe Friedman, Hinda Guterman**

Translator's note:

Izaak Kovalsky

[Col. 1201]

The Colorful Organizer Att. Eliyahu Rudnitzki

Taken from the Autobiographical Lexicon in the Pinchas of Vilna "Yekapo", 1931

Related by Moshe Shalit

Translated by Anita Frishman Gabbay

Edited by Rhoda Miller

Eliyahu Rudnitzki was born in Kaltinian, Vilna province in 1892. He was the son of a wealthy family of wood merchants.

Like all the children in those days he started his studies in a traditional cheder, later to a Kibbutz of Porushim and later to the Vilna Russian Gymnasia of P. A. Kagan, which he completed in 1913.

After completing the Gymnasia he left for Germany to study medicine in the Heidelberg University.

A year later the First World War broke out and he had to return to Kaltinian.

In the first years of the war he was restless at home, so in 1915 he left for New Sventzian, where he began work in a branch of Yekapo (Jewish Community Relief of War Victims) and Aze. (another help organization) The main work in those days was the evacuation of the homeless by rail: those from Panevezys, Onikst, Utian and New-Sventzian to the Penza-Tamboz and Tzernigover provinces.

[Col. 1202]

Eliyahu Rudnitzki

In 1916 he went to Gluboke because of the war situation, where he remained in contact with the semski– soyuz (union) and the soyuz–gorodov (union).

Eliyahu decided to continue his studies and left for Petersburg, where he came to the Psycho Neurological Institute.

He couldn't concentrate on his studies as he became committed to Zionist activities during his student years. In May 1917 he became general–secretary of Z. K. in Petersburg and in the same year left for Moscow where he became the secretary of the Zionist party. He also was active in Zeirei Zion, which was only a small branch of the larger Zionist organization.

[Col. 1203]

At the same time he resumed his studies in the Moscow University. However now he began his studies in the Judicial faculty.

After the Brisk peace treaty, May 1918, he returned home to Kaltinian. However, he went to Vilna to take over as publisher of the newspaper "Last News."

In Vilna he became one of the most devoted contributors to the city's cultural establishment. He was chosen by the Vilna Jewish community as their representative where he spent and devoted many of his years.

In 1919 he was the delegate chosen to represent Yekapo at a conference in which he held an executive position.

In the same year he was chosen as a city councilman for the Vilna city council, which he held with honor until 1928.

He also worked with much devotion in the Folks–Bank. In 1928 he became its director.

[Col. 1204]

In addition, he was also associated with the bank–branch in Warsaw.

In 1928 he was the director of the students' council in Vilna. In 1930 he ended his judicial studies in the Vilna University and became a practicing attorney in the city.

He remained president for more than seven years of the Zeirei Zion party in Vilna. In May 1930 he was chosen as the president of the Vilner "Shul–Kult."

Advocat Eliyahu Rudnitzki was one of the most popular personalities of the Vilna province. When the Second World War broke out he escaped deep into Russia and in the time of Sigorski's regime he became involved in affairs in Teheran, the main city of Iran, as a representative of the refugees.

After the war he fulfilled his lifetime dream and made Aliyah to Eretz Israel.

Here he worked in the Histadrut and was a member of "former citizens of Vilna in Israel."

He also published an important book about Russia. He died in 1951.

May his memory be blessed!

[Col. 1203]

The Figure of a Talented Educator

Heshel Gurewitiz

Translated by Anita Frishman Gabbay

It is difficult to get used to the idea, the devoted and outstanding teacher, Neche, is no longer with us. It is simply difficult and unbelievable to write about the gruesome and unimaginable death that tore these brilliant and intelligent souls from our midst, who were carried on the *black wings of death*, in indescribable torture and inhumanity; these were our bright personalities, simple folk– teachers and folk– intelligentsia, like our teacher who spent many years devoted to passing on her intelligence to the children in the Yiddish Shul, to raise healthy Jewish minds for a future generation of young people. To plant the seeds of a Jewish people and Jewish culture, she received her qualifications as a teacher in the Sofia Gurewitch Gymnasia in Vilna, then completed her pedagogic course in Hebrew under the direction of Dr. Tcharne, and afterwards with great idealism, courage and holiness, she carried the work– load of the school on her shoulders.

[Col. 1204]

She endured all the sufferings of hell during Hitler's occupation. In 1944, I believe she was in Vaivara as a slave labourer–in a German work camp–where they robbed her of her two children and her old mother, Raiza Tabacavitch: they all perished in the death camp of Aushwitz.

Her first husband was Berel Axelrod, a teacher and a devoted community leader. The Germans murdered him at the Ninth Fort in Kovno.

[Col. 1205]

After this gruesome tragedy she survived alone together with her sick sister. They were both deported to the concentration camp Stutthof.

Shortly before liberation her sister died and she remained alone. Herself sick, she began to wander through Poland looking like skeleton, saved from this great catastrophe.

The injustice in the ghetto, the life in the camps, the gruesome deaths of her beloved nearest and dearest impacted her well– being. She remained steadfast and resolved to save herself. She immediately began her work with the Lodz Jewish committee where she implemented schools and kindergartens for the survived Jewish orphans.

One couldn't live in these areas of destruction any longer and the survivors decided to leave Poland and continue to wander in order to arrive in their Jewish homeland.

Neche joined the flight, first she arrived in Germany and from there to Austria. She couldn't live without her work and started a weekly paper, called Aufgang (Rise Up) which soon became the voice of the refugees who were then located in Austria.

[Col. 1206]

She didn't only edit the weekly newspaper, she wrote most of the articles and announcements herself and established her own literary style.

Besides this, she took upon herself the task to document the Polish and Lithuanian atrocities.

Besides her historical and literature achievements, she was active in the refugee–school named after Theodore Herzl. She helped organize children's performances and she put her efforts towards maintaining high pedagogical standards at the school. She gave her heart and soul for the improvement of the lives of those Jewish orphans.

In 1947 her second husband, Melech Bacaltchik was invited for a conference at Yad Vashem in Jerusalem.

Neche and Melech went to Jerusalem. Later they didn't find any possibilities for work so they accepted the invitation of the Johannesburg Jewish Folk–shul and both left for South Africa.

With complete devotion and fire she began her work to educate. She loved her scholastic work in which she found some peace after the nightmare of the Holocaust.

Before her time, age 49, she was taken away from her dear and beloved work. She died June 1, 1953.

We shall never forget her. May her memory remain with us forever!

[Col. 1205]

As A Russian Prisoner of War in Kaltinian

Yerachmiel Korb

Translated by Anita Frishman Gabbay

In 1916 the Germans brought me to Kaltinian to manage a turpentine factory. As a specialist I earned 30 phenig a day because I was a Russian prisoner of war. This was the payment for each prisoner of war.

[Col. 1206]

Besides food, every two weeks I received raw produce in New– Sventzian, enough to last for five days. I already had a wife and a child. On one hand I was very happy that I was living in my district together with my family. But, where can we get food? I already took precautions, thanks to my protectia that I bought knowing certain people, but I saw the hunger around me.

[Col. 1207]

In the Vilna province people went around with their bellies swollen from hunger. Sventzian also suffered from hunger. Why did I come here to see the suffering of our Jewish people? Why did they bring me from Germany? The person that brought me here from Germany was the director, the boss of the forestry trade, had warehouses and turpentine factories in the whole region.

He was a man with a golden character and loved the Jews. He hired the wealthy wood merchant, Gershon Rudnitzki, to be in charge of transporting wood products on the river Zemiane.

I then made the acquaintance of Gershon Rudnitzki and with the other Jews of Kaltinian. The wood merchant and all the Jews from this shtetl sustained all the newly arrived hungry Jews of the region. In addition packages of food were sent to Sventzian. He employed not only Jews from Kaltinian, but other Jews from New– Sventzian.

Thanks to Rudnitzki I was made in charge of the turpentine factory. I made a very good wage. The boss knew about this. One time he said to me: “I am very pleased that you are earning a living, but don't get richer than me.”

The second richest wood merchant of Kaltinian was the in– law of Rudnitzki–Hirshe Kremer. He was a religious Jew and in his spare time read a page of Gemara. He didn't have business in forestry only in our region, but also throughout Russia. In the time of the First World War he didn't have any business. But his son Eliahu Kremer provided the Germans with all sorts of mushrooms and berries and with this gave many Jews the means to earn a living. We can say, thanks to these two Jews, many survived and didn't die from hunger. In my life I didn't see such a shtetl where Jews were so intelligent and charitable as in Kaltinian.

[Col. 1208]

I still have to mention a relative from the merchant Rudnitzki family by the name Mordechai Mavitch, or we used to call him Motel the Rav. He could have been a Rabbi, he was a bookkeeper for Rudnitzki and later for Kremer. He was from a poor family from Zarazai.

His father was a single maker, but their son studied Torah and culture. He was a good person with an honest face, a nice black beard and dark intelligent eyes.

There were more wood merchants, like Popiski and others. The others of the shtetl were employed as transporters by these merchants. The shtetl barely had any Jewish craftsmen besides one tailor and a glass maker. In later years the shtetl of Kaltinian had beautiful workshops, fields and bean stalks.

It is difficult to remember every Jew in Kaltinian, therefore I can only mention several of the families.

C. Katz held the post office position in the shtetl during the time before the First World War. He was an intelligent man and had several daughters and a son Eliahu who was a chisel- worker for the German supervisor. He was quite young and got along with everyone, not only Jews but also the Christians from the region. He was loved by the local people. In the years between the two world wars be became involved in wood industry and lived in New Sventzian. It didn't seem important that his whole life he had a friendly relationship between himself and his Christian neighbours, when his wife and child tried to save themselves and hide in the corn fields, the Lithuanian neighbours ran after them and murdered them.

He was also athletic and the director of the firemen in New- Sventzian.

The second family was Abraham Itzhak Guterman, he was a wood transporter and an intelligent man. He had a good sense of humor and often studied a page of Gemara in his spare time.

Today the shtetl is empty of Jews.

I bow my head for these Holy souls, for the pure, intelligent people of Kaltinian.

[Col. 1209]

Rabbi the Gaon Yosef Kahaneman

Heshl Gurwich

Translated by Anita Frishman Gabbay

Edited by Janie Respitz

Involved with his entire soul in Gemara–nigun, in rabbinical teachings and in everyday affairs with the communities of Vidz, Kaltinian and Ponevezh until Bnei Brak.

It is impossible in such a short article to describe the colorful life of the great scholar Gaon Rabbi Yosef Kahaneman who in every decision made for the well– being of his people and community conducted himself with great moral clarity. Here, in short, I will speak proudly about his greatest achievements by bringing help, moral and material, and about his deeds that he performed while serving as Rabbi.

Rabbi Yosef Kahaneman was born in Kuli (Kuliai), Lithuania, studied in the Telz Yeshiva and in 1911 he married the daughter (Feige Rubin) of the renowned Rabbi of Vidz, Rabbi Leibele. When Rabbi Leibele took over as leader of the Rabbinate in Vilkomir, his son in law, Rabbi Yosef Kahaneman became the Rabbi in Vidz. At that time the students in the Vidz Yeshiva came also from all the nearby towns. Many of those students who graduated from this Yeshiva became great Talmudic scholars.

In 1915, when the Germans arrived in our region, many families from Vidz left their homes just like others of the region. The Vidz Rabbi and many families left for Ignalina and lived there in great hardship. He didn't have his own house and lived with his family in a corner of the Synagogue (House of Prayer).

At that time the scholars in Kaltinian who had studied in the Yeshiva in Vidz, decided to bring the Rabbi and his family to Kaltinian. Rabbi Shloime Yosef Katz took him into his own large home and Rabbi Kahaneman took part in all the shtetl's affairs, even though he was not the official Rabbi.

The German military regime opened a Centrale warehouse (mill) to exploit the forestry industry of the surrounding forests. A German foreman was in charge of operations who developed a great friendship with Rabbi Yosef Kahaneman and thanks to his intervention the well– known wood merchant Reb Gershon Rudnitzki received the entire administration of cutting and exporting wood to Germany.

[Col. 1210]

Rabbi H'Gaon Yosef Kahaneman

This work had a positive effect on the lives of the people of Kaltinian and they would be spared from hunger that lingered everywhere in the region. The workers and managers who were employed in this wood industry were given extra food rations.

The rumors from this "abundance" spread to the other towns where a shortage of food was found, so the Jews from the other towns came to Kaltinian. The newly arrived Jews were well received by the Kaltinianers.

[Col. 1211]

Not only the Jews from the surrounding towns, but from all over Lithuania, which suffered from hunger, came to come to Kaltinian in search of food. In the military barracks of Podbrodz and Poligon, the regime confined these masses that were driven from the war zone. There were many Jews amongst the refugees. The Jews of New–Sventzian were the first to organize a help committee for the Jews in Poligon. The first that came to their aid were the Jews of Kaltinian. At that time Rabbi Yosef Kahaneman showed great ability and talent to organize a humane help committee for the Jews of Poligon. He went to the head German of the wood Centrale to allow the Jews to take the small train from Kaltinian to Ponevezh, which was an area that produced more and it would be easier to obtain food. In Ponevezh, because the Russians left in haste, many Jewish homes were empty. Thanks to Rabbi Kahaneman, those homeless and hungry Jews found a new life.

This news reached the many hundreds of hungry Jews all over, and Kaltinian became the help and welcome center, where every passerby received shelter and a good meal. Every home in Kaltinian received these refugee families.

In 1919 Rabbi Kahaneman left Kaltinian and became the Rabbi in Ponevezh, where he developed a new branch of his work. He built other religious institutions.

There were 25 synagogues in this shtetl, and besides the reading of the day, they also read three portions of the Talmud.

A fruitful Jewish life pulsated here. He was also a deputy in the Lithuanian Sejm (parliament), also a member of the presidium of the council of Rabbis of all Lithuania and active in the Agudas Yisroel party

The Jews of the Lithuanian shtelach were murdered, tortured and shot. It was one of the largest miracles that the Rabbi was protected from the hands of the murders and was brought to the shores of Eretz Israel.

[Col. 1212]

In 1944 for the first time the Rabbi looked at the naked mountain in Bnei Brak and homesick he said: "it would be beautiful to build a Yeshiva here." A Jew was standing nearby, a simple Jew, with firey seriousness, as in a prayer answered: "Rabbi, I will give away all my plots on this mountain in order to build your Yeshiva here."

The Rabbi didn't expect it for nothing, and the Jew accepted a low price, on condition that they build this Yeshiva within the year.

A lot of hard work and energy went into this Torah work, which today has about 1000 students, besides the 400 young women in a separate Gymnasia.

The large Yeshiva was not the end of fulfilling his life's work: Rabbi Kahaneman founded a home for rescued and orphaned children of the Holocaust, children from abused families,and with his fruitful instruction renewed, "Yarchei Kallah"[Yarchei means month, Kallah means assembly], a Talmudic age– old tradition of studying Torah for two months (Elul and Adar when agricultural activity was at a low) when large masses of worshippers, as in ancient times of the Amorites, in the large Yeshivas of Sura and Pumdita. The students returned to their communities to refresh and bolster their Torah knowledge, thus strengthening their ties to Yiddishkeit. Today in Bnei Brak religious pupils from all streams and from all corners of the world come here to study.

Rabbi Kahaneman gave a lot of energy and initiative for the memorial monument and its site of construction to commemorate the destruction of the people of Lithuania: etched are the towns of Kaltinian, Ponevezh and many others of Lithuania. Over 700 headstones will stand on the site according to his plans. On each stone the name of the Kehilah (community) will be engraved, the date of her founding and the date of her destruction. The survivors will have a place to come to gather to remember those that perished and say Kaddish for them. In the Arun Kodesh, that will be built mountain, the saved Torah scrolls and Religious books that were rescued from Lithuanian schools and Synagogues stairs will lead to a shrine (cave)– the memorial of the words of all the lost Jewish communities in Lithuania. Special record books (Pinchas) from all the Lithuanian towns which were lost will be found here. A special archive committee was set up to restore this.

[Col. 1213]

It will also contain all testimonies of the holocaust written in many languages about the destruction of Lithuanian Jewry. In this depository will be gathered the books and manuscripts of scholars of more than 650 years of life in Lithuania.

When I write these few words, the Rabbi is close to eighty, and he is still studying without glasses. His gaze and voice are still youthful. The Rabbis's illustrious appeal stretches far and wide. In the Ponevezh Yeshiva in Bnei Brak he created a great learning center. Students from all countries came to study here. In the days of “Yachei Kallah” many Rabbis and simple Jews come together, merchants and professionals, regular worker and military workers, teachers and officials, old people, young men from other Yeshivas and students from high schools. They set aside their work and worries of the entire year and take their seats, each with their group, in the halls or under the free skies, and at a specific hour one of the heads of the Yeshiva welcomes the newcomers and looks for new meanings of simple and complicated words of the Tractaite that will be learned and discussed in the new year, just like in old times, 2000 years ago, in the same Bnei Brak where there once stood the historic Torah–fortress, which was defended by Rabbi Akiva.

[Col. 1214]

In those times Bnei Brak was still a small village and Jews from faraway, from the Jezriel Valley, the Galilee and Judean Hills, from across Jordan (south). Peasant–stock and scholars who from early morning till late at night were immersed in Torah study. Rabbi Kahaneman created a center here in Bnei Brak for eternal continuity, with an absolute connection with its past Jewish history and traditions. This he did with his great warmth which he brought with him from his old home of Kaltinian.

[Col. 1213]

A Heroic Family

Beile Garshin

Translated by Anita Frishman Gabbay

The family Guterman lived in Kaltinian, the family was Reb Abraham Yitzhak, whose trade was a fisherman.

He was of medium height, broad shouldered with strong and healthy hands, which day and night worked with the fisherman's boats and dragged nets full of fish.

Life in the open nature, on the rivers, that meandered through fields and forests, developed his personality, strong as steel. He wasn't afraid of storms or strong winds or bad weather.

[Col. 1214]

He was a picture of health due the clean air and pure life he led. In his free time he sat and read a page of Gemara, or a book that he loaned from the library. He was happiest when he could read his Gemara or a chapter from the Mishna, and even when he sat in the fisherman's boat he reviewed what he had learned and thought over the tracts and questions. He belonged to that group of Jews, their hearts fluttered with each devotion and there was a thirst for more learning. He was drawn to faraway places, unknown lands, which he couldn't reach and had to satisfy himself with just reading about them.

[Col. 1215]

He loved to read late into the night. He was stingy to allow himself the use of the kerosene–lamp, so as not to burn for very long he prepared long, thin kinelech (match–like candles), from dried out wood and when they burnt out, he lit another.

Another of his characteristics was to take the side of the weak and to find ways to alleviate the suffering of the poor, showing how the Torah can enhance your life and ease the pain of your suffering.

He noticed how the Christians, on happy market days, would look for ways to agitate or make trouble for the Jews, so Rabbi Abraham Yitzhak would suddenly appear with his strong hands: the crowds dispersed and this avoided any grievances or attacks.

When the Polish regime was in Kaltinian after the First World War and they celebrated their freedom by robbing and beating Jews, Rabbi Abraham Yitzhak and his younger son Berl went out and kicked them out of the shtetl.

The elder Rabbi Abraham Yitzhak escaped from Kaltinian during the shooting by the Lithuanian bandits and swam across the Zemiane river, arrived in New–Sventzian and was later deported with all the Jews to Poligon. He was murdered in the massacre of Poligon and buried in the mass grave together with the thousands of Holy people from the region.

Rabbi Abraham Yitzhak's son Berl, was exactly like his father, he couldn't remain silent when he witnessed injustice. Wherever there was a conflict, when a poor man was in trouble, he made sure the truth be upheld.

[Col. 1216]

Berl Guterman, his children Afroim and Tzirka, wife Chaia with her sisters: Hena and Sura Katz

The horrible intervention for Jewish respect and standing up for the poor and abused, was handed down from Rabbi Abraham Yitzhak not only to his sons but also to his grandchildren. Zalman's son, Dovid (Dudke) through his ideals became a Communist and fought against the Polish regime. He often found himself in Polish prisons.

When the Second World War broke out, he ran to Soviet–Russia. He fought in the Soviet army and then on his own free will decided to help the partisans of the regions where they fighting the enemy.

He was parachuted into a forest and attached himself to a partisan brigade where he fought a blood battle against the Hitlerite army. He was captured, tortured and shot to death.

Berel's son Efroim, (Efroimke), fought a Holy battle in the ranks of the Soviet Army.

[Col. 1217]

The Destruction of Kaltinian – In Those Dark Days

(Kaltinėnai, Lithuania)

5°34'/22°27'

By Rachel Milontchik

Translation by Anita Frishman Gabbay

June 22, 1941 the Germans attacked the Lithuanian–Soviet territories. The panic in our shtetl was great, many refugees from Lithuania began to arrive in order to save themselves in Russia, but to arrange this was already too late. The Germans encircled the shtetl on all sides, and life grew more difficult from day to day. The Lithuanians took over and began to target the Jewish people: they attacked them in the streets, they robbed their shops, and dragged Jews to various work details.

Several days later we learned that the Jews of Lingmian suffered a terrible fate and the entire shtetl was murdered in a gruesome manner. Things got worse for us. On July 8, without reason, they arrested Mashe Rochin(Yitzhak Yosef's daughter), Yoel's wife, z"l with her niece, Chana Beila Kharmatz (Charmatz). They brought them to the edge of town and shot them. These were the first casualties in our shtetl. Friday July 11, 1 o'clock at night, they surrounded the shtetl, gathered several families, took them to the edge of town near the lake and shot them.

Those murdered were: my father Avraham–Leiba Milontchik, Rochel and Yitzhak Milontchik's children, Shasel Volovitch and her children, Chasia, Shloime and Esther. Esther married A Sventzianer lad, she was pregnant and after the slaughter, they found her alive with her dead child.

That same night, those that were murdered were Ruben Trak with his wife, he attempted to resist and struck a policeman with a knife. Aidel Kovalski with her children, Laia and Benyamin Rufeitz, Chana Eidel Guterman with her children.

[Col. 1218]

Abraham Yitzhak Guterman, her husband remained alive. Later he was murdered in Poligon. As it was told, he was a man of 80 years old, he swam across the river and escaped to New Sventzian, but from there he was later sent to Poligon.

In the second week, those murdered were: Yacov Moishe Tabacovitch, Berel Tabacovitch, and Dovid Rufeitz.

The remaining Jews stayed in Kaltinian until the deportation to Poligon, where they were murdered with all the other Jews from the Sventzian region.

In Svir, I met up with Berel Volovitch and his wife and Berel Guterman's family. Chaia, Berel Gutermans wife, and her daughters were murdered on the way to Sventzian. Berel died in a lager (work camp) in Estonia. Chana Rufeitz died in the liquidation of the Vilna Ghetto. Berel Volovitch and his wife returned to check on their daughter they left behind with a Christian in Nemencine. The gentiles sold them out and they were shot. They were buried next to the house of the Christian.

Dovid Guterman, at the outbreak of the war, was serving in the Polish army and from there was fortunate to escape to Russia. In 1943 they sent him into the Kazian forests by parachute. There he was appointed commander of a special division. In the division "Spartak" he fell in battle when the Germans blockaded the Kazian forests.

Those that were saved were: Neche Tabacovitch, Beila Garshein, Yosef Abrahmovitch, Yoel Rachin, Shmuel Katz, Gershon Katz and wife and child, and Chana Portnoy.

This is all that remained from the Jewish community of Kaltinian.

[Col. 1219]

Those who died in Poligon: Motel Movish with his wife Rochel Katz and their children, Devoirele and Hirshele. Alter Tabacovitch and his wife Baila. Sheina Tabacovitch,

Binyamin Volovitch and his family, Ben–Zion Volovitch and his family, Shifra Rufeitz–Rudnitzki and her child. Garshein's family Motel and Mera. Chloine Gavenda and his wife Batia Raiza and daughter Eitel. Abraham Yitzhak Guterman, Eitel Gavenda, Shalom Tuvia's daughter, Rafael Katz and his wife Dina and daughter, married to Yacov Tabacovitch , and her child Yitzhak–Elia. Eliahu Kurapatkin's family, his daughter Rivka and her husband Natan Beigel and their child, Leia'le. Henia came to Kaltinian with her husband where she gave birth to a child and they all perished in Poligon.

[Col. 1220]

The Mass Graves in Ponar and Poligon

by Neche Tabakhowitz–Bakaltchuk

Translated by Anita Frishman Gabbay

Two mass executions swallowed up thousands of Jews: Ponar and Poligon. Ponar wiped out the community of “the Jerusalem of Lithuania” and Poligon, the community of the Sventzian region.

In the years prior to the war, in the “good” times Ponar was a train station with many trains passing through. Passengers were not in any danger, as many Jews, on those fields and even the fields of Poligon, used these as meeting places, where thousands of Jews passed through (vacationed).

Often the Russian and Polish soldiers gathered here, where they set up tents in the town and carried out their yearly military manoeuvres.

The Hitlerite beasts used these fields as mass graves for thousands of living Jews. In the fall of 1941, thousands from Sventzian, New–Sventzian, Podbrodz, Kaltinian, Ligmian, Ignalina, Haydutishok, Gaviken, New–Daugelishak, Old Daugelishak, Stayatishok, and Maligan were either shot or buried alive here.

The “long train to their deaths” were carried out by the Lithuanian bandits. Their hands are stained with Jewish blood, just like those of the Germans.

Until today I cannot forget the caravans with thousands of Jews, dragged around, terror stricken, crammed as “glued” together with hopelessness in their eyes.

Most of them were innocent and pure, and for all that had already happened to them; they wished for only one last thing: that death should come quickly...

Everyone wanted to become the first victim, in order not to see their nearest and dearest meet their end in front of their eyes.

[Col. 1220]

It took 10 days for those animals to complete their gruesome acts of terror. For 10 days the 8000 Jewish people lived in the most horrible conditions in the barracks of Poligon, until their turn finally came for their deaths. They willed the end should come quickly.

Over 400 Lithuanian bandits helped the Hitlerite beasts with this extermination. The day of the murder the Rabbi Kimkhi of New Sventzian wrote: "Shema Israel, Jews", it is God's will and I will be the first to go to "Kiddush Hashem"! (I will finally meet my maker).

Right after those words the beast–like slaughter began. The murderers didn't want to waste bullets so they threw the young children, still alive, into the pits. The execution was too horrendous to watch. Everyone stood in his row anxiously awaiting his turn which was not soon enough.

For two days, October 8 and 9, 1941, this devastation lasted. Long after covering the pits, movement and sounds were coming from them, the earth of this mass brother's–grave was still moving. Christian recounted the story that the earth moved for several hours after the mass execution.

There, in that mass grave, I lost my nearest and dearest, my beloved young children: Devoreh'le and Yosel'le. The well of tears in my eyes are all dried up and there are no more tears! My heart is wounded and will never heal!

Their memory should not be forgotten by Jews, and each generation should pass on to the next generation what the Nazis have done!

[Col. 1221]

A List of the Jewish Families in Kaltinian Before the Holocaust

by Ada Katz

Translated by Anita Frishman Gabbay

Rudnitski, Gershon, a well-known forest merchant his wife Sura, children: Eliahu, Zlata, Leizer, Leib, Yitzhak, Berel, Shifra, Rivka, Ezriel

Kremer, Hirsh, a well known forest merchant his wife Devorah, chidren: Yosel, Zlata, Eliahu, Roze, Rochel, Liza, Rivka, Gitel, Yitzhak

Katz, Shloime Yose, an innkeeper with a beer shop(factory) his wife, Devoreh, children: Zlate, Alter, Rochel

Faive Yitzhak Popiski, a forest merchant his wife Yocheved, Chaim, Aharon, Shloime Mordechai Hertz

Katz, Abraham Yitzhak, post office his wife Gitel, children: Feige, Beila, Ida, Mirta, Eliahu

Kurapatkin, Eliahu, a peddlar his wife Chana Aidel, children: Zale, Berel, Eliahu, Hinda, Baila

(8 in book) Rudnitzki, Chone, forest merchant and owner of a grocery store his wife Chana Rive, children: Zlate, Sure, Raizel, Shifra, Eliahu, Motel, Yitzhak Meir

Mabacovitch, Natan, a miller and merchant his wife Hinda, children: Rivka, Sheina, Itel, Chaia Laia, Baila, Alter, Yacov, Berel, Hirsh

Mabacovitch, Yacov (Hirsh), forest merchant and farm worker His wife Reizel, children: Berel, Shimon, Yosel, Neche, Teibe

Itze Yacov the Shamash his wife Mashe

Volovitch, Faive Yitzhak, a butcher and farm worker his wife Teibe, children: Ben–Zion, Berel, Moshe, Rivka, Benyamin, Baila

Portnoy, Dovid, a tailor his wife Raizel, children: Nechame Tobe, Reichel, Chane, Zalke

Rufeitz, Yehoushe, a wagon driver of wood his wife Laia, children: Ruchel, Zalmen, Binyamin, Dovid, Chana

Movish, Motel, a bookkeeper in the wood trade his wife, Rochel, children: Eliahu, Leib, Shloime Yosef, Shimon, Hirsh, Devorah

Gavenda, Sholem Tuvia, a fisherman

Zak, Itze Ber, a blacksmith his wife Sura, children: Yacov, Henoch

Milontchik, Shmuel, a tar shop Gitel, Yitzhak

Milontchik, Leib, worked in forestry his wife, Hiena, children: Iser, Rochel, Braine

Gavenda, Chloine, a chimney-sweep, his wife Beitye–Raize, children: Feige, Chaia–Sura, Itel

Volovitch, Bentze, butcher and wood trade his wife Sose, children: Shloime

Garhin(Garshein), Motel, manufacturing and watcher–maker his wife Riva Mera, chidren: Dovid, Rochel, Beila

Katz, Rafael, the bath attendant his wife Dina, children: Shmuel, Rochel, Gershon

Henia Munia, a daughter Riva

Ruditzki, Yechiel, a shopkeeper his wife Rochel, children: Laia, Ahroine

[Col. 1223]

Lingmian – The Life and Beauty in Our Shtetl

(Linkmenys, Lithuania)

55°18'/25°57'

By Zvi Zar [son of Ethel]

Translation by Anita Frishman Gabbay

With awe and dread, with respect and admiration, with sorrow and heartache, I take my pen in hand in order to write about our heartfelt shtetl Lingmian. This should serve as a monument to perpetuate our Yiddish "kibbutz", a murdered Jewish community, a Jewish shtetl, that evaporated in fire and smoke, together with those wonderful people that were murdered in the most barbarous ways.

Not one trace, not one memory of this former little shtetl remains. No documents can be found anywhere about its origins and its development. Even the former residents did not leave any written memoirs to tell about its glory, nor any writer gave any accounts of its way of life. What we know about her, we were told in our youth by the older generation. Just from those few words we can catch a glimpse of her beauty and daily routine, so that our children and grandchildren and all future generations can have a small idea, what a dear "family" we lost with the destruction of the shtetl, we, her children, and together with us the children of Israel and all the people in the world.

The writer of these few lines, who remained in the "land" (Israel) and is one of the few that remained from Lingmian, believes it is his Holy duty to tell us how the community of Jews existed and lived with pride and devotion before its destruction.

It is one's duty and a “mitzvah” (great deed) to forever remember them, our nearest and dearest, in a Yiskor book, about their lives and during the Holocaust. May their memory be a blessing, “Yisgadal Ve'yiskadash”... (opening words of the Kaddish prayer...“Magnified and sanctified.”)

[Col. 1225]

Lingmian, a small shtetl in the Vilna province, great in respect and blessings, simply didn't have anything with what and with whom to praise/brag or have any pretensions of grandeur. All the Jews were simple and honest, hard– working, who had to work hard and with great difficulties to earn their piece of “bread”.

Partizanka (female partisan)
Mira Minaizki–Grinshpan

There were no factories or large shops in the shtetl. There was no electricity, no water mill and no train station. However, the shtetl was close and dear to us. We loved our small town, our homes, our beloved ones and our friendly Jewish neighbours, the bare forest, the endless fields and deep lakes, that surrounded the shtetl.

The first Jewish families settled here over 100 years ago. These families first lived in the nearby villages and on the “noble” estates. My grandfather Avraham and my grandmother Elka originated from a village by the name: Pokevne. They were considered amongst the earliest settlers of Lingmian.

I remember this shtetl from my early childhood years. I remember when I sat by the dim candle in the Synagogue, rocking back and forth as I read from the Gemara: “ Our Rabbis, said that Abaye* claimed”...father of the Jewish Talmud (Little Father, after his grandfather)

From those years, every road and every alley is woven with memories and "fantasies of our youth".

The desire to build and educate myself drove me in my later years to a larger world, however, wherever I went, I never forgot my small birth–shtetl.

Until today I can still see before my eyes the wooden houses with the straw roofs, which defined it more as a village than a shtetl. We didn't even have our own market day like in the other shtetelach of the region. Only once a year we celebrated a fair and this was on the holiday of the "Troitze". (Christian holiday)

As this shtetl was blessed with many fields, and lakes, most of the population was employed either in the wood or fish business.

[Col. 1226]

The Jews of Lingmian leased the abundant lakes from the nearby estate owners and after a generation they became professional fish–mongers. The lakes contributed to the economic situation of the shtetl.

The second means of economic activity were from the Baranover forests. In Lingmian lived the wealthiest wood merchant of the Vilna province, Meir Gavenda, who had business dealings in Hamburg and sent his relatives to Danzig as his representatives.

The wood commerce gave many people a livelihood, they were called: "Voszhakes". (Russian word=trucked wood back and forth)

For many months they were gone from their homes and lived in a collective, deep in the forests. However, they always stayed close to their Judaism, prayed and studied, ate "kosher" and obeyed the Sabbath and holidays.

As a child I heard a story, bandits attacked the Jews in the forest and wanted to steal their horses. This happened on a Shabbos day and the Jews were at their Tehillah prayers, the bandits observed how the Jews were wrapped in their Tefillim and prayed. The eldest of them became so enthralled, he gave an order not to harm the Jews; servants of the Holy God. The bandits left and later the Christians told a story of a miracle that happened to the "Voszhakes" in the forest.

Besides fishermen, Voszhakes and wood merchants, Lingmian had Jewish blacksmiths, shoemakers, butchers, and of course, shopkeepers, small merchants and pedlars.

All the wealthier Jews of Lingmian took care of the needs of those less fortunate around them.

The well– known sage and young Gaon, Efraim Zar, came from Lingmian. Our shtetl was also known for the religious Rabbi Akiva, who was a great teacher of the "Sha's" (Shisha sedarim, the 6 volumes of the Mishna and "verdicts/decisions and determinations that important Rabbis published answering questions posted to them) ".

This is how the Jews led a quiet and honest life for many years, until the wild German barbarians invaded our nest and all our beautiful "birds" were murdered in a gruesome manner.

[Col. 1227]

Jewish victims that were murdered by the Lithuanians, in Lingmian

The Jews of the Lingmian community were erased by those murders under God's skies.

The Holy and the Pure will forever remain etched in our hearts and in every generation we will not forget them.

The pedlar from Lingmian

It was a hot summer day, not even a leaf stirred, a branch did not move. The old windmill, which was next to the stream by the Lidekener nobleman's estate, stood before us, we could still see the broken boards from the former walls and the remains of the shingle roof.

Through the stretch of huts which divided the fields from the gardens of the shtetl, we could see a bent over, white bearded Jew "dragging" his body with a patched- up sack on his shoulders.

This was Mordechai Nachman, the pedlar from Lingmian. He was wearing large, stuffed boots, a torn coat and on his head–a hat, which barely had any color left.

The sun stung his eyes and large droplets of sweat were pouring down his weary, creased face.

With his parched lips he quietly said his Tehillah, a psalm...

[Col. 1228]

It got very hot and Reb Mordechai Nachman searched for a shady spot under a tree, and stopped to pray “Shachrit” . (the morning prayer)

Slowly he placed his sack, which was packed with ladies' trimmings, pins and needles, glass beads, fine green smelling soaps, ribbons, strings, buttons, rings and other colorful objects.

He went over to the nearby water where he washed his hands and wiped them on a handkerchief. Then he took out a yellow, torn Tallith and wrapped himself in it. From a suede sack he pulled out his Tefillim, turned to the east and started his “davening” (praying) with great zeal.

When the hooligans approached the stream and saw the white bearded person, they became frightened and started to cross themselves.

One of them recognized him and started to scream:

–Oh, Jesus, this is only a sinning Jew from the shtetl.

One little gentile bent over immediately grabbed a few stones and threw it at him. A second one taunted the dogs: a third one hurled dirty curses at him.

Reb Mordechai Nachman didn't stop his “Shachrit”, with tears in his eyes he yelled: Hear our voice... and he continued with his psalms, the hooligans eventually got fed up with him and they left to enjoy their pranks elsewhere.

When he finished praying, he put back his Tallith and Tefillim in his patched– up sack, he washed his hands in the nearby water. He took out a small piece of black corn bread with a little salt, he sat on a stone and ate his breakfast.

He gathered some dry branches, made a fire and baked some potatoes which he had with him. He filled himself up with water, said the after– meal prayer, and again he put his sack on his shoulders to continue his journey.

He crossed over lakes and fields, passing peasants, who didn't receive him in a friendly manner and several hours later arrived at the edge of the village, Zezdrele.

He went from hut to hut, knocked on doors and propositioned the peasants to buy his merchandise.

[Col. 1229]

In a house with colored curtains, he encountered a young gentile woman, with a red kerchief on her head and knew instantly she was preparing to get married.

Her laid out the merchandise on the table and knew this time he would be lucky. She chose an apron, a ring, a piece of soap, a necklace and other small items. But she didn't have any money to pay for these items.

She went to the shed, and brought back several pelts and proposed to make a trade.

However, this was not enough.

Meanwhile the mother of the bride entered the house. She proposed to give this Jew a bundle of onions, a sack of flour, some barley and a little flax.

The pedlar left very satisfied.

God helped him. He had enough to return home. It was Friday, Mordechai Nachman decided not to make any more stops in other villages and to return home. This time he can prepare a fine Shabbos, thanks to mercy of the Almighty.

He didn't pay attention to the fact that he had to carry such a heavy sack on his shoulders, he increased his pace. With "such" a sack he wanted his wife and children to enjoy the fruits of his labour.

The sack pinched his shoulders but he didn't pay attention. He must return before the blessing of the Shabbos candles, it would be even better if he arrived in time to take his bath in the market square.

The entire week he slept in the sheds, slept in his clothes and didn't eat any cooked meals. He was longing for a warm bed and a cooked soup.

Oh, how lucky he would be if he found short–cut and he arrived home earlier than expected.

He "shleps" his bundle and asks God that, the very least, it should not rain. And luck is with him from all directions.

It is a beautiful day, not a cloud in the sky. He arrives in the shtetl before the sunset and decides not to eat or rest, but to hurry to the bath.

[Col. 1230]

When he got closer to his house he noticed his loveliness, Esterel, waiting by the door. She looked thin and overworked.

Seeing him she immediately ran over to relieve him of his heavy sack, Itzikel also ran out of the house, a thin little boy, barefoot and pale and went straight for the sack. He wanted to know what father had brought home.

Mother understands his look and says to him that we are lucky to have father return to us in good health. They all enter the house and start kissing each other. Separately he embraces his small daughter Surke'le.

Esther, his wife, wants to prepare the table immediately and give him his meal. He excuses himself and says he want to go to the bathhouse.

He took out a patched, but clean shirt from the drawer, in white linen, a towel and soap and left in a hurry for his bath.

It was very slippery in the bath, tight and dark.

Over the black coals trickled cold water, naked Jews poured pails of cold water over the hot coals to make more steam.

Mordechai Nachman threw off his clothes and eagerly immersed himself in the steam bath.

An entire week he roamed around in mud, and now he needs to sweat! So that his body is cleansed from the dirt! With a "broom" in his hand he is enjoying his time - Oiy, oiy,oiy, such a bath...

When Mordechai Nachman left the bath, one could hardly recognize the sloppy pedlar. He was dressed in his Shabbos coat, clean and combed, a Jew like all the other Jews. It was getting late, he took his Itzikel and his Siddur (prayer book) and left for the Synagogue.

There all his neighbours and friends greeted him with a warm "Shalom Aleichum" and welcomed him as his week was off to a good start " (this was a good fortune for him) .

—Baruch Hashem (Blessed be God) , the pedlar greeted them.

After the prayers he approached the Rabbi and greeted him with a "Gut Shabbos" and then left quietly for home.

[Col. 1231]

The floor of his house was covered with yellow, clean sand. Two small candles were burning in the metal candleholders, Izikel and Surk'ele were impatient with hunger, waiting for their Shabbos meal.

Reb Mordechai Nachman said the "Kiddush" and was fortunate to eat his first cooked soup of the week. He prayed again. The candles burnt out and the house became dark.

The family of this poor pedlar, content and always happy, went to sleep.

He got up early the next morning, content, and went off to the synagogue to pray with delight and to thank God, who has not forsaken him and provides for him.

The Holy Shabbos soon ended, and the difficult, weekly, routine began once again on Sunday.

Reb Mordechai Nachman began his weekly wandering through the villages with the sack on his shoulders.

Only in the summer days was this "ideal" way of life suitable for a pedlar. It became more difficult when winter approached, with its cold, strong frosts and deep snow.

Reb Mordechai Nachman knew he had a false sense of security.

When all the roads were covered in snow and a storm was brewing, the frost stung bitterly, one had to have a strong faith to continue in such conditions.

He had this strong will and fortitude of character. On such a winter morning, he said out loud: "Father–father, take pity on me" and left in the freezing cold. Nothing seemed to bother him.

One day he left, with his torn boots filled with straw and rags, bound with pieces of sack, covered his head until his eyes, dressed in an old coat, took a stick in his hand and his sack on his shoulders and left on his journey.

[Col. 1232]

Esther and the children, with tears in their eyes, begged him to take pity on himself and on them and not to go. The roads were invisible. How can he go out in this weather, no living being can survive outdoors.

He didn't give in. – God is our father, and thus calmed them. One cannot sit at home and die of hunger. "God and Peace". We must go and earn our piece of bread.

– Stay in good health, my children, good health to you Esterel, and he left the house.

He quickly made his way through the shtetl, fearful that he could encounter someone. He passed the last home on Goyisher Street and came to the wide– open fields.

First, the road wasn't too bad, then a large whistle and the wild wind stabbed at him. Soon the snow started to fall and the roads and alleys were buried.

He didn't see anything besides snow and a blanket of white. The wind whistled, jabbed and entered his body from all sides.

He couldn't see the road and had to continue with his instincts that this direction would lead him to the small town. The wind howled and the hurled large piles of snow. The pedlar felt he was sinking, and it became more difficult to lift his boots out of the heavy snow drifts.

He felt his strength leaving his body, but he didn't give in. He is a Jew, with strong beliefs, and how can he be weak in front of God?

He preached to his wife and children that God is the father, and he is in his hands. This is the way it will be, there can be no other way.

He was a follower of the commandments, he was on his way to earn a piece of bread, in order to save his family from hunger.

Reb Mordechai Nachman relied on God's will and continued on his way, as a true believer that God will "take care of him".

Not a living soul was seen.

[Col. 1233]

Not a soul, not a wagon. No one to ask if he is going in the right direction.

Outside a "frost is burning", but sweat is pouring from him. Before he knew the direction, now he was getting lost but he can't turn back, he will not be able to find his way home..

– Oy, God in heaven, Father–father, help a poor Jew, take pity on him.

Thus goes the pedlar, still saying his Tehillah (prayer) in his quiet manner.

Suddenly a white horse appeared next to him, with a rider and a rifle on his shoulders. He was dressed in a thick fur coat and a sheepskin hat nearly to his eyes.

The pedlar at first thought this was a dream, but suddenly he recognized him.

This is the "leshnik", from the nearby forests. He knows him very well. In the summertime he was even at his home, where he sold his daughters strings of colored beads and rings.

The "leshnik" looked him over, shook the snow off his sheepskin hat and suddenly yelled out with pity: –oh, Jesus– Maria, where are you going in this cursed weather? The wolves are going to eat you!

The "leshnik" thought awhile and then said–today you should not have left your house. This is a certain death for you. You will be snowed under or be eaten by wolves–good, so what do you propose?– Reb Mordechai asked him with tears in his eyes. What can I do now?

– You must return to Lingmian and I will show you the way. You will still manage to return to your shtetl before sundown.

Then the "leshnik" took from his bundle a long piece of bread, a piece of cheese and gave it to the pedlar.

[Col. 1234]

– You will bring this home to your children. We will make a trade with your goods. Now every minute counts. You must go home at once.

He turned around with his horse and showed the pedlar every step. They arrived at some trees, and pointed out the Lidekener hamlet, and when he arrived there he could easily find his way to his home.

Mordechai tied his head scarf tighter around his head and thanked the "leshnik" for his help and left for home.

The wind was now on his back and this made his return easier. He reached the trees and from there he already knew the way to Lingmian, a few hours later he was home.

Esther and the children were very worried and when they saw him back home, they all jumped for joy.

Mordechai Nachman unbundled himself from all those rags and brought out the bread and cheese.

They all attacked the "bargain" and asked where this came from?

After eating and warming himself, he began to tell of his great miracle with great enthusiasm, what the "one above" did for him.

The "leshnik" that saved him, was a sign from above, which came exactly at the right moment. He was spared from a certain death and he must go pray "Gumel".

Several days later the frost eased, and the pedlar once again left to the nearby towns to sell his wares.

In this manner the years went by, summer or winter, the pedlar could be seen with his sack on his shoulders through fields and forests, roads and alleyways.

This was a difficult existence, but was able to provide for his family and didn't need the assistance of others...

When the Hitlerite–beasts arrived and destroyed Lingmian and everything in its path with fire and blood, Mordechai Nachman together with his family and all the Jews, met their fate.

[Col. 1235]

"Troitze"–The Green Holiday

Lingmian did not have a market day the entire year. Only once a year a fair took place. This was the day the Christians celebrated their holiday, which they called "Troitze".

This holiday always was after Shavouth, and that is why it was called the "green holiday."

At night, before the fair, the excitement started. A great "tumult" started on the square next to the church. The Christian shopkeepers from the parish were already running around and setting up their wares for the fair next day.

The whole shtetl participated, the words of the speaker was heard from all directions, the clapping of the participants, the clanging of dozens of bells, neighing of horses, and the air of the whole shtetl was filled with "disorder".

The shtetl became alive, young and old were on their feet. Everywhere there was a noise of wagons and people, action and disorder.

Merchants arrived from the entire region. Different wares were displayed on tables which attracted people from all over. Leib'ke, with one eye, from Smorgon, would come and sell those famous "beigeles". (sweet rolls that were famous near and far) . Many Christian wagons arrived very early. Christians crawled out of their wagons to shake the straw off their clothing. The peasant women wore large shawls, the gentile lads–in fancy, shiny boots and the gentile girls–in patterned, colored dresses, with red aprons and necklaces on their necks.

The music from the harmonicas and the singing from the market players was heard through the entire village.

The fair began with a large Huh–Hah! Crowds of Christian men and women descended on the shops and stalls. Woman and men were taking leisurely walks, hand in hand, through the streets cracking nuts and seeds.

In a corner, next to Bune Gilinski's house, seated young woman looked over their wares. Hens, geese, cheese, butter, honey, eggs and other things. In another corner, next to the high cross (church) other peasants were selling their goods, like pig–hair, strings of dried mushrooms, and homemade baked goods.

[Col. 1236]

Next to Shloime Yankel the tavern–keeper's house, peasant women sat eating black berries, "pozemkes", radishes, and other vegetables. Next to the stall of Leike the Smorgoner, bread and onions were sold.

Yoske the cutter (barber) stood with a leather case and was sharpening a razor–knife and shaved the peasants. Not far from Brunem's, next to the old shochet, stood Chaim the tar maker selling his black sticky tar to the peasants. His beard and payot (sidelocks) were stuck and his face looked like a "negro".

Next to the iron gate sat a Gypsy woman, throwing cards and telling everyone's fortune.

All the Lingmianer shops were packed with customers and at least once a year we made a good amount of money.

Flies were buzzing overhead and the children were crawling beneath their parents' feet.

Here and there peasants created a scene and cursed everyone's fathers' fathers.

The shtetl smelled of people and horses, of tar and gasoline, of garlic and onions, of flowers, fruit and vegetables.

This lasted until sundown. When it got dark the stalls were disassembled, the horses were harnessed, and everyone left in the direction of their villages and homes. Everything settled down in Lingmian, quiet, until the next year, for another fair to take place.

Simche Hirshe in the Shtetl

When Shimche Hirshe arrived, the shtetl was filled with joy and in a festive mood. It seemed, that every tree and every street was overjoyed together with all of its Jews. That day everyone forgot his problems and worries, they all took part to celebrate the holiday of the Torah.

It was even wintery outside, the "mud" was increasingly becoming deeper, winds were blowing, but in all the homes the sun was shining.

On that day, even the town's watchmaker smiled with pride. During all the holidays, year– round, he went around bitter and angry at everyone.

[Col. 1237]

The official festivities were carried out with great ceremony and singing throughout the streets. The leader of this day, naturally, was the teacher and mayor of the shtetl, Reb Akiva. His relatives were the teacher Reb Shimon Volak, an important Jew, a scholar, with a red spot on his face. On Simchat Torah the red spot grew brighter than usual.

Reb Akiva's second helper was the Transporter, Reb Chaim Yitzhak. The whole year he transported merchandise to all the shopkeepers and he never considered himself a great "Tzadik" (man of learning) . It was whispered in the shtetl, that he did not obey all the commandments. Simchat Torah all was forgiven. The whole day he sang and danced and showed his love for the Torah like all the Jews.

A very important role in all these holidays, was the Chasid Bertzik, the tall one. That day he played a wonderful role.

The preparations for Simchat Torah took place several days prior. Several volunteers went from house to house to collect various articles. Jews would give cakes, pletzeles, tzimmes, taigelach, tarts that were prepared this for this special day.

Everyone gave, old and young, rich and poor. Even Feiga, the fat one, who everyone labelled the "cheap Jewess in the shtetl," for this celebration she did not refuse. Young people went to bring these goods and they amassed so much food that after the holiday there were leftovers.

Everything was then sold and the proceeds went to the synagogue.

The Simcha started in the evening before the actual day of rejoicing. The synagogue was packed with people. The Chazzan sang the first passage and the entire audience repeated with great enthusiasm. Jews with Sefer Torahs in hand danced and sang. When they came to the part: "help for the poor", the clamouring was already at its peak in the synagogue.

[Col. 1238]

The Simcha lasted until very late at night. In the dark streets, drunk Jews could be seen tapping on the houses in order to find their way home.

This was a traditional Jewish holiday. It was said in the entire region, and with just cause, if Simchat Torah did not take place in Lingmian, one would never experience such a wonderful and cheerful folk (people) holiday in their lifetime.

It is no wonder, that all those holidays remain engraved in our memories.

Nata the Shoemaker–the Undertaker of the Shtetl

Nata was well known in the shtetl. He was a short Jew, with a pointed grey beard. Most of the time he wore a white coat with holes and torn from years of use.

He considered himself a specialist in boot–making. But when he finally, with luck, sewed together a pair of boots for a client, it never was the right size, either too large or too small.

He lived in a low house with small windows, without land. When Tuvia the fisherman, the Lingmianer giant, had too bend over when he entered his house.

Natan was often found sitting on a small bench, banging the small nails and singing the popular folk song:

"Hammer, hammer, bang, bang a nail and another nail, we have no bread at home".

It was a catchy tune, but very sad when Natan sang it, it was true, that quite often there was no bread in his home. Misfortune came from all sides. Nevertheless, Natan was happy, always in a good mood. Honest words and jokes came from his mouth.

When the community saw that Natan was unable to make ends meet, help arrived from the shtetl, and from here on things got better.

Still, he held on to his "airs" and would say to the rich folk: –Jews, don't be cheap, you will not take anything with you to the grave".

[Col. 1239]

When he was questioned in a dispute: – Natea, how do people live in the other world?

– The life they make, that is their face that will represent them–he didn't back down and answered in such a manner. But he then added:

– Sure. It's been several days, I don't have any Chometz left in my house, the container for the matzo is prepared in the corner and the flasks for mead and wine are in another corner. Like you can see, I have a great God who will help me.

The Blacksmiths of Lingmian

We were blessed with 3 blacksmiths in Lingmian. All 3 were giants in their own style. Their fingers were like their pliers and their fists were like hammers. They were not only physically giants, but also giants in their spirituality. They also had other means of earning a living. Each one had a strong personality. They served the entire region from the shtetl Taragin to Kaltinian, about 24 kilometers away. No blacksmiths of the region could compete with them. All 3 were both good tradesmen and honest. In short, the peasants and the entire community didn't have more than an axle to repair or a wagon to make, and so went the work of the blacksmiths of Lingmian.

One of them was of simple pedigree, not a big "learned" person, and we used to called him: Ahron –Moishe, we didn't proceed with the Reb title, as was the usual custom when addressing an elderly Jew.

The Jews also called him by the wife's name, calling him: Ahron–Moishe, Raske Rutke's. The peasants labelled him with the name: "Faika Nasas", which in Lithuanian translates, crooked nose.

He could barely pray and say Tehillim. Four o'clock, in the afternoon, he would run to the synagogue, to say his Tehillim and pray with the first minyan.

As a blacksmith, he mostly received basic repairs of (peasant) wagons and wagons of the "Vozsakes", that brought the wood from the forests. He worked skillfully and the peasants waited weeks for his handiwork, so he alone could do the job.

He was broad shouldered, with a long yellow overgrown beard, barely making his face visible.

[Col. 1240]

He walked with a heavy gait, the earth trembled under his feet.

He went to Cheder for a short time and started working with his father in his workshop. He loved to work therefore making Shabbos and holidays endless for him.

He couldn't wait for Shabbos to end, and right after Ma'ariv, he would run home, quickly said the Havdalla, ate, took off his Shabbas attire and returned to his workshop, next to his anvil.

The second blacksmith of Lingmian, was already a different person. We called him Reb Hirsh Leib, and the addition, Reb, wasn't just out of habit. We honored him, as he was a man of learning and was well versed in Gemara and translations.

Reb Hirsh Leib (a blacksmith)

He learned his blacksmith trade while still a young student in Vilna and there he often attended the Synagogue of the "Tiffereth Young Men"

He was also a giant, broad shouldered, with a large forehead, with an overgrown full beard. Smart eyes protruded from his face, his lips emanated a sweet smile, he greeted everyone with a "good morning". Everyone loved him and respected him.

He was an outstanding craftsman and harnessed the horses, made axels for the wagons and all the wealthy noblemen were his steady clients.

On Sundays at the Church, the peasants lined up outside his workshop and the sounds of the horses could be heard throughout the shtetl. It happened, that a fight would break out amongst them, angry, and Reb Hirsh Leib had to interfere and make peace amongst them.

Amongst the Jewish folk he was held in high esteem. He didn't only teach Torah with simple folk, he was also a community activist, one who dealt with the public needs in disputes. He had time for everything. He was involved in all the shtetl's activities. He would run to the synagogue to lead prayers and to the Mikvah to do repairs. He was the father of all the orphans in the shtetl and the provider of all the widows, a blessed person who didn't expect praise, a truly devoted townsperson, the best one can describe in words.

[Col. 1241]

After the First World war, when Lingmian didn't have a Rabbi, all he wealthy folks came to Reb Hirsh Leib, to be the interim Rabbi in the shtetl.

Reb Hirsh Leib didn't want to burden (financially) the Rabbinate, so he chose to work half days at his workshop.

In this manner, Lingmian had a Rabbi a blacksmith and everyone was pleased with this arrangement.

The third blacksmith of Lingmian was also an interesting person. We called him Reb Yitzhak Nepucha, this was a Jew who knew the "Zochar" very well, a "Tikun–Hatzut" Jew, to whom other rabbis had great respect and valued his interpretations of the laws.

He was also a giant, tall and thin, with a thin black beard and a high forehead, always lost in deep thought, as it was said in the shtetl, he wanted to enter the next world and focused on the next life.

Besides all these things he was also a master of his trade. Next to his workshop stood many beautiful "Britczkes", lavish coaches that belonged to the wealthy noblemen.

Every Friday he closed his workshop at exactly 2 o'clock, both summer and winter. As he was a Kabbalah–Jew, he went very early to prepare for the Sabbath.

Many wonderful stories were told about Rabbi Yitzhak Nepucha in the shtetl, one especially resonates like a legend.

One time, it was told, that the old prince from the Pokever estate ordered a fancy wagon, the princes from the region wanted to present the prince this gift for his 70th birthday. That particular day fell on a Friday and the parade for the prince was scheduled for Sunday. What shall he do? It was a few hours before his Kaballah–Shabbos and the carriage was not ready.

[Col. 1242]

Reb Yitzak, from this great angst burst out crying. He was truly sorry for the old prince, who was also a true friend of the Jews. From time to time he gave a (measure) of wood to the synagogue. Erev Pesach, he already prepared sacks of potatoes for the poor of Lingmian.

The prince was at the mayor's house playing chess. Someone told him that the blacksmith finds himself in a difficult predicament and doesn't know what to do.

The prince got up and immediately got on his horse and went to Reb Yitzhak's workshop. When he saw the blacksmith sitting and crying he got very frightened and asked him: what tragedy happened to you? He told him the story that he promised to complete an important job and wanted to complete it as promised, as suits a very important prince, but very soon arrives a "special guest" and he cannot complete the task.

With every word the prince understood the entire story.

– Tell me, if so, who is the guest? Who is coming?

– This is our Holy Shabbat, answered the blacksmith

The prince thought it over and then answered.

– Actually, Sunday is a very important holiday for me, my entire family will be visiting and I would very much like for them to see the wonderful gift from the noblemen, but God's "calling" is more important than my birthday.

Close your shop and go prepare yourself for the Sabbat like you always do.

Reb Yitzhak Nepucha was deeply moved by the gentle words and thanked the prince. When they said their goodbyes, the blacksmith said:

– Blessings from our Holy Sabbath, that you didn't allow to stand in your way, you will be blessed with a long life, like any man in our region has never been honored before.

[Col. 1243]

The prince lived another 30 years and he died at 102 years old.

The prince loved to tell the story on each birthday that his long life was attributed to Reb Yitzhak Nepucha the Jewish blacksmith, who had given him the "blessing".

Reb Yitzhak Nepucha donated a beautiful "gift", which he nurtured his entire life; every week he gave 10 percent of his earnings to the poor of the shtetl. This is how he conducted himself, according to the laws, earning him a place in the next world.

After Ma'ariv he didn't go home, he stayed in the synagogue to study and until late you could hear his beautiful Gemara "nigun" (melody) .

When the young people would return late at night from a meeting or a play, you would always meet Reb Yitzhak on the way, coming from the synagogue.

Erev Yom Kippur it was customary to go to Reb Yitzhak Nepucha to ask him for his blessings for the new year.

He married his daughters to each Sefer and Gemara scholar. He was also a Gemara scholar. When he died, his day of mourning was declared "a day of sorrow" in Lingmian. The Melamdim (teachers) closed the Cheders and requested all the students to participate in the funeral. The shopkeepers closed their stores, the fishermen didn't go out into the lakes: young and old, women and children, everyone came to give him his last "koved" (pay their respects) . Even Christians from the entire region assembled and were led by the prince of the Pakavner estate, who praised the virtues of the Jewish blacksmith to all his followers.

Rabbis from the surrounding shtetls arrived, as well as the eulogizer, to honor him as if he was the greatest "Gaon".

One of the Rabbis began the eulogy with the following words: A" cedar" tree fell (reference was used: the trees used by King Solomon to build the Temple) amongst the Jews–...

The three blacksmiths were an example how one can live "with Torah and with work".

[Col. 1244]

Fishermen of Lingmian

Lingmian was surrounded by many lakes. Each side had its own name, like, Zezdrele, Ultaksne, Pashekst, and other names according to the hamlets which lay at the edges.

The most beautiful, which was clear from stones, and wasn't deep; the young people came in the summertime to swim and the wives came to wash their clothes and beat them with a special stick on a grate all year long, was call Zezdrele.

This bank was very interesting. It stretched lengthwise and from it many fields on which grew high, old Berozes (name for a tree) . The entire area was filled with singing of various types of birds. The air was pure, so pleasing to smell and breathe.

Not far from the bank was the Bath. This was an old bath house, with small smoked up windows with a crooked shingle roof, and with the so–called "podmur", which was full of holes and cracks.

Friday after lunch, the Jews of Lingmian came to prepare their duty for the Sabbath.

There was much activity during the summertime along the bank of the Zezerele, day and night. Friends and girls, gentile boys and girls, had their love trysts there, singing, playing and dancing.

At night the people of the surrounding hamlets lit the bank with lanterns, and on these lanterns many fires were lit, to deter the wolves so they wouldn't come to eat the animals who were grazing on the luscious fields.

The important people of these banks were the fishermen. For them the lake was the principle source of income. From the banks they cast their nets. From the fishing they supported their families.

For these Fishermen the bank had another name. Here they lived the entire week, they ate, they drank, they slept. For them this was not a place to enjoy pleasurable moments, it was just their work–place. A place of income.

The Jewish fishermen of Lingmian were interesting persons and it is difficult to describe.

One of them was called Tuvia. He was a tall man, with a yellow beard and large brows over small eyes, and his entire face was full of summer–spots. He was very difficult, he often had disputes with the helpers and even fought with some and it would take a while before peace was re–established.

[Col. 1245]

With one thing Tuvia was full of himself, that, when he was young he had spent some time in Sweden and this he could never forget. He brought back a hat and plastic (synthetic) shoes. Friday night he actually put on all his fine Swedish clothing and appeared in the synagogue like a true "lord".

Saturdays he paraded around the shtetl with his coat and fine shoes and his face shone with pride.

A second, interesting fisherman, was Berke, Raitze's, they called him by his mother's name, as his father Leizer, z'l, died while still a young man. Raitza, the widow, continued in the fish business after her husband's death, raised Berke and trained him in the fish business.

She taught him, sent him to Cheder and he wasn't particularly interested, he was a different type. He knew how to sing and dance, belonged to the shtetl's youth groups and took part in all the meetings, at simchas and also sad occasions. In the summertime, Berke's singing broke the silence of the Lingmian nights, which came from the direction of the lake and was known to all:

"Karasnaya Davitza,.... (Russian or Polish song...)

A third fisherman of Lingmian was called Yoske Lipa Mates. Or Yoske the fighter. He was of medium weight, broad–shouldered, with a red face with fiery eyes. He was hot tempered, not one Goy of the shtetl could feel his might with his fat hands.

When we saw the authorities next to the old inn in Lingmian we knew that they were searching for Yoske, for his "good deeds".

The day of the fair, "Troitze" in Lingmian, Yoske didn't go to his work on the lake, in case, the Jews of the shtetl needed him to deal with troublemakers.

[Col. 1246]

Another fisherman was the well– known Lipa Mate, the Tehillim–person. His face was overgrown with a white, thin beard. He had broad shoulders, a red nose and long payot (side locks) and was considered the oldest of the fishermen. He controlled the fishing nets very well, made sure no problems and had his own song, which he always sang when working.

He was the leader at the services, the Tehillim reader, before Ma'ariv in the synagogue. That is the reason we actually named him : Lipa the Tehillah–reader.

The head–boss of the fishing industry in Lingmian was the wealthy Reb Meir Gavenda. He leased the lakes from the nobles and employed many Jewish fishermen.

Meir Gavenda came from a hamlet, next to Lingmian, and as a young man came to the shtetl and later became successful in the forestry industry.

The fish he transported to the larger towns. In the last years he lived in Vilna and even there he became a successful merchant.

Meir Gavenda's sons were all well– known wood merchants.

The dress code for the fishermen were always the same. They all wore long, rubber boots, and overalls covered with a coating in order the water not penetrate and wet them. Besides this they wore heavy overcoats, made of a material to keep the cold and humidity out. The “sermege” was tied with cord.

Going to the lake, they carried a small case with a piece of black corn bread, a “pot” to cook some fish.

Each one had his own taste and beloved fish. Tuvia, only cooked “platkes”, Berke Raitze's and Yoske the “fighter” loved “shli'en” (type of fish), Lipe Mate, only small fish.

Yoske used to say, that'shle'in” increased a man's life. If he is healthy and has the strength, it is only thanks to the “shle'in”.

[Col. 1247]

When the fishermen came ashore and sorted their fish and then hung out the nets. Later they each took their pot and cooked their fish.

When they finished eating, they took off their boots and hung them from the trees to dry out.

In the summertime Berke spread himself out on the field and played his whistle, which he made himself from a soft branch. Mote Lipa, after the meal, said several passages from the Tehillim. Tuvia oiled on the nets, quite late they fell asleep and slept in the open air.

Tuvia, around 6 in the morning, started screaming: get up, you lazy ones, it is already late, the sun has long been out.

They got up quickly, said their prayers, ate and went back onto the lake. A new day began.

This is how the fishermen of Lingmian lived without any free time, working dy and night, however they were happy, glad to make a living.

They were hard working, simple peasant folk, loved by all the Jewish and Christian folk.

Shloime Yankel the Tavern–keeper, and the Miracle that happened to him

It was Friday evening. It was quiet and still around Shloime Yankel's tavern. The peasants of the region had left in all directions. The place around him was empty. On the street, next to his tavern, there were the remains of straw and horse dirt.

It became dark. Shloime Yankel and both his sons left for the synagogue. In the large hall, the Shabbos lights glittered. On the long beautifully laid out table there were fresh baked challahs, covered with a cloth, which was a gift from the son in law Chaia Hodel.

Laia'ke, the tavern keepers' wife, with her 6 daughters sat around the table, in their Shabbos attire, and waited, that the father with his sons return from praying.

[Col. 1248]

Soon 3 men entered and said, "Gut Shabbos".

Shloime Yankel was a learned Jew and everyone in the shtetl respected him. Two fiery smart black eyes, peeked out from his wide forehead. The thick and messy bear gave him a rabbinic face.

Leah'ka, his wife, was the opposite of him. Thin and small, with sharp eyes, she became known for it, that each year she gave birth to another daughter.

Coming home he immediately greeted her with delight , "Shalom Aleichem, Queen of the Sabbath, Queen of the House", walking around the large room, from one wall to another.

A beaker with wine was ready for the Kiddush. Everyone waited, for him to finish and go to the table.

Suddenly the "Shabbos–Goya" (Christian lady who looked after lighting the fire on Shabbos) Staschike, barely catching her breath, frightened and screaming: "noblemen are coming, very important guests".

Shloime Yankel made a sour face and asked Laia'ke, his wife, to escort them to the guest room in order to rid himself of them. It is Shabbos and he doesn't want to sell them anything.

Before all was said, the guest showed up in this eating room and Shloime Yankel immediately recognized them as the noblemen from the Lidekener estate.

They entered the house like gazelles, with hunting rifles on their shoulders and muddy boots. Leike couldn't get a word in and they, not waiting for a separate invitation, sat themselves down at the Shabbos–prepared table and I could do anything about it.

The aromatic gefilte fish, the fresh challahs and the flask of wine immediately went to their senses.

They were ravenous, one grabbed a challah and torn it in half and without hesitation, began to eat.

Staschike, tried, with all her goodness to beg them, that they should go to the guest room, that the Jews must continue with their Shabbos preparations.

The noblemen had a good laugh. They were very comfortable here in this spot and no special guest room was necessary.

[Col. 1249]

When they finished the challah, they asked Laia'ke to bring a flask of beer.

With tears in her eyes, she told them that on the holy Shabbat, she couldn't sell them any beer.

One them pounded on the tables with his fists, the candle lights shaking, and said:

—cursed, Jewess, bring a few flasks of beer, if not, we will make trouble for you.

Shloime Yankel and his two sons stood in the corner the entire time, with bloodshot eyes, fearful to utter a word.

The noblemen were insulted by the Jewish "chutzpa" and started breaking glasses, plates, hurling insults and even wanting to shoot their rifles.

When one of the noblemen ran to his eldest daughter and started to bother her, Shloime Yankel started to yell and make a commotion:

"Murderers, ruffigans"

These screams of the family could be heard on the other side of town.

Their bullets tore through the sky. At one moment we thought that some Jewish blood would be spilled.

Suddenly all stopped. The bells of the church suddenly began to ring, and at that moment the drunkards left, as if thunder had struck them.

They became very nervous and left the house, mounted their horses and left the shtetl.

Shloime Yankel's family became anxious from fright of death and the from mess they left behind.

The Shabbos ended and the family couldn't believe what had just happened and how they were saved. Sunday morning, their poor Christian neighbour, Jozepke, came by and told them the entire story.

Friday night he heard the commotion and came running, looked through the windows to see what was happening.

He noticed the Tavern–keeper and her family were in a difficult predicament, breaking glasses and attempting to molest their daughter, we wanted to run for help. But he noticed that the hooligans were no ordinary ruffians, but the young noblemen of the Lidekener estate, he saw their hunting rifles and in the courtyard stood the beautiful horses with their adornments.

[Col. 1250]

The Tavern keeper brought out some brandy for Jozepke and thanked him heartfully for his concern. He also sent a separate heartfelt thanks to the priest.

Many years had passed and still the story of this great miracle was told throughout Lingmian; that Friday night at Shloime Yankel's.

Reb Afroim the "White Head"

Reb Afroim who was known to all in the shtetl by the name "the white head", he was considered to be one the most beloved "noble" (wealthier class) of Lingmian. He was not only a great scholar amongst Jewish scholars, he also had business skills and could read and write Russian. Everyone went to him to write an address or a letter in Russian. It was a rarity 40–50 years ago in a Jewish shtetl and therefore people had great respect for him. He was a tall man, with curly, long payot and black, intelligent eyes, which peaked through his large brows. His pointer finger was yellow from tobacco, he was always dressed in a black frock: his rubber boots were smeared with oil. He was very devout and led his life according to the Schulchan Aruch and used to say, an honest Jew must live according to the (Jewish) law.

Reb Akiva, the devout mayor and Shmuel Michal, the skeptic looked up to him as a great leader but he didn't reciprocate these feelings. He owned a large house, with a glass porch. In the courtyard there was a large stable where the peasants kept their horses.

[Col. 1251]

His livelihood was derived from two things: he was in the transportation business and he owned a brewery where he sold beer and one could get drunk. Every Sunday his house was filled with commotion and cooking. Peasants came on Sundays to the shtetl Church from the surrounding hamlets and used this time to buy various stuff from the Jewish shopkeepers. They also frequented the brewery.

One time a very interesting story happened to Reb Afroim. This was during the holiday, "Troitze". The entire shtetl was in a "tumult". Hundred of peasants arrived from the region, they were near and around his ale house, the smoke from the fire in the lanterns were suffocating in his house. Reb Afroim busied himself in the shop, overseeing that no one disappear without paying.

One time, he noticed a package in a corner. He bent over, picked it up and put it in his pocket. With great surprise he said the blessing: thank you God for this present. He went into a nearby room and took out this package of money and to his great surprise saw several hundred rubles. Reb Afroim jumped for joy. Such a small thing, this present! On such a clear day, a miracle from the heavens...

Several hours barely past after he found this package, when suddenly Reb Itze the Innkeeper burst into his shop. Reb Itze lived in a hamlet, which lay on the road from Puptishak–Otian (Utian) , where he owned an Inn. When the small train was installed and passed through the hamlet, a station was built, Reb Itze started a business where he sold fruit, pig–hair, and fur pelts. He often went to the markets and fairs to buy goods.

When Reb Itze arrived at the brewery at night he was white as chalk. His forehead was covered with a cold sweat. His black beard was completely disheveled and large hot tears poured from his eyes. He was delirious and was barely able to tell Afroim the terrible tragedy that occurred to him that day.

[Col. 1252]

Going to the fair he took with him a large sum of money to buy merchandise. When he was ready to pay the peasants, he realized that he had lost his money someplace. He searched everywhere but couldn't find his money. Suddenly he remembered he was in the brewery and decided to come here, maybe someone had found his money?

Reb Afroim calmed him down, and said in a cold an indifferent manner:

– The truth, I don't want to lie to you, I actually found the money. This package lay here on my floor. There were many people in my house today and anyone of them could have found the package of money. If the package was meant to have been lost, then the found package belongs, according to Jewish law, to the finder.

Reb Itze started to scream and beg:

– How do you not have any pity on me and my children? You are a thief, you have no heart. What is your piety worth? Your teaching, you do not have a Jewish heart?

Reb Afroim didn't want to back down. He lived according to the (Jewish) law and will follow the orders of the (Jewish) court.

Reb Itze gave him some offers, Reb Itze offered 5, then 10 rubles, but Reb Afroim saw that he couldn't rid himself, so he wanted to go before the Rabbi to settle the matter.

Reb Itze had no choice, so after Mincha, they both left to the Rabbi. Reb Afroim took the Shulchan Aruch from the "Olmer", looked into the passages, and happily said to himself approaching the Rabbi:

– Don't be afraid of anything. The court is on my side.

The Rabbi heard both sides of the story, and then called Reb Afroim into a nearby room and said something to him. Soon Reb Afroim left the room with anger and fire in his eyes and again yelled at the Rabbi:

[Col. 1253]

– Rabbi, I demand a trial. The court will be on myside and the "gift" will be mine.

Reb Itze Leizer the Innkeeper could no longer hold back and started to yell:

– This is a trick. Reb Afroim does not possess a Jewish heart. He knows well that this is my hard–earned money. How can a religious Jew be such a miserable person? Without this money I cannot return home. I am now an unlucky man. Rabbi, take pity, tell him to return the "gift".

Reb Afroim refused and declared:

– I lived my entire life according to the law and now I demand a court of law.

Itze Leizer's quarrels were heard through the shtetl and crowds gathered around the Rabbi's house, they all felt sorry for the unlucky Innkeeper and insisted Afroim to make the right decision, he should not be so stubborn. The end was, that both "Tzadakim" (men of learning) left the Rabbis house, but the "gift" still was with Afroim. He approached the crowd and quietly said:

– Jews, you need to have faith. There is a God and Itze Leizer will soon get his money back.

After this incidence it was talked about in the shtetl, that Reb Akiva the religious mayor, discussed the matter with Reb Afroim , the lawful verdict he will obey. His advice was that his wife should return the money in installments. And this is how it finally ended. The gentle Chaia–Riva (wife of R'Akiva) returned the money in this manner.

Reb Akiva–The Religious Mayor

With respect and love, with great esteem we must describe to all our beloved and important personality of our shtetl, Reb Akiva Aizikovitch, who we named the religious mayor.

The affair started many years ago. A representative from Sventzian arrived in Lingmian and brought an interesting announcement.

[Col. 1254]

They were planning to build a small train to tie Sventzian to Poneveshz, therefore they needed to build a station in Lingmian. Our shtetl welcomed progress in this manner, and we nominated one of our own as the mayor of the region. He will institute many reforms, means for growth and other necessities. The shtetl and village folk will no longer need to manage their affairs with the Sventzian authorities.

Quick as lightening, the idea was spread in the entire region and the occasion was a rejoicing for all, it didn't take long and Reb Akiva Itzikovitch was chosen as the mayor of the region.

Reb Akiva Aizikovitch, the mayor of Lingmian

He was a Jew, a great Talmud scholar, a son of a Schohet (ritual slaughterer) from Paliush, and a son– in– law of the known Tzadik Reb Yitzhak Nafcha. He was a tall and well– built young man, with intelligent eyes and was always well dressed, with a patriarchal beard. He was good–hearted, full of humour and from his mouth he spoke truthful and important words. He was a source of information and a Torah scholar, from his father and his father– in– law he inherited Torah and humour. For every occasion he recited the words of the Torah, passages from the Gemara and Midrash.

He was respected in the entire community and everyone came to him for advice. He was at every conflict, and everyone wanted him to preside, as everyone knew that Reb Akiva was the essence of honesty and practicality. For his rule of law everyone had the utmost respect and admiration.

He was also considered an expert in forestry–trade and even the noblemen came to him to discuss the issues of forestry and wood trade.

He knew Russian perfectly, writing, reading and speech and owned a large cupboard full of different books. Religious and worldly, current events and literary. He was all known to be a brilliant chess player: a personality in every sense of the word.

[Col. 1255]

Every Shabbos he invited a guest to his home, and he knew how to choose specifically a magid (preacher) or a mesholach (rabbinical emissary), learned person, in order to have someone to talk about Torah topics all day Shabbos.

He had a large family and was not close to being wealthy. However, he gave charity generously. his wife was also a great charity doer/donor and brought up his 5 daughters in the spirit of modesty , doing good deeds and devoted to their Yiddishkeit.

He had a beautiful tradition where every Friday, Kabbalat Shabbos, he gathered the youth of the shtetl to recite to them "Shir Ha'Shirim" (song of songs) .

It was said that in all the world's literature, there was never a more beautiful, spiritual, sweet and holy song than "Shir Ha'shirim". In addition he read to us various psalms and proverbs/fables. He especially liked to say to us:

– He would love to give such an interpretation: SH'CHORA ANI V'NAVA–I am black and lovely.

You know children, it means that Jewish life in the Diaspora is as black as the earth, Nava–Lovely means however, when we arrive home in the land of Eretz Israel, our lives will be beautiful and blessed.

At the High Holidays, Rosh Hashana and Yom Kippur, Reb Akiva was the leader in the shtetl services. He went up to the "Bima" with great anticipation, dressed in a white "kitel" (coat) , and wrapped in a Tallith with silver threads. The shofars were decorated and he stood up to have a "fight/war" with the Devil.

When he started chanting "Hear Oh Zion..." amongst his worshippers, the women were separate, he broke out in heart–wrenching tears.

It was also his turn to recite the Yom Kippur Tehillim with the audience. The entire shtetl, young and old, came to pray with him the passages of the Tehillim. Even the heretic, the free–thinker, Shmuel Michal, couldn't pass up the opportunity to say Tehillim with everyone, so he could join them: "Do not leave the others...."

In short, Reb Akiva was a master of an honest community activist, who was an honest and virtuous man," Do not separate yourself from the community" (Talmud, Avot 2,4)

[Col. 1256]

He was considered the "crown jewel" and brought glory to himself, the shtetl of Lingmian and the whole region.

Every Jew who was lucky and blessed to hear Reb Akiva praying in the large wooden synagogue of Lingmian will never in their entire lives forget him.

His blessed memory will be engraved in our hearts for glory and fame forever.

From Both Sides of the Border

From 1924–1928, fate suddenly smiled upon Lingmian and the shtetl became famous throughout the world.

Newspaper– correspondence and writers of the largest Jewish newspapers and even Jews from all parts of Poland and Lithuania, sought every piece of news from our small shtetl.

The result of this was the community became involved either in a political–historical or in a national way.

After the first world war, when borders shifted from time to time and new administrations took over, many of the people were making the best of the situation, the border near us, finally stabilized between Lithuania and Poland.

Our small shtetl of Lingmian as a result was divided into 2 parts. The larger part belonged to Poland and the smaller–to Lithuania.

The fate was that the Jewish cemetery would be the "neutral zone" and accessible for both communities.

Both communities were on good terms, but the border between them was strict and it was difficult to cross from one part to the other.

For the Jewish population this was a great tragedy, both from social side and from the economic side.

The Jews lived together for many years, worked and traded and suddenly we were" cut in half" and caught between 2 administrations.

Children were torn from their elderly parents, brothers and sisters, one from another.

Families were torn apart and this came without warning. We didn't have the time to talk this over and how we were to live together.

[Col. 1257]

Several years past and the Jews of Lingmian sought out different ways and ideas to solve the problem of reuniting and with the relatives and friends on both sides of the border.

In the end we came up with a brilliant idea. As the cemetery was the neutral zone, Jewish custom was on Tish A'bav, Jews went to the cemetery to pay respects to their deceased relatives.

We asked the Polish regime to allow the Jewish people to visit their relatives' graves once a year. And thanks to the intervention of the senator Rabbi Rubinsten of Vilna, the permits were received.

Immediately the same procedure was followed by the second side, requesting permits from the Lithuanian regime, which also agreed. Nothing more, understandably, was needed. And the cemetery was the place, where friends and relatives could visit once a year peacefully and speak with one another. This was a “special” day both in Poland and Lithuania.

Several weeks before the meeting, preparations were already being made, for this historical meeting. The shopkeepers arrived in Vilna with their various goods, knowing that thousands of guests would assemble there that day. They will need to eat and they will surely bring gifts for one another.

Etel, the baker, began her baking several days prior, especially that famous bread. Dobe and Moishe baked a large quantity of their delicious “beigelach”. Shloime Yacov the Tavern keeper prepared the beer and appetizers. Everyone was involved in these preparations, just like for an important holiday.

The religious Jews were not so happy with this idea, because they knew, that this reunion would not be according “Jewish law” with the “day of mourning”. But they came to terms with this “sin” and a lot of them came along as well to visit their relatives from the other side.

Tish B'av, exactly 6 oclock in the morning, the soldiers, the “green” and the “yellow” from both sides took their places, as they were called in the shtetl, because the Lithuanian soldiers wore yellow uniforms and the Polish, green ones.

From both sides of the border the Jews descended upon the cemetery.

[Col. 1258]

All at once, the politics of the 2 regimes were forgotten. The cemetery on that day was filled with long separated relatives, fathers, children and grandchildren, brothers and sisters, friends and mothers, who didn't see each other for many years. They cried and they laughed.

Here and there they sat in groups on the ground, between the tombstones, a tablecloth was spread out, they brought out their gifts that brought for one another. They ate, made a “L'Chaim”, and spoke about everything and everyone.

The Jewish merchants of Lingmian also profited nicely on this day. They all did well. The peasants of the surrounding villages also took advantage of this day and brought their wares and fruits of many colors to the cemetery.

They spent the entire day running from one friend to another, from one group to another. Everyone knew each other, everyone was a friend. Here one met a friend from their childhood, and there a student from the Folk–Shul, with whom they sat on the same bench.

This lasted until late in the evening. When it was dark, the soldiers, the green and the yellow, reappeared.

[Col. 1259]

This was the warning sign, that we had to say our goodbyes and return home. Each in his direction. The border closed until the next year.

Several years passed this way with the yearly meeting, until both regimes, instead of visiting their relatives' tombstones', they saw “living” Jews, and soon their permits were rescinded and the meetings were stopped.

Again the Lithuanian–Polish border was hermetically sealed, and to our great misfortune, it opened when the second world war broke out, which brought death and destruction for both the Polish and Lithuanian Jewry.

My Grandfather's House–the “Pekerne”

My grandfather's house stands before me, which we called the “pekerne”.

My grandfather Reb Abraham was born and raised in a hamlet called “Pokevne”, 5 kilometers from Lingmian.

A meeting at the cemetery of Lingmian, of Lithuanian and Polish Jews The family of Chaim Faiva Shutan, New–Sventzian, Elperin family and Tzikinski family

Sitting below: **Chaim Faiva, Guta Shutan, Yacov Shutan, Raitze Elperin**
Sitting: **Lieve Shutan, Leibe Chaim Elperin, Eidel Elperin, Chana Elperin, Liba Elperin, Perel Elperin**
Standing: **Chana Shutan–Fishman, Chana–Laia Elperin, Mina Muler, Chana Elperin, Muler, Meir Muler, Loibe Svirski, Shimon Svirski, Itele Elperin, Dina Muler, Tzeikunski Raiza, Feige Elperin, Peretz Zeikunski**

My grandmother Elka, was born in a hamlet "Krivashele". They were counted as amongst the first settlers of the Lingmian community. They had a wooden house, which stood on a small hill, on the road to Utian (Utena) . This was a typical village hut, without a floor, covered with straw roof and with small windows. Before you entered, it was fenced off for the wagon and Bunen's horse. In a corner stood a thin goat.

Near the door stood a large and deep oven, without a chimney. When it heated up, it filled the room with smoke and we choked in the house, the smoke covered the walls, and they always looked like they were painted with black oil "paint."

In the middle of the house was the wooden table of gathered planks of wood, surrounded by long, wide benches, which we called "sapzenes". (probably served as sofas)

Not far from their house ran a tired stream, where frogs always croaked.

[Col. 1260]

Grandfather was a short Jew, with a white beard with deep black eyes. He was broad shouldered and had the appearance of a wealthy man.

Grandmother Elka was a slender Jewess, tall with a pale face, and bright blue eyes. Her smiling face always was filled with goodness and love.

Every Wednesday grandfather left for New–Sventzian to the market, where he brought his various goods from his village, like, flax, pig–hair, peas and so forth. Returning home he brought pots made out of lime, kettles and other household articles. He then spent the entire week going from hamlet to hamlet selling these wares. He already had his loyal customers and sold to them on "loan" or traded them for produce. From this he had a difficult but steady income.

Grandmother Elka,
one of the first settlers of
Lingmian

Grandmother Elka was considered the midwife of Lingmian. No one knew where she learned her trade. In those times she didn't attend any Gymnasia nor was she ever in a hospital. She was nevertheless an excellent midwife and delivered the children of the shtetl.

Every month she went to visit the religious mayor and present him with an update of the children, who were born that month.

According to her information he recorded it in his ledger. She didn't receive payment for this work. When the patient was a poor woman, she would bring her some soup afterwards.

Grandmother Elka was a shining light, she was known for her charity throughout the region. Every poor person, whether a teacher or an orphan, knew that a warm bed and good meal was readily available.

Often she gave up her own food and her last piece of bread. She made a wedding for all the poor girls in the shtetl, helped widows and raised orphans.

[Col. 1261]

No one knew how difficult my grandfather worked to earn a living, going from hamlet to hamlet. He ate at the peasants' only a piece of black corn bread followed by cold water.

He had to be careful going from hamlet to hamlet, as the earthenware pots were fragile, breaking easily.

It is hard to imagine that such a poor family had the means to still give charity and look after orphans and still managed to lead such a beautiful and well defined Jewish life.

Erev Shabbos, grandfather beamed with “nachos” (pride) . The community also helped him. When grandmother lit the Shabbos candles and did the blessing, tears ran from her eyes.

Friday evening, grandmother looked like a princess. She wore a black silk shawl in honor of the Sabbath and lit the kerosene lamp.

She loved her grandchildren very much. Once, when my father was sick, she said to me: Hirshenke–go pray and ask God to make your father well.

Two things that brought honor to my grandfather and grandmother in their quiet, simple and charitable life: 1–good deeds–they helped everyone and loved everyone, 2–they served their God and commandments–with love and life. “Glory and glory to the Holy One!”

My Brother, the Genius

Our shtetl was widely known throughout the entire region with her young “Gaon”, who studied in the Radin Yeshiva of Cheifetz–Chaim and was known as the Lingmianer genius.

This was my brother Afroim.

Even as a young boy, all the teachers already knew that this child was growing into–a Gaon. After the early death of our father, he studied with the renowned teacher of our shtetl, Reb Akiva. Afroim was a great scholar and studied late into the night.

Onetime mother woke from her sleep and caught him studying and called out to him:

– Enough, child, it is so late, go to sleep.

Afroim called out to her with his gentle smile: “Maminke, learning is never enough, the Talmud is a deep ocean, without a bottom and without a “shore”.

Ha'Gaon Afroim Zar

[Col. 1262]

Soon Afroim, aged 14, saw there were no more teachers for him in Lingmian and left the shtetl for the Radin yeshiva of Cheifetz–Chaim to continue his Torah learning (larger shtetl had teachers of higher learning) . All the Yeshiva lads were older than him, but he didn't get lost (he felt comfortable amongst them) . He knew his strength and would surpass them in his studies. The head of the yeshiva saw his talents and loved him like “the eyes in your head”.

Quite soon, the Yeshiva noticed that this young lad was a genius. Everyone treated him with respect and wanted to study with him.

The years flew by, he went from teacher to teacher and grew up to become a great Torah scholar.

At 22 years old he became the head of the Novorudker Yeshiva. (maybe Novagrudek)

At 25 years he left for the great center of Rabbis in Vilna and there Rabbi Chaim Oder Grodzenski called him: “Ha'Goan Ha'Tzair”.

When World War 11 broke out, he joined his family and all the Yeshiva “bocherim” (lads) in Vilna and hoped, from there that he would be able to immigrate to a larger and freer, democratic world.

To our immense heartache, he was unable to save himself from the Hitlerite animals. They brought him to Ponar together with all the Rabbis, Doctors and all the important people of the city.

My brother Afroim was a tall and thin young man. He had beautiful blue eyes, a wide forehead and was always in a good mood and tolerated all men, people of different nations and religions.

His teachers said, he possessed a phenomenal memory which was a blessing and therefore his teaching of the Talmud, its comprehension and explanations were so valuable.

[Col. 1263]

He didn't limit himself only to the Talmud, he read books by important writers and lecturers. Separately, he admired greatly our national writer Chaim Nachum Bialik, who also was a Yeshiva –bocher (lad) from Volozhin.

In the Rabbinic world there was a day of mourning, when the news came, that Afroim, the genius, perished in Ponar.

The Tehillim–Sayers (preachers)

Shabbos, after Schlosha Seudah, is considered a sad day by every Religious Jew. In the Jewish soul, this was a day of soul–searching, about good deeds and bad. Between Shabbos–keit (obeying the Shabbat) and weekly events. No one wanted to throw themselves in the bustle of the work week. Everyone knew that the week meant dragging those sacks on their backs throughout the long roads, from village to village in order to earn a small piece of bread for themselves and their families. The week days were filled with hardships and anxiety.

Every Jew searched for a different way to prolong the Shabbos. If only for a short time. And there many such ways. The most important of them were: you have to learn Torah until sunset or say Tehillim.

Therefore in Lingmian a group Tehillim–sayers became very fashionable. Saturday evening they all gathered at the synagogue and with great devotion, said "sentence" after "sentence" (psalms) , this "band of psalm–sayers".

The leader of this group was the fisherman Reb Lipa Mate.

He was a healthy Jew, with a wide forehead and grey eyes. Afterwards he worked on the lakes and was known as a successful fisherman. The whole week it was difficult for him to find a minyan, listen to a Kiddush or a portion of the Torah. It was said in the shtetl, that he didn't have time to "eat a Jewish word".

So Lipa Mote, on the Shabbos, after 3 Seudath, immersed himself. It was felt that he found his true soul during these hours of higher spiritual immersion.

[Col. 1264]

Several others gathered around Lipe Mota, devout Tehillim sayers, these were hard working, simple Jews, like: Aharon Moishe, Feife Gases, Tuvia the pedlar, Eliahu the tailor, Moishe the orchard–tender, and Chaim the butcher. Lipe Mota was a very spiritual leader. It was said, that before he began his "blessed are those who walk the righteous way–ASHREI TMIMEI DERECH", he quietly whispered a prayer.

The start of the Tehillah was as follows: Beloved God, I am not a scholar. I didn't have the opportunity to study Torah like all the other children. Nights are spent wandering through villages and fields, crossing over roads and alleys, and I don't have the means to serve and honor you like other Jews. Help me today. Cleanse my heart and my soul, so I am prepared to sing praises to you from the Tehillim, together with all the Jews. I want to be like the green grass on your great field, like a drop of water in your wide ocean. Take away all my sins that stand in my way and allow me to be the leader of these simple Jews.

Suddenly, as if he awoke from a deep dream, with great enthusiasm, he began to recite one after the other and they all followed. The entire synagogue was filled with a new energy. A feeling of spiritual holiness filled the air. The sadness of the prayers lessened. A group of Jews were always present to honor the Shabbat.

In those times, even the scholars and the intelligent folk were jealous of the so called Tehillim–sayers, who wouldn't allow others to read Ma'ariv. When one wanted to smoke a cigarette, or go to their shops, Lipe Mota didn't interfere. With great patience he continued to uphold the holy Shabbat, even for another few minutes.

He considered himself a preacher, as a writer holds a pen in his hand.

In Lingmian Ma'ariv was prayed much later than in other shtetls. This was because of Mote Lipe, who we called with respect, The Tehillim–sayer.

[Col. 1265]

Ethel and Her Six Sons

Rabbi Shmuel Pliskin (Baltimore)

Translation by Meir Razy

Ethel's house stood at the top of a hill that, as a child, I thought was a "high mountain." A magnificent building stood on the side of this hill. It was the only Beit Midrash in Lingmian. Ethel's house was not large, but we, the children of the town, considered it a palace, and Ethel was the mistress of that palace.

Her husband, Rabbi Eliyahu, had died in his prime, leaving her alone with six young orphans. All those who knew him still remember his fine qualities. He was a humble man; a handsome black beard surrounded his full, pale cheeks. The eyes showed tenderness and kindness. He was tall and his athletic body projected courage and bravery. His voice was pleasant and always expressed friendship and love. And suddenly this powerful and handsome tree was cut off from both our town and his poor wife, the righteous Ethel, who was left a widow with six sons.

The tragedy, however, did not suppress or break her spirit. On the contrary, this great disaster became the impetus which strengthened her spirit and body. She decided to raise her children despite all obstacles.

It is true that her ready, natural laughter became more gloomy. However, her face showed a spirit of steel and her black eyes glistened and expressed determination. She was ready for any endeavor or task, but only if it would be useful in the education of her children.

No task was too difficult for her. She baked and cooked, washed and ironed, all so that her six children would not starve. And what was most astonishing about her was that despite all the hard work and daunting worries, she always had a funny joke or just something nice to say.

[Col. 1266]

She spent little time worrying about her own life. She gave her children the best of everything but she paid particular attention to their education and schooling. She would not allow any of them to stop their studies in order to help her support the family.

After completing their studies in the local "Cheders", she sent them to the best Lithuanian Yeshivas and her aspiration was for her sons to rise up the ladder of Torah and wisdom and knowledge.

It is no wonder that this woman was famous throughout the region as a wonderful mother. For her contribution to the Torah education of her children, the public metaphorically crowned her with a crown of glory. Their praise matched her family name, Zar, or "Zer", the Hebrew word for wreath or crown.

Her eldest son was Shmuel Leib, who later became known as Dr. Shmuel Leib Zar, the famous director of Yeshiva University in New York. He was a professor of Literature, Biblical Studies and a well–known scientist.

He was the first to succeed in connecting the world of Torah to the world of science. He not only served as an example for all his brothers but also for many of his friends and fellow students.

Shmuel Leib was born on the 17th day of Adar, 1893 in Lingmian. His first teacher was a Melamed from Utena, Lithuania. His second teacher was one of his relatives, Rabbi Ya'akov of Tauragnai. He then moved on to the Cheder of Rabbi Shimon Ze'ev Hacohen Katz, who was already considered a "special" educator. He truly opened the treasures of Torah and wisdom to the talented young man and instilled in him a passionate love for the people of Israel and for the idea of Jewish Nationhood.

This great Rabbi Shimon Ze'ev, the illustrious Melamed, happened to be my uncle, (husband of Feiga Beila, my mother's sister), and I had the privilege of knowing him. He was a gifted teacher and educator and all the wealthy people in town sent their children to study with him.

[Col. 1267]

Rabbi Shimon Ben Yehuda Leib Katz

When the talented young man Shmuel Leib arrived at his Cheder, Rabbi Shimon Ze'ev immediately recognized the wonderful qualities of this new student and began to encourage and support him.

Shmuel Leib was even made the study partner of the Rabbi's son for one study session (=semester). This distinction was a hint of what was to come in the future. Everyone considered him special as the Rabbi himself had wanted to teach his own son in the company of Shmuel Leib.

The young Shmuel Leib moved from Lingmian to the Vidz Yeshiva where he studied under the Gaon Rabbi Leib, who himself later moved and became the head of the Rabbinate of Vilkomir. It is interesting to note that Rabbi Yosef Kahaneman who succeeded Rabbi Leib in Lingmian became known as the Rabbi of Ponevezh and founded the Yeshiva in Bnei Brak and Old–age Homes in the State of Israel.

Shmuel Leib went to study in Ponevezh with the teacher known as "the Gaon Rabbi Shlomo Ezra". He was known to recruit only the most talented scholars, those who would be able to understand his innovations and his method of Torah interpretation.

From Ponevezh Shmuel Leib moved to Seduva, to the Yeshiva of Rabbi Yosef Bloch, where he studied for more than five years. Later, Rabbi Yosef was called to succeed his father–in–law, Rabbi Eliezer Gordon, in Telz. When the famous Gaon Rabbi Aharon Baksht arrived at Seduva, the young Shmuel Leib was appointed as his assistant at the Yeshiva. (Rabbi Aaron Baksht was also widely known as Rabbi Arzik Iveyer).

Rabbi Meir Tzvi Jung was the Rabbi of Uhersky Brod (today in the Czech Republic) at that time. He was gathering young Lithuanian men and preparing them to become Rabbis in the Jewish communities of Austria–Hungary. In addition to Jewish studies he would also teach them foreign languages (German and Latin) as well as secular studies: arithmetic, history, etc.

Shmuel Leib was one of only three young men chosen from all of the Lithuanian Yeshivas for this privilege. Thus, the eldest son of Ethel Zar arrived at the city of Vienna, the capital of the Austro–Hungarian Empire. He devoted five hours a day to his Jewish studies and the rest of the day to general studies. Professor Silverman, Rabbi Jung's brother–in–law, became Shmuel Leib's patron and his studies supervisor.

Later, Rabbi Meir Zvi Jung moved to serve as Chief Rabbi of British Jewry and settled in London. Shortly thereafter he invited Ethel's son, Shmuel Leib from Lingmian, to join him in London. There, he was a guest at the Chief Rabbi's house.

[Col. 1268]

Shmuel Leib arrived in Baltimore, USA in 1914, and was accepted as a student at the Faculty of Medicine. His goal was to become a physician and not to use the Torah knowledge and expertise as his income–producing profession.

Professor Reed, who was the head of the Institute of Medicine, advised his new student to change his course of study and transfer to the faculty of Law. Shmuel Leib followed the advice of his teacher and enrolled there.

In 1919, less than five years after his arrival in the United States, Shmuel Leib was invited to come to New York and become the head of the Yeshiva named after Rabbi Yitzhak Elchanan (=the institute was later renamed Yeshiva University). At the same time he began to teach Talmud, Jewish History, Hebrew Literature and Bible at the University. Soon after he was awarded his Doctorate degree and his name became recognized both as a scientist and researcher.

This son of Lingmian is now considered one of the key people who helped advance New York's Yeshiva University to its current status as a leading Jewish–centered, higher–education institution.

Professor Shmuel–Leib Zar

Dr. Shmuel Leib Zar has been involved in most of the activities of the Jewish national religious circles in America. More than once he served as a faithful emissary to the Diaspora. He spent some time in Europe after the Second World War and helped organize the survivors and their immigration to the land of our forefathers.

Dr. Zar married the daughter of Rabbi Mordechai Gifter. His father–in–law was a native of Seduva, Lithuania. His son is a well–known physician in New York and his daughter Esther is the wife of Rabbi Avraham Zoref of Baltimore (head of the Yeshiva in Brooklyn).

This is the brief history of eldest son of Mrs. Ethel Zar, the widow of Rabbi Eliyahu of Lingmian.

[Col. 1269]

The second brother, Yehuda–Yudel, chose a different path in life. He arrived in the United States a long time before Samuel Leib. He set foot in the New World before the outbreak of the First World War. Yehuda worked hard to support himself and moved from place to place and from job to job until he found his place in the field of drama. He was a talented actor in both the Jewish and English theaters.

As soon as the Jewish Legion was created in 1915, Yehuda volunteered for the Legion and was sent to England. His desire was to fight for the liberation of the Land of Israel from Turkish occupation.

Upon his return to England after the war, he studied optics and began distributing eye–glasses, first in Ireland and then in Scotland. Eventually he moved to London where he continued his entrepreneurship.

Ethel's third son chose yet another way of life. His name was Nissan, and he too studied in different Cheders and Yeshivas. Eventually he became a schoolteacher. Over the years he became known as an excellent speaker and devoted all his energies to the Zionist movement and the settlement of the Land of Israel. In addition, he wrote and published articles in the Jewish press.

The Jewish immigration movement grew especially quickly once the Russian Government began pushing the Jews out of their traditional occupations. Nissan emigrated to South Africa where he opened a large and successful general store. He was considered one of the most successful Jewish merchants in the country.

Most of the Jewish community in South Africa is of Lithuanian origin. Nissan is a much respected activist within the community and well–known as an educator, a writer and a public speaker.

Ethel's fourth son, Rabbi Zvi (Hirschel), immigrated to Eretz Israel and is involved with the organization of the Sventzian district expats. He dedicates a great deal of time and energy to the memory of his hometown, which was utterly destroyed by the German oppressors and their Lithuanians cohorts during World War II. He is the only one of Lingmian's survivors who documented the history of the town, its life and institutions, its people and its leaders. In doing so he erected an eternal monument in the form of a book, in memory of our martyrs, the Jews of Lingmian. These were simple and hard–working people, people who studied Gemara and recited the Psalms, murdered and massacred for no reason other than their Jewishness.

Zvi, Ethel's fourth son, began studying in Hebrew Cheder at the age of five. At the age of 7 he was sent to the teacher Binyamin Abba, a bookbinder, and with him studied Chumash (=the Torah) and Rashi (interpretations). His mother then sent him to study in the small Yeshiva (= a Yeshiva for younger students) in the town of Utena, Lithuania when he was only 9 years old.

[Col. 1270]

The arrangement for out of town students consisted of being fed at assigned homes each day of the week ("eating days"). He used to sleep at a relative's home who owned a bakery. Since her apartment was very small, the boy from Lingmian slept on sacks of flour.

At the age of 12 he moved from Utena to Ponevezh, where he attended the Great Yeshiva under the direction of Rabbi Meir Nathan. There, too, he was fed through the "eating days" arrangement and slept in a dormitory with the other students. He continued his studies and all his teachers and instructors praised him and his work.

The boy wanted to expand his knowledge and three years later he moved to Vilna. Although only fifteen years old, he was accepted at the famous Yeshiva of Ramailis. The spirit of "Enlightenment" was all over Vilna in those days and the young man from Lingmian got the taste of it. Zvi was influenced by the general atmosphere that engulfed the Vilna youth and started reading secular books in the Strashun Library.

Modern Hebrew literature made a significant impact on his life. He started writing and publishing articles in the daily press describing the various types of people he met in the alleys around the synagogues and in the famous Schulhoff district in Vilna.

This, of course, became known to the Head of the Yeshiva, Rabbi Pinchas, and the boy was expelled. Zvi immediately became a regular visitor to the library and diligently continued reading the books.

Meanwhile World War I broke out and the young man was taken as a forced laborer by the German army. He suffered from hunger and cold for the next 18 months.

After the war, he joined Tze'irei Zion (=The Youth of Zion) and was busy working day and night for Zionist causes. He saw no future for Jewish life in Europe and all he wished for was to immigrate to Eretz Israel.

In 1925 he finally managed to achieve his dream and immigrated to Eretz Israel. He had not forgotten his hometown and his mother, Ethel, the most precious person in his life. Immediately after World War II, he devoted himself to helping the survivors. He was elected to the Association of former residents of the Sventzian district.

The fifth son, Shimon, naturally studied in the Cheder and the Yeshiva, but all he wanted was to help his mother. He stayed at home and was the only son who did not move away from his beloved mother. The only time he was separated from his mother was when he was drafted into the army.

He married Libba–Ahuva, the youngest daughter of Rabbi Akiva Itzikowitz and his wife Ethel. He made his living as the owner of a shop he received from his father–in–law.

Rabbi Akiva Itzikowitz was the son of a Shochet, Rabbi Chana from the town of Paliush. He emigrated to the United States and served as a Shochet in Kansas City for many years.

[Col. 1271]

Shimon, too, did not stay in Lingmian for many years. He took his family and his dear mother to South Africa where he found a decent living.

Mrs. Ethel Zar passed away in South Africa. The modest, hard working woman saw all her orphan children rise both in social and in economic status. Her soul remains remembered forever!

Ethel's sixth and youngest son was Ephraim. He probably was smarter and more educated than all his brothers. He was a good–looking youth, tall and dignified, almost an image of both his father and his mother. All who knew him predicted a brilliant future.

Ephraim was only three years older than me. He studied in the Cheder of Rabbi Yosef Walman and later moved to the Melamdim Rabbi Binyamin Horowitz and Rabbi Shimon Ze'ev. He soon became known as a prodigy.

Rabbi Shimon Ze'ev was offered the position of the treasurer in the company of the forest merchants the Gilinsky brothers, his previous students. Ephraim then went to study with the Gemara Melamed Rabbi Israel Chaim Hurwitz (who later served as the Rabbi and Shochet of Lingmian).

This Rabbi and teacher was my stepfather. He was killed, along with my mother, by the defiled Germans together with the rest of the town's Jews. Let G–d revenge their death!

Once the great Rabbi Yosef Kahaneman visited Lingmian and noticed the talented young Ephraim. He liked the boy and when he was called to sit on the rabbinate in the community of Ponevezh and to lead the Yeshiva of the Gaon Rabbi Itzela, he immediately invited Ephraim to study Torah in his Beit Midrash.

Ephraim accepted the invitation from Ponevezh and shortly after arriving at the Yeshiva he became known, once again, as a young genius.

[Col. 1272]

I too had the privilege of studying at the Ponevezh Yeshiva. I arrived there about three years after Ephraim, who was already loved and accepted by all the Yeshiva students.

From Ponevezh we both went on to the Chafetz Chaim Yeshiva in Radin. There we found hundreds of young men sitting day and night, studying Torah and wisdom. Even among them the young man from Lingmian immediately distinguished himself and was recognized as being intelligent, both well–versed and well–rounded. His way of studying amazed all his acquaintances and teachers and the son–in–law of the Chafetz Chaim, the Gaon Rabbi Zachs SHALITA, chose him specifically as his study partner.

In 1936 he married the daughter of the Rabbi of Horodyszcze and was immediately appointed as Rosh Yeshiva in the city of Nowogrsdek. He was only 22 years old at the time. A few years later, a large assembly of Rabbis convened in Vilna and Rabbi Chaim Ezer Grodensky referred to him as “the young genius.”

His new methods of understanding the Torah, his special way of study, his sharpness and his fame, made his name known all over Poland.

At the outbreak of the Second World War he moved with all his students to Vilna and hoped that he would be able to escape to the free world.

To our dismay and great pain he was unable to carry out his plan. In the early days of the German occupation, he and hundreds of other Rabbis and Yeshiva students were taken to the vicinity of Ponary, where they were all executed by human predatory animals.

The House of Israel, wherever it is, should mourn this great loss to our nation. This destruction removed a significant community, rich in Torah and culture, that promised glory to future generations.

Be the memory of this righteous man and genius, Rabbi Ephraim Zar of Lingmian, blessed forever.

G–d will revenge his blood!

[Col. 1273]

The Esteemed Scholar Rabbi Efraim Zar (May his named be avenged by God)

Rabbi Khayim Khaykl Greenberg

Translation by Janie Respitz

The greatness of the great scholar from Lingmian, Rabbi Efraim Zar lay in knowledge and sharpness. He was considered the best student of the Chafetz Chaim in the Yeshiva in Radin.

Even outwardly he made a big impression on everyone. His stately appearance, kindness, virtuous traits and comprehension, his wonderful memory and deep intellect, his knowledge and intelligence spread his name among all the yeshivas. Everyone was in awe of him and people talked about him with love and respect. I heard from my Rabbi, the esteemed scholar from Vilna Rabbi Khayim Ozer, may his name be a blessing, interesting praise. He said Rabbi Efraim from Lingmian was like a cupboard filled with books. This was in fact the truth. In Rabbi Ephraim's personality there were many characteristics that made him one of the greatest Torah scholars of our generation. He combined the power of Torah and strict piety with the strength of perseverance and love of humanity. He was a rare genius and everyone saw a great future for him in the rabbinic world.

Besides learning he was loved by all as a dear friend and brother.

His home in Vilna, on Zavalne Street was always open. Refugees, rabbis and students from the Yeshiva were always warmly received with a kind word, comfort, and advice and material aid.

During the Soviet occupation when everyone ran deep into Russia and were saved in Vladivostok, Japan and China, he remained in Lithuania. This is where he met Hitler's beasts, and together with thousands of others he was killed in Ponar.

May his soul be bound in the bond of life!

[Col. 1274]

The Jewish population of the town when it first emerged was very small. The Hasidic community was comprised of merely tens of followers. You could not earn a living as beadle of the shul. Therefore his wife supported him and sold dairy products. She made cheeses. Like many women in those days, she would go to the train station and sell her cheese to passengers. Worn out from their difficult life, they never complained. Quietly and piously they worked hard at their individual jobs.

The Beadle of the Hasidic Shul in Ignalina with his wife

[Col. 1275]

The Economic Situation in Lingmian Between the Two Wars

According to the Pinchas of Lithuania, Yekapo register, 1931

Translation by Anita Frishman Gabbay

Of the 150 families of Lingmian, 50 were Jewish.

Before WW1, Lingmian was a lively city of trade. The main product was fruit, mainly cherries, mushrooms and berries.

The trade of these products was sold on a large scale.

In the shtetl there were several important large Jewish merchants who dealt in flax and other produce. Another important source of trade came from fish and lobsters.

Then, by 1914, there were over 130 Jewish families, about 25 shopkeepers and dozens of artisans.

Everyone earned a living and in hindsight, everyone in Lingmian made a good living.

In 1915, when the Germans occupied our region, many Jewish families fled to Russia. Only part of them returned when the area was returned to the former regime.

In 1919, Lingmian became the border between Lithuania and Poland. The border went right through the city and the cemetery found itself both on Polish and on Lithuanian territory.

It happened that in one family, part had to enter the cemetery through the Polish gate, the other through the Lithuanian gate. The Lithuanian regime was very strict, and made sure no one used the wrong gate.

All the fields belonging to the Christian population were on the Lithuanian side and every day, in order to work their fields, they had to get special permission from the Sventzian authorities to cross the border.

Also the animals that left for the fields needed a different “pass”. In the evening, the border patrol reviewed their list to check who returned to their shtetl.

Until 1929 no one was able to enter the shtetl without this special pass from the Sventzian mayor. Life in the shtetl was similar to the days when the front existed, a war was going on.

At night, when the sun went down, a signal using the chiming church bells was given, and this meant it was strictly forbidden to leave your home until five the next morning.

If someone was caught in the streets after hours, he was arrested by the military patrol and he had a hefty fine to pay.

It is understood that this way of life for ten years eventually ruined the shtetl. In this type of situation it was difficult to arrange a market day, as was organized in the other shtetls. The situation was more difficult in Lingmian, even the peasants didn't have the means with which to attend Church on Sundays

Eventually everyone got used to not coming to Lingmian. It is no wonder that the shopkeepers of Lingmian barely made a living. The bakeries and the Inns closed. The merchants closed their shops. No one wanted to get permits and pay taxes, it was worthless.

Having no choice, a small barter–trade between towns emerged, but earnings were smaller.

In the village we bought some products, flax, groats, a calf, butter. The Jewish tradesmen sold the Christian folk various products such as trimmings, pottery, and textile–goods.

Earnings were small. The labour was very tiresome and the tax collectors added to our problems when they came for their tax. Other ways to pay the tax was with a cow, a horse, a cushion, corn meal or other such things.

In the end, the younger generation began to leave the shtetl. Many immigrated to America and Africa and the rest to Eretz Israel. The only ones that remained were the poor people home with these poor souls who found the situation very difficult.

Thanks to the help of our American friends many souls were saved from starvation and poverty.

[Col. 1277]

Dukstas

(Dukštas, Lithuania)

55°32'/26°20'

[Col. 1279]

On Polish – Lithuanian Soil

Chaim Grade

Translated by Janie Respitz

—Were you only from straw and moss
That the wind , without vestige could carry you away?
My poor Sabbath, my holy ecstatic week,
Who will now recite the mourner's prayer for you?
The market place is full with merchants and villager's wagons,
The fairs are bustling and joyfully noisy,
The village virgins bow to the stone Jesus,
As if they were thanking him because there were no longer any Jews.

Fathers dreaming, your stringy beards
Are now the autumn spider webs, that hang in the air,
They hang like harps on the river banks of Babylon…rusty
On willows bent over Polish – Lithuanian soil.
A flood of water, that ends, leaves no signs
As our settlement here has been abandoned,
Only I see, on the porches of our occupied homes –
A shadow of the side locks that are blown and scream in the wind.
I search on the road for the prayer shawl I spun
From stories of our Shtetl, cemetery legends and worker's songs.
If I could only find a piece of my torn prayer shawl –
I would spin it again.

[Col. 1281]

The History of the Town of Dūkštas

By B. Davidowitz

Translation by Meir Razy

The town was named after the close-by Dūkštas estate that belonged to the well-known land-owner in the area, the Polish aristocrat Zechan. The town, located between the two big cities of Vilnius and Dvinsk, was founded around 1860 with the completion of the railroad linking Warsaw and Leningrad (St Petersburg in those days).

The earliest Jewish residents in Dūkštas were Shneur Zalman Levin and the Kopilovsky family. Shneur Zalman Levin was a very respected timber trader who was my maternal grandfather. The Kopilovsky family was also engaged in timber trading. Several Jew who rented forests in the surrounding area followed. The Jewish community was founded by about ten families whose businesses were based on the forest, wood and timber. When they moved from their plots of forest to the town, they wanted to maintain their presence on their leased forest land. As a consequence, they left their sons or married daughters living on the estates of the land-owners.

The number of trains passing through Dūkštas increased rapidly and the increased business helped build up the Jewish population of the town. Various branches of commerce developed in the town thanks to the local train station.

The train would often bring cars loaded with flour, oil, barrels with salted fish, groceries and other commodities needed for the town and the surrounding rural population.

The Jews took advantage of this opportunity and began exporting local commodities. They bought beef, pork, grain and fruit from the peasants and from the land-owners and shipped it all to the big cities. This trade greatly improved the economic situation and created new opportunities, making the whole district very attractive to new settlers, especially Jews.

The Jewish population grew every year and reached about 600 by the end of the 19th century. This was a relatively large number for towns in those days. Jewish merchants soon opened many shops in town: grocery, textile, notions, leather goods, etc.

[Col. 1282]

The proximity of the train station brought occasional traders and visitors to the town. Travelling agents and other passengers needed places to stay, sometimes even for several days and some Jews took the opportunity to open hotels and restaurants. The hospitality industry developed rapidly and employed many families, directly or indirectly providing related services.

Meanwhile, the timber trade of the Levin family was growing. Hundreds of workers and porters were busy in this industry. The booming economic situation attracted hundreds of small craftsmen and merchants and a large, well-established Jewish community developed in the town of Dūkštas.

Rabbi Schneur Zalman Levin, the richest man in the community, was elected as its leader. He brought in a Rabbi, a slaughterer and providers of other religious services and the town developed a traditional Jewish character. Later on, his eldest son, Rabbi Abba Noah Levin, succeeded him as the leader of the community. This is how the Levin family helped shape the town for many years and became the main influence on its social and economic life.

[Col. 1283]

Nothing in town would happen without first consulting the distinguished Levin family. Dūkštas became a kind of tiny monarchy of the Levins.

The economic situation prospered until the First World War. Merchants from Riga and St Petersburg, Vilnius and Warsaw arrived at Dūkštas and various types of trade flourished. Companies trading in flax, geese, beef, fruits and crabs were established and the standard of living of the local residents continued to improve.

The Jewish community decided to build a magnificent synagogue. Each resident donated generously and secured a “place” for him and his whole family in the synagogue (a place was called “a shtat” in Yiddish).

The Jewish population continued to expand and it became clear that one synagogue could not accommodate the crowd. A second synagogue was built, smaller but beautiful and convenient. They were called “the Great Synagogue” and “the Little Synagogue”.

The good name of Dūkštas attracted emissaries from Yeshivas, wandering Jewish preachers (=Magid), cantors, and various other religious types. These guests needed a place to stay, “a hospitality house” as was the custom in every established community. All the lumber and building materials were naturally donated by Rabbi Aba Noah Levin, the wealthy merchant.

A large–size, tiled fire–place was built inside the hotel so the guests could sleep on it during the long, cold winter nights. Rabbi Abba Moshe, a poor Jew, was appointed as the caretaker of this hotel. He was given a free apartment in lieu of salary for his work.

This man was the official Torah Reader in the Great Synagogue. He was paid on Holidays and other occasions by placing a plate on the table so that people would leave a few coins in it on their way out.

In addition, he also had a side job as a MELAMED, teachings young children the prayers and Torah. However, his multiple callings he did not earn enough to support his family.

The town of Dūkštas stood in a favorable location: two rivers flowed near it. Lake Disna, which provided an endless supply of high quality fish, was about 3 kilometers away. It was also a wonderful place of entertainment for the town's young people. On summer evenings, the younger generation would flock to the row boats and would joyously sing and dance for hours on the shore.

On the other side of the town was another large lake, called the Dūkštas Lake. The townspeople, even the elders, used to go there and bathe in its water on hot summer days, especially on Fridays. Everyone would eagerly await the end of the “Counting” when bathing was forbidden (=the forty nine days between Passover and Shavuot). Immediately afterwards, all the residents, no matter their ages, would rush to bathe in the river and swim in its cool, fresh water.

[Col. 1284]

The lake lay about a mile from the town and many would come by their cart. The youth preferred, of course, to walk.

The road to the lake was both pretty and interesting. Fertile, fresh, crop–bearing fields of wheat stretched on both sides. Thick forests, where all kinds of berries, mushrooms and nuts could be found in abundance, stood not far away. Flocks of young man and young women, teenagers, boys and girls would go to the forest during the month of Menachem Av (=July and August) and return home with baskets full of nuts, fruit and various berries. The trips to the river and the lake, walking together into the nearby forests, always gave the participants unforgettable and enjoyable experiences. To this day, it's hard for me to forget those wonderful times.

These were the glorious days of childhood. I remember, for example, how we would play all kinds of games, running and jumping along the way and having fun until sunset.

Sometimes it is hard to imagine that all this was erased and destroyed, that all this life was ravaged and disappeared from the face of the earth.

And while I am reminiscing, other pictures hover in front of me. I can see an interesting picture that took place almost every morning in those days:

I see Jews, early–risers, rushing before dawn to the synagogues for morning prayers. I see the shadows of their figures, holding prayer shawls and Tefillin under their arms, rushing to serve the Creator. They enter the synagogue, wrap the prayer shawls around themselves, place the Tefillin and sing a hymn. As the house of G–d fills up - morning prayers are heard throughout the whole universe.

The children of Israel used to go to a Cheder at an early age in Dūkštas. There were always good, wise Melameds in town, and the standard of learning was high. Study time in all the Cheders was from morning till evening and sometimes even until late at night. Some of the Melameds knew Gemara and had a special higher status. It is interesting to note that almost no attention was paid to the study of the Bible in those days.

A modern teacher arrived in town just before World War I. He taught Bible, History, Hebrew and Arithmetic to the children. Some of the parents were frightened by the horrible "Epicurus" and removed their children from his school.

[Col. 1285]

The young people who wished to benefit from a more general education had to leave town in order to pursue their studies. They moved to the bigger towns and cities. Some of them even entered university. Among them were some members of the famous Levin family.

On the eve of World War I a big fight broke out in the town, after the city Shochet (=slaughterer) passed away. Rabbi Abba Noah Levin immediately brought another Shochet from a nearby town but the general public did not like him. Rabbi Aba Noah was already losing his power over the community in those days and a number of the homeowners dared to oppose his choice.

Among the "rebels" were: Rabbi Avraham Shmuel Reeves, Israel Lurie, Mendel Podvitz, Shaul Bar Shinovitz, my own grandfather and my father. They argued that the new slaughterer was not well–versed in the SHAS (=Mishna) and his Jewish knowledge was based solely on the "Ein Yaakov" book (an interpretation of the TALMUD, published 1516). They wanted to disqualify him as a professional because of this "flaw".

The whole town was divided into two rival camps: one camp included the large and powerful Levin family and all the artisans, the workers and the officials who depended on the Levin's businesses. They were careful about supporting their source of income. The other camp included most of the homeowners (=middle class) and the independent merchants. The disagreement lasted for a long time but when the First World War broke out, the public had other, more important concerns.

The warfront was not far from the town and trains carrying wounded soldiers would often pass through the train station. The Jewish public desired to help the unfortunate wounded. My brother, Israel Davidovich, and his friends, Idelman and Podvitz, organized a special team providing the injured soldiers with warm milk and fruit. Help was given to every wounded person, regardless of whether he was a Christian or a Jew.

This activity did not last for long as my brother was soon drafted into the army. Soon afterwards most of the town's Jews were forced to relocate. Only a few Jewish families stayed in Dūkštas, among them the Levin family. They hid on the farm of a Christian peasant. The peasant family cared for the forest land the Levins had bought from the Polish nobleman.

The town was almost completely destroyed during the war years, only ruins remained. Houses were demolished and robbed; sometimes the robbers ripped even the doors and windows and stole the wooden panels off the walls.

When the fighting was over and the armistice was signed, the residents began returning to the ruins of their homes in order to rebuild the town. However, the four years of the war instilled a new spirit in the Jewish population and there was a desire to change and modernize their way of life. The youth began to get organized, a modern new public library was built and most importantly – they decided to create a Jewish school where the language of instruction would be Yiddish.

This matter, of course, was not easy to do. There was no building suitable as an educational institution in the entire town. There was no source of even a minimal budget either, but they still insisted on setting up the school despite all the difficulties.

[Col. 1286]

There is a popular Hebrew saying: "If you put your mind to it, you can accomplish anything". Well, we put our mind to it and started looking for a building. As the Great Synagogue remained almost intact, we decided to set up the school in the Women's Section of the synagogue. The organizing committee included Bezalel Levin, Lippman Levy, Tzipa Levin, Elijah Himmelfarb and several other public figures.

After finding the building, we encountered another problem no less challenging. It was difficult finding suitable teachers. Not every Jewish teacher was willing to teach in Yiddish. After much effort, two uncertified teachers were finally found. One was Gluz, a good teacher who was well versed in Russian and German literature and had a good knowledge of Biblical Hebrew, however he had no organizational skills. Except for teaching his classes he didn't understand and didn't want to understand anything. He was always immersed in reading books and sometimes did not even notice when someone entered his house.

The other teacher was a totally different type. His name was Motil Gilinsky and he was brimming with energy and initiative. He was the son of a painter from the nearby city of Sventzian. The whole town, both students and their parents, were enchanted by him from the minute he arrived in town. Unfortunately, he did not stay in Dūkštas for long. He left town when the Teachers' School was opened in Vilnius and went on to continue his studies. At the seminar he acquired the nickname Batke, that is "father". That nickname stayed with him for the rest of his life.

After he graduated from the Teacher's Seminar he moved on to Warsaw and managed the sanatorium "Madam" for many years. He returned to his hometown of Sventzian at the outbreak of World War II. After the liquidation of the ghetto he was transferred to the Vilna Ghetto and from there to Estonia. There, he was killed along with thousands of other Jews.

The Yiddish School was located in the Women's Section of the synagogue for many years. The public opposed this and the school management rented two rooms from an old Jewish woman, Frida Hamburg. Her narrow, small apartment could not accommodate all the classes and the children had to study in two shifts. The children and the teachers suffered from this arrangement but they managed to hold on despite the poor conditions.

Frida Hamburg and her family. Her apartment housed

the Jewish school

[Col. 1287]

Over time, a Drama Club was established by the school's management, and all of the income from the performances was dedicated to improving the school and its financial state. With the initiative of the Asher brothers and Schneur Segal, they bought a plot of land and started building a suitable, spacious building for the school.

A festive inauguration ceremony was held in 1930, with many guests from all around. Notable guests were: Senator Dr. Tzemach Shabad of Vilnius and A. Klianski, a member of the Managing Committee of the Jewish Schools Organization[T.I.S.H.O]. The school provided quality education and many of its graduates successfully attended high schools and the Seminary in Vilnius.

Nine years passed. World War II broke out and all that effort and toil was lost. Dūkštas found itself under the Soviet rule for two years. Life was not easy, but at least it was possible to live. People found it difficult to get used to the new arrangements of the Soviet rule as everyone had been used to their individual freedoms and private initiatives. No one could imagine that it was still “the lesser of two evils” that was awaiting them.

[Col. 1288]

A memorial at the grave in the Zagrin Forest

The Germans entered the town in August 1941 and the Lithuanian murderers arrived with them too. A month later, almost all of the Jewish population was taken to the Zagrin forest and murdered by these human animals.

This is how the light of the community of Dūkštas has extinguished forever. A Jewish town, working, functioning, cultured and social was erased from the face of the earth.

G–d shall revenge the blood of all the inhabitants of Dūkštas. Their memory will be forever cherished in the history of the Jewish Nation.

[Col. 1287]

The First Hebrew School

By Shmuel Dobkin

Translation by Meir Razy

I had the great privilege of being among the teachers of Torah and knowledge in several of the Jewish communities in the Sventzian district near Vilna. There, I was involved in the education of young children, teaching love for the nation of Israel and the Land of Eretz Israel.

Whenever I remember that distant time that has already sunk into oblivion, all those little towns, their Hebrew schools, their students and their parents, their businesses, their livelihoods and the zeal of their labor appear once again before my eyes.

From the outside these towns seemed very similar in almost every respect: economically, culturally and socially. However, once anyone closely examined their life they noticed that each town had its very own character and special unique features.

[Col. 1288]

Of all these towns, the one that remains in my heart to this day and stands out for me, is Dūkštas, the community that left me with many fond memories. My memories from Dūkštas are embedded in my heart as the most profound experiences I have ever had in my life, both as a teacher and an educator.

It was a primordial experience in two senses: this was the beginning of my work as a teacher in a Hebrew school and I was the first teacher in that school. So I was privileged to be among the founders of the national Hebrew education in the Diaspora and of the Zionist youth movement. I went through the initial struggle of establishing the Hebrew School in Dūkštas and was among those who shaped its character and outlined its path to the future.

The town of Dūkštas was located near two borders: on the one side – the Lithuanian border and on the other – the border of the state of Latvia.

The town, one long street of wooden and stone houses, sat on a hill. A number of small alleys branched out from the main street.

[Col. 1289]

Two beautiful synagogues in the middle of the town served the community. The rich and affluent residents prayed in the Great Synagogue while the small synagogue served the so–called laymen and the poor. Public opinions were formed and public affairs were decided in the Great Synagogue.

The market and almost all the shops were located down the street. Local farmers came to the market once a week, bringing their best produce for sale. They bought their own supplies and other necessities in the market as–well. Most of the town's residents made their living from trading during the market day.

The TARBUT School

The railway that linked Riga with Warsaw passed through town and was the economic engine of its development. A narrow railroad linked Dūkštas to the towns of Braslav–Druya. The train station was a significant factor in the expansion of the wholesale trade, especially in flax, grain and timber.

One of the most famous companies in the area was named after its owners and founders: Kovarsky – Himmelfarb. Other important companies were those of the Luria brothers, Aaron Kacherginsky and Levin. Dozens of accountants, bookkeepers, and various clerks manned the offices of all these companies.

The railway station was not only an economic factor, but also a cultural and social one. Travelers would bring the latest "big–world" news as well as the "Jewish–world" news to town. Here the townspeople met acquaintances and friends from near and far and this expanded their knowledge and opened the news of the world's progress to them.

The train station hummed with activity during most of the day and evening, busy with travelers and visitors. Young people and residents who assembled there during their leisure time, especially on holidays, added to the commotion.

The Dūkštas Jewish community was not large, yet it had a vibrant cultural and social life. Although the residents were busy during most of the week with their work and businesses, they still found time to engage in public and cultural affairs.

[Col. 1290]

In this respect, the town earned a good reputation throughout the region and in various matters it even became an example to other towns.

In 1927 I was invited by the distinguished businessman, Mr. Bezalel Levin, to serve as the first teacher and educator at the newly established Hebrew School. We met for the first time in Vilna and I learned that just a few months earlier a few parents and community leaders decided to open a local Hebrew School. From the conversation with him it became clear to me that they were not satisfied with their children's education in the Yiddish school. They did not want their youth kept away from "national" values. In general, Yiddish education opposed Zionism and instilled animosity towards it and its goal of returning to Zion.

The founding of the Hebrew School surprised the leaders of the Yiddish School who, for several years, opposed the new educational institution.

I had many hesitations when Mr. Bezalel Levin tried to recruit me for this endeavor. I was a young man at the time, I had no experience in public and political struggles and I feared that I would not be able to take on the responsibility. On the other hand, I was full of ambition and ideals and the "fight" against those who rejected Zionism attracted me.

Mr. Levin apparently understood my hesitation and encouraged me and by the end of our conversation I expressed my agreement to the proposal. I took on this challenge as the goal of my life.

I arrived in Dūkštas on a cold, windy winter night and was greeted by the members of the school board, representatives of Zionist youth associations and some students, at the train station.

My first stop was at the home of Rabbi Asher Davidovich, the teacher of Jewish Studies at the school. He was a good man and a loyal friend who greeted me with happiness and an open heart. His wife, who exhibited cleverness, wisdom and nobility, took care of me so my first feeling was that I was joining a loving community.

I started teaching at the school the next day. The institution was in a rented building at the end of the main street. The walls had not yet been plastered and all the surroundings were indicative of the huge challenge ahead of me.

The kids sat quietly and were so nice that I forgot all about the difficult task and the struggle ahead of me. The first day passed in exhilaration. The children were attentive and industrious and that made me all more want to fight and overcome any challenges.

In addition to Davidovich I found another teacher at the school. He was Leib Opeskin of Vilnius, who died later as a partisan in the Vilnius (Vilna) ghetto during World War II. He was a very educated Jew who had a poetic and gentle soul.

[Col. 1291]

Although he himself was a graduate of the Yiddish School, he immediately joined the effort to develop the Hebrew School and with all his energy he developed a superb pedagogical study plan.

We found that the pro–Yiddish camp was telling parents that many subjects cannot be taught in Hebrew. As a result, we decided in our first meeting, to prove to the Yiddish camp that they were wrong and misleading in this matter and that the children would actually achieve no less in Hebrew than in Yiddish. And, perhaps even more!

After raising the pedagogical level of the school, we turned our efforts to improving its finances. We found that the financial situation was not sound and we had to look for additional sources of income. To that end, we occasionally performed children's stage–plays and all the income was devoted to improving the school's financial foundation.

Over time, our shows became famous and the public eagerly awaited them. Of course we put a lot of effort into rehearsals. We were forced to work in the afternoons and evenings and the outcome of our labor benefited the school in many ways. The shows were educational, artistically successful and added fairly decent amounts of money to the meager budget.

The audience did not forget our first Purim show for a long time. The hall was filled to the brim. Parents, acquaintances and neighbors attended. There were brothers, sisters, grandparents and even just plain city people who wanted to hear a live spoken Hebrew word. The play made a great impression on the public in town and even the Yiddish circles were amazed and cheered. For many, hearing Hebrew sparked tears.

Our success was so great that we were invited to appear that summer in the nearby towns Ignalina and Rimshani. There, too, the performances were greeted with enthusiasm and appreciation.

Our school started attracting many young people. An excellent library of Hebrew and Yiddish books was created through the initiative of Mr. Bezalel Levin. Soon after, we started a marching band that paraded through the streets of Dūkštas on Lag Omer. The residents welcomed us with applause and love and the band advertised our school throughout the district of Sventzian.

The great success attracted the attention of the Polish authorities who started to look for ways to restrict us. They used all kinds of excuses. One time they did not like the principal. Another time – one of the teachers. There was always some flaw or offence in our work. After they had run out of all these reasons, they announced that the building was not appropriate for an educational institution. The threat was loud and clear. Unless we would find another building, we would not receive a license for the next school year.

[Col. 1292]

The founders and the leadership immediately began exploring various options in order to build a proper school building. Mr. Levin was able to purchase a spacious lot on a pretty hill, surrounded by meadows and fields. Then they began looking for financial means to start the construction work.

A loyal and dedicated member of the board, Aaron Kacherginsky, who was a successful timber merchant, was able to collect building materials from donors. It is interesting to note that even his Polish forest–owners acquaintances helped by donating timber and other building materials for free.

The result of all this effort was that in the fourth year of our school, during the holiday of Chanukah, we were able to celebrate the dedication of the new school building in a large public ceremony. Distinguished guests from out of the town arrived for this important celebration. Among them were Rabbi Yitzchak Rubinstein, Rabbi Klinbaum who was a leader in the Mizrachi Movement, Yerachmiel Korb who was the chairman of the Jewish community in nearby Ignalina and many other community workers from across the region. There was a real atmosphere of holiday in the town and happiness and exhilaration was felt in every home.

I had to leave Dūkštas and move to another educational institution about a year later. The departure was difficult for both me and the students and their parents. I felt that I had acquired many devoted friends in the town. I have since lived in several Polish cities and managed eventually to immigrate to Eretz–Israel, but throughout the years I kept in contact through letters with the people of Dūkštas. I was interested in everything that was happening to them. I was happy to receive their letters and keep up with the progress of the school in Dūkštas. I had the feeling that my labor was not in vain, I had worked hard and now, here were the fruits.

The correspondence continued until the outbreak of the Second World War. A few years later I could only mourn the destruction of the community and eulogize the murder of all my acquaintances and friends, all devoted and faithful.

BEITAR Youth

Sitting: **Bluma Hamburg, —,**
Standing: **Yacov Fludman, Rochel Shor, Shneur Korb, Reisenberg,—, Bluma Hamburg Beit Mendel, Basia Shvil**

Writing these memories inspire me and bring me satisfaction but, they also bring me pain and grief. Inspiration and satisfaction because it was one of the brightest periods of my creative life: pain and grief because everything was ruined and lost by human animals. Nothing is left.

Their memory shall remain etched forever in the history of the revival of the Jewish Nation. May G–d keep their souls forever.

[Col. 1293]

My Little Shtetle

By Ruben Hamburg

Translation by Anita Frishman Gabbay

My little shtetle Dukst were I was born and where I spent the best years of my youth, comes back to me now as if in a long lost and beautiful dream.

Until today, I remember every detail of my little shtetl. I can see the streets with their shops, the marketplace with tens of stalls, the mill with the electric power, the 2 Jewish Folk schools, the synagogue and the miniamin, the Holy aura during the "Days of Awe" (Yom Kippur), and other holidays, the Zionists and the "Yiddishists". All this is so near and dear to me and stands before my eyes.

I remember my little town with its beautiful nature, with her lakes and forests, hills and valleys, each placed where we used to play or stroll during the Shabbath. I remember those frosty winter days, when we used to sled down the higher hill, this was always a wonderful time for us, the children of Dukst.

It amazes me that I remember my dear home, without my dear and wonderful parents and without my entire family, which were so closely knit to each other.

My heart pines for them and my eyes are filled with tears, like flood waters from the Sea, and I think that there is no one to remember the Kushlins, the Segals, the Himmelfarbs, the Zainmans, the Shapiras, the Gedods, the Levines, the Rosenbergs, the Gurewitches, the Arons. I, alone, remain from my Hamburg family.

[Col. 1294]

Everyone perished at the hands of those murderous beasts! My sister Lipka perished in Vilna when she left the Ghetto. My cousins Bluma and Sara–Elka were shot on the way to the forest, where they wanted to reach the Partisans. My parents with my younger brother Smerele, died in the Dukst forest together with the Jews Malak, Rimsana, Turmant, Zarasai.

In Dukst, 20 people were hacked to pieces, amongst them my young friends.

From this "Action" very few remained.

From this moment on, my will to survive became my obsession. Besides this, my sister Bluma was still alive, as well as my cousins Sara–Devora Berman, who had at the right time left for America. My aunt Chaia Kushlin with her sons Abraham and Sneour.

Those who saved themselves by fleeing into the forests and fighting alongside the Partisans in bloody battles are most thankful.

The part of the Dukst community that remained was very small, one can say they were almost annihilated.

In the Dukst forests you can find our "Dear Brother's Grave" and this is what remains to remember our dear little shtetl of Dukst.

It was a very little shtetl. Jews lived side by side like one large and extended family. You couldn't distinguish who was a relative and who wasn't. We all lived like brothers and sisters, until the wild and barbaric beasts arrived and slaughtered these good and innocent souls. I, together with those who survived, will always keep their Memory alive.

[Col. 1295]

The Cultural – Communal Life

Soreh – Dvoyreh Berman / Hartford, United States

Translation by Janie Respitz

Dukssht began to develop as a town when it was decided to build a large train station in the region. Jews were dispersed throughout all the villages in the region like: Kaniuk, Drishkun, Ligun and others. They lived a lonely life. They believed a community could be built around the train station and began to move to Duksht.

They all built their homes around the train station.

One of the first Jewish residents in the new community was actually my great grandfather Moishe Kaniuker, or Moishe Hamburg. He moved there with his sons: Abba – Nakhman, Yisroel and Leyb. Following him other families arrived including the family of Reb Shneour Zalman Levin, from whom all the Levins and Davidovitchs in town descended.

Another early Jewish resident was Reb Lipeh Rappaport, whose son Anshl became an important socialist leader in France.

Besides the Jews from the villages, many Jews moved to Dushkt from surrounding towns. They believed it would be easier to earn a living close to the new train station. They were right. Many Jews benefited from the station.

Among the Jews in Duksht who earned a good living were: Ruven Eidelman, Yehuda Leyb Podvitch, Shaul Ber Shinavitch, Zundl Tzinaman, Yisroel Feldman, Yisroel Luria, and all the Tarnesses and Bloshteyns.

Slowly, a Jewish community grew around the station.

[Col. 1296]

A nice House of Prayer was built, a Rabbi was hired and Duksht became a Jewish community like all the others in Sventzian province.

The first Rabbi in Duksht was Rabbi Dov– Ber Abigil. He arrived as a young man and remained his whole life. When he died his position was taken over by his son–in–law Rabbi Borukh Spivak who was a great scholar.

Duksht was always proud of its Rabbis and they were loved throughout the region. Rabbi Abigil was even a student of the well–known Rabbi Meir Simkha. The story in town was Rabbi Meir Simkha gave him a prayer book as a gift with the following inscription: "One should know what is written here".

In the early years Duksht suffered a fire which destroyed the town. In those days no one was insured and as they say, everyone was left with only the shirt on their backs. But, no one lost faith. They quickly rebuilt the town and returned to a normal life.

[Col. 1297]

The story went that when people did not even have a piece of bread, they still sent their children to their teacher, and made sure he lacked nothing so the children could continue learning.

Duksht was situated topographically on a hill. This did not help much as the town was often deep in mud. It was referred to in the region as the "Duksht Marsh".

My mother, may she rest in peace, Taybe (nee Epshteyn), would recount how when she arrived in Duksht from the Lithuanian city Vilkovsky, she had to get used to wearing boots all the time. At home, only peasants would wear boots, not Jewish women.

In time, the main streets were paved and they even built wooden sidewalks. The town now looked nice and people forgot about the past marshes.

Until the outbreak of the First World War, Jews lived in tranquility. They were satisfied and happy. A few months after the war began the front moved closer and the Jews had to leave all their belongings and evacuate their homes. The majority wandered to Ukraine and deep into Russia. Meanwhile the Christians destroyed and stole their belongings. The few Jewish families which remained tried to guard the Jewish homes, but they too were eventually chased out by the Germans and they settled in Utian and Ponevezh.

In time, all the Jews from Duksht became refugees.

The large family of Leyb Hamburg with their relatives: Doytch, Rozentzveig, Ahkenazi

After the war, when they returned home, they had to start from scratch. They had to rebuild their homes and look for livelihood. But our Jews did not lose their courage or faith. With great trouble they rebuilt and found a way to earn a living. Some more and some less but everyone found his way. Almost all who left returned.

After the war the Jewish population increased not only in numbers but in quality. Some important well- off people arrived like: Aharon Katcherginsky, Noteh Luria, Yakov Kovarsky and others.

[Col. 1298]

They brought new colour into the communal and economic life of Duksht. Duksht was reborn and once again had a great reputation in the region.

Aharon Katcherginsky has the town to thank for two large economic endeavors. He built a steam mill and was the first to provide the town with electricity. He had a strong will. When Katcherginsky decided to do something, everyone knew he would not rest until it was accomplished. This is what happened with his dream of providing the town with electricity. Within a few years there was electricity in all the homes and in all the streets.

Communal life began to develop after the First World War. The youth were particularly involved. Firstly, a Jewish Folk – School was established thanks to the energy and initiative of Zalman Feygelson, Lipman Levin and Eliyahu Himilfarb.

[Col. 1299]

The school quickly became associated with the centre of all the Jewish schools in Vilna.

From the first day, the economic situation of the school was not well founded. They received subsidies from the central school organization as well as tuition from the parents. However this did not cover all the expenses.

The students decided to form a drama club and all proceeds from performances would go to the school.

The leaders of the drama club were: Lipman Levin, Tzipe Levin, Eliyahu Himlfarb, Leyb Kushlin, Malka Bloshteyn, Esther Feldman, Soreh Levin (Davidovitch), Hirshl Gurvitch, Motl Kalrin, Motl Levin, Shloimeh Katcherginsky, Binyomin Davidovitch, Asher Segal and others.

The drama club from Duksht soon acquired a great reputation throughout the province. All of their performances were well received. They strove toward two goals: the town now had a Yiddish theatre and they now had the financial ability to support the Yiddish school.

The drama club from Duksht performed plays by: Sholem Asch, Sholem Aleichem, Yakov Gordin, Dovid Pinsky as well as translations from general literature.

Thanks to the initiative of Bezalel Levin a Jewish People's Bank was also founded which had the colossal responsibility for the economic development of the town. Its first board of directors was comprised of: Bezalel Levin, Aharon Katcherginsky, Abba Levin, Yoel Luria, Yosef Rives, Pinkhas Daytch and Avrom Segal.

In later years, the bank saved many shopkeepers and artisans from a big crisis.

The Jewish public library helped build the communal and cultural life in town. It contained many Yiddish, Hebrew, Russian and Polish books. There were always many readers and they raised the cultural level of the town's youth.

When the struggle began throughout Poland between the Hebraists and Yiddishists a second Jewish school was founded. The language of instruction in the new school was Hebrew and it belonged to the Tarbut organization. Its founders and leaders were: Bezalel Levin, Binyomin Davidovitch, Moishe Luria, Shloimeh Katcherginsky and Moishe Doytch.

[Col. 1300]

Later, a branch of "HeChalutz" was founded. They opened a carpentry workshop which taught many young people a good trade. Besides this, "HeChalutz" rented land from a Christian and planted vegetables. This garden provided income, but more importantly, taught the youth to work the land.

Duksht was considered a Zionist town. Often speakers would come from Vilna and Warsaw and provide propaganda on behalf of The Jewish National Fund and The Jewish Agency.

Youth from top to bottom: **Borukh Noyman, Dovid Gravitch, Yakov Feldman, Kanovsky, Shneour Korb, ____**

I remember a speaker called Garbovsky who made a big impression on his listeners. After his talk many wrote out pledges for the Zionist fund.

There was also a division of Mizrachi in Duksht. All the Zionist organizations were represented. It was said that our town played a large role in the building of the Land of Israel.

This is how our town was active until the outbreak of the Second World War. First our town was occupied by the Red Army. Then it was given over to the Lithuanian Republic.

At that time I took advantage of the opportunity and left for Kovno. I then had the opportunity to leave and join my husband who was in America.

This is the reason I was saved, but I left behind my entire family. They were all later killed by the bloody hands of the German and Lithuanian beasts.

Today I live with my husband and two children in Hartford, in the United States. We will never forget our nearest and best who were murdered in Duksht.

Their memories will be eternally engraved in our hearts.

[Col. 1301]

My Students and Their Parents

by Zlateh Katcherginsky

Translated by Janie Respitz

As soon as I graduated from the Vilna Teacher's Seminary, they sent me to work at the Dukstas Yiddish School (Tsisho). It was late summer when I arrived at the Dukstas train station where a few “dirty” barefoot children greeted me. When I asked the children why no members of the parent's committee came they explained they were waiting for me in town because coming to the platform cost 20 groshn, and this was a lot of money...

A few minutes later I had the honour to meet Dovid Beer, the chairman of the parent's committee and with a few other miserable Jews â€“ fathers of the children from the Tsisho School.

Walking to town they told me there were 90 children in the Yiddish school, recruited from the poorest families. The Hebrew school had the children from the wealthiest families.

There was a life and death "battle" between the two schools. The fight between Hebrew and Yiddish was no laughing matter. The sent me to "my room". To my surprise, it was a corner of a kitchen, closed off with a brown curtain. When I protested, they insisted this is where I had to live, because the homeowners sent their child to our school, they don't pay tuition. Instead, they house the teacher...If I refuse to live there, they may, God forbid, send their child to the Hebrew school...With such an argument, I had to agree.

The school year began. I taught 8 classes a day, organized a drama club, read their papers and lost my temper at meetings. After a while, the town deeply entered my heart.

[Col. 1302]

This was a town of hungry, unemployed Jews. They only ate meat on the Sabbath (the ritual slaughterer cam every Thursday to slaughter a sheep). The few who were better off had stores. The rest lived off "miracles". Some would deal in flax, dragging sacks to the train, travel to a marketplace. But more often than not, they walked around empty hands in their pockets. The most interesting was, each person from Dukstas had strong feelings about his preference toward Hebrew or Yiddish.

In the Hebrew school and Yiddish school, parents had to pay tuition. Both schools were private, without government subsidies. The third school in town was a Polish public school that did not charge money. In spite of this, everyone sent their children to the Hebrew or Yiddish schools. All the Jewish holidays were celebrated with great fanfare. This was looked after by the leaders of the schools Shloimeh Katcherginsky (Hebrew) and Dovid Beer (Yiddish). The children of Dukstas performed the finest plays, sang beautiful songs and sewed the finest costumes for Purim.

Graduates from the Yiddish school

Seated: Bluma Hamburg, Esther Levin, ___, female teacher, male teacher
Standing: Ushpal, Shapiro, Bluma Hamburg, Boruch Noyman, Konyavsky, ___.

[Col. 1303]

The Emergence and Development of the Economy

by Shloimeh Katcherginsky

(Dedicated to the memory of my mother Rokhl – Feygeh, may she rest in peace)

Translated by Janie Respitz

My beloved, dearest mother, my best and dearest friend,
Who knows if the sun shines on you face? (Folksong)

Let these lines also serve as a dedication to my mother, Rokhl – Feygeh, who simply saved me, and later, in an horrific manner was killed in the hills of Ponar near Vilna, around the 7th – 9th of September 1941.

You mother, may your memory be a blessing, are the one I have to thank for my salvation, as well as my sister Miriam and her son Aharon, who live today in Israel.

On a summery May day in 1924, I arrived with my parents, sister and brother, at the small town of Dukstas, in the northern province, often called “Polish Siberia”. Not looking at my young age, the local organizers quickly involved me in the bubbly communal life. Most of all I owe thanks to Bezalel Levin, of blessed memory, the leader of the Zionist movement in town.

Right from the start I became involved in the town, up until the destruction, which brought about the downfall of the town at the beginning of World War II.

Fate decided that I, a newcomer, would be one of the only survivors of the Jews of Dukstas. It has fallen upon me to eternalize the memory of this lovely town and describe it in this memorial book the life and death of its Jewish population.

It is difficult to write a "memorial" about a life which was so cruelly annihilated, a community of our nearest and dearest friends so deeply etched in my memory. I know this is my obligation. I will therefore make the greatest effort to erect this historic tombstone in memory of the Jews of Dukstas who were murdered.

[Col. 1303]

The Town of Dukstas was founded in 1863 when the railway was built between Warsaw and St. Petersburg (Leningrad). The town was built on rented land that belonged to the farmers of the surrounding villages: Kanyuk, Gerutsishky, and Drishkun. The houses were built by Jewish settlers that previously lived in the surrounding villages and courts. The first Jewish settlers in Dukstas were: Ruven Adelman, Ziskind Shapiro, Mordekhai Karb, Shneur Levin, Elkhanan Segal, Rafalov, Luria, Rivas, Davidovitch, Hamburg, Aran, Podviz, Daytch, Tzinman, Mordekhai Gurvitch and others. The town stood on hilly, clay soil, surrounded by swamp that would overflow in the spring and fall, making communicating with the town very difficult. After many years, wooden sidewalks were built and partly paved roads which helped improve the situation.

[Col. 1304]

The town was situated between 2 borders: 3–4 kilometres from the Lithuanian border and 20–22 kilometres from the Latvian border, surrounded by kilometres of forests, lakes and orchards. Thanks to the newly built train station, Dukstas became an important central point for the surrounding towns and villages. Everyone had to come to bring or receive their merchandise.

[Col. 1305]

The first Jews to settle brought their previous village businesses. They would travel around to the villages and sell their goods. Business slowly developed. The train station and the geographic situation provided great opportunity for the development of the town.

It was no surprise that by the 1880s a large trade began in wheat, flax and lumber. The entire region was populated by many rich farmers and noblemen who brought their goods to Dukstas. Due to the large amount of dealings, two market days were established: Wednesday and Friday. After selling their products at the market, the farmers would purchase the following items in town: salt, kerosene, leather, haberdashery and textiles.

This helped local business and strengthened the economic situation.

The most important wheat, flour and flax merchants in the early years were the following families: Holland, Rafalov, Chazan, Rivash, Tarnas and others. The leather and iron businesses were run by: Padvidz, Eidelman and Hamburg. Lumber merchants: Levin, Feytl Kapelovsky, Luria, Davidovitch and Hamburg.

The above mentioned merchants would buy large plots forest directly from the noblemen and provide the following: timber, paper ...This work required many for manual labour therefore providing income for man Jews and around the town. In connection to this, new professions emerged such as woodsmen, records keepers of the lumbering operations, shipping clerks ...One could often see piles of chopped wood waiting for transport near the railway between Dukstas –Ignalina and Dukstas –Turmont, as well as at the train station. During the day the railways were busy with passenger and freight trains.

[Col. 1306]

Often, late at night you could see hundreds of Jewish farmers loading raw materials on to freight cars. Sometimes 30–40 cars were added to freight trains. This trade continued to develop and helped improve the economic situation of the local population.

A second very important business was geese. The families involved were: Motl Gurvitch, Bloshtyen and Tarnes. The geese would be purchased in remote areas and brought by the flock, day and night, many kilometres. Special ponds were prepared for them in Dukstas. They would later be exported in special train cars, mainly to Germany.

By the beginning of the 20th century a fruit business developed, at first only strawberries, then apples and pears. The fruit merchants would rent orchards in the surrounding area from farmers and noblemen. They would hire pickers and export the fruit.

The fruit business grew after the First World War when there were many more orchards in the area. The produce was sent first to St. Petersburg, then to Katovitz, Warsaw and other cities in Poland. The biggest fruit dealers in town were the Segal brothers, Motl Gurvitch, Aran and Hamburg. Besides them there were other smaller dealers.

In connection with this business merchants and middlemen would come to Dukstas from far away cities, and would often linger the entire season. Therefore, over the next few years a few modern hotels and restaurants were opened: Rappaport, Shvil and Gurvitch.

Even the situation of the artisans improved. Instead of wandering from village to village looking for work, they settled in one spot and eventually opened workshops.

Among the first artisans in town were: Yehuda – Levi Bercovitch the tailor, Pinkhas Daytch and Nakhman, both shoemakers.

[Col. 1307]

The meat business was also developing, previously in the hands of the Aran and Telent families. Soon the Eynhorns joined. This business gave work to many Jewish wagon drivers, like Ziskind, Shapiro, Dovid–Shloymeh Ginzburg, Kraytzer, Blond Yudl and Moshe Yosl Furman.

After the First World War

The First World War suddenly ruined the economic development of the town. The battles took place not far from Dukstas and almost the entire Jewish population ran away to Russia. A large part of the town was destroyed. All the financial success from hard work was lost. After the war, people began slowly to return, but many did not and remained in foreign places where they found new opportunities to earn a living.

Dukstas began to rebuild anew. The wheat and lumber business began again. The firm "Kovarsky – Himelfarb" concentrated on doing business in wheat, flour and flax. They opened branches in surrounding town such as Braslav, Druye, Gluboke ,Disna and others. In later years, they were based in Vilna and Warsaw.

This firm hired many Jews as employees, middlemen, agents, foremen and simple workers. After the war, old friends joined them including the brothers Yisroel and Noteh Luria, Aharon Katcherginsky, Tuvyeh Karlin, Abba –Yosef Bloshteyn, Tzinman, Karasin and others. The Levin firm dealt in lumber.

One of the biggest lumber merchants in those years was Aharon Katcherginsky, a new resident who quickly familiarized himself with the town and soon became an active member of the community. He also became the owner of the mill and in 1929 built a power plant which brought electricity to our town for the first time. Understandably, this was important for all the residents of Dukstas, Jews and Christians alike. The electric lights in town stimulated future development, in the social activity as well as physical appearance.

[Col. 1308]

Nature also made the town pretty as it was surrounded by green fields, thick forests and large lakes that encompassed many kilometres. The waters sparkled and provided a harmony of colours depending on the changes in weather. It is no wonder, groups of kids, in their free time in the afternoon, would go out into nature and enjoy the beauty. Some would sail, others would walk in the forests, and others would enjoy a relaxing walk through the fields. They widened the boundaries of the town and dreamt and hoped for their future.

Practically speaking, some of the residents understood how to take advantage of the beautiful nature surrounding the town and took to fishing. These fishermen would go out in the summer late at night and in the winter very early in the morning do carry out their hard work. It was particularly hard in the winter when the lakes were frozen and covered with thick layers of ice and snow. They would make cracks in the ice and using special nets and other tools the fish would be caught, gathered in ice cellars, packed in baskets with ice and transported to the central cities of Poland. The people doing this work were the brothers: Gdud, Arans from Rimshan, Gavenda from Ignalina and others. There were also crayfish in the surrounding lakes which were packed in specially prepared baskets and transported to the biggest cities in the land. The Bloshteyn family took part in this.

The iron business lay in the hands of Yosef Rives, Reuven Feyglson and Moishe Luria. The leather business was run by: Yisroel Feldman, Eliezer Hamburg, Drisviyatsky, and Kurland. The textile industry was run by: the Luria family, Gurvitch, Feldman, Levin, Rosenberg and others. The owners of the larger food businesses were: Notl Luria, Motl Gurvitch, Zundl Tzinman, Tzipe Rosenberg, Frayda Hamburg.

[Col. 1309]

Dukstas was quickly rebuilt. Even though the town was only 3 kilomtres from the Lithuanian border, it still was able to become a leading centre in the region, with tight business connections with merchants in Vidz, Apse, Braslav, Druye and other towns.

After the war, another railway was built, connecting Dukstas with Druye. It was a small train which daily bring many cars of wheat, flax and lumber that provided a livelihood for many Jewish families. This expedition was run by the firm Zalman –Leyb Segal.

A significant amount of Jews worked in the mill and sawmill that belonged to Katcherginsky. In season, many worked in the fruit business packing crates of apples. This way, many peddlers and wagon drivers earned extra income.

The coachmen earned a livelihood from transporting cargo, as well as passengers, especially on market days in the surrounding towns.

It is worthwhile to tell about on episode concerning one such coachman, the Blond Yudl. Yudl was a middle aged man with a pointy small yellow beard, thin face, resembling a teacher more than a wagon driver. Even his horse was thin and could barely stand on his legs, reminding us of Sholem Aleichem's story "The Mare". But the horse brought Yudll a livelihood. Yudl mainly transported passengers from the Dukstas station to Vidz, a distance of approximately 28 kilometres. This trip would often take place at night, the roads were not paved, and in the fall he would ride through thick mud. Such a trip would take 7–8 hours.

Midway, they would come across the Volhynia Lake where all the coachmen would drive down the hill to allow their horses to drink from the lake.

One day, Yudl was taking new passengers who were unfamiliar with the area. When he went down the hill, as usual to bring his horse to drink, the passengers became frightened and asked why he was taking them to a lake. Yudl responded, telling them he was taking a shortcut. It is true they will get soaked, but it's not worth for him, at such a fare, to travel on dry land. If they pay the difference, he would be happy to take the longer, dryer route.

[Col. 1310]

This was, of course , an episode. In reality, Yudl was an honest Jew, with a sense of humour, always in a good mood. A true people's person.

From an economic standpoint, Dukstas had nothing to complain about. Nobody suffered from hunger, and everyone earned a living.

Culture and Education

Until the First World War all the Jewish children in Dukstas received the same education as everywhere else. Only in Cheder. (Religious school). The well– known teachers were: Zilig Shloymeh, Shmuel Feyvish, Itche Yosl, and the ritual slaughterer Shmuel –Hirsh. The older boys, the one's after Bar Mitzvah were taught by Reb Dov Ber Avigail.

At the beginning, Itche Yosl did not live in town. He would come to Dukstas to teach temporarily. Later, he moved with his family to town.

By the end of the 19th century, Abba Eidelman, the son from a well–known family began to revolt against the Cheder and its teachers. His father beat him and he had to run away. His ideas quickly spread and he found many supporters.

Abba Eidelman pursued his worldly education abroad and became a famous artist.

An important personality, particularly among the workers was Shaul Rappaport. I will provide a short biography in later writings.

These two individuals mad a large impression of the youth of Dukstas. Many strove to escape the Cheder and study in the outside world. In the end, some of the distinguished families decided in good faith to send their children to study in Dvinsk or Vilna.

The first families to send their children to study away from home were: Sinovitch, Podvidz and Holland.

[Col. 1311]

These high school students would return home for vacation and Jewish holidays, bringing with them winds of change.

In 1902, the first speech on Zionism was delivered. Thanks to him, a Zionist organization was founded in town. The first members were: Eidelman, Podvidz, Hollender and Abba – Shimon Davidovitch. The branch in Dukstas only had a few members and belonged to the Vilna Zionist division.

In those days, the Levin family brought in a teacher from Dvinsk to teach their children. He organized a branch of the Bund, which attracted some of the Zionist youth.

Under his influence, the Bund became quite strong in town. After the revolution of 1905, he worked illegally. His activity became even stronger.

In 1905 the first Jewish library was founded. Its leaders were: Binyomin Kopolovitch, Shimon Davidovitch, and Efraim Eidelman.

Thanks to these books, many of the youth began to read about secular subjects. There were many progressive clubs, where Hebrew newspapers were read: "HaTzfirah" and "HaMelitz".

The news and sensationalized stories spread with lightning speed throughout the town.

An important communal worker in these years was Shneur Zalman Levin. He served as a middleman between the Jewish community and the local authorities.

After the First World War, with the emergence of the Polish Republic, one of the leaders from the Bund, Feyvish Gilinsky became well- known. He was from Dukstas. In the 1930s he sat as a councilman on the Warsaw city council, and was one of the founders of the Medem Sanitorium.

After the war, an intensive communal and cultural life began to flourish.

One of the first secular Jewish schools in the province was founded, setting an example for other towns.

[Col. 1312]

The initiative of starting a secular Jewish school was taken on by: Lipman Levin, Bezalae Levin, Asher Segal and Zalman Feyglson.

The first teacher in the Yiddish school was Motl Gilinsky from Sventzian, who while in the seminary, received the all telling name "Batko".

At the same time, once again Zionist thought began to spread in town. In 1924 the "Hechalutz" (the Pioneer) was founded and a half year later, "HaChalutz Hatzair" (the Young Pioneer).

The pioneers would take part in difficult physical work and were admired by Christians and Jews. No one could comprehend how such children from wealthy families would chop wood and work in the fields with the workers.

Eventually, like everywhere else, two fronts were established: the Zionist and anti–Zionist. Among those who opposed Zionism were: Bundists, Communists, and Yiddishists. At first, those opposing were much stronger, but with time, Zionist ideas developed deep roots among the Jewish population and the majority of the youth were taken by these ideas.

A group of young people in front of the house of the medic Teller

In 1926 a Hebrew school was founded in town. At first it was affiliated with Mizrachi (religious Zionists) and then to "Tarbut".

[Col. 1313]

The founders of the Hebrew school were: Bezalel Levi, Aharon Katcherginsky, Moishe Luria, Yisroel Feldman, Eliezer Hamburg, Yosef Shvil and others.

One of the first teachers in the Hebrew school was Shmuel Dobkin from Svir.

The budget of the school was subsidized mainly from tuition, paid by the parents. This did not cover the expenses, forcing them to look for additional income. To achieve this, the Zionist youth helped out: collections, performances, lotteries and tag days.

Here we can see great devotion from the members: Yisroel and Hirsh Gurvitch, Mordekhai Karlin, Musia Kamraz, Shloymeh and Nokhem Bloshteyn, the Gurvitch brothers, Binyomin and Soreh Davidovitch, Rokhl Katcherginsky, Rodeh Luria, Basia Gurvitch, Bluma Hamburg, Khaya Karasin, Nekheh Luria, Shayneh Davidovitch, and the author of these lines.

Rokhl Katcherginsky

Bluma Hamburg

Every Zionist sympathizer took upon himself a moral obligation to support the newly founded school, in different ways depending on possibilities and talents.

The top organizer and founder was Bezalel Levin, one of the founders of Zionist ideology in our town. I will dedicate a few lines to him later on in my memoir.

[Col. 1314]

Soon all the Zionist organizations and parties concentrated around the Hebrew school. A cultural club was founded called "Ben – Yehuda's Corner", which attracted a lot of young people. Every member of the club accepted the obligation to speak Hebrew to each other. This club founded a brass orchestra. It was led by Hirshl Gurvitch, who had been a member of Hechalutz, and later a founder of Betar. His assistant in the orchestra was Mordekhai Karlin, known to all for his artistic talents, especially as a comic.

The above mentioned gave all their energy and free time to communal work. A handful of people, without money, without an appropriate building, without textbooks, without an association with a central organization, but with stubbornness and enthusiasm, founded the Hebrew school.

Tarbut orchestra and Zionist activists

First row bottom from right to left: **Hirsh Gurvitch, Shloimeh Katcherginsky, Zelig Feyglman, Tzadok Feldman, Khone Aron**
Second row: **A. Opeskin, Bezalel Levin, Shmuel Dobkin,____, Milyeh Segal, Aharon Kagan, Yisroel Gurvitch**
Third row: **Mikhaek Feldman, Shayneh Davidovitch,**
Fourth row: **Hinda Hamburg, Bayleh Aron, Esther Feldman, Esther Tabakhovitch**

Besides the mentioned difficulties, it was also difficult to gain permission from the authorities. They had to intervene with the curator and school inspector. Only with the intervention of Senator Rabbi Rubinshteyn did they succeed in obtaining a temporary permit to open the school for the academic year 1926/27. As they did not have a building, they took over the women's shul. In order to gain support from the religious community, they called the Hebrew school “Mizrachi School”.

[Col. 1315]

The first year they begin with very few students. With time enrollment grew, and the school continued to develop. Within a year, they left the women's shul and rented a room in the home of Dovid Sloimeh Ginsburg. They did not remain there long. By 1929 they built their own building.

The Opening

The opening of the school was celebrated with great fanfare. Senator Rabbi Rubinshteyn and the leader of Mizrachi, Rabbi Kleynshteyn came from Vilna.

The guests were led from the train station, accompanied by the Tarbut Orchestra, to the home of Aharon Katcherginsky. With the help of Rokhl Katcherginsky, known for her great hospitality, the important guests were well received. Also present were our local rabbi, Rabbi Avigail, Bezalel Levin and others.

There was a celebratory mood in town. Young and old came out to share in the joy. Many guests arrived from the surrounding towns, including the Zionist leader from Ignalina, Yerakhmiel Karb(Korb) and others. The celebration took place in the new building at beautifully set tables.

In honour of this event, the children, for the first time, performed in Hebrew. The local teachers, with patience and perseverance, never abandoned their work even under the hardest conditions, and sometimes waiting months for minimal pay. Among them were: Shmuel Dobkin, Aharon Beker, Fliskin,Mina Minkovitch and others.

"Teachers, volunteers and Zionist youth

First row bottom, right to left: Esther Tabakhovitch, Mikhael Feldman, Nekhe Luria, Beyleh Aron
Second row: Khone Aron, Leyb Gravitch, Moishe Daytch, Nokhem Bloshteyn
Third row: Shneur Davidovitch, Shloimeh Bloshteyn, Segal, Aharon Beker, Soreh Hamburg, Mordekhai Levin, Shmuel Dobkin, Shloimeh Katcherginsky, Peretz Kagan, Avrom Segal

[Col. 1316]

Until 1931 the school was officially associated with "Mizrachi", in connection to the department in Vilna. Later they belonged to "Tarbut" which was based in Warsaw.

The Hebrew school had a drama club that performed on Purim, Pesach and other Jewish holidays. It was always difficult to find an appropriated hall. There were none in the Jewish community. They had to approach the Polish community. There were two: "Ludov" and "Agnisko". There was always a competition between the Hebrew and Yiddish school (of which I will discuss later) to get the better hall.

The children's performances in Hebrew were particularly successful, prepared with great effort by the teachers and parents. The administrative tasks and decorations were enthusiastically done by all involved with the school. The income and donations were key. Such events always gave the feeling that something important was accomplished among the people and strengthened the belief and continuity of the old Hebrew language.

"Tarbut" School 1937/38 Children, parents and volunteers

[Col. 1317]

The Hebrew school existed in Dukstas for 14 years, from 1926 –1940, when the Red Army arrived.

During that time, the grown up graduates carried the Zionist ideal and spread the pioneering spirit.

With the outbreak of the World War and the entry of the Red Army, we saw the demise of one of the most beautiful cultural achievement – the Hebrew school.

The Yiddish School

The Yiddish school was founded right after the First World War, representing the basis of cultural life in town, for the entire Jewish community, no matter which party affiliation. Its existence is thanks to a group called "crazy about it". Members of this group included: Bezalel Levin, Feyglson, Leybe Kushlin, Lipman Levin, Eliyusha Himlfarb, and the Segal family. In two small crowded rooms at Frayda Hamburg's, Jewish children got their first taste of the Yiddish classics, history and other subjects within the framework of a 6 class Folk –Shul. Teachers were found, who with great effort, under difficult circumstances, instilled the Yiddish word into the souls of the young Jewish children in town.

The school was associated with the centre in Vilna, but supported itself through various efforts: tuition, events and private donations. Thanks to the devotion of its supporters, they managed in 1930 to build a nice building, which resulted in improved local relations and led to further growth and development. The school had a rich library, which provided the opportunity to learn about Jewish and secular culture. The drama club also displayed great talent with the help of: Abba Levin, Dovid Beer, Mendl and Mordkhai Hamburg, Yosef Shapiro, Yudl Gefen, Leyb Bloshteyn, Malka Bloshteyn, the female teacher Lev–Gefen, Yisroel Levin and others.

The school remained active until the outbreak of the war between Russia and Germany, and together with the Jewish population of the town, ended its 22 year existence.

[Col. 1318]

People's Bank

One of the most constructive economic initiatives in town was the People's Bank, which was founded right after the First World War by the businessmen: Zalman Fyglson, Abba and Lipman Levin, Bezalel Levin, Yoel Luria, Abba–Yosef Bloshteyn, Pinkhas Daytch, Yosef Rivesh and others.

The People's Bank in Dukstas joined the central committee of Jewish People's Banks in Warsaw. Its fundamental capital was based on the income of the local Jewish residents and long term loans they received from Vilna and Warsaw.

The bank made loans available to everyone in town. The conditions were comfortable: a low percent at small monthly rates. In such conditions small business and artisans got the help they needed to exist.

This was a clean economic institution but often political party antagonism would sneak in causing bitter fights between two camps: the Zionists and Yiddishists. Above all, in the elections for council and the People's Bank. Each side wanted to ensure a majority. The general meeting would take place in the synagogue and always drew a large crowd.

A member of the central committee would come: Kliansky or Mekhanik. Neither one was a Zionist. This played well for the anti-Zionist camp in town. Many unaffiliated would vote for them.

After the elections, everyone would forget their differences and bickering and return to sitting together at one table working for the benefit of this important institution.

Over the years the People's Bank in Dukstas underwent various periods. There were times of prosperity and crisis. The leadership did everything to encourage development in order to help the Jewish community. They sacrificed their days and nights and very often their health and money.

In order to increase credit, they would make an appeal to the people. These appeals always had positive results.

[Col. 1319]

In 1939, with the outbreak of the Second World War, and the region was now part of Lithuania, the People's Bank did not stop its activity. It now joined with the central bank in Kovno. This was a prosperous time for the bank because they received a lot of support from the central institution in Kovno.

This honeymoon did not last long. By July 1940 Lithuania was occupied by the Soviets and became part of the Soviet Union. The People's Bank in Dukstas was closed. The entire archive and inventory was sent to Kovno.

[Col. 1320]

This was the demise of tone of the most positive, worthwhile institutions in town.

To conclude I would like to provide a list of those who played an active role in the bank from its founding until its downfall: Zalman Feyglson, Bezalel Levin, Abba Levin, Lipman Levi, Leybe Levin, Soreh Levin- Davidovitch, Leybe Hamburg, Binyomin Davidovitch, Soreh Hamburg, Abba - Yosef Bloshteyn, Asher Segal, Aharon Katcherginsky, Yoel Luria, Moishe Luria, Mordekhai Gurvitch, Yisroel Gurvitch, Mordekhai Hamburg, Pinkhas Daytch, Yosef Rivesh, Yoel Feldman, and the author of these lines.

[Col. 1319]

Communal Activists and Personalities

by Shloimeh Katcherginsky

Translated by Janie Respitz

Rabbi Dov Ber Avigail

Rabbi Dov Ber Avigail was the Rabbi of Dukstas for many years. He was physically weak, small in stature with a straggly beard, yet he possessed a large soul. He was a kind, learned, God fearing Jew.

He was satisfied with basic material needs. He did not worry about this world; he strove for a better afterlife.

When passing legal judgement he displayed an enormous amount of patience, always finding a way for both sides to compromise. This is why so many came from all over for his advice, even other Rabbis.

He passed away in 1940, having had the honour to be buried in the Jewish cemetery.

Dov Ber Avigail was considered was one of the most popular Rabbis in the entire Vilna province, during the period between the two World Wars.

Before his death he passed on the position of chief rabbi to his son–in–law Rabbi Borukh Spivak. He did not foresee his community living out its last years, and the horrific destruction that stood at the threshold.

Rabbi Elkhanan Segal

Khone, as he was called, was one of the first Jewish residents of Dukstas. He had two sons: Reuven, who died in the First World War, and Zalman Leyb, killed by Hitler's murderers.

[Col. 1320]

Rabbi Elkhanan had branches of his family in Poland and Lithuania. His proudest moments were when all his grandchildren and greatgrandchildren gathered and he could recount episodes of his life. Having lived 108 years, he had lots of stories to tell. He had a special style of storytelling keeping the attention of his listeners. He was and honest, passionate Jew. Until his last days, he never missed going to synagogue to pray. He would walk there three times a day. The people of our town called him "not long ago", because that is how he began all his stories.

"Not long ago, when I began to go to Cheder...". Everyone knew chapters of his biography.

Until his last day he was fresh, happy, energetic and fully aware. He was never sick and had trouble understanding physical pain of others.

When one of his grandchildren complained of a toothache, Khone, who was over 100 angrily said "how can bones hurt?"

No wonder he was considered an interesting type, not only in Dukstas, but in the surrounding area. Everyone marveled about this healthy old man.

[Col. 1321]

Jews and gentiles respected him, and showed him a special love. He died a natural death and was buried in the Jewish cemetery before the arrival of Hitler's murderers.

Bezalel Levin

A son of a Rabbi, he studied and was raised in religious schools, later on his own, obtained a secular education.

Arriving in Dukstas after the First World War he devoted himself entirely to communal work, often neglecting his own interests.

First of all, he was one of the founders of the Yiddish school. A few years later he became one of the most important Zionist leaders in town. Thanks to him," HeChalutz" was founded in Dukstas in 1924, followed by The Jewish National Fund and The Jewish Agency. The crown of his activity was the founding of the Hebrew school. He devoted days and nights for its development, attracting new workers and sympathizers. In connection with the Vilna division, without fear he opposed all disturbances and with pride achieved his idealistic goals.

A man of rare energy, full of courage and stubbornness, he devoted his best years to furthering Zionist thought and always dreamed how to make it a reality.

In 1935, he managed, with great effort to emigrate to Israel, "illegally" as a tourist, with the plan to eventually bring his wife Bayleh and their son Hillel. His plan was never realized. Being very lonely, he got sick and died three months later.

The news of his death impacted Dukstas greatly. Not just his family, but the entire Zionist movement. For many years his memory encouraged and energized his followers to continue the Zionist work he began.

His grave is in the Nachalat Yitzchak cemetery in Tel Aviv.

[Col. 1322]

Aharon Katcherginsky

Born in Rimshan, a small town near Dukstas. Before the First World War he went to Russia and lived in Snavsk, in the Chernigov region. Already in those years, he became involved in Zionist activity and other philanthropic institutions. Especially close to his heart was the Radom Yeshiva of Chefetz Chaim, of blessed memory, who he befriended during the years 1919/21, when he was one of the lumber merchants in the city and a partner in the power station, and found time to help support the Yeshiva.

In 1921, Aharon and his family left Russia, and as a Polish citizen, returned to Poland. Travelling with him on the same train were some students from the Yeshiva. The Chafetz Chaim, of blessed memory came to the train and made a special blessing. In 1924, together with his wife and three children, he settled in Dukstas and quickly became involved in Jewish communal affairs, administration of the People's Bank, representing the Zionist camp and always showing interest in the workers. He helped organize all Zionist activities and all communal philanthropic events.

In 1926, together with Bezalael Levin, he was the first builder of the Hebrew school. He dedicated a lot of energy to the project as well as time and money. He was particularly involved in build a new building for the school. He served as an example to other residents of the town, donating large sums of money.

Thanks to his business connections, he was able to get donations from some Christians, receiving lumber and other building materials for the Hebrew school.

For 13 years of his life in Dukstas, 1924–1937, he was one of the most prominent community – personalities. After a brief illness he passed away in May, 1937.

[Col. 1323]

His death did not only orphan the Katcherginsky family, but also the Zionist movement in town, and above all else the Tarbut school, which he loved dearly and was connected to with heart and soul.

The entire Jewish community came to his funeral, where they laid him to his eternal rest in the Dustas cemetery.

Moishe Luria

At first Moishe Luria was a wheat and flax merchant. Later he owned an iron company. He gave a lot of his time, energy and money to raise the cultural level in town.

His beloved institution was the Hebrew school. He gave his soul to the school. From the first day he was one of the most active volunteers and builders. In his Zionist work he knew of no compromise in the battle with those who opposed Zionism. In the fall of 1941 he was murdered by Hitlers' beasts together with his wife Rodeh and son Khone.

Yisroel Gurvitch

The son of Mordkhai Gurvitch. A well know merchant in town from before the First World War, and a hotel owner after the war. Yisroel was one of the first members of “HeChalutz” in Dukstas and participated in all Zionist activities. He was very helpful in the founding of the Hebrew school. He was always ready when called upon by the Zionist movement to develop its ideals. He worked for the meeting of The Jewish National Fund and the Jewish Agency. His entire life he dreamed about Eretz Yisrael and waited for an immigration certificate to realize his dream. Hitler's bandits and the Lithuanian hooligans ruined his dreams. The murderers killed him together with his wife Basia, their son and the entire Jewish community.

Zionist leaders from Dukstas, New–Sventzian, Ignalina, at the opening of the Hebrew school

[Col. 1324]

School Volunteers at "Tarbut"

Moishe Daytch, Bluma Hamburg, Shloimeh Katcherginsky, the male teacher, the female teacher, Yisroel Gurvitch

Betar Organization

Bottom: **Hirsh Gurvitch**
Standing first row: **Yakov Feldman, Lipke Rosenberg, Bluma Hamburg, Rokhl Shur, Dovid Gravitch**
2nd row: **Yakov Hamburg, Bluma Hamburg, Shneur Karb, Khaya Kurland, Sholem Tabakhovitch**

[Col. 1325]

Hirshl Gurvitch

The second son of Mordkhai Gurvitch. He was the founder of the Tarbut Orchestra and its conductor, with special musical talents. Founded Betar in town to which he devoted much time and energy. One of the talented artists who participated in the theatre performances dedicated to the Hebrew School. He married just before the war in Marchinkantze, Vilna province and was killed by Hitler's murderers.

Meir Katcherginsky

Meir Katcherginsky was one of the first graduates of the Hebrew school. Later went to Vilna to study at the Tarbut High School, and was one of the founders of " Ha'Shomer HaTzair" in town. He also worked hard to establish Ha'Shomer in other towns. His youthful enthusiasm and devotion toward his ideals helped him leave home and join a Zionist training camp first in Myadel and then in Grokhov, near Warsaw.

During the war he was in Gluboke with his wife. Like everywhere else, there too he displayed great enthusiasm and tried to help friends by preparing false passes to cross over to the Aryan side. Helping him with this work was the Yiddish poet Shmerl Katcherginsky. (Killed in a plane crash in 1954).

From Gluboke, together with his wife and a friend, disguised themselves as White Russian police, and on bicycles arrived in Vilna, where he worked as a blacksmith in a smithy. A Lithuanian bandit from Dukstas recognized him and turned him in to the Gestapo.

Meir Katcherginsky

[Col. 1326]

He was horribly tortured in Lukshik jail, in an attempt to make him turn in his wife and friends. He held firm and stubborn and did not say a word. The wild animals poked out his eyes, and with great cruelty, tortured him to death. He was 26 years old.

Let his name always be remembered together with all the other martyrs and heroes who were killed by Hitler's beasts during the Second World War.

The Feldman Family

Yisroel Feldman and his five sons: Yoel, Mikhael, Tzadok, Moishe and Yankl and his daughter Esther were active in the Zionist communal life in our town. They supported the Hebrew school and donated money to all Zionist activities. The youngest brother Yakov died tragically before the war. He was a graduate of the Hebrew school and was to immigrate to Eretz Yisrael just before the outbreak of the war. A month before his departure he went to Vidz to say goodbye to family. There he was attacked by young Polish anti-Semites who killed him. The rest of the family was eventually killed in Dukstas, Vilna and Braslav.

Eliezer Hamburg

One of the first to switch his children from the Yiddish school to the Hebrew school. His daughter Bluma had great artistic talents, belonged to the drama club and took part in all the Zionist performances.

Eliezer (Lozer) was one of the most devoted volunteers for the Hebrew school. His daughters Bluma and Soreh were in the Vilna Ghetto. Together with a group of 17 people, they escaped to the forest planning to join the partisans. On their way, near Svir forest, they were killed.

Yisroel Davidovitch

A son from an established Jewish family in town. His father Asher was a devoted Zionist volunteer and the first teacher of Jewish Studies in the Hebrew language. Yisroel was one of the first pioneers to emigrate to Eretz Israel right after the First World War. Slowly he brought the rest of the members of his family. He was one of the founding members of Kibbutz "Ramat Rachel" near Jerusalem. The first to arrive were his sisters: Bayleh, Yaffa and Miriam. Later, his brother Binyomin with his whole family, followed by his sister Khava-Rokhl and son and daughter.

[Col. 1327]

Their parents emigrated in 1935. Some of the family settled in Nes Tziona, and others in Netanya. The old man Aher and his wife died in Nes Tziona and are buried there.

Yisroel, of blessed memory, died in 1962. Not long before he died he was helpful with his knowledge of the history of Dukstas.

Rappaport Shaul

A well-known socialist leader .He was born in Dukstas in 1865 and died in France in 1942. Right after Cheder, he went to study in Vilna, leaving behind his brother Khayim-Moishe to study with local religious teachers.

Already in his youth he stood out as an activist. In 1883 he joined the Revolutionary Socialist Party. In 1887, together with Lenin's brother participated in a conspiracy to attack Czar Alexander III. Lenin's brother was sentenced to death and Rappaport escaped to France where he later became a citizen. He joined the French Socialist Party, aligning himself with the extreme far left wing. He was a relentless proponent of Marxist theory. He wrote for the French Socialist press.

During the First World War in 1917/18 he was sentenced by a military court to three months of arrest for his speaking out against the government of Clemenceau. He wrote a pamphlet in self– defence which caused a big sensation.

He joined the French Communist Party in 1921. The party had to be thankful to him for their victory at the party congress.

From 1922–1924 he published the newspaper“Revi –Communist”. In 1926 he was invited to Russia and received with great fanfare. He also worked as an editor of the Marxist column for the newspaper “Humanity”. The Moscow Trials in 1929 in Russia led to his departure from the Communist Party. In 1930 he wrote and open explanation.

[Col. 1328]

In 1922 a Russian White –Guard tried to assassinate him. This resulted in his daughter being wounded.

The Paris Yiddish newspaper “Arbeter Tzeitung” published his autobiography in 1930–33. His last two works were dedicated to the Jewish question, under the title of “At the Crossroads” and “Historical Writings”.

Among his many published works are: “The Social Qustion of Ethics” (1895)

“La Revolution Mondiale” (The World Revoultion) 1923

“La Philosophie sociale de Pierre Lavroff” (The Social Philosophy of Pierre Lavroff) 1901

“La Philosophie de l'histoire de Prouthon” (The Philosophy of History of Prouthon) 1904

“Socialisme gouvernmental et socialism revolutionnaire” (Governmental Socialism and Revolutionary Socialism) 1910.

“Jean Jaures” 1910 with an introduction by Anatol Franz

“Marx and the Dictator of the Proletariat” 1920, in Yiddish.

Torture, Murder and Destruction

The large brothers –grave of Jewish martyrs lays spread over a field between the roads from Dukstas to Zarasai in the so–called Dukstas forest. There were no survivors from the “Umshlag Platz” except a few that were saved from the grave by hiding in the forest: Bluma Hamburg–Zilbershteyn, Khaya Kushlin and Reuven Hamburg (Saved himself in Russia). They collected limited material. They received the news of what happened from the Dukstas Christians who witnessed the deaths of the Jews.

Sixteen days after the war began the Red Army arrived in Dukstas. A short time later, power was handed over to the Lithuanians, who remained under Russian supervision until the outbreak of the Russian–German was of June 22, 1941.

[Col. 1329]

Two days later, the Lithuanian bandits began to rob Jewish businesses, divided the Jewish goods and possessions among themselves and began their sadistic cruelty and murder. One of the local Lithuanian bandits, a former owner of a bakery and restaurant, Antony Umbraz, was nominated as one of the leaders of the town. The first murders of Jewish youth were carried out by him. He also began the business of taxation. Officially the commander of the town was a German, but in practice the leaders were Lithuanian collaborators. Besides this bandit others who "excelled" with cruelty were the Sharke brothers, Abelevitch, Mikulen and others.

A few days later these sadistic murderers showed their true colours and began their horrific work. Jewish children of various ages, together with Moishe Daytch, of blessed memory, one of the Zionist activists in town, were pitilessly killed.

The following were killed in this first operation: Sonia, Hirshl and Avrom Segal; Nokhem and Mikhael (Mikhkeh) Teller; Moishe Levin (son of Abba Levin); Bebik Hamburg (son of Eliezer Hamburg); Avremke Levin (son of Dovid Levin);Yishayahu Telent; Yisrolke Shapiro (son of Hirshl Shapiro); Shneur Tbabkhovitch; Yakov Hamburg; Shmuel (Mulke) Rosenberg, (son of Tzipe Rosenberg) and Moishe Daytch.

The names of the others killed in this operation are unknown.

The murders were done in the open. Each one was tortured in a different way, on the streets, in the marketplace, or the roads to surrounding villages.

Avrom (Avremke) Segal was tied to the back of a wagon and dragged with his head on the ground by galloping horses over the paved streets. Arriving close to the Jewish cemetery, the Lithuanian bandits shot the bloodied, tortured martyr and left him in the open field.

His sister Sonia was tortured publicly near the police station. Mikhke Teller was cut up alive in front of his father, the local Medic, Shloimeh (Solomon) Teller, the father who was forced to be present, attacked one of the murderers, and began to choke him. A second bandit shot the medic together with his other son Nokhem, who came to help. This is a short description of the methods of murder carried out in those times. The Jews of our town were still living in their own homes and had to witness these terrible tragedies.

[Col. 1330]

A few days later he increased tax collection. All methods were "Kosher".

A Jew from the town of Rimshan (about 8 km. from Dukstas), Solitan, hid at the leader of the bandits, Antony Umbroz, at the cost of 200 gold ruble (a large sum in those days, especially for a Jew from a small town). The moment the money ran out, he was shot.

By August 1941 the Jews were taken from their homes, permitted only to take the minimum amount of possessions. One group – apparently the wealthier – were brought to a half–island on Lake Disner called "Ostrov", and the second group to the Jewish bathhouse and the surrounding homes called "Azhutovineh". The Jews were isolated and any contact with Christians was punishable by death.

Remaining without money or possessions, the majority of the Jewish population lived off the mercy of a few Russians who in different ways managed to bring food into the so–called Ghetto.

Crying over graves

[Col. 1331]

The Jews from both places "Ostrov" and "Azhutovine", women and men, worked on the railroad line between Ignalina and Turmont, forced to walk many kilometres a day.

The beginning of September that same year, the Jews were brought to "Antonova", a good estate, which was owned by the noblewoman Navahanska, 3 kilometres from town.

In cold rain, with minimal humane conditions, in an open field, men and women were locked up for three weeks. They continued to be taken to the same work. Despite the difficulty of the work and the far walk, the majority of the Jews were interested. True, the guarding by the Lithuanians was very strict, but from time to time they managed to make contact with the Christian population, and through various means, receive food, most important, bread for one's family. They paid for the produce with clothing and valuable objects that had not been stolen. The Lithuanian officers would receive their part for these "transactions".

A few tradesmen from among the Jewish population were useful in town as shoemakers, tailors, and stitchers. They were "happy" as their material situation was better. Even their "normal" life ended on September 21st, 1941.1941 16 Lithuanians arrived in "Antanova". Promising better conditions, they took everyone to a field. Under stronger supervision, in the dark of night, they took women, children and men without telling them where they were heading. Small children and the sick were taken by wagon. On the way the drivers were in a good mood. Late at night they stopped in a potato field. Not only did they allow everyone to cook and eat the potatoes, the allowed them to take a supply. Early in the morning, Lipke Gdud's wife, Bezalel's daughter gave birth in the wagon. One of the guards, out of "pity" killed the baby. Having witnessed this murderous act, Shimon Tabakhovitch began to strangle the bandit. Three other bandits jumped on him and shot him.

[Col. 1332]

Visiting the mass grave in 1944

The last road travelled by the Jews of Dukstas led to Zarasai, a town in Lithuania about 25 kilometres away. Midway, in the Degutch forest, they stopped. This was the meeting place of all the Jews from the surrounding towns. The cruelty soon began. By the afternoon of September 22nd, they began to separate children from their parents. Machine guns stood in all corners of the field.

[Col. 1333]

The Lithuanian barbarians together with their German partners, in broad daylight, murdered thousands of children, women and men. The Christian forest guard witnessed this horrific tragedy. He was not in a position to recount all he saw, but he did tell this short version:

"That day, when a stream of men, women and children arrived from all around to the big field which was surrounded by a dense forest, they locked me, the forest guard in a room, and threatened to kill me if I came out during the day. Through a crack in the wood, I climbed into the attic and saw a black crowd of people. At every corner of the field were machine guns. They divided men, women and children into rows, and shot them as they walked. Mothers who refused to give up their children were shot with their children in their arms. Suddenly, people began to run around naked, not knowing where. They ran and fell. Not one man was saved from this fire".

The town of Dukstas remained standing in its old place. The houses were not destroyed in the war. A few houses were burned accidentally when the Russians entered in 1944.

During my 4 hour visit in town in the fall of 1944, I met the same non–Jewish faces with their fake smiles and false compassion. Each one with his newly acquired wealth from stolen Jewish possessions and revolting bragging about how many Jews they managed to save.

[Col. 1335]

I sought out the direct Lithuanian murderers, but to no avail. The bandits escaped to surrounding areas and continued to rob, but not the Jews. There were none left. I found only one Jewish family in town, Hamburg–Zilberman.

Broken and without hope I walked through the former Dukstas Jewish streets, visiting the old Jewish corners, I found no trace of the past.

An autumn wind blew from the surrounding fields and chased me with cold and terror. Depressed, I left Dukstas on the next freight train leaving behind the judgement of history.

To close the historical overview, a period of only 78 years, I had to write rise and fall of the Jews of Dukstas. I am sure I did not write about everyone and everything. More would have been written if there had been more witnesses.

My deepest gratitude goes to my friends who helped gather some of the information, especially Reuven Hamburg, Bluma Hamburg–Zilberman, Nekhe Luria, Leyb Bloshteyn, Yisroel Dvidovitch of blessed memory, and my sister Miriam Wasserman.

The grave of Dukstas and the surrounding towns

[Col. 1335]

Do Not Cover, Earth, Their Blood...!

by Miriam Katcherginsky – Wasserman

Translated by Janie Respitz

Tragic and horrific were our experiences which we will never tire of recounting and we will not stop remembering the loss of our mothers, sisters and brothers.

As long as we are alive on this earth, as long as we are still breathing, we will continue to see, in every drop of dew the tears of our mothers, and in every whisper of wind we will hear the prayers of our fathers and the reading of Psalms by all the simple Jews on their way to their death in the Dugutch forest.

We will forever be the children of the Holocaust who walk barefoot on the ashes and search for the flame of all those simple, yet devoted Jews from our town of Dukstas. Their song will ring in our ears for eternity, from the burnt out small synagogues, clubs and houses of prayer and study, the echo from the Psalms sung out by our fathers and great grandfathers.

Wherever we may find ourselves, we will hear the voice of all the bones of Dukstas and we will remember the holy words they said to us on usual and dreadful days.

The ruins of our town have cooled and are extinguished, but wherever we go we will forever carry the hellish flame from our destroyed and washed out town.

Those hellish fires will never be still or extinguished. They tug and twist in the quiet words that we bring like prayers, a contribution to the memorial book for the murdered Jews of the Sventzian region.

There are no towns, entire worlds destroyed and no words for the tragedy and nor words for the deep pain. Entire generations lost their lineage in the blood soaked earth. The silent skies reflect their glances, the winds carry their ashes and their souls fly in all spaces like the wings of white doves.

All the forests rustle in a lamenting cry for the thousands of martyrs. All the hilltops remind us of the heaps of children's shoes, all the caves – in the gloomy ghettos.

We will never forget, never, we will never forget you, fathers and grandfathers, mothers and sisters from our dead home, Dukstas, our dear town. The cry of blood will never be silenced, which was absorbed in the ground of the forest Degutch.

[Col. 1337]

Podbradz, Lintop, Kimelishak

[Col. 1339]

The Last Prayer

B. Mordekhai

Translated by Janie Respitz

Father removed his Tefilin today and let out a big sigh,
It rocked the stillness in the house like a heavy bell.
Like a black bird, his hand trembled the half – wrapped head piece.
An asthmatic answered from the rain outside.
Your sighs, father, are like thin swords, that sharply cut your limbs.
Oh, cry out, the storm of your painful years,
Silence is calling from years of talk, voice – the walls are dark, more screaming
Leaking from all corners in the silent frost.
Oh, tear out the storm from your heart, so a stone can also hear
A wild tempest from your blood should blow the world apart.
These are everyone in the town's troubles
How to save people from a sinking ship.
But quietly, father won't shout today, he won't even speak.
The screams are stuck like a fire in his limbs.
Autumn winds are blowing in the streets, the last prayer in town
And chestnut trees in the yard are confessing their sins.

1934

At the Flames

B. Mordekhai

Translated by Janie Respitz

Today I make a blessing, the grandchild of Guli Sefarad[1], in all the markets and streets I whisper the blessing,
Thank you, lord: they take me again to all places to burn,
A sign: after hundreds of years of slaughter they have not broken me yet,
A sign, I am alive – and my life is a light that not all can carry
And at the pyres I warm my hands and sing from The Song of Songs,
About eternal blossoming, eternal growing, eternal youth, full of strength,
He who throws me in the fire, will burn his own brains.
And I, purified, open all paths to capture people's brains.
I am no longer writing the Book of Lamentations – rather I am giving offering teachings, new prophecies,
(Because even the seeker from Trevir – Karl Marx, is, like Jesus of Nazareth, one of my brothers)
Hey! Throw me into the flames – the grandchild of Guli Sfarad laughs at fire.
Flames alone, and his steps are pyres for all the thorns.

1934

Footnote:

Could be a reference to the Inquisition

[Col. 1341]

The Establishment and Development of the Shtetl

Aharon Bavarski

Translated by Anita Frishman Gabbay

Podbrodz was one of the small shtetls in the Vilna province. Since the great catastrophe [Holocaust] that descended upon the Jewish people from all these towns, it is now our Holy duty to *shine a light* from whatever source and from whomever remains to tell their story, about those inhumane events that led to its demise. Writing about how we survived will serve as a memorial to all the Jewish communities that existed there for generations but ended in genocide and destruction.

On a large piece of land that stretched from Vilna to the former Russian border, at the train station that tied Warsaw and Petersburg, the shtetl of Podbrodz was founded in 1863–1865. The rivers Zemiane and Duvinke cut through the shtetl in one direction, and the train line cut through in a second direction. The Sosnove forest surrounded the shtetl on all sides and it became a suitable place for *dachas* and *pensiones*. Through the entire length of the shtetl a highway passed that tied Vilna to Sventzian.

Because of the short distance, 50 kilometers, Podbrodz was called the “father's bedroom” of Vilna. It was actually true, as the summer homes were occupied by Jews from Vilna and the *dachas* in Podbrodz were famous throughout the entire Vilna township.

The population was comprised of Jews, Poles, Lithuanians, Russians, one Karaite and one Tatar.

[Col. 1342]

There was no need for a special count of the population, as we are told. One could sit down with a glass of tea, take a stroll through the shtetl and count the Jews. We went from street to street, alley to alley and could point out each one by his name, take a count and total the amount of Jews in the shtetl.

The large bridge over the Zemiane river, on the side ran the river Duvinke

[Col. 1343]

Understandably, we could do it this way, as we knew each young and old person.

This count started at Tzufrinker on Vilner Street, as we arrived in the shtetl from the Vilna side, until Shmuel Chaim Mirski; on the way we didn't have to include Odeskin, the goyish convert. He even spoke Yiddish and called Jews for a minyan, especially to say Kaddish when his father died. He even knew how to say a blessing: "*Baruch ata...* king of the universe" *shine a light* fundamentally he was a non– Jew and we didn't have to include him in our count.

From Mirski we had to walk for some time until we arrived at the "brasgunes" (this could be a family name=Brashgun)–a family that spoke with a weird clinging sound, like the clanging of bells that hung around the horses' necks in the wintertime.

From there we went to Arianer Street until Shloime the *volik* (type of boot) maker and then back to Berl Fine.

At Berl's we had to be vigilant and remain very still, because he was a Jew who took great care of his health. We couldn't make a wind passing his house. God forbid he caught a cold in the winter.

[Col. 1344]

He used to take sand from his pockets and throw it in front of him in order not to fall. He was a very cautious Jew!

From there we continued along Vilner Street, passing the Inn, until we came to the boss of the shtetl, Reb Israel Bratanishki. Here, next to his house, we purposely rested in order to hear his Torah reading. He was a Torah great scholar, an authority in *Shas and Paksim.* He was always busy during the holidays, sitting and teaching a page of Gemara with great enthusiasm.

Rabbi Israel Bratanishki always found a way to help a fellow Jew in a difficult situation, whether with charity or with friendly advice.

On the way we also have to mention another boss, who we called Abramke "Feigel", at Simchat Torah he got so drunk he barely managed to make his way home.

From there we had to cross the small bridge, also to Boyarel (could be the name of another small village). There we found Rabbi Leibe Lapp, sitting on the porch of his house. It gave him great pleasure to sit for hours staring at the Zemiane river.

Not far from Rabbi Leibe Lapp lived Fishel the tailor. He was a Jew with a majestic beard and a constant smile on his face. He would stand, with his small Tallit humming a beautiful nigun (melody) while cutting his fabric.

Picture of Fishel Rudnitzki, which was printed in the daily newspaper, "The Forward", famous in America.

It shows a picture of a typical tailor in a Lithuanian shtetl, working and studying in his leisure time, doing both with great enthusiasm. What brought out these fine Jewish melodies that surrounded him as he was working, these melodies filled with of longing and sadness?

[Col. 1345]

Pilsudski Street

A Polish officer photographed him and the picture was printed in the New Year in the *The Forward.*

From Fishel we had to take a left turn and go in the direction of the mill.

Not far from the water mill, at the edge of the town, under a small hill, was a small house where Shloime the *gribener* (one who likes to ruminate) lived.

Going back we had to pass the same small streets because there was no other way to reach the large bridge. On this route we could encounter Rabbi Sheftlin sitting and reading a book. In my days, he was already in his eighties. He was still lucid and lively. He played chess and checkers, studied a page of Gemara and even read a modern book or novel. He was well versed in Russian and loved to listen to a concert. It was a pleasure to have a conversation with him. He always had a joke or a witticism, a Jew of great aspirations, he was a combination of the old and the new generation.

From him we arrived at Kaisener (King) Street, until Doctor Raizshefski, and then we arrived at Pilsudski Street, which was considered our main street (boulevard) of the shtetl.

There was Taibe–Golde's hotel, if only I could stop by. From here we passed Sender Kagan (an), the pharmacist Kavkin, and the watchmaker Luvatzki.

Before we crossed the railroad I could remember that Leizer the Melamed [teacher] also lived there, an interesting personality.

After the railroad tracks, we had to continue on the left side. On the right of the station only the Gentiles lived.

[Col. 1346]

On this left side lived Meike Krol, a tall, broad and heavy–set young man who was known in the region as a man of great strength. The Jews of the shtetl were very proud of him and his presence made us feel more secure. Even the Gentiles feared him and didn't want to antagonize him.

From Meike Krol we continued further to Sventzianer Street and finally at the end we reached the cemetery. This was a good sign, we finally ended our count. In the final total of old young, men and woman, the total number was about 960 Jewish souls.

The Religious Life

There were 2 Beit Midrashim and several small minyanim, where all the Jews assembled for Saturdays and holidays. In the Beit Midrash we got to meet our friends and receive the latest news (gossip) of the shtetl and from the outside world.

Quite often we heard a sermon by Rabbi Perski or from a teacher who arrived as a guest in the shtetl. Rabbi Perski was a Jew, a Talmud scholar, very talented with a sharp wit.

From the religious community we also must mention the Chazzan and the 3 Shochets.

The life of the Beit Midrash revolved around learning or to *hand out a fat [large] Aliyah.* (Aliyah=honor bestowed when a sum of money was pledged).

The honor at the *Niehlah prayer*, at Yom Kippur, [the Aliyah] was reserved for the Shklaravitch family. Iser the butcher always bought the portion "*you showed him* shine a light".

The Beit Mamidrash played an important role in the lives of the children. They studied with Rabbi Zimel–Itzik. They reserved their pranks for Purim when they shot and murdered *Haman.*

Way before the holiday of Purim, the youth started preparing locks, picked mushrooms, fixed nails and prepared for the great "battle" against the Jewish enemy of Persia.

When we started to read the *Magillah Esther*, we all waited impatiently, until they read the portion reminding us of about the terrible times for Israel.

[Col. 1347]

As loud as the Torah reader screamed the name "*Haman*", the entire Beit Mamidrash fell into a disorder (a thunder), the walls seemed to shake! Now the children took the opportunity to fight and denigrate the terrible enemy *Haman*.

Another holiday that included the youth was Simchas Torah. We sang and danced, drank and ate, but we also had to rally for an Aliyah, which made us feel worthy and somewhat older.

Yom Kippur provided the shtetl with a different atmosphere. Even the Gentiles feared the night of Yom Kippur which they called, "*strachna natz*", the scary night.

Tisha B'av, the Beit Mamidrash became a meeting place where the young people "threw nuts" and passed this sad day playing.

On the day of the holiday *Beit Hashoeva* [the water drawing festival] the orchestra of the firefighters, comprised only of Jews, played.

Even Zionist activities were conducted in the Beit Midrash. All the Zionist speakers and activities took place here. The "Aliyah" was often given as a donation to the Keren Kayemet or the Keren Hayesod.

When the Jewish world celebrated an important national holiday, such as, the Balfour Declaration or the opening of the University in Jerusalem, a celebration took place in the Beit Midrash. Opposite, when the state regime issued a warning or the Arabs attacked or carried out a massacre, the synagogue became a place of mourning or protest.

In the large synagogue there was a recluse [*who devoted his time to sacred study*], the children looked at this weird person and ridiculed him. As he didn't seem to know his real name, they called him, *porush* [recluse]. This created a form of entertainment for the children.

The second Beit Midrash was only a Gemillut Hesed, which shared the synagogue space and the handouts took place here. No memories or special remarks can be remembered from this one.

[Col. 1348]

The Folk Shuls

Of all the Jewish institutions of the shtetl, the Folk–Shul played the most important role. During the First World War, during the German occupation, the Jewish children studied in the state school. After the war, when the Poles occupied our region, Podbrodz founded a Jewish school. It was in a dacha of a rich Jew from Vilna, by the name Kamin. It was a summer house and didn't have ovens in all the rooms. The children and the teachers suffered from the cold during the winter. During a frost, it was difficult to study.

Summer and spring were very suitable for learning, but at that time the house needed to be vacated, so the vacationers from Vilna could use it.

The school suffered many hardships. The teachers were paid only for 10 months, 2 months they went without pay.

Yiddish Folk–Shul 1928

In the second year, another building was found. They rented Yudel Epstein's second floor and it was easier to study in the wintertime.

In my memory remains engraved the teachers Dobke and Vilentchik whose devotion and love I will never forget.

The Yiddish school didn't last long. The difficult economic situation, in the beginning of the 1920s, the lack of books, supplies and teachers, led to the liquidation of the Jewish school.

[Col. 1349]

I actually remember, when the help committee handed out tablets and pencils, while notebooks and pens were not available. Every 2 students received 1 tablet. I had to share with Toine Epstein. She didn't want to share and this is the situation I had to deal with.

After the school closed the students took private lessons from Beker, in Shilnochike's that later became a hotel. Only rich and select children left for Vilna and studied in the Real–Gymnasia and the middle school of Sophia Markovna Gurewitz.

The situation lasted several years, in 1924 finally the “Tarbut School” was founded in Abrashe Krol's house, on the second floor.

Tarbut 1924

Below: **Ring, Loibe Krol, Guta Mirski, Yehudit Feler, Chaia Shapira, Moishe Mirski, teacher, Chana Blitz, Rochel Patashnik, Tzila Lubotski, Leib Orman**
Above: **Leia Mirski, Aske Gordon, Aharon Bavarski, Abraham Charmatz, Yitzhak Vilian, Shabtai Mirski, Ben-Zion Eingelzin**

Ha-Chalutz 1925

Below; **Sara Kovarski,—, Mirski, Danishevski, Motel Shmidt, Elka Cheifetz, Chana Blitz,—**
Sitting: **Ben-Zion Aronovitch, Ezriel Patasnik, Bankover, Nachman Bavarski, Ruven Bavarski, Michal Bavarski, Nate Mirski**
Standing: **Yitzhak Blitz, Avraham Abramovitch, Meir Blitz, up above: Rivkind, Schmidt, Dovid Lapp, —, Patasnik**

[Col. 1350]

1926, Freedom and Preparation for Life in the Land

Motel Schmidt, Shapira, Abraham Abramovitch, Nachman Bavarski, Israel Epstein

The first teachers were: Kopelovitch, Danishevski, Blitz and the female teacher was Helena.

Many children also studied in the Polish school, in *Boyerel*, which was on a high educational level. These were the children whose parents didn't raise them with a Zionist passion.

The Tarbut school had a colossal influence on the development of all the Zionist organizations like Ha' Shomer Ha'Zair, He'Halutz, Tzeiri Zion, He'Halutz Ha'zair and others.

Thanks to the Tarbut Shul, the Jewish people renewed their interest in Zionism and the Hebrew language.

Tarbut school 1930

Right to left: sitting: **Sonia Charmatz, Esther Rifkind, teacher, —, —, —, —, Keila Ring, Ita Kalanski, Cana Charmatz, Charmatz, Fraida Brataniski, Asher Leizerovitch, Leizer Mirski, Yekutiel Eingelzin, Elihu Shilan, —, Shaoul Lapp, Leizer Trachtenberg, Elihu Krol, Tuvia Lubitch, Abraham Mirski, —**

[Col. 1351]

Tanach and Hebrew were taught by Kopelovitch and Polia Danishevski, who was a graduate of a Hebrew gymnasium and spoke a fluent Hebrew. He uncovered the beauty of the Hebrew language for his students, which was unknown on a daily basis at that time.

Hanan Blitz, the first graduate from Podbrodz at that time, gave the Jewish children a good foundation for mathematics, geography and biology.

The teacher Helena, a Jewish maiden, taught Polish and excelled in the Polish language and literature.

All these above–mentioned teachers laid a foundation for "worldly" schools in the Hebrew language and everyone in the region knew that Podbrodz had an excellent Tarbut school.

The school instilled in each one of us the Zionist spirit. The teachers taught us the love for Eretz Israel. I will never forget when the University in Jerusalem was opened, we celebrated in our shtetl this wonderful holiday! The children arranged the special day in the forest on a hill.

The first Tarbut school existed only 2 years, and closed due to its large deficit. A few years later it was reopened, thanks to the help from the "culture center of Tarbut".

Participants

Below: **Slove Lapp, Chaia Naradski, Noite Epstein, Mirele Kopelovitch, Feige Skurkovitch, Feige Mirski, Glas, Sara Reitenberg, Shabtai Mirski, Abraham Charmatz, Moishe Mirski, Zav Bratanishki, Moishe Lapp, Fani Rabinovitch, Devoirah Feler, Chaia Vilian, Chana Charmatz**

[Col. 1352]

The new school was in a better building, next to the Folk–Bank.

The first Aliyah to Eretz Israel from our shtetl started. The first were: Natke Mirski, Nachman–Lew Bavarski, and Yerachmiel Patasnik. The leadership of the Zionist clubs were taken over by the Bar Mitzvah youth.

Hashomer Hazair

Sitting: **Israel Gordon, Lapp, Leizer Trachtenberg, Shaoul Lapp, Leizer Mirski, Yechutiel Eingelzin, Yose Schklaravitch,**
2nd row: **Abraham Gordon, —, Leizervitch, Abraham Charmatz, —, Fenke Socnovitch, Ahron Bavarski, Monia Charmatz, —, Shaike Charmatz**
3rd row: **Sholem Schklaravitch, Berl Eingelzin, —, Ester Trakinski, Chana Charmatz, Leia Charmatz, Zev Bratanishki, Sura Reitenberg, Yehudit Zak, Ester Rifkind, Leifer, Sura Vilian, Chaia Narotzki, Mina Leizerovitch**
On top: **Teiba Charmatz, Ben-Zion Ain Ziporah Orman, Ruven Patasnik, Chana Baltvinik, Ziporah Malaravitch, Devorah Feler, Feiga Skurkovitch, Elisva Skurkovitch, Rochel Patasnik, Feiga Mirski, Tzilah Sparber, Chaia Mirski, Hene Lapp, Nite Epstein, Itzhak Vilian, Leib Blitz, Chaia Blitz, Moishe Lapp, Israel Feler, Shabtai Mirski, —, Glaz, —, Linde**

The school's existence became easier. The never ending question of teachers and books was addressed. The youth groups helped to maintain the school financially. The parents paid according to their means. Funds were raided through gatherings, lectures, a flower-day, and others, the most important: the plays by the drama club.

Several committees were comprised of 16 and 17 year old boys and girls, friends of Shomer Hatzair. At first it seemed strange that the elders didn't form a committee, but we got used to it and this created a new experience for us.

The Public Library [folk–library]

The public library was the institution in Podbrodz which they were the proudest, it possessed over 4000 books and benefitted not only the children but also the adults.

The books were in Yiddish, Polish, Russian, Hebrew and German. Surrounding its foundation many discussions and struggles were fought. Each side wanted to have a greater influence over the library. Again the Yiddishists versus the Hebraists, each group trying to influence the management with their representation in the membership.

The management of the library was involved with cultural undertakings, for example, literary evenings and discussions. Thanks to its existence, many of the young people had the opportunity to distance themselves from the atmosphere of the older generation.

The library provided usefulness to the thousands of vacationers each summer. For 3 months every year there was constant activity. The guests, who were from the larger cities, expressed their gratitude for such an important library and made it famous in the region.

First the library was in a rented building. Later, "bricks" were collected and thanks to the financial assistance of *friends*, a new building was built. At that time this was an unknown thing in the whole province. First, we never dreamed of possessing our own library building!

The hall also served as a theatre. From then on we didn't have to move the benches from the fire station and then return them. Even though we made do with the other "locale", it was not an ideal situation.

The building was a rarity in those times and Podbrodz was unique in this way, this building and theatre became well known in the entire region.

[Col. 1354]

The Drama Club

Like in all the other towns, the youth of Podbrodz needed a cultural outlet and the drama club provided such an atmosphere. Each performance infused new life and enthusiasm in this forgotten shtetl. Most of the plays were in Yiddish, several later on in Hebrew.

The most popular plays were from Sholem Aleichem and Gordin.

The youth devoted themselves to this amateur– theatre, they found either interest in performing or simply used it as a meeting place; this was a fundamental inheritance for the Jewish people, to see theatre.

Also from an artistic point of view, it didn't fall short. Podbrodz was proud to possess several talented people, who had the "talent" to perform in larger city theatres.

Many of the summer vacationers came to these performances which they were accustomed to as they lived in larger cities. They were full of praise and the reviews were very positive.

Alihu Licht was the director for many years. Everyone remembers until today," Kuni Lemel", "The Lottery", "Tuvia the Milkman"," Seven Hanged", and others.

Two students participated with enthusiasm: Hoita Epstein and Ben Zion Eingelzin who played in Osip Dimov's "The singer of sadness".

Often people arrived and the tickets were sold out. The hall was always filled, head to head. Sometimes the performance played twice, and from time to time we displayed our talents in other shtetls. The drama club was an important work of art in the region and our amateur–artists were praised wherever they went.

[Col. 1355]

The Orchestra

Right after the First World war the youth of Podbrodz organized a string orchestra. Slowly we accumulated the necessary instruments, especially, mandolins and guitars and then we began to play. The musical talents were: Chaim Lunefski, Abrasha Skrolovitch, Chaim Fine and the 3 Bavarski brothers. Abrashka played the *klavir* [piano], the others the mandolin, guitar and balalaika. The ensemble played for 5 straight weeks, even with the Ukrainian Theatre of Rudenka when they visited Podbrodz.

Often concerts with rich classical music took place, they even played folk music (popular Yiddish songs). It is incredible to imagine that these musical and talented young people never saw a note.

At that time no one owned a radio in our shtetl, in select homes we could find a gramophone.

We were afforded the opportunity to listen to music on account of this "ensemble", we also had a military orchestra which played the entire summer in the forest. Thanks to this military orchestra, our own "fire–fighters" orchestra was founded. All the participants were Jews, they were: Shmuel Gavenda, who played the bass, Yosef Mirski, the clarinet, Arke Gordon was the tenor, Pinka Shapiro was the baritone and 2 bar–mitzvah boys played on a small and old *baraban* (military drum).

The fire– fighters orchestra played during all the parades in the shtetl and for all the simchas (celebrations, Jewish and non–Jewish).

The 2 teachers, the sisters Ida and Roza Shapiro, made it possible for a conservatory of music to be founded in Podbrodz, where they taught *klavir* (German= piano).

This shows the artistic heights the youth in the shtetl achieved.

This is how we lived and the developed the shtetl Podbrodz in the Vilna province. We built important cultural institutions with our own efforts and determination, a small ring in a larger chain of Jewish life in all of Poland.

Firefighters

Below: **—, Ischayu Rudamin, Chaim Fine, Abraham Gordon, Faiva Lubitch, Aske Gordon, Shapiro, Ischayhu Lapp,—, Abrasha Shklaravitch, Leib Zilber, Burmitch, —, Peretz Lapp, Israel Epstein**
Standing: **Ben Zion Abramovitch, Kovarski, Chana Yavitch, Yerachmiel Trackinski, —,—,Ezriel Potashnik, Michal Bavarski, —,—, Abraham Abramovitch, Dovid Lapp, —, Abraham Gordon, Chaim Lunefski, —,—,—,— ,Yitzhak Zilber, Shmuel Krol, Yitzhak Blitz, Idel Kulback, Mule Narodzki**

[Col. 1356]

Orchestra 1920

Sitting below: **Tzvi Aronavitch, Suzan, Yosef Bavarski, Yulke Rifkind,—, Oske Gordon**
Middle: **Shmuel Krol, Dovid Lapp, Esterel Lapp, Gita Vilian, Rivka Shapiro, Feiga Katz,—, Yehudit Kravtchinski, Ida Shapiro, Roze Shapiro**
On top: **Alter Epstein, Meir Gordon, Yuntche Luefski, Shulamit Lunefski, Yosef Shapiro, Chaim Lunefski, Idel Kulback**

[Col. 1357]

Our Way of Life

by Ben-Zion Lapp

Translated by Anita Frishman Gabbay

On a hill, near the ...., stood the old and large synagogue. In the summer you could see through the open windows of the synagogue, Fishl the tailor, standing and holding a Gemara in his hand and singing such beautiful and melodious tunes. You could also see Moishe the Blacksmith asking a question to the Rabbi Israel Bratanitski and he shows him with his finger in the Gemara, while deep in thought, looking at the stars and stroking his beard.

Because of Podbrodz's beautiful and rich nature, it became a very well known summer vacation spot in Poland. In the summertime (before the first World War), thousands of summer residents arrived here, even from St. Petersburg and Riga. In and around the nearby woods, beautiful and modern pensions were built. Amongst those of the providers were the blacksmiths, the bakers, the fishermen, the haberdasheries, and others.

Besides this, there were other summer homes built in the woods, which were rented out either for a month or a week. The revenue alone from these summer homes(Dachas) would provide income in addition to all products which had to be provided. These summer rentals would provide a very good income for the shtetl folk. Butchers would deliver meat to these summer homes, Bakers-breads and other baked goods, storekeepers-others necessary articles, peasants-fruit and vegetables, handworkers would come to repair clothes, shoes and other things. Shopkeepers would bring eggs and poultry, butter and cheese, ...Many families earned a living from this.

In the summer evenings you could hear music, singing and other sounds coming from these summer homes.

[Col. 1357]

Most important, the coffee-house of Shapira was packed, where you would eat "Marozhina" (ice cream).

The summer residents would often make outings to the green and yellow lake, which was located several kilometers from the shtetl. There they would spend their leisure time fishing. Even from these excursions, many Jews earned a living.

A second and noteworthy way of earning a living, came from the Military Barracks that encircled the shtetl. About 8 kilometers from the shtetl was a large Military fortification, which until 1914 was named: Alexanderovitch fortification. Everyone came from near and far, as this was the largest Military fortification in Russia.

A lot of Jews did business there, stalls made from wooden boards, food stores, restaurants and other things. Also, the handworkers from the shtetl came to the fortification: like watchmakers, shoemakers, barbers, and others.

This produced great envy amongst the non- Jewish population and an order was given forbidding the Jews to provide any kind of service to the Military. The shtetl Jews immediately found an answer to this disaster. They sought out friendly Christians and immediately resumed their business using their names.

After the first World War a military base still remained there and the Jews were still the main suppliers of meat and bread.

Before the first World War "The Bund" in our town played an important role about the political and way of life.

[Col. 1359]

Quite often speakers would come to meet in our shtetl in someone's home, in the summertime they would conduct these meeting in the nearby woods.
In those days there was also a Jewish library in our shtetl, many books were scattered throughout the homes of our shtetl.

When pogroms against the Jews broke out in Russia, this also had an impact on the Gentile population of our shtetl and in Podbrodz the atmosphere was also hostile. The Jewish youth found out about this and organized a counterattack. They immediately raised money and bought revolvers, iron capsules with explosives, and placed them all around the Jewish streets of the shtetl. The entire Jewish youth banded together and waited for a signal, in order to prevent an attack on the Jewish folk.

At that time I was still a very young boy, but I remember to this day how Mendke Katz, fired a shot in the air, as a warning to those who were preparing to attack us, that Jews were prepared to arm themselves and this would be a warning not to bother with us.

This had a great impact on the Christian population and as a result the program in Podbrodz did not take place.

This was the effect "The Bund" had after the first World War and was organized in our shtetl. Later many left for the larger towns, others immigrated to America and the numbers of the "Bund" were depleted.

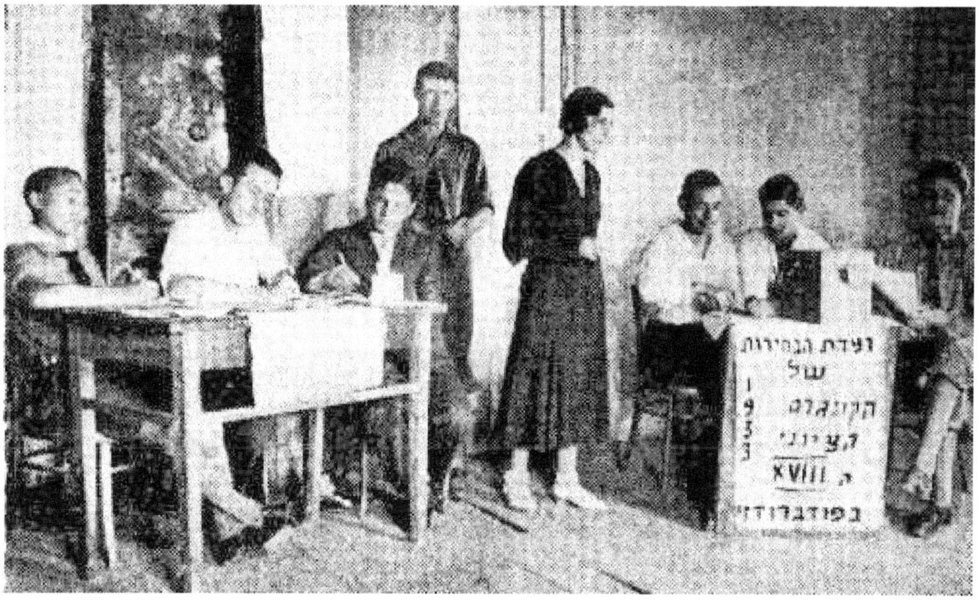

Congress-volunteers in July 23, 1933
Ben-Zion Sklarovitch, ___, Shalom Sklarovitch,______, Aharon Bavarski, Aharon Trachtenberg

[Col. 1360]

The Zionist calling beckoned the Jewish youth and most of them dreamed that they would meet in Eretz Yisroel and end their days there. Only Aharon Engelson and his wife Chaia Surel, until the very last hour of their lives, were Bundists, and met their end by the Lithuanian and German bandits.

After the first world war, a large "Halutz" movement took place: we went to "Hakhshara" (pioneer training camps), raised funds for "Keren Kayemet", and helped found the "Tarbut-Schul" and other things. The most important Jewish institution in the shtetl was the public library with its own building, its guiding light was Rabbi Chaim Lonefski, the director, who was devoted to this institution.

He made a living from watchmaking and photography, but he often left his work because of his love for the library. Entire nights he would spend there, in order to organize these books, to number them and to catalogue them, post events, go to Vilna to buy books, to bring lecturers and other things.

During the Nazi occupation, Chaim Lonefski, was one of the first to fall into those murderous hands.

A Flower Day for the Keren Kayemet

Below sitting: **Krol, Golda Kraftshinski, Rebecca Shapira, Ben-Zion Lapp, a teacher, Krol**
Standing: **Neme Mirski, Rebecca Blazman, Raya Silber, Meir Eingelson, Pina Krol**
On top: **Mina Mirski, Zvi Aronovitch, Narodski, Sura Ring**

[Col. 1361]

Rabbi Moshe Perski

by Nathan Perski

Translated by Meir Razy

Rabbi Moshe Perski

Rabbi Moshe Perski was the Rabbi of the Jewish community of Podbrodz (Pabrade, Lithuania) in the district of Sventzian between the two World Wars. He was known as God-fearing, a bright scholar and excellent preacher who possessed many other good qualities. He did not limit himself to the world of Halacha but also dealt with public affairs and led his community honestly and with a firm hand.

He was born in the city of Minsk. His father, Rabbi Benjamin, was a Jewish scholar, a Mishnah scholar and a strict follower of the Jewish traditions. Rabbi Moshe was educated in a Cheder and was one among the many Yeshiva students in that great city. Later he studied for many years at the famous Yeshiva of Volozhin and was considered one of the most prominent students by this great Yeshiva's leaders. He continued studying there for several years even after he was ordained as a Rabbi and after starting a family in the town of Karelichy, near Novogrudok, supported by his father-in-law.

His life was not easy. When the First World War broke out, as the town of Karelichy was on the front line, his family was displaced along with all the other Jews. As a student of the Yeshiva he was unable to find a paying job to support his family. His “merchandise” was his knowledge of the Torah, which was not a desirable commodity during the hard times of the war.

Many Jewish refugees gathered in the city of Novogrudok. The grocers and merchants who brought a little money with them started small businesses while the young scholar and his family were destitute and hungry. Indeed, those early years of the First World War were years of hardship and suffering, hunger, deprivation, despair and depression. The bitterness that accumulated in the heart of the young Rabbi nibbled at his psyche and stirred his spirit.

In 1916, Rabbi Moshe Perski was appointed as a Dayan (=Judge) and the head of the Yeshiva of Rabbi Reines in the city of Lida. His students and associates at the Yeshiva grew fond of him but his financial situation was quite strained. The well-known Reines Yeshiva was destroyed during the war and had to be rebuilt but, who was interested or had the financial means to study during the war years? The town was captured by the Russians, then the Germans and then given to the Poles while pogroms were always close-by. Who was available to study Torah in such terrible years?

[Col. 1362]

At the end of the First World War Rabbi Moshe Perski was appointed Rabbi in the town of Podbrodz, near Vilna (Vilnius). The town was beginning to recover from the war. While its Jewish residents were not property-rich, most of them were engaged in small trading and crafts and many of them started to flourish. It was a progressive, cheerful and full-of-life town; full of warmth and vigor, blessed with an educated and largely Zionist-oriented youth. The town was close to Vilna and the spirit of openness that came out of Vilna encouraged parents to give their children a proper general education. There was no demand for traditional Cheders in the town. One by one the Cheders were closed down and were replaced by modern secular schools: the older one was the Yiddish School and the newer one was the Hebrew TARBUT School. The majority of the graduates of the elementary school system turned to high schools In Vilna while others joined various Yeshivas.

Concerned about the education of the younger generation, Rabbi Moshe Perski worked hard to establish a religious school in the town. He fought vigorously against the Yiddish School until it was closed and he even established a national religious school next to the Hebrew TARBUT School. The religious school's approach was “nationalistic” too. It taught using the Hebrew language and provided a general education, albeit traditional. The teachers were devout Jews who had received a good secular education in addition to their Jewish education. Over the years, that religious school was also closed and the Rabbi's efforts turned towards maintaining the traditional character of the TARBUT School. He made sure that the school's Judaism studies were kept to a high standard and that its Judaism teachers were Torah scholars and observant Jews. And indeed, the townspeople were educated in the spirit of tradition and nationalism. Most of them were enthusiastic Zionists and many of them immigrated to Ertez Israel as Pioneers many years before the Holocaust that hit our people in Poland and other countries. A number of these townspeople, many of who live in Israel today, occupy important positions in various fields.

Rabbi Moshe Perski was admired by all the members of his congregation. They respected him for his wisdom and deep knowledge of Judaism, for his acumen, his honesty, his courage and his dedication to the needs of the community.

[Col. 1363]

Jews would attend his lessons every evening in the synagogue. They were the "SHAS Company" who studied Talmud with the Rabbi. Others took classes in "Ein Yaakov" (an interpretation of the TALMUD, published in 1516) and others listened to the Legends of the Sages on Saturday nights in the Beit Midrash. His clear explanations attracted many listeners. His excellent sermons attracted large crowds who enjoyed his combination of Halacha, Midrashim and Legends.

The quotes that he inserted in the sermons and his melodic delivery captivated the audience. Not only orthodox Jews gathered to hear his sermons, but also secular Jews and the young people who usually would only come to the synagogue on High Holidays. People who heard the Rabbi's sermons felt a profound and memorable experience. Even if they did not agree with the ideas he was preaching, his words fascinated and penetrated deep into their souls. Rabbi Moshe Perski's sermons were great cultural events in town and the synagogue was packed. Old and young, men, women and teenagers flocked to hear to him.

While adhering to the Torah and Jewish tradition, Rabbi Moshe Perski pursued general education and culture as-well. He wanted the younger generation to adhere to the values of Jewish culture and tradition but also felt they should be exposed to the world's general knowledge and culture at the same time. Torah and general education, in his opinion, should be tightly bound together. He dedicated his entire life to educating the younger generation.

[Col. 1364]

Rabbi Moshe did not limit himself to religious studies and was very active in the public life of the town.

He was a tough adversary to his opponents, mostly various public figures. He relentlessly fought for his views and often angered many officials in his town. This did not deter him, sometimes alone, from insisting on his principles. He fought with the upmost zeal to remove any non-Zionist influence from the affairs of the community and, using his rhetorical skills, he successfully pushed his political opponents out of any important public positions. Who else was able to convince the public that his views were the correct ones? He maintained the national and traditional character of the town and defended its institutions regardless of the interests of the rich and powerful. Even his opponents respected his dedication to the Jewish religion and his commitment to national ideas.

Rabbi Moshe Perski served as the Rabbi in Podbrodz for almost twenty five years during the interwar period. He was full of energy, passion and belief in his endeavors. He studied the Talmud and the other Holy books day and night. He cared for the public more than he cared for himself and his family. He lived a humble life and was always sensitive to the wants of others and assisted those in need.

His powers left him during the terrible years of World War II and he died at the young age of 58. The memory of this righteous man will be forever blessed.

[Col. 1365]

My Father Rabbi Israel Bertinski, May God Avenge His Blood

by Mordechai Bartana

Translated by Meir Razy

My father, my father, Israel!

Which of your many eminent qualities shall I choose in order to describe you? You were honest in your way of thinking and in your actions, you kept away from intrigues and distanced yourself from any quarrels or arguments. You were a man of truth, careful not to say any falsehood and you taught us, your sons, to always stick to the truth, even if it would hurt us. You were humble despite your vast knowledge of the Talmud, GEMARA and the other holy books. You were open to modern literature and to world events. You refrained from seeking honor, although honor pursued you and the whole community chose you as its leader and spokesman. You were a source of advice and resourcefulness to the townspeople. Many shared their personal secrets with you and trusted you to be their arbitrator and judge.

But above all I see your kindness, which had no limit, towards every person and every being. While you were the head of the entire community, the poor and oppressed considered you as their father or brother. You did not have to open your hand to them because your hand was always open to every person in need. You shared all your possessions with those in need. You gave dowries to poor brides, you sent poor, sick people to hospitals at your expense. You created stores and workshops for those on the brink of failure. You were the leader of all public affairs in town and every matter, major or minor, was settled through your guidance.

The elementary school, 1922

[Col. 1366]

You paid a large part of the "Tarbut" School teachers' salaries, the school that you helped set up in town. You helped build the new synagogue – it is difficult to list all of your many, many good initiatives and deeds. Your numerous businesses (distribution centers for flour, tobacco, oil, petrol, groceries, shoes. leather, etc.) employed many of the town's people, and this fact made you stay even though you were planning to immigrate to Eretz Israel in the early 1930s. Your employees knew that they would lose their jobs and the cornerstone of the strength of the community if you left their town.

Rabbi Israel Bertinski

You were rich but you did not exploit your success for your own benefit. You always dressed modestly and treated each person like a brother.

You were distinct in town, different from everyone else in your nature, your temperament and your behavior. You were like a fortress, supporting every person who approached you. You were quiet and temperate. I have never heard you get upset or angry with anyone. If you were ever hurt by someone you always got past it, and the only response was: “He doesn't understand” and you moved on. You educated us in the same spirit and never hit us or punished us for our actions. This is why we took all your observations and opinions very seriously and were very careful how we behaved.

You taught us, your children, from our earliest years of life to speak the truth and only the truth. You were a great educator. You never demanded of us things we could not do. You tried to fulfill your children's requests and I do not remember a single instance that you replied to our wishes negatively. When you did not like something, you tried to explain its negative side to us and then you would summarize: “I don't think so, but you yourself can decide whether or not to accept my opinion.”

[Col. 1367]

You were wise. You encouraged your children to emulate your actions, your dress and your behavior. When relatives commented that they were surprised that you had not prevented your sons from doing something, you would normally reply: “If my children are similar to me in their nature, then when they grow up they will try to avoid doing anything wrong and be honest people. And if, G–d forbid, they are not like me in their nature, then my "bans" will not help and when they grow up they will only resent me."

Your workday always started with a wake–up call early in the morning. You prayed in the first Minyan and then you taught the attendants the daily page of the Talmud. Then you worked at your many businesses until noon. You were in contact with the largest flour mills in Poland, with food factories, with oil and tobacco suppliers both in Poland and abroad. You usually devoted the afternoon to the needs of the public. This you did through your memberships in public institutions such as the community leadership, the beadles of the synagogue, the management of the bank, the School Board Parents Association and so on. It was only after the night prayers that you found time for yourself and your family.

Your home was always open to all, and poor travelers dined at your table almost every day. Various people visited our home in the evening for their private affairs. They sat around the table with you and in the center of it stood a large samovar. Everyone drank tea, tasted the pastries and explained their claims to you. Occasionally you would meet with one of the visitors in private. Every person came out of your home satisfied, whether they came for advice or for help.

A special virtue was your secret almsgiving ("Matan baSeter"). You searched for people in distress and secretly helped them.

The Christians too respected and loved you. When the Russians conquered the town at the outbreak of World War II, the workers, both Jews and non–Jews alike, recommended your appointment as secretary of the Labor Association to the Communist authorities. This, even though you were the richest man in town! You held this position until the German destroyers, may their name be blotted out, entered the town and you died along with all the townspeople of Pabradė and the surrounding area. This came to pass in the Ghetto of Kamelishki on the Sabbath, the 12th day of Cheshvan 5703 (October 24, 1942). You were only 58 years of age. Along with you died your son, my brother Jacob, a pure, humble, knowledgeable Torah scholar; a wise man who had a compassionate heart for every creature. He was only 28 years old.

[Col. 1368]

And your son Shlomo Zvi, my 17–year–old brother, innocent, good–natured and pure. And my good sister Frieda, humble and devoted to any needy person as well as to her husband, Moshe Tanchum, my cousin. G–d will avenge them.

My father, Rabbi Israel, son of Rabbi Shlomo Zvi Bertinski and Golda of the Kemach family, was born in Nemenčinė. My grandfather was famous as a scholar and his name was well known all around the region. He had ten sons and one daughter, all of whom produced large families in Poland, Lithuania and Russia.

Except for my three uncles who immigrated to the United States before World War I, and me, (I immigrated to Eretz Israel in 1935), the only survivors of my grandfather's family were my brother Ze'ev and my sister Miriam. Both survived the Holocaust in ghettos, camps and forests. Everyone else – uncles, aunts, dozens of cousins were all lost along with six million of our people.

May G–d avenge their blood.

The Bertinski Family: Frieda, Marisha, Shlomo–Zvi, Mordechai (in the back)

[Col. 1369]

The Economic Situation of Podbrodz

From the "Pinchas of Lita" Yekapo, 1931

Translated by Anita Frishman Gabbay

In the 1930's the folk of the Podbrodz region was comprised of 30,000 souls, of which there were no more than 900 Jewish souls.

Over forty percent of the Jewish population was involved in shop keeping and small trade. Thirty percent were artisans, and the remaining thirty percent didn't earn a living.

The economic situation worsened in the last few years. The important market day, which took place every Monday, grew smaller than in former years. As in all the other shtetls, markets were opened all over. Only the peasants of the neighbouring hamlets came to Podbrodz.

Strangers also frequented the market, set up their stalls and undercut prices. They brought cheaper merchandise of inferior quality and our economic livelihood grew smaller. The Jewish merchants couldn't compete.

The main crisis for the Jewish shopkeepers was when the large Christian cooperative was opened, the Rolnik, rich in merchandise, attracted the entire peasant population.

The cooperative was well connected to the Christian Folk–Bank (People's Bank), which was rich in capital and gave credit at low prices.

The bank had over 1000 members. Each person had to have credit of 50 zlotes in the bank and also buy for the same amount in the cooperative. This way he was obliged to buy everything he needed in the cooperative.

This cooperative Rolnik, added another crisis to our situation. Speakers came and started agitations amongst the Christian folk, to buy only from Christian shops.

The cooperative also gave them merchandise on a credit at very preferential rates. All transactions were settled through the bank. The cooperative therefore never lost money, as the Christian Folk–Bank always rescued the cooperative if the need arose.

It is no wonder the Jewish shopkeepers were helpless in such circumstances.

To add to their economic problem, many cooperatives as well as Christian shops opened in the larger towns. It resulted in a loss of trade for the Jewish shops and Innkeepers.

In addition, the surrounding area was sandy and not prone to cultivating fruit. The peasants ability to buy anything was limited, therefore not having means to purchase goods. They spread false rumors that the Jews are sucking the economy with anti–

Semitic slurs, “Svai do svego.” The peasants soon believed this and stopped frequenting the Jewish shops.

The result is clear, eighty percent of the Jewish shopkeepers have a very small income. We can say if the loss in earnings of a shopkeeper is 25–30 zlotes a week and his wage is 300 zlotes a week, it is hard to live on this. Added to this are the taxes which are very high and definitely affects the bottom line.

After the taxes and other deductions, the shopkeeper is left with 15 zlotes a week. It is a pittance and result in a catastrophe for the Jewish shopkeeper.

One can imagine if the situation is so diminished for the shopkeeper, how the smaller tradesmen and artisans are faring. In the last years before the War, many Christian blacksmiths, shoemakers and tailors arrived in our small villages. Everyone's earning suffered and there was not enough money to buy a piece of bread. All lived in poverty and need.

Most of the Jewish folk took to gardening and working from their homes. Each one grew potatoes and vegetables which saved them from starvation. Very few Jews had money to buy a cow or chickens, so milk and meat were scarce.

Podbrodz was known for its beautiful scenery, for its summer–homes and beautiful forests. In dacha–season the economic situation improved. About 300 vacationers arrive in the area, and all the residents prepare to sell their various products. The income increased from prior days.

The dacha–season also brought a joyful atmosphere to the region. Our hearts were happier and more joyful. The big heartache is the dacha–season doesn't last more than 3 months, and when the students begin their studies, the shtetl become quiet and sad again.

The Polish military added to the economy in Podbrodz, stationed not far from town. We made a living from these soldiers even though they had their own military shops.

The bakeries also pay heavy taxes and we cannot envy them.

How can we survive in such a manner? The answer is quite simple. Most of the help comes from America.

[Col. 1371–1372]

Destruction and Holocaust

The Decline and Fall of Jewish Life in Podbrozie

(Pabradė, Lithuania)

55°00'/25°47'

By Ben Zion Lapp

Translation by Yocheved Klausner

Podbrozie belonged to Poland until the first of September 1939, when the Second World War broke out. On the 17th of September, the Soviet army marched into town. On the 28th of October, the same year, the Soviets gave up the entire region to Lithuania, and our town was occupied by Lithuanian troops. In June 1940 the Soviet army returned and remained there until the outbreak of the German–Soviet war.

On June 22, 1941, the Germans began bombing the Lithuanian cities Vilna and Kaunas, and our town Podbrozie was bombed as well. The target of this air attack was not only the military objects in our area, but also the important railroad junction. The first German air attacks caused terrible panic among the Jewish population.

The Jews packed their belongings and fled the town to acquaintances among the farmers in the surrounding villages. They believed that in the villages they will not be troubled as in town. The next day, however, they realized that it was not safe in the villages either. We heard, for example, that in the village Karkaziski, some 3 kilometers from town, Lithuanian officers broke into the house of the Jewish family Schmukler and shot both brothers Leizer and Moshe, and in another village Lithuanians shot the brothers Mirski and Chaim Zaken.

Myself, my wife, my father and my father–in–law, my wife's sisters and her brother–in–law, together with the Werfel family – we all went to a village not far from our town, to the home of a Christian acquaintance. Suddenly we observed, through the window, several Lithuanian officers who stopped our host and asked him whether he was hiding Jewish refugees.

We dropped to the floor and tried to be as quiet as possible, and the Lithuanians did not notice us. After a few minutes our host came in, pale and frightened, and when he realized what we had done, he said that we saved ourselves from certain death – for the time being. He had assured the Lithuanians that there were no Jews in his house, that all the Jews had run away. The question was, however, what will happen if they would demand to enter the house and search it.

We all realized that the village was not a suitable hiding place and we decided to return to Podbrozie. On the way we were stopped by Polish hooligans who tried to steal our horse and our belongings. We began asking for mercy and thanks to a Christian acquaintance that came to our rescue they let us go and we continued our journey home.

By that time the town was without regular governing authorities and deserters from the former Lithuanian army ransacked the place. Only on 29 June was Podbrozie formally occupied by the German army. The civil administration was given to the Lithuanian police, which was manned mostly by hooligans and murderers. They soon demonstrated what they were capable of: they would enter the Jewish houses, forced the Jews out and drove them to the army barracks and there they shot them on the spot.

Thus perished: Chaim Levenski, the tinsmith Chanan Schneiderowitz, Kopel Sklyarowitz, Idel Kolbak, the Lieberman brothers and others.

[Col. 1373–1374]

On July 15th the Lithuanians shot over 60 people, among them were: the old rebbetzin [the rabbi's wife] with her two sons, 70–year–old Israel Baruch Bawarski and his niece with her husband and children; Yitzhak Silber with his wife and child; Leibe–Nachum Glass with his wife and four children; Tadd with his wife and children; Abrashe Sklyarowitz with his wife, son and daughter; Kivelewitz with his wife, and several other families.

They were driven to a small forest near the mill, where a pit had been dug beforehand, and shot them upon arrival. Welvel Abramowitz, the old rebbetzin's son, was the sole survivor. He managed, miraculously, to escape from the very grave. Later, he became a partisan and after the war he returned to Podbrozie.

Right after the executions, official restrictions against the Jewish population were issued. At first it was demanded that all Jews wear white patches on the front and the back of their clothes. Later it was changed to yellow patches. Jews were not allowed to walk on the road or on the sidewalk, but only in the gutter and in single file, like animals. Jews were not allowed to shop in the market, not allowed to trade or have any negotiations with Christians and other such atrocities.

The private clinic of the Jewish dentist Kune Suzanne was closed and all the medical instruments taken. The Jewish doctor Reizhevski was forbidden to treat Christian patients. Jews were ordered to give all their radios to the authorities. In general, even those who were still alive were made to feel the hand of the German wild beast.

One day an order was issued, that all Jews – men women and children – gather on the square near the police building. All were certain that it would be the last moment of their lives, that the entire Jewish population will be murdered. Gloom spread over town, sobbing was heard in every corner.

After everybody gathered in the square, the military commandant came and made a speech. He explained that every Jew must work, that without work they will not receive food, and so on.

Right after his speech, a large number of Jews were sent to repair a road not far from town. Others were sent to the forest to chop trees, still others to the army barracks to clean the toilets.

Soon a “Judenrat” was formed, its object being to carry out all German orders concerning the Jews. In particular, the Judenrat would assign people to work and collect the imposed “contributions.”

Several days later, a new order was issued, requesting all the Jews to move to a ghetto, which was to be located in the two Christian streets: the Arnian and Bayarel Streets. The residents of these two streets were to occupy the vacated Jewish homes.

Christians began streaming to the houses of their Jewish acquaintances, each trying to “catch” a better house, with good furniture and riches.

Many Jews dug large pits in their gardens and hid boxes full of household objects, in the hope that they will sometime return to their houses. Others gave all their belongings to Christian acquaintances, hoping that they will be returned in better times.

Some of the Christians, however, asked the Jews to give them their valuable possessions, squarely telling them “what do you need these things, all of you are going to be shot anyway...”

Meanwhile, rumors spread – horrible rumors. Christian neighbors reported that in the surrounding villages and towns all Jews were slaughtered. In Njemenczin, for example, the Jews were taken to a place outside town and all were shot.

Christians, who came to Podbrozie on market day, would cross themselves when they still spotted some Jew. Often we heard them talking to each other, saying that it was a miracle that so many Jews are still alive in Podbrozie.

Receiving all these terrible news, we in the ghetto began to think of ways to save ourselves. The Judenrat collected money in order to try to bribe the Lithuanian police. We asked them at least to let us know when they planned to liquidate the ghetto.

In this gloomy atmosphere we lived in the ghetto 26 days, from the 1st to the 26th of September 1941. Friday, 26 September, we heard that they were going to liquidate the Podbrozie ghetto. All Lithuanian teachers, post–office workers, forest watchmen and tens of hooligans and underworld people were mobilized, to help chase out the Jews.

[Col. 1375–1376]

We decided to escape to Belarus, where the situation was not as dangerous as in Lithuania. Many of the Podbrozie Jews arrived thus to Kimelishak, Svir, Michaelishak, Lintop etc. Some were caught and shot right away.

I and my family, together with the Feller family, 9 persons in all, decided to hide in a cellar of a neighboring house in the ghetto. The door of the cellar we covered with hay. When the police came to look for Jews, they did not notice us, luckily. We heard them entering the house and looking around.

Shortly after we hid in the cellar, we heard shots and loud cries and weeping, mostly of women and children. We realized the slaughter of the Jewish population had begun.

We remained in the cellar the night between Friday and Saturday and the entire day Saturday. The second night we began thinking of going out of our hiding place to look for some food – the entire time we had not had even a sip of water. We all crawled out through a hole in the wall. It was a very dark night and we walked through the fields until we reached the house of a Christian that we knew, Gajdamowitz Gaspar. The Feller family went to another Christian, Stalewski, where they had left the day before their 6–months–old child.

At midnight we knocked on his door. His sister opened, and seeing that we were still alive, she fainted. They took us in and we told them how we were saved, but the wife explained that they were afraid to hide Jews in their house.

Her brother overheard our conversation. He got out of bed and dressed, then came out to us and asked us to follow him. He led us into a small shed and there we spent the night.

In the morning he brought us food: bread, eggs and hot coffee. We all opened our eyes in wonder. He explained, that for the time being we must not leave our hiding place, because death is lurking everywhere. Later the situation will perhaps improve. He led us into a place covered with hay and we remained there all day Sunday.

Sunday night, Gaspar brought the Feller family to join us. Stalewski had flatly refused to give them shelter.

The entire week we hid – all 9 of us – in the hay. Gaspar made great effort to bring us food. We noticed, however, that his entire family was very agitated, worrying that perhaps their neighbors would suspect anything. About a week later, Gaspar's uncle came running and very distressed: he told us that we must leave as soon as possible and run away, because the Germans and Lithuanians are searching the entire region, looking for hidden Jews.

Frightened, we all crawled out of the hay. Gaspar was already waiting for us in the courtyard. He took us aside and told us that the old man, his uncle, is simply afraid to hide us. But Gaspar had prepared for us a plan: one family will remain in the same place and the other will hide in a shack nearby. He will bring us food every day, but his own family must not know.

So we separated from the Fellers and went to our new hiding place. Often Gaspar would bring us some food. In this place we spent over five weeks.

One day, Gaspar came in and brought the news about the annihilation of the Podbrozie Jews. For the first time we heard what had happened and how horribly the 8,000 Jews in the Swenciany region perished.

We all admired the goodness of heart and the devotion of the Christian young man. When he was alone at home, he cooked for us a pot of potatoes and brought it to us. The neighbors probably (and hopefully) thought that he was carrying out food for the pigs or the horses.

In time, we told him where we had buried our money and valuables. He went there and dug them out – and brought us everything. We wanted to give him part of the money as a reward, but he refused categorically: "You – he said – will need it more than I."

[Col. 1377–1378]

News reached us, that in Belarus the situation was a little calmer, so we thanked him for all he did for us and told him that we have decided to leave for Lyntop [Lyntupy]. He told one of his friends and both took their wagons and took us to Lyntop.

There we realized that Lyntop is about to be annexed to Lithuania as well, so we didn't wait and started on foot toward Svir. On the way we were caught by the Belarus police. The news about this reached the Svir Judenrat and they bribed the chief of police and we were released.

And so we became official residents of the Svir ghetto. We went to work, like all of the Svir Jews, to chop wood, carry stones and other jobs. In the Svir ghetto, it was possible to buy food products, and we decided to send a messenger to Gaspar and ask him to send us some money.

In a few days the man returned and brought money and some other things.

We were not hungry any more, since we were able to buy food products. But together with the money we received through Gaspar the terrible news that the family of Doctor Reyzhewski, Berl and Ben–Zion Eingeltzin and Jonah Kevin with his family – all were murdered in the Barany village.

At about that time, tragedy struck Svir: a large group of young Jewish men were sent to work in a neighboring town, and soon we heard that all of them were murdered.

I was transferred to work in another village and I was able to bring my family with me. We didn't stay there long, since we were soon transferred to the Michalishok ghetto. From there we were sent to Vilna, where I worked at the railroad.

During that time, the Svir and Michalishok ghettos were destroyed and most of the Jews were murdered at Ponar.

One day I found out that my wife's father and sisters were hiding in a village 60 kilometers from Vilna and we managed to correspond with them. They sent us a cart and we went there. A Christian friend prepared for us a special hiding place under the roof of a stable.

We spent there about two weeks and we were glad that we had found a shelter with the help of such a good man, when suddenly terrible news hit us again, like a thunder: not far from us, a hiding place with many Podbrozie Jews was discovered. In the group were Feige Barawski with two sons, Chaia–Rivka Munitz and her son, Shmuel and Tzviya Shmidt and their child. All were shot, including the Christian man who had helped them.

This tragedy made a frightful impression on the Christians, who helped to hide Jews. All became terribly frightened, and "our" Christian not less than the others. He was scared, and we had to leave our hiding place.

We didn't know where to go. During the day we stayed in the forest, at night we would walk through the fields, looking for food and a place to rest.

Finally we found another Christian, who agreed to hide us in an attic for 25 poods [1] of grains a month. Soon, however, he changed his mind and we had to leave. It was raining on that day. Not far from the place there was a large swamp with tall trees, so we went there, and at night we would go looking for food. Some of the Christians in the neighboring villages, who were aware of our plight, had pity on us and would bring us food from time to time.

Finally we arrived at another village, where one of the farmers agreed to hide us. We remained there for a longer time, until Polish partisans came looking for arms. Seeing the partisans, we quickly fled to a nearby wood, because we had heard that the Polish partisans, as well, used to murder Jews.

We stayed a few days in the wood. It was raining and we suffered much. Suddenly, Polish partisans stormed the place and began shooting at us. My wife and her two sisters fell dead. They shot at me as well but did not hit me and I managed to run away. I found a little ditch and I hid there – it was full of water. I waited until it was dark, then I crawled out and began to walk, alone, not knowing where I was or where I was going.

[Col. 1379–1380]

After days of wandering and misery I arrived at a small village, and without asking anyone's permission I climbed into a small attic over a stable, where I spent the night. I had no food at all, not even water. Nevertheless, I decided to remain there the entire day. When night came, I climbed down and began walking again, until I reached the home of the Christian who had given us shelter before. He took me in and I stayed there for three weeks, all alone. He treated me quite well.

One morning, my host came running and said that troops of the Soviet army were stationed in the village. It was simply unbelievable that I was free, that my troubles and suffering has come to an end.

I went out of my hiding place and made my sorrowful summing–up: my wife and her two sisters remained lying in the little wood; my wife's father died in the village and was buried in a fox's den. All my dear and beloved have perished.

I was the only one left alive. What shall I do now? Where shall I go? I decided then and there that I shall do everything in my power to reach Eretz Israel. My wish came true: I live now in Haifa.

Translator's Footnote:

pood = a Russian unit of weight

[Col. 1379]

This is How I Was Saved

Eliyahu Likht

Translated by Janie Respitz

On the sad day of June 22nd 1941 I woke in the morning as usual and went to work as the manager of the bakery. Even though it was very early, the feeling on the street was unusual. Groups of people were standing on the street telling of sensational news which they had just heard on the radio. According to the reports, Hitler had attacked the Soviet Union and the larger cities of the Soviet Union were bombed from the air. Everyone was confused and did not know what to do.

[Col. 1380]

Truth be told, we always assumed war would break out between Germany and the Soviet Union, but no one thought it would happen so soon.

When I arrived at the bakery I met the baker who was panicking. No one knew what to do. No one thought about working. I tried to encourage everyone by telling them it was our obligation to get back to work. I did not succeed in calming the crowd. Everyone was talking only of one thing. How can we save ourselves? Every hour is crucial, they insisted. We must run away as fast as possible.

[Col. 1381]

I realized I had no choice and went home to discuss with my wife what we should do.

At noon, we heard Molotov's speech on the radio, and we no longer had any illusions. Molotov stated that German airplanes were bombing the peaceful cities of the Soviet Union such as Vilna, Kovno, Kiev and others.

I immediately decide with my wife to leave town. Our intention was to leave temporarily: until this will pass...we packed a few belongings and with the help of our neighbour Borukh Blushinsky we got a wagon and immediately set out on our wandering march. We eventually arrived in a village called Redzie.

The famers in the village received us warmly, even showing pity for our fate. Every day a farmer we knew went to town to find out what was going on. One day he returned and informed us Germans were patrolling the town but the administrative powers were given to the Lithuanians.

At this point we did not yet know of the mass murders the Lithuanians were carrying out in many towns, and we decided to return home. Returning with us were Blitz, Nosn Shapiro, Yisroel Bratanisky, my mother and brother–in–law.

When we arrived at a small forest, not far from Podbrodz, Lithuanian bandits suddenly jumped out from behind the trees and with murderous eyes wanted to begin shooting at us.

Luckily, their elder asked who we were and where we were headed. He then gave an order to allow us to go.

[Col. 1382]

Arriving back in town we soon became acquainted with the new "Regime". Near the bakery a long line of Jews stood waiting for bread. A few Lithuanian police carried out their orders like this: they hit Jews over their heads with their rifles. Upon seeing this I returned home sad and broken. I felt with all my senses, difficult times were approaching.

The next morning, the regular German army entered Podbrodz. Right beside our house, a truck stopped and a German officer got out, grabbed a few Jews passing by and ordered them to bring water to wash his truck.

I was one of those "fortunate" water carriers.

Our fate was that no less, we had to accommodate the German military deputy commander. Within a week he began to give orders in town. He gave the command that all Jews must gather at the police station within an hour. When I arrived I immediately saw that all the guards were Lithuanian police.

A short time later "our" commandant arrived on a motorcycle accompanied by a Lithuanian honour guard. He made a speech and told us everyone had to go to work. Whoever does not work will not receive food...

After his speech he had the police register all the Jews according to age. I stood among the middle aged workers. He then shouted at me to join an older group. I later he realized he actually did me a favour. My job was to be a cook in the hospital.

A few days later notices were hung in all the streets stating Jews had to wear white bands with the Star of David. Jews were not permitted to walk on the sidewalks. They had to walk in the gutters on the sides of the street. They were also not permitted to walk in groups, just alone.

A day later they changed the order from a white band to a yellow patch to be worn in front and in back. He then called for the establishment of a Judenrat to help the Germans carry out their orders.

[Col. 1383]

Everyone in town suggested I sit on the Judenrat. At first I wanted to escape such an "honour", but Yisroel Bratanisky convinced to take the position. He appealed to my sensibilities and convinced me to not to turn down this important responsibility. As long as the commandant lived with us I could be very useful to the town. In the end, I became a member of the Judenrat and was elected secretary.

The other members of the Judenrat were: Ben–Zion Vilian – chairman, Yisroel Batranisky – treasurer, Meir Blitz, Dovid Suzan – vice– chairman, Nosn Shapiro and Blushinsky.

At a secret meeting it was decided Blitz would bribe the German commandant, and I, the Lithuanian. The other members had to meet with other high police officials.

The plan was to try and get them to tell when there would be an operation against the Jews, so we could plan to escape. A few days after the Judenrat was chosen the order was given that all Jews in Podbrodz had to live in the ghetto. The Lithuanian police chose two Christian streets. This is where all the Jews would be concentrated. At first they allowed people to bring as much as they could carry; later, they allowed Jews to take all their possessions.

We later learned, he was just answering to the S.S. In any event, the Jews would have to leave everything behind.

This is how the new chapter of Jewish communal life began in the ghetto.

In attempting to house the Jews who were thrown out of their homes, the members of the Judenrat had their work cut out for them, dealing with scandals and screams. One wants to live here and the other – of course, there. Everyone believed he was maltreated and others were better off.

My family and I settled in with Rayzl Bavarsky in a house on Biarel Street. Our neighbour was Ben–Zion Vilian, the chairman of the Judenrat.

[Col. 1384]

One house was chosen as the place to hold our meetings, receive people and take care of communal business.

Meanwhile we received the horrific news of mass slaughtering of Jews in Lithuanian towns. The town of Malat was 50 kilometres away. A farmer told us that on a market day when he was there, they shot all the Jews. This was the first we heard of mass murders and panic ensued in the ghetto.

The Judenrat immediately held a meeting and it was decided to bribe the military commandant. We bought a gold watch and sent Blitz to the high ranking German officer.

At first, when Blitz put the watch on the table the commander was insulted, but he calmed down quickly and took the gift. Meir told him the Jews appreciate how he restrains the brutality of the Lithuanian police.

The deputy commander lived in our house. I spent some time with him. Thanks to this we were able to save Leyzer Trachetenburg from a sure death. The deputy commander received wonderful fabric for a suit...

The chairman Ben–Zion Vilian had another "system" to befriend the police. He would pour them a drink and learn a lot from them.

This role suited him. He was a cold calculating person, smart and bold. In a glance, he knew who he was dealing with.

However, this did not help. Our ghetto only existed for a short time. One day a Christian acquaintance came and told me a secret. They wanted to kill all the Jews.

–Don't wait. Run away wherever you can.

–Where should we go? – I replied. There are Germans everywhere. Death looms everywhere.

The Christian did not leave it alone. "If you want, you can find a solution to save yourself" he said. Go into the forest and dig a trench. Live there with your family. I'll help you. I promise I will not let you starve. I'll bring you food.

[Col. 1385]

When I told my wife what my good Christian friend said she answered: You fantasized about this non–Jew. Digging a trench and hiding in it is foolish.

In a short time we realized he was right. The healthy and logical plan of this farmer was more practical than our intellectual ideas. Unfortunately we paid for our blindness. If only we had listened to him.

A few days later I met the same Christian. He told me, in the town of Niementshin about 25 kilometres away; all the Jews had been shot. We immediately sent someone to verify this. It was true. That same night, Blushinsky and his wife escaped from the ghetto.

Friday, September 26th at noon we noticed two nice cars driving into town. Two high ranking German officers emerged. We approached our "people" but could not get any information. We later learned they came to plan the operation to take all the Jews to Poligon.

We did not know what to do. Jews began to gather and with the fear of death asked what they should do.

Ben–Zion Vilian thought for a while. With an ice cold expression he turned to everyone and said these words which I remember clearly:

"I advise we send all women and children out of the ghetto. Let each one escape to wherever possible. The main thing is to hide from the patrols. Do not let them notice a thing. After they leave, the men will follow. Jews, don't panic. This will only spoil our plans of escaping."

[Col. 1386]

The crowd did not even wait for him to stop speaking. People began to run around the ghetto in a great rush. The Lithuanian police noticed the upheaval but did not have orders to begin the operation.

I entered our house and told my wife to take our 18 month old daughter Dvoyraleh with her to Kimelishk Street. I would soon join them there.

My wife stared at me in silence and began to dress. My brother–in–law Yitzkhak came with me.

An hour later I joined them. We went into the forest and later arrived at an estate Novo – Misla, 2 kilometres from our town.

A Christian from the estate promised to take us further. Meanwhile he took us all to his barn. His wife took Dvoyraleh with her to an onion warehouse and played with her there.

Later, that Christian brought us to a farmer not far from Kimelishok, whose address we got from Blushinsky before he escaped from the ghetto. The farmer was afraid to let us into his house. Even just to warm up a bit. We learned from him where Blushinsky was hiding and went to him. That Christian received us well and even allowed us to spend the night. However, we did not find Blushinsky there.

The next morning we left for the village Talushan where we finally met Blushinsky. He was hiding at Duchnovich's, the mayor of the village.

Blushinsky was very happy to see us. Thanks to his recommendation, a neighbour of the mayor agreed to hide us.

People in the village knew some Christians were hiding Jewish families from Podbrodz. The Christians were afraid and we decided to leave that village.

In the darkness of night we all left for Pastazhine and went straight to a Christian acquaintance Dombrovsky.

It is worthwhile to remember this man.

[Col. 1387]

He risked his life many times trying to save Jews. We stayed with him for a longer period and he helped us sell some things so we could have some money to live off.

He told us in White Russia Jews were living calmly in the ghetto. Mass murders had not taken place. We began to make plans to go there. Blushinsky planned to go deep into Lithuania where the operations against the Jews had already ended. It was worse to go where they had not yet occurred.

One day a few acquaintances arrived and suggested we go to Baran where the family of our town doctor Rayzhevsky was hiding. At this time we experienced a miracle from heaven. We agreed to go to Baran. I asked if we could postpone our departure because on that day, Dombrovsky was slaughtering a cow and I wanted to have at least one good meal. My wife was very angry with my foolishness and let me have it.

The whole thing lasted about an hour and a half. We finished eating and were preparing to leave. Suddenly we heard shots from a machine gun coming from Baran.

We delayed our departure and a few hours later a Christian came and told us the Dr. Rayzhevsky's entire family was shot together with everyone visiting them.

This is a perfect example that people were not saved due to intelligence of heroism, but simply blind luck saved many Jews.

Meanwhile a Christian came and told us S.S personnel were going from village to village looking for Jewish refugees. That same night, Blushinsky ran deep into Lithuania, just as he had planned. We wrapped Dvoyreleh in a blanket (it was 30 degrees) and left for the forest.

It was a clear starry night. We sat down in the snow not knowing what to decide.

Suddenly Dombrovsky came to us.

[Col. 1388]

At that moment he fell upon us like an angel. We were desperate. We believed only two choices existed for us: to die of cold and hunger in the forest or give ourselves over to the S.S.

Dombrovsky took us to his friend on a nearby estate. We arrived there around two o'clock in the morning. The owner was a Russian and Dombrovsky whispered something to him and he then led us in to a warm place. They brought some straw and laid it out on the floor. We were tired and broken. We fell into the straw like sheaves and fell asleep.

In the morning his wife brought us hot potatoes and we ate until we were full.

We remained there an entire day and could not decide where to go next. The owner of the estate agreed we could stay for a few more days. What would we do after?

At night I went out to get a bit of fresh air. Suddenly I noticed strange shadows lingering among the trees. At first I was frightened. Then I realized there was no need to be afraid. They were: my mother and brother–in–law Bratanisky and the whole family.

It turns out they were also hiding in Baran. After the incident with Dr. Rayzhevsky they too ran to Dombrovsky who told them where we were hiding.

The owner of the estate received us all. We realized he hated the Germans as much as we did.

We remained there for a few weeks. One night around 11 o'clock we heard voices and shouting from many drunkards. Our host came in and quietly whispered to us these were young Christian boys looking for Jews.

We knew the Germans promised 1 kilo salt and 1 kilo sugar for every Jew. Our host did not disappoint. He invited them into his house, gave them a drink and the gang left.

[Col. 1389]

We were saved, but not calm. If we were to be discovered we would be killed together with the owner of the estate.

We decided to go to the Kimelishok ghetto. What will be will be.

I wrote a letter to a friend in Kilmelishok and our host sent it. The question was whether they were prepared to take strangers into the ghetto.

Eight o'clock that evening, the peasant harnessed the horses and took us to Kimelishok. As there was not enough space for everyone in the wagon, the men and young women walked on foot. We planned on where to meet.

I went through the forest in search of a shortcut. I had been in the forest many times in my life. I don't know what happened that night, but I got lost. After a few hours I ended up where I began. All the others walked behind the wagon.

Our host arrived and our planned destination. Everyone stopped and waited for me. They waited and waited and I did not show up. Our host decided to go looking for me.

When he found me he hurled a few Russian curses my way for looking for a shortcut, and brought me to the others in the forest.

The night was dark and we continued on our way. When we arrived in town a member of the Judenrat was waiting for us. He took us to a small house and we all went to sleep.

The owner of the estate returned home.

Sleeping on the floor I suddenly felt someone caressing my head. It was my brother–in–law Yisroel Bratanisky who murmured: Eltzik, Eltzik, is it you? You are alive?

I saw him standing there and crying. He told me they were sure I had been killed.

[Col. 1390]

I heard him whisper a prayer to God, that I was saved. This is how this new period of our life began, our experiences in Kimelishok ghetto.

In the morning we began to get organized in the ghetto. The conditions in the ghetto were not strange to us and we quickly got used to them. Our friends in Kimelishok received us warmly. Because of us they were afraid.

The authorities gave an order they were not permitted to register strangers in the ghetto. The Judenrat was held responsible for this. Nevertheless, they gave me work and treated me equally.

One day, as I was going to work as usual outside the ghetto I suddenly recognized a familiar Lithuanian police officer. Apparently they sent him from Podbrodz to Kimelishok. As he had received a lot of money and gifts from me I wanted to meet him.

Once again he accepted gifts and remained silent about us being in the ghetto.

Meanwhile, things were happening in the ghetto that made us take up our walking sticks once again. They gathered all the Jews in the market place and made a speech about work and being useful. This scared us.

They also began to talk about soon liquidating the ghetto. I thought the best thing for us would be to obtain Aryan documents. I met a friend who prepared to passes for me and my wife. I was registered as a Pole and given the name Adam Kozlovsky. My wife was now called: Evalia Sosnovska.

I immediately wrote to my good Christian friend Kozlovsky near Podbrodz. He agreed to take my wife and child and promised to find me work.

Until today my wife cannot forget this kind Christian. This was a man with a gentle, delicate soul, which was very rare to find. Such people must be venerated. He did such good thing for Jews never looking for profit.

[Col. 1391]

He should be inscribed among the Righteous Gentiles.

Even after I liberation he was insulted when I offered him money. He stated:

–I saved Jews because my conscience told me to. I did it for God, for history and for humanity.

After I left my wife and daughter I received a document from the municipality and began to work outside the ghetto. I often sent a messenger to my wife to find out how they were doing. In her letter to me she wrote how she was lacking nothing. Yet she was not comfortable living as a peasant woman among Gentiles.

Slowly I advanced in my work and became a master of the first order. I rented a room in a Christian home and brought my wife to live with me. I worked as a specialist in the forest and my wife worked with all the Polish women. At night we would meet and return to our home.

More than a month passed and nothing suspicious occurred. One day the village magistrate came and asked to see my papers. I took out my pass and showed it to him. He took a good look and then wanted to put it in his pocket. I protested and energetically told him I had to keep the documents. If not, I would lose my job.

He told me to go with him to the municipality in Kimelishok and there things would be straightened out. I certainly did not like that idea. I began to speak with him softly and him not to cause me hardship. The outcome: he received a shot of whisky and a few Rubles and left me alone.

Another incident occurred one night when Russian partisans knocked on the door of the Christian's house. He did not open the door and the knocking became louder.

Finally he crawled out of bed, went to the door and asked who was there. I listened to the conversation and learned they were Russian partisans.

[Col. 1392]

In a juicy Russian they asked him to open the door immediately. Otherwise his home will go up in smoke. He opened the door and begged for mercy that they not rob this poor peasant. They replied that Russian partisans don't steal. They asked that he willingly give them food for their comrades. He gave them eggs and fat. They thanked him and warned him not to tell the authorities Russian partisans had come to him.

The situation for me and my wife became serious again. We knew if the Germans would know the Christians were helping the partisans, they would burn down the village.

Meanwhile, they liquidated the Kimelishok ghetto. We decide not to remain in the region.

I remember the day of the liquidation very well: it was the 13 day of Cheshvan)November 3, 1941). That day I lost my closest and dearest.

I must describe all the details of the liquidation of the Kimelishok ghetto. I went with Elke Krol to find out how our families were doing. He too had a mother, sister and many friends there. On the way we stopped in at a forest watchman who knew us very well. He and his wife received us well, gave us food and deeply regretted the situation of the Jews.

We sat there for a half hour and wanted to continue on our way. Suddenly his wife ran in and began to shout: They are killing the Jews of Kimelishok. They are shooting everyone!

We sat there frozen. She began to comfort us.

–My dears, run away from here as fast as possible. Perhaps you can save yourselves.

We did not waste time and ran to our families in the village. Elke Krol was so disturbed it was impossible to calm him down. We barely made it to the village and immediately told our closest:

–We must run to the forest right away. They are liquidating Kimelishok ghetto.

We managed to pack a few things and food and ran to the nearby forest.

[Col. 1393]

Lying among the trees we heard the shooting from the machine guns. We knew the Jews of Kimelishok were being shot. We thought we would go insane from pain and fear.

We lay in the forest with silent, sad stares and hurting hearts until nightfall. When it was completely dark, Yoske Blitz suggested he go to Dombrovsky and ask him what to do. It was the middle of the night, no one would see him and he did not feel it was dangerous. I wanted to go with him but he would not let.

I remained with my family in the forest. I decided to go to our Christian acquaintance and him what to do. He advised I go to his relative who lived about 10 kilometres from the forest. He hoped we would be able to hide there for some time.

We followed his advice and in the darkness set out to this Christian. We arrived dead tired and broken.

That Christian man chased us from his house. He was afraid to risk his life.

We returned to the previous Christian and crawled into an abandoned bath, where we lay for a few days.

After a few days, the region became calmer and the Christian suggested my wife and daughter go to his brother. We put a shiny cross around her neck. We said goodbye and cried. I remained all alone.

When my loved ones left I was very sad. For a few hours I thought I was going crazy. Then I took my pack with my few belongings and headed where my eyes led me.

I did not know the roads very well. I wandered without direction. When I had enough I went to Dombrovsky, the only Christian I knew in the region. He took me to the forest where Yoske Blitz and his family were hiding.

[Col. 1394]

I remained with them for a few weeks. One day Yoske proposed he and his family would go deep into Lithuania and I should go to the Christian who was hiding my wife and daughter.

Blitz hired a wagon and made plans to leave. When the coachman arrived, I asked if he could take me to the village where my wife and daughter were. It was a dark night, and we all set out on the road.

The Christian received me with a bitter expression but did not send me away. A few days later his brother arrived and brought us a lot of food.

Since my wife looked Aryan and spoke excellent Polish we decided she should not hide. We would tell the people in the village she is from Warsaw; her husband was killed and she had nowhere to live. She came to the village where she has relatives.

What difference did it make to our daughter? She would play with the Gentile children in the village.

I was the only who had to hide. It would not be so terrible for them.

The Christian agreed and I remained there for six months.

At that time, big acts of sabotage were being perpetrated by the partisan divisions. They took down trains, burned bridges, and attacked German warehouses. There were raids throughout the region.

The Christian was afraid and hid me in a trench. The trench was so narrow and low, I couldn't even sit up. I crawled in on all four. There was a small hole on the side which I used as a sort of window.

One day the Christian brought me a Polish newspaper. Through the light coming through the hole I read news from the front. I read the entire newspaper as this was the only way to pass the time. I would read it from all sides and then begin again. Reading by the hole became a type of sport, an enjoyment.

[Col. 1395]

While in the trench I slowly became a politician and strategist orienting myself with the situation on the fronts. I knew Hitler and Goebel's speeches by heart.

From time to time my wife would come and bring me food. I would tell her the news and it appeared all my commentaries were correct.

After a while I tired of the sport of constantly reading Hitler's press and tried to spend my time doing other things.

I wrote riddles, collected expressions and finally attempted to write poems. When my wife would visit, I would read her my “literature”.

In my poetry I described my life in the trench and my hopes for liberation.

My daughter had just turned four. In honour of her birthday I wrote a poem.

One day, I serious discussion took place between me and my wife as to who would liberate us. My wife believed the Americans and British would liberate us. I held by my convictions that it would be the Soviets.

One cold day in January, the Christian came and asked me to come to his house at night. He had very important news.

When I went in, his brother was there. He showed me various newspapers which described the defeat near Stalingrad. This news cheered me up and began to believe there would be a victory over Hitler.

It appeared, these leaflets were dropped from Soviet planes and they ridiculed Goebel's lies.

When I heard this latest piece of news I kissed the good Christian and said:

–If this is true, the sun has begun to shine on us! And that is how it really was. The Germans began to retreat from all fronts. One could feel the despair in the German press.

[Col. 1396]

Another chapter in our suffering is about the upbringing of our little daughter.

When we ran away from Podbrodz ghetto she was only 18 months. She learned Polish fluently. You could not distinguish here accent from gentile children. Nevertheless she was depressed and felt insulted. The Christian woman was not mean and cared for her well, but she failed to understand our daughter's little heart.

The Christian women called her the noblewoman because she could not get used to their food. Every day they ate beans and peas. She got tired of it and did not want to eat.

She played with our host's daughter. One day she pushed her and the gentile girl fell on a stone and was badly hurt. Her nose bled and her parents were afraid.

They took her to a doctor. Our luck was it was not a serious injury.

This incident put us in danger because they told our host my wife was responsible. With difficulty she managed to calm them down.

Among other stories that I told my Christian friend, I had hidden a lot of gold and after liberation I would pay him handsomely.

My wife was angry that I told this lie but I explained I had no choice.

Another problem was when the woman of the house went away and asked my wife to feed the children.

Once she asked my wife to give her daughter potato pancakes with bacon. Our daughter had to watch with envy how she fed the Christian girl and nothing remained for her.

Dvoyrele had a great instinct and felt she must resolve everything and concede.

In short, there was nothing to be jealous of her.

[Col. 1397]

Meanwhile the Germans kept facing defeat. The Christians told us how the Red Army is getting closer to our region. The German front was trembling. The gigantic wild beast was leaving city after city and village after village.

When the Christian brought me a newspaper I immediately saw the news that the army is methodically retreating from Dukstas. I was amazed.

Dukstas was three stations from us, only 80 kilometres away. Was this not a mistake? Is it possible? It was hard to believe.

I waited impatiently for my host to come feed his horse, and could finally learn the truth.

I burned with fever: every second was like an eternity. Finally I learned this was really our Dukstas and the Germans were running like demons from all fronts.

My heart was beating strongly. I felt the big hour was approaching, the hour of liberation.

"Being liberated", no one who had not lived through the Hitler years could conceive what these two words mean to a Jew who hid for years from the Nazi animal claws.

"Being liberated" meant going from darkness to light, just like our sages said: "From darkness to great light".

This was our only dream, everyone's fantasy, our wish and desire.

One day, in the end of June 1944, my host suddenly knocked on the secret little door. He told us the Germans had retreated and the Soviets were 30 kilometres from our village. The problem was the Germans were burning villages as they were retreating. He wanted to escape with his family to the forest and wait there for the Red Army to arrive.

I remained lying in the trench startled. What would we do? We can be burned alive here in the trench.

I discussed it with my wife and we decided to take Dvoyrele and run to the forest, but not with the Christians.

Truthfully, it was very hard for me to walk.

[Col. 1398]

I had been lying in the trench for almost 14 months, and simply could not move my legs. Nevertheless we dragged ourselves slowly deep into the forest and found a hole to hide in.

As my wife said, I looked like a real bandit. I walked in big torn boots, a pair of patched dirty pants, a jacket full of holes, and on my head a cap with a twisted visor. I looked like a wild animal.

I thought Dvoyrele would be afraid and not want to go with me. But she actually snuggled up to me and would not leave my side the entire time.

Suddenly we heard loud shots not far from our small forest. We lay as if electrocuted. We then heard soldiers passing, speaking German. We trembled with fear.

After 14 months in hiding, now, on the eve of liberation we can fall into their hands.

The Germans did not notice us. We later learned it was a German punishment division searching for hiding partisans.

At night, once it was dark, I sent my wife to look for the Christians and ask them what we should do. She returned to say we must return to our hole. It was safer there than in the forest.

Did we have a choice? A few hours later I was back in my hole. I remained only for a few days.

One day I heard shots from canons and machine guns. It was around noon .I heard the noise of trucks on the highway.

I felt my heart exploding from joy. I waited for this hour for three and a half years and it finally arrived. The damned Nazis were leaving the village.

The canon –music lasted for six hours, and then all was quiet. I felt the dead silence in the entire region. In the evening my host came knocking and told me the Germans were gone. They disappeared. Everyone was awaiting the Red Army.

[Col. 1399]

The next morning he returned and told us the Red Army was 1 kilometre from the village. I jumped out of my hole. I began to shake his hand not knowing how to thank him for the good news.

The Christian advised me to crawl back into my trench. We still should be careful. I did not want to lie in there any longer.

OK, good. Do as you please.

It was July 4th,1944. I went into my host's house and was ashamed. We were saved, but we lost are best and closest. What will we do now? Where will we go?

I sat down on a bed and started to cry...My wife comforted me and said we should say goodbye to the Christians and return to Podbrodz. Perhaps we will find someone there.

We all cried. Then we took Dvoyrele and headed through the forest toward Podbrodz. Half barefoot and dishevelled we looked like real beggars. We were sad and as we walked could not say a word.

We stopped to rest a couple of times. My feet really hurt. Finally we saw our hometown from a distance. We did not feel happier. We felt we were nearing the destruction, the ruins of our homes.

Podbrodz was considered one of the nicer towns in Vilna province. We all loved it and we were sad. Why are we going there? To whom?

[Col. 1400]

We approached the town and a stream of tears flowed from our eyes. We took control of ourselves and came to the first street. Everything blackened before our eyes even though the sun was shining.

We saw destroyed houses, broken windows and doors, scorched beams and ruins. No end to the ruins...

What is there to say? Podbordz looked like a cemetery. A dead silence ruled all the streets. Here and there we saw a Christian passing by who looks at us in great wonder, like we returned from the dead...

We stopped a Christian and asked if other Jews had returned to the town. He told us that in Eltzik Gordon's house we will find a few saved Jews. We went straight to Eltzik's house on Post Street and found him, Ben–Zion Valian and a few more Jews.

There is no poet who can describe how we felt at that first meeting. It was a non-describable experience.

We were barely able to speak. We all sat there and cried, cried over the horrific destruction we encountered.

The destruction of the individual, the destruction of all of Israel...

Remnants at the First Reunion in Haifa

Seated: **Golda Shapiro, Miriam Shapiro, Sholem Raytenburg with Miriam's child, Esther Flexser with her child, Khana Zilber, ____, _____, Soreh Kirshon (Bavarsky), Soreh Rivkind-Lapp, Khane (Trakinsky) Rivkin, Miariasha Bratanisky, Mordekhai Bar-Khone, ___ Grunia (Norman) Patashnik,___, Riva Blushinsky**
Standing: ___ **(Shkurkovitch) Shokhet, Eliyahu Gordon, Ben-Zion Lapp, Avrom Rivkind, Aharon Kuritzky, Mirsky, Dr. Shni**

[Col. 1401]

The German Commander

Meir Blitz

Translated by Anita Frishman Gabbay

August 12, 1941 the Germans flooded our district. When they arrived in Podbrodz they immediately caught Jewish men and sent them for forced labour. One of them was shot. In another evening, with the help of the Lithuanian bandits, they forced about 270 men from their beds and shot them near Tishkevitch's mill.

The rest remained in their homes and no want moved around in the streets. The doors and windows were shut and we peeked through the cracks.

As our house was on Sventzianer Street we were able to see the motorized army passing. It seemed to us, their numbers were endless. We felt that death and destruction had arrived.

I brought in water and my wife Sonia wanted to light the *samovar.* Suddenly she started to squabble and scream "run quickly and fetch the doctor."

I immediately ran to Dr. Rezshevski and brought him home. A short while late we heard a whimper from a new Jewish life. She had to arrive at such an evil time.

I went out to tell our friends the good news. They gave me a weak *Mazel Tov.* I learned from them that harsh decrees against the Jews were announced. Soon we will no longer be allowed to walk on the sidewalks and after five, we were to remain in our homes.

Besides this, all the Jews must wear yellow patches with a *Magen David* on the front and back.

[Col. 1402]

A short while passed and new decrees were issued. All the Jews had to live in a ghetto. They enclosed all the Jews within two streets and the lack of space was unbearable.

As my father had a concession of beer and lemonade, he was invited to the commander.

They told him that the Lithuanians vouched for him, he didn't dilute the bottles and was an honest Jew. Therefore he will receive a permit to deliver beer and lemonade to the German army.

As they didn't allow us to have a horse and buggy, we managed with a two wheeled cart. My brother Leibke and I had to deliver our supplies to the commandant.

My first meeting with the commandant didn't go so well, my heart was beating and my nerves were rattled. Leibke remained with the cart and I gathered my strength and brought the first crate to the commandant. On the way I pushed my patch into my jacket so he wouldn't notice who I was.

He counted the quantity of beer and lemonade I brought and I was ready to leave. Suddenly I noticed that he was unshaven. This was a wonder to me. A German not shaving, there must be a reason?

I said to him a matter of fact tone–"Why are you not shaven?" He looked at me strangely and politely answered

"I don't have a razor."

[Col. 1403]

So I said to him, if you allow me, I will bring you soap to shave. He looked with strange eyes again and I thought to myself, I can do some business here with this *yekke* (German).

At the speed of lightening Leibke and I returned to the ghetto with our cart and told our story about a business opportunity. At that moment I put into my pocket six bars of shaving–soap and six bars of *toilette–soap* and I returned to the commander.

The yekke didn't know what to do with me. He asked me to sit and offered me some champagne. Word for word he told me that he is a teacher, has a wife and two children and is a *Volk–Deutsch* from Czechoslovakia. He is going to fight for a greater Germany, but is very uncertain if he will live to see the end. He is lonely and wants to return to his wife and children.

I strongly felt that this commander could at some point save our lives.

One time in the middle of the night, an escaped Jew from Malat arrived in Podbrodz and told us that all the Jews had been murdered there. A terrible panic broke out in the Podbrodz ghetto. All the Jews came running to me to ask the commander clearly if he could help us.

The next morning I left to his office to carry out my talk. I asked if he received any letters from his family and what news they were sending?

He was in a good mood and told me one of his colleagues was quickly leaving with a pass and he would love to send a gift to his family. He didn't know what to send. I quickly answered and told him I will bring him a package in several hours.

In the speed of lightening.

I returned to the ghetto, and gathered women's' clothing, playthings for the children, a gold watch for him.

When I brought the commander the package he looked at me as if I was some sort of king. He didn't know how to thank me.

[Col. 1404]

When I told him this was a gift from the Podbrodzer Jews and I was also a Jew, he became entirely confused. He grabbed his gun and wanted to shoot.

I remained calm and sweetly said that we wanted to offer this as a gift for his wife and children. What is the catch? Didn't he deserve this? Their father and husband is going to murder them and they give him a present? Why should he receive a token of appreciation from them?

He settled down, put down his revolver, asked me to sit down on the sofa and excused his behaviour.

I asked him to hide the gifts quickly, as no one should notice them. I told him that I will bring him nicer things.

Slowly he gained my trust and he told me his life story and hopes for the future. He told me he was a Social–democrat and is a Nazi out of duty. What else could he do?

Word by word he told me that Hitler will not only destroy the Jews and Russia, but also Germany. He doesn't believe in Nazi idealism. As Hitler was successful in his early years of the fighting, in the end Hitler will lose the war and the end result will be greater than in the First World War.

Hearing such a confession I told him of our situation. The Jews of Maliat were murdered. The Jews in Podbrodz also await such a fate. No one knows what tomorrow will bring. We all believe that he is a good person and under his watch he would not allow such a slaughter.

He thought deeply, seconds of silence and finally said:

"As long as I am here, nothing will happen to you Jews."

I returned to the ghetto to tell the Jews of my conversation. Everyone felt the sun started to shine again over the Jewish heads.

Several days later, they actually felt the German actions grew milder. Jews went to work and received more food to live on. Life was somewhat easier than before.

[Col. 1405]

We started to hope for better days. This ideal lasted only for several months. One time I received an invitation to see the commandant. In a few days the Jews will be divided and deported and a new commander will arrive in Podbrodz. He warns us to run away as this will be the S.S. and it will be more difficult for the Jews.

[Col. 1406]

The good times now ended, in a few weeks the murder–spree started for the Jews of Podbrodz that brought death and destruction. Only a few managed to survive.

The Jewish community of Podbrodz was erased from the map.

[Col. 1405]

In the Valley of Death

Hadassa Rosen–Shapira

Translated by Meir Razy

I came to Podbrodz in 1939 with my parents Nehama and Mordechai Rosen and my sister when I was just a little girl. I do not remember much about the people of Podbrodzie and their life, but my soul is linked to the name of this small town because I went through the saddest chapter of my childhood in this town. I would like to tell my story about this short period.

When I think of the town of Podbrodz I can see the big bridge, below the river flowed, and then the little bridge, next to the synagogue [which stood on a hill, towering over the area of Jewish streets and alleys]. I walked this route every day, crossing the little bridge and then the big bridge on my way to the TARBUT School in our town, where my father was a teacher.

We would always go with a group of kids with schoolbags, happy and cheerful. When we reached the big bridge we would pause for a few moments at the railing and look at the slowly flowing river, whose water was so clear and whose green banks served as a beautiful and impressive frame. In winter the snow covered the frozen river and then it appeared to us in all its beauty. Laughing and cheerful we watched nature's magic and our happiness was limitless.

[Col. 1406]

I remember Rabbi Fishel the tailor, from whom we rented a room in his apartment on Boyarleska Street. He was a tall, handsome, white bearded Jew who always smiled and hummed a song. He was very energetic and loved life. I even remember the day he married his second wife. To this day I can see his smiling eyes and kind, expressive face.

Behind our house was the narrow alley called Malinova Street, where the Silver family, whom I loved visiting, lived. That family managed to escape the Germans' claws but their hearts were mourning for their son Moshe'ke. It was a beautiful little house with unique double windows. Every winter Hannah Silver used to sew mushrooms on cloths of different colors and placed them between the two windows. Each mushroom had a white leg and a red body embroidered with white dots and they were planted into the snow–white cotton. Two windows, two mushrooms in each one. Each winter I would run to Hannah Silver and ask her when would she "plant" the mushrooms and Hannah would smile and say only when the first snow falls.

We were waiting for the first snow that brought cheerful snowball games and competitions of creating the most beautiful snowman, the many trips down the mountain to the middle of the river, skiing and running that would fill our hearts with joy. We were happy indeed.

[Col. 1407]

But the time of happiness soon ended with the arrival of 1941, the start of the most horrific and shocking chapter in human history, especially for the Jews. The Germans crossed the Russian border on June 22, 1941. German airplanes appeared over the roofs of our town and bombed it. The Germans entered the town of Podbrodz the following day. Horror captured the Jewish inhabitants of our town and they wandered about frightened and depressed. The Germans did not leave much time to think and make plans. After several days they instructed all the Jews of Podbrodz to move into a crowded ghetto that spanned just Boyarleska and Orninska Streets. Our family moved into a small room near the synagogue. The migration of Jewish families from the central streets into these two small streets created unbearable conditions – a large number of people had to share one small room. Slowly, people started adapting to the harsh conditions, knowing that new edicts will probably come soon. Then came the law that all Jews from the age of 10 must wear a white ribbon with a yellow Star of David on their sleeves. However, a few days later the Germans thought that a white ribbon on the sleeve was indeed too beautiful and was not degrading enough to human dignity, so the new order was to carry two yellow badges large enough to be noticed from a distance with the letter "J" in the middle to signify "Jude", one on the back and the other on the chest. At the same time they put up posters all around town stating that dogs and Jews are strictly prohibited from the sidewalks. Violation of this "law" would be punished by being shot on the spot without a trial.

Jews were taken to forced labor every day. The work was supervised by Germans holding clubs in their hands and each one of them tried to excel in beatings and other cruelties.

The children's' world was turned completely upside down. Schooling was forbidden and we grew older within a few days. We paid close attention to adult conversations, laughter disappeared, happy games stopped and one concern was in our hearts: Why do the Germans want to destroy us?

One night the Germans took 40 people out of their homes and ordered them to dig pits in the forest. The Lithuanians told them that these were part of a defensive line. When the Jews finished their work they were released, but after midnight the Germans took the forty, their wives and children from their homes, led them to the pits and shot them. Among them were some people I still remember: Nahum Glaz with his family, Abramowitz – the mother and her two sons, Velvele, and others.

In the morning we learned about the previous night. Rivka Lazarovich, a neighbor's daughter, entered our home and said that Velvele Abramowitz had escaped death and is hiding in their home. He said that many Germans and Lithuanians surrounded them, ordered them to stand with their back to the pit and shot them, but he managed to escape in the darkness. The impact of this event was shocking in the Podbrodzie ghetto but everyone was helpless.

[Col. 1408]

Rumors about events in the nearby towns began to arrive. They were heartbreaking and people refused to believe the horrors the Germans had done to us. Humanity had not known such horrors in all its existence.

We had not settled into the ghetto for a long time. It was a Saturday night, three days before Yom Kippur, when suddenly there was a commotion in the ghetto. All Jews were ordered to gather in the synagogue. We felt that something terrible was about to happen. The Germans cheated and lied to the Jews while leading them to death, a different lie in each ghetto. We were told that we were being taken to the labor camp in Polygon, not far from Podbrodz.

Most of the Jews realized that the situation was hopeless but they all stood helpless, waiting. Some who had acquaintances among the Christians in the area, decided to flee to them.

I remember my father sitting thoughtfully for about fifteen minutes, talking to Mom, looking at me and at my younger sister. Suddenly Dad got up and said “We have to hide until the rage passes.” Suddenly the door of our apartment was opened with extraordinary ferocity and three armed Germans stood in the doorway, shouting “You must be in the synagogue in five minutes, dirty Jews”. Mother said she will take a loaf of bread with us. “You don't need food. Hurry!” They left. We glanced out the window for a moment and saw a group of armed German murderers pushing Jews toward the synagogue. We left the house, Mom held my sister's hand while Dad and I walked first. Dad leaned over to me and told me that we would try to climb up to the attic of the synagogue, not inside. We climbed the ladder into the attic and hid there. Daddy camouflaged the opening and it was hard to notice it. All night we trembled with fear of being found. We heard the cry of the Jews gathered inside the synagogue but, unfortunately, we could not help them.

In the morning we heard someone crawling toward the door. We were startled at first but then we noticed other Jews who were looking for shelter and we let them in. And so we shared the hiding place with the Lazar Ring family, a father, two girls and a boy, Eliahu'chik Patashnik, Zalman Lapp, one blonde woman, I cannot remember her name, with a baby, about a year old. And there were a few other Jews I did not recognize.

Through the cracks of the planks we saw how the Jews were loaded onto wagons and those who did not hurry were beaten to death with rifle stocks. This picture, which I saw through the cracks of the planks, will remain etched in my memory forever.

We saw the convoy, accompanied by Germans, started moving. I pressed my face to the floor and cried quietly. Here they are going away and disappearing from my sight. It was early morning and shortly after we heard a barrage of gunfire. Trembling, a cold chill gripped us. This was how the Jews of Podbrodz were massacred.

At that time I felt a sense of guilt that I was safe in hiding and over there my friends, whom I lived with, were being killed. The kids whom I studied, played, and roamed with. All of them existed but will not be anymore. The echoes of their footsteps were already silenced in the distance and will not return. My thoughts were accompanied by thunderous gunshots.

[Col. 1409]

We were in the synagogue's attic. Saturday passed and then Sunday. It was the dawn of Monday. We had no food or water except for a single loaf of bread my parents brought with them from home. My father distributed daily tiny portions from this loaf of bread to twenty people. “MAZAL u–BRACHA (Luck and blessing) went into this loaf of bread” I heard my father say. Everyone sat silent or shocked during the first day. The conditions were very difficult, especially for the little baby, who cried and cried incessantly and there was nothing to help calm him. I felt so bad for him. Such a small baby and he had to endure so much. His crying was really heartbreaking. His mother held him in her arms and pressed his tiny head to her face, stroked him while bitter tears streamed from her eyes. This somewhat pacified him for a few moments as the mother's tears flowed into his small mouth and he drank, but when the mother's eyes went dry and her fountain of tears emptied, the baby continued to cry. The adults began to think that the baby should be silenced. The mother too realized that he may be endangering the lives of twenty people and said: “Please, if I am doomed to sacrifice my son for the sake of saving twenty souls, take him and do as you please, but not by my hands! No! No! No!”

However, no one stepped forward and the crying of the little baby grew day by day, and his voice was heard by the preying animals who had not yet consumed enough Jewish blood. Suddenly we heard a noise come from the street. I heard snippets of conversations, loud punching. Then three of the planks fell and dropped on the attic floor and four armed, cruel Germans stood in front of us.

Our breath froze in its midst and even the baby stopped crying, as if he understood the meaning of those moments. “Do you have any weapons?” they shouted. We had no weapons. “Remove the ladder” one German ordered.

We went downstairs, some jumped, some crawled, and some were thrown by the Germans. Everyone stood and waited, surrounded by Germans and Lithuanians.

Suddenly the mother approached one of the Germans and begged him: “You must also be a father to children, release him – the child, and hand him over to someone who will raise him. Please, what is the fault of a baby?” But the murderer's hardened heart did not move. He replied: “Now he is a little baby and tomorrow he will grow into an older JUDE and therefore he must die” and he burst into a satanic laugh.

Grieving and full of despair we climbed on the wagons that some Polish peasants brought there by the German's command.

The Germans and the Lithuanians rejoiced – they trapped another group of Jews while we were mourning and trembling next to each other, looking at the street that continued its everyday, usual life.

Is this our end? I could not believe it. Dad, Mom and my only little sister, how can we say goodbye?

[Col. 1410]

And where were they taking us? My mother was crying bitterly, kissing my head, face, and hands, my father hugged my sister and his lips constantly muttering: “My children, my dearest children.”

Suddenly my mother erupted with a heartbreaking cry, we were all shocked: “Anton, take my children! Take them Anton!” and Anton, an acquaintance, a peasant, a tall, broad–shouldered man who happened to be in the street, covered his face with his hands and cried softly. But the whole street and the strolling people were indifferent to my mother's bitter cry.

The wagons rolled down the street and I looked at every passer–by and pondered: what made us different from all other people? Everyone was alive, free to go as they wished, why are we doomed to die? Why?

We passed the Boyarleska Street, and here is the intersection with the Malinova Alley. My feet had passed there many, many times, running and playing games with friends, with my parents. Was all that just a dream and the reality is different? Is the "real" reality us being led to die in a nearby grove?

Here is our house. Where is Rabbi Fishel the tailor? He would forever chant his cheerful melodies. Here is the home of Rabbi Persky, whom my father visited occasionally. He will never visit there again. Here, in the house on the other side of the street, lived Mosheke Zilber's grandmother. Everything is empty, the doors of the Jewish homes are broken, and there is no living soul in them. The life of a Jew is a wasteland, anyone can end it! Here, at the end of Malinova Street is the home of the Silver family. The windows are open and no one will ever look through them. And I closed my eyes and in my imagination I saw red, not artificial, but real mushrooms growing in the grove, in the forest.

Here is the grove. "This will be our grave", the thought pierced my heart.

"Get off the wagons!" a shout was heard. Hence everything flashed before us. Suddenly I saw guns pointed at us, pistols drawn and a barrage of thunder shocked our ears. I sat on the ground, buried my head in my mother's lap. I heard screams, moans, gunshots. I still felt alive and rolled into the pit. I laid there clinging to the bottom, clawing at the ground.

The shots stopped. I briefly lifted my head and saw a German walking and shooting the wounded. Once again I clung more firmly to the moist soil, hoping to look dead. I had never seen a dead person before but this must certainly look like it, close to the ground and not breathing. I stopped breathing. The killers, meanwhile, left and I was left not shot – but not alive either. The very fact that I kept thinking proved to me that I was actually alive.

Here, not far from me, are my father, mother and sister lying dead. And I thought my mother would never die! Mother is Eternity. And here is the end of things that I had never expected or anticipated. I lost everything dear to me. Where will I turn now? I had no close relative, no savior.

[Col. 1411]

I raised my head again. It was dark. Probably a whole day passed by while I was lying down. What do I do now? I have nothing left but to go and turn myself over to the Germans. I saw no other way out and within me stirred different feelings of life and death. It is worthwhile to live. The day will come that life will be good and freedom will be proclaimed. And another voice pointed to the dead bodies. Dead bodies around me and everywhere I go I will be stepping over dead bodies. My parents, too, were swallowed by death.

I fell asleep. I had a dream. And in my dream I could see my mother, sitting in her own chair, with a deep sadness on her face, all wrapped in black and blood-red tears were streaming from her eyes. As soon as she noticed me she smiled and said, "My child, go away from here, far, far away. Do not be afraid, be brave. There are a lot of bad people in the world, but I believe you will find good ones who will help you, people with a good heart. Be brave my child and go!"

I woke up, trembling with fear and cold. With strange feelings I got up and went with some confidence in my heart.

I came up to the mill near the forest. One village boy recognized me as a Jew and told me to leave. He handed me a slice of bread. I took a bite of it and left.

In the distance I saw peasants digging potatoes. I joined and started digging with them. The peasant woman was happy to have free help, but she was also afraid. Every person who comes into contact with a Jew has signed his death sentence. I pleaded with her to take me to her house and from there would continue on my journey alone. The woman asked for a fee, and I had no money. I remembered that coming out of the house my mother had dressed me with two dresses on top of each other. I took one and handed it to her.

We had to go through town to get to her home. A lot of Germans were walking around the street and she warned me that I would follow her, but from a distance, fearing that if the Germans would recognize me they will shoot her too.

With trembling feet and aching heart I began to walk as I looked ahead. I glanced at our house one last time, glanced toward the synagogue, passed through the Great Bridge, and then left Podbrodz, silent and with a mourning heart.

This is how I started my own struggle for existence, for life, the struggle of a single Jewish girl facing a cruel and hostile world, totally controlled by the Germans for the time being.

I had many difficult experiences throughout my wanderings, sleeping outdoors during many rainy and cold days, hungry and distressed for days and with a constant fear of all other human beings.

I remember that on one of those bleak nights, sitting down near the woods, I prayed to God that not a single human would appear in the dark of night. I was not afraid of wolves and other predators, hoping that if I will plead with the wolf not to rend me it will understand and if it would not be very hungry it will surely let me live.

[Col. 1412]

But I expected no such mercy from a human.

I wandered and dreamed of a day when Jews would not be persecuted and Jewish children would have a warm home and bread to eat.

With the cross on the chest

One morning I arrived in a small village. I went into a barn and hid without permission from the landlord. And so lying on the straw I felt my enormous loneliness again. I wished I knew what my fate would be. I wished I would not be discovered here for at least two days as my legs hurt from walking. Hungry and tired, I felt my strength leaving me.

A loud knock on the door woke me up. The owner came in and was amazed to find me in the barn. He came close to me, sighing, as a sorrowful participant, and ordered me to leave.

I had to wander again. It was dusk as I walked through the woods and the shadows of the trees appeared to me to be like living animals. I felt cold, pressed myself against a tree and closed my eyes.

At dawn I began walking again, not knowing where I was heading. Where does the road lead? To whom? I did not know.

I noticed the roofs of a village in the distance. I approached, entered a house and greeted the inhabitants. I stayed there for a longer period, I learned their customs, I attended church. I crossed myself at the appropriate times, I knelt when everyone did and I said "Amen" after the priest's prayer. I almost froze when my landlady told me I should go for confession! They spoke about the confession with a lot of respect and admiration. I did not know what to tell the priest in a confession so I delayed it from day to day.

I was sure I would probably fail even though the customs did not seem too complicated to me. And then came my fall.

Every time when the family sat around the table for dinner then crossed themselves. I also did it, reluctantly and uncertain, with my finger clenched to a fist. My hosts looked at each other and I felt as if my world was being destroyed. The landlord turned to me and said: "You know, Marisha (this was my name at that time), that a decent Christian intersects with his open hand extended to his head, then to the left shoulder, then to the right and then the hands are close to each other. Who are you anyway? You are not Christian! Go away from our house!" I left, but I learned a lesson in Christianity.

I carried a cross on my chest and hoped it would rescue me while secretly I prayed to G–d not to punish me for carrying a cross.

On many nights when I could not fall asleep, I would turn from side to side and fight with myself, a hidden struggle between Christianity and Judaism. It was a deep pain that they had inflicted on us.

[Col. 1413]

In the morning I felt like flying, daydreaming, and trying to estimate how much longer I would be able to hold on.

Again I continued on my way. I was a shepherd. I was collecting wheat and tying bundles following the harvesters in the field even though my legs were injured and sore. I worked hard beyond my own strength.

Several years passed. Rumors started that the end of the war was coming soon and then one day, while we were working in the field, we suddenly saw a Soviet tank. I froze in my place. I understood the meaning of that moment. This is the day of freedom, as many expected, and I was sad remembering my parents who did not survive to see it.

The war was over and again I was lonely and deserted. The sadness did not leave me. I do not belong to anyone and our fate as children, orphans of war, was bitter when millions of people celebrated the triumph and returned to their homes and families, while I stood mourning, without knowing what to do and where to turn. The end of the war did not end our hardship and troubles.

At that time, we were orphans of humanity [the human race], not just orphans without parents, we were persecuted for living[Jewish] and it seemed to us that the whole world was foreign to us.

I arrived in Podbrodz on one of the postwar mornings. Here is Boyarleska Street. Here the deserted synagogue stood with its windows shattered and its doors open to the wind. There are no more Jews to come and pray here. Most Jewish houses stood empty and robbed. Christian families lived in some of them.

[Col. 1414]

I entered our house. I came across a Christian woman rummaging through the closet, which was already mostly empty. I peeked through all the corners and wielded all my strength and courage not to cry. Here stood my sister's bed. Here is where my father used to sit and read a book. The woman turned her head to me, probably thinking that I was a Christian girl.

"You can come in and search. There is enough for both of us. People say that many Jews remain. They may return one day and demand their properties. But who is stupid enough to give it back? They had many large possessions, those Jews."

I had no ability to tell her what was in my heart. I left her as she continued to mumble to herself with tears streaming down my eyes.

I went to the grove. The trees have grown a bit since then. Here's the place, yes, this is the place. Many mushrooms grew here and grass covered the area. I bowed my head and kissed the ground. I left Podbrodz the next day, accompanied by a deep pain.

And then two Jews came to our village one day looking for Jewish children. Men whose names I still cannot remember, but they were the first ones to give me a spark of hope, a spark of desire for a new life. They were the first to plant hope of a better future in my heart. They took me to a children's home in Vilnius (Vilna). I will never forget the experience of seeing a Jewish home again, a house where Jewish children were loved and welcomed.

I felt there was someone who cared about us. That I once again belong to someone, that I belonged to the Jewish people.

[Col. 1415]

In the Hand of the Murderers

by Zev Bartana (Kibbutz Amir)

Translated by Jerrold Landau

My brother Yaakov awakened me in the early morning and told me that Hitler had ordered his army to attack the Soviet Union. They were announcing this now on the radio. I woke up quickly and went to the restaurant where I worked. In the meantime, nothing unusual was felt. At 8:00, Molotov announced on the radio that the Germans had crossed the border of the Soviet Union. Airplanes appeared the next morning and dropped bombs. Their intention was to damage the railway station and railway tracks. Everyone moved eastward throughout the day, some by vehicle and some by foot, for the trains were no longer working at this point. At the beginning, I thought that I should also retreat along with the Red Army, but since it was very difficult to take leave of my home, I remained with my family.

We decided to go to a village, to the home of a farmer acquaintance. We reached the village toward evening. I sat next to the house of the farmer, and behold, several vehicles appeared. They apparently did not notice that we were Jews, for they asked me in Russian: "Perhaps you have seen Germans here?" From their accent, I realized that they were Lithuanians. After I responded negatively to their question, they continued on their way. The Germans only reached us in the evening two days later.

The first victim was Chaim Zak, who traveled from the village to the town and was murdered by the Lithuanians. There were two more victims the next day – the brothers David and Eliezer Mirsky. The Lithuanians found them hiding in the field and murdered them.

In the meantime, the relationship changed with the family of the farmer with whom we were hiding. They began to curse us, stating that all the Jews were Communists, and the like. We had no choice but to leave. We decided to return to Podbrodz (Pabradė).

[Col. 1416]

Father and I walked by foot and succeeded in reaching Podbrodz. This was on Friday evening. The German and Lithuanian murderers were in control of the town. On Saturday they arrested seven Jews: Idel Kulbak, Yosef and Avraham Liberman, Rabbi Mianiszok, Kopel Szklerowicz, and two others. They immediately took them out to be killed. The entire day was passed in fear. On Sunday morning, two Lithuanians came to us. They began to search. They took everything that came to their hands, and finally took us as well: that is me, Father, our neighbor Zelig Szapira, Yudel Szklerowicz, Yona Lewin, and the son of the rabbi of Švenčionys. The Lithuanian Siaulists[1] took us downward behind the city, where they informed their superior that they had captured a Jewish gang that was conducting an anti-Fascist gathering. They placed us in a room where there was already a number of Jews, including Leib Nachum Glaz, and one Pole, Wasilowicz, who had been the principal of the public school in Podbrodz during the Soviet era. Leib Nachum Glaz, who was our relative, greeted us with weeping and told us that we were going to be taken out to be killed. They took people out every morning and shot them. We began to get used to the idea that the next day we would no longer be among the living. At 4:00 a.m. the door opened and a young captain with two soldiers called from a note the names Belski, Wasilowicz, and Glaz to come out with them for their final journey. Aharon Belski tried to commit suicide. When he did not succeed, he took off his shoes and said that they be given to his wife and two children, if someone remains alive. "I can also walk barefoot to death," he said. Wasilowicz asked that they bring a priest for confession. The captain thought a bit and agreed to his request. After a bit of time, the priest came, and they entered the next room. The confession took some time.

Then an unexpected miracle took place:

A German captain with the rank of Polkovnik (colonel) arrived and issued a command not take anyone to be killed without a permit from the Germans. (It was said that the Polkovnik lived in the home of the Wasilowicz family. Perhaps the pretty daughter influenced him to become involved with this situation). The verdict was suspended, and we remained afraid of what was to come. That night, the Lithuanian murderers came to our house and pillaged everything that came to their hands. My brother-in-law Moshe Tanchum and my brother Yaakov escaped. After the murderers emptied the house of all the valuables they found, they said to my sister Frida that if she wishes to free us, she must join us in prison. My sister went with them, and they brought her to the edge of the city, where they removed her gold watch and marriage ring.

[Col. 1417]

My sister began to escape, and the Lithuanians shot at her, but did not hit her due to the darkness. She went to a Polish woman acquaintance and requested that she give her a place to sleep, as she was afraid to return home. They next day, my sister turned to a Pole name Brozowski who had a connection with the Lithuanian police. With the help of a bribe, the head of the Lithuanian police gave my sister a letter to the Siaulist camp, asking to transfer us to the civil police for interrogation.

A policeman with a bicycle and my sister on foot went to the military prison where we were. They ran so as not to be too late...

The letter had its effect, and even the German command decided to transfer us to the civilian police. Despite all this, they held us until the next morning, and only then did they take us out and transfer us under heavy guard, surrounded by policemen with guns aimed at us, to the civilian prison which was two kilometers away. Many German soldiers marched along the route and shouted: "Jews! Communists! Shoot them." This is how we arrived at the police station. The small room of the prison was filled to the brim with Jewish, Russian, and Polish prisoners. Dr. Rajwaski was among them (he was accused of offering medical assistance to the Russians). There was not a drop of air to breath, but food was permitted to be brought to us, and we were also allowed to talk to family members and to breathe a bit of fresh air in the police station yard.

I had the idea to escape, and I had the ability to carry it out, but I did not do so because of Father and the other Jews. In the evening, Dr. Rajwaski asked Father to recite the deathbed confession with him, for he had heard that a German had issued a command to take him out to be killed. It was difficult to describe those frightful moments. Dr. Moshe Rajwaski and the other Jewish prisoners repeated the words of the confession after Father. In the meantime, another day passed, and we were freed on Friday evening with the help of Lithuanian acquaintances and a large bribe. After Father and I returned home, a Lithuanian policeman arrived and said that they had freed us in error, and demanded that we return with him to the prison. He only left us when we gave him some objects from our house.

One night, the Lithuanians took 67 Jews – children, women, young and elderly – outside the city next to the flourmill and murdered them.

Among those murdered were: Rebbetzin Ethel Abramowicz and her sons Avraham and Leibka, Yitzchak Zylber and his wife and daughter, Yisrael Baruch Boworski and his family, and others. Only one person, Zev Abramowicz, the Rebbetzin's third son, succeeded in escaping from this group. We learned that before the murder, Yitzchak Zylber and others stood up for their lives with stones and sticks, but the Lithuanians succeeded in overcoming them and killed them.

A few days later, all the Jews were gathered by the police. They issued a command that from that day on, all Jews from ages 14 to 60 were required to go out to work. We were till standing in the police station trembling, when they brought Dr. Rajwaski's son who had been a Soviet police captain. They captured him in the forest. In the meantime, frightful news reached us from the nearby cities such as Yanishok [Joniškis], Inturke, and Molėtai, where they had liquidated all the Jews. A Lithuanian farmer told us that in Molėtai, approximately 1,500 Jews were gathered in the cemetery, where they were shot. They even let the rabbi address the gathering before their deaths.

[Col. 1418]

In the Podbrodz Ghetto

From time to time, word spread that they were going to liquidate the Jews that night. One day, a command was received that all the Jews must gather in the ghetto that had ben set up between Orangi and Bauarlaski Streets, and that the Poles who lived on those streets would be transferred to the houses which the Jews had abandoned. It was forbidden for the Jews to remove furniture from their homes. They could only take a few belongings. Therefore, the Jews began to distribute their property to the Poles that they knew. The crowding in the ghetto was terrible. Once a week, permission was granted for them to go out to the market for a few hours to purchase food. The Germans also set up a Judenrat, whose main job was to provide bribes to the Germans and Lithuanians. One day, about ten city notables were arrested. A large sum of money and valuables was demanded as ransom. We made an effort and gave over everything that we had to free the prisoners.

At that time, the Lithuanians burned the splendid library. The smoke of the burning books and the ash covered the town. The Poles watched this lowly act with open joy.

The Liquidation of the Nemenčinė Ghetto

One Sabbath, about three weeks before Rosh Hashanah of 1941, a Pole appeared in the ghetto and said that he had been driving on the road leading from Vilna to Podbrodz, and saw that they were taking the Jews of Nemenčinė to be killed. After a few hours, the refugees of Nemenčinė reached us and said that all the Jews of that town had been awakened before morning. They were gathered near the market and told that they were being taken to the Vilna Ghetto. Along the way, they brought them to the forest where large pits were already prepared for them. The Germans and Lithuanians shot at them, and only a few succeeded in escaping. Among those murdered were all of Father's large family, including: Uncle Yaakov Bratniski, his wife Ethel, their daughter Chaya-Henya with her husband, their daughter Rasha, their son Shlomo Tzvi, and the rest of their children. His 12-year-old daughter Mariasha succeeded in escaping from the pit, with her hand injured, and she reached the Michalishok Ghetto. Also killed were my uncle Mordechai Bratniski, his wife Esther, their daughters Chaya-Ita and Mariasha, their son Shlomo Tzvi, and many tens of other relatives.

The Liquidation of the Podbrodz Ghetto

I returned from my work in the hospital and sensed an unusual movement of Lithuanians, forest guardians, police, and many Poles. A German guard stood on the bridge over the Zemiana River. This was on a Friday, a few days before Rosh Hashanah of 1941, about two weeks after the liquidation of the Nemenčinė Ghetto. I ran to the Judenrat to inform them of this unusual movement. Along the way, I met the wife and children of the head of the Judenrat, as they were leaving the city. I asked them what they knew, and they said that it was best for the women and children to go out to the forest.

[Col. 1419]

Yaakov Bartana

I arrived home and found an acquaintance of my father there who came to warn us to escape. In the meantime, pandemonium of mass escape broke out in the ghetto.

Father, my sister Freda and her husband Moshe Tanchum, and my sister Mariasha decided to go to the farmer acquaintance who warned us. My brother Shlomo Tzvi and I decide to go to White Russia. We sneaked out of the ghetto and reached the bridge over the river. The German who guarded the bridge arrested us. I took out my work permit and told him that the doctor had asked us to come for night work in the hospital. After a few minutes, Pinchas Krol with his sister Lyuba and her daughter arrived. Even though the permit was for an individual, the German permitted us to cross the bridge. We already did not walk on the road but rather on the path at the river bank until we reached the hospital. We asked the doctor to go to the ghetto and see what was going on. The doctor went and returned about an hour later, and informed us that everything was normal in the city. However, his Polish wife told us that we should wait. After the doctor left, she told us that they were hauling the Jews to the synagogue. She advised us to go down to the cellar of the hospital and even to hide in her house. We went out with the doctor's wife in the direction of her house, but a Pole met us along the way and shouted: "Despicable Jews, you are going to hide with the doctor..." We left the doctor's house and went to a different Polish acquaintance, where we remained until evening. From there, we went to the forest. After walking for several hours on the dark forest paths, we reached the border between Lithuania and White Russia. Polish guards stopped us there. To our joy, some of them knew us, and permitted us to continue. Toward morning, we knocked on the door of a Russian named Kulka, who took us in willingly.

On Saturday morning, they took them to Poligon. There, they gathered all the Jews of the Švenčionys area, and murdered them within a few days. After a week, Kulka transferred us to another Russian, but he was afraid to keep us, because in the house of the Pole Jozefowicz, Jews from Podbrodz – Shmuel and Tzvia Schmidt and their families – had been caught. The Lithuanians murdered them and also killed the Pole who hid them. We separated from Pinchas Krol, who went to search for his family. We wandered from place to place for several days. We slept in pits in the forest until I arrived at a farmer acquaintance who received me nicely, and told me that my family was not far away from there, in the village of Baran. We went through the fields under the cover of night, and arrived in the village in the morning.

[Col. 1420]

I met my family in a house at the edge of the village. The joy that we were all together was great. We found a place with a farmer in the village of Baran who agreed to build a double wall in a storehouse in exchange for a sum of money. The entrance to the hiding place was through the roof. We also succeeded in bringing into this place my cousin Mariasha, the daughter of my uncle who had been saved from the Nemenčinė Ghetto. After several days, Grandmother Rachel Licht also came to us. The family grew, and we were now nine people in the hiding place.

The Killing in the Village of Baran

A Jew named Avraham had lived in the village of Baran for decades in a small, two-room house with his family of six. He barely had any land, and he earned his livelihood from commerce and also from helping farmers with agricultural work. Avraham was loved by the farmers of the village and the area, and accepted as an honest, goodhearted man. With the liquidation of the ghettos in the towns of the area, Jews came to his house, and he received them and shared the little bit of bread and potatoes that he had. A sick, tired

Jew rested at his house for several days. Some Jews remained in Avraham's house, including Dr. Moshe Rajwaski and his family, including his wife Sonia, his daughter Beila, and his daughter-in-law Mina, who had escaped from the Podbrodz Ghetto. One day, Father's brother-in-law Yona Lewin came to us. We were standing and talking when suddenly a farmer women entered and said: "There are Germans in the village!" Without thinking, we ran to our hiding place. Yona Lewin jumped from the house to the forest, where the Germans caught him. We sat in the hole, and did not know what was taking place outside. After about half an hour, we heard shots. Toward evening, the mistress of the house opened the entrance to the hiding place, and told us that the Germans had killed all the Jews in Avraham's house, except for Avraham himself, who was not in the house at the that time. Thirteen Jews were murdered together: Dr. Moshe Rajwaski, his wife Sonia, his daughter Beila, his daughter-in-law Mina, Avraham's wife, his son and two daughters, Father's brother-in-law Yona Lewin, the brothers Berl and Ben-Zion Ajngelcyn, Yisrael and Yosef Zak. The Germans ordered the village chief to bury them. The farmers removed all valuables from them and buried them in a communal grave next to Avraham's house.

Our farmer was afraid to keep us in our hiding place, and we also could not continue to live behind the wall in the crowded situation. We decided to go to the Kimlishok [Kamelishki] Ghetto, where several hundred Jews still lived. This was on Saturday, December 31, 1941. We set out in the evening on tortuous paths. We wandered through the forests, and since we did not know the way to Kimlishok, we went in the estimated direction. Suddenly, we heard a voice calling out. We did not see anything in the darkness. We thought that Germans or Lithuanians were certainly attacking us. A commotion began, and we started to escape in every direction. It was dark, and there was a strong wind and a storm in the forest. Fear afflicted the hearts. We ran as long as we still had strength, and lost track of each other. I remained only with my cousin Mariasha. We reached some village after traveling for an hour. We entered the home of one farmer. During the conversation, I discovered that the wagon driver of Kimlishok was staying there. He was about to return. I spoke to the wagon driver and gave him a wristwatch. He agreed to take us to the Kimlishok Ghetto. We saw images of people from afar about five kilometers from the town. The wagon driver beat his horses and began to escape. I thought that they might be my family members. I asked the wagon driver to stop the wagon, and asked from afar in Yiddish: "Who are you?" It became clear that the images were my brothers Yaakov and Shlomo Tzvi, and my sister Mariasha. We took them onto the wagon, and reached the Kimlishok Ghetto. Father, my sister, and brother-in-law arrived in the ghetto toward morning, trembling from cold and fear of the murderers who were wandering along the roads. It was only through a miracle, after looking death in the face, that they succeeded in escaping from their hands alive.

[Col. 1421]

In the Kimlishok Ghetto

The small town of Kimlishok is situated approximate 80 kilometers from Vilna. Public transport did not connect it to the district city. It had several tens of Jews. Along with the refugees, the numbers reached approximately 200. At first, the ghetto was not fenced off, and it was possible to enter and exit. The ghetto was only later fenced off. On Wednesdays, the market day, it was permitted to go out for two hours to purchase food.

We went to work every day, especially in cutting down trees for the Germans. The winter was especially cold, and from time to time, we succeeded in sneaking in wood for heating in the ghetto. My brother Yaakov always claimed: It is forbidden for us to work for the murderers! He avoided the forced labor to the extent possible, with the recognition that it was forbidden to assist the German murderers by working for them. He regarded helping the murderers of our nation in any way as a sin. Once, the guards caught him failing to fulfil his work, and beat him with deadly blows. However, even after that he did not change his ways. This was a clear case of passive opposition to the murderers by individuals in the death camps and ghettos.

In May 1942, news spread that the Jews of the Kimlishok ghetto were to be transferred to Lithuania. Escaping began. I went to the village of Baran, to the farmer Wiski, and I remained there for about a month. When I found out that the Lithuanians were not behaving badly, I returned to Kimlishok and again went out to work. One day, an order arrived that the ghetto must give over 30 young people for work with the Germans. I was among them. The Lithuanian police took us by foot in the direction of Michalishok. We arrived in the town toward evening. The next day, the "Todt" people arrived. Other Jews from the Michalishok ghetto arrived, and brought us to a far-off village. There were already groups of Jews from the town of Svir that had been brought there earlier. We worked at building the railway line. Poles who were imprisoned like us worked with us. After some time, a group of about 80 Jews from Baranovichi arrived to us in Michalishok. They were isolated, hungry, tattered, and worn out, lacking everything. We did everything to help them, but some of them died of hunger. One day, shots were heard. It became clear that they had taken eight gypsies and shot them in the grove next to us. After some time, they brought about 100 more Jews from the Ashmyany Ghetto. They were young men and women, whom we met at work. From them, we found out about the liquidation of the Ashmyany Ghetto.

[Col. 1422]

The Jews were transferred to be killed at Kovno and Ponary. At that time, I received a note from my father in the Kimlishok Ghetto, in which he asked me if I can find him potato peels, for the hunger was great in the ghetto.

The Liquidation of the Kimlishok Ghetto

On Saturday, October 24, 1942, 13 Marcheshvan 5703[2], S.S. brigades came, surrounded the ghetto, took all the Jews to the forest, and shot them. This took place so suddenly that only few had time to escape.

In this manner, I lost my beloved, dear, family members, may G-d avenge their blood. They included: my righteous pure father Reb Yisrael, age 58; my brother Yaakov, age 28, my sister Frida, age 26, my brother Shlomo Tzvi, age 17, my brother-in-law Moshe Tanchum, age 28, my cousin Mariasha, age 13 and other family members: Rachel Licht, Reizel Licht, Meir and Leah Ajngelcyn and their children Shmuel-Zev, Mariasha-Fruma, and others. Freda Lewin and their children Roza, Chaim, and tens of other of our relatives, may G-d avenge their blood. A few days later, I learned that my little sister Mariasha was saved, and was in the Michalishok Ghetto. She came to me from there. I hid her in the camp for about a week without the Germans knowing. However, from fear that they would find her, I took her out of the camp, and she went to a farmer. Our camp was fenced off at the end of December. I noticed here and there that the end was approaching, especially in that the guarding became stricter, and the work became more and more difficult. They did not spare us from death blows. I decided to escape. With a promise to the captain of the camp to bring him a present of valuable objects that I had hidden with a farmer in a far-off village, as well as liquor, I received an exit permit for three people, for Reuven Licht and Chanoch Mirsky of Podbrodz who were with me. Mirsky refused to go with us, so Licht and I left the camp. This was in January 1943. We were chased from place to place, and wandered from farmer to farmer. We slept in abandoned bathhouses. In the meantime, my sister Mariasha joined us. At times, we were very close to death. We were starving, and we swallowed everything that came to our hands. We were dressed in rags. Spring arrived. This was after Stalingrad. Discomfort was felt in the area because of the partisans. The farmers did not want to allow us to cross their threshold due to fear of the Germans. It was only possible to travel during nights. We hid in the forest during the day. Finally, after wandering between villages, a farmer permitted my sister to remain with him for a few days. I went to find a hiding place. I found a hiding place in a pit in the barn of a farmer. After several days, I found out that my sister was forced to leave the hiding place of the farmer due to slander. Along the way, a farmer came across her in a sled, and asked her where she was going. My sister told him that she was an orphaned Polish girl from Vilna, and was going to seek work. The farmer agreed to take her with him, and she worked at every hard job with him in the farm, and slept in the pen. The farmer's wife recognized that she was not a Pole but rather a Jew, and sent her out of their house. Thus my sister Mariasha wandered again in the forests until she reached me in the pit one night without the farmer knowing about her. Thus, we were together for some time and we starved together. At the end of December 1943, the situation became very tense. The white Polish partisans[3] who belonged to the Armia Krajowa wandered about the area, coming several times to my farmer. They murdered every Jew whom they came across. Out of fear of the Polish murderers, we decided to go to another place.

13 Cheshvan 1942, 170 martyrs of Kimlishok, Boistritz, Podbrodz
Moshe Epstein, Freda Bozorski, Malka Solsiacki

I wish to tell here about two incidents in which we met the murderers almost face to face.

In the Barn Attic

After much wandering, a farmer named Wyszko, an acquaintance of ours from before the war, agreed to hide us in his attic, under the condition that his family members not know about this. We slept on the hay in the attic, open to rain and snow, for about three months. At night, the farmer would sometimes bring us crumbs of dry bread or a few potatoes.

One Saturday, we heard voices in Russian demanding horses from the mistress of the house, and immediately threating to shoot her on the spot if she does not bring them a horse. We were sure that these were partisans, and since we had wanted to contact the partisans for some time, we thought that we should go down and join them... However, suddenly we heard the sound of motorcycles, and busses full of Germans spread through the village. The "partisans," who were collaborators with the Germans, placed machine guns in the center of the city. The farmer and his household locked the door of their house immediately and fled from the village, fearing that they might find us and kill them as well. The Germans made a thorough search through all the houses, barns, and warehouses of the city. When they reached the house of the farmer, they broke the lock of the house, searched the house, and took everything they found. Then they entered the barn, and searched in every corner. Had they raised their eyes upward, they would have certainly found us. Only a bit of straw separated between us, between life and death... The Germans remained in the village for three days. During that time, they murdered the Janiszki family whom they found hiding there. We lay hovering between life and death for three days...

[Col. 1424]

After the Germans left the village, the farmer forced us to leave his farm. We were sent out in the evening hungry and weakened from fear. We could not stand on our feet. My sister literally crawled. We reached a grove and slept there. Germans passed on the road, but did not notice us due to the darkness. Only during the next night did we succeed in reaching the village of Magon [Magûnai] weakened to death and with injured feet. A farmer acquaintance had mercy on us, and let us hide with him for a few days.

Meeting with Partisans

In the meantime, my sister broke out in skin injuries. We decided that she would go to the farmer acquaintance and ask him to go to the pharmacy in Podbrodz to get some medicine. On the way, my sister went to a farmer acquaintance to rest a bit and ask for some food. The farmer received her nicely and told her that Russian partisans are with him in the threshing floor. My sister saw a chance to connect with the partisans, and was happy with the meetings. The partisans recommended that my sister go with them. She agreed on the condition that they accept her brother – that is me – to go with them. She told them that I am in a far-off forest, and we would be able to meet here, with the farmer two days. The partisans agreed, and my sister hurried to tell me of the meeting. I had a suspicion in my heart that these were disguised Germans or Polish murderers connected with the Germans. Therefore I decided not to go to the meeting at the designated time, but rather the following evening. We arrived at the grove near the designated village toward morning. We approached the farmer's house at dawn. We did not recognize the farmer, for he was wounded all over. It became clear that the previous day, that was the day designated for the meeting, the "partisans" came, and wanted to shoot the farmer and his family when they did not find us. In the meantime, they beat him with deathblows. The villagers managed to save the farmer and his household through pleas and gifts, with the pretext that they would find us and give us over to them within a few days. These "partisans" were Polish murderers connected with the Germans.

Despite the great suffering that we had caused to the farmer, he gave us a bit of food. We quickly disappeared from the place. Before we went, I requested a favor from the farmer's wife, and she promised to fulfil my request. I had photographs of my family members. I wrote a farewell letter to my brother Mordechai who was living in the Land of Israel. I added the photographs, and requested that the Polish farmer send them to my brother's address after the war.

Assistance from a Former Member of the Polish Government

We again wandered through the forests together with Reuven Licht. One night, we left my sister Mariasha in an abandoned bathhouse, for her feet were badly wounded, and she could not continue walking under any circumstance. In the middle of the night, my sister woke up from her sleep very perplexed at the image of a woman lighting a match. She quickly recognized this woman as Pesia Schmid-Kulbak, who was also hiding in abandoned bathhouse. The next day, my sister joined me, and, together with Reuven Licht, we found a shelter in the threshing floor of a farmer for a month in exchange for a leather coat that we gave him. From there, we moved to another farmer who housed us in a pit that he had dug in the pigsty. He covered the pit with boards, and spread straw upon them. It was constantly dark in the pit. At night, the farmer would bring us a meager amount of bread and also a bit of water. After a few months, we were forced to leave this place as well, for the Germans had surrounded the village, and murdered all the Jews that they found. We hid in an attic of a shed in another village for some time, without the owners knowing. At night, we would steal potatoes from the pig trough, which the farmer provided in ample amounts. We were jealous of the pigs...

[Col. 1425]

We were tired of our lives. The will to fight for this terrible life was lost. Our life was under threat at any moment. At that time, we found a pit in the forest, and hid there for about a month. At night, my sister would go out to the farmers in the area and sometimes bring a bit of food. In the meantime, Polish partisans from the Armia Krajowa arrived in the forest, and we were forced to leave the place. We decided to turn to a Pole who had been a delegate to the Polish parliament before the war, and lived in a nearby village. He received us very nicely. We requested that he help us obtain various items that we had hidden before the war with farmers in the area so that we could sell them and subsist from them. The Pole agreed. On Sunday, when they went to church, my sister drove with his wife and returned with a few of our valuables toward evening. The Germans who met them thought that my sister was a Polish girl.

Now we had valuable objects that we could sell so as to be able to continue somehow to live. In exchange for blankets that my sister had brought, the former parliamentary representative agreed to hide us in his house for a month. He placed us in the attic of the barn, and provided us with food. This was the only month during the war when we were more or less satiated. We were forced again to set out on our way after a month. Even though the liberation was not far off, and the farmers saw that the Germans were losing the war, the dangers to our life did not abate. We chose to return to a farmer with whom we had once hidden. We reached him at night. He received us nicely. After we gave him our remaining belongings, he agreed to hold us in the same pit in the barn for three months.

We were satisfied, for it seemed that the place was more secure, and we also sensed that the war would end shortly. Reuven Licht came to us after some time. The farmer agreed to keep him with us in the pit in exchange for the additional belongings that we promised to give him.

From time to time, the Polish bandits caught Jews and murdered them. They caught Sara Krol with her children, Reuven and Chana Glaz, Shinka Belski and her children, Itza, Rivka and Chaya Szapira, and Abba Gordon, and murdered them.

[Col. 1426]

The Liberation

We were afraid to leave the pit for even a moment. One night, the Germans arrived with their wives and children and slept in the city. This was the last wave of them. We felt that the day of liberation was approaching. The next day it was quiet, and we began to hear echoes of artillery. We went out a bit, and sat all night. The next day, the farmer came and told us that the Russians had entered the village. Despite that, we slept for another day in the pit, in order to be certain that we would not fall into some sort of trap... Then we left the pit. We were torn and tattered, weak and tired, forlorn and alone. We began to walk to Podbrodz. We met those who pillaged and murdered. They were going about free, walking calmly and with security. They were also the rulers of the city. We entered our house through the window, as it was locked with a lock.

Toward the evening, a Pole entered and asked: “Why did you enter the house, for I have purchased it along with its furniture from Lithuanians?” They did not imagine that anyone would survive. They had done everything to finish the task completely.

We took an oath to take revenge. We reported several hooligans, pillagers, and murderers to the Russian N.K.V.D. There were trials, but it was very difficult to judge them solely for murder of Jews. It was necessary to testify that they also murdered Russians or gave over partisans to Germans. Only those who did the murderers will receive their punishment. In one case, I was at the trial of a Polish hooligan. The trial took place in Vilna before a field court, and the judges were only army captains. I testified that this hooligan turned Jewish Communists over to the Gestapo and murdered them. The army captain was not embarrassed to ask me: “Did he only catch Jews?” I responded, “No! He also caught Communists!”

Life on the accursed ground became abhorrent to us, and almost all the survivors of Podbrodz left at the earliest opportunity. Most made aliya to the Land. Jews also left for America and Canada. My sister and I went through a long journey to the Land, via Russia, Lithuania, Poland, Germany, France, Haifa, and Cyprus. We remained in a camp of the rulers of the Land, our British "friends." We then spent a month in Atlit[4], and we were finally free in the Land of Israel.

I was able to participate in the War of Independence.

Translator's Footnotes

Lithuanian collaborators.

There is a typo in the text here. It says 5713 rather than 5703 (5713 would correspond to 1952-1953).

See "White Poles" in this article: https://ipfs.io/ipfs/QmXoypizjW3WknFiJnKLwHCnL72vedxjQkDDP1mXWo6uco/wiki/Soviet_partisans_in_Poland.html.

See https://en.wikipedia.org/wiki/Atlit_detainee_camp.

[Col. 1427]

Poems

Meir Blitz (Toronto)

Translated by Janie Respitz

Dedicated to my family: Yitzkhak, Etl, Sonia, Nadia. Our children: Yunke, Herman, Yoske, Ella, Moishe. Our grandchildren: Shloimeleh, Nekhama– Yehidisleh – my heart and "bitter song" is a gift.

My Town in Blood

Near the mountains of Podbrodz, from the Polish slaughter
Death was celebrated in the beaks of black bloody ravens.
The first victims of Hitler fell like sheep.
The sun warmed, smiled and shone –
And we – the victims – doomed.

The Germans, Lithuanians, surround the town.
Death is a "Gift" the remnants inflict.

We spit in the face of death.
Our bones prolonged our fate.
A little in Svir, a little in "Lipes" (Kimelishok ghetto)
We breathed, trembled and continued to chase our troubles.

My heart breaks for Khayke, for Leybke.

For the slaughtered district of "Sventzian".
A mother "Nekhameleh", your heart is a bleeding wound.
Over and over.
In Khayke's and Leybke's last call
Your heart has burned in your body.

Also my brother and I breathed the tar
In the forests of Vilna.
We chewed troubles for long months and years!
We barely breathed, and suffered with our children.
We prevented them from starving and freezing!

When Hitler's kingdom of a thousand years! –
Together with him his Aryan friends became a *pile of shit.*
Remember our mothers! Collective memory!
Not erased! Not lost!
On Canada's soil! In a town near Moishe and Etl.

She lives! – She breathes! –
For many more years!

Near a Lake

Near a lake, near a Lithuanian
Stand two huts,
There lies my past, dark,
They remind me of my life.

Far from the village stands a forest,
We are cold, I freeze.
In the marsh stands a hut
Without a window, not even a door.

People live in this hut,
Among them a baby, a small child.
What do they live off? What do they hope for?
They now live in the claws of the Nazis?

Days, months and years rush by
They all become citizens of the forest.
They rock the little girl and sing her a song
About a world that is cursed for Jews.

[Col. 1428]

Instead of a Tombstone

In memory of my mother, my father, Reb Yisroel Bratanisky, Boreh Blushinsky, and all that died in Kimelishok, September 1943.

Oh, shadows far away, near the Vilna aster city gate,
This is where I was born, not far from the gate,
Hardened generations, stationed at the wall,
A memory, far away and grey.

My father, the strong man – Reb Motl! Rabbi Mote! –
Until today the blanket drenched in water,
The slaps on my back, my rear end, my soles,
When I innocently tore my coat playing ball.
Oh mother, Nekhamele! Your glance from up high,
Oh mother Nekhamele! Your sighs supressed.
Your Meirke wailing from under the blanket
In the corner a plucked chicken is moaning.

Afterwards your moralizing, mother Nekhamele! –
The delightful richness of colour and fantasy,
Your pearls of speech, your teaching me, mother,
Together in a corner where a wounded eagle fell.

Your years were cut short, oh mother!
In Lipe's garden near the fence busy resting,
The beginning of the end of Hitler's victims,
The ropes around the necks were tightening.

When the Lithuaninan and German axes
Cut the Jewish community forever
I met you Mitzke in "Vengravitz" forest,
My own – "Etke" two non– extinguished bullets
Shone through rags, lonely in terror.

The memory of spinning pulls at me,
My cradle, my youth, not far from the Vilna city gates,
The shout from the ghetto Podbrodz – Kilmelishok,
Hardened in Lipe's kingdom near the gate,
Instead of a tombstone, your smile, oh mother, Nekhameh!

Bunkers

We are proud of you, heroes from the ghetto!
We feel how rigid the guns are in your hands.
You kill the murderers! You fire you veto!
You lived to take revenge! You lived the moment!

We are with you in the dark bunkers,
We feel the heat and smoke,
The heroes mow down the cadets,
The bandits who howl loudly like wolves.

Days and nights are consumed by fire,
A few proud Jews against the Nazi army,
All are fighting for and dreaming about a free youth
That would know of no moans or pain.

We are sitting far from you, in forests and swamps,
We are searching to make contact with the ghetto and the forest,
We are striving for freedom, to no longer be scoundrels,
The enemy dead, his destruction is coming soon.

[Col. 1429]

In Zemlianke

In the narrow Zemlianke – smoke,
The weeds are soaked in tears,
We sit around and heavily sigh,
About life, nothing to explain.

We are about to leave on our way
To search for a small piece of bread,
It is raining buckets
The bread is tied to death.

Kaddish
(Prayer for the Dead)

There, far in the forest
Stands a willow, quietly divided into branches,
Here lies my father's grave
Not far from the shores of the lake.

He fell at night
Silent shadows encircled him
The waves of the lake
Quietly whispered a silent Kaddish.

The willow often cries
Slapping and rocking in the wind,
Sometimes the sun kisses him splendidly
When she sets in flaming red.

My father lies there in his grave,
My father lies there in his eternal rest,
A dear father, a loving Dad,
You fell like as a hero!

Graves

The bells ring in the evening
Echoing far away
It hurts me, it pains me,
I spent my childhood there.

My youth,
Was spent there
My life,
Buried at the door.

On the east side,
In the red of morning,
I buried you,
My mother, my dearest, near a fence.

In the west in the distance – quietly on a hill,
A tree grows, with green needles,
Father's smile...a cool wind,
Tearing at my heart to that place...to that place...
The bells ring in the evening!
Carries your trembling away!
My mother near the fence,
My father, there in the forest, near the shores of the lake.

[Col. 1430]

Our Home – Ash Trenches

All the doors were closed and locked,
I run to look for my wife and child,
I leave all – I look where is better,
The steps, striding in the wind.
Our home spits fire,
Our home – trench of ash
We run like mice from the burning barn
Broken, disheveled, frightened and dead tired.
The Zhemaniye[Zemlianke] does not want to know us any longer,
Drowned in Jewish blood,
The enemies are delighted! The eyes are beaming!
All's good for them!

Clouds

Raised in the forests and swamps,
Without a tomorrow, without a home,
Summer – the tent, winter – mud hut,
Snakes and wolves were our friends.
The dark nights lasted long,
Our suffering and pain lasted long,
Grandfather, father and mother, thought,
How can we bare the hunger?

Finally the hour of light arrived,
From the swamps and forest, back to town.
The hill, the house, a grey dream,
We want to kneel and bow.

Our town is empty, our dream dismal,
Surrounded by evening shadows, veiled,
The grass on the graves barely trembles,
We are all withered, but alive.

A Refugee – Song

Frolic, frolic, angry winds,
Today is your time,
Darkness, our lives
We again not free.

After concentration camps and crematorium,
After so many rivers of blood,
Again parliaments, directives,
Everything hidden in fat skin.
Our struggle in the forest was trampled on,
Seas of blood taken away with the wind,
Just the enemy is affectionately caressed
Gentle and nice now.

Go look for justice among diplomats,
Woe to the fate of refugees,
They only know about weapons and cannons,
But not of righteousness and morality.

[Col. 1431]

Not a Sign nor a Hint

by B. Mordechai

Translated by Jerrold Landau

Not a sign, or a hint, or an innuendo from anywhere
The thin star is extinguished somewhere, and the heart clenches,
Only flocks of darkness graze in the skies
And angry jackals on agonized nights,
Only the damaged moon casts a lost glance
Before it sets, and with it, the solution.

From morning to evening, the day is so long.
The journey on paths that I had never been on before.
As if everything was from some dream.
And as if I never had a brother or a sister,
As if thousands of years have already past.
Time has caressed their hand, I am refreshed from their voices.

The silence is deep. There is no sign in it, no image.
Evening casts its shadows like camels

Meeting the heavens. Afterward a gloomy night
Will knock on the doors of the horizon, and who will open for it?
Woe to me! I have already forgotten how my father smiled
But his tears – I will see. I will never forget.

I cannot forget, and cannot believe
That his smile will not suddenly appear to me in the door.
For the hand of the murderer was raised, and G-d
Did not come in a storm, and did not plug the breach.
For my little brother screamed out for naught, the child
And his screams piece the heavens and the earth.

I will awaken at night; a voice screams out from my blood.
I will tear open the eyes, perhaps
The awaited miracle has arrived, when I see it I will believe,
Their hands are so close to me, and their voice is so close to here.
From morning till night I wait for the dream
In which they live with me, and will live forever.

[Col. 1433-1444]

Lintup

(Lyntupy, Belarus)

54°51' 25°53'

Our Shtetl

By Mordekhai Kentsianski (Max Khenchynski)

Translation from Yiddish by Dr. Sonia Kovitz

Donated by Irene Mauber Skibinski

Lintup was a small *shtetele* in Sventzian district, where more than 70 Jewish families lived. The *shtetl* was surrounded on all sides by a large thick pine forest. Most of the bathhouses in the shtetl belonged to the well-known Count Bishevski. He also owned several estates in the region, as well as sawmills, alcohol works, and turpentine factories. He was a liberal person, a serious philanthropist, and a community leader. Just before the outbreak of the World War II, he was 80 years old

The landowner Bishevski was on good terms with the Jews, and the managers of all his businesses were Jewish. He was therefore sharply criticized by the Polish anti-Semites, but he had few dealings with them. In the Lintup area, all his businesses were managed by Uri Shapiro, a peace-loving man, a generous host, and an outstanding community leader. All Bishevski's Vilna businesses were also managed by a Jew, who hid the landowner during the period of Soviet rule. The Soviets wanted Bishevski in order to send him off to Siberia or even kill him.

The Jewish *kehile* [community] was not big in size, but it had all the important institutions. In Lintup there was a beautiful *beis medresh* [synagogue], *gemilus khesed* [interest-freeloan] society, *hakhnasas orkhim* [hospitality] society, library, and *tarbut* [secular Zionist school where Hebrew rather than Yiddish was spoken].

The Bishevki estate

Almost all the *shtetl* Jews were favorably inclined toward Zionism and fervently gave money to be invested in *keren kimes* and *keren hisod* [Zionist organizations] and in all Jewish national funds generally. The Jewish young people joined [Zionist groups]: *hakhaluts* [the Pioneer], *hakhaluts hatsair* [the Young Pioneer], and *tseirei tsion* [Young Zion]. The best of them studied in the *gymnasia* [high school], and one of Shapiro's sons even studied in France.

An ebullient social life pulsed in the *shtetl*. Almost every Jewish family subscribed to a daily paper and most of the young people borrowed books from the library. A major role in religious, social and cultural life was filled by Rabbi Yudkevski, for whom the entire Jewish population felt great respect and *derekh erets*. He was highly esteemed by the Christians as well, and was a good friend of the town's mayor, Bielovski [translator's note: alternate spelling used elsewhere by the author is Bialoveyski].

We were indebted to the rabbi for the establishment of the *gemilus khesed* fund, over which I had the privilege of presiding as chair for many years. In addition to me, the rabbi's colleagues in the gemilus khesed were Dovid and Khaim Katskovitsh, Borukh Matskin, and Uri Shapiro.

Lintup Drama Club

"The Orphan Chasya." Yudel Pamevitsh, Khayah Beynis, Tsile Tsiblin-Kharmats, Beyle Yavitsh, Berta Strachansky, Lyuba Mauber, Sholom Shapiro

z"l, Moshe Mauber, Abram Sandak, Khayah Shteynhart, Asher Shapiro

In 1924 Dovid Katskovitsh and I established the Jewish town library. I served also as a representative on the City Council, was in the Marske League [?], on the Parents' Committee of the *tarbut* school, and a member of the Fire Brigade.

One of the main community leaders of the *shtetl* was Abram Asher Gilinski. In his younger years he studied in the Slobodke Yeshiva [in Kovno] and returned home well versed in *talmud* and *poskim* [halakhic decisions]. He was not only an outstanding *baal tefilah* [prayer leader] and *baal kriyah* [public reader of the Torah], but a *baal tsedakah* [leader in charitable works] and a generous host. Every itinerant *magid* [preacher] and *meshulakh* [emissary raising funds for Jewish causes] knew that with Gilinski he would find a warm bed and something good to eat.

A fine *shtetl* householder was Reb Leyb Yakov Sarafan, who made his living as a butcher. He was solidly built with wide shoulders and he overflowed with humor and witty sayings. Everyone liked to visit his butcher shop because he was always making jokes. On *shabbos* and *yontif* he would *daven* at the *omed* [cantor's lectern]. He especially liked to be given a "juicy" *aliyah* [*fete aliyah*: to be called up to bless the Torah reading on some special occasion].

The Jewish population depended mainly on small business and crafts for a livelihood. A large number of Jews were engaged in the wood and timber trades. Others were employed in factories and the turpentine works. General contentment prevailed, whether due to economic or to cultural and social conditions.

And so the years flowed by until the cursed and terrible days of June 1941.

Disaster

Immediately upon the outbreak of the German-Soviet War on June 22, 1941, a heavy black cloud cast its shadow over Lintup. In the very first days, the Lintup Jews paid with the lives of two beloved family members. The two brothers Moshe and Yudel Mauber were murdered by the villains—randomly, without a reason, without a why or a wherefore.

Several months later Lintup paid very heavily when the bestial criminals slaughtered the entire family of our renowned Rabbi Yudkevski. The terrible event happened as follows. The rabbi lived, as everyone knew, in the same building as Mayor Bielovski, who was on friendly terms with the Jews. When the Germans gave the order that all Jews must hand over their radios, the rabbi and other respected householders often went to listen to the radio in Bielovski's home. This was strictly forbidden. A Jew must under no circumstances enter a Christian home, above all, not to listen to the radio. One time the rabbi happened to be sitting in the mayor's apartment when one of the Enemies of Israel walked in. The man immediately left to inform the police.

A big raid took place right away. The rabbi with his family—the *rebbitsin* [rabbi's wife] Khanah and their nine-year-old son Mendele—were taken to Postav. The mayor wasn't allowed to go free either; his house was searched and he was arrested. A few days later the news came that the rabbi and his wife were in great danger. Immediately there was great panic in the *shtetl*. A large amount of money and valuables was collected and the decision was made to send it to Postav to bribe the police and to free the rabbi.

A young man and a girl, Abram Rein and Frume-Basya Rudnitski, set off for Postav to carry out the dangerous mission.

They dressed as landowners, rented a small cart of the type used by landowners, and left for Postav. It was a cold, wintry early morning and along the road they came across an overturned sleigh. They gave some money to a policeman to help get it righted. Scattered over the snow around the sleigh were bloody *b'godim* [specifically Jewish clothing]. Suddenly they recognized the rabbi's silk *bekeshe* [fur-lined coat], *talis katan*, and wide-brimmed *kapelush* [hat]. A drunken man told them that the rabbi and his family had been murdered. They quickly turned around and drove home, bringing us the terrible news. It is hard even to conceive of the mourning that gripped all the Jews of Lintup on that day. In this event we had a preview of the destiny awaiting the Jewish people.

A few days later Mayor Bielovski was released from jail. He came back deeply griefstricken and let us know that we, *khas'vesholem* [heaven forbid], should have no illusions. In his opinion the Hitlerists would destroy all the Jews and all of us should expect the worst.

*

Barely a week after the death of Rabbi Yudkevski, the police liquidated the Lintup ghetto. We were told that all the Lintup Jews would be transported to Sventzian. We immediately considered all the options and succeeded in creating a work camp where the "useful" Jews could be held and put to work. Since the *shtetl* offered for this purpose the sawmill, the *smolarnia* [place where pitch is burned], several courtyards, and the woodcutting operation in the nearby woods, out of all the town's Jews the "productive element" that remained alive was around 100. The rest were transported to Sventzian.

Life in the camp was extremely hard. People were beaten and chased and sometimes struck with truly murderous blows. One time some Jews were harnessed to a wagon and ordered to pull it to the railway line. When one of them paused a moment, the Germans whipped him with sharply pointed rods. Nevertheless, some Jews endured and persevered and it was perhaps only thanks to this camp that they survived. In a short time, though, all our illusions ended and the work camp was liquidated.

*

The reason for the liquidation of the Lintup work camp was as follows: on the night of the 18th-19th of December 1942, a group of Russian partisans unexpectedly attacked the

Lintup woods. They set fire to several important military objectives and for several hours engaged in a tenacious battle with German troops. We were sitting in the camp and with delight saw all of Lintup on fire, and flames coming from our enemy. Revenge sprang up in our hearts. We knew well that we would soon pay dearly, but nevertheless we were gratified and didn't think about what the morning would bring.

At dawn our camp was surrounded by the Lithuanian police, who began to shoot at the workers without a goal or a warning. The first to fall were Yosef Rudnitski and his brother's son. The police chased us straight into the open field, where peasants with sleighs were already waiting for us. They packed us in like cattle and drove us toward the forest. We hadn't gone even 200 meters before we saw long narrow graves. We instantly realized what that meant for us.

Not far from the graves were masked gunmen. We couldn't get out of the sleighs and there was an onslaught, a hail of bullets. When I saw the first victims fall, I started shouting to everyone to run. I made a break from the sleigh and with all the strength I possessed I leaped and set off running into the woods. Bullets were flying over my head. I ran and fell, ran and again fell. Finally I found myself deep in the woods. I was so exhausted that I simply could not move from the spot. I burrowed into the snow and decided to rest for a while. I began to catch my breath and think about what to do next.

When it became very still and I didn't hear any more of the terrible sounds of shooting by the villains and the cries of their dying victims, I got up and walked deeper into the woods. I walked without a goal and without a path until I arrived in a little village. There I discovered that in addition to me, a few other Jews from the Lintup work camp had survived. I found there in the woods Abram Rein, Moshe Gilinski, and Hirshe Kharmats.

Together we went back to the site of the horrible murders and there, by the fresh mass grave, we swore to take revenge for the spilled blood. Then we decided to go to the Sventzian ghetto. But I separated from my two friends and told them that first I wanted to go and find out whether any of my family might still be alive. What I had in mind was that possibly some of them had been taken in by Christians in the area. I asked here, asked there, but no one had any news about the members of my family. So I decided to head for the Sventzian ghetto too.

I was feeling deeply discouraged and bitter and didn't even notice that I was walking along the main highway just as in the former good times. By the time I realized my mistake, it was already too late. Directly ahead of me three large trucks filled with German soldiers suddenly appeared. I started to run into the woods, but they saw me and sprayed the woods with a hail of bullets.

Luckily they didn't want to go further into the woods. I covered myself with the branches of a pine tree and stayed there for several hours, not moving from the spot. Meanwhile a thick snow fell and completely covered me from my head to my feet. Probably the snow saved me since it covered my tracks.

When it became quiet, I stood up, shook off the snow, and set off walking again. After some time passed I oriented myself and went in the right direction to find my way to Sventzian. I followed the route through the night and arrived at the Sventzian ghetto.

*

To my great happiness, in the ghetto I found my daughter Basya and son Leybele, who had been wounded in the leg. At first my only thought was to go into the woods and join the partisans there, but my children wouldn't let me. My son was wounded and unwell and my daughter was so completely exhausted she couldn't take another step. So by necessity I too stayed in the Sventzian ghetto. But I could feel the unrest among the young people, who wanted to escape into the woods and take revenge on the brutal enemy. Mikhelson felt the same strong unrest that I did.

In the end 27 young people left the ghetto and went into the woods. The group would have been a lot larger if we hadn't been deluded by the Vilna commandant Gans. He made a special effort to come to our ghetto in order to assure us that the Sventzian Jews were not in danger. He said we would be taken to Vilna and Kovno and placed in various work camps. People let themselves be convinced. There were even some optimists who saw a good sign in the fact that the liquidation of the ghetto would be carried out by Jewish police instead of by Germans or Lithuanians.

I hadn't the slightest confidence in Gans and tried extremely hard to convince my children to leave the ghetto and hide in the woods with me. They simply would not come to the same conclusion. In the end it came down to all of us being transported to New Sventzian. Special railroad cattle cars were waiting for us there. My intuition instantly told me that these cars would take us not to life but to obliteration and extinction.

At the very last minute we succeeded in getting away from the railway station. The following people escaped with me: Moshe Gilinski, Abram Rein, Hirshe Kharmats, Ber Fisher from Heydutsishok, and one other person, Khaim Leyb from Sventzian. For the next three weeks we wandered around the woods, fields and villages. Wherever we would spend the day, we would not stay the night in case they came looking for us. So there was a practical purpose in our wandering.

We decided to lead our lives as partisans and survive by our wits. Near Strunvits we broke into a large dairy that provided dairy products to the German army. We smashed all the machines with a hatchet and ruined all the prepared dairy products.

Through a Christian I tried to establish contact with my children, who at that time should have been in the Vilna ghetto. She brought back the horrible news that they had never gone to the Vilna ghetto, that the entire transport had been murdered on the edge of Paneriei [the Ponary Forest south of Vilna].

From that time on my sole thought was to find all possible ways and means to take revenge. With my entire soul in a furor I threw myself into battle and together with my friends, went back to the Lintup area to find all the peasants who had helped the Germans. We set fire to their houses, stole their sustenance, and most importantly, their weapons. In a short time we were well-armed and the entire area was afraid of us. Because of their fear we prolonged our activity there. Then we began to search for a way to join the regular partisan detachment.

At this time Hirsh Kharmats became seriously ill. He had an abcess that required an operation. I myself had to conduct the operation. We hid in a barn and there I cut out the abcess with a razor blade. When he recovered, we were contacted by the partisan organization. Eventually we were accepted into the Suvorov detachment of Markov's brigade.

In Battle

In Markov's brigade, a proposal emerged to organize a special Jewish division called “Revenge.” A young man from Vilna, Katzenelenbogen, and I were appointed as the leaders of the division. In all, the division numbered 30 young Jewish men. This was not a large number, but all the same we carried out a series of very important assignments. We blew up bridges, burned villages, killed Germans, and earned in partisan circles a name for ourselves as bold heroes.

Our detachment was then located four kilometers from Miadl. We in fact commanded the entire area. We were free as birds and woe to any German who entered that zone. With us in the forest lived entire families—husbands, wives and children. They all benefited from our protection and we considered ourselves one large partisan family.

We carried out all our assignments in the middle of the night. One time our task was to go to the Lintup forest and investigate the large German garrison that had been established there. We were eight Jews divided into two teams. Not far from the forest we found two small bathhouses and we hid there. The owner of the bathhouses noticed us and, no doubt realizing that we were Jews, must have immediately informed the Lithuanian police. In a few hours both bathhouses were surrounded by a large number of policemen, who fired at us in a hail of bullets. In one of the bathhouses were Yehoshua Gertner, Leyb Gurvitsh, Simke Levin from Sventzian, and Hirsh Kharmats from Lintup. They ran out of the bathhouse and were killed. However, Yehoshua Gertner first managed to throw a grenade and killed a lot of the heinous Lithuanians.

We saw this from the other bathhouse and also threw grenades into the group of Lithuanians. This created a great confusion there. We of course made use of the opportunity and ran for the forest. We managed to take with us Moshe Gilinski, who was hit by a bullet.

We succeeded in escaping and returned to our base. I gave headquarters an account of the brigade and proposed that we should dissolve the special Jewish division. I made it clear to them that anti-Semitism was very strong in all the villages, and that some

Christians should be sent in each group in addition to Jews. Headquarters agreed and the Jewish division was dissolved.

A few days later a group of 12 partisans was sent out to find the provocateur who had informed against us to the Lithuanian police. The group found him and carried out to perfection the *psak din* [sentence of the court] against him. After that we were entrusted with various other important assignments in Markov's brigade. It is important to tell about one of them especially. Once we were walking at night through a thick forest when we happened to come upon the Vilna-Polotsk Highway. Suddenly we noticed something glimmering opposite us and it seemed to us that it might be a wolf. We stopped and stood there, quietly consulting each other about what to do. On the other side of the highway evidently our talking could be heard because shooting broke out directed at us. We realized a large force was located there and we chose not to enter into battle with them. We had to retreat. Such cases happen, but in my life as a partisan it happened only this one time. On the way back all of us swore on our lives to expel the Germans from the entire forest.

*

Meanwhile the regular Soviet Army came closer to our district. This was in the first months of the year 1944. We received an order to blow up all the bridges and railroad lines in order to make a normal retreat more difficult for the enemy. We were supposed to make sure that the Germans would have no way to take back their plunder with them to Germany. We carried this order out with accuracy, happiness and enthusiasm. We felt that with each kilometer that the Red Army came closer, they were bringing to us Jews, more than to everyone else, blessed freedom.

Finally the long-awaited moment arrived. The regular Soviet Army took command of our area and expelled the German forces. We were free.

In the first days we couldn't accustom ourselves to the new situation. We didn't know what to do or where to go. We knew that our homes were destroyed and that we would not find anyone alive there. We also could not imagine being face to face with the neighbors who had spilled Jewish blood and taken part in theft and the “actions.”

Finally we decided to go to Lintup. Our hearts wanted to fantasize that perhaps we would find someone there of our families or friends or acquaintances.

*

I returned to Lintup together with Moshe Gilinksi and Abram Rein. There we found Frume-Basya Rudnitski with her two nieces. They were all that remained of our Lintup Jewish *kehile.*

Our first task was to dig a mass grave for the 100 martyrs who had fallen in the first work-camp. We also brought there the body of Hirshe Kharmats. Then we went six kilometers from the *shtetl* and buried the bodies of the four friends whom we had honored there a few years before.

Over the mass grave we placed a gravestone and wrote on it that these were all that remained of the good and dear Jews of Lintup.

The Soviets offered me a good government post, but I decided not to accept it because I felt that I could not live on the ruins and among murderers.

I went into the depths of Poland and from there I wandered through various Jewish refugee camps, until finally I came to *erets yisroel* and I now live in the old historic town of Safet.

The destroyed shtetl

[Columns 1445-1446]

My shtetl

Its Houses and Streets May Be Plain but It Is Splendid

By Tsilia Matskin-Tsiblin

Translation from Hebrew by Dr. Sonia Kovitz, appreciation for the assistance of Itzhak M. Itzhaky and Eilat Gordin Levitan

Donated by Irene Mauber Skibinski

My trip to Lintup after ten years

Lintup is a typical *shtetl.* In the autumn, the mud sticks to your shoes. When the first snow falls, people are happy that everything is covered with a clean white blanket. Later in the freezing cold, everyone impatiently longs for spring.

The layout of the *shtetl,* surrounded by a forest with streams, is picturesque—so beautiful that you would think an architect designed it. But the Jews' lives were gray—they worked hard six days a week running after *parnosse* [making a living]. In the *beys hamedresh* on *shabbos* the bitterness of a week of quarreling was lifted from their shoulders. Every Tuesday farmers would come from all over to the market, and the noise was overwhelming. At the end of the day everyone would sit at home and calculate how much they and their neighbors had made.

I made *aliyah* to *erets yisroel* in 1924. Ten years later, in 1934, I came back to Lintup for a visit. Nothing had changed, except that many friends who had been Zionists dreaming of making *aliyah* to *erets yisroel* were now Communists and sitting in jail. I went to visit three of them. They were surprised since they didn't know I was coming, and were amazed to see me. The Polish guard treated me with respect.

The antagonism of the Christians toward the Jews was widespread. Wild slander and provocation by speakers full of hatred and venom was heard in the market. At night the Jews were afraid to go out, and hooligans would throw rocks at the windows of Jewish houses. Despite all this, a group of boys and girls from the Christian school visited me and even brought me and my daughter all kinds of gifts. When I remarked on how much the times had altered the relations between Jews and non-Jews, they replied, “Not everyone here has turned into an animal.”

Rabbi Prutovitz had seven children at home and his salary was barely able to support them. One after the other they left Lintup to go to Vilna. Of all of them, only one son survived. Mikhal lives in Haifa; one daughter, Esther, lives in Kfar Mala; and the second sister, Sarah, lives in America.

In the family of the *shokhet* Zilber, there were three sons. One of them, the older son, Bentsion, survived and lives in Lud.

Of the four Gilinski brothers and three sisters who lived on Sventzian Street, two survived: one brother is in Israel and one sister in America.

Of the family of Mordekhai Kentsianski [Max Khenchynski], his wife and children perished in the Shoah. He came to Israel and died in Sfat.

My family—my father Sholem Matskin, my brother Borukh and his wife—died in April 1943. My brother Borukh's daughters are in Israel; his only son is in Warsaw.

Of the Katskovitsh family, I don't know their exact fate but they are gone—two brothers and two sisters and their families. One of the sons survived and is in Lintup.

Of the Rudnitski family, two daughters survived.

Of the Sarafan family, not one survived.

Of the family of Yudel Mauber, the mother and daughter survived. The daughter studied medicine in Russia.

Of the Kharmats and Khaimovitsh families, not one survived. The two Yavitsh families (my uncles) perished, with their sons and daughters and grandchildren.

Of the Leyzerovitsh family, two of them live in Israel.

Of the well known Shapiro family, one son survived and is in France. The rest perished. Of the Shteynhart family, not one survived.

Of the Levin family, their daughters and sons with their families perished, and many many more.

Regarding the suffering that these people went through, we must write about this with our blood and let the blood endure in the light.

[Columns 1447-1448]

Shlomke – Pioneer from Lintup

By A. Kril

Translation from Hebrew by Dr. Sonia Kovitz, with appreciation for the assistance of Itzhak M. Itzhaky

Donated by Irene Mauber Skibinski

In the old cemetery on Trumpeldor Street in Tel-Aviv a lonely stone is standing. No one has visited on memorial days since the first yahrzeit in the year 1921 [1928]* because his parents who were left bereaved in the little village of Lintup, near Svencionys, were murdered [in the Holocaust]. When I come every year on the memorial day of Khaim Arlozorov, I visit this stone and stand for several minutes reading the lines inscribed on the stone.

Here rests
A devoted soldier in the company of the workers
In the land of the pioneer,
Sholom ben Yisrael Uri Shapiro z"l
From Lintup in Vilna District.
He was cut down in the flower of his youth
On the 9th day of the month of elul.

We called him Shlomke as a nickname. He was given this name by his friends because he was a lovable guy. He belonged to the 5th platoon of Kibbutz ha-Kovesh. When the platoon arrived in erets yisroel early in 1926, they got off the boat and came to Lemak-ha-Shevah in Petakh-Tikvah, to the orchard located between the farm of the female workers and Camp Yehuda. This area was a temporary settlement of seven groups, the largest of which was ha-Kovesh.

When the 5th platoon arrived, among them Shlomke Shapiro z"l, we had already taken over the dining room, a big wooden building used as a meeting hall. There were also small wooden shacks to live in. The good-hearted Shliomke, totally devoted to work and to the community, came with his friends that first evening to my tent, which was the central gathering place for the sons of the villages around Svencionys. In his hands he had two containers of teyglakh, a delicacy of baked dough dipped in honey, and buttery cookies which his beloved mother had prepared for the trip.

A friend from the Khodotsishki family took care of providing a bottle of wine, and on the wooden box that we used for a table, the delicious treats were spread out, with plenty for everyone. And so this friend from Lintup was absorbed into our family, the family of pioneers. We sat until a late hour and heard Shliomke tell us what he had gone through, how he managed to leave his parents' home and emigrate to erets yisroel. Everyone liked him immediately.

On days of famine and through an epidemic of a disease of the tongue, Shliomke remained optimistic and happy with his lot. The shovel stayed “glued” to his hands when he went to dig the ground for the planting of new trees, always with a smile on his face. He was always looking for a way to help his friends, and always participated in group discussions on the the future of the kibbutz and plans for a permanent settlement.

At the end of the harvest and the beginning of the major new plowing for the next year, he was the leader of the group. In the evenings he kept his shovel under his bed so he wouldn't have to use a different one—his hands were accustomed to this one. I recall how during the great famine he once came into my tent and said with a smile, “Listen Kril, now I'm even willing to eat bread and onion... if we just had bread.” His friends joked about the things he said. Shlomke found a way to handle even starvation with humor.

When the diseases started—no one knew their name—Shliomke walked around healthy and took care of his friends. And then suddenly one sunny day he came back from the orchard with sickness in his face. His temperature climbed without stopping. We called the doctor to come, and found out he had typhus of the stomach. He was transferred to the government hospital in Jaffa, and when I visited him, I saw his temperature had come down. I thought he would be coming back to us. But suddenly at night an emergency message arrived that we had lost Shlomke.

One of our dearest friends, Shlomke Shapiro, was no longer among us. He was only 21 years old when he was taken from everyone dear to him.

At the grave of the pioneer Shalom Shapiro z"l, Tel-Aviv, Trumpeldor Cemetery

***Translator's note:** The Hebrew year in the original is tav-resh-pey-aleph representing 1921, but the final digit, aleph (1), may be a typographical error, since Shlomke didn't arrive until 1926 according to this account. He died about a year later so tet (8) is most likely the intended final digit.

[Col. 1449]

Kimelishak

(Kamelishki, Belarus)

54°51' 25°53'

Kimelishak, a Village Transformed into a Splendid Shtetl

Leah Aharon Kuritzki

Translated by Anita Frishman Gabbay

Edited by Rhoda Miller

Until October 17, 1942 our small shtetl led a splendid existence. Four generations of Jews grew up here until the wild Nazi beasts arrived and sowed their destruction, all our nearest and dearests, grandfathers and grandmothers, mothers and fathers, brothers and sisters and our beloved young children were murdered and wiped from this earth.

To this day there are very few that remained to tell the story of how the shtetl was founded and how it developed. I see it as my Holy duty to write and brag about the things I learned during my Cheder–years and which I heard from my grandfathers, father and mother.

Through the flatlands of Lithuania and White–Russia there were kilometers of thick, lush green forests that cut the landscape, from Podbrodz, Michaelishok and Bistritz. Within this triangle of about eighteen kilometers from the Podbrodz train station was a long narrow village, surrounded by sharp stones. The wooden houses were covered with straw roofs. This village was called Kimelishak.

Next to the town meandered a stream which went as far as lake Niemen, on whose waters sailed many boats transporting the wood–products from our rich forests to all the towns of Europe.

Passing through the village, next to the road which led us to *moniantek sviranec* (Svir mountain), a new landscape appeared before our eyes where we saw different styles of houses. They were built in the modern style and they were covered with shingles, tin or other materials, but not straw.

[Col. 1450]

Not far from these home the sidewalks, comfortable and wide, made of wood stretched alongside. These homes belonged to the Jewish folk, which developed the shtetl into a splendid one.

In the center of town was the market square with its old Church standing nearby, surrounded by a wooden fence.

The main streets were called: Church Street, Prener Street and Sviranker Street. Each street also had side streets, the so–called "little streets." At the end of town, behind the forest, was the Christian Cemetery, the *Magilnik*.

When the Polish revolt of 1863 was over, the Tzarist regime declared to confiscate the Polish homes and divide the land amongst the poor. Thanks to this change the small town of Kimelishak was founded in that area.

[Col. 1451]

Many Jewish *Yeshuvnikes* (from the word Ishuv=collective farm) lived in the surrounding area. They rich folk of the noble estates employed them; mill keepers, craftsmen, Innkeepers and tradesmen. They lived far from a Jewish community, separated and their dream was to live amongst fellow Jews.

These original *Yeshuvniks* were the first founders of Kimelishak. In 1873, my great grandfather happened to arrive here, Rabbi Moishe Yankel Kuritzki, z"l.

His parents previously lived in Haydutishok, when he was 13 years old they left for a small village Apushin, at 16 years he married and opened a *kleitel* in that village.

Slowly the young man found a better profession. He was a procurer of meat for the Russian garrison, not far from his village and he delivered various products for the workers who were laying the tracks for the Vilna–Petersburg railway.

In Apushin he bore five sons and three daughters. The eldest son Elochim married a girl from Niemencine, and moved to Sviranek. The second son Meir married the daughter of the Sol(er) Rabbi and moved to Varnian.

The third son married Esther–Raize Levin from Sventzian and moved to Kimelishak.

Arriving in the village our grandfather found one Jewish family, Eliahu Garberovitch who came from Pren and already owned an Inn and a restaurant. Many peasants frequented his establishments. Especially every Sunday it was full when the Christians came to pray at Church. At the same time they brought fruit and other produce which they sold to the Innkeeper. He earned a comfortable living this way.

Slowly the Jewish community grew and by the 1900s there were approximately 30 Jewish families in Kimelishak.

[Col. 1452]

It became known throughout the region that the priest was secretly converting Jews. Often Jews arrived to seek help to rescue those converted Jews.

Grandfather Gershon told us how he saved Jewish girls from this shame. At that time you risked your life. The gentiles were angered and if they knew the truth, they were prepared to kill us. I was still a young boy when this took place and I was very frightened. My grandfather seemed a true Jewish hero to me, I respected and loved him.

It seems to me that business was done on those Sundays. They took advantage of bringing their produce and went home with various products they bought in return.

The community survived from these Sundays and holidays, it was their primary means of livelihood.

Although the church bells and Christian holidays brought us our income, we, children, have unhappy memories. When the bells started ringing, we suddenly had bad thoughts. Mainly, I remember, we were frightened when a Christian funeral took place. We closed our shutters, pulled down the curtains and hid in our homes. We children peaked through the cracks. Our hearts were sad.

In the weekdays the shtetl was very quiet. The Jewish shopkeepers sat on their porches and talked politics or read a newspaper.

When the shtetl grew larger, we organized a weekly market day, like in all the nearby towns. This took place every Wednesday, hundreds of small wagons arrived laden with products. The peasants brought eggs, hen, butter, cheese, fruit and vegetables, calves and horses, and other animals.

[Col. 1453]

The shtetl was filed with noise. All the Jews were overworked and exhausted. One bought a sack of corn, another a sack of wheat. We children loved to watch in bewilderment how the hens were bought. An old Jewish woman took a hen from a wagon, and blew into its behind to see if the hen had enough fat.

I remember the two brothers Sender and Menachem Stripunski who were considered large traders in eggs and pig–hair.

Chana stood with her little wagon and sold her *polive* and other things. She traded her products for things to eat.

Faivele the foreman traded in calves. Other Jews sold bread, candies, fruit and lemonade.

Asher Gimnanski dealt in other things. He had large spinning– machines in his store. The peasants brought him the wool of the shorn sheep. Here they spun the wool on his spinning wheels and they prepared the yarn for the long winter days and nights.

Max Beckenteyn had a beautiful shop. His store was always full with gentile boys and girls. One could dress from head to toe in his shop, everything from hats, clothing and footwear.

For the market day, the nearby brewery of Sviranek sent hundreds of bottles of beer.

In the old tavern of Eliahu Garberovitch the gentiles got very drunk. By nighttime, there were many drunkards in the shtetl. Most of the time it entailed lots of noise, other times they broke into fights...

When it got dark everyone started to return to their towns, the market square emptied. The shopkeepers of the shtetl counted their proceeds of the day and had to wait for their next market day.

The shtetl Cheder must be mentioned, it brought culture and knowledge to our shtetl.

[Col. 1454]

In my time the Cheder was in the women's section of the synagogue, the *schochet* was also our teacher. He was tall and thin with a black beard. Often when he was caught by a gang of gentiles, he suffered many blows from their hands.

It is very interesting, in our shtetl there were almost no *beggars*. When we had one in the shtetl, he was often just passing through. The residents all made a living, some less, some more than others. Even the craftsmen studied a page of Gemara every night. I can still see before my eyes Rabi Itzhak Meir the shoemaker catching another page of his Gemara in the synagogue. Sitting next to him was always Lipa the blacksmith and Afroim the tailor.

Of the better known rich folk of the shtetl was Rabbi Gershon Kuritzki. He inherited his intelligence from his father Rabbi Moishe Yankel. Both he and his brother Meir were involved in the timber business ad were the first to build beautiful homes in the shtetl.

Rabbi Gershon Kuritzki,
one of the founders of the shtetl

Their business was very successful and even sold their merchandise as far away as Danzig. The eldest son Dovid married the daughter of Hanoch Ginzburg and settled in Sventzian. He owned a manufacture–facility. He was able to make Aliyah to Eretz Israel and died at his daughter Chaia in Kibbutz *Gevat.*

Mainly the Kuritzkis were known throughout the region for their intelligent offspring. Max Kuritzki finished the Vilna Teachers' Seminary. Idel Kuritzki finished his pharmacy studies in Kiev.

At Meir Kuritzki's home, the writer Dan Kaplanovitch spent many years. He was the later writer of the Vilna newspaper, "*Times.*"

[Col. 1455]

Besides the Kuritzkis, Rabbi Afroim Reznik was another owner(boss) in the shtetl. He was smart and learned. Other important Jews in the shtetl were: Rabbi Asher Gimszanski, Max Beckensteyn, and the pharmacist Rudnick.

Until World War One the Jews of Kimelishak lived a quiet and orderly life.

Erev Yom Kippur, 1915, the Germans took control of the entire Vilna province. Many Jews became refugees and thus their wander–years began in all directions with their belongings on their backs. Our family also decided to flee. We dragged ourselves for a year, from village to village, then my parents decided to return home and whatever will be will be. We could no longer live in our former house. Arriving in our shtetl we learned our home was turned into a field–hospital. The Christians took our furniture and we had to rebuild from the beginning.

Slowly other families returned and the shtetl began to turn itself into a Jewish one.

The war ended and a Jewish–American committee was founded, which helped the returning refugees re–establish their businesses. A soup kitchen was opened for the impoverished folk and provided inexpensive meals or were given free to those in need. This kitchen saved many Jewish children from starvation. Many packages and money arrived from America to help the Jews get back on their feet.

The Founding of the Yiddish Folk–Shul

A Gemilut Hesed Bank was also founded and actually, my grandfather Rabbi Gershon Kuritzki, z"l was its first president. It got a lot of support from the Vilna "*yekapo.*"

The political climate after the war was very fragile. The regimes changed very often.

[Col. 1456]

A group of students and their teachers of the Yiddish Folk–Shul

First came the Russians, then the Poles, then the Lithuanians, and again the Poles. This affected our shtetl. When the Polish regime stabilized, our shtetl Jews began to rebuild their trade and their lives.

Meanwhile the children grew older and educating them was necessary. Whoever had the means sent their children outside the shtetl. Jewish children from Kimelishak studied in Sventzian an Vilna. When they came home a drama club was founded, which performed various plays. This opportunity also allowed us to found a library and a "*poszarne kamande." (Gymnastic club)*

The students and gymnasts brought new life to our shtetl and elevated Kimelishak to a higher cultural platform.

[Col. 1457]

In the meantime branches of the "he'chalutz" also developed in the shtetl. A group of the youth left for training and later made Aliyah to Eretz Israel.

Kimelishak was counted as a Zionist shtetl. Many Jewish children studied in secular schools, they were even brought up with the Zionist idealology.

During a holiday, the Jewish youth went for an outing to the "old tree" that the Christians used to call (tree worship=old believers) that dated back to pagan times, it was three meters thick. In the summertime we went to the Vilya to swim. Another delight for us, we sat on a boat and floated on the lake. These meetings didn't last long. The young people didn't have much opportunity in the shtetl and left in many directions. Most left for Eretz Israel,

Firefighters 1928

From left to right sitting: **Yacov Gesheit, Volf Rudnitzki, Max Beckensteyn**
Standing: **Siame Garberovitch, (commander), Leib Rudnitzki, Shabtai Feinberg, Yacov Garberovitch, Ahron Gimzanski, Yacov Hadash, Shimon Garberovitch, Leizer Rudnitzki, Chaim Pruzan**

The large tree on the *Yorzimkin* hill
Hanoch Garberovitch (on the right)

[Col. 1458]

The shtel became empty and sad.

Every Halutz dreamt and hoped to establish themselves and bring over their parents, brothers and sisters. In the meantime World War Two approached and many were unable to save themselves. October 17, 1942, the Jews of Kimelishak perished and from this old Jewish community there remained only destruction and mass graves.

Departure of Dovid Kuritzki for Eretz Israel

Sitting from right to left: **Belal Kuritzki, Dina, Dovid and Genendel Kuritzki, Alme Feinberg, Motel Kuritzki, Ahron Kuritzki,__, Abraham Kuritzki, Bluma Kuritzki, Monia Kuritzki, Batia Gershovitch, Shabtai Feinberg, Dovid Huritzki**
Standing at the back: **Lipa Kuritzki, Leib Kuritzki**
On the ground sitting: **Lusia, Chaim, Esther Kuritzki**

We, Kimelishak Jews, are left with the legacy to remember our lost Jews and remind our children never to forget.

Their memory shall be engraved in our hearts forever.

God will rise in their blood!

[Col. 1459]

In Calm Days

M. Kuritzki–Shulzinger

Translated by Anita Frishman Gabbay

Edited by Rhoda Miller

Kimelishak was a tiny village, approximately fifty kilometers from Vilna, thirty– five kilometers from Sventzian, fifteen kilometers from Podbrodz, eighteen kilometers from Michalishok, and six kilometers from Bistritz. In all there were about thirty– five Jewish families.

This shtetl was full of beautiful scenery. All the houses were beautifully painted with grey windows and roofs. Next to each home was a garden sprinkled with flowers. Along the main street was an alley of tall trees. The road was well built and covered on both side with covered sidewalks, often not seen in those days in small towns. All the residents greeted each other with pride and wonder of their shtetl.

The main industry of the Jews was shop keeping and small trade. Jews owned two bakeries and a pharmacy. Besides this, the Jews were involved in all types of craft. All the tailors, shoemakers and blacksmiths were basically Jews.

[Col. 1460]

There were several wealthy families amongst the Jewish folk, Rudnitzki, Beckenteyn, and Gimzanski.

In the last years before World War Two, the Jews suffered from heavy taxation which ruined the economic situation for the Jews. The tax collectors emptied the Jewish homes of their last possessions and sold them at auction.

The local anti–Semites played an important role in the ruination of Jewish economic life, they incited the local population to boycott the Jewish shops. There were episodes, when gentile lads overturned Jewish stalls in the marketplace and spread anti–Semitic leaflets amongst the Christian folk.

In spite all the shenanigans, a cultural and spiritual environment remained in our small shtetl. The young people had modern clothing, almost all were members of the Folk–Library and read Jewish and worldly literature.

Part of the Jewish youth participated in sports. The drama club had a very good reputation, which performed many interesting plays. The roles were always performed by good, culture– orientated people.

At the pharmacy of the Rudniks

From right to left: **Monia Kuritzki, Chaim Yudel Grodzenski, Ahron Gimzanski, Yacov Garberovitch, Leib Rudnitzki, Dobe Pruzan, Rochel Rudnik (the pharmacist), Betia Rudnik, Leizer Rudnitzki, Shmuel Kuritzki, Shimon Garberovitch, Yudel Kuritzki**
Sitting: **Chaim Pruzan, children of the shtetl**

New winds started to blow into Jewish life with the arrival of the Halutz and Halutz Ha'tzair. Kimelishak had to thank the Sventzian young man, Moishe Kuritzki, who especially came to Kimelishak to form this branch.

Thanks to his initiative evening courses began in Hebrew and in Yiddish history.

The "Halutz" locale was always packed with young people who sang and danced or just met for interesting conversation and companionship.

[Col. 1461]

We often went to these meetings and returned with new information and new Israeli songs. Part of the youth left for *Hacshara* (preparation) and this gave them the opportunity to make Aliyah to Eretz Israel.

Often members from the interior, from Warsaw and from Vilna, came to visit. This enlivened our shtetl and many came to listen to our guests' speeches.

The older generation had their own forms of entertainment. In the synagogue, where they often fought for an *Aliyah* (*an honor*), a bet with a friend or a page of Gemara.

In general the older folk lived a quiet and intertwined existence. They all lived as if they all belonged to one large family. When there was a wedding or a Bar mitzvah, the entire shtetl shared in the joy. The same was, if God forbid, a tragedy occurred, they all grieved and cried together with the bereaved family.

[Col. 1462]

In 1939, when our shtetl was occupied by the Soviet regime, Jewish life slowly worsened. The economic situation, however, was not so bad. Many Jews got involved in good jobs with the Regime or with the cooperatives, the shopkeepers got used to the high taxes but they were also happy, that Hitler's bandits had not yet arrived here.

Overnight we all became devoted Soviet citizens, and some of us relaxed. Even the citizens said a blessing: thank God from delivering us from Polish anti–Semites.

These quiet days did not last long. Barely two years past, and the heavy and dark Devil descended upon us.

[Column 1461]

The Economic Situation in Kimelishak

According to the Pinchas of Lita, Yekapo, 1931

Translation by Anita Frishman Gabbay

In Kimelishak lived 140 families, only 36 were Jewish ones.

The main income of the Jewish families came from shopkeeping. There was a surplus of shops. The competition amongst them was great and the earnings were small.

The Regime thought that the Jews were earning a splendid living and therefore the taxes were high.

Besides the high taxes, the Jewish trade became somewhat of a hidden nature(illegal). When a Jewess went to the market with her basket to barter, she also had to buy a pass, even if her merchandise of little significance. Her earnings at the end of the day was several groshen, of small importance.

Many foreign tradesmen arrive at market day, who undercut the prices. The profits of the shopkeepers of Kimelishak were small.

Several Jewish craftsmen also lived in Kimelishak, they barely made a living. In the surrounding towns there were many Christian craftsmen and they stole many of the clients from the Jewish craftsmen.

To our misfortune, the last summer brought a poor harvest and the peasants became impoverished and did not have the means to tailor new clothing or buy new shoes.

Earning a living became more difficult from day to day. The youth were leaving the shtetl and the old folk were waiting for miracles or help from their American relatives.This is how the economic situation played itself out in a faraway place like Kimelishak.

[Col. 1463]

Destruction and Holocaust

M. Kuritzki-Shulzinger

Translated by Anita Frishman Gabbay

Edited by Rhoda Miller

June 22, 1941, at the outbreak of the German–Soviet war, a flood of pain, suffering and blood *rained* on our heads, in Kimelishak as well. In the first days of the war the Jews suffered at the hands of brutal and wild outbursts. An empowered Christian *Haman* ran through the streets robbing and plundering. Overnight, the Jews felt that they became the target of every hooligan and bandit. They hid in their cellars or in their attics, and were frightened by every shadow.

In the daytime barely a Jew was seen on the streets. In the first few weeks we had enough food in our homes and no one was in the mood to go outside. Basically, we all sought various ways to procure food products. We felt that tomorrow will bring hunger and need.

After a long meeting, it was decided to rent some healthy Christians, to pay them well, in order to provide protection for the Jewish population.

Shortly after, we found out that these Christians hired hooligans to attack the Jews in order to demand more money from us Jews.

Once they also spread a rumour, that the shtetl was going to be set on fire. There was a terrible panic in all the homes. Everyone went to sleep in their clothing, we all packed some necessities and prearranged places where to escape to in case of an emergency.

Actually, a miracle happened, the village priest tricked the folk. The church bells rang, church officiants led a procession and created such a mystical atmosphere for the Christian folk that they forgot about their desire to burn the Jewish homes.

We passed the time with such panic, and to mention the priest again, he often stopped many of the hooligan attacks against the Jews. In his church sermons he repeatedly spoke about the love for humanity and requested his religious believers to respect their neighbours.

[Col. 1464]

At every troublesome moment, the Jews ran to the priest to intervene. He quickly lost his power and later did not officially have ways to continue with his help.

In the first weeks all the trouble came from the town's residents. No one could believe the Hell that was to encompass us, especially when the German Army marched in.

Kimelishak was a village off the beaten path, far from the main towns, therefore the Nazis arrived here not so early in the occupation. This didn't matter as our fate was the same as in all the other towns of the region.

The first Aktion that was ordered in our town, was somewhat a strange one: Christians were forbidden to greet their Jewish neighbours and no contact with them whatsoever.

A few days later, a new order was issued: Jews must clean the streets and were not allowed to go to the marketplace.

An order came to us that our mothers had to sweep the streets of the shtetl. We barely got used to this when a new order was issued, Jews needed to wear yellow patches with the Magen David on the front and back of their clothing.

One evening at home, when I was sewing the yellow Star, Sosia Feinberg came in. I cried:

Sosia said to me:

“What are you crying for? We have to wear the Star with pride, this is nothing shameful. This is our national symbol, our end will be, that our Magen David will outlive the Black Iron Cross (*Hackenkreuz*).”

[Col. 1465]

His words lifted our spirits and we calmed down.

Soon another situation arose where they sent Jews for forced labour. German soldiers went from house to house, chased the Jews onto the street, and like animals, chased them to work.

One time a German soldier shot a dog in the street, he came into our house, and made my mother hurry out to bury the dog. If she refused him he would shoot her.

Mother left and buried the dog in the garden. She said that this sadistic act alone describes what was to come.

She was right. Life grew more intolerable. Every roar from a motor threw the shtetl in a panic. Our hearts stopped beating when a motorcycle or a car rolled into the shtetl. We all knew this meant another tragic episode.

One time several motorcycles arrived to fool us in think they came for the cows, we didn't care about robbers. We heard worse, the Jews in the neighbouring villages were being slaughtered. They were slaughtering Jews like animals.

We welcomed all the refugees and did our best to help them with whatever means we had. We basically shared every piece of bread with them. We shared our home with Rivka Kimkhi, the New Sventzian's Rabbi's daughter– in– law. She stayed six weeks with us and then left for Svir.

Another order came, a ghetto in Kimelishak needs to be made for the Jews. They gave us two days to arrange this and move our belongings.

[Col. 1466]

It was our luck to bribe the police and we were able to remain in our home, and the ghetto started directly from our house. The Garberovitch family lived with us, whose son Yacov was very well connected with all the Christian youth. Thanks to him we managed to keep the ghetto open and not fenced off like in the other ghettos.

Without a fence we could leave to buy necessary food products. We traded different articles and clothing for food.

Many refugees came to us again in the winter months. They were hidden in the woods, but during the freezing winter they could not endure and came to warm themselves in the Kimelishak ghetto.

The lack of space was unbearable. There was no place for them to sleep. Food was not sufficient. Our children didn't have enough to eat and suddenly they had to share their little rations with strange mouths.

They all escaped in summer–like clothing and lacked what to wear.

We did our best to share everything we had with them. We all gave them our last piece of clothing.

The frost was unusually bitter and all the roads were covered with thick white snow. The Germans didn't seem to care and drove the Jews to work in spite of the conditions. One froze his feet and one froze his ears. Epidemics spread in the ghetto.

Many refugees stayed in the synagogue and it was overcrowded, they lay head to head. The filth was great, lice and pox spread. They lay on rotten straw and many sick people lay between them.

A ray of hope came to us in one of those days. We found out that the Germans received a terrible blow at Stalingrad. We were thrilled with the good news that came from the front and we started to believe in Hitler's defeat. The question was, were we going to survive?

Erev New Year Hitler's henchmen held a rally and declared, the Jews will not live to see the end of the war.

[Col. 1467]

A few days after New Year the German soldiers arrived in Kimelishak and ordered the Jews into the streets for an *Apel.*

We knew very well, from the refugees, what this meant and the ghetto was in a panic. We were certain, this was our last day. Many prepared to escape to the forests.

The frosty weather burned, and few escaped. The most part went to the *Apel.* To our good fortune, the officer called us only for a speech and demanded we work harder.

We were not convinced sitting in the ghetto meant waiting to die. Everyone made plans for their escape, but where to and to whom? Everyone looked for a friendly and Christian acquaintance who would accept to hide us.

Our good fortune we owe to the Christian mayor of Kimelishak who was quite a trustworthy and upstanding person. We owe him our gratitude. He allowed the Christians to come to us in the ghetto for black market trade, allowed us to go to the nearby villages to buy food to save us from starvation.

A second mayor came shortly after. He was a tyrant, the exact opposite, he immediately ordered the ghetto to be fenced all around and all the windows which faced the street, barricaded.

From then on it was very difficult to leave the ghetto.

Winter ended and spring, 1942 arrived. Such a miserable spring! At least it became easier to sneak out of the ghetto and buy some food. We hid either in the bushes or the woods and under the darkness of the night we left to the Christian to buy food. Our whole life depended on buying food.

In spite of all, spring was a marvelous wonder, the beautiful nature gave us the will to live.

We had four to five bake–ovens in the ghetto for about ninety families.

[Col. 1468]

It meant that the oven had to be heated five to six times a day in one house. The heat was overwhelming, the smoke choked us and everyone sat barricaded inside, like prisoners under lock and key, not being allowed to go out for some fresh air.

My mother was known as a good woman and all came to her to bake bread. We had three rooms, but thirty souls lived with us, ten per room. We thought things couldn't get worse.

Then we started to understand what awaited us. As long as we were alive we considered ourselves fortunate.

The men of the shtetl left for work in the surrounding villages. I worked in the canteen with men from Michalishok and Svir.

The summer months of 1942 passed this way. The peasants started to harvest their fields, autumn approached and when we thought of the weather our hearts became sad. We all had a bad omen that something evil was coming our way. We talked amongst ourselves. Death was near, quickly approaching. Basically, we hoped for another miracle.

Many bought potatoes, cabbage and beets from the neighbouring villages and began to prepare supplies for the winter months. The living soul wanted to believe that his life will be spared and he will need these supplies.

When the autumn winds started to blow, we learned about the selections that took place in all the other shtetls. They selected the young ones and strong work–worthy and left them in the labour–camps. The others were led to unknown places. By then we all knew and we sought the means and where to flee.

A decree came to us in Kimelishak, an *Apel* twice a day was mandatory. No one was allowed to leave the ghetto.

The ghetto was filled with sorrow. We all felt the end was near. There was no longer a drop of hope. Fall was a difficult one, rain, mud, and cold, where can we run in such conditions?

[Col. 1469]

It was on a Wednesday, market day, a German automobile arrived and the mayor and the commander were taken away. This was our sign of death.

Several hours later a Christian arrived at our home and told us, pits, long and narrow, are being dug near the shtetl. Among the village folk they spoke about the shooting of all the Jews.

There was a mess hall in the shtetl for officers and other city officials. This is where I worked for several days.

Shabbos, October 22, I suddenly heard shots. Someone arrived and spoke in Lithuanian. I didn't understand, but I had the feeling that the Jewish slaughter began.

I hid in a small room, and five minutes later the Lithuanian police arrived and said all Jews must return to the ghetto.

I left the room and returned to the ghetto, which was already surrounded by Lithuanian police called up for duty, chasing the Jews from their homes and go to the *Apel.*

In our home, behind the shop was a cellar. During the days of the ghetto we stored our potatoes there during the winter months. It was empty now, except for a few broken crates that lay in the corners.

I immediately thought to go to the cellar. I called my mother and together we hid amongst the boards. Mother's foot hurt and she was wearing boots and warm clothing.

[Col. 1470]

Shortly after, Bracha Kagan, from Vilna, joined us in the cellar. She lived in our home and knew about the cellar. She was a rich Jewess and stuck a lot of gold in her hair.

We remained hidden, minute by minute passed like an eternity. We heard the shooting and fear entered every ounce of our being. We even heard some entering our house, banging and dragging things!

Several hours passed and then dead silence surrounded us. We lay there until it got very dark outside. Then we left, our house was demolished. Everything was either stolen or broken. In all corners nothing remained of our memories of everything good. It was not important, I looked for several things for mother and myself, dressed warmly and we snuck out of the shtetl.

We heard footsteps and thought, the ghetto was perhaps being guarded. We decided to leave through a back window, which led to the garden. As the gate was closed with chains, I quietly removed them and we left the shtetl. In the darkness no one noticed us and we finally arrived in a small village. Here we knew a Christian acquaintance and he permitted us to come into his home.

From him we learned the entire situation. All the Jews of Kimelishak were murdered. They were led to the pits that had been previously prepared and were ordered to undress. They were shot naked.

The blameless execution of our community took place October 22, 1942. This is now our *Yartzheit.* (yearly memorial)

May these pure souls be forever remembered and blessed! God avenge their blood!

[Col. 1473]

Haydutciski, Dzikevinetz, Stoyatzishok, Maligan

[Col. 1475-1476]

And There Was

(Adutiškis, Lithuania)

55°09'/26°36'

Shimon Kantz

Translated by Janie Respitz

And there was...and there was a city Haydutzishok which grew not only because of her own Jewish rooted reality but also from the surrounding forests, towns and villages, with their Jewish farmers, Torah scholars and dreamers of Zion; those who passionately worked their fields and those, who day and night sat by a dim light of a kerosene lamp and studied; with the wagon drivers who loved the noise and their youthful idealism which during the week seemed like dream, not on the muddy ground but almost in heaven and until today have left us as a legend. But what will be told here is far from legend. Their heroic lives and martyr deaths. The earth their wagons stood on was not a dream, the sky that filled their eyes with light, the air, the landscape, the shadows from the dark forest, the noise from the rushing rivers, the gold of the open fields, the storms of the shining spring, and the sadness of the weeping autumn, the silence of winter's snow, the sorrow of unending distances, the blessed work of an entire week and the broad glow of Friday night tables; the warm candles and mother's blessings, filled with compassion, with a love that formed all worlds, blessed with father's song: Peace unto you, angels of peace. All – the simple Jews with the upset faces who carried the suffering of the sunset and the flame of all goods, from travelling stage-coaches, fairs of all weekly Jewish scents, and those who split the heavens with Torah and prayer – everyone believed there was order in the world, until the black night arrived and wiped out everything. Only the few who survived cry over the destruction at the rivers of the world. Every record is a reminder of the horrors and awakes the sadness of the third destruction, for us and for future generations. Oh my Jews, Saints from Haydutzishok, from Maligon, Vidz, Mior, Kazian, Kobilnik, and Pastov! A few of your children have survived and live in various corners of the world. As far as they wandered they carry with them not only the black sadness and pain, but also the desire that their children and grandchildren will understand the ascension of the souls of their grandfathers and they will read the simple words told here about that life and the horrific deaths and will understand, feel and perceive how many tears and how much pain lie in the letters.

[Col. 1477]

Jewish Haydutishok

Itzhak Perlis (Yagur)

Translated by Ettie Zilber

In memory of my Haydutishok families: Disner, Zivov, Santockis, Chadash many of whom died in the years 1941–1945

Edited by Rhoda Miller

Itzchak Perlis (Yagur)

A four cornered market square, from which stretched three streets and from those, a few smaller streets, the so–called alleys. That's the way Haydutishok looked.

In the middle of the market stood a small round building called the *Klatchmes* (could refer to the Inn=*krechme*) and in a corner a white row of old houses, built of lime and un-baked bricks, which stood on high curved posts packed together.

The town was built many generations ago on previously–standing remains that might have been part of a lord's courtyard.

As it turns out in the Czarist times, many Jewish families moved here from the outlying villages when the decrees for Jewish lessees and saloon keepers affected them.

It was very common, in the previous century, to chase the Jews out of the villages. Those Jews were the first to come to settle in Haydutishok.

Mainly, they engaged in trade and dairy, but over time, as in other places, some came to the shtetl and slowly established a Yiddish community, which by the First World War numbered about 300 families.

In the marketplace and on the main streets there were absolutely no trees. Only in later years, a couple of Jews found it necessary to plant a few trees near their houses.

[Col. 1478]

In the yards behind the houses, there were fruit trees and a few Jewish residents would also plant a variety of greens in their gardens.

The old Jews said the reason for its great poverty of trees, that in the past, the shtetl had many goats and they destroyed all the trees. Nevertheless, I myself don't remember any goats raised in our town.

A few hundred meters from the market was the so–called non–Jewish street, where mostly Lithuanians lived. There stood small huts with straw roofs, but in front of each house there were tall and small trees. Nicely fenced garden flowers were dotted with wonderful plants, yellow and dark red Dahlias, Nasturtiums, mint, beans and peas. All together it truly smelled so good, with its pleasing and heartwarming aroma.

On the other side of the town, was another hamlet, Gaydishok, a long village street, full of gardens and vegetables. Only 20 Jewish families lived there, for example, the Kutnikes, Patashniks and others.

Aside from that, Haydutishok allowed itself a *Kaydershe* street, where Lithuanians, White Russians and mainly many *Kidrim* (Tatars) lived. They worked at manufacturing pelts and they actually developed a reputation for their outstanding skills.

The Beit Midrashim– (houses of learning)

In Haydutishok there were four houses of learning: the old *shul*, the *shtibel*, the new minyan and the tailors' *cloiz* (house of study). As it turned out, the old *shul* and the *shtibel* were the oldest buildings in town and their style was similar to the style of the newer building in the Market Square.

[Col. 1479]

The new minyan was built of wood with thick walls from unbaked bricks and lime. The *shul* was built a few decades before the First World War.

According to the number of worshippers, the places of honor took up the new minyan. Their worshippers were not actually part of the religious circle. Only a few dozen Jews from the older generation prayed there and were educated by the older old–fashioned group, and simply some religious people, like T.B. Leibe Kloines (Solomiak), Mendel Gordon, the certificate maker, Mendel Yafe, Yosel Gordon, Kloine Gurwitz, etc.

On the Eastern side, however, a lot of young chatty people sat, who would bring shortened modern Tallit. They were not great followers of Halacha or commandments, and would come together to pray only on Saturday and holidays.

From time to time, in the new minyan, community meetings and concerts would take place by the cantors who would pass through. Various *Maggidim* [preacher/orators] would also hold their lectures there, and all the envoys from the *Keren Hayesod*, *Keren Kayemet* and even envoys from the *Histadrut* would talk about Zionist themes and topics.

The new minyan tolerated everyone. The Shamash, Shmuel–Itshe Alsfei, who was a liberal person, should be thanked for this. Sometimes he was a Melamed, and after that when the modern public schools were established, he became a teacher in the Yiddish, and later, in the Hebrew school, but in addition, he also was involved with sextonship. He was, by the way, a very good reader.

During his entire tenure, he was a man with a progressive view of all questions about Jewish life. He was soaked in the old Yiddish culture, a big expert in Tanach [Bible] and in the interpretations of *Rashi, Ibn Ezra, Radak, Shadal*, and was even well read in German Bible–critique. In addition, he was also knowledgeable in Hebrew and grammar. The well–informed used to say that he once was a *maskil* [highly educated] about whom it was said, "*hatzit v'nifga*" [he was curious and got hooked unintentionally].

In any case, this was an educated man, full of wisdom. However, his economic situation was always very bad. Regarding affairs of this world, he was a type of 'dummy' and therefore a big pauper.

The gathering of the worshippers in the old shul was already quite solid. Mostly older Jews prayed there and from the tradition and order of the prayer, they felt the good strong hand of the Gabai, Shimon Reichel, the brick–man, who was an ambitious Jew, an aggressive one who liked to hold control over all the community issues.

[Col. 1480]

His tragic end was very characteristic of him. Travelling together with all the other Jews to Poligon, he was accosted by a Lithuanian bandit and he took away his fur coat. His intrinsic pride wouldn't let him get over the 'cheekiness' of this *shaygetz* (non–Jew) without resisting and he let him have a burning punch in the face. The Lithuanian hooligan immediately shot him, and Shimon Reichel, the Gabai, paid for this with his life. But he salvaged his honor.

The most religious "group" of the Chabadniks prayed in the shtibel. There was strong control of the tradition, of the customs and set of the prayers and not just anyone was allowed to come up to read [from the Tanach].

Between lunch prayer and evening prayer, they would study a page of Gemara. Among the worshippers in the *shtibel* there were Rabi Haim Zalman Shapira, Yosel Lurie, Mendel Bar Abel, Shimon Leib Svirski, Heshel Kurlantzik, Zalman Patashnik, etc.

The tailor's study house was located on Vidzer Street, in a small wooden shtibel. All the shopkeepers or just newcomers, the sons– in– law who arrived occasionally in town, prayed there.

The tradition of the prayers in the tailor's study house was pure Mitnaged style. In all the other prayer houses in town – a Chasidic one.

Usually Haydutishok was considered a Chassidic town. The tradition was according to Chabad – Lita and everyone was considered Lubavicher Chassidim. Until in later years everyone celebrated the festival in Kislev, in memory of the liberation of Rabbi Shneur Zalman of Lida.

Haydutishok did not hold the Polish and Galizianer Rabbis in high esteem and our Chassidim would talk about the Rabbis – owners of the miracles as if about simple common people.

The Chassidic passion in the later years declined strongly and the Haydutishok Chassidim even allowed themselves to perform less pious acts.

The story about which they spoke in the entire region, played itself out in this manner: Haydutishok was receiving the Koidanover Rabbi, Reb Nechomtche Ferlov. Our Chasidim made all the preparations, prepared a nice table with all good things, lit the lights in the windows and travelled to the train to receive him personally. But the Rabbi never came that evening.

[Col. 1481]

The Chasidic world was not flustered, they sat back in the sleds and travelled back to the town in song and enthusiasm, as if nothing happened and pretended as if the Rabbi was travelling with them. Before they realized that the Rabbi did not come, all the good things and drinks from the tables disappeared. The Chasidim did not give up on the good snacks.

And a few days later, the Rabbi really did come, but then the Chassidim only sat around the table and listened to Torah, sang Chassidic songs, but they could not partake of *'shirayim'* (eating the honorable remnants of the Rabbi's food.)

The Economic Situation

There were two things that Haydutishok was famous for in the region: for its trade and for its mockery. Haydutishokers flax–traders and Haydutishoker clown sect were very well known in the entire area.

It was in this order: in winter they were involved in the flax trade and in summer with clown work.

Usually, the many grocery stores stood vacant in Haydutishok the entire week. The storekeepers would sit on small benches and read a newspaper or a book or just looked out into space.

Their income was made only on the market day, which took place every Thursday. Hundreds of peasants would travel in and set up either on the market square or in all the neighboring streets.

The peasants would sell various agricultural products, but the main articles were: flax, grain/cereal, potatoes, hides/pelts, pig hair, etc.

After selling their products the peasant would leave with their cash, visit the stores to buy materials and, by the way, also get good and drunk in the taverns.

The summertime markets, when the peasant was busy with their field work, were mostly very weak... large markets took place only in the autumn and in the winter. The largest income would be during autumn, when the peasant had to buy all their necessary things for the winter. The Jewish shopkeepers would then bring in money for clothing, boots, tools, etc. in these days a terrible commotion took place in the town, without exaggeration, thousands of people would plod along in the deep and thick mud.

In the general chaos various people would seek out the long–bearded "Russians", the various bagel sellers, the dozens of "bargain" sellers and the haberdashers.

All these market stores would travel to Haydutishok from the entire area and even from the furthest places. They had a custom of selling their merchandise with loud voices and in this way would scream and call out all the merits that they ascribe to it. The fundamental thing that they would show, as you can imagine, is that it is a big bargain, very cheap, half free and many peasants actually allowed themselves to be convinced and grabbed the bargains.

They were all, as you would say, completely foreign, dangerous shopkeepers. Most of the Haydutishoker Jews made their living by dealing with one important product. This was flax.

The flax trade was the vital foundation of the town. The reason was, what the flax from Haydutishok region was very similar and of an outstanding quality. They would stock it from the furthest places and they would export it even overseas/out of the country.

The Jewish flax–merchants of Haydutishok were familiar with all the towns and they would actually divide the week so that they would be able to visit them.

Every Monday they would travel to Postov, Tuesday to Vidz, Wednesday to Sventzian or Kazian and only on Wednesday did they stay home.

In summer they rode around on the wagon and winter with the sled and that is how they wandered from market to market, in order to earn a living for the family.

They brought the flax to Haydutishok and then they would have to stock it, sort it, cultivate, process it, pack it and finally transport it to the big exporters. That's the way the flax–industry earned a living, not just for the dealers and workers, but also for the dozens of employees like accountants, bookkeepers, foremen, carriers, packers.

In this way hundreds of people worked through the entire winter. That's why Haydutishok was converted into a revenue town in our region and, in the early days, the economic situation was actually not bad.

[Col. 1483]

The Haydutishok flax merchants were divided into various categories:

merchants who dealt on their own and were connected directly with companies overseas/outside the country.

Fraslers or middlemen who bought for the bigger merchants

Klingers (or hawkers, those that called out) brought the peasants to the sales place to negotiate the price and get their fees according to the sale price.

The season for the flax trade stretched out from after the [High] Holidays until Pesach. During the season, everyone, child and grownup, was strongly engaged, even thirteen and fourteen year old boys were involved in the trade and wanted to earn whatever they could, just to help the parents and ease their fight to earn a living.

The time between Pesach and the High Holy Days was a quiet one. The people removed themselves a bit from the trade and shops and devoted themselves to other issues.

The big traders at that time made all the preparations for the new season. They would relieve the peasants of their supply of super–phosphate and this way they were able to earn a good living.

But after the town quieted down, it would be quite often that one could see how young people sat in the middle of the day on benches in the marketplace, doing nothing and just clowning around

This was the so called "cucumber, fresh potatoes and milk products season" and in this time everyone was busy with parties and politics.

The business owners had a very difficult life on the economic front. Especially the tailors and shoemakers. For them the slowdown of trade in the town had a reverse influence. The people in the town simply stopped having clothing and shoes made. They searched for the latest fashions and travelled to Vilna for shopping.

The business owners slowly lost all their clients and simply didn't have any way to continue their livelihood. Therefore in our town 2 classes were established and the process developed in a sharp format, just prior to the Second World War.

In the First World War the familiar banishment of the Haydutishok Jews took place. Except for two families, all the Jews were sent out of the town with the excuse that they were located too close to the front. But the non–Jews were not sent away.

[Col. 1484]

Immediately, various committees were started, which organized the banished Jews in the surrounding town of Lithuania. After the end of the first World War the situation in our neighborhood was far from being stable. The power changed every month and sometimes even each week.

Polish, Bolsheviks, Lithuanians and again, Poles. Afterwards, there were the so–called "Middle–Lithuanians" which was established by General Zheligavski and finally he allied with Poland.

Little by little, the situation for the Jews started to turn around and in place of their burned wooden houses they built two story buildings of red brick and thus restored their lives, and renewed their old relationships with the neighboring non–Jews.

Because of the special ethnographic structure of our neighborhood, the signs of rising antisemitism, which was raging in Poland in the first years of its existence, were not noticed.

The small number of Poles in the town was made up mainly of officials. They were happy that the local minorities (Lithuanians, White Russians, Russians and Tatars) didn't bother with them and they were even friends with the Jews. The Jewish residents lived with an illusion of safety and stability.

As children we loved to play in the vacated trenches and especially we would often go to the German military cemetery, where we would get together for hours and enjoy reading the engravings on the hundreds of burial tombs.

We heard about the million victims from the war, about the plagues, epidemics and the hunger and that the world has become smarter and that there would be no more wars. We also were assured (convinced) by our elders and therefore enjoyed dreaming and hoping that it would be like that.

The feeling of stability had such an effect that the youth raced to action and together with construction of the slums and they began renewing the social–cultural life in the town.

The Betei–Midrashim and Chederim were no longer considered important for the youth and they were destined for a new life, for new ideas, and new ideals.

[Col. 1485]

Salvation came from the big Jewish center of Vilna, from which all neighboring towns sucked their culture.

In the early years after the World War in Vilna a big network of Jewish public schools and gymnasium (secondary school) were developed, with the Jewish foundation–language, a Jewish teacher seminar, a technical school, a professional ORT school, and others.

This specific culture movement had a tremendous influence on the entire province and, of course, also on Haydutishok.

Vilna was also the center of various committees and organizations which developed a wide– branched help– network in the province like Yekapo, Aze, Cooperative Folk– Bank and other help societies.

The leader and businessmen from all these institutions were good, devoted ordinary people, who had progressive inclinations and believed, that only the Jewish (world) school would be able to renew the national cultural upbringing of the young Jewish generation. They understood that the old half–religious lifestyle from before the war completely lost its influence on Jewish social life and new times began to search for new ways to implant the love of Jewish folk into the Jewish culture by the Jewish youth.

[Col. 1486]

The Vilna societal activists travelled around the province and disseminated their ideas and beliefs among the Jewish masses. They founded Jewish schools everywhere and, of course, Haydutishok was not opposed to this and a Jewish secular school was founded.

In its first years, the school didn't have any political mission and its leaders naively believed that Jewish children must study in a secular school which is free from the old guardians like Rabbis, Gabais, Melamdim, etc. They felt that such a school must be in the mother–tongue of our children, that means, that the fundamental language must be Yiddish.

Only in the later years, inside the walls of the public school, political themes entered and the big cities became nests of Bundism and Communism.

The ideology of the later Jewish school was a type of strange mishmash of various political factions, like Folkism, Bundism, Democracy, and Communism. We had everything together and gave it a name with a significant expression: Yiddishism.

"Tarbut" School 1925

Razeh Kuritzki, Nechama Abel, Rivka Lapide, Rachel Broide, Hana Matzkin, Chava Gitlitz, Sheine Katz, Roche Malka Abel, Sheine Volatzki, Zalman Kutnik, Shabtai Abel ——Zelde Svirski, Tirzah Perevaznik, —Dobe Gitlitz —Batya Kutnik, Beile Kotnik, Hillel Volatzki, Lovke Kanfer, Pinchas Matzkin, Moshe Abel, Michael Perevoznnik, Chana Svirski, Gendl, —Shlomo Yochelman— Nachman Abel, Gershon Katz—Abigdor Dan, Yakov Svirski, Lerer, Aliahu Volatzki, Yosef Girlitz, Lerer Lachovitzki - Henech Kutnik, Chaim Perevoznik -Taybe Katz, Rishe Abel

[Col. 1487]

The Yiddishists admittedly had no united, positive ideology; it was however, against Zionism, against Eretz Israel and against Hebrew.

The first teachers of the Yiddish school were mainly leftovers from the big revolutionary movement in Russia. A large portion of them were Bundists, Socialists, *Sejm–ists*, very nice and devoted people, but they had a completely negative attitude toward everything that smelled of Eretz Israel, Zionism and Hebrew. This fact would upset the Zionist circles and they started rebelling against these anti–national and anti–Zionist movement–methods.

Meanwhile, the Jewish families who were sent out of Haydutishok, those who during the war years lived in Kovner Lita (area around Kovno), turned back toward it. They brought us in Haydutishok the ideas and ideals from the then Zionistic and Hebrew "*storm and pressure*" era in Lita (Lithuania).

[Col. 1488]

Students From the "Tarbut" School 1932

Chaim Israel Svirski, Efraim Shapira, Nachman Abel, Moshe Abel, Tchernotzki Hirsh, Perevoznik Michael, Abel Shalom, Brayne Vlaichor, Tirza Perevoznik, Chaim Gordon, Tzepelevitz Yosef, Shlomo Yachelman, Patashnik Israel, Bracha Zeiger, Arieh Volatzki, Chava Gitlitz, Rivka Broide, Zahava Tshernotzki, Shuel Perlis, Zelde Svirski, Leib Lapide, Eliahu Lobatzki, Etel Abel, Yehudit Abel, Chana Perlis, Taybe Kanfer, Yehudit Zeiger–Ezra Shapira, Chana Svirski, Gittel Yafe, Reuven Ginzburg, ——Yehudit Abel, Gittel Lapide, Taybe Broide, Pese Gershtein, Berel Ychiltshik

One of the head leaders of the Zionist circle was the student Yerachmiel Katz, who didn't rest, still had great difficulties until he broke through the ice and he established a "Tarbut" School in Haydutishok. He was also its first teacher.

Immediately on the first day of its existence, the Tarbut shul had to start a difficult, stubborn fight, really like "life or death" with the *Yiddisher* school.

The entire town was divided into two camps and the feud was very sharp. In many families, the fight disturbed the *peace in the home* and it started fights even between children and parents, between brothers and sisters.

[Col. 1489]

The fights between the Yiddishists and the Zionists was reminiscent of the old fight, which once took place between the Chassidim and the Mitnagdim. It was sharp, bitter and held on, in various forms, until the outbreak of the Second World War.

The reality of the 30's was overshadowed by the weight of the “Tarbut” shul and it could be said that she won the fight.

Until the current day it is a wonder about the colossal strength and the dynamic risk which sprouted from that little, poor and desolate soil of our town.

The schools found themselves in buildings which were more similar to barns than to houses. They didn't earn any economic foundation for their existence. There were no textbooks or maps. The teachers would, for months at a time, not receive any salary.

At that time, on the other side of town there was a lovely Polish government school which was prepared to accept Jewish children. But, in fact, there was not even one Jewish kid who came near it, even without paying tuition.

Both the Yiddish and the Hebrew schools existed from three sources: tuition from the parents, performances, and from not paying salaries for the teachers...

The shows would be organized a few times each year and each school had its own dramatic circle (group).

The rehearsals would last a few weeks and when it was well prepared, they would rent a hall and begin selling tickets.

The tailor's house of study (small synagogue) was the first to be rented as a hall. Later they went to Adam Kurtzin on the non–Jewish street, and thereafter in store of Mayer Ahron Reichel. In the later years they would also often rent the hall of the Polish city–hall.

Usually when the Zionists would organize a show, the Yiddishists did not *stand still* and immediately got organized and vice versa. If both sides would not get along with each other, in one evening there could be two spectacles and the competition harmed both sides.

From the artistic standpoint the theater performances were very weak and could not afford a large troop.

[Col. 1490]

The public enjoyed these performances and squealed with pride.

After the shows they would visit the buffet, dance, conduct a raffle and the beloved attraction was to hear the *fli–flost* (name of dance=fly). All these things brought in quite a considerable revenue which helped save the schools from their eternal crises.

The children's–evening was another charming event which would take place at least twice a year: Hanukah and Purim. The "Tarbut" school would perform in Hebrew and mostly about the Land of Israel or about a historical theme. Although the audience understood little, everyone took pride in the sputtered Hebrew, which was so lively and fluent–sounding in the children's mouths.

The themes from the Yiddish school were very different. They would be devoted to organizing a *Mendele* evening, a *Peretz* academy or even a lecture about the *Chernowitz* conference.

Due to the rise of Polish antisemitism, the economic foundation of the Jewish life dropped. The land actually slipped out from under the feet of the Jewish residents.

In just this situation, the youth, which was raised with the Yiddishist spirit, didn't know what to do or where to go.

The graduates of the Hebrew school, in hindsight, felt much happier, because they had a goal in life. They all were organized in the Zionist youth organization "Hehalutz," (pioneers) "HaHalutz HaTzair" (the young pioneers). Their ideal was to immigrate to Eretz Israel and change their lifestyle completely, transferring their lifestyle to more productive labour.

Trusting in the principles, dozens of boys and girls went to Hachshara (agricultural training) in Volyn, Bialystock region and far into Poland. There they met up with the bitter Jewish reality and returned to Haydutishok with a full wide outlook on Jewish life and with a strong decision to leave the Diaspora and the hopeless village life.

Therefore, the "Hehalutz"–organizations blew in new winds into the backward villages and with it a big revolutionary mission for the Jewish youth.

The immigration of each Halutz (pioneer) became one of the most important events in the life of our small village. It demonstrated a radical solution for the youth, as well as for the entire Jewish population.

[Col. 1491]

It would be difficult to imagine this colossal revolution without the Hebrew school, without the devoted teachers from the "Tarbut" school and without the education which was absorbed the love for Eretz Israel and for its Jewish history.

Despite the divisions between the Zionists and the Yiddishists, in our village there was an entirely other division. In the village, there was a Rabbi, a slaughterer, a lot of Judaica, a stall for selling yeast, a lease on the bath house, a stall for slaughtering and a legalized Jewish community

The community also owned its property: a bath, a slaughterhouse, a cemetery and a piece of land. It needed to calculate its income and expenses and always had accounts with Rabbi On, and, by contrast, with the bathhouse attendants. Very often it also had to sue, and from time to time the aggrieved [parties] would throw an insult and each side kept track of it.

in Haydutishok there was a Gemilut Chesed fund, which offered loans without interest for poor business owners and small shops. It was also had a Folk–Bank and a sports organization.

The Jewish community also had to take care of the Fire station, for the firefighters, who were Jews, and their base was actually in the school yard.

Football Association 1928

Left to right: **Kuritzki Mendel, Gurevich Yehuda, Abel Zalman, Volatzki Yona, Abel Nachman, Svirski Chaim, Perevoznik Bar–Zion, Carlin Yehoshua, Yafe Avraham,**
Shmidt Berel, Tshak Moshe, Patashnik Shmuel, Yafe Gershon

[Col. 1492]

From time to time we had to take care of our relations with the *Vojt* (mayor) from the *Gemina* (province) and with the police commandant. There was a Sunday rest– decree and often all types of sanitary commissions would walk around and create problems for the Jewish population. With all these officials, the Jews had to find a way to soften their stubbornness with various means.

At one time, the regime had a desire to move the market outside the village, and this would have, of course, totally destroyed the Jewish commerce. The excuse was that according to Skadcavski's law, they had to beautify the look of our town and the market doesn't fit [in the plan]. The community then employed all strategies and they succeeded in decrying the evil decree.

It is worthwhile to stop separately and tell about one important Jewish character. He lived in my mother's neighborhood and was called: Hanoch Kuritzki. He was unique in Haydutishok, because he hated two things: trade and business.

His yard was filled with trees and flowers. He had a pair of cows, a horse and even a dog.

In summer he rented some land (*desiaten*, a measure, as in acrage of land) and rode to work on his own horses. He would express his scorn regarding business and considered himself the only Jewish peasant in the village.

He was a smart Jew, a Zionist, he was very interested in Eretz Israel and, above all, with the development of agriculture.

As it happened, the Second World War found me in Warsaw, where I then was working in the center of "He'Chalutz".

Running away from Warsaw, I rolled around over bombarded stations and at last, dejected, went toward Vilna. But my end goal was Eretz Israel.

Once, on an October night, I decided to visit my mother and travelled to Haydutishok.

I arrived in the village in the middle of the night. Near the station a fire was burning and around it sat a few Red Army men singing.

Gershon Katz, my childhood friend, was walking around with a red band on his sleeve and with a gun on his shoulder. He was a military man. When he saw me, he immediately said that I made a big mistake coming here. He promised to meet me at dawn and better explain his meaning.

[Col. 1493]

My mother was moved by surprise. She thought that I had finally come home to remain with her during these turbulent times.

Very early in the morning, Gershon Katz knocked on the door and warned me to run away as soon as possible, because they are looking for me and if they find me, I would surely be arrested.

Gershon was once a friend from "He'Chalutz Hatzair" [youth pioneers] and I had absolutely no doubt that his information was right.

Meanwhile, Abraham Eliahu Abel also came in and cried like a small child. Gershon also started to cry; the same morning we also visited Eliahu Volotzki and Rafael Yafe.

My mother understood that there was no other choice and that I had to leave as soon as possible. Dripping with tears, she packed a package with warm clothes and I immediately started on my way.

[Col. 1494]

That early morning was my last meeting with my mother and with Haydutishok. My mother's tears and my devoted friends from that moment on became my best companions during the difficult years.

After long wanderings I achieved my goal and I finally arrived in Eretz Israel.

I will never forget those dripping tears from that October morning.

The horrific slaughter in Poligon made those tears Holier and dearer.

[Col. 1493]

Haydutishok– a town of honest toil and hard labor

Michal Patashik

Translation by Dr. Ettie Zilber

Edited by Anita Frishman Gabbay

With pain and sadness these words are being written: once there was a town, which the Jews called Haydutishok and the Poles called Haydutzishki. Once, because it no longer exists, this town was located in Poland, 120 kilometers from Vilna, the "Jerusalem of Lita", and belonged to the Svencionys region [poviat=county or district], the provincial town of Sventzian was about 30 kilometers northeast of Vilna. To the south [of Haydutishok] was Postov [Pastavy], 30 kilometers to the south east; Vidz [Vidzy] was 10 Kilometers to the north [from Haydutishok]; and Komai, 12 kilometers to the southwest; Maligan [Mielagėnai] and the Jewish village Stayatzishok [Stajetiškė] were 4 kilometers away, a small village Dzikevines was 3 kilometers from our shtetl.

[Col. 1494]

Haydutishok lay on a hilly area and right through the middle of the town flowed a river by the name of Kamaika, because it started from the town of Kamai.

The story of the town was only a few hundred years, according to how the old Jews would tell it, and added to this, some witnesses told us about the old cemetery which lay on the hill in the middle of the town. On this very point the Jewish settlement developed.

[Col. 1495]

In our time, almost nothing was left of the tombstones in the old cemetery. From old age and over time, they all fell over and were covered with sand and stones. The site was fenced–in and it was considered a holy place.

Haydutishok started to develop after the Yeshuvniks [farmers] from the surrounding areas arrived, according to a *law* from the old Czarist regime they had to leave [expelled] their villages. They then moved into the town and slowly, a Jewish community grew out of the village on both sides of the river Kamaika.

In Haydutishok, before the First World War, there were up to 300 Jewish families. But the front stopped next to the town and it became dangerous for its inhabitants, the Germans also needed the Jewish houses, that's why in the year 1916 the Jews were all sent out (except for 2 families – Yaffe and Perevoznik) to other Lithuanian towns, further from the front–line. After the war, in 1918, the Jews returned to their old home and rebuilt their destroyed houses.

Postovy street and the bridge over the Kamaika river

From 1918 to 1921 the returning Haydutishoker Jews still suffered greatly because during these three years there were battles in their neighborhood and often the regime would change between Bolsheviks, Poles and Lithuanians.

[Col. 1496]

Before the Second World War, the population of Haydutishok included over 2000 persons, more than half were Jews, including 200 Jews who lived in the Jewish village Stayatzishok. They officially belonged to the Haydutishok Jewish community. The population was comprised of Jews, Lithuanians, Poles, Russians, White Russians, *Shtarovern* [could be Karaites] and Tatars. The Jews lived in the center, and this town therefore had a real Jewish character. The entire time until the outbreak of the Second World War in 1941, the Lithuanians lived with the Jews in very friendly relations. The Lithuanian minority, which during the Polish Republic felt oppressed, sympathized with the Jews. Just after Hitler's attack, these same Lithuanians showed their real face.

Economic Life

The Haydutishok Jews made a living through commerce, artisanry and fieldwork [farming]. Among the artisans there were tailors, shoemakers, quilters, glaziers, blacksmith, tinsmiths, milliners, bakers, hairdressers, millers, carpenters and voliak [type of boot]-makers. Of the "*free*" professions [professionals] in Haydutishok there was: a Jewish doctor as well as Polish doctor and a government hospital for the entire region.

[Col. 1497]

In the economic realm, our town was proud of its dam and powered water mill, which belonged to the Meir and Cloine Friedlender brothers. The mill family increased in size with 2 more families of Haim Halperin and Moshe Shmukler. The mill also provided electricity for the town, and for this reason, it also powered a sawmill and an oil factory.

In addition, Haydutishok had a Jewish brick factory, a factory of soda and lemonade. In later years they also set up a Jewish auto transport business which produced a very nice revenue.

The most important economic industry which provided the Jewish residents of Haydutishok its income was its commerce in flax and grain. In this realm, Haydutishok earned an excellent reputation in the entire region, and it became the center for all the neighbouring towns, like Postav, Vidz, Kazian, Sventzian and some smaller villages, where large markets took place and all the flax then flowed back towards Haydutishok.

[Col. 1498]

There were middle–men and agents who traded the half raw–material, local agents who transported the flax weekly in dozens of wagons to all the factories all over Poland and also Europe. The cultivation of flax gave employment to hundreds of male and female peasants from the region, thereby giving a livelihood to dozens of wagon drivers, porters, intermediaries and others. The important flax and fruit agents were Reuven Kuritzki and Tczernatzski.

In addition to this well–established flax trade, a trade developed with grain, pelts, various threads, wool, mushrooms, meat, blueberries, eggs, chickens, fish and wood. All around, there were large forests and lakes which contributed to the wood and fish trade. In the town there was a slaughterhouse which belonged to the Jewish community. In season, the Haydutishoker agents would transport dozens of wagons with super–phosphate. There were many Jewish shops and groceries, all sorts of businesses, hostels for the traders and agents who came here from all over the country. A poorhouse, where poor people passing through had a place to spend the night also existed.

[Col. 1499]

Almost all the Jews in town had their own homes and many had gardens with vegetables, potatoes and fruit trees. Families also had small economies like a cow, chickens, geese and turkeys.

The Folks bank and the Gemilut Hesed [loans without interest] fund played an important role in the economic life of the Jews in the town.

Cultural Life

Until the First World War the Jewish children studied only in religious Cheders and traveled for studies to other places where there were Yeshivas. Only a small portion of them studied at Russian government schools or with private teachers who would come from the big cities. After the First World War, when the Haydutishok Jews came back to their homes and life began to seek a more cultural level, immediately a modern Jewish elementary school was established and later when the town became larger, a Tarbut school was established. Two libraries with hundreds of books, two drama clubs, which often organized theatrical performances, literary evenings, lessons and lectures on various themes, were founded.

The Jewish Wind Orchestra

In the year 1935, 10 men got together from all strata of the Haydutishok community and they decided to establish a Jewish Bloz [wind]–Orchestra. The 10 men were: Berel Shmid, Itzhak Yaffe, Leibe Kuslin, Michael Oistreich, Zalman Abel, Avraham Eliahu Abel, Melech Shtrikovski, Yichiel Yochelman, Eliahu Volatzki and Michal Patashnik. Each of them signed a commitment [took a loan] to buy the instruments, taking into account that in time the orchestra would pay it back. They travelled to Vilna to the store with musical instruments of H. Dintzes, they bought 3 clarinets, 2 altos, a tenor, a baritone, a bass, a drum, and a pair of cymbals —all of the best quality. They assembled all the youth who wanted to study. They took the local organist from the Christian church as their teacher. They studied well and after a short while they started putting on performances with great success and even played at various celebrations and weddings, [Jewish and Christian], wherever they were invited. After a while they earned back [the money] for their studies.

[Col. 1500]

A Jewish fire command station with over 60 volunteers and fire equipment functioned. The leadership included: Shmuel Yehuda Katcherginski, Ben Zion Ferevoznik, Melech Strikovski, Rafael Yaffe, Gershon Yaffe and Michal Patashnik. The firemen would also go around and put out fires in the surrounding villages.

The religious life was concentrated around the four Betei Midrashim with dozens of Torah scrolls and thousands of religious books for study. The rabbi of the town, Rabbi Elchanan Mashitz and the ritual slaughterer, Rabbi Moshe Lev, who also contributed to the religious life of the community. Each night the melodies from the Gemara studies would be heard throughout the entire town.

Jewish Elementary School, Teachers and School–Administration, 1922

From right to left: above **Moshe Perevoznik, Zalman Abel, Feigel, Feigel, Feigel, Sheine Abel, Hana Yaffe, Miriam Perevoznik, Tirza Perevoznik, Sheine Volotzki, Zelda Svirski, Feiga Shapira, Hava Patashnik, Zalman Kutnik, Leah Reichel, Zelda Kutnik, Hana Perevoznik, Dr. Plotkin, Ben Zion Perevoznik, Yoel Alsfein, Araham Yafe, —,Yakov Bass, Pharmacist Reuven, Pesach Volatzki, Yerachmiel Lubatzki, Yona Volotzki, Teacher Aronovitz, Michal Gavenda, Miriam Patashnik, Haim Svirski, —, Shmuel Patashnik, Moshe Abel, Gitel Patashnik, Miriam Chaikin, Etel Abel, Ester Perevoznik, Baile Kutnik, —, Gershon Yafe, Mendel Blatt, Moshe Bass, Chana Svirski, Shalom Bass, Itzhak Feigel, Liove Reuven, Bebke Reuven, Muse Bass, Batia Kutnik, —, Breine Patashnik, Israel Patashnik**

Firemen

Rafael Yaffe, Ben Zion Ferevoznik, Gershon Yaffe, Novak, Hirsch Perlis, Chaim Halperin, Michal Patashnik, Moshe Svirski, Nachum Gordon, Yosef Blatt, Shalom Shapira, Reuven Yochelman, Benyamin Gitlitz, Zundel Patashnik

Zionist Youth, 1922

Standing: **Tzchernotzki Israel, Svirski Batya, Perlis Hirsh, Reichel Israel, Perevoznik Yehuda, Kuritzki Yosef, Volak Chaykel, Katz Yerachmiel, Gordon Meir** Sitting: **Shapira Etel, Reichel Libe, Gurvitch Chiene, Perlis Lipe, Yaffe Rafael, Abel Nechama, Katcherginski Miriam**

[Col. 1501]

The Zionist activities were lively. Branches of almost all the Zionist organizations and parties existed in the shtetl. The youth trended towards Halutz [pioneers], Hachalutz HaTazair [young pioneers] and Shomer Ha'tazair [young guards]. They would travel to train and aspired to immigrate to Eretz Israel, but unfortunately, not all were able to fulfill their ideal; over 50 boys and girls managed to come to Eretz Israel and they blended into the routine life–style of the "workers".

The War 1939

The outbreak of the war between Germany and Poland immediately paralyzed life in Haydutishok. Many Jewish youth were immediately mobilized into the Polish army. Five youths: Israel Patashnik, Israel Oistreich, Moshe Bass, Beinish Shapira and Meir Disner were killed in battle.

On September 18, 1939, Haydutishok was occupied by the Red army and private enterprises were nationalized –as well as large houses and warehouses. Stores were â€˜bought out' at the lowest prices, and after some time, all private enterprises and shops were liquidated on their own. Thereafter, in the beginning of 1940, three flax–traders were arrested: Henech Perevoznik, Meir–Ahron Reichel and Itzhak Yaffe. A few months later their families were transported to Siberia together with the families of Berel Shmidt, Henech Kuritzki, Shmuel Yehuda Katcherginski and Hertzl Reichel, who was from Kazian, but in the later years lived and had a shop in Haydutishok.

[Col. 1502]

Shmuel–Yehuda Katcherginski and Hertzel Reichel remained hidden with their families and remained alive. After saving themselves they decided to return to Haydutishok. A month before the German attack on Soviet Russia, their families together with the family of Henech Kuritzki, returned to Haydutishok; in a few months they would join all the Haydutishok Jews on their last road [death]. The older and sick Henech Perevoznik couldn't last long in captivity. [Siberia] The other two after serving a year were sent back to their families in Siberia. Yitzhak Yaffe died there later. Also, the wife of Meir Ahron Reichel, Mania, died during the transport [either on the way to Siberia or the return from Haydutishok= unclear]. After the end of the war, travelling through Poland, Berel Shmid died by the hands of the Polish murderers. All the others had the honor of seeing the restoration and revival of the State of Israel.

During the time of the Soviet regime in Haydutishok, the youth were taken into the Red Army, who, according to their age. [the required military service in that time]. Also, other youth and even entire families ran alongside the retreating Red Army in the first days of the war [World War II]. Not all managed to come back. In those days, Lithuanian youth from the town and from the neighboring villages immediately organized themselves and attacked small groups of the retreating Red Army [it is possible many Jews were killed in those first days=undocumented], murdered them and took their guns and ammunition.

Editor's notes: col. 1493–1494: distances of surrounding towns need to be verified Ferevoznik=Perevoznik, editor not certain how the name was actually spelled

[Col. 1503]

Haydutishok in the First World War

Yakov Abel, ben Shimon (Ein Shemer)

Translated from Hebrew by Dr. Ettie Zilber

Edited by Anita Frishman Gabbay

Chapter 1

September 1915. The pressure of the German military on the Russian forces continued to increase. The penetration of the Russian army at the eastern front [Prussia] blocked the advancing army[German] but they[Russian] suffered defeat with many casualties. This was their downfall, well known to the Czar, near Tanenberg.

Right afterwards, the German army penetrated deeper into Lithuania and captured Kovno, with her famous fortress, and the entire region.

The Russians retreated in chaos and in haste. The Germans continued to attack and advance to Vilna and its environs.

The Jewish towns in the area of Sventzian passed from hand to hand. The Cossacks took advantage of the situation and demonstrated their heroism by pouncing upon defenseless Jews and pillaged their property.

In the nearby town of Postavy, a pogrom took place against the Jewish population. Postavy refugees escaped to Haydutishok and told us about the events that took place in their town. Fear overcame the Jews [of the town] when they heard what took place in the nearby community.

After a few days Haydutishok remained without any government, neither civil nor military. The

Pristav [inspector or commissioner] and the police left the town together with all the officials of the government in great haste. All the Jews were in fear, shock and distress. The disaster of Postavy reminded them of the days of Kishinev [anti–semitic progrom].

A few days passed, one morning in the days of autumn, suddenly, they informed us that dozens of wildly carousing Cossacks were heading towards the town.

The Jews immediately began to leave their homes and searched for places to hide in the nearby villages. Many escaped to Stoyatishok, an agricultural village. Others left for Dzhikevines, where a few Jewish families were located.

And here a miracle took place, the Cossacks didn't have the time to execute their plot. A non–Jew came running into town and told the Cossacks that he saw a German soldier–patrol wandering in the area. The Cossacks didn't delve to investigate or demand proof, immediately when they heard from this non–Jew the word "*Nimtz*", they disappeared "like a smokescreen" on their horses, and the Jews of Haydutishok were saved from a terrible calamity.

[Col. 1504]

The Jews who abandoned their homes and managed to take with them just a few small packages of food products, started to return slowly to the town from the nearby villages and hid themselves behind locked doors and shuttered windows.

The threat of death passed, with a prayer in their hearts! The town, God forbid, could not remain without the necessary authorities and the Cossacks need to be prevented!

Chapter 2

It was during the eve of Yom Kippur, in the morning hours. The German advance–party entered in military order, with bayonets mounted and started to organize themselves in the market square. The first platoon was the mounted *Hussars.*[horse=cavalry].

The Jews peeked out of the cracks of their windows and doors and watched as they jumped down from their horses, looked at the maps and discussed something among themselves. After a short time, a flow of German soldiers entered the town from all sides: infantry, artillery, cavalry. They flowed like ocean waves in a storm, endlessly. All these heavy enormous troops passed through the first streets of the town and it seemed as if they had no intention of stopping and remaining permanently.

Some Jews dared to poke their noses outside the house and learned that, to their great surprise, the German soldiers were hungry, thirsty and were in a state of exhaustion

After about an hour, we realized that they were breaking into the warehouses and stores and taking everything that came into their hands. They were especially searching for all sorts of food products. Since it was Erev Yom Kippur, they found nourishing and abundant foodstuffs. They gorged on all the *challas* and the *kaparot* [chickens used for the Yom Kippur ceremony] and actually devoured everything they found.

[Col. 1505]

The Jews found themselves in a bad situation, just before the *feast* to *'break the fast'*. The soldiers came in waves, some leaving and others entering. They conducted careful and detailed searches, but without threats or aggressiveness. The looting was not accompanied with violence. Among the soldiers there were even some who paid for the products with the German Mark, which no one knew its value at the time.

After a brief discussion, we realized that they were in retreat from the Vileyka front where they suffered a terrible defeat. They planned to set up camp in the area of the forest region near Haydutishok, since our city was just on the border of the front–line that was established and settled, and continued all the way to Dvinsk (Dinaburg) in Latvia. There were no changes at this line until the outbreak of the Russian Revolution in 1917.

From the other side of the line, the Russians established a defensive line and for more than 3 years, the two camps conducted stubborn and irritating trench warfare without moving or dislocating one another, *even one foot*, despite the heavy attacks that took place from time to time.

Slowly Haydutishok was changed into a very important strategic point for a main military base near the front. The town was chosen as a military center for the rear, and as an emergency station for those injured in battle.

In order to hospitalize the sick and injured the Germans confiscated 3 synagogues with 'years in the chain of Jewish history' that were located in the town. The Germans put up a barbed wire fence in order to divide the hospital and the only synagogue which they left for the use of the worshippers. Despite the inappropriate proximity, there were no disturbances or special actions by the soldiers toward the crowd of worshippers.

Meanwhile the rainy season arrived, the animals and the soldiers servicing the base were in need of appropriate lodging. Those in charge of civil affairs in the commander's administration decided to confiscate all the public buildings and here and there also some private houses.

This was considered an [life altering] order and many Jews were forced out of their homes and remained without a roof over their heads. The congestion in the buildings was suffocating. Each family absorbed tenants and additional tenants and only residents from the small and dilapidated shacks didn't have the benefit of neighbors or neighbors of neighbors.

The Germans also put farmers into barns and in warehouses and many soldiers stayed in their homes.

Usually all of these confiscations were conducted politely and in a very fair manner. Just here and there someone suffered some violence and evilness and of course there was no shortage of evidence of their distinct antisemitism.

[Col. 1506]

Chapter 3

From the first day of the entry of the German army into Haydutishok until the last minute before the big expulsion there was a complete night curfew, that began in the early evening hours. All the citizens suffered from this, even the Christian residents would close their houses.

Throughout the entire time and at every hour of the day there was a policy of “no exit and no entry to the town” without a special pass from the commander.

These passes were given only in extraordinary and very urgent cases and mainly for public needs. That's the way, for example, we received a pass to travel to Sventzian on Erev [night before] Pesach to bring flour to bake *matzot.*

The difficult and worrisome problem was the question of “what will we eat.” On this subject of provisions, the situation got worse from day to day. All the food products which were stored from the beginning of the war, continued to disappear. Even the storehouses of the farmers were empty. A great portion of the harvest from the fields were smashed and robbed at the outbreak of the war. If someone succeeded in bringing into town a bit of produce, he paid dearly for it.

Only after great efforts could flour be acquired in exchange for gold and its value continued to escalate in those days. Many families suffered from malnutrition and lack of food, were it not for the soldiers and tenants, they would really have died of starvation.

It turns out that, interestingly, lodging the soldiers in their homes this time saved the situation. In those days the army received excellent supplies and they were given an abundance of food. The entire population was fed from the army divisions' leftovers. The Germans fed the horses brown sugar and this commodity quickly captured the attention of the citizens.

The general situation remained very bad, despite everything, because, it was impossible to earn a living over a long period of time, for a population of about 2,000 people. They survived only from the leftovers of the soldiers' food.

Chapter 4

From the moment the military authorities entered the town they started to concern themselves with quotas of workers from among the citizens. They demanded forced labor of all the men from an early age and wouldn't exempt even the most elderly.

The forced labor was characterized by snow removal from the railroad tracks, cleaning of the streets, digging trenches, but also building sidewalks on the main streets and making various improvements in the town.

All the citizen workers were sent to the army according to a certain order. In order to carry out the demands of the army and to ensure that the order would be fair, the commander of the militia appointed a citizen and *dumped* the job of supervising the work. At the head of the militia was Yudel Hartzen.

The civilian workers did not receive any payment for their work. Only by chance, did some enjoy food from the leftover food or from other products.

Christian residents were also taken for this slave labor and the Jews served as translators. In this respect the Yiddish language helped them a lot and thanks to that they found a common language with the Germans.

[Col. 1507]

Chapter 5

The commander officially recognized the local Rabbi, Rabbi Popol [may his memory be a blessing], as the only leader of the Jewish people. He was accepted and loved by all strata of the local population and also the Christians related to him with respect. He had deep knowledge of German language and culture and was considered by the military authorities an important civilian personality.

When the army entered Haydutishok, for some reason the family of Rabbi Popol came out of their permanent apartment and was lodged with us.

I was then a young boy of 12 and I was very proud of our new tenants and I saw this as a special honor that was granted to us.

From time to time high officers came to the Rabbi to consult with him about all types of issues or to give him instructions for various requirements, and I would watch with pride how they would salute the Rabbi with a full military salute.

Rabbi Popol slowly converted into an important intermediary for the Jewish population. The peace was disturbed by the horrible question: what would be the fate of the Jews of Haydutishok if these living conditions continued for a long time?

Once when he stood in front of the commander, General Von Etzel, who lived in the priest's house next to the church, he reached out to him regarding all perspectives of the Jewish problem. The General suggested something extremely far–fetched.

From a military standpoint, the General's opinion was appropriate, he wanted the Jews to agree to leave the town voluntarily.

The town was located on the main front–line and they[the townsfolk] could possibly be injured when the battles restarted.

The German General promised Rabbi Popol to find safe places for his people in other occupied areas of central Lithuania.

The military authorities would make contact at with the heads of other Jewish communities and would travel with them to take care of their absorption and lodging [for the Jews of Haydutishok].

Rabbi Popol responded strongly to the General's suggestion and expressed his opinion that it sounds like a general expulsion of all the Jews. The Rabbi proved also that this proposal contains clear discrimination for the non–Jewish population.

The General, who was known as a Jew–hater, justified himself and said that the Christian citizens didn't cause the authorities any significant problems. The large majority of them were farmers who worked their land and the question of supplies didn't constitute any obstacle for them.

It was our bad luck, during those days, a young soldier was caught spying and passing information to the Russians and during his interrogation he reported that one of the Jews from Haydutishok collaborated with him.

Until today we are not sure whether this was a plot and used only as a deception. For the German command the soldier's information was enough to be suspicious of the Jews and to be vigilant.

[Col. 1508]

This spying issue decided the fate and the military expelled all the Haydutishok Jews as fast as possible.

The order was given and the authorities decreed that all the Jews had to leave the town without exceptions.

Despite this, two families received passes to remain; they were the Yaffe and Frabuznik families. One acquired the release because he was seriously ill and the other for a birth.

From the beginning they were given passes only on a temporary basis, but afterwards they remained.

These two families, Yaffe and Frabuznik, were used throughout the war like gatekeepers for the whole Jewish community.

Chapter 6

The expulsion was carried out in the month of June 1916. The Jews of Haydutishok were torn from their town in two large columns. Those expelled received permission to take their possessions without limit. Actually, they couldn't take everything and many were impoverished as they were forced to leave valuable property in their homes.

The two columns travelled in transport trains accompanied by military guards. Mid–way the guards became strict and they didn't allow anyone to leave the wagons.

The first column was brought to the area of Vilkovishk, Virblin and Kibert. The second convoy came to the towns: Mariampole, Pren and Viblvirishuk.

The Jews of these towns already knew in advance about the arrival of the exiles. At the train stations various activists waited for them and immediately took care to house and feed them.

All those who were expelled were given the name 'refugees' and throughout all the years this was the way the Jews of Haydutishok were recognized by the Jewish veteran population.

Chapter 7

Only part of those who were expelled returned to Haydutishok at the end of the First World War. Many remained in Lithuania even afterwards and integrated nicely into the life of the Jewish community in the state of Lithuania [which was established at that time].

The returnees to Poland quickly rebuilt their homes and slowly started their economic renewal.

At the outbreak of the Second World War, when the area was transferred to the Red Army, many families were reunified. But the claws of Hitler's animals caught them some years later and brought upon the Jewish community in Haydutishok death, destruction and extermination.

The bones of the victims of Haydutishok are laid to rest in the mass grave of Poligon, where they were slaughtered, together with Jews of the entire province of Sventzian by these *filthy* [bastards]. Only a few of us succeeded in escaping and they are here with us in the State of Israel.

[Col. 1509]

Between the Two World Wars

Rafael Yaffe, Rehovot

Translated by Anita Frishman Gabbay

Edited by Rhoda Miller

Our town which in the Russian language was called Gaydusciski, in Polish, Hayduscisk i, and in Yiddish, Haydutishok, was situated 118 kilometers to the north–east of Vilna, along the train line of Vilna to Podbrodz, Lintup, Postov, Gluboke and Krulevzhine.

A small river ran through the town called Kameika. Thanks to the water mill that belonged to the Friedlander family, together with its dam, made the lake appear much larger.

According to older generations, the story was that this land was the estate of a noble family and only at the beginning of the 18th century, the land was parcelled and divided and the first peasant farmers settled on this spot.

[Col. 1510]

The settlement enlarged itself and by 1914, before the First World War, the population was about 2000 souls, Lithuanians, White–Russians and Jews.

There were about 300 Jewish families, who were mostly shop keepers, sellers of various goods, artisans and particularly, agents in the flax trade.

The flax industry employed almost the entire folk. Whether Jewish or Christian, this trade employed the largest part of the population.

In 1916 the entire Jewish population was evacuated and sent to Lithuanian towns, mostly in Mariampole and its surroundings.

The iron bridge on the river Kamaika

[Col. 1511]

The Haydutishoker Jews already felt the might of the Germans and saw the destruction they could "bestow" on the Jewish folk.

In 1919 some families returned. But the war continued along with different regime changes. This caused hunger and deprivation.

Slowly Jewish life returned. The economic situation renewed itself and life slowly returned to normal. The flax trade was centralized in Haydutishok, warehousing, transport, processing, etc. blossomed. The export of flax became an important commodity all over the world.

They also provided raw materials which was sent to many Polish factories. There it was processed, sorted and cleaned, all the raw flax from the entire region.

Representatives of the Folk Bank of Haydutishok, 1912

Right to left: **Yosef Feigelson, Pesach Volatski, Yehutiel Perlis, Moishe Yacov Kuritzki, Abraham Kuritzki, Dovid Yoel, Ruben Kuritzki, Heshel Kurliandtshik**

[Col. 1512]

Thanks to the development of this industry, many depended on it for their primary source of income. The Jews were the traders, foremen and merchants, the Christians were the shakers and the packers. In high season the industry employed thousands of workers.

Each firm had their own Christian workers and were on friendly terms with them, we even invited them to our simchas, we thought these relationships would last forever.

Several Polish families also established themselves in Haydutishok. They were civil servants or police. Even some White Russians arrived.

Most of the Poles were either open or "masked" anti–Semites. They were jealous of the economic success of the Jewish people. Heavy taxes were levied but the Jews couldn't object.

[Col. 1513]

Haydutishok had the same ideals towards culture–building [cultural development] as all the other towns of the region.

In 1922, T.I.S.H.A. [organization for Yiddish schools] from Vilna founded a Yiddish folk shul. A devoted following, led by the pharmacist Ruben Brash, centered around the school.

Special mention to its devoted founders: Pinchas Ruben, Pesach Volatzki, Peretz Yaffe, Shabach Solomyak, Lipman Gordon, Shmuel Yehuda Katcherginski and others, who gave their heart and soul for the continuation of the Yiddish language and culture. At the same time a Yiddish library was founded, which was endowed with a large collection of important Yiddish texts and also literature [Yiddish] from the broader world.

At the end of 1922, the Vilna Jews arrived and founded the Tarbut school on the same platform as the other Tarbut schools in Lithuania.

Yerachmiel Katz stood at the head of its Hebrew instruction, who now is the director of a middle–school, "Hugim", in Haifa.

The other founders were: Yerachmiel Katz, Elihu Volatzki, Israel Reichel, Rochel Kurlandtshik, Rafael Yaffe, Zalman Abel, Berel Fisher, Feiga Svirski, Yerachmiel Lubatski, Yacov Svirski, Yehoushe Ferevoznik Bertha Kuritzki and other sympathizers for the development of its youth, to teach them Hebrew, to become pioneers and to build "our" own land in Eretz Israel. A meeting of all the Zionist organizations was organized and it produced positive results. During the holidays our initiative to implement our plan began.

The youth went from house to house to convince the parents to send their children to the Tarbut school.

Many were receptive, others laughed: "You want to teach them the Holy tongue? Do you want them to become Rabbis?"

In a matter of two weeks, thirty five children registered and we did all we possessed to make the start of the school year a success.

[Col. 1514]

The difficult part was to find a suitable building and appropriate teachers.

Luckily we found a devoted and sympathetic teacher from a Hebrew school, Abraham Abel, z"l. He gave us a building, now the question was "how to repay him?" The building served as a school and in the evenings we held group meetings of Tzeirei Zion and Ha'Halutz. Later the library was added with many Hebrew books. The Zionist library was founded after many difficulties, with the proceeds from evenings, meetings and lotteries [to raise funds to buy the books].

Most of the children of the town studied in the Hebrew school and were fortunate to make Aliyah and thus were rescued from the tragedy that descended upon our Jewish people.

A Zionist spirit was instilled and a direction to further our Jewish identity was promoted.

Many were saved because of this.

Histradut Tzeirei Zion

Left to right: on top: **Moishe Ferevoznik, Yerachmiel Katz, Yehuda Ferevoznik, Yerachmiel Lubatzki, Meir Fridlander, Leib Reichel, Yehoushe Ferevoznik**
Sitting: **Basia Kutnik, Etel Ichiltchik, Sheina Shneiderovitch, Beti Kuritzki, Rochel Kutnik, Zalman Abel**

A Gemillut Hesed bank also existed in Haydutishok, thanks to Avigdor Dan, Chaim Pesach Gantovnik and Yosef Gitlitz, to which they devoted much of their time. Thanks to them they helped many unfortunate Jews overcome either bad luck or other unfortunate situations.

[Col. 1515]

The Gemilut Hesed helped mostly workers, artisans, medium wage–earners and the poor and widowed families.

In later years, a mixed committee of Zionists and Yiddishists founded a "wind" orchestra.

It was comprised of: Berel Shmid, Abraham Elihu Abel, Yitzhak Yaffe, Zalman Abel, Rafael Yaffee, Michal Patashnik, Leib Kushlin, Michal Oistreich, Elihu Katz, Melech Strikufski.

We should also mention those families, righteous and devoted, who tirelessly gave of their time to the Tarbut school, the Zionist organizations, the Keren Kayemet and the

Keren Hisud; they were, Abraham Kuritzki z'l, Yoschev Rash from Keren–Hisud, the Heshel Kurlandtchik family, the Roni Volotzki family and his son Elihu, Yoschev Rash from the “parents' committee”, the Shimon Reichel family, the Mendel–Ber Abel family, the Abraham Abel family, son of Abraham Katz and many, many others.

An episode of the first Aliyah from Haydutishok in 1924, Itel Ichilchik, now in Moshav Herut, Tel–Mond [Sharon plain, Israel] 1924; one beautiful summer evening we said our goodbyes at the train station, the friends of Halutz and Tzeirei Zion returning home were singing songs on top of their lungs and were arrested by the police. They were detained the entire night for disturbing the peace.

The orchestra helped the community with all its performances, special evenings, and various presentations, making sure they were a success.

Haydutishok also had their own Jewish fire–fighting society which had a dual duty to fulfill.

First it needed to provide immediate help when a fire broke out, second its mission was to serve when there was local unrest, like attacks or pogroms.

It is important to note the episode with the fire–fighters: in 1870–1880, there were huge fires in the shtetl, and after one such great fire, the firefighters of Sventzian donated a *pompe* /machine that needed to be dragged by hand and also a *pessel* [water–carrier] to carry water. Eventually we managed to buy another machine, which was wheeled on three wheels, and another few water carriers on two wheels.

[Col. 1516]

Before the First World War the involved were: Hanan Yoel, Chaim Pesach Gantovnik, Avigdor Dan and others. Every summer we learned the lively pazarnikes [firefighters=they used to sing lively songs as they worked].

After the First World War we got new equipment, like a motorized machine/pompe, which drew water from the river and reached the market square. We also built a new building for these machines. Again we should mention the devoted volunteers: Peretz Yaffe, Meir Reichel, Shmuel Yehuda Katcherginski, Rafael Yaffe, Chaim Pesach Gantovnik, Meir Gordon, Abraham Elihu Abel, Zvi Perlis, Ben–Zion Perevoznik, Gershon Yaffe.

Later it [fire–fighting] was “ripped out” of our Jewish hands and taken over by our bloody enemies, the Lithuanian hooligans.

This is how life unfolded in the shtetl until the year 1939.

Before the outbreak of World War 11, Poland mobilized an army and 32 young Jewish men from Haydutishok were conscripted. Six died in this short time, which was in the first weeks of September 1, the battle between Germany and Poland.

Their names were: Israel Oistreich, Moishe Bas, Israel Patashnik, Beinush Shapiro, Ezriel Kuritzki and a son of Hillel Disner.

The Jewish soldiers who returned home, recounted, that our friends fought valiantly against the blood–thirsty enemy and instinctively felt they were fighting against the greatest and most brutal enemy the Jewish people would ever encounter. This was a short but bitter battle between men and wild beasts, which descended in the "middle of the night" [without warning].

The Polish–German war didn't last long. The Polish army capitulated very soon and the nightmare unfolded upon the Jews of Poland!

September 18, 1939, the mechanized Russian army marched into Haydutishok. At first the Jewish people welcomed them with open arms, as we were scared of the Germans and we considered the Red Army as liberators of those Nazi beasts.

[Col. 1517]

The first days we were hopeful that they were our saviours.

The Sovietization of the shtetl began and we started to endure difficulties.

Slowly all the shops were emptied. We sold the goods at low prices and the money we earned was not sufficient to buy anything.

The flax, grain and fruit trade was handed over to the newly–opened cooperatives and the former merchants had no choice in this matter.

The "former rich–Jew" homes were seized, and they [the Jews] had to resettle into tight quarters outside the shtetl.

On the other hand, the "so–called proletarian" part of the Jewish population was pleased. They immediately got regime–posts and became policemen, administrators, trade officials and officers in the political parties.

From the other side we can underline some humane facts. A Jewish lad, who was the commander of the police, came to review and look for stolen/hidden merchandise. He barely looked and left without revealing anything.

This was only one of the incidences. On the other side the "former bosses" were sent to "work" in a different place and one didn't know what the next day would bring [for the former wealthy entrepreneurs].

April 10, 1940, many divisions of police and N.K.V.D. from Russia arrived at the train station of Haydutishok. This meant the beginning of a great disaster.

April 11, 1941, thirteen "wagons with chimneys" arrived at the train station, that how these transport–wagons were called. They had ovens. We began to tremble, and instinctively felt that something important was going to happen.

We didn't know what and when. The former “so called rich ones” got together to make a plan, they all knew very well the difficult journey they were about to embark on.

[Col. 1518]

That day was muddy, raining, a dreary Friday, my last day in Haydutishok.

First they gathered all the “rich people” and made them clean the mud off the streets and from the market square and clean the snow from the railway lines.

A good [Hagas] friend warned me to leave the shtetl but I wanted to face our situation, I didn't want to run away.

The Action was to take place at 12 midnight, we were going to be deported to Siberia.

Together with my wife we started to prepare some useful things as well as food, said our goodbyes to our nearest and dearest and waited for the police to come for us like those “guilty of a crime”.

We didn't sleep that night and waited for them to come and take us. The night seemed endless, daylight came and no one arrived. About 1 o'clock in the afternoon a police with several soldiers came to us. No one went in, no one went out. The process started when they read from a list, although the officer knew my entire autobiography, [he made himself stupid and asked] he questioned me: where do I live, how old am I, my father's name, my mother's name, and other things. In the end he showed me some respect and told me the administration decided to send me to another place in Russia. We were allowed to take 100 kilograms with us. He told us to get ready and he accompanied us to the train station.

The whole procedure took less than 2 hours, the soldiers had rifles and they pushed us along with bayonets, just like criminals.

April 13, 1940, Friday, Shabbat, twelve at night: these were the Jews of Haydutishok that were deported:

Mendel Yaffe's family, himself 74 years old, his son Abraham and daughter Chana

Peretz Yaffe's family, his wife Leia and children Afroim and Avraham

Rafael Yaffe's family and wife Shifra

Gershon Yaffee's family and wife Sima

Berel Shmidt's family and wife Ester and children, Kopel, Abraham and Moishe

[Col. 1519]

the last one the son–in–law and [mistake=should be of] the daughter of Mendel Yaffee)

Feiga Ferevoznik (wife of Henech Perevoznik)

Yehoushe Perevoznik with wife Henia and children Sheina and Chana

Moishe Lozer Pereoznik with wife Esther

Mania Reichel (wife of Meir–Ahron Reichel)

Vita Kuritzki and daughter Roza

Bertha Katcherginski and children Yosef and Teibele (the last one– wife and daughter of Henoch Kuritzki=unclear, Bertha or Taibele)

The departure from our friends and family was so disturbing, like a scene at a funeral of a dearly departed.

In the end we departed. Our belongings were thrown into the wagons and we walked alongside. The soldiers were pointing their rifles at us like we were the most dangerous criminals.

Our younger brother Gershon and his wife joined us along the way. When Gershon saw the rifles pointed at us he stopped, and stubbornly insisted he would not continue unless the rifles were placed on their backs.

The commander of the group decided to comply, as he saw that Gershon was very stubborn.

We passed the streets and the market place, our friends saying their last goodbyes through stares or a blinking of an eye.

Two scenes remain etched in my memory; my father–in–law, Elihu Katz, z'l, standing at his door shaking his head, hoping that we will survive and signalling to stay strong.

The second, our Polish friend Dashkevitch, with whom we lived in friendly relations. When we crossed the bridge, he [Dashkevitch] waited for us, when he saw us he took off his hat, cried like a child and yelled: "*Oy, Boze Mei, Boze Mei.*"

We couldn't answer him as we walked like statues and were afraid to be beaten.

When we arrived at the train station, we were greeted by closed wagons, packed with people and luggage, surrounded by soldiers. Our watchman opened a door and threw our packages into the wagon and then pushed us in.

[Col. 1520]

The space was overcrowded. There was no water and no place for personal necessities.

There were fifty–four people in our wagon, women and children all screaming and crying in loud voices. The other wagons were also filled to capacity with the same crying and screaming. We overnighted at the station and from that first evening we knew our new lives were going to be filled with cold, thirst, hunger, and darkness [gloom]. Sunday morning a friend approached us and gave us something to eat. They told us it was very difficult to reach us and bring us this food and other items.

The wagons remained in the station until twelve o'clock Sunday. We later found out we were waiting the arrival of the transport from Sventzian and Lyntup.

When the transport arrived, our wagon was attached to the others. The military stood guard, with machine–guns and stretched out rifles. They stood on both sides of the railway tracks to make sure that none of the civilian population dared to free us.

A large crowd leaving the church also assembled.

They stopped to watch our departure to Siberia, the crowds stood lined–up on all the platforms.

About one in the afternoon we started to move from the Haydutishok station, passing the melancholy landscape, our depressed streets and houses; this was our last memory fading before our eyes. Everyone started to wail, tears were flowing and the sounds pierced the entire region. The crowds also started to scream, wail and cry in sympathy with the deported.

[Col. 1521]

Far until the Komai station, thousands of people waited and greeted the passing train. The screams from within the wagons mixed with the protests of those left behind created a terrible commotion and angry protest against the brutal treatment.

The people [also the Christians] instinctively felt that they were saying their last goodbyes and they will never see us again.

[Col. 1522]

That day, Sunday, is very difficult to describe but even harder to forget.

That was my last day in Haydutishok and in such a tearful manner I had to depart from my beloved home of my birth.

No one could predict, at that time, that those remaining will suffer a far worse fate than those deported and will be murdered in various sadistic and non–human [bestial] ways.

[Col. 1521]

In Your Streets– Haydutishok

Shabtai Abel, Ein Shemer

Translated from Hebrew by Dr. Ettie Zilber

Edited by Anita Frishman Gabbay

Our town Haydutishok was a neighbor, equidistant between the towns of Sventzian and Postavy; Postovy to the east and Sventzian to the west. The town of Vidz neighboured to the north and the Lintupy train station wrapped around the town and closed her[Haydutishok] off from the south. The entrance to the town was from the south side, from the train station, the line that led from Vilna to Krulevchine.

The town [Haydutishok] benefitted due to the continuous connection with Vilna and with other Polish towns, which gave it an advantage over all the towns in the area.

The train station fulfilled an important economic and commercial function in the life of the town, and due to this, merchants arrived and goods exited the town, mainly flax, to Vilna and abroad.

The town was built on two hills. Between these two hills stretched a wide valley through which flowed the river Kamika. Forests and lakes did not surround the town. The view was not poetic, the plain *was an arm* from which many villages stretched, all with Jews. Evidence of this is seen when every veteran family of the town was named according to their village of origin. These were the families Matzbot, Mekomai, Meshoilan, Medzikvinsh, Mazhetz, Menorkvitz; the nearby village Stoyatzishok was completely settled by Jews, farm workers and village people, until the days of the Holocaust.

The Kamaika River in Haydutishok

The Christian population was made up of 3 nationalities: the area of Sventzian was Lithuanian, the area of Postovy, Belorussian and the third group, Pure–Russians[velicorussians] or panies in Yiddish. The Jewish population came in contact with all and spoke 3 languages.

[Col. 1523]

After the occupation of Haydutishok by the Poles in 1921 the Polish language was added. This language was easy for the Jews of Haydutishok. The language of the Haydutishokers could not differentiate between the *–sh* and the *–s*. There were significant educated people who added the Polish language, but the – sh and –s came in shades of their own.

We, the youth in the 1920s, learned Polish in school as the national language. It was very difficult for us to get used to it, perhaps because we couldn't stand the Polish authorities. Lack of adjustment to the people of authority and to the language of the country caused a desire for independence of language and nation–hood. That was the time of the *flowering* of the Yiddish and Hebrew languages. Even the signs on the shops and businesses were written in two languages Polish and Yiddish. From here started the directive to teach the children in the *Tarbut* school and of the *T.H.I.SH.A*, (Central Yiddish school organization). The Polish government elementary schools opened their gates free to all Jewish children but found no resonance among any Jewish child, not even the poorest child was caught in this net.

Like in all towns at that time, the market was in the middle of the town. This was the economic and business center. It was a large field which was covered in rocks, encircled by homes and shops. There were grocery shops, iron and textiles shops. Large and small shops; on market day, each Thursday, the shops would fill up with buyers, especially farmers from the area.

Market days and some annual fairs maintained the income of the townsfolk. In addition to stores, trade in linen took place in the market. Near the farmer's wagons, the merchants, the peddlers, the agents gathered, testing, breathing and lifting the flax to the sun. After the purchase they brought it to the warehouses. There they sifted and cleaned it. Hundreds of Christian girls from nearby villages and from the shtetl's Christian population worked during the winter season in these warehouses.

This was the industrial branch of the town. The linen was packed in large rolls by special machines. This was difficult work and only young people would do this work.

In the beginning of the 1930s, a number of Jews also worked in this industry, mainly from the "Leizer Nate" family, a family of laborers and porters, also the younger generation who apprenticed for the pioneer youth movements who were proud and blessed by it's difficult labour [duty to fulfill for their training to immigrate to Israel].

The packed linen was transported in wagons to the train station by Jewish wagons from Vidz street.

The flax industry created an important industrial atmosphere in the marketplace, especially during the winter season. The calls of the porters, wagon drivers, workers and managers filled the entire market.

[Col. 1524]

The eyes [attention] of the anti–Semitic Polish authorities were on this market in Haydutishok – for the worst. From time to time a rumor would be spread that they will move it to Gaydishok, the neighborhood across the river. For years it was an unresolved fight between the east and west, and the Jews feared its relocation.

In the marketplace the majority of the shops were owned by Jews. Only in one corner were Christian stores located whose roofs leaned on columns.

In the middle of the market there was a well with a hand pump, which was called *flomp*. This pump usually did not work and in the winter the field nearby was covered in ice and it was very dangerous to get to it. Near the well stood a pole on which there was a warning bell and they used it as a warning in case of fire.

The descent into the valley started from the marketplace to the east, “the downhill.” [Yiddish]. The wall of the house of Rabbi Pesach Vilotzki on one side and our house on the other side stood at the beginning of this descent. A steep descent in the middle of the town was *renowned.*

Those poor wagon drivers and the neighboring farmers would work hard to overcome this descent! On the way down, they had to restrain the horses and on the way up it required the energy of a man and an animal in order to reach the top [reference to a pregnant lady]. Only the experienced wagon drivers, like Yankel Abel and Baruch Shapira, moved materials to the station and from there they continued by cursing the dangerous descent.

Screams and shouts, shouts and calls, would echo every day and every hour from this place, but the height of “happiness” came when we, the youth, were overjoyed when a steam engine at the Fridlender station arrived. Forty horses were strapped to that steam engine. The horses were recruited from the nearby villages and were used for plowing, they didn't know how to work in a team, as a collective. Each one pulled in their own direction and immediately got what was coming to him [a beating] by the farmer near him.

The slope was like a gigantic realization of a vision to industrialize the town. Of course, when the steam engine was brought, after great efforts, the town's gain was realized. This steam engine put an end to the oil lamps in the town and it was now the age of electricity. This was actually a very special kind of electricity, pale and weak, but, it was, nevertheless, electricity.

But this slope did not cause only hardships and mishaps. It was really also a place for games and fun. On long winter nights, convoys of youth went to slide on sleds, everyone was stretched out on their back and with one pull they reached the valley, that started near the house of Rabbi Noach Frebuznik, owner of the seltzer factory, and continued until the house of Rabbi Alter.

The mountain itself that was spread over the slope was very steep, exposed, not built up, and a blocked cave was found at the foot of the slope. The people told many stories about that mountain. According to the stories there was a cemetery and it was forbidden to build on it. the children would carry out many, so called, battles to conquer the mountain. In their imagination it was really Mount Tabor [in Israel=many battles were fought].

[Col. 1525]

Almost all the townspeople pumped water from the well, for those who were not willing to pump water, they hired a Christian woman to bring it with poles and pails. With a rope connected to the pail, they would pump the water from the well, which was deep and full. The water was green, really like the river, while nearby, on the eve of Pesach they would bring this water to bake the matza and then would soak the Pesach “cutlery” in it.

A second well was next to the home of Alter the blacksmith who was called by the name "Alter Tekes Brunes [the black one]." The water was amazingly clear and all the *Mehadrim* [*strictly kosher*] would pump from it. While pumping they would bathe in the river which flowed toward the stream or they went in to have a little fun with friends from the movement, the children of Alter the blacksmith, Nachman Vlibteka. They immigrated to Palestine in the 1930s and both are no longer alive.

From the valley that ended near the homes of Rabbi Shimon Reichel and Alter the blacksmith, two streets stretched: one to *Hakadarim* street, a neighborhood of *Tatars* who dealt in leather works and in gardening, and the other to the bridge and further to Gaydishok.

[Col. 1526]

Here was an entirely different world. Gaydishok was a neighborhood built on the other hill of the town. It was all planted with trees, gardens and orchards. The population was mixed: Christians and Jews lived all together. But even the Jewish families took care of their gardens and orchards. The Bass family had a garden of large fruit trees and Patashnik family had a large vegetable garden, this was really a garden[farming] neighborhood, the Christian church was seen high above, surrounded by a large brick fence and inside was a large garden that was called "the priest's garden" which extended to the banks of the Kamika. Big dogs would guard the garden in case anyone would enter to pick its fruit. Nevertheless, our sons *dared* enter, swimming in the river and sneaking into the garden to take their booty.

We loved to travel in Gaydishok every Shabbat crossing the bridge, we took great pleasure with each house and street. From there we would usually also go to the village nearby Gaydishok on the way to Postavy, to a large village that was called Neidorf. We were so envious of the residents of this village. The houses, the gardens and the field, its serenity caused us envy and we wanted to imitate them.

In the town itself there were no trees growing at all. The only tree grew on Vidz street which started from the market square and continued to the Jewish cemetery. This street didn't have anything notable about it. Its houses were low and next to them there was a walkway of broken wood, and those coming and going kept their feet off it. It was always full of mud. But for us, poor Vidz street was like a magnet. The *Tarbut* schools and T.I.SH.A. [Central Yiddish school organization] were actually nearby. The branches of "Hechalutz [pioneers], "He'chalutz Ha'ztair [young pioneers]" and also "Hashomer Hatzair [young guard]" had a great time on this street, and as evening arrived sounds of singing or lectures would be heard. Regional meetings of Hechalutz and Hashomer Hatzair would take place on this street. The majority of residents were *Delet Ha'am* [the door of the people]; artisans, wagon drivers, porters, who showed respect for the youth. They were happy to see their children in the Tarbut school and in the youth movements. We would go out on trips to the open fields which stretched out far from the town, wonderful fields of linen and grain. We loved to hide inside the tall–standing grain. A sea of crops would remind us of Bialik's song "*in the field*". We yearned for these fields and based on this poet we would also ask: who cultivated all of this?

Hechalutz=Pioneers 1930

Abel Nachman, Perlis Shmuel, Broide Rachel, Perlis Lipman, Tzrontzki Zvi, Zeiger Bracha, Matzkin Michal, Katz Gershon, Perlis Itzhak, Ferbuznik Yehuda, Matzkin Chana, Katz Sheina, Broide Rochel(?), Svirski Zelda, Abel Moishe, Reichel Sura, Ferbuznik Miriam, Abel Shabtai, Ferbuznik Tirza

[Col. 1527]

The longing to build Eretz Israel became overpowering at that moment. We knew that only in Eretz Israel we would be able to cultivate fields, they would belong to us; poor Vidz street and the fields around it raised our desire to fulfill our pioneering dream and many of us decided to immigrate and start a new life.

The second place for fun, was served by the "little trees", to read books and play games in the summer—the grove of these trees were spread out on both sides of the Kimieka.

Because of the dam which stopped the water near the Fridlender station, the river was very narrow in this place and made it an ideal place to bathe to our young hearts' content, we took off into the fields and picked peas and beans. Many times this harvest ended in a surprised escape from the non–Jew who chased us furiously, accompanied by dogs and an iron bar in his hand and murder in his eyes. We would disperse in every direction and find shelter on the other side of the "little trees" which bordered Gaydishok.

"Tarbut" School 1925

From right to left: **Tirza Frebuznik, Zelda Svirski, Michal Frebuznik, —,—,Rivka Lapida, Rosa Kuritzki, Zahava Tzernotzki, Chava Gitliz, Rachel Broide, Sheine Katz, Sheine Volotzki, —,—,Michal Prebuznik, Miriam Fremont, Breina Glichor, Libe Abel,—,Doba Gitlitz, Chana Svirski, Masha Abel, —, Gershon Katz, Mina Meizel, Basia Kutnik, —, —, —, —, —, Leia Abel, Pinchas Matzkin, Sheine Katz, Shalom Shapira, —, —, —, —, —, —, Hillel Volotzki, Nachman Abel, Yakov Svirski, Eliahu Volotzki, —, teacher, teacher, teacher, Lekovitzki, Zvi Perlis, —, Yosef Gitlitz, Gendel, Taibe Broida, Taibe Katz, —, Risha Abel, —**

[Col. 1528]

There was one corner of Gaydishok that we would visit infrequently. It was the Christian cemetery. It interested us mainly because of the military section with the German soldiers who were killed on the front in the First World War. It was a very well maintained section decorated with flowers. Row and rows of crosses, in surprising order, stood. In the middle of the section there was a luxurious grave with a monument in honor of Rutmister who died and was buried there. Here and there were also individual graves of Russian soldiers that the German army brought for burial. These graves had no names and written on them was only "here was buried a courageous Russian soldier." These interactions with the graves of the German soldiers gave us material to think about the recent past and about the results of all wars. We could not imagine that there would be an outbreak of another horrible war seven times as horrible and it would bring on its wings a total destruction, destruction and loss of a third of our people and in addition would tear out the *foundation of the buildings* [Jewish community] that our forefathers established with their hard work and sweat over hundreds of years.

[Col. 1529]

The Youth Movement in Haydutishok Did Not Disappoint

Shabtai Abel, Ein Shemer

Translated from Hebrew by Dr. Ettie Zilber

Edited by Anita Frishman Gabbay

In all the conferences and meetings of our townspeople pulsated the one essential question: what drove us to achieve our dream? Where was the *stream* from which we drew the energy to leave our parents' home years before the storm and immigrate to Eretz Israel?

The one and only answer: our inspiration came from the Zionist youth movements, "Hashomer Hatzair" and "Hechalutz Hatzair." These movements filled us a deep feeling of hopefulness [in this town] and affinity. We had a feeling of a new movement, and thereby we rejected the 'way of life' in the towns of Poland and Lithuania. It pushed us to immigrate to Eretz Israel, whatever happens it will be "in our own land".

The Zionist movement took us out of the *degenerate* village life to fulfill and complete our pioneer yearnings.

In front of my eyes ten years of the development of the Zionist youth movements in our town from 1925 to 1935 passed. These were 10 years of education of children and youth in preparation to separate themselves from a life of idleness to one of work and creativity. For this reason we went out for agricultural training, we pushed ourselves to do physical labor, we learned a profession, we worked in agriculture, we spent time in nature with the main goal to establish a new home in our ancient homeland.

[Col. 1530]

The youth movement was the antithesis of village life. And that was why our fathers and older brothers, also good Zionists, didn't understand us, made fun of us and fought us.

But our stubbornness and endless dedication positioned the youth movements as the center of our lives [in our town].

The Pioneers 1931

—,Hillel Vilotzki, Liba Abel, Hana Svirski, Hava Gitlitz, Tirza Frabuznik, Zelda Svirski, Michael Frabuznik, - Arieh Vlotzki, Moshe Probuznik, Zahava Tzernotzki, Itzchak Perlis, Michael Prevoznik, Zvi Tzergotzki, Shmuel Shapira, Chaim Gordon, Tova Katz, Miriam Frabuznik,—, Moshe Abel, Nachman Abel, Bracha Zeiger, Rivka Lapida, Yirachmiel Sutzkever, —, Haim Svirski, Israel Patashnik, Perlis Chana, Baile Abel, Yehudit Abel, Taibe Broide, Shmuel Perlis, Reuven Ginzburg, Shlomo Yudelman, Yehudit Zeiger, Lubka Kanfer

The hand of the movement was in everything: in the organization of the schools, in the parties, in the fundraising, and in going out to the agricultural training and for immigration. Finally, the movement gained the trust of our parents and an agreement was formed between us and them. Finally, they also understood that we found the right path. It helped so much to send letters from Eretz Israel and maintain connections with those who remained in the town.

Unfortunately and painfully, they realized too late and they couldn't manage to get out from under the *claws of the voracious beast*– the filthy Germans.

But the youth movements didn't disappoint us even during that horrible period [Holocaust], they invigorated the spirit of revolt in the ghettos which showed the young people that were trapped, the way to the forests and to the Partisans.

The Zionist youth movement fulfilled a brilliant function even afterwards through the period of illegal immigration, the majority of its 'students' immediately joined by immigrating to Eretz Israel, joining the ranks of the Hagganah [army] and battled with their blood and their lives to establish the State of Israel.

[Col. 1531]

Avraham Eliahu Abel Z"L and His Public Work

by Shabtai Abel

Translated by Jerrold Landau and Ettie Zilber

My brother, Avraham Eliahu, was the fifth in our family. He was born in 1900, studied in the Cheder of Meir Leib and at 12 years old he was sent to the Yeshiva in Vidz. There he studied diligently [Gemara, Rabbinic decisors and Tosafot] under the Director of the Yeshiva, the renown, the smart and diligent – Rabbi Leib. They used to say about Rabbi Leib that he would disparage the *great sages* [Ha'Gaonim] [of the generation] and that they could barely learn even one page of Humash. Because of this Director, the Vidz Yeshiva was renowned throughout the region. Together with Avraham Eliahu many boys from our town studied in this Yeshiva. The learning that Avraham Eliahu received in Vidz affected him deeply for the rest of his life. There he received his spiritual foundation that guided him throughout his life.

At the outbreak of the First World War, when in 1916 the Jews of Haydutishok were chased out, including our family, we settled in Mariampole, Lithuania. The difficult living conditions in this new place, and worries about making a living, of our father Menachem-Dov, didn't allow Avraham Eliahu to continue his studies. He knew the Hebrew language very well and was familiar with its ancient and new literature, its grammar, and he continuously read new literature. He loved Bialik and the national poems of the period of renaissance. And he was also one to keep the Jewish traditions. He loved the Jewish people's customs and holidays profoundly, he was respectful of the Jews who guarded his 'God' with their deep spiritual bond.

Similarly, our firstborn brother Yishayahu Haim (z'l), studied in the Lubavich and remained all his life true to the Chasidic Lubavicher romanticism.

I remember on holidays, especially during the days of Sukkot, all of us, [Yishayahu Chaim] the Lubavicher Chasid, an honest and innocent man, Avraham Eliahu, leaning towards "Mizrachi", and I, the youngest son of elderly parents, a man from "Hashomer Hatzair"—we all met in the succah for a [Kiddush] benediction, and that was surprising, in that despite the differences in our opposing world views [of the three brothers] we all respected one another. There was no hatred or animosity between us. The reason was: love of one's fellow Jew. Each one loved his people in his own way. Avraham Eliahu was the best of us.

He was particularly careful in obeying the Jewish laws governing interpersonal relations. He was very careful to avoid any damage to the property of a fellow Jew or gentile.

[Col. 1532]

He was disgusted and protested against any misleading of one's fellow. He followed the straight path in an unparalled way. He was not a passive upright person, but rather, he fought openly and with strength for justice and propriety, and did not tolerate any compromise in that area.

Never in his life did he come in conflict with people, even those who were involved in the common good, but who he suspected were looking after their own interests.

With all of this, he was not one of the delicate people who avoided all communal affairs.

He was an industrious communal activist in many areas and set a real example for the entire region. He was active with the *Tarbut* school in the town, he was one of the members of the administration of the people's bank and even participated in the administration of the firefighters.

At the beginning of the 1930's, he joined the civil administration and advocated for the worker's unions, advising them to take progressive new approaches and to improve their business. He always strived for excellence in all the tasks that he accepted, he dedicated himself with all his energy, he demanded responsibility from others that participated in these institutions. His public functions in these institutions stemmed primarily from his feeling of communal responsibility, but his heart and soul was devoted to his involvement with the "Keren Kayemet."

He was the deputy of the "Keren Ha'Kayemet L'Israel" [Jewish National Fund] for many years. He loved the Keren and collecting money for it, he wouldn't miss an opportunity or an event for the Keren. "HaKeren Hakayemet" bound him to Eretz Israel, its settlement, its pioneering spirit; everything to do with the Land was the center of his being.

Through this work he came in close contact with all the youth movements in the town, members of "Hashomer Hatzair" and the "Halutz Hatzeir", he appreciated the dedication of the young members to the Keren Ha'Kayemet, loved every Zionist [without differentiating between the person's Zionist style. He would invite the veteran Zionist of the town, Reb Avraham Kuritzki to meetings and gatherings for the Keren Ha'Kayemet on the 20th and 26th of Tammuz, and would honor him with delivering the opening and bestow on him many other honors. He himself distanced himself from any honor and prominence. As stated above, he leaned toward the *Mizrachi*, but he was close in his heart to the Working Land of Israel- 'Eretz Yisroel haOved'. He was a working man, loving work, and honoring the worker. He was secretly distraught that most of the people of his age became middlemen and contractors in the flax trade, and shopkeepers.

He was[broad boned] and healthy and didn't exclude himself from hard work, all his days he gave of himself and worked hard together with all the family members in our bakery. At the end of his days his situation improved by marrying Dvora Kurlantzik, the daughter of Reb Heshel Kurlantzik, owner of the largest wholesale store in the city. But these good days did not last long. With the entry of the Soviets into the city in 1939, he returned to the bakery and continued the hard work together with our sister Tzvia and her husband (Z"L)

His entire life he dreamed of immigrating to Eretz Israel. Already in Lithuania in 1920 with the original awakening of the "He'Chalutz" movement he went out with groups of youth to Hachshara[training] at the Jewish farm near Mariampole.

[Col. 1533]

The days of these trainings lasted half a year. They left a deep impression on him for the rest of his life, and many of his friends immigrated to Eretz Israel. He strove with all his heart to follow them.

As has been mentioned, those days were days of great national awakening, his friends in Hachshara would appear at our house on Saturdays and holidays and would sing the songs of Zion, arguing, getting excited and returning at night to the farm and their hard labor.

Luck did not hold out for Avraham Eliahu, he was called up for the military for the young Lithuanian army. This prevented him from immigrating to Eretz Israel. In 1924 our family returned to Haydutishok[which was returned to Polish rule] together with the entire region of Sventzian. He remained in military service and only after one year "snuck across" the Poland-Lithuania border and joined the family. (only our brother Yakov remained in Lithuania and immigrated from there to Eretz Israel in 1929, a short while before the outbreak of the events.)

Right after his arrival Avraham Eliahu dedicated himself to rehabilitating the family and the house. He encouraged me, that since I only finished the "Tarbut" school in the town, to continue studying in the Teachers' college of Dr. Charna Boilena. He supervised my studies and enjoyed my accomplishments in Hebrew studies. He loved the Hebrew language and with the appearance of *Hayom* as a daily newspaper, he subscribed immediately and would read it from front to back.

In 1929 there were outbreaks of bloody events in Eretz Israel which caused deep trauma. His great love and concern for Zion arose with a double fervor, and he continued to rise and join the builders. Our brother Yakov who had already found his place in Bet Shemen, started to prepare the necessary paperwork. His immigration [to Eretz Israel] did not work out for a variety of reasons.

In 1934 he married Dvora Kurlantchik, entered into family life and after 2 years a son was born, Mendel Be'er (after the name of our father Z"L who died the night after Yom Kippur 1934).

In 1935 I immigrated to Eretz Israel, on Saturday night [of Chazon-the night after the Sabbath prior to Tisha B'Av]. I said goodbye to my family, to my sisters Tzvia and Sheine Rivka, to Yeshayahu Chaim and to Avraham Eliahu, I didn't know that this goodbye would be forever. Avraham Eliahu beamed with happiness, although he would not accompany me in my voyage to Eretz Israel, his feelings about immigrating and his 'envy' of me, he hid deeply, deeply within his soul.

[Col. 1534]

With the outbreak of World War Two the gates closed and the world stopped. The Zionist work ended. His short letters from this period that arrived in Eretz Yisroel, I remember one saying of his: just from bread alone man will live, which means that we should work hard in order to earn our daily bread. Of course, he didn't mention and didn't write about the Zionist vision or his aspiration to immigrate [make Aliya].

On the day of the mass murder, through the Intermediate Days of Sukkot 1941, he marched together with all the people of the town towards death in the fields of Poligon- he was one of them.

With every strand of his soul he was connected to the community. His Jewish pride was nourished by the enterprise of the community, its construction and labour, its development and growth, its protection and struggle and the courage of the *Yishuv [refers to the Jewish people living in the Pre-State Land of Israel]*.

It was at the celebration of the Hebrew school, where he appeared at an amateur performance (as was customary in the towns) and he sang from deep in his heart the song: "if I had the strength, I would run through the streets of the town and scream: *geula* [redemption]."

He invested his entire soul in this song. This was the song of his life. He wanted with all his soul to redeem himself from the deterioration of life in the shtetl, from the diaspora and aspire for a new life in Zion. There is no doubt that he marched to his death in Poland and in his heart he sang "redemption" and "Hatikva [hope]" - and he was then only 41 years old.

This article should be dedicated to his pure and refined soul. May his memory be a blessing.

[Col. 1535]

About the Hebrew School and the Zionist Activity/Action

Shimon Abel, Kibbutz Ma'anit

Translated from Hebrew by Dr. Ettie Zilber

Edited by Anita Frishman Gabbay

My town, Haydutishok, is engraved into my memory for all eternity. In the years of my youth I suckled the air of her environment, her streets and her houses.

Engraved in my soul I remember the hills, the “Kamaika” river that winds its way between those hills, where I swam in the summer and skated in the winter. I admired the vast fields of grain which stretched from village to village and its orchards, past the flour mill, which on Shabbat days were vibrant with children and young people.

The years of my childhood and youth were spent in rich and vibrant social and cultural activities. In those days we established a drama group and we donated the proceeds towards a library, orchestra, the Keren Hakayemet, Keren Hayesod, etc.

[Col. 1536]

The youth movement “Hashomer Hatzair” and “Hahalutz ha'tzair” planted the “ideals” of the Eretz Israel labor movement. These youth movements put us to work in all the Zionist activities and paved the way for youth immigration to Eretz–Israel.

After trips to the fields we would return to the town, to its shops, its markets and its businesses. These trips proved to us the anomaly of our lives in the town and we then started to understand the big difference that exists between business and the field[agriculture].

There were three schools in Haydutishok: the Polish government school, in which only a very few Jewish children studied.

On Vidz street, between the rickety wooden buildings was the Tarbut school. In another wing of the "Tailor's Cloize" [study house] in the second wing were four rooms that were used for six study classes. Both the teachers and the students studied and learned in difficult conditions, however, many graduating classes came out of this school. With the youth activities, and after many efforts by the parents, they decided to construct a permanent building for a school which greatly improved the conditions for studying. A similar situation also existed in the third school, which used Yiddish as the language of instruction and was affiliated with the network of schools of the *T.I.SH.A. (Central Yiddish school organization).*

[Col. 1537]

How did schools exist financially in our town? The tuition was set according to the economic ability of the parents. The school Board together with the parent council decided the tuition. Many parents paid only a token tuition, because they simply had no possibility to pay, and the result was that there was not one Jewish child in the town who was left out the school.

There were many active clubs and the school concentrated all the youth groups around it, as well as its intelligensia. No effort was too difficult for them to establish the school.

“Hehalutz” 1932

From right to left: **Ginsburg Reuven, Chaim Farbuznik, Avraham Patashnik, —, Taibe Broide, Yehudit Abel, Nechama Zeiger, Roza Lifshistz, —, —, Arieh Lapida, Israel Patasnik, Yehudit Abel, Shalom Sutzkver, Lipka Shapira, —, —, Ezriel Lubotzki, Sheina Katz, Israel Lubotzki, —, Yerachmiel Sutzkever, Shalom Yochelman, Taibe Kanfer, —, —, Leib Kanfer, —, Gittel Yafe, Chaim Israel Svirski, Yehudit Zeiger, Michaela Abel, Hana Perlis, Gittel Lapida, Shapira.**

Inside the walls of the school building they found a sheltered space for all the youth organizations, and likewise for the Hebrew library. Lectures, celebrations and special culture evenings took place frequently there. Throughout all the streets echoed Hebrew songs that came from the school building. The spiritual experiences and longing for Eretz Israel was developed there. The Zionist vision and its fulfillment were wedged within its walls. And, in addition, this institution was dear to us and remains deeply engraved in our hearts.

[Col. 1538]

In our town it is difficult to speak about the “classes” in simple terms, there were people of means and high status, and also *DELET–AM,* workshop owners and small shopkeepers.

What was interesting was that actually it was the poor children who constituted the majority of the "Tarbut" school students. The Yiddish school whose mandate was in the Yiddish language, reconciled themselves with the diaspora life in the town. How did this school die?

From the majority of those who immigrated to Eretz, most were from the "Tarbut" school and only after the Second World War, some who studied at the T.I.SH.A. (Yiddish) school arrived.

"Tarbut" School

Michael Ferevozhnik, Sheina Katz, Zahava Tchernatzki, Rivka Lapida, Mina Meizel, Rosa Kuritzki, Zelda Svirski, —, Chana Svirski. Nechama Abel, Roche Malka Abel, Feigel, Sheine Katz, Rochel Broide, Itzhak Meisel, Leib Volotzki, Sheine Volatzki, Chaim Svirski, Chana Matzkin, Itzhak perlis, Shlomo Matzkin, Shmuel Perlis, —, —, —, Mee Ferman, Feigel, Feigel, — ,Moshe Abel, Lipe Perlis, Taibe Katz, Teacher ,—,Yerachmiel Katz, Rachel Kuliandtzhik, teacher Lachavitzki, —, Reuven Ginzburg

[Col. 1539]

Characters from Our Town

Shimon Abel, Ma'anit

Translated from Hebrew by Dr. Ettie Zilber

Edited by Anita Frishman Gabbay

A. Rabbi Chaim Zerach

I only knew Rabbi Haim Zerach from his melodies which echoed before every Shabbat and holiday, and especially on the Yamim Ha'norim [Days of Awe=Yom Kipur].

I heard his name from my father Rabbi Yishayahu–Chaim (Z"L) who continued to pray according to the leadership of Rabbi Chaim Zerach. They both did not understand the notes but when father would tell me, that this is the exact way Rabbi Chaim Zerach did it, I knew that the style was correct and there was no room for any doubt.

The entire audience in the *shtibel* [prayer house] would hum the melodies of Rabbi Chaim Zerach with adherence and enthusiasm.

From my youth my ears absorbed that "style", and I was blessed that my father was honored to become his successor on earth and to sing exactly like Rabbi Chaim Zerach, the: "*I am the poor man*" on Yom Kippur.

My father was a Chabadnik through and through. And every Shabbat he would read from the book of secrets and hints. But when the Yamim Ha'norim approached he would dedicate himself by listening to melodies, pleasant and enthusiastic, and would prepare with awe and humility for the lofty job that will be given to him – to be the public emissary to the people of Israel.

This, too, he received as an inheritance from his Rabbi and his educator Rabbi Chaim Zerach Z"L.

B. Rabbi Yossi Bar Alsfein

Rabbi Yossi Bar Alsfein served as a nursery school teacher. In the days when my father was young, may he rest in peace, his house stood on the mountainside in one of the narrow lanes off Vidz Street. It was a poor and dilapidated house and one time it totally collapsed. Rabbi Yossi Bar got injured under the wreckage.

Soon the house was raised anew and stood in all its glory on the edge of the slope. It was pleasant to look at the surrounding area and to see the winding Kamaika river.

In the field of education, Rabbi Yossi Bar was fortunate to have an appropriate successor because his son Shmuel Itzhak became one of the best teachers in the elementary school.

The son, like his father, was known to be very knowledgeable, sharp and smart and became famous as possessing a deep understanding of the world of the Bible.

Rabbi Yossi Bar's only daughter, Rivka, was a very admirable character among the Zionist youth. Her only ambition was to go Eretz Israel and get involved in the life of the Land.

Unfortunately, not one of Alsfein's family managed to escape the claws of the Nazis.

[Col. 1540]

C. Friedlander Family

This family settled far away from the center of the village and by that they already made themselves different than the rest of the Jewish population.

The father of the family spent a long time in South Africa and for some reason came back to Europe and settled in Haydutishok.

Evidently, he managed to bring some fortune with him because he immediately built the only flour mill in the area and constructed a water turbine on the river, something that was never seen before in our area.

His heirs, sons and daughters, continued with this blessed project and even expanded it. They were the ones who brought the electric light to the dark village and with that helped in the development and progress of the village.

To this day, I still remember the incredible experience that I had when the Friedlander's brought the first *locomobile* [car] from England. And 18 teams of horses were required to transport it from the train station to the flour mill. I imagine that there was never a more incredible sight than that!

All the citizens of the town, Jews and Christians, old women and babies, everyone congregated on both sides of the road and accompanied the procession with joy and excitement.

Also, the first day in which Haydutishok received its electricity is embedded in our memory. It was a day of real festivity. The day when we exited from darkness to bright light! In short, the Friedlander home was very advanced and cultured in all respects. That family was also very generous, and every poor and needy person received support in time of need

This extended and large family was completely exterminated by the Nazis and not even one soul remained.

D. Gitlitz Family

In all aspects, the Gitlitz home was a Zionist home. All the members of the family were dedicated and involved with every Zionist endeavor, especially when they worked [with love] for KKL [Israel National Fund] and the *Tarbut* school.

Even though they all worked very hard, they had a hard time making a living, nevertheless, you could always hear singing and playing music, sounds of joy and happiness from this house.

The son Benyamin was known for his artistic talent and there wasn't one show in town without his participation.

From this distinguished family, only one of the daughters managed to survive and she lives with us in the State of Israel.

[Col. 1541]

Rabbi Gershon Zak Z"L

by Yaacov Abel

Translated by Meir Razy

Gershon Zak

Tall and straight, his beard meticulously combed - his Hasidic long coat, flawless - his traditional Hasidic boots, always polished and shining. Rabbi Gershon Zak was a well-built, handsome man.

His noble appearance stood out everywhere: in the house, on the street, in the synagogue. I had the privilege of being a child of a relative as-well-as a neighbor, and served as his "partner" for his physical training. Whenever I entered their home, whether for an errand or on my own initiative, this serious and strict Jew took a long, thick leather strip that always lay in the wardrobe, passed it under my arms and carefully lifted me with one hand up to the ceiling and back down to the floor. He repeated this exercise 10-12 times. This was very puzzling and scary at first, but this "sport" made me very proud to have helped him.

Rabbi Gershon, like the vast majority of the Jews of Haydutsishok, was a Chabad Chassid, a Lubavitcher Chassid, a strict and fanatical, stubborn and consistent man. He brooked no compromises under any circumstances, with anyone or under any conditions. And this was so in his personal life and in public or social matters.

It is no wonder that with such extremes he was always involved in strong, fierce and bitter quarrels, and from time to time he caused bitter disagreements and in-fighting. It was said of him that there were always two sides in Haydutsishok. All the Jews of the town were on one side and on the other side was Rabbi Gershon with a number of his associates.

One of the great controversies in the history of the town which was legendary some 50 years ago, was the dispute over Rabbi Fogel. That rabbi was nominated as the Chief Rabbi of the town against the opinion of Rabbi Gershon and a number of other zealots, including my grandfather Z"l. Things deteriorated into fights, physical blows and hatred among the community members. The rabbinic court apparently ruled against his opinion, but Rabbi Gershon did not accept this ruling and the dispute continued for a long time until Rabbi Fogel left.

[Col. 1542]

The rabbi who came after him to serve in Haydutsishok, Rabbi Poppel ZT"L, was a friend of Rabbi Gershon, close to and respected by him as well as by all the Jews of the town.

Our family relocated together with the family of Rabbi Poppel and Rabbi Gershon to Mariampole, Lithuania.

Rabbi Gershon was very satisfied when Rabbi Poppel was appointed as the Chief Rabbi of Mariampole. His joy was complete and he was delighted when his friend, Rabbi Poppel, was chosen as a delegate to the first parliament of an independent Lithuania as a representative of ultra-Orthodox Jews.

While he was an extremist and fanatic, Rabbi Gershon was also involved with people -he did not limit himself to the confines of the synagogue. As a young man he roamed even farther away and sailed to the United States where he stayed for several years. It was said about him, and we do not doubt this story as the truth, that during all his years in America he did not eat meat. This was not because he was a vegetarian or that there was some shortage of kosher meat. It was only because the Kashrut was not done according to the Chabad customs.

Rabbi Gershon had several different businesses. The commerce and business brought him into close contact with people, mostly women and girls. He was a ritual slaughterer in the town but his trade did not seem to provide him with a decent living. So he set up several machines for making socks, a very essential commodity in small towns at the time. He employed many young women from the local community, usually from poor families. Just before the First World War, he also began trading with leftover textiles, and most of his clients were women too.

He did not shake hands with women and would not share a ride in a vehicle with women.

Several times, as a little boy, I eye-witnessed his bravery and his strict beliefs. Rabbi Gershon and his wife Karina Nechama had two sons and two daughters. The youngest son was Meir, who died in Israel about seven years ago. As a boy he studied and worked in the town of Dvinsk, where his sister Zvia lived after her marriage. He would visit his parents on Saturdays and holidays. One Friday, the train was late and Meir arrived at his father's house after the lighting of the candles. He came home apprehensive about the mishap and tried to justify himself to his father. However Rabbi Gershon did not extend a hand to him and did not want to hear any justification. He instructed his wife not to talk to the boy. This boycott remained until after end of the Shabbat.

[Col. 1543]

During the First World War, the Jews of the town feared the Cossacks. Rabbi Gershon was also alarmed by this risk and, gathered his strength and courage, he provided a refuge for the young daughters of Israel.

The house of David Kacerginski, who lived in the next alley, had a large storage room with a door the opened from the inside. Rabbi Gershon selected this storage room as a shelter for the women and daughters of Israel. He stood by that door with an axe in his hand and guarded them.

Rabbi Gershon died at a ripe old age in Mariampole, Lithuania.

May his memory be blessed.

R' Shimon Reikhel–the Brick Layer

Chanoch Ben–Sarah

Translated by Anita Frishman Gabbay

One of the interesting figures in Haydutishok was Reb Shimon Reikhel, who everyone called the brick–layer. This knick–name was well known across many villages of the region.

He was born in Postov and brought up there, after his wedding he moved to Haydutishok, where he lived with his large family for more than 40 years.

He was a tall Jew, with a dark beard, a healthy face and fiery intelligent eyes. He loved to work, he was always overworked and loved to engage in conversation.

Reb Shimon Reikhel was considered in the shtetl as one of the few manufacturers. Several kilometers from Haydutishok, on an open field, he built a gigantic oven and manufactured tiles and mortar. He worked with a huge furnace and was able to produce 40,000 tiles in one shift. He didn't own the land and he purchased the lime (clay) from his Christian neighbours.

Besides being considered a rich man and a manufacturer, he still exerted himself like a dark, uneducated peasant. He alone placed the tiles in the oven and then fired them up. This was a difficult job and much strength was needed to place the tiles in the oven. This hard work didn't deter him, the other way around, he was always pleased and felt rewarded.

Even in those times, seldom was there such a hard and devoted personality.

[Col. 1544]

Very few Jews, especially the wealthy ones, didn't work at physical labour. Most of the Jewish folk were employed–as known–with shop keeping and small trade.

In the tile workshop also worked his two sons: Leibe and Israel. Besides them, he employed another 20 people, a large percentage were Jews. One of his best masters was Hershel Tzernatzki, who was from Dzhikevines.

Also Jewish girls worked transporting the tiles. Two of them were Hirshele's [Tzernatzki] sisters: Slove and Tzipe.

When a branch of “Halutz” was established in Haudutishok, many *Halutzim* also worked in his tile factory. He beamed with pride. He couldn't stop wondering how children from wealthy Jewish families did such menial and physical labour.

For the town *Halutz,* the tile factory served as a *Hackshara* (preparation) training. The youth of the shtetl therefore were able to prepare themselves for a future, more physical way of life in Eretz Israel. Many *Halutzim* thought that in the land of Eretz Israel hard work would be a necessity and in this way it was practise, to fire and produce tiles.

Reb Shimon never argued with his workers. He was loved by all, Jews and Christians, and they had great respect for him.

[Col. 1545]

He set an example, he didn't work less than his workers. They didn't see him as the rich man, the boss, or the manufacturer. Just a regular worker like the rest of them.

He sold the tiles throughout the entire region and had many close relationships with all the merchant clubs(associations) of the Haydutishok county. Known for his honesty and good character throughout the towns, he was often requested to serve as a representative in various societies.

He was quiet and very respected, shy. All knew that one could come for a loan at his home, or charity. He had an open hand and an open home. There was seldom a Shabbos, when there wasn't a guest, a Magid, a scholar or just someone passing through, they all knew they could have a meal and a bed.

From his own tiles he built a 2 storey house beneath the hill which and was considered one of the most beautiful buildings in Haydutishok.

The years passed by and in this way Reb Shimon established himself and made a good living.

In 1915, the front closed in on Haydutishok and the Jewish folk of Haydutishok had to evacuate. Reb Shimon and his large family resettled in Dzhikevines, a small village where Jewish peasants lived.

There were many Jewish beggars and he took care of them in the same manner as for his own family.

A year later they were thrown out to Lita (Lithuania). Reb Shimon went to live in Pren, as told by his daughter Sara (now Shuster from Ramat Chaim)and in his home he developed a true social help–society, whoever needed help knew his address. In his name the money arrived from the *Joint* and only he was entrusted to divide the proceeds amongst the refugees.

His daughter recounts his trustworthy character trait:

In a cold, winter day he left with his sons to bring wood from the nearby forest. He forgot, that in his bosom–pocket he hid some bank–notes, which he had to divide among the workers.

[Col. 1546]

At night, when he returned home, he noticed he lost the important package in the forest.

The event bothered him like *thunder* on a bright day. In several minutes the first white hairs appeared on his head. He raised his hand and couldn't stop brewing:

"This money does not belong to me, what should I do?" Not long after pondering, he dressed and returned to the forest to look for the lost package.

His good fortune ensued, a Christian saw him and asked, are you looking for a package containing some bank–notes? It showed immediately that this was an honest Christian, and she returned all the money. Not one bank note was missing.

Shimon then told everyone, this woman was his saviour angel. He would never recover from such a loss!

During these additional years in Pren, his daughter told a second important tale. There was a woman with 5 small children among the workers? Her husband was in America and she was alone to raise them.

Suddenly the woman got sick and died several days later. Shimon immediately took the 5 orphans into his home and looked after them like a true father.

A second daughter from America writes another interesting episode:

Smerl, Raske's Zalman, a terrible epidemic broke out in the house. Three children died within a week. The doctor immediately demanded the home be painted and sterilized. There was no painter in the shtetl that wanted to enter the house. They were all frightened and did want to whitewash the house.

Reb Shimon spent his entire life as shingle maker, he never painted, nor did he know how to whitewash, but when he heard the story, he didn't think too long and took a pail of slaked lime and a brush, left and whitewashed the infected house.

Everyone saw him as a hero and they were impressed by his devoted and courageous character.

[Col. 1547]

He became famous in the region because of his good deeds, his virtues became legends.

Besides all these deeds he was also an ardent Zionist and dreamt his whole life to make Aliyah to Eretz Israel.

He was also a conscientious person with broad vision and outreach, a true man who looked after the needs of the community. His entire life he served as the Gabbai of the old Synagogue, he held the position of leader of the shtetl and was the overseer and head–boss of the cemetery.

As Haydutishok didn't have the means for a bath, he built one with his own funds, a very beautiful bathhouse.

Every night he sat in the Synagogue and prayed Tehillim with his own, sad nigun (melody).

[Col. 1548]

His singing was followed by large crowds.

His sad fate was a gruesome and terrible one. Also a Holy one! When all the Jews of Haydutishok were led to Poligon, he wrapped himself in his broad silk Tallit and led a prayer. A Lithuanian hooligan approached him, made fun of him, and wanted to steal his Tallit. Reb Shimon resisted and the hooligan shot and wounded him. Several days later the Christians found his body laying near the railway tracks.

This is the way Reb Shimon the brick maker lived and died. Holy and devoted!

May his memory be blessed!

[Col. 1547]

Rabbis, Slaughterers, Teachers and Scholars

Rafael Yaffee

Translated by Anita Frishman Gabbay

At the end of the nineteenth century, a quarrel broke out between the slaughterers and the Rabbi. Understandably, each side had its followers, and eventually a bitter struggle unravelled.

The dispute flared up before the reading of the Shabbat Torah. It went as far as reaching the court of Jewish law (Beit Din), where the greatest Rabbis of the region presided.

In the end one Shochet was reprimanded: one had to leave the shtetl together with the Rabbi and a new Rabbi came to replace him, Rabbi Fafel, z"l.

Rabbi Fafel remained in Haydutishok until 1916, until the known expulsion of the Haudutishoker Jews and Rabbi Fafel became the Rabbi in Mariampole.

[Col. 1548]

Later he became so famous and was appointed as a deputy to the Lithuanian Sejm, in Kovno.

Rabbi Fafel was a Jew of great wisdom, with a pure heart. He also knew Russian and German and was popular among his Lithuanian deputies.

After the First World War the Jews started to return to Haydutishok and started to look for a new Rabbi. The task wasn't an easy one, after a Rabbi such as Rabbi Fafel, it was a difficult to find a suitable candidate to represent the Rabbinate of Haydutishok.

Many Rabbis came to our shtetl to fill the position, they held talks and interviews.

[Col. 1549]

At that time two groups fought bitterly.

On one side were the very religious, mostly the Elders. On the other side were young elements, who only wanted a progressive Rabbi, with worldly views and a knowledge of languages.

Finally, the young won and in 1925 Rabbi Elhanan Moshitz arrived in Haydutishok, the son– in– law of the Rabbi of Vileyka.

He was a young man of twenty something years, sharp and intelligent, well versed and was immediately loved by the townsfolk. Even the Elders gave their blessing and made peace with him.

Rabbi Moshitz was especially known for his Saturday sermons, which drew large crowds. He solved Jewish problems with worldly and political solutions and the young people of the shtetl hurried for his Saturday services in the synagogue, especially to hear his sermons.

Rabbi Elhanan Moshitz remained the Rabbi of Haydutishok until the destruction arrived. In 1941 he went to his father–in–law in Vileyka and was murdered there by the German beasts.

May the memory of the righteous be a blessing!

After the First World War, a new Shochet also arrived in Haydutishok. He was Rabbi Moishe Leib, the son– in– law of Tabariski from Svir. He was a pleasant young man, with a warm Jewish heart, a great philanthropist and a lover of books. There was never a day, when a poor person didn't sit at his table.

The Shochet's house was open for every unfortunate soul. Whoever was in a difficult situation, went to the Shochet and explained his troubles. Rabbi Moishe Leib set out immediately to everyone in the shtetl to collect some zlotes (money).

The Shochet was involved in all the affairs of the townsfolk, with young and old, poor and rich, everyone respected him and loved him.

In 1941, when the Germans entered Haydutishok, his father–in–law Tabarishki from Svir sent a special carriage to bring him back to Svir, which was in White Russia; we thought that it would be quieter there than in our Lithuanian shtetls.

[Col. 1550]

But Rabbi Moishe refused to go. He answered his father– in– law: “What will be will the Jews of Israel, will be will the Rabbi of Israel”. He was murdered with all the Jews of Haydutishok In Poligon. May his memory be blessed!

Teachers (melamedim)

In 1909 I began my Cheder studies. We had several Cheders in Haydutishok with well-known teachers.

Moishe Hirsh Ferman. The Shamash of the old synagogue, was then an elderly Jew, with a white beard and taught about 12 boys in his Cheder. We learned our Aleph– Beth here, Chumash and the Prophets.

His Cheder was in a small house, next to a pit, on a narrow street where Henoch Kuritzki lived. We studied from eight in the morning until late at night.

At mid–day the Rabbi went to the synagogue to take a break and catch a nap. For us children this was an opportunity, we went outside to the pit and played and played.

The second well known teacher was the Shamash from the new synagogue, Elihum Zalman, a middle– aged Jew with a black beard. His Cheder was in a small street where Rubin Kuritzki lived, which also was next to a pit. There was not much difference between these two Cheders.

Both Shamashim had similar methods of teaching.

The third teacher was Rabbi Mendel, the Shamash from the Hasidic Shtibel (house of prayer); his Cheder was in a rather large room, in Asne Kuritzki's house.

I studied here for about 2 semesters, that is about a year.

The house was on Vidzer Street near the stream, and often in the summertime we went into the water to bathe.

The Rabbi had a cane which was braided from leather. When one was late he received several whacks from the cane.

Rabbi Mendel had his cane wrapped around his left hand, in the right hand he held a paddle made of wood, about 25 centimeters long.

[Col. 1551]

After ending 2 semesters at Rabbi Mendel's, I was sent to another teacher, a young man, who knew the whole Tenach from memory. They called him by his family name, Berl Matzkin.

I studied Chumash, the Prophets, grammar, arithmetic and other subjects from modern books. He told us current events and was considered a very progressive teacher.

His Cheder was on the street of Abraham Kuritzki. There were about 15 young boys studying with me, some were Abel, Patasnik, Katz and Perlis.

Every Thursday we had to recite everything we learned that week, this was a good method and we received a lot of praise. He was considered a good pedagogue among all the teachers. I studied 3 semesters with him and was very pleased.

My third Rebi was Meir Leib, an older Jew with a long white beard. He was a scholar and only took students versed in Gemara.

He didn't have a cane or a paddle. Instead he used his hand or fist and give us a whack in the face. This left a trace, a warning for the entire week.

Besides his teaching, his wife went to the market on Thursdays to barter. She bought eggs, and this day was like a holiday for us children. We could breathe easier or play in the garden and even run home to eat a warm meal.

We also have to remember the teacher Rabbi Shmuel Yitzhak Alsfein, he was considered a scholar and a genius. He taught Tenach and grammar to the older children. Besides being a teacher, he was also the Torah Reader in the New Synagogue.

When the Yiddish Folk Shul was founded he taught Hebrew to the students.

He was also murdered with the Jews of Haydutishok in Poligon.

Until the first world war, the former Shochet, Gershon Zak had a Talmud Torah in his house, where poor children studied, for the most part, orphans.

Every Friday a collection was made for the Talmud Torah.

At Israel Abramovitch's house there was a Cheder for Gemara students. He was very well–versed and only accepted the brightest students. He was very strict and conducted his students with a severe discipline.

[Col. 1552]

There were another 2 Cheders in Vidzer Street, at the Shochets, Gedalia and Meir, where the students had many breaks. The slaughterers had to go often to the slaughter–house and this gave the students a lot of free time to play or bath in the nearby stream.

In Haydutishok we also had a special teacher for girls, called Shneur, he taught arithmetic and Yiddish writing. He even went to the children's homes and gave private lessons. He didn't make much a living from this.

A year before the first world war in Haydutishok, the teacher Israel Abramson founded a different sort of Cheder, a reform–cheder. He was well educated and owned a business of shoes and boots. All of a sudden he decided to become a teacher. He rented a large and airy room, bought special tables and benches for children; hired teachers specializing in Russian, mathematics and geography and always dreamed of turning this Cheder into a modern Folk–Shul.

He considered himself a modern pedagogue and didn't allow the punishment of children by beating them. He either put the student in a corner or expelled them from the class.

The outbreak of World War One ended his dreams.

Besides the Melamdim we also had female teachers, I for example, studied Russian with Fania, who later married Yudel Fisher from Svir. She lives in Israel now.

A second teacher was Chaia–Sora, Soieyvitch, also the *monopoltchik's* (some business owner who had a monopoly, perhaps referring to Chaia–Sora) daughter.

The amount of Melamdim, teachers, male and female, shows us that Haydutishok had very high standards of education.

[Col. 1553]

There were rarely any illiterates in the shtetl. Everyone knew how to read and write.

Many of the Jews of Haydutishok considered themselves great scholars. In the Beit Midrashim, Torah and Gemara was studied day and day. Amongst these scholars we should mention the children of Mendel Gordon, now in Brazil. Leib Solomyak was also a scholar. No one remained from his family. His nephews live in Israel and in South Africa.

[Col. 1554]

We also have to mention Chaim Zerach Zar, Chloine Yosel's, Chloine Gurwich, Shloime Dovid, Yosef Chaim, Meir Kuritzki and Israel Abramovitch.

Before the First World War many young people left to study in the yeshivas, others went to study in Russian gymnasiums.

[Col. 1553]

Our Drama Club

Rafael Yaffe

Translated by Anita Frishman Gabbay

After the revolution of 1905, Haydutishok produced a progressive generation of young people. They founded a library which was a great source for Yiddish, Hebrew and Russian books. Lectures were held but their main energy was devoted to the drama club.

The first play, which was performed in 1910, was *Mekhiras Yosef*, "The Selling of Joseph". For months everyone practiced their roles. Then we were busy acquiring special clothing for the costumes, in Ruven Kuritzki's shed we prepared a special stage. Then we went to Sventian to get special permission from the authorities.

When all was ready, the Christian folk came to us with a warning and forbade us to proceed with the performance as the Jews wanted to desecrate the name of Jesus.

Nothing helped, even with our assurances, this was nothing more than a play!

A group of young people from the Folk–Shul

Zalman Abel, Michal Patasnik, Slava Tzernatzki, teacher Rozenfeld, Chaim Swirski, Mashe Fisher, Chana Feigelson, Sara Lunofski, teacher Filovski, Yosef Abramavitch, Rochel Tzernatzki, Liba Hochman, Etel Perevoznik, Gershon Sheitel

Then we called the priest to help out. He was an intelligent Christian and understood modern ways, it would be ridiculous not to allow the play to go on. He called some from his parish and they deleted several lines and took care of the police officer as well.

[Col. 1554]

The police watched over the play and the first performance was welcomed with great enthusiasm.

The drama club in Haydutishok, from that time forward, became famous throughout the region. Later we put on these plays: The Lottery (Sholem Aleichem), The Slaughter (Di Shkhita), The Trial Wedding, the Family, and others.

After the war, the drama club was founded by the Folk Shul. These plays were important sources of income for the school, otherwise the deficit of the 2 schools would never be never ending.

[Col. 1555]

The Jewish Folk Shul

Gershon Yaffe and Shneur Zalman Abel

Translated by Anita Frishman Gabbay

A Jewish Folk Shul was founded in Hauditishok in 1921, without the help of the central Yiddish school organization (T.I.S.H.O).

It was an exemplary school with high pedagogical standards and a good reputation in the region. Her first teachers were: Rozenfeld, Filofski, Aronovitch, Tzintzinatus, and a few locals, Yacov and Michla Kaplan.

The first administrator was the teacher Rozenfeld and later in 1931, the school administration was taken over by Yacov Kaplan.

The founder of the school in 1921 was the pharmacist Rubin, Pesach Volatzki, Peretz Yaffe, Shevakh Solomyak, Yeruchmiel Lubatzki, and Yitzhak Rudnitzki.

The directors of the school–committee in the last years were: Shevakh Solomyak, Gershon Yaffe, Abraham Yaffe and Ben–Zion Perevoznik.

This school had 6 classes (grades)–and boasted, a wonderful children's library with over 600 books. The first graduation was in 1926. Her graduates left for Vilna to further their studies in the *real–gymnasia* (University) and Teachers' Seminary.

When the school was founded in 1921 it stood on Vidzer Street, in the house of Shmuel Kuritzki. Later it relocated to Gurwich, then to Yitzhak Rudnitzki, and then to a Christian house on Sventzianer Street.

In 1936 the school received a warning, that if a suitable building is not found for the coming year, its status would be revoked.

This came from the Polish Ministry of Education. Everyone understood, the warning was serious, and the friends of the school decided to build a new building.

[Col. 1556]

They started to ask for donations.

A few thousand *zlotes* were donated by the T.I.S.H.O. The building cost was more than 30,000 *zlotes*, a sum to be paid by the shtetl's inhabitants.

The administration organized several fundraisers: recitals, plays, etc. and eventually raised enough money to erect a magnificent building on Tatarska Street.

In 1937, when they laid the first stone, a lively ceremony was organized, where all the important guests from surrounding shtetls came. Also the central school organization from Vilna, who sent two important delegates, school officials and speakers, our friends, Attorney Sternikov and Barontshuk. Also in attendance for this festive evening was the secretary of TISHO in Vilna, Fine.

Graduates, 1931

1st row: **Abraham Yafe, Gitel Fisher, Ben–Zion Perevoznik, Teacher Ida Fisher, Zalman Abel, Sara Abramovitch, Gershon Yaffe, Chana Perevoznik, Sheina Abel**
2nd row: **Gitel Patashnik, Chana Patashnik, Ester Perevoznik, teacher Feiga Shapira**
3rd row: **Slova Tzernatzki, Miriam Patashnik**

The building of the Jewish Folk–Shul

[Col. 1557]

All the participants greeted and addressed the school–committee of Haydutishok to thank them for their help to build the Jewish school.

[Col. 1558]

In 1938, a year later, the Jewish folk of Haydutishok had the fortunate opportunity to prepare the dedication of the building.

In those days everyone was proud of this achievement and conducted themselves in the same manner as preparing for a holiday, they walked around with their heads held high, full of pride for their shtetl.

Later it was not easy to maintain—it had one year of glory in its own building. After so many problems, tireless work and devoted efforts, the Jewish children studied here only one year.

In 1939 with the outbreak of World War Two, the entire cultural life of the shtetl was ruined, and in the front line, of course, was the school.

Who could have imagined in 1938 that our lives would be destroyed, everything will be lost in flames and in blood!

Yiddish Folk–Shul

1st row: **Steinhard Abraham, Marmur Fruma, Patashnik Israel, Marmur Hirsh, Matzkin Chana, Katz Shietke, Abramovitch Sheina, Yocelman Pesach, Matzkin Liba,—,Faives, Rudnitzki Yona, Groman Itze**
2nd row: **Chaikin Shifra, Rudnitzki Miriam, Charmatz Gershon, Feigelson Fraida, techer Berensteyn, teacher Soleiveitchik, Yocelman Abraham, Oistreich Matla, Perevoznik Yudel, Gordon Abraham Bina, Strikovski Mendel**
3rd row: **Pomerantz Heikel, Abramovitch Shapiro Sholem, Marmur Merel, Barensteyn Moishe, Feigelson Lipa, Polikanski Rochel, Amdurski Elka, Feigelson Masha, Yocelman Leizer, Matzkin Reizel**

[Col. 1559]

The Big Fire

Nachum Kuritzki

Translated by Anita Frishman Gabbay

I was born in Haydutishok in 1875.

Until today I remember the big fire in our shtetl in 1880, when I was 5 years old.

The blaze was so strong that I will never forget it.

It was a Saturday evening, somewhere a wedding was taking place, I was asleep when I heard the commotion and screaming: Alert! Alert! Fire!

My mother quickly ran in and dressed me and took me out into the street.

The picture, that was in front of me, as I said, I cannot forget until today.

Our neighbour's house was on fire, Zalman Raske's (or Roskes). My mother brought me to my grandfather, who lived in a far– away street.

In that fire almost the entire Vidzer street burned, as far as the bridge.

I remember more details from the second fire.

I was 11 years old, as it was in 1886.

At the time in Haydutishok, there was a Jew who we called Chloine, the *kvetcher* (complainer). The origin of this name I don't know.

It was a hot Shabbos afternoon, his son went into the attic, like the custom, to catch a Shabbos *drem* (nap).

At the same time, at the neighbours house, in the attic, there were 2 young girls napping, which had a small window facing the street. When they got up from their nap, they saw through the window Chloine's house in flames.

[Col. 1560]

The flames were spreading to their roof and everyone was yelling to them to jump out of the window. One of the girls jumped down and injured herself. The second was burnt alive.

That Saturday afternoon, more than half the shtetl burned down. The flames in several hours engulfed over 300 houses, most of them, Jewish homes.

It was fortunate, that there was a brick building that belonged to Yosel Leibl's (could be mistaken for Lavin), they managed to extinguish the fire here and only a small part of the building was gone.

From that fire I can remember an interesting episode: A Jewish tavern owner lived in Gaydishok. When he saw from a distance that a fire broke out in Haydutishok, he came running to rescue. His wife and children saw and also came running. They knew many of the townsfolk and also gave help to the affected townsfolk. They were carrying furniture from the homes, then they were carrying water.

No one from the tavern owner's family noticed the flames were reaching Gaydishok, and there houses were also burning like in the center of our shtetl.

[Col. 1561]

When the fire was completely out, and nighttime arrived, they left for their home and realized their home disappeared. Not one item of theirs was saved. The main tragedy was, the tavern owner had invited some of the homeless to stay with him, until God will provide and they can rebuild. It is difficult to understand, how the homeless felt when they arrived to Gaydishok, seeing that the tavern owner's fate is worse than theirs. The family stood on the spot and the homeless had to help them.

[Col. 1562]

I remember my mother giving me two cushions to bring to the tavern owner.

After that fire, a fire–brigade was founded in Haydutishok. Straw roofs were no longer allowed. All the people rebuilt. Such large fires no longer occurred.

[Col. 1561]

Simple, Good–Hearted and Unforgettable Jews From Haydutciski

A page of memories of Jewish Haydutishok

Israel Witzentovski, Australia

Translated by Anita Frishman Gabbay

I wandered through many shtetls and shtetelechs during the panic and confusion created, at the end of 1939, when masses of refugees from occupied Poland ran across borders in search of a home, feeling the thunder under their feet. All the roads were flooded with refugees, full of fear in their eyes. One another asked themselves: "where? And who will welcome us and put a roof over our heads? And what about work?"

The storm took me through unfamiliar towns and roads further and further away. Winter arrived, harsh, with bitter frosts and snowstorms. I barely made it to Lintup, where I arrived one evening. An angry February wind blew through the streets, unfamiliar surroundings greeted me and I didn't know where to go. Together with another Jew, Ben–Zion Apter, a Braslav Chasid and also a refugee, we entered the Beit Hamidrash.

It was after Maariv and the assembled were in deep conversation. They received us in a friendly manner and asked where we came from. Ben–Zion's hands were swollen from cold and hunger, someone brought food and hot coffee. But to invite us home to sleep, no one spoke! They were all afraid of the news brought by the unwelcome guests.

The entire night we slept on the bench in the Beit Hamidrash. In the morning Jewish gendarmes arrived and with anger they sent us to the train transport, which was arranged to take us in an unknown direction.

[Col. 1562]

Someone said we were going to Donbas, in the coal mines. Others said to Siberia. I didn't have the desire to go to any of these place so I got off at the next station. This was Haydutishok.

In the evening, an unknown, cold world! The frost was eating through my bones and my stomach was growling from hunger. I looked at the houses, standing low and covered in fresh snow, appearing worn out from generations of use. "Which door should I knock on? Will I receive the same welcome as in Lintup? and from the other towns? will my fear deter me because of my earlier unpleasant welcome, will they close their doors on me again?"

It seemed to me that I heard an old nigun floating over the roof–tops in that frosty and lonely evening, it reminded me of praying so I went to the Beit Hamidrash.

The warm and wonderful eyes looked at me, they made a circle around me, questioning me with warmth and trust.

Soon a Jew approached me and told me he was the representative of the shtetl. The eyes underneath his brows looked over my clothing and quietly said:

[Col. 1563]

"You are in torn clothing and surely you must be exhausted. My idea, is that you rest now. We will provide you with a job, a house and you will return to your former self. Later you will decide what you will do."

"Yes, but in the meantime, what do I do?"

"We will soon see."

He brought me to a Jew called Kuritzki, and they sat me at a table and fed me a warm meal.

After I ate I took my coat and wanted to return to the Beit Mamidrash, where I imagined I would spend the night. The wife of Kuritzki said in bewilderment: "why are you leaving? and where to?"

"I don't want to disrespect you, but I am a stranger!"

"Why are you speaking like this? You are amongst your own kind, among Jews! You will not go out into this cold!"

She prepared warm water and the first time in months I washed and slept in a clean bed.

The next morning I left for the Beit Mamidrash with Kuritzki and after davening he invited me back to his home for breakfast. A neighbour came in and asked "from where I came?" When he heard I was from Warsaw, he told me he had a son in Warsaw, Henoch Todres, who worked in the scientific institute. We soon discovered that Henoch was a good friend of mine, and this Jew was so pleased to receive this firsthand news about his son.

The Jew didn't leave my side, he went with me like a long lost relative, took me to Josef Gordon, an 80 year old butcher, with a long beard, who lived with his wife in a welcoming home. There were no children and they gave me my own house (could be room), and welcomed me as their own child.

I remained in Haydutishok for a few years, worked and bartered, and earned enough for food. But Shabbos I was required to eat at the same table as the old married couple. The warmth and welcome radiated from them.

I told them over and over again the same stories about Jews all over the world and felt their great love they carried deep in their hearts for all their fellow Jews. I had met them by some miracle in the course of that week. When I spoke he was so enthralled, he felt he was living each of my stories.

[Col. 1564]

A meeting in 1938 of the Yiddish Folk–Shul

Right to left: **Israel Katzenellenbogen, Yitzhak Rudnitzki, Yudel Volotzki, Ben–Zion Perevoznik, Yitzhak Yofe, Berl Smidt, Gershon Yofe, Abraham Yofe, Michal Patasnik, Berta the teacher, Bialer the teacher**

I closely observed the way the Jews of Haydutishok lived. They welcomed many refugees, worn out, broken and in rags, but they received them with open arms in a true spirit of friendship and brotherhood. Like their own relatives!

They refugees were homeless and lost, and could not believe the kindness and warmth of the Jews of Haydutishok. They felt so at ease they didn't want to continue further.

Even the young people, the Kommosol– affiliated, closed their eyes to the severe communist rules and helped them receive a document, a paper, that permits the refugee to work like a free person in order to earn a living.

[Col. 1565]

I remember one late winter night, when the shutters of the homes were locked, through a crack in the shutter and only a speck of a red light shone through, Katzkel Becker was rushing through the quiet streets. Quietly he knocked on the shutters, he was collecting money for a refugee who was arrested. He was engaged in an illegal trade, so he, Katzkel Becker, put up most of the money and when he was released he brought him to his home, fed him, boarded him until he got back on his feet.

Students of the Tarbut School, 1931

Shloime Yochelman, —Yehudit Yocelman, Rishke Abel, Batia Abel, Yehudit Zeiger, Avraham Bina Gordon,—,Shloime Lifshitz, —,Taibe Katz,Ruben Ginzberg, Chaim Disner, —, teacher,—,Itzhak Perlis, Chaim Leib Hochman, Israel Patasnik, Avraham Lipa Shapira, Shmuel Yitzhak Alfsfein, Leib Lapida, Sholem Shapira, Israel Lubotzki, Chaim Yocelman, Beila Abel, —,—,—,—,Shalom Yofe, Nechama Zeiger, —,—,––,Litl Lapida, —,—,Avraham Patasnik, Pesia Gerstein, Ahron Mashitz, Meir Konfar, Shapira, Gitl Yofe, Chana Mashitz, Henia Yocelman

"Where are you, my dear brothers from Haydutishok? I see you constantly before my eyes, I hear your voices and feel the pride of your Jewish words!"

I see myself at your Shabbat table that glowed with so many Jewish candles, its glow was so holy and pure, those times were bittersweet, "more sweet", if I dare say so! My blood is boiling with your memories!

[Col. 1566]

During all my wanderings, through all the hardships of seeing the destroyed shtetls, in times of fear and pain, the echo of your words greeted and calmed me. I will never forget your deeds of brotherly love and all that you did for me.

I know, I will no longer see you, you were tortured and murdered and thrown into the mass graves of Ponar and Poligon, but forever, until the end of my days I will carry your spirit inside my heart as my memorial for your welcoming Jews which I encountered during my difficult wander–years.

[Col. 1567]

Dzhikevines, a Settlement of Jewish Farmers

Henoch Drutz

Translated by Anita Frishman Gabbay

Dzhikevines was a little hamlet, no more than 3 kilometers from Haydutishok. In between there was another little hamlet, Stortzun. A Russian saying goes: small, but smart. This describes Dzhikevines–small, beautiful, friendly and intimate.

Fields and forests, streams and valleys, surrounded this hamlet. In the summertime, the 20 families traded in fruit, vegetables, pigs, wheat, corn, oats, cherries, peas and most important, flax. These were very plentiful here. The land was soaked with “milk and honey”.

Not more than 20 families lived here, 5 of them Jewish. These Jews were actually peasants, they worked the land. Each family owned a 10–Dusiat, about 110 Dunas of land. They all earned a living mainly from the flax–which grows like thin sticks and doesn't need to be cut, just torn with its roots, dried thoroughly and then beat to release the seeds.

[Col. 1568]

The seeds served a double purpose. Part was left as seeds and the rest made wonderful oil. The dried sticks of flax were tied into bundles and were shipped to the textile mills. Besides the flax industry, the lush fields produced an abundance of other produce: corn, wheat, and all kinds of grains.

Around each house, the peasant had his own yard filled with fruit trees. Besides this, each family owned a shed, a few cows, hens and geese.

In the winter, when there was no work in the fields, the peasants, Jews and Christians, occupied themselves with the “Voske”. They drove to the train station bringing assorted goods back and forth.(transportation or trade). From the Jewish families in Dzhikevines, 2 brothers became very well known in this trade in the region: Chaim and Hirshe Tchernatsky. They had 2 large and intermarried families: Chaim had 4 sons and 5 daughters; Hirshe, 5 sons and 2 daughters.

[Col. 1569]

Rabbi Chaim's house was quite impressive and had its own synagogue. All year round the Jews prayed here on Saturdays and holidays. Only for Rosh Hashana and Yom Kippur, the Jews went to Haydutishok where they prayed in the old synagogue. For the small children they hired a Melamud (teacher) who was also the Torah Reader. The older children drove or went by foot to Haydutishok where they studied in various cheders. The Dzhikevines Jews were famous in and around Haydutishok for their warm hearts and their open hands. Every Thursday they arrived in the shtetl to sell their produce and to buy housewares, cloth and trimmings, and baking goods. It was also an occasion to buy fresh bagels at Rabbi Shneur Kuritzki's bakery for the children.

Nighttime, when the market ended, when the Dzhikevines' Jews barely had enough time to harness their horses, the poor Haydutishoker Jews would gather around them. They knew for sure that these Jewish peasants would give them some alms(money for the needy).

On this site and in the courtyard of the old synagogue, the poor people came to beg and also use the facilities of the synagogue for shelter.

Every traveller or student, passing through Haydutishok, knew that the nearby settlement were good Jews and heeded the commandment of Feeding the Needy.

On the way to Dzhikevines, you could always see people travelling in that direction. It wasn't only on Saturdays that you found a Dzhikevines Jew eating with a poor man at his table. Relations between the Christian and Jewish peasants were very friendly. The Jews thanked God that they were brought here and were blessed with good health and good fortune. This was the way they lived, until one time a tragedy struck at Rabbi Chaim's home. Like I mentioned, he had 5 daughters and 4 sons. The oldest was Zlata and the youngest, Sarah.

When it was time for marriage, Zlata, was to have a large wedding at her home. Many guests were expected to arrive from the whole region. The groom's family was also large.

[Col. 1570]

A month before the wedding there was much turmoil in the shtetl. Baila, Rabbi Chaim's wife, was known as excellent housekeeper and organizer. Her cooking and baking were works of art. Baila, at last, was marrying her eldest daughter, and there was no rest day and night. She wanted to present her daughter with a grandiose wedding, to be remembered by all children and their children. Baila fried “tagelach” (small pieces of dough), cooked, baked tortes and lekach (sweet cakes), made her own wine from apples. She was so happy that she was able to prepare such a feast “fit for a king” (pooh, pooh)[against the evil eye]. There was no doubt that this was such a beautiful wedding for Chaim of Dzhikevines. The Chuppah (ceremony) was scheduled on a Tuesday in the evening. It was a cold and rainy spring. Sunday was a downpour. Baila didn't pay attention to this. She ran from neighbour to neighbour, house to house, she trudged through the muddy fields, God forbid anything should go wrong before the wedding! Baila caught a very bad cold. Monday in the morning she came down with a very high fever. A doctor arrived immediately from Haydutishok, who diagnosed her with a lung infection.

No special remedies were available in those days. Baila suffered all of Monday and in the evening got worse. In the middle of the night she died, exactly before the wedding.

Difficult, very difficult to see this! There were no telephones. They didn't know how to reach the in–laws, to tell them not to come.

Very early in the morning, some friends went to the Rabbi in Haydutishok to ask his advice. He told them to postpone the wedding by a week until the bride gets up from sitting Shiva (mourning the dead).

Instead of preparing for a wedding and to greet the groom, they had to prepare for a funeral. All the peasants, Jews and Christians, harnessed their horses to bid farewell to this good and righteous Baila.

[Col. 1571]

At the cemetery, the wailing and screaming of the 9 children could be heard in the entire region. On the way to the funeral they were met by the in–laws, who knew nothing and could not understand such a tragedy–a few of their wagons were approaching the funeral with music and dancing.

[Col. 1573]

Stayatishok

(Stajetiškė, Lithuania)

55°11'/26°31'

Rachel Gan–Tov (Gantovnik) Voliak, Hadera

Translated by Anita Frishman Gabbay

Stayatishok! I want to sing my praise for you, in the same time I want to cry for you! I want to remember you forever! Your memory should never be forgotten! People should read these few pages and know, that there was a Yiddish shtetl where Yiddish peasants existed (they were farmers) and took pride in their work, just like the Christian peasants who were in our shtetl. But now, no one is left!

Stayatishok, I haven't seen you in so many years. Your economic situation was not very good, your women toiled day and night, not to clothe their own families, but for others. Your cows were so thin, and very little milk was produced. The fields were laboured so primitively and yielded little.

[Col. 1574]

In those difficult years my grandfather told us they called us "Yeshuvniks" (people who worked the land). They (the Jewish folk) were ashamed of us. We worked hard and were barely able to support our families. We were always envious of the "city" folk, who earned their "bread" with greater success.

I saw you, Stayatishok, for the first time, as it appeared to me, you were a large and beautiful flowering garden!

Your fields overflow with abundance, your cows produce a lot of milk. The gardens are full of different plants, your barns and sheds, at the end of the summer, are filled with all kinds of fruit and grains. Your women weave and spin for themselves, and not for others. Your children were clothed and the walls of your homes are covered with beautiful woven tapestries.

I remember, as if it were today, when I arrived at my grandfather's house as a guest. It was in the 1930s. I bent over to have a small conversation with Rabbi Nechama, one of the farmers. Stayatishok, he said, is our America today, the only thing missing, is the education of larger cities and that Jewish children must attend the Gymnasium (schools of higher learning) elsewhere.

I then thought, I would like to change places with them!. If only I could go to the Gymnasium in Sventzian for a few days with my friends, Yentka, Hinda, Ruchel, and attend lectures in mathematics and physics: sit in on Dr. Kovarski's Latin lectures, to learn Caesar and Avidush(?) by heart. If only I could wear that white headscarf and go to the fields to cut corn!

Shmuel Voliak with his family

[Col. 1575]

The stream in the middle of the shtetl

If only: I would drink cold water from the stream and eat black bread and jam with a full appetite. In the evenings, I would strut around bragging how much pleasure this gave me and I was looking forward to sleeping in a barn on fresh hay!

Seven summers I saw you, my dear Stayatishok, and I can never forget you! Forever you shall remain in my memory, I will always love you!

I loved your warm homes with those straw roofs! I loved your hills and valleys, your fields and meadows with flowers that grew like tall sticks, your barns filled with freshly plowed and stacked hay.

I loved your children that ran around barefoot in the summertime, and with much heartache, I remember you, Dear Children!

I close my eyes for awhile, and I can still see you, running to swim in the river at night! Dinahla, Yosela, Lipkes' and Shepsels' 6 children, Baruch, Itzele's Zamele, and Esterke!

And more and more...I didn't forget anyone! I remember you once more: how you were running to gather the flowers in the fields while you were singing and dancing, these are my countless memories of us and I still cannot believe, you are no longer with us!

I cannot allow myself to believe that your fate was so unthinkable!

My heart aches for you, that you could not survive to live in our land (Eretz Israel)! If your parents would have understood, their homes were built on foreign soil, this calamity might not have happened. As every tree that they planted did not belong to them, it could be ripped from its roots at any moment! They didn't understand, the same as other Jews from much larger shtetls, our Destiny would be such. Stayatishok Jews, plain and honest Jews!

[Col. 1576]

You didn't bargain, you didn't fool around, you didn't cheat anyone! You were so dear to me and how I understood you!

Even till today, you are etched in my Memory together with the last Rosh Hashana of 1941. I can still hear the wailing and the praying from the women's' section. Did you not pray hard enough to God to avoid this horrible fate? Your requests were so simple (God in Heaven!!)

"I don't want your money, I don't need beautiful clothing and expensive trinkets, just let me remain in my little hut with my husband and small children!"

The melody (nigun) from the Torah reader was beautiful and full of enthusiasm!

This is how we said our good–byes to you, Stayatishok, for the very last time, the last Rosh Hashana, and the next day, Friday Shabat T'Shuva, we left you forever!

The fire burnt brightly (Rebeccala warmed her small body and slept for awhile) [her daughter]. Everyone sat deep into the night, enmeshed in their troubles. Stayatishok, Stayatishok, I thought! Remain strong! I am saying good–bye to you forever!

[Col. 1577]

The Yiddish Town on the River Suwalki

Israel Gan–Tov (Gantovnick)

Translated by Anita Frishman Gabbay

Stayatishok was a small Jewish shtetl, several kilometers from Haydutishok in the Sventzian region, Vilna Province. It was surrounded on all sides by high mountains, fields and lakes and all the surrounding residents benefited from the beauty and the sweet smelling flowers. Through the shtetl a small river ran through the middle called "Suwalki".

The story of this small shtetl is very interesting. In 1863, when it is still a Polish town, Czar Nicholas declared a manifesto in which he told all the poor peasants to divide the land amongst themselves, which he confiscated from the wealthy folk.

Stayatishok was a noble estate then, which belonged to a Polish nobleman. The Czarist regime confiscated this estate and invited the Jews to settle here. They each received 11 hectares of land, and in a short while, in 1865, 30 Jewish families established themselves here.

The lives of our grandfathers in those early years were quite difficult. The machinery for agriculture was very primitive. Wooden tools and ploughs were used, the production yield was poor, so they barely made a living.

[Col. 1578]

Many men from the shtetl, as well as women, went to work in neighbouring villages, especially in Haydutishok. This is how the shtetl developed.

Slowly, our livelihood improved. We raised cows and horses. We had our own vegetables, eggs, milk, and potatoes. On a day off work we went to the train station in Haydutishok to earn a few rubles and in this way our daily lived started to improve.

Erev Yom Kippur, 1915, the German army arrived in our town. Right away we knew that the German–Russian front was only 1 kilometer away from Stayatishok. The Germans confiscated our Jewish cows and horses in the first days of the war. Soon afterwards they took away all the produce and left the peasants in hunger and poverty. All men, 14 and over, were taken away for forced labour. The sweat (hard work) of those previous years were lost. Stayatishok was destroyed and barely survived.

In 1917, the Russian Revolution broke out. Many battles were fought between the Russians and Germans, between the Polaks and the Bolsheviks, between the Polaks and the Lithuanians and all this ruined our economic situation. Many homes were burnt and in some more years later, even the land was difficult to cultivate.

[Col. 1579]

1929 the Stayatishok land workers

First in 1920, when it was clear, that Stayatishok was under Polish regime, the peasants started another revolt. A few years later, new homes were built and rebuilding anew in Stayatichok began. Many families who left during the famine started to return.

In 1925, the economic situation for the Jews began to improve. The fields produced a healthy crop, a new generation of young people appeared and they helped out the older generation. Many peasants began to trade in flax, oats, hay, eggs and milk products. One person also built a mill. Life was normal again, and the same was for all the other shtetls.

[Col. 1580]

Slowly this little shtetl developed its Jewish cultural identity. There was a modern Cheder(school) with a good teacher, although some children went to the Tarbut School in Haydutishok. Several boys and girls also studied in the Sventzian Gymnasium (also, a school).

The youth started to feel the unrest brewing. One realized that studying was not the only answer. We all started to dream of going to Eretz Israel. Even in this small shtetl, a branch of "Halutz" was founded. There were about 25 men and women. One must note that almost the entire shtetl was Zionist, they all dreamed of working the land in Eretz Israel for their own benefit, not for the Polish state.

A Gemilut Hesed Bank was founded (help for the needy) in order to provide loans when the harvest was bad and when the peasants needed some means to survive. We provided many opportunities for a Jewish existence in the shtetl.

[Col. 1581]

1936 The Haydutishoker Rabbi Elhanan Mashitz carrying the Sefer Torah, Left from him is the son in law, the old Vileiker Rabbi (celebration for the writing of the Sefer Torah)

Chaim Gantovnik and his family

[Col. 1582]

We also had a beautiful synagogue, where Jews prayed and also studied the Gemara, from morning to evening. Until today, it is difficult to understand how Jewish peasants, after a hard days work, could come to the synagogue and study.

These Jewish peasants were very devoted Jews.

In our shtetl there was a neighbour who also took the role of Rabbi. He was also a great leader. The older Rabbi was religious, the younger one had a more conservative approach. All together they lived an honest Jewish life in this shtetl. Until the outbreak of World War II, Sept. 1939....

R'Chaim Gantovnik

R'Chaim Gantovnik was born in Stayatichok in 1873 and all his life he worked in this shtetl. He was used to hard work and for many years he was active in the Gemilut Hesed Bank, with which he helped many needy get back on their feet. He played an active role in the synagogue as well.

He was a quiet man, never angry with anyone, never insulted anyone. He was loved by all the people in our Jewish shtetl. He and his wife Baila and son Eliahu were murdered on Kislev 1942, in the Postov Ghetto.

[Col. 1583]

Maligan on the Mountain and in the Valley

(Mielagėnai, Lithuania)

55°15'/26°26'

Gershon Braslavski

Translated by Anita Frishman Gabbay

Maligan was in the district of Sventzian, Vidz and Haudutishok, and was surrounded by thick forests. Half of the shtetl was on a mountain, the other half in the valley, through which flowed a small stream into a larger lake.

As the area lent itself to great abundance of produce from the land, many folk made a living as Jewish farmers.

The Jewish families were about 25 in total. The Jewish folk were shopkeepers, farmers and craftsmen. Most important the Maliganers were known for their blacksmiths and tinsmen.

Maligan was 20 kilometers from Sventzian, and 14 kilometers from Haudutishok: the only communication for many years was a wagon and a horse. Shortly befor WW11, a passenger–auto was the means of transportation between Sventzian and Vilna.

Besides this, many folk used the train station in Haudutishok, 14 kilometers away.

Besides Jews, Lithuanians Russians and Polaks also lived in Maligan. Prior to WW11, the situation between the Jews and the rest of the population was very friendly, and no one had the foresight that some would turn into bandits, hooligans and robbers.

Young Jewish folk from Maligan taking a trip on the river

[Col. 1584]

A group of young Jewish folk during an outing in 1937

[Col. 1585]

The Jewish children went to Cheder and Yeshivas like in all the other shtetls. In later years the children went to study in Sventzian and Haudutishok.

[Col. 1586]

A smaller portion of the children went to the Polish "Povshne" school.

The older generation was religious and followed all the religious traditions. Everyone seemed to be in a good economic situation.

Children–young and old during a Zionist evening in Maligan

In Honor of My Shtetl

Boruch Gontovnick, Montreal

Translated by Anita Frishman Gabbay

In a valley, between flowing rivers,
I was brought up,
By a father who not very rich,
But a righteous peasant, standing before my eyes!

I felt very at home there,
With my friends and beloved ones,
We played together,
In the shtetl, this little one!

Green fields, covered with flowers,
From forests to rivers–such a pleasant aroma,
Around and about, everything smelled,
Of our endurance of hard work, with courage and honor.

[Col. 1586]

Jewish peasants, with long beards,
Plowed and seeded their fields,
With the knowledge, to work their land,
Their sweat would bring forth an appetite–to eat black corn bread.

Healthy Jews, with callouses on their hands
Went to the meadows with their baskets,
With a joyful "nigun" they cut and shook the grain,
Working hard, they were not ashamed!

The huts were covered in straw,
The fields spilled over with abundance,
Our fathers seeded these fields,
With barley and oats and peas and beans.

The houses, with balconies, covered in moss,
We ran barefoot as children in the gardens,
For many years we carried this heavy burden,
And that is how our mothers lived.

[Col. 1586]

Postov

(Pastavy, Belarus)

55°07'/26°50'

Translation by Anita Frishman Gabbay

Postov, Vidz, Mior, Kazian, Kobylnik

These small shtetls are often mentioned in their regards to their daily lives and destruction of the Jews of Sventzian and Haydutishok, the folk from Vidz, Mior, Kaltinian, Kazian, and Postov were so closely knit and intertwined, and thanks to the YEKAPO book we can detail their daily lives and desperate times. We are also able to present detailed information how they were slaughtered and disposed of in the mass graves of Poligon, Ponar fields and forests and other places near their shtetlach.

*The murdered body of Yitzhak Yavnovitch of Kobylnik was thrown into Lake Narach, believing his Christian friend was helping him escape. This is his memorial (uncle of Anita Frishman Gabbay), son of Shlomo Yavnovitch and Raitza Gilinski Yavnovitch of Kobylnik.

[Col. 1587]

The total population of this shtetl was about 3000 people. The Jews were about a third of the total, barely 1000 in total.

Like in all the other shtetls in the area the way of life for the Jews was similar: shopkeepers, small merchants and warehousing. In the last years, life was very difficult.

Two Christian cooperatives opened: the first one, Polish and the second one, White–Russian. They both created a lot of trouble and a difficult economic situation for the Jewish population.

The Polish cooperative was called “Vigoda”.It was supported by the state and the bank “Gospodortkva Kravienga” . It occupied a beautiful brick building right in the middle of the town, on the “High market” place, it sold all types of groceries, clothing materials and trimmings for manufacture and dressmaking, shoemaking and leather goods. In the last years (before World War 11) they also included iron and building materials and equipment used in agriculture.

In order to sell this machinery, the cooperative brought a technician from Vilna in order to teach the peasants how to use this equipment. This alone brought a lot of people to this cooperative.

As this Polish cooperative "Vigoda" was affiliated with the rich "Peoples Bank", they gave the people very cheap prices and very favorable credit and repayment loans. It is no wonder that this created a bad situation for us (the Jews).

[Col. 1588]

Both cooperatives badly undercut the profits of the Jewish shopkeepers. After awhile, they found two wealthy Jews to sell machinery and from this were also able to make a good living.

They (the Jews) were completely ruined. Traditionally, the phosphate industry was mainly in Jewish hands. This went into the hands of the cooperatives and the officials of the province endorsed it.

The Christian folk were advised to buy only in the cooperatives. A strong order came from the state officials to buy in the cooperative: Vigoda:, and the official gave the cooperative a guarantee that their loan would BE repaid and the workers wages would be deducted from the loan. With this help from the state–officials, the cooperative also increased its appeal to other buyers.

The only Jewish shopkeepers left were the wealthier ones, which were also known as "lazy" or slow payers. The state did not want to give them any guarantees. The Jewish stores undertook to purchase various goods, and at higher prices and now were not able to repay. When these Jewish shopkeepers tried to repay their debt, they found themselves in a more difficult financial situation. Not only was the Polish cooperative their competition, but also the White–Russian.

[Col. 1589]

The White–Russian (Belarusian) cooperatives attracted their own people from all over the area. They also decided to open branches in all the other Postov districts. In the shtetl there were many Christian shops and manufacturing warehouses. There was great loyalty amongst the Christian folk to buy from their own for patriotic reasons.

The lives of the Christian shopkeepers were still better than those of the Jewish ones. This was not their sole livelihood, they also owned plots of land and made a very good amount of money from agriculture. Their stores were run by their wives and children.

The shtetl market took place once a week, on Mondays. The shopkeepers brought small amounts of goods, and strangers arrived on this day, and they brought the prices down(they brought cheaper quality goods). In Postov the flax and cattle industry became smaller, so the small merchants bought their merchandise from the larger merchants in Glubboke and Haydusishok, so their profits were very small.

Because of this, the trades became less important.

Our shopkeepers, because of this situation, start selling other items:

like pig–hair, fur pelts, and goats, and other things, but It didn't help the economic situation.

[Col. 1590]

What is happened to the shopkeepers, was not better for the (handworkers) tailors and shoemakers. The shoemakers were also in difficulty: they mainly repaired shoes. What's interesting, that all the Jews who worked for the state, were let go, so we had to endure the hardships imposed by the "Svoida–Svenga".(state run retail shop)

As a result, one wonders, why Postov became completely destroyed during the first world war, everything had to be rebuilt. This was our fate, and no one in the shtetl had other options. Without capital(money) there was no way for the shopkeepers and handworkers to compete against the cooperatives and other Christian shops. This created great poverty in our shtetl and thus created "Bread for the Needy." They received bread and wood. A small sum maintained about 35 families....

Others receive funds from America and in this manner they managed to survive.

From the YEKAPO register, 1931, Pinchas of Vilna

[Col. 1590]

Vidz

(Vidzy, Belarus)

55°24'/26°38'

Translation by Anita Frishman Gabbay

A shtetl of about 450 families, 230 of which were Jewish. More than fifty percent were shopkeepers. There were at least 120 Jewish shops. The rest of the Jews were small merchants and workers. Life was difficult. Market day was every Tuesday. Other shopkeepers arrived from surrounding shtetlach and sold their goods at cheaper prices.

Two Christian cooperatives opened, and the Jews eventually became their clients. These cooperatives sold for cheap credit and had their own bank. They were backed by the town and the state. They also paid almost no taxes. Many of the Jewish stores were liquidated and they were ruined. They lost everything, but still had to pay taxes. What were the remaining 60 merchants in our shtetl that remained to do? So they begin processing, they buy flax and grains, and then sell to the small shops, but their profits are small, putting more duress on the townspeople.

[Col. 1591]

The peasants don't feel the need to work any longer, as the flax industry changes. The cooperatives buy the raw material and send it for processing to Poznan. This ruined the flax trade for the Jewish flax merchants, eventually the entire industry was in Christian hands. Jews can no longer compete. The Jewish processors who are self financed, cannot sit by and watch their livelihood go into the hands of the rich cooperative who by any measures is taking over this trade and is controlling it with their own central committee. The cooperative is very successful, as it is linked directly with the flax–central of the region. Also the seed merchants are faced with a similar competition.

[Col. 1592]

A cooperative from Braslav comes to our shtetl on market days and buys the entire crop. As they own their own ale–factory(brewery), they can afford to pay higher prices and this puts our industry at risk. All of these things put our livelihood at risk, these trades that were for so many years in Jewish hands.

The handworkers suffered in the same manner. Larger cities were providing merchandise, therefore our handworkers lived in poverty.

Something interesting happened in our shtetl. Some wealthy family came to collect money to provide for such a family, who had many children, and couldn't afford to buy wood for the winter months. We later found out that this was the well known tailor's family, who couldn't afford to buy bread for his family.

In Vidz there were also many Jewish transports (waggoneers) that brought the merchandise from the railroad station in Dukst to Vidz, a distance of 27 kilometers. Now, lesser amounts of merchandise were brought and we lost our profits.

YEKAPO 1931 register, Pinchas of Lita

The Beginning of the Problems

by Shlomo Ichiltchik

Translation by Anita Frishman Gabbay

A week of worrying and fright in our shtetl Vidz passed before the German army arrived in 1941. We endured the sinister actions of the Poles, White–Russians, Lithuanians and Russians. In June 1941 they rounded up 200 Jews from Vidz and took them to the Maroger Lake, 2 kilometers from Vidz, on the way to Dukst and there they slaughtered them.

In this manner, small groups were taken away, on the pretext that they were going to take them to work, and there they were murdered. This terror continued until November 1941. When the German regime arrived, at first they did not feel the need for a large ghetto in Vidz, just to rearrange the people, from:

Braslav, Ofsa, and Glubokie. In Vidz, about 200 "useful" Jews remained, and in the spring of 1942, the Germans enlarged the Vidz Ghetto with 2000 people: they were brought from Droisk, Duvina, Kazian, Ofsa and others. The healthy ones were selected and sent to different work camps: like Dukst, Podbrodz, Ingalina, New Sventzian and others. At the end of 1942 the Vidz ghetto was liquidated and they were all sent to Sventzian. Only 50 Jews remained (in Vidz). Before the liquidation of the Vidz ghetto a group of young people organized themselves: Zelman Zilber, Noach Swirski, Leah Swirski, Yitzhak Ginsberg, Hiena Kuritzki and others.

[Col. 1593]

With courage and revenge! They left for the Kazian forests, where they joined the Partisans and started their fight against the Christians, who were helping the Germans, burnt their home and warehouses, tore down telephone communications and attacked German garrisons.

In 1942 I was sent to Glubokie, with other Jews, to work in a spinning mill. I lived there for some time and from there escaped to Vidz. Staying in Vidz for a short while, I was sent to work in New Sventzian. I worked on the railroad in New Sventzian.

The Liquidation

I found out from a Jewish policeman that came to liquidate the Sventzian ghetto, that Vilna and Kovno was next on the list. Wagons were being prepared for transport, I then decided not to get into the wagon, to remain on foot. With me was Zvi Beliak from Braslav. We then crept into a small unseen corner of a wagon and remained there until we arrived in Vilna, not seen. We met in Vilna a railroad worker who told us that they were taking everyone to Ponar, instead of Kovno. Now we had to make a plan to escape, but we were seen by a Jewish policeman, and brought in a wagon where we met Gens and Dessler.

Gens sat awkwardly, his hands behind his bent head. Seeing me with Zvi Beliak, he started screaming at us: How did you get here? And I answered: Don't scream, we know everything that is happening here...you sent some of our friends in the police wagon into the Vilna Ghetto". Six of our friends were detained, which Zvi and myself rescued from New Sventzian by tearing off the tarps from the wagons, they were: the brothers Asher and Shlomo Feigl from Vidz, Barke Ulman from Braslav, Israel Wolfson from Svenzian, Motke from Duvine, and Israel Solitan from Vidz.

[Col. 1594]

Gens, realized that he was being fooled by the Germans. Instead of sending the Jews to Kovno, they were being sent to Ponar. He decided to save the 6 Jews. Gens did us a favor. He sent us into the Vilna Ghetto.

In the Vilna Ghetto

We all meet up again, and we decided to join the Partisan organization. The Vilna Partisan Organization had their own set of rules, they must take action! We requested that they admit us and undertake an active role in the fight in the nearby forests against the Germans. We started to organize quietly amongst ourselves: our first endeavour was: to obtain guns. We used our own money and bought a revolver. Later we made contact with a young man from Vilna, who had contact(connections) with the Lithuanian policemen. Zvi left the ghetto with this friend to buy guns. Coming back they encountered a German agent. Frightened of being arrested, Zvi took out his revolver and was about to shoot, but the revolver jammed. Zvi was arrested alive and brought to the Gestapo. The other one managed to escape.

Zvi was tortured in a horrible manner, but did not give up any of his friends. Later we found out, the Germans were besides themselves. (from no information)

The Jewish police were constantly watching our every move, although we still decided to go to the forests and rearm ourselves. Two Sventianers came to Vilna from the forest: Yitzhak Rudnitski and Itzike Gertman, who brought us a map of the area and introduced us to the Partisaners. At the right moment, Moishe Shutan also arrived at the Vilna Ghetto. Ruven Miadzialski from Sventzian, who was to go with us to the forest, remained behind to see his friend Moishe Shutan. We decided not to wait and left. Leib Falant led the way, a brigadier from a New Vileika group, and after some time we arrived at the Kazianer forests.

[Col. 1595]

Mior

Translation by Anita Frishman Gabbay

This is a little shtetl of 150 families, only 10 were Christian. In other words, this was a Jewish shtetl. Mior used to be the major center for the flax trade. In those days, Mior was a lively town where many came for trade and the folk made a good living.

In 1930, events turned around and the center for the flax trade moved to Poland. Many families suffered. Also, the cooperative "Rolnick" opened up and conditions worsened. To add to these problems, the cooperative received the monopoly for gasoline and salt. Most of the women of the shtetl went to shop there. Things are going well, and they decide to build a new building in the center of the market. Even the other Jewish shopkeepers must shop in the cooperative, for such products as salt, gasoline, flour and seeds.

The "Rolnick" gives the products on credit, and even allows the people to pay 3 zlotas a week. With these measures alone, they won over the poor folk. Besides the "Rolnick" there were 2 other Christian cooperatives in our shtetl. One for the rich, one for the peasants. Besides this, another Christian opened another shop and sold very cheap products.

[Col. 1596]

The Christian didn't need the shop to exist, he was a rich peasant, and had lots of land.

Market day was on Monday, but few goods came here for the townsfolk. Other shopkeepers came to sell their wares at cheaper prices: bakers, manufacturers, leather merchants and others.

This brought misery to the existing shopkeepers. The taxes were so high that it wasn't worth the effort.

Our warehouses and other business were in a terrible state, barely providing us with support.

The peasants prefer to sell their produce and deal with the cooperatives.

Some of the Jewish families made a good living from selling baked goods. Even they were taxed, and we are hindered from all sides to prevent us from competing. We don't want to get sick from this. All kinds of tricks are used, they even use them on our butchers. These shops were also heavily taxed and in the end, it was not worthwhile to keep them open.

Finally, the city council confronted our wood and forestry industry. They started to exploit this industry for themselves and eventually drove out the Jewish interests. This affected the agents, foremen and others.

All the industries started to fall apart, and the Jewish folk could not see any way to make a living. They were able to work but they didn't know what to do.

This is how the economic situation in our little town of Mior unfolded.

YEKAPO, 1931 Register, Pinchas of Lita

[Col. 1597]

Kazian

(Kozyany, Belarus)

55°18'/26°52'

Translation by Anita Frishman Gabbay

This small town had about 200 families, of which 50 families were Jewish. There were 17 Jewish shopkeepers and 13 Jewish handworkers. Market day was every Wednesday. Very little products were available, as many arrived bringing goods at cheaper prices. It is interesting, that even the Christian cooperative closed here. It was run by a weak woman and they couldn't afford to hire a supervisor.

The Jewish folk were very poor and barely survived. There are 5 warehouses in the shtetl and they were involved mainly to bartering, they traded combs, needles, soap, pins and pig–hair, flax and other things, the police tried to confiscate these goods (probably black–market dealing).

Several Jewish families went into the wood trade, but soon the regime went into the lumber business and this put an end to this Jewish livelihood.

[Col. 1598]

The Jewish bakeries and butcher shops had to pay high taxes, which led to debt. From all sides our situation worsened, and all were left helpless. Our impoverished community wanted to start paving the roads, but this required money. Every day we run one to another for handouts. It is a sad state of affairs, as no one has the extra cent (groshen).

Half a year later, a terrible fright broke out in our shtetl. A great fire broke out the in the center of town, where the nicest homes and shops were found, all were destroyed by fire and smoke. Many of the merchandise was lost. Until this day the town could not rebuild itself. They took out loans and tried to build anew, however, they fell into debt.

All this led to very bad times for the shtetl and there was no hope for the future.

[Col. 1599]

From Vidz we were brought to Sventzian. When the Sventzian (ghetto) was liquidated in 1943, together with my parents and brother, we were brought to the Vilna Ghetto. We were a group of 12 people in the Vilna Ghetto, which were my brother; Israel Solitan, Shlomo Ichiltchik, Motl Feigl, Borke Ulman, and others. We all left the Ghetto to the forests led by a group of Sventianers that came to help us leave and join the others in the forests.

When we arrived in New Vileika we received the yellow badges. Not knowing the roads, we wandered around for about a month, travelling at night and hiding during the day. Finally, with much misery, we arrived at the Kazian forests, and here we joined the Partisan group.

YEKAPO 1931 register, Pinchas of Lita

In the Kazian Woods

by Israel Ichiltchik

Translation by Anita Frishman Gabbay

At the end of June 1941, the first part of the mobilized German army arrived in our shtetl. They were first met by an organized resistance of White–Russians and Poles, the commander was Solski, the priest Nachanowitch, and the doctor (barber surgeon) Koniascik.

In November 1941, 28 Jews were assembled and taken under the bridge on the way to Vashevitze, where they were ordered to dig ditches and then they were shot. A few ran away. The Jews dug their own graves. Those who survived were: Nate Esterovtch, Yehutiel Reichel, Israel Ichiltchik and Josef Swirski, who later had the idea that the order came from the leader Solski.

In March 1942 a group of Jews were sent to Vidz, but some were left in Kazian as they were considered useful workers.

I left Vidz for a small town Osierov and from there I went to the woods and met up with Russian groups. A Christian friend of mine helped me, not having any arms(revolver)he introduced me to an organized Otriad, "Sportok". I became involved with this Christian Fufkevitch from Pletarova and sent him to bring my wife Chana Solitan and Asher Bitushunsky from Vidz. The Christian was captured and arrested, and the letter was found... He was shot, but Asher Bitushunsky managed to flee to the woods.

November 22, 1942, the Germans started to attack the woods. Most of the group of the Spartok Otriad managed to go in the direction of Polotsk. The ones that remained behind from the small surrounding towns were: Kazian, Yadi, Miori, and Zamashe, organized an attack with Leib Voliak from Stayatitshok. 500 Germans were then in Kazian. They shot into the woods and tried to capture the Partisans.

Not far from us were hundreds of Gypsies.

[Col. 1600]

The result was that the Gypsies and a small group of Jews from Sharkovtzina, Yadi, and Pohost were killed in these attacks.

May 3, 1943, Russian groups started to return to the Kazian woods and regrouped the Otriad Spartok and amongst them there were some Lithuanians from the Markov brigade from Sventzian. Our small Jewish group with Leib Voliak also fought with the other Otriads.

In the same month of May, the Russian group took out of their Lithuanian division all those that were born in our region and parachuted them into the Kazian forests with full military authority, to bring medical supplies and help, especially because the well known communist of New Svencionys, Afroim Guterman was amongst them. An attack against the Germans with these fighters was immediately organized. As I knew this area quite well, the military commander took me along as a scout to help navigate the forest.

During an offensive attack Afroim Guterman was caught by the Germans. We did not want to be caught alive by the Germans. I was on such an attack with very important Russian military against the Germans, when we came across a wagon. In this wagon we found the mutilated body of our dear Svencioner comrade Afroim Guterman.

In the summer of 1943 we fought a bitter battle against the Germans, were we lost our dear leader Leib Voliak, who was responsible for many German casualties as well. Together with him we lost the sick sister Braina Hochman from Kazian.

Together with others, I took part in many more important attacks against the German garrison in Kazian and Vosevitche. We killed many of them and destroyed and burned their trains and barracks.

In the month of August, a group of young people arrived from the Vilna Ghetto, brought by Sventzianer, New Sventzianer and Vidzer young fighters.

[Col. 1601]

Kobylnik

(Narach, Belarus)

54°56'/26°41'

Translation by Anita Frishman Gabbay

The population of this town of about 800 folk was comprised of about 300 Jews. The livelihood for these people was made up largely by trade and stores. As not far from this shtetl was the large lake called Narach, many Jews made a living from fishing. In the shtetl there were 11 fishermen.

The stores were barely providing a living. First there was an abundance of stores. In addition, there existed a Christian cooperative, which competed aggressively with the Jewish stores, and then 2 Christian private stores opened. The cooperative was supported by the bank :"Casa Stepshtika" a loan and credit bank for the district. The two Christian storekeepers, however, still made a good living, had lots of merchandise, gave credit and favorable loans to be paid over a period of time.

Understandably, the situation for the cooperative and the two private stores was far better than for the Jewish shopkeepers and also they enticed the best clients even amongst the Jews.

The market takes place every Tuesday. Many unknown people from other towns come here in order to barter and purchase merchandise. These people brought to the market leather goods, fancy goods and trimmings, fabric, baked goods and ingredients for baking as well as groceries. Their products were of an inferior quality and were able to lower their prices. Their profits were in cash, so they don't lose anything.

Everyone thought, that in the market they were purchasing bargains and they didn't concern themselves with the quality of the goods.

[Col. 1602]

The honest shopkeepers, in addition to all their other problems, had to pay a heavy tax, thus eventually ruining the Jewish shopkeepers. Remember, the Postover administration, in hindsight, was responsible for levying those heavy taxes and made it very difficult for the Jewish shopkeepers to continue (this showed the anti– Jewish sentiment).

Also, the fishermen did not have it easy. They didn't possess winter nets, because this type of winter net would cost about 2000 dollars and no one could afford it. Even summer nets, which cost about 300 dollars, were owned by only 3 Jewish fishermen. Therefore, they used the peasants to go out with them and they paid them either with half the catch or a small daily wage. A lot of the fishermen bought their fish from the

Christian fishermen and do not go to the lake themselves. Slowly, this work was taken over by the Christians and eventually they become the fishermen, who then brought the fish into town and become the middlemen, that was previously done by the Jewish fishermen. This is how the money–making was transferred from the Jewish folk.

The trade of furs, pig–hair, and other things now became the small money producing industry. It is sad for the Jewish tradespeople. Their lives were difficult and they barely made a living. Mainly the dressmakers and shoemakers maintained their way of life. In all the nearby villages, the same thing happened, the Christians monopolized all the trade and thereby the Jewish population was left without work.

Altogether, this produced a great crisis, along with those unthinkable events to come, and this was the end of our little town.

This is an excerpt from the Pinchas of Lita "YEKAPO", 1931

*Kobylnik Yiskor Book is now under the name "Narach"

[Col. 1603-1604]

The Melody of Our Fathers and Grandfathers

Translation by Janie Respitz

No vestige has remained from these small rural Jewish settlements. But throughout the world, the children and grandchildren of those wonderful Jewish farmers carry the melody of their fathers and grandfathers in their blood, as they recount the words of the first century Rabbi, Rabbbi Shimon Ben Eliezer:

"Adam did not taste anything until he began to work. It is said about him: God placed him in the Garden of Eden to cultivate and protect, and only after did he allow him to eat from all the trees in the garden. Man must make an effort to work, and only then will God send the blessing".

The good village Jews worked hard all week. On the Sabbath they would go to pray in Heydutzishok and delight in the words of the passing preacher who with great enthusiasm for their hard work would sing: "Rabbi Tarfun said: The Almighty would not allow his Divine Presence to rest upon the Jews until they did their work, as it is said: "When they make me a Temple, I will rest among them".

Rabbi Yehuda Ben Batira said: He that has no profession, what should he do? Let him search. If he has a ruined house or a devastated field and busies himself with that, it is said: For six days you shall work at whatever it is you have to do – just do it. To this end Rabbi Yishmael Bar Rabbi Nakhman said: Work is twenty – six generations older than Torah. There were twenty – six generations from Adam until the giving of the Ten

Commandments. Therefore, the one who profits from his own efforts is on a higher level (closer to God) than a God fearing man".

This is how these quiet, simple Jews soaked up pride from their work and blessed their children with the brightness of the preacher's enthusiasm and love.

In the village, they were farmers. In town – warm, heartfelt Jews who carried with them, wherever they went, their love of labour and toil.

[Col. 1605]

Holocaust–Destruction and Death

Haydutzishok During These Terrible Days

(Adutiškis, Lithuania)

55°09'/26°36'

Nekhe Volotzki

Translated by Anita Frishman Gabbay

I was not born in Haydutzishok. I married a young man from a shtetl and we came here only in 1935. I familiarized myself with the townsfolk and immediately I felt like a Haydutzishker daughter.

I fell in love with the people and the shtetl. There was a high cultural standard amongst the young folk. Many noteworthy institutions existed here, friendly and inviting. There was a wonderful library, a horn–orchestra, a drama club, 2 Folk–Schuls, and several Zionist organizations.

This did not last very long. The second World War broke out 4 years after I arrived, and within a month, our world was upside down. Everything that the people built with all the strength in their bodies, was in disarray.

Already under Russian rule, the Jews lived in constant fear for the days ahead. A lot were deported to Siberia, a lot were imprisoned. One was a Zionist, the other a Bolshevik!

June 22, 1941, the “thunder” arrived: Hitler had arrived.

[Col. 1606]

My husband and I were in Svir and we decided to return home. On our way home we already felt what Hitler's Regime had in store for us! We were stopped several times, searched, nevertheless, we made it home.

We arrived at Itzhak Potasnik's home to a warm welcome. We stayed with him for 3 weeks. Everyday the men went to Yozek Kracovski's warehouse, a good Christian who gave them food and promised to help us in whatever manner he was able. If there wasn't any work to be done, he told the men to pretend they were working by bringing the same bundles of flax in and out the warehouse.

The priest Bunevitch also helped the Jewish folk. One Thursday, when a progrom against the Jews was to take place, the priest held the crazed crowd back. The day dragged on, and on Sunday after lunch, Moishe Smuckler ran into our house. He worked in the mill and came to tell us a ghetto was being prepared on Vidzer Street.

Several Christians arrived at our home with sticks and clenched fists: we must leave our home in 2 hours and move into the ghetto. We put as much clothing as possible on our bodies, we still believed that we would need them. Everything was left behind, which the Christians robbed and took away. The ghetto was extremely crowded, a small room was packed with 15 people. Food was scarce. And still this was not the worst! Some Christians told us that we will be led to a camp (barracks) and be shot.

[Col. 1607]

We lived in this ghetto for several weeks, and on a Thursday before its liquidation, a Christian friend of ours came to us to let us in on a secret: all the Jews were going to be killed in a few days. He says: escape as soon as possible! That is how it happened! Friday in the morning we snuck out of the ghetto and ran with Grachovski to Svir. During the day my husband Eliahu saw the roundup of the Jews from Stayatishok. His heart told him that the ghetto would be the worst place to remain. He went to the priest to plead with him to help us.

The priest, like I said, was friendly toward the Jews. He asked that my husband remain in his home, while he went to get news from the streets and about the activities in the ghetto. He came back quickly and confirmed: do not return to the ghetto. He brought him to Gravoski where we found the entire Smuckler family (that worked in the mill), where they were awaiting Gravoskis' reurn from Svir. When he returned in the evening, Gravoski told us all was quiet in Svir. He asked that we leave immediately, not even to spend the night.

Shabbos, very early in the morning, my husband and the Smuckler family and Michel Potasnik arrived in Svir. In the meantime, news arrived that all the Jews of Sventzian district were sent to Poligon. We sent a friendly Christian to verify the truth. He returned and this was validated. He asked that one of us accompany him back to Svir, but no one wanted to go–"Hitler is everywhere" they replied.

[Col. 1608]

Only one woman with a child agreed to go with him and actually, they survived. We all left for a small town near Svir, where an uncle of mine lived and we stayed with him about 6 months, from Erev Yom Kippur to Purim. We found out about the gruesome tragedy on KolHamoed Succoth, what happened to our people. The folk told us 8000 Jews were all shot in the woods of Poligon.

It is unbelievable to absorb this now, how did we survive those days under such conditions?

We were stronger than iron that we were able to endure such horrific ordeals!

We spent the entire winter in Svir, more or less it was quiet, and in the spring, the murdering started again. We found out that the Jews from Kurenitz were shot, and also from another shtetl. We felt we were sitting on a volcano!

In the meantime tragedy struck Sheina and Moishe Smuckler: they had a sister in Dolhinov and suddenly they wanted to go to her, the entire Dolhinov community was massacred. They were caught there and shot with the others (in Dolhinov).

All this news came as a shock and from then on we decided not to remain in the ghetto. The question: where to go, where to hide? Either find a Christian or go to the forests! I went off to find a friendly Christian, one would hide me and my son, another one would hide only my husband. Everyone was afraid. I returned to the Svir ghetto to my husband, we made our plans, and at the first opportunity we made a plan to escape to our Christians. Our days were numbered: that same evening a policeman, our friend, came to us and told us to leave right away. An order came to deport all the Jews from the ghetto and the surrounding region. We jumped out of bed, quickly got dressed and left from the back door that led us to the riverbank. Our house was next to the lake, luckily for us.

[Col. 1609]

We travelled in the darkness, lengthwise along the bank in the direction of the town, where our cousin, Korosin, lived. With great difficulty we arrived only to find out their families were all in the Svir ghetto. We waited impatiently until it became light out, and sent a message to them in the ghetto to escape right away. People in Svir thought we were creating an unnecessary panic and fear, and they didn't believe us. We decided whatever the outcome, not to return to Svir. I went with my son to one Christian, my husband to the other, and we hid there. After a week, we wanted to know the outcome of the Svir ghetto, so we begged our Christian to bring us some news. He returned and brought me a letter from my cousin, "Do not return here". The Lithuanians took over control of the Svir ghetto several weeks later.

Several months passed in this hideout, when a partisan attack occurred nearby on a German commander, who was driving from Sventzian to Lyntup, captured him and shot him.

The forests and surrounding shtetls were overrun by German military. Our Christians became too frightened to hide us. I then begged the Christian to keep only my son, my husband and I decided to return to Svir. In Svir it was again somewhat quiet again, the Jews were sent to work in the surrounding towns. My husband made arrangements to work in a town, not far from where my son was. Every Sunday, our Christian came to this town with our son, who we could see in the distance. You can imagine we paid the Christian very well for this

[Col. 1610]

This is how we lived in the shtetl Komorova until we found out that all the Jews from Svir and Michaelishok are going to be deported.

Our tears were endless. No one knew where death lurked. We had to decide instantly whether to remain or to go to Michelishok. Our hearts told us not to go. We couldn't remain in the shtetl either, so we returned to the Christian who had our son, and with great difficulty arrived safely. Three months passed, our Christian gave us information that the Jews from Michaelishok were sent to Vilna. Later we were informed they were all sent to Ponar woods where they perished.

We remained 6 months like this, hiding between the 2 Christians. In 1944, 6 weeks before the arrival of the Red Army, the partisans located my husband and took him to the forests with them. I had no news. He did not return.

Together with my son, I was freed by the Red Army. Where should I go? There was no place for us, our dearest and finest were all slaughtered.

We started to wander again through roads and fields, but the end of the road led us here (Eretz Israel).

This is a small part of the entire story, what I lived through. The memories are still disturbing and it is difficult to concentrate on the pain and suffering we endured, and the enormity of the crime against humanity.

Rivers of tears flow from my eyes, when I take my pen in my hand and want to write. In short, I want to remember and honor the names of those nearest and dearest, whom the Hitlerite bandits robbed from me.

With heartache and tears I remind myself daily! Holy be thy Names!

God shall revenge for their spilled blood!

[Col. 1611]

The Painful Last Road of the Hayduskitzer Jews

Michel Potasnik

Translated by Anita Frishman Gabbay

As soon as the Red Army fled Haydutishok and even before the German Army arrived, the Lithuanian hooligans took control of our shtetl. The Jews felt this great unrest. Part of them left their homes and together with their families went to their acquaintances in smaller towns. At first they were welcomed, but later on they were asked to leave: this happened all over like an "order" from God.

In the meantime, the peasants discovered the guns and ammunition that the Russians left behind, and the descent into chaos began. In the beginning, these attacks occurred in the evening, but shortly after, they became emboldened and these attacks on Jewish homes took place in broad daylight. First, the attacks were on the empty homes, later they attacked the homes with rocks to make the Jews run away.

The peasants from our neighbourhood arrived with their wagons, as if it were market day, robbed the home and off they went with wagons loaded with our possessions. This lasted until July 2, 1941, when the German military arrived in our shtetl.

Also, in nearby Vidz, about 30 kilometers away, the same robberies occurred. The robberies were not sufficient, murders were also taking place. In a matter of 10 days, between the Red Army leaving and the Germans arriving, these Lithuanian bandits murdered 200 Jews. The Jews of Vidz fled and some arrived in Haydutishok.

When the Germans arrived, 10 hooligans in police uniforms took over our shtetl. These police recruited more Lithuanian hooligans from our shtetl and the surrounding area and the destruction began. They started with the synagogues, Sefer Torahs and books, which we held in such high esteem. They started to arrest the Jews that fled from Vidz, and every day they took a few to the outskirts and shot them. Women were raped before they were shot. The Jews of Haydutishok were warned if they would hide amongst the Christians, all would be shot, even the Christians. When the interim authority arrived, they freed the remaining hostages from Vidz, who returned to Vidz.

[Col. 1612]

When there were no more Jews from Vidz left, the Lithuanians started attacking the Haydustikzer Jews: they arrested 3 Jewish boys under the pretext that they were Communists. These were: Gershon Charmatz, Chaim Gordon and Abraham Yocelman. After a few days in prison, they were brought to the edge of town to be shot. In the last minute, Gershon Charmatz offered a bribe, A. Yocelman overtook his shooter and fled, receiving only a bullet wound. Then he fought with the Partisans and eventually arrived in Eretz Israel. The third friend, Chaim Gordon, was shot through and through like a sieve, all the bullets for the 3 of them found their way into Chaim's body. Chaim was the first Jewish resident of Haydutishok to be shot, the second, Israel Lapida, the baker. When the Germans confiscated foodstuffs and other goods from the Jewish homes, they said the baker was hiding his goods from them. Israel was shot outside his home. Besides murder, the Hitlerite sadists invented various ways to torture and torment these poor Jews: in a few minutes they requested a pail full of water be brought from far away, not to spill a drop, the Jew was clocked, and God forbid, 1 additional second cost him! Jews had to fill sacks with heavy weights and run! God forbid they stopped to catch their breath! Beatings with sticks were commonplace. On a chosen day, the Lithuanians rounded up the Jews, old, young, men women, children, in the market square. Seeing this, the peasants ran with sacks thinking these Jews were going to be killed. Robbery was on their mind. But the German commander who was new to the shtetl, wanted only to record each Jew and to demand that items, such as guns, radios, etc. should be turned over to the authorities in 2 hours time or else they would be shot.

[Col. 1613]

All the towns folk, age 14–60, and women who didn't have small children, had to report for work at 6 a.m. every day. Jews were not allowed on the streets from 7p.m to 5 a.m: every Jew had to sew on the front and on the back of his coat a yellow patch with the letter"J". On every house a board with a Yellow Magen–David had to be posted. Those who did not obey had 1 option: Death!

When the German military advanced to other shtetls, they left in place 5 local representatives to keep order. These were: Faivel Rakovski, Leon Rimsha, Faivel Fashun, Ilitz Shidlovski. These 4 were from our town, Together with the 10 Lithuanian policemen who arrived earlier, they were in charge. Also, they left 5 Germans who took such pride in how well their work was being performed.

New edicts were issued each day! A Jew cannot live under the same roof as a Christian. The Jew cannot leave the shtetl without a pass. Jews were not permitted to eat meat or butter.

The Jews obeyed and arrived for work on time: they had to repair the roads under Lithuanian supervision. Every Jew still had his Goy, which he trusted! There were those that brought the Jews food, whiskey to be used as bribes, (used to bribe when a Jew was about to be shot). It didn't always work, especially when it came to torture.

[Col. 1614]

When a hooligan was angry with a Jew, he went to the police, threw the Jew in prison in a dark cellar, beat him so badly that later he to be wrapped in wet sheets. When a Jew got sick, he wasn't allowed to visit the Christian doctor, only if he got a "pass" from the "good hearted" police. Bread was baked in our own premises.

Every Thursday was market day, and the Jews were not permitted to attend in the first days. Later, with bribes, Jews could come for 1 hour, 12–1, knowing that the Christians were finished their shopping. A whistle to commence and when to end was used. If the Jews didn't leave at once, they were beat by the hooligans with rubber hoses. One crisis after another! The mighty hand of these Lithuanian bandits, our former neighbours, decided to enclose us in a ghetto. August 15, 1941, within 2 hours, we were ordered to vacate and move into the ghetto on Vidzer street. It was overcrowded, but we used every inch: stalls, barns, sheds, attics. Lucky it was still warm outside. Arriving in the ghetto, our once friendly neighbours were still inspecting what we were carrying with us, what pleased them, they stole. All that was left in our homes were robbed by the marauding peasants. Even in the ghetto, they arrived with wagons and policemen, and continued to rob us. They even gave the simple peasant the robbed booty. Every hooligan chose for himself a cow, a goat. The time was moving along, and in the third month, Erev Rosh Hashana, Monday and Tuesday, the few old Jews were released from work and found a place in the ghetto to conduct a service and to cry to the Almighty. We were not allowed to go to our beautiful synagogue, and 3 days after, Erev Shabbos, the ghetto was made smaller.

[Col. 1615]

Pressure mounted, we were squeezed in so tightly, cordoned off and surrounded by Lithuanians with guns: if we dare leave we would be shot. After blessing the Shabbos candles, 200 Jews from Stayatitchok were brought into the ghetto by Lithuanians and the next morning at 10, they herded them into the market square. Peasants with wagons and were waiting to transport the Jews, only the sick, elderly and small children were allowed to ride, the others had to go by foot. They were only allowed to bring with them a small bundle with small things. The peasants even stole these small bundles!

Also on this morning other horrible events took place: Yitzhak Yacov Zeiger was shot because he was protesting to the commander about the mass roundups of the Jews from the ghetto.

This was the fate of the Haydutsker Jews, their last road. They walked 50 kilometers to the thin forest of Poligon, near to New–Sventzian.

On the way, the strength of Shimon Reichel gave up, he stopped in the middle of the road to rest, the Lithuanian behind him shot him. He walked with his Sefer Torah in hand all this way. This is how many perished. Finally they arrived in Poligon late at night, and shoved into wooden barracks. The stench was unbearable. All the Jews from the region were assembled here: from Sventian, New Sventzian, Haydutishok, Ignalina, Podbrodz, Kamelishak, Daugelishak, Maligan, Kaltinian, Stayatishok and others. For 12 days they suffered, worse than animals, and Chol H'Hoed Succoth, Jews were released in groups, taken to freshly dug pits and shot with machine guns.

[Col. 1616]

It took 3 days to completely annihilate 8000 Jews in this manner. The helpers didn't bother to look if they were dead or wounded. They dumped the earth on the living souls and still several days later the earth was seen moving in this brotherly mass grave. Some managed to escape, some got shot. These were: Raizel Barenstein with her 2 children, Moishe and Rochel, Rochel Rudnitzki with her daughter Miriam and Rochel Chait. Two days later they shot Chaia–Faiga Fisher, who was sick in bed In Haudutishok, at a Christian hospital, where she was brought with a special pass a week earlier.

Zundel Potasnik managed to escape to Postov, there he was shot in the middle of the street by a policeman, who did not recognize him as a Postov resident. Those that perished while fighting with the partisans: Chaim–Leib Gordon, Berl Fisher, Shmuel Potasnik, Shalom Abel, and others. And many more perished in the lagers and ghettos.

This was the fate of the entire region. When the Germans left and the Red Army arrived, 2 Jewish brothers came out of hiding: Leib and Wolf Katcherginski. They went into town, but they didn't recognize anyone so they left for Lodzenel, a few kilometers from Haydutishok, where they knew some good Lithuanians from earlier days. They were attacked and murdered in a horrible manner. Few of the Haydutchiser Jews survived. I alone, sick, hungry and half- naked through the shtetls of Svir, Kobylnik, and finally Myadel. Together with the Jews of Myadel, we all decided not to wait till the Murderers arrived to kill us, we decided to escape to the only friendly place on earth–the forests (Narach).

[Columns 1617-1624]

The Story of the Holocaust in Shtayatsishok (Stojaciszki)

by Israel Gantovnik

Translated by Daniel Wolfe

Donated by Simon Kreindler

It was the 23rd of August. A week before the war. A large part of the Polish Jewish youth was mobilized. A terrible panic occurred among the Jews in the small towns. The war was going on for three weeks when, on September 19, the Red Army entered Shtayatsishok.

A part of the mobilized youth immediately returned home. Another part went with the Red Army deep into Russia.

The brothers Yehuda and Meyer Lapida did not return nor go deep into Russia. Yehuda was killed in battle and Meyer was severely wounded by the Nazis. He was captured and they killed him. The Lapida family was the first to suffer such severe casualties.

With the occupation of the Red Army, the economy of the shtetl was not too bad.The farmers were able to work their farms harder than ever and everyone was able to make a living.

Only political items had to be hidden. We burned all the archives of the Zionist organizations. A lot of Jews got assorted government posts and were very happy.

Our shtetl did not fall into the hands of the German Army. For nearly two years we were able to catch our breath until that terrible day, the 22nd of June 1941.

On that day, at six o'clock in the morning, Moscow radio reported that that Germany broke the German-Russian pact. This caused a panic among the Jewish population in general and of course in our shtetl.

The Lithuanian population (gentiles) received the news with great joy and were dancing in the streets. As the Russian Army withdrew, the population started to rob all the arms that were in storage. They immediately started their own militia which fought against the retreating Russian Army.

The leading criminal of the area was Feyoss Rokovski, a Lithuanian from Adutzishik. His group started harassing the Jews. Within the first few days there was a casualty, Gordon's son.

Eight days later Hitler's army entered the shtetl in the morning and pasted posters declaring laws against the Jewish population.

We learned that all Jews are to wear yellow patches in the front and back, each bearing the Star of David. All Jews fourteen years and older had to go on forced labor.

The Germans immediately revealed their sadistic nature. The soldiers caught ten Jews and ordered them to pull a large wagon with a very heavy load. The Germans were on both sides of the wagon carrying large wooden clubs. If any of the Jews faltered, the soldiers hit them over the head with the club.

The weeks passed in this manner. Finally, the Germans left our area because the front moved eastward. In Adutzishik the Germans left a Lithuanian civilian government. The head of this government was a young Lithuanian, a terrible anti-semite, Feyoss Rokovski. In Shtayatsishoks the criminal Joseph Senkowicz was designated the head of the shtetl. Ha became the boss of the area. He confiscated all the cows from the Jewish farmers and gave them to the gentiles in the area.

This was not the end of our agony. On the 20 of September 1941, there was a conference of all the German appointed government heads in Shvintzan (Swincian). The head of the Vilna province proposed that all Jews be rounded up and sent to Poligan. Only Jews with essential skills were to exempted from this proposal. Only the head of the Shvintzan governnent agreed to exempt Jews with essential skills.

On the eve of the Sabbath, September 26th, ten Lithuanian police came to Shtayatsishok. They told all the Jews to go into the street and take with them a three day supply of food. In a few hours they were marched to Adutzishik. In addition to the Shtayatchik Jews, there were over 8,000 Jews from the Svintzan area here. On Chol Hamoid Succoss they were all murdered. Very few were able to escape or be rescued.

Shmuel Katzyonah, Hodeh Abel and Chana Wollak hid in the field. They were caught and shot to death. Rudnitzky was shot to death as he was running away from the shtetl. Only sixteen Jews were able to hide. They were: Eliyahu Gedod and his son Tzvi, Leib Wollak, David Gordono, Chanuch Kahan, Paysach Wollak and his wife Chana, his son Abraham and daughter Shayneh, my father Chayim Gontovnik, my mother Bayleh, brothers Eliyahu and Abraham, my sister Ethel, my wife Rachel, my daughter Rebecca (26 days old) and myself, Israel Gantovnik.

Everyone ran in different directions. Late in the evening we started looking for one another. Around eleven o'clock in the evening we met. We discovered my father and brother Eliyahu were missing. We waited a few hours for them, then decided to go through the woods at night in the direction of White Russia. On the way we came upon two Jews from our shtetl, Sholem Gantovnik's son Israel Itzchok and his daughter Miriam.

At four o'clock we approached a village not far from Vidz. A Russian gentile farmer whom we knew lived here. We decided to knock on his door to have pity on us and hide us in his attic for the day. He was startled. It was not easy to hide thirteen people. We spent the day with him and when it became dark we went on our way.

Early Sunday morning we arrived in Katzian. The Katzian Jews greeted us warmly and we were taken in by various families. Early Tuesday, my father and brother Eliyahu whom we hadn't heard from arrived here too.

In few days we heard that the situation in Opseh was better than in Katzian. We decided to leave and go there. We had to travel over 50 kilometers.

We arrived in Opseh erev Yom Kippur. The Opseh Jews greeted us warmly. Here we met Jewish refugees from Ignolineh, Doksh, and Adutzishik.

In a few weeks they found jobs for all of us and we remained in Opseh for a half year. In March 1942, there came an order for the roundup of all the Jews. They were to be sent to Vidz.

We decided that this was not a good situation so we left for Postoy. For three days we plodded through deep snow, through fields and forests until we finally arrived in the Postoy ghetto.

We immediately saw that we had made a mistake. The Postoy Jewish Council was afraid to take us in. With great reluctance they finally decided to take my wife, my child and myself because they had pity on the infant. The other Shtayatchisok Jews said goodbye to us and left for Donilovitsh. None of us realized what a sad day this was, for we did not realize that we would never see each other again.

The Postoy Jewish Council made us feel that we were useless. We remained there until the 17 of June 1942.

At the beginning of June they started killing all the Jews from the Postoy area. This brought on a terrible panic in the Postoy ghetto. On the 16 of June we learned that all the Jews in the area were to be killed. We decided to leave Postoy and continue our wandering.

The 17 of June was a rainy day. This saved our lives because it was easier to flee. The rain did not let up for the entire day. We bundled our little child and wandered through fields and forest back towards the direction of Shtayatchisok. The next morning, the 18 of June we came upon the village of Yakomenish, 3 kilometers from Shtayatchisok.

We knocked on the door of a gentile we knew, Favel Borok. He greeted us very warmly and allowed us to hide in his barn. We stayed there for entire day. In the evening, when our daughter started crying, he told us that he was afraid and suggested that we go to the Shvintzan ghetto. It was quiet and safe there.

Did we have a choice? So we left for Shvintzan. The Shvintzan Jewish council told us categorically that they could not under any circumstances take us in. They didn't even have a tiny room for us.

I found an old hovel and repaired it myself. I made a room from it and the problem of housing was solved.

It turned out that in this ghetto there were 40 illegals. We had to be careful of the Lithuanian police. I saw there was no future in this so we left for Tsurklishok.

I told the administrator Jan Chaltzki who I was and proposed to him that I work the land. He appealed to the German Work Council and in a few days he appointed me his landworker. A short time after I got employment for my brother Abraham and my sister Ethel who arrived from the Shvintzan ghetto.

Our situation improved. We had enough to eat and we were no longer illegal. Understand that we had to thank the kindhearted Chaletzki for this.

Meanwhile there was a shock throughout the ghetto. It was encircled with barbed wire. There was only one entrance and exit. The police became much sterner.

By the end of the summer, the Vids ghetto was liquidated and any remaining Jews were brought to Shvintzan. It became overcrowded. Rumors passed that there was a plan to liquidate all the ghettos.

I discussed the situation with my brother and sister. We decided not to wait but to leave quickly. Our daughter was fourteen months old at this time.

We waited for a dark night, wrapped my daughter well and left by way of a large forest in the direction of Lintov.

In the middle of the night we came upon a town. It was very cold and we wanted to get our child out from the bitter cold. We knocked on a gentile's door and asked him to have pity on us. He let us into his house. They were friendly people and gave us a warm welcome.

We ate, warmed up and wanted to continue further. The farmer said that with such a small child we could not get very far. He suggested that we leave the child with him. We couldn't make up our minds. All this time we had the child with us; now we should separate ourselves from her? It was very difficult to arrive at such a decision. He presented us with a good argument. So, with a heavy heart, great sorrow and pain we finally decided to rescue Rebecca and left her with him. We took note of the name of the village and the name of this good family. The name of this village was Mili. The names of the family were Aniskenza and Matrona Burlokov. They had a daughter Zeena and a son Fyodor. They ware Russian Staravyaran who were not enemies of the Jews.

After leaving our child, our hearts were bitter. We left for the nearby forest and waited until nightfall. At night we started for Tsirlishok in order to find out what happened in Shvintzan. It turned out that it was quiet there and no harm was being done to the Jews. Chaletzki suggested that we continue at the work we were doing. We heeded his advice and remained there until February 1943.

Meanwhile, we received good news about the war. The German army was badly defeated at Stalingrad. The Red Army captured Kharkov and was approaching Vitebsk. Everyone began to hope that freedom was approaching. But simultaneously the situation in the Shvintzan ghetto became horrible. The head of the Vilna ghetto told us that all Shvintzan ghetto Jews will be transferred either to Kovno or Vilna.

We later found out what happened to them. The Kovno transport took them to the Ponar forest where they were slaughtered.

But my wife Rachel, brother Abraham and sister Ethel could not be talked into going on to the Kovno transport. We all left in the direction of Shtayatchisok. To our good fortune we came upon some good gentiles who had pity on us and hid us. I must note their names: Marcal Tsolko from

Shtayatchisok and Mazayeh Kazimir from Djikevenish. They placed their lives in danger in order to save ours.

On the seventh of July the Red Army came and freed us. We returned to our shtetl and learned that only seven Jews survived out of 350 in Shtayatchisok.

We decided not to remain amongst this death and destruction. We returned to the village of Mill to get our daughter.

We made aliyah to Eretz Israel.

This is only a brief story of a doomed Jewish shtetl. I want to honor all of our dear best friends and families who were tortured to death. I also want to honor all those friendly gentiles who imperiled their lives in the face of the Nazis.

Rachel Gantovnik's story. (Wife of Israel Gantovnik.)

The days were clear and bright and the sky was blue. It was Friday, Shabbos Tsuveh. There were little frosts in the morning and evening. The women were preparing tzolant. Some were in the midst of their housework. Suddenly shouts were heard throughout the shtetl, "Take bread for three days and get into the street!" These were the shouts of the drunken police who came to chase the Jews out of the shtetl.

There were more shouts, tears and screams from one end of the shtetl to the other. "Where are we going?" cried Chiyenneh Layeh. "Where are they chasing us with our small children? My children have no shoes for the winterl"

'Where are they taking us?" asked Reb Chayim quietly. "I have lived here my entire life. Where are they sending us? That which I own, I earned with my ten fingers. Even my house I built myself. To leave would be equal to death."

Then Reb Chayim became quiet. In his entire life he never had an argument nor insulted anyone. Thanks to his perseverance and skill his business grew and prospered. He couldn't understand the hatred of these German murderers. He said, "I have no place to go from here." He sat quietly and prayed. To this day I could recall his prayers. To this day I cannot forget them.

"Where are these killers taking us?" asked Reb Nochim. "I'm not going anywhere! This is my last word. They will not chase me out of my house!"

He remained in his house. He didn't have the strength to go. He sat alone, alone and by himself he cursed the shtetl Shtayatchisok. Two days later, on Sunday, the police (Joseph Senkowicz) came and shot him in the field. To this day his grave is in that Shtayatchisok field.

"What do these murderers want from us? cried Dvayrah. I have suffered so much these past few years. Finally I have a bit of money saved, oh how I denied myself over the years!"

Dvayarah was left a widow with two small children, Abraham and Maysheh. She alone had to run the farm. Alone, with very little strength she plowed the fields, sowed the seeds and drove the cows to the fields. There wasn't anyone to relieve her. She lived in a broken down house outside the shtetl. With her last few pennies she paid to send the boys to chayder. When Abraham was a Bar Mitzvah he also became the boss. He began working the farm. He no longer ran to play with the children. He knew that the responsibility of the house was on his shoulders. He worked with his mother day in and day out. While everyone was asleep Abraham was working the fields. He was usually ahead of everyone. His cows were feeding before everyone elses'. His work was on a par with the adults'. Drayrah became old and bent from this heavy work. She never allowed herself to eat well because she was saving money for a new home. Their butter and eggs were sold in the village. A few years went by. Abraham and Maysheh became adults. They built a new house closer to the shtetl, near the hill next to Reb Nochim and Reb Haymen. Now they started to live better. They ate and dressed better. Dvayrah would llft her hands daily to God and say, "I thank you God for the miracles you have bestowed upon me."

"Where shall I go now? How could I leave my beautiful palace? How can I throw away everything for which I worked so hard and saved so long? Oh God, Oh God! What do these terrible people want from me?"

This could be heard from a distance. It was tragic and heart rending.

“Save yourself Jews, there is a fire burning (holocaust)” Liebeh screamed. Oh how Liebeh and Shmuel suffered until their children grew up!

“And Brankeh, who is studying at the gymnasium, Liebeh would boast. “And Yehudis can sew and weave very well; and is also a good housekeeper; and both are beautiful.”

Brankeh, I remember you to this day with your black braids and burning black eyes. When I asked you what you can learn from the books you were, reading, you would tell me all about them.

I heard cries and screams in the distance. I still hear them to this day.

Leib, the big one with ten children said goodbye to his house. He stood a long time at the doorway kissing the mezuzah. “Oh how I want to save my house just as I want to save Shtayatchisok!” he cried.

In our house we had no idea as to what was going on. We thought they were coming to rob us, so we hid a few things. Suddenly, our door flew open and my sister-in-law Ethel came running in wearing a coat over her shoulders and boots without socks.

“Children, don't be afraid, God is with is. They came to take us to Poligan where we will die of hunger. Let's run away and God will help us. “Quickly children, the police are ten meters awayl”

Fortunately, we were all at home. I, Abraham and Shayneh. I thought that in White Russia they would not send us to a camp. None of us could imagine that they would send us to our death. My mother and father lived in Shtayatchisok for seven years... We moved into my grandfather's farm after his death. He had three cows, some sheep, chickens, ducks and geese.

I saw my father lean against the book cabinet and started to cry. It was the first time I ever saw him cry. “How do I leave my home? How could I leave Shtayatchisok? How do I leave my books?”

In one sac he placed a loaf of bread, a shirt and a few books. My mother tried to appease him. “You shouldn't cry because we are leaving. God will help us. I saw her place a Chassidic sidur in his sac.

I was very confused. I didn't know how I was going to meet my husband Israel. But Ethel assured me that we would meet on the path late at night. He did not, under any circumstances want to leave at midday. We would escape by a hidden trail. He knew the direction we were to go. He said that we were to go towards Beyellow Russia (White Russia), Kazian and Postov where more Jews could be found. I couldn't find a kerchief for my head so I took a nightgown. I only found one shoe. So I left with a shoe on one foot and a heavy sock on the other. In my briefcase, I placed all my papers from the teacher seminar in Vilna and from the Jewish gymnasium in Vilna. I always saved them. They were very dear to me.

While Rebecca was asleep Ethel took her. Our little Rebecca! How much more will she suffer? We ran through the fields. From the distance we could see smoke rising from Shtayatchisok and a trail black with people wailing and screaming. The cries and the screams from the children accompanied us the entire way. From every direction we could hear the crying of the cows and sheep and the barking of dogs. Everything at this point was in a state of chaos. My father, speaking to Abraham said, "We are leaving Shtayatchisok. Who knows if we shall ever return? This story has continually repeated itself throughout the history of the Jews. Ever since the Diaspora. Ever since the wandering of the Jews began. In every generation there was a new decree for banishment. But God always helped us. This time there is a terrible storm on unfriendly soil. What worth do we have to these murderers? We are like sheep bleating in the wind. Maybe we should have gone with the rest of the Shtayatchisok Jews? I don't know. Where shall we run to. The Germans are everywhere!"

Late that night we met in the woods. My brother in law Reb Chayim, sister in law Bayleh, father in law Eliyahu, my son Abraham and my husband Israel.

Under no circumstances did Reb Chayim want to leave his home. With great difficulty his children led him out of his house. "Whoever wants to go, should go; I will not leave," he argued. "I have nowhere to go!"

It was dark and cold in the woods. Rebecca did not stop crying. I had nothing with which to cover her. Abraham was carrying her in his arms and rocking her, but it did not help. As we went further, she cried harder and everyone else was crying with her. It was decided that we should start a fire in order to warm her up. I tried to breast feed her but she wouldn't drink.

She was very cold and wet.

Woe is me!, Woe is me! We are living through such wonderful times "said Reb Chayim sarcastically. "We have sinned! We should have sold everything and moved to Eretz Israel" said Reb Paysach.

"Now it is too late!" replied my father.

[Col. 1623]

The Sad Shabbos

Jews of Shtayatsishok Leave the Village Forever

Rachel Gan – Tov (Gantovnik)

Translated by Anita Frishman Gabbay

The days were so beautiful and clear, the sky was a beautiful shade of blue. Friday, Shabbos Tsuvah, after Rosh Hashana, the days were bright and clear. Everyone was preparing for the Sabbath, the women were preparing their "Cholent" (baked beans and meat, kept in the oven overnight). Some folk were still at work. The ovens in some homes were still warming, suddenly a large sound was heard throughout the village: 3 days worth of bread and go into the streets! This was the message of those drunken policemen who came to take us away from our village.

[Col. 1624]

A panic, lamentation, from one end of the village to the other!

– – Where shall we go? – said Hiena Leah – where are they chasing us with our small children – my children don't have any winter shoes! Where do they want to bring us? – – said Rabbi Chaim, quietly. I lived here all my life with my wife and children, and with my 10 fingers worked for everything I have, I even built my house, leaving this home is like death to me.

[Col. 1625]

Rabbi Chaim was quiet, he never fought with anyone his entire life, nor insulted anyone. Thanks to his hard work, his livelihood improved and his situation was comfortable. He couldn't understand the rules that the Nazis were enforcing! He said – I have no where to go! He sat quietly amongst his religious books and continued saying his "Tehilim". The sounds are still ringing in my ears until today: his beautiful melody and I cannot forget!

"Where are they taking us, these beasts? – said Rabbi Nachum. I am not going anywhere! That is my final word! They are not throwing me out of my house!

He remained in his home. He no longer had the strength to go. Until Sunday, for 2 days, he sat alone, bereaving his Stayatishok! The police came and shot him, and until today, his grave is in the fields of Stayatishok.

"What do these animals want from us," – – Devorah said. We laboured for so many years before we finally came into a little money. Oy, Devorah, Devorah, how I admired you! How I bear your pain!

Devorah remained a widow with 2 small children, Abrahamele and Moishele, alone she had to run her business. Alone with her frail health she laboured, she cultivated, she brought the animals to the fields. There was no one to help her. She lived at the ?, a broken down house. With her last few groschen, she sent the children to cheder. As soon as Avramke had his Bar Mitzvah, he took over as boss. He helped with the business. He no longer ran to play with the other children, he knew the burden of the household was now upon him. He worked day and night with his mother.

When everyone was still asleep, Avramke was in the fields. His animals were always fed before the others, his fields were reaped before the others. He was considered an equal amongst the elders, and was always willing to help.

Devorah became old and haggard before her time, due to her hard labour. She wouldn't allow herself to eat better, in order to save every cent to build a better home.

The butter and the eggs were sold in the village.

[Col. 1626]

Several years past and Avramke and Moishele grew up. They built a new home closer to the village, on the hill next to Rabbi Nacuhman and Rabbi Chaim. soon as they started to live better, eat better and get some new clothes. Devorah got up every morning and raised her hands to God: Dear God, thank you dear God, for the blessings that you have brought to me"!

– – Where do you want me to go now? Why do you want me to leave my beautiful palace? Why should I throw everything away? That I slaved for! For what? For what? What do our enemies want from us? I heard from a distance her pain and heartache.

– – "Save the Jews, a great fire is burning!" – Livke was screaming. Livke and Shmuelke, with their 6 children. How much hardship she endured till those children got older. And Bronke, who is studying in the Gymnasia, who Livke was always bragging about. And Yehudit, thank God, who sews so well, and knits so well, now can help in the household chores. And both are so beautiful!

Bronke, I remember you until today, with your black braids and fiery eyes. You told me about the books you read, which you described to me, and I asked you, what can one learn from each book.

I heard the screaming and pleading from a distance, and still hear it today!

Leibe the big one, with his 10 children, said goodbye to the synagogue, stood for a long time kissing the Mezuzah.

...Oy! how I don't want to give you up, oy, how I don't want to give up my Stayatishok" – he was saying to himself.

We, in our home, could not imagine what was happening. We thought they were coming to rob us, so we managed to hide some things. Suddenly the door opened, and my sister in law Ethel burst in, a coat on her shoulders, wearing boots without stockings.

Children, don't be frightened! God is with us, they came to take us to a work camp, in Poligon, we will surely die there of hunger. Let's run away, and God will help us. Children, quickly, have pity, the police are 10 meters away.

At that moment we were all at home, I, Avraham and Sheina, too bad, I thought to myself, may be there in White Russia, they are not being sent to labour camps. Maybe it's not as bad there, like in Vilna. No one was going to protect us. Mother and father lived here in Stayatishok for 7 years, after the death of grandfather, he didn't want to leave the business in unknown hands, so they moved from Sventzian to here. After a few years they had 3 grown cows, sheep and hens, ducks and geese.

[Col. 1627]

I saw my father, for the first time, crying. How can I leave my home? How can I leave my Stayatishok? How can we leave the Holy Books?

In one sack he put a piece of bread and a shirt and in the other sack, some books (maybe holy bible). Mother was trembling and said: Do not cry on the way. God will help us. I saw that she placed her Chasidic Siddur in one of the sacks, I was very emotional and scared that I wouldn't know how to meet up with Israel(her husband), but Ethel assured me, that late at night, we will all meet on the road. Under no circumstance did he want to meet in daylight. He will leave through the edge of town, knowing the direction we were heading. In the meantime, we are heading to Belarus, Kazian, Postov, wherever Jews are still to be found. I couldn't find a head scarf, so I pulled out a house coat, I couldn't find my second shoe, so I left with 1 shoe and 1 Volek (boot), and luckily, my papers were prepared earlier. My certificate from the Teacher's Seminary of Vilna, the certificate of the Sventzianer Jewish Gymnasia, and the other certificates from the Jewish school. I kept them always close by as they were always so dear to me. Rebeccela, our 3 week old child, was grabbed out of her carriage still asleep by Ethel. How much she still had to live! We ran out of the house leaving the door open. We ran through the fields, from a distance, one could see the mass of black people, like smoke. The crying and the screaming greeted us on the way. We all cried silently.

[Col. 1628]

The sounds of the animals and the sheep, the howling of the dogs, came from all directions.

My father spoke to my brother Avraham. We are leaving our home, our Stayatishok. Who knows if we are going to return? History keeps repeating itself, since we left our own land, we will continue to wander. In every generation we are faced with new obstacles, but God always helps us, but this time a great storm is coming towards us on foreign soil, we do not have a say in these matters, like a mighty wind(tornado). It could be, that we should have joined the crowd, where all the Jews are going. We don't know whether we will have a place to hide, everywhere there are Germans – said our father.

Late at night we all met in the forest: my in – laws, Rabbi Chaim and Baila, my brother in laws Eliahu and Abraham, and with my Israel.

Rabbi Chaim did not want to leave his home. With great difficulty, the children had to force him to leave with them. Where shall I go, he said?

The forests were cold and dark. Rebeccala didn't stop crying. There was nothing to rock her in. Abraham held her in his hands and rocked her, nothing helped. It made things worse, and we crying with her. We started a fire, to warm ourselves. I tried to nurse her, but was unable. She was completely frozen and wet.

Oy, oy, said rabbi Chaim, this is what we lived for! These are great times for Rabbi Pesach! We have sinned! We should have sold everything and gone to Eretz Israel.

Now it's too late! Opportunity was lost! Answered my father.

[Col. 1629]

The Destruction of Maligan

Gershon Braslavski

Translated by Anita Frishman Gabbay

Suddenly in 1939 the population of Maligan was enlarged. Many refugees arrived here and they were warmly received. They remained until the outbreak of the German – Soviet invasion in 1941.

When the Hitler Army and their Lithuanian helpers arrived, the young people decided to go deep into Russia. I was one of them, my 2 sisters, my brother in law, 2 cousins Rosa and Sonia Teitleboim, Meir Kovarski, Dovid Ravitch, Chaia Sura Svirski and a Yitzhak, whose family name I can't remember.

This was on a Tuesday, the third day after the war started. We picked ourselves up and decided to run away. In our hearts we knew that we would not survive the Hitlerite Regime. The old generation would not listen to our warnings.

When my mother discovered our plan, she bid us farewell and peace, but she would not join us.

– – – You are young, she said – and you must run away. It is not a good plan for us to go wandering around (she was only 59 years old).

By chance my father was not at home that week. He was away on business, at Taraseitzkin in Sventzian, with whom he dealt with in large quantities of hay from the entire region. My father left with merchandise and didn't manage to return home. I never had the chance to say goodbye to my father.

Heina Teitlboim and her family

[Col. 1630]

On the way, this left me with a very unsettling feeling. My thoughts kept me thinking that it was not correct to run away, leaving behind my mother and father.

After 4 kilometers away, I decided to return to the shtetl to bring my mother with us. My sister and her husband had to wait for me in the forest. She was overjoyed to see me, but wouldn't come. She gave me a ring with my father's monogram as a souvenir, and begged me, if they were murdered, not to forget to say Kaddish for them.

We kissed again, cried and then I left to join the others in the forest. After this I never saw my nearest and dearest again.

We met up an hour later and left for Polotsk by foot, arriving tired and hungry. We didn't stay long, we continued our journey deeper and deeper into Russia.

After much pain and suffering, hardships and wandering, we managed to remain alive.

In 1945, when Russia took control of the region, we decided to return to our shtetl of our birth.

Yitzhak fell in battle and the only ones to return to Maligan were myself, my sister Surel and Chaia Sura Svirski. We found complete destruction and only 1 living Jewish soul.

We were told how the complete Jewish folk of Maligan were murdered.

We learned about the horrors and fate of our parents. Our father returned from Sventzian several days later and together with my mother, they left to a Christian friend, who hid them in the fields between the potatoes. They remained till Khoel Hamoed

Succoth. As soon as he found out that the Jews from the shtetl were being deported, they decided to go with the entire folk. This was their gruesome end with the others in Poligon. There bones are in the mass grave – amongst the bones and corpses of thousands murdered from the Sventzian district.

[Col. 1631]

Pesach Braslavski before the shooting

According to our neighbour Roketch, he took pity on my parents and gave them some bread. The Lithuanians found out and they went to the house and burned it down. They also shot his father.(Roketch). Three homes and the synagogue remained, but later the Lithuanians destroyed everything that was left.

[Col. 1632]

One Christian friend, who had worked for us, gave us a description who took part in the robberies of Jewish homes and goods, who murdered Jews, and where the Jewish goods could be found. I didn't wait long, and went to search for Jewish goods amongst the Christian homes. I was able to find some of our belongings as well as those of other Jews. I decided to report this to the N.K.V.D. and as a result several Christians were arrested and sent to Siberia.

Four days later I found out that the Christians were going to murder me on the road. Once before, they tried to trick me, offering me some whiskey to make a L'Chaim, but I got suspicious, and refused the offer. They were going to poison me. So now it was no longer safe, I had to make a plan to leave.

This was now official, they were out to murder me.

I still had a little hope. From a fellow Christian, when I had arrived to my cousin's house in Disna, my parents before their death found out that we were all safe and had crossed the border and arrived in Bobruisk.

After receiving all this information, I left for Vilna, then Poland, then to Germany and I finally arrived in Eretz Israel.

[Col. 1633]

The Liquidation of the Postover Ghetto

Translated by Anita Frishman Gabbay

The liquidation took place December 25, 1942. There were still 1500 Jews in the ghetto. At 3 in the morning, screaming and disorder was heard. An order came from the police that the Jews were to leave the ghetto. The children were woken up. The Jews already had a feeling what this meant. They were ordered to make rows of four. Everyone assembled, men women, old and young, and the Germans order the people to march to the train station. They all knew what this meant, several, under darkness, started to run. Others followed and the Germans started shooting. The weaker ones were already shot on the way to the train station.

[Col. 1634]

Postov, dug up corpses

To the mass grave, that had been prepared in advance, few Jews that were still alive were there. The mass grave was covered with the earth that was set alongside the pit. The "Mass Brothers Grave" is on the other side of the train station, at the end of Zelmianer Street.

The mass grave of murdered Jews of Postov, which was opened when the Soviet Army arrived

[Col. 1635]

Magnified and Sanctified

Translated by Janie Respitz

I figure that all we presented here is merely a drop in the ocean, but everyone who will turn page after page will experience his own lamenting.

In every line that has been written, our sadness can be felt and every word carries the holiness and purity drowning in suffering.

The voice of every survivor from Sventzian, New –Sventzian, Ignalina, Old and New – Dugelishok, Lingmian, Kaltinian, Kimelishok, Podbrodz, Lintup, Stayatzishok, Maligan, Dukstas and Haydutzishok and all the other surrounding small towns: Paliush, Gaviken, Tzeikin, Dzikovinesh, and smaller settlements like Vidz, Miori, Yadi, Postov, Kobilnik – is a source of tears.

In each voice thousands and thousands of names are breathed, of those who were once cradled in a dream of a sunny life and who, at the hands of inhumane murderers were tortured, murdered and burned.

These are the holiest of holiest upon whom we recite the mourners prayer in a voice that calls out: Amen. May God's great name be blessed forever, in all worlds, unto eternity.

In our Kaddish (mourner's prayer) there is the pain and complaint, our helpless suffering and our burning hatred, the blood that is drunk in the terror of the darkest nights.

Through the unsurmountable mountain of pain, that hides for us the macabre reality, at the chasm of the unending terror and suffering that carried out this reality, our shout should be lifted, and shout not stop demanding and prevent sleep for the indifferent and their lives should resemble a flung stone, which will terrorize people and themselves.

That world which has been lost to horrific murder, twisted and hardened, did not see and did not hear the desperate cries from the ghettos, from Poligon and Ponar – they should always feel the shame, the guilt for these brutalities.

May the murderers be punished, who are still walking around this world. May their horrific sins be washed away with their dirty blood.

The cries that emanate from this memorial book, the tombstone for twenty–three Jewish towns from the Sventzian region, should never stop ringing in our ears and should never be silenced for generations to come.

[Col. 1637]

In the Death Camps

[Col. 1639]

Two of One Hundred Thousand

Shimon Kantz

Translated by Janie Respitz

...One of a thousand, two of a hundred thousand, where those who were saved in order to tell the generations the pain suffered by our sisters and brothers, and also to show generations to come that our people was not destroyed. For the few who survived the horrors of Hitler's death camps, one day was like three years. They are now in a position to tell about their experiences in the ghettos and camps. The responsibility has fallen upon them to carry the burden that not even Jeremiah had to withstand, to bear witness to the pain and atrocities are people endured. With their own eyes they saw entire towns destroyed together with their parents who were hung and choked in gas chambers. They also bore witness to hidden graves in Poligon and Ponar. We listen to them talk about it and watch their lips break, as if they are kissing a corpse, and it sticks in their throat like an unsung song, with holy words, "Father – Mother"; like a stone like pain in their hearts; like a cry which is more silent than mute...We read the lines written here by Etya Rudnitsky and Leah Holtzman, and are feeling everything they are not talking about, that they can't talk about, that they don't want to talk about because the wounds have not healed. The bleeding has not stopped, and a man who is still bleeding cannot relate everything clearly. Every torn word contains thousands of unsaid words, because no one is capable to recount the experiences of a day in the camps.

[Col. 1641]

From Kimelishak Through Hitler's Death Camps

by Etya Rudnitsky – Teitlman

Translated by Janie Respitz

A soon as the German army arrived on June 21st, 1941, they began to attack us. Even our Christian neighbours from surrounding villages did not spare us and began to rob Jewish homes. The Ghetto was ready before Rosh Hashana.

Mid–summer, 1942, around July, I, together with a group of young people which included refugees, was saved from slaughter and sent to a work camp, between Kiene – Ostrovitz, near Vilna. Our job was to build a railway for the “Todt” company. It was difficult work. We were happy not be sitting in the Ghetto and hearing bad news every day about the killings. Their treatment of us at work was not too bad. Besides the food they gave us daily, from time to time we received food from home. Our “good” situation did not last long. By the end of 1942 the Jews of Kimelishak Ghetto, which included people who had escaped from Podbrodz, Niemencine Podbrodz, Mikhalishok, Bistritz, Svir and other places – were exterminated. Two small girls brought us the news, Baylinke Epshtein and another one whose sister was with us.

Our situation worsened. We no longer received aid. We needed warm clothing for the winter and could not get any. Also the German's treatment toward us got worse. They brought Jews from Baranovitch, among them were doctors, engineers, teachers...We saw how our “good” Germans tortured them as they worked, and they dropped dead from hunger and suffering.

I knew my mother and my sister Masha were miraculously saved from the slaughter, and were in Ashmene Ghetto. I ran away to meet them in Ashmene. My luck did not last long. March 1943, they began to liquidate all the Ghettos in the Vilna region.

[Col. 1642]

The liquidation was carried out by the Vilna Jewish police, led by Gens. They were divided in two groups, one was sent to Vilna, the other to Kovno. We were brought to Vilna Ghetto. The “Kovno” transport was killed in Ponar. This is how we were once again, miraculously, saved from death.

Our situation in Vilna Ghetto was very difficult. We wandered around not having a regular place to sleep. We were hungry, dressed in rags and barefoot. In those days I learned from a couple of survivors, the Kiene camp where I had worked was liquidated and all the Jews were exterminated.

Suddenly, there were new orders. All the Jews from the provinces who were in Vilna were being sent to Estonia. In the middle of summer 1943, they confined us without food or drink. This work, once again, was carried out with cruelty by the Jewish police. A few days later, they brought us to the train, confined us to large dirty freight cars, threw in a few loaves of bread with jugs of water and locked the doors.

Through a small window we saw we were travelling past Podbrodz and New–Sventzian. After a few days, the train came to a stop. When they opened the doors we heard an unfamiliar language. We were in Dorpat Estonia.

From the train station they made us walk to a camp which was called: Vaivara.

[Col. 1643]

In the camp we found our neighbour, a wealthy man from Kimelishak – Aharon Gimzansky. He looked like a skeleton and asked for a piece of bread. We were all hungry and could not help him. We later learned they threw him into the Baltic Sea because he could no longer work.

In the evening they took our group to another camp called Vivikane. The barracks stood deep in the forest. There was no light or water. Broken from our journey we went to sleep. In the morning we began to “organize” and see who was among us. I met Kovalsky from New – Sventzian, and Nomkin and his wife from Sventzian. As our representative we chose Aronovitch, a Jew from Mikhalishok, a really nice guy. The camp was run by Estonians and an S.S officer.

The authorities did not like our choice of leader, Aronovitch, and replaced him with someone who did everything they asked. He was a former underworld guy who knew how to please them.

The Estonians did not treat us terribly. We worked in the forest and the mines. Our lives “normalized”. We had a doctor, the well- known Dr. Fried from Vilna. We hoped: Perhaps we will be able to survive here?

One morning as we stood for rollcall, they took all the children away from their parents. The cries and screams from the children and their parents still ring in my ears until today. I will never forget that horrific scene.

The same day, as I was working in the forest, I saw them lead a line of small Jewish children on their final walk. A Jewish woman from Ashmene witnessed this scene and went mad. Together with a woman from Brodz, I tried to bring them potatoes I received from an Estonian woman. I was beaten up.

From dawn until late at night we were not permitted to rest from our work for a minute, – besides the curses and beatings from our oppressors – hungry, worn out, on our last strength. There were many who remained lying with glazed over eyes, where beating from the oppressors no longer helped. Sometimes I was envious that they had already died.

This went on day after day, without change, constant bloody horror, under unbearable edicts, one more horrifying than the next. Then they chose three hundred men, from the heathiest and strongest, and we believed the explanation they were being sent to work elsewhere. We soon learned they were burnt alive in Klooga Camp.

[Col. 1644]

In Vaivara Camp working in the forest

As hard as it may be to comprehend, we still had a glimmer of hope we would be rescued.

There were no grounds for this hope. Everything pointed to the fact that sooner or later we will be killed. Day in and day out, people dropped dead at work, at night roll–calls, – but we hoped, in and unclear hopefulness, that we ourselves could not acknowledge, that we would courageously fight to survive.

Months passed. It was the end of 1943 and it seemed to us that our hope was useless. We began to notice signs that our murderers were uneasy and afraid. The Nazis became meaner, crueler, and unsure, as if they were frightened.

We did not know the reason, but we took it as a sign the Germans were experiencing defeats. We were cut off from the outside world and had no idea what was happening on the fronts. Our instincts did not fool us. From the east, a wave of aggressive Red Army units was nearing and the German "heroes" were running like poisoned mice. They lacked train cars to carry out important military objectives. They did not have enough ships to transport their own people. However, their hatred of the Jews was so great, even in the most difficult moments, they found wagons to chase out the Jewish slaves, while continuing to torture them, to Germany, and did not evacuate them, but murdered them on the spot, like the Jews of Klooga Camp, where they shot the Jewish inmates on a prepared pyre. When the Red Army arrived a few days later, they were shocked to see thousands of half burnt bodies, still lying on the wooden boards. Our camp was luckier. We were evacuated.

[Col. 1645]

Suddenly, the command came, unjust, during a snowstorm. The snow was deep and covered the roads. We walked with our blankets and small bags on our backs all night and the whole next day without a rest, enduring curses and beatings.

We were only able to stop and catch our breath when we had to clear the road for German military. We would fall into the deep snow like cut down trees.

The guards began to beat us with clubs and forced us to march on. We barely made it on the second night to our new camp, Ereda.

In the camp there were half –circle huts mad from asbestos. We had to bend down to enter the huts. We entered exhausted and on the dark, everyone sought out a board to sleep on. I lit a match, and was horrified with what I saw. The barrack was full of corpses. They were laid out like boards. I ran out.

In the camp there was a special group of workers whose job it was to burn the corpses. The smell of those burned entered our lungs. The sanitary conditions were terrible. We had no water. When we received a bit of tea we did not know if we should drink it or use it to rinse our faces and hands. We received 150 grams of bread. It was overcrowded. It was so cold our hair would freeze to the wall. We were covered in lice and abscesses.

We suffered greatly under the Camp leader, Shnabel, and his Jewish helpers. Khayt, a Jew from Vilna was particularly bad. He would often surpass the German Camp commander. People were falling like flies. The German Dr. Botman dealt with the over crowdedness it by sending a large transport of people into the field to freeze to death. Later, they brought them back to us to be burned.

[Col. 1646]

In the spring, when the sun got a little warmer, a Typhus epidemic broke out. People were dying en masse. The living envied the dead. When the S.S. wanted to be entertained, they would choose a few people and torture them to death. This would calm them down.

Luckily, together with my mother and sister, I was sent to another camp, Kivioli. Compared to Ereda, the new camp was paradise. The barracks were made of wood, and there was light and water. The immediately shaved our heads. They packed our hair and sent it to Germany.

They took us often to bathe and the food was better. The work was hard, but the Jewish camp leader was Segal, a very nice Jew from Vilna. We met our friend Abraham Kuritzky. Here too there were many edicts: selections and torture.

After a few months they brought us to another camp, Sonda. This was a small camp with a few hundred Jews. The camp elder was a Jew from New–Sventzian, Yonah Katz. He did not treat us too badly.

Summer 1944

We are hearing a lot of bombing. We were very happy. But here too, there were selections. At one selection we had to hide our mother in a toilet. That's how she remained alive.

After a few months in Sonda, they evacuated the camp. On a hot summer day, they shoved us into freight trains and locked the doors. When two young boys tried to escape, they caught them and shot them on the spot.

I don't know how long we traveled. But after a few days the train suddenly stopped. They opened the doors and we saw the sea. A terrifying German with face of a murderer shouted: “Everyone out!” We were sure they were going to drown us in the sea.

They took us to the port and put us on ship. On the ship we found inscriptions in many languages: Russian, Polish, Yiddish, French and others. They all warned we were being taken to our death.

A few hours later, more transports arrived to the ship. They packed the people in like herring. It is impossible to describe what took place.

[Col. 1647]

After sailing for 4–5 hours, we arrived at a port. From there they took us to a camp Stutthof.

The entrance to the camp was filled with flowers. Inside the camp was hell on earth. Before entering the camp they took us to a bath house. They took away our belongings and gave us camp uniforms. We were skin and bones with no hair. We could not recognize one another. We laughed and cried. This is how we entered the camp.

The huge area of the camp was lit with electric lights. Nighttime was as bright as day. The conditions were terrible. In the morning we had rollcall where we had to stand for hours. In the morning they gave us bitter coffee and bread. Lunch – one bowl of soup for two people, and in the evening, a small piece of bread. We were not sent to work, but all day they would chase us like dogs and beat us. Our leaders were women – German S.S women. They tortured us with the help of Russian and Jewish women. The Jewish Kapos were not embarrassed with their handling of us.

Besides the torture, there was a crematorium in Stutthof where thousands of people from various countries were killed.

There was a special place with mountains of glasses, shoes, children's shoes and clothing. I was in Stutthof for a short time. Unfortunately my sister and I were separated from our mother. After liberation, we learned she died of hunger.

In the Fall of 1944 they took 300 women from Stutthof to a labour camp near Danzig – Rusashin. The conditions in this camp were better. Everyone had a place to sleep and a cover. Each day we received 250 grams of bread and one portion of soup.

We woke up every morning at 4 o'clock to go to work. We worked hard all day and had to endure the persecutions of the S.S women.

[Col. 1648]

Winter, the beginning of 1945. An order came. We were to leave the camp.

On a cold morning we set out in the snow wearing rags and wooden shoes. We walked for a few days, hungry and frozen. From time to time they gave us a piece of bread – sometimes, a few potatoes. At night we slept in cold barns with wet, frozen feet.

Each day our group became smaller. The road was covered with corpses of Jewish men and women.

After a few days we arrived in Strelentin and went to sleep on the ground. We remained there for a few weeks. They barely gave us any food, and we had no energy to move our legs. We lay there waiting to die.

The defeat of the Germans was nearing, but would we survive?

We were ordered to leave the camp. They gave us large portions of bread and we set out at night. A wet snow was falling. The snow stuck to our wooden shoes. I could not walk any further. The S.S female guard hit me and shouted: "Walk faster, the Russians are approaching". I took off my wooden shoes, advised others to do the same, and we continued walking barefoot all night. At dawn they took us into a barn and blocked the doors.

Inside we found people lying in their own filth. There were many dead among them. In the morning Russian prisoners came and removed the dead.

A few of the healthier women went to the gate and tried to open it. No one stopped them. My sister and I also went out. Suddenly there was a cry: "the Russian army is coming!".

The cries were mixed with joyful shouts: We are free!

March 10, 1945, we were few, sick, broken shards, freed, leaving the majority behind, dead in the barn, in the region of Loenberg.

[Col. 1649]

In the Hell of Hitler's Camps

by Leah Svirsky – Holtzman

Translated by Janie Respitz

In 1944, me my mother and my eleven year old sister Chaneleh were in a "prison camp" near Kovno. My mother worked at her profession, a dentist. I worked as her assistant, so we were always in the camp and not sent put to work like all the other Jews.

On March 27th, 1944, I was in the laundry barrack which stood about 10 metres from the main 3 story camp building. Suddenly I noticed through the window, how the German and Lithuanian guards were running around.

In such situations, our first reaction was that we must be together. I wanted to run to my mother and little sister, but I found myself standing at the exit in front of a locked door. On the other side of the door stood an armed guard.

I looked out the window and saw them open the gate to the yard. Large black trucks were driving in. I watched as armed soldiers threw people into the trucks like bags of flour.

My mother, Rochel Svirsky – Khanukhovitch

Meanwhile, a few wild murderers opened the door to the laundry, and began to throw dirty laundry around, poking at it with their guns – thinking they may find children hiding. Finding nothing, shouting obscene curses, they left and locked the doors behind them.

[Col. 1650]

Once again I stood by the window. The trucks drove away. Only one stood with open doors and I saw our Chaneleh being taken away with other children and a woman. Chaneleh was wearing a brown fur coat and a blue knit hat.

The last truck drove off and life in the camp returned to "normal". The door to the laundry was opened and I ran, like from a Fury, across the yard, and fell upon my mother. She hugged me, kissed me and cried. She told me how she hid the child under a bed and warned her not to move until the danger passed. But the murderers came with dogs, and pulled the frightened child from her hiding place. Mother took Chaneleh by the hand and went together with her, but they did not allow this. "You can still work, you are strong". The big dog jumped on my mother and pushed her to the ground. By the time she stood up a minute later, there was no sign of Chaneleh in the room.

*

June 1944, the front line was nearing Lithuania and the Germans were retreating, we again awaited our death. But no, they took us with them. After a few days and night of traveling in a closed train car, not knowing where or when, we arrived in Stutthof, the well–known concentration camp near Danzig. As we got off the train they led us to a big place, where we sat all day under the burning hot sun, each one holding his bag and awaiting his fate.

My mother did not leave my side and said: “No one else from our family is alive, just the two of us. We must never leave each other. Not even for a minute”.

Suddenly we heard a command:

[Col. 1651]

“Strip naked, leave everything behind, and go in a group to the baths”.

We already knew what the Germans meant by “a Bath”. We had already heard about the gas chambers in Auschwitz and Treblinka. But there could be no talk about resisting. We stuck together and went in, when it was our turn, into the long narrow room, filled with naked bodies. There were showers on the ceiling and taps to turn on the water on the walls. We knew the “showers” were there to spread the gas that would soon kill us. People were panicking. Mother pulls me closer to her and we were saying our goodbyes without words, and waiting. Here and there we hear a woman shout: “I'm choking! I can already smell the gas!” Suddenly we hear a noise in the pipes. Our hearts stood still for a second, and then we felt a stream of hot water...

Again my mother pulls me close: “my child, we are alive!...”

*

[Col. 1652]

After a few weeks in Stutthof, there was a selection. They gave us some rags to cover our naked bodies, and they sent us to a labour camp to dig trenches for the army. The camp was on Polish territory, in the region of Poznan. We lived in tents. As long as it was warm, it was bearable. But as autumn passed and winter arrived the suffering became unbearable: 10 hours a day of forced labour, hunger and the worst, frost on our half naked, partially barefoot bodies. My mother withstood it. She dug with the shovel all day, making an effort to feel this was the “norm”. If not, her back would be broken by bloody smacks, which happened more than once; we lived an entire day on a bowl of soup and a piece of bread, and slept on the frozen ground. In the morning we had to get up and tear our frozen hair from the ground.

She withstood and survived all of this. Today, this all belongs to the past, like our old home in far away Sventzian. How deep Sventzian was engraved and baked in her heart can be understood from the following: In her last days in Tel Aviv, when she had already lost consciousness, I asked her: “Mother, how are you?” She responded: “Good, my child. The Jews of Sventzian are taking care of me, watching over me, making sure I am okay”.

[Col. 1651]

We Begin the Day of Anguish

Translated by Janie Respitz

The moon barely begins to pale
And fresh snow covers the earth
The wind is chasing the dawn
The first greeting of the day.

On all the roads, wherever
It's always the same scene
It's chasing and carrying, the frost burns
And we have shovels in our hands.

We walk straight, five in a row
We step through the deep snow,
We suffer in the darkness
Our hearts long for joy.

We don't hear any ringing
But songs from the church
There is no ray from the sun
The day of anguish has begun.

All around us is dark, dull and pale,
Our feet are frozen, bare and wet. Our
bodies – skin and bones
Our hearts are hardened like stone.

[Col. 1652]

Your persecutor stands over you
Watching every movement and turn
Beats you blindly, without pity.
You ask: Why, how have I sinned?

My body has become accustomed,
Long forgotten how to rest,
There is no ray of light
Apparently , this is how it must be.

The clock will soon strike three
The day passes slowly,
This day is already over
But many more just like it will come.

From troubles, anguish, cries and suffering,
We are often lacking a piece of bread,
Mysteriously the future shines,
We must live with the present.

[Col. 1653]

Heroism

[Col. 1655]

Our Heroism

Heshl Gurvitch

Translated by Janie Respitz

...The Jewish heroes from the region of Sventzian tell about their daily battle they fought in the ranks of the various partisan units within the regular Lithuanian division. In simple language, in plain words, the heroes, these heroes recount their experiences. They give the facts of their great heroism, both physical and spiritual. If physical heroism ended with defeat, the end of spiritual heroism is always victory. These heroic fighters continued in the heroic traditions of our people. Physical resistance has always been in our lives, which has always been surrounded by a sea of hatred, wickedness and murder! When they forced the Jewish tenant farmer to dance, he did not pay attention to the humiliation and did not lose his self– respect. Deep in his heart he disdained the wild, powerful but intellectually inferior nobleman. The peddlers showed amazing heroism as the Christian shepherds threw stones at them. They would not even stop their prayers. These Jews who lived in a Christian setting, and the innkeepers who kept the Sabbath would continue to perform good deeds under the mocking laughter of their neighbours. However, even in this wild situation, the neighbours knew the Jews would not turn the other cheek. More than once, they felt the punches of the Jewish boys when the hooligans wildly fell upon unprotected Jews. These were the Jewish boys in Sventzian throughout the years. The non–religious boy would stand up to the military power as they confiscated the last prayer house in New – Sventzian, just as he would dare to call for a boycott of the German school which made Jewish children learn on the Sabbath. The Jewish boys were raised in this spirit. In the most horrific times, they breathed the air of magnificent spiritual heroism. With a glance of the hill of Jewish corpses, they looked to a higher mountain – the one where the sun shines on a proud equal Jewish people. I hold great honour respect for the Jewish heroes of this time of slaughter. Your heroic struggle possesses the large, superhuman splendor of the Maccabees and all the martyrs of the times. It is the splendor that was shown in all periods among the revolutionaries of the Sventzian region, Zionists, Socialists, dreamers and fighters for a better world. Your heroism, partisans and fighters on the front, is the eternal light in the history of life and death in the cities and towns on the Sventzian region. You, heroic warriors from burnt homes, proud vanquishers of death, will be remembered for centuries. We will remind ourselves and repeat the holiest oath, the words of our partisan poet: "And where a spurt of our blood fell on the earth, there our courage and our spirit have rebirth".

[Col. 1657]

Heroic Deeds

by Sh. Buszkanitz

Translated by Jerrold Landau

When a historian comes to search for material on the terrible Holocaust that descended upon the Jewish nation, including the frightful destruction of the Jews of the district of Švenèionys, he will certainly stand astonished and surprised at the pages of splendor of the sublime Jewish might, of the bravery of the Jews of Švenèionys and its district, bravery without any chance of victory; battles lost from the outset, but brave battles of Jewish heroes against the Nazi German death machinery – a battle for the honor of the Jewish nation.

The Jewish youth in the region of Švenèionys, who sensed the Holocaust and annihilation even before it was perpetrated in the ghettoes and the fields of Poligon and Ponar, did not want under any circumstance to make peace with the murder. Immediately after being confined to the ghettoes, many searched for the possibility of escaping and fighting against the Nazi invasion. They directed their steps to the forests to join the partisans.

Many of them sacrificed their lives and did not merit to celebrate the great victory over the Nazi enemy. It is our duty, people of arms and fighting, the few who survived, to perpetuate their might – how they disrupted and struck the enemy on the military communication arteries, and even caused many losses; how we were a fighting people even during the years of the war and the Holocaust.

How many treasures of bravery are hidden in the battles of the dwellers of those forests? Through their efforts, and by setting up their area in the forests of White Russia, a district called "Garatch", a distance of hundreds of kilometers from the city of Vilna, they were able to provide help and guidance to the Jews of the ghetto, to the members of the F.P.O (the organization of fighters of the Vilna Ghetto), and to all those who wished to transfer to the camp of fighting and revenge. With the help of the partisans, the vast majority succeeded in reaching the forest of the fighters. Along with this, they supported the honor of the fighters and avengers of the Vilna Ghetto in the eyes of nations of the world.

S. Katzerginski writes:

"The heart began to beat a new pulse from when it became known one day that several partisans from the forests of Byelorussia arrived in the ghetto – lads who were in the ghetto just a few weeks previously. They stated that many of the Jews were in the forest and that they excel in bravery, instilling great fear on the farmers and even on the Germans.

Who are these partisans?! You know them, oh Švenèionys natives: Yeshika Gertman, Moisheke Shutan, Itzka Rudnicki[Rudnitzki], Yisraelke Wolfson, Motke Feigel, Mote-Heshke Buszkanitz, Moshe Yehuda Rudnicki,[Rudnitzki] Davidka Jochai, and others. They reached here on a mission from the commander of their unit, Fyodor Grigorovich Markov, to deliver a letter to the F.P.O people of the Vilna Ghetto.

In his letter, Markov writes them that they should come to the forest with all the Jews.

"Many wish to see the partisans, but they act discreetly for various reasons, and do not reach them. All their connections are only through the F.P.O group, and with their close friends.

On the morning of August 24, 1943, 40 armed Jews went out as a work group with the yellow patch on their clothes – if one looks carefully at them, one would notice Yeshika (a partisan from Švenèionys) and other recognizable people from the Vilna F.P.O. among them. There were women among them, and brothers and sisters of the partisans who were already in the forest and waiting for them there.

The command of the F.P.O decided to send additional groups accompanied by partisans, but the information will arrive from the forest. The call of this daring action was:

We will go from here – to the forest, to the forest!

Here we will perish in any case...

Let us fall in honor, in battle..."

In this section, we will perpetuate the deeds of bravery while everything is still in the memories of the fighters who returned from the front and the strong partisans who went out to the forests to avenge the spilled blood, the blood of brethren screaming out from the vale of perplexity so as to not forget the destruction of the nation and the battle against the cruel enemy.

[Col. 1659]

With Weapons in Our Hands

Moishe Shutan

Translated by Anita Frishman Gabbay

The outbreak of the Soviet – German War. It was still summer, the youth were carefree and were enjoying their time, when suddenly this came to an abrupt end: to leave our homes and flee with the Soviet military or stay under German rule? Our young intuition told us that we should flee, as far away from the Germans as possible.

On the other hand, we wanted to take our families along, father – mother, sister – brother. This however was impossible – a difficult weight! No one had the will or the strength to leave their families to die. Basically, we remained. Only some managed to flee with the Red Army. Most remained in their shtetl.

Our hearts were greatly saddened. We wandered the empty and bare streets with heavy hearts.

[Col. 1660]

I returned home and sat on the large stone in front of our home and Yoske Rudinski, Dudke Yokhai, Itzka Rudinski, Ishike Gertman came by. It became clear to all of us we all had the same concerns, the same worries about the future.

What shall we now do? How are we going to survive? Ishike said:

Friend, do not lower your heads! (accept defeat) Don't loose your willpower! We will have to fight for our lives. Today we all have to prepare ourselves to fight. We know we have to fight and therefore we have to organize ourselves.

The First Days in the Ghetto

We the young people of Sventzian and the surrounding region did not have good feelings about the Germans. We already heard from others about the German concentration camps and their activities, the ghettos that tens of thousands of Jews were thrown into. The truth, one never imagined that such atrocities toward mankind would actually occur. We then decided it would be impossible for Jews to live with the German occupation, and our only way was to fight with all our might.

In the evening, a young group of friends assembled to discuss our plans and ideas for organizing our fight. Together with Ishike Gertman, Itzke and Yosef Rudnitski and Dudke Yokhai, we were the organizers of this group. We were isolated from the world and we had to know what was happening around us:

[Col. 1661]

We suffered under the Germans occupation as well as the Red Army.

We decided to organize a radio – contact, so that news would reach us from all sides.

The radio apparatus was assembled by Avraham Gertman, and Itzike Tatin brought us this apparatus and in no time, we were able to hear the news from all the other countries.

The news from the radio and the call for action, gave us incentive and strength to endure this situation. We spread the news amongst our group, at first hoping that the war would soon be over.

Our radio gave us the update of the difficult battle between the Russians and the Germans, and about the horrendous events taking place amongst the Jewish population. From other sources we discovered that the ghettos were liquidated and many Jewish communities were destroyed and murdered. Thousands of Jews were being liquidated.

All those, that believed that the Sventzianer Jews would not meet the same fate, soon knew they were living with false hope. So this is exactly what happened, the fate was the same for all the shtetls and shtetlach. An order came to send all the Jews of Sventzian to the camps in Poligon. They only left the "useful Jews", about 500 people.

We were thankful to one another not to be caught by the Germans.

When they ghetto was established, we came out of hiding and snuck into the ghetto with everyone. We quickly learned that all the Jews who were in Poligon were slaughtered and physically tortured.

The thought of the Poligon Massacre shook the Sventzian Jews in the ghetto and a heavy gloom hung over our heads. Amongst us young people, the idea to avenge the dead was declared and now we were going to take our revenge! Our hatred grew deeper and stronger now. Our will to fight to the last drop of blood festered.

One person who was in the workplace, at the "Depot", was Godel Gilinski, who worked there, and told Itike that there were a lot of guns there. We sent several friends, in order to bring back as many guns to the ghetto as possible. Several of them joined the work detail at the warehouse and brought guns back; rifles, hand grenades and chains, which we hid in every corner.

[Col. 1662]

Our group began to slowly expand, the following: Gershka Bak, Rivka Miadzolski, Berka Yocai, Shulka Michalson, Mote – Heske Bushkanitz, Kuske Ligumski, Motke Feigel, and Feivke Chait from New Sventian, who escaped from Poligon at the last minute. The survivors of our group: Berke Yokhai, Feivke Chait and I. (Moishe Shutan). Our thoughts were to enlarge our arsenal and to hide our conspiracy.

At first everything went along quietly, until a great tragedy struck our group. Shaulka Michelson, in his former house, told us that several revolvers were hidden. Two friends of ours snuck out of the ghetto, late at night, and brought the revolvers back to us. The next morning, Dudke Yokhai, Gershka Bak and Rivka Miadzolski went outside to clean and inspect the revolvers. Accidently the gun went off and wounded Gerhon Bak severely. The bullet went through his mouth and neck. The shot fired was heard in the ghetto, and everyone soon found out. The Judenrat who were in charge were displeased. Gershon was hospitalized and Rivka, at first hid, but they found her.

A policeman was watching over Gershon and Rivka was arrested. We were very anxious that our group and activities would not be revealed.

A meeting of our group was immediately set up and we didn't know whether we should remain in the ghetto or escape to the forests. Everyone of us was concerned, but the two arrested, under torture and pain, did not reveal anyone of us.

[Col. 1663]

After 3 days of torture, they were both shot. May 16, 1942, a wagon of Lithuanian police arrived, took Gershon from the hospital and Rivka from the prison in chains (also Surke Levin, who was put to death because she insulted a Lithuanian policeman). They were all led in the direction of the cemetery. The grave was already prepared, they stood at the edge, all 3 were shot and thrown in.

After this incident, our secret was out. We went to the Judenrat to help us, to assist us with able bodies (young people) ready to fight.

Two friends, Faivka Chait and Berka Yokhai, were given the task of working with the Judenrat. Moishe Gordon and those two, were delegated to get money from the Judenrat in order to buy guns. They warned Moishe Gordon, that if the police found out what the Judenrat was ordered to do, they would pay with their lives. The head of the Judenrat gave us the money and we bought the guns. The main person in charge was Chaim the tanner, who had friendly relations with the Tatars, and brought our organization many guns and ammunition. Again our Partisan group was armed and was joined by new volunteers: Itzke Teitz, Moishe – Heskel Milutin, the brothers Shimke and Ruvke Levin, Yoske Flexser, and several others from the nearby shtetls, who were now in Sventzian. The organization had to make decisions: some believed we should remain in the ghetto. Those that wanted to remain, didn't want to leave and encounter the German enemy. This was not an option for us, to remain in the ghetto and fight. But the majority wanted to leave the ghetto and go to the forests where we could actively engage in fighting the Nazis. After long negotiations, it was decided to send 2 friends to make contact with Partisan organization in the forests.

[Col. 1664]

They left for a small village, which according to our information, these partisans came from time to time. We came back empty handed, no contact was made.

We made several attempts, contacted different Otriads, but unsuccessfully.

Suddenly, our entire region was threatened with an order. 3 Germans officers, sitting in a car, were attacked, successfully by a Partisan group. A note was left on the spot, that this attack was carried out by Markov, who was known to belong to the Otriad in the Narach region.

As punishment, the Germans arrested 100 men, Poles, White Russians and amongst them, Moishe – Yitzhak Zeidel and Yankele Gurwitch. They were all shot.

After this, our organization understood what was to come shortly thereafter. All that we previously heard about the Partisans, now became a reality. The name Markov, which we all knew, was now before us. Even before the war he was a well–known personality in Sventzian.

He was a White–Russian, and he worked as a teacher in the Jewish school. Known for his Communist ideals, he was sent to prison for 4 years during the Polish Regime. His activities gave us the desire to make contact with him.

Life in the ghetto became more difficult. We had to increase the number of workers, there was no room to breathe and the hunger increased, and many diseases spread. Our lives were at their worst.

The Jewish Judenrat of Sventzian couldn't meet the demands and bribes, couldn't help with the epidemic, and were forced to seek the help of Gens, the leader of the Jewish police of the Vilna Ghetto.

A shorter while later, Gens arrived at the Sventzian Ghetto and called a meeting: the Jews were all going to be deported, either to Vilna or Kovno. The reason, the Germans said that the Sventzian ghetto was too close to the Partisan groups!

[Col. 1665]

Our group didn't trust Gens, we knew well that he misled many. Our organization discussed what to do: we should not remain in the ghetto and await deportation! We all decided to go to the forests. We divided ourselves into groups, 5 per group. Between March 5 – 6, we were going to sneak out one at a time and meet in a designated spot in the Ligumer forest.

All our groups made it to the forest. The brothers Shimon and Rubin Levin, who knew this area well, were our guides. They knew a Christian peasant in the area, and it was decided to go to him. He received us in a friendly manner, but got alarmed when we asked to remain in his barn. We had to come up with a new plan. We decided to go to the Zcherklishker forest and make our base there. As soon as it got dark, we left the barn and went in the direction of Zcherklishok. When we arrived, travelling by night, we began to look for a suitable spot.

It was cold that night. We made a fire and sat around, wondering our fate and how to find food. We sent out a few friends to the nearby village, to see what products they could bring back.

Another group, to which I belonged, decided to return to the ghetto to find out what was going on. Besides this, we wanted to rescue some more Jews. The Jews were already on their way. The order for overseeing this mass evacuation of Gens', was led by Solak Dessler, who came with other Jewish police from Vilna to oversee mass evacuation.

[Col. 1666]

Amongst the Jewish police, was our friend, Averbuch. We learned he was part of the Partisan Organization, called the F.P.O. and from him we learned that this organization existed in Vilna.

Aberbuch told us to gather our group and guns and come and join the F.P.O. in Vilna. We sent out 2 friends with the transport to Vilna, to make contact with the F.P.O and to get a sense of acceptance: these were Itzke Rudnitski and Ishike Gertman. My sister and I decided to go to Vilna by foot.

In the Vilna Ghetto I found many from the Sventzian district, all with similar ideas, to leave the ghetto for the forest where we can fight the bloody enemy!

We immediately started to organize our departure, but we also had to make contact with those that remained in our former spot.

I and Isike Gertman were chose and we left for New Sventzian and Sventzian. On the way we encountered Shaulke Michelson and Berke Yokhai. From them we found out about the group in the woods, which were attacked by the Lithuanian police. On account of our scout, the Christian Goige, our group fled to another location. We also were told to contact Peretz Grozel in Sventzian and he will tell us the new location of our base.

We met Peretz late at night and he took us to our new base. We found them in good spirits, as they made contact with a Soviet Otriad, the head was Vaskai Charnai (Vaskai the black one). The group was to meet Vaskai in the Baronover woods, where they will be introduced to the Markov Brigade.

[Col. 1667]

At the given time, Vaskai led our group to Sidiaken, the commander of the Stofaiev Otriad. Sidiaken was known by the name "Yosnamayare". He received us warmly, asked that we rest for several days and then he would begin to send us on missions. A few days later he told us that we couldn't use our guns against the Germans, that we had to provide ourselves with rifles. (he ridiculed us) We decided a group of us should return to Sventzian to buy guns with our money and the others went to Markov, these were Itzke Gertman and Israelke Volfson. That is how our group was divided. We wanted Markov to know about the group was in a difficult situation. Besides, I and Itzke Farus returned to Vilna to deliver a letter to the F.F.O. from Sidanken.

Vittenberg questioned us about life in the woods and if we should bring more Jews out of the Vilna Ghetto. In order to make sure this was not a trick, the F.P.O. decided to send their own to Sidianken to find out his intentions. Aberbuch told us several days later, that the F.P.O. decided not to send more people to the forests, but to remain in the ghetto in order to defend those that had to be left behind. Meanwhile, Itzike Gertman and Isroelka Volfson also arrived in the Vilna Ghetto. They told us that Markov wants more Jews to be sent out of the Vilna ghetto to the forests. We saw that we could not get our way with the F.P.O and decided to take matters in our own hands.

Chaim – Hirske Levin, who was formerly the head of the Sventzian ghetto police, made a plan with some friends to escape to the forest and meet at a designated place, but when the time arrived, he found himself alone at the train. He therefore returned to the ghetto, at the gate he was met by the police, arrested and thrown into prison. He drew his gun, begging to be released, but without success, thereby shooting and wounding the policeman.

[Col. 1668]

A great tumult resulted. Even Gens arrived with many police, and Chaim – Hirsh was shot on the spot.

The Jews in the ghetto were informed that the Sventzianer partisans with guns were willing and able to take the young folk into the woods from the ghetto. Suddenly, there was an urgency to find these Sventzianer partisans. Gens arranged to call for a meeting after this tragic episode, to plead with the Jews to remain, not to make things worse. A raid took place, but they were still looking for us.

In the end, they brought me to Gens, Soliak Dessler (his superior) by his side, into his office where he asked me:

– – You want to rescue Jews by taking them to the forest? Tell me? Can Jews survive in that environment? 100, 200, and even 500? Here they have work, and thanks to this, the ghetto can exist. You want to lead the old, sick and children to God knows where, whom the Germans will murder immediately? I will not allow this. Do you know what is happening around us? What is happening on all fronts? We don't know what tomorrow will bring. It can be, that the Germans might run away and we will all survive in the ghetto. It is being said that the Red Army started a massive campaign. Our fate is to endure a little longer. There are still 20,000 Jews in the ghetto. We should not shorten the existence of the ghetto even by 1 day. I will fight for each day. Later I will be responsible for the story of the ghetto.

– – Herr commandant, I said to Gens – why did you bring us here, convincing us through Averbuch, that we should come here with our guns and now you want to detain us?

– – I called you here – Gens answered – because I need loyal people here, especially with guns, in case, at the right moment, there is an uprising!

[Col. 1669]

I know about the existence of the F.P.O. I know there will be a time where I will need them. I know their hideouts, I am turning a blind eye. When they plan to attack the ghetto, we will all need to count on one another. Then we will all fight together".

We were face to face during our conversation. Later Dessler reappeared.

– – Herr Commandant – I said again, – – we will not change our minds. We do not have confidence in the Vilna Ghetto. Just like the Germans destroyed all the ghettos, they will do the same here. Our main goal is to lead out as many Jews as possible. To the forests and set up a base for them. As many as possible, and together with other groups, we can join the fight against the enemy to take "Revenge".

After several minutes, I continued my talk with Gens. We came here as partisans on Markov's orders to bring as many Jews as possible to the forest, and if you don't allow it, you are to blame.

Then Dessler mixed into the conversation:

– – What do you think, we are against the Jews going to the forest? We are against the fight of the partisans? Peace and quiet. Gens was once a partisan. We would like go to the forests as well, but we cannot leave the ghetto unprotected."

Gens again counter-attacked me.

– – Do you personally know these people that you want to lead into the forests? Are you certain they all want to leave? Are you absolutely certain, that the police Boyarski and Rudnitski, who are close to you, will leave with you? Now we will address them.

Gens called in the watchman and sent him to bring the two mentioned policemen.

They soon arrived, white as the walls!

Gens asked if they knew me. The two said no, pretending not to know me as they were not aware what was happening.

I interrupted and said –

[Col. 1670]

Don't worry. Nothing will happen to you. Everything will work out.

Gens answered:

– – Herr, my friend, take these people wherever you desire. You have to know, all the guns and documents shall remain in the ghetto. Otherwise a large scale exodus can occur.

– – No, not like this – I answered – – – without guns we will not leave. I am telling you the truth, I have nothing against you, but what are we to do without guns?

– – Good, Gens said, do as you please –

– – Another thing, I said, our friends are in your prison, I must bring them with us.

Gens replied in anger –

– – Take all of them, but I beg you, I don't ever want to see you here again –

I replied – Herr Gens, you are also a military person, what would you do if you received an order from your superior? You would certainly obey! That is exactly what I am doing, being a soldier in the Partisan Army! My commander is Markov. If he orders me to return here, I will certainly obey this order!

Gens replied – if you return, you must advise me first –

Another thing, I beg you, we need medicine and cigarettes for the partisans in the forest –

Gens smiled and looked over to Dessler.

– – Good, you can obtain these things as well –

Early the next morning, our entire group met at the gate of the ghetto, the gate guard, Levas, took our passes and let us leave. At the end, 25 men left.

We left as "workers" and went to the train station. We went into a wagon, that was taking workers to New – Vileika. At the first chance we left the wagon and disappeared into the thick forest. We went in the direction of the Lake Narach. We travelled by night, hid in the daytime and after 6 days we arrived at the Markov Brigade in the Narach forest. Isheke and I became close to Markov. He questioned us about the situation in Vilna and the underground activities in the ghetto.

[Col. 1671]

He was especially interested in the work of the F.P.O.

Markov's plan was to unite all the Polish, Lithuanian and Jewish partisans. He requested the two of us return to Vilna, to ask Vittenberg (as per Markov's request) to send the F.P.O. fighters to the forest. He requested we seek out the Polish and Lithuanian units and they should unite with Markov and keep in regular contact. In order to carry out this mission, he gave us a Russian partisan to lead the way. We left and on the way we met a Lithuanian partisan otriad who told us there was unrest in Vilna. They arrested the leader of the Polish and Lithuanian underground organizations and near Vilna there were horrible things happening.

25 kilometers from Vilna, we came across a peasant who let us stay overnight and fed us. In the morning, he packed a wagon with wood, I dressed like a Christian peasant, and the two of us left for Vilna. Isike stayed behind, awaiting my return. As soon as I arrived I contacted Averbuch to make contact with the F.P.O and tell them what Markov requested. This was the day of Yitzhak Vittenberg's trial, which started, when the Lithuanian underground leader Koslovski was arrested by the Germans. They tortured him endlessly, and eventually he gave up the leaders of the F.P.O., led by Yitzhak Vittenberg. When Vittenberg was arrested, led bound in chains, his followers managed to free him and Vittenberg hid in the ghetto. Gens arrived at their headquarters and relayed the message from the Germans: hand over Vittenberg or the entire ghetto will be murdered. Many discussions ensued. Everyone knew that Vittenberg's life was at stake. It was a difficult decision to make, but it was the only thing to do: Vittenberg had to turn himself in to the German police.

[Col. 1672]

When things settled down, I approached the headquarters of the F.P.O with Markov's plan, to bring the fighters to the forest. In principle, it was decided. If they were to leave, only as an entire group. If only one group left, Gens would stop the other groups.

Gens received me like an old friend. I again submitted Markov's plan (also, I gave him Markov's greetings) and he said – men I don't have to spare, but if the F.P.O. want to send their men, I will allow it.

I met with Sonia Madaisker, and the next evening 3 representatives went to Gens. These were Abba Kovner, Shmuel Kaplan, Henia Barovski and I. Long discussions took place, and finally Gens agreed to let all the groups leave. His only demand was to leave all personal documents.

July 22, 1943, the first group, under Yosef Glazman's leadership, left the ghetto. Their guide was Ishike Gertman. By the Lavarishker bridge, they encountered a German military unit. Shooting started. Some were killed and part were captured by the Germans. Of them, Glazman and Gertsman escaped and after many days arrived in the Narach forests.

[Col. 1673]

As a result, the F.P.O. were not interested.

I, on my own, organized another group to leave with me. In the end Alexander Bogen, Sholomke from Lodz, Yudke Rudnitski, Motke Feigel went back into the ghetto and brought other groups to the forests. Rudnitski successfully brought out the Vilna writers: Abraham Sutzkever and Shmerke Katcherginsky and other young and ambitious fighters.

[Col. 1673]

Eli[1]

by Nechama Shutan

Translated by Dena Mann

In memory of my grandparents

Daughter of the partisan Moishe Shutan

My God, you could have saved them
My god, you could have rescued them
The six million
Who fell into the hands of the Nazis

You had their faith in your hands
To you alone did the pray
In each place their feet touched the ground
They had your name on their lips

And you didn't save them
And you didn't stretch your hand to help them
And the six million perished

May their memory be with us forever

Translator's footnote:

My God

[Col. 1673]

This Is How We Fought...

Fragments of a larger work about the struggle of the Sventzian Partisans

Moishe Shutan

Translation by Anita Frishman Gabbay

Edited by Rhoda Miller

Ishike arrived in Sventzian from Vilna after a long night of travel by train. He was tired and went straight to bed, but he couldn't fall asleep. He overheard his father talking about the London radio reporter's alarming news,

[Col. 1674]

the Germans were amassing large military armies on the Russian Border. "Least of all we need another war!" Three days later, at Bagin, the Germans crossed the border. The German airplanes bombarded Russians cities and villages. The first news in Sventzian came from the radio: the Germans attacked city hall!

[Col. 1675]

That evening, columns of retreating Red Army militia passed through Sventzian, we noticed many white heads amongst them, bandaged and wounded soldiers.

One set of news after another was racing non– stop.

The German military arrived in Kovno by train, then they occupied Vilna. The Lithuanians joined the Germans. Russian townsfolk were fleeing together with workers of the Russian Regime, and many Jews were fleeing with them.

Many fleeing Jews turned back (they felt remorse leaving their families behind) and on the way they were shot by Lithuanian bandits.

In terror and in awe we waited for the arrival of the Germans.

At Abraham Gertman's house, on New–Sventzian Street, five of our friends were sitting in the shade of the large old trees, they were preparing themselves for the new school year, instead they were greeted by war.

Ishike Gertman was only 19 years old when he finished the Yiddish Folk–Shul. He was above medium height with an energetic face, grey eyes and red hair. His father, Abraham Gertman, was a shoemaker, patching shoes, barely making a living and was also involved in community affairs and world politics.

The entire responsibility of the household lies on Isike.

Dudke Yocai, a pupil at the Gymnasia, tall with a long pale face and hot–tempered black eyes, inherited a sharp mind.

His father Chaim Yocai was a tailor, overworked and barely made a living.

Yoske Rudnitski, short with a small round face, always smiling was full of humour. His father Pesach Rudnitski was a wagoner, day and night he brought merchandise from Sventzian to Vilna and back.

Moishke Shutan, one year older than Yoske, of medium height with black hair, dark eyes, was ambitious and one of the best students in the Gymnasia. His father, Shmuel Hirsh, went from shtetl to shtetl, buying and selling merchandise in the markets.

The youngest amongst them, Itzke Rudnitski, barely 14 years old, was a ray of sunshine, fair with somewhat curly hair and dark grey eyes. He was a student in the first class of the Gymnasia. His father, Israel–Moishe was a Chazzan who remained stuck in the Warsaw Ghetto together with his mother Chaia.

The talk amongst them now was to run away to Russia.

Moiske believed that they should remain here to fight. Ishike was of the same opinion as Moishke.

Two days later, in the evening, the Germans and their tanks arrived in Sventzian. Their panzer units rolled through with their insignias, the black crests with the iron–cross on

[Col. 1676]

their dark grey tanks. They opened fire on the Soviet transport airplanes from the Poshmener hill, who were dropping parachutes with canisters of fuel for the hundreds of Russian tanks stranded on the road that were low in fuel (benzene).

This was useless. The German army arrived the next morning. Young German soldiers overflowed the tanks and panzer automobiles. They moved without stopping, their army was strong and we knew their forces were unstoppable.

Suddenly, fire broke out of nowhere. A soldier appeared out of nowhere. The automobiles stopped, soldiers with rifles and machine guns jumped from their automobiles and threw themselves on the ground, with their hands on the barrels of their automatic guns and rifles, which were pointed at the long row of people waiting in line for bread that had been promised to them.

The men ran away. The Germans suddenly realized that a Russian unit caught a German soldier on his motor cycle and forced him to ride in a suicide mission. Arriving in the middle of the town they saw the advancing German columns and they jumped off the moving motorcycle and sprayed the Germans with bullets.

The soldiers disappeared and the poisoned Germans returned from their chase empty handed. Next to the store, where earlier the rows of people stood for their bread, no one was there, only three beaten Russian soldiers, without weapons waiting to be taken into captivity.

The Germans opened fire on them and they dropped dead on the sidewalk.

Mid–day, German gendarmes were seen on the streets of Sventzian together with the other wild hooligans, wearing white armbands. These were the Lithuanians, hooligans, and other underworld figures (mafia).

The Hebrew Station from Jerusalem

A terrible nightmare fell upon the Jewish population in Sventzian. Several days later the Lithuanians rounded up twenty–five Jews who were falsely accused, together with some Russians, and were shot. Then another six Jews were sent to work and after work they were shot.

One cause for alarm followed another. The Lithuanians, like animals in heat, ran around the streets catching Jews

[Col. 1676]

to pull the wagons instead of using horses, they cut and ripped beards, robbed them and then shot them. Not one day passed without incident.

Isike's father, Abraham, went around drunk (or in a stupor). He witnessed the murder of the three Russian soldiers.

When Abraham was 5 years old during the time of the Russian revolution, he ran through the street yelling: "*Daloi, Nicholai*", he no longer feared death; he came across a hidden radio (radios were illegal), brought it home and Moishke, his next door neighbour, helped him install the apparatus to hook it up to electricity and hide the electric wires. Everyday they listened to the news from Moscow.

One day they heard a Hebrew station from Jerusalem. It consumed them to hear the news and understand what the Jews of Eretz Israel knew. They invited a friend, Yodke

Shapiro, who they knew from the Halutz Ha'Tzair and knew Hebrew, to translate the news. No good news was transmitted.

The Aktion of the Hundred

Ishike understood, hearing the screaming, that something terrible was happening outside. He went to the window with his father and saw, Dvorah Ozschinski in her night dress, barefoot, running through her garden, screaming with all her strength: "Save me!"

The Lithuanian bandits took her husband from his bed, told him to take a package with soap and other things, and said they were taking him to work. He managed to tear away and escape. They ran after him and captured him in the garden, hit him with their rifle–buts on his back and head.

Then Ishike saw Amilka, Zalman Gurwitz's servant, approaching the gate of their house, in her long black dresss with her long silver cross on her breast, blocking the policemen's way and said:

—"Jews don't live here."

That day the Lithuanians gathered 100 Jews and sent them to Poligon. They took them away in wagons, the Jews were frightened out of their minds. The wailing was heard throughout the streets.

The Plan to Resist

Moishe Gordon arrived in a terrible state at the Tailor's Kloiz and recounted the frightening news:

—"The whole of Sventzian and its surrounding villages

[Col. 1678]

are being evacuated, all the Jews, young and old, will be sent away. Not one Jew will remain. To Poligon! Let us save ourselves, let's run away!"

The Jews listened, downtrodden and broken, either alone or in small groups they left in the middle of the night, as far away from this horrible nightmare as possible. And where to? Perhaps it is quieter in the other shtetls?

Abraham didn't want to run. In all the occupied zones where the Germans were located, the same fate awaited. Ishike stood in the darkness and hid packages in a pit in the garden, all the things his father told him to hide. This was Abraham's plan. His whole life he spent working to acquire these items. People wanted to buy these things from him, but he didn't want to sell them.

—"We have to resist"–called out Moisike, looking how Isike was straightening the earth with his feet, —"I work in the *Abramke* (warehouse). There must be a lot of guns there that the Germans gathered in the fields after the Russians fled. We have to attack the work camp, steal the weapons, burn the city and run away into the forests."

This is how the plan of an organized resistance was born—without a plan, without help or assurance, only with the will not to surrender.

Godel

After the Jews were taken to Poligon, the Germans left a small ghetto of 80 men in the shtetl. The entrance was Shul–Holf Street with a gate and a sign "Ghetto," with barbed wire encircling the Shul–Hof with all her alleys and houses. On the door of Abraham Tzepelovitch's house hung a sign, *Judenrat*, the main room led to three smaller rooms, on the doors were written: "ghetto–police, work–detail, and *Judenrat*".

Godel Gilinski, more than 50 years old, tall and good humored, painted signs which the Germans and Lithuanians needed in the ghetto. He looked at the other painters with regret, as he didn't feel as they did. His worst fear was for Ishike, who spent the entire day talking about the impending fight.

Godel was a quiet man who worked diligently and pretended not to hear Ishike's words which impacted him. Three ghetto policemen arrived and patiently waited for the volunteers "who willingly would come forward to go to the work detail that the Germans arranged? Godel was the first one to speak out:

[Col. 1679]

—"I am going!"

With scared glances, we looked at Godel, warning him by making signs with our fingers not to go, we will never see him again.

Godel returned. But that same evening he sat at the desk by the hot stove, he mulled over his work that day in the *Avramke*, it didn't bother him that the Germans yelled or the Lithuanians were picking on the old Jews. He surveyed the barrack that was surrounded by a wooden fence and barbed wire. Here were the guns and ammunition that he was focused on.

He sat anxiously waiting for Ishike.

Ishike arrived like a "storm" and went straight to talk to Godel:

—"I am returning from Litvin and gave him back the signs. He is not so full of himself (turned up nose). It seems, the loss at Moscow cooled him down." He turned the radio on, from the Moscow station, all seemed quiet, only small local battles are being fought.

Ishike took out a loaf of bread from his opened coat, broke off a piece and gave it too Godel saying:—"He gave me a whole bread."

Godel took the bread and immediately called out:

—"At the *Avramke* is an entire warehouse full of guns, we have to get our hands on them and find a way to smuggle them out."

—"How"–Ishike looked at him with wonder in his eyes!

Godel spoke while thinking.

—"Make sure, that your friends are sent to work there!"

The *Avramke*

The *Judenrat* was wondering:

—"Why are the young people lining up to work in the *Avramke*?"

Shimke, the German overseer, was happy that all the old workers were being replaced by the younger ones. It is already two weeks they are working here, but the Germans don't leave their side.

One time in a watch–room of the Lithuanian police, the telephone rang. He called Yoske Rudnitski, who was at the dairy farm, they spoke Lithuanian and called the foreman of the dairy farm. But Yoske said to the German, that the German supervisor was wanted on the phone. So the German officer told him to go fetch him.

When Shimke's small frame with his crooked feet arrived at the watch–room of the police, Yoske screamed out:

[Col. 1680]

—–"Now!"–

No more words were needed. Itzke Rudnitzki and Gershke Nodel disappeared into the barracks. It barely took several seconds and they jumped through the windows on the other end of the barrack. They left with three Russian rifles and buried them quickly in the snow next to the barrack.

In a corner of the warehouse were broken crates that used to contain ammunition. Twice a week, before the end of the work shift, peasants arrived to collect them with a horse and sleigh to bring the broken boxes to the overseer in town. The peasants threw the empty boxes into the sleigh.

A short while after, Iszke and Gershke asked for a pass to leave, and when they left the overseer yelled out to them to help the peasants with the loading of the wooden crates.

Both of them froze in their tracks! Under their coats, in their pants, were hidden the rifles which reached their knees. They could barely take a step. How will they be able to mount the sled? Cold sweat poured from them. The German lost patience, started cursing, and at that moment, Moiske and Yoske jumped onto the loaded sled and the German got flustered:

—"Not you, them!"

—They don't feel well"–Moishe said quietly–"we will help load the wood."

The officer noticed the pale faces, signalled with his hand and they jumped on the sled.

The other workers lined up in a row, and returned to the ghetto. Itzke and Gershke went with them. Hidden in their coats were the two Russian rifles.

The First Meeting

That day was a cause for celebration. The celebrants were the two brothers, Berke and Dudke Yocai. The first meeting took place in their house. In their honor, their father Chaim brought several bottles of *samogan* and a bottle of spirit.

Between the men, sat Chaike, a young girl with half blond hair, who helped hide the guns. Next to her sat Isike, spirited with a smiling face. A new friend, Itzik Teitz, a wonderful lad, was now speaking, a devoted and honest being, who Moiske invited to join the organization. Itzke is talking about keeping the conspiracy a secret, which was the first requirement of this illegal organization. Until now everything was handled between us, with discretion. There needed to be a control over all the activities, an exact discipline was needed.

[Col. 1681]

Chaim got involved, telling about the First World War when he served in the artillery and a leader was necessary. But, in time, all showed their own initiatives.

Afterwards, Shaielke Michelson spoke. He told us that together with his father, they hid pistols in the cellar where the new Lithuanian police commander is now living. The guards were watching day and night.

Several of our friends volunteered to retrieve the guns from the cellar.

One after another they slid in the darkness through the streets where the police commander lived. There was a small window leading to the cellar. The opening looked rather small, how shall we enter?

We contemplated a short while, soon the three shadows found their way in.

They had to remain in the cellar until morning, with great angst. Cold entered their bodies, but they couldn't move from their spot. The smallest noise could give them away.

Very early in the morning, when the street began to fill with noise, the three volunteers, Yitzke Teitz, Shaielke and Dudke, began their work. They chiselled into the hard brick until noon, but they barely chiselled half a brick. The work was going slowly and with difficulty. Therefore, they didn't sleep the entire night, their thirst was painful. They wanted to stick out a hand and lick a little snow. But no one did it. When night fell, they managed to tap the hidden revolvers.

It was already late at night when they crawled out of the cellar, carrying the package of bullets and four new pistols. They avoided the Lithuanian guards and crawled through the barbed wire fence back into the ghetto. Once there, they breathed a sigh of relief.

The next morning, Dudke Yochai, Rubka Miadzolski, and Gerske Bak, crawled up onto the roof of a house that bordered the ghetto and sat there sewing cases for the revolvers.

Gershke positioned himself as the watchman. Gershke sat and cut the leather with a knife that he brought with him. Rudke played with the newest "Walter" (gun).

[Col. 1682]

He held the revolver in his hand and was speaking in an angry tone:

—"How can one survive?"–he said to Gershke, holding up the revolver–" to encounter some Germans and end their lives. To take revenge for my father and my mother"...

In that moment the gun went off and Gershon was wounded, a thin stream of blood poured from his mouth.

Rubke remained standing, frozen. He suddenly came to and immediately put Gershke on his shoulders and carried him off the roof. He brought him to his house, to his aunt Mina, where he lived. A tragedy occurred, Rubke was besides himself and Berke was attending the wounded friend. The doctor arrived and turned Gerske on his side, tapped his neck and felt the bullet. One cut was sufficient and the bullet could be removed.

The doctor, Niame, also served in the *Judenrat,* and he wanted an account of what happened to find himself in this situation. He said:

—"An operation will come with complications, we have to do this in the hospital. I am bound by an oath, and I must report this incident"...

The doctor left.

Gershke's mother and father arrived, the noise increased. News spread to the Jewish ghetto police.

Rubke stood frozen. He heard Berke saying to him, "run away" but he didn't move an inch. He was taken away by the Lithuanian police.

Rubke

From the bath house ran a small canal lengthwise, through which the collected rainwater ran to the small stream. This was next to the ghetto. The canal was now empty and the participants of the organization were laying in the ditch discussing what to do now. After Rubke's arrest a new edict was issued. The *Judenrat* had to bring many gifts to the criminal, the Lithuanian–chief, to beg forgiveness for the blameless young men who went on the roof to find old things and instead they found a revolver. They didn't know how to handle a gun.

Rochke, from Zarasai, who worked for the chief Lithuanian, said that Rubke with the wounded Gershke are being cruelly tortured. They wanted to break them.

[Col. 1683]

Suddenly, Rachke Rudnitzki appeared, who came here with her young brother Itzke Rudnitzki from Warsaw, when the Polish–German war broke out. She lived with her uncle Pesach in the ghetto, she often saw him leave with his nephew Yoske, watched him whispering with friends and somehow knew he had guns. That evening, she followed him in the darkness.

Lying hidden, she heard their decision to leave the ghetto and she decided to interrupt them. The lads were angry at her spying and hearing their conversation, then without hesitation she said:

–"You are not doing us a favor by fleeing at this particular time. The trial has not yet ended, you can't leave the ghetto, the two friends of ours did not break, and until now they have not spoken. When you will need a resistance, you will not be alone. I, and many others, will be ready to help you."

In the end, Itzke and I, together with Rochke (Rachke) returned home.

Nothing materialized of this decision to leave and everyone left for his own home. Only two men remained under guard.

In the *Judenrat*

Chaim–Hirsh, in normal times would have remained at his father's trade–a painter, he was now the head of police in the ghetto, under him were five policemen who carried out all his orders.

After the incident with the revolver shooting, he called Berke Yocai and Faivke Chayt (from New Sventzian) to him .

—"Do you know, with your playthings you are endangering the ghetto?"

—"We guarantee you, such a thing will no longer happen."

—"So nice, on your behalf, but the safest insurance will be to hand over the pistols which you can't openly have."

The talk became more heated minute by minute. Berel warned him they were bastards and responsible for the death of Gershke and Rubke, who were shot by the Lithuanians.

Chaim–Hirsh agreed, but this had to happen, in order that the other families remain alive.

Hearing the screaming, the other members of the *Judenrat* came running, Moishe Chaikel's. At that moment Chaim–Hirsh requested the police, arrest the two men. In a split second, Berel jumped from their arms to the wall, and in his hand was a shiny black revolver. Everyone stood in shock. The only calm one was Chaim Hirsh, who tore open his jacket, showing his hairy chest, and said, "Shoot! We are all going to the Almighty and you are a murderer amongst the few Jews that remain in the ghetto."

[Col. 1684]

Berel was overcome with rage. His voice was loud and clear: "From now on we declare that you will no longer collect gold and valuables for the Lithuanians and Germans. You will give us the money to buy guns. You have until tomorrow evening to accumulate 30 thousand rubles."

Guests from Vilna take the Jews out of the Sventzian Ghetto

March 1943

When the Sventzian ghetto was liquidated, new policemen arrived from the Vilna Ghetto with other hooligans, and divided the people into two categories. 1–The representatives of the *Judenrat*, other important people and some with *protectia*. They were to go to the Vilna Ghetto.2 The others were going to the Kovno Ghetto.

In the Tailors synagogue, where those of the Sventzian ghetto came together to pray, they were wrapped in their coats waiting for the representative of the Vilna Ghetto to arrive, Gens, perhaps he will give us a clue where the others were resettled.

Yacov Gens came in the company of several police commanders. With a fast military gait, he went through the mass of Jews to the podium.

—"in my ghetto"—with a quick tone of voice–"we don't go around with bowed heads (declaring defeat). Sadness is our enemy. We need to be hopeful, we need to keep working, In the Vilna Ghetto we have enough workplaces, meeting places, theatres and other cultural institutions. We have to remain in good spirits against all odds, with hopefulness and endurance; we must live and survive."

No one dared open their mouths. After a quiet moment, Berel Charmatz began to sing with enthusiasm:

—"We believe you, that you are bringing us to Vilna. How certain are you, that the guards are not bringing us to Kovno, and we will we actually arrive here (in Vilna)? Are you sometimes misled by the Germans?

This outburst spun before Gens' face, he disappeared shortly, then he called out:

[Col. 1685]

—"Jewish brothers! The Germans are emptying the ghettos of the provincial shtetls, which are close to the partisan–zones of the larger towns. I am ready to go to the Kovno Ghetto together with you all, but don't make any difficulties in the resettlement. Help us carry out the orders of the German military."

The Group of Fighters Depart from the Ghetto

In Haim Yocai's house, all the friends from the group assembled to take their orders to leave the ghetto.

Only half a year earlier, in the fall 1942, the group agreed to leave the ghetto for the forest, motivated by an alliance with the partisans (the ones who were already established) at a convenient time. This was their final hour, everyone agreed the time was right.

The last one, at the departure, Chaim Yocai said:

—"I want to say my goodbyes with you," his voice was trembling and upset, —"dear children, let us make clear and settle our accounts, those that remain alive, will no longer find a Chaim in Sventzian. All the ways of return are cut off for us. I am sure, that you will not give up your lives on any account, I want to see you succeed. I am fortunate to see my two sons amongst you, and I believe, that you will look out one for another, will stay together, like with your own brother"...

The old soldier couldn't endure and started to cry, tears filled with emotion, dripping down his pale, punished soul.

One by one the shadows slid through the fence passing the ghetto–hospital, the bath, the city square of former times.

Waiting, were those that arrived earlier, quiet, crouching, listening carefully for the Lithuanian guard.

We approached the fence in small groups, someone noticed an unknown person, that was Pertzke Grazel, who didn't belong to our group. He didn't obey our orders and he didn't want to return to the ghetto.

Stretched out in a row, several paces between each one, we left in the night, through the side streets and alleys, through mud and swamps.

We were twenty– two in all, with several rifles, pistols and grenades. Shimke Levin and his brothers were leading the group. They knew the roads well and knew where to go. Ishike looked at the poor souls and with a heavy heart and thought: here is our tiny handful, the remains from our shtetl Sventzian, a community of 400 years! Will a miracle save them? Will they survive the bitter fight, what lies ahead?

[Col. 1686]

We stopped at a shed overgrown with branches. Shimke and his brother Rubke left to go somewhere. It was endless waiting, and sadness filled our hearts. Eventually they returned to the group. We followed them quietly and after half an hour we reached a barn close to the forest. Two men remained as guards, the rest went into the barn and arranged themselves in the straw.

Tired, after the long journey, they fell into a deep sleep.

The next day they remained in the nearby hamlet. The peasant fed them and when night came, the same peasant came to them to bid them farewell, shook everyone's hand and wished them a safe journey.

Again we wandered in the dark night, fleeing like birds, away from death, to freedom. The Tzirklishker forest where they arrived, wasn't large, only four kilometers square, very dense with pine and leafy trees, amongst them the white *Bereozes* (a tree). The air was filled with humidity and fumes from rotten left over leaves. Snow still lay between the trees and we heard the running stream at a distance. We immediately began our work, sawed, chopped and soon between the trees and bushes we arranged three bunkers.

In the Forests

It rained the entire night. Soaked till their bones, four partisans dragged their feet with difficulty through the swampy earth. Besides the rifles, wrapped with rags, each one carried on their backs a sack with food, which was also soaked. The wetness and cold entered their bones. They were tired and without energy from the long road but sweat rolled from their faces.

Perz'ke went first with his "torn" head, his thoughts of the previous days gave him additional willpower. He was still thinking how they didn't want to bring him along when they left the ghetto. Now they will all see the usefulness that he brings to the group. They all wore boots, only Froike wore shoes, soaked with water. From the wetness, his skin rubbed off between the toes of his feet, each step was painful for him. He was the last one, not complaining. Pertzke felt how Froimke was suffering and thought, on the way we can get a pair of boots from a rich peasant for Froimke.

[Col. 1687]

This night was darker and more difficult than the others. We didn't know if we could survive. Perzke stood still, thinking they were lost. We have to turn back, after an hour of walking, he stopped and thought. Berel lost his patience and took over the leadership. With his compass in hand he forged ahead and Perzke and the others followed.

After a short way they got into an argument. Berel didn't wait long and sprung over the ditch. A dog started to bark. They all froze, listening in all directions. A fire pierced the darkness, then a shot was heard.

They quickly jumped back over the ditch and started running. When the shooting stopped, they stopped and took off their wet sacks and sat down exhausted to catch their breath.

Berel was embittered and said with a bent over head, "to fall upon the Germans was the last thing they needed." When daylight appeared, Perzke brought the group to the forest.

Rainy days came day and night, filled with bitterness. When night arrived they went into their bunkers and went to sleep on the beds of straw and branches, two men stood outside watching the fire, which wasn't far from their bunkers and stood guard.

Yoske and Itzke Rudnitzki, when it got light outside, went to start a fire. They gathered stone, rubbed them, blew on them with their last breath but the wet branches would not light up. Pertzke found some branches someplace, which were seeped in benzene, and lit them. All of us followed and gathered these branches and threw them on the fire. We dried our clothes, which released a lot of steam. Peretz took potatoes from his sack and place them under the burning branches.

The rain slowly let up. Then we remembered the two girls, who were amongst us, standing with their modest smiles and combing their wet hair. Our hearts were filled with a new longing. Ishike sang a known "nigun" (melody) with his own words:

–"You will cry, long after mother–father.

–"We are going, we are leaving for the front.

[Col. 1688]

–"The enemy is before us, so near"... The girlish voices and the deep voices of the men joined in and the tune was carried far into the forest.

Back to the Ghetto

A week in the forest went by this way. The weather grew worse. One day was worse than the next. We were on guard duty. We left to the nearby villages to obtain more food products. No contact with the partisans was made until now. How long would we have to wait? Ishike was the most impatient of the group. It was clear that this forest was too bare and we couldn't hide very well without been caught. We started to look at the map for a better forest and the consensus was the Baranover forest.

One time amongst the trees, we noticed a middle–aged gentile dressed in a peasant winter coat and winter hat, pulled over his face, —"who are you?"–Berel said, with his pistol in his hand.

The gentile was angry, but smiled. This was Goyge, the forest–watchman. From the onset of the war he knew that the forests were filled with partisans. From his hut, which was several hundred meters from the forest, many nights he saw the shine of the fires and heard shots fired. But he didn't want anyone to see him, especially the prying eyes of his group of woodsmen. When the peasants started talking about the hidden groups in the forests, robbing at night, he wanted to warn the partisans what was going on in town. Soon the mud will dry out, and the peasants will come to bring their cut wood out of the forests.

On Berel's orders they all left, just Berel and Faivke stayed behind in Goyke's hut and discussed everything Goyke had told them, whether this was the actual truth. He reassured the group (of partisans), that in a week's time, that the partisans (the ones the group was looking for) will come to him.

The partisans were overjoyed and decided in one week's time to go to the Baranover forests. (Barashniker). Only Ishike was impatient and asked in a loud voice:

—“Perhaps, we should check what is going on in Sventzian?”

Everyone stayed silent. But Ishike and Moish'ke, armed with revolvers, left at night on their own.

[Col. 1689]

It was a black night. They used their hands to tap and find their way. The broken branches cracked under their feet, they tripped on fallen branches, picked themselves up and continued. They finally reached the hill and there was the shtetl. They soon arrived at the lake next to the ghetto, stood before the barbed wire, which they left behind not too long ago.

In the lonely calm, they crawled through the wire fence and approached the closest house, Pesach the *Tanes* (prayed at Yom Kippur for forgiveness). Emptiness appeared through the open doors and windows.

In a minute the entire scene became crystal clear: no more Jews were left in Sventzian.

After several minutes of frozen silence, they crawled back under the wires and went back to the forests. Ishike then decided to go in the direction of Vilna, perhaps there he would find some remnants of the Jews of Sventzian, which were promised to be resettled there. Moish'ke followed quietly.

The Fight with the Train–Police

Early in the morning they approached some homes near New–Sventzian. A door suddenly opened and there appeared an elderly gentile wearing a uniform of a train worker.

Ishike greeted him. His stared at his blue armband with the black iron cross (Nazi symbol), which he wore on his left arm.

—“Give me your armband”–Ishike called out.

The peasant looked at him with shocked eyes, but Isike continued.

—“For a free Poland”–

The peasant looked around with suspicion, took off the arm–band, showing solidarity with Moish'ke:

—“One for all.”

The train worker soon came out with a second armband.

With the armbands with the iron–cross they went through the streets of New–Sventzian, to the train station. We didn't enter through the main door, but through a side door used by the train workers. Passenger wagons with German soldiers were on their way to the front. An echelon of soldiers and train workers were running around with their green and red tickets.

[Col. 1690]

This was the main artery where the soldiers left for the Leningrad front.

Ishike and Moihke were standing near the police station, waiting for a train to Vilna. A German soldier with a rifle on his shoulder noticed their dirty shoes and creased clothing. The two partisans had their hands in their pockets gripping their revolvers.

At last the train arrived, on route to Vilna, and they sat down amongst the passengers. The Lithuanians, with their large egos, greeted the Germans and others in a friendly manner. The Polish people, who were sitting in the wagon, had unhappy faces. The Jewish partisans kept to themselves, not wanting to arouse suspicion. Who would imagine that these two train workers were Jews?

The train remained at the New–Vileika station, seven kilometers from Vilna. A train worker passed the window, where Ishike was sitting, stood there awhile, looked at Ishike's Polish military hat and said: “a control!” Ishike looks around and sees the Lithuanian police checking the train tickets.

—“Train workers?” said the first policeman passing Ishike, sitting next to Moishke, but the second one said,

—“Where do you come from?”

—“From Ignalina.”

—“Documents.”

As they didn't have any documents they took them off the train to the police station where they met a head police officer. He angrily shouted:

—"You know, you can't travel without documents".

—"You are able to work only at the Ignalina station."

—"Hands in the air!"–the Lithuanian police said.

We are caught–thought Ishike, as the policeman was tapping Moishke under his arms, on his chest, soon he will touch the pockets of his coat and will feel the revolver. What should we do?

Ishike sprung instantly on top of the policeman and placed his hands around his throat. Moishke helped with the attack on the Lithuanian, who suddenly came to. He couldn't free his neck from Ishike's hands, he managed to roll through the open door onto the station with Ishike entwined. The German soldiers, who noticed the fighting, came running and were enjoying a good fight, a train–police and a train worker fighting! Ishike, with all his strength, hit him on the head and he passed out. He let out a deafening scream. Ishike released him from his grasp, thought, straightened himself out and went through the crowd and pointed out:

[Col. 1691]

—"A Lithuanian swine."

The Germans, in great spirits, opened the way for Ishike to pass to the ramp of the train.

In a short time, the policeman woke up from his fainting spell and started to scream:

—"Where is he? Catch him. This is a bandit, a spy!" The German soldiers laughed at the beaten and bloody policeman.

Ishike went through the German passenger–cabin, went into the end train. He heard a commotion from behind. Revolver shots were heard overhead. Ishike took out his revolver, turned around, saw the Lithuanian police only a hundred meters from him. The German soldiers were running after him.

Ishike ran out between the sleeping cars to the other side and saw the river, the Vilenke, and saw a bridge made from two boards. He was eager to reach the bridge, but saw the Lithuanians running towards him. They will soon catch him. He went down on his knees, readied his revolver and fired a shot. With Ishike's first shot, the policeman held his stomach and fell down.

In the blink of an eye, Ishike ran over the bridge and disappeared in the bushes on the other side of the river.

He kept running until the shooting stopped, and after that, he resumed his footsteps and left for the direction of Vilna. One in the afternoon, he arrived at Kailis' second block, alone, without Moishke. He entered the gate, where a Jewish policeman stood guard and told him Moishke had arrived half an hour before him and told him, "Ishike died."

"Moishke is alive! Who is with him to celebrate the joy of that moment?"

The Attack by the Germans and Lithuanians at the Base in the Zirklisher Forest

Several days earlier, Goyge united the Jewish partisan group with the Russian partisan group. They agreed to meet in the Baranishker forest (Baranover).

That day Goyge got up quite early. It seemed to be a beautiful day, there were no clouds in the sky. Goyge was pleased that he introduced his band of friends to the Russians. It would be more advantageous for both groups, the forest wasn't so large and the neighbourhood was unfriendly.

[Col. 1692]

That which frightened him so much, finally came! Half a kilometer from his hut, on the Polyane, he saw the Germans creeping –it made him very nervous!

In one breath he sprung from his house, leaving his frightened wife and children. First he went slowly, but when no more Germans were in sight he started to run. Coming to the stream, he saw the peasants mulling around, they did not know what was to come. He made it across, and when he arrived at the first watch–gate, he screamed:

—"Police, run away!"

There was no time left to warn them! They formed a row and Shimke Levin led the group. After him was Berke Yocai, the last one was Pertzke Grazel.

In ten minutes a thunderous shooting began in the forest. The shooting occurred directly over the area where the bunkers lay, which they just left behind. The echo of the bullets and machine guns greeted the fleeing Jewish partisans.

The Unforgettable Meeting

When Ishike and Moishke didn't return to the base after several days, Berke Yocai and Pertzke Grazel left for Sventzian to find out what happened to them. The ghetto was empty. Berke decided to go to Kube the Tatar, who had worked with his father in the tailor shop. He also wanted to learn the fate of the deported Jews.

To his great surprise, he found his father at Kube's. He was hidden in the attic of the tailor shop.

Berl wanted to take his father into the forests with him, but life there was not easy, who knows if he would be able to survive there. He said:

—"Not now, later. When we will be established with the partisans, I will come for you and bring you with me."

Late at night they returned to the Tzirklishker forest. They were counting the hours with great anxiety.

Shaoulke Michelson couldn't relax. He knew his mother and father were hidden by gentiles and wanted to see them to say his goodbyes. Dudke Yocai wanted to go with him, also he wanted to see his father. Pertzke Grazel liked to wander about so he went with them as far as Sventzian.

[Col. 1693]

Shaoulke was in a hurry, from Sventzian to his parents hiding place was still a distance, and eventually he had to return to the Tzerklisker forest.

Dudke met his father, and together with Shaoulke they continued further.

Night was pitch black. Quietly Dudke and Shaoulke shuffled through the grass of Sahlinski's fields, Dudke stoped, grabbed Shaoulke, and someone called out:

—"Who goes there?"

The answer came from nearby with a familiar voice.

—"Dudke."

—"Ishike, Moishke!"

They recognized each other in the darkness. They didn't bring any good news from Vilna.

They Jews that were taken to Kovno, were murdered at Ponar. The other Jews were sent to the Vilna Ghetto. "The youth are searching for guns, they want to go to the forests. We have to help them."

Dudke told them they were relocating to the Kazianer forests the following day. Now he wants to see his parents. One sack is filled with food for his parents. In the other—a radio, which he exchanged with a gentile for a rifle. They were informed about the German and Lithuanian attack on their former base, and they barely escaped death. Dudke then added:

—"Hurry, we can still catch Pertzke in the tailor shop. He will also come to the new site in the Baranisker forest, where we will meet up with Markov's brigade."

The Fight at the Baranishker Forest

Mate–Heshke Bushkanyetz was chosen to meet with the leader of the Russian partisans, Voske, Markov's lieutenant. He was wearing a black leather vest, his pants were tucked into his Russian boots and was outfitted from head to toe with an automatic, a "*nagan*", a knife, grenades and bullet–sacks.

His good– natured face smiled, greeted us like an old friend, then lay down to sleep. He was tired from the long journey.

[Col. 1694]

After his sleep, Voske gave us details about the attacks which recently took place in the forests, how the Germans destroyed a complete battalion and with their artillery shot the partisans.

After lunch Voske told everyone to get ready.

We knew it was still early, but no one dared to contradict Voske.

Berke Yocai was checking his revolver, and after releasing his lock, he accidently shot Nacke Svirski, from Vidz (who left the Sventzian ghetto with his sister); he ran several feet and fell to the ground.

Everyone was unnerved.

The first one to run over was Voske, who saw the bullet had entered his right foot and immediately started to bandage him.

He then requested a stretcher made from branches, on which they placed Nacke and continued on their way.

Close to a cross–way, that cut through the road, Voske stopped, asked everyone to sit and rest and together with two men he left on a side road.

Less than an hour later they returned with horse and wagon, put Nacke in the wagon on fresh straw and continued on their journey.

The peasant didn't stop observing the young men and girls, who were marching not far from the wagon.

Three in the afternoon we arrived at the edge of the forest and Voske freed the peasant with the horse and wagon.

After another short rest, Voske took five volunteers to get another wagon.

They passed the stretch of field near the village huts with their straw roofs. Coming closer, he left two men behind to stand guard, and with the remaining went into the village, and knocked on the second door.

Not a living soul was in sight. Moishke and Israelke Wolfson were standing watch. From far next to the furthest hut of the village they noticed harnessed horses and large wagons. They crawled closer and noticed these were policemen who had already seen the partisans. Quickly they turned around, looked for Voske, who gave the order to return immediately to the forest, taking the same route that brought them to the village.

[Col. 1695]

Running one kilometer, the partisans had to increase their pace. The police that were chasing them did not shoot any bullets. The partisans didn't want to lead them to the forest. It was clear–they wanted to capture them alive.

Voske took his automatic gun from his shoulder and screamed:

—"Lie down!"

Lying on the ground, Voske didn't take his eyes off the police, who were closing in on them.

He said:

—"We will not be taken alive! Do not waste any bullets. Each bullet should count."

The five Jewish partisans were lying in a half circle next to Voske and were waiting the approaching policemen.

Amongst the partisans who remained in the forest was Berke, sitting uneasy, he couldn't forgive himself for the useless shooting that wounded Noahke. Yoske Rudnitzki didn't leave his side. Yoske looked at the fields, where Voske and the group had gone.

Suddenly he noticed from a distance six of his group running, and behind them, the policemen. He yelled out to Berke, who quickly understood the situation and gave an order to the others:

—"Spread out under the bushes!"

The police were soon close by, running to the forest, directly across from them. We heard the pounding of their feet.

—"Fire!"–yelled Berel.

The shooting of the rifles was soon muffled by the sounds of the fire.

Itzke Teitz had two grenades, and he threw one at the fleeing police.

We heard the groans of some wounded police. The others threw themselves to the ground.

The Lithuanians were angry from the sudden onslaught, and started shooting blindly with their guns. We could feel their surprise from this attack.....crawling through the ground they started their retreat.

Voske heard the shooting and saw the Lithuanians falling on the ground, not knowing exactly what happened, he managed to reach the forest.

When they reached the forest, it was dark outside. They were still far from their group of friends and it was useless to look for them in the dark. They now learned what happened here. Voske was hopeful and pointed out that the remaining partisans will surely make their own way to the Kazian forests, and together with the five, he left the forest.

[Col. 1696]

In the Heat of the Partisan Fight

It happened as Voske had predicted. The rest of the group made their way to the Kazian forests. They carried Noachke on the stretcher, leaving the village where the police were located. Late at night they arrived at another village.

Berke and Itzke slid quietly to a hut and knocked on the window; the woken– up peasant was told to dress and was requested to show them the direction.

The peasant was very frightened, he said the whole village was full of police. His pleading didn't help, in a short while he was dressed and outside.

The police in the village *smelled* the partisans. Several shots were fired and the sky lit up like daytime. Without stop the air was filled with rocket fire.

The peasant was running and the group after him when they came to a river, the peasant said that there was a small bridge nearby, but probably being watched by the police. There could be another crossing point over the river, but it was farther away.

—"On our way"–Berel commanded!

They passed through muddy fields and swamps. It took days to arrive, the swamps were getting deeper, every step was laboured. Their feet barely made it when suddenly they saw the crossing, exactly as the peasant had predicted. Here the water was shallow. Holding on one to another they went into the ice–cold water which reached their necks. No one complained, there were no disappointments. The three girls, with their last strength, held on to each other, bit their lips and crawled into the water.

Frozen, congealed from cold and frost, they arrived to the other side. This was the entrance to the Kazianer forests.

After sending two volunteers, the group came to the single hut with a barn. They got undressed, twisted their wet clothes and put them back on. Later they went to the peasant and begged for food. They reorganized themselves to continue further—to the forest.

[Col. 1697]

The peasant saw the exhausted and wet men and women and said:

—"What's your hurry? I will heat up the oven and you will dry your wet clothing. Don't be afraid, you are in the partisan–zone. The Germans and Lithuanians won't dare cross over to this side of the river."

We calmed ourselves, ate, allowed ourselves to enjoy a little brandy with the peasant and then departed for the forest. When we arrived, first, we lit a fire, then dead–tired we fell asleep.

The sleep was a short one. Berel looked at the map and said:

—"According to Voske's words, we are still about 20 kilometers from the partisan–base. The entire route is through the forest."

Finally we arrived at the first partisan watch post. We didn't know the language and we told them they were from Sventzian and were following Voske's orders, Markov's lieutenant.

They let us through.

This occurred several times before they finally reached the main base of the *Tzapeviev* Otriad (brigade).

Here we met up with Voske and our other five friends.

***Sediakin*, the Commander of the Tzapeviev Brigade**

Washed and rested the group assembled in a row and were greeted by the Russian partisans.

In front of them stood the commander *Sediakin* of the *Tzapeviev* Brigade, broad–shouldered, in his thirties, a bright warm face, blonde and hairy. He recited the charter and we repeated word for word.

Later he held a speech:

—"It is said, that Jews are cowards. I don't believe this, when I arrived in the forest there were Jewish partisans here already. Leib Voliak is in my Otriad, the entire region is afraid of him. He is a fine example of your fight and struggle. Itzik Blat, Boris Feigelman, and other Jewish heroes are here in our brigade, take an example from them. But the minimum a partisan must own, is a rifle. You don't have any guns. I am giving you an order— go out and find some guns."

He left and we remained near our "*zemliankes*" (underground hiding places) and thought over the commanders orders.

[Col. 1698]

Berke Yocai had connections with the Tatars. Through them he obtained pistols. We thought, with their help, we could obtain more rifles. We have to return there which is closer to Sventzian.

Ishike couldn't remain still, he wanted to fight with Markov" Brigade. Markov was not at this camp, he was in the Naratcher (Naroch) woods. Ishike left for those woods, Israelke Wolfson went with him.

Moishke devised another plan which he presented to the commander. He was in a difficult situation. The partisans are many kilometers from Myadel, where a partisan can't stick his nose in. How can a young man go the 200 kilometers through unfriendly territory to Vilna, swarming with Germans? He will certainly die on the way!

Moishke tells him of an underground–organization in Vilna, in the ghetto, they have guns, even explosives. (FPO) He will bring them out of the ghetto to the forest, and enlarge the partisan army!

Sediakin becomes very interested and after a long deliberation he gave his answer.

Moishke became bolder and asked for a letter, so that the Vilna group (FPO) would believe that he is coming on behalf of the partisans.

But the others (FPO) have a different mandate, they want to revolt in the Vilna Ghetto. In the forests we can be more effective than to undertake an uprising in the ghetto.

Sediakin took a piece of paper and wrote his letter. Moishe requested his stamp. They wouldn't believe him. *Sediakin* stood his ground:

—"This is enough! Nothing is missing. If the German find this letter with the official stamp...they will think we are sending spies."

Moishke stood his ground. In the end, *Sediakin* said:

—"Bring me the letter, half a stamp, I will give it to you."

Jewish Mazel

On the same day, in the evening, a group of eight men, together with Berel left for Sventzian.

Berel led the group. In the middle–the two girls. The last, at the back, was Moishke.

The group was armed with two rifles, two revolvers and an *Atrezanke.* Next to Berel was a scout, a young peasant from a nearby village.

Suddenly the scout stood still, kneeled and called out in fright:

—I hear driving!

Before Berel had a minute to think, the peasant ran away. Pertzke and Moishke ran after him.

[Col. 1699]

They ran a hundred meters but the peasant vanished. They stood at the edge of the forest and heard unfamiliar voices coming from the place they left Berel.

In the darkness they crawled back to that place and noticed two trucks. They were speaking Russian, asking which brigade they belonged to and why they were on this road? Berel didn't know what to answer them. Someone yelled:

—"Are you partisans? We, together with our commissar, are going to tell you who the real partisans of the *Tzapaievz** (very anti–Semitic partisan leader) Otriad are, you are a bunch of thieves, you are running around like "old women", hand over your weapons!"

The other partisans, who travelled with the commissar, pounced on our young ones (our group) and in a split second they beat them with their rifle buts.

Berke started to scream, but with all the commotion no one heard anything.

[Col. 1700]

Beaten, Pertzke and Moishke approached the group, who were standing in bewilderment and didn't know what to do.

Itzke was the only one that didn't have his revolver taken away. They didn't notice him. Berke gritted his teeth:

—"I will teach them a lesson, this commissar, I will report him."

He wanted to cry.

They continued further, over the muddy roads, in semi darkness.

Moishe felt the commander's (Markov) letter, which he hid in the breast pocket, he wanted to feel safe, instead he felt his heart aching, as if a heavy stone was squeezing his heart.

Moishke and Itzke said their farewells when they reached Sventzian.

Arriving in New–Sventzian, he put on the armband with the black iron–cross and sat down in the train, back to Vilna.

[Col. 1699]

Partisans are Coming

Shmerke Katcherginski

Translation by Anita Frishman Gabbay

When we were in the (Vilna) ghetto, we found out that several Jewish partisans from the White–Russian forests came, together with the Jewish workers, into the ghetto; some of whom had been previously here.

It created much discussion amongst the Jews.

In their name (partisans), they said that many Jews were now in the forests, who are turning out to be exemplary fighters; the peasants in the region were frightened of them and even the Germans were uncomfortable with their existence!

Who are these Partisans?

I am also looking for them and discover that amongst them are my friends from Sventzian: Ishike Gertman, Yitzhak Rudnitski, Moishke Shutan and Heske Bushkanyetz.

[Col. 1700]

They came here with orders from the Brigade commander Feodor Grigoravitch Markov (a former teacher at a Sventzianer Polish school before the war).

They had to give Gens a very important letter. Markov wrote to him, that he, Gens, should come to the forest and bring lots of Jews with him, with all their belongings (mainly money and jewelry), with which he will buy ammunition and guns. If Gens did not answer Markov's letter, the group will bring as many people as possible out of the ghetto.

This started a search party for the partisans. The newcomers (partisans) continued their resolve and didn't give up. They didn't want to communicate with any unknown persons.

[Col. 1701]

Their own ties were with the F.P.O.* representatives or those known to them.

The F.P.O. had their own ideas how to lead the fight and all the members were of the same opinion.

Until Vittenberg's death, it was forbidden to let anyone of the F.P.O. members go to the forests: their idea was to remain together with all those Jews, old, sick and young, who could never make it to the forests or survive in them.

We already heard about the living conditions of the partisans in the forests. Ishike Gertman related to me his own experiences of the life in the forests.

His stories were like out of "a thousand and one nights". Ishike told me and others, that Markov was a very intelligent man and would give special protection to writers. He convinced me to join the group that he was leading into the forests.

To tell you the truth, I didn't need much convincing: to go to the forests as a free man was very enticing. However, my will and Ishike's advise was not enough.

At that time I was very committed to this organization of which I was very active participant, and a very disciplined member, like all the others. Sutzkever and I tried to interest our new commander Uri (Abba Kovner), but without success, and besides us, there were many in the ghetto, and we had great influence amongst the people.

[Col. 1702]

Our departure could have negative effects on those remaining.

So we had to wait for a later group, each group had to await their turn to leave.

August 24, early in the morning, through the courtyard at 3 Kerenski Street, which was outside the ghetto, a group of 40 men made their way out, disguised as "workers" with yellow patches on them.

When we carefully inspected them, we recognized Ishike, Sheresevski, Glazman, Itche Matzkievitch, the Gordon brothers and Chaim Lazar, all the known personalities of the F.P.O.

There were others amongst them, mainly women, brothers and sisters of the partisans who were already in the forest and through the scouts wanted their own families to join them. The distance was long to reach the Narach forests, about 200 kilometers.

In a few days, news after news arrived: one worse than the other: they were all captured: they were all shot: Dessler revealed to us, peasants noticed the group and advised the police.

A little later we found out the entire story.

The group decided to rest for awhile in the forest and they didn't notice the night–watchman, and they quietly resumed their journey. At the long, wooden bridge over the Ashmien river, they were attacked by machine guns. Over 20 men were struck dead, amongst the saved ones were Ishike Gertman, Glazman and Lazar, who arrived at Markov's brigade after many days of wandering.

[Col. 1701]

In the Glow of the Burning Night

The name Boris was the partisan name of our Sventzianer friend Berel Yochai, he was the oldest son of his father, Chaim the Garber (tailor), who then was in his third year of service. It was only a year, when he left the shtetl and the brigade commander of the partisans was already proud of him, "how he had grown", like he grew wings just like a true eagle!

Also, his father, Chaim, who was in the same detachment, didn't recognize his own son. He looked to the sky with his eyes, beaming over his son's radiance (fame), and his heart was overwhelmed with joy.

[Col. 1702]

The father trembled at his son's fame (against the evil eye) Other than from Leib, from whom he didn't receive anymore money, he relied on his son Bere.

Boris (they took Russian names in the partisan detachments) can't remain still, he wanted to "fly" and "storm through the air". He is amongst his terror group, where he is the commander. Ivan Smirnov, Kolie Petrov, Volnie Lavrinovitch, Yosef Flexser and Yitzhak Rudnitski, the last 2 are Sventzian youth who are now both in Israel.

"With such a group of fine fighters I will not be afraid to venture anywhere"–he is most certain.

[Col. 1703]

"With Boris we will even jump into a fire", one speaks with the other.

It is now June, lying on the small green mountain, they cannot get enough pleasure from the sun. Like small cats rolling around joyfully in the earth, they are basking in the sun with exposed bodies!

Night!

Summer is gone, on a dark evening, the "Gestapo" took away the mother and the young sister. Now, Boris (Bere) begin his nightmares; when the sky turned black from the poison. Going out for his kill, he storms through the darkness, as if he wants to break through, rip apart and see—"perhaps, perhaps, he can find his loved ones".

In four days, it will be a year, in four days Boris and his group will assemble and plan to annihilate the 15th echelon. (division of Germans).

The detachment commander praises him, how wonderful, that in 2 weeks you must carry out this attack.

—Comrade commander, Boris, saying his goodbyes, you can add to my account the nights of June 27 and 28 as " the destruction of the 15th echelon"!

Now, the commander bursts out laughing, today is the 24th. So, only a few days are left.

—But–Boris does not quit, but everyone understands what the "but" means–

The entire otriad remains in uncertainty...

Only 4 days: we have to destroy the entire battalion!

No one wanted the other to know their thoughts:

—What if Boris does not succeed? And the group will be left without him?

There were hardships everywhere: the Hitlerites, the Samorovtes, and Whites (Russians).

Berel Yocai–at the explosion of a railroad

[Col. 1704]

Boris was difficult, no one could keep up with him. He knew only one thing: to look at his compass and blow up railroad lines.

No road was inaccessible to him, no hiding place. If he had to pass through a bare forest, so what? This is how they have to cut through.

And if a stream doesn't let them pass, so what?

Just by determining the water table from afar, Boris tied the automatic guns and the dynamite on his head and they cut through the water and crossed over.

The compass tells them to go through mud, —Boris obeys, and the night, the night is pitch black. Only the squeaking and the swamps lets you know that one is following the other. Ivan and Yosef are touching each others boots, to make sure that they are not stuck in the mud.

—"Only our hats remained dry", joked Kolya and Itzik.

Volya is the most practical of the bunch. He bound his boots with studs around his feet.

And Boris is ahead of everyone–he turns and looks and looks, what is he looking for in the dark?–and suddenly he sees his mother and his sister. He hears their screaming. He hears them being tortured. He seems to think that they are calling out to him for help. But he can't help them.

Boris walks quicker, as if he is chasing the murderers, to tear his mother and his sister from the arms of these murderers.

The hatred lingers in every corner, in every village. But Boris is now is now on familiar ground, the place where he was born. He knows this region in and out, with closed eyes.

He doesn't care about the garrisons, the villagers, the police–watchmen, he plows through wasted fields, through swamps and over fallen trees–storming through everything. (like a madman)

Early in the morning. The sweat is pouring from the fighters, they stop to rest. They are only 4 kilometers from the railroad line. The day passes, he (Boris) is deep in thought.

Trains are passing in the distance, as if they are mocking them: look, we are here, so what are you going to do to us?

Boris is nervous. He is sobbing from "heartache" just like the "locomotive". –we will see, who will have the last laugh!

The last 4 kilometers were the hardest. Afraid (the Germans) of the partisans, the shooting from the wagons came from both sides, in the event that anyone come close to them (the Germans). The partisans are creeping among the shadows of the trees and creep deeper into the area where the shootings are taking place, in the cover of night.

[Col. 1705]

Suddenly a bunker appears. The patrols are marching and believing that they are closely guarding the railroad lines, as well as searching for mines. It is now clear to the partisans: the dynamite has to be placed only when the train is closer by. When they are sleeping, otherwise the work would be for nothing! The watchman will find him.

Night.

When they brought his mother and his sister from the prison, Boris reminds himself, and when they led his mother and his sister to their deaths! He can't forgive himself, that he allowed this to happen!

He is now standing at the edge of the forest.

If only another 100 men, he would attack them like an animal on attacks their prey, taking delight from their kill, and would blow up the wagons, the garrison and all those responsible for killing mothers and small sisters.

Today, on the Yortzheit (anniversary of the death) of his beloved ones, it must take place! He can't bring them back to life, but to save other mothers, daughters, fathers and brothers from death, he still can do that! When he is thinking of this revenge, a "sweetness shines through him", that he is about to" bestow" on these murderers.

Boris, however, knows that the most difficult part is yet to come.

The earth is covered with branches and cut down trees. We can't go now, as everything will snap under our feet. Every sound would be heard.

Meanwhile a garrison is approaching.

– A death to a death (these murderers)–says Boris under his breath, leading his young group amidst the noise and heading toward the railroad line.

– No one can hear anything, the branches breaking under their feet, the garrison flies by and they are left standing in the middle of their road covered in darkness.

The locomotive disappears from sight.

His heart is beating faster.

Everyone must remain in his tracks, not even take a deep breath! Boris is fuming! How is he in this predicament? It seems to him that no more trains will be passing tonight, and his mission would not proceed as planned...

All at once, a signal is heard, wheels were rolling and approaching. Boris gives a sign and the dry branches are breaking, without pity, under the boots of the partisans.

This is how they ran from the hill barely catching their breath.

All around them, like on the move, the watchmen are marching in all directions with their brightly lit cigarettes.

[Col. 1706]

Something in Boris' heart is stirring: "now we shall take out the entire battalion of Hitlerites, with tanks full of fuel! An end! An end to everything! We shall make a "mish–mash" out of everything". (a kasha, i.e. soup of buckwheat)

The partisans were ready and eager, like animals drawn to their flesh (prey), with wide–open blaring nostrils, something to smell (savour)! It seems that they are too eager with anticipation, but they must be very cautious! Or else this will be their end!

The murderers will again sow death and destruction!

The darkness is pierced by a little rain.

Boris is delighted, the watchmen can no longer wander about. The rain becomes louder, the pieces of wood are flying about and hitting them in their faces, the oncoming train cannot be heard.

—Everything ready–he breaks out into a sweat. He doesn't feel the bitter cold, backwards, he is overtaken by a heat–wave! The rain is pouring without stop.

Suddenly.... a dark light appears, a miracle, like seeing pale dead pale fingers spread over the tracks!

——We are placing them–Boris hurries us to crawl up the little hill with all our might, even if we have to use our teeth and nails.

The station of the railroad is in front of us, the eyes of the locomotive become" wider and closer" like they were waiting to destroy us!

The wheels are approaching, wild and restless!

—Take care! Take care!–I come to terms with death. I'm on the way! I placed the dynamite, Flexser pushes the 2 capsules and the demolition cords.

Boris controls.

—Good! Now give me the 2 others. Vania, come here. Like a strike of lighting all is in place. The chamber is in place, the demolitions–threads are stretched over the rail–lines waiting for the locomotive to pass over them.

—Comrade, commander——screams Shmirnov–the train will blow you up.

And so. The train is "racing like he is about to capture the enemy", moving forward with its massive speed.

Boris checks the capsules again with his hands, and shouts: "Leave, now comrades!"

They roll down the hill, run to the forests, as quickly as they could, faster and faster.

Suddenly a mass explosion and thunderous noise destroys the railroad and sounds like a lightening strike hit the earth.

Several seconds pass.

[Col. 1707]

—To the forests—hollers Boris.

The night sky suddenly lit up with a colorful explosion and pierced the darkness of the forests.

The debris of the explosion continues falling and the sounds of the wagon cars were still rumbling in its magnificent fire of the explosion.

[Col. 1708]

Boris stops running. He takes pride in this explosive evening. He is overjoyed and pleased. He looks at the rails where death is everywhere.

He understands that this same death, on the same night, is the same gruesome murder that robbed him of his mother and sister.

The Revenge on this Bright Day

Translated by Janie Respitz

...then, Freidrich Olin appeared in Sventzian. He was now a count. A dark, chequered suit, recently pressed, his patent leather shoes stepping lightly, quietly shining from far away.

The only one wearing a gaudy silk bowtie, that waves before him and states: Freidrich Olin has arrived!

The count just realized, the Commissar of Sventzian, Gustav Von Bek, his deputy Grill and the chief gendarme Kril were on their way to Lintup to shoot...

For Freidrich it was all the same, it did not matter who would carry out the assassinations. The order was laconic: 500 heads.

That dark night, ripped from their warm homes, were workers, teachers, doctors, students and pupils. In their place remained the cries of women and children...

The next day, Freidrich rode in his taxi, with a rested, powdered face. Lost in his thoughts, he elegantly tipped his hat to an acquaintance. What a lovely smile emanated from his lips.

The taxi continued on its way to the cemetery, and the sun shone on him.

The arrested were already lying on the grass near the graves, face down, surrounded by armed Gestapo and police. He walked around carefully (making sure his shoes and pants would not get soiled in the mud), quietly, thinking, waving his manicured long, shining fingers and suede gloves, while wiping his sweaty brow with a handkerchief. The scent, not from the cemetery, was of eau de cologne. He marveled at the tomb stones, the lovely granite. He was also familiar with that. He remembered that in his library in Magdeburg he had many interesting art books.

[Col. 1708]

The tombstones and the engravings clouded the gentle face of Olin. He remembered, finally...no, he caught himself, watching a bird above, not him. He was still young. He feels, thank God strong. He forgot this morning to ask for his boxing gloves to strengthen his body.

He did not want to disturb the quiet mood of the cemetery, but he was forced to.

–You sir, as he looked on the covered grass, are lying too much on your side.

– And you sir, a bit closer please.

– Please Miss, hold your hands higher on your back!

He was gentle and kind to the accused.

–Nu, he said. The Gestapo knew from his look that he was ready.

–Aha! He remembered something important.

He took broad steps near the graves, and was soon standing beside his taxi.

A loving, calm smile was on his face. He held a sparkling new camera.

Now we can really begin, he thought to himself. Everyone understood and held their fingers on the triggers.

Freidrich looked for a higher, more comfortable spot for himself. He climbed onto a dark piece of granite, and sat down. The light was perfect. He turned his head toward the armed men, raised his right hand in a Heil Hitler, and dropped it swiftly...

In the town and the villages the inhabitants were shocked by the sudden shooting. Women fainted, tore out their hair. Children cried in fear. Men clenched their fists while tears dropped.

For Freidrich, this was nothing new.

[Col. 1709]

He didn't even twitch a brow when the hurricane of fire poured out on all the innocent people. Even then, he did not lose his calmness...Oh pardon, not true, the almighty helped his body, turning in all directions. Freidrich Olin was now reading a sensational novel, which he did not have in his rich library in Magdeburg. He now sees a suspense film never seen on screen. He is enraptured. Suddenly, he stood by the cross – the lens noticed one who was shot running far away. His glasses are splattered with pieces of bloody marrow. Freidrich forgets about making a production.

The camera works on:

A woman was caught on a cross, climbed on to a cold stone and fell back onto the mound of graves.

A man clenched his fists. Red poison spilled from his open mouth. He ran toward Freidrich:

Olin shuddered, but calm down – the man is lying split open on a stone.

A young girl shivered in the air:

–A shame, – she could have been useful.

The shooting is quiet. The green underfoot is now boiling red. Freidrich does not rest. The camera continues to work. The lens is looking for new scenes, perhaps a quivering corpse.

The wheels quietly roll back to town. The sun reflects off his diamond rings. Thoughts. A man like Freidrich is always thinking. It's annoying. If there was a sound technician at the cemetery as well as a photographer there would have been something to hear as well as see.

As in an amusement park, the machines swing and rock over the graves.

From the windows of the houses, pale faces look out and in fear see:

The shiny blue taxi drips red, as if red tears...

Shimon, can't be compared to the culture commissar. He is of lower stature, not as much education, and the son of poor parents.

He was happy when he was able to study at the University. His parents were also pleased:

Shimon is studying. He will be an engineer – they said with respect about their son.

[Col. 1710]

For him as well as millions of others, fulfilling this dream was ripped away from him.

He wandered deep into Russia, and threw his passion into the holy war against the German occupiers who were annihilating his people.

Shimon goes to his hometown where he had left his parents as well as many relatives and friends. The horrific remnants which the Hitlerites left on Lithuanian soil did not allow him to rest. – Revenge! – was now his desire.

He wandered around his quarters in Tashkent whispering to himself and his friends:

–I won't rest until I accomplish my goal!

*

In the golden forest green of the occupied Lithuanian soil, Shimon's beautiful head shone among the partisans.

A realized dream: Shimon is walking on home turf. He is returning to his base, sitting in mud huts with the partisan who are his old friends in silence. Their blood is boiling. With their own eyes they witnessed the murdered and the slaughtered...

It is no wonder that the occupiers are sitting on Lithuanian soil as if on a fiery volcano. Guarded trains go by – and fall into the valleys. They guard dignitaries, armed guards. Factories are burned, bridges are destroyed. Partisans take revenge!

Shimon is irritated, but you can't see it on his face. No one can see what's in his heart, except his commander who notices his nervousness and nail biting:

–So Shimon, – the commanders words tear into him – Are you ready?

Shimon was insulted that this question was posed to him, and from whom? Doesn't the Comrade Commander know that such a question is superfluous?

The commander realizes this and understands why his fighter is sad. He lovingly puts his arm around him:

–Have I really insulted you, Shimon?

The young man felt embarrassed. How could he think like this? The commander's affection and hug pleased him. If only he wasn't so shy, he would tell his commander...no,

[Col. 1711]

If he could, he would open his heart – and the commander would see what a stormy volcano was seething within:

Comrade Commander! For our tortured people, for those who were murdered – I shall kill and the enemy will be defeated. I promise you, Comrade commander, Olin will not escape my hands!...

Both are silent, their hearts are pounding.

The young man was embraced by his kind commander. They both stepped through the narrow paths among the huts. The pre–Spring sun shone on their dark heads, dipped into their hearts and left a shiver. A memory of a Spring which passed and a new one coming.

The road was silky white. Two sleighs pulled by eagle–like horses rushed by.

Four guys – partisans, ride as in a dream – though the reality is harsh and terrifying.

They do not feel the ride. They do not see the tops of the golden trees. They do not feel the loving sun rays of dawn.

The horses gallop and in the sleighs, dead silence, as if no one was there. Apparently, due to nerves, the fighters harnessed their horses firmly and taut.

–Partisans are travelling?

No one said anything.

They were wearing patched peasant furs and heavy peasant coats on top, hats over their eyes, with no expression on their faces. Shaggy. What would happen if their pockets were searched?

The fighters think about this. So, nothing would happen except strange hands going into their pockets. There was no need to do this.

The route was calculated. Every detail – in every point. And...they arrived in Sventzian.

They slow down. They crawl into the travelling line of other horses, until they come to a stop on Gedimin Street, in front of the Commissariat.

Each one has his note and his pack.

Everyone surmises what the notes are for. That means – forced labour in Germany. It means getting sent to the Front. For women – to be prostitutes on the front.

What is in the pack?

Olin's motto is – bacon!

The peasants must bring him gifts.

[Col. 1712]

It's good to bring a pig, butter, eggs, sour cream, cheese, a chicken. (His relatives in Germany are very grateful for the "splendid packages" he sends them).

–Lately, – complained a peasant– these gifts don't help much...he complains and screams...

–His wife must drive him crazy– joked Shimon.

–His wife, – smiling to his friend Vitek – should give him some advice...

–It's worse for the partisans – grumbled an old man.

–So far, in Sventzian, he does not have to fear them.

–Don't you know, children, fear has big eyes – advised the old man.

–Shshsh...the door is already open!

The people pushed in and sat on the benches in the dark corridor.

*

Lithuanian – called out the commissar – hearing the nationality of his client.

Freidrich was disappointed in the Lithuanians. "This is also a nation? Lithuanians? Did you ever hear such a language?"

Olin knows French (he was in Paris in 1940), Polish (he was in Warsaw in 1941), his Russian is not bad (he was in Moscow). He thought he would soon be in London...New York...but for now he was stuck in Sventzian. If he had to be stuck in the sticks, he would not let the partisans rest. He also had to watch out for the advancing Bolsheviks.

–Lithuanian – he repeated – with a teasing smile.

–Lithuanian! – said Shimon again – and feels like the volcano inside of him is about to erupt. He gets hold of himself and says "this is not the time. I will lure him into the corridor, and there, together with Vitek, Itzik and Ugol, in front of all the peasants, we will carry out his sentence. If Olin only knew what I had in my pockets...if Olin knew who I am. To the devil, – his deputy does not see either, he is also entering into our plan."

Freidrich senses that his client is not a common peasant. His proud answer puzzled him. He looked directly into his face:

–It seems like the same garbage – thought Olin – like all the others, long messy hair, but why does he think he's so big? Just because he was born in Sventzian – he laughed to himself.

[Col. 1713]

–Do you have bacon? – He asked Shimon in his shining uniform.

–Yes sir, – Shimon bowed – I brought you a full bag. I couldn't carry it myself.

–A whole bag, you say? – Olin livened up.

–Heinrich!

– He grabbed the telephone receiver, come down, I need your help.

Shimon is also happier. His plan is unfolding. He will be like a cat to me.

Heinrich opens the door:

–What is it Freidrich? I'm ready and so is my Mauser.

Freidrich laughed:

–Put away your Mauser, I need your throat!

–My throat is already ready! – whined Heinrich.

–Good...very good. Come my love...you see this gentleman – Freidirch elegantly pointed at Shimon – this gentleman brought us a beautiful gift.

–Perhaps also some moonshine? – Heinrich gently placed his hand on Shimon.

–No sir, I was afraid the bottles would break on the road –Shimon quivered. He was afraid the German would feel his weapon.

–It doesn't matter. It doesn't matter.

The German go through the offices into the corridor. Shimon was right behind them.

The peasants stand up, remove their hats and bow.

–Please gentlemen, here is the sack – Shimon points to the corner.

Freidrich and Heinrich pick up the sack from both sides:

–Wow, this is heavy, what's inside? Bacon, you say?

–Bacon sir! A whole pig and something else. –

Freidrich wants to untie it. The fighters stand ready, their hands hidden deep in their pockets, waiting for the order from the commander, for Shimon to begin. This appeared to be the right time. While they were bent over the bag, shoot a few rounds.

Shimon wants to play a bit with them. They wanted the peasants to see what sort of gift he and his friends brought for the Germans.

–To the devil – complained Freidrich – Heinrich, go bring a scissors.

Before Heinrich could turn around, Freidrich managed to untie to knot. He opened the sack:

[Col. 1714]

–Straw, well packed – praising Shimon.

The peasants were very curious to see what the gift was.

Freidrich removed the straw, put his hands in the sack and pulled something out:

–What kind of brick...

But before he turned around, Shimon was holding his gun in both hands. Shimon extended his right hand toward his red neck, and through clenched teeth said:

–Here is your gif! –Bang! There was a burst of fire together with the crack.

Freidrich fell on his back onto Shimon's armed left hand.

Heinrich came running from the office with the scissors. Shimon's right hand was free. He shot Heinrich. He fell onto a broken chair.

The peasants ran in fright to the door.

–Remain! Shouted Vitie, and blocked the door.

–No reason to run away friends – Itzik calmed the peasants.

–Comrade commander, he's still alive!– shouted Anton, pointing to Freidrich.

–He's still alive? – Shimon shot Olin in the face.

–You don't like Lithuanians, you swine? Eh? This you received from a Lithuanian, and a Jew...I'm also a Jew!...

Itzik came running:

–Permit me – comrade commander – one series.

–Shoot him my brother – said Shimon, granting permission.

–Take this, you rascal, for my parents, – as Itzik's gun went off.

–Give him one from all of us – the peasants were becoming bolder.

–Give him one for my daughter – called out the old man.

–Take this for his daughter– shouted Anton – and shot him again.

–Those taking revenge were not stingy. Shimon looked at the bandits again. "All is in order".

–Exit comrades! – Our mission is complete.

*

The road was silky white.

Two sleighs pulled by eagle swift horses were rushing back, back to the forest. Going home...

[Col. 1715]

Gestapo and police run to the place where they thought they heard shooting. The horses are flying, carrying through the air, the disheveled fighters. They threw away their used peasant coats. Their disheveled hair waved in the wind. They kissed and hugged one another.

The sun faced Shimon like a lit torch.

[Col. 1716]

He took a deep breath of the frosty air and exhaled:

–Long live revenge!

The burning souls of his friends lit up the surrounding forests. The words echoed in the dazzling white snow:

–Long live revenge!

Zazier Forest Brigade "Zhalgiris" April 1944.

[Col. 1715]

How We Recruited New Fighters

Yitzhak Rudnitski

Translated by Anita Frishman Gabbay

When the German–Polish War broke out, I was in Warsaw with my parents. In December 1939, my sister Chaia and I left Warsaw and were searching where to go; we arrived in Svenztian which was still under control of the Czarist regime. In June 1941, like many young Jewish men, I had the opportunity to escape to Russia. Suddenly, without being prepared, the German Army arrived with its thunder! We barely noticed when the Red Army left the shtetl, which they left in disarray.

A group of us, being the young ones, met and decided to make a plan: to organize ourselves in the event that we should have to fight. We set up a radio apparatus and luckily, in this manner, were able to get news and updates from the front. From these communications we learned about the murderous actions of the Germans against the Jews and captured folk.

When we learned of the German plan to lead the Jews of Sventzian to Poligon, I and Moishke Rudnitski left for Glubokie. We stayed half a month, and when we learned the ghetto in Sventzian was still functioning, we returned to Sventzian. We resumed contact with our former friends of our group to do everything possible to go to the forests.

[Col. 1716]

The question was: where can we obtain guns and ammunition?

When we found out that the "Akranka" were some Jews were working was full of guns and ammunition, we decided to several of our friends on this work detail to secure these guns for us. We worked there several weeks and were successful to smuggle some guns back to the ghetto: we had then rifles, ammunition and hand grenades.

We had to seek out making contact with the partisans already in the forests, but this was not successful. We therefore needed to find our own place in the forest, a group of 20 of us left Sventzian. The first night we walked about 30 kilometers, and when daylight came, we decided to set up our temporary base, in the Tzerklishker forest.

Life was very difficult, we were in an unknown place, without supplies and without preparation. Neighbours were unfriendlyb& we were in constant fear and danger!

In time, we got used to our situation, we became friendly with our neighbours, which were simple peasants, who were sympathetic to our cause against the Hitlerite bandits and wanted to help us.

[Col. 1717]

Slowly, we got used to our way of life, we even managed to carry out several actions on our own initiative against the White–Russian partisans and steal their guns.

They feared us in this region, so in this manner, we got our food provisions when we carried out these raids. When we discovered that the Sventzian Jews were going to be deported, we decide to infiltrate the ghetto to find out the plan for them.

Once there, we made contact with a Jewish policeman from the Vilna Ghetto, who was a representative of the F.P.O.. It was decided that Ishike Gertman and I join the transport of Jews going to the Vilna Ghetto and that Moishke Shutan and his sister should go there on foot.

In the Vilna Ghetto we had to arrange for a meeting with the representatives of the F.P.O. In the Vilna Ghetto, they proposed to us: their main goal was to organize their fight from within the Gupa ghetto (the ghetto was in 2 parts). At that time, there was the Warsaw Ghetto uprising, so they proposed to us to bring our group from the forests into the ghetto and unite with their Vilna group in the ghetto.

We told them, we were of a different opinion, according to our beliefs, all the young people should be sent into the woods and fight together with the partisans.

[Col. 1717]

The next morning we found out the Jewish police were looking for us. Ishike and I left our revolvers with our group, and went into the street to see what to do.

They arrested us and brought us to the Police Commissar, Natick Ryng, who warned us: we know everything about your partisan groups and we should hand over our guns.

Understandably, we lied and said we didn't have any guns.

He called several policemen, who beat us very badly with sticks and threw us into the ghetto prison. We remained 3 days, when some of our friends managed to get our release. Several days later, Ishike and I left the ghetto as “workers”. Once outside the ghetto, we separated from the group, tore off our yellow patches, and in the evening jumped on a wagon train full of coal, which was going to New– Sventzian. We got off at Sventzian and by foot we crossed the town and left for our base in the Tzerklishker forest.

[Col. 1718]

Our base was upside down, our friends were no where to be seen. We didn't know what happened to them nor what to do.

Standing around and thinking, we suddenly heard footsteps. We took out our revolvers and were prepared to shoot. Can you imagine our joy, when we saw, amongst the branches, our friend Shimke Levine.

He told us that they received word, that the Germans were going to attack the base, so he left for the village to get more information. In the meantime, the base was attacked by the Germans, our friends fled, and when he returned he was alone. He hid at a peasant's house, and from him learned that we had returned to the base.

Together with Shimke, we left for Chaim the Garber, where we found Berke Yochai, and Shaoulke Michalson. They brought us to the new base of our Sventzianer friends.

At our new base, we were informed that they were met by a group of Markov's brigade, who was led by Vaske Tzharnai, (Vaske the Black). He took Israelka Wolfson with him and told us when he returned, he would take our entire group to the Tstopiever Otriad.

Sidiaken was the commander of that otriad. He clearly told us that those with guns could join his otriad, the others were on their own, they had to obtain guns before joining his group.

I remained in the Tsopiav Otriad for 2 months, and on May 18, 1943, they took me the Lithuanian partisan–otriad, “Zalgurim”.

My first order that I received was to go with the partisans(of) Stavienas and Stankevitchis to carry out political work in the nearby villages.

This was important work, as we had to recruit new fighters for our otriads, we had to spread our literature to the peasants and new recruits. We were targeting the young people.

July 2 they sent me to New–Sventzian in order to make connections with Koslovski, leader of the underground communist party.

In a short time, the Lithuanian partisan otriad, “Vilnius” was founded and I joined them.

[Col. 1719]

In this otriad they gave me a special name, Lolia Kunitzki, and this is how I was then known is the partisan organizations. I remained here until the liberation, for almost a year. In a period of this year, I carried out various raids, the most important was the destruction of 11 large and 3 smaller battalions of German soldiers.

[Col. 1720]

After liberation, I returned to Sventzian and found a total destruction, a ragged city. The Jewish community was murdered. Everything was empty and wasted. I couldn't bear to see this destruction and decided to continue wandering about, as far away from the graves and mass– murder sites.

[Col. 1718]

The Heroes in the Forest

Alexander Bogen

Translation by Anita Frishman Gabbay

I want to add my comments about the heroic and fierce struggles of the Sventzianer Partisans, about their bravery and about the way they organized to rescue the youth from the Vilna Ghetto which they brought to fight alongside the partisan army in the forests.

In the F.P.O. of Vilna many agonizing days were spent: whether to fight the Nazis from within the ghetto or to fight the Nazis from the forest? The youth of Sventzian had to convince me that it would be better from the forests! They came to the Vilna ghetto to lead us to the Narach forests, which the F.P.O. was against.

When the first group would arrive successfully in the Narach forest, led by Ishike Gertman and Yosef Glazman, then it would be decided to send more groups. This group was attacked on the way and half was murdered. This made it more difficult for the F.P.O. to allow more fighters to leave the ghetto. They Sventzianer partisans did not accept defeat readily, and continued their talks with the F.P.O. to allow fighters to leave. Several groups left, but they still encountered difficulties on the road. These groups arrived at the Narach base. This activity continued until the liquidation of the Vilna Ghetto. These who excelled in their work: Isike Gertman z'l, Moshe Shutan, Moishe–Yitzhak Rudnitski, Shlomo Ichiltchik, Motke Feigel and others.

[Col. 1719]

I asked one of the former and well known Sventzian partisans, Motke Heske Bushkanetz, to tell me about his activities (he had a count of 12 destroyed German divisions).

Leave me alone, he said, we destroyed them and that's the important thing. He thought that I would not pursue this talk any further.

After lengthy pleading, he finally gave in.

I started to write, "I Motke Hershke"... and he answered me angrily.

[Col. 1720]

You are writing "I"...there were many like me...

He was very modest and this showed his character.

Young men came to the Vilna ghetto to persuade the partisan organization.

It is important for this story to continue, young men risked their lives to travel 200 kilometers through the forests, trying to avoid the German garrisons and to avoid being attacks, travelling day and night?

Who sent them?!

They took it upon themselves to risk their lives to save as many lives as possible.

[Col. 1721]

They, these young souls, who were the “scouts” or the “messengers”, were truly the unsung heroes of this terrible time in our history. Therefore I want to stop and discuss the history of Sventzian.

It's a small shtetl near Vilna, with its own rabbis and freethinkers, with Chasidim and progressive youth, with organizations and schools, with many different folk people, with a love for Hebrew and Yiddish. In one word–a real Jerusalem of Lita in miniature.

Sventzian was so immersed in its cultural traditions and in the atmosphere of Vilna, she was actually a part of her, as part of Jerusalem of Lita.

The importance lies with all the fighters of the partisans, especially those that lie in the fields of White–Russia, their final “resting place”; the story is about all the young fighters that fought so valiantly and risked their lives to rescue the young lives from the Vilna Ghetto. Those who survived stand before our eyes every day, as well as those that perished.

These young fighters were just children when the war broke out, and these children fought with their hearts and souls against a mighty enemy to save their Jewish brothers and sisters.

The Judenrat had to send able bodied men to work in the Sventzian ghetto. As there was no communication between the partisans and the Jewish community in the earlier stages of the war, the Judenrat had difficult choices to make. They often went to labour themselves. No one knew what the real intent of the Germans were. Godel Gilinski went as one of those workers. After one such work detail, he noticed a black market for illegal weapons. He met with Isike Gertman who said:” you want to fight the Germans?” There are guns here, this would be our opportunity to acquire them!”

So the plan was set in place. The workers went to work, these were: Yitzhak and Yoske Rudnitski, Gershon Godel, Kuske Ligumski, Moshe Shutan, Ruben and Froike Miadzolski, and Gershon Bak. They left work limping and with swollen stomachs. This is how they slowly accumulated guns.

[Col. 1722]

Yitzhak and Moshe Yudke Rudnitski, as well as Motke Feigel, engaged themselves with the Judenrat in order to find out the happenings in the ghetto. They met in the Yocais's home, where all the decision– making was done. The older Yocai was a tanner, a very important Jews, with hands of a true craftsman. Berka and Dudke were his sons. Rubke and Shimke Levine knew the streets and hide outs in the whole region.

The beginning was difficult–until we were able to establish contact with the partisans. We suffered for a while. Until late 1943, our lives continued in this manner. We trekked through the mud and we smuggled potatoes into the ghetto. How long can we eat only potatoes?

Eventually, we met up with the ordinary partisans.

The commander of the Stafaiev Otriad was Sidiaken, a Siberian with a long blond mustache, who laughed at us when we showed him our 5 rifles:– you need to get more guns–we were stunned and didn't know what to say.

Moshele Shutan answered: we have to go to Vilna and join forces with the F.P.O.in the Vilna Ghetto. Isike Gertman and Israelka Wolfson soon arrived to the ghetto. Isike was delivering an order–a letter from Commander Markov, to send all the young abled persons to the forests.

The message was not well received. The route was a long and terrible one, full of danger, full of police and Gestapo.

Three scouts were sent out of Sidianken's Otriad, they went to New Sventzian, where Moshele (Moshe Shutan) left the group and the other two, Israelka and Isike, dressed as peasant gentiles and boarded a train for Vilna.

The train, when it reached the station didn't stop. Israelka peeked outside and saw a Gestapo–man holding the head of a dead person.

[Col. 1723]

Several Lithuanian with rifles were standing there as well, for a review. Isike descended first, Israelka followed with fear. The head officer screamed "Halt"!

Isike put his hand in his pocket and increased his speed. A shot was heard. Isike yelled to Israelka to run faster. Isike ran and slid under the wagon and scrambled over the tracks, running for his life. A great commotion ensued, the Germans were shooting everywhere. But Israelka ran over one, two, three, four, five tracks, between the wagons like a wounded cat until he disappeared, like the earth swallowed him up. 15 minutes passed, he was laying in a corner near the hill on his stomach, the Germans close by, and Israelka had his grenade in his hand. The Germans got tired and this saved the 2 young lads from Sventzian. Isike did the same "cat–dance". They left for the road shortly afterward.

The ghetto was the same as before. Rows of slaves left for work detail every day into the town. The Jews endured many hard and difficult labours. There were two sets of uniforms, yellow and green. The Jewish police from part of the ghetto would speak often with the Lithuanian police of the other side.

In the ammunition camp a young lad was shot. His name was Zalman Tiktin. He wanted to steal some ammunitions.

Tuvia Bieliak, from Vidz, was arrested for carrying a gun. The Gestapo tortured him without mercy, but he didn't reveal anything, he eventually died.

Gens, the head of the Jewish Ghetto police, was uninformed.

If you were found smuggling flour or grains, a beating took place.

Keitel took young women (girls) who had to undress and he spanked them for his pleasure.

Beginning of July 1943, Vidas and Koslovski were arrested, 2 associates of the ghetto.

[Col. 1724]

Great unrest followed. Keitel, the head– commander of the ghetto, gave an ultimatum to Gens: to bring Vittenberg into custody (head of the F.P.O.). July 16, 1943, the workers did not go to work, the gates were locked. Men and women gathered in all the streets. The directors were frustrated and angry.

What happened?" From mouth to mouth, one word was uttered, "Vittenberg"! Rumors were flying. One said he escaped, the other that he fought till the end. No one knew the truth. The police made it clear: capture Vittenberg or the entire ghetto will be punished.

Truly, this was only a matter of time, life in the ghetto was very fragile.

Zagoiski with 2 other policemen representing the Judenrat met with the partisans of the F.P.O. The Judenrat wanted to hand over the young one(s), but the partisans said" no." Some said not to make decisions when in a heated argument. Think clearly! These arguments went back and forth. Only the F.P.O. had the right to make the final decision: perhaps the fight should take place now! It was a big moral dilemma!

Vittenberg gave himself up and was eventually killed. July 22, 1943, a few days after Vittenberg's death, Iske Gertman led the first group of partisans out of the ghetto. That evening we received news that they were attacked at Lavarishok, from 50 partisans , only 14 survived. Dessler, the Jewish police, certainly had his hand in this! The Gestapo found passes from the Vilna ghetto amongst the dead partisans. Day and night the ghetto police were everywhere, the Sventzianer partisans were in great danger. We had to rescue them while we could.

The house on 11 Rudnitsker Street was blocked, nailed the door shut. Moshele(Moshe Shutan) snuck in a crevice between the walls and held his breath.

[Col. 1725]

Footsteps were heard. An electric lamp shone over the walls.

– Anyone here?"–a Jewish policeman shouted. They turned to retreat, but another police said–anyone found?–"No".

– “Wait a minute, what is that in the corner?”

Shooting started, Moshe had no alternative but to give himself up.

– “I give up, I have no gun, please believe me, dear police”

They searched all over, then took him to the criminal– police: they were expecting him. Zeidel was waiting for him, in his previous years he was a criminal, and was promoted by the Germans to this high post in the criminal–police. Moshe was searched and they found 2 papers, 1 a pass, the other a letter from Commander Markov.

– “Who wrote this?” –Moshe, a prisoner in chains, remained silent. They beat him and his eyes swelled. Moshe, through the corner of his swollen eyes noticed Nusbaum peaking into the room.

Nusbaum threw a glance at Zeidel, and interrupted the beatings. Nusbaum was an elegant man, who didn't like violence.

It had been 2 hours they were chasing Isroelka Wolfson from roof to roof, and Nusbaum was angry at this. He was surrounded on one house, he had a gun, the problem was if he shot, what would they do to the rest of the people in the ghetto?

Nusbaum , deep in thought, said to Moshe–what shall we do?

[Col. 1726]

– “Do nothing–my commander!”

– “Yes, young lad, I will stop this aggression right away!”

Nusbaum looked at Zeidel and asked why he beat up the arrested one(Moshe).

He was quiet like the wall,—–Nusbaum said—what is the matter with you?–

Moshe, the 18 year old partisan said he will only answer to Gens alone, boldly.

Gens, at his desk at Rudnitski Street, spent a sleepless night, he wanted an answer from Dessler: what is happening?

A knock on the door, 4 police accompanied Moshe and he stood before Gens, looking him straight in the eye:

Gens said – “Tell me, tell me!”

Moshe stood in his place and the second time Gens asked him, he approached Gens and sat down.

– “Do you know what shall happen to you” – said Gens.

– “Herr Commander, I am a partisan, I am here because Markov, the partisan Brigade

Commander ordered me to come to the Vilna Ghetto and leave with other fighters.

If a hair on my body is touched, they will descend upon the ghetto from the forests!

They 2 ghetto leaders were upset.

– “Do you know what a disturbance you caused. You want to take out a few dozen young people, but what will happen to the thousands?” Gens said.

I will tell you, but first Dessler must leave the room. Dessler was rattled, his fat face grew pale like a ghost, how this young lad had the “Chutzpa” to speak of him like this:

– “What's going on?”

– “Who is in charge, you or Dessler?, Moshe said with boldness and clarity.

– “Dessler takes orders from me(Gens)”, he answered.

[Col. 1727]

Dessler saw that this was getting nowhere, swearing he left the room.

[Col. 1728]

Two hours passed, after many long discussions, the next morning, Moshe and his young partisans left the ghetto heading towards the Narach forests.

The Vilnius Otriad

Mote Heshel Bushkanetz

Translated by Anita Frishman Gabbay

Leaving the Sventzian Ghetto our group organized 2 bases in the Zerlisher forests. We had 2 main goals: to obtain food for our men, and to meet the leader of the Partisan army. This was not easy. We had to endure a lengthy procedure in order to make contact.

Finlly we came across a partisan group led by Voska Starnai,(the black one). He led us to the Kazian forests where we met the Otriad “Stopoviet”. The commander of this otriad, Sidioken, only enlisted those who brought guns with them. Those without guns, had to find a way to obtain guns.

Yoske Flexer, Berke Yocai, Peretz Grodel went in the direction of Sventzian to obtain guns for our group. The sisters Ester–Feige and Raske Chait came along with us, who were going to New–Sventzian, to the Lithuanian Koslovski where they hid before coming to us in the forests. The sisters remained with Koslovski and we returned with our weapons.

[Col. 1728]

In the Baranover woods, not far from Haytutishok, the Lithuanian otriad “Vilnius” was based, and they received us in a friendly manner. From an earlier group we found our friends: Berke Yocai, Pereta Grodel,, Yosef Flexser, Chaia Yocai, Faivka Chait, Rochel Feige–Kromnik, Yitzhak Rudnitski.

Here the Lithuanian Communist Ofevela was the commander of the Vilnius Otriad, the group comprised of about 100 persons. This also included Russians, White–Russians and Lithuanians: the Russians were previously in the Red Army and when it fled, they joined the partisans to fight the Germans. This otriad carried out many important missions against the Germans in which our group took an active roll and excelled in every mission.

One important offensive was against the electric grid of Sventzian. The group was led by Arbanovitch, in which our friends also participated. These were: Berke Yocai, Itzke Rudnitski, Yoske Flexser and I. (Heshl Bushkanetz)

We arrived 11 at night and hid in the Christian cemetery of Sventzian. Here we prepared our explosives and other ammunitions that we brought.

[Col. 1729]

We sent out 2 scouts to make sure the road was clear and there were no hidden enemies.

They returned, all was quiet, the roads were clear so we began to make our way slowly and quietly to the electric station. We had grenades in our hands, guns on our shoulders, we carried the explosives and when we arrived, we immediately blew up the telephone lines. Two men worked inside, we entered and placed the explosives, we dragged the 2 workers out with us and fled about 50 meters, when we heard the large explosion. The whole shtetl went black!

We freed the 2 workers and left for a nearby village. We spent the night with a peasant that we knew, and in the morning we sent him back to Sventzian to bring us updates. He returned and told us the explosion the previous night disabled the electric grid and blew out all the windows of the nearby houses. The word was that partisans did this! Panic in the shtetl resulted. It also created difficulties for the general population of the shtetl.

We carried out another attack on the town of Fodiasinki, not far from Lyntup, our group was only 6 men. We hid here and we were told by the peasants that 21 Germans arrived in Fodiasinki and confiscated all their food and produce. We decided to go to the edge of town and murder these Germans.

[Col. 1730]

We left and hid in the nearby woods, near the road. When we saw the wagons loaded with the goods approaching, we opened fire and killed 3 Germans. The others ran away.

We took rifles and other goods, this was a big deal for us. But this wasn't our main focus. We were more interested in blowing up trains on the tracks.

I was fortunate to take part in 10 missions. They took place in different regions, the most important was the one that went from Podbrodz to New–Sventzian. Also another successful mission was on the station Fahulianka, which was not far from New–Sventzian. The commander of our otriad chose five men to blow up the train full of Germans coming from Vilna. I was also in this group.

It was a cold winter night, we were making our way through the snow in the forest, it was in complete silence. It took us longer making our way through the snow and we lost our way. When we got to the station we had to exit the forest and found ourselves in a difficult situation. However we managed to hide behind a hill next to the station. We lay there quietly awaiting the sound of the train. We knew now everything depended on our swift and immediate action.

Slowly we heard the train approaching. Like the speed of light we ran to the railroad and we laid our explosives. With all our strength we ran back to the forest.

[Col. 1731]

From a distance we saw the explosion which sounded like a great thunder.

The soldiers in the train started shooting, fortunately the shooting from the train didn't reach us as we were already deep into the forest.

I was involved in another mission in small village Girdon, which was near Haudutishok and Sventzian and I proved myself again to the partisans. They shot at a partisan group...

We took away a lot of food products from the peasants, clothing as well as guns. We burnt the entire town to the ground and went back to the forest.

[Col. 1732]

In our Vilnius Otriad we remained until liberation. When the Red Army freed our region we left the forest and started to make our way back to Sventzian.

In our group was: Chaim and Berke Yocai, Itzke Farus, Yitzhak Rudnitski, Yosef Flexser, Peretz Grodel, Shaul Michalson, Rebecca Levine, Faivka Chait, Froimke Miadzolski, Moishe Shutan and I (Heshsl Bushkanetz). With great heartache, missing were: Isike Gertman, Shimke Levine, Yoske Rutnidski, Dudke Yocai, and Israelka Wolfson. They all perished at the hands of the Nazi murderers. Other partisans also returned, they were: Shimon Bushkanetz, Yudel Ambros, Ber Swirski, Moishe Itke Rudnitski, Rochel Feige Kromnik and Raska Chait.

We all had the same opinion: We did all that we were able! We shall take revenge for all of our spilled blood!

My Survival as a Partisan

Ber Swirski, z'l

Translated by Anita Frishman Gabbay

Together with the Sventzianer Jews I was brought to Poligon. Thanks to Chaim the tanner, who was a "useful Jew", I was freed. He had the right to take his family with him so I became part of his family. In the same manner, my brother Meir was let go. We didn't want to remain in the ghetto, so the next morning my brother and I left for Lyntup, then Svir and onto Glubokie. There we were fortunate to get two revolvers and some hand grenades and decided not to remain in the Glubokie Ghetto.

As we heard, that in the village of Niever, near Myadel, the center of partisan activities were in that area, so we left in that direction.

[Col. 1732]

At night we arrived in a village and pointed our guns at a peasant to harness his horse and bring us to Niever. He had no choice, so he brought us and we disembarked nearby and went by foot the short distance. On the way we encountered a partisan agent who told us to wait until evening. We were told by him that Jews from the forest arrived at night, at this villiage Niave, to replenish their supplies and to take these things back to the forest. They will surely lead us to the partisan group!

[Col. 1733]

And this is exactly what happened: we waited till dark, the Jews arrived to buy their food products and then we joined them to go back to the forests with them.

A few days later, a commander Of the Miadvadova Brigade arrived, to recruit young people for the partisan brigade. I decided to join them. The Miadvadova was part of the larger Sventzianer Russian Army.

He was sent specially, parachuted into the White–Russian forests, to find recruits for the partisan army.

His brigade had about 800 people. They were mostly white–Russians who escaped from their German units and joined, there were also a few hundred Jews in this unit. Many attacks against the Germans were carried out. The first one that I took part in was the attack on Dukshitz.

[Col. 1734]

We encircled Dukshitz on all sides, when we went in and with the help of some Christians, we were shown who the helpers of the Germans were. Our intention was to burn their homes and we did it successfully. Our brigade became famous because of so many successful attacks. One such attack was against regular German military. For two years we fought in this Dukshitzer region. Later we were sent to the Ashmiener region.

Here we fought many horrible battles against the German occupiers. Just before the Red Army arrived, we occupied the village of Ostrovietch. We stayed here until the Soviets arrived and then handed over this village.

Our brigade after liberation by the Soviets was held in high esteem and people wrote many accounts about us.

The Soviet Regime gave me an excellent review and gave me a medal, “Soviet Cross”, for my service and devotion.

[Col. 1733]

Jewish Heroes in the Partisan Unit "Mastityel"

Recorded by Michel Potasnik, from Abraham Yokelman and Abraham Bina Gordon

Translated by Anita Frishman Gabbay

Abraham Yokelman

In August 1942, Abraham Yokelman together with a group of 10 Jewish friends left the Glukokie Ghetto. They went to the forests nearby Myadel, where they met up with the Partisan Otriad "Mastityel" which means "Nekama"(Revenge). There were dozens of Otriads(divisions) and together there were about 1500 people in the forests. The number of Jewish Otriads were comprised of about 300 people, who came from the entire region.

[Col. 1734]

They came from Dolhinov, Danilevitch, Postov, Kurenitz, Kobylnik and other towns. The mission of these Otriads, that stretched from Minsk to Postov, was each unit to undertake their own campaign (attacks) against the German enemy, to cause as many casualties and disruptions to the Germans as possible so that they had limited access to the shtetls and destroy all German garrisons in the area.

The main focus of the Jewish Partisans was to rescue their fellow Jews, that were still alive in the ghettos. That was the first offensive was against the German military garrison in Myadel, which was organized by the Jewish Otriad called “Diada Vosiv”. This took place November 4, 1942, when the last 85 Jews were still locked up in the Myadel ghetto and their first mission was to free them. About 2 months earlier, about 100 Jews escaped from the ghetto to the forests and enlisted to fight with the partisans. Their main goal: free the imprisoned 85 Jews. The garrison was destroyed, the Jews were freed and the ranks of the Otriads were enlarged.

[Col. 1735]

In the same month of November 1942, Abraham Bina Gordon arrived in our Otriad. He brought with him guns, and mainly, he had strong personality and the will to fight, which became an inspiration to the others. After the liquidation of the Postov Ghetto in December 1942, the people from Haydutishok came to our Otriad to fight with us: Gershon Berenstein, the brothers Leib and Velvel Katcherginski, Tanchum Gordon, Israel Rudnitski and Sholem Shapiro.

In the same month, we went to destroy a division of German gendarmes on the way to Kazistshe, near Postov. The group of 5 Partisans included Abraham Yocelman and Abraham Bina Gordon. It was such a successful attack, and they managed to take away many guns and ammunition. Many gendarmes were killed.

In the winter of 1943, the Otriad moved their headquarters closer to Minsk. In March, we attacked the market in the Flaznianer region, where there was an automobile transport full of German soldiers that were being sent to the front and we carried out an attack with great precision and success.

Abraham Bina Gordon

The military transport was almost destroyed.

In the spring, the Otriad returned to the district of Old–Vileika, with another plan to attack the garrison at Luban, 7 kilometers from Vileika. The Geman military which was comprised of Ukrainian combatants suffered a terrible blow and and the Jewish fighters were a force to be reckoned with. The Jewish partisans were now well–known and admired by the Jews in the region. The Jewish partisans surrounded the ghetto, which housed a liquor factory, and emptied their entire stock. Also, 100 cows and horses and many food products: a great victory and especially important, the bounty, which was a dire necessity for the hidden Jews in the forest. Abraham Gordon took part in dozens of such attacks, and thanks to his excellent skills and leadership. He took credit for blowing up the large bridge and the Lubiner Germans no longer had contact to Vileika.

[Col. 1736]

July 21, 1943, Abraham Bina Gordon, was part of a group that struck another ammunition and German military unit, between Podbrodz and Galadnia. After blowing up another railroad station, they encountered another German unit on horseback. They were chased and eventually they made their way to the town of Baltzik, between Lintup and Konstantinova. There they hid from the Germans who were pursuing them and hid in a farmhouse to rest, thinking the Germans lost sight of them. Tired, they sadly fell asleep, but the Germans followed their footprints and found them in their hideout. The Germans started shooting and the Jewish partisans jumped out of bed, quickly dressed, and reorganized themselves. They killed 6 Germans, but 3 of them(Jews) were wounded and they quickly returned to the forest.

In the same month(July), the Jewish Otriad blew up the railroad line Moledechno–Polotsk. In August 1943, a group including Abraham Gordon blew up the railroad near Krivitch, that brought heating fuel to the front.

September 1943, the Germans planned to destroy the corridor from east to west that the Partisans were using. They laid down explosives all along the way, but the Jewish Otriad still managed to attack them. The Germans were defeated, the whole time they were shooting blindly. The skilled Partisans shot 50 Germans, and took 50 as hostages.

Another attack on the Germans by Jewish partisans in Ludvinova, on the border of the Kurenitz railroad terminal and the intersection of Krulevetzchnina and Moledechno took place, where a large German detachment on a train was destroyed. Gordon's group also blew up the Sonoker(Sanok) bridge and murdered the entire Germans detachment.

April 24, 1944, the same group blew up another German patrol that was bringing wood from Galadinia to Lintup.

May 7, 1944, the same group blew up a patrol between Podbrodz and New–Sventzian. Going through the town of Dvorzani, between Podbrodz and Kobylnik Abraham Gordon and his group encountered a group of White–Russian police and a bitter struggle enfolded. 4 police were killed, 6 were wounded.

[Col. 1737]

January 1944, the same group planned an attack on the German garrison at Varlov, between Dokshitz and Lepl. The plan succeeded, the Germans suffered great losses, many were dead and many wounded.

[Col. 1738]

In February 1944, the Germans began their massive blockade against the Jewish Partisans. Many lengthy battles followed and bitter fighting between them, many casualties occurred on both sides. Abraham Yocelman who took part in all these attacks excelled in his devotion to the cause. The struggle was face to face combat, everyone fighting for his life. Shalom Shapiro, the much loved Haydishoker, fell in one of these horrible battles, which was carried out by the German garrison from Komai.

Summer 1944, the Russian army entered the Sventzian region, freed the region and requisitioned the partisans to join the Russian military.

[Col. 1737]

Rise Up and Fight

Leah Svirski–Holtzman

Translated by Janie Respitz

Jewish people, rise up and fight!
Too long have we been oppressed;
We won't be slaves, our rights we will claim,
And we will never, never forget.

Too long we've been slaves, dejected, depressed,
We must tear apart the chains that bind us,
Like heroes so bold, our blood has been spilled,
Revenge we must take–one for the other.

The enemy has gained much profit from our work,
Yet he is never satisfied,
Don't keep still about this–but get going, quick!
Who says that our good cheer has run dry?

Everyone says that we Jews are cowards,

Let's show them that this isn't right!
Now marching we'll go, to battle the foe,
So that our tomorrow will be bright.

Now is no time to dance or to sing,
Nor is it now the time to laugh;
You who are young, rise up! jump and run!
This will surely make things better fast.

Fearless and brave, we march, forward on,
In the ghetto, there is no more to do,
In battle we will fight, and vanquish their might,
Let the blood of our enemy flow!

But should the foe's strength prove greater than our own,
And nothing will help, all is futile,
Then think what you must: that our cause has been lost
Let us still die like heroes in the battle!

Written when the partisan group left the Kovno Ghetto for the Rudnitzker Forests, 50 Kilometers from Vilna.

[Col. 1739]

Only the Two of Us Remained

Leah Yosef Flexser

Translated by Anita Frishman Gabbay

November 1943: I found myself in the "Vilnius Otriad" of the Lithuanian Partisan Brigade. The commander, Kazimir, called our commissar to his headquarter to give the order to blow up the German military unit at New Sventzian and disrupt the communication system at Sventzian. He chose 6 men, myself, Faivel Chait, Moriak Siniak, Miska Galobov, Rozes.

We quickly made preparations for our departure. We packed our backpacks with bread, and especially explosives, we inspected carefully the bullets and dynamite and when everything was in order, we departed for this dangerous mission. Shortly after, we began dragging ourselves through the muddy woods, leaving behind us our "zemliankes"(holes in the ground covered with grass and twigs used as shelter), our fellow partisans and the forests: all our familiar surroundings. We were heading toward the "mouth" of our enemy, some 70 kilometers away. A road full of enemies and many hardships.

—"What do you think?"–I ask Faivka, is the commander Fumfetitch actually joining us in this attack?" This was the first time he joined another division.

No one ever questioned the commissar before. We never saw him partake in any of the major attacks. Would he find an excuse not to join us?

We arrived sooner than expected at the town of Vileti, near the Baranover woods, and at the very last minute our commander made an excuse that he had to remain in the village. We were put under the command of Rozos and ordered to proceed further.

[Col. 1740]

The commander wished us luck and a safe return. Then he vanished between the small houses of the village. Rozos was an energetic lad, bold and nimble, but his weakness was he liked to drink. When such a major offensive was to take place, we had to hope for the best. Meanwhile we went further. By the evening we crossed through 10 kilometers of the Baronover woods, which were between Haydutishok and Postov. We didn't stop to rest, we went single file passing all the shtetls along the way, we had to make sure not to be seen by anyone.

When daylight approached, we sought out a hideout for the day, there were no forests in sight. We trembled from the cold. We were dreaming to find a place even for a few minutes to warm our cold bodies. We soon approached a small house and knocked on the door. "Oy, children, oy, beloved ones, a peasant greeted us, you are surely tired and cold. But this is a tiny shtetl and the neighbour! Do you understand me? We decided to continue on, on the edge of a small wooded area we found a hut. The owner received us warmly, and even made us tea and gave us something to eat: we drank and ate and warmed our tired and frozen bodies.

[Col. 1741]

The old woman brought us straw and made us a place to sleep. We placed a watchman by the door and fell down into the hay, like we were dead, into a deep sleep.

Lunchtime the owner woke us up and invited us to lunch with him.

—"Lunch is ready and there is also a little brandy!–

In the evening some Lithuanian guests arrived at the owner's house. Seeing us and Rozos, we talked with them and things got friendly. He (Rozos) took out his gun and wanted to show them how it was made. He wanted to show off and shot in the air several times. The woman and child got frightened and stated to cry. This started to make everyone uncomfortable. It was dark out, so we decided not to linger here any longer. We started our trek again. The roads were difficult, it was hard to cut through the fresh snow. Saniak had torn boots and couldn't continue. Rozos decided to get some boots in town. One stupidity followed another!

We approached a house which was set apart from the others, lit up with high steps, tall windows and a tin roof. As it appeared, we came across the richest peasant of that town, "the American" as he was called. Before we were able to explain the reason we arrived here, he knew very well the Partisans needs , several litres of "samorgon" were already set for us on the table, as well as food. Moriak's eyes began to sparkle as he looked around, and Rozos couldn't believe his good fortune. Rozos didn't wait for an invitation, and before long was sitting at the table with his group. Just Faivka understood the need to be suspicious and worry for our lives.

—They want to kill us! these neighbours, Faivka said angrily, and went outside to keep watch. We remained seated and ate and drank with great appetite.

From the "samorgan" our heads became heavy, our bodies relaxed. We all knew that Rozos asked the peasant woman for hay and a place to sleep. I and Faivka, with clear heads, knew we had enemies!

[Col. 1742]

Taking orders from the commander, who was not thinking straight and responsible for the whole group, did not sit well with us.

In the morning our watchman woke us up alarmed: Get up, the Germans are in town! Quickly we got up and snuck out of town to the forests. This was a forest that was not good protection: thin and sparsely forested so the light penetrated easily. We ran through quickly, reached another peasants house, and again asked for shelter till it got dark outside.

He told us a search team of Germans from the Haydutishok garrison were in the area and searching for "Bandits"as they called us. The Germans were told no one was here and therefore left the village.

We calmed down a little, and we had to make a plan to leave as soon as possible without anyone seeing us. But it was already too late, the Germans appeared out of nowhere: running to the forest was impossible, the Germans were going to attack us here, in this house! We took out our grenades and decided to rescue ourselves. The Germans encircled the house and opened fire on us. The bullets made holes in the house, and the house started burning. The roof was also burning. The shooting escalated and the burning planks were falling on us. We ran out of time to think, our end was near! The 5 of us were lying on the floor next to the door. Rozos screamed, "jump!" As I was next to him, it fell on me to initiate the first attempt! I had no choice, with a rifle and a grenade in my hand, crouching, I jumped through the door, and a hail of bullets came towards me. I suddenly felt a bullet hit my foot, on all fours I managed to drag myself through the snow to the pit 50 meters away. As long as the Germans were focused on me, my friends managed to escape from the burning house, and soon joined me in this small pit. What will become of us? What shall we do? Our lives were in great danger!

[Col. 1743]

The Germans, letting down their guard upon seeing such a small group, started shouting "Hoorah, hoorah!", slowly approaching our pit. Upon Rozos' orders, we took out and threw our grenades and started shooting. Several were killed, the others got scared. This small "miracle" gave us renewed hope to rescue ourselves and time was of the essence. Minute by minute, we were still at great risk, our bullets were running low. We had a few guns, but the Germans had machine guns. We needed to prove a point!

We noticed that the Germans left a small part of the forest unprotected and we decided to make a run for that part through the field. Rozos got up. He was the first. Quietly we got up and I got another bullet in my foot. The pain got worse and the blood was flowing in my boot.

Meanwhile I saw Moriak, also wounded. I received a third bullet. This time on the right side. I was overcome with weakness and I could hardly move. I was in deep despair and thought I would not survive and begged Moriak, who was behind me, to shoot me so that I would not be captured alive.

[Col. 1744]

A few minutes later, Rozos received a head wound. Moriak yelled to me to continue. I gathered my last strength and crawled on one hand and foot. Our luck continued to worsen. Bullets were flying, but missing their target. Under the hail of bullets we crept further until we reached the small river Loschiska, we jumped in, holding our rifles over our necks, where we remained until nightfall. We knew this village and the river very well, as we had often visited this region. Nightime arrived and we found a shed nearby and quietly made our way. I could barely stand. Moriak was a sight, bleeding, making me feel not as bad. We thought we heard sounds, we lay still. 10 minutes seemed to us like an eternity. We thought the beasts had left.

Finally it became silent! We had survived! We had no where to go, no where to hide. To gather our strength took great effort, but we managed to arrive at a small hut, near the Baranover forests and begged, once again, for shelter. We were hungry, weak, our wounds were not bandaged, but we had survived! What about the others? Where were they, dead or alive?

In the morning, like a ghost from the cemetery, Faivka Chait showed up and we learned about the fate of the others. He told us, when he saw Rozos dead, us wounded, they remained in the pit and vowed to fight till their last drop of blood(end). He suffered endlessly, his machine gun jammed, he saw a little water in the pit and crawled on his knees It was deep enough to immerse himself and hide, just his head was above the water and covered with small twigs, he waited for the right time, with a grenade in his hand. The Germans were attacking Miska and Siniak, and from his hideout he saw them killed; it suddenly became quiet and the Germans thought everyone was killed. With a wounded hand, swollen, Faivka lay still in the water till evening, and with all his strength left his spot when there still a little light. At night he left for the Baronover forests. On the way, passing the village to find a scout to lead him, he was told that a bloody battle took place only four hours earlier in which the Germans surrounded and killed 6 partisans.

[Col. 1745]

After many days of wandering, we arrived at our Otriad base and we found out, that the commissar, Fumfetitch was put on trial: how he tricked us to stay behind and why he wasn't on the mission with us! The outcome was that only he alone, should have led the mission and to lead our group to battle.

[Col. 1746]

Three more times he went with us to Sventzian with 15 kilograms of explosives, the fourth time, he went out and blew up the train station.

He was demoted from a commissar to a regular partisan.

Also, interesting, was the fate of Moriak. Two months after we were saved, we learned that he was put on trial in a village, found guilty and was shot to death.

This is how only 2 from our group survived, myself and Faivka Chait. This is the story, that I decided to name: Only two of us survived.

[Col. 1745]

Moshe Shutan–The Partisan's Delegate to the Vilna Youth

by Rivka Kovarski-Gordon

Translated by Anita Frishman Gabbay

In 1943, short of deciding what to do when the Vilna ghetto was to be liquidated, the F.P.O. (Partisan Organization in Vilna Ghetto) had a decision to make: to fight the Germans in the ghetto or leave for the forests and to fight the Germans alongside the other partisans.

[Col. 1746]

Two reasons for not starting the fight in the ghetto: their were few guns, and most of the Jews were against the F.P.O. They thought that life in the ghetto would remain quiet if the partisans didn't interfere. If the F.P.O. would start to fight, they would have both the Jews and the Germans against them. Therefore they decided to go to the forests. September 1943, I decided to join a group with 30 others to go in the direction of the Narach Lake. We arrived in the evening in Subota by the "cheap houses". Our scout, a Sventzianer, Moshe Shutan met us there. He came from Sventzian, sent by the Sventzian partisans to lead us. He was very brave, as he had to make the trip Narach-Vilna, and Vilna-Narach, where death lingered with every footstep. Four days we were on the road, as we travelled only at night, resting by day. Moshe Shutan knew the roads very well, so after 4 days, we arrived without incident.

Motel Kovarski - The Partisan Scout

[Col. 1747]

Motel Kovarski was born in New-Sventzian, his father was Noach and his mother was Chaia. Later the family moved to Vilna. In 1940 he got married in New Vileyka and when the German military arrived in 1941, the Jews of the region and New Vileika were scattered to a nearby hamlet of New Vileika, "Vilutshin".

The first day they took the strongest men to a field. They started to dig pits, and when they were ready, the German and Lithuanian bandits took the Jews to the pits and shot them.

[Col. 1748]

Motel was amongst the first group, he started to run. Others saw, and started running as well. The Lithuanians started chasing them and shot them. Motel knew this region very well, so he managed to escape and find a Christian friend and found refuge in his cellar. Lying in the dirt, he thought, “if they capture me”, he would rather drown himself than surrender. After spending the night, the peasant woman brought him into the house, washed him, fed him, dressed him in men's clothing and led him to the Vilna ghetto.

Knowing the ghetto well, he organized two groups with guns, and led them out. Cunningly, he led his group to work in New Vileika, and from there he led them to the “Narach” woods.

His wife and child were murdered in Vilutshin. He didn't want his father to remain alone, so he was sent to Estonia with the others. His father Noach was killed in a work camp in Estonia. When the Germans began their retreat, Motel together with other Jews from Vilna and surrounding shtetls were sent to Germany, and he then finds himself on the “ famous cemetery” of the Jewish people (concentration camps).

[Col. 1747]

The 16th Lithuanian Division

(Memories and Episodes)

Yitzkhak Viduchinsky

Translated by Janie Respitz

Twenty years now separate us from the Second World War. It is not surprise that even those who participated have forgotten many details. Dates, names of places and names of friends from the front escape me. Together with that, we have forgotten episodes, some important, serious, and useful to present a broad, clear historical work about the Lithuanian Division during the Second World War.

[Col. 1748]

It is also clear as day, that everyone that experienced the war and survived – experienced the entire journey with the Lithuanian Division – is a book unto itself. Our goal is to eternalize in this memorial book of the Sventzian region, the participation of Jewish youth in the ranks of the regular army, the heroic episodes, the heroic deaths of our friends from the towns on the battle fields, in the ranks of the Lithuanian Division against Hitler's Germany. They were perhaps the first and most heroic in the battles against Hitler's army.

[Col. 1749]

Sventzian. Saturday night, June 21st, 1941. On Vilna Street behind the Orthodox Church an outdoor dance party was underway, organized by the Soviet authorities for the youth. Young couple were twirling to the tunes of the Levin Brother's Orchestra on the round dance floor. It smelled of fresh pine resin, and some would trip on the planks of wood. Shloimeh Lifshitz, the active volunteer used all his free time to help organize choirs, drama clubs and orchestras for sheer entertainment. He was the head of the Regional club. When the dancers stopped to catch their breath, Shloimeh Lifshitz announced that the next day, June 21st, a concert will take place in the village Kochonovke, down by the lake about 5 kilometres from Sventzian. That night the dancing went on until 10:00. The sky was covered with thick black clouds. With the sudden change in weather all the dancers and observers went home.

No one even thought, the black clouds and angry wind were signs of a horrible destruction that was approaching over our heads. No one, on that evening thought about the arrival of a horrific national tragedy. The worst in the history of the Jewish people.

Sunday, at dawn when the sun was rising, the first victims from our region fell as a result of Hitler's bombing. The morning train from Vilna to New–Sventzian brought the first casualties of Hitler's bombs.

Not considering the unexpected and surprising news, the Sventzian authorities ordered to carry out the plans for the concert. The string orchestra had been rehearsing songs for the concert. At the exact same time Molotov, officially on the radio, announced the unexpected attack by Germany on the Soviet Union, we left for Kochonovke. Understandably, the concert did not take place. No one was in the mood for song and dance. The authorities were waiting for orders from higher up. From the first minute, all the connections were cut.

[Col. 1750]

By the afternoon the first refugees from Lithuania were marching through Sventzian toward Polotzk. Large Lithuanian truck and buses were filled with Jews, especially young people. They brought the first reports: The Germans were chasing at great speed, through Lithuania to Russia, destroying everything on their way.

From Sventzian to New–Sventzian, from Ignalina to Daugelishok, from Podbrodz and Kaltinian, Tzeikin and Kimelishok, from all the towns and villages where there were Jews, they made groups of sisters and brothers, relatives and friends, and sent them east. Parents were telling their children to run, some children dragged their parents along. It was a horrible, crazy mishmash. People ran forward, some turned back. In rovers, wagons but mainly on foot, people ran, really ran. Vidz was burning, Disne was heavily bombed. They ran forward, out of breath towards Polotzk. Many of our friends stopped in Polotzk like "unwanted elements". Everyone received a bullet, now not from above, but from below, from the NKVD. We all turned around, and miraculously continued running to Vitebsk.

In Vitebsk, our town troops looked at themselves, at their nakedness. "Where to, and what next? The Germans are on their way."

Train cars filled with coal, with wood. Our guys sat on the roofs and they were scattered throughout cities deep inside Russia. Some in the Tatar Republic, some in the Ural region, but the majority went to Uzbekistan with the thought and calculation that for us who were naked, the warmer regions of Russia were better, perhaps we will not freeze. Within a few weeks, many of us were dispersed thousands of kilometres from home.

By the end of 1941, the beginning of 1942 the mobilization of the Lithuanian division began. Many refugees, including the writer of these lines went to the military command and asked to be sent to the front. Everyone wanted to participate with a weapon in his hand in the fight against the German murderer.

There were regions and places where the soldiers came to the local authorities and asked to volunteer in the Lithuanian division (Reuven Muller for example), those who did not have their geographical bearings, and until it became clear, worked in a labour camp. In Gorkov province, in a town called Balachna, the 16th Lithuanian division was formed. Thus began the gathering of Lithuanian citizens, refugees, the majority called up according to an official summons. There were many who came on their own free will, directly to the headquarters of the division.

[Col. 1751]

In quarantine in the registrar's headquarters friends who had been dispersed in the days of the bombing were reunited. With great joy they hugged, kissed and shared stories of their experiences.

At headquarters, Shmerl Maimon from New –Sventzian, a Lieutenant, sat on the distribution commission. Every day, new transports would arrive. A new division was formed of three infantry regiments, an artillery regiment, anti – tank division, military engineers and other support units. The people obtained military knowledge with great enthusiasm. Military preparations came at a fast tempo. They often went out for tactical training. Out in the field we realized 80% of the soldiers were Jews from Vilna and other Lithuanian cities. There was also a large percentage of Jews among the officers. There were some small divisions where 99% were Jews and the commands in exercises, theoretical and practical, were given in Yiddish.

That summer was very hot. Military preparations were hot and intensive. Who would have believed, there in Balachna – Gorkev province, after a day of difficult military training, Lithuanian military units wearing Red Army uniforms would march and sing Zionist songs. This is how it was. It was a proud message to the world that we were present and ready to fight with courage.

In August 1942 the division received orders to be prepared to march toward battle. Our marching route was: Balachna, Gorky, Moscow, Sierpuchova and Tula.

The Germans had just been chased out of Tula. The houses were still smoking. There were barricades and installations on the streets of Tula against tanks. Here we saw, for the first time destroyed cities and villages wiped off the earth. We stood in the region of Tula, in the historic town of Yasnaya Polanya, where Leo Tolstoy is buried. Everything was burned and smashed.

This was the exact time the Germans were preparing their great offensive against Moscow. The 16th Lithuanian division was complete and ready for battle.

In December 1942 the division Joined the 3rd army – Bransk front. At this time the fighting began in Stalingrad. Then we received orders to go out to the first line. In the village of Sukmanova they handed out winter equipment and off we went.

[Col. 1752]

It was a difficult winter, freezing cold and lots of snow. We could not see the roads. From the 14th – 19th of February, for four nights, we walked 70 km a night towards the front. These were incredibly difficult marches. Passing burnt villages, dying German soldiers, burning tanks. The city Ruski –Brod had been wiped out.

Lagging behind was the commissary unit together with the most important things you need in battle: nourishment and ammunition. The decided place to begin our fight against the Germans was the Alexeiyev region. (old Economichne, Ivanovka, Protasova). One day before the battle, when some members of the unit were hiding in an open field, the Germans greeted us with a bombardment from 20 airplanes. There were some wounded and killed.

The Germans were strategically well placed on a hill which they covered in water so it would freeze, become icy and hard to reach. This was a strategically important point. We found ourselves lacking food and bullets. When our division was ordered to begin our attack on the enemy, they were at a great advantage with their strategic position and ammunition. During this bitter struggle our units displayed bravery. For 6 days we stormed the enemy's position. On the 28th we received an order to reinforce and take a defensive position.

In the battles we suffered serious losses. Fighting heroically, those who fell were Yehuda Troytze from New– Sventzian, Shaleh Bank from Ignalina, Yikhasriel Itzikson, and Mulka Shapiro. Leybke Kovarsky, Avremke Vilkomirsky, Ziske Shapiro, Khayim Avintelsky, Dovid Gurvitch and Shimon Gurvitch were seriously injured.

In the months that we stood on the defensive line, the battles continued. Day and night we warded off German attacks. There would be 4–6 attacks per day. Besides this we would carry out intelligence operations. We “studied” the German units, how many there were and their locations. We brought back prisoners' “tongues”. *[Col. 1753]*

Shimon Gurvitch **Dovid Gurvitch** **Khaim Svintelsky**

During the above–mentioned time, the 16th division belonged to the front led by General Rokosovsky of the 48th army of General Romaneneko. This was one of the most important and terrible time. The Germans brought forth their very best, the newest mechanized equipment, and the best airplanes. The Lithuanian division remained in Panskoye, Nikitovka and the Alchovka region.

When the difficult battles began in the air and on the ground, it was like one big fire. This was part of the large German offensive on Moscow. Here is where they received their first serious blow.

Until July 23rd, 1943, the Lithuanian division held strong, and even advanced 120 km. They succeeded in freeing 60 inhabited areas, received many trophies, obtaining 12 large warehouses of weapons and chemical equipment, fuel and more. On their way to the village of "Litva" the Lithuanian division was sent to the reserves.

Many Jewish boys were injured in these battles. Others fell heroically. Quite a few were from our area. Their names will be mentioned in a separate list.

2018 fighters were rewarded for their heroic deeds with orders and medals. The majority were Jewish boys and girls.

The 12th of August 1943. The division was on a break in Tula: in the forests around Tchtokino and Yasna Polina. Units were completed with men and technical equipment.

We were visited by a Lithuanian dance and song ensemble. How happy was I when I recognized Taybele Kuritski among the dancers and singers. With her lovely voice, she filled the hearts of the soldiers with joy and courage. Taybele was also happy to be with us, the familiar surviving "compatriots". We sat with Taybeleh on the railroad tracks (the ensemble lives on the train), cooked kasha in a military pot and remembered the not so long ago past. We remembered those who were killed in our division. We talked about the vague news we were hearing from our one time homes.

[Col. 1754]

From October 6 – 23 the division fought every day.

On the 28th of November we were on the Nevel highway in Vitebsk. There were difficult battles with the German motorized detachments. All the detachments of the division joined the battles and the Hitlerites were chased further west. On the way to Gorodok (White Russia), they were surrounded by a large German force. This ended another well planned encirclement by German forces on the White Russian front.

Around July 20th, 1944, the division arrived in the Sventzian region: Tveretch, Ignalina, and surrounding towns and villages with very familiar roads, forests, fields and lakes.

It was dawn when our unit walked past Ignalina. The sun was just rising and with sleepy rays, touched all of us. Even in the most difficult and worst minutes of battle against the Germans, our hearts did not pound so hard and we did not feel as nervous as we did now, on the sandy, quiet road to Ignalina at daybreak.

I walked behind the wagon pulled by two German horses. It seemed they were heading toward Dukstas, deeper into Lithuania. Here was the slaughterhouse of Ignalina. The town was now behind us.

[Col. 1755]

I ran to my commander. He was far from poetic sentiments. The years on the front hardened us physically and emotionally. We would often think: How could we ever drink tea from a glass again? How could we complete a sentence without cursing at least four times?

I really don't know, how in that moment I found these words to say to my commander: " This sandy town , which you see – surrounded by lakes, is where I spent my earliest years, wrote my first poem and fell in love for the first time...allow me, Comrade commander, to spend a few minutes listening to the dead silence of the town of Ignalina".

I received a half hour and two companions. At first I rejected the requirement of having companions. I felt a moment of weakness. My heart was beating loudly.

The main thing, Kolya and Nikolai – two young friends from Ivanova in the Lithuanian division – accompanied me. We quickly walked through the yellow sand of Ignalina. When we came to the wooden cottage that was once the Yiddish school, I just stood there. The doors and windows were boarded up. I soon noticed, the cottage, from bottom to top was wrapped in black cloth with black crepe. I was evidentially hearing voices. My ears were ringing with voices of children, with whom for six years, within these four walls, played and studied with me. I heard laughter and crying, a horrible cry and sighing...

I removed my rifle from my shoulder, shot in the air and stood at attention. Without saying a word, Kolya and Nikolai did the same. Apparently, the expression on my face told them everything.

I caught a glimpse of Yisroel – Noyakh's lake, its still glimmer. From where did the white swan come? Nervously, the swan began to move around in the middle of the lake, as if he lost something, as if he was searching for something, as if he was lost. Until this day I can't explain where the swan came from – a symbol from tranquil beauty and gentle innocence?

[Col. 1756]

We quickly moved on. We walked through the marketplace. I saw our old house, our nest. We stood in silence. My heart that had hardened like steal and stone began to soften. Thoughts were racing through my head. I was remembering Friday nights and Saturday nights. The days of Pesach, celebrating Simchat Torah in the Hasidic shul and Yom Kippur at the other shul; frosty nights on the balconies of the wealthier homes. Stormy discussions between "Yiddishists" and "Hebraists". It was if a fast film was playing before me and my head was spinning. I felt like I was about to fall. Beards clean shaven and with long beards. Weddings, circumcisions, Bar – Mitzvahs. Poverty and joy accompanied by town jokes.

Years of life ran by in seconds. The town was dead. There was not a Jew in sight.

An unfamiliar Christian passed by and looked at us with fear through his glassy eyes. Who knows, maybe he is also guilty of this dead silence that now rules?!

"What do you know, dear friends, comrades, Kolya and Nikolai about the vibrant life that once cooked in this small town of Ignalina?"

We don't move on, we don't run. Just one more look at the glass porch. This is where the first songs were composed together with our first loves .Time passes and I feel my heart is going to explode.

The silence in Ignalina was broken by the three shots from our guns with which we honoured the dead. Honour to my nearest and dearest!

We arrived in the region of the city Shavl, practically without any conflicts. The destruction we found on our way depressed us. The will to fight became stronger in all of us, to take revenge on the murderers of our people. Our commander Lisenko was killed near Shval. He was buried with the Oder "Hero of the Soviet Union". He said to us: "You are on your turf comrades, keep it and take revenge!"

Binyomin Zelikovsky excelled as a hero in all the battles of our division. It is not for nothing his uniform was decorated with Orders and medals. But it was fated, as we battled across the Dubiseh River, an enemy's bullet entered his heart. His grave is not far from the bridge, over the Dubishe River on the highway Shavl – Kielmi. Chasing the Germans from Shavl, where a bitter battle took place due to the strategic railroad to Riga, we saved a few Jewish families. Tired and hungry, they appeared as if they came out of a grave. These Jewish families made use of the little time we remained in Shavl, awaiting further orders, and helped us with whatever they could. Dovid Ravitch from Maligan brought laundry for the rescued families, Mitzieh Ushpal gave up his bread, and Reuven Muller brought whatever he could find as did others. Everyone ran to the division and tried to help.

[Col. 1757]

Binyomin Zelikovsky

The next step for our division was to rescue Zhemaytiye and Klaypedeh. The Hitlerites used their largest tanks, the "Ferdinands" and the "Tigers", large detachments of aviation.

With tremendous bravery, all the German attacks were defeated. We went forward, capturing entire divisions with German prisoners.

In October the battles began over Klaypedeh and the highway between Tilzit and Klaypedeh. The famous tank division named for "Herman Goering" and the Tilzit military school were there. Other motorized military divisions were there at the same time as the Lithuanian division.

On October 31st, the division received the Order of the Red Flag – for bravery in the battles at that time at Klaypedeh – Tilzit.

Hirsh Ushpal – Hero of the Soviet Union

At this point many soldiers and officers received high rewards, Orders and medals. The highest honours, the Order of the Gold Star and Hero of the Soviet Union was given to one of the fighters in our division, Hirshke Upshal from Daugelishok in our province. Our division was now named the "Klaypedeh Division".

[Col. 1758]

Two more Jewish soldiers who received the "Hero of the Soviet Union" title should be mentioned: Shuros and Vilensky.

From our entire division there were six who received the highest Order and title the "Golden Star" and "Hero of the Soviet Union". It is worth pointing out that out of the six there were: one Ukrainian, one Russian, one Lithuanian and three Jews.

Hirshke Ushpal ran away from Daugelishok to a Tatar village in Kazian, with a brief stop in Vitebsk. Most of those who escaped our town went to Vitebsk. They attempted to find work digging peat, or carrying sacks of food from warehouses. The quick attack by the Germans made it impossible to stay there for long.

One in the Tatar village, Hirshke threw away his torn shoes, and put on their national clothes: but the shoes were made from hemp and tied with cloth bands always fell off his feet.

During the fighting in White Russia, being always among the first, Hirshke Ushpal was badly wounded. It took him a long time to recover. When he returned to his division he threw himself with even more bravery and devotion into the attacks on the front.

At night, as soon as we buried our canon and lay down to rest an alarm suddenly sounded: the tank unit of the "The Goering Division" attacked our canon! This unequal fight in the middle of the night was struck down. When it got a little quieter, everyone wondered how we survived? At dawn, we suddenly heard the German language and saw Germans standing nearby in disguised coats. It did not take long before we turned our canon on their group and shattered them. A panic ensued among the Germans. Taking advantage of this we turned our fire on the German tanks. Some of us were wounded and Hirshl Ushpal took on the responsibility of servicing the canon. Three remained beside the canon. They threw grenades and shot. They shot at the large tank detachment and the troops who attacked us. Before the battle ended we received a command to aim our fire at another sector. The command was carried out and bullets began to hit the heavy tanks. They were destroyed.

[Col. 1759]

Hirshl Ushpal remained with few bullets and no contact. Everything was torn apart. In the middle of the night the German spies snuck over to our canon. He didn't stop to think and with a bullet from the canon ended this attack. In the morning he saw the results from this shot – dead Germans!

For three days he burned German tanks with his canon and filled the area with dead Germans. On the fourth day help arrived.

His reward for this battle – "Hero of the Soviet Union".

No the journey continues to Latvia.

The Lithuanian division captured positions near Kurland. This is a swampy, muddy region, without roads or highways. We had to build roads from wood and planks in order for a truck to drive through. These were difficult months of fighting with a bitter enemy who did not want to surrender, even after capitulation.

Siomkeh Shultz (the husband of Giteleh Brumberg form Ignalina) was sixteen and a half years old when they stole his last bag of rags from under his head. This was in Tashkent, the end of 1941. Tired and hungry he lay down on the asphalt near the train station with his bag under his head, an old jacket by his side.

When the sun rose and he awoke, his bag, jacket and documents were gone. The Uzbekistan militia investigated. With his broken Russian he explained he was a refugee from Lithuania. It took time until they figured out what was Lithuania and where was Lithuania. The miracle was, they knew a Lithuanian agent who was looking for citizens for the Lithuanian division. Shultz was more than happy to meet the agent and join the Lithuanian division.

He was assigned to the anti–tank division. During the fighting it became evident that not only was he a good fighter, he could also lead. In 1944, on the Shalv front, Shultz was sent to intensive officer's course. As an officer, Siomkeh arrived in Kurland.

It was a cold night when Shultz met up with his front comrades. The anti–tank canon stood on the front line fully ready. His comrades received him with great joy. He had not received any orders. It was pouring rain and impossible to get to headquarters. He spent the night in the trenches. He did not sleep. Spies from both sides make use of such rainy nights. Siomkeh went out to look around and check up on the soldier guarding the canon. The guard had fallen asleep. He pointed out to him how on such nights, anything could happen and he must be aware of every rustle.

[Col. 1760]

Shultz remained with the guard and suddenly heard a rustle, not a usual sound. He noticed of group of twenty Germans a few metres from their canon. He quickly began to fire at them with everything they had. Upon hearing the shots, his comrades ran out of the trenches. The German did not succeed. Shultz received another Order for this effort.

Leybl Teitz was the commander of an anti–tank canon. This was in Kurland. The Germans opened fire on his position because his cannon was always on target, always shooting, never even lifting their heads. Under such fire, the servicemen ran away. Leybl Teitz was left alone.

Allow me to quote from a high placed official about his bravery. In the fourth session of the highest Soviet council in the Lithuanian Republic, General Major Matziuskos said:

“Comrade Deputies, I would like to tell you a few facts about bravery which our soldiers and commanders displayed fighting in our Lithuanian division. While in Kurland, Comrade Teitz displayed great bravery as the commander of a canon. His group, with the canon, grenades and automatic weapons, defeated 4 attacks by the enemy.

Leyb Teitz

[Col. 1761]

After that, the Germans brought in their "Tiger" tanks. Comrade Teitz bravely fought them as well. Even after he was seriously wounded, he continued fighting and succeeded in destroying two "Tigers".

Dying from his wounds, Teitz said: "I carried out my last order".

He continued to talk about these heroic acts at the Central Organ of the Lithuanian Republic.

In the newspaper "Soviet Lithuania", August 4th, 1945 the following appeared:

"Four horrible attacks by the Germans were warded off by the Commander Comrade Teitz and his unit. Seriously wounded, Teitz did not leave the battlefield. Displaying great bravery he destroyed two more German tanks".

Sergeant Leyb Teitz from Sventzian never saw his last order fulfilled. The high Order "Fatherland War First Rank" was sent to his family in his memory.

Victory Day was celebrated in the mud of Kurland. Early morning, May 9st, 1945, they began to receive phone messages from infantry units saying that German were flying white flags on their rifles.

Shooting started from both sides with coloured rockets. The Germans capitulated! Victory and the end of the war!

[Col. 1762]

Zalman Gurdos

Here are the surviving members of the Lithuanian division from our town: Khaim Svintelsky, Zalman Gurdos, Shimon Gurvitch, Hirsh Ushpal. Some came out not wounded at all. The rest were wounded a few times while others had pieces of iron and shrapnel in their hands and feet.

They all received honours: medals, Orders, words of gratitude from general headquarters. Each one fought with his unit as a hero. Each one brought honour to his people and revenge for those killed. Today, I believe the majority of surviving Jewish fighters live in Israel.

A List of the Heroes Who Died in the 16th Lithuanian Division:

[Col. 1761]

From Sventzian: Ginsburg Abba, Leyb Kovarsky, Yisroel Tzikinsky, Hirsh Vilkomirsky, Leyb Teitz, Olke Gurvitch, Shloimeh Katzizne, Dovid Gurvitch.

From New-Sventzian: Yehuda Troytzeh, Shloimen Tzinman, Zalman Broydeh, Yitzkhak Shmulevitch, Zalman Rudnitsky, Gershon Katz, Dovid Guterman, Mikhael Yaffe, Hirsh Ring, Shneur Guterman, Kasriel Itzikson, Yitzkhak Hellershteyn, Pesakh Liber.

[Col. 1762]

From Ignalina: Gedalyahu Brodsky, Shaleh Bank, Mula Shapiro, Gershon Segal, Leyb itzikson, Khaim Yosef Fraydenzon.

From Daugelishok: Hirsh Berman, Yisroel Abelevitch, Meir Kesl, Grisha Bas.

From Lingmian: Binyomin Zelikson.

From Maligan: Yitzkhak Glezer.

Eliyah Katzizne

Olke Gurvitch

Abba Ginzburg

Yisroel Abelevitch

[Col. 1763]

In the Battlefield

by Mule and Leib Troytze

Translated by Anita Frishman Gabbay

Yehuda Troytze

After a year after the evacuation, after much suffering, we arrived in Uzbekistan and Kokand. We worked here in a "kolkoz"(cooperative farm) and until they mobilized us into the Lithuanian Division of the Army.

Amongst those were: Yehuda Troytze, Shlomo Tzinman, Moishe Tzinman, Mickah Yofe, Pesach Liber, Zelman Broida, Yacov Abelevitch, Moishe and Dovid Ring, Asher Katz and the writers of this article (Mule and Leib Troytze).

At the outbreak of WW11, in 1941, Yehuda together with his brother Mule and many other young Sventzianers ran away, like: Avrahmke Gubieski, Ruvke and Yankele Abelevitch, Zamke Broida, Asherke Katz, Moishe and Dodke Ring, Shlomke and Moiske Tzinman, Michke Yafe. Some went by transport, others went by foot to Old Sventzian, where they got horses and wagons, and continued their flight. We fled through all the villages until we arrived at the Russian border. Day and night, we didn't eat and we didn't drink, we were under the threat of the bombardments and shootings and frightened of the Polish bandits. At the border we stole horses, and had to run for our lives until Polotsk, where we got on a train, modern and convenient, until we arrived in central Russia. From here we were sent to a village to work in the forests. This was a very difficult labour.

Our Yehuda was one of those that kept the group together, who helped in a time of need, intervened in quarrels. Everyone had a special place in their hearts for him because of his intelligent demeanour and the way he truly sympathized with our dire conditions. He undertook the most difficult work.

[Col. 1764]

We didn't remain here very long, the Germans were quickly approaching and we had to evacuate again, further away.

We ran as far as Tashkent and there they sent us to a village in Kokand (city in Uzbekistan) to another “kolkoz”. One evening, Moishe Gaviser arrived and proposed for us to cross the border, and through Iran, make our way to Eretz Israel. Several ideas arose, the majority were frightened and remained in the “kolkoz”. The older people from the kolkoz were taken into the army, amongst them our dear brother Yehuda. Here he got separated from his brother Mule and was sent with the Lithuanian division to the front to fight against those wild –Hitlerite murderers, the Germans. On the front he excelled and was assigned to a tank unit, in which he became a sergeant.

In a bloody battle he got wounded, they wanted to send him for an operation. He didn't want to leave his comrades in such a difficult battle, so he demanded they operate on him on site; they operated and he returned to the battle on the front lines.

In one of the bitter battles, being the first in the tank division, he encountered a mine and was blown up together with the tank.

In that moment we lost our dear and beloved brother who will remain forever in our hearts.

Honor to his memory!

The 16th Lithuanian division was eighty percent Jewish soldiers.

[Col. 1765]

After a short study course, which took place in Balabne, the division was sent to the Tuler Oblast, around Yosne Polania, the village where Lev Tolstoy was born.

After that the 5th royal guard division tore through the front, the 16th division was sent to her help out; this was a very difficult march. Winter was a very cold one, all the roads were covered with snow, the artillery and the food transports were halted, due to poor access. Finally the food arrived, each soldier got a thin watery soup with a little flour with and 2 pieces of sugar (candies) a day. In this manner we had to survive and continue our painful march.

Also, special airplanes dropped some food packages, otherwise, we would have starved.

Finally we arrived at the Illavsker front, which was around the village of Alexzeievke, where we came across the German army for the first time.

The Germans were trapped near Alexzeievke and we received our orders at to attack the bloody enemy at once. We were starving and exhausted from the long march, from the cold and the snow.

My brother Yehuda was then in the 156th flank of the peoples' army.

[Col. 1766]

He was the commander of a division which had tanks. Because of the harsh winter conditions, because of the snow, which covered all the routes, the tanks weren't able to advance. The Germans noticed this and immediately ordered an attack against our division.

Yehuda didn't give up and advanced with all his strength. His losses were great. This fight was not on an equal one, the Germans outnumbered us and were better equipped. Slowly all our food products and ammunition were depleted. We really didn't have anything to fight with.

On this front, next to Alexzeievke, many of the young Jewish men from Sventzian died, and also, the commander, my dear brother, Yehuda Troyze.

Here fell our dear, holy youth from Sventzian, New Sventzian, Haydutishok, Ignalina and other surrounding shtetls.

Their outstanding deeds were later decorated by the Red Army who praised their will and endurance; how valiantly they fought against those murderous Germans.

All of us, who had the honor to fight alongside them, we will never forget their memory!

[Col. 1765]

In Battle with the Bloody Enemy

Moshe Zinman

Translated by Anita Frishman Gabbay

Sunday, June 22, 1941 the war between Germany and Soviet– Russia broke out.

The train from Vilna arrived late because it was bombarded on route. Among those that arrived were many wounded. There was a great panic in our shtetl.

Monday, early on the 23rd, German airplanes flew over our shtetl and dropped bombs on the small train bridge, that went from Kaltinian to Paneyvesz. The link with Vilna was broken.

[Col. 1766]

We were scared for additional bombardments so many of the shtetl inhabitants scattered to farms on the outskirts, that belonged to Jews; where Chaim Faive Shutan, Hirsh Rutsteyn, Shloime Gubeski and others lived.

Early Tuesday morning some friends came to me to run away with them together with the retreating Russian soldiers.

[Col. 1767]

In the morning Moishke Zak came to tell us the Soviet deserters along with the police left the shtetl. I didn't want to listen, took my rover and left for Sventzian.

Shloime Zinman

On the road I met some friends, who changed their minds and turned back from Sventzian. Amongst them Mole Gavenda, Binyamin Rabinovitch, and others. In Sventzian I encountered those from New Sventzian. Together with my brother Shloimeh, Yehuda and Mule– Nachum Troitze, Abraham Gubeski, Gershon Shep, Ruben and Yacov Abelavitch, Zamke Broide, Zalman Gordos, Moishe and Dovid, Berl Ring, Asher Katz, and Michke Yafe we continued. The officers from the N.K.V.D. helped us get horses and off we went to Polatzker territory.

We rode through Maligan, Vidz, Luski, Yiod, Sharkovszizne. At Disna, the previous border, we crossed over to the Russian side, we went to a *kolkoz* and spent the night.

In this collective farm the border–police surrounded us and wanted to arrest us. We told them we were escaping from the enemy and we want to help the Soviet Regime in their fight against Hitler and Germany. They released us and we left for Polatsk. We took the train there to Smolensk.

We lost (was killed) Ruvke Abelevitch in Smolensk. From Smolensk we took the train to Bielov Tulsker *Oblast*, and from there they sent us to a forest where they exported wood. Some of us worked in the forest and the others worked transporting the wood on horses.

After five weeks we had to begin our trek again as the Germans were advancing.

We finally arrived in Tashkent after a long journey by train. Seeing the deluge of refugees lying on the streets near the station, we decided to continue our journey. We arrived at Samarakind where they sent us to a collective farm. After some time they mobilized us into the Army in its Lithuanian division.

[Col. 1768]

In the Lithuanian Division

My brother Shloimeh, myself, Yudkeh Troitze, Michka Yofe, arrived in the Lithuanian Division at Balachna, near Gorki where we met Chaimke Rabinovitch, Afroike, Berl Guterman, Yitzhak Hellerstein, Kasriel Itzikson. This was the 156th flank, later we found in the 249th flank: Itzke Shloimevitch, Zamke Rudntzki, (from Kimelishak) Israel Portnoy, my nephew, in the 187th flank, Zale Guterman's two sons, Sneur and Dovid, Hirshke Ring, Berel's son Gershke Shep, Yacov Abelavitch and Zamke Broide. Zamke Broide got sick with typhus and died.

In the artillery flank of the Lithuanian Division we found the three Karpas brothers, sons of Shalom: Ezriel, Faive and Hirshe Itzke.

The 16th Lithuanian Division was comprised ninety percent of Jews from the Lithuanian region. Yiddish was the language that bound us. The lead command was comprised of Russian, Jewish and Lithuanian men.

After some military training, they sent us to the front in 1942, we went immediately to battle against the enemy.

My brother Shloime, myself and Yudke Troitze remained together the whole time. I was wounded on the Feb 26, 1943 in both legs. My brother Shloime took me on his back and brought me to the field hospital. Here I got my first medical attention and then I was sent to Gorki.

Through different means , while I was in the hospital, I searched for news of my brother. In the end I learned he and Yudke Troitze fell in battle.

Those from New–Sventzian that fell were : Shloime Zinman, Yudke Troitze, Yitzhak Hellertein, Yitzke Shloimevitch, Zamke Rudnitzki, Michke Yofe, Gershon Shep, Shneur Guterman, Kasriel Itzikson, Hirsh Ring.

Dudke Guterman was dropped by parachute into the forests of Kazian to fight with the partisans , where he later fell in battle. For my fighting at the front I received a medal from the Soviet Regime, loosing both feet.

This is how our Jews of New–Sventzian died with honor against the bloody enemy!

[Col. 1769]

Battles of Resistance and Struggle

Shimon Bushkanyetz

Translated by Janie Respitz

The city was already filled with police posts and the roads were guarded to ensure Jews would not run from the military action that was to begin in the morning. This is why we left town at 2:00 in the morning. Through meadows and swamps we avoided the dangerous guarded points. We came to the fields of Tzerklishok and headed towards the town of Lintup. It was a dark autumn night, Shabbat Tshuvah (the Shabbat between Rosh Hashanah and Yom Kippur), September 27th, 1941.

Following me were my mother, Khaya and Golda. Carefully, like an experienced woodsman, we came out of the forest at Lintup in order to hear and see the movement around Smolarnia at the highway not far from town.

All was quiet in Lintup, forced labour, yellow badges, so be it... but we walked toward Svir. The walk which we could have done in a day, took us a week, due to caution.

I remember, Wednesday night, Yom Kippur, at the time of Kol Nidre, a mother and son, the guard of the Olshev forest, brought us hot potatoes and buttermilk. The pious woman Leah–Soreh asked: “My dear children, should we fast or not?...Where is God in heaven?” Under the glow of the half–moon we had the traditional meal, as it was essential for our health and wellbeing. We were like stone, without prayer, accompanied by two Christian shadows, which left us late at night.

The last outpost to inform us on what is happening in town, if it is worthwhile to visit or even stay for a short while, was the watermill in Stratze, which still belonged to a Jew named Abrasha, Moishe Gordon's brother–in–law. The Gordon family still remains here, not knowing what to do next.

[Col. 1770]

The winter of 1941–42 we were in Svir. The Jewish community took in refugees as best they could from Sventzian and surrounding towns. Shloime Rabinovitch was the teacher for the refugees.

By the end of winter we were notified that Svir, Mikhalishok and Kimelishok would fall under the Lithuanian administration's governing council. Now instead of the Polish – White Russian liberal police and administration, it would be Lithuanian.

Thanks to our connection to the Sventzian Ghetto and Golda's family, which she had visited 3 times that winter, we decided to move to Sventzian.

March 1943

The Ghetto is about to be liquidated. The Vilna police, led by Fried, were in charge of this operation.

The selection: Vilna – Kovno in these last days was in full swing.

The first transports left through New – Sventzian April 1st and 2nd. The transports to Kovno left April 3rd and 4th.

On the last day a delegation came from Vilna: Genz, Dessler, Drazin, Auerbuch. The last one knew Khaya personally. When he saw her he became overwhelmed from the surprise encounter and said: "You can't go...this path leads to death."

She runs to the train and hears it start to go. She changes direction and runs to the bridge, hoping to find me on the passing train. Luckily, I was standing at the door and saw her waving her hands. Without stopping to think, I jumped off the train and ran to her.

She shared with me what she had been told and I ran straight to save my mother who was on a wagon transport to New – Sventzian. I found her near the city and took her out. Through side streets we come back to Khaya and I take my mother directly to a Christian friend Balinsky, with the hope he will find us a place outside of town. We both say goodbye to them and leave the city.

[Col. 1771]

We spent a week with the Christian Baltushevitch, near the Blakish forest (owned by: Skrutkovsky). We heard shooting at the nearby cemetery. The Christian told us they gathered all the Jews wandering about from Sventzian and shot them. Among them were:

Efraim Shpiz's wife, the daughter of an Orthodox priest from Pravoslav who converted; Khana Gurvitch Nelkin, Yeshayahu Liberman and his wife Eva, Svirsky Moishe and Rokhl (Zaydl) and others which the Christians could not identitfy. Our Christian, a father of 10 children was afraid and informed us he was not prepared to put his whole family at risk and asked us to leave. We then prevailed upon his wife who knew the Christians hiding our mother, to go to them and inquire about her fate. She returned and told us the same horrors they were experiencing were also happening at Balinsky's in the city. They saw and heard how they were searching for Jews, and the punishments given to those hiding Jews. Being honest people, they dressed our mother in peasant clothes and brought her to their family in a village called Vielitchky near Lintup where she sat in a warehouse. Antony Butzyuta, who I knew from before promised his relative from the city he would protect her as much as possible.

We left toward Pushtche, the larger forests where the partisans spent days and nights wandering to and from their bases.

The Christians in the area were my acquaintances from before. Pietrovksy form Vintzentova, Pietrukha from Tzirklishky, Kaziemyakin Ivan Ivanovitch, Shilkis, Gudelshek, Visaky, Rinkian, Kaptarun, Vigodke, and all the villages were familiar to me. I knew who to hide from and who would protect me.

I spent the day in the forest or in an acquaintance's barn. He provided for me without worrying about payment or possible punishment. They all knew if they would betray a Jew, revenge would be taken by the Jews in the forest, armed and organized in the Russia detachments.

A few months passed before we decided to visit mother. At night, in a farmhouse among the marshes of Kaptarun – Velitshky. The Christian asks us what will be, and how long will this last? With the best intentions, he cannot keep her for long. We promised him we would soon join the partisans in the forest and take our mother with us.

[Col. 1772]

At that place we learned Golda came from Vilna and is in Sventzian being hidden by Christians. I immediately sent her a letter asking her to come to us. There is place in the forest. We will wander together. The forest is big and in danger, every tree is a protector.

My forest address was precise, the Lintup highway – near Vigodke is where we met and recounted our last few months. Golda recounted:

She arrived in the Ghetto on April 4th with the Vilna transport. On the same day they heard shooting from Ponar and the same evening they began to receive the sad news from those who managed to escape. Instead of going to Kovno, they brought everyone to the mass graves in Ponar. Under a hail of gunfire the following managed to be saved: Furman and his wife Lyuba (Mikhlson), Vermeses two children (6–8 years old), Zhenya

Zaretsky (Gurvitch) and her little brother, Sholem Matzkin, Zaydl, Lishansky Dov and other Jews from Vidz who were in the Sventzian ghetto whose names are not known.

The Jews from Sventzian in the Vilna ghetto saw the fate that awaited them in Vilna ghetto.

After a few days partisans from Sventzian appeared in the ghetto, which only two weeks earlier had been with us in the ghetto. With cheerful greetings from the forest they told us of a strong, well organized force, among them, many Jews.

Mayshke Shutan, Ishike Gertman, Itzke, Misha –Yitzkhak, Yisrolke Volfson, Mate – Heshke accompanied the groups and led them away. My brother Motke was one of the active collaborators with those from Vidz: Salitan, Yekhiltzik, Bielak.

The Vilna Jewish police greatly hindered this operation. Because Motke disappeared from the ghetto they arrested my father and mother, tormenting and investigating them. The jail on Lidske Street was full with those arrested. They arrested me as well. What saved me was a false identity card with another name. When I was released, the forest representatives promised to take me with them, but when they told me Shimke, my sister Khaya and my mother were in the region of the town, I decided to go find them on my own.

[Col. 1773]

I left the ghetto with Motl Kovarsky's group, going to work in New – Vilayke. From there I took a train to Sventzian.

When I got off the train in New – Sventzian I met Christian acquaintances who told me things were quiet. No one payed attention to who was coming and no one was searching for Jews, since there were none anyway.

For a few months, Khaya, Golda and I wandered in the region. We often visited our mother, taking her from one place to another.

Mother was well looked after. She was fed and lived in a warm house, sometimes too warm, having to stay, most of the time near the large oven in the farmer's house. Me, Khaya and Golda – varied: a barn in a field, a bath in the river or a pond, forest or the district around the familiar villages.

Ivan Ivanovitch Kaziemyakin, Fiedula from Tzirklishek, Pietrovsky from Vintentztova Shilkes, Manula and their colleagues surrounded the forest in the partisan zone. They were the liaisons who instructed the groups where to spend their days and nights according to instruction from headquarters.

When the Gendarmes visited a nearby farm where we were hiding, the Christians helped us go to the forest. Another time, when the army came to the village Rinkian, searching for youth to send to German to work, we ran with them to the forest and hid together.

February 1944

Ivan Ivanovitch said to me: "You know, Simke, today's the day. Last night, a group slept at my place led by Black Vaska. With him was Vaska Zubov, who knows you from Sventzian. They will linger near Minelishok, at his parents'. He promised me, if I go with them, they will also take your family to the forest. They will work for a detachment there, where they will be safer than here."

I listened to my Christian friend and in the darkness of night left with Khaya and met up with the entire group at the Zubars. I explained my situation and promised to come with my weapons the next morning, after I take my sister to my mother and Golda who were waiting for her.

I arrived on time and left with the group toward the train tracks of Vilna – Dvinsk, near Ignalina Kretanky.

Laden with explosives, we all walked past Sventzian to Rashkutan and stopped near Krasnobarky in Bielanisky at my Christian friend's Mikhael Karla whose house stood beside Kretan Lake. We remained there for a few days. Twice from there we crossed the frozen lake, carrying out successful missions.

[Col. 1774]

The great satisfaction from our first operation is indescribable. Hearing the moans and cries of the Germans we breathed easier feeling the sweet taste of revenge for the innocent spilled blood of our loved ones.

Together with my group we carefully retreated from a hail of bullets from the train guard and lit a flare in order to cause a diversion. "Simke – you are not a Jew – said Vaska the former adjutant of the Markov Brigade – rarely does one of you go first to a giant job and feels, like me, like a proficient saboteur".

Our group completed our mission. We had one casualty. Sadly, when a second group of partisans came on the same dark road that night, with the same motives, they thought they were shooting at the enemy and mistakenly shot Kirila, the diversion agent of our group.

On our way back, we found horse drawn sleigh in the village and took the corpse of the partisan to the forest to bury him with honour in the cemetery of the "Tchepayev" division.

On a side road, at Pietrovsky's partisan shelter, at the edge of Tzirklish forest, my family waited: My mother, Golda and Khaya. This time I decided to take them to the forest to the base of the division.

Six horses harnessed to a sleigh travelled over the frozen ice of "Narotch"(Narach) to the village of Hatovitch, and from there to the division.

The commander Sidiakin (his nickname: Yasnaya Maria), a true Siberian Russian, a high ranking officer in the Soviet Army, happily received our harnessed transport. He bowed his head when he saw Kiril was dead.

[Col. 1775]

I settled my family in the point where most of the people from Sventzian in the division gathered from the forests near Myadel and Narotch(Narach). A nearby Komsomol base which had been attacked and burned by the Germans now came back to life with the influx of people from Sventzian: Jews from Kurenitz, Myadel as well as Jews from Vilna, not organized in the armed divisions, they received more protection thanks to the newly arrived partisan family which was armed and known by the name "Tchepayev". Among others in the group were: Berl Gurvitch, Gitl, Dvoyreh, Yekhilkeh Taytz, Khanan Opeskin and Yehuda Shapiro from Podbrodz, Henia Shaytl and Khatzkl Kaltun from Sventzian.

*

Diversion groups don't sit in the forest, they are called to holy work.

Vaske and his group are on their way, laden with dynamite, to the train tracks: Vilna – Dvinsk in the region of Sventzian. The train tracks are always heavily guarded by German patrols every 100 metres. Due to the fierce cold, the Germans walk back and forth heavily dressed. The partisans are dressed less heavily. When they see Germans, they turn around and jump in the darkness over the train tracks and lay the dynamite and detonators.

The operation was successful, we run from the explosion, the locomotive and all the wagons on the side, downhill – head down and feet up...from the sudden tear all around was lit up. The strong explosion awoke the guards who began shooting in all directions, not know where the diversion came from. Watch points were lit in order to find the "criminals". Flares were shot, mine throwers and other weapons to not cease being fired. Now we have to control our own fear. Our retreat must be sure; we have to be able to quickly hide behind a tree, or a small hill. On the other hand, we are very happy seeing from far the help we have provided for the front by disturbing the transport to and from the front.

Our group annihilated tens of echelons, and thousands of troops and ammunition. We heard the cries of the wounded soldiers and their dying moans from faraway, lying under a tree or in the white snow, wearing a white jacket to camouflage – our spirits were lifted with the joys of revenge.

[Col. 1776]

*

After our plan was executed, our group went to the trustworthy farmers, rested after a week of difficult work, heated a bath and washed.

We gathered at my friend Mikhael Garla's from Bielanishok, near Lake Kretan, not far from Raskutan. Not far away lived the murderer Nimayke, on a farm near Krasnaborke. We visited him as we were passing and loaded his horse and wagon with Jewish baggage that were in big boxes.

In order to avoid Sventzian we went out to Stanislavove and destroyed tens of thousands of eggs from the gathering point for front needs. Many farmers were killed, and others learned the account was not settled, for their collaboration with the Nazis.

The 8th of March we were back in the forest. It was joyful at the base. Women's Day was being celebrated. The division called "Maxim Gorky", made up of 10–12 men, performed various folk tunes and played instruments; of course there were accordions.

This took place in an underground structure that was built especially for cultural work and other events. It is hard to believe, if you did not experience it, winter in the forest, in occupied territory, we carried on courageously with our lives and did not fall in despair, and awaited a better tomorrow.

At headquarters there was a special group of writers and poets, cultural activists. Every day – a short update of the latest news from the front. In the forest we received radio news from Moscow. Announcements about our daily operations were printed and distributed among the partisans.

It is hard to believe; we built a hospital for the sick and wounded partisans, operated on and cared for by doctors. Specialists knew their place was in the fighting forest. A dentist, with the help of a peasant's spinning wheel, pulled teeth, cleaned and filled cavities with cement.

A produce – division – men and women, organized a brigade according to their professions, and carried out useful work for life in the forest. There were tailors, shoemakers, bakers, hairdressers and others who helped the partisans.

[Col. 1777]

The Commissar met us at the meeting point, acknowledged our preparedness and sent us with necessary supplies to the forest. One dark night, we occupied Hatdutciski Road on the corner of Bliakishk, and confiscated from all the Tatars' leather goods. This was used by the partisans to make shoes and coats. On a larger attack we tore out telephone connections, stole 8 horses, confiscated 15 shot pigs, clothing, shoes and boots and in peacefully brought everything to the forest, even though we were few in numbers. They were afraid of the robbing partisans; among them was "Simka" from Sventzian.

The cooperative in Old – Strunoytz was filled with various products prepared for the front. In the light of day, we loaded it on our wagon and brought it to the forest.

*

The Lithuanian village Daukshi, after Nieverishki (5 kilometres from Sventzian) often impeded our operations. The dogs would bark and their guards, in the darkness of night would shoot in all directions scaring the partisans in their search.

After a day of rest in Bielanishok near Kretan Lake, which we swam with ammunition to the train track, we spent a few days on the other side of Ziemiane after destroying 3 German echelons, and decided to rest in the village Daukshi...

In the evening, when it was still light, we approached the village, surrounded by guards so no one would leave, we entered the village magistrate and demanded all the weapons to be handed over to us within a half hour, if not, we burn down the entire village. They immediately gave us 8 guns and ammunition.

We took the weapons and went to the fields, avoiding the city Sventzian, toward the forest. After a night of walking in the region of Komai, we noticed suspicious movement which I almost payed for with my life.

In order to see what was happening, together with Peysakh Magid (a partisan from the Vilna region) who was participating in our march, I went to check if our whole group could pass through the village. Before we approached they began to fire a round of bullets from a machine gun. We threw ourselves on the ground to avoid the bullets and returned through the trenches on both sides of the road.

[Col. 1778]

Peysakh Magid managed to return to the group, but I lost the group. They thought I was wounded. It was too dangerous to come rescue me. They began their return to base without me. It was announced at headquarters that I was killed. Even if I was only wounded, the Germans would surely finish the job.

For two or three days the division whispered...that Simke was killed. The sad news also reached my family, except my mother.

Nevertheless I had double weapons, an extra gun from the Daukshi robbery, I ran for three days and arrived at the base, and met my family at the horrible moment when a partisan was preparing to tell my mother her son is no longer alive...

*

With lowered eyes and heartfelt prayers and blessings, my old mother, the smart Leah – Soreh said goodbye to the group of partisans which her only son had to leave the forest and begin a dangerous path. She would be afraid when the group would arrive late and miss the time for her "walk" to the railroad track.

Her fear was well founded: the entire way was filled with danger, the diversion work was dangerous. The enemy and death loomed at every step.

Ignoring this, we the diversionists drove the Germans crazy. They placed a guard every one hundred metres along the tracks and we planned accordingly.

In the last minutes before the echelons arrived, we placed explosives along the track and ran back as quickly as possible. The explosions and the flying train cars rang like music in our ears.

*

Arriving in the village Rinkian we met our acquaintance Gutvirt: Neautz Valdek, a friend from earlier times. He received me warmly and asked me to get down from my horse. He confided he had something to show me in his barn. I went with him and saw with my own eyes two friends from Sventzian: Mikhlson Yokhanan (Yokhke) and Taybe Luria.

[Col. 1779]

They told me about their wanderings, the places they hid. The Christian told them that I pass through often and promised them he would connect them with me at the first opportunity.

Seeing their situation, I told them they can return with me to the forest where there were many Jews from Sventzian , including their nephew Shaul Mikhlson who was serving with me in the same division. They agreed to go with me as they had been waiting for this opportunity. They were tired from wandering and hiding.

Ten days later, when we finished our plans, I went to the farmer Neautz to take the couple to the forest. Unfortunately I found upheaval. Vladek told me that Yokhke went out one night to get a Mauser he had left behind in the village Milvuke, and ran into partisans. When they shouted: Stop! He ran. They shot and killed him.

When Taybke heard from the farmer Yokhke had been found dead, she had no patience to wait for me. She joined a group of partisans passing through. According to him, she was with Pedul in Tzirklishok. I went immediately to find her in that group.

I actually found her. After much discussion I was able to take her way leaving her short gun as compensation.

Taybke came with us to the base in the forest and remained with my6 family until liberation. Today, she lives in Raanana Israel.

The Miadl German Garrison had its boundaries from one side of the huge Narotch Lake and the surrounding forests on all sides filled with partisans. They placed guards at many observation points to prevent an attack from the forest. The garrison was practically harmless, sat as if in a ghetto.

The Germans lived here better than at the front, swimming every day, doing nothing and waiting for better days when a more powerful force would arrive and clean out the forest.

[Col. 1780]

The partisans, to the contrary, were sure they would not disturb. But when a liaison officer announced a Postov garrison was coming to Miadzal to preapare a big blockade of the forest, the headquarters of the Voroshilov Brigade sent out the fighting Tchepayev division to carry out the sentence.

With Sidiakin at the head of the entire division they decided on the village Pasienke as the strategic point to await the German expedition.

Military trucks arrived, led by a tank...

The partisans met them with unexpected fire. The tanks responded with all types of weapons.

We had favourable positions but the commander protected hi heroes and wanted to give an order to retreat.

Krupski fell, Leonid shouted he was running out of bullets from the last disc of the machine gun, Kasarevsky's machine gun was already standing. Tzibuksky is wounded, the situation is becoming serious.

Sidiakin is not shot. He walks from one place to another and suddenly gives a command: “Follow me, “Yasnaya Maria” Abramov! Bikov! Koyre! Up on the hill...Tolstofyatov, Dukshtulsky – lie down in the bushes...Seres! Timoshenko! Near me”...

Sokolov and Leonov, attack the enemy from both sides!

Within minutes, all was carried out under the fire of the enemy's bullets.

“Fire! Yasanya – Maria!”

Sere's machine gun (F.P.O Vilna) and Kuria continued to fire and did not allow the tanks to budge. The self–confidant German and Lithuanian military fell like sheaves, like wild policemen.

The tanks, the Panzers were still shooting, unwilling to give up.

The battle burned on. The partisans crawled through the fire to take weapons from the dead and wounded Germans, and began immediately to work with their found weapons: automatics and machine guns which were badly needed in the forest.

Onward! Commanded Kudriavtsev and stormed Sidiakin.

“For victory!” – shouted the fighters – Forward, forward!

Twenty dead Germans remained on the battlefield, five were taken prisoner, rifles, automatics, and two banged up trucks. One truck was driven through the forest to the“Tchepayev” base by the partisan from Sventzian, Shaul Mikhlson.

[Col. 1781]

Those who interrogated the prisoners were: Yudl Shapiro (Podbrodz) and Yisroel Wolfson (Sventzian).On the first of May 1944 all the partisans celebrated. According to plan, we all left the forest and went to Kobilnik, on the other side of the lake.

The Germans had already left the town because a strong group from the forest burned the town and forced them to retreat. The town was the regular passage to the forest which belonged to the partisans.

We occupied the two main roads from Komay to Postov and from Svir to Kobilnik, considering perhaps the enemy could come and disrupt our celebration. The entire division was at the marketplace under the loud speakers which played what was happening at the same time in red Square at the Kremlin.

A fiery speech from the Duma was presented by the commissar of our division, calling for battel, encouraging the forest and ensuring victory.

The mood was lifted. We continued the celebration in the forest.

Our diversion group did not return to Kobilnik. Vaske had a new plan.

*

The Red Army was preparing a big offensive in Vitebsk, and commanded the partisans behind the lines of the enemy to cover the entire forest, from the north to the far south and prevent the return of the enemy's army. On June 22nd, 1941, Hitler began. On June 22nd, 1944, the Red Army returned the favour. On the night of June 21st all the divisions went out to all possible train tracks and bridges and destroyed them. Special units shot the German guards and captured their weapons. The diversionist (saboteurs) displayed their special talents in these explosions.

In those hot days, after the rail battle, occupied the Baranov forests near New – Sventzian and worked night after night on the Zhemanye the help of fishermen, who in the dark night would transport our loads and await a new operation.

[Col. 1782]

The Germans were afraid to enter the forest in New– Sventzian. They believed powerful forces were in the region, but in fact we were only 5 men: Black Vaska, Vaska Zubov, Kostia, Shienke and me (Simke).

On July 4th we met the first Soviet Army in the forest. Large groups and parts of the enemy's military remained stuck, without any contact. The partisans had to disarm the Germans and send them to military points where special commandos dealt with them. In this operation, Yisroel Wolfson, a partisan from Sventzian lost his life.

We “freed” the Germans from Myadel ghetto. They threw down their weapons. I remember how one tall officer who I interrogated following instructions from headquarters, kept repeating during our discussion: “I want to be with you.. serve you forever”. This Nazi dog wanted to be a Canaanite slave for a Jew.

Coming from the forest – At a fresh grave in Sventzian. Shimon, Khaya and Golda, Moishe Ginzburg and Zalman Motzkin. The granddaughter Leah in the middle.

[Col. 1783]

The Great Operation

Yitzchak Arad–Rudnitzki

Translated by Jerrold Landau

Indeed, everything has passed, everything has ended. The previous week, from the day when we found out about the Nazi attack on Russia until the arrival of the first German soldier in Sventzian, was a week filled with events and disappointments. The week passed. We are again in their hands. They have caught me again. I was in their hands more than two years ago in Warsaw. I escaped from them. I crossed borders and dangers. I thought that I had thereby freed myself from them. But no, they have caught me again. Enough, there is nowhere to escape, we must fight and battle with them. But how can we fight, with what will we fight, what are the chances of fighting, what will the future bring... Many questions to which we will not receive an answer – and from whom could we get an answer. We must find it ourselves.

*

I am returning to Sventzian, but to what Sventzian? Where are the Jews of the town? Where is the life, where are the children and old people, where are they all, where are the thousands of the Jews of the town...? I know the answer, everything is known to me. Two months passed from that morning when they informed the Jews of Sventzian that they were concentrating all the Jews of Sventzian and its region in Poligon. Time passed as a dream, a frightful and terrible dream. The escape to Glebokie, the perils on the journey, life in Glebokie, the terrible news of the annihilation in Poligon – news that we did not want to believe, and the return to Sventzian – to what was left of Sventzian. What remained? The "Shul Hoif" [Synagogue Yard] with several tens of wooden houses. A wire fence surrounded several houses. There was a gate with a Lithuanian guard. In all these were several hundred Jews, afflicted with despair and fear.

Where are they taking us? For what purpose? I stood next to the gate of the valley, together with Gershka Bak, for several minutes. Suddenly, a number of Germans burst into the ghetto... And here was me, Gershka, and three other young Jews walking, being taken, but to where? "Gershka," I whispered, "if we turn to the direction of the Jewish cemetery, we can begin to run and to escape. It is better that they shoot us while running than while standing next to a grave." No, we did not turn toward the cemetery. They brought us to "Ocharonka." There, before my eyes, I saw what I was looking for the entire time, weapons. Our job was to clean the pillaged weapons, load them on a vehicle, and transfer them to the train in Novo– Sventzian. They guarded us carefully. A German soldier did not take his eyes off us. It was sufficient for me for the German to turn aside for a brief moment and look outside, and the "Otorzanka" (a short gun without no butt and a sawed–off barrel) was in my pants. I put bullets into my boots in the same manner.

I felt that I had weapons. What would happen if they caught us at the end of work or when we returned to the ghetto? What would happen to me? No, it was clear, they would kill me immediately. But what would they do to the rest of the Jews? There was no time to think, we had to work, only that the time should pass. It was difficult to work, difficult to bend down, for the barrel of the Otorzanka pushed into the belly. It seemed to me that the German noticed the outline of the hidden weapon. Time flowed slowly, slowly. Work finished, and they would or would not catch us. But why would they search the Jews, for they would not dare to steal weapons. They would not think of this. We marched back to the ghetto accompanied by a German. We approached the gate. My tension increased. No, the German brought us inside, and the Lithuanian did not search. I have a weapon... The future appeared rosier to me. This was the first weapon in the Sventzian Ghetto.

[Col. 1784]

Gershka and Dovka were not there. Early in the morning, we heard several shots from the direction of the Jewish cemetery. After a few hours, the ghetto found out that they had taken both of them along with Sarale Lewin to be shot. They were the first victims of our group. The previous three days had passed over us and the ghetto like a nightmare. At that moment, Ruvka had the loaded gun with Gershka next to him, and stated in a trembling, angry voice, "Would it be that there was a German next to me..." The bullet came out and hit Gershka. The shot was heard outside the ghetto, on the Aryan side. The Judenrat informed the Germans of the incident (the information was that two lads went onto the roof of an abandoned house, found a gun there, and the bullet came forth when they lifted it up). The two were arrested. Within a few moments, the entire ghetto knew about the existence of a partisan organization in the ghetto. We knew about the inquisition methodologies of the Germans and the torture that was hard to endure. We suspected that Ruvka and Gershka might break down and inform them [the Germans] of everything. At that time, we were already a group of 15 people, and we all had weapons. The aim was to encompass all the Jewish youth of the ghetto, to arm them with weapons, and to be prepared for the spring, to go out to the forests and to begin the battle as partisans. We were also prepared to fight in the ghetto in the event of a sudden aktion by the Germans. With the news of the arrest of Gershka and Ruvka, and the news that spread through the ghetto of the existence of a fighting organization in the ghetto, it was clear to us that we could not continue in the ghetto. Each of us had to bring their weapons and set out to the forests that very night. Everyone appeared at the designated spot on time, but most of the people of the ghetto came along with us. They all said one thing, "You will go, and when they find out, we will all be killed." We knew that there was truth in those words. At that time, we thought that the Gestapo would extract the knowledge of our existence from Gershka and Ruvka through torture. Then, if they would find us, they would take other Jews in our place. The choice was before us, we for life and the ghetto for death, or we for death and hundreds of children, women, and ordinary innocent Jews for life. We decided to remain, place ourselves in danger, and not to endanger the others. The weapons were hidden, and each of us waited in our houses for the arrival of the Gestapo. Ruvka and Gershka did what we did not expect. Despite the harsh torture, despite the promises and enticements to keep them alive if they would tell the truth about the source of the weapons and who else in the ghetto has weapons, the Gestapo did not succeed in extracting anything from their mouths. Very few stood and did not break down with the torture of the Germans, but Ruvka and Gershka, 17–year–old youths, stood bravely. The hatred of the Germans and the faith that we would avenge the blood helped them in their stance. Even as they stood by their grave, next to the group of shooters, they did not break. Thus they fell as heroes...

[Col. 1785]

We marched in a line. In the forest to which we desired the entire time, of which we spoke for months underground, we were in it, breathing the clear air. The aroma of spring was in the air. There was still snow here and there, and lots of mud in the melting snow. We were outside, outside the fence of the ghetto, in the forest. The forest will now be our home, for how long? Who knows? Yes, until the Nazis are expelled from here, until we take our revenge. Several hours earlier, we stood in the ghetto. We gave a final kiss to our dear ones, a shake of a hand, Shalom, who knows when we will see each other again. Goodbye ghetto, goodbye my dear ones, we are marching to fight, to take revenge.

*

The pack was heavy on the back, 12 kilograms of T.N.T. explosive material. How precious was the load, a German train with soldiers and equipment would fly in the air? The weight was heavy, but who thought about this. The rattle of the approaching train could be heard from afar. No, for this one we would not have enough time to place the load. Another one will come. The five of us walked, with the commander of the squad in front, me behind him, and three more behind me. We were all armed with P.P.Sh. sub machine guns, pistols, and grenades, and we had a mine to damage the train.

This railway line was vital for the Germans. It supplied everything for the Leningrad front. The forest ended, and the line was about 100 meters in front of us. We chose a section of the forest that reached close to the tracks, especially since it would be easier to retreat.

We knew about two German bunkers next to the railway line. There was a distance of about 600 meters between them. We planned to plant the mine between them. There was a German foot patrol along the tracks, between the bunkers. We approached the tracks carefully. The squad commander and I were in the center with the load. One person was keeping guard on the right and one on the left. The fifth remained a bit rearward to secure the flank. I climbed the slope of the mound. The place was excellent; if the explosive material exploded, the train would be derailed.

Here are the railway tracks. I looked right and left. No patrol was visible. I placed my ears on the railway track. Noise was heard, apparently a train was approaching. We had to work fast, digging a small pit between the two railway tracks, placing the load of T.N.T. placing the mechanism, covering it with earth, and everything was as it was before. We heard the steps of the patrol approaching. Indeed, a train was approaching. Who would arrive first? We ran backward, in the direction of the forest. The train continued to approach. It seemed to me that there should have already been an explosion. Why did it not explode? Doubts began, perhaps we placed a defective mine, perhaps the mechanism did not work, perhaps... And then a light lit up the entire area, and a powerful explosion was heard. The train flew in the air, and rolled down the slope. Tens and perhaps hundreds of Germans were killed and wounded. Military equipment was destroyed. This was my first train (of 16 that I took down).

*

We marched in silence on the winding road in the forest. The forest was dark even though the sun had not set. The day before we had marched on the same path, the entire Partisan Otriad of about 100 people. Today, we were only five partisans: Pepka, the unit commander, me his deputy, and three others.

[Col. 1786]

The task was short and clear, to “liberate” Semyonov from prison in the hospital of Sventzian, and extract him from there, alive or dead.

Semyonov fell prisoner to the Germans when he was wounded. He was expert in the negotiations that took place at that time between the Lithuanian partisan commanders and the Lithuanian army forces in the German ranks. This was after the German defeat in Stalingrad, and the Lithuanian collaborators looked for ways to leave the Germans and join the victorious side. There was a suspicion that Semyonov was liable to disclose the details of the business under the pressure of Gestapo torture. The command given to the Vilnius Otriad was to extract the wounded Semyonov from German hands. Yesterday, there was a plan that the entire Otriad would attack and extract him. At the list minute, we found out about a strong Lithuanian force near the hospital, and it was clear that an attack with the force of the entire Otriad would not succeed in extracting him. The five of us volunteered to attempt to quietly penetrate the city and free Semyonov. We took advantage of the daylight hours to approach Sventzian through the forests and groves. It was the middle of the summer, and we had approximately four hours of darkness to extract Semyonov and retreat to the forest. We neared Sventzian about a half hour after dark. Penetrating the town was difficult. We had to pass between two positions, about 100 meters from each other. We heard the Lithuanian soldiers singing and chatting in the positions. The place, with every house and every path, was well known to me. Here was the hospital. Within a few seconds, we liquidated the sentry at the door of the hospital. We knew that Semyonov was on the second floor, but we did not know in which room. We also knew that another sentry, a Lithuanian guard, slept next to the door of the room. We broke into the stairwell, Pepka first, and me after him. We reached the second floor. I turned left, and Pepka turned right. Suddenly, an image in white, a nurse, moved before me. “Where is the wounded partisan?” I shouted to her. Rather than responding, she fell and fainted. I ran into the second room, encountered a doctor, and he responded to me, after being pushed hard with the barrel of a gun into his belly, that the partisan was on the other side of the hall. I turned there and saw Pepka leading a Lithuanian guard with his hands up, and two others were dragging Semyonov. I sneaked upward, and a Lithuanian guard was there, the existence of whom we did not know. Running upward, I lowered all my P.P.Sh. onto his head, and he fell, wallowing in his blood. I exited, and then heard the alarm in the nearby police camp. The retreat was slow, and we had to carry Semyonov by the hand. Each moment, we waited for a pursuer to capture us.

To our good fortune, the police reported that a large force had penetrated Sventzian to free Semyonov. At the moment that the alarm was sounded, they prepared for defense, and did not think about pursuing us. We were again in the forest at the break of dawn, where the people of the Otriad waited for us. Few believed that we would emerge alive from this action. That which the entire Otriad could not succeed in doing was carried out by five volunteer partisans.

[Col. 1787]

The Anger of the Martyrs and Heroes

Shlomo Kovarski

Translated by Anita Frishman Gabbay

I survived the gruesome internment of the Vilna ghetto, took part in the fighting in the forests of the Sventzian region and after many years of wandering after the war, through faraway cities and lands, I carried deep within me the heartache of the martyrs and heroes. My heart forever carries this heavy burden. Deep in my memory these horrors will remain with me and will never cease to haunt me.

The spirit of my people haunts me: they are still “swimming before my eyes”, the lost towns and hamlets of the Sventzian region.

It shall haunt us forever and all people as a reminder of our Jewish brethren!

The entire history of the Jewish people is a story of incomprehensible struggles, with strength and determination of enormous proportions, together with the struggle from within for different values. In the matter of a few hundred years in Eastern Europe a large Jewish center developed. Generations came and went, each with its own challenges and its struggles for survival. Each town created their own identity, with its own personalities who were involved with various institutions and community renewal. This uniqueness was produced with their own unique idealism.

This is how the Jews lived in their small shtetls of Eastern Europe, developing their culture and its institutions, leading colorful lives until the "catastrophe" befell them and wiped out years of civilization. This "catastrophe" wiped out 6 million Jewish lives all at once, most of the East European Jewry.

It was not a passive resistance against those Hitlerite murderers, many battles of resistance took place in the ghettos, in the work camp, and in the forests, with devotion and passion.

Small and large groups, organized Jews both for political or for personal reasons, obtained guns and ammunition and carried out these battles.

[Col. 1788]

There was no organized group in Poland, as we know, but many revolts took place. This awoke young Jews everywhere, they took part in these revolts. They didn't want to be led to their deaths, like "sheep to the slaughter". They wanted to fight with honor. Although their strength was weakened after such terrible living conditions and meager food rations, the Jewish people fought with all their strength to inflict as much damage on the Hitlerite animals as possible. They organized sabotage and divisive activities in these ghettos and work camps that diminished the German military potential.

Many of the young people went to the forests to join the partisans where they fought heroically with much success, inflicting many disruptions against the German war effort.

Many ambushes took the lives of our Sventzianer youth who were part of the first groups that went to the forests. They joined the fighting battalions and received much praise and many awards for their heroic battles. They fought the enemy and took revenge against our bitter enemy that spilled the blood of our brothers and sister, mothers and fathers, destroying our people. They risked their lives by going to the Vilna Ghetto, joining the partisan divisions, bringing fighters and many others from the Ghetto to the forest to the bases of the various battalions. Hundreds of Jewish fighters, daily, went to carry out these dangerous attacks to inflict as much damage and carry out their holy duty of revenge for all the spilled blood.

Do not forget! Do not forget! This was the last words of the partisan fighters. This last call until today, remains in our hearts:

Do not forgive these murderers who are still around in the world, the helpers, whose hands are washed in Jewish blood.

Do not forget to tell future generations about the righteous and almighty struggle of the Jews in the most horrific time in the history of the Jews.

[Col. 1789]

The Heroes Who Have Fallen [in Battle]

Translated by Jerrold Landau

Hirsch Charmatz

He was born in 1910 in the town of Lyntupy to his parents Yaakov and Malka. He worked in business. His family perished in the slaughter in Lyntupy, on December 19, 1942. He escaped from Lyntupy on the day of the slaughter and reached Sventzian. From there he escaped to the Narocz [Narach] forests with three survivors from his town. This was the area of the Markov partisan brigade. They joined a group of Lithuanian partisans, who took their guns and stripped them of their clothing and boots. They succeeded again to obtain several guns from farmers through various means.

They were accepted into a Jewish brigade that was composed of Sventzian and Lyntupy natives. The brigade leader assigned spying and scouting tasks to the Jewish group. To this end, some of the brigade went out under the command of Avraham Rein to the areas of Lyntupy and Sventzian. They entered the home of a farmer named Birt, who received them cordially, but secretly sent his daughter to inform the Germans in the town of Lyntupy. The Germans surrounded the house and set it on fire. The lads burst outside in a flurry of fire. Hirsch Charmatz was among the four partisans who fell in battle in a desperate act of defense. The others were Leib Gurwicz, Ishika Gertman, and Simka

Lewin. That night, their friends returned and buried them in a communal grave. After the war, they were transferred to the grave of the martyrs who were slaughtered in the town.

Yisrael Wolfson

He was born in 1926 in Sventzian, near Vilna, to his parents Avraham and Perl. He completed seven grades in the Tarbut School.

During the years of occupation, he visited the ghettos of Postov and Glubokie. He was active in obtaining weapons, and he was in contact with a group of youths in Sventzian who were preparing to escape to the partisans in the forests. He escaped to the forests in 1943 with a group of Sventzian youths, and was accepted into the Markov brigade of the Chapoyev [Tzapaiev] unit, which was stationed in the forests of Kazian [Kažinė].

He was sent by his command to the Vilna Ghetto. From there, he returned to his base with a group of Vilna youths.

Among other things, he participated in the attack on the stationary force of Komai, which ended in a decisive victory with the bombardment of several trains, etc.

He fell in battle a few days after the liberation (July 1944) in a combing operation against retreating Germans.

Leib Woliak

He was born in 1916 in the village of Stajetiškė in the area of Sventzian to parents working in agriculture. He was educated in the Tarbut School and was active in Hechalutz.

He lost his entire family in the slaughter that the Lithuanians perpetrated in Poligon during the first months after the German invasion.

He fled to the city of Kažinė. He took advantage of his work in chopping trees in the forests to search for traces of partisans. A group of Russian prisoners of war to which they joined along with three other youths of Kažinė removed their weapons and stripped them of their clothes. They only succeeded in escaping and returning to Kažinė in the cover of the darkness of night.

[Col. 1790]

After a few weeks, he fell into the hands of the guards who had accepted them as partisans. They brought him to the village of Paltro and ordered him to dig a pit for himself. He hit one of the guards over the head, pushed the second one aside, and sneaked away running wildly. The guards opened fire and wounded him. His friends found him in a pool of blood, transferred him to Kažinė and later to the Vidz Ghetto where he recovered from his wounds.

The third time he went out to the forests with a group of youths and organized a Jewish partisan brigade under his own command, numbering 50 fighters. When the Spartak unit arrived from the east in June 1942, the Jewish group under the command of Woliak was joined to that unit.

He has several successful ambushes and battles against groups of guards and small garrisons to his name. These provided more weapons for the hundreds of fighters who joined the brigade.

Commissar Ponamarov commended the wonderful command of Woliak to the unit after an ambush against an S.S. commander group and guards who attacked the partisan base. Thirty Germans were killed in the deathly fire of the ambush. Eleven were taken prisoner. The booty of weapons and arms was large and variegated.

The Jewish division under his command excelled in the attack of the brigade against the stationary guard of Kažinė. As natives of the town, they served as guides. They surprised 40 Latvians and took them prisoner.

During the time of the German siege on the forests of Kažinė (November 22, 1942), when the unit retreated eastward, Woliak remained with his brigade to protect the unarmed Jews. At the risk of their lives, they obtained supplies and secure places for the Jews during the winter season of 1942–1943. Thanks to him, most of those Jews survived until liberation.

When the Spartak unit returned in the spring of 1943, they granted the Jewish brigade freedom of action against the murderers and collaborators of the population. Thirty murderers whose hands were sullied with Jewish blood were killed in punitive actions, and their farms were set on fire.

His crowning action was the burning of the railway station in the village of Petrovitch and the killing of the local garrison. Other groups had failed at this objective.

Woliak and his group stumbled upon an ambush on their way to one of their actions. All 15 partisans fell after battling against the enemy that outnumbered them tenfold until their weapons were used up.

Ponamarov, the Commissar of the unit, eulogized him as follows, “the best, most faithful partisan, wo excelled as a friend, a partisan, and a commander has fallen.”

He was granted three emblems of excellence after he fell. His memory remains forever etched in the minds of hundreds of Jews who survived the war in the forests of Kažinė thanks to him.

[Col. 1791]

Gershka Bak

He was born in Sventzian in 1925 to Yitzchak and Rivka. His father was a glassmaker. He completed seven grades in the Tarbut School.

He worked in the Vita–Lager armaments warehouse during the time of the occupation, and took advantage of every opportunity to take weapons and ammunition for the underground youth of the ghetto.

He was injured in the ghetto from a bullet that escaped from a gun in the hands of his friend Reuvke Miadzolski while they were busy digging hiding places in the roof of a house for guns that had been stolen from the Germans. Both were turned into the Gestapo by the Judenrat.

The two of them endured cruel tortures for ten days and nights, and did not give over any information about the underground or the source of the gun.

He transmitted a message through a girl who worked in the police, saying, “I did not disclose anything. I did not turn in anyone.”

They were both shot in the cemetery of Sventzian on May 16, 1942.

David Guterman

Ephraim Guterman, Shlomo Jochelman, Peretz Czepelowicz, Leib Kanfer

He was born in Kaltanėnai near Nowo– Sventzian in 1917 to parents who worked in agriculture. He was a graduate of the public school, a sportsman, strong, and a member of the Polish Communist Party. He was imprisoned by the Polish authorities in 1934, and moved to work in Warsaw at illegal Communist publishing after he was freed.

He was in the Polish army at the outbreak of the war in 1939. He participated in battles against the Germans, displayed bravery on the front, and was injured badly. He transferred from the Polish front and reached Russia. He fought in the ranks of the Lithuanian brigade on the Ural–Kursk front. He went through a special course, and in December 1942 or early 1943 parachuted from Moscow – with a Lithuanian brigade – to the forests of Kažinė, where he organized a partisan movement on Lithuanian soil. He was one of the organizers of the Spartak unit, and was appointed as commander of a special division and a sabotage group in one of the brigades of the unit. He carried out numerous sabotage operations resulting in the killing of many Germans. He became known as a hero throughout the entire area, and was praised by all the partisans. He earned many emblems of excellence.

[Col. 1792]

During the German hunt in the forests of Kažinė, he participated in a desperate battle of 20 people against the superior force of the Germans. Since the group had no other way to retreat, he volunteered to cover those retreating with his machine gun.

His machine gun did not stop shooting until the group succeeded in escaping from the enemy. After the last of the fighters disappeared from the battlefield, he began to run, but he suddenly realized that he had no energy to advance. He realized that he had been wounded badly. He remained alone on the battlefield. His machine gun continued to rain fire on the enemy. He detonated all the grenades that he had with him. They exploded, and several Germans were killed. However, he was surrounded by the Germans at the same time. He did not have even one bullet with him that he could have used to end his life. Wounded badly, he fell into the hands of the enemy soldiers. They brought him to the nearby village, gouged out his eyes, and exhibited him to instill fear.

Death relieved him from inhuman torture.

Leib Gurwicz

He was born in Sventzian in 1914 to his parents Kopel and Chava, who earned their livelihood from commerce. His father was one of the 100 townsfolk who were taken by the Germans apparently for labor, but were really taken to be killed.

He escaped from Sventzian with his mother and wife Rivka Feigel, and were saved in Poligon. A daughter was born to him during that time. He gave her over to a Christian acquaintance.

He lived together wish his family in the Vilna Ghetto for some time. From there, they escaped to the Narocz forests. He joined a kernel of a group of Jewish partisans that was organized by Alexander Bogen [1] (the well–known artist, who lives in Israel), having been confirmed by the commander of the unit, Markov.

He participated in many actions, and fulfilled dangerous scouting and spying roles in Lithuania, along with others. They had to cross paths central roads, and railway tracks that were guarded well by Germans.

On November 14, 1943, he was in a group, commanded by Avraham Rein of Lyntupy, who were tasked with following after the movements of the German army on the roads, and obtaining weapons and other supplies. When they reached one village near Lyntupy, they entered the house of a farmer named Birt. He received them cordially, and secretly sent his daughter to inform the stationary force in Lyntupy about the presence of partisans in his house. Germans and Lithuanians arrived in the village after a short while, surrounded the house in which the Jewish partisans were located, and rained fire upon it. The partisans returned the fire, and a bitter, desperate battle broke out. The Jewish fighters attempted to break out of the house in self–defense.

Three succeeded in escaping from the Germans and fleeing to the forest, while four died as heroes. Leib Gurwicz attacked a German machine gunner and killed him. The machine gun stopped, but he fell dead.

Yeshaya Gertman, Hirsch Charmatz, and Shimon Lewin fell along with him.

His mother, wife, and daughter survived, and live in Israel.

[Col. 1793]

Shayka Garber

He was born in 1920 in Sventzian, region of Vilna.

He was a partisan in the Voroshilov brigade, in Markov's unit. He was sent by Markov to Vilna several times for special missions. Due to this, he made contact with the survivors of the Vilna Ghetto, and took several of them out to the forest.

He participated in many battles and actions of the brigade.

In the autumn of 1943, he was in a group that was sent to carry out a mission in Lithuania. When the group was near Kobylnik, it was attacked by soldiers of the Lithuanian fascist army, and he fell in battle as a hero.

Yeshaya (Ishika) Gertman

He was born in Sventzian in 1921 to Avraham and Reizel. His father was a shoemaker, and active Bundist.

His entire family perished in Poligon. Alone and forlorn, he joined an underground organization and excelled in "extracting" weapons from the German weapons factories in which he worked. In March 1943, he was with a group of 24 youths who left the ghetto with their weapons and reached the Lyntupy forests. At that time, there was not yet even one partisan unit in those forests. Since there was no possibility in the forests, they set out for the Vilna Ghetto. There, they made immediate contact with the F.P.O. group, which advised them to join the organization in the ghetto. The people from Sventzian only agreed to collaboration with respect to going out to the forests. In the interim, the Jewish police found out that there were Jewish partisans in the ghetto who had arrived from the forests. They traced after them, and arrested him along with Yitzchak Rudnitzki, a member of the Sventzian group. At the police station, the captain, Natan Ring, demanded that they turn over their weapons to the police, otherwise a bitter fate would await them. The two refused to fulfil this order, and the captain summoned the police who beat them seriously over their heads with rubber batons. They were transferred to the ghetto jail, unconscious and bleeding. They were freed after strong intervention from the command of the fighting organization.

After being freed from jail, he left the ghetto and went to the Narocz forests, where he was accepted into the Chapayev brigade, Markov unit.

He was the messenger of Markov, the commander of the Byelorussian unit, to the Vilna Ghetto, with a command to the leader of the Jewish fighting organization to transfer themselves with all of their weapons to the forests.

Several times, he served as a guide to groups that were setting out to the forest.

At the beginning of 1943, he joined the Jewish group headed by Alexander Katzenelbogen (Alexander Bogen, the well–known artist, living today in Israel), which was expected to concern itself with provision of its own weapons. He joined a battle against the Germans who attacked the groups in the village of Melniki, when it was returning from a scouting mission. There, they succeeded in forcefully extracting several guns from Polish farmers.

On November 14, 1943, he was in a group commanded by Avraham Rein of Lyntupy that was surrounded by German forces around Lyntupy. In the desperate battle that ensued, he died as a hero by his own shot after all his ammunition was exhausted, as he did not want to fall alive into the hands of the enemy. Four Jewish partisans fell in that battle, and three succeeded in escaping and returning to the forests.

[Col. 1794]

Shimon and Rachel Levin

There were born in Sventzian to Menachem–Mendel and Esther. Shimon was born in 1908 and Rachel in 1913. They were saved from the slaughter at Poligon where their parents perished, and escaped together with their younger brother Reuven.

They wandered about among farmers they knew in the area of Gudeliszki until the liquidation of the Sventzian Ghetto. When the organized group left the ghetto, Shimon served as their guide, and as one of the advisors of the first base in the forest. His knowledge of the paths of the area and the forests often prevent armed clashes with police forces who had come to liquidate the first kernel of Sventzian natives – the partisans and Jews. When Rachel got sick and died due to the lack of medical attention in one of the isolated buildings at the edge of a village in the area, the two brothers took her out and buried her at the edge of the forest, without the farmers of the area knowing about it. After this tragedy, the two brothers continued to wander about the area without being able to distance themselves from Rachel's grave.

I recall that when I stayed with my sister Chaya in the bathhouse of the village at the edge of the forest of the farmer P. Shilkis, Reuven and Shimon entered in the middle of the night, also to rest a bit and sleep. They had not dreamed of meeting us or of other people of the remove area in such an abandoned building. They informed me of the death of Rachel, who had been a childhood friend of my sister Chaya.

Later, the two brothers joined the Voroshilov brigade in the forests of Myadzel. They joined the Bogen group. While spying in the area of Lyntupy– Sventzian, Shimon fell in battle along with four of his comrades. They were buried not far from Rachel's grave, and this was after two months.

Yosef Rudnitzki

He was born in 1921 to Pesach and Sheina. He graduated from the Tarbut School and prepared to continue.

In the ghetto, he worked at acquiring weapons from the German warehouses in which he worked at forced labor. He was one of the faithful participants in the groups of youth of Sventzian who prepared to escape to the forests and join the camp of fighters.

He left the ghetto with them in March 1943, and joined the Voroshilov partisan unit under the command of Markov. Later, when the Jurgis unit was founded, he joined the Vilnius Otriad.

While on route to fulfil a task on Lithuanian soil, they were attacked by an ambush of soldiers of the Latvian fascist army. Yosef fell in the desperate battle that ensued, thereby avoiding falling into the hands of the enemy alive.

David (Dudka) Jochai

He was born in 1926 to Chaim, a tanner by trade. He joined an organized group to go out to the forests as a fighter along with his older brother Boris.

How great was the joy that their father Chaim succeeded in escaping from the death train to Vilna and Ponar, and reached them.

His desire and thoughts for the future, when the war would end, were to not leave his elderly father, and to be an aid to him during his old age. Fate had it opposite. Chaim was bereaved of his son of old age, and he mourned for his faithful son.

[Col. 1795]

While he was alive, he participated in many battles and sabotage actions of the Chapoyev brigade, to which he belonged and displayed bravery. His name went before him.

He fell in battle during an attack on the stationary force and in a combing operation against the Germans.

Shalom Mechkin

He was born in 1926 to Yaakov and Leah. He graduated from the Yiddish public school. He continued with his studies during the time of Soviet occupation. He worked at obtaining weapons, and was connected with the group of youths of the ghetto who were preparing to escape to the partisan forests.

The group abandoned young Shalom at the last minute, and he was forced to go with his grandmother Sara–Rivka to the slaughter at Ponar. However, fate brightened for him, and he succeeded in escaping, and in arriving in the forests of Kažinė through his own efforts. He joined the fighters in the forests. He participated in many battles and sabotage operations.

During the German siege of the forests of Kažinė, he was surrounded by Germans, and he fell as a hero in battle.

When the people of Sventzian who were transferred to the Vilna Ghetto saw the partisans from their town marching at the head of the F.P.O. fighting groups which decided to transfer to the forests of fighters, and leaving the ghetto, they too joined the battle to forge a path to the forests. They expressed deep sorrow on not having done this while there was still time, while living in the Sventzian Ghetto. They decided to set out on the paths and roads without direction or a guide.

Many of them reached the partisan base in the forests of Narocz, and even went to the partisan base in the forests of Kažinė.

There were also incidents of opposition, as follows:

A large group reached the river and were forced to cross the bridge before dawn, when suddenly an ambush of strong fire hit them from three sides. Our people returned the fire. Both sides suffered losses. It is unfortunate about those who were lost, and who fell in battle before reaching the forests.

The forests were surrounded by German guards and a stationary force that attacked with cannons, automatic weapons, and even airplanes. The battle was difficult and heavy. The organized partisans prepared for this, and left the dangerous places while there was still time so they could hide in secure places. Our group stumbled into a German guard before reaching the base, and did not succeed in preparing secure spots. It was forced to fight and fall in battle, without selling their lives for cheap. They received full price – a soul for a soul.

We will remember the heroes who fell in battle!

The names of the partisans who fell in battles and other circumstances:

Pesach Goldberg, Pinchas Shulgeifer, Sheina–Lea Shulgeifer, Akiva Numkin, Mordechai Bak, Reizel Bak, Chaya–Esther Rudnitzki, Meir Katz, Gittel Katz, Esther Garber, Beila Michelson, Batya Kowarski, Gita Leifer, Chaim–Leib Gordon, Yochanan Michelson, Meir Swirski*, Berl Solomiak, Chanan Opeskin, Shmuel Bushaknitz, Reuven Miadzolski.

*this is not the same Meir Swirski of Kobylnik [see Kobylnik Yiskor book]

[Col. 1796]

Pesach Goldberg

Told over by Chana Goldberg

Pesach Goldberg was born in 1901 in Lida. He married Ella Szuta in Sventzian. His wife and three children were taken to Poligon together with all the Jews of the Sventzian region. Only he remained in the small Sventzian Ghetto. The Jews sent him with a wagon of bread to those imprisoned in Poligon. At the same time, he helped us leave there.

At the liquidation of the Sventzian Ghetto in 1943, he and his family were sent to Vilna. When the Sventzian youths who had already found their way to the partisans arrived in Vilna with the purpose of taking Jews out to the forest, Pesach Goldberg connected with Shlomo Ichiltchik and Motka Feigel, who took us to the Narocz forests, where Pesach had already joined the Jewish Nekama [Revenge] Otriad, led by Yosef Gluzman [Glazman].

On a certain day, the Germans set up a blockade around the partisans . At the time of the assault, the forward group of the Otriad succeeded in breaking through, and advanced toward the direction of the Kažinė forests. However, they were noticed by the Germans, and were all killed.

Only Pesach Goldberg's daughter Elka survived from the entire group of forty people.

*Shalom Yavnovitch, son of Shlomo Yavnovitch and Raitza Gilinski of Kobylnik, died in the forest on Tuesday August 25, 1943 during the German siege of the Partisans. [see Kobylnich [Narach] Yizkor book. This is the late uncle of Anita Frishman Gabbay

Translator's Footnote:

See https://en.wikipedia.org/wiki/Alexander_Bogen

[Col. 1797]

Children Saved from Satan's Hands

[Col. 1799]

Saved Children

The editors

Translated by Janie Respitz

...Of all the sadness, the worst sadness was a mother's, when being chased by a terrifying death, left her children with strangers, with a glimmer of hope they would survive. From all the tortures, the most horrific to witness with one's own eyes, was the cruelty in which the Nazi murderers tortured these young souls. When we read about the tragic, painful and miraculous experiences of those who managed to survive, it is astonishing: How in the world did the Taybeles, Estherls, Moishelehs find the courage and wisdom to escape the hands of the murderers that awaited them? The children of Sventzian region experienced exactly what the adults did, the violent ways of horrors of war, torture, sorrow and loneliness. The same curses chased after and them, and they found no rest. But how often were they stronger, smarter and more tenable than the adults?! This is how they remained child –pure and innocent. For years these innocent babies were carried through the storm of fire, blood and hatred. While millions of children around the world enjoyed sun and light, the same sun brought Jewish children darkness and tragedy. The sun was used as a tool in the hands of the wicked, so they could discover the steps of the children that ran away and managed to escape. Hundreds of evil men would chase after one hungry child. From thousands of children from the cities and towns of Sventzian region, very few survived. Except for one or two, the enemies succeeded in poisoning their childlike hearts and fill their heads with hatred towards Jews, their own Jewish mothers and fathers, who returned from this difficult nightmare, from the giant mass graves. Huge praise must be bestowed upon the Kovarskys, the Garshins and others who performed the holy act of saving Jewish children who survived from Satan's hands. These young people returned from the battle fields, understood the great fortune, that there were surviving Jewish children. With great humanity and national responsibility, they sacrificed and fought for revenge, to defeat the stained enemy at its own race, to resurrect the longing for parents, help them to rediscover themselves, and to once again merge with the Jewish people, its tradition and history.

[Col. 1801]

My Fight to Save the Children

Sender Kovarski

Translated by Anita Frishman Gabbay

The fight was difficult and complicated. This fight was against the fanatic–religious Christians, with whom we fought for Tachum Ester's son. He was raised a Christian together with their own daughter. Many Christians remained under the influence of the local priest, who advised against returning Jewish children.

When Itzhak Yocnes returned to Sventzian, he told us what Chana Ester (Rabotnik) had told him, about her in–laws child that is in Christian hands. We immediately began our search and found this child, who was with the Christian we knew, Kutchinska: with whom we started to negotiate with in order to return the child to us.

She said no close relative survived the war and therefore there is no one to make demands.

We then, with much kindness towards her, provided papers and promised her a large cash reward. This didn't produce any results–she became angry and through the priest, she would not release the child into Jewish hands. The priest told her that she would commit a "sin", even though the child was born a Jew. Kutchinska found out and became emboldened, that the Sventzian law ruled against Yocnes from getting his daughter returned to him (also held by a Christian family). Our begging did not produce any results.

In those days (after the war), a woman from an organization from Poland came to Sventzian, who undertook to help find missing Jewish children (who were rescued by Christians).

[Col. 1802]

We sent her to Kutchinska, to meet with her as the child's mother's sister, and to return this boy! Kutchinska almost threw her out of her house and from this time onwards, she kept her house locked. She would not allow any further contact between the boy and a Jew!

Several months passed, the few survived Jews were preparing to depart Sventzian to Poland and from there to other countries. We still continued our struggle: one day I went to Kutchinska, bringing sweets, but the door was locked. I presented myself as Sender, son of Leizer Kovarski, her former neighbour on Vidzer Street, and she asked me to approach her window and I said–"I come to you with good intentions, with sweets for the children, with some money and you won't welcome me into your home?"

In the end I convinced her and she let me in. I made her understand that my aunt Funes' child was her nephew, and she wanted to turn the process over to the judge and the child would be taken from her. Should we get a judge to decide this matter or is it not better to settle this matter in good faith, between us? I propose a solution, which will be beneficial to both her and a dowry for her daughter.

"Why do I need a dowry? The boy will get older and he will become my daughter's husband!" Her words torn my heart out! With great heartache I spoke of the great injustice that had been perpetrated against the Jewish people. You robbed us of everything and now you want to rob us of our Jewish children?

[Col. 1803]

She tried to respond–she found the child on the street and saved him from death! She understands my pain, but the priest won't allow it...I tried to go into the room where the boy was, but the door was locked. Through a crack I saw a small boy with dark, scared eyes looking towards the door. A blond girl was sitting next to him, and he began to cry, "Mamusia", I don't want to go to those "black" (dirty) Jews! They want to kill me!

The anger within me grew and I said to her: you will be held responsible for this!

She broke into tears and weakened her stance...I left 10,000 ruble and asked her to sign a paper, that she is giving the child of Chana Ester to his aunt Feige Rubin.

Crying, she asked me to postpone the signed paper for later, but when she opened the door both children ran to her. The boy didn't stop crying. She calmed him down and instructed him to go with his uncle. She dressed the boy. It seemed he didn't even own a winter coat. It was a frost outside. I took off my winter coat and wrapped him in it. I carried him through the streets to the home of the Flexser family, where the woman from Warsaw was waiting, whom I presented as the aunt of this child.

Laden with gifts I returned to Kutchinska and with some other Christians as witnesses, she agreed to sign the paper that she agreed to return the child of her own free will.

That same evening, a Vilna ensemble performed a concert in Sventzian, after which I returned to the Flexser house to check up on the child. First, they tell me the child cried endlessly before going to sleep. Then, the Christian, Kutchisnska, came by and took him in her hands, promising to take the child for the evening and return him in the morning.

I became embittered, and the first thing the next morning, as she hadn't returned the child, I went to her. No one was home. The neighbours who were witnesses, went to the priest. After several long hours, they returned, the priest said to return the money and gifts and take back the child!

Like a lunatic, not knowing what was best, I ran to the church to talk to the priest, to appeal to his emotions and to his wisdom! When I entered the courtyard, I saw the priest through the window, sitting with other people, drinking tea. I thought I would see Kutchinska and the child, but they were not there.

[Col. 1804]

I scuffled through the maze of buildings, the cold entered my body. I wanted desperately to find a place to warm myself, but I couldn't abandon my mission. My heart told me that he child was somewhere in one of these buildings.

Suddenly, a building, where the watchman lived, a side room was lit. Quietly I approached the window, where I saw Kutchinska with both children. The little boy was crying and she was consoling him. I heard: she will never leave him again, and in a few days when the Jews are gone, she will return him to her home.

I vowed to follow her to her home and kidnap this child!

I didn't go to work the next morning, waiting in my hideout, kept watch on the house. I noticed Kutchinska and the priest entering the house. As I was standing around in such difficult circumstances, I decided to take another approach with the child, trick the child.

On the third day I went to Kutchinska to enquire about the well- being of the child. She became disoriented when she saw me. The child was not with her, but she wanted to keep the gifts and money and wanted me to returned the signed paper and was willing to return the child.

I told her the aunt had already left for Poland and the money was to be used for Kutchinska to buy clothing and other necessities for the child. The aunt's only request, she begged that the child not be raised in the Church and with its anti-Semitic tendencies! Kutchinska was overjoyed and left immediately to seek out the priest and relay our encounter.

At that time, a young man was living at the Flexser's house, who worked for the NK.V.D. I told him the story of my intent to kidnap the child once he returned to Kutchinska's. I left with some sweets, but when I arrived at Kutchinska's, the door was locked. At that moment, the N.K.V.D. man knocked at the door and lied to her that he was sent from the court of Vilna and that he had the signed document that she received 10,000 ruble for the return of the child. He held her accountable that she stole the money and the child! He was going to take her to court.

[Col. 1805]

Kutchinska became pale from fright and after many tears and pleading, opened the door and gave me the crying child.

Together with Moshe Shutan, the cousin of Chanele Goldberg (now my wife), and Yehuda Sorski, we took the child to the train, which was going to New–Sventzian. There the Bitusunski family, the woman Rubin, were waiting the survived child of the funes' aunt (?).

Rivka Bitushunski washed the child, fed him and put him to bed. At the Bitusunski's house, there was also little Teibele, who was also returned from a Christian family. This child also survived a terrible war and understood the needs of this little boy. Their fate had ben similar. She sat next to him and said: don't be scared of your aunt, she is very nice and sweet, and she brings me wonderful toys!

The little boy stared at her with wounded eyes and she said to him again, “I was in the same situation as you are.” She was with strangers and was also very frightened to be returned to the Jews! Now she is happy and the Jews are very kind to her and bought her many beautiful things. He relaxed, then fell asleep.

Three in the morning, we left with the sleeping child on a train for Vilna. There we went to Liba Gurevitch–Gershonovitch.

In the days to follow, Feiga Rubin was ready and available to help me retrieving more children. She took the children from the orphanage and accompanied them to Poland.

Returning to Sventzian, my brother told me that the authorities were searching for me. I was being accussed of kidnapping a child with many lies! I left immediately to the authority who showed me the charge filed against me by Kutchinska. He was bewildered when I showed him the paper signed by Kutchinska and the 2 witnesses, that she willingly handed over the child. I told him the priest was meddling in our affairs. He was bewildered, he wanted to cancel the trial, but was under pressure, so the trial had to proceed and I had to appear at the precinct every 3 days until the day of the trial.

[Col. 1806]

If there was going to be a trial, I wanted to finish with it as soon as possible, in order not to delay my trip to Poland. After hounding them, the trial took place 3 weeks later.

It was a Tuesday morning, at the courthouse the priest and a large group of his Christian followers, assembled. I was all alone. None of my friends nor my brother were present. I didn't even have a lawyer to represent me! I didn't want to lose the trial by their very organized one. The judge opened the proceedings: I planned the kidnapping of a child that Mrs. Kutchinska had saved and had risked her life for this Jewish child! Her lawyer said, “In the name of Hela Kutchinska”, that I entered her house by force, threatened to murder her and the papers were signed under duress of death. The witnesses and authorities were all falsified and I took the child with force and falsehoods!

Now it was my turn to defend myself, I asked Kutchinska 2 questions: can you tell the judge who are the people who signed the papers ? and can she name the persons who helped her carry the 5 parcels she received from me? The lawyer asked the judge that these questions should not be answered. The head judge threw out his request, and Kutchinska had to provide the names of her neighbours: Kantorovitch and Vitkofski. I remain steadfast, that the witnesses signed these papers of their own free will and Kutchinska agreed willingly to hand over the boy. It was the priest who later objected!

In my final argument, I placed the blame on the fate of the Jewish people and the mass destruction that the Germans created. I praised my fellow Christians that I hold in my highest esteem, who in those dark days risked their lives to save a Jewish child! My upbringing was the same as the Christian values, as that of Hela Kutchinska's. The money and gifts were showing our deepest and sincerest appreciation for the humane deed she performed of saving a Jewish child from death!

[Col. 1807]

She showed deep understanding for my wish that the child be returned to his mother. The misfortune arose when this religious woman went to the priest and confided in him: he said–return the child to the Jews? For this you saved him? He wanted to convert this child into a Christian child! This kind woman is being influenced by these fanatics! Hela was a pawn in the priest's hands, he is using her to bring up this child to become an enemy of the Jews! He is the cause of this antagonism and doesn't want the aunt to have access to this child, who wants only to see the child of her murdered sister and bring him gifts. This was a terrible blow to the aunt, who suffered from loosing her entire family and the only one left is this boy.

When I came to Mrs. Kuthinska's house she insulted me by calling me “cursed Jew!”, She terrified the boy saying that Jews were the “Black Devil”. This was like a knife in my heart!

After all that we suffered, does a saved Jewish child have to become an enemy of the Jewish people? To be raised by a priest to instill this hate in him and against the Jewish people? Are this the values of a Christian?

I believe in my heart that Ms. Kutshinska is not guilty in all of this, even though it breaks my heart. She is blessed with a kind and good heart. She is poisoned by the priest and the actions of these fanatics, that is why I didn't want the money returned. I am willing to give her additional support that she will need in the future. We trusted her when she said she would return the child in the morning, and when she didn't show up that morning we knew that the priest was influencing her decision.

The lawyer tried to interrupt my speech. He said I was insulting people who had nothing to do with the trial. He underlined that the priest was the leader of the Christian community and his integrity is sanctioned by the Soviet regime in the region. After this interruption, I was told to proceed with my speech. I painted a picture of our despair, our desperation, our lives were uprooted in Sventzian, the murders in Poligon of 8,000 innocent lives that were thrown into a mass–grave. Here also lies the mother of this child!

[Col. 1808]

My ears are still ringing from the cries of this murdered mother! “Save my son! Don't allow him to become an enemy of his people!” I felt the tears running down my cheeks and I almost collapsed from the anguish I was portraying. The attendants ran to me with fright and the judge asked whether we should end the all my strength and begged for the trial to continue, I didn't want to lose this trial.

I called the witnesses who signed the paper, and they said they knew what they were signing.

So, I asked them, when did they learn that Kutchinska changed her mind... and they answered, from the priest. He said, “Do not return the child to a Jew!”

After painting the picture, the trial proceeded and eventually the aunt was granted custody of the boy. The judge told Mrs. Kutchinska that her grievances were agaisnt the aunt.

The demands were thrown out.

After I arrived in Poland, I became involved again with the fate of the Jewish children. I was in contact with the woman to whom I had given the child, she was a representative of “The Organization of Finding Hidden Children” in Poland and she was involved with a religious party. From here, I was informed, that the child was sent to Switzerland, then to Eretz Israel. I felt relaxed and calm, and when I reached Eretz Israel I wanted to know what happened to this child. I searched all the orphanages and other institutions, without any success. I never found out what happened to this child, at least he came to Eretz Israel.

[Col. 1809]

This is the Story of Teibele (Anka)

Aryeh Anat, (son of Zeev Popiski)

Translated by Jerrold Landau

The town of Nemenčinė is situated on both sides of the river, on a sand route, along the wide slope, between ridges of hills covered with tall pine trees, as you go from the city of Vilna toward Dvinsk [Daugavpils], approximately 21 kilometers past the bridge over the Viliya River on the north bank.

A few years prior to the outbreak of the Second World War, a tall, thin, broad–shouldered, jolly youth arrived from the town of Kaltanėnai. His name was Berl Wolowicz. He came to work in Aharon Popiski's flourmill, that was once there. The place of the mill, Hamarna, was about four kilometers from Nemenčinė, over the river on the south bank.

A Jewish family named Endelman lived in that town. They had an only daughter, short and pretty, named Rachel.

When he was among the local lads and girls one Sabbath, Berl noticed the young, beautiful Rachel, and began to court her seriously and persistently, until one bright day, he decided to get married and build his own home among the Jewish people. This was in 1938, one year before the outbreak of the Second World War. They had a daughter nine months later, called Teibele.

Teibele was only just over a year old at the outbreak of the war between Germany and Poland in September 1939.

Before the town was conquered by the Nazi troops, the local Lithuanian and Polish "fine youth" had already pillaged. Jewish lives were a free–for–all, and their property was for pillage and plunder. Any Jew who had a friend or acquaintance in a nearby village searched for a hiding place. They would pay the villager money in order to take them in and hide them.

Four kilometers from this town, in the forests, there were several isolated houses, about a kilometer apart from each other, called Podksziosz. A farmer widow named Marcinkiewiec lived in one of those houses next to the forest. This farmer always made her purchases from Rachel's parents' store. Berl and his wife went to Podksziosz with their little daughter. They went to Marcinkiewiec' isolated house in the forest and knocked on her door. After a long wait, noise was heard from inside the house and the voice of the woman was heard, asking "Who is there?" "It is I, Rachel, the daughter of the merchant from the town of Nemenčinė. Open the door for us," she pleaded to the farmer women who was peeking out the window with suspicious eyes.

[Col. 1810]

Yona Wolowicz (Teibele) [1]

The door opened for them, and Rachel explained the reason of their visit to her. The women did not make it too difficult for them, but it was possible to discern from her words that she needed money in order to arrange the matter in the best way possible. Of course, Berl and his wife Rachel understood the subtle hint, and placed their money and gold jewelry in her hands.

She hid them in the attic, behind the bales of straw, so that nobody could see. Three days later, they were transferred to a hiding place in the forest, some distance from the house. The hiding place was a sort of long pit, as tall as Rachel was when standing, so that Berl had to "stand" in a sitting position. There was a layer of hay thick enough to sleep upon. It was on a small hill. There were young pine trees around, the branches of which merged with each other, almost like a mist above the ice. Above the hiding place, covered with branches and weeds, there was a sort of chimney to the skies, covered completely so that nobody could notice.

Before they entered the hiding place the woman gave them a thin rope, so that she would be able to give them the necessary food. One end of the rope was tied to a pine tree, hidden so that it was almost impossible to notice.

As was agreed, she brought them food and drink once a day, after dark, when all the neighbors were in their houses.

[Col. 1811]

Day after day, at the same time, after darkness had spread over all creation, the woman would pack a package of food, leave the house through the back door leading to the yard, as if she was going to feed the animals in the barn. She would go around the yard, peer in the darkness, stop for a moment to look and hear whether someone would appear suddenly to disturb her from carrying out her holy task of offering help to a friend in need. When she was certain with all her senses that nobody could see her, she disappeared between the barn and the storehouse into the direction of the hiding place in the forest.

Every evening, she set out for the forest, each time through a different exit point so that she would not catch the attention of anyone, and also so that she would not leave a noticeable trail from trampling too much on the grass and weeds of the forest, for an enemy and adversary might catch her in her disgrace and annihilate her from under G-d's heavens along with her meager property for offering assistance to Jews.

After about two months, on a Sunday when she was in church in the town of Nemenčinė, as she was exiting to the street after the services, her ears caught on to some snippet of conversation as one was saying to the others: “What do you say about Marcinkiewiecowa?[2] They say that she needs multiples of her normal quantity of food.” The first took hold of the shoulder of the second and brought her close, as if she wanted to trust her with a deep secret: “They say that she... got rich from Jews.”

The conversation continued about the property of Jews, about gold, jewelry and other valuables, about the danger lurking with hiding Jews, and about the annihilation of them from the face of the earth. The farmer woman stood astonished the entire time overhearing the conversation, with flames spitting fire in her heart and soul. She returned home in a depressed mood. She sat and thought about the oppressive things that the two women were discussing. This means that it was no longer a deep secret, and how long would it take until it reaches the ears of the police and their dogs? I will inform them [the Jews] tonight about what has happened, to prevent both their and my complete annihilation. She made a firm decision.

A quiet discussion in an oppressive atmosphere took place between the farmer and the Wolowicz family. Finally, the village woman agreed to take their daughter Teibele to her home and raise her and protect her until the day would come... They were forced to leave the hiding place and to wander around the forests of the area in constant hunger, with barely a moment of rest, from fear and uncertainty.

They would visit their small daughter from time to time after sunset, in the dark. Their caution was insufficient, however, and one evening before it was completely dark, when they were going to visit their daughter they ran into a young girl who recognized that they were Jews. She followed them secretly and saw where they went in. The young girl hurried straight to the police and informed them about what she had seen with her eyes, and the isolated house into which they entered.

Berl and Rachel were at the table in the house of the farmer women. They were sitting on a wooden bench, facing the two front windows. Suddenly, Berl noticed a person appearing from the trees of the forest, apparently carrying weapons. They got up quickly, placed their daughter on the clay floor, and each ran through a different door in the corridor of the house. They ran in different directions, thinking that one of them might survive and raise their young daughter, so that she would not remain alone and orphaned in the frightful world, and would not be alienated from her people.

The gunshots from the Lithuanian militia first hit Rachel. She fell, wallowing in her blood, and died on the spot. They only injured Berl as he was fleeing from them across the threshing [where the grain stock is trampled to detach the kernels] floor, hiding among the bales of hay. They did not leave him be – their victim who was escaping with his wounded body. They removed him from his hiding place, and, with blows to his head with a gun, murdered him in a cruel, frightful manner. They did not receive a Jewish burial. They were buried as donkeys where they fell.

[Col. 1812]

These are the words told by the Christian farmer woman, the only light in the great darkness of that time.

Y. Avicz Relates:

I returned to the city of Vilna from the far–off depths of Russia in April 1946. From the Jews whom I met, I found out that there is a sole survivor from the entire community of the town of Nemenčinė, and he knew that the daughter of Berl and Rachel Wolowicz survived thanks to the dedicated, pleasant stance of the village women Marcinkiewiec. After the murder of her parents, the men of the Lithuanian militia entered the farmer woman's house and wanted to murder the girl as well. She fought against the criminal murderers with her strong arms, hands, and fingernails. With full force, she avoided giving her over to their hands, sullied with the blood of pure, innocent martyrs. Finally, when she saw that they would overcome her, she preached to them Christian morality, saying that Jesus their Messiah will not forgive or pardon them for the sin that they were about to carry out in murdering the girl, whom she had baptized about a half year earlier. She was prepared to die together with her, and would not let them murder a tender, pure Christian soul. They backed off after the reproof, but decided to imprison her and the child.

She endured seven levels of hell with inquisitions and torture at the Lukiškės jail[3] in the city of Vilna – and she won! She was freed with the girl after two and a half months, and returned to her isolated house.

One summer day, I went out to the town of Nemenčinė to meet with the aforementioned Jew, named Dov. He survived thanks to the belongings that he gave over to a farmer in return for hiding him. He knew the parents of the girl, and knew the place where she was located. Therefore, he agreed to meet me at the house of the widow in Podksziosz, to take back the daughter who was my relative.

Forlorn in the forest, by Rivka Ben–Sira

[Col. 1813]

When we entered, we greeted her as is customary there, and told her who we were, and what I wanted as a relative of the girl. She told us about the entire tragedy that took place before her eyes, and how she literally saved the little girl from the talons of the murderers, stressing especially the word "little." We asked her directly regarding the matter: "What sum of money do you ask for?" The farmer thought a bit and said,

"100,000 rubles." After some negotiations, we left the house without positive results, and returned to Nemenčinė as we had come.

I began to visit that house weekly. I became friendly with the girl and won over her heart and her pure, tender 248 limbs[4]. We became very close. I won her over to the extent that if was late in coming, she would stand outside waiting eagerly.

Teibele's appearance was frightful and terrible: she was thin as a stick due to malnutrition, and as short as a baby. She only wore a cloak on her body, and lice swarmed upon her. I bought her new clothes.

Once, when I was sitting in conversation with the farmer women, I raised the question of her education: "You will be forced to send her to study, and of course, she will need new, clean clothing, and from where will you get such? I have a recommendation: I will support her with everything during her period of study, and she will live with you during the vacation. Do you agree? If you are afraid that I will take her from you, come along with me. I will pay all expenses."

She responded: "I cannot give you a clear, decisive answer now on the spot, for various personal reasons. Therefore, we will deal with this issue next week, on Sunday after I return from church services." I agreed to her words, with the hope that I would finally succeed in convincing her.

At 10:00 [a.m.] on Sunday, I set out on a wagon to my intended destination, her house in Nemenčinė– Podksziosz. I saw that the farmer woman was standing on the porch, pacing to and fro. I got off the wagon, approached her, and greeted her as always, as was customary amongst the villagers. Her response was cold and almost hate–filled. As I attempted to go up the stairs of the porch in the direction of the door, the woman jumped opposite me and against me as a wild beast and stood in the opening of the door. Her elbow on the side blocked the entire width of the door. I was surprised at her sudden change of attitude toward me, and I was unable to guess why.

"What happened, Mrs. Marcinkiewiecowa?" I asked with great surprise. "This is the way you are. You repay a good deed with a bad. You are like your Dov!" I took advantage in a hiatus in her flurry of words and asked her an innocent question: "What did I do wrong?" The woman refused to speak to me at all. When I recommended that I enter so we can discuss, she responded: "You will not enter, and your feet will not cross the threshold of my house anymore!" When I swore with everything that was dear to me and to the soul of the girl Anka that I know of no connection with Dov Benin, aside from him showing me the place where the girl was located, her heart softened, and she agreed to let me in to the house, to discuss, and to clarify the chain of events during the time of my absence.

The women said as follows: Last Monday, Dov came to me in a drunken state, barely standing on his feet. He said to me: "We will take the girl into our hands for better or worse. The law is on our side, as you are guilty of anti–socialist education and external improper care that is likely to damage the tender soul of the girl. I will bring representatives of the government her to show them her physical and spiritual state, and the court will put you in jail for cruel treatment." I remained seated in my place without able to move or to utter anything. After a few minutes, I she continued: "This is your thanks for my deeds, as I stood against the beasts and did not permit the Satanic murderers [to perpetrate their deed], and took my life in my hands in front of them."

[Col. 1814]

I had not expected to hear such a shame and embarrassment. I sat as if on thorns and scorpions. My flesh and soul were burning like a flame, and my face turned red from embarrassment and shame as to what a drunk "person" could do, and could destroy within a moment. The women continued: "It would be better, do a good deed for her parents. Take them out of the donkey grave, and bring them to a Jewish burial." My tongue stuck to my palate from the reproof of this upright, honest, and proud woman, one of the Righteous of the Gentiles. My soul was singed from her degrading and disparaging words to a Jew, a drunkard. I stood up from the table with my head dizzy, and went toward the door. I blessed her with great peace. I did not receive a response from her.

I traversed the four–kilometer distance from Podksziosz to Nemenčinė on foot with great speed. My anger toward Dov was burning so strong, as I wished to give him the overflowing portion coming to him. To my great disappointment, I did not find Dov at home. I waited at his house for a long time, and he did not return. I returned to the city of Vilna with a broken, tormented heart.

My sublime, high objective, to return a daughter of Israel to the bosom of her nation, seemed finished. In any case, I tried through letters to urge her to remain in touch with me, but I never received an answer. I was astounded at the good, dedicated woman, and her embittered stance – to the extent that I recognized her uprightness and clear thought. It was not her own thoughts, for there were foreign, inimical ideas operating around her.

I had no rest from this matter for two months. I attempted to get in contact with Dov several times by travelling to Nemenčinė to meet him, but I always returned as I had come, with his absence from his house. I asked his neighbors and acquaintances if it was possible at all to ever find him at home? There response was always short and consistent: "We only have seen him for a few moments." I even remained once until late at night, and he did not return. It is possible that he was evading me, knowing what had taken place through his tongue. After a few months, as I was sitting in my room toward evening, the door opened, and a tall, handsome man stood before me, stated my name, and removed an envelope with my family name on it from his coat pocket.

I nervously opened the envelope. I removed a thick piece of paper from it, upon which was written:

My dear friend, relative, and fellow townsman!

From my letter you can see that I am living, alive, and functioning in this world. I survived, and my daughter Danka (Dvorale) is with me. My husband and sons fell victim, among the first in the slaughter in Ponar near Vilna. I know that Teibele, the daughter of Berl and Rachel Wolowicz, is found around Vilna, in Nemenčinė. Help the special messenger to go to her place, and bring her to me. I hereby beg in all forms of request to give to one of the Righteous Gentiles full and dedicated assistance.

I hope that you will do everything in your power to ensure that this objective will succeed. I thank you from the depths of my heart. May G–d repay you for your deeds.

Your friend and relative:

Signed: Bilha Gurshin

[Col. 1815]

In order to be sure that this was not a trap set for me, and to find out if Bilha had indeed sent it, I asked him for details about her appearance, town, and relatives. He told me everything as if he was one of the townsfolk. I chatted with him to find out as well if he was to carry out his mission on a voluntary basis, or for money. He got very angry when he realized my thoughts: "Do you need money, I will give you what you need."

I set the table with liquor, bread, and herring. We drank *lechayim* [a toast]. To his questions, I told him how he could find the place where the girl is located if Dov refused to give him the needed assistance. He left me in a high spirit, and disappeared into the darkness of night.

Bilha Gurshin Relates:

Anka was walking hand in hand with a Russian on the streets of Vilna, going toward the railway station. They were chatting, and he bought her sweets and some toys. Then, the railway station was in front of them. There was still some time until the train left for Bialystok, therefore he went to the first–class restaurant in the railway station and purchased a meal for her. She ate unwillingly, and between each swallow, she turned her head to all sides. Who knows what was in her tender, stormy soul? The train arrived at a fortuitous moment. They went out to the platform to travel. The little one was stubborn, and refused to ascend the steps of the car.

He sat with Anka in the compartment of Russian soldiers. They were chatting, discussing all kinds of levity and laughing out loud. One asked: "Why is the girl so bitter?" "We have gone a long distance, and she is very tired," was his answer. In the meantime, a second soldier began to take interest in her. He took advantage of him [apparently the one guarding Anka] passing the time by looking in a newspaper so intently that he did not see how Anka had disappeared.

As if from a snakebite, he got up from his place to move from the door of the compartment to the hallway of the car. He passed through and counting people with measured steps, peering into each compartment through the glass of the door. At the back of the wagon, he noticed a group of men and women standing and speaking in anger: "Who is this, who snatched a Christian girl and is trying to transfer her to the accursed Jews?" Anka stood among them and pleaded to them, pouring out her heart: "Good people, save me from the Jews, they kidnapped me from Podksziosz. I have 20 zloty. Take them and bring me back to my mother and my brother Tomek."

Were it not for his superior, who knows what might have happened?

This time, as they were sitting in the compartment, Anka sat next to the window and her temporary guardian behind her in the seat next to the door, with crossed legs covering the width of the compartment to the bottom of the second seat, so as to prevent easy access.

They arrived in Bialystok at a propitious time, and went to the house of Bilha Gurshin. He told her everything that had happened during the journey, being thankful that he had finished: "I spoke to her heart in a good way, and turned her attention to the good fortune waiting for her with her aunt. From my senses, I realized that my words were not absorbed in her tender mind, and her thoughts were directed toward the environment and house in which she grew up and was educated. I also realized that the poison of hatred and disgust for anything connected to Jews had struck deep roots in her soul. Anka sat bitterly, turned into herself, without uttering a word from her mouth. It was impossible to talk to her and to find out about the turmoil afflicting her. At times, she groaned from the depths of hear heart, and uttered the one word: "Home to my mother." The tears in her eyes and the occasional groans had an immeasurably bad effect on me. I knew that I was doing a positive thing by returning a girl to her nation and people, and providing her with a more progressive and free education without the previous dark ideas. My conscious was completely clear.

[Col. 1816]

A new period began. There was jealousy over every small thing between her and my daughter. I became the judge, and Anka did not always like my verdict. Neighbors alerted my attention because they saw Anka wandering about the outskirts of the city as if she was searching for something hidden. I was forced to open my eyes and supervise her more carefully, which stole from me precious time that was needed to earn our livelihood. I also had to instill new ways in her, ideas looking toward the future as a Jewish child, and to encourage her to forget the spirit of life in which she grew up and was educated. A bundle of difficulties and challenges were poured over our head.

One day when I returned from visiting acquaintances, I did not find Anka at home. I asked my daughter, the neighbors, and acquaintances from the house and the nearby area, but nobody saw her. What do we do now? Where can we look for her without help from the police? Having no choice, I turned again to my employer, who had influence with government authorities, to encourage them to search for Anka. He calmed me, saying: “”Everything will work out. Only patience and calm nerves are needed.”

They searched for her for three days, and found her with a certain Christian woman in a remote suburb of the city. She did not give her over easily. She demanded a comprehensive investigation as to where I got her from, and believed the words of the girl. With the force high level police, they took her out from the crowd of inciters and transferred her to the police station in the area of the city in which I lived.

On a Sunday morning, I was summoned to the police station to identify the child and take her home.

I endured the seven levels of hell with vengeful cross–examination until my eyes saw Anka's face before me. Anka refused to approach me. A policewoman intervened and said, “Friends, pay attention! The girl claims that this is not her mother. Her true mother is in a remote village near Vilna called Podksziosz. Perhaps we should wait until we investigate to find out if the words of the girl are true. Do we have time to investigate the mother?” The head of the division did not agree to extra headaches for his superiors. Hand in hand with Anka, with a heart full of happiness, we walked toward the exit of the police office and went out to the road swarming with masses of people after church services. Anka took the opportunity and began to shout out for help, asking people to save her from the Jews who kidnapped her from Podksziosz and transferred her to who knows where. “Good, merciful people save a Christian girl from a Jewish woman!” was the last shout I heard from her. Suddenly, I was surrounded by a stormy, angry crowd, headed by a young woman burning with murderous wrath toward the Jewish people. She grabbed Anka's hand, which I was holding, and removed it from my hand. She put her other hand on my shoulder, as if to distract me. The stormy crowd were in ferment and shouted in a commotion: “Death to the accursed Jewess! Kill the despicable person! She is certainly preparing for their Paschal offering – with the blood of a Christian girl for matzos.” No explanation or papers that I showed them could influence them. A cold sweat covered my body, and a shiver went through my flesh as I saw death before my eyes once again – despite the fact that I had become used to it for a long period of five years of Nazi conquest, when I was a wanderer, without any rights of existence on Earth. Then, I desired to remain alive and I won. I decided this time as well to remain alive and to somehow escape from the wild crowd desirous of a vain sacrifice. I turned to one man who seemed more settled than the rest and said to him: “You know what I am telling you, come to the nearest police station, several tens of steps, and we will determine whether or not my words are true?” “Right, right! We will indeed go to the police, but you will go with us, without trying to escape and flee.” Anka and the woman disappeared during those moments. I did not despair, and I was firmly determined to free her from the unknown woman and bring her back to the bosom of my family. This time as well, I was forced to turn to my acquaintance. He related to me in such a good, merciful way, that I have no words to thank him for his sublime deeds.

[Col. 1817]

I was not at home when one of the N.K.V.D men came to inform me to appear at their office on a certain street the next day regarding the claims of the girl. Nobody dissuaded me from going. My acquaintance advised me to go, so as not to arouse the slightest suspicion, and he would make sure that everything would be arranged to work out positively. I appeared at the office of the captain of the inquisition at the address in the notice at exactly the right time. I went through several obscure administrative procedures, meant to instill their fear upon you, before I reached him. When I appeared in the designated place, it was as if he did not see me. He paced back and forth, making you wait for something unknown. Suddenly, it was as if he woke up. He turned to me face to face, and asked an incidental question as if he did not sense your presence. He shouted: “What are you doing here, and what do you want?” I took control of myself, put on my good spirit without getting flustered over the drastic approach against me, and presented him his notice. He lowered his head, raised his eyebrows, and surveyed me from top to bottom with his inquisitive eyes. “Hmm... This is you? Why did you not appear at the time designated in the notice?” I was indeed self–assured at that time, but.. he did not permit me to continue with my explanation. He said in a questioning and commanding voice: “Since when does a Russian captain, especially of the N.K.V.D. have to wait for any person? You could not come before the time and wait for me!” I was quiet. “Why are you quiet? I have means at my disposal to make you talk?”

“Do you know that Anka claims that you have kidnapped her from her mother who lives in Podksziosz, and that you are unrelated to her. If it is proven after the investigation that the girl is telling the truth, do you know how many years of prison you will receive. Ten years of harsh labor!” “The girl is mine. Here are her official papers. However, at the time when I was in dire straits, on the verge of annihilation, with a strong will to put an end to my life, I made sure she would survive.” I informed him of the terrible, frightful things I had endured. I noticed that he trembled, and a chill passed through is body. He suddenly rose from his chair, and said with a trembling voice: “You are owed a medal for your strength of survival! Take your child, and be happy.”

“Anka! Anka!” he called loudly. The side door opened, and Anka was brought straight to me by a policewoman. “Please, strong fighter, take your desired one and your happiness. Be healthy, so that we do not have to bother ourselves again.”

Anka was with us in the home again.

Once when the teacher punished a portion of the class for not doing their homework, Anka was among them. When they took them out from the class, she disappeared from the school and did not return home. Certainly the teacher had forgotten who Anka was, and from where she had come. I had warned the teacher more than once about negligence in this matter, with regard to punishing this child. In order to draw her near, a completely different approach, more from the heart, a soft approach, with an understanding of her soul was needed.

I went to my acquaintance, as usual, to once again save the girl from the talons of the detractors. However, this time he almost refused to fulfil my request due to the danger involved in interceding with the authorities. He explained to me that the investigation was liable to become complicated: "I hereby advice you as a friend, take her to somewhere far off, and thereby prevent a bundle of problems for both me and you. This is the last time that I will get involved."

I gave her over to a Christian woman in the city to raise her, educate her, and to ensure that she would be weaned away from the place from whence she came. After about two months, I transferred her to the city of Łódź, and went to visit her every two weeks in the children's home. A special Jewish committee took care of the children, transferring them onward to Israel or America.

My daughter and I moved to live in Łódź about a half year after Anka was transferred there. I dedicated myself to her here, in the new place, for a full year, until she was sent via France to Israel with olim.

Moshe and Shifra Relate:

When we were informed about Anka, who is Teibele, via a letter from Bilha Gurshin, our happiness was immeasurable. We waited for more than a year until our financial investment reached fruition. Anka–Teibele arrived in Israel via France, through the Youth Aliya. From the family of olim, she went straight to the home of my sister Rivka.

Our household was happy with the new guest–daughter. There was nothing that Anka asked for that was not provided.

She was freed from the army in 1959 and went to study in a teacher's seminary in Jerusalem. She only completed one year. During the summer vacation, she met her mate, Ari Weinberger from Brazil, who had come to Israel on a visit. They got married.

Translator's Footnotes:

Teibe (or diminutive Teibele) is the Yiddish form of Yona – both meaning “dove”.

The ‘owa’ suffix to a name in Slavic languages implies a female.

See https://en.wikipedia.org/wiki/Luki%C5%A1k%C4%97s_Prison

A traditional Jewish number for the bones of the body (not accurate of course, but used colloquially and also used in the prayer for recovery of the ill).

[Col. 1819]

My Mother Commanded Me to Live

By Arie Anat (son of Zeev Popiski)
As told by Dvora Rozenzweig-Vinokur

Translated by Jerrold Landau

Dvora Rozenzweig-Vinokur

This took place during the time when the gas chambers were functioning in full force in all the cities of Poland, daily suffocating thousands upon thousands of people from all countries of occupied Europe, ripped apart and torn asunder by the Nazis and their disgusting, dedicated assistants: Ukrainians, Latvians, Lithuanians, and Poles. They suffocated them and burned their bodies to ash, scattering it over the four corners of the earth. The bodies of our dear parents were burnt in the crematoria next to the gas chambers. How did it happen that I remained alive? How?... My mother commanded me to live! Do not ask how I emerged alive from the frightful Sodom? Behold, I am one of those whom death skipped over, perhaps it forgot about me completely, not paying attention to such a baby as me, as it was hovering and sweeping over the impure land with its great work of complete destruction.

There was one great miracle: my mother held me with her teeth and sharp nails, and did not allow me to be offered as an offering to the angel of death.

We overcame them... My mother commanded me to life! Miracle, miracle, miracle! A miracle in every place! We set out on paths, through forests and fields, in the darkness, cold, howling wind and pouring rain.

Death was Always a Shadow Close to Me

In my memory, I will rummage through the stories of my mother, and I will write about everything that we endured during our time of wandering, from the time of my birth.

I was born at a time when death reigned in full force on the Jewish street, and mercilessly swallowed up entire communities in the district of Švenčionys and region of Vilna.

I first saw the light of the world in the town of Vidz. At that time, a war was being waged on the battlefields between the children of light and the children of darkness, taking many victims.

From then, death did not leave me be for a moment. It hovered around me, in my proximity, against me, with each and every step, wishing to annihilate me.

This was the end of the summer of 1941.

When the Vidz ghetto was liquidated in 1943 before I was two years old, all the Jews of the town were transferred on foot to the district city of Švenčionys, from where they would shortly transfer all the Jews to work in the city of Kovno.

We were loaded onto transport wagons like chased animals. The wagons were packed with no space. It was hard to maintain a stance due to the great crowding, and the lack of sufficient fresh air to breathe. The first victims were the sick, the weak, the elderly, and the children. They would faint, suffocate, and die while standing.

[Col. 1820]

There were hours and hours of travel... Suddenly there was the creaking of breaks. The train stopped, and there was the sound of shouting in German, Polish, Lithuanian, and Latvian. A mixture of languages as Babel, with some sort of commands being heard: Open the doors! Exit! Exit! Shouting was heard from the evildoers, accompanied by whipping on the "flesh" [1] and bones of those tortured, sticks on the shoulders, and butts of guns on the heads of those who did not hurry to exit and jump off the wagon... Were we in Kovno? Mute glances were exchanged between the people. With their look of astonishment, they understood the "workplace" as they saw the gigantic pit in front of them, surrounded by a wire fence.

As they jumped out, before they had figured out what was going on, and as they were being prodded toward the pits, the heavy machine guns were already rattling and spewing forth hellfire. The "work men" murdered and annihilated wagon after wagon, without fear of punishment or G–d.

Did a miracle not happen? When a person is found in the valley of beasts, the vale of murder in Ponar, and escapes under a shower of shots, with bullets shrieking and zooming around him, over his head, and he escapes onward and onward?

Under the wings of the raven by Rivka Ben–Sira

[Col. 1821]

My father ran holding me in his arms, while my mother held my four–year–old brother's hands. When my father realized that shortly my mother and brother would fall behind, he slowed his forward pace a bit, transferred me to her arms to make it easier for her, and took my brother in his hand to make it easier for her. The machine gun bullets, sowing death, hit them, and they both fell.

My brother wept so bitterly: "I still want to live, Mother," he pleaded. His voice got weaker and weaker. The hands of the murderers silenced him with a second shot.

I cried and cried. My mother took me in her arms, nestled me against her body, and with her remaining energy fled from that place, from the death in the vale of death of Ponar and the accursed surroundings.

I was not yet two years old.

Two other women were running with their daughters. A bullet grazed the head of one of them. She fell, with her small arms raised upward. Her cry of “Im...” [2] remained fixed in the cold air. Her hand was extended toward her fleeing mother, calling out for her help: “Don't leave me.” It remained hanging in the air for another moment, and then suddenly fell forever, with no end, to the end of days.

The mother continued to run and escape from death, without looking behind her, without turning her face. On the second side of the grove there were fields, meadows and fruit trees before the autumn. Above our head there was a clear sky and the sun that was warming and caressing, even in the coolness. Bu the light? How much light was it spreading? So much light...

Light!? It was our enemy in body and soul, betraying us and turning us over to our enemies! It was death! To us, darkness and blackness – was light! Without it, it would be impossible to exist and to escape from death.

My mother and I were one body and one soul. She dug under the tall bushes in the grove until the wrath would pass.

We began to walk, to walk and to set out in the dark to where our eyes directed us – only to escape from there with our remaining energy, as far as possible from this “workplace”... to the endless place.

My mother moved toward the town of Daugeliškis in the area of Švenčionys. We hid during the day, and walked slowly but in a wearying way during the night, without food, as our energy waned.

Suddenly a wagon hitched to a horse moved, with Lithuanian farmers in it. They peered out from the side, as if from the ground, noticed her, and attempted to forcibly load her onto the wagon. With her remaining strength, my mother resisted those who “were concerned.” The corpulent, stout Lithuanian hit her over the head with a fist, shocked her, and tossed my mother onto the wagon as a valueless object, as if tossing sack of hay.

He brought her to the local prison, to the German guard in the town, in the home of her brother–in–law. They were discussing amongst themselves: “Is this not Moshe's sister–in–law?” Each of them had their own theory. They decided to transfer her from this world to the world of truth, so that there would not be a living witness to their deeds and iniquities.

Sunday was their holiday, the holiday of their creator and messiah. My mother's ears heard a vibrant discussion amongst friends: “It is not appropriate to dirty our hands on a holiday,” said one. Their firm decision was to kill her the next day.

In the darkness of the windowless room, it was hard to find a remedy or salvation. My mother did not rest. As an animal in a trap, she paced to and fro, and felt the walls and the porthole above. That was the only escape from death, so that she could save our lives again this time from the talons of the wild beasts.

[Col. 1822]

Her gaze fixed upon the iron trellis of the porthole. The space between the second last bar and the one beside it was slightly wider than the others. She decided to endanger herself and make an attempt through the diagonal, facing downward.

She removed her worn–out, simple clothes and created a sort of rope. When she saw that it was not long enough, she also took off her cloak, tore it into wide pieces, and added to the rope. She tied me to one side, and tied the second side to her left hand. Like the leaping of a wild cat, she jumped upward and grabbed one of the bars with her right hand. She attempted to move her head through the trellis, but did not succeed. She turned to and fro, leaned a bit to the side, and her head went through the diagonal opening. Her thin body and bones somehow moved through. She tied the rope to the trellis, and lowered herself quietly and slowly onto the wooden floor. With several steps, she crossed the hallway to the next room. The room of the diary keeper was empty of people. She took the bench, brought it to the door of the prison room, climbed up, and untied the knot in the rope. The rope was in the hands of my faithful mother. She raised me upward, and brought me through the trellis.

My mother ran like a madwoman through yards, jumped over fences, crossed fields, and went straight to the adjacent forest to hide from the Lithuanian "human" beast. We escaped through the thicket of the forest: escaping from an enemy and adversary who was liable to pursue us. My mother heard the ringing of bells. The alarm bells of the firefighters? Yes, yes, they were ringing! They were summoning all the destructive angels against us. There they were, the accursed dogs, almost next to us. They were searching and foraging through every shrub and thicket of trees. One more small step... They literally tread on our bodies. A miracle!... They skipped over us and moved on. We were saved! Soaked to our bones, with my mother's feet bleeding and deathly frozen, we knocked on a door with light. There was a house in front of us, alone and forlorn, built in a corner between the trees of the forest. She knocked on the door delicately. Who is there? The voice of a man was heard, and the door opened. The man did not permit us to enter. Her pleas and entreaties to his Christian heart to at least let us dry off and warm up were to of no avail.

We began to wander again. The tribulations, difficulties, suffering, and hunger were with us again. I was bloated from hunger and cold. Our legs and feet were scratched and wounded, without appropriate care or a secure spot to heal them. When we found a heap of hay or straw covered with a roof and semi enclosed with wooden walls, or even with bales of wheat that were forgotten or remained in the field before they were taken in, at the edge of the forest and the meadow or next to the river, we were the happiest in the world.

How good for us was the darkness in the hay? We could rest, strengthen our dry bones, and sore, tired feet.

It was as if her eyes were fixed on one point, a bit further than the village, to an isolated house among the trees, separate from the forest. Perhaps it was a bathhouse? We walked toward the house on our failing feet. Then we were inside. It was a bathhouse. It still had some heat, which caressed our face and bodies. What joy was on Mother's face: the water in the large iron basin was still warm. Mother stripped me and herself to our birthday suits. We bathed and enjoyed the rare opportunity. A piece of soap rolled out from a corner under the bench. Mother washed and scrubbed me with soap. Herself, she only washed in in the warm water to spare the soap, leaving it to wash our dirty, filthy clothing, which was full of lice.

[Col. 1823]

As she was so busy and occupied with cleaning, and happy with such a rare opportunity, she completely forgot where she was, and the inimical, murderous environment. Suddenly, her ears heard a faint, barely audible creak. Then, there was knock on the door that had closed on itself from the power of her pull. A shudder passed over her flesh and skin. Her eyes wearily turned toward the open door, where a Lithuanian was standing with a hunting rifle on his shoulders. He was shouting and threatening to turn us over to the German police. Her pleading and begging on bent knees and hands wrapped around his boots and feet softened him, as he placed his eyes on Mother's ring. He extorted her last memento of her wedding – a gold ring with a diamond. We remained alive that time as well. It was simply a great, rare miracle in the frightful den of beasts.

The winter progressed in its full strength. It was freezing, and snow covered all existence. The paths, roads, trees of all types, fields and meadows were all covered in white. We were cold, hungry, and oppressed in body and soul.

Could we maintain a stand to fight with two mighty enemies? Having no choice, my mother slowly got used to her new situation. She prayed with her soul that wet, soft snow would fall. The footprints of our bare feet could not be covered and left a trail for the enemy. In wet, soft snow, it was possible to erase them with a pine branch tied behind her. We made our way at night from place to place, without resting after searching for food for our hungry mouths, as we were up to our knees in snow. From time to time, mother stood for a few seconds and rubbed my hands and feet in snow so they would not freeze.

It was before nightfall. The cold sun had not yet set behind the forests, and the voice of youths, joyous and happy, could be heard almost next to us. We were finished! There was no time to escape. Mother placed herself in the snow, with me below, covering me. They almost passed us, but suddenly the last of the group shouted to the rest: "Look, there is someone frozen under the snow!" Mother trembled from cold and fear together. The end of our suffering and tribulations was at hand, and there was no way to prevent it. The youth approached and tried to turn her around and lift her up, to see if she was alive or dead. She panicked when she saw him. He calmed her, saying, "Don't worry, we will not do anything to you, we are also persecuted by the Germans. We are from the underground." With amazed eyes , he looked at Mother and said, "You are Moshe's sister–in–law, are you not?" Mother asked him to bring something to eat. He promised to do so. After a short time, he brought a jug full of milk and a half a loaf of bread, about two kilos. Mother pleaded with him to bring clothes, a pair of old shoes, but he refused, and explained: "You know our people, and how depraved and denigrating are the times. They know and recognize everyone's clothes. They would even recognize someone's shoelace. They could figure out whose clothes it is from the buttons... Don't be angry, and don't tell anyone that I gave you even this little bit of help."

One night, when we were at the edge of the forest, we heard voices in German. Their coarse and arrogant laughter did not bode well. There was no way to escape from the place. Mother took me, and we both fell into a sewer pit full of snow. We sunk, and sunk...

It was dark in the forest, the area, and the roads. One could move and search for a distant settlement or an isolated house to live, to seek a morsel of dry bread.

[Col. 1824]

Behold we were next to a house. A giant dog attacked my mother, biting and barking. She did not let up from her, and I was screaming. Mother fell down without strength. It seemed that the end had arrived, and her minutes were numbered. Soon, the dog would tear her body to bits.

A voice calling his name from the darkness distracted him. It left my wounded, bleeding mother alone, and disappeared to the voice that called him.

Before us was a tall village man, wearing a coat as was customary in the winter, and with boots on his feet. My mother pleaded and wept before him. "You are a good–hearted man, a savior and rescuer. You saved me from the claws and teeth of your faithful dog. Do me another favor, have mercy on us, and give us something to eat. The dog exhausted our last energy. We are starving to death." Without saying anything, he returned to his adjacent house, and brought a full loaf of bread, large, and fresh, under his shoulder. He gave it to my mother. Before he gave it over to her hands, my mother noticed that there was a knife with a long blade tucked into his boot. She thought: certainly the knife is for us. The bread under his arm is only to trick us so that we will not escape. He turned around and went back to his house, closing the door behind him as he entered. He certainly did not hear my mother's blessings.

We set out again on the roads, with bare, wounded feet. Night after night, week after week, persecuted more than before, as if the circle of tribulations and difficulties was closing in around us. We had no way of escaping the trap. My mother had no more resourcefulness to maintain our stand under these circumstances in this hateful environment. She decided to go to the ghetto in Vilna.

As we crossed the long path, we found ourselves around a village. We were surrounded by Polish Christian youths, shouting, "Look, look! Here are two forlorn, dismal Jewish women. Death to them for killing our messiah!" The calls were repeated over again, and incited the rest of the group to come. A "rescuer and redeemer" in the form of an adult villager came and saved us from them.

We were in the Vilna ghetto, where "life" still took place. People were taken to work in distant places, by foot, tens of kilometers per day back and forth. My mother was among them, and I was left alone in the common house, without special supervision. I knew how to "arrange things" and hide myself in all sorts of "holes." The adults, good people, had pity on my and gave me some of their meager food, a morsel the size of an olive. I would look in their eyes while they were eating, and saliva dripped form my mouth.

How happy was mother when she greeted me on her return from work and saw that I was still alive, in a hidden corner so that nobody would see. One morning, when she went out to the physical labor, she returned to the block as she had left, saying with sadness and sorrow: "They did not go out to work today. Something unusual has taken place."

I was the only small child together with the adults in the block. It seemed to me that no other children were still alive. When my mother realized that there was no escape, and that she would have to go on the way of all flesh, to the gate of the ghetto, to the gathering place for the "selection" she covered me with a sheet, tied the four corners with one knot, like a package. She left a little space open for breathing, and descended the states of the building, with her "package" behind her shoulders.

In the concentration and selection area, who for the rod and who for "mercy," the young people who were still strong and healthy were sent to one side. Women, older people and weak people were sent to the other side.

[Col. 1825]

We were behind the "sorting." The living "gathered material" still moving, passed through the gate according to the command of the Jewish ghetto police. The "package" on my mother's shoulder, with me inside, began to rebel and to throw herself to all sides, since there was not sufficient air and she was suffocating. I burst out in wailing. My Mother, hearing what was happening behind her ears, opened it with her hands, and widened the airhole a bit. She sensed inquisitive eyes on her, and looked around. She did not lose her composure. She left the line, and leaving the line was not simple. Somehow, she pushed herself between the crowd of those being sorted with her elbows and her "package." My mother found herself outside the sorting, and ran quickly through the slope of the hill to the grove. None of the guards said anything, paid attention to her actions, or looked at her. They did not stop her.

We were among the trees of the grove. The trees were naked and frightening. Here and there, a yellow leaf that had not yet fallen was still hanging from a branch. A cold, stormy wind whipped them incessantly until destruction. The trees also hated the yellow color and tried to toss them down. Next to the trees, there were still small piles of yellow leaves that the wind had heaped up. Mother gathered the small heaps into a single large one, and dug a sort of long pit in the melting snow and mud. She covered the two "forlorn creatures" with the yellow leaves.

This was the only time that the yellow color protected Jews and became a redeemer, savior, and helper.

We were in the cellar, in a hiding place with two other women and their children. Complete silence pervaded there, as a cemetery. The quiet and silence was interrupted by the crying of a baby. The baby's mother tried to calm it and stop its wailing. She tried again and again, but the baby continued to wail in a louder, shriller voice. The mother got upset, and was afraid that the wailing would turn everyone into the hands of the enemy. She took the pillow from the baby's head, put it over its mouth, and silenced the baby forever.

There was complete silence in the cellar. The hiding place was a cemetery. And the mother? She survived... for how long?

We escaped from the hiding place. Bullets from guns again shrieked over our heads and around house. There was almost no escape from them.

The woman escaped together with us, and advised my mother quietly: "Cast her aside, and it will be easier for you. You no longer have the energy to run and carry her on your shoulders. Cast her away and save yourself!"

A fifteen–year–old girl fell beside us, severely injured. She was lying on the ground, tending to her wounds. Her voice weakened as she pleaded with her mother: "Do not leave me in my groaning. Help me, take me with you. I am young." The mother ran onward and onward, moving in all directions. She advanced a few more steps and fell on the cold ground with full force.

Broken and weakened from the tribulations, hunger, and escapes, fighting for her life, my mother had no more energy to maintain herself. She decided to put an end to her suffering. One dark night, she brought me to the edge of an isolated village and left me alone in the garden next to the house. She covered me with the rest of her rags that she removed from her body, frozen with frost. She quickly disappeared, so that nobody would notice her with a wicked eye. She stood a distance away and looked, to see if I would be taken in by the residents of the adjacent house. She wanted to die with a quiet, calm heart, and a clean conscience.

I cried and wailed bitterly, pleading, "Mommy, Mommy! Where are you? Why did you leave me?" The door of the adjacent house opened, and a woman appeared next to me from the darkness. She looked on me with pity, lifted me with her arms, and brought me into a large, spacious room in the house. The light of the lamp spread weak rays along its length and width. I was with a Polish family.

[Col. 1826]

The next day, a problem arose in the family: What to do with me, whether or not to inform the police? The woman said: "Perhaps she is a Jew?" The husband reacted in a slightly more humane way and said: "It does not matter to me who she is! We will raise her as a Christian girl, and this is the commandment."

My light hair, blue eyes, and the Polish language that mother had taught me throughout the time of our wandering helped me, and did not fail me. They took me for a gentile foundling, and I remained with those Poles until after the war.

My mother, standing before the gallows, changed her mind at the last minute and escaped from the dangerous place. Death was in her own hands. She never forgave herself for losing her mind, not having any recourse, and for the travesty that she perpetrated against me and my future. As she was alone and childless, she never rested. She secretly came out of her hiding place at any appropriate time to see me from afar.

I became a member of the villager family. They loved me very much, and dedicated themselves to my care, with their heartfelt, good attitude. My clothes were always clean and nice. I prayed every morning to Holy Mary, kneeling on my knees toward the icon that hung over the bed. Of course, I completely forgot my entire past. My throat and tongue uttered all the hate, venom, curses, and invective that I learned in this Polish home. I became on of them. My mother was completely forgotten from my heart and memory, and left my soul.

Despite their positive relations, my "mother" did not hesitate to punish me with a rod on my naked body for every small misbehavior. She had no mercy on me, even when tears came from my eyes like streams of water, and bitter pleas came from my mouth. I loved my "father" more, because he never punished me. One day, he fell ill, and died after a while. They dug a grave next to the house. Every day, I lay over his fresh, pleasant grave and wept bitterly, pouring my heart out to him. I recited prayers and pleas to the Creator for the elevation of his soul. I loved him very much, and made decorations around his grave so it would be orderly and neat. I planted flowers on top, and protected it so that it would not be damaged. I went to church services with the family, and sang in the church choir. The priest would chat with me privately on occasion, and teach me Christian doctrine and morality. He comforted me, saying that a day would come when it would still be good for me. He knew that I was the daughter of Jews, and he never said anything that might crush me.

When I was four years old, my "mother" took me to the house of the priest, asking him to baptize me with the holy water. The priest spoke to her softly and nicely, explaining and promising to forgive her for this sin in particular. When he saw that the woman was stubborn, and did not understand is innuendo, he said to her openly: "I will not baptize this little girl as long as the war has not ended, and we do not know who her parents are." The women left the house of the priest with a clear conscience. She was calmed for the time being. Having no choice, she waited impatiently for the fortuitous moment that would come.

Since my mother was alone and childless in an area that was unfamiliar to her, she decided to seek refuge in the next village over to where I was, with a poor women, who was alone, isolated, and widowed. She had a young child, and was pregnant herself.

[Col. 1827]

She lived in a gloomy hut at the edge of the village, somewhat far from the houses. One night after dark, she knocked on the woman's door and begged her to take her into her house, where she would be a great help to her in her tribulation and difficult life. The women agreed to my mother's request, and housed her in the attic, where there was straw. She gave her her husband's coat to cover her body against the cold that pervaded outside. My mother knew how to sew very well, therefore my mother advised the women to advertise that she would take on hand sewing jobs, fine and good. The widow did so.

My mother became a sewer, secretly without anyone knowing. The widow closed the door by placing a large crate against it. She covered the windows so nobody could see. During the time that my mother sewed clothes and garments for the women of the village, the widow stood guard. Shen she saw someone approaching the path to the house, she took the place of my mother, taking the thread and needle in her hand as a sewing expert. To measure the dress, my mother would peek through a crack in the ceiling located at a place facing the area they were measuring the dress. She looked carefully, with a discerning eye, lest, heaven forbid, there be an error that would require an additional repair. When the customer left, she came down and returned to the room. She fixed what was necessary with a professional hand. There was light and joy in this gloomy hut. The poverty turned into abundance and a plentiful food. They were not hungry as in previous days, and there was also heating wood in the yard. This ideal situation continued for several months until... one bright day, when my mother was in the attic after figuring out the measurement of the customer, my mother detected the agreed upon sign was given – opening and closing the iron gate of the heating stove twice – indicating that there was no danger. My mother came down from the hiding place and stood in the room in front of the strange women. From her great surprise, my mother remained fixed to the wooden floor. The customer was surprised by the appearance, and did not believe what she saw before her eyes. She crossed herself in the customary fashion, saying, "Oh Jesus and Holy Mary! What am I seeing? You are hiding a Jewess? Have the Germans not been looking for her for several weeks already? Is this not for sure!" She shouted loudly, and left the house, slamming the door.

My mother, unable to move and escape, stood in the room as a dreamer. I am finished, she thought to herself. The village woman left after a few minutes. My mother escaped after her, running toward the forest to trick and mislead her.

My mother returned from the forest only when it started to get dark, and hid behind the house, calling out to the widow and consulting with her about what to do now. She explained to the woman that it is not appropriate to endanger her life and that of her family in order to save a Jewess. Therefore my mother said, "I have decided to leave you and to become a wanderer once again." No!" said the woman with an iron will." Remain together with me. We will trick them, and we will yet see good." She moved my mother to a secret place, farther from the house. When the widow returned, the village mayor and his men came to her house, claiming that she would bring tragedy and destruction on them all if the matter were to become known to the Germans. They strongly demanded of her to place my mother far away, so that she would not even be seen in the area. "I distanced her from my house and my area," answered the woman in a firm voice!

Humane, tolerant feelings continued to pulsate in the heart of the widow. After an interruption of a few days, they began work anew.

[Col. 1828]

They were sevenfold cautious of every step. The widow measured and marked up the clothing for repair herself. My mother only sewed, mainly at night to the light of a lantern.

The widow went into labor. The labor was especially difficult, and her screams reached the heavens. My mother urged her to fetch one of the women of the village to help her. She refused to listen and call someone to help, lest she endanger my mother's life.

The German troops were being defeated. They were attacked on all fronts from the east and west, and were pushed backward toward Germany. Liberation neared our area. The city of Vilna and its area was also liberated from the enslaving yoke and boot of Nazi Germany. My mother emerged from her hiding to the light of the liberated world, in order to liberate me from the strange, inimical environment, and to return me to my people.

I had become a Christian in all limbs of my body and soul. I hated Jews as did the Poles, with a blinding, burning hate, as I received from my "mother's" kerchief. I swallowed the venom, hateful poison, curses and invective as the truth. My mother moved to live in our village. She attempted to draw me near to her and talk to me at any occasion, to explain to me and remind me of the events that we endured together. At times, I listened with great patience, but for the most part I escaped from her. Finally, I escaped to another village, about ten kilometers away, because of her.

When my mother saw that I had disappeared, being five and something years old, she went to the Christian woman's house to inquire about me and to find out why I was absent from the street. "Your daughter escaped from you, is afraid of you, and I do not even know where she went and where she is hiding." Her response was brief and curt. My mother pleaded with her and explained that she should understand her soul. Finally, when my mother realized that her words were for naught, and would not move her from her inimical stance, she threatened to start a court case against her for hiding a child that was not hers, in an improper, negligent situation, with hunger. The Christian woman became afraid, and brought me back to her house from the village. My mother's joy cannot be described in words. She was the happiest woman in the world when she saw me on the street again, playing with the children as in previous days.

Passover was approaching. My mother brought me matzos to eat. I took one matzo from her and ran to street. When the children saw the matzo in my hands, they all shouted: "Throw away that matzo! It was kneaded and baked with the blood of Christian children!" I dropped the matzo. The children ran and each picked up a piece of it, chewing and eating it. I escaped home. She cursed my mother with the worst words of denigration that I had ever heard, on account of the embarrassment from the children, because of the matzo that she brought me. I fled from her.

My mother once again discussed with the Polish women, to convince her to give me over to her hands, or else she would approach the state solicitor. The Polish woman stood her ground: "No! This is not going to happen. You can approach anyone you want! I will not give up the girl whom I have raised and cared for under any circumstance! Do not attempt to convince me, for your efforts will be for naught. This is my daughter, and I will not give her up under any circumstances. Furthermore, there is no law in existence that will force me to give her over to your hands!"

My mother thought about how to break the strong will of the Polish woman. Suddenly, my mother got up and said, "You know what? Perhaps the priest will adjudicate between us?!" She agreed at first, but she almost regretted it on the way to the house of priest, as she recalled his words:

[Col. 1829]

"We will wait for the baptism until the end of the war. Perhaps her parents will survive, and will come back to take her."

This time, my mother used sharp words of reproof against her, that literally burnt her flesh and soul: "You don't trust your priest? All that is holy in the Christian religion? I, a Jewess, recognize his uprightness and justice, and I have full faith in him." From great embarrassment that a Jewess reproved her in public and declared that she does not believe, she remembered the words of the priest and agreed to give me to my mother's hands.

It was no simple matter for my mother to separate me from the family that I had gotten used to, and was one of. My mother expended many explanations and countless speeches until my lack of trust in her dwindled.

How many new birth pangs did my mother and I endure until she convinced me, and I agreed to leave the village, my “mother” whom I loved, and the entire environment in which I was raised, How much spiritual and other difficulties did I endure until my mother saw the first fruits of her efforts, and her face shone with enjoyment and happiness. Her efforts were not in vain. She returned me with my heart and soul to the nation to which I belonged and into which I was born!

My mother won over my heart and soul once again as in past days, and we once again became one body and soul. Thanks to my mother, I am again with my people, my birth heritage, amongst my brothers and sisters. My national pride returned to me, and my Jewishness rose to life with greater strength and full consciousness of our eternal destiny.

My homeland and I – we both rose to live through tribulations, difficulties, and persecutions, which we overcame.

My mother commanded me to life!

She maintained me literally with her fingernails and teeth, and did not allow me to be given over to the murderers who were thirsty for Jewish blood: the Poles, Lithuanians, Latvians, and Ukrainians, may they be cursed, and may their names be blotted out forever!

Translator's Footnotes:

It is not clear why flesh is in quotations in the text, but my guess is that the author is hinting that the tormented people were more bones than flesh at this point.

The first syllable of the word for Mother.

[Col. 1829]

The Yachnes Twins

Communicated by Sender Kovarski

Translated by Anita Frishman Gabbay

Sonia and Yitzhak Yachnes had to give away their twins when the Sventzian Ghetto was liquidated. They were born at the beginning of the war. They left them with a poor Christian family for a large amount of money. They were led to Vilna with the rest of the folk, where Sonia died and Yitzhak survived the many work camps in Estonia and Germany. He was liberated in Dachau and with the survivors he left for Italy with the hope to make Aliyah to Israel.

In Italy, he was reunited with the survivors of Sventzian, whose help he needed to find out the fate of his twins that he left with the Christian family. After a while he received an answer, one daughter was at the same Christian he left them with, and agrees to return her, the other daughter was given to another childless Christian family.

The Jewish survivors did not wait long for Yitzhak Yachnes's answer, they took the child from the Christian, which was left at the Jewish orphanage in Vilna.

Yitzhak left immediately to find the second child. Not long after arriving in Sventzian, he discovered the whereabouts of the Christian family.

[Col. 1830]

When he arrived at the village, and inquired about the child, he was told she belonged to them. She gave birth to this child and she forbade Yitzhak from entering her house.

Yitzhak wasn't deterred and didn't leave the village. He got acquainted with a neighbour, he promised him money to keep watch, that the Christian woman should not try to escape with the child. This kind neighbour told Yachnes that the child was brought to this village in 1943, and this fortunate couple told all the villagers that the child was a sister's child.

Going back to Sventzian

Shoshana Yachnes in the Army

[Col. 1831]

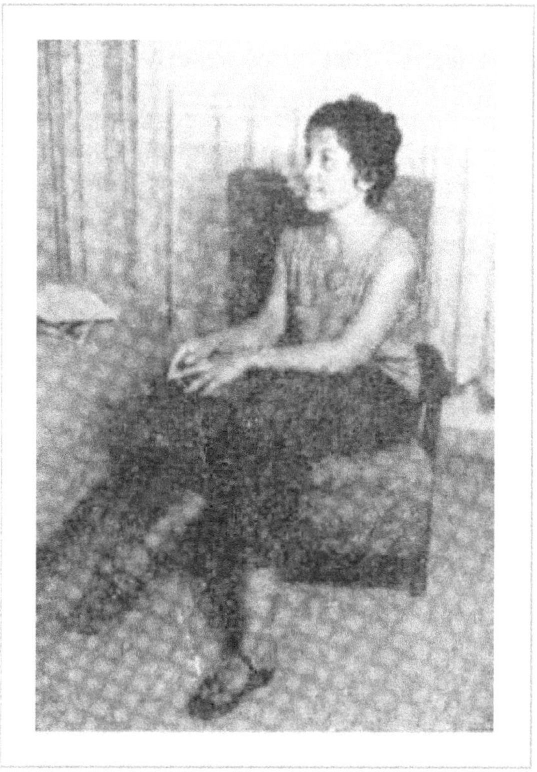

Fruma Yachnes

Yitzhak Yachnes went to seek help from the mayor, but he didn't want to get involved and referred him to the court, which gave an order, that the Christian cannot leave the village with the child. She had to wait for the trial.

Yitzhak believed that as the father the court will bring justice. This child was given to the Christian family to be rescued from death by Hitler's murderers.

[Col. 1832]

The court didn't care about the father's rights and gave the child to the adopted parents. They verdict was in order to protect the child from going to a new environment.

Yitzhak didn't accept defeat, he appealed to the court in Vilna. During the process, he rendered a heart wrenching speech, he recounted his life – threatening experiences that he lived through, that his strength came from finding his children. His speech made a great impact. The court pronounced that the child should live with the Christian family until age 18, then she can make her own decision where to go.

Yitzhak appealed again, this time to the Russian high court of appeals, and this time he was awarded the return of the child. When Yitzhak left to take back his child, the Christian fled the village with the child. Thanks to the help of those Jews who were still in Sventzian and New Sventzian, and especially with the intelligent Nechama Tzinman, they eventually found the hiding place.

The Jewish youth led an organized effort, they rescued the child. Together with the other daughter, Yitzhak and his daughters left for Eretz Israel, all 3 of them, where they are till today.

[Col. 1831]

"Righteous Gentiles" Have Saved My Child Esther

David Soroka

Translated by Anita Frishman Gabbay

My child, Esther, was born in Vilna in 1940. When the Germans arrived and set up the ghetto, we were living on Shavelski Street. Our house maid, Jadzhe Lukovska, who worked for us for many years, had to leave us. Gentiles were not allowed to work for Jews and if they found her in the ghetto, she would be punished as well. At the beginning, when they were taking young children from their parents, Jadzhe came to us to take the child with her. She assured us, that if we remained alive, she would return the child.

[Col. 1832]

With heavy hearts, we decided to give her the child, to rescue her from death.

My wife didn't want to let the child leave her hands, but I warned her of the hardships and dangers. In the end, I convinced her and made the arrangements to bring the child myself to Jadze.

[Col. 1833]

Esther Soroka with her husband and child[1]

As I went to work outside the ghetto every day, I left with my child hidden under my coat and went through the gate. No one noticed.

Jadzhe Lukovska waited for me by the church on Rudnitzker Street. She was so happy when she saw me with the child and took her from me.

I left for work at the ? and when I returned at night, I passed through Small–Stephen Street, where Jadzhe lived. Approaching her house, I heard the crying of the child, Mame, Mame. My heart was aching from fright and I quickly decided to return without seeing her.

When the Vilna Ghetto was liquidated in 1943, my wife and I were sent to work at the Fur Factory in Kailis, and Jadzhe found a way to bring our child so that we can see her from a distance.

[Col. 1834]

When they liquidated Kallis, we were sent to Kovno, where I remained for 6 weeks, then I was sent to Stuthof. My wife remained in Kallis several more weeks, and then was sent to Ponar with the remaining Jews.

After the liberation, I returned to Vilna to look for the child. Everywhere I encountered anger, and it took a long time before I found out that the priest of the Rudnitsker Church, his parish and amongst them Jadzhe Lukovska, my former maid, all left for Poland.

I left for Lodz, and from there, together with a friend, we left for Woltsh, near Bydgotsz. This was 1946, when the Kielcer Pogrom occurred, and travelling by train was a death trap. Finally, and with great difficulty I arrived, only to learn that Jadzhe had died 2 months earlier. My question, where is my child?

I came across a woman and she showed me through a window, a child playing in the garden and she called out to her, "Teresa, your father is here!" She came running, and took a look at me and said,—but this is a Jew! My father is on the front! She ran back to play and I stood paralyzed in my spot!

I stayed overnight with this Christian and the next day the priest summoned me to him. He was very friendly and told me the child was not converted:

[Col. 1835]

..."a lot of Jews were saved in my Church. I saw and suffered your pain and anguish what I saw around me, a folk that is washed in blood, we cannot force their children to be converted!"

David Siroka when he took back Esther

I remained in the village for several days in order to gain the trust of this child. In the end I was able to take my child with me to Lodz. At the train station, the Polish neighbours, their children and the priest who played with my Esther, all came to say goodbye. I wanted to give the Christian woman more money, but she answered me–we wanted to save your child from the hands of those bloody murderers, not for money".

[Col. 1836]

We arrived in Lodz and it took a while to distance her from her Christian beliefs. We finally made Aliyah to Eretz Israel after 3 hard months at sea on the "Exodus", enduring more difficulties.

In the end, my Esther became a real Israeli child, grew up and married. Today she is a mother of 2 children.

Translator's Footnote:

I believe the identification of these people is wrong

[Col. 1835]

My Child Kept Me Alive

Rivka Feigel-Falant

Translated by Anita Frishman Gabbay

When the war broke out between Germany and Russia, my husband Leib and his family wanted to escape to Russia. But, as I was pregnant, the family decided to remain at home, as it was risky for me to travel. The first 3 months we remained in our homes. All at once the "tumult" started: the Jews of Sventzian were to be deported. We were frightened. The first would be the men. So my husband Leib Gurwitz and my father Peretz Feigel ran away to White Russia, to hide in Konstantinova, near Svir, in the turpentine factory of Faiva Yonishki. I waited for a miracle, that perhaps we would not have to escape. But the day of the evacuation arrived quickly, a Saturday morning; they chased the Jews from their homes to be sent to Poligon. Not paying attention to the orders, as I was in the last stages of pregnancy, I decided to save myself together with my sister- in- law Chava Gurwitz. We ran by foot to Lyntup. The next morning a decree was issued to arrest all the newcomers that arrived from other shtetls and to send them back.

They gathered 38 people from Sventzian and sent them back. A miracle happened: a Polish policeman from Lyntup noticed that I was pregnant and came to me and said: Scream, that you are having labour pains! I listened to him and went to the S.S. man and he told me to go to the hospital. Instead, I and my sister- in- law went back to Lyntup. After 4 days in Lyntup, with the help of a Polish doctor and a midwife, I gave birth to my daughter Esther. This was October 4, 1941.

[Col. 1837]

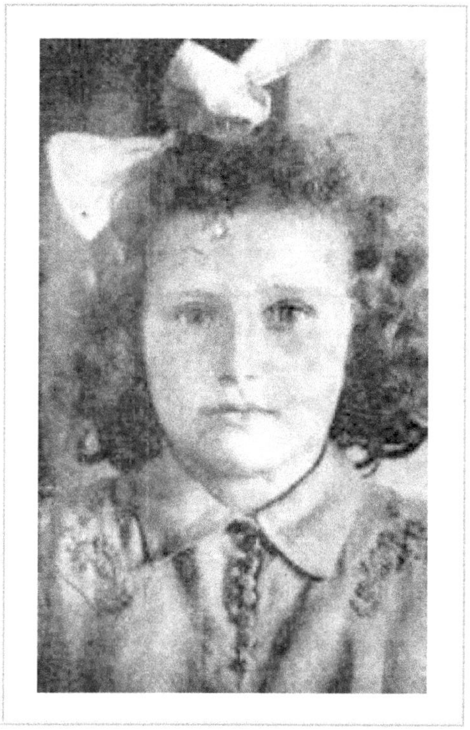

Esther Gurwitz–daughter of Rivka Feigel

After 3 months in Lyntup with my husband father and sister– in– law, we returned to the Sventzian district where the "necessary" Jews still remained. These were Jews working for the Germans and we hoped that we would be amongst those to remain "useful". We remained like this until February 1943, amongst the "useful" ones, but the time came that we also going to be liquidated, sent either to Vilna or Kovno. My father, hearing the news, said to us: you are young and you must save yourselves. I advise you to give your child to a Christian family for safekeeping and it will be easier for you to find hiding places. In the beginning I didn't want to listen to my father's advise, but slowly, it became clearer, that we will all die together! If we want to save the child, and hopefully if we remained alive, we could take the child back.

We found a childless Christian family in a small village that took pity on us. With a broken heart and flooded with tears, I handed over the child to the Christian. But after 3 days she returned Esther to us. She was too scared to keep her and we had to find another home for her. In the end, we found a poor Christian with a young son the age of Esther, and with the help of some money, she took our child.

As long as we were in the Sventzian ghetto we left frequently to see her, even when they brought us to Vilna we didn't cease contact with the Christian and kept in contact. We remained in the Vilna ghetto until September, then, through Moishe Shutan, we were sent with a group of 20, to the Narach woods.

[Col. 1838]

Our contact with our child was cut off. We got news from time to time through the Lithuanian partisans. One time we heard that the Christian wanted to give our child to the Germans. Her neighbours told her that we were in the woods with the partisans, and it wouldn't end well for her. The partisans will take revenge on her!

It was Christians who brought food to our child from time to time. They knew all that was going on, and the Christian with whom we left Esther, was in a difficult economic situation. The Germans took her husband for forced labour to Germany, and if not for her father, who became a beggar, she wouldn't have survived.

On the advise of the priest, she converted our child and gave her the name, Krisia Tragadeiti, from the word “tragedy”.

My husband Leib Gurwitz died November 14, 1943 during a partisan raid. I remained with the partisans until the liberation. When it became clear that liberation was close, I had an idea, if my Esther is alive, and the Red Army is in Sventzian, I would retrieve my Esther (and found my sister– in– law Chava Gurwitz, who also came out of hiding, at the Christian,) to take her back with me. We had no difficulty getting back our child, she (the Christian) really did not have the means to keep her. She(Esther) didn't recognize me, but we got reacquainted very easily. There was no motherly love nor enough food to eat at the Christian's home. She was three and a half and didn't feel any closeness. She immediately gained my trust and wandered into my arms.

My good fortune was overwhelming, that my dream to bring my child to Eretz Israel with me came true, where I got the means to raise her, educate her in Yiddishkeit and give her a better future. Her grandmother lived to see these joys and together we brought her to the “Chuppah” (wedding ceremony).,

[Col. 1839]

We Shall Remember Until the Last Days of Our Lives

Dr Shlomo Stein z"l, New York

Translated by Anita Frishman Gabbay

My Dear shtetlach of the Sventian region, remembering you, I become overwhelmed with a longing, bathed in pain; I find it difficult to remember and to put down on paper the memories that shine from our childhood years, that was so abruptly interrupted in New Sventzian, Sventzian, Svir, Haydutitchok and Michaelishok.

I remember my place of birth, Sventzian, its friendly and brotherly existence!

Sventzian, your brightness with all its intellectual people I remember, Rabbi Aharon Tzinman and his family; Svir, where my mother was born, where my grandfather Rabbi Schmuel Hirsh Soleveitchik and many of my relatives lived; Haydutitchok and Michaelishok, where I spent time as a 17 and 18 year old, as teacher in the nearby Tarbut–Schuls, I will never forget you and will forever keep your memory and language alive. Day and night I am filled with tears when I think of you. It pains me and I cannot be at peace, that our beautiful way of life, which was rich in tradition of our Jewish folk went up in smoke. That gruesome picture of the mass grave in the Baronover woods does not let me rest, the "Rakarnia" on the Ziemiene (river)— which remains before our eyes as a gruesome symbol (a pain in our hearts) of the destruction and death of our community, words that cannot describe the suffering, pain and loss caused by this enormous tragedy!

My heart is crying and aching for the "righteous", for my dear and beloved, for the "sweet and innocent ", for the Holy murdered souls; for our beautiful life and for a generation that is lost, for those wonderful people, who will always remain in our hearts from those beautiful and brotherly shtetls, that were, without mercy, destroyed and erased!

Let this book shine an everlasting light to remember those pure and holy souls and let it be a reminder, every day to our last dying breath, to remind others, what that "Amalek" did to them!

[Col. 1841]

Landsmanchaft: Sventzian

Sventzianer Relief in New York

Brania Forus – Chasid, New York

Translation by Anita Frishman Gabbay

In 1906 a young man from Sventzian by the name of Belal Levinson arrived in New York. He was the son of Rivka and Meir, one of the well known families of Sventzian. Arriving in America he met up with those Sventzianers who came in 1900, among them: Sheina Richman, Chana Heyman, Abraham Bromberg. Levinson also remembers in the early 20's, a young man from Sventzian who arrived from a wealthy home, religious and honest. His ambition was to study in America, later his plans fell apart. He worked during the day, and studied at night. After earning some money, he decided to open a small factory in the center of New York and started to manufacture character – monograms for ladies clothing.

His factory became the center of many activities. We got letter from many Sventzianers from all over the world. He always helped, and was very beloved by all.

Poverty, need and despair drove Sventzianers to leave and wander all over the world, eventually some arriving on the shores of America.

Between 1905 – 1914, before the first World War, there were already here: Harry Beigel, son of Itze – Zelman the tailor, Harry Norek, son of Mordechai, Yosel and Aharon Jakobson, sons of Hirshl the Melamed, Frank Klatzko, son of Schaia the butcher. Lewis Isackson, son of the grocer, Chana Heyman, Max Grin (Green), son of Chaim, Harry Breiner and Harry Rich (Richman).

The above mentioned group of Sventzianers decided to organize in 1918, with Charles Levinson's help, the Sventzian Landmanchaft Society in America.They formed a committee to provide help and resources to their fellow Sventzianers. After World War 1, help in Sventzian was desperately needed.

Charles Levinson and the idea of the organization, set an example for other such relief societies. They elected Chana Heyman as its first President, and the finance secretary, Charles (Belel) Levinson, who was the primary source of help, and he carried the burden mostly upon himself. Being young in spirit, and young in years, the group enthusiastically and energetically began their mission. The goal – – to help Jewish Sventzian. After the war, the Jews started immigrating to North and South America to flee the poverty and hopelessness of the shtelach of Russia and Poland, amongst them many from Sventzian. Charles Levinson reached out to his fellow Sventzianers, and with help even from South America, managed to bring about 450 Jews to America.

[Col. 1842]

Bellel – Charles Levinson

Help came from other organizations and the work that was being done was meaningful and necessary. A Jew, that should be mentioned, is Harry Gordon – a brother of Hirshl the shoemaker from the Schul – Hof, open – handed and very generous helped our Sventzian Relief Organization. The name of Charles Levinson grew in name and fame every day.

[Col. 1843]

He became the heart and the symbol of the organization. He was never too tired to answer the numerous appeals and letters from all over the world. From this organization others were founded as well: the Talmud Torah, the Yiddish Folk Schul, the Yeshiva, Refugee Help, Clothing for the Needy, both Beit Midrashim (synagogues), the Tailor's Kloiz and the Bath in the Schul – Hof and Free Loan Society.

Thanks to the Sventzianer in America, a People's Bank (Gemilut Chesed) was founded in the new synagogue. Packages were sent to individuals for Rosh Hashana and Passover, they were given wood to tide them over those cold winter months.

In 1937, the Sventzian Relief Organization was officially renamed : "The American Friends of Sventzian". In 1938, it celebrated 20 years of existence. A journal was published and good wishes from friends and organizations from all over the world were sent to celebrate the 20 year anniversary. The celebration was mentioned by the American representatives and those who were mentioned were: Charles Levinson, Yosef Jacobson, Moris Teitz, Max Oster, Shimon Siroka, Harry Sneider, Yosef Richman, Harry Gordon, Max Richman, Harry and Rose Beigel, Mrs. Rose Rabinovitch, Harry Gurwitch, Yacov Beker, Rebi Milken, Aharon Jakobson, Sam Rifkind, Frank Klatzko, Mrs. Mirski, Herman Shapiro, Mrs. Bella Goldman, Tzilia Tomson, Rose Chit, Rose Amber, Tzilia Katz, Rose Osofsky, Shragovitch family, Hillel Kopelovitch, Meir Kantorowitch, Dora Kessner, Ida Miller, Frances Lagorna.

[Col. 1844]

The Workmans Circle, 321, also organized a branch of the Sventzianer relief, which also provided cultural as well as institutional help, such as medical, burial and other things necessary to sustain a good quality of life. This branch comprised of: Y. Max Breicher, Mr. and Mrs. Ozinski, Zina Stein, Israel Siroka, Meir Blumberg, Charles Charmatz, Abe Glick, Mr. Bromberg, Mina Trotski, Aida Oster, Annie Katz, Mrs. Sirokin, B. Golstein, Rose Lifton, Abraham Radni. For many years the secretary for this branch was B. Vidutchinski. A devoted individual, who passed away in 1960 and this branch was then dissolved.

After the death of Chana Heyman, the presidency was taken over by Yosef Jacobson. The protocal - secretary was Harry Oster. The role of finance - secretary was never handed over to anyone else. Charles Levinson had always, with great efficiency and devotion, carried out his duties.

[Col. 1845]

In 1938 when the reorganization and renewing of the Sventzian committee took place, Harry Oster became the new president, son of Moishe Benjamin the Melamed, a practical person, who conducted himself in his work with logic and tact. He held this position for 10 years. Until his last breath he carried out his duties with honor and devotion.

A void was created, until Mrs. Osofski, who was working in the Vilner society as secretary, in 1938 started to work with our Sventzianer society and then became its secretary. She conducted her job with great devotion.

The women were for many years active in relief work, they organized themselves in 1940 and became known as "The Woman's Auxillary". This idea came from the daughter of Kalman Shutan, Rose Ginzberg. They called her the "mother of the organization". The first women who were involved were: Aida Oster, Annie Katz, Rose Lifton, Rose Rabinovitch, Lena Jacobson, Rose Beigel, Aida Norek, Tzene Teitz, Bella Goldman, Mrs.

Osofski. They attracted a lot of people and worked diligently raising money for different needs, and collected articles which were sent to needy Sventzianers in Europe.

Standing: **Michael Oster, Harry Oster, Bellel (Charles) Levinson**
Sitting: **daughter of Levinson, Mrs. Bromberg, Avraham Bromberg**

Rose Ginsberg

Aida Oster was one of the “Ladies Auxiliary's” presidents. In 1958 this group dissolved because of sickness and old age.

With the outbreak of World War 11, all contact with Europe was interrupted. Our Sventzian was caught in this hell of fire and was completely destroyed. The call for help to the free world was not heard!

Rich America always absorbed immigrants, amongst them Sventzianers. The Sventzian Relief Society always gave help to our needy fellow immigrants, seeking out the sick in hospitals, in their homes, providing the necessities as well as welcoming them and providing financial assistance.

In 1945, after the Liberation, the committee received calls for help and letters from their needy brothers from Sventzian who managed to survive the war, and with brotherly love, assistance was provided. Food parcels and clothing were sent to those who barely survived and were now living in post war German, Italian and Austrian camps.

[Col. 1846]

When the time came and things were getting back to “normal” and we came to our senses, we began to heal from this horrible nightmare and time was needed to heal these open wounds of our enormous loss, the Sventzianers began to work together with other organizations. The task at hand was urgent, we couldn't leave our brothers and sisters to rebuild their lives in a “blood soaked” land: rescue was of utmost importance and our work was needed especially at this time.

The American Government, together with Jewish and American organizations, undertook to bring the remnants of European Jewry to America. The first ship of immigrants arrived on our shores on April 1946. On this ship was Chaiala Forus, and Folevski and her husband. These were the first of the newly arrived Sventzianers who managed to survive.

Another newcomer, Frieda Ligunski, from Sventzian, and her husband made a very difficult journey through Siberia, Japan, China, to finally reach American shore in 1944. These were the first newcomers.

Later the mass immigration took on a different character, amongst the thousands who arrived, these were the Sventzianers: Dr. Niame Toraseitski, Avigdor Levin, Dora Pomerantz, Brania Forus – Chasid, Dina and Kapel Sirotka, Monesh Sirotka, Tzdek Charmatz, Hirsh Bleichman, Efraim Miadzolski, Luba Gershonovitch, Pesia Lantzman, Chaim Swintelski, Chaia Cutler – Fridberger, Rocha – Feiga Kramnik – Hit, Guterman Abraham, Sura – Tema Bak – Ring. Moishe Kurlandtzik, one of the last, arrived from Poland was Dr. Kovarski's son Liove with his wife and child. Others were scattered in South America, Canada and other places, names which I cannot remember.

A special committee was formed with the help of Hirshl Beigel, son of Itze – Zelman the tailor. The task on hand for these newly arrived was of great importance and special attention was needed. He arrived in 1913 and like every immigrant to America, he knew the hardships.

As our organizations were already established, these new Sventzianers soon found a new home and quickly integrated in their new way of life.

Few families were in constant contact with the Relief Society in New York. They were: Hersh Ushpal, Guterman, Bronia Chasid, Frieda Fradkin and Tzdek Charmatz. For the Remembrance ceremonies, a large percentage were Sventzianers.

In 1948, after the declaration of the new state of Israel, many of the survivors left the camps in Germany to rebuild their lives in their new homeland. The new Olim endured many hardships in those first years. Broken, physically and spiritually, they had to adapt to their hostile environment. In those days the Sventzian Relief Committee in New York endured the outpouring of grief and those Olim were thankful to receive whatever help or warm words in that time of need.

[Col. 1847]

Charles Levinson, with his warm and constant correspondence, always as organized help. One way was sending over 40 parcels a year to the needy in Israel, and with Heshl Gurwitz coordinating in Israel, a relief society was also set up there. A Gemillut – Hesed Bank was ready in 1951 to give loans to the needy Sventzianers to get them back on their feet after suffering the worst of humanity and had to flee their broken homes of Sventzian. In addition, they organized a dedication – a memorial stone to the 8,000 brothers and sisters who perished in Poligon, erecting a "Brother's Grave " Memorial, as well as remembering them with a Yiskor Book – all that was needed to help in order to meet their needs.

Many challenges were encountered in the last 10 years. Every year the membership dwindled. They got older, weaker and sick, many died and it became increasingly difficult to continue, and by 1962, only 120 remained. 25 – 35 persons would attend a meeting. The president, Harry Sneider, son of Mendl – Shmuel, took over in 1956 from Sam Rifkin, who was in office for only a year.

[Col. 1848]

Harry Sneider, born in Vilna, raised in Sventzian, came to America in 1903. Until 1922 he lived in New – Haven, Connecticut, and when he arrived in New York in 1922 be began his work in the Vilna Branch, in the Workmen's Circle and became its protocol – secretary. He is involved until this day. Shortly after he arrived, he became involved in the Sventzian Relief Committee, and became Treasurer during many presidencies: Ike Jacobson, Israel Siroka and Sam Rifkin.

He was by nature a quiet and honorable person, and was very dedicated in our society with energy and enthusiasm. His duties – to supervise all the secretaries – Mrs. Osofski, who celebrated her 50 year relationship with vivaciousness and vitality. Her excellent protocols were exemplary : Treasurer, Harry Ozinski, was an honest, philanthropic and devoted individual. His role started in 1956 and he carried out his duties with love and devotion; Charles Levinson, the founder and finance secretary of the organization, became weaker and sicker in the last years, but rarely missed a meeting, finally in 1958 his feet made him retire. The job was transferred to Meyer Kanterovitch. He was not one of the early Sventzian immigrants, he came much later. He worked very diligently.

Working for the Sventzian Relief Committee was: Hershl Beigel and his wife were devoted to the work as well. Distinguished and with an open heart, he worked quietly and endlessly. Loved and respected by all. Harry Beker, also should be mentioned with great respect for all that he did, with deep pockets; Louis Isakson, Harry Noirek, Max, Breicher, Ike Jacobson, Abraham Guterman, Tzduk Charmatz and others.

The women to be mentioned: Rose Liftov, dedicated and selfless, sister of Abraham Guterman was the first and most active in the "Ladies Auxillary" and all the other organizations of Relief. Mrs. Sneider, the wife of the President, Mrs. Ozinski, always welcomed us into their homes. From the more recent arrivals, there worked: Mrs. Bronia Chasid and Frieda Fradkin. Thanks to them, the organization under the presidents, Harry Sneider, Harry Beigel, Harry Noirek, Harry Beker, Abraham Guterman, Tzudek Charmatz, Rose Lifton, Rose Osofski, founded a separate committee to work for the interests of the Yizkor Book Project.

[Col. 1849]

A hearthy thanks to Rabbi Ushpal, a son of a Sventzian Rabbi, for his contributions to the writing of the Yiskor Book about the religious way of life in our shtetl. And thanks to his importance – this gives us great respect here in America.

In conclusion, let us not forget those holy people who recently perished.

[Col. 1850]

In the last few years, these dear ones left us (died):

Moishe Meir Levinson, brother of Charles Levinson, Chana Herman, Yosef Jacobson, Harry Oster, Ben Zion Vitutchinski, Barney Woods, Israel Siroka, Shimon Siroka, (brother of Israel), Rose Ginsberg and her husband (founder of ladies auxillary), Aharon and Len Jacobson, Yosef and Ethel Richman, Avraham and Frank Bromberg, Alter and Lena Goldstein, (Harry Beker's sister and her husband), Maurice Trotski, Sheine Matle Teitz, Nathan Sneider, Israel Yosef Lifton, Avraham and Esther Zalkin, Boris Stein, Dovid Leib Rothstein, Molly Weisman, Rabbi Aharon Gordon (from Michaelishok), Dzeni Sneider (Mr. Sneider's first wife), Hyman Rabinowitch, Moishe and Alte Herman, Avraham Ber Lifshitz, Leah Tomson, A. Klatzko, Nachum Moishe Saks, Harry Gordon, Aida Noirecki, (Naradski), Abe Glick, Leiba Ber Mordechai Grin, Ben Hurwitz, Mendelevitch, Herb Bernard Stolpher, Sam Stolpher, Rabbi Meyer Blomberg, Yacov Leib

Saks, Lifa Reines, Luba Grin, Schlomo and Betty Rothstein, Tuli Grosman, Azia Batkin, Avraham Segal, Yosef Goldman, Lena Farus – Artuganov, Yacov Veks, Aida Vidutchinski, Charles Levinson (Bellel), the Rabbi Boruch Leib Minkin.

Sventzianer Relief in New York, America

Sitting: **Mrs. Charmatz, Breicher, Mrs. Oster, Ozinski, President Sneider, Mrs. March, Harry Beker, Jacobson**
Standing: **Charmatz, Guterman, Mrs. Vidutchinski, Freida Fradkin, Bronia Chasid, Harry and Rose Beigel, Harry Noirek, Mrs. Sneider, Kantorovitch, Secretary lady, Maurice Yunge**

Note: Sheina Richman married Avraham Bromberg in Sventzian in 1896

The wedding cake in the previous photo, is actually a cake for their 50th wedding anniversary, celebrated in New York

The 3 men standing sang at their wedding in 1896, and again at their anniversary party

Information by Alan Schorr

[Col. 1849]

Our Aid Committee in South Africa

Mania Tzkinski – Yaffe (Cape Town)

Translated by Anita Frishman Gabbay

Through Sisela Pupiski – Tabachovitch of Johannesburg, I found out that a letter from Heshel Gurewitz of Tel – Aviv arrived, telling us about the relief work that was begun for the Jews that survived Hitler's destruction.

We immediately assembled a meeting of our landsleit from New – Sventzian that were in Cape Town and we formed a committee, in which were found these devoted individuals: Binyamin Yaffe – President, Mania Tzkinski – Jaffe – Treasurer, Belal Kaplan – Secretary, Zelig Rutseyn – assistant, Ahron Yitzhak Malaravitch – assistant, Teiba Rutsteyn – Tzinman – assistant.

We threw ourselves into this work with great urgency and we immediately started sending packages to the camps for which we had received addresses. The funds from the Sharit Plitah were not enough, the requests were larger and additional help was needed, so we had to make a plan. Social gatherings were organized in private homes and they were very successful.

[Col. 1850]

At these events we sold various items and this helped raise a lot of needed money. The first such evening took place in the home of Ruchel and Ahron Yitzhak Malaravitch. Later at the homes of Sisi and Binyamin Yaffe, Nechama and Shneur Walman, Chaia and Zelig Stein, and Mania and Abraham Yaffe.

Our numbers grew as a result and we raised many funds for these unfortunate souls.

The Relief – Society was directed through Cape Town by a small number of people who where so devoted to this cause: Riva Rudnitski, Chaia and Zelig Rutsteyn, Nechama and Shneur Wolman, Shein and Josef Zak, Ruchel Madaiski, Isaiah and Silva Wolman, Nechama's son, Eliahu Madaiski and his wife, Ruchel's son, Dr. Eliahu and Besia(Pesia or Vesia) Rutsteyn, a son of Chaia and Zelig Rutsteyn, Belel and Yehudit Kaplan, a son in law of the Rutsteyn's, Eliezer and Henia Rudnitski, a nephew of Riva Rudnitzki, Teibel and Motel Tzinman, Mania and Ahron yaffee, Binyamin and Sisi Yaffee, Ruchel and Aharon Yitzhak Malaravitch, Rivka and Pesach Rogov from Lita, Raizel Shapira from Ignalina, Bluma and Binyamin Schvabski from Lingmian and Yosef Sadur from Sventzian.

[Col. 1851]

In 1950, the work was delegated through the Israeli society by our friend, Hirsh Zar, to tie the two organizations together with our South African branch. A Gemulut Hesed (loans to help the needy) was founded to help the refugees rebuild their lives and homes in Eretz Israel. The branch set up in Johannesburg was aided by: Zelman and Keila Steingold, Zisla and Shimon Tabacavitch, Chaia Maida Kuritzki, Myron and Ezriel Goldberg, Leizer Swirski, Mania and Alter Azinski, the Katzkelevitch and Berzak families, Nisan Zar, Shimon Zar, Shaul Vilkomirski, and Shmuel Braverman.

I must underline, that the families with their children involved themselves with this relief work, even though they were born in South Africa and had no connection to the old home.

[Col. 1852]

In 1951, I arrived in Eretz Israel, and the Gemillut Hesed was founded, in memory of those who perished in Poligon.

Besides Hirsh Zar, others came to visit us in South Africa: Yitzhak and Mania Zak and Yehudit and Yacov Michelson. Their requests for help strengthened our involvement.

Of course we wanted to help more, but some had no ties to our former landsleit.

Zelig Rutsteyn was very involved and we must always remember him for his devotion and love for the cause. His death was a great loss for not only the landsleit in South Africa, but for all the Svenzianers all around the world.

[Col. 1853]

Zelig Rutsteyn loved everything about his roots from New – Sventzian, and he would give his life and soul for his home of his birth. A separate fund, in his honor, was established in the Gemilut Hesed by his South African friends, of which he was the founder and builder. With all that we possess, we will remember....

New – Sventzian in Cape Town

Sitting: Riva Rudnitzki, Yehudit Kaplan, Zelig, Chaia Rutsteyn, Ahron Yitzhak, Ruchel Malaravitch
Standing: Abraham, Mania Yaffee, Beni Yaffee, Charlie Kaplan, Josef, Sheina Zak, Teiba Rutsteyn – Tzinman, Motel Tzinman, Beni, Raizel Shapiro, Leib Yaffee

[Col. 1854]

A reunion with Yehudit and Yacov Michelson in Cape Town

Sitting: Sisi Yaffee, Mania Yaffee, Yehudit and Yacov Michelson, Chaia and Zelig Rutsteyn, Riva Rudnitski, Taibe Tzinman
Standing: Beni Yaffee, Abraham Yaffee, Sadur, Ahron Yitzhak and Rochel Malaravitch, Josef and Sheina Zak, Fruma Malaravitch, Motel Tzinman

[Col. 1853]

The Good Will of a Group

Heshel Gurewitz, Tel Aviv

Translated by Anita Frishman Gabbay

When we remember South Africa, we are talking about Johannesburg and Cape Town, we are talking about those Jews of South Africa who where originally from Lithuania. The ties actually begun in 1914, a short time before the outbreak of World War I.

Nechama, the oldest daughter of Ali and Riva Rudnitski, the well known baker with her loved cakes from New Sventzian bakery on Kaltinianer street, soon left our shtetl to join her relatives in South Africa. Meanwhile the war begun and immigration stopped.

After the war, the bad economic situation of our Jewish folk and the anti - Jewish politics encouraged more folk to leave their beloved shtetls and to immigrate overseas. At that time the entire Rudnitski family left New - Sventzian, old and young, together with all their in - laws and made their home in Cape Town, and created a "nest" where they welcomed later arrivals from New - Svenzian. Later more families arrived: Binyomin and Ahron Yaffee, and the Malaravitch and Tzinman (Zinman) families.

[Col. 1854]

This handful of Jews remained true to their old home and after the war they were ready to help the survivors with necessary help. After World War 11, a Relief Society was set up and packages were sent to the various lagers in Germany.

They joined forces with Eretz Israel's "Former Residents of Sventzian" to facilitate the help that was needed and received all the necessary addresses. The first immigrants to South Africa understood the need to lay the foundation of the Gemillut Hesed Bank, in order to provide the basic necessities of life for our survived brothers and sisters! Our group didn't wait long, as soon as we received the request, a committee was formed. This was formed in 1951, with a special memorial to those murdered in Poligon, which was named "Gemillut Hesed in Memory of our Perished Family in Poligon". Also, on the same note, our devoted and gentile member Zelig Rutsteyn, may his memory be blessed, should not be forgotten, the son in law of the Rudnitski family and a brother of Chana and Devorah Rutsteyn who were tragically murdered in Poligon, as well as the family of Mania Tzikinski – Yaffee.

[Col. 1855]

In Cape Town we survived to see another wonder: the Lithuanian family Rogov, became involved in our relief society and with great devotion and enthusiasm, with no ties to our Sventzianer region. Eventually we all were known as "Lithuanians".

It is amazing to see what a small handful from New – Sventzianers could achieve, if there is will and kindness.

We need to give thanks to our friends in Cape Town, and all the others from South Africa: the families Rudnitskis, Rutshteyn, Yaffes, Malaravitch, Tzinmans, Zaks, Altman, Kaplan, Mrs. Chaia Stein, who follows in her husband's footsteps with open arms to help the Sventzianer Jews.

[Col. 1855]

The Founding of the "Association of People from Sventzian" in Israel

Heshl Gurvitch

Translated by Janie Respitz

In September 1939 when Hitler began his military march into Poland, I saw it as the beginning of a march of destruction on 3 million Jews. In 1941 after the outbreak of the German–Soviet war, it was clear to me that it was not just Polish Jewry, but Lithuanian, White Russian and Russian Jews that were facing destruction. We did not yet know exactly what was happening. Only in 1942, when the papers began to write articles about sabotage and military diversion on the train line between Podbrodz – New–Sventzian, unrest began to grow and we began to worry about our families in those towns. We understood the Hitlerites would take revenge on the rebels and make the civilian population responsible, and the first scape goat will be the Jews.

Days, weeks and months passed and we began to receive horrific news about mass graves of Jews. The Jewish press began calling for protest gatherings. In 1943 I wrote me article "And us?" where I already felt the premonition of frightful mass murder which would take place in Poligon.

Then came the joyful Soviet victory in Stalingrad. Moscow radio was reporting daily on liberated cities and towns. Our hearts beating fast we listened carefully and flinched hearing the name of a familiar town. The liberation of our region began in 1944. Every day the extent of the destruction became clearer.

*

The Polish army under General Anders came to the Land of Israel and we learned about the suffering of Polish and Lithuanian Jews who escaped to Russia. Together with my comrade Shloime Velner, we approached the chairman of the workers in the Land of Israel, Meylekh Noyshtat, may his memory be a blessing, and asked him to organized aid for Jews who survived in Soviet Russia. Despite the material difficulties in the country, the workers' organization in the Land of Israel succeeded in collecting useful and important things, and send packages to the addresses we had. The British mandate authorities limited the size and value of the packages, but the Jewish workers at the post office and the port turned a blind eye and helped us smuggle out large and valuable packages. The names Kandinav and Aviezer Pedro must be mentioned here for their outstanding gentleness and kindness in this work. Such transports were sent on numerous occasions and many people were saved from hunger and death.

[Col. 1856]

*

After the First World War, Vilna and the surrounding area belonged to Poland. The whole region possessed a certain beauty, authentic traits that united us in Israel as well. We wanted to start an aid organization for Jews in that region that were saved from the great destruction. Having been an active worker with YEKAPO in Vilna, together with Khaim Kapeolvitch from Vilayke, the present chairman of the Vilna Farband (Labour Zionist Organization), began to organize the committee for Vilna province. With great difficulty, we were able to send out our first appeal in June 1945 for the Jews of Vilna and the surrounding region.

I succeeded in bringing Berl Yoel from Svir, chairman of the Svir Farband, and a few other Jews from Vilna province, to work with us. I was thinking of organizing the work on a broader front in order to encourage the survivors, to provide means for them to return to the equilibrium, material and spiritual, physical and psychological. But the Vilna committee showed a tendency to limit itself to elementary philanthropic aid. We made use of Reb Moishe Svirsky, of blessed memory who was a representative in the most important Jewish institutions in the country. Thanks to his efforts, packages for survivors were sent by the “Joint” through Teheran. Packages were sent this route for survivors in Sventzian, New– Sventzian, Ignalina, Svir and Kobylnik.

[Col. 1857]

Hirsh Zar

Dovid Kuritsky, of blessed memory

Avrom Rabinovitch, of blessed memory

Moishe Levinson, of blessed memory

[Col. 1858]

At this time we learned about the horrifying mass murders in Poligon and I decided we must begin broader relief work for the Jews in Sventzian region, whose fate was tied to the memory of their murdered relatives in the mass grave near New–Sventzian. Thanks to my dear friend Yitzkhak Broydes, of blessed memory, who was at the time secretary for the union of artisans in Tel Aviv, I received a hall to hold a meeting. A vote took place at that meeting. Those elected were: Reb Avrom Yitzkhak Rabinovitch, of blessed memory, Reb Dovid Kuritzky, of blessed memory, Reb. Moishe Levinson, of blessed memory, and long years to: Hirsh Zar, Avrom Kril, Leyb Pupisky, and the author of these lines. It was voted on and decided to carry out taxation. The money collected would go to sending packages to Jewish survivors in the Sventzian region. At the same time we widened our relief work in helping those Jews return to a normal life.

There were those who opposed sending packages as it was not sure they would arrive. I believed that even if some got lost, those that did arrive would greatly help lift the spirits of those Jews and give them the feeling they are not alone.

Soon immigrants began to arrive who told us how meaningful the packages were, both for material needs and morale. These packages also helped rescue a Jewish child from Christians. I would like to mention the help we received from friends and comrades in Cape Town, South Africa. I contacted them when I began the relief effort sending packages to Russia. Sventzian Jews in Africa responded to my requests with warmth.

Leyb Pupisky

Avrom Kril

Heshl Gurvitch

[Col. 1859]

Jewish survivors were wandering through the cities and towns of Poland, until they arrived in D.P camps in the Germany where they were supported by the "Joint". Our job was weakened. The gates to the country were locked. The Jews fought hard to open the doors to immigrants.

Together with our hard work we decided we had to eternalize the memory of the martyrs of Poligon, those who died in the Ghettos and the heroes who fought with the partisans and on the front. Sender Kovarsky from Sventzian came to mc and suggested we do something to remember the heroic battles fought by Jewish youth from our region, and were not mentioned in the Vilna books. We decided to start a separated group that would include everyone from around Sventzian. After much effort, a new association was founded whose main goal was:

To eternalize the martyrs from our region; and to create an interest free loan fund.

We had to begin to collect material for a memorial book which was to include all the Jewish towns of the Sventzian region.

We approached our friends in South Africa. We delegated Hirsh Zar to explain the importance of these goals.

In 1951 Mania Tzikinsky – Yaffa came from there to Israel. She was helpful in setting up the free loan called: The Martyrs of Poligon. Thanks to Yitzkhak and Mania Zak and Yehudit and Yakov Mikhalson who travelled to South Africa. Their visit helped to encourage donations, and the fund was started with 1,000 Israeli pounds. It was harder to convince the Sventzian committee in New York, but they too began to send aid.

My experience in communal work during the First World War taught me we should accept material help people give on the spot. We received our first large donation from the estate of our friend Sholem Berman, of blessed memory, who passed away, thanks to his cousin Yekhiel Berman, who passed up his portion of the inheritance for our free loan fund of our association. We also began to create endowment funds. Thanks to initiative of Moishe Mikhalson a yearly membership fee was proclaimed. We also held a special meeting for the fund and were pleased at the warm response to our appeal. Confidence in our organization was growing. People were leaving sums in their wills.

[Col. 1860]

We are witnesses of deep human relationships which should be mentioned. I would like to stress the devotion of Mrs. Yehudit Mikhalson who donated large sums and encouraged others to do the same.

On her deathbed, Mrs. Rokhl Svirsky – Khankhovitch asked her husband to donated 500 Israeli pounds to the fund. Mrs. Menukha Yisraelovitch brought 500 Israeli pounds and said: “I'll give more!” Mrs. Fanny Fisher gave 500 Israeli pounds and exclaimed: “When I get compensation from my children, I'll bring you the money”. Shmuel Gurvitch – Ben – Zerach donated 500 Israeli pounds in honour of his wife. I knew his situation and tried to talk him out of it. He told me: “You must take the money!”

There were many other examples of lesser and greater sums. Everyone understood the importance of our work.

Yakov Mikhalson of blessed memory – member of the board of directors

With veneration and honour I would like to mention Mr. Harry Beker from America. A Jew in his eighties, with a sick wife, he ran to the American committee of Jews from Sventzian, and donated the largest amount to our fund than any other in America. With admiration I would like to mention the heartfelt relationship with Bezalel Levinson, of blessed memory, Yisroel Soroka, of blessed memory, and may many more years be granted to: Harry Shneider, Izinsky, Mrs. Dr. Minkin, Bronia Khasid.

It was more difficult to get people to realize the importance of our work on the memorial book. We did not get discouraged and continued our efforts. Right after our association was founded, with the help of the lawyer Yisroel Gurvitch, you worked closely with the well–known historian Yakov Lechinsky, and a questionnaire was distributed. Each member of the association had to answer.

[Col. 1861]

It was hard to get people to write. Many of the people were not used to holding a pen in hand. It was hard for them to find the words to describe the pain in their hearts. Yisroel Gurvitch would not give up. He went to visit the people, invited some to come to him, spoke with them and wrote their stories.

Finally material was collected about towns. With much effort the material was reworked, but we were still lacking the professional hand to construct the book. We were lacking an editor, and more importantly, we were lacking the money needed to publish the book. When the approached the office of Yad VaShem in Tel Aviv, they wondered how we could take on such a large project without money. They told us we would never succeed in publishing such a book.

Understandably, this was not encouraging. All sides were telling us to not to cover so many towns. Our hearts were hurting: You will eternalize all these poor towns? If we would not do it, who will do this holy work? We could not forget about it and we continued step by step.

Time was flying by. The more time passes; more and more material is collected. The content is becoming richer and so are we thanks to due paid by our members and donations from guests from abroad. We finally decided to contact the editor Shimon Kantz, and the work of compiling and editing was progressing. According to his instructions, missing material was found and the book finally began to be published.

[Col. 1862]

If the free loan fund was mainly supported by friends from abroad, the memorial book, this huge historical work, the tombstone for the murdered from the region of Sventzian, was published as a result of devotion of our friends in Israel.

I would like to thank our friend Shimon Bushkanietz for his dedication in collecting material about Sventzian; Sender Kavarsky for his enrichment of the portion on heroism, struggle and uprising.

Thank you to Avrom Kril, Yitzkhok Viduchinsky, and Ruven Muler, for helping to collect material about Ignalina and Dugelishok; Leyb Pupisky and Yisroel Gurvitch, of blessed memory, for New- Sventzian; Mikhal Patashnik, Zalman Abel, Rafael Yaffa for Haydutzishok; Zvi Zar for Lingmian.

Thanks to all our friends who wrote and collected documents and memoirs, and di everything they could to enrich our memorial book.

Let us express our gratitude to the lawyer Yisroel Gurvitch, of blessed memory, who laid the foundation for this book.

Thanks you to Dr. Henekh Drutsh for supplementing various materials. Thanks to Leyb Pupisky for his detailed map: Destruction. And for continuing for 20 years to serve our committee with council.

Special thanks go to Mr. Shakhneh Tzeplovitch – Achiasaf for helping us with his professional advice and warm relationship to our work.

Thank you to Moishe Mikhalson and Aharon Svirsky, Berl Kharmatz and Berl Zak, and Yitzkhak Gurvitch for their friendly respect they showed toward our work.

Board of Directors in 1959

Standing: **Berl Kharmatz, Moishe Mikhlson, Aharon Svirsky, Zakman Abel, Sender Kovarsky**
Seated: **Shimon Bushkanietz, Mikhal Patashnik, Heshl Gurvitch, Hirsh Zar**

[Col. 1863]

The Committee of the Organization of Jews from Sventzian in Israel 1965

We thank our American friends: Bronia Khasid, Freda Fradkin, Guterman, Harry Beker, Beygel, Kharmatz and Rabbi Ushpol, the president Harry Shneider – for their help for this book.

Allow me to express my gratitude to my wife Nekhama for her devotion in helping me overcome all the difficulties in my many years of work on this memorial book which a look at as a tombstone over the large mass grave in Poligon.

Of course there will be those who will come with complaints and criticism of omissions and mistakes. There is no light that does not cast a shadow. But we must be aware of great difficulties we faced on the road to publishing such a large undertaking. We began with a small building that grew into a large palace. This is the satisfaction for our efforts. We thank the publishing house "Ha Merkaz" and their staff for their guarded loyal work. Elkhanan Toker and Zve Shamri, the son–in–law of Khaim Zelig Lukner from Sventzian for their friendly realtions.

Let it be noted here:

When the Jewish National Fund began its program of planting six million trees on the Judean Mountains, we, the Jews from Sventzian and vicinity joined the program and planted 1200 trees with the inscription: Sventzian and Vicinity.

Mikhal Patashnik at the erection of a memorial plaque on Mt. Zion in Jerusalem

[Col. 1865]

The trees were planted by the Israeli relatives of the martyrs.

*

In the Chamber of the Holocaust on Mt. Zion in Jerusalem, together with the bloodied, torn Torah scrolls, the soap made from Jewish corpses, and the tens of other objects from that horrific time, stand memorial plaques from all the destroyed Jewish communities. We, the Jews from Sventzian and vicinity, were among the first to place such a plaque.

*

This is the work we did to eternalize the memory of the martyrs from our region, a memorial for the mass grave in Poligon.

I have been involved in this work for twenty years. I would like to personally thank all our friends in Israel, Africa, America and the whole world for the help and trust they bestowed on me. Without them, this work about life and destruction of the Sventzian region would not have come to be.

My request to you, our friends throughout the world is:

"Continue not to forget our martyrs!"

[Col. 1866]

Shmuel Gurvitch – Ben– Zerach at the plaque in the Chamber of the Holocaust

Forest of the Martyrs in the Forest of the Millions in the Judean Mountains

Standing: **Greenblat Anna, Nekhama Gurvitch, Shoshana Volatzky, Shifra Yaffa, Rafael Yaffa, Leyb Pupisky, Dovid Katz, Kayla Milner, Shifra Kovarsky, Moishe Abel**
Kneeling: **Sender Kovarsky, Zalman Abel**

[Col. 1867]

The Man from Sventzian in Argentina

Heshl Gurvitch

Translated by Janie Respitz

Yakov Murmis

When the historian Ginzburg wrote about Leon Bak from Sventzian he characteristically referred to the Jews from Sventzian as: intellectuals.

The Sventzian intellectuals are spread out throughout the world, and are clearly defined by their heartfelt Jewish folksiness and an attachment to the region they were born. One of these is Yakov Murmis, who from 1917 until today, lives in Argentina. He is one of the lucky ones who managed to bring his family there as well. Yakov Murmis brought his whole family to Argentina, his brothers: Zalman, Dovid and Yosef, his sisters: Sofia, Riva and Temeh. His mother died of old age in Buenos Aires.

Yakov Murmis arrived in Argentina young and full of hope, facing lots of opportunity. However it was not easy for him to adjust to the new way of life. He had all the lovely traits of the simple, modest Sventzian Jew, but thanks to his energy and initiative he was able to overcome the hardships and conquer material and spiritual obstacles. A source of courage for him was his dear life's partner Bazilia, who came from Russia. The joy of family life was the basis for his future endeavors.

Yakov Murmis became involved in a variety of communal organizations. He was active in the biggest and most important Jewish institutions in Argentina. He was active in the Joint from its first years, and became president. He was active in the League Against

Tuberculosis, and the Russian - Yiddish library. He served as vice-president of the hundred year old institution - The Jewish Congregation, and treasurer of B'nai B'rith. There was not one Israeli organization he did not work with.

[Col. 1868]

This is the life of Yakov Murmis. Born in Jewishness, raised in honesty. This is how he raised his children. His son Oscar served as a deputy in the Argentinian parliament. His second son, Miguel is a professor at a university in Buenos Aires.

It was a great joy for me to meet him in Israel after not seeing each other for 57 years. I remembered going to school together in Sventzian. Years changed his appearance and characteristics that I remembered, but his smile remained the same. He spoke about the heartfelt warmth he absorbed from his hometown, and carried with him over great distances over many years. His hair is grey, but Yakov Murmis is still running the marathon, with an inextinguishable flame in his heart, which gives us much confidence, that as chairman of the Sventzian Society in Argentina he will continue to offer solidarity and help. Help in eternalizing the memory of the martyrs from our towns.

Our representatives in Toronto, Canada are: Mary Gilinsky and Meir Blitz. In Colombia, Cali: Yitzkhak Gilinsky. In Barankville: Yakov Gantovnik.

Meir Blitz

Yakov Gatovnik

[Col. 1869]

He Deserves Our Thanks

Aviezer Pedro

Translated by Meir Razy

Mr. Yehoshua Gurevich appeared at my workshop for some business one morning. My eyes lit up and I spontaneously embraced him. It was as if I had met with a good angel who had come from a world that was very different from this world. This very feeling often made me want to pick up a pen and try writing about the days of the Holocaust when I worked in the post office in Tel Aviv.

I remember those days when I was a clerk in the package section of the Tel Aviv post office. I noticed Mr. Gurevitz many times among the people standing in line. As with unusual patience, he would wait for his turn. All of Mr. Gurevich's packages were sent to Russia. After many days I dared to ask him if he had a business of sending packages to Russia. To my surprise I learned that he was doing all the work as a volunteer and had devoted a great deal of time searching for the remaining Jews who had fled from Lithuania to Russia. He felt as if each package would save an entire family that would come to Israel and build the country and continue the tradition of the family lost in the European Holocaust.

I remember how the humble Mr. Gurevich showing me one of the packages and saying to me: “I received this address last night from acquaintances and I believe that I am saving an entire family and that a day will come when they will build their home here”.

Translated by Janie Respitz

[Col. 1870]

He believed that his parcels contained not only food and clothing, but also gave hope and belief that there were other Jews in the world who were making efforts to bring these recipients to Israel, to settle and thrive in the Land of Israel.

Sometimes I wonder if Mr. Gurevitz's natural modesty and humility was too restricting. If he or other institutions had published his activities, then more people might have joined forces to rescue Jews in various ways, hundreds and thousands of Jews.

Even today, when Mr. Gurevitch is busy with his work and everyday worries, he continues to provide help and does not limit his involvement and time in helping survivors.

Drama club in Sventzian directed by Borukh Rozental

Standing: **Yitzkhak Ogulayk, Leah Shutan, Goldman, Shmuel Vidushinsky, Freda Gurvitch**
Seated: **Zalman Eidelman, Mereh Kovner, Borukh Rozental, Klara Markelevitch**
The child: **Leyzer Levin**

This photograph is an addition to the portion entitled "Sventzian" This is a group from the Sventzian drama club, led by Borukh Rozental. He was an old school activist in the Poalei Zion, but remained non–partisan in the drama club. The main goal was to bring art, joy and elevation to the Jewish population in Sventzian. Under the leadership of Borukh Rozental the drama club pursued this goal with respect and the performances, prepared with great effort and love for Yiddish culture, were on a high level and very successful. This is thanks to the initiative, devotion and intelligence of Borukh Rozental.

The Institutions of the community must thank Mr. Gurevitch for all his actions and praise his work. Let us wish him that the rest of his life, for many years to come, may be healthy and that he will take pleasure in the success of all the people he helped save. He was their stronghold and source of encouragement and hope during their great tribulation.

[Col. 1871-1872]

A Reunion of Sventzianers in Tel-Aviv, Oct. 9, 1960

Sitting: **Heshl Gurwitch, Nechama Tzinman, Rochel Levin, Dovid Levin, Raizel Umbros, Sheina Kovarski-Shpigel, Chaia Rudnitzki-Levin, Yacov Tabakhovitch, Yacov Michelson, Yehudit Michelson, Chaia Zak**

Standing: **Rivkah Levin, Dovid Katz, Fani Fisher, Genia Kovarski, Israel Gurwich, Nechama Gurwich, Raizel Landsman, Rochel Katz, Shifra Kovarski, Henech Kovarski, Klara Yavitch, Freida Rudnitzki, Devorah Zak, Tzila Kisberg**

Standing: **Sholem Katz, Shimon Gendel, Miriam Shutan, Shloime Sneider, Fruma Rozofski, Moishe Tzinman, Henech Kovarski, Ruth Katz, Mule Troitze, Vera Troitze, Levi Zak, Michel Shutan, Nisen Las, Meir Ligumski, Yehuda Ligumski, Dedalihu Zak, Berl Tzinman, Berl Zak, Yitzhak Shutan, Binjamin Ligumski, Hillel Zak, Yitzhak Gurwich, Ruben Abelavitch**

A Reunion of Jews from Ignalina and Daugelishok, Tel–Aviv, Oct. 9, 1960

Sitting: **Natan Shapira,—, Laizerovitch, Doba Kreitzer, Eliezer Shapira, Ruben Muler, Ela Soleiveitchik, Fani Fisher, Chana Leia Elperin, —, Shneider**
Standing: **Levitan, Leib Korb, Moishe Korb, Eliezer Levitan, Shmuel Segal, Yitzhak Vidushinsky, Ester Vidushinsky, Yitzhak Segal, Gitel Brumberg, Velvel Kril, Mina Muler, Heshl Gurwitz, Elihu Gilinski, Simcha Dubinski, Shmuel Gilinski, Aharon Gilinski**

[Col. 1873-1874]

Reunion in Haifa: Podbrodz, Kimelishak, Bistritz

Below: **Zav Ber–Chana, Baruch Blushinski, Rivka Blushinski, Yehudit Feler, Sara–Leia (Rifkind), Ben–Zion Lapp**
2nd row: **Ahron Bavarski (Sharnovitch), Ben–Zion Vilian, Sara Ring, Golda Shapira, Boruch Shapira**
3rd row: **Devorah Feler, Miriam Shapira–Shank, Esther Flexer (Rifkind), Grunia Potashnik (Orman), Sara Kirchon (Bavarski), Basia Lapp, Elihu Gordon, Velvel Abramovitch, Chana Zilber**
4th row: **Zvi Mirski,—,—, Sura (Reitenberg),Shaul Lapp, Elihu Licht,—, (Fisher), Boruch Naratzki (Lofer),—,Shmuel Krol, Henia Shapira**

Reunion of Sventzianer in Tel–Aviv, Oct. 9, 1960

Sitting right to left: **Shalom Katz, Chaia Rudnitzki–Oenstein, Zenia Zaretzki–Gurwitch, Rochel Pres–Kovarski, Sheina Kovarski–Ulpan, Ester feigel–Kuritzki, Gershon Kuritzki, Basia Luria–Mirinov, Chana Gurwitch, Shmuel Gurwich–Ben–Zerach, Shachne Levin, Dovid Tzepelevitch, Dr. Moishe Kuritzki**

2nd row: **Shalom Kuritzki, Mordechai Zeidel, Ben–Zion Bak, Elihu Kovarski, Yacov Michelson, Heshl Gurwich, Yitzhak Shibavski, Chana Rabotnik–Shlanski, Rochel Cohen–Svirski, Miriam Rosenberg, Sender Kovarski**

3rd row: **Leia Kovarski, Yosi Bushkanetz, Golda Feigel–Bushkanetz, Moishe Ginsberg, Chia Bushkanetz–Ginsberg, Pesia Kurlandtshik–Shapira, Etel Shibovski–Vilenski, Yocheved Bushkanetz–Ben–Zirach, Libe Gurwich–Konopinski, Chana Goldberg–Kovarski, Rosenberg LaiaSvirski–Koltzman (Holtzman)**

4th row: standing: **Elihu Bikson, Sara Katz, Teme Michelson–Shutan, Dora Kisberg, Liba Zar, Elke Goldberg, Rivka Teitz, Teiba Ovtzinski, PesiaTeitz–Koniak, Henia Gurwitch, Leizer Levin, Shifra Leifer–Korb, Rivka Katcherginski, Basia Katcherginski–Etzmon, Ester Lukner–Tzripruni, Leia Garshein, Chaim Charmatz, Shoshana Lukner–Shmri, YehuditKuritzki–Margalit, Ber Charmatz**

Standing last: **Moishe Shutan, Yitzhak Rudnitzki–Arch?, Israel Pliner, Yeshahu Volfson, Rivka Kovarski,– Vaintroib, Abraham Matzkin, Ester Shutan, Yeshaihu Rutshtein, Dov Lishanski, Menachem Kotler–Haloi, Shloime Charmatz**

[Col. 1875-1876]

20 years of the Yiddish Folk–Shul of New Sventzian in 1936

Sitting: **Baler Yocheved, Dr. S. Kapelovitch, Epstein Rosa, Gordus Yitzhak, Guterman Chaia, Epstein Chaim, Levenstein Feige**
Standing: **Katz Lipman, Zak Lipman, Elperin Moishe, Elperin mania, Gordon Leizer, Kavarski Esther, Abelevitch Boruch, Katcherginski Isher**
Standing: **Boler M, Rutstein Chana, Boyarstein Aharon, Levenstein Hirsh**

Date unclear 1907 or 1917
Halutz

[Col. 1877-1878]

The artists Soreh Gorshin, Rivka Volovitch - Ben - Sirah and Yehoshua Heshl Kovarsky were born in Sventzian and their works eternalized their hometown in the old traditional way and its decline. The paintings of the well–known artist Heshl Kovarsky can be found in museums in America and in private collections. One of his famous paintings belongs to a member of our book committee Sh. Akhiasaf. The beauty of the life in his hometown of New– Sventzian had a great influence on the artist and he eternalized it with his paint brush. He spun the motifs of life in the Svntzian region in his series of paintings entitled "World Creation". The sculptor Soreh Garshin was born in Sventzian. She survived Hitler's death camps and sculpted the woman's head right after liberation. The motif of Jewish continuity repeats itself in many of her works. The drawings of the original artist Rivka Volovitch - Ben–Sirah, born in Kaltinian, are penetrated by the horrors of the Holocaust. Her exhibitions in Israel were widely visited and opened up hearts and provided a source of tears for the incomparable destruction that befell our region.

...after Liberation
Sara Garshein–Teitz

In times of sorrow
Rivka Volavitch–Ben–Zerach

[Col. 1879-1880]

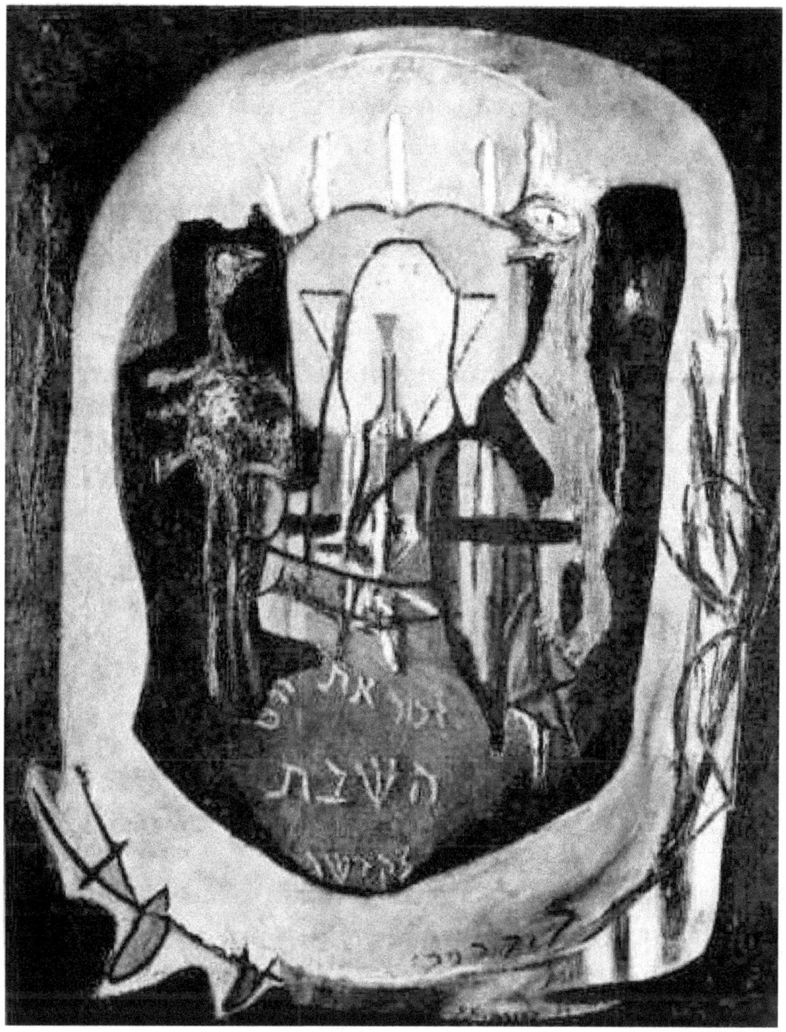

Shabbos in the shtetl
Yehoushe Kovarski

[Col. 1881-1882]

Upon completion of this memorial book we received the sad news about their deaths.

Dr. Hanoch Drutz–Svirony z"l

Translated by Meir Razy

Dr. Hanoch Svirony, the cultural coordinator of the Histadrut (=The Workers' Union) in Ra'anana, died on Thursday at the Beilinson Hospital at the age of 56.

A native of the town of Svir in Poland, he was educated at the Hebrew Gymnasium in Vilnius (Vilna). He completed his journalism studies at the University of Berlin in 1933 and worked as a reporter for the "Die Zeit" newspaper, published in Vilna. in addition, he also wrote for Hebrew periodicals that were published in Kovno, Lithuania.

He immigrated to Eretz Israel in October 1933 and was a reporter for Yiddish newspapers published abroad. In 1938 he went to Basel, studied philosophy and history in the university and earned a PhD. Upon his return to Eretz Israel he became a teacher of literature and history in high schools until about seven years ago.

Noble and humble was Svirony and the sense of inner nobility left its mark on his entire being, on his professional and public work, for he was energetic and had a will to carry out what he had taken upon himself. He showed the same devotion in editing the memorial book of the community of Svir, his hometown. He also worked, with great skill and sensitivity, on the preparation of the memorial book of the Sventzian region.

A mortal illness suddenly overwhelmed him and most untimely terminated his life and all his educational, cultural, and public works.

Reb Moishe Svirsky of blessed memory

Translated by Janie Respitz

On February 3, 1965 (the first day of Adar 5725) Reb Moishe Svirsky, of blessed memory, passed away in Tel Aviv. Under the influence of the movement "Narodnaya Volya" (the People's Will), Reb Moishe Svirsky left his home in Sventzian and came to Vilna with the intention of joining the folk and working towards the idea which was later called: Socialist Revolutionaries. This is how he arrived at Zionism as the first thing one must do to free the people, as a Jew would be to free the oppressed Jewish nation. This can be how Zionism came about.

In Vilna, Svirsky joined the group "Ha Tchiya" (The Resurrection) and devoted himself to the Zionist movement. In 1924 he immigrated to the Land of Israel.

Yosef Brumberg, of blessed memory

Translated by Janie Respitz

Yosef Brumberg, of blessed memory died suddenly on January 2, 1965 in Philadelphia.

Yosef Brumberg returned from Russia after the First World War and settled in Sventzian where his family lived.

Yosef Brumberg was influenced by socialist thought (active in the Bund). He did not give up when the Poles occupied Sventzian region, and the minority rights of the Jews were secured under the Treaty of Versailles. Yosef Brumberg became involved in cultural activities in Sventzian, reinforcing the existence of the Yiddish school and one of the founders of the Yiddish language high school.

[Col. 1882]

Yosef Brumberg was forced to leave Poland. With the help of Nosn Kovarsky and Dr. Klumel, he immigrated to the Land of Israel in 1926. The situation in the land was difficult due to unemployment, and lack of opportunity to earn a living. I met Yosef Brumberg leaving his work pulling up stones. He said: "Talking about workers is easier than being a labourer. Talking about workers' problems is easier than reading about them."

He returned to Poland in 1929 and became the director of the Medem Sanatorium for children outside of Warsaw. When Hitler invaded Poland, he ran with his wife Lola and their son to Vilna. Thanks to the American Workers Committee, he left Vilna for America with his family and worked for the Workers Committee in Chicago.

His quest did not end there. He studied and explored. Yosef Brumberg was never happy, more and more culture, never satiated with culture, education and knowledge. Yosef Brumberg participated in this memorial book with an article about his cultural work in Sventzian.

Itzkhak Porus of blessed memory

News arrived from America: Itzkhak Parus died in a horrible accident on December 20th, 1964 in New Zealand at the thriving age of 40. At a very young age, Yitzkahk Porus joined the Partisans which was organized in 1943, by with Yitzkhak Rudnitsky, Ishikeh

Gertman and others in the Naratch forest. As a partisan he fought against Hitler's beasts. After liberation, together with his girlfriend Liza, also a partisan, he left Sventzian and wandered with difficulty until they reached his relatives in New Zealand.

[Col. 1883]

God shall remember
The souls of the martyrs from VIDZ

Translated by Meir Razy

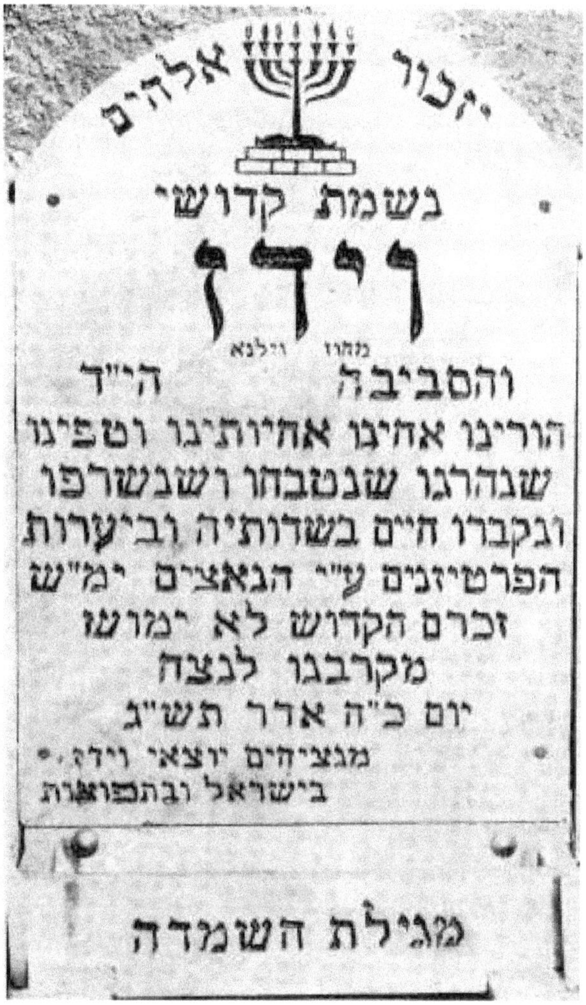

God shall remember
The souls of the martyrs from

VIDZ

In the Vilnius district
And it surrounding area, God shall avenge the blood of
Our parents, our brothers, our sisters and our children
Who were killed, were slaughtered and were burned,
And were buried alive in the fields and forests of the
Partisans by the Cursed Nazis!

Their holy memory will not be forgotten
From among us forever
The 25th of Adar 5703

The Commemorators of the Jews of Vidz
In Israel and the Diaspora

The Scroll of Extermination
The gravestone in the Holocaust Memorial Basement - Mount Zion, Jerusalem

Names of those who died over time:

Gandel Chaya	Farber Batia	Kocher (Kutcher) Yoseph
Gandel Beinush	Kacherginsky Mordechai	Kamrez Yoseph
Reiner Yaakov	Kacherginsky Moshe	Katz Rivka
Reiner Slawa	Strobin Yoseph	Katz Tzadok
Weiner Chaya	Fishman Zilberman Sheina	Pinchov Kalman
Farber Shmuel	Fishman Israel	Dubinsky Shmuel
Farber Dan	Zilberman Bracha	Barishnikov

[Col. 1887]

Those Remembered...

Heshl Gurvitch

Translated by Janie Respitz

It was difficult, immensely difficult to collect and collate the material about this huge tragedy, the incomparable destruction that befell the Jews of our region.

In this region Jews lived from the beginning days and like all others on that land, were deeply rooted there. They planted the seeds of bread and were nourished every day of their lives.

The land in the Sventzian region was always still, but the Jews living there were always restless, living in two spheres: the outside material world and the inner spiritual world, of a pure human intellect and an undying Godlike soul, which was the true purpose of life.

This is what we wanted to portray in this memorial book, to show the world what was annihilated in the hellish fires of the biggest satanic extermination of all time.

This was a past Jewish world of holiness and bravery, which was uplifting even in the days of the horrific destruction, and has no comparison in all of human history thereby making it really unbelievable.

Here is a list of the names of the thousands who Hitler's Lithuanian murderers threw into graves, not quite killed, still alive. Those whose blood will never stop screaming and demanding:

Revenge should be great for the innocent spilled Jewish blood!

The large cemetery of their names will as their holiness and bravery remain engraved in our memory forever!

Note: The names were collected by the representatives of the town. The editor is not responsible for misspelled or missing names.

[Col. 1885]

Remember...

[Columns 1889-1902]

Svencionys Necrology

(Švenčionys, Lithuania)

55°09' 26°10'

Transliterated and Donated by Steven Weiss z"l

Surname	**Family members**
א Alef	
ABRAMSON	Aba Lazer, wife: Recha Reyzle, son: Shlomo Itzchak
ABRAMSON	Sabbatai, wife: Sarah (Tsefelvitz)
ABRAMSON	Israel, wife: Bella, daughter: Hilah (Weiner)
ABRAMOVITZ	Zesne, son: Yosef
OGILNIK	Itzchak, wife: Ida, children: Esther, Sarah 3
UMVRATZ	Leah
USHPOL	(Harav) Shlomo Eliehu, wife: Chaiya Rechel, daughters: Bayta, Etta,Myra, Dinah
USHPOL	Mordechai, wife: Shifrah and children
USHPOL-ZAYGER	Chana and children
OVITZINSKY	Leah
OZINSKY	Avraham, wife: Etta Leah
OZINSKY	Berah Moshe, wife: Henya
EINHORN-KATZ	Etel, daughter: Livba
EDELMAN	Zalmen, wife: Rivka, children: Shimon, Moshe
ESTHER	Moshe Binyamin, wife: Chana, children: Ephraim, Gilda
ESTHER	Tenachum, wife & child: Baruch
OPESKIN	Yosef, wife: Batya Malcha, children: Chanan, Mordechai, Recha Feyga, Chana, Freydel, Israel
AIKEN	Avraham, wife: Rechel (Shutan), child: Leiba
AIKEN	Moshe, wife & children: Sarah, Zelda, Lazer, Etel

AIKEN	Sinder, wife: Mariah, children: Moshe, Meyna
AIKEN	Chalvina, wife: Sonya, son: Saul
AIKEN	Aflikant, wife and child
AKERMAN	Yovel, wife
ASHVARISHITZ	Akiva, wife: Shifra

ב Bet

BASIS	Alter Hilel, wife: Sheyna Sarah, children: Meyna, Chaya, Israel
BASIS	Shmuel Noteh, wife: Chaya Leah, children: Moshe, Chana, Blumah,Feygah, Heynda, Yichael
BOCK	David, wife: Chana, children: Chayim, Zovel, Feya + 2
BOCK	Yosef, wife: Chaya, son: Mordechai
BOCK	Itzchak, wife: Rivka, children: Gershon, Gita
BOCK	Leib, wife: Meyna
BOCK	Mordechai, wife: Reyzel
BOCK	Pesach, wife and 4 children
BOCK	Rivkah (Kavarsky), children: Feyga, Mordechai
BARON	Shochat, wife: Gilda (Goldis), and children
BARON	Shmuel, wife Bryna (Gurvitz), child: Masha
BOSHKANITZ	Mendel, wife: Riva, son: Shalom, Shimon
BOSHKANITZ	Shmuel Volf, wife: Nachma, 2 children and grandmother
BOSHKANITZ	Heynda, children: Avraham, Shrivka, Slava
BOSHKANITZ	Shalom, wife: Gitel, child: Pesah
BOSHKANITZ	Moshe Hirash, wife: Rechel, daughters: Chana, Sheyna, Meyna, Grunia
BOSHKANITZ	Shmuel, wife: Sheyna, sons: David, Naftali
BOSHKANITZ	Aaron, wife: Sonya (Levin), child: Bati
BAYGLE	Avraham, wife and child
BAYGLE	Etta Sima
BAYGLE	Yehudi, wife and children
BAYGLE	Yosef, wife: Triza, child: Leiba
BAYGLE	Yaakov, wife: Leiba and children

BAYGLE	Itzchak, Zalmen, wife: Tayva, daughter: Leah
BAYGLE	Tsipa, and children (Bengas)
BAYGLE	Reyzel, and children (Bengas)
BILKAVITZ	Itzchak wife: Michel, children: Ayzik, Aaron, Sarah (grandmother)
BILKAVITZ	Moshe, wife: Heyne, children: Rechel, Yehudi,
BINDER	Emanuel, wife: Kreyna, son: Eliezer
BIKAVITZ	Avraham, wife and children
BIKAVITZ	Bunim, wife: Leah, daughter: Busya
BIKAVITZ	Hirash, wife: Sarah and children
BIKSON	Zalmen, wife: Masha, daughters: Reyza, Dreyza
BIKSON	Tsipa
BAYLEN	Avraham, wife: Rechel, daughter: Sima
BAYLEN	Dvora, mother Esther and child
BLOCH	Reyzel
BLEIKMAN	Zalmen, wife: Bluma
BLEIKMAN	Chaim, and sister Bunya
BLEIKMAN	Meyna (Shutan) , daughters: Yochvad, Myra, Sarah
BLEAKER	Alter, wife: Esther, sons: Chaim, Feyvish, Hirash
BECKER	Shmirel
BERLIN	Moshe Mendel, wife: Gneydel, children: Leah, Moshe, Heyne, Sarah, Dvora, Itzchak
BRUDNE	Aaron, wife and child
BRUDNE	Grisha, wife: Reya and children
BRUDNE	Moshe Itzchak, wife: Teyva
BROYDA	Chana Teyva
BROYDA	Rocha Etta and children
BRUMAN	Moshe Chaim, wife: Chaya, daughter: Chana
BRUMAN	Shimon, wife: Mosse and children
BRUMBERG	Avraha, wife: Malcha
BRUMBERG	Boris, wife: Fanya, children: David, Yulia

BRUMBERG	Moshe Itzchak, wife: Sarah, children: Rivka, Beryl, Yehudit, Herschel
BRUMBERG	Recha Leah
BRUMBERG	Shimshon, wife: Esther, children: Clara, David, Fruma, Aaron
BRECHER	Saul, wife: Reyzle, children: Gedlihu + 6
BREZGIN	Sonya
BRENNER	Mordechai, wife: Sarah Myra (Gilinsky) and child
BRESLER	Gutman, wife: Leah, children: Sarah, Shlomo

ג Gimmel

GOVISER	David, wife: Fruma, children: Rechel, Dav, Nachum
GOVISER	Mordechai, wife: Malcha (Weinstein), child: Shmuel
GOVIND	Shlomo, wife: Ziva (Druts) and children
GOLDSTEIN	Chayne, children: Eliehu, Feyga
GOLDBERG	Etel
GOLDBERG	Pesach, wife: Elke, daughter: Stira
GOLDIS	Dav, wife: Golda, daughter: Chaya
GOLDIS	Chaim, wife: Zshenye, children: Yosef, Sarah
GOLDIS	Moshe, wife--children: Zelda, Mordechai
GOLDMAN	Eli Moshe, wife: Gitel
GOLDMAN	Itzchak, wife: Chaya, daughters: Chana, Golda
GOLUBAK	Aba, wife: Rechel (Levin), child: Leiba
GANTOVINIK	Yaakok, wife: Sheyna, and children
GOPSTEIN	Chaim, wife: Chana and Motel
GOPSTEIN	Golda
GORBATZKI	Feyvel, wife and child
GORBATZKI	Yerachmel, wife: Milcha, children: Sheyna, Batya and noch 4
GERBER	Esther
GERBER	Reuben, wife: Sheyna, daughters: Rivka, Chene, Elke, Esther, Yehudit
GERBER	Rechel and mother
GORDON	Avraham Ben-Zion, wife: Sarah, son: Leib
GORDON	Aba Shlomo, wife and 5 children

GORDON	Eliehu, wife: Bat-Sheva, children: Beryl, Yerachmel, Raphael, Pesya + 2
GORDON	Gershon, wife: Alta, children: Hirash, Tsipa, Ezriel
GORDON	Dov, wife: Cheyne, children: Yenta, Sarah
GORDON	Cheykel, wife: Etel, children: Zorach, Avraham, Itzchak, Henye
GORDON	Chaim Leib, wife: Radel (Seitel) and children
GORDON	Yosef, wife: Dora (Libisky) and children
GORDON	Yaakov, wife and children
GORDON	Itzchak, wife-- son: Godlia, Moshe
GORDON	Yeshehu, and wife
GORDON	Lazer, wife: Yehudit (Ginzburg)
GORDON	Mendel, wife and sons: Hirash, Zundel, Zalmen
GORDON	Moshe, wife: Batya and son
GORDON	Nachum, wife: Chaya Etel (Levenson), daughters: Miriam, Esther
GORDON	Nachma
GORDON	Akiva, wife: Esther, children: Chaya, Shmuel
GORDON	Pinkas, wife and four children
GORDON	Fruma Chaya, sons: Shimon, Shmuel
GORDON	Shimon, wife and daughter
GORDONSON	Moshe, wife: Dova, children: Yosef, Nachma, Yehudit
GUTERMAN	Moshe Leib
GUTERMAN	Shlomo, wife: Leiba, children: Chanan, Mordechai,Myra
GURVITZ	Uri Chaim and wife
GURVITZ	Alter, wife: Zeyla, daughters: Chasya, Gitel
GURVITZ	Benny, wife: Chaya, sons: Zorach, Yeshika, Yaakov
GURVITZ	Gershon, wife: Sarah
GURVITZ	David, wife: Feyga, children: Avraham, Rechel
GURVITZ	Heschel, wife: Frieda, children: Mendel, Shalom, Moshe, Rechel, Leah
GURVITZ	Hirash, wife and 4 children
GURVITZ	Yosef, wife: Tsipa, children: Leib, Bracha, Nachma
GURVITZ	Israel, wife: Bluma

GURVITZ	Leib, wife: Malyoseye (Abramovitz) daughter: Esther
GURVITZ	Leib, wife: Chaya, children: Leah
GURVITZ	Mendel, wife: Luba, child: Nelli
GURVITZ	Mendel, wife: Esther and children
GURVITZ	Moshe, wife: Hodel and son
GURVITZ	Kopel, sons: Leib, Elke
GURVITZ	Shmeril, wife: Zeyla, daughter: Meyna
GITTELMAN	Frieda, daughter: Chana
GILDEIN	Reuben Hirash, wife: Alta and children
GILINSKY	Ben-Zion, wife: Yittel, children: Etel, Feyga, Eliezer
GILINSKY	David, wife & son: Godel
GILINSKY	Zalmen, wife: Chana (Shapiro) daughter: Chava
GILINSKY	Moshe, children: David, Tsipa, Rechel, Itzchak
GILINSKY	Mordechai, wife: Heynde (Glickman) and 4 children
GILINSKY	Mordechai, wife: Zisla
GILINSKY	Zvi, wife: Hona, daughters: Rivka, Mosse
GILINSKY	Shalom Leib, wife: Sarah Gitel
GINZBURG	David, wife: Yochbad, children: Mordechai, Shlomo, Itzchak, Moshe
GINZBURG	Chaskel, wife: Chasia, children: Eliezer Batya
GINZBURG	Aaron Yoel, wife: Bella and children
GINZBURG	Eliehu, wife: Pesya, children: Dvora, Luba, Etel, Yosef, Motel
GINZBURG	David Leib, wife and children
GINZBURG	Zov, wife: Esther, children: Sonya, Aba,
GINZBURG	Chana and Sonya
GINZBURG	Yaakov Leib
GINZBURG	Itzchak, wife: Halana, son: David
GINZBURG	Itzchak, wife: Feyga, daughter: Beryl
GINZBURG	Mendel, wife: Chaya Feyga, children: Zorach, Kreyna, Rivka
GINZBURG	Mordechai, wife: Motele (Murmis) and children
GENDEL	Baruch Shalom, wife Bluma, children: Chaim, Etel Zelda

GENDE	Sarah, daughter: Chana
GLUCH	Ayzik, wife and child
GLUCH	David, wife Dina and 2 children
GLAZER	Itzchak Meyer, wife: Leah, son: David
GERTMAN	Avraham, wife: Breyna, children: Yeshik, Rechel, Lazar, Hirash, Moshe, Bella, Etel
GERTMAN	Golia & Reysa
GERMANISKY	Feyga (Nachimovitz)
GEFFEN	Mordechai, wife: Lipsha
GROVITZ	Shmuel, wife: Freida (Shutan)
GROZUL	Tsipa, children: Alter, Leib, Henya, Chaya
GROZUL	Aaron Zelig
GROZUL	Yichel, wife: Rechel
GREENFELD	Chaim David, wife: Sarah
GREENFELD	Bera Leib, wife: Rechel and children
GREEN	Nach, wife--children Mayer, Leah
GREEN	Mayer, wife: Rechel (Flechser), children: Sarah, Leib
GREEN	Hone

ד **Dalet**

DOVROMESLOV	Nach, wife: Gitel, daughter: Myra
DOVROMESLOV	Yenta
DEITZ	Israel, wife: Clara (Markelevitz), son: David
DEITZ	Shlumit, son: Yeshehu
DRUTS	David Moshe, wife: Chana (Desitnik)
DRUTS	Beryl, wife: Dina and children
DRUTS	Yosef Mayer, wife: Slova, son: Daniel
DRUTS	Shalom Yaakov, wife: Batya
DRUTS	Zalmen, wife: Tila, children: Eliehu, Batya
DRUTS	Eliehu, wife: Sheyna and children
DRUTS	Reuben, wife: Sarah and children

ה Hey

HOCHMAN	Peretz, wife: Rivka, son: Shlomo, Avraham
HEYZEREKER	Sonya: children: Berka, David

ו Vav

VOLPSON	Avraham, wife: Perel, children: Israel, Sima, Rechel
VOLPSON	Aba, wife: Bella (Soroke), childre: Shimon, Sima
VOLOZKY	Itchak, wife: Heynda, children: Israel, Friedel
VOLOZKY	Israel, sister Friedel
VOLOZKY	Shmuel, wife and children
VOLIK	Yehuda and sister
VOLIK	Pesach, wife & children: Leib, Avram, Sheyna
VIDUTSHINSKY	Leon, wife: Polia
VILKAMIRSKY	Leib, wife: Ida, children: Bella, Yaakov, Grisha, Kayla, Dvora
VILKAMIRSKY	Zalmen wife and children
VILKAMIRSKY	Chaim, wife: Rechel and children
VILKAMIRSKY	Yaakov, wife: Katia and children
VILKAMIRSKY	Israel, wife and children
VILKUMIRSKY	Saul, wife: Yenta, son: Chaim
WEINSTEIN	Rivka, children: Moshe, Batya
WEISKUNSKY	Ben-Zion, wife Yenta, children: Batya, Hirash
WEISKUNSKY	Ketriel, wife and daughters: Leah, Shlumit
WEXLER	Yaakov, wife: Batya (Weiskunsky) and children
WEXLER	Mendel, wife: Feyga
VARMAS	Mayer, wife: Cheyna, children: Masha, Shlomo

ז Zayin

ZALKIND	Nachma and children
ZANARSKY	Moshe, wife: Esther, son: Binyamin
ZAK	Leiba, daughter: Zelda
ZAK	Mates, wife: Tila and children

ZOROCHEVITZ	Yaakov, wife: Dvora, children: Yeshehu, Esther
ZORETSKY	Myra, children: Shlomo, Berka, Chaim
ZOR	Ben-Zion, wife: Neche, children: Yosef, Masha, Zeyla, Miriam
ZOR	Mordechai, wife: Chana, children: Zovel, Sheyna, Bat-Sheva
ZOR	Riva Leah
ZEIDMAN	Henoch and 2 sisters
ZEIDMAN	Leib, wife and children
ZEIDMAN	Moshe wife and children
ZISKIND	Yaakov, wife: Yochved (Boshkonitz) and children
ZILBERMAN	Henoch, wife: Yochved (Flekser) child: Zovel
ZEIDEL	Aba, wife: Chaya Golda (Gurvitz) and children
ZEIDEL	Binyamin, wife: Slova (Solomik) and children
ZEIDEL	Itzchak, wife and children
ZEIDEL	Lazar, wife: Kune Feyga
ZEIDEL	Mendel, wife: Nachma, son: Avraham
ZEIDEL	Moshe, wife: Nachma (Kril) and children
ZEIDEL	Feyvish, wife: Chana, children: Nachum, Sarah, Batya, Chava
ZETEL	Itzchak, wife: Meyna and children
ZEITEL	Meyna

ח **Chet**

CHADESH	Chaim, wife: Bat-Sheva (Kyle)
CHAIT	Miriam, children: Israel, Leiba
CHAYUT	Etta
CHAYUT	Latel, children: Feyvish, Gota, Batya

ט **Tet**

TARASEYSKY	Perach, wife: Leza, daughter: Nina
TARASEYSKY	Rivka
TEIZ	Alter, wife: Chaya, children: Betslal, Pesya
TEIZ	Betslal, wife: Sheyna (Karmatz), child

TEIZ	Shmuel, wife: Chaya Pessia, sons: Lazar, Leib, Tuvia
TEIZ	Sheyna and Leiba
TELENT	Eliehu, wife: Sonya and children
TROYZE	Rodel and husband
TSHOSNIK	Ben-Zion, wife: Rechel, daughter: Leah
TSHERNOZKY	Gitel and Sheyna
TSHORNEVRADKY	Yente, Rechel, Rivka

י Yod

JAVITZ	Avraham, Itzchak, wife: Batya and children
JAVITZ	Alter, wife: Batya and children
JAVITZ	Chaim, wife: Tsipa and children
JAVITZ	Chana
JAVITZ	Yaakov David, wife: Reyza Batya
JAVITZ	Yaakov, wife: Rechel and children
JAVITZ	Leila, wife: Sarah
YOCHI	Chasia, son: David
YOCHNES	Sonya (Vilkamirsky) son: David
YOSELSON	Rechel
JACOBSON	Leah, children: Leib, Avraham, Yektiel,

כ Kaf

KATZKELEVITZ	Bella
KATZKELEVITZ	Binyamin, wife: Dova
KARMATZ	Chana, children: Sara, Yehuda, Batya
KARMATZ	Henya and Hirash
KARMATZ	David, wife: Chana and children
KARMATZ	Yosef, wife: Chene, sons: Avraham, Itzchak
KARMATZ	Leah, children: Yosef, Neche
KARMATZ	Mordechai, wife: Sarah, children: Itzchak, Leib, Chana
KARMATZ	Moshe and wife

KARMATZ	Feyga, children: Yehudit, Batya, Michla, Avraham, Zev
KARMATZ	Riva Dvora
KARMATZ	Shalom Moshe, wife: Leah, son: Gershon, 2 daughters
KATZ	Dov
KATZ	Chaim, wife: Esther, sons: Moshe, Hirash
KATZ	Yaakov, wife: Chaya Genisya (Gilinsky) child: Saul
KATZ	Mayer, wife: Lena (Javitz) daughter: Gita
KATZ	Fruma
KATZ	Shlomo Yankel, wife: Frieda
KATZ	Shmuel, wife: Galia, child: Genia

ל Lamed

LANDAU	Yeshiehu, wife: Pesya, daughter: Slova
LANDSMAN	Shmuel Hirash, wife: Bella
LOPE	Reyzel (Kalton) and children
LOBATZKY	Leib and mother
LOLINSKY	Yehuda, wife: Sonya, children: Henoch, Feyga, Henya, Reyzel
LOLINSKY	Ephraim, wife: Emma (Kopelevitz)
LOLINSKY	Zalman, wife: Mosse, daughter: Henya
LOLINSKY	Leib Henoch, wife: Reyna
LOLINSKY	Feyva Yosef, wife: Dova, daughters: Zirel, Meyna
LOLINSKY	Mendel, wife: Leyza and children
LOSTIKMAN	Mayer, wife: Reshel, children: Itzchak, Beryl, David
LOKNER	Chaim Zelig, wife: Chana Pesya, children: Zorach, Aaron
LOKNER	Moshe, wife: Feyga and children
LURIA	Ayzik, son: Shimon
LURIA	Michel, wife: Sonya
LURIA	Mendel, wife: Rechel and children
LURIA	Zvi, wife: Zirel, daughter: Leah
LIBERMAN	Heynda, son: Lipa, Shlomo
LIBERMAN	Yeshiehu, wife: Yeva

LIBMAN	Chaya Leba, daughter: Rechel
LIBISKY	David and wife
LIGOMSKY	Chana, wife: Sarah Leah
LIGOMSKY	Henoch, wife: Dvora, children: Reuben, Dova, Batya
LIGOMSKY	Zalman, wife: Esther, children: Michal, Myra, Leah, Yakutiel
LIGOMSKY	Shalom, wife: Gitel, children: Baruch, Bella
LIGOMSKY	Ephraim, child
LIPKIN	Avraham, wife &
LIPKIN	Batya
LIPSHITZ	Jeremia, wife: Chene, children: Dina, Avraham, Moshe
LIPSHITZ	Shlom, wife & (Ayzen), child
LIPPSHITZ	Sabbatai, wife: Leiba Feyga (Solovitsik), children: Chene, Shlomo, Yaakov
LEIFER	Yaakov, children: Alter, Gitel, Chaya
LISHANSKY	ben-Zion, wife: Bella, children: Avrahm, Moshe, Zelda, Zev
LEVIN	Baruch, wife: chana, children: Sarah, Mordechai, Zalma
LEVIN	Gitel (Feygel), daughter: Dvora
LEVIN	Chaim David, wife: Masha and child
LEVIN	Chana, wife: Leiba, children: Chaim, Hirash, Rechel
LEVIN	Teyva, wife, Chava, daughter: and 1 daughter
LEVIN	Yaakov, wife: Mania, children: Leah, Nachman, Shula
LEVIN	Israel, wife: Chaya (Solovisky) and children
LEVIN	Israel, wife: Rivka
LEVIN	Mayer, wife: Hodel and children
LEVIN	Mendel, wife: Esther, children: Shimon, Rechel
LEVIN	Mordechai, wife and children
LEVIN	Nach, wife: Dvora, son: Shimon
LEVIN	Nachma
LEVIN	Feyvish, wife: Leiba and child
LEVIN	Frieda
LEVIN	Reydel (Brumberg) children: Zlata, Shimon

מ Mem

MASHOVITZ	Israel Eliehu, wife: Lika
MASHOVITZ	Moshe Yosef, wife: Chana, children: Eliehu, Sarah, Leah
MANKOVITZ	Yaakov, wife: Sarah (Gordon) and children
MATSKIN	Dova (Kril) children: Roshke and Elka
MATSKIN	Chaim, wife: Sarah Rivka
MATSKIN	Tuvia, wife: Sheyna and children
MATSKIN	Yehosha, wife: Fruma, son: Shlomo
MATSKIN	Yaakov, wife: Leah, children: Shalom, Chana, Beryl
MATSKIN	Motel, wife: Leyza and children
MATSKIN	Kalman, wife: Chava Gitel, daughter: Etel
MARGOL	Zeyla (Kavarsky) children: Dvora, Leah, Mordechai,
MARKEN	Hesha
MARCUS	Itzchak, wife: Zelda, children: Shmuel, Leib, Miriam
MUNITSH	Chana and child (Sarak)
MUSIN	Aba, daughter: Chana
MOROSHKIN	Shmuel, wife: Leah, children: Chana, Zelig, Chaya, Yochved
MURMIS	Eli-Tsadik, wife: Rivka, children: Sima, Batya, Shlomo
MIDZOLSKY	Daniel, wife: Chana Meyna, children: Reuben, Rechel, Leah
MIDZOLSKY	Ben-Zion, wife: Sarah, children: Rechel, Reuben
MIKELSON	Leah, son: Yochnan
MIKELSON	Bella
MILSHTEIN	Hirash, wife: Reyzel, children: Uri, Motel, Gedelka, Rechel, leah, Grandmother: Sarah Rivka
MALEMED	Itzchak Moshe, wife: Dvora (Ayzinsky)
MELNIK	Yaakov, wife: Bat Sheva and children
MARGLIT	Itzchak and Eliehu
MARGLIT	Shmuel, wife

נ Nun

NADEL	Kalmen, wife: Zisla, children: Chana, Mendel, Gershon

NAROTSKY	Moshe Hirash, wife: Michla and children
NIEMKIN	Zechria, wife: Feyga, sons: Akiva, Yosef
NELKIN	Mayer, wife: Chana
NEMZER	Yeshiehu and wife

ס Samech

SUCHER	Eliehu, wife: Mari and children
SUCHER	Hirash, wife: Sarah, Leah and children
SUCHER	Shimon, wife: Dina, children: Hirash, Sarah
SARSKY	Henoch, wife: Leah, children: Shumel, Etel
SARSKY	Chana, children: Mari, Hirash
SARSKY	Katzkil, wife: Chana and children
SOLOVEITSHIK	Baruch, wife: Leah Feyga
SOLOVEITSHIK	Yosef, wife: Miriam, children: Avraham, Leib, Itzchak, Leah
SOLOVEITSHIK	Reuben, wife: Leiba and children
SOLOMIK	Leah Feyga
SOLOMIK	Yoel, wife: Chana, daughter: Leah
SOLODOCH	Nach
SAROK	Velvel, wife: Chaya Dova
SAROK	Moshe, wife: Teva, children: Dova, Rechel, Chana
SAROK	Sheyna and children
SAROK	Yaakov, wife: Henya and son
SAROK	Baruch, wife: Chana, children: Nachma, Dreisa
SEAGLE	Yehuda, wife and children
SWIRSKY	Dov, wife: Chava, children: Myra, Yoel
SWIRSKY	Zalmen, wife: Chana, son: Eliehu
SWIRSKY	Yosef, wife: Batya
SWIRSKY	Yaakov, wife: Penny, children: Mayer, Jonah, Meyna. Dov
SWIRSKY	Leib, wife: Bella (Matzkin), child: Ephraim
SWIRSKY	Moshe, wife: Rechel (Zeidel), child: Leah
SWIRSKY	Rechel, daughter: Chana

SVERDLOV	Rochel, daughter: Yocha
SUZAN	Reuben, wife: Chana (Vidutshinsky) son: Itzchak
SWINTELSKY	Avraham, wife: Etta, sons: David, Leib Mendel
SWINTELSKY	Zev, wife: Leah, children: Mordechai, Zvi, Mordechai
SWINTELSKY	Yosef, wife: Chaya, sons: Chaim, Israel
STERIPINSKY	Gershon, wife and child
SIROTKE	Yerucham, wife: Sonya, daughter: Fanya, Reyzel
SIROTKE	Tsherne (Baygel), son: Tuvia
SLOVIN	Hirash, wife: Neche, children: Israel, Beryl, Moshe
SMORGANSKY	Avraham, wife: Sheyna, son: Yosef
SEGOLOVITZ	Yaakov, wife: Esther, children: Mari, Mendel, Noteh, 1
SPECTOR	Itzchak, wife: Nachma, children: David, Reyzel 4

פ Peh

PODGRUNT	Itzchak
POTOSHNIK	Yeshiehu, wife: Reyzel (Cohen)
POSTOVSKY	Yehuda, wife: Henya, sons: Binyamin, Shmuel
PORTNOI	Hene and mother
FARFEL	(Rosh-Yeshiva) wife and children
FARUS	Eli Leib, wife: Manya, children: Rechel, Rivka, Hirash
FASHUMENSKY	Yaakov, wife: Bryna, child: Yosef
FASHUMENSKY	David and Avraham
FASHUMENSKY	Fishel, wife: Feyga, children
FUTERMAN	and family
FEYGEL	Yosef, wife: Mariesh
FEYGEL	Peretz, wife: Esther
FEYGEL	Chaim Baer, wife-daughter
FEYGEL	David, wife: Leah and children
FEYGELMAN	Baer, wife: Chaya, child
FEYLOTOWITZ	Binyamin, wife: Sonya (Becker)
FISHER	Dvora (Lerilin)

FLENER	Reuben, wife: Mania (Vidutshinsky)
FLENER	Zalmen, wife: Fanya (Goldstein) daughter: Chaya
FLENER	Pesya and Meyna
FLEKSER	Chana
FLEKSER	Shimon, wife: Zelda, children: Miriam, Zevel
FELDMAN	Itzchak Leib, wife: Feyga Henye, son: Shlomo
FELDMAN	Mendel, wife: Batya and children
FERES	Zelda
FEKEL	Mendel, wife: Feya, son: Itzchak
FERDER	Chana
FERMANT	Yaakov, wife: Moseh, son: Moshe
FRIEDMAN	Hirash, wife: Berta, son: Leib and daughter

צ Tzadik

TSEIKINSKY	Itzchak, wife: Pesya, children: Chaya, Reuben, Beryl, Shmuel
TSEIKINSKY	Bella
TSEIKINSKY	Ephraim, daughter: Chaya
TSEIKINSKY	Moshe
TSEIKINSKY	Reyzel, son: Israel
TSINMAN	Sheyna Leiba, son: Dr. Betslal
TSEPELOVITZ	Avraham, wife: Bella, daughter: Chava
TSEPELOVITZ	Zalman, wife: Alta and 2 sons
TSEPELOVITZ	Yehuda, wife Alta and 2 sons
TSEPELOVITZ	Yosef, wife: Sarah Bluma
TSEFNAS	Reuben, wife: Frieda (Katz), sons: Yehuda, Chaim

ק Kof

KAGAN	Aaron, wife &
KAGAN	Gitel
KAGAN	Golda and children
KAVNER	Zelig, wife: Leah, daughters: Rechel, Chaya

KAVNER	Meyna (Avtzinsky), daughters: Berta, Rechel, Fanya
KOVALSKY	Yeshiehu, wife: Chava (Zeidel) and children
KOVARSKY	Aaron, wife: Sonya
KOVARSKY	Eliehu, wife: Sima, children: Gershon, Luba
KOVARSKY	Binyamin Dr., wife: Polya, daughters: Lena, Pera
KOVARSKY	David, wife and children
KOVARSKY	Zalmen, wife: Chana Reyza
KOVARSKY	Zalmen, wife: Leah, daughter: Batya
KOVARSKY	Chava (Levin), children: Meyna, Sheyna
KOVARSKY	Chana
KOVARSKY	Yoel, wife: Sonya, son: Aaron
KOVARSKY	Yosef, wife & son: Mordechai
KOVARSKY	Lazar, wife: Matla, children: Teyva, Motel
KOVARSKY	Lazar, wife: Feyga, sons: Leib, Reuben
KOVARSKY	Matehu, wife: Pesya (Baygel), daughter: Chana
KOVARSKY	Feyvish, wife and children
KOVARSKY	Reuben, wife: Tzira Leah
KOVARSKY	Sarah Bella, son: Israel
KOTLER	Nach, wife: Chana, child: Henya
KOTLER	Raphel, wife: Leah
KOTSHERGINSKY	Israel, wife: Reyzel
KOTSHERGINSKY	Yaakov, wife: Etel, children: Chava, Meyna, Sarah
KOTSHERGINSKY	Moshe, wife: Asne, children: Pesya, Gita, Sheyna
KOTSHERGINSKY	Polya, son: Israel
KOTSHELNIK	Eliehu, wife and children
KOTSHELNIK	Rochel
KOTSHELNIK	Sarah and daughter
KOLTON	Moshe, wife: Rechel
KOLTON	Alter, wife: Sarah Leah, and 2 children
KANTOROVITZ	Velvel, wife: Rechel Leah, daughter: Chaya

KOPELEWITZ	Yaakov Dr., wife: Rechel (Taraseysky), son: Kalman
KOPELEWITZ	Nachum, wife: Sarah, sons: David, Yosef
KOTZNE	Shlomo, son: Mendel
KURITSKY	Alikum, wife &
KURITSKY	Beryl, wife: Feyga, children: Rechel, Shmuel, Chaim
KURITSKY	Motleh, Chana
KURITSKY	Mendel, wife: Chava Liba, daughters: Gita, Teyva, Sarah
KURITSKY	Moshe, wife: Dina (Katz), children: Eli, Chaim
KURITSKY	Moshe, wife: Yochved
KURITSKY	Shlomo, wife: Btya, children: Rechel, Pesya, Yochved, Leib
KURLANDTSHIK	Shlomo, wife: Rivka, daughter: Esther
KURLANDTSHIK	Gershon, wife: Moroyshe, children: Leah, Feyga, Jonah
KURLANDHIK	Mordechai, wife: Feyga (Stalfer) children: Itzchak, Chaya
KURLANDSHIK	Yechatzkel, wife: Rechel (Zak), children: Motel, Chaya, Meyna
KIDUSHMAN	Zev, wife & sons: Hirash, Itzchak + 2
KYZBERG	Avigdor, wife: Zeyla, children: Pira, Moshe
KYLE	Mordechai, daughter: Shlumit, Chaya
KLOVER	Alter, wife and children
KLOVER	Eliehu, wife: Bella
KNEL	Honeh
KESTIN	Sabbatai, wife: Leah (Cohen), son: Mordechai
KESSEL	(Leher) wife, child
KESSEL	Israel, wife: Alta, children: Nayma, Nadya, Meyna
KROMNIK	Chana Reyzel
KROMNIK	Yaakov, wife: Rivka, children: Yeshiehu, Henya, Chaya, shlomo, Yetta
KROVTSHIK	Sheyna
KROK	Yehuda, wife: Bella, children: Rivka, Yosef, Rechel, Moshe
KREITZER	Shlomo, wife: Bat-Sheva, children: Hirash, Rechel, Moshe
KRIMELISKY	David, wife: Sonya, son: Yochnan

ר **Resh**

RABATNIK	Moshe, wife: Sarah, son: Manshe
REISEN	Moshe, wife: Haneh
ROCHIN	David, wife: Chana, children: Reske, Eliehu
ROCHIN	Nachum, wife: Teyva, children: Leib + 2
ROSENSTEIN	Lipa, wife: Rivka, sons: Hirash, Kalman
RAPPAPORT	Chana Leah, daughter: Pesya and child
RUDNITZKY	Eliehu, wife: Henya
RUDNITZKY	Binyamin, wife: Leah, children: Noteh, Esther
RUDNITZKY	Israel Moshe, wife: Chaya (Karmatz)
RUDNITZKY	Pesach, wife: Sheyna, sons: Yosef, Itzchak
RUDNITZKY	Shimon, wife: Masheh and children
RUDNITZKY	Tenachum, wife: Pesya
RUTSTEIN	Avraham, wife: Batya, daughters: Sarah, Feyga
RUTSTEIN	Leib, wife and children, grandmother: Bella
REIZEVSKY	Grisha, son: Shmuel
REICHEL	Baer, wife: Reyzel, children: Etta, Mendel, Halal, Reuben
REIN	Leib, wife: Tamara
REIN	Itzchak, wife & daughter: Masha
REINEG	Henoch, wife: Ziva, children: Baer, Itzchak, Teyva, Zelda
REINEG	Yehosha
RITZMAN	Zalmen
RITZMAN	Ben-Zion, wife: Batya, daughter: Feyga
RITZMAN	Nachum Leib, wife: Deisel, children: Itzchak, Etta
RITZMAN	Pinkas, wife: Chasia, sons: Eli, Mendel

ש Shin

SHOCHNOVITZ	(Lita)
SHOLOVSKY	Chana, children: Chanan, Rechel
SHAPIRO	Binyamin, wife: Bella, sons: David, Yehuda
SHAPIRO	Baer, wife: Leyza, children: Eliehu, Meyna, Teyva
SHAPIRO	Zev, wife: Zelda, children: Zeyla, Eliehu

SHAPIRO	Leib, wife: Sarah and son
SHAPIRO	Maer, wife: Perel (Bock) and children
SHAPIRO	Mendel, wife: Chasya
SHAPIRO	Pesach, wife: Bella, children: Zovel, Reuben
SHAPIRO	Shalom, wife: Nachma, son: Ben-Zion
SHAVITZ	Yehosha, wife: Miriam, sons: Moshe, Zalmen, Avraham
SHOCHER	Yiddel, wife: Chava, Henoch, Sarah, Michla
SHOCHER	Beryl
SHUTAN	Heshel, wife: Zeyrel, son: Alter
SHUTAN	Chanan, wife and children
SHUTAN	lipa, wife: Reyzel
SHUTAN	Leyba Ayzik, wife: Chana, daughters: Rechel, Heynda
SHUTAN	Moshe, wife: Chaya (Baygle), children: Tuvia + 1
SHUTAN	Kalmen, wife: Steyrel, daughter: Genesia
SHUTAN	Rechel Leah, daughter: Myra
SHUTAN	Shmuel Hirash, wife: Reyzel, daughters: Sarah, Cheyna, Nachma, Liba
SHULGEIFER	Sheyna Leah and children
SHULGEIFER	Aba, wife & son: Yerachmiel
SHULGEIFER	Pinchas and child
SHULMAN	Leah Shose
SHUSTER	Leib, wife: Leiba Bella,children: Mashe, Engele
SHUSTERMAN	Shmuel, wife: Zeyrel and children
STEIN	Yaakov, wife: Leyza (Levin) son: David
STEIN	Avraham, wife: Berta (Levin) and children
SHIBOVSKY	Avraham, wife: Elke
SHIBOVSKY	Yaakov, wife: Esther (Gurvitz) and children
SEITEL	Elikum, wife: bella, Chaim, Zeyra
SHIKMAN	Rechel (Kuritzky), child: Miriam
SHEYNOK	Ayza Yisa, wife: Bella
SHEYNOK	Israel Moshe, wife: Sonya and children

SHEYNOK	Shmuel Michel, wife and children
SHEYNOK	Sarah Cheyne and children
SHLASBERG	Frieda and mother
SHMIDT	Beryl, wife: Esther and children
SMOLGOVISKY	Pesach, wife: Sonya and children
SHNEIDER	Widutshinsky Dora, children: Itzchak Shlumit
SHNEIDER	Shmuel Nisan, wife: Rechel
SHNEIDER	Itzchak Leib, wife: Tsipa, children: Heshke, Bella, Israel
SHNEIDERVITZ	Rechel, daughter: Rivka
SHNEIDERVITZ	Reuben, wife: Esther
SHNEIDERVITZ	Katzkel, wife: Sonya and children
SHNEIDERVITZ	Sarah Bluma
SHERYL	Leah and children
SHPITZ	Shmuel, wife and daughters: Chana, Reyzel, Alta
SHPITZ	Mendel, wife: Feyga, daughter: Tsipa
SHPITZ	Yehuda, wife: Chaya, son: Moshe
SHPITZ	Ephraim and wife
SHROLOVITZ	Yaakov, wife: Sarah and children

[Columns 1903-1908]

New Svencionys Necrology

(Švenčionėliai, Lithuania)

55°10' 26°00'

Transliterated and Donated by Steven Weiss

Surname	Family members
א Alef	
ABELOVITZ	Baruch, wife: Sarah Rivka, children: Bella, Moshe
UMVRASH	Moshe, wife: Bella
UMVRASH	Itzchak, wife
UMVRASH	Beryl, wife: Sheyna, child: Eliehu
OVITSHINSKY	Kapel, 2 daughters, 2 sons
USHPOL	Shumel, wife: Sarah (Kovarsky)
AZBEL	Leib, wife: Yehudit, son: Michel
AYZIKOVITZ	Shlomo
ISAACSON	Yechtriel, wife: Malcha, children: Bella, Rechel, Shoshana
OPMAN	Dvora (Kovarsky), child: Yaakov
ב Bet	
BAYIK	Itzchak, wife: Batya
BANK	Hirash, wife: Myra, daughter: Malcha
BANK	Israel, wife: Esther
BASS	Mayer, wife: Chaya Rechel Shutan
BOCK	Eliehu, wife &
BOCK	Baruch, wife: Manya, children: Zelda, Bella
BOCK	Yaakov, wife: Liba, children: Hirash, Leah
BOCK	Motel, wife: Matla, child: Beryl
BOCK	Sarah (Ginzburg), children: Chana, Sarah, Golda

BOCK	Shlomo, wife: Chana, child: Chaim
BOCK	(from Berlin David), children: Moshe, Dvora
BIKSON	Hirash, wife: Sonya, child: Shlomo
BOYRSTEIN	Dova, child: Hoda
BITSHVANSKY	Fruma, daughter: Hynde
BERMAN	Hirash, wife & 2 children
BERMAN	Chana Sima
BERMAN	Shmuel, wife and child
BROYDA	Zorach, wife &
BROYDA	Mayer, wife: Frieda, children: 3
BROYDA	Moshel, wife: Chaya Rosha, child: Leib
BROYDA	Noteh, wife: Bella, children: 3
BROYDA	Shmuel, wife: Alta, children: Hirash, Zalmen
BROSLAN	Eliehu, wife and 2 children

ג Gimmel

GOWENDE	Lazer, wife: Bella, child: Shmuel
GORDON	Heschel, wife: Manya and children
GORDON	Chaya, husband Shochat, children: 2
GORDON	Chaim, wife: Esther
GORDON	Yodel, wife: Dvora and child
GORFEIN	Zalta, husband Moshe, children: 2
GORFEIN	Chava
GUBESKY	Shlomo, wife & children: Zalmen, Esther
GURVITZ	Eliehu and family
GURVITZ	Henoch, wife: Sonya, children: Esther, Shmuel
GURVITZ	Hirash, wife: Chaya Feyga
GURVITZ	Loleh, wife: Riva, children: Bluma, Leah, Sheyna, Leybel
GURVITZ	Motel, wife: Batya, child: Chaim
GURVITZ	Moshe, wife: Esther, children: Yerachmil, Shachne, Miriam
GURVITZ	Shlomo, wife: Frieda, son: Gershon

GILDEIN	Hirash, wife and child
GILDEIN	Yosef, wife: Menucha, children: Golda, Geler, Pesya, Muter
GREENFELD	Baer, wife: Reycha Swirsky and child

ה Hey

HELERSTEIN	Lazer, wife: Lyza, children: Itzchak, Bluma

ו Vav

VOLBERSHTER	David, wife: Heynda
VOLIN	Moshe, wife: Liba (Kovarsky), child: Velvel
VOLPSON	Chana and family
VOLPSON	Itzchak, wife: Myra, children: Feyfga, Shlomo, Moshe, Gabriel, Motel
VOLPSON	Feyva, wife: Zisla, son: Beryl
VIDLANSKY	Avraham, wife: Reyna (Bock), child: Chana
VINIK	Avraham, wife: Ganya, child: Kalman

ז Zayin

ZAK	Eliehu Gershon, children: Yosef, Moshe, Reyzel
ZAK	Lipman, wife: Eta, daughters: Tsirel, Myra
ZAK	Moshe and son
ZAK	Motel, wife: Dvora
ZOR	Mendel, wife & children: Bella, Itzchak, Yente

ח Chet

CHARMATS	Mendele, wife: Sarah and child
CHADESH	Mendel, wife: Elke, children: Alta, Moshe, Yehuda, Leib
CHAYDKEL	Mayer, wife: Chana, children: Michel, Freida
CHAIT	Asher, wife: Teyva, children: 2
CHAIT	Moshe, wife: Sheyna
CHAIT	Morris, wife and 2 children

ט Tet

TOVAKOVITZ	Batya, daughter Yente

TELENT	Eliehu, wife and 2 children
TROYZE	Nachum, wife: Chaya, son: Yodel
TSHORNEVRADKY	Dvora, son: Avraham
י Yod	
YOVITZ	Avroshe, wife &
YOVITZ	Ozer, wife: Bella, children: Katya, Tsipa, Heschel
YONISKY	Golda and husband
YONISKY	Lazar, wife: Dina, children: Tsirka, Chaim
YAFFE	Yosef, wife: Slova, children: Michel, Avraham, Eliezer, Bat-sheva
YOKISHKY	Michel, daughter: Michel
ISRAELOV	Yerucham, wife: Menucha, children: 3
כ Kaf	
KATZKELEVITZ	Eliehu Mayer, wife: Etta Malcha, children: Moshe, Ephraim, Yosef, Yerachmil, Shmuel, Chana, Batya
COHEN	Yosef, wife: Rechel
KATZ	Avraham, wife and child
KATZ	Avraham, wife: Zelda (Salteisky) child: Yocha
KATZ	Heynde, husband and child
KATZ	Velvel, wife: Myra, children: Bella, Asher
KATZ	Velvel, wife: Rechel, daughter: Sheyna
KATZ	Yaakov, wife: Batya, children: Itzchak, Sarah
KATZ	Yerachmiel, and wife
KATZ	Yeshiahu, wife: Lyza
KATZ	Lazar Itzchak, wife: Nachma: daughter, Rivka
KATZ	Lipman, wife: Esther
KATZ	Moyleh
KATZ	Matot, wife: Dvora, child: David
KATZ	Nachum, wife and child
KATZ	Elke and 2 children
KATZ	Feyva, wife: Bat-Sheva

KATZ	Sheyna Rivka and family
KARPAS	Avraham, wife: Sheyna

ל Lamed

LIEBMAN	Avraham Leib, wife: Chana
LEGUMSKY	Moshe, wife: Dova, children: Bella, Chana
LEFENHOLTS	Yosef, wife: Rechel
LEVENSTEIN	Hirash, wife: Feyga and 2 children
LEVENSTEIN	Chazkel, wife: Glika, son: Itzchak
LEVENSTEIN	Rivka (Yosemovitz) and family
LEVENSTEIN	Shlomo, wife: Sarah
LEVIN	Mendel, wife: Bella Pera, son: Aaron
LAPIDUS	Henoch, wife and children
LAPIDUS	Rechel, children: Beryl, Yosef, Feyga, Paya, Leib

מ Mem

MALEROVITZ	Beryl, wife and child
MALEROVITZ	Motel
MALEROVITZ	Tsipa
MATSKIN	Shlomo, wife: Rivka (Pupisky), child: Chanala
MULLER	Henoch and family (Svir)
MULLER	Moshe, wife: Rechel (Svir)
MILNER	Itzchak
MILNER	Motel, children: Myra, Abigale
MAYMAN	Batya
MAYMAN	Zalmen and Shmerel
MIRMAN	children: Hirash, Beynish, Frieda
MEISUTSHINS	daughter
MEISHELES	Zelig, wife

נ Nun

NACHUMSON	Reuben, wife: Sarah, children: Feyga, Shlomo

NEMENTSHINSKY	Dvora and children

ס Samech

SALTISKY	Yosef Leib, wife: Yochved
SALTISKY	Mayer, wife: Chana, child: Feyga
SALTISKY	Matus, wife: Bluma, children: Sheyna, Yocha
SALTISKY	lipa Lazer and children
SALTISKY	Melech
SALTISKY	Fishel, wife: Fruma, child; Yocha
SOLOVITSHIK	Aba, wife and children
SWIRSKY	(Torpentine)
SWIRSKY	Chaya Sarah, daughter: Chana
SWIRSKY	Chaya, and husband
SWIRSKY	Rosha, and husband
SEGALOVITZ	Chaim Leib, daughters: Pyra, Heynde
SEGALOVITZ	Golda and child

ע Ayin

ELPERIN	Eliehu, wife: Chaya, children: Sarah, Itzchak
ELPERIN	Itzchak leib, wife: Hesha Myra
ELPERIN	Yosef and wife
ELPERIN	Moshe, wife: Tanya and child
ELPERIN	Moshe, wife and child
ELPERIN	Shlomo, wife: Bella, daughter; Sonya
EPSTEIN	Chaim, wife: Reyza, children: Fanya, Sonya

פ Peh

POTOSHNIK	Yosef, wife: Nachma, 3 children
POSTOVSKY	Mendel, wife: Rechel, daughter: Dova
PORTNOI	Yedel, son: Yerachmiel
PORTNOI	Israel, wife: Sarah
PUPISKY	Ben-Zion, wife: Rochel, son: Itzchak, mother: Yente

PUPISKY	Velve, wife: Chasia, son: Tsadok
FINEGROIT	Zacharahu, 2 daughters, son: David
FEYGEL	Eliehu, wife: Shifra, 2 daughters
FINE	Aaron, wife and children
FINE	Chaim, wife and daughter
FINE	Yosef, daughter: Manya
FISHMAN	Yaakov, wife: Chana Shutan, children: Avraham, Itzchak
FLEISHER	Yahon, wife: Esther, children: Rivka, Miriam

צ **Tzadik**

TSYNTSONOTUS	Reyza, 2 daughters
TSINMAN	Yosef, wife: Chava Rechel
TSINMAN	Mendel, sons: Shlomo, Avraham
TSEIKINSKY	Esna, husband and children
TSEIKINSKY	Moshe, wife: Dvora, daughter: Chaya
TSEPELOVITZ	Hirash, wife: Batya (Kovarsky) and children
TSEPELOVITZ	Henya, (Milner)
TSEPELOVITZ	Chaim, wife: Nachma and children
TSEPELOVITZ	Chaim Eliehu, wife: Sonya and children
TSEPELOVITZ	Leib Shalom, wife: Rechel, son: Beryl

ק **Kof**

KOVARSKY	Avraham, wife: Fanya, son: Israel
KOVARSKY	Eliehu Yosef, wife: Myrel, children: Reyzel, Chava, Sarah
KOVARSKY	Heschel, wife: Sarah
KOVARSKY	Zalme, wife: Chana Leah, son: Yosef (Vilna)
KOVARSKY	Itzchak, wife: Sheyna, children: Leah, Esther, Henoch
KOVARSKY	Motel and family (Vilna)
KOVARSKY	Nach, wife: Chaya (Vilna)
KOVARSKY	Sarah Cheyna, sons: Heshel, Yankel
KOVALSKY	Yosef, wife: Rechel, children: Masha, rivka, Motel

KOVALSKY	Itzchak, wife and children
KOTSHERGINSKY	Yasse, wife: Feyga, (Shutan), daughters: Bella, Miriam
KOTSHELNIK	Leib, wife: Rechel, children: Itzchak, Gedalia, Feyga, Zlata
KULBOK	Shmuel, children: Eliehu, Frieda
KURITSKY	Beryl and wife
KIZBERG	Sonya, daughter: Teyma and husband
KLOTSHKA	Avraham, wife: Dvora, children: Sarah, Tsvia, Moshe
KLOTSHKA	Yaakov, wife: Esther
KAMCHAI	Ha Rav, wife: Bracha, son: Noten
KAMCHAI	Yehosha, wife &
KAMCHAI	Tsipa and child
KRUZ	Sarah
KREMER	Yosef, wife and 2 sons

ר **Resh**

RABINOVITZ	Avraham, wife and child
RABINOVITZ	Yehosha, wife: Gita and child
RABINOVITZ	Yaakov, wife: Bella, son: Binyamin
RUDNITZKY	David and wife
RUDNITZKY	Yodel, wife: Bat-Sheva, daughter: Etta
RUDNITZKY	Yaakov, daughter: Bella
RUDNITZKY	Motel, wife: Reyzel and children
RUDNITZKY	Nachma, husband and children
RUDNITZKY	Shlomo, wife & children: Reuben, Banya, Beryl
RUTSTEIN	Hirash, mother: Chasia, wife and children
RUTSTEIN	Chana
RUTSTEIN	Yaakov Tuvia, wife: Chasia, son: Hirash
RUTSTEIN	Myra
REINEG	Beryl, wife: Chana and 2 children
REINEG	David, daughter: Myra
REINEG	Itzchak and family

REINEG	Yoktiel, wife: Dvora and 2 children
REINEG	Leib, wife and children
REINEG	Shlomo, wife: Pesya, child: Chaim

ש Shin

SHOCHER	Alta and family
SHOCHER	Glika, husband and child
SHOCHER	Velvel, wife: Teyva and children
SHAPIRO	Chava
SCHWARTZ	Yaakov and wife
SHUTAN	Gershon, wife: Tsila, children: Yaakov, Reuben, Malcha
SHUTAN	Chaim Feyva, wife: Rechel Gitel
SHUTAN	Yaakov, wife: Gita and 2 daughters
SHUTAN	Moshe Itzchak, wife: Zelda, children: Keyla, reuben
SHUTAN	Noten, wife: Reyzel
SHUTAN	Raphael, wife: Gitel
STEIN	Yosef, and wife
STEIN	Moshe, wife and children
SHEYN	Heschel
SHLOPOK	
SHMUELOVITZ	Sabbatai, wife: Perel, children: Itzchak, Yosef, Sarah
SHMUELOVITZ	Bryna, children: Rosha, Lipa
SHIFF	Nachum, wife: Heynde, children: Gershon, Mayer, Zovel, Itzchak, Dina
SCHREIBMAN	Reycha, daughter: Bella, son: Pesach

Please Note: Page numbers refer to the original Yizkor book and not this translation

[Columns 1910-1914]

Ignalina Necrology

(Ignalina, Lithuania)

55°21' 26°10'

Transliterated by Beryl Baleson

Page numbers reference the Original Yizkor Book

Family name(s)	First name(s)	Gender	Marital status	Father's name	Mother's name	Name of spouse	Remarks and additional family	Page
א **Alef**								
IVANTER	Isaac	M	married			Alta	child	1909
IVANTER	Alta	F	married			Isaac	child	1909
ILITAVITCH	Yehuda	M	married			Sarah Leah	5 children	1909
ILITAVITCH	Sarah Leah	F	married			Yehuda	5 children	1909
EINHARN	Joseph	M	married			Fraida	2 children	1909
EINHARN	Fraida	F	married			Joseph	2 children	1909
ITZICKSON	Velvel	M	married			Yenta		1909
ITZICKSON	Yenta	F	married			Velvel		1909
ITZICKSON	Isaac	M	married			Pearl		1909
ITZICKSON	Pearl	F	married			Isaac		1909
ITZICKSON	Ethel	F		Isaac	Pearl			1909
ITZICKSON	Laiv	M		Isaac	Pearl			1909
ITZICKSON	Raiza	F		Isaac	Pearl			1909
ITZICKSON	Faiga Ethel	F						1909
ASTERINSKY	Haya	F						1909
ASTERINSKY	Isaac	M						1909
EFESKIN	Isaac	M	married			Rivka		1909

EFESKIN	Rivka	F	married			Isaac		1909
EFESKIN	Abraham	M		Isaac	Rivka			1909
EFESKIN	Rachel	F		Isaac	Rivka			1909
EFESKIN	David	M		Isaac	Rivka			1909
ARAN	Israel Noah	M	married			Golda		1909
ARAN	Golda	F	married			Israel Noah		1909
ARAN	Benjamin	M		Israel	Golda			1909
ARAN	Abraham	M		Israel	Golda			1909
ARAN	Sima	F		Israel	Golda			1909
ARAN	Reuben	M		Israel	Golda			1909
ARAN	Meir	M		Israel	Golda			1909
ARAN	Bentzion	M		Israel	Golda			1909
ARAN	Fishel	M	married			Hana		1909
ARAN	Hana	F	married			Fishel		1909
ARAN	Pesiya	F		Fishel	Hana			1909
ARAN	David	M		Fishel	Hana			1909
ARANAVITCH	Benjamin	M	married			Rivka	2 children	1909
ARANAVITCH	Rivka	F	married			Benjamin	2 children	1909
ב Bet								
BANK	Abraham	M	married			Deborah		1909
BANK	Deborah	F	married			Abraham		1909
BANK	Shaul	M		Abraham	Deborah			1909
BANK	Isaac	M		Abraham	Deborah			1909
BANK	Yehoshua	M	married			Yenta		1909
BANK	Yenta	F	married			Yehoshua		1909
BANK	Rivka	F		Yehoshua	Yenta			1909
BARANCHUK	Joel	M	married			Hana	child	1909
BARANCHUK	Hana	F	married			Joel	child	1909
BARNSTEIN	Nehama	F	married					1909

BODAVITCH	Basiya	F					Sister of Masha & Raiza	1909
BODAVITCH	Masha	F					Sister of Basiya & Raiza	1909
BODAVITCH	Raiza	F					Sister of Basiya & Masha	1909
BORMAN	Jacob	M	married			Braina	2 children	1909
BORMAN	Braina	F	married			Jacob	2 children	1909
BITSHONSKY	Hananya	M	married				child	1909
BITSHONSKY		F	married			Hananiya	child	1909
BITSHONSKY	Yehiel	M	married				child	1909
BITSHONSKY		F	married			Yehiel	child	1909
BITSHONSKY	Moshe	M	married				child	1909
BITSHONSKY		F	married			Moshe	child	1909
BEGIN							Unclear if individual or in family	1909
BECKENSTEIN	Heniya	F						1909
BECKENSTEIN	Hana	M			Heniya			1909
BARMAN	Israel Moshe	M	married			Batya	child	1909
BARMAN	Batya	F	married			Israel Moshe	child	1909
BARMAN	Shaina	F						1909
BARMAN	Shaina	F						1909
BARMAN	Rachel	F			Shaina			1909
BRADSKY	Miriam	F						1909
BRADSKY	Fraida	F			Miriam			1909
BRADSKY	Gedalyahu	M			Miriam			1909
BROMBERG	Nehemia	M	married			Sarah		1909
BROMBERG	Sarah	F	married			Nehemiya		1909
BROMBERG	Reuben	M	married			Sarah		1909
BROMBERG	Sarah	F	married			Reuben		1909

BROMBERG	Moshe Isaac	M	married			Saniya		1909
BROMBERG	Sonia	F	married			Moshe Isaac		1909
BROMBERG	Rivka	F		Moshe Isaac	Saniya			1909
BROMBERG	Bera	M		Moshe Isaac	Saniya			1909
BROMBERG	Yehudit	F		Moshe Isaac	Saniya			1909
BROMBERG	Hirsh	M		Moshe Isaac	Saniya			1909
BROMBERG	Aharon	M	married				2 children	1909
BROMBERG		F	married			Aharon	2 children	1909
BROMBERG	Moshe	M	married				2 children	1909
BROMBERG		F	married			Moshe	2 children	1909

ג Gimmel

GAVENDA	Hena	F						1909
GAVENDA	Hinda	F						1909
GAVENDA	Hana Rivka	F						1909
GAVENDA	Yonah	M						1909
GAVENDA	Joseph	M	married			Alta	2 children	1909
GAVENDA	Alta	F	married			Joseph	2 children	1909
GAVENDA	Faivish	M	married				3 children	1909
GAVENDA		F	married			Faivish	3 children	1909
GAVENDA	Shlomo	M	married			Tzvia	child	1909
GAVENDA	Tzvia	F	married			Shlomo	child	1909
GAVENDA	Shmuel	M	married			Faniya		1909
GAVENDA	Faniya	F	married			Shmuel		1909
GAVENDA	Liba	F		Shmuel	Faniya			1909
GAVENDA	Raiza	F		Shmuel	Faniya			1909
GAVENDA	David	M		Shmuel	Faniya			1909
GALPERIN	Sima	F						1910

GARDAN	Shaina	F						1910
GARDAN	Yekutiel	M						1910
GARDAN	David	M		Yekutiel				1910
GARDAN	Joseph	M		Yekutiel				1910
GARDAN	Noah	M		Yekutiel				1910
GARDAN	Sarah	F		Yekutiel				1910
GEDUD	Eliyahu	M	married			Pesiya		1910
GEDUD	Pesia	F	married			Eliyahu		1910
GEDUD	Liba	F		Eliyahu	Pesiya			1910
GORVITCH	Abraham	M	married			Sarah Leah	2 children	1910
GORVITCH	Sarah Leah	F	married			Abraham	2 children	1910
GORVITCH		M	married			Dabe		1910
GORVITCH	Dobe	F	married			Herzl		1910
GORVITCH	Sania	F		Herzl	Dabe			1910
GORVITCH	Ita	F		Herzl	Dabe			1910
GORVITCH	Noma	F		Herzl	Dabe			1910
GORVITCH	Mattel	M	married			Hinda		1910
GORVITCH	Hinda	F	married			Mattel		1910
GORVITCH	Faiga	F		Mattel	Hinda			1910
GORVITCH	Liba	F		Mattel	Hinda			1910
GORVITCH	Laiv	M		Mattel	Hinda			1910
GORVITCH	Moshe	M	married			Tzira	3 children	1910
GORVITCH	Tzira	F	married			Moshe	3 children	1910
GEIDIGER							whole family	1910
GILINSKY	Aba	M	married					1910
GILINSKY		F	married			Aba		1910
GILINSKY	Hana	F		Aba				1910
GILINSKY	Abraham	M	married			Hana		1910
GILINSKY	Hana	F	married			Abraham		1910

GILINSKY	Eliyahu	M	married			Rachel	child	1910
GILINSKY	Rachel	F	married			Eliyahu	child	1910
GILINSKY	Asher	M	married			Hana		1910
GILINSKY	Hana	F	married			Asher	maiden name RING	1910
GILINSKY	Bera	M	married			Haya		1910
GILINSKY	Haya	F	married			Beriya		1910
GILINSKY	Gittel	F		Beriya	Haya			1910
GILINSKY	Hayyim	M		Beriya	Haya			1910
GILINSKY	Faiva	M		Beriya	Haya			1910
GILINSKY	Deborah	F						1910
GILINSKY	Hirsh Laiv	M	married			Alta		1910
GILINSKY	Elta	F	married			Hirsh Laiv		1910
GILINSKY	Shmuel Isaac	M		Hirsh Laiv	Alta			1910
GILINSKY	Heshel	M	married			Rivka Sarah		1910
GILINSKY	Rivka	F	married			Heshel	maiden name DUBINSKY	1910
GILINSKY	Zalman	M	married					1910
GILINSKY		F	married			Zalman		1910
GILINSKY	Taiba	F						1910
GILINSKY	Raiza	F			Taiba			1910
GILINSKY	Joel	M	married			Leah		1910
GILINSKY	Leah	F	married			Joel		1910
GILINSKY	Ita	F		Joel	Leah			1910
GILINSKY	Isaac Gershon	M						1910
GILINSKY	Isaac	M					In list written as Gilinsky possibly in error	1910
GILINSKY	Israel Wolf	M						1910
GILINSKY	Israel	M	married				child	1910

GILINSKY		F	married			Israel	child	1910
GILINSKY	Leah	F					2 children	1910
GILINSKY	Liba	F						1910
GILINSKY	Mera	F			Liba			1910
GILINSKY	Meir	M	married			Lota	3 children	1910
GILINSKY	Lota	F	married			Meir	3 children	1910
GILINSKY	Moshe	M	married				children	1910
GILINSKY		F	married			Moshe	children	1910

ד Dalet

DAGIM	Israel	M						1910
DAGIM	Jacob	M		Israel				1910
DAGIM	Hinda	F		Israel				1910
DAGIM	Gittel	F		Israel				1910
DUBINSKY	Isaac	M	married			Ethel		1910
DUBINSKY	Ethel	F	married			Isaac		1910
DUBINSKY	Faiga	F		Isaac	Ethel			1910
DUBINSKY	Yishayahu	M		Isaac	Ethel			1910
DUBINSKY	Shlomo	M	married			Hiena		1910
DUBINSKY	Hiena	F	married			Shlomo		1910
DUBINSKY	Shmuel	M		Shlomo	Hiena			1910
DUBINSKY	Osnat	F		Shlomo	Hiena			1910
DVAZSHETZ	Abraham	M					child	1910
DROTZ	Berel	M	married			Sarah	2 children	1910
DROTZ	Sarah	F	married			Berel	2 children	1910

ה Hey

HAMER	Jacob	M	married			Rachel		1910
HAMER	Rachel	F	married			Jacob		1910
HAMER	Berel	M		Jacob	Rachel			1910
HAMER	Eidel	F		Jacob	Rachel			1910

HAMER	Shlomo	M		Jacob	Rachel			1910
HAMER	Haya	F		Jacob	Rachel			1910

ו Vav

VANANSKY	Berel	M	married			Rachel	child	1910
VANANSKY	Rachel	F	married			Berel	child	1910
VIDOTSHINSKY	Yudel	M	married			Palia		1910
VIDOTSHINSKY	Palia	F	married			Yudel		1910
WEINSTEIN	Shmuel	M	married			Sima		1910
WEINSTEIN	Sima	F	married			Shmuel		1910
WEINSTEIN	Hasiya	F		Shmuel	Sima			1910
WEINSTEIN	Abraham	M	married			Deborah	child	1910
WEINSTEIN	Deborah	F	married			Abraham	maiden name SOLOVEICHIK. One child	1910

ז Zayin

ZARGA	Mordechai	M	married			Boniya	2 children	1910
ZARGA	Boniya	F	married			Mordechai	2 children	1910
ZEIDMAN	Nahum	M	married			Baila		1910
ZEIDMAN	Baila	F	married			Nahum		1910
ZEIDMAN	Tzirel	F		Nahum	Baila			1910
ZEIDMAN	Haya	F		Nahum	Baila			1910

ח Chet

HAYAT	Berel	M	married			Sarah Leah		1910
HAYAT	Sarah Leah	F	married			Berel		1910
HAYAT	Taiba	F		Berel	Sarah Leah			1910
HAYAT	Rabbi Moshe Aharon	M	married			Malka		1910
HAYAT	Malka	F	married			Moshe Aharon		1910

HASID		M						1910

ט Tet

TSHESLER	Mordechai	M						1911
TSHESLER	Batya	F		Mordechai				1911
	Hana	F		Mordechai			maiden name TCHESLER. One child	1911

י Yod

ICHILCHIK	Lipa Laiv	M	married			Sarah	child	1911
ICHILCHIK	Sarah	F	married			Lipa Laiv	child	1911
ICHILCHIK	Moshe	M					child	1911
ISRAELAVITCH	Abraham Jacob	M						1911

כ Kaf

KATZKELAVITCH	Berel	M	married			Heniya	child	1911
KATZKELAVITCH	Heniya	F	married			Berel	child	1911
KATZKELAVITCH	Sarah	F		Berel	Heniya			1911
KATZKELAVITCH	Hasiya	F		Berel	Heniya			1911
KATZKELAVITCH	David	M		Berel	Heniya			1911
KATZ	Aba	M	married			Tila		1911
KATZ	Tila	F	married			Aba		1911
KATZ	Nehama	F		Aba	Tila			1911
KATZ	Saniya	F		Aba	Tila			1911
KATZ	Israel	M		Aba	Tila			1911
KATZ	Uri	M						1911
KATZ	Zalman	M	married			Baila	child	1911
KATZ	Baila	F	married			Zalman	child	1911
KATZ	Berel	M		Zalman	Baila			1911
KATZ	Nehama	F		Zalman	Baila			1911
KATZ	Hana	F						1911

KATZ	Israel	M						1911
KATZ	Joel	M						1911
KATZ	Mirel	F						1911
KATZ	Taiba	F			Mirel			1911
KATZ	Rachel	F			Mirel			1911
KATZ	Deborah	F			Mirel			1911

ל **Lamed**

LANDE	Rachel	F					maiden name SOLOVEICHIK. 2 children	1911
LANDE	Saniya	F			Rachel			1911
LAFER	Michael	M	married			Leah	3 children	1911
LAFER	Leah	F	married			Michael	3 children	1911
LIBERMAN	Hana	M					3 children	1911
LEIBSTEIN	Israel	M						1911
LEIBSTEIN	Haya	F		Israel				1911
LEIBSTEIN	Yerachmiel	M		Israel				1911
LEIBSTEIN	Joseph	M		Israel				1911
LOCKNER	Mina Zalata	F						1911
LOCKNER	Sarah	F			Zelata			1911
LOCKNER	Abraham	M			Zelata			1911
LIGOMSKY	Leah	F						1911
LURIA							whole family (2 children)	1911
LEVIN	Aharon	M	married			Batya		1911
LEVIN	Batya	F	married			Aharon		1911
LEVIN	Hirsh	M					child	1911
LEVIN	Joseph	M	married			Osnat	2 children	1911
LEVIN	Osnat	F	married			Joseph	2 children	1911
LEVIN	Jacob	M	married			Dina	2 children	1911
LEVIN	Dina	F	married			Jacob	2 children	1911

LEVIN	Isaac	M					4 children	1911
LEVIN	Moshe	M		Isaac				1911
LEVITAN	Betzalel	M	married			Leah	2 children	1911
LEVITAN	Leah	F	married			Betzalel	2 children	1911
LEVITAN	Groniya	M						1911
LEVITAN	Velvel	M	married			Shaina		1911
LEVITAN	Shaina	F	married			Velvel		1911

מ **Mem**

MEGID	David	M						1911
MEGID	Esther	F		David				1911
MULLER	Esther	F					maiden name GILINSKY	1911
MULLER	Meir	M	married			Dina		1911
MULLER	Dina	F	married			Meir		1911
MULLER	Max	M	married			Liba		1911
MULLER	Liba	F	married			Max		1911
MUNITCH	Bluma	F						1911
MUSHKIN	Nachmia	M						1911
MILCHIKER	Mendel	M	married			Yenta		1911
MILCHIKER	Yenta	F	married			Mendel		1911
MILCHIKER	Laizer	M		Mendel	Yenta			1911
MILCHIKER	Saniya	F		Mendel	Yenta			1911
MILCHIKER	Rivka	F		Mendel	Yenta			1911
MILCHIKER	Raizel	F		Mendel	Yenta			1911
MILCHIKER	Isaac	M		Mendel	Yenta			1911

ס **Samech**

SARACKA	Baruch	M	married			Hana		1911
SARACKA	Hana	F	married			Baruch		1911
SALAVEITCHIK	Mendel	M						1911
SALAVEITCHIK	Abraham	M						1911

SALAVEITCHIK	Aharon	M	married			Hinda		1911
SALAVEITCHIK	Hinda	F	married			Aharon		1911
SALAVEITCHIK	Hirsh	M		Aharon	Hinda			1911
SALAVEITCHIK	Slava	F		Aharon	Hinda			1911
SALAVEITCHIK	Hena	F		Aharon	Hinda			1911
SALAVEITCHIK	Bentzion	M						1911
SALAVEITCHIK		F		Bentzion				1911
SALAVEITCHIK	Berel	M	married			Raiza		1911
SALAVEITCHIK	Raiza	F	married			Berel		1911
SALAVEITCHIK	Nehama	F		Berel	Raiza			1911
SALAVEITCHIK	David	M	married			Ela		1911
SALAVEITCHIK	Ela	F	married			David		1911
SALAVEITCHIK	Shmuel	M		David	Ela			1911
SALAVEITCHIK	Deborah	F						1912
SALAVEITCHIK	Zalman	M	married			Sarah Esther		1912
SALAVEITCHIK	Sarah Esther	F	married			Zalman		1912
SALAVEITCHIK	Baila	F		Zalman	Sarah Esther			1912
SALAVEITCHIK	Haya	F						1912
SALAVEITCHIK	Isaac	M	married			Haya		1912
SALAVEITCHIK	Haya	F	married			Isaac		1912
SALAVEITCHIK	Baniya	M		Isaac	Haya			1912
SALAVEITCHIK	Israel	M	married			Rivka		1912
SALAVEITCHIK	Rivka	F	married			Israel		1912
SALAVEITCHIK	Mina	F		Israel	Rivka			1912
SALAVEITCHIK	Moshe	M	married			Dina		1912
SALAVEITCHIK	Dina	F	married			Moshe	maiden name DUBINSKY	1912
SALAVEITCHIK	Shmuel	M		Moshe	Dina			1912
SALAVEITCHIK	Moshe Joseph	M	married			Ita Raiza		1912

SALAVEITCHIK	Raiza	F	married			Moshe Joseph		1912
SALAVEITCHIK	Faiga	M	married			Hinda		1912
SALAVEITCHIK	Hinda	F	married			Faiva		1912
SALAVEITCHIK	Gedalyahu	M		Faiva	Hinda			1912
SALAVEITCHIK	Reuben	M	married			Sarah		1912
SALAVEITCHIK	Sarah	F	married			Reuben		1912
SALAVEITCHIK	Slava	F		Reuben	Sarah			1912
SALAVEITCHIK	Abraham	M		Reuben	Sarah			1912
SALAVEITCHIK	Reuben	M	married			Ela		1912
SALAVEITCHIK	Ela	F	married			Reuben		1912
SALAVEITCHIK	Haya	F		Reuben	Ela			1912
SALAVEITCHIK	Shmuel	M		Reuben	Ela			1912
SALAVEITCHIK	Kayla	F		Reuben	Ela			1912
SALAVEITCHIK	Shlomo	M						1912
SEGAL	Gershon	M						1912

ע Ayin

ELFER	Jacob Tuviya	M						1912
ELFER		F		Jacob Tuvia				1912
ELFER		F		Jacob Tuvia				1912
ELPERIN	Laiv Hayyim	M	married			Pearl		1912
ELPERIN	Pearl	F	married			Laiv Hayyim		1912
ELPERIN	Hanan	M		Laiv Hayyim	Pearl			1912
ELPERIN	Ethel	F		Laiv Hayyim	Pearl			1912
ELPERIN	Masha	F		Laiv Hayyim	Pearl			1912
ELPERIN	Sarah Raizel	F						1912

ELPERIN	Shmuel	M		Raizel			1912
ELPERIN	Hana	F		Raizel			1912

פ Peh

PASTAVSKY	David	M					1912
PASTAVSKY	Velvel	M					1912
PASTAVSKY	Hana Ravka	F					1912
PASTAVSKY		F		Hana Rivka			1912
PASTAVSKY	Laiv	M				3 children	1912
FEIGEL	Abraham	M				2 children	1912
FEIGEL	Hayyim	M				5 children	1912
PERLMUTTER	Hayyim	M	married		Rachel	2 children	1912
PERLMUTTER	Rachel	F	married		Hayyim	2 children	1912
FREIDENSON	Hayyim Joseph	M					1912

צ Tzadik

TZIDIRAVITCH	Berish	M					1912
CINMAN	Aharon	M				3 children	1912
CINMAN	Tuviya	M					1912
TZEIKINSKY	Isaac Eliya	M	married			3 children	1912
TZEIKINSKY		F	married		Eliya	3 children	1912
TZEIKINSKY	Abraham	M					1912
TZEIKINSKY	Daniel	M					1912
TZEIKINSKY	Rivka	F					1912
TZEIKINSKY	Raizel	F					1912

ק Kof

KAGAN	Haya	F					1912
KAGAN	Ita	F		Haya			1912
KAGAN	Shhifra	F		Haya			1912
KAGAN	Hasiya	F					1912

KAGAN	Israel	M	married			Heniya	2 children	1912
KAGAN	Hebiya	F	married			Israel	2 children	1912
KAGAN	Laiv	M					2 children	1912
KAGAN	Reuben	M						1912
KARB	Yerachmiel	M	married			Miriam		1912
KARB	Miriam	F	married			Yerachmiel		1912
KARB	Shprinza	F		Yerachmiel	Miriam			1912
KARB	Israel	M		Yerachmiel	Miriam			1912
KORITZKY	Abraham Eliyahu	M					child	1912
KORITZKY	Henoch	M						1912
KORITZKY	Jacob	M						1912
KORITZKY		F		Jacob				1912
KORITZKY	Laizer	M						1912
KORITZKY	Laibel	M						1912
KORITZKY	Meriya	F						1912
KORITZKY	Pesiya	F						1913
KORITZKY	Reubem	M						1913
KORITZKY	Gershon	M		Reuben				1913
KORITZKY	Rivka	F						1913
KORITZKY	Saul	M						1913
KORITZKY	Shlomo	M						1913
KORITZKY	Shmuel	M						1913
KIDESHMAN	Gershon	M	married			Esther		1913
KIDESHMAN	Esther	F	married			Gershon	maiden name KRIL	1913
KIDESHMAN	Laiv	M		Gershon	Esther			1913
KIMBERT	Joseph Avihdor	M						1913
KIMBERT		F		Joseph Avigdor				1913
KIMBERT	Laizer	M	married			Batya	2 children	1913

KIMBERT	Batya	F	married			Laizer	2 children	1913
KIMBERT		M	married			Haya	child	1913
KIMBERT	Haya Mina	F	married				child	1913
KRAVITCH	Bluma	F						1913
KRAVITCH	Menucha	F			Bluma			1913
KRIL	Hillel	M	married			Rasha		1913
KRIL	Rasha	F	married			Hillel		1913
KRIL	Zalman	M						1913
KRIL	Hirsh	M		Zalman				1913
KRIL	Simcha	M		Zalman				1913
KRIL		F		Zalman				1913
KREITZER	Shlomo	M	married			Batsheva		1913
KREITZER	Batsheva	F	married			Shlomo		1913
KREITZER	Hirsh	M		Shlomo	Batsheva			1913
KREITZER	Rachel	F		Shlomo	Batsheva			1913
KRIMILISKY	Alter	M	married			Rachel		1913
KRIIMILISKY	Rachel	F	married			Alter		1913
KRIMILISKY	Yenta	F		Alter	Rachel			1913

ר **Resh**

RABINOWITCH	Hayyim	M	married			Baila	2 children	1913
RABINOWITCH	Baila	F	married			Hayyim	2 children	1913
ROTSTEIN	Abraham Isaac	M						1913
ROTSTEIN	Hayyim	M		Abraham Isaac				1913
ROTSTEIN	Reuben	M		Abraham Isaac				1913
ROFITZ	Shlomo	M	married			Haya Mina	child	1913
ROFITZ	Haya Mina	F	married			Shlomo	child	1913
RITVA	Mordechai	M					4 children	1913
RITVA	Shaina	F					3 children	1913

RAICHEL	Zakman	M						1913
RAICHEL		F		Zalman				1913
RAICHEL	Aharon	M						1914
RAICHEL	Dabe	F		Aharon				1914
RIMER	Hayyim Joseph	M	married			Pearl	2 children	1914
RIMER	Pearl	F	married			Hayyim	2 children	1914
RING		M	married			Mirel	2 children	1914
RING	Mirel	F	married				2 children	1914
RING	Haya	F					child	1914
REIN	Sarah	F						1914
REIN	Kayla	F						1914
RAPAPORT	Joseph	M	married			Sarah		1914
RAPAPORT	Sarah	F	married			Joseph		1914
RAPAPORT	Nehama	F		Joseph	Sarah			1914
RAPAPORT	Taiba	F		Joseph	Sarah			1914
RAPAPORT	Isaac Joseph	M						1914
RAPAPORT		F		Isaac Joseph				1914

ש Shin

SHAPIRA	Shaina	F						1914
SHAPIRA	Shmuel	M						1914
SHALKAVITCH	Abraham	M						1914
SHALKAVITCH	Shimon	M					2 children	1914
SHALKAVITCH		F				Shimon	2 children	1914
SHOR	Pinchas	M	married					1914
SHOR		F	married			Pinchas		1914
SHUTAN	Abraham	M	married			Pesiya		1914
SHUTAN	Pesiya	F	married			Abraham		1914
SHUTAN	Ephraim	M		Abraham	Pesiya			1914

SHUTAN	Hava	F		Abraham	Pesiya			1914
SHUTAN	Sarah Rivka	F		Abraham	Pesiya			1914
SHUTAN	Hanan Haya	M	married			Sarah Rivka	2 children/ In list written as first name "Hana" possible error	1914
SHUTAN	Sarah Rivka	F	married			Hanan	2 children	1914
SHINTOP	Ezriel	M	married			Rivka	2 children	1914
SHINTOP	Rivka	F	married			Ezriel	2 children	1914
SCHNEIDERAVITCH	Hayyim	M	married			Baila		1914
SCHNEIDERAVITCH	Baila	F	married			Hayyim		1914
SCHNEIDERAVITCH	Deborah	F		Hayyim	Baila			1914
SCHNEIDERAVITCH	Shaina	F		Hayyim	Baila			1914
SCHNEIDERAVITCH	Hayyim	M	married			Kraina Sarah	3 children	1914
SCHNEIDERAVITCH	Crsaina Sarah	F	married			Hayyim	3 children	1914
SCHNEIDERAVITCH	Mera	F					3 children	1914

[Columns 1913-1916]

Daugielishki Necrology

(Naujasis Daugùliškis, Lithuania)

55°22'/26°18'

Transliterated by Beryl Baleson

Page numbers reference the Original Yizkor Book

Family name(s)	First name(s)	Gender	Marital status	Father's name	Mother's name	Name of spouse	Remarks & additional family	Page
א Alef								
ABELAVITCH	Joseph	M	married			Dina	4 children	1913
ABELAVITCH	Dina	F	married			Joseph	4 children	1913
ABELAVITCH	Laiv	M	married			Nalka		1913
ABELAVITCH	Malka	F	married			Laiv		1913
ABELAVITCH	Haya	F		Laiv	Malka			1913
ABELAVITCH	Braina	F		Laiv	Malka			1913
ABELAVITCH	Israel	M		Laiv	Malka			1913
ABELAVITCH	Shlomo	M		Laiv	Malka			1913
USHPAL	Abraham	M	married			Haya Pesa		1913
USHPAL	Haya Pesa	F	married			Abraham		1913
USHPAL	Rivka	F		Abraham	Haya Pesa			1913
USHPAL	Yekutiel	M	married			Haya		1913
USHPAL	haya	F	married			Yekutiel		1913
USHPAL	Shmuel	M		Yekutiel	Haya			1913
USHPAL	Necha	F		Yekutiel	Haya			1913
USHPAL	Liba	F		Yekutiel	Haya			1913
USHPAL	Hava	F		Yekutiel	Haya			1913
USHPAL	Shaul	M	married			Esther		1913

USHPAL	Esther	F	married			Shaul		1913
USHPAL	Yochevet	F		Shaul	Esther			1913
USHPAL	Velvel	M		Shaul	Esther			1913
USHPAL	Hana	M		Shaul	Esther			1913
ARON	Aba Zelig	M	married			Shaina	his son-in-law & grandchildren	1913
ARON	Shaina	F	married			Aba Zelig	her son-in-law and grandchildren	1913
ARON	Faiga	F		Aba Zelig	Shaina			1913
ARON	Shaina	F		Aba Zelig	Shaina		Possibility first name is different	1913
ARON	Yehuda	M	married			Musa	3 children	1913
ARON	Musa	F	married			Yehuda	3 children	1913

ב Bet

BERMAN	Alter	M	married			Ela		1913
BERMAN	Ela	F	married			Alter		1913
BERMAN	Hirsh	M		Alter	Ela			1913
BERMAN	Tzvia	F		Alter	Ela			1913
BERMAN	Batya	F		Alter	Ela			1913

ג Gimmel

GORDON	Hirsh	M	married			Rivka		1913
GORDON	Rivka	F	married			Hirsh		1913
GORDON	Masha	F		Hirsh	Rivka			1913
GORDON	Haya	F		Hirsh	Rivka			1913
GORDON	Kayla	F		Hirsh	Rivka			1913
GORDON	Isaac	M		Hirsh	Rivka			1913
GORDON	Hana	F						1913
GORDON	Ethel	F			Hana			1913
GORDON	Pesa	F			Hana			1913
GORDON	Ita	F			Hana			1913

GORDON	Haya	F			Hana			1913
GORDON	Israel	M	married			Haya		1913
GORDON	Haya	F	married			Israel		1913
GORDON	Hirsh	M		Israel	Haya			1913
GORDON	Hasia	F		Israel	Haya			1913
GORDON	Moshe	M						1913
GORDON		F					Mother of Moshe Gordon	1913
GORDON		F					Sister of Moshe Gordon	1913
GAITZIN	Rachel Baila	F						1913
GAITZIN	Shlomo	M			Rachel Baila			1913
GAITZIN	Sarah	F			Rachel Baila			1913

ד Dalet

DOITCH	Gershon	M	married			Ita	3 children	1913
DOITCH	Ita	F	married			Gershon	3 children	1913

ו Vav

VINAKOR		M	married			Deborah	child	1913
VINAKOR	Deborah	F	married				child	1913
VINAKOR		M					his aunt	1913
VINAKOR		M					his aunt	1913
VINAKOR		M					his aunt	1913
VINAKOR		F					Mother of three brothers Vinakor	1913

ז Zayin

ZAGAJI	Aba Hirsh	M	married			Rivka		1914
ZAGAJI	Rivka	F	married			Aba Hirsh		1914
ZAGAJI	Liba	F		Aba Hirsh	Rivka			1914

ZAK	Bentzion	M	married			Shulamit		1914
ZAK	Shulamit	F	married			Bentzion		1914
ZAK	David	M		Bentzion	Shulamit			1914
ZIV	Melech	M	married			Malka	2 children	1914
ZIV	Malka	F	married			Melech	2 children	1914
ZILBER	Mendel	M	married			Gita		1914
ZILBER	Gita	F	married			Mendel		1914
ZILBER	Aba	M		Mendel	Gita			1914

ל Lamed

LEVIN	Zelig	M	married			Ela	7 children	1914
LEVIN	Ela	F	married			Zelig	7 children	1914

מ Mem

MELAMED	Moshe	M	married			Bat Sheva		1914
MELAMED	Bat Sheva	F	married			Moshe		1914

פ Peh

FAIGEL	Hayyim	M					7 children	1914
FAIGEL	Yerachmiel	M	married				3 children	1914
FAIGEL		F	married			Yerachmiel	3 children	1914

צ Tzadik

CINMAN	Zalman	M	married			Yochevet	his son-in-law and grandson	1914
CINMAN	Yochevet	F	married			Zalman	maiden name LIPSCHITZ. With her son-in-law and grandson	1914
CINMAN	Rachel	F		Zalman	Yochevet			1914
CINMAN	Shulamit	F		Zalman	Yochevet			1914
CINMAN	Tzirl Miriam	F		Zalman	Yochevet			1914
CINMAN	Shlomo	M		Zalman	Yochevet			1914
CINMAN	Jacob	M	married			Leah		1914

CINMAN	Leah	F	married			Jacob		1914
CINMAN	Shmuel	M		Jacob	Leah			1914
CINMAN	David	M		Jacob	Leah			1914

ק **Kof**

KAGAN	Faiva	M	married			Ita	2 children	1914
KAGAN	Ita	F	married			Faiva	2 children	1914
KORITZKY	Velvel	M	married			Kayla		1914
KORITZKY	Hayla	F	married			Velvel		1914
KORITZKY	Joseph	M		Velvel	Kayla			1914
KORITZKY	Berel	M		Velvel	Kayla			1914
KORITZKY	Moshe	M						1914
KORITZKY	Moshe	M	married		Gita	Hesha		1914
KORITZKY	Hesha	F	married			Moshe		1914
KORITZKY	Gita	F					Mother of Moshe	1914
KORITZKY	Hinda	F		Moshe	Hesha		Sister of Moshe	1914

ר **Resh**

RODNITZKY	Hana	M	married			Chiena		1914
RODNITZKY	Chiena	F	married			Hana		1914
	Rivka	F	married				maiden name RODNITSKY. With her husband	1914
RAIN	Haya Feiga	F						1914
RAIN	Pesa	F			Faiga			1914
RAIN	Nehama	F						1914
RAIN	Baila	F			Nehama			1914
RAIN	Zusman	M			Nehama			1914
	Sarah	F					Sister of Isa	1914
	Isa	F					Sister of Sarah	1914
GURVITCH	Pesa	F						1915
ZAIDEL	Moshe	M	married			Nehama		1915

ZAIDEL	Nehama	F	married			Moshe		1915
ZAIDEL	Arye	M		Moshe	Nehama			1915
KATZ	Abraham	M					family	1915
KATZ	Ita	F					family	1915
KATZ	Fruma	F			Ita			1915
KATZ	Velvel	M	married			Baila	family	1915
KATZ	Baila	F	married			Velvel	family	1915
KATZ	Joel	M					family	1915
KATZ	Mair	M					family	1915
LIPENHALZ	Jacob	M	married			Sarah		1916
LIPENHALZ	Sarah	F	married			Jacob		1916
LIPENHALZ	Laiv	M		Jacob	Sarah			1916
LIPENHALZ	Pesa	F		Jacob	Sarah			1916
LIPENHALZ	Henech	M		Jacob	Sarah			1916
PASTAVSKY	Isaac	M	married			Michla		1916
PASTAVSKY	Michla	F	married			Isaac		1916
PASTAVSKY	Batya	F		Isaac	Michla			1916
PASTAVSKY	Moshe	M		Isaac	Michla			1916
PASTAVSKY	Mattel	M		Isaac	Michla			1916
PASTAVSKY	Shaina	F		Isaac	Michla			1916
KRIL	Moshe Isaac	M	married			Zelda		1916
KRIL	Zelda	F	married			Moshe Isaac		1916
KRIL	Nehama	F		Moshe	Zelda			1916
KRIL	Alter	M		Moshe	Zelda			1916
KRIL	Hava	F		Moshe	Zelda			1916
KRIL	Ita	F		Moshe	Zelda			1916
KRIL	Deborah	F					maiden name MATZKIN	1916
KRIL	Ela	F			Deborah			1916

KRIL	Rasha	F			Deborah			1916
ש Shin								
SHARPMAN	Mairam	M	married			Nehama		1916
SHARPMAN	Nehama	F	married			Mairam		1916
SHARPMAN	Zalata	F		Mairam	Nehama			1916
SHARPMAN	Michla	F		Mairam	Nehama			1916
SHARPMAN	Braina	F		Mairam	Nehama			1916
SHARPMAN	Leah	F		Mairam	Nehama			1916

[Columns 1915-1918]

Dukstas Necrology

(Dukštas, Lithuania)

55°32'/26°20'

Transliterated by Beryl Baleson

Page numbers reference the Original Yizkor Book

Family name(s)	First name(s)	Gender	Marital status	Father's name	Mother's name	Name of spouse	Remarks & additional family	Page
א Alef								
	Abigil	F					Rabbi's wife	1915
USHPAL	Hirsh	M					his family	1915
ITZIKSON		M					family	1915
AIDELMAN	Hirsh	M	married			Matla		1915
AIDELMAN	Matla	F	married			Hirsh		1915
EINHARN	Moshe	M	married					1915
EINHARN		F	married			Moshe		1915
EINHARN	Abraham	M		Moshe				1915
EINHARN	Rachel	F		Moshe				1915

ARAN	Elchanan	M					family	1915
ARAN	Ber	M	married			Raiza	family	1915
ARAN	Raiza	F	married			Ber	family	1915
ARAN	Joseph	M	married			Fraida	family	1915
ARAN	Fraida	F	married			Joseph	family	1915
ARAN	Joseph	M	married			Rivka		1915
ARAN	Rivka	F	married				maiden name FAIGELSON	1915
ARAN	Isaac	M					his family	1915
ARAN	Joseph	M	married			Henia	children	1915
ARAN	Henia	F	married			Joseph	children	1915
ARAN	Liber	M						1915
ARAN	Nahum	M	married			Nehama	family	1915
ARAN	Nehama	F	married			Nahum	family	1915
ARAN	Shimon	M					his family	1915
ARNSTEIN	Mendel	M					family	1915
ASHKENAZI	Mordechai	M					his family	1915
ASHKENAZI	Bentzion	M					his family	1915
ASHKENAZI	Isaac	M	married			Hode		1915
ASHKENAZI	Hode	F	married			Isaac		1915

ב **Bet**

BODAVITCH							Uncertain if individual or with family	1915
BIR	David	M	married			Malka		1915
BIR	Malka	F	married			David		1915
BIR	Yehuda	F		David	Malka			1915
BIR	Ber	M		David	Malka			1915
BLASTEIN	Aba Joseph	M	married			Haya		1915
BLASTEIN	Haya	F	married			Aba Joseph		1915

BLASTEIN	Shlomo	M		Aba Joseph	Haya			1915
BLASTEIN	Nahum	M		Aba Joseph	Haya			1915
BLASTEIN	Peretz	M		Aba Joseph	Haya			1915
BLASTEIN	Wolf	M		Aba Joseph	Haya			1915
BLAIMAN	Reuben	M	married			Gita		1915
BLAIMAN	Gita	F	married			Reuben		1915
BLAIMAN		M		Reuben	Gita			1915

ג Gimmel

GEDUD	Betzalel	M					family	1915
GEDUD	David	M					family	1915
GEDUD	Zelig	M					family	1915
GEDUD	Jacob	M	married			Shaina		1915
GEDUD	Shaina	F	married			Jacob		1915
GURVITCH	Hirsh	M					family	1915
GURVITCH	Israel	M	married			Batya		1916
GURVITCH	Batya	F	married			Israel		1916
GURVITCH	Mola	M		Israel	Batya			1916
GURVITCH	Mordechai	M	married			Sarah		1916
GURVITCH	Sarah	F	married			Mordechai		1916
GURVITCH	Neta	M	married			Sarah		1916
GURVITCH	Sarah	F	married			Neta		1916
GURVITCH		F		Nata	Sarah			1916
GINSBERG	David Shlomo	M					family	1916
GINSBERG	Hirsh	M					family	1916
GALIAT	Isaac	M					family	1916
GALIAT	Reuben	M					family	1916
GEFEN							whole family	1916

GEFEN	Yodel	M				Esther		1916
GEFEN	Esther	F				Yudel	maiden name LAUW	1916
GURAVITCH	David	M						1916
GURAVITCH	Hayyim	M					family	1916
GURAVITCH	Feiga	F					family	1916
GURAVITCH	Shmuel	M					family	1916
GURAVITCH	Laiv	M	married			Rachel		1916
GURAVITCH	Rachel	F	married			Laiv	maiden name BAK	1916

ד Dalet

DAVIDAVITCH	Abraham	M	married			Rivka		1916
DAVIDAVITCH	Rivka	F	married			Abraham		1916
DAVIDAVITCH	Matla	F		Abraham	Rivka			1916
DAVIDAVITCH	Mordechai Aharon	M						1916
DAVIDAVITCH		M	married			Rivka	The children are girls	1916
DAVIDAVITCH	Moshe	F	married			Moshe	The children are girls	1916
DAVIDAVITCH	Shniar	M						1916
DAITCH	Moshe	M	married			Hana	children	1916
DAITCH	Hana	F	married			Moshe	children	1916
DAITCH	Joseph Laiv	M						1916
DAITCH	Pinchas	M	married					1916
DAITCH		F	married			Pinchas		1916
DAITCH	Tzadok	M					family	1916
DAITCH	Eliezer	M					family	1916
DRISVIATSKY							whole family	1916

ה Hey

HALPERIN	Hana	M						1916

HAMBERG	Eliezer	M	married			Tzvia		1916
HAMBERG	Tzifa	F	married			Eliezer		1916
HAMBERG	Bluma	F		Eliezer	Tzifa			1916
HAMBERG	Sarah	F		Eliezer	Tzifa			1916
HAMBERG	Berel	M		Eliezer	Tzifa			1916
HAMBERG	Esther	F		Eliezer	Tzifa			1916
HAMBERG	Laiv	M	married					1916
HAMBERG		F	married			Laiv		1916
HAMBERG	Mina Hadel	F						1917
HAMBERG	Mendel	M	married			Fraida		1917
HAMBERG	Fraida	F	married			Mendel		1917
HAMBERG	Lioba	F		Mendel	Fraida			1917
HAMBERG	Mordechai	M	married			Esther	children	1917
HAMBERG	Esther	F	married			Mordechai	maiden name FAIGELSON. With children	1917
HAMBERG	Sarah	F						1917
HAMBERG	Jacob	M			Sarah			1917
HAMBERG	Necha	F			Sarah			1917
HAMBERG	Hinda	F			Sarah			1917
HIMELFARB	Anshel	M	married			Niuta		1917
HIMELFARB	Niota	F	married			Anshel	maiden name LEVIN	1917
HIMELFARB	Pesach	M	married			Shaina Liba		1917
HIMELFARB	Shaina Liba	F	married			Pesach		1917
ו Vav								
WEINSTEIN	Tzvi	M	married			Bella		1917
WEINSTEIN	Bella	F	married			Tzvi	maiden name ARAN	1917
ז Zayin								

ZACKAVITCH	Shlomo	M	married		Hana		1917
ZACKAVITCH	Hana	F	married		Shlomo		1917

ט Tet

TABACHAVITCH	Jacob Meir	M	married		Hana		1917
TABACHAVITCH	Hana	F	married		Jacob Meir		1917
TABACHAVITCH	Isaac	M				family	1917
TABACHAVITCH	Shalom	M					1917
TABACHAVITCH	Shimon	M					1917
TABACHAVITCH	Shnior	M					1917
TELENT	Yudel	M				family	1917
TELENT	Shnmuel	M				family	1917
TELENT	Abraham	M				family	1917
TELER	Shlomo	M	married			children	1917
TELER		F	married		Shlomo	children	1917
TELER	Nahum	M		Shlomo			1917
TELER	Michael	M		Shlomo			1917

כ Kaf

KAGAN	Aharon	M	married		Esther	children	1917
KAGAN	Esther	F	married		Aharon	children	1917
KAGAN	Hirsh	M				family	1917
KAGAN	Shmuel	M	married		Pesa		1917
KAGAN	Pesa	F	married		Shmuel		1917
KAGAN	Pesa	F					1917

ל Lamed

LURIA	Aida	M					1917
LURIA	Joel	M					1917
LURIA	Mina	F					1917
LURIA	Moshe	M	married		Rada		1917
LURIA	Rada	F	married		Moshe		1917

LURIA	Hanan	M		Moshe	Rada			1917
LURIA	Neta	M	married			Faiga		1917
LURIA	Faiga	F	married			Nata		1917
LURIA	Ela	F		Nata	Faiga			1917
LURIA	Gita	F		Nata	Faiga			1917
LEIBAVITCH	Laizer	M					family	1917
LEIBAVITCH	Fraida	F					her family	1917
LEVIN	Aba	M	married			Leah		1917
LEVIN	Leah	F	married			Aba		1917
LEVIN	Moshe	M		Aba	Leah			1917
LEVIN	Esther Faiga	F						1917
LEVIN	Bila	F						1917
LEVIN	Hillel	M			Bila			1917
LEVIN	David	M	married			Leah		1917
LEVIN	Leah	F	married			David	maiden name RIMER	1917
LEVIN	Abraham	M		David	Leah			1917
LEVIN	Hirsh	M	married			Braina		1917
LEVIN	Braina	F	married			Hirsh		1917
LEVIN	Luba	F		Hirsh	Braina			1917
LEVIN	Ela	F		Hirsh	Braina			1917
LEVIN	Yekutiel	M	married			Miriam		1917
LEVIN	Miriam	F	married			Yekutiel		1917
LEVIN	Yerachmiel	M		Yekutiel	Miriam			1917
LEVIN	Leah	F					her family	1917
LEVIN	Mordechai	M					family	1917
LEVIN	Shnior	M					family	1917
	Abraham	M	married			Masha	children	1917

מ Mem

MILLER	Masha	F	married			Abraham	children	1917

ס **Samech**

SALTAISKY	Joseph	M					family	1917
STARAVITCH	Isaac	M	married			Sima	children	1917
STARAVITCH	Sima	F	married			Isaac	children	1917
SMALKIN	Gershon	M	married					1917
SMALKIN		F	married				maiden name KOSHLIN	1917
SMALKIN		M		Gershon				1917
SEGAL	Hirsh	M	married			Shaina	children	1917
SEGAL	Shaina	F	married			Hirsh	maiden name KAGAN. With children	1917
SEGAL	Zalman	M	married			Rachel		1917
SEGAL	Rachel	F	married			Zalman		1917
SEGAL	Sania	F		Zalman	Rachel			1917
SEGAL	Abraham	M		Zalman	Rachel			1917
SEGAL	Shmuel	M		Zalman	Rachel			1917
SEGAL	Shnior	M						1917
SEGAL	Asher	M						1917
SEGAL	Ita	M						1917
SEGAL	Sarah	F						1917
SEGAL	Abraham	M					family	1917
RABBI SPEVAK		M	married			Rada	Rabbi	1917
SPEVAK	Rada Abigil	F	married				Possibility Rabbi Spevak's wife's maiden name "ABIGIL"	1917

פ **Peh**

FAIGELMAN	Zelig	M					family	1917
FAIGELMAN	Hana	M	married			Hena	family	1917
FAIGELMAN	Hena	F	married			Hana	family	1917

FINGERHOIT							whole family	1917
FLISKIN	Moshe	M					family	1917
FELDMAN	Israel	M	married			Sarah		1918
FELDMAN	Sarah	F	married			Israel		1918
FELDMAN	Joel	M	married			Haya	children	1918
FELDMAN	Haya	F	married			Joel	maiden name HAMBERG. With children	1918
FELDMAN	Michael	M					family	1918
FELDMAN	Moshe	M					family	1918
FELDMAN	Mordechai	M					family	1918
FELDMAN	Tzadok	M						1918

צ **Tzadik**

TZUKERMAN							whole family	1918
CINMAN	Gesia	F						1918
CINMAN	Laiv	M					family	1918
CINMAN	Shlomo	M					family	1918
CINMAN	Shimon	M	married			Hana	children	1918
CINMAN	Hana	F	married			Shimon	children	1918

ק **Kof**

KAVARSKY	Haya Sarah	F						1918
KATSHARGINSKY	Meir	M					child	1918
KATSHARGINSKY	Fiaga	F					family	1918
KAMARAZ	Moshe	M	married			Hena		1918
KAMARAZ	Hena	F	married			Moshe		1918
KAMARAZ	Batya	F		Moshe	Hena			1918
KAMARAZ	Shlomo	M		Moshe	Hena			1918
KAMARAZ	Musa	F		Moshe	Hena			1918
KARASIN	Aharon	M				Haya		1918
KARASIN	Haya	F				Aharon		1918

KARASIN	Sarah	F		Aharon	Haya			1918
KARLIN	Mordechai	M					family	1918
KARLIN	Raicha	F						1918
KRITZER	Hayyim	M	married			Batya		1918
KRITZER	Batya	F	married			Hayyim		1918
KRITZER	Miriam	F		Hayyim	Batya			1918
KRITZER	Rachel	F		Hayyim	Batya			1918
KRITZER	Abraham	M		Hayyim	Batya			1918
KRITZER	Sarah	F		Hayyim	Batya			1918
KRITZER	Shaina	F		Hayyim	Batya			1918
KRITZER	Reuben	M	married			Hana	family	1918
KRITZER	Hana	F	married			Reuben	family	1918
KARLAND	Shmuel	M	married			Rivka		1918
KARLAND	Rivka	F	married			Shmuel		1918
KARLAND		M		Shmuel	Rivka			1918
KARLAND	Haya Sarah	F						1918
KOSHLIN	Zalman Isaac	M					family	1918
KOSHLIN	Jacob	M	married			Shaina		1918
KOSHLIN	Shaina	F	married			Jacob		1918
KOSHLIN	Laiv	M					family	1918
KOSHLIN	Musa	F						1918
KOSHLIN	Mordechai	M						1918
KONAVSKY	Abraham Michael	M					family	1918
KONAVSKY	Isaac	M					family	1918
KONAVSKY	Pesa	F						1918
KONAVSKY	Rivka	F						1918
KONAVSKY	Reuben	M						1918

ר **Resh**

RAIZENBERG	Tzifa	F						1918
RAIZENBERG	Shmuel	M			Tzifa			1918
RAIZENBERG	Luba	F			Tzifa			1918
RAIZENBERG	Rafal	M						1918
RAIZENBERG	Sima	F						1918
RAIZENBERG	Laiv	M						1918
RAIZENBERG	Hasia	F						1918
RAIZENBERG	Necha	F						1918
RAPAPORT	Haya Batya	F						1918
ROSHKEVITCH	Mordechai	M						1918
ROSHKEVITCH		M					Brother of Mordechai	1918
RIVAS	Joseph	M					family	1918
RIMER							whole family	1918

ש Shin

SHAPIRA	Abraham	M					family	1918
SHAPIRA	Ephraim	M					family	1918
SHAPIRA	Ber	M					family	1918
SHAPIRA	Henoch	M	married			Fradel	children	1918
SHAPIRA	Fradel	F	married			Henoch	children	1918
SHAPIRA	Joseph	M	married			Aida		1918
SHAPIRA	Ida	F	married			Joseph		1918
SHAPIRA	Zelig	M		Joseph	Aida			1918
SHAPIRA	Fraida	F		Joseph	Aida			1918
SHAPIRA	Zelda	F		Joseph	Aida			1918
SHAPIRA	Jacob	M	married			Pesa	children	1918
SHAPIRA	Pesa	F	married			Jacob	children	1918
SHAPIRA	Leah	F					family	1918
SHAPIRA	Liba	F						1918
SHAPIRA	Moshe	M	married			Alta		1918

SHAPIRA	Alta	F	married			Moshe		1918
SHEVIL	Joseph	M						1918
SHLASBERG	Isaac	M					family	1918
SHLASBERG	Hirsh	M	married			Shaina	family	1918
SHLASBERG	Shaina	F	married			Hirsh	family	1918
SHERMAN	Zalman	M	married			Esther	family	1918
SHERMAN	Esther	F	married			Zalman	family	1918
SHOCHAT	Shmuel	M					family	1918
SHOR	Hirsh	M					family	1918

[Columns 1915-1916]

Ceikiniai Necrology

(Ceikiniai, Lithuania)

55°16'/26°16'

Transliterated by Beryl Baleson

Page numbers reference the Original Yizkor Book

Family name(s)	First name(s)	Gender	Marital status	Father's name	Mother's name	Name of spouse	Additional family	Page
א Alef								
GORDON	Shmuel	M					2 children	1915
GILINSKY	Abraham	M	married			Deborah	child	1915
GILINSKY	Devorah	F	married			Abraham	child	1915
GILINSKY	Liba Haya	F						1915
פ Peh								
FAIGEL	Haya	F						1915
FAIGEL	Sima	F			Haya			1915

צ Tzadik								
TZAIKINSKY	Moshe	M	married			Hana		1916
TZAIKINSKY	Hana	F	married			Moshe		1916
TZAIKINSKY	Aharon	M		Moshe	Hana			1916
TZAIKINSKY	Deborah	M		Moshe	Hana			1916
TZAIKINSKY	Eliyahu	M		Moshe	Hana			1916
TZAIKINSKY	Yerachmiel	M	married			Hasia	2 children	1916
TZAIKINSKY	Hesia	F	married			Yerachmiel	2 children	1916
ש Shin								
SCHNEIDERAVITCH	Tzirel	F						1916

[Columns 1919-1922]

Koltiniany Necrology

(Kaltanėnai, Lithuania)

55°16' 26°00'

Transliterated by Beryl Baleson

Page numbers reference the Original Yizkor Book

Family name(s)	**First name(s)**	**Gender**	**Marital status**	**Father's name**	**Mother's name**	**Name of spouse**	**Remarks and additional family**	**Page**
א Alef								
ABRAMAVITCH	Shaina	F					maiden name TABACHAVITCH	1919
AGRANIN	Shmuel	M	married			Gita		1919
AGRANIN	Gita	F	married			Shmuel	maiden name KRAMER	1919
ITZKAVITCH	Hana	M	married			Rivka		1919
ITZKAVITCH	Rivka	F	married			Hana		1919
ITZKAVITCH	Hirsh	M		Hana	Rivka			1919
AXELROD	Berl	M	married			Necha		1919

AXELROD	Necha	F	married			Berl	maiden name TABACHAVITCH	1919
AXELROD	Deborah	F		Berl	Necha			1919
AXELROD	Moshe	M		Berl	Necha			1919

ג Gimmel

GAVENDA	Haluina	M	married			Batya		1919
GAVENDA	Batya	F	married			Haluina		1919
GAVENDA	Faiga	F		Haluina	Batya			1919
GAVENDA	Tzifa	F		Haluina	Batya			1919
GAVENDA	Nathan	M	married			Rivka	child	1920
GAVENDA	Rivka	F	married			Nathan	maiden name KORAPATKIN. A child	1920
GAVENDA	Shalom Tuvia	M						1920
GAVENDA	Ita	F		Shalom Tuvia				1920
GERBER	Siama	M	married			Rivka		1920
GERBER	Rivka	F	married			Siama	maiden name KRAMER	1920
GERBER		F		Siama	Rivka			1920
GERBER		F		Siama	Rivka			1920
GARSHIN	Mordechai	M	married			Rivka		1920
GARSHIN	Rivka	F	married			Mordechai		1920
GUTTERMAN	Abraham	M	married			Hana		1920
GUTTERMAN	Hana	F	married			Abraham		1920
GUTTERMAN	Hinda	F		Abraham	Hana			1920
GUTTERMAN	Baila	F		Abraham	Hana			1920
GUTTERMAN	Berel	M	married			haya		1920
GUTTERMAN	Haya	F	married			Berl		1920
GUTTERMAN	Tzirel	F		Berl	Haya			1920
GUTTERMAN	Tana	M		Berl	Haya			1920

GUTTERMAN	Zala	M	married			Batya		1921
GUTTERMAN	Batya	F	married			Zala		1921
GUTTERMAN	Shniur	M		Zala	Batya			1921
GUTTERMAN	David	M		Zala	Batya			1921
GUTTERMAN	Zalman	M		Zala	Batya			1921
GUTTERMAN	Malka	F		Zala	Batya			1921
GLAZER	Zlata	F					maiden name RODNITSKY	1921
GLAZER	Israel	M			Zelata			1921
GLAZER	Rishel	F			Zelata			1921

ו Vav

VALAVITCH	Bentzion	M	married			Ita		1921
VALAVITCH	Ita	F	married			Bentzion		1921
VALAVITCH	Frieda	F		Bentzion	Ita			1921
VALAVITCH	Berel	M	married			Rachel		1921
VALAVITCH	Rachel	F	married			Berl		1921
VALAVITCH	Shasa	F						1921
VALAVITCH	Shlomo	M			Shasa			1921
VALAVITCH	Braina	F			Shasa			1921
VALAVITCH	Hasia	F			Shasa			1921
VALAVITCH	Berl	M			Shasa			1921
VINAKOR	Shmuel	M						1921
VINAKOR	Shlomo	M		Shmuel	Baila		List in brackets written "Baylis"	1921

ט Tet

TABACHAVITCH	Alter	M	married			Baila		1921
TABACHAVITCH	Baila	F	married			Alter		1921
TABACHAVITCH	Jacob	M	married			Rachel		1921
TABACHAVITCH	Rachel	F	married			Jacob		1921
TABACHAVITCH	Hirsh	M		Jacob	Rachel			1921

TABACHAVITCH	Nathan	M						1921
TABACHAVITCH	Baila	F		Nathan				1921
TABACHAVITCH	Haya	F		Nathan				1921
TRAK		M	married			Aida		1921
TRAK	Aida	F	married				maiden name KAVALSKY	1921
TRAK	Vitka	F			Aida			1921
TRAK	Malka	F			Aida			1921

כ Kaf

KATZ	Eliyahu	M	married			Raiza		1921
KATZ	Raiza	F	married			Eliyahu		1921
KATZ	Abraham Isaac	M		Eliyahu	Raiza			1921
KATZ	Leah	F		Eliyahu	Raiza			1921
KATZ	Rafal	M	married			Dina		1921
KATZ	Dina	F	married			Rafal		1921

מ Mem

MAVSH	Mordechai	M	married			Rachel		1921
MAVSH	Rachel	F	married			Mordechai		1921
MAVSH	Joseph	M		Mordechai	Rachel			1921
MAVSH	Deborah	F		Mordechai	Rachel			1921
MAVSH	Laiv	M		Mordechai	Rachel			1921
MAVSH	Eliyahu	M	married			Hana	2 children	1921
MAVSH	Hana	F	married			Eliyahu	2 children	1921
MILONTCHIK	Laiv	M	married			Hiana		1921
MILONTCHIK	Hiana	F	married			Laiv		1921
MILONTCHIK	Braina	F		Laiv	Hiana			1921

פ Peh

PORTNOY	David	M	married			Raizel		1921
PORTNOY	Raizel	F	married			David		1921

PORTNOY	Nehama	F		David	Raizel			1921
PORTNOY	Shaul	M		David	Raizel			1921
PUPISKY	Aharon	M	married			Faiga		1921
PUPISKY	Faiga	F	married			Aharon		1921
PUPISKY	Gitel	F		Aharom	Faiga			1921
PUPISKY	Abraham	M		Aharom	Faiga			1921
PUPISKY	Hayyim	M	married			Saniya		1921
PUPISKY	Saniya	F	married			Hayyim		1921
PUPISKY	Rivka	F		Hayyim	Saniya			1921
PUPISKY	Taiba	F					maiden name TABACHAVITCH	1921
FRIEDMAN	Moshe	M	married			Rachel		1921
FRIEDMAN	Rachel	F	married			Moshe		1921
FRIEDMAN	Jacob	M		Moshe	Rachel			1921
FRIEDMAN	Golda	F		Moshe	Rachel			1921

ק Kof

KAVALSKY	Grisha	M	married			Sarah		1921
KAVALSKY	Sarah	F	married			Grisha		1921
KAVALSKY	Mordechai	M		Grisha	Sarah			1921
KAMINSKY	Shmerel	M	married			Rosa		1921
KAMINSKY	Rosa	F	married			Shmerel	maiden name KRAMER	1921
KAMINSKY	Yasha	M		Shmerel	Rosa			1921
KORAPATKIN	Haya Sarah	F						1922
KORAPATKIN	Melech	M			Haya Sarah			1922
KORAPATKIN	Gita	F			Haya Sarah			1922
KORAPATKIN	Shimon	M	married				children	1922
KORAPATKIN		F	married			Shimon	children	1922
KRAMER	Deborah	F	married			Hirsh	Rabbi's wife	1922

KRAMER	Eliyahu	M	married			Liuba		1922
KRAMER	Liuba	F	married			Eliyahu		1922
KRAMER	Isaac	M						1922
KRAMER	Joseph	M	married			Rosa		1922
KRAMER	Rosa	F	married			Joseph		1922
KRAMER		M		Joseph	Rosa			1922
KRAMER		M		Joseph	Rosa			1922

ר Resh

RACHIN	Joel	M	married			Masha		1922
RACHIN	Masha	F	married			Joel	maiden name RODNITSKY	1922
RODAITZKY	Yehiel	M	married			Rachel		1922
RODAITZKY	Rachel	F	married			Yehiel	maiden name PUPISKY	1922
RODAITZKY		F		Yehiel	Rachel			1922
RODAITZKY		F		Yehiel	Rachel			1922
RODNITSKY	Eliyahu	M	married			Rosa	2 children	1922
RODNITSKY	Rosa	F	married			Eliyahu	2 children	1922
RODNITSKY	Gershon	M	married			Shifra		1922
RODNITSKY	Shifra	F	married			Gershon		1922
RODNITSKY	Rivka	F		Gershon	Shifra			1922
RODNITSKY	Ezriel	M		Gershon	Shifra			1922
RODNITSKY	Berl	M		Gershon	Shifra			1922
RODNITSKY	Hana Rivka	F						1922
RODNITSKY	Isaac	M	married			Nadiya	3 children	1922
RODNITSKY	Nadiya	F	married			Isaac	3 children	1922
RODNITSKY	Leah	F						1922
RODNITSKY	Meir	M	married			Rachel	child	1922
RODNITSKY	Rachel	F	married			Meir	child	1922
RODNITSKY	Mordehai	M	married			Faiga	2 children	1922

RODNITSKY	Faiga	F	married			Mordechai	2 children	1922
RODNITSKY	Rivka	F						1922
RODNITSKY	Shlomo	M			Rivka			1922
RODNITSKY	David	M			Rivka			1922
RODNITZKY	Rachel Daba	F						1922
ROPAITZ	Leah	F						1922
ROPAITZ	Leah	F			Leah		Possibility first name is different	1922
ROPAITZ	Haya	F			Leah			1922
ROPAITZ	Hana	F			Leah			1922
ROPAITZ	Zalman	M			Leah			1922
ROPAITZ	Benjamin	M			Leah			1922
ROPAITZ	David	M	married			Shifra		1922
ROPAITZ	Shifra	F	married			David		1922
ROPAITZ	Elchanan	M		David	Shifra			1922

ש Shin

SHAPIRA	Zelata	F					maiden name KRAMER	1922
SHAPIRA	Eliyahu	M			Zelata			1922
SHAINBERG	David	M	married			Zelata		1922
SHAINBERG	Zelata	F	married			David	maiden name RODNITSKY	1922
SHAINBERG		M		David	Zelata			1922
SHAINBERG		M		David	Zelata			1922

[Columns 1921-1926]

Podbrozie Necrology
(Pabradė, Lithuania)
55°00'/25°47'
Transliterated by Beryl Baleson

Family name(s)	First name(s)	Gender	Marital status	Father's name	Mother's name	Name of spouse	Remarks	Page
א Alef								
ABRAHAMOWITZ	Ethel	F						1921
ABRAHAMOWITZ	Abraham	M			Ethel			1921
ABRAHAMOWITZ	Leav	M			Ethel			1921
ABRAHAMOWITZ	Bentzion	M			Ethel			1921
AVITSHINSKY	Kaliya	M	married			Hasiah		1921
AVITSHINSKY	Hasiya	F	married			Kaliya		1921
INGELSTEIN	Aharon	M	married			Haya Sarah		1921
INGELSTEIN	Haya Sarah	F	married			Aharon		1921
INGELSTEIN	Leah	F		Aharon	Haya Sarah			1921
INGELSTEIN	Hanah	F						1921
INGELSTEIN	Jacob	M	married			Hesiah		1921
INGELSTEIN	Hesiah	F	married			Jacob		1921
INGELSTEIN	Berel	M		Jacob	Hesiah			1921
INGELSTEIN	Bentzion	M		Jacob	Hesiah			1921
INGELSTEIN	Yekutiel	M		Jacob	Hesiah			1921
INGELSTEIN	Meir	M	married			Leah		1921
INGELSTEIN	Leah	F	married			Meir		1921
INGELSTEIN	Mariasha	F		Meir	Leah			1921
INGELSTEIN	Haya	F		Meir	Leah			1921
INGELSTEIN	Hayyim	M		Meir	Leah			1921
INGELSTEIN	Shmuel	M		Meir	Leah			1921
INGELSTEIN	Feiva	M	married			Dobe		1921
INGELSTEIN	Dobe	F	married			Feiva		1921
ALAKSAR	Mordehai	M	married			Taibe		1921
ALAKSAR	Taibe	F	married			Mordehai		1921
ALAKSAR	Hayyim	M		Mordehai	Taibe			1921

ALAKSAR	Joseph	M		Mordehai	Taibe			1921
EMETH	Moshe	M	married			Rivka		1921
EMETH	Rivka	F	married			Moshe		1921
ASTRACAN		M	married					1921
ASTRACAN		F	married					1921
ARMAN	Sender	M	married			Hanah		1921
ARMAN	Hanah	F	married			Sender		1921
ARMAN	Leib	M		Sender	Hanah			1921
ARMAN	Beila	F		Sender	Hanah			1921

ב Bet

BAVARSKY	Esther	F						1921
BAVARSKY	Batya	F			Esther			1921
BARVARSKY	Shmuel	M			Esther			1921
BAVARSKY	Be'er	M	married			Fesiya		1921
BAVARSKY	Fesia	F	married			Be'er		1921
BAVARSKY	Gutman	M						1921
BAVARSKY	Haya Sarah	F						1921
BAVARSKY	Israel	M						1921
BAVARSKY	Nata	M	married			Feiga		1921
BAVARSKY	Feiga	F	married			Nata		1921
BAVARSKY	Joseph	M		Nata	Feiga			1921
BAVARSKY	Feiva	M	married			Feiga		1921
BAVARSKY	Feiga	F	married			Feiva		1921
BAVARSKY	Abraham	M		Feiva				1921
BAVARSKY	Hirsh	M			Feiga			1921
BAVARSKY	Shlomo	M	married			Leah		1921
BAVARSKY	Leah	F	married			Shlomo		1921
BAVARSKY	Hayyim	M		Shlomo	Leah			1921
BAVARSKY	Batya	F		Shlomo	Leah			1921
BAVARSKY	Shlomo	M		Shlomo	Leah			1921
BAVARSKY	Hearch	M		Shlomo	Leah			1921
BATVINIK	Alter	M	married			Yenta		1922
BATVINIK	Yenta	F	married			Alter		1922
BATVINIK	Elchanan	M		Alter	Yenta			1922
BATVINIK	Feiga	F		Alter	Yenta			1922
BARNAMAV	Hanan	M	married					1922

BARNAMAV		F	married			Hanan		1922
BIKSAN	Yerucham	M	married			Gitel		1922
BIKSAN	Gitel	F	married			Yerucham		1922
BIKSAN	Sarah	F		Yerucham	Gitel			1922
BIKSAN	Nahum	M	married			Sheina		1922
BIKSAN	Sheina	F	married			Nahum		1922
BIKSAN	Hasiah	F		Nahum	Sheina			1922
BIKSAN	Israel	M		Nahum	Sheina			1922
BLOCK	Hannah	F						1922
BLOCK	Sonia	F			Hannah			1922
BLOSHINSKY	Isaac	M						1922
BLITZ	Mordehai	M	married			Nahama		1922
BLITZ	Nehama	F	married			Mordehai		1922
BLITZ	Leiv	M		Mordehai	Nehamia			1922
BLITZ	Hayah	F		Mordehai	Nehamia			1922
BRATANITSKY	Israel	M						1922
	Freida	F	married	Israel		Moshe	Maiden name BRATANITSKY	1922
BRATANITSKY	Jacob	M		Israel				1922
BRATANITSKY	Shlomo	M		Israel				1922
BRATANITSKY	Hirsh	M		Israel				1922
BRIN	Isaac	M	married			Hayah		1922
BRIN	Hayah	F	married			Isaac		1922
BRIN	Hanah	F		Isaac	Hayah			1922
BRIN CROOK	Ita	F						1922
BRIN CROOK	Sarah	F			Ita			1922

ג Gimmel

GARDAAN	Mordehai	M	married			Gitel		1922
GARDAAN	Gitel	F	married			Mordehai		1922
GARDAAN	Sarah	F		Mordehai	Gitel			1922
GARDAAN	Hayah	F		Mordehai	Gitel			1922
GARDAAN	Rachel	F						1922
GARDAAN	Geiva	M			Rachel			1922
GARDAAN	Leiv	M	married			Baila		1922
GARDAAN	Beila	F	married			Leiv		1922
GARDAAN	Aharon	M	married			Sania		1922
GARDAAN	Sanya	F	married			Aharon		1922

GARDAAN		M		Aharon	Sanya			1922
GARDAAN	Feiga	F						1922
GARDAAN	Nianak	M			Feiga			1922
GARDAAN	Aba	M						1922
GARDAAN	Meir	M		Aba				1922
GARDAAN	Abraham	M		Aba				1922
GARDAAN	Israel	M		Aba				1922
GURVITCH	Tuvia	M	married			Tzifa		1922
GURVITCH	Tzifa	F	married			Tuvia		1922
GURVITCH		F		Tuvia	Tzifa			1922
GURVITCH		F		Tuvia	Tzifa			1922
GILINSKY		M	married			Sarah		1922
GILINSKY	Sarah	F	married				Maiden name LIEBERMAN	1922
GINDLIN	Joseph	M						1922
GLASS	Yehuda	M	married			Mera		1922
GLASS	Mera	F	married			Yehuda		1922
GLASS	Reuben	M		Yehuda	Mera			1922
GLASS	Leiv	M		Yehuda	Mera			1922
GLASS	Freida	F		Yehuda	Mera			1922
GLASS	Jacob	M	married			yacha		1923
GLASS	Yacha	F	married			Jacob		1923
GLASS	Leiv	M	married			Esther		1923
GLASS	Esther	F	married			Leiv		1923
GLASS	Rachel	F		Leiv	Esther			1923
GLASS	Dina	F		Leiv	Esther			1923
GLASS	Dud	M		Leiv	Esther			1923
GELER	Ephraim	M	married		Hava			1923
GELER		F	married			Ephraim		1923
GELER	Hava	F						1923
GELER	Hayyim	M		Ephraim				1923
GELER	Haya	M		Ephraim				1923
GELER	Rachal	F		Ephraim				1923

ד Dalet

DENDE		M	married					1923
DENDE		F	married					1923

ה Hey

HALPERIN	Kodesh	M	married			Leah		1923
HALPERIN	Leah	F	married			Kodesh		1923
HALPERIN	Hayyim	M		Kodesh	Leah			1923
HAPTKA	Nehama	F						1923

ו Vav

VILLIAN	Hirsh	M	married			Reiza		1923
VILLIAN	Reiza	F	married			Hirsh		1923
VILLIAN	Isaac	M		Hirsh	Reiza			1923
VILLIAN	Sarah	F		Hirsh	Reiza			1923
VILLIAN	Hayyim	M						1923
VILLIAN	Gita	F		Hayyim				1923
VILLIAN	Mark	M						1923
VILLIAN		F	married					1923
VINER	Moshe	M						1923
VINER		M		Moshe				1923

ז Zayin

ZACK	Hayyim	M	married			Freida		1923
ZACK	Freida	F	married			Hayyim		1923
ZILBER	Hanah	F						1923
ZILBER	Fruma	F						1923
ZILBER	Moshe	M					Brother of Mera	1923
ZILBER	Mera	F					Sister of Moshe	1923
ZILBER	Isaac	M	married			Rivka		1923
ZILBER	Rivka	F	married			Isaac		1923
ZILBER		F		Isaac	Rivka			1923

ט Tet

TAD	Shlomo	M	married					1923
TAD		F	married			Shlomo		1923
TAD	Nehama	F		Shlomo				1923
TAD	Hillel	M		Shlomo				1923
TAD	Hayyim	M		Shlomo				1923
TORISKY	Joseph	M	married			Liba		1923
TORISKY	Liba	F	married			Joseph		1923
TAITZ	Fina	M	married			Raizel		1923
TAITZ	Raizel	F	married			Fina		1923
TRAKINSKY	Arye	M						1923

TRAKINSKY	Ela	F		Arye				1923
TRAKINSKY	Sasha	M		Arye				1923
י **Yod**								
YAVITCH	Ashia	M	married			yenta		1923
YAVITCH	Yenta	F	married			Ashia		1923
YAVITCH	Shlomo	M		Ashia	Yenta			1923
YAVITCH	Hayyim	M		Ashia	Yenta			1923
YAVITCH	Leah	F						1923
YAVITCH	Hirsh	M						1923
YAVITCH	Moshe	M	married			Rachel		1923
YAVITCH	Rachel	F	married			Moshe		1923
YAVITCH	Kayla	F						1923
YAVITCH	Shimon	M	married				Possible personal name different	1923
YAVITCH	Hena	F	married				Possible husband's personal name different	1923
YAVITCH	Hasiya	F			Hena		Possible father's personal name different	1923
YUDELOVITCH		F					Mother of the son	1923
YUDELOVITCH		M					Son of the mother	1923
YEVIEROVITCH	Shmeul	M					Possibility personal name different	1923
YEVIEROVITCH	Shmuel	M					Possibility personal name different	1923
כ **Kaf**								
KARMETZ	David	M	married			Rivka		1923
KARMETZ	Rivka	F	married			David		1923
KARMETZ	Moshe	M		David	Rivka			1923
KARMETZ	Abraham	M		David	Rivka			1923
KARMETZ	Haya	F		David				1923
KARMETZ	Tema	F						1923
KARMETZ	Fafe				Tema			1923
KARMETZ	Henech	M			Tema			1923

KARMETZ	Yehuda	M	married			Mera		1923
KARMETZ	Mera	F	married			Yehuda		1923
KARMETZ	Abraham	M		Yehuda	Mera			1923
KARMETZ	Haya	F		Yehuda	Mera			1923
KARMETZ	Tzipa	F		Yehuda	Mera			1923
KARMETZ	Yacov	M			Rachel			1923
KARMETZ	Rachel	F					Mother of Jacob	1923
KARMETZ	Joseph	M		Jacob				1923
KARMETZ	Haya	F		Jacob				1923
KARMETZ	Ita	F		Jacob				1923
KARMETZ	Mayrim	M	married			Haya		1923
KARMETZ	Haya	F	married			Mayrim		1923
KARMETZ	Malka	F						1923
KARMETZ	Hanah	F			Malka			1923
KARMETZ	Nathan	M	married			Bonah		1923
KARMETZ	Bonah	F	married			Nathan		1923
KARMETZ	Joseph	M		Nathan	Bonah			1923
KARMETZ	Gershon	M		Nathan	Bonah			1923
KATZ	Israel	M	married					1923
KATZ		F	married					1923
KATZ	Yacov	M		Israel				1923
KATZ	Rachel	F		Israel				1923

ל Lamed

LUP	Abraham	M	married			Nehama		1923
LUP	Nehama	F	married			Abraham		1923
LUP	Aida	F					Maiden name SHAPIRA	1923
LUP	Aita	F						1923
LUP	David	M			Aita			1923
LUP	Moshe	M			Aita			1923
LUP	Zalman	M			Aita			1923
LUP	Rachel	F			Aita			1923
LUP	Sania	F			Aita			1923
LUP	Hena	F			Aita			1923
LUP	Gela Reiza	F						1923
LUP	Shachna	M			Gela Reiza			1923

LUP	Rivka	F						1923
LUP	David	M	married			Yacha		1923
LUP		F	married					1923
LUP		M	married					1923
LUP		F	married					1923
LUP		M	married					1923
LUP		F	married					1923
LUP	Lipman	M						1923
LUP	Hanan	M					Grandson of Lipman Lup	1923
LUP	Fruma	F					Granddaughter of Lipman Lup	1923
LUP	Salave	F					Granddaughter of Lipman Lup	1923
LUP	Badana	F					Granddaughter of Lipman Lup	1923
LAFER	Beila	F						1923
LAFER		M			Beila			1923
LAFER		M			Beila			1923
LAFER	Haya	F						1923
LAFER	Joseph	M						1923
LAFER	Isaac	M		Joseph				1923
LUBATZKY	Hillel	M	married			Reiza		1924
LUBATZKY	Reiza	F	married			Hillel		1924
LUBATZKY	Fruma	F		Hillel	Reiza			1924
LUBATZKY	Ela	F	married				Possibility family name different	1924
LUBATZKY		M	married			Ela	Possibility family name different	1924
LUBITCH	Matel	M	married			Malka		1924
LUBITCH	Malka	F	married			Matel		1924
LUBITCH	Sheina	F		Matel	Malka			1924
LUBITCH	Feiva	M	married			Sarah		1924
LUBITCH	Sarah	F	married			Feiva		1924
LUBITCH	Sarah	F		Feiva	Sarah		Possibility that her name or that of her mother is different	1924
LUBITCH	Tuvia	M		Feiva	Sarah		Possibility that the name of her mother is different	1924

LUBITCH	Batya	F		Feiva	Sarah		Possibility that the name of her mother is different	1924
LONEVSKY	Hayyim	M	married			Stiral		1924
LONEVSKY	Stiral	F	married			Hayyim		1924
LIEBERMAN	Abraham	M					Brother of Abraham and Leah	1924
LIEBERMAN	Joseph	M					Brother of Abraham and Leah	1924
LIEBERMAN	Leah	F					Sister of Abraham and Joseph	1924
LICHT	Rachel	F						1924
LICHT	Raiza	F			Rachel			1924
LICHT	Esther	F			Rachel			1924
LAZEROVITCH		M	married					1924
LAZEROVITCH		F	married					1924
LAZEROVITCH	Abraham	M	married			Marisha		1924
LAZEROVITCH	Marisha	F	married			Abraham		1924
LAZEROVITCH	Rivka	F		Abraham	Marisha			1924
LAZEROVITCH	Asher	M		Abraham	Marisha			1924
LAZEROVITCH	Fraida	F						1924
LEVIN	Jonah	M	married			Freida		1924
LEVIN	Fraida	F	married			Jonah		1924
LEVIN	Haikel	M		Jonah	Fraida			1924
LEVIN	Raizel	F		Jonah	Fraida			1924
LEVIN		M	married				The father	1924
LEVIN		F	married				The mother	1924
LEVIN		M						1924
LEVIN	Joseph	M	married			Raichel		1924
LEVIN	Raichel	F	married			Joseph		1924
LEVIN	Elchanan	M		Joseph	Raichel			1924
LEVIN	Haya	F		Joseph	Raichel			1924
LEVIN	Jacob	M						1924
LEVIN	Tzemach	M	married			Braina		1924
LEVIN	Braina	F	married			Tzemach		1924

מ Mem

MALIARAVITCH	Haya	F					Sister of Rivka	1924
MALIARAVITCH	Rivka	F					Sister of Haya	1924
MALIARAVITCH	Rachel	F						1924
MARIANOV	Hana Leah	F						1924
MARIANOV		F			Hana Leah			1924
MEHIFIT	Eliyahu	M						1924
MEHIFIT	Gitel	F						1924
MEHIFIT	Liba	F			Gitel			1924
MEHIFIT	Hava	F			Gitel			1924
MEHIFIT	Tzipi	F			Gitel			1924
MEHIFIT	Leiv	M			Gitel			1924
MUNICH	Leiv	M	married			Haya		1924
MUNICH	Haya	F	married			Leiv		1924
MIRSKY	Neta	M	married			Hana		1924
MIRSKY	Hana	F	married			Neta		1924
MIRSKY		F		Neta	Hana			1924
MIRSKY	Neta	M	married			Golda		1924
MIRSKY	Golda	F	married			Neta		1924
MIRSKY	Haya	F		Neta	Golda			1924
MIRSKY	Mina	F		Neta	Golda			1924
MIRSKY	Disa	F		Neta	Golda			1924
MIRSKY	Abraham	M		Neta	Golda			1924
MIRSKY	David	M	married			Ela		1924
MIRSKY	Ela	F	married			David		1924
MIRSKY	Haya	F		David	Ela			1924
MIRSKY	Hinda	F		David	Ela			1924
MIRSKY	Lazer	M		David	Ela			1924
MIRSKY	Abraham	M		David	Ela			1924
MIRSKY	Joseph	M	married			Raya		1924
MIRSKY	Raya	F	married			Joseph		1924
MIRSKY	Neta	M	married			Rachel		1924
MIRSKY	Rachel	F	married			Neta		1924
MIRSKY	Lazer	M		Neta	Rachel			1924
MIRSKY	Daniel	M		Neta	Rachel			1924
MIRSKY	Feiga	F		Neta	Rachel			1924
MIRSKY	Shmuel	M	married			Fiea		1924

MIRSKY	Fiea	F	married			Shmuel		1924
MIRSKY	David	M		Shmuel	Fiea			1924
MIRSKY	Leizer	M		Shmuel	Fiea			1924
MIRSKY	Feiga	F		Shmuel	Fiea			1924
MIRSKY	Sarah	F		Shmuel	Fiea			1924

נ Nun

NARATZKY	Abraham	M	married			Taibe		1924
NARATZKY	Taiba	F	married			Abraham		1924
NARATZKY	Raika	F		Abraham	Taiba			1924
NARATZKY	Hava	F		Abraham	Taiba			1924
NARATZKY	Zelig	M	married			Zelda		1924
NARATZKY	Zelda	F	married			Zelig		1924
NARATZKY	Heimel	M						1924
NARATZKY	Jacob	M	married			Ita		1924
NARATZKY	Ita	F	married			Jacob		1924
NARATZKY	Raiza	F		Jacob	Ita			1924
NARATZKY	Haya	F		Jacob	Ita			1924

ס Samech

SILAN	Isaac	M						1924
SARAPEI		M					Son	1924
SARAPEI		F					Daughter	1924
SALAWEICHIK	Josaph	M	married			Haya		1924
SALAWEICHIK	Haya	F	married			Joseph		1924
SALAWEICHIK	Berel	M		Joseph	Haya			1924
SALAWEICHIK	Moshe	M		Joseph	Haya			1924
SALAWEICHIK	Faiga	F		Joseph	Haya			1924
SUZAN	David	M	married			Nadia	Brother of Koniya	1924
SUZAN	Nadia	F	married			David		1924
SUZAN	Koniya	F					Sister of David	1924
SOCKANAVITCH	Nechemia	M	married			Hana		1924
SOCKANAVITCH	Hana	F	married			Nehemia		1924
SOCKANAVITCH	Batya	F		Nehemia	Hana			1924
SIDERSON	Joseph	M	married			Hada	Brother in Law of Rachel	1924
SIDERSON	Hada	F	married			Joseph		1924
SIDERSON	Moshe	M		Joseph	Hada			1924

SIDERSON	Hayyim	M		Joseph	Hada			1924
SIDERSON	Shlomo	M		Joseph	Hada			1924
SIDERSON	Ela	F		Joseph	Hada			1924
	Rachel	F					Sister in law of Joseph SIDERSON	1924
SEGAL	Bane	M						1924
SEGAL	Joshua	M						1924
ע **Ayin**								
EPSTEIN	Dina	F						1924
EPSTEIN	Yehuda	M	married			Shifra		1924
EPSTEIN	Shifra	F	married			Yehuda		1924
EPSTEIN	Israel	M	married			Dina		1924
EPSTEIN	Dina	F	married			Israel		1924
EPSTEIN	Isaac	M		Israel	Dina			1924
EPSTEIN	Daniel	M		Israel	Dina			1924
פ **Peh**								
PATASHNIK	Eliyahu	M	married			Malka		1925
PATASHNIK	Malka	F	married			Eliyahu		1925
PATASHNIK		F		Eliyahu	Malka			1925
PATASHNIK	Hayyim	M						1925
PATASHNIK		F				Hayyim		1925
PATASHNIK	Isaac	M	married			Breina		1925
PATASHNIK	Braina	F	married			Isaac		1925
		M					Grandson of Isaac and Braina Patashnik	1925
PATASHNIK	Shlomo	M	married			Fraida		1925
PATASHNIK	Fraida	F	married			Shlomo		1925
PATASHNIK	Ezriel	M		Shlomo	Fraida			1925
PATASHNIK	Esther	F		Shlomo	Fraida			1925
PATASHNIK	Shmuel	M	married			Yenta		1925
PATASHNIK	Yenta	F	married			Shmuel		1925
FAIGEL	Gnesia	F						1925
FAIGEL	Ela	F			Gnesia			1925
FAIGEL	Rochelle	F			Gnesia			1925
FAIGEL	Yehuda	M			Gnesia			1925
FAIGEL	Abraham	M	married			Mera		1925

FAIGEL	Mera	F	married			Abraham		1925
FAIGEL	Ela	F		Abraham	Mera			1925
FAIGEL	David	M		Abraham	Mera			1925
FAIGEL	Meir	M		Abraham	Mera			1925
FINE	Hayyim	M	married			Baila		1925
FINE	Baila	F	married			Hayyim		1925
PAISATSHINSKY	Tzila	F						1925
FISHER	Nathan	M						1925
FISHER		F					Mother of Nathan	1925
FISHER		M					Brother of Nathan	1925
PERLMAN		M	married				Father	1925
PERLMAN		F	married				Mother	1925
PERLMAN		M					Son	1925
FEHLER	Israel	M						1925
FEHLER	Yehudit	F						1925
PERSKY	Isaac	M						1925

ק Kof

KAGAN	Sender	M	married					1925
KAGAN		F	married			Sender		1925
KAGAN		F		Sender				1925
KALINSKY	Lasa	F						1925
KALINSKY	Ita	F					Granddaughter of Lasa	1925
KALINSKY	Ela	F					Granddaughter of Lasa	1925
KALINSKY	Yehudit	F					Granddaughter of Lasa	1925
KALINSKY	Sheina	F					Granddaughter of Lasa	1925
KASAVSKY	Joseph	M	married			Nehama		1925
KASAVSKY	Nehama	F	married			Joseph		1925
KAPELMAN		F						1925
KATSHARGINSKY	Laizer	M	married			Masha		1925
KATSHARGINSKY	Masha	F	married			Laizer		1925
KAVARSKY	Israel	M						1925
KOLBACK	Eidel	M	married			Rivka		1925
KOLBACK	Rivka	F	married			Eidel		1925

KOLBACK	Nehama	F						1925
KIVELEVITCH		M	married			Taiba		1925
KIVELEVITCH	Taiba	F	married					1925
KIVELEVITCH	Leah	F						1925
KARAVATSHINSKY	Rachel	F						1925
KARAVATSHINSKY	Eliyahu	M						1925
KARAVATSHINSKY	Mendel	M						1925
KARAVATSHINSKY	Meir	M						1925
KARAVATSHINSKY	Yehudit	F						1925
KRAL	Fina	M	married			Sarah		1925
KRAL	Sarah	F	married					1925
KRAL	Sarah	F		Fina	Sarah			1925
KRAL	Leiv	M		Fina	Sarah			1925
KRAL	Ela	F		Fina	Sarah			1925
KRAL	Yachna	F		Fina	Sarah			1925
KRAL	Feiga	F		Fina	Sarah			1925
KRAL	Rivka	F		Fina	Sarah			1925
KRAL	Abraham	M		Fina	Sarah			1925
KRAL	Masha	F						1925
KRAL	Maniya	F			Masha			1925
KRAL	Julia	F			Masha			1925
KRAL	Reiza	F						1925

ר Resh

RAZEN	Mordehai	M	married			Nehama		1925
RAZEN	Nehama	F	married			Mordehai		1925
RAZEN	Tzvia	F		Mordehai	Nehama			1925
RODAMIN	Yehusha	M	married			Rachel		1925
RODAMIN	Rachel	F	married			Yehusha		1925
RODAMIN		F		Yehusha	Rachel			1925
RODAMIN	Joseph	M	married			Miriam		1925
RODAMIN	Miriam	F	married			Joseph		1925
RODAMIN	Yehudit	F		Joseph	Miriam			1925
RODAMIN	Sarah	F		Joseph	Miriam			1925
RODANITSKY	Velvel	M	married					1925
RODANITSKY		F	married			Velvel		1925
RODANITSKY		F						1925
RODANITSKY		F						1925

RODANITSKY	Isaac	M	married			Rachel		1925
RODANITSKY	Rachel	F	married			Isaac		1925
RODANITSKY	Faiga	F			Rachel			1925
RODANITSKY	Fishel	M						1925
RODANITSKY	Kalman	M	married			Mariasha		1925
RODANITSKY	Mariasha	F	married			Kalman		1925
RODANITSKY	Ye'hezkel	M		Kalman	Mariasha			1925
RODANITSKY	Rachel	F		Kalman	Mariasha			1925
RODANITSKY	Joseph	M		Kalman	Mariasha			1925
RODANITSKY	Shachna	M	married			Rada		1925
RODANITSKY	Rada	F	married			Shachna		1925
RODANITSKY		F		Shachna	Rada			1925
RIVKIN	Joseph	M						1925
RITLER		M	married					1926
RITLER		F	married					1926
RING	Shlomo	M	married			Pesa		1926
RING	Pesa	F	married			Shlomo		1926
RING	Hayyim	M		Sjlomo	Pesa			1926
RING	Laizer	M	married			Baila		1926
RING	Baila	F	married			Leizer		1926
RING	Batya	F		Laizer	Baila			1926
RAIBACH	Laizer	M	married		Tzesna	Haya		1926
RAIBACH	Haya	F	married			Laizer		1926
RAIBACH	Tzesna	F						1926
RAIZ	Meir	M			Haya			1926
RAIZ	Haya	F					Mother of Meir and Maida	1926
RAIZ	Maida	F			Haya			1926
RAIZEVSKY	Dr. Moshe	M						1926
RAIZEVSKY	Saniya	F		Moshe				1926
RAIZEVSKY	Shosa	F		Moshe				1926
RAIZEVSKY	Bella	F		Moshe				1926
RAIZEVSKY	Mina	F		Moshe				1926

ש Shin

SHACHANAVITCH	Jacob	M	married			Esther		1926
SHACHANAVITCH	Esther	F	married			Jacob		1926
SHACHANAVITCH	Hayyim	M			Esther			1926

SHACHANAVITCH	Moshe	M			Esther			1926
SHACHANAVITCH	Shepsel	M			Esther			1926
SHACHANAVITCH	Feiga	F			Esther			1926
SHACHANAVITCH	Braina	F			Esther			1926
SHAPIRA	Zelig	M						1926
SHAPIRA	Haya	F		Zelig				1926
SHAPIRA	Fina	M						1926
SHAPIRA	Mina	F						1926
SHAPIRA		F			Mina			1926
SHAPIRA		F			Mina			1926
SHAPIRA	Berel	M	married			Sarah		1926
SHAPIRA	Sarah	F	married			Berel		1926
SHAPIRA	Feiva	M		Berel	Sarah			1926
SHAPIRA	Aharon	M		Berel	Sarah			1926
SHAPIRA	Nathan	M	married			Leah		1926
SHAPIRA	Leah	F	married			Nathan		1926
SHAPIRA	Saniya	F						1926
SHAPIRA		M			Saniya			1926
SHTEINMAN		M						1926
SHTEINMAN		F						1926
SHTEINMAN		F						1926
SHTEINMAN	Nachum	M	married			Leah		1926
SHTEINMAN	Leah	F	married			Nachum		1926
SHTEINMAN		F		Nachum	Leah			1926
SHMUKLER	Laizer	M	married			Leah		1926
SHMUKLER	Leah	F	married			Laizer		1926
SCHNEIDEREVITCH	Elchanan	M	married			Haya		1926
SCHNEIDEREVITCH	Haya	F	married			Elchanan		1926
SCHNEIDEREVITCH	Ethel	F		Elchanan	haya			1926
SCHNEIDEREVITCH	Sarah	F		Elchanan	Haya			1926
SCHNEIDEREVITCH	Tzipi	F		Elchanan	Haya			1926
SCHNEIDEREVITCH	Moshe	M	married			Devorah		1926
SCHNEIDEREVITCH	Devorah	F	married			Moshe		1926
SCHNEIDEREVITCH	Taiba	F		Moshe	Devorah			1926
SCHNEIDEREVITCH	Faiva	M						1926
SCHNEIDEREVITCH		F		Faiva				1926
SCHNEIDEREVITCH		F		Faiva				1926

SHMIDT	Shlomo	M					1926
SHMIDT	Haya	F		Shlomo			1926
SHMIDT	Mina	F		Shlomo			1926
SHMIDT	Shmuel	M					1926
SHMIDT	Shaina	F					1926
SHMIDT	Dara	F	married				1926
SHMIDT		M	married			Dara	1926
SHMIDT	Jacob	M					1926
SHMIDT		M					1926
SHMIDT	Mordehai	M	married			Nata	1926
SHMIDT	Nata	F	married			Mordehai	1926
SHMIDT	Saniya	F					1926
SHMIDT		F					1926
SHMIDT	Shlomo	M	married				1926
SHMIDT		F	married			Shlomo	1926
SHMIDT	Shmuel	M	married			Tzvia	1926
SHMIDT	Tzvia	F	married			Shmuel	1926
SHMIDT		F		Shmuel	Tzvia		1926
SHPARBERG	David	M	married			Sarah	1926
SHPARBERG	Sarah	F	married			David	1926
SHPARBERG	Bana	M			Sarah		1926
SHPARBERG	Tzila	F			Sarah		1926
SHPARBERG		M			Sarah		1926
SHORKAVITCH	Riva	F					1926
SHORKAVITCH	Faiga	F			Riva		1926
SHKLIARAVITCH	Kapel	M	married			Haya	1926
SHKLIARAVITCH	Haya	F	married			Kapel	1926
SHKLIARAVITCH	Batya	F		Kapel	Haya		1926
SHKLIARAVITCH	Yacha	F		Kapel	Haya		1926
SHKLIARAVITCH	Mera	F		Kapel	Haya		1926
SHKLIARAVITCH	Abraham	M	married			Helena	1926
SHKLIARAVITCH	Helena	F	married			Abraham	1926
SHKLIARAVITCH	Guta	F		Abraham	Helena		1926
SHKLIARAVITCH	Jacob	M		Abraham	Helena		1926
SHKLIARAVITCH	Yehuda	M	married			Gitel	1926
SHKLIARAVITCH	Gitel	F	married			Yehuda	1926
SHKLIARAVITCH	Moshe	M		Yehuda	Gitel		1926

SHKLIARAVITCH	Batya	F		Yehuda	Gitel			1926

[Columns 1927-1928]

Lintup Necrology

(Lyntupy, Belarus)

55°03'/26°19'

Collected by Kh. Matskin-Brauman

Translation from Yiddish by Dr. Sonia Kovitz

Donated by Irene Mauber Skibinski

Surname	**Given name**	**Family members**
ב Bet		
BAK	Elye	wife: Beyle, children: Shmuel, daughter
BUKOVSKI	Max	wife: Sorah, children: Khavah, Zelde
BERKI	Zalman	sisters and brothers
ג Gimmel		
GOTMAN	Frume	son: Moshe
GILINSKI	Abram	wife: Teybe, children: Sonye, Khayah, Zlate, Aharon
GILINSKI	Aharon	wife: Sonye, children
GILINSKI	Leyzer	wife: Khanah
GILINSKI	Dovid	wife: Dinah
ח Chet		
KHANAH	[no surname]	
KHODOS	Zelde	husband and children
ט Tet		

TSHERNOTSKI	Pinkhas	wife and children: Leyb, Yakov

י Yod

YAVITSH	Rive Zlate	
YAVITSH	Motl	wife: Masha, daughter Beyle
YAVITSH	Yakov	wife: Rokhl and child.
YUDEVSKI	Rabbi Leyb	wife: Khavah, son Mendel

כ Kaf

KHAIMOVITSH	Mere	children: Yakov, Berl
KHARMATS	Hirsh	[this name is listed twice exactly as transcribed here]
KHARMATS	Hirsh	wife and child
KHARMATS	Motel	wife: Khayah and child
KHARMATS	Malkhah	daughter Rivke
KHENTSIANSKI		Lyube, children: Khayah, Leyb, Khaim, Aharon, Yosef

ל Lamed

LEYZEROVITSH	Fayve	wife: Reykhl, children: Freyde, Khaim
LEYZEROVITSH	Tsivye	children: Shefes, Etl, Berl, Khayah
LEYZEROVITSH	Zalman	wife: Beyle, children: Leyb, Tsife
LEVIN	Levi	wife: Feyge, children: Raye, Abram, Sorah, Zelde

מ Mem

MAUBER	Yudel	children: Liepe, Meilach, Monya, Boris (Borukh)
MAUBER	Moshe	wife: Rokhl, children: Ester, Hirsh, Zalman
MAUBER	Sule Pese	
MEIR the smith	[no surname]	wife: Bunye
MATSKIN	Sholem	
MILIKOVSKI	Ruven	wife: Khanah Rokhl

נ Nun

NODL	Leybe	wife: Shprintse

ס Samech

SANDAK	Abram	wife: Lube and children
SVIRSKI	Berl	wife: Lube, children: Motl, Yakov
SVIRSKI	Refael	wife: Berte
SANDAK	Dovid	wife: Leah and children
SANDAK	Libe	daughter: Kreine
פ Peh		
POSHEMENSKI	Mine	children: Khaim, Leyzer, Yitzkhak, Leyb, Fayve
ק Kof		
KATSKOVITSH	Leyb	wife: Rivkah, children: Basye, Ester, Reyze
KATSKOVITSH	Khanah	
KATSKOVITSH	Khaim	wife: Malkhah, children: Dovid, Moshe, Basye, Feyge, Itl, Motl, Pinkhas
ר Resh		
RIMER	Yitskhak	wife: Tsivyeh and children
RUDNITSKI	Abram	
RUDNITSKI	Mendel	children: Pese, Sime, Khayah, Ite
ש Shin		
SARAFAN	Hene	children: Mirl, Feyfe, Khayah, Khanah
SARAFAN	Yakov	wife: Rivke, children: Hirsh, Khayah
SARAFAN	Leyb Yakov	wife: Bas-Sheve
SARAFAN	Leyzer	wife and child
SHAPIRO	Aharon	wife: Khanah, daughter: Miriam

[Columns 1927-1930]

Kiemieliszki Necrology

(Kamelishki, Belarus)

54°51' 25°53'

Transliterated by Beryl Baleson

Page numbers reference the Original Yizkor Book

Family name(s)	First name(s)	Gender	Marital status	Father's name	Mother's name	Name of spouse	Remarks and additional family	Page
ב Bet								
BECKENSTEIN	Max	M	married			Liba		1927
BECKENSTEIN	Liba	F	married			Max		1927
BECKENSTEIN	Jacob	M		Max	Liba			1927
BROMBERG	Shimon	M	married			Esther		1927
BROMBERG	Esther	F	married			Shimon		1927
BROMBERG	Fruma	F		Shimon	Esther			1927
BROMBERG	Kayla	F		Shimon	Esther			1927
BROMBERG	David	M		Shimon	Esther			1927
BROMBERG	Aharon	M		Shimon	Esther			1927
ג Gimmel								
GERBERAVITCH	David	M	married			Rivka		1927
GERBERAVITCH	Rivka	F	married			David		1927
GERBERAVITCH	Jacob	M		David	Rivka			1927
GERBERAVITCH	Sima	M					with family	1927
GIMZANSKY	Asher	M	married			Rasha		1927
GIMZANSKY	Rasha	F	married			Asher		1927
GIMZANSKY	Aharon	M		Asher	Rasha			1927
GIMZANSKY	Luba	F		Asher	Rasha			1927
GIMZANSKY	Meir	M		Asher	Rasha			1927

GLAT	Moshe	M	married			Pesa		1927
GLAT	Pesa	F	married			Moshe		1927
GLAT	Baruch	M		Moshe	Pesa			1927
GLAT	Leah	F		Moshe	Pesa			1927
GARADZANSKY	Hana	F					In the list name shown as GARADZENISKY aparently in error	1927
GARADZANSKY	Faiva	M	married			Rivka		1927
GARADZANSKY	Rivka	F	married			Faiga		1927
ו **Vav**								
WEINSTEIN	Moshe	M	married			Rachel		1927
WEINSTEIN	Rachel	F	married			Moshe		1927
WEINSTEIN	Simcha	M		Moshe	Rachel			1927
WEINSTEIN	Leah	F		Moshe	Rachel			1927
VAINER	Hayyim	M	married			Yacha		1927
VAINER	Yacha	F	married			Hayyim		1927
VAINER	Leah	F		Hayyim	Yacha			1927
VAINER	Faiga	F		Hayyim	Yacha			1927
ז **Zayin**								
ZORER	Pesa	F						1927
ZORER	Shaina	F			Pesa			1927
י **Yod**								
YANAVSKY	Moshe	M	married			Sarah		1928
YANAVSKY	Sarah	F	married			Moshe		1928
YANAVSKY	Eliyahu	M		Moshe	Sarah			1928
כ **Kaf**								
KATZKALAVITCH	Shmuel	M	married			Baila		1928
KATZKALAVITCH	Baila	F	married			Shmuel		1928
KATZKALAVITCH	Malka	F		Shmuel	Baila			1928

KATZKALAVITCH	Moshe	M		Shmuel	Baila			1928

ס Samech

STARIPONSKY	Isaac	M	married			Malchel	3 children	1928
STARIPONSKY	Malchel	F	married			Isaac	3 children	1928
STARIPONSKY	Moshe	M	married				child	1928
STARIPONSKY		F	married			Noshe	child	1928
STARIPONSKY	Sarah	F						1928
STARIPONSKY	Berel	M			Sarah			1928
STARIPONSKY	Sarah	F						1928
SANTATZKY	David	M	married			Alta	3 children	1928
SANTATZKY	Alta	F	married			David	3 children	1928

ע Ayin

EPSTEIN	Menahem	M	married			Haya		1928
EPSTEIN	Haya	F	married			Menahem		1928
EPSTEIN	Esther	F		Menahem	Haya			1928
EPSTEIN	Shaina	F		Menahem	Haya			1928
EPSTEIN	Mera	F		Menahem	Haya			1928
EPSTEIN	Baila	F		Menahem	Haya			1928
EPSTEIN	Sender	M	married			Leah	5 children	1928
EPSTEIN	Leah	F	married			Sender	5 children	1928

פ Peh

FEINBERG	Alta	F						1928
FEINBERG	Alexander	M			Alta			1928
PROZIN	Hayyim	M	married			Daba		1929
PROZIN	Daba	F	married			Hayyim		1929
	Leah	F					Not clear if she is the sister of Hayim PROZIN or his wife Daba	1929
PROZIN	Mula	M		Hayyim	Daba			1929

PROZIN	Shlomo	M		Hayyim	Daba			1929
PROZIN	Hana	F		Hayyim	Daba			1929

צ Tzadik

TZLAV	Yechazkel	M	married			Gaiga		1929
TZLAV	Faiga	F	married			Yechkel		1929
	Liba	F					Not clear if she is the sister of Yechezkel TZLAV or his wife Faiga	1929

ק Kof

KRETZMER	Hayyim	M	married			Braina	Slaughterer	1929
KRETZMER	Braina	F	married			Hayyim		1929
KRETZMER	Pesach	M		Hayyim	Braina			1929
KORITZKY	Abraham	M	married					1929
KORITZKY		F	married			Abraham		1929
KORITZKY	Betzalel	M	married			Dina		1929
KORITZKY	Dina	F	married			Betzalel		1929
KORITZKY	Abraham	M		Betzalel	Dina			1929
KORITZKY	Mula	M		Betzalel	Dina			1929
KORITZKY	Mattel	M		Betzalel	Dina			1929
KORITZKY	Lusiya	F		Betzalel	Dina			1928
KORITZKY	Batya	F						1930
KORITZKY	Aharon	M			Batya			1930
KORITZKY	Jacob	M	married			Hasiya		1930
KORITZKY	Hasiya	F	married			Jacob		1930
	Yenta	F	married	Jacob	Hasiya		maiden name KORITZKY. With husband	1930
KORITZKY	Yudel	M	married			Bluma		1930
KORITZKY	Bluma	F	married			Yudel		1930
SHAPIRA	Laiv	M	married			Frieda	child	1930

SHAPIRA	Frieda	F	married			Laiv	child	1930
KORITZKY	Lipa	M	married			Sarah		1930
KORITZKY	Sarah	F	married			Lipa		1930
KORITZKY	Baruch	M		Lipa	Sarah			1930
KORITZKY	Laizer	M		Lipa	Sarah			1930
KORITZKY	Simcha	M		Lipa	Sarah			1930
KORITZKY	Moshe	M	married					1930
KORITZKY		F	married			Moshe		1930
KORITZKY	Mondick	M		Moshe				1930
KORITZKY	Meir	M	married			Nehama		1930
KORITZKY	Nehama	F	married			Meir		1930
KORITZKY	Masha	F		Meir	Nehama			1930
KORITZKY	Moshe	M		Meir	Nehama			1930

[Columns 1929-1934]

Hoduciszki Necrology

(Adutiškis, Lithuania)

55°09'/26°36'

Transliterated by Beryl Baleson

Page numbers reference the Original Yizkor Book

Family name(s)	First name(s)	Gender	Marital status	Father's name	Mother's name	Name of spouse	Remarks & additional family	Page
א Alef								
ABEL	Abraham	M	married			Hesha		1929
ABEL	Hesha	F	married			Abraham		1929
ABEL	Yehudit	F		Abraham	Hesha			1929
ABEL	Abraham Elia	M	married			Deborah		1929

ABEL	Deborah	F	married			Abraham Iliya		1929
ABEL	Mendel	M		Abraham Eliya	Deborah			1929
ABEL	Berel Zerah	M	married			Kraina		1929
ABEL	Kraina	F	married			Berel Zerach		1929
ABEL	Reuben	M		Berel Zerach	Kraina			1929
ABEL	Moshe	M		Berel Zerach	Kraina			1929
ABEL	Faia	M		Berel Zerach	Kraina			1929
ABEL	Leah	F		Berel Zerach	Kraina			1929
ABEL	Gedalyahu	M	married			Sarah	2 children	1929
ABEL	Sarah	F	married			Gedalyahu	2 children	1929
ABEL	Zalman	M	married			Hana		1929
ABEL	Hana	F	married			Zalman		1929
ABEL	Berel	M		Zalman	Hana			1929
ABEL	Yehoshua	M	married			Tzirel Leah		1929
ABEL	Tzirel Leah	F	married					1929
ABEL	Isaac	M	married			Pesa		1929
ABEL	Peas	F	married			Isaac		1929
ABEL	Israel	M		Isaac	Pesa			1929
ABEL	Shaina	F		Isaac	Pesa			1929
ABEL	Rachel	F		Isaac	Pesa			1929
ABEL	Yishayahu Hayyim	M	married			Yenta		1929
ABEL	Yenta	F	married			Yishayahu Hayyim		1929
ABEL	Batya	F		Yishayahu Hayyim	Yenta			1929

ABEL	Michla	F		Yishayahu Hayyim	Yenta			1929
ABEL	Yishayahu	M						1929
ABEL	Baila	F		Yishayahu				1929
ABEL	Jacob	M		Yishayahu				1929
ABEL	Shlomo	M	married			Raicha	4 children	1929
ABEL	Raicha	F	married			Shlomo	4 children	1929
ABEL	Shalom	M	married			Liba		1929
ABEL	Liba	F	married			Shalom		1929
ABEL	Haya	F		Shalom	Liba			1929
ABEL	Shalom	M	married			Grunia		1929
ABEL	Grunia	F	married			Shalom		1929
ABRAMAVITCH	Shalom	M	married			Faiga		1929
ABRAMAVITCH	Faiga	F	married			Shalom		1929
ABRAMAVITCH	Shmuel	M		Shalom	Faiga			1929
ABRAMAVITCH	Joseph	M		Shalom	Faiga			1929
ABRAMAVITCH	Hayyim	M		Shalom	Faiga			1929
ABRAMAVITCH	Hana	F		Shalom	Faiga			1929
ABRAMAVITCH	Shaina	F		Shalom	Faiga			1929
AVASREICH	Israel	M	married			Shaina		1929
AVASREICH	Shaina	F	married			Israel		1929
AVASREICH	Michael	M	married				2 children	1929
AVASREICH		F	married			Michael	2 children	1929
AVASREICH	Ita	F						1929
EINHORN	Liba	F			Ita			1929
ALSFINE	Shmuel Isaac	M	married			Ita		1929
ALSFINE	Ita	F	married			Shmuel Isaac		1929
ALSFINE	Rivka	F		Shmuel Isaac	Ita			1929
ALPERAVITCH	Shlomo	M	married			Rachel		1929

ALPERAVITCH	Rachel	F	married			Shlomo		1929
AMDURSKY	Shmerel	M	married			Leah		1929
AMDURSKY	Leah	F	married			Shmerel		1929
AMDURSKY	Elka	F		Shmerel	leah			1929

ב Bet

BASS	Sania	F						1929
BASS	Moshe	M			Sania			1929
BASS	Yacha	F			Sania			1929
BASS	Jacob	M	married					1929
BASS		F	married			Jacob		1929
BASS	Shalom	M	married					1929
BASS		F	married			Shalom		1929
BASS	Musa	F	married				child	1929
BASS		M	married			Musa	child	1929
BAK	Laiv	M	married			Miriam	2 children	1929
BAK	Mariam	F	married			Laiv	2 children	1929
BARENSTEIN	Raizel	F						1929
BARENSTEIN	Moshe	M			Raizel			1929
BARENSTEIN	Faiga	F			Raizel			1929
BLATT	Hana	M	married			Liba		1929
BLATT	Liba	F	married			Hana		1929
BLATT	Joseph	M	married			Malka		1929
BLATT	Malka	F	married			Joseph		1929
BLATT	Bentzion	M		Joseph	Malka			1929
BLATT	Bracha	F		Joseph	Malka			1929
BLASS	Mendel	M	married				child	1929
BLASS		F	married			Mendel	child	1929
BROIDE	Hirsh	M	married			Aida		1929
BROIDE	Aida	F	married			Hirsh		1929
BROIDE	Taibe	F		Hirsh	Aida			1929

BROIDE	Abraham	M		Hirsh	Aida			1929
BROIDE	Taibe	F						1929

ג Gimmel

GALPERIN	Hayyim	M	married			Leah		1929
GALPERIN	Leah	F	married			Hayyim		1929
GALPERIN	Rivka	F		Hayyim	Leah			1929
GALPERIN	Rachel	F		Hayyim	Leah			1929
GANTAVNIK	Hayyim Pesach	M	married			Rachel		1929
GANTAVNIK	Rachel	F	married			Hayyim Pesach		1929
GANTAVNIK	Hirsh	M		Hayyim Pesach	Rachel			1929
GANTAVNIK	Pinchas	M		Hayyim Pesach	Rachel			1929
GANTAVNIK	Tzipe	F		Hayyim Pesach	Rachel			1929
GARDAN	Kayla	F						1929
GARDAN	Ezriel	M			Kayla			1929
GARDAN	Mendel	M			Kayla			1929
GARDAN	Mattel	M	married			Pesa		1929
GARDAN	Pesa	F	married			Mattel		1929
GARDAN	Hayyim	M		Mattel	Pesa			1929
GARDAN	Rachel	F		Mattel	Pesa			1929
GARDAN	Raizel	F						1930
GARDAN	Fraida	F			Raizel			1930
GARDAN	Hena	F						1930
GARDAN	Velvel	M	married			Hana	2 children	1930
GARDAN	Hana	F	married			Velvel	2 children	1930
GARDAN	Zalman	M	married			Rachel		1930
GARDAN	Rachel	F	married			Zalman		1930
GARDAN	Shmuel	M		Zalman	Rachel			1930

GARDAN	Simcha	M		Zalman	Rachel			1930
GARDAN	Esther	F		Zalman	Rachel			1930
GARDAN	Hayyim Laiv	M	married			Rada		1930
GARDAN	Rada	F	married			Hayyim		1930
GARDAN	Simcha	M		Hayyim Laiv	Rada			1930
GARDAN	Yonah	M						1930
GARDAN	Joseph	M	married			Hasia		1930
GARDAN	Hasia	F	married			Joseph		1930
GARDAN	Jacob	M	married			Pesa	3 children	1930
GARDAN	Pesa	F	married			Jacob	3 children	1930
GARDAN	Laizer	M	married			Ita		1930
GARDAN	Ita	F	married			Laizer		1930
GARDAN	Nahum	M		Laizer	Ita			1930
GARDAN	Hayyim	M		Laizer	Ita			1930
GARDAN	Lipa	M	married			Leah		1930
GARDAN	Leah	F	married			Lipa		1930
GARDAN	Tzerna	F		Lipa	Leah			1930
GITLITZ	Benjamin	M					Brother of Boniya and Dauba	1930
GITLITZ	Boniya	F					Sister of Benjamin and Dauba	1930
GITLITZ	Dauba	F					Sister of Benjamin and Boniya	1930
GLAICHAR	Shlomo	M	married			Miriam		1930
GLAICHAR	Miriam	F	married			Shlomo		1930
GLAICHAR	Joseph	M		Shlomo	Miriam			1930
GLAICHAR	Moshe	M		Shlomo	Miriam			1930
GLAICHAR	Aba	M	married			Yehudit	child	1930

GLAICHAR	Yehudit	F	married			Aba	child	1930
GLAICHAR	Asher	M	married			Hinda		1930
GLAICHAR	Hinda	F	married			Asher		1930
GLAICHAR	Abraham	M	married			Batya		1930
GLAICHAR	Batya	F	married			Abraham		1930
GLAICHAR	Hirsh	M		Abraham	Batya			1930
GLAICHAR	Joseph	M		Abraham	Batya			1930
GLAICHAR	Geladyahu	M		Abraham	Batya			1930
GLAICHAR	Hana	F		Abraham	Batya			1930
GLAICHAR	Hinda	F		Abraham	Batya			1930
GLAICHAR	Rivka	F		Abraham	Batya			1930
GLAICHAR	Hiena	F		Abraham	Batya			1930
GLAICHAR	Hena	F		Abraham	Batya			1930
GENDEL	Jacob David	M	married				3 children	1930
GENDEL		F	married			Jacob David	3 children	1930
GENDEL	Lipa	M	married					1930
GENDEL		F	married			Lipa		1930
GENDEL	Nathan	M		Lipa				1930
GENDEL	Yehiel	M		Lipa				1930
GENDEL	Haia	F		Lipa				1930
GARSTEIN	Aivish	M	married			Tzvia	2 children	1930
GARSTEIN	Tzvia	F	married			Aivish	2 children	1930
GRUMAN	Abraham	M	married			Esther		1930
GRUMAN	Esther	F	married			Abraham		1930

ד **Dalet**

DAN	Avigdor	M	married			Leah		1930
DAN	Leah	F	married			Avigdor		1930
DAN	Shlomo	M		Avigdor	Leah			1930

DAN	Yonah	M		Avigdor	Leah			1930
DAN	Taibe	F		Avigdor	Leah			1930
DAN	Jacob	M						1930
DISNER	Hillel	M	married			Ethel		1930
DISNER	Ethel	F	married			Hillel		1930
DISNER	Hayyim	M		Hillel	Ethel			1930
DISNER	Meir	M		Hillel	Ethel			1930
DISNER	Hana	F		Hillel	Ethel			1930
DISNER	Hinda	F		Hillel	Ethel			1930

ה Hey

HACHMAN	Cloina	M	married			Tamar		1930
HACHMAN	Tamar	F	married			Cloina		1930
HACHMAN	Jacob	M		Cloina	Tamar			1930
HACHMAN	Leah	F		Cloina	Tamar			1930
HACHMAN	Haya	F						1930
HACHMAN	Musa	F			Haya			1930

ו Vav

VALATSKY	Eliyahu	M						1930
VALATSKY	Haya	F						1930
VALATSKY	Felix	M					grandaughter of Haya, possibility that name of family is different	1930
VALATSKY	Bira						grandaughter of Haya, possibility that name of family is different	1930
VALATSKY	Yehuda	M	married			Pesa		1930
VALATSKY	Pesa	F	married			Yehudit		1930

VAINER	Cloina	M						1930
VAINER	Gila	F						1930
VAINER	Joseph	M			Gila			1930
WEISSPAPIER	Zalman	M	married			liba		1930
WEISSPAPIER	Liba	F	married			Zalman		1930
WEISSPAPIER	Levy	M		Zalman	Liba			1930
WEISSPAPIER	Rachel	F		Zalman	Liba			1930
WEKSLER	Yehoshua	M	married			Rivka	3 children	1930
WEKSLER	Rivka	F	married			Yehusha	3 children	1930

ז Zayin

ZAR	Zelda	F						1930
ZAR	Alikum	M			Zelda			1930
ZAIGER	Isaac Jacob	M	married			Pearl		1930
ZAIGER	Pearl	F	married			Isaac Jacob		1930
ZAIGER	Mana	M	married			Dina		1930
ZAIGER	Dina	F	married			Mana		1930
ZAIGER	Bracha	F		Mana	Dina			1930
ZAIGER	Nehama	F		Mana	Dina			1930
ZAIGER	Hillel	M	married				2 children	1930
ZAIGER		F	married			Hillel	2 children	1930

ח Chet

CHAIKIN	Yonah	M	married			Miriam	2 children	1931
CHAIKIN	Mariam	F	married			Yonah	2 children	1931
CHAYOT	Haya Mirel	F						1931

ט Tet

TADRES	Neta	M	married			Hana		1931
TADRES	Hana	F	married			Neta		1931
TADRES	Henoch	M		Neta	Hana			1931

TADRES	Salava	F		Neta	Hana			1931
TADRES	Tzipora	F		Neta	Hana			1931
י **Yod**								
YACHELMAN	Isaac	M	married			Musa		1931
YACHELMAN	Musa	F	married			Isaac		1931
YACHELMAN	Reuben	M		Isaac	Musa			1931
YACHELMAN	Pesach	M		Isaac	Musa			1931
YACHELMAN	Henoch	M		Isaac	Musa			1931
YACHELMAN	Shepsel	M	married			Rivka		1931
YACHELMAN	Rivka	F	married			Shepsel		1931
YACHELMAN	Daniel	M		Shepsel	Rivka			1931
YACHELMAN	Henoch	M		Shepsel	Rivka			1931
YACHELMAN	Yehiel	M	married			Mina		1931
YACHELMAN	Mina	F	married			Yehiel		1931
YACHELMAN	Laiv	M		Yehiel	Mina			1931
YACHELMAN	Moshe	M						1931
YACHELMAN	Yehuda	F		Moshe				1931
YACHELMAN	Hena	F		Moshe				1931
YACHELMAN	Hayyim	M		Moshe				1931
JOFFE	Isaac	M						1931
JOFFE	Yishayahu	M	married			Pesa		1931
JOFFE	Pesa	F	married			Yishayahu		1931
JOFFE	Shalom	M		Yishayahu	Pesa			1931
JOFFE	Gitel	F		Yishayahu	Pesa			1931
YUNGELSAN	Haya	F					child	1931
YICHILCHIK	Aba Laiv	M	married			Golda		1931
YICHILCHIK	Golda	F	married			Aba Laiv		1931
YICHILCHIK	Berel	M		Aba Laiv	Golda			1931
YICHILCHIK	Benjamin	M		Aba Laiv	Golda			1931

כ Kaf

KARMATZ	Hirsh	M	married			Hena		1931
KARMATZ	Hena	F	married			Hirsh		1931
KARMATZ	Gershon	M	married			Haya		1931
KARMATZ	Haya	F	married			Gershon		1931
KARMATZ	Abraham	M	married			Hinda		1931
KARMATZ	Hinda	F	married			Abraham		1931
KARMATZ	Nehama	F		Abraham	Hinda			1931
KARMATZ	Shaina	F		Abraham	Hinda			1931
KVAT	Isaac	M					2 children	1931
KATZ	Idel	M	married					1931
KATZ		F	married			Idel		1931
KATZ	Gershon	M		Idel				1931
KATZ	Beba	F		Idel				1931
KATZ	Eliyahu	M	married			Rivka		1931
KATZ	Rivka	F	married			Eliyahu		1931
KATZ	Sarah	F		Eliyahu	Rivka			1931
KATZ	Zalman	M	married			Baila		1931
KATZ	Baila	F	married			Zalman		1931
KATZ	Abraham	M		Zalman	Baila			1931
KATZ	Gita	F		Zalman	Baila			1931
KATZ	Hana	F						1931
KATZ	Haya	F			Hana			1931
KATZ	Yacha	F						1931
KATZ	Mirel	F						1931
KATZ	Gershon	M			Mirel			1931
KATZ	Rivka	F						1931

ל Lamed

LAPIDE	Israel	M	married			Rachel		1931

LAPIDE	Rachel	F	married			Israel		1931
LAPIDE	Laiv	M		Israel	Rachel			1931
LAPIDE	Gita	F		Israel	Rachel			1931
LAPIDE	Hava	F		Israel	Rachel			1931
LUBATSKY	Yerachmiel	M	married			Kayla		1931
LUBATSKY	Kayla	F	married			Yerachmiel		1931
LUBATSKY	Israel	M		Yerachmiel	Kayla			1931
LUBATSKY	Azriel	M		Yerachmiel	Kayla			1931
LUBATSKY	Ita	F		Yerachmiel	Kayla			1931
LURIA	Betzalel	M	married			Golda		1931
LURIA	Golda	F	married			Betzalel		1931
LURIA	Benjamin	M		Betzalel	Golda			1931
LURIA	Jacob	M		Betzalel	Golda			1931
LURIA	Gitel	F	married				possibility that family name is different	1931
LURIA		M	married			Gitel	possibility that family name is different	1931
LAUW	Moshe	M	married			Sania	Slaughterer	1931
LAUW	Sania	F	married			Moshe		1931
LAUW	Dina	F		Moshe	Sania			1931
LAUW	Haya	F		Moshe	Sania			1931
LEVIT	Liba	F						1931
LEVIT	Zalman	M			Liba			1931
LEVIT	Moshe Laiv	M						1931

מ **Mem**

MATSKIN	Asher	M	married			Ita		1931
MATSKIN	Ita	F	married			Asher		1931
MATSKIN	Hana	F		Asher	Ita			1931

MATSKIN	Baruch	M	married			Haya Rivka	2 children	1931
MATSKIN	Haya Rivka	F	married			Baruch	2 children	1931
MATSKIN	Baruch	M	married			Hinda		1931
MATSKIN	Hinda	F	married			Baruch		1931
MATSKIN	Hirsh Laiv	M	married					1931
MATSKIN		F	married			Hirsh Laiv		1931
MATSKIN	Shlomo	M		Hirsh Laiv				1931
MATSKIN	Golda	F		Hirsh Laiv				1931
MATSKIN	Rachel	F		Hirsh laiv				1931
MATSKIN	Salava	F						1931
MATSKIN	Isaac	M			Salava			1931
MATSKIN	Shlomo	M			Salava			1931
MATSKIN	Pinchas	M			Salava			1931
MATSKIN	Meir	M			Salava			1931
MASHITZ	Rav Elchanan	M	married				Rabbi	1931
MASHITZ		F	married			Elchanan		1931
MASHITZ	Aharon	M		Elchanan				1931
MASHITZ	Moshe	M		Elchanan				1931
MASHITZ	Sarah	F		Elchanan				1931
MASHITZ	Hana	F		Elchanan				1931
MARMUR	Nehama	F						1931
MILNER	Moshe	M	married			Deborah	2 children	1931
MILNER	Deborah	F	married			Moshe	2 children	1931
MILSTEIN	Betzalel	M	married			Ela	3 children	1931
MILSTEIN	Ela	F	married			Betzalel	3 children	1931
MILSTEIN	Taibe	F						1931
MILSTEIN	Hana Laizer	M			Taiba			1931
MINKIN	Liv	M	married			Rachel	2 children	1931

MINKIN	Rachel	F	married			Liv	2 children	1931
MINKIN	Isaac Mendel	M						1931
ℶ **Nun**								
NITZARG	Gutman	M	married			Fera		1931
NITZARG	Fera	F	married			Gutman		1931
NITZARG	Faivish	M		Gutman	Fera			1931
NITZARG	Shmuel	M		Gutman	Fera			1931
NITZARG	Baruch	M		Gutman	Fera			1931
NITZARG	Yehuda	M		Gutman	Fera			1931
NITZARG	Hana	F		Gutman	Fera			1931
NITZARG	Shaina	F		Gutman	Fera			1931
ס **Samech**								
SALAMIAC	Musa	F						1931
SALAMIAC	Shevach	M			Musa			1931
SAVERSKY	Haya Rachel	F						1931
SAVERSKY	Taibe	F			Rachel Haya			1931
SAVERSKY	Jacob	M	married			Sarah Rivka		1931
SAVERSKY	Sarah Rivka	F	married			Jacob		1931
SAVERSKY	Moshe	M	married			Miriam		1931
SAVERSKY	Miriam	F	married			Moshe		1931
SAVERSKY	Shimon	M		Moshe	Miriam			1931
SAVERSKY	Shimon Laiv	M	married			Daba Leah		1932
SAVERSKY	Daba Leah	F	married			Shimon Laiv		1932
SOTSKEVER	Moshe	M	married			Yenta	3 children	1932
SOTSKEVER	Yenta	F	married			Moshe	3 children	1932

STRAVITCH	Jacob	M	married			Faiga	1932
STRAVITCH	Faiga	F	married			Jacob	1932
STRAVITCH	Rachel	F		jacob	Faiga		1932
STRAVITCH	Deborah	F		Jacob	Faiga		1932
STRICKAVSKY	Melech	M	married			Miriam	1932
STRICKAVSKY	Miriam	F	married			Melech	1932
STRICKAVSKY	Mendel	M		Malech	Miriam		1932
STRICKAVSKY	Hayyim	M		Malech	Miriam		1932
STRICKAVSKY	Tzadok	M		Malech	Miriam		1932
STRICKAVSKY	Malka	F		Malech	Miriam		1932

פ Peh

PATASHNIK	Reuben	M	married			Farada	1932
PATASHNIK	Farada	F	married			Reuben	1932
PATASHNIK	Shmuel	M		Reuben	Farada		1932
PATASHNIK	Zondel	M		Reuben	Farada		1932
PATASHNIK	Israel	M		Reuben	Farada		1932
PATASHNIK	Hava	F		Reuben	Farada		1932
PATASHNIK	Braina	F		Reuben	Farada		1932
PATASHNIK	Isaac	M	married			Luba	1932
PATASHNIK	Luba	F	married			Isaac	1932
PATASHNIK	Israel	M		isaac	Luba		1932
PATASHNIK	Abraham	M		isaac	Luba		1932
PATASHNIK	Geldalyahu	M		isaac	Luba		1932
PATASHNIK	Zelda	F		isaac	Luba		1932
PATASHNIK	Sarah	F		isaac	Luba		1932
PALIKANSKY	Moshe	M	married			Rasha	1932
PALIKANSKY	Rasha	F	married			Moshe	1932
PALIKANSKY	Rachel	F		Moshe	Rasha		1932
FISHER	Berel	M	married			Fruma	1932
FISHER	Fruma	F	married			Berel	1932

FISHER	Shimon	M		Berel	Fruma			1932
FISHER	Henoch	M	married			Haya		1932
FISHER	Haya	F	married			Hanoch		1932
FISHER	Israel	M		Henoch	Haya			1932
FISHER	Shaina	F		Henoch	Haya			1932
FISHER	Tzirel	F		Henoch	Haya			1932
FISHER	Nehama	F						1932
FISHER	Gitel	F			Nehama			1932
FAIGELSON	Joseph	M	married			Haya		1932
FAIGELSON	Haya	F	married			Joseph		1932
FAIGELSON	Lipa	M		Joseph	Haya			1932
FAIGELSON	Henoch	M		Joseph	Haya			1932
FAIGELSON	Fraida	F		Joseph	Haya			1932
FAIGELSON	Masha	F		Joseph	Haya			1932
PERLIS	Haya Leah	F						1932
PERLIS	Hirsh	M	married			Esther	child	1932
PERLIS	Esther	F	married			Hirsh	child	1932
FARMAN	Jacob	M	married			Hana		1932
FARMAN	Hana	F	married			Jacob		1932
FARMAN	Pesach	M		Jacob	Hana			1932
FARMAN	Henoch	F		Jacob	Hana			1932
PEREVAZNIK	Hirsh	M	married			Haya		1932
PEREVAZNIK	Haya	F	married			Hirsh		1932
PEREVAZNIK	Bentzion	M		Hirsh	Haya			1932
PEREVAZNIK	Yehuda	M		Hirsh	Haya			1932
PEREVAZNIK	David	M		Hirsh	Haya			1932
PEREVAZNIK	Henoch	M						1932
PEREVAZNIK	Laiv	M	married			Leah Mera	2 children	1932
PEREVAZNIK	Leah Mera	F	married			Laiv	2 children	1932
FRIEDLANDER	Meir	M						1932

FRIEDLANDER	Cloina	M					1932

צ Tzadik

TZAK	Laiv	M	married			Faiga	1932
TZAK	Faiga	F	married			Laiv	1932
TZAK	Moshe	M		Laiv	Faiga		1932
TZAK	Hana	F		Laiv	Faiga		1932
TZEFELAVITCH	Zalman	M	married			Baila	1932
TZEFELAVITCH	Baila	F	married			Zalman	1932
TZEFELAVITCH	Israel	M		Zalman	Baila		1932
TZEFELAVITCH	Haikel	M		Zalman	Baila		1932
TZEFELAVITCH	Joseph	M		Zalman	Baila		1932

ק Kof

KAZIEL	Velvel	M	married			Gita	1932
KAZIEL	Gita	F	married			Velvel	1932
KAZIEL	Gidalyahu	M		Velvel	Gita		1932
KAZIEL	Hana	M		Velvel	Gita		1932
KATSHERGINSKY	Noah	M				Baila	1932
KATSHERGINSKY	Baila	F	married			Noah	1932
KATSHERGINSKY	Daniel	M		Noah	Baila		1932
KATSHERGINSKY	Melech	M		Noah	Baila		1932
KATSHERGINSKY	Asher	M		Noah	Baila		1932
KATSHERGINSKY	Hana	F		Noah	Baila		1932
KATSHERGINSKY	Shasa	F					1932
KATSHERGINSKY	Laiv	M			Shasa		1932
KATSHERGINSKY	Velvel	M			Shasa		1932
KATSHERGINSKY	Taibe	F			Shasa		1932
KATSHERGINSKY	Rachel	F			Shasa		1932
KATSHERGINSKY	Shmuel Yehuda	M	married			Betty	1932
KATSHERGINSKY	Betty	F	married			Shmuel	1932

						Yehuda		
KATSHERGINSKY	Taibe	F		Shmuel Yehuda	Betty			1932
KATSHERGINSKY	Joseph	M		Shmuel Yehuda	Betty			1932
KAMERANTZ	Isaac	M	married			Leah		1932
KAMERANTZ	Leah	F	married			Isaac		1932
KAMERANTZ	Haikel	M		Isaac	Leah			1932
KAMERANTZ	Sarah	F		Isaac	Leah			1932
KANFER	Aharon	M	married			Sarah		1932
KANFER	Sarah	F	married			Aharon		1932
KANFER	Meir	M		Aharon	Sarah			1932
KATZENELENBOGEN		F	married			Israel	2 children	1932
KARANAVITCH	Mana	M	married			Liba		1932
KARANAVITCH	Liba	F	married			Mana		1932
KARANAVITCH	Masha	F		Mana	Liba			1932
KARANAVITCH	Rachel	F		Mana	Liba			1932
KOTNIK	Bera Laiv	M	married			Ita		1932
KOTNIK	Ita	F	married			Bera Laiv		1932
KOTNIK	Zelda	F		Bera laiv	Ita			1932
KOTNIK	Batya	F		Bera Laiv	Ita			1932
KOTNIK	Henoch	M						1932
KOTNIK	Zalman	M						1932
KOTNIK	Rachel	F						1932
KOTNIK	Zelda	F						1932
KUSLIN	Laiv	M	married			Shaina Rivka		1932
KUSLIN	Shaina Rivka	F	married			Laiv		1932
KUSLIN	Rachel	F		Laiv	Shaina Rivka			1932
KORITZKY	Asna	F						1932

KORITZKY	Esther Bluma	F						1932
KORITZKY	Esther Michla	F						1932
KORITZKY	Henoch	M	married			Vita		1932
KORITZKY	Vita	F	married			Henoch		1932
KORITZKY	Raza	F		Henoch	Vita			1932
KORITZKY	Isaac Mordehai	M	married			Batya		1932
KORITZKY	Batya	F	married			Isaac Mordehai		1932
KORITZKY	Raiza	F		Isaac Mordehai	Batya			1932
KORITZKY	Rachel	F		Isaac Mordehai	Batya			1932
KORITZKY	Liba	F		Isaac Mordehai	Batya			1932
KORITZKY	Melech	M	married			Liba		1932
KORITZKY	Liba	F	married			Melech		1932
KORITZKY	Moshe	M		Melech	Liba			1932
KORITZKY	Mendel	M	married			Haya Faiga	2 children	1932
KORITZKY	Haya Faiga	F	married			Mendel	2 children	1932
KORITZKY	Shmuel	M	married			Shifra		1932
KORITZKY	Shifra	F	married			Shmuel		1932
KORITZKY	Abraham	M		Shmuel	Shifra			1932
KORITZKY	Haya	F		Shmuel	Shifra			1932
KORLANDTSHIK	Heshel	M	married			Ethel		1932
KORLANDTSHIK	Ethel	F	married			Heshel		1932
KLAR	Mendel	M	married			Pesa	child	1933
KLAR	Pesa	F	married			Mendel	child	1933

ר **Resh**

RABINAVITCH	Yechezkel	M	married			Tzvia		1933

RABINAVITCH	Tzvia	F	married			Yechezkel		1933
RAZIN	Tzemach	M						1933
RAZIN	Hana	F		Tzemach				1933
RAZIN	Mania	F		Tzemach				1933
RODNITZKY	Isaac	M	married			Rachel		1933
RODNITZKY	Rachel	F	married			Isaac		1933
RODNITZKY	Marim	F		Isaac	Rachel			1933
RODNITZKY	Pinchas	M	married				3 children	1933
RODNITZKY		F	married			Pinchas	3 children	1933
RAICHEL	Israel	M						1933
RAICHEL	Laiba	M		Israel				1933
RAICHEL	Braina	F		Israel				1933
RAICHEL	Cloina	M	married			Baila		1933
RAICHEL	Baila	F	married			Chloina		1933
RAICHEL	Moshe	M		Cloina	Baila			1933
RAICHEL	Israel	M		Cloina	Baila			1933
RAICHEL	Masha	F		Cloina	Baila			1933
RAICHEL	Laiba	M	married			Michla		1933
RAICHEL	Michla	F	married			Laiba		1933
RAICHEL	Jacob	M		Laiba	Michla			1933
RAICHEL	Leah	F		Laiba	Michla			1933
RAICHEL	Mania	F	married			Meir Aharon		1933
RAICHEL	Rivka	F						1933
RAICHEL	Sarita	F			Rivka			1933
RAICHEL	Shimon	M	married					1933
RAICHEL		F	married			Shimon		1933
RING	Yehuda	M	married			Miriam		1933
RING	Miriam	F	married			Yehuda		1933
RING	Pesach	M		Yehuda	Miriam			1933

RING	Braina	F		Yehuda	Miriam			1933

ש Shin

SHIAT	Rachel	F						1933
SHAPIRA	Isser Hertz	M	married			Mina		1933
SHAPIRA	Mina	F	married			Iser Hertz		1933
SHAPIRA	Shalom	M		Iser Hertz	Mina			1933
SHAPIRA	Haya	F		Iser Hertz	Mina			1933
SHAPIRA	Ita Leah	F						1933
SHAPIRA	Bainish	M			Ita Leah			1933
SHAPIRA	Faiga	F			Ita Leah			1933
SHAPIRA	Ephraim	M	married			Shifra		1933
SHAPIRA	Shifra	F	married			Ephraim		1933
SHAPIRA	Menashe	M		Ephraim	Shifra			1933
SHAPIRA	Baruch	M	married			Raizel		1933
SHAPIRA	Raizel	F	married			Baruch		1933
SHAPIRA	Hana	M		Baruch	Raizel			1933
SHAPIRA	Jacob	M		Baruch	Raizel			1933
SHAPIRA	David	M	married			Bet Sheva		1933
SHAPIRA	Bat Sheva	F	married			David		1933
SHAPIRA	Yehuda	M		David	Bat Sheva			1933
SHAPIRA	Hana	F		David	Bat Sheva			1933
SHAPIRA	Rivka	F		David	Bat Sheva			1933
SHAPIRA	Zalman	M	married			Braina	2 children	1933
SHAPIRA	Braina	F	married			Zalman	2 children	1933
SHAPIRA	Hayyim Mattel	M	married			Pesa		1933
SHAPIRA	Pesa	F	married			Hayyim Mattel		1933
SHAPIRA	Yehuda	M	married			sarah		1934

SHAPIRA	Sarah	F	married			Yehuda		1934
SHAPIRA	Joseph	M						1934
SHAPIRA	Isaac	M	married			Baila		1934
SHAPIRA	Baila	F	married			Isaac		1934
SHAPIRA	Yehiel	M		Isaac	Baila			1934
SHAPIRA	Abraham	M		Isaac	Baila			1934
SHAPIRA	Tuvia	M		Isaac	Baila			1934
SHAPIRA	Fruma	F		Isaac	Baila			1934
SHAPIRA	Rivka	F		Isaac	Baila			1934
SHAPIRA	Gelka	F		Isaac	Baila			1934
SHAPIRA	Sarah	F		Isaac	Baila			1934
SHAPIRA	Yishayahu	M	married			Miriam		1934
SHAPIRA	Miriam	F	married			Yishayahu		1934
SHAPIRA	Shimon	M		Yishayahu	Miriam			1934
SHAPIRA	Moshe	M		Yishayahu	Miriam			1934
SHAPIRA	Hana	F		Yishayahu	Miriam			1934
SHAPIRA	Mair	M	married			Pesa	mother and 2 children	1934
SHAPIRA	Pesa	F	married			Meir	mother and 2 children	1934
SHAPIRA	Michael	M	married			Shaina		1934
SHAPIRA	Shaina	F	married			Michael		1934
SHAPIRA	Raizel	F		Michael	Shaina			1934
SHAPIRA	Leah	F		Michael	Shaina			1934
SHAPIRA	Taibe	F		Michael	Shaina			1934
SHAPIRA	Menashe	M	married			Mina	child	1934
SHAPIRA	Mina	F	married			Menashe	child	1934
SHAPIRA	Daube	F		Menashe	Mina			1934
SHAPIRA	Deborah	F		Menashe	Mina			1934
SHAPIRA	Hinda	F		Menashe	Mina			1934
SHAPIRA	Moshe	M	married			Sarah		1934

SHAPIRA	Sarah	F	married			Moshe	1934
SHAPIRA	Ezra	M		Moshe	Sarah		1934
SHAPIRA	Moshe	M	married			Hinda	1934
SHAPIRA	Hinda	F	married			Moshe	1934
SHAPIRA	Abraham	M		Moshe	Hinda		1934
SHAPIRA	Moshe	M	married			Sarah	1934
SHAPIRA	Sarah	F	married			Moshe	1934
SHAPIRA	Neta	M	married			Sarah	1934
SHAPIRA	Sarah	F	married			Neta	1934
SHAPIRA	Gita	F		Neta	Sarah		1934
SHAPIRA	Isaac	M		Neta	Sarah		1934
SHAPIRA	Pinchas	M	married			Taiba	1934
SHAPIRA	Taibe	F	married			Pinchas	1934
SHUBITSH	Israel	M	married			Masha	1934
SHUBITSH	Masha	F	married			Israel	1934
SHONTOP	Laiv	M	married			Faiga	1934
SHONTOP	Faiga	F	married			Laiv	1934
	Raicha	F					1934
SHTEINHARD	Moshe	M	married			Nehama	1934
SHTEINHARD	Nehama	F	married			Moshe	1934
SHTEINHARD	Haya	F		Moshe	Nehama		1934
SHTEINHARD	Marim	F		Moshe	Nehama		1934
SHAITEL	Isa	F					1934
SHAITEL	Sheps	M			Isa		1934
SHAITEL	Gershon	M			Isa		1934
SHMUKLER	Moshe	M	married			Shaina	1934
SHMUKLER	Shaina	F	married			Moshe	1934
SHMIDT	Berel	M					1934

[Columns 1933-1934]

Stojaciszki Necrology

(Stajetiške, Lithuania)

55°11'/26°31'

Transliterated by Beryl Baleson

Page numbers reference the Original Yizkor Book

Family name(s)	First name(s)	Gender	Marital status	Father's name	Mother's name	Name of spouse	Remarks & additional family	Page
ABEL	Bentzion	M	married				child	1933
ABEL		F	married			Bentzion	child	1933
ABEL	Hada	F						1933
ABEL	Tzerna	F			Hada			1933
ABEL	Jacob	M	married			Haya	3 children	1933
ABEL	Haya	F	married			Jacob	3 children	1933
ABEL	Cluina	M	married			Shasa		1933
ABEL	Shasa	F	married			Cluina		1933
ABEL	Shmuel	M	married			Esther		1933
ABEL	Esther	F	married			Shmuel		1933
ABEL	Idel	M		Shmuel	Esther			1933
ABEL	Israel	M		Shmuel	Esther			1933
ABEL	Malka	F		Shmuel	Esther			1933
BAIGEL	Laiv	M	married			Pesa	child	1933
BAIGEL	Pesa	F	married			Laiv	child	1933
BAIGEL	Raiza	F						1933
BAIGEL	Israel	M			Raiza			1933
BAIGEL	Shmuel	M	married			Esther	2 children	1933
BAIGEL	Esther	F	married			Shmuel	2 children	1933
GEDUD	Abraham	M	married			Liba		1933

GEDUD	Liba	F	married			Abraham		1933
GEDUD	Aba	M		Abraham	Liba			1933
GEDUD	Jacob	M	married			Sarah		1933
GEDUD	Sarah	F	married			Jacob		1933
GEDUD	Meir	M	married			Malka	2 children	1933
GEDUD	Malka	F	married			Meir	2 children	1933
GEDUD	Eliyahu	M	married			Leah		1933
GEDUD	Leah	F	married			Eliyahu		1933
GEDUD	Tzvi	M		Eliyahu	Leah			1933
GEDUD	Meir	M		Eliyahu	Leah			1933
GEDUD	Nehama	F		Eliyahu	Leah			1933
GEDUD	Rivka	F		Eliyahu	Leah			1933
GLASS	Eliezer	M			Sarah			1933
GLASS	Shmuel	M			Sarah			1933
GLASS	Haya	F			Sarah			1933
GLASS	Sarah	F						1933
GROISDORF	Shlomo	M	married			Lipsha	3 children	1933
GROISDORF	Lipsha	F	married			Shlomo	3 children	1933
GANTAVNIK	Baruch Isaac	M	married				6 children	1933
GANTAVNIK		F	married			Baruch Isaac	6 children	1933
GANTAVNIK	Gedalyahu	M	married			Rachel		1933
GANTAVNIK	Rachel	F	married			Gedalyahu		1933
GANTAVNIK	Zalata	F						1933
GANTAVNIK	Reuben	M			Zalata			1933
GANTAVNIK	Hayyim	M	married			Sarah		1933
GANTAVNIK	Sarah	F	married			Hayyim		1933
GANTAVNIK	Eliyahu	M		Hayyim	Sarah			1933
GANTAVNIK	Israel	M	married			Baila		1934
GANTAVNIK	Baila	F	married			Israel		1934

GANTAVNIK	Shalom	M	married			Kieana		1934
GANTAVNIK	Kieana	F	married			Shalom		1934
GANTAVNIK	Moshe	M		Shalom	Kieana			1934
GANTAVNIK	Israel	M		Shalom	Kieana			1934
GANTAVNIK	Miriam	F		Shalom	Kieana			1934
GANTAVNIK	Shimshon	M	married			Ita Shaina		1934
GANTAVNIK	Ita Shaina	F	married			Shimshon		1934
GORDON	Tzvi	M	married			Esther		1934
GORDON	Esther	F	married			Tzvi		1934
GORDON	David	M		Tzvi	Esther			1934
VALIAK	Cluina	M	married			Shasa		1934
VALIAK	Shasa	F	married			Cluina		1934
VALIAK	Laiv	M	married			Eida	7 children	1934
VALIAK	Eida	F	married			Laiv	7 children	1934
VALIAK	Laiv	M	married			Sarah	2 children	1934
VALIAK	Sarah	F	married			Laiv	2 children	1934
VALIAK	Nahum	M	married			Raichel		1934
VALIAK	Raichel	F	married			Nahum		1934
VALIAK	Raizel	F		Nahum	Raichel			1934
VALIAK	Nehemya	M	married			Fruma		1934
VALIAK	Fruma	F	married			Nehemya		1934
VALIAK	Braina	F		Nehemiya	Fruma			1934
VALIAK	Esther	F		Nehemiya	Fruma			1934
VALIAK	Faivish	M	married			Baila	2 children	1934
VALIAK	Baila	F	married			Faivish	2 children	1934
VALIAK	Shmuel	M	married			Liba	6 children	1934
VALIAK	Liba	F	married			Shmuel	6 children	1934
VALIAK	Shepsel	M	married			Glicka	6 children	1934
VALIAK	Glicka	F	married			Shepsel	6 children	1934
SALAVEITSHIK		M	married			Esther	3 children	1934

SALAVEITSHIK	Esther	F	married				3 children	1934
SALAVEITSHIK	Isaac	M	married			Rachel		1934
PEREVASNIK	Rachel	F	married			Isaac		1934
PEREVASNIK	Pinchas	M	married				2 children	1934
PEREVASNIK		F	married			Pinchas	2 children	1934
KATZIZNA	Shmuel	M	married			Sima		1934
KATZIZNA	Sima	F	married			Shmuel		1934
KATZIZNA	Faiva	M		Shmuel	Sima			1934
KATZIZNA	Sarah	F		Shmuel	Sima			1934
RODNITSKY	David	M	married			Frada	child	1934
RODNITSKY	Frada	F	married			David	child	1934
SHPAIER	Joseph	M	married			Sarah Gitel	3 children	1934
SHPAIER	Sarah Gitel	F	married			Joseph	3 children	1934

[Columns 1935-1940]

Widze Necrology

(Vidzy, Belarus)

55°24'/26°38'

Transliterated by Beryl Baleson

Page numbers reference the Original Yizkor Book

Family name(s)	First name(s)	Gender	Marital status	Father's name	Mother's name	Name of spouse	Remarks & additional family	Page
ABELEVITCH	Israel	M	married			Sarah		1935
ABELEVITCH	Sarah	F	married			Israel		1935
ABELEVITCH	Haya	F		Israel	Sarah			1935
ABELEVITCH	Yishayahu	M		Israel	Sarah			1935
ABELEVITCH	Tzirel	F		Israel	Sarah			1935

ABELEVITCH	Jacob	M		Israel	Sarah			1935
ABELEVITCH	Aba	M	married					1935
ABELEVITCH		F	married			Aba		1935
ABELEVITCH	Michael	M		Aba				1935
ABELEVITCH	Herzl	M	married			Slava		1935
ABELEVITCH	Slava	F	married			Herzl		1935
ABELEVITCH	Jacob Laizer	M	married			Haya	child	1935
ABELEVITCH	Haya	F	married			Jacob Laizer	child	1935
ABELEVITCH	Laiv	M	married			Vichna		1935
ABELEVITCH	Vichna	F	married			Laiv		1935
ABELEVITCH	Meir	M						1935
ABELEVITCH	Hasiya	F						1935
ABELEVITCH	Batya	F						1935
ABELEVITCH	Israel	M						1935
ABELEVITCH	Michael	M	married				2 children	1935
ABELEVITCH		F	married			Michael	2 children	1935
ABELEVITCH	Ethel	F						1935
ABELEVITCH	Hinda	F						1935
ABELEVITCH	Bracha	F						1935
ABELEVITCH	Sarah	F					male relative	1935
ABRAMSON	Eliyahu	M	married			Sarah		1935
ABRAMSON	Sarah	F	married			Eliyahu		1935
ABRAMSON	Faiga	F		Eliyahu	Sarah			1935
ABRAMSON	Esther	F		Eliyahu	Sarah			1935
UGAL	Shaul	M	married			Rivka		1935
UGAL	Rivka	F	married			Shaul		1935
OSIAN	Laiv	M	married			Ita		1935
OSIAN	Ita	F	married			Laiv		1935
OSIAN	Shmuel	M		Laiv	Ita			1935

OSIAN	Benjamin	M		Laiv	Ita			1935
OSIAN	Shemerihu	M	married					1935
OSIAN		F	married			Shemerihu		1935
AHARONAVITCH	Israel	M	married			Sarah	3 children	1935
AHARONAVITCH	Sarah	F	married			Israel	3 children	1935
EINHORN	David	M						1935
EINHORN	Bentzion	M		David				1935
ELKENITZKY	Abraham	M	married			Batya	child	1935
ELKENITZKY	Batya	F	married			Abraham	child	1935
ESTHERINSKY	Hanan	M	married			Deborah	child	1935
ESTHERINSKY	Deborah	F	married			Hanan	child	1935
ASHKENAZI	Taiba	F						1935
ASHKENAZI	Rachel	F						1935
BANK	Eliyahu	M	married			Hana		1935
BANK	Hana	F	married			Eliyahu		1935
BANK	David	M		Eliyahu	Hana			1935
BANK	Ephraim	M		Eliyahu	Hana			1935
BANK	Nahum	M		Eliyahu	Hana			1935
BANK	Geniya	F						1935
BANK	Hirsh	M	married			Gitel		1935
BANK	Gitel	F	married			Hirsh		1935
BANK	Jacob	M	married			Batya	3 children	1935
BANK	Batya	F	married			Jacob	3 children	1935
BANK	Leah	F					3 children	1935
BANK	Mordechai	M	married					1935
BANK		F	married			Mordechai		1935
BASIN	Shmuel Neta	M	married				3 children	1935
BASIN		F	married			Shmuel Nata	3 children	1935
BASEL	Israel	M	married				child	1935

	Jacob							
BASEL		F	married			Israel Jacob	child	1935
BASEVITCH	Isaac	M	married			Leah		1935
BASEVITCH	Leah	F	married			Isaac		1935
BASKIN	Yishayahu	M	married			Faiga		1935
BASKIN	Faiga	F	married			Yishayahu		1935
BASKIN	Batya	F		Yishayahu	Faiga			1935
BASKIN	Haya	F		Yishayahu	Faiga			1935
BAK	Aba	M	married			Batya		1935
BAK	Batya	F	married			Aba		1935
BAK	Necha	F		Aba	Batya			1935
BARISHNIKOV	Shmuel Isaac	M	married			Leah		1936
BARISHNIKOV	Leah	F	married			Shmuel Isaac		1936
BARISHNIKOV	Sima	F					Maiden name GLAICHER	1936
BARISHNIKOV	Shalom	M			Sima			1936
BINDERMAN	Michael	M	married					1936
BINDERMAN		F	married			Michael		1936
BINDERMAN	Raizel	F		Michael				1936
BINDERMAN	Israel	M		Michael				1936
BLECHMAN	Abraham	M	married					1936
BLECHMAN		F	married			Abraham		1936
BLECHMAN	Berl	M	married			Yacha	child	1936
BLECHMAN	Yacha	F	married			Berl	child	1936
BLECHMAN	Shmuel	M	married			Geniya		1936
BLECHMAN	Geniya	F	married			Shmuel		1936
BLECHMAN	Rivka	F		Shmuel	Geniya			1936
BELMAN	Zelig	M	married			Deborah		1936
BELMAN	Deborah	F	married			Zelig		1936

BELMAN	Hanoch	M		Zelig	Deborah			1936
BELMAN	Koniya	M		Zelig	Deborah			1936
BELMAN	Raizel	F		Zelig	Deborah			1936
BELMAN	Moshe	M		Zelig	Deborah			1936
BELMAN	Hana	F		Zelig	Deborah			1936
BELMAN	Golda	F		Zelig	Deborah			1936
BELMAN	Vichna	F		Zelig	Deborah			1936
BELMAN	Hena	F		Zelig	Deborah			1936
BELMAN	Israel	M	married					1936
BELMAN		F	married			Israel		1936
BERNATAR	Salava	F						1936
BERNATAR	Liba	F						1936
BERNATAR	Hirsh	M						1936
BERNATAR	Shifra	F						1936
BERNATAR	Shmuel	M						1936
BEREZ	Jacob	M	married			Ethel		1936
BEREZ	Ethel	F	married			Jacob		1936
BEREZ	Nachman	M	married					1936
BEREZ		F	married			Nachman		1936
BEREZ	Pinchas	M	married			Braina		1936
BEREZ	Braina	F	married			Pinchas		1936
BEREZ	Pesach	M	married			Golda	2 children	1936
BEREZ	Golda	F	married			Pesach	2 children	1936
BEREZ	Shlomo	M	married			Zlata		1936
BEREZ	Zlata	F	married			Shlomo		1936
BEREZ	Shmuel	M		Shlomo	Zlata			1936
BEREZ	David	M		Shlomo	Zlata			1936
BEREZ	Hanan	M		Shlomo	Zlata			1936
GUTKIN	Mordchai	M	married			Tzirel	2 children	1936
GUTKIN	Tzirel	F	married			Mordechai	2 children	1936

GOLDIN	Eliyakum	M						1936
GOLDIN		F					mother of ELIYAKUM	1936
GALTZ	Mina	F						1936
GALTZ	Hana	F			Mina			1936
GANTOVNIK	Eliezer	M	married			Rachel		1936
GANTOVNIK	Rachel	F	married			Eliezer		1936
GANTOVNIK	Betzalel	M		Eliezer	Rachel			1936
GAPSTEIN	Baruch	M	married			Maniya		1936
GAPSTEIN	Maniya	F	married			Baruch		1936
GAPSTEIN	Laiv	M		Baruch	Maniya			1936
GORDON	Masha	F					2 grandchildren	1936
GORDON	Hirsh	M			Masha			1936
GURVITCH	Joseph	M						1936
GURVITCH	Shimon	M						1936
GURVITCH	Sarah Liba	F						1936
GURVITCH	Shevach	M	married			Mina	2 children	1936
GURVITCH	Mina	F	married			Shevach	2 children	1936
GINSBERG	Raichel	F						1936
GINSBERG	isaac	M			Raichel			1936
GLEICHER	Benjamin	M	married			Rachel	child	1936
GLEICHER	Rachel	F	married			Benjamin	child	1936
GLEICHER	David	M						1936
GLICKSMAN	Shmuel	M						1936
GLICKSMAN	Hayyim	M		Shmuel				1936
GNESIN	Gitel	F					child	1936
GNESIN	Shlomo Isaac	M			Gitel			1936
GENDEL	Hirsh	M	married			Nehama		1936
GENDEL	Nehama	F	married			Hirsh		1936
GENDEL	Gita	F		Hirsh	Nehama			1936

GENDEL	Miriam	F		Hirsh	Nehama			1936
GENDEL	Shaul	M						1937
GELLMAN	Esther	F					sister of Mina. 2 children	1937
GELLMAN	Mina	F					sister of Esther	1937
GELLMAN	Gitel	F						1937
GELLMAN	Hayyim Laiv	M						1937
GELLMAN	Tzadok	M						1937
GELLMAN	David	M						1937
GELLMAN	Baruch	M						1937
GELLMAN	Raizel	F						1937
DAITCH	Israel	M	married			Hinda		1937
DAITCH	Hinda	F	married			Israel		1937
DAITCH	Esther	F					Maiden name STARAVITCH	1937
DAITCH	Yehudit	F			Esther			1937
DAITCH	Taibe	F			Esther			1937
DAITCH	Laiv David	M						1937
DAITCH	Tzipa	F						1937
DAITCH	Masha	F						1937
DAITCH	Necha	F						1937
DAITCH	Meir	M						1937
DUBINSKY	Aba	M	married			Rachel		1937
DUBINSKY	Rachel	F	married			Aba		1937
DUBINSKY	Haya	F		Aba	Rachel			1937
DUBINSKY	Sima	F		Aba	Rachel			1937
DLAT	Pesach	M						1937
DLAT	Yehuda	M						1937
DLAT	Gedalyahu	M						1937
DLAT	Hasiya	F						1937

HABERMAN	Laiv	M	married			Esther		1937
HABERMAN	Esther	F	married			Laiv		1937
HABERMAN	Meir	M		Laiv	Esther			1937
HABERMAN		F		Laiv	Esther		In List written in brackets "TZEFLAVITCH"	1937
VASKIN	Moshe	M	married			Hasiya		1937
VASKIN	Hasiya	F	married			Moshe		1937
VAINONSKY	Aharon	M	married			Deborah		1937
VAINONSKY	Deborah	F	married			Aharon		1937
VINAKUR	Shmuel	M						1937
VAZGEL							Not clear if individual or in family	1937
VALATZKY	Gershon	M	married					1937
VALATZKY		F	married			Gershon		1937
VALATZKY	Joseph	M		Gershon				1937
VALATZKY	Moshe	M		Gershon				1937
WAINSTEIN	Frieda	F					Maiden name SEGALAVITCH	1937
VIDOTSHINSKY	Sarah Rivka	F						1937
VIDOTSHINSKY	Haya	F						1937
VIDOTSHINSKY	Frieda	F						1937
VIDOTSHINSKY	Isaac	M						1937
ZARCH	Hanan	M	married			Hana		1937
ZARCH	Hana	F	married			Hanan		1937
ZARCH	Leah	F		Hanan	Hana			1937
ZARCH	Gitel	F		Hanan	Hana			1937
ZUBAVITCH	Zalman	M	married			Rachel		1937
ZUBAVITCH	Rachel	F	married			Zalman		1937
ZAIDMAN	David	M	married			Shva		1937

ZAIDMAN	Shva	F	married			David		1937
ZAIDMAN	Leah	F		David	Shva			1937
ZAIDMAN	Shalom	M		David	Shva			1937
ZAIDMAN	Moshe	M		David	Shva			1937
ZAIDMAN	Gela	F		David	Shva			1937
ZAIDEL	Isaac	M						1937
ZIV	Pinchas	M						1937
ZIV	Leah	F		Pinchas				1937
ZIV	Rachel	F		Pinchas				1937
ZILBER	Merl	F						1937
ZILBER	Gedalyahu Zalman	M			Merl		possibily relating to two people - GEDALYAHU and ZALMAN	1937
ZLATKIN	Shimon	M	married			Lata		1937
ZLATKIN	Lata	F	married			Shimon		1937
ZLATKIN	Tzila	F		Shimon	Lata			1937
ZLATKIN	Rachel	F		Shimon	Lata			1937
ZLATKIN	Rashel	F		Shimon	Lata			1937
ZLATKIN	Shazeniya	F						1937
ZLATKIN	Hayyim	M			Shazeniya			1937
ZLATKIN	Golda	F			Shazeniya			1937
	Hayyim Michael	M	married				Beadle of the synagogue and his wife	1937
HIDKAL		F					child	1937
TVARETSHKY	Zalman Be'er	M					2 children	1937
TVARETSHKY	Haya	F						1937
TVARETSHKY	Sima	F			Hana			1937
TVARETSHKY	Yehuda	M			Hana			1937
TVARETSHKY	Hayyim	M	married			Miriam	2 children	1937

TVARETSHKY	Miriam	F	married			Hayyim	2 children	1937
TVARETSHKY	Raphal	M	married			Malka		1937
TVARETSHKY	Malka	F	married			Rafal		1937
TVARETSHKY	Hayyim	M		Rafal	Malka			1937
TVARETSHKY	Yekatriel	M		Rafal	Malka			1937
TEMPELMAN	Isaac	M	married			Bella		1937
TEMPELMAN	Bella	F	married			Isaac		1937
YICHILTSHIK	Abraham Moshe	M	married			Nehama		1937
YICHILTSHIK	Nehama	F	married			Abraham Moshe		1937
YICHILTSHIK	Isaac	M		Abraham Moshe	Nehama			1937
YICHILTSHIK	Jacob	M						1937
YICHILTSHIK	Mariasha	F		Jacob				1937
YICHILTSHIK	Miriam	F		Jacob				1937
YICHILTSHIK	Liba	F						1937
YICHILTSHIK	Isaac	M						1937
YICHILTSHIK	Gutman	M						1937
YICHILTSHIK	Raizel	F						1937
KANANKIND	Hinda	F					Maiden name SALTAISKY. child	1937
KANANKIND	Hayyim Noah	M	married			Fruma		1937
KANANKIND	Fruma	F	married			Hayyim Noah		1937
KANANKIND	Hanan	M	married			Batya	child	1937
KANANKIND	Batya	F	married			Hanan	child	1937
KAGAN	Moshe	M	married			Fraida		1937
KAGAN	Fraida	F	married			Moshe		1937
KATZ	Abraham	M	married			Ida	child	1937
KATZ	Aida	F	married			Abraham	child	1937

KATZ	Hana	F						1937
KATZ	Meir	M	married			Golda		1937
KATZ	Golda	F	married			Meir		1937
KATZ	Isaac	M		Meir	Golda			1937
LUBATSKY	Ita	F						1937
LUBATSKY	Berl	M			Ita			1937
LUBATSKY	Zelda	F			Ita			1937
LUBATSKY	Yerachmiel	M						1937
LUBATSKY	Naomi	F						1937
LUBATSKY	Yishayahu	M						1937
LUBATSKY	Moshe	M						1937
LUBATSKY	Saniya Frada	F						1937
LIAKAVITSHKY	Isaac	M	married			Osnat		1937
LIAKAVITSHKY	Osnat	F	married			Isaac		1937
LIAKAVITSHKY	Lioba	F		Isaac	Osnat			1937
LIAKAVITSHKY	Sarah	F		Isaac	Osnat			1937
LIPKAVITCH	Joseph	M	married			Mera		1937
LIPKAVITCH	Mera	F	married			Joseph		1937
LIPKAVITCH	Isaac	M		Joseph	Mera			1937
LEVIN	Isaac	M					his parents	1937
LEVIN		M	married				father of ISAAC	1937
LEVIN		F	married				mother of ISAAC	1937
LEVIN	Haikel	M	married			Boniya		1937
LEVIN	Boniya	F	married			Haikel		1937
LEVIN	Mina	F		Haikel	Boniya			1937
LEVIN	Shachna	M		Haikel	Boniya			1937
LEVIN	Berl	M		Haikel	Boniya			1937
LEVIN	Jacob Hanoch	M	married			Hana Daba		1938
LEVIN	Hana	F	married			Jacob		1938

	Daba					Hanoch		
LEVIN	Nata	M	married			Eliya		1938
LEVIN	Eliya	F	married			Nata		1938
LEVIN	Hana	F					Maiden name MILIKAVSKY	1938
LEVIN	Lipa	M	married			Niota		1938
LEVIN	Niota	F	married			Lipa		1938
LEVIN	Saniya	F		Lipa	Niota			1938
MAGILNIK	Berl	M	married			Saniya	2 children	1938
MAGILNIK	Saniya	F	married			Berl	2 children	1938
MAGILNIK	Zalman	M						1938
MAGILNIK	Yerachmiel	M						1938
MALIATSHKY	Jacob David	M	married			Kara		1938
MALIATSHKY	Kara	F	married			Jacob David		1938
MALIATSHKY	Saniya Bluma	F						1938
MALIATSHKY	Masha	F			Saniya Bluma			1938
MALLERAVITCH	Berl	M						1938
MALLERAVITCH	Joseph	M		Berl				1938
MALLERAVITCH	Hana	F		Berl				1938
MALLERAVITCH	David	M						1938
MATZKIN	Joseph	M	married			Zisla		1938
MATZKIN	Zisla	F	married			Joseph		1938
MATZKIN	Yehuda	M	married			Rivka	child	1938
MATZKIN	Rivka	F	married			Yehuda	Maiden name SHAPIRA. child	1938
MONITCH	Abraham	M	married					1938
MONITCH		F	married			Abraham		1938
MONITCH	Asher	M						1938
MONITCH	Pinchas	M						1938

MONITCH	Alta	F						1938
MONITCH	Baruch	M						1938
MONITCH		M					brother of Baruch	1938
MONITCH	Berl	M	married			Sarah		1938
MONITCH	Sarah	F	married			Berl		1938
MONITCH	Hertz	M						1938
MONITCH		F					mother of HERTZ	1938
MONITCH	Hayyim	M						1938
MONITCH	Zisa	F						1938
MONITCH	Berl	M						1938
MONITCH	Hayyim Eliyahu	M	married					1938
MONITCH		F	married			Hayyim Eliyahu		1938
MONITCH	Joseph	M		Hayyim Eliyahu				1938
MONITCH	Laizer Jacob	M						1938
MONITCH	Hoda Leah	F						1938
MUSKIN	Fraida	F						1938
MUSKIN	Hirsh	M			Fraida			1938
MUSKIN	Nina	F			Fraida			1938
MUSKIN	Nehemiya	M	married			Gita Leah		1938
MUSKIN	Gita Leah	F	married			Nehemiya		1938
MUSKIN	Rafal	M		Nehemiya	Gita Leah			1938
MUSKIN	Lifa	M		Nehemiya	Gita Leah			1938
MUSKIN	Sarah	F		Nehemiya	Gita Leah			1938
MORMINSKY	Hayyim	M	married			Batsheva		1938
MORMINSKY	Batsheva	F	married			Hayyim		1938
MORMINSKY	Velvel	M		Hayyim	Batsheva			1938
MORMINSKY	Laiv	M		Hayyim	Batsheva			1938
MORMINSKY	Yerachmiel	M		Hayyim	Batsheva			1938

MORMINSKY	Jacob	M		Hayyim	Batsheva			1938
MORMINSKY	Pinchas	M	married			Matla		1938
MORMINSKY	Matla	F	married			Pinchas		1938
MORMINSKY	Moshe	M						1938
MORMINSKY	Mosiya	F						1938
MORMINSKY	Reuben	M						1938
MORMINSKY	Rachel	F						1938
MORMINSKY	Berl	M						1938
MORMINSKY	Sarah	F						1938
MORMINSKY	Rivka	F					Maiden name MIRANSKY	1938
MORMINSKY	Lana	F					Possibly the family name is different child	1938
MIASNIK	Shmuel	M	married			Rachel	child	1938
MIASNIK	Rachel	F	married			Shmuel	child	1938
MAIZEL	Abraham Moshe	M	married					1938
MAIZEL		F	married			Abraham Moshe		1938
MAIZEL	Berl	M	married			Shperintza		1938
MAIZEL	Shperintza	F	married			Berl		1938
MAIZEL	Eliezer	M		Berl	Shperintza			1938
MAIZEL	Bisiya	F		Berl	Shperintza			1938
MILIKAVSKY	Gitel	F						1938
MISOSHTSHIN	Isaac Jacob	M	married			Gitel		1938
MISOSHTSHIN	Gitel	F	married			Isaac Jacob		1938
MISOSHTSHIN	Ezriel	M	married			Lioba	2 children	1938
MISOSHTSHIN	Lioba	F	married			Ezriel	2 children	1938
MELLMAN	Berl	M						1938
MELLMAN	Joseph	M						1938

MELLMAN		F					sister of Joseph	1938
SALAVEICHIK		F					Maiden name EVENSON. 2 children	1938
SALITAN	Isaac	M	married			Ella		1938
SALITAN	Ella	F	married			Isaac		1938
SALITAN	Moshe	M		Isaac	Ella			1938
SALITAN	Yerachmiel	M		Isaac	Ella			1938
SASNAVIK	Sarah	F						1938
SASNAVIK	Shmuel	M			Sarah			1938
SARKIN	Abraham	M	married			Bluma	child	1938
SARKIN	Bluma	F	married			Abraham	child	1938
SWIRSKY	Baruch	M	married			Hinda		1938
SWIRSKY	Hinda	F	married			Baruch		1938
SWIRSKY	Hasiya	F		Baruch	Hinda			1938
SWIRSKY	Aba	M	married			Kraina		1938
SWIRSKY	Kraina	F	married			Aba		1938
SWIRSKY	Hanoch	M		Aba	Kraina			1938
SWIRSKY	Berl	M		Aba	Kraina			1938
SWIRSKY	Rachel	F		Aba	Kraina			1938
SWIRSKY	Fruma	F		Aba	Kraina			1938
STARABIN	Velvel	M						1938
STARABIN	Miriam	F						1938
STARABIN	Sarah	F						1938
STARABIN	Liba	F						1938
STARABIN	Pesach	M						1938
STARABIN	Malka	F						1938
STARABIN	Hayyim	M	married			Pesia	2 children	1938
STARABIN	Pesia	F	married			Hayyim	2 children	1938
STARABIN	Kayla	F	married				Possibly the family name is different. 2	1938

							children	
STARABIN		M	married			Kayla	Possibly the family name is different. 2 children	1938
STARABIN	Rivka	F					2 children	1938
STARAVITCH	Abrasha	M					child	1938
STARAVITCH	Gruniya	M						1938
STARAVITCH	Mordechai	M					child	1938
STARAVITCH	Velvel	M	married			Raizel	child	1938
STARAVITCH	Raizel	F	married			Velvel	child	1938
STARAVITCH	Pinchas	M	married			Lioba	child	1938
STARAVITCH	Lioba	F	married			Pinchas	child	1938
SEGALAVITCH	Reuben	M						1938
EVENSON	Aba	M	married			Haya		1939
EVENSON	Haya	F	married			Aba		1939
EVENSON	Yehezkel	M	married				child	1939
EVENSON		F	married			Yehezkel	child	1939
EVENSON	Rivka	F					child	1939
PATASHNIK	Laiv	M	married			Miriam	possibly they are parents of his wife and her parents	1939
PATASHNIK	Miriam	F	married			Laiv		1939
FEIGEL	Eliezer	M	married			Michal		1939
FEIGEL	Michal	F	married			Eliezer		1939
KATZ	Rachel	F		Eliezer	Michal		Maiden name FAIGEL	1939
FISHERMAN	Laiv Isaac	M	married					1939
FISHERMAN		F	married			Laiv Isaac		1939
FISHERMAN	Meir Be'er	M						1939
FISHERMAN	Shlomo	M						1939
FISHERMAN	Yenta	F						1939

FISHERMAN	Gitel	F					child	1939
FLEXER	Shlomo Hayyim	M						1939
FLEXER	Saniya	F						1939
FLEXER	Moshe	M						1939
PETSHENISKY	Abraham	M	married			Shaina		1939
PETSHENISKY	Shaina	F	married			Abraham		1939
PETSHENISKY	David	M		Abraham	Shaina			1939
PETSHENISKY	Shmuel	M		Abraham	Shaina			1939
FELDMAN	Hayyim	M	married			Fraida		1939
FELDMAN	Fraida	F	married			Hayyim		1939
FELDMAN	Isaac	M		Hayyim	Fraida			1939
FELDMAN	Geniya	F		Hayyim	Fraida			1939
PEKAL	Fia	F					2 children	1939
FERMANT	Levy	M						1939
FERMANT	Hayyim	M						1939
FERMANT	Haya	F					Maiden name KATSHERGINSKY	1939
FERMANT	Reuben	M						1939
FERMANT	Rachel	F					mother and child	1939
FERMANT		F					mother of the child	1939
FERMANT		M					mother's child	1939
FEREVAZNIK	Hana	F						1939
TZVEIGARN	Zisel	M	married			Leah		1939
TZVEIGARN	Leah	F	married			Zisel		1939
TZVEIGARN	Joseph	M	married			Hana	child	1939
TZVEIGARN	Hana	F	married			Joseph	child	1939
KATSHERGINSKY	Abraham	M						1939
KATSHERGINSKY	Abraham	M						1939
KATSHERGINSKY		M					brother of Abraham	1939

KATSHERGINSKY	Gitel	F						1939
KATSHERGINSKY	Berl	M						1939
KATSHERGINSKY	David	M						1939
KATSHERGINSKY	Rivka	F						1939
KATSHERGINSKY	Taiba	F						1939
KATSHERGINSKY	Shaul	M						1939
KATSHERGINSKY	Hasiya	F						1939
KATSHERGINSKY	Berl	M						1939
KATSHERGINSKY	Shimon	M						1939
KATSHERGINSKY	Mendel	M						1939
KATSHERGINSKY	Hana	F						1939
KATSHERGINSKY	Rachel	F						1939
KATSHERGINSKY	Zalman	M						1939
KATSHERGINSKY	Deborah	F						1939
KATSHERGINSKY	Moshe	M						1939
KATSHERGINSKY	Hayyim	M						1939
KATSHERGINSKY	Haya	F					Maiden name KLOMEL	1939
KATSHERGINSKY	Jacob	M	married					1939
KATSHERGINSKY		F	married			Jacob		1939
KATSHERGINSKY	Gedalyahu	M		Jacob				1939
KATSHERGINSKY	Tsheska	F		Jacob				1939
KATSHERGINSKY	Isaac	M	married				child	1939
KATSHERGINSKY		F	married			Isaac	child	1939
KATSHERGINSKY	Shlomo	M	married			Rashel		1939
KATSHERGINSKY	Rashel	F	married			Shlomo		1939
KATSHERGINSKY	Meir	M	married			Hada		1939
KATSHERGINSKY	Hada	F	married			Meir		1939
KATSHERGINSKY	Shmuel	M		Meir	Hada			1939
KATSHERGINSKY	Hinda	F		Meir	Hada			1939

KATSHERGINSKY	Zelig	M		Meir	Hada			1939
KATSHERGINSKY	Rachel	F		Meir	Hada			1939
KATSHERGINSKY	Hayyim	M		Meir	Hada			1939
KATSHERGINSKY	Nehama	F		Meir	Hada			1939
KATSHERGINSKY	Moshe	M	married				child	1939
KATSHERGINSKY		F	married			Moshe	child	1939
KATSHERGINSKY	Shevach	M	married			Miriam	2 children	1939
KATSHERGINSKY	Miriam	F	married			Shevach	2 children	1939
KATSHERGINSKY	Shlomo	M	married			Batya		1939
KATSHERGINSKY	Batya	F	married			Shlomo		1939
KATSHERGINSKY	Hana	F		Shlomo	Batya			1939
KATSHERGINSKY	Masha	F		Shlomo	Batya			1939
KATSHERGINSKY	Gershon	M		Shlomo	Batya			1939
KATSHERGINSKY	Shmuel	M						1939
KAMINSKY		M	married			Raza	Dentist	1939
KAMINSKY	Raza	F	married				Dentist's wife	1939
KAMINSKY	Jacob	M			Raza		Dentist's son	1939
KAMERAZ	Hirsh	M						1939
KAMERAZ	Helena	F						1939
KAMERAZ	Raza	F						1939
KAMERAZ	Shalom	M						1939
KAMERAZ	Frada	F					not clear whose child she is	1939
KRAV	Hirsh David	M	married			Hada		1939
KRAV	Hada	F	married			Hirsh David		1939
KRAV	Shlomo	M		Hirsh	Hada			1939
KRAV	Mordechai	M	married				2 children	1940
KRAV		F	married			Mordechai	2 children	1940
KORITZKY	Abraham	M						1940

KORITZKY	Aharon	M		Abraham				1940
KORITZKY	Leah	F		Abraham				1940
KORITZKY	Tzirel	F		Abraham				1940
KORITZKY	Gita	F		Abraham				1940
KORITZKY	Rafal	M	married			Gita		1940
KORITZKY	Gita	F	married			Rafal		1940
KORITZKY	Haya	F		Rafal	Gita			1940
KORITZKY	Moshe	M		Rafal	Gita			1940
KLOMEL	Zalman	M						1940
KRUT	Shaul	M	married			Cieana		1940
KRUT	Cieana	F	married			Shaul		1940
KRUT	Gitel	F		Shaul	Cieana			1940
KRATKA	Emma	F						1940
KRATKA		F			Emma			1940
KRETSHMER	Meir	M					brother of Reuben	1940
KRETSHMER	Reuben	M					brother of Meir	1940
RAZIN	Tsherna	F						1940
RAG	Abraham	M	married			Yacha		1940
RAG	Yacha	F	married			Abraham		1940
ROZENBERG	Hayyim Eliezer	M						1940
ROZENBERG	Gitel	F						1940
ROZENBERG	Pesiya	F						1940
RAFKIND	Benjamin	M	married					1940
RAFKIND		F	married			Benjamin		1940
RAFKIND	Gershon	M		Benjamin				1940
RAFKIND	Gesiya	F		Benjamin				1940
RAFKIND	Haya	F		Benjamin				1940
RAFKIND	Rivka	F		Benjamin				1940
RAFKIND	Pesiya	F		Benjamin				1940

RAPP	Isaac	M	married			Esther	2 children	1940
RAPP	Esther	F	married			Isaac	2 children	1940
RITVA	Hayyim	M						1940
RITVA	Batya	F						1940
RITVA	Aidel	F						1940
RITVA	Rivka	F						1940
RITVA	Bracha	F						1940
RAICHEL	Hayyim Asher	M	married					1940
RAICHEL		F	married			Hayyim Asher		1940
RING	Yekatriel	M	married			Gita		1940
RING	Gita	F	married			Yekatriel		1940
RING	Moshe	M		Yekatriel	Gita			1940
RING	Luba	F		Yekatriel	Gita			1940
RING	Reuben	M	married			Fraida	2 children	1940
RING	Fraida	F	married			Reuben	2 children	1940
SHAPIRA	Abrasha	M	married			Gitel		1940
SHAPIRA	Gitel	F	married			Abrasha	Maiden name MUSKIN	1940
SHAPIRA	Jacob	M						1940
SHAPIRA	Sarah	F						1940
SHAPIRA	Ela	F						1940
SHAPIRA	Bentzion	M						1940
SHAPIRA	Solomon	M	married			Mera	2 children	1940
SHAPIRA	Mera	F	married			Solomon	Maiden name GURVITCH. 2 children	1940
SHAPIRA	Reuben	M						1940
SHUB	Meir	M	married		Hana	Yenta		1940
SHUB	Yenta	F	married			Meir		1940
SHUB	Isaac	M		Meir	Yenta			1940

SHUB	Hana	F					Mother of MEIR	1940
SHULHOIFER	Hillel	M	married			Salava		1940
SHULHOIFER	Salava	F	married			Hillel		1940
SHULHOIFER	Sarah	F		Hillel	Salava			1940
SHULMAN	Taiba	F						1940
SHULMAN	Meir	M						1940
SHULMAN	Abraham	M						1940
SHULMAN	Israel	M						1940
SHULMAN	Sarah	F						1940
SHULMAN	Aidel	F						1940
SHULMAN	Haya	F						1940
SHUNTOP	Eliezer Isaac	M						1940
SHUNTOP	Taiba	F						1940
SHUNTOP	Moshe	M						1940
SHUNTOP	Leah	F						1940
SHUNTOP	Laiv	M						1940
SHTALTZ	Israel Joseph	M	married			Haya		1940
SHTALTZ	Haya	F	married			Israel Joseph		1940
SHTALTZ	Hayyim	M		Israel Joseph	Haya			1940
SHTALTZ	Rachel	F		Israel Joseph	Haya			1940
SHTALTZ	Leah	F		Israel Joseph	Haya			1940
STEIN	Isaac Joseph	M	married			Leah		1940
STEIN	Leah	F	married			Isaac Joseph		1940
SHAIBEL	Mendel	M	married			Rachel	2 children	1940
SHAIBEL	Rachel	F	married			Mendel	2 children	1940

SHAIBEL	Laiv	M	married				1940
SHAIBEL		F	married		Laiv		1940
SHAIBEL	Reuben	M					1940
SHAIBEL	Abrasha	M		Reuben			1940
SHER	Meir	M	married				1940
SHER		F	married		Meir		1940
SHER	Liba Mera	F	married			Possibly the family name is different. 2 children	1940
SHER		M	married		Liba Mera	Possibly the family name is different. 2 children	1940
SHERMAN	Nehama	F					1940
SHERMAN	Joseph	M					1940
SHKLIAR	Laiv	M					1940
SHKLIAR	Aidel	F					1940
SHKLIAR	Nissan	M	married			brother of Shaul. child	1940
SHKLIAR		F	married		Nissan	child	1940
SHKLIAR	Shaul	M				brother of Nissan	1940

[Columns 1935-1936]

Mielegjany Necrology

(Mielagėnai, Lithuania)

55°15'/26°26'

Transliterated by Beryl Baleson

Family name(s)	First name(s)	Gender	Marital status	Father's name	Mother's name	Name of spouse	Page
EPSTEIN	Raza	F					1935
EPSTEIN	Isaac	M			Raza		1935
EINHORN	Leah	F					1935
EINHORN	Bat Sheva	F			Leah		1935
EINHORN	Tzvi	M			Leah		1935
EINHORN	Sarah	F			Leah		1935
EINHORN	Naomi	F			Leah		1935
BAIGEL	Isaac	M	married			Leah	1935
BAIGEL	Leah	F	married			Isaac	1935
BAIGEL	Meir	M		Isaac	Leah		1935
BAIGEL	Liba	F		Isaac	Leah		1935
BAIGEL	Sarah	F		Isaac	Leah		1935
BRASLAVSKY	Pesach	M	married			Yenta	1935
BRASLAVSKY	Yenta	F	married			Pesach	1935
BRASLAVSKY	Bentzion	M		Pesach	Yenta		1935
GOLDSTEIN	Yehuda Laiv	M					1935
GOLDSTEIN	Jacob	M	married			Haya	1935
GOLDSTEIN	Haya	F	married			Jacob	1935
GOLDSTEIN	Shlomo	M		Jacob	Haya		1935
GOLDSTEIN	Getxel	M		Jacob	Haya		1935
GOLDSTEIN	Taiba	F		Jacob	Haya		1935
GLAS	Fraida	F					1935
GLAS	Isaac	M			Fraida		1935
GENDEL	Joseph	M	married			Fraida	1935
GENDEL	Fraida	F	married			Joseph	1935
GENDEL	Rivka	F					1935
GENDEL	Batya	F		Joseph	Fraida		1935
GENDEL	Baila	F		Joseph	Fraida		1935

GENDEL	Tuvia	M		Joseph	Fraida		1935
GENDEL	Shmuel	M		Joseph	Fraida		1935
GENDEL	Noah	M	married			Doba	1935
GENDEL	Doba	F	married			Noah	1935
DALAT	Hana	M	married			Liba	1935
DALAT	Liba	F	married			Hana	1935
DALAT	Katriel	M		Hana	Liba		1935
DALAT	Isaac	M		Hana	Liba		1935
TAITELBAUM	Tzvi	M	married			Ethel	1935
TAITELBAUM	Ethel	F	married			Tzvi	1935
TAITELBAUM	Pinchas	M	married	Tzvi	Ethel	Ida	1935
TAITELBAUM	Ida	F	married			Pinchas	1935
TAITELBAUM	Kiena	F					1935
TAITELBAUM	Merle	F			Kiena		1935
LOURIE	Tzvi	M	married			Tzirel	1936
LOURIE	Tzirel	F	married			Tzvi	1936
LOURIE	Leah	F		Tzvi	Tzirel		1936
SWIRSKY	Abraham	M	married			Haya	1936
SWIRSKY	Haya	F	married			Abraham	1936
SWIRSKY	Mina	F					1936
SWIRSKY	Braina	F			Mina		1936
TZAIKINSKY	Eliezer	M	married			Sarah	1936
TZAIKINSKY	Sarah	F	married			Eliezer	1936
TZAIKINSKY	Tzirel	F		Eliezer	Sarah		1936
TZAIKINSKY	Meir	M	married			Haya	1936
TZAIKINSKY	Haya	F	married			Meir	1936
KAVARSKY	Abraham	M	married			Haya	1936
KAVARSKY	Haya	F	married			Abraham	1936
KAVARSKY	Nehama	F		Abraham	Haya		1936
RAIF		M	married				1936
RAIF		F	married				1936
RAIN	Shaina	F					1936
RAIN	Eliyahu	M			Shaina		1936
RAIN	Moshe	M			Shaina		1936
RAIN	Golda	F			Shaina		1936
RAICHEL	Abraham	M	married			Raiza	1936
RAICHEL	Raiza	F	married			Abraham	1936

RAICHEL	Hinda	F		Abraham	Raiza		1936
RAICHEL	Mordechai	M		Abraham	Raiza		1936
RAICHEL	Laiv	M		Abraham	Raiza		1936
RAICHEL	Hanan	M		Abraham	Raiza		1936
RAVITCH	Baila	F					1936
RESNIKAVITCH	Shalom	M					1936
RESNIKAVITCH	Jacob	M		Shalom			1936
RESNIKAVITCH	Dabe	F		Shalom			1936

[Columns 1939-1942]

Koziany Necrology

(Kozyany, Belarus)

55°18' 26°52'

Transliterated by Beryl Baleson

Page numbers reference the Original Yizkor Book

Family name(s)	First name(s)	Gender	Marital status	Father's name	Mother's name	Name of spouse	Remarks and additional family	Page
א Alef								
ABEL	Tzina	F	married				Rabbi's wife	1939
ABRAMSON	Hayyim	M					Slaughterer	1939
ABRAMSON	Rivka	F		Hayyim				1939
ABRAMSON	Aba	M		Hayyim				1939
ESTHERAVITCH	Neta	M	married			Rachel		1939
ESTHERAVITCH	Rachel	F	married			Neta		1939
ב Bet								
BEIGEL	Malka	F						1939
BEIGEL	Reuben	M			Malka			1939
BEIGEL	Shlomo	M			Malka			1939
BEIGEL	Shulamit	F			Malka			1939
BERZON	Pesach	M						1939
ג Gimmel								
GUTKIN		M	married			Rashel	2 children	1939
GUTKIN	Rashel	F	married				2 children	1939
GREIZDORF	Aharon	M	married			Noima		1939
GREIZDORF	Noiman	F	married			Aharon		1939
GREIZDORF	Rivka	F		Aharon	Noima			1939

GREIZDORF	Esther	F						1939
GREIZDORF	Yishayahu	M	married			Lea		1940
GREIZDORF	Leah	F	married			Yishayahu		1940
GREIZDORF	Rachel	F		Yishayahu	Leah			1940
GREIZDORF	Pinchas	M	married			Rachel	2 children	1940
GREIZDORF	Rachel	F	married			Pinchas	2 children	1940
ה **Hey**								
HACHMAN	Bainish	M		Mendel				1940
HACHMAN	Hana	F						1940
HACHMAN	Liber	M			Hana			1940
HACHMAN	Shmaryahu	M			Hana			1940
HACHMAN	Laiv	M	married			Batya	2 children	1940
HACHMAN	Batya	F	married			Laiv	2 children	1940
HALPERIN	Israel	M	married					1940
HALPERIN		F	married			Israel		1940
HALPERIN	Rachel	F		Israel				1940
HALEVI	Sarah Pesa	F						1940
ו **Vav**								
VALKAVSKY	Alter	M	married			Sarah		1941
VALKAVSKY	Sarah	F	married			Alter		1941
VALKAVSKY	Moshe	M		Alter	Sarah			1941
VALKAVSKY	Sender	M		Alter	Sarah			1941
VALKAVSKY	Baila	F		Alter	Sarah			1941
ז **Zayin**								
ZALKIND	Hayyim	M						1941
ZALKIND	Rina	F		Hayyim				1941
ZUBAVITCH	Eliezer	M	married			Sarah		1941
ZUBAVITCH	Sarah	F	married			Eliezer		1941
ZUBAVITCH	Nehama	F		Eliezer	Sarah			1941

ZUBAVITCH	Gutman	M		Eliezer	Sarah			1941
ZUBAVITCH	Zalman	M	married			Liba	children	1941
ZUBAVITCH	Liba	F	married			Zalman	children	1941

ח Chet

HADASH	Jacob	M	married			Sarah	2 children	1941
HADASH	Sarah	F	married			Jacob	2 children	1941
HADASH	Yekutiel	M	married			Rivka		1941
HADASH	Rivka	F	married			Yekutiel		1941
HADASH	Hayyim	M		Yekutiel	Rivka			1941
HADASH	Yudel	M		Yekutiel	Rivka			1941
HIDKEL	Abraham	M	married			Sarah		1941
HIDKEL	Sarah	F	married			Abraham		1941
HIDKEL	Hillel	M		Abraham	Sarah			1941

י Yod

YECHILTSHIK	Asher	M	married			Lipsha		1941
YECHILTSHIK	Lipsha	F	married			Asher		1941
YECHILTSHIK	Shlomo	M		Asher	Lipsha			1941
YECHILTSHIK	Meir	M		Asher	Lipsha			1941
YECHILTSHIK	Israel	M		Asher	Lipsha			1941
YECHILTSHIK	Gaiga	F		Asher	Lipsha			1941
YECHILTSHIK	Ber	M	married			Sarah	2 children	1941
YECHILTSHIK	Sarah	F	married			Ber	2 children	1941
YECHILTSHIK	Hirsh	M	married					1941
YECHILTSHIK		F	married			Hirsh		1941
YECHILTSHIK	Ethel	F		Hirsh				1941
YECHILTSHIK	Nachman	M		Hirsh				1941
YECHILTSHIK	Laiv	M		Hirsh				1941
YECHILTSHIK	Laiv	M	married			Sarah		1941
YECHILTSHIK	Sarah	F	married			Laiv		1941

YECHILTSHIK	Miriam	F	married				Possibility family name different. With children	1941
YECHILTSHIK		M	married			Miriam	Possibility family name different. With children	1941
ל **Lamed**								
LEVIN	David	M						1941
LEVIN		F					Mother of David	1941
LEVIN	Hirsh	M	married					1941
LEVIN		F	married			Hirsh		1941
LEVIN	Isaac	M	married			Radel	2 children	1941
LEVIN	Radel	F	married			isaac	2 children	1941
LEVIN	Moshe	M	married			Malka		1941
LEVIN	Malka	F	married			Moshe		1941
LEVIN	Liber	M		Moshe	Malka			1941
LIPSHIN	Yehoshua Hayyim	M						1941
מ **Mem**								
MILNER	Haya Rivka	F						1941
נ **Nun**								
NATKAVITCH	Hiena	F						1941
NATKAVITCH	Jacob	M			Hiena			1941
NATKAVITCH	Sender	M			Hiena			1941
NATKAVITCH	Aida	F			Hiena			1941
NATKAVITCH	Pearl	F			Hiena			1941
	Nahum	M	married			Faia	daughter	1942
	Faia	F	married			Nahum	daughter	1942
ס **Samech**								

SVIRSKY	Zalman	M	married			Masha		1942
SVIRSKY	Masha	F	married			Zalman		1942
SVIRSKY	Abraham	M		Zalman	Masha			1942
SVIRSKY	Braina	F		Zalman	Masha			1942
SVIRSKY	Joseph	M	married			Shaina		1942
SVIRSKY	Shaina	F	married			Joseph		1942
SVIRSKY	Esther	F		Joseph	Shaina			1942
SVIRSKY	Tzvia	F		Joseph	Shaina			1942
SVIRSKY	Joel	M		Joseph	Shaina			1942

פ Peh

FAIGEL	Hana	M	married			Gela		1942
FAIGEL	Gela	F	married			Hana		1942
FAIGEL	Hirsh	M		Hana	Gela			1942
FAIGEL	Abraham	M		Hana	Gela			1942
FAIGEL	Sarah	M		Hana	Gela			1942
FRESMAN	Abraham Asher	M	married			Tzvia	2 children	1942
FRESMAN	Tzvia	F	married			Abraham Asher	2 children	1942

צ Tzadik

TZIMER		M	married			Sarah		1942
TZIMER	Sarah	F	married					1942
TZIMER	Rachel	F			Sarah			1942
TZIMER	Baruch	M			Sarah			1942
TZIMER	Joseph	M			Sarah			1942
TZIMER	Bracha	F			Sarah			1942
TZIMER	Zundel	M			Sarah			1942
TZIMER	Berl	M			Sarah			1942

ר Resh

RAICHEL	Berl	M	married			Raiza		1942

RAICHEL	Raiza	F	married			Berl		1942
RAICHEL	Reuben	M		Berl	Raiza			1942
RAICHEL	Mendel	M		Berl	Raiza			1942
RAICHEL	Ita	F		Berl	Raiza			1942
RAICHEL	Hertz	M	married			Hinda		1942
RAICHEL	Hinda	F	married			Hertz		1942
RAICHEL	Velvel	M						1942
RAICHEL	Laiv	M		Velvel				1942
RAICHEL	Zalman	M	married			Saniya		1942
RAICHEL	Saniya	F	married			Zalman		1942
RAICHEL		M		Zalman	Saniya			1942
RAICHEL		M		Zalman	Saniya			1942
RAICHEL	Hayyim	M	married			Rachel		1942
RAICHEL	Rachel	F	married			Hayyim		1942
RAICHEL	Joel	M		Hayyim	Rachel			1942
RAICHEL	Laiv	M	married			Leah		1942
RAICHEL	Leah	F	married			Laiv		1942
RAICHEL	Yechezkel	M		Laiv	Leah			1942
RAICHEL	Hava	F		Laiv	Leah			1942
RAICHEL	Shmuel	M	married			Batya		1942
RAICHEL	Batya	F	married			Shmuel		1942

ש **Shin**

STEIN	Abraham	M	married				children	1942
STEIN		F	married			Abraham	children	1942
STEIN	Isaac	M	married			Tzerna		1942
STEIN	Tzerna	F	married			Isaac		1942
STEIN	David	M		Isaac	Tzerna			1942
STEIN	Esther	F		Isaac	Tzerna			1942
STEIN	Golda	F	married				Possibility family name	1942

							different	
STEIN		M	married			Golda	Possibility family name different	1942
SHAPIRA	Berl	M	married			Hinda		1942
SHAPIRA	Hinda	F	married			Berl		1942
SHAPIRA	Malka	F		Berl	Hinda			1942
SHAPIRA	Hana	F		Berl	Hinda			1942
SHAPIRA	Rivka	F		Berl	Hinda			1942
SHAPIRA	Deborah	F		Berl	Hinda			1942
SHAPIRA	Braina	F		Berl	Hinda			1942
SHAPIRA	Bentzion	M		Berl	Hinda			1942
SHEINUK	Shmuel	M	married			Haya		1942
SHEINUK	Haya	F	married			Shmuel		1942
SHEINUK	Rachel	F		Shmuel	Haya			1942
SHEINUK	Hillel	M		Shmuel	Haya			1942

[Columns 1941-1944]

Kobylnik Necrology

(Narach, Belarus)

54°56' 26°41'

Transliterated by Beryl Baleson

Page numbers reference the Original Yizkor Book

Family name(s)	First name(s)	Gender	Marital status	Father's name	Mother's name	Name of spouse	Remarks and additional family	Page
א Alef								
EINBINDER	Rabbi Yehuda Laiv	M	married				Rabbi	1941

EINBINDER		F	married			Yehuda Laiv		1941
ALSFINE	Mendel Laiv	M	married			Gisiya		1941
ALSFINE	Gisiya	F	married			Mendel Laiv		1941
AXELROD	Eliyahu	M					family	1941

ב **Bet**

BATVINIK	Moshe	M	married			Haya		1941
BATVINIK	Haya	F	married			Moshe		1941
BATVINIK	Joseph	M		Moshe	Haya			1941
BORGIN	Hayyim Meir	M						1941
BERGER	Shabtai	M	married			Nehama		1941
BERGER	Nehama	F	married			Shabtai		1941
BERGER	Israel	M		Shabtai	Nehama			1941
BERGER	Moshe	M		Shabtai	Nehama			1941
BERGER	Mina	F		Shabtai	Nehama			1941
BERGER	Hana	F		Shabtai	Nehama			1941

ג **Gimmel**

GORDON	Abraham Laiv	M	married			Haya		1941
GORDON	Haya	F	married			Abraham Laiv		1941
GORDON	Eliyahu	M		Abraham Laiv	Haya			1941
GORDON	Hava	F		Yishayahu Joseph			children	1941
GORDON	Baila	F		Yishayahu Joseph				1941
GORDON	Fruma	F					In list written in brackets "Yishayahu Gordon". 3 children	1941

GORDON	Saul	M	married			Dabe		1941
GORDON	Dabe	F	married			Shaul		1941
GORDON	Jacob	M		Shaul	Dabe			1941
GORDON	Gaiga	F		Shaul	Dabe			1941
GALDZAGER	Abraham	M	married			Baila	Slaughterer	1941
GALDZAGER	Baila	F	married			Abraham	3 children	1941
GANTAVNIK	Meir	M	married			Gitel		1941
GANTAVNIK	Gitel	F	married			Meir		1941
GANTAVNIK	Yehuda	M		Meir	Gitel			1941
GANTAVNIK	Hayyim	M					Brother of Bila	1941
GANTAVNIK	Bila	F					Sister of Hayyim	1941
GANTAVNIK		F					Brother of Hayyim and Bila	1941
	Laiv	M	married			Aida	Family name unsure. In list written "GILAN"	1941
	Ida	F	married			Laiv	Family name unsure. In list written "GILAN"	1941
	Hayyim	M		Laiv	Aida		Family name unsure. In list written "GILAN"	1941
	Asher	M		Laiv	Aida		Family name unsure. In list written "GILAN"	1941
	Leah	F		Laiv	Aida		Family name unsure. In list written "GILAN"	1941
	Matla	F		Laiv	Aida		Family name unsure. In list written "GILAN"	1941
GLAT	David	M					family	1941
GERSHTER	Moshe	M	married			Tamara		1941
GERSHTER	Tamara	F	married			Moshe		1941

GERSHTER	Shlomo	M		Moshe	Tamara			1941
GERSHTER	Hirsh	M		Moshe	Tamara			1941
GRINBERG	Jacob Beinish	M	married			Mina		1941
GRINBERG	Mina	F	married			Jacob Beinish		1941
GRINBERG	Laiv	M		Joseph Bainish	Mina			1941
GRINBERG	Hana	F		Joseph Bainish	Mina			1941
GRINBERG	Esther	F		Joseph Bainish	Mina			1941

ד Dalet

DANISHEVSKY	Baruch	M	married			Menucha	3 children	1941
DANISHEVSKY	Menucha	F	married			Baruch	3 children	1941
DIMENSTEIN	Esther	F	married				Wife of the cantor	1941
DIMENSTEIN		M	married			Esther	cantor	1941

ה Hey

HILFMAN	Shmuel	M	married			Hana		1942
HILFMAN	Hana	F	married			Shmuel		1942
HILFMAN		F		Shmuel	Hana			1942

ו Vav

VAINER	Israel	M						1942
VAINER	Alter	M	married			Faiga		1942
VAINER	Faiger	F	married			Alter		1942
VAINER		M		Alter	Faiga			1942
VEXLER	Yishayahu	M	married					1942
VEXLER		F	married			Yishayahu		1942
VEXLER	Shaina	F					Maiden name. With family	1942

ח Chet

HADASH	Joseph	M	married			Baila		1942
HADASH	Baila	F	married			Joseph		1942
HADASH	Haya	F		Joseph	Baila			1942
HADASH	Isaac	M		Joseph	Baila			1942
HADASH	Laiv	M	married			Asna		1942
HADASH	Asna	F	married			Laiv		1942
HADASH	Mina	F						1942
HADASH	Moshe Zelig	M	married			Rivka		1942
HADASH	Rivka	F	married			Moshe Zelig		1942
HADASH	Tzipora	F						1942
HADASH	Shaina	F						1942
HADASH	Rivka	F					2 children	1942
HADASH	Sarah	F						1942

ט Tet

TADRES	Ita	F						1942
TARANTSHIK	Hirsh	M	married			Sarah		1942
TARANTSHIK	Sarah	F	married			Hirsh		1942
TARANTSHIK		F		Hirsh	Sarah			1942
TARANTSHIK		F		Hirsh	Sarah			1942
TSHERNATZKY	Israel	M	married			Dina	2 children	1942
TSHERNATZKY	Dina	F	married			Israel	2 children	1942
TSHERNATZKY	Fraida	F						1942
TSHERNATZKY	Jacob	M			Fraida			1942
TSHERNATZKY	David	M			Fraida			1942
TSHERNATZKY	Gedalyahu	M	married			Sarah Rivka		1942
TSHERNATZKY	Sarah Rivka	F	married			Gedalayahu		1942

TSHERNATZKY	Yochevet	F		Gedalyahu	Sarah Rivka			1942
י **Yod**								
YAVANAVITCH	David	M	married			Boniya		1942
YAVANAVITCH	Boniya	F	married			David		1942
YAVANAVITCH	Baruch	M		David	Boniya			1942
YAVANAVITCH	Laibel	M		David	Boniya			1942
YAVANAVITCH	Joseph	M	married			Rachel		1942
YAVANAVITCH	Rachel	F	married			Joseph	GANTAVNIK	1942
YAVANAVITCH	Michael	M	married			Matla		1942
YAVANAVITCH	Matla	F	married			Michael	HADASH	1942
YAVANAVITCH	Shlomo	M	married			Raiza		1942
YAVANAVITCH	Raitza	F	married			Shlomo		1942
YAVANAVITCH	Shalom	M		Shlomo	Raiza			1942
YAVANAVITCH	Isaac	M		Shlomo	Raiza			1942
YANAVSKY	Zelata	F						1942
YANAVSKY	Yehoshua	M			Zelata			1942
YANAVSKY	Gitel	F			Zelata			1942
YANAVSKY	Dvasha	F			Zelata			1942
YANAVSKY	Eli Joseph	M	married			Raizel	3 children	1943
YANAVSKY	Raizel	F	married			Eli Joseph	3 children	1943
YANAVSKY	Hershel	M					family	1943
YANAVSKY	Hayyim Jacob	M	married			Sarah Rivka		1943
YANAVSKY	Sarah Rivka	F	married			Hayyim Jacob		1943
YANAVSKY	Yishayahu	M					family	1943
YANAVSKY	Moshe	M					In Kobylnik during the war. With family	1943
YANAVSKY	Moshe	M	married			Gisiya		1943
YANAVSKY	Gisiya	F	married			Moshe		1943

YANAVSKY	Shmuel	M		Moshe	Gisiya			1943
YANAVSKY	Faivish	M	married			Sarah		1943
YANAVSKY	Sarah	F	married			Faivish		1943
YANAVSKY	Haya Liba	F		Faivish	Sarah			1943
YANAVSKY	Pinchas	M	married				3 children	1943
YANAVSKY		F	married			Pinchas	3 children	1943
YANAVSKY	Shlomo Laizer	M	married			Haya	3 children	1943
YANAVSKY	Haya	F	married			Shlomo Laizer	3 children	1943
YABLANAVITCH	Merel	F						1943
YABLANAVITCH	Eli Joseph	M			Merel			1943
YABLANAVITCH	Tzviya	F			Merel			1943

ל **Lamed**

LOSHNATSKY	Shabtai	M	married			Rashel		1943
LOSHNATSKY	Rashel	F	married			Shabtai	LEVITAN	1943
LOSHNATSKY	Shmuel	M		Shabtai	Rashel			1943
LOSHNATSKY	Isaac	M		Shabtai	Rashel			1943
LOSHNATSKY		F		Shabtai	Rashel			1943
LAZEROWITCH	Hayyim	M	married			Liba		1943
LAZEROWITCH	Liba	F	married			Hayyim		1943
LAZEROWITCH		F		Hayyim	Liba			1943
LIPSHITZ	Liba Malka	F					LEVITAN	1943
LIPSHITZ		F			Liba Malka			1943
LEVITAN	Dina	F						1943
LEVITAN	Isaac	M	married			Frieda		1943
LEVITAN	Frieda	F	married			Isaac		1943
LEVITAN	Israel	M		Isaac	Frieda			1943
LEVITAN	Meir	M		Isaac	Frieda			1943

LEVITAN	Abraham	M		Isaac	Frieda			1943
LEVITAN	Faiga	F		Isaac	Frieda			1943
LEVIN	Fraida	F						1943

מ Mem

MAKAVSKY	Laiv	M	married			Liba	Rabbi	1943
MAKAVSKY	Liba	F	married			Liba		1943
MAKAVSKY	Abraham	M		Laiv	Liba			1943
MASHITZ	Isaac	M	married			Tzipora		1943
MASHITZ	Tzipora	F	married			Isaac		1943
MASHITZ	Shmuel Hirsh	M		Isaac	Tzipora			1943
MILKMAN	Michael	M	married			Mina		1943
MILKMAN	Mina	F	married			Michael		1943
MILKMAN		F		Michael	Mina			1943
MILKMAN	David	M		Michael	Mina			1943

נ Nun

NARANSKY	Laiv	M	married			Frieda		1943
NARANSKY	Frieda	F	married			Arye Laiv		1943
NARANSKY		F		Arye Laiv	Frieda			1943
NARANSKY		F		Arye Laiv	Frieda			1943
NARANSKY		F		Arye Laiv	Frieda			1943
NARANSKY	Michael	M		Arye Laiv	Frieda			1943
NARANSKY	Shlomo	M	married			Braina		1943
NARANSKY	Braina	F	married			Shlomo		1943
NARANSKY	Baila	F		Shlomo	Braina			1943

ס Samech

SVIDLER	Esther Leah	F					TSHERNATZKY. 3 children	1943
SVIRSKY	Herzl	M						1943

פ Peh

FAIGELMAN	Tuviya	M	married			Haya Sarah		1943
FAIGELMAN	Haya Sarah	F	married					1943
FAIGELMAN	Moshe	M		Tuviya	Haya Sarah			1943
FAIGELMAN	Sarah	F		Tuviya	Haya Sarah			1943

ק Kof

KAGAN	Laiv	M	married			Pesa	2 children	1944
KAGAN	Pesa	F	married			Laiv	Maiden name ALSPIN. 2 children	1944
KAPLAN	Yehudit	F					TADRES	1944
KAPLAN		M			Yehudit			1944
KORNITSKY		M					In list written - Christian from ZNAKATSH	1944
KIEVSKY	Abraham	M	married			Haya Sarah	2 children	1944
KIEVSKY	Haya Sarah	F	married			Abraham	Maiden name GLAT. 2 children	1944
KIRMAILISKY	Laiv	M					family	1944
KIRMAILISKY	Baila Dabe	F						1944
KIRMAILISKY	Faivish	M					family	1944
KLOMEL	Haya Sarah	F						1944
KLOMEL	Gitel	F			Haya Sarah			1944
KLOMEL	Miriam	F			Haya Sarah			1944
KLOMEL	Isaac	M	married			Rivka		1944
KLOMEL	Rivka	F	married			Isaac		1944
KLOMEL	Abraham	M		Isaac	Rivka			1944

KLOMEL	Biala	F		Isaac	Rivka			1944
KLOMEL	Niosa	F					Dentist	1944
KRAVTSHINSKY	Isaac	M	married			Batya	4 children	1944
KRAVTSHINSKY	Batya	F	married			Isaac	4 children	1944
KROKAV	Kiena	F						1944
KROKAV	Heshel	M			Kiena			1944
KROKAV	Israel	M	married			Haya		1944
KROKAV	Haya	F	married			Israel		1944
KROKAV	Ariye	M		Israel	Haya			1944
KRIVITSKY	Hana Dvsasha	F						1944
KRIVITSKY	Laiv	M					family	1944
KRIVITSKY	Abraham	M					family	1944
KRIVITSKY	Gershon	M	married					1944
KRIVITSKY		F	married			Gershon		1944
KRIVITSKY	Zelig	M		Gershon				1944

ר Resh

RAIDER	Hayyim	M	married			Aida		1944
RAIDER	Aida	F	married			Hayyim		1944
RAIDER	Slava	F		Hayyim	Aida			1944
RAIDER	Esther	F		Hayyim	Aida			1944

ש Shin

SHTEINGART	Joseph	M	married			Batya		1944
SHTEINGART	Batya	F	married			Joseph		1944
SHTEINGART	Jacob	M		Joseph	Batya			1944
SHTEINGART	Boniya	F		Joseph	Batya			1944
SHAPIRA	Shraga	M					Teacher. With family	1944
SHNEIDERAVITCH	Batya	F						1944
SHNEIDERAVITCH	Isaac	M			Batya			1944

SHNEIDERAVITCH	Sarah	F			Batya			1944
SHNEIDERAVITCH	Haya	F			Batya			1944
SHTEINGART	Reuben	M	married			Saniya		1944
SHTEINGART	Saniya	F	married			Reuben		1944
SHTEINGART	Raizel	F		Reuben	Saniya			1944
SHTEINGART	Haya	F		Reuben	Saniya			1944
SHTEINGROV	Raizel	F						1944
SHPITZ	Hayyim	M					family	1944
SHAPTAN		M					Teacher. With family	1944

[Columns 1943-1950]

Postav Necrology

(Pastavy, Belarus)

55°07' 26°50'

Collected by Rokhl Broydo and Beyle Akh-Yosef

Translation from Yiddish by Dr. Sonia Kovitz

Donated by Irene Mauber Skibinski

Surname	Given name	Family members
א Alef		
ABRAMSON	Mendel	wife: Yehudis, children: Shaul, Sonye, Izke
ADANITSH	Yitskhak	wife: Khanah, children: Mordekhai, Ruven, Yakov, Yisrael
AVERBUKH	Borukh	children: Miriam, Berl, Sonye
AVERBUKH	Teybe Leah	
IZYKSON	Zalman	wife: Itl, children: Yitskhak, Rokhl
EYNHORN	Asher	family

EYNHORN	Moshe	family
AYNBINDER	Yehoshuah	wife: Dvorah, children: Rivke, Khayah
ITSLER	Leyb	children: Yisroel, Rafael, Khaim Yitskhak, Leah, Feyge, Yakov
ITSLER	Abram	family
OSLEROVITSH	Sheftl	family
ב Bet		
BASE	Yakov	wife: Ester nee Estrin
BAK	Meir	wife: Khanah, children: Velvel, Yakov, Nakhman, Miriam
BARON	Feyge, Libe	
BARKAN	Diske	sister: Dvorah
BUNIMOVITSH	Abram Yosef	wife: Dvorah, kinder: Shlomah Dovid, Feyge, Moshe Meir
BEYGEL	Abram	wife: Fanye, children: Motl, Rivke
BLOKH	Roze nee Meymin	daughter: Edzye
BROYDO	Malkhah	family
BROYDO	Nakh	family
ג Gimmel		
GOBER	Merl nee Tseplovitsh	daughter: Yokhved
GOLOMB	Tsivye nee Rokhman	
GURVITSH		mother, children: Frume, Brayne, Shmuel, Yosef
GURVITSH	Sholem	wife: Lyube and children
GILINEV		family
GINDIN	Shmuel	wife: Ester, children: Mendel, Freydl, Khaya, Sonye
GELVAN	Hirshl	family
GELVAN	Simkhah	family
GELVAN	Khaya	family
GLEZER	Dov Ber	wife: Khanah, children: Teybe,

		Yakov, Khayah, Dovid, Rezke
GLEZER	Tsvi	wife: Golde di shneyder [seamstress]
GENDEL	Nekhomah	son: Benyomin
GENDEL	Tsvi	wife: Matle, children: Mordekhai, Teybe, Shmuel
GENDEL	Keyle	family
GENDEL	Yerakhmiel	family
GENDEL	Yosef	family
GENDEL	Sender	wife: Khavah nee Feygel
GENDEL	Sorah Leah nee Gendel, wife of ... SOKOLINSKI	
GENDEL	Beryl der melamed [teacher]	
GENKIN	Simkhah	family
GENKIN	Yitskhak	wife and son: Nakhman
GARBAROVITS H	Khaya	daughter: Sonye
GREYTON	Shmuel Hirsh der shokhet [Kosher butcher]	wife

ד Dalet

DALUS	Rokhl nee Dalus, wife of Kalman FISHMAN	
DOYTSH	Meytke der shneyder [tailor]	family
DLOT	Aharon	wife: Rive Esye, children: Yitskhak, Shmuel
DLOT	Leyb	family
DLOT	Fayvish	family
DLOT	Shmuel Khaim	family
DROTS	Abram	wife: Sheyne nee Rivkind, daughter: Khayah Disye

ו Vav

VAYNER	Zlate	family
VAYNER	Moshe	son

VAYNER	Eske	
VAYNER	Pinkhas	family
VAYNER	Sorah nee Vayner, wife of Yehoshuah Leyb PERMAN	
VAYNER	Dove nee Vayner, wife of Yerakhmiel PERMAN	
VOYNONSKI	Hilel	wife: Rashl and children
VOYNONSKI	Khayah Rokhl	daughter: Sheyne
VISKUNSKI	Shmuel	wife: Dvorah and son
VEKSLER	Natan	
VEKSLER	Leah	children: Perl, Itl
VEKSLER	Sorah Zelde nee Veksler, wife of … LEVIN	
VEKSLER	Gronye nee Veksler, wife of … STROVITSH	
ז **Zayin**		
ZAGA	Mordekhai	wife: Tsile and children
ZOLITSKI		
ZASLAVSKI	Misha	wife: Sonye
ZEYGMAN	Yehoshuah	family
ZEYGMAN	Yekhiel	family
ZEYDEL	Abram	family
ZEYDEL	Itse Yakov	family
ZEYDEL	Yisroel Eliahu	wife: Leah, child: Moshe Leyb
ZEYDEL	Leyb	wife and children: Shimshon, Leah, Gedoliahu
ZEYDEL	Mikhal	wife: Slave nee Shapiro
ZEYDEL	Moshe	wife: Reyzl
ZEYDEL	Luk	wife: Sorah, children: Khanah, Etl, Shlomah, Yakov Gershon
ZEYDEL	Sholem and wife	
ח **Chet**		

KHATSKEL	Ayzik	wife: Libe Gitl, child: Khavah
KHODOS	Gershon	wife: Sorele and children
KHODOS	Zelig	family
KHODOS	Moshe	daughters: Reyzl, Sorah
KHODOS	Mole	wife: Khayah nee Sherman and children
KHODOS	Motl	wife: Feyge Leah, children: Zelig, Sime
KHODOS	Meir der shames [synagogue caretaker]	daughters
KHODOS	Nakh	family

ט **Tet**

TAUBES	Mikhal	wife: Dvorah, child: Sorah
TAUDRES	Notl Khaim	wife: Khanah, children: Khayah, Slave
TAUDRES	Tsfureh nee Taudres? [question mark in original], wife of Zalkind RABINOVITSH	

י **Yod**

YAGEL	Velvel	sister: Khayah
YAGEL	Rokhl	husband
YOFFE	Shmuel	wife: Khayah Sorele, children: Pesye, Abram
YUNGELSON	Yosef	family
YUNGELSON	Nakhum	family
YUNGELSON	Ester nee Feygel	daughter: Leah

כ **Kaf**

KATS	Khaya Beyle nee Shapiro	family
KATS	Yosef	family
KATS	Leyvik	
KATS	Mendel	wife: Tonye, son: Zev

ל **Lamed**		
LUBOTSKI	Ester	
LUBOTSKI	Shimon	family
LUBOTSKI	Brayne	family
LEVIN	Sorah Zelde nee Veksler	children
LIFSHIN	Aharon	wife: Risye, children: Monik, Shmuel, Ester
LIFSHIN	Rokhl Rivke	
מ **Mem**		
MANDELMAN	Simkhah	wife: Tile
MANPIL	Hinde	wife: Sorah nee Sokolinski
MEYMIN	Leyb, wife: Khanah	
MEYMIN	Roze nee Meymin wife of ... BLOKH	
MILSHTEYN		wife and children
MELER	Leyzer	
MELER	Yekhiel	family
MESTER	Abba	wife: Tsforah, children: Diske, Khaya, Basye, Abram Moshe
MESTER	Yisroel	
MESTER	Abram, wife: Rivke, children: Yakov, Lipe	
MESTER	Yakov, wife: Sonye, son: Zelke	
MESTER	Libe	
MESTER	Rokhl	family
MESTER	Khayah nee Mester, wife of Eliahu PERSKI	family
נ **Nun**		
NAKHUM	Nakhum der shokhet [kosher butcher]	wife
ס **Samech**		
SANDLER	Yitskhak	

SOSNOVIK	Two sisters	
SOKOLINSKI		family
SOKOLINSKI	Sorah Leah nee Gendel	son: Yakov
SOKOLINSKI	Sorah nee Sokolinski, wife of Hinde MANPIL	
SVIDLER	Khatskel	family
SVIRSKI	Abram	family
STROVITSH	Gronye nee Veksler	
STROVITSH	Abram and son	
STRACHANSKI	Yitskhak	wife: Rashe (Resil), children: Yakov, Leyb, Sonye
STRACHANSKI	Leyb	family
STRACHANSKI	Henye	
STRACHANSKI	Rivke	husband

ע Ayin

ESTRIN	Yosef, wife: Rivke, son: Mendel	
ESTRIN	Binyomin	
ESTRIN	Ester nee Estrin, wife of Yakov BASE	
ESTRIN	Mashe nee Estrin, wife of ... SHUB	

פ Peh

POLIAKOV		brothers
POSTAVSKI		family
PIGAVSKI		family
FEYGEL	Dvorah	son: Shmuel
FEYGEL	Tserne	children: Sholem, Velvel, Khayah
FEYGEL	Khene	wife: Teybe, children: Paltse, Simke
FEYGEL	Khaim Meir	family
FEYGEL	Khava nee Feygel, wife of Sender GENDEL	
FEYGEL	Abram	family

FEYGEL	Yekutiel	family
FEYGEL	Shayah	family
FEYGEL	Zalman	family
FEYGEL	Mordekhai	family
FEYGEL	Eliahu	
FEYGEL	Ester nee Feygel, wife of ... YUNGELSON	
FEYGEL	Leah	family
FISHMAN	Kalman	wife: Rokhl nee Dalus and children
PLATKIN	Fayvish	family
FELDMAN	Abram	family
PERGAMENT	Avrashe	wife: Tsile, children: Ronye, Aharon
PERGAMENT	Abram	family
PERGAMENT	Khavah	children: Gege, Khanah
PERGAMENT	Shlomah Dr.	family
PERMAN	Yehoshuah Leyb	wife: Sorah nee Vayner and children
PERMAN	Yerakhmiel	wife: Dove nee Vayner and children
PERSKI	Eliahu	wife: Khayah nee Mester and children
PEREVOZNIK	Tsviah	children
FRIDMAN	Zev	wife
FRIDMAN	Yakov	wife: Etl, children: Abram Itse, Khenokh
FRIDMAN	Moshe	
FREYDIN	Rabbi Yehudah Leyb	wife: Gronye, children: Natan, Malkah
FRISHMAN	Dovid	family

צ Tzadik

TSUKERMAN	Moshe Ber	family
TSEPLOVITSH	Abram	wife: Lyube, son, Shlomah
TSEPLOVITSH	Eliahu	wife: Basye, children: Nakhum, Khanah, Nemi
TSEPLOVITSH	Basye	wife of Khaloyn, children: Khayah

		Sorah, Moshe Ber, Iser
TSEPLOVITSH	Zalman	
TSEPLOVITSH	Khaim Eliahu	wife: Sonye, children: Rivke, Moshe
TSEPLOVITSH	Khayah Sorah	wife of Yerakhmiel, children: Khanah, Pesye, Soyetke, Tsvi, Tsirl
TSEPLOVITSH	Yosef	
TSEPLOVITSH	Yisroel	
TSEPLOVITSH	Leyb Sholem	
TSEPLOVITSH	Motel	wife: Khanah, daughter: Sforah
TSEPLOVITSH	Meir Yakov	
TSEPLOVITSH	Mendel	wife: Iske, children
TSEPLOVITSH	Moshe Dovid	son: Yakov
TSEPLOVITSH	Nakhum	daughter: Rokhl
TSEPLOVITSH	Tsvi	wife: Basye nee Kovarski, children: Shmuel, Nakhum, Nemi
TSEPLOVITSH	Merl nee Tseplovitsh, wife of ... GOBER	
TSEPLOVITSH	Shimon Dovid	wife: Genye and children
TSEPLOVITSH	Shmuel	wife: Henye, children: Leyb, Leah, Aharon
TSEPLOVITSH	Shimon Gershon	wife: Fanye, children: Zelig, Sime, Khaim
TSEPLOVITSH	Yitzkhak	family
TSEPLOVITSH	Khanah	family
TSEPLOVITSH	Khavah	
TSEPLOVITSH		wife and children from Moshe
TSEPLOVITSH	Basye	family
TSEPLOVITSH	Khayah Sorah	daughter: Rivke
TSEPLOVITSH	Motl	wife and children: Shmerl, Yerakhmiel
TSEPLOVITSH	Ruven	wife
TSEPLOVITSH	Shimon	wife: Sime, children: Pesakh, Rokhl
TSEPLOVITSH	Rafael	wife: Sonye, daughter: Lutsye

ק **Kof**		
KURITSKI	Nekhemah	sons: Ben Tsion, Khenokh
KLYOT	Benni	family
KOVARSKI	Basye nee Kovarski, wife of Tsvi TSEPLOVITSH	
KREMER	Leah	husband and children
KREMER	Leyb	wife: Tsife
KREMER	Sonye	
ר **Resh**		
RABINOVITSH	Zalkind	wife: Tsfureh (nee Taudres?) [question mark in original]
RABINOVITSH	Shmuel, wife: Hinde Dvorah, daughter: Shoshonah Khayah	
RUBINSHTEYN	Doctor	wife
ROGOV	Khaim Yitskhak	wife
ROKHMAN	Tsivye nee Rokhman, wife of ... GOLOMB	
RUDNITSKI	Ester	family
RUDNITSKI	Dvorah	daughter
RIVKIND	Sheyne nee Rivkind, wife of Abram DROTS	
RIVKIND	Yekutiel	son: Yitskhak
REYKHEL	Brayne	son: Abba
REYKHEL	Dvorah	
REYKHEL	Hertsl	wife: Gitl, children: Asnah, Siome
REYKHEL	Velvel	son: Shmuel
REYKHEL	Yehoshua	wife: Rivke, children: Ester, Khaim
REYKHEL	Yakov Leyb	children: Rokhl, Khanah, Khayah, Yisroel Nakh, Tsfureh
REYKHEL	Yakov	
REYKHEL	Yitskhak	daughter: Khayah
REYKHEL	Yisroel Ber	family

REYKHEL	Leyb and children	
REYKHEL	Meir	[wife?:] Khanah, daughter: Sorele, family
REYKHEL	Mikhal Zote	
REYKHEL	Mendel	wife: Fanye, son: Sev
REYKHEL	Moshe	wife: Miriam
REYKHEL	Edzye	family
REYKHEL	Shmerl	wife: Khanah, children: Vikhne, Libe, Yakov, Yehudah
REYKHEL	Abram Khaim	family
REYKHEL	Khaim Aharon	wife: Leah and children

ש **Shin**

SHAPIRO	Alte nee Feygel	children: Yehudis, Sorah, Nakh
SHAPIRO	Gershon, children: Natan, Rokhl, Yisroel, Sorah	
SHAPIRO	Khayah Dinah	
SHAPIRO	Yakov	family
SHAPIRO	Yirmiahu	wife
SHAPIRO	Khaya Beyle nee Shapiro, wife of … KATS	
SHAPIRO	Slave nee Shapiro, wife of Mikhal ZEYDEL	
SHERMAN	Khayah nee Sherman, wife of Mole KHODOS	
SHVARTS	Aharon Dovid	wife: Leah, children: Khanah, Khaim
SHVARTS	Khene, wife: Manye and children	
SHVARTS	Yakov Leyzer	family
SHUB	Mashe nee Estrin	son: Mendel
SHUBITSH	Dovid Shlomah	wife and daughter: Khanah
SHUBITSH	Zisl	wife: Alle, children: Lyonke, Sorah
SHUBITSH	Yeshiahu	wife: Musl, children: Yisroel, Reske
SHUBITSH	Pesakh	wife: Khasiah and children

SHULKIN	Esne	and children
SHUSTER	Leyb	wife: Frume, children: Khayah Alte, Shoske
SHNEYDER	Aharon Velvel	
SHNEYDER	Asher Leml	wife: Sforah, daughter: Pesye
SHNEYDER	Yitskhak	family
SHKLAROVSKI		family

[Columns 1949, 1951, 1953]

Nemencine Necrology

(Nemenčine, Lithuania)

55°09' / 26°10'

I spoke to the women who helped collect the necrology for Nemencine in 1956 when she came to Israel. This is the explanation of the Yishiva:

The Yishiva was not a permanent Yishiva. It was a house that a widow had donated when she died to a Yishiva. In 1939 when WWII started in Poland, a group of Yishiva Buchers who had escaped from another town lived there, and were taken out and executed on Saturday 20th September 1941 with most of the Jews of Nemencine.

Rita Friedman, Israel

Head of household	Family
א Alef	
Eizgor	wife: Mashe; daughters: Fania, Sheina
Engiolczyn Zev	wife: Shluma; children: Hersh, Beryl
Engiolczyn Abraham Yitzhak	wife: Esther; children: Hana, Chaim, Nachman
Andeman Moshe	wife: Sara; children: Miriam, Feige, Mordeckhai,Michael,Reize
Andeman Keile Yente	
Aranovitz Avigdor	wife: Teibel, children: Peretz, Yosef
ב Bet	
Baron Chaim	
Baron Tzipe	and family
Bloshinski Michle	
Borstein Feive	
Borstein Fishel	wife: Shasel, children: Pasia, Bracha
Borstein Shalom	wife: Pasia
Beirak Abraham	wife: Ettel; children: Mania, Beile, Shimeon, Yakov

Baronstein Shmuel	daughter: Teibe
Baronstein Sara	children: Moshe, Yakov, Shlomit
Brataniski Ber Velvel	wife: Feige
Brataniski Yakov	wife: Ettel; daughter Chiya and husband children: Reise, Teibe, Marisha, Shlomo Hersh, Beile
Brataniski Yitzhak	wife: Ettel and family
Brataniski Mordechkai	wife: Esther; children: Hana Ette, Marisha, Shlomo Hersh
Brataniski Shmuel	wife and son

ג Gimmel

Gold Max	wife: Rifka; children: Eida, Louisik
Gordon Chaim	
Gordon Tuvia	wife: Tzipe; and child
Gordon Meyer	wife: Esther, daughter Sheineleh
Gordon Musia	and child
Gordon Shlomo	wife: Keine, children: Yikutiel, Sheine
Gordon Shmuel	wife: Beile, children: Yisrael, Moshe
Gdud	wife: Hana son Mordeckai
Guravic Rachel	and Husband, son: Yitzhak and his wife
Glaz Hana	husband, children: Chaim, Rachel
Gluch Abraham	wife: Dera; son Yakov
Gluch Eizick	duaghter: Sheineh
Gluch Dan	wife: Dina; daughter Hesia
Gluch Hana	children: Chaya, Hinde, Rifka
Gluch Welvell	wife: Keine
Gluch Chaya	daughter Hesia
Gluch Yhezkel	wife: Rifka, children: Hinde, Shimeon
Gluch Sender	wife: Sara; daughter Hinde
Gluch Pinkhas	wife: Dara; son Yakov
Gradzienski Yakov Yosef	wife, children: Bracha, Rueven

ד Dalet

Dubitzki Yakov	children: Meyer, Leipe
Dubravskai	
Deitch Shalom	

ו Vav

Wolowitz Beryl	wife: Rachel

ז Zayin

Zak Heshel	wife: Miriam; son Leib
Zlatkawitz Benyamin	wife: Feida son Moshe
Zashor Reize	daughter: Genasia

ח Chet

Chen Metel	wife: Rachel; and child

ט Tet

Taub Shmuel	
Teitz Yosef	son Moshe
Taal Meir	wife: Leah, children: Kopel and child
Trapetchnick Meir	wife: Esther, children: Freida, Hersh
Trakinski Rashel	
Trakinski Yisrael	wife: Ettel; children: Shabtai ,Elke, Moshe, Dina
Tshenobrodke	wife: Miriam, children: Dvora, Chaiya

י Yod

Yaniski David Shlomo	wife: Keile; children: Yisrael, Shimeon
Yaniski Feive	wife: Batya; and son
Yoker Leib	wife: Sarah, daughter Batya

כ Kaf

Kaachim Ahron	

ל Lamed

Lashenski Yitzhak	children: Chaim, Menia

Leifer Michael	wife: Rachel; children: Moshe, Yitzhak, Beinish, Abraham, Miriam, Mine, Yisrael, Mordeckhai
Leibman Ahron	wife: Hessia; children: Moshe and child
Leibman Shmuel	wife: Shluma
Lewit Golde	son Michael
Lewit Yosef	and family
Levin Hanan	wife: Leah, children: Nachman, Chaim, Nachum
Lewinson Sara Leah	son Shabtai
Lewinson Abraham	wife: Gittel;two children
Lewinson Batya	childen: Pesia, Chiya
Lewinson Leib	children: Yisrael, Dishe, Shlomo
Lewinson Moshe Asher	wife: Eide; son Natel
Lewinson Shlomo	wife: Leah; son Yitzhak

מ Mem

Magun Sarah	
Margolis Yakov	wife: Miriam; children: Ettel, Moshe
Margolis Meir	
Miedzianski Beile	children: Chaim Yosef, Leib
Meidzianski Yoshua	wife: Esther, children: Yakov, Chiya

נ Nun

Natik Yakov	son Alter
Nodzen Dvorah	children: Reuven, Shnier
Nievieczynski Yhuda	wife: Chiya, children: Shulamit, Eite, Rachel
Niemenczynski Abraham	wife: Miriam, children: Masha, Yosef, Yakov
Niemenczynski Beile	children: Abraham, Naomi and child
Niemenczynski Daniel	wife, three children
Niemenczynski Hersh	wife: Chiya
Niemenczynski Hershel	wife: Heishe; son: Gershon
Niemenczynski Zelda	2 children
Niemenczynski Yakov	wife: Ettel; and children

Niemenczynski Yhizkel	wife: Rachel, children Masha with two children
Niemenczynski Feive	
Niemenczynski Fishel	wife, three children
Niemenczynski Fredl	children: Velvel, Tzvia
Niemenczynski Tzadok	wife and two children
Niemenczynski Rashel	
Niemenczynski Rachel	and family
Niemenczynski Shlomo	
Nirke Yitzhak	wife: Bracha
Nirke Yosef	wife: Grunia, children: Efraim, Leib

ס Samech

Sapir The Rabbi Gedalhou	wife: Hana

פ Peh

Pageralski Chana	daughter Rachel
Pazniak Malka	children: Gita, Fruma, Yitzhak, Nisan, Yisrael
Pazniak Yitzhak Yisrael	two sisters
Fine Mendel	wife: Michle, two children
Fine Yisrael	wife: Sarah, daughter Bracha
Fine Yikutiel	wife: Beile, children: Tzemach, Yosef, Sara, Rachel
Fine Golda	children: Sheina, Rachel
Fine Metel	wife: Malka, children, Shein, Michael, Nachama, Leah and her husband Meir
Fin Yakov	children: Alter, Elte
Finkel Moshe	wife: Chaya; children: Yisrael, Sara
Pelshdetein Moshe	wife: Emma
Farawazki Ahron	wife: Dvora
Farawazki Leibe	son Yhushua
Prazan Yakov	wife: Reizel; children: Moshe, Mina
Prazan Shlomo	wife: Sara; children: Chaya, Shmuel
Prazan Sara	and her children

ק Kof

Kowarski Abraham David	wife: Sara; son Moshe
Kowarski Yhishua Yakov	wife: Beile
Kalmanowitz Gershon	wife: Chana Batya; son Berele
Klein	son Abraham
Kemach Abraham	wife: Pesia; children: Yonatan, Moshe
Kienski Tzila	children: Michle, Leiba
Kienski Teibe	children: Yikutiel, Elihou, Berel
Kienski Michael	wife: Tsherna
Kravatchuk Abraham	wife: Nachama; two children
Kravatchuk Yhuda	wife: Rifka; daughter: Frieda + a child
Kravatchuk Yitzhak	wife: Batya; son Natle
Kramer Bracha	husband and children
Kramer Velvel	wife: Sara; daughter Miriam
Kramer Leib	wife: Chaya; two children

ר Resh

Rantel Leobe (Kowarski)	daughter Yehudit
Ratkawski (Grinburg) Pesia	
Rudaszewski Lipe	wife: Miriam; children: Leib, Abraham
Rudaszewski Mina	Flimanik Shlomo
Rudaszewski Shlomo	wife: Dvora; Children: Hanoch, Chaya, Leib
Rudin Elhiou	and wife
Rudin Chaim Yitzhak	wife and two children
Rudin Shimeon	wife: Rachel; children: Hillel + a child
Ross	father, mother, two children
Reize	wife: Reizel; children: Esther, Shmuel, Chanan

ש Shin

Shapiro Efraim	wife: Dreizel; son Chaim
Shapiro Moshe	daughter: Miriam

Shmuelovitch Esther	Chana and husband
Snipiliski Asher	wife: Leah; children: Hersh, Mena
A Yeshiva of 100 Students (names not recorded)	

[Col. 1959]

Dates of the murder of the Jews of the Sventzian region

Translated by Anita Frishman Gabbay

1.	Sep. 1, 1939	Start of WWII
2.	Sep. 17, 1939	The Soviet military arrives in the Sventzian region
3.	Jun. 22, 1941	Germany and Russia at war
4.	Jul. 1941	The Lithuanians murder all the Jews of Lingmian
5.	Jun. 1941	25 Jews of Sventzian murdered by the Lithuanians
6.	Jul. 1941	18 Jews of New-Sventzian murdered by the Lithuanians
7.	Jul. 23, 1941	43 Jews of New–Sventzian murdered by the Lithuanians
8.	Jul. 20, 1941	102 Jews of Sventzian murdered by the Lithuanians
9.	Jul. 1941	28 Jews of Ignalina murdered by the Lithuanians
10.	Jul. 1941	The first roundup of Jews of Daugelishak
11.	Jul. 1941	The first roundup of Jews of Dukhst
12.	Sep. 22, 1941	The Jews of Dukhst were murdered
13.	Aug. 1941	The roundup of Jews of Lyntup
14.	Jul. 1941	The roundup of Jews of Podbrodz
15.	Sept. 27, 1941	The entire region of Jews sent to Poligon
16.	Oct. 8–9, 1941	Liquidation of the Jews in Poligon
17.	Jun. 1941	The Jews of Vidz were murdered
18.	Sept. 1941	The Jews of Yodi were liquidated
19.	Sept. 1941	The Jews of Nemenciene were liquidated
20.	Nov. 1941	28 Jews in Kazian were murdered
21.	Oct. 22, 1942	Liquidation of Kimelishok, Bistritz, Podbrodz
22.	Aug. 1942	Liquidation of Miori
23.	Dec. 25, 1942	Liquidation of Podbrodz
24.	Apr. 4, 1943	Liquidation of Sventzian and Vidz
25.	1941–1942	Liquidation of Kobylnik and district

26.	Jul. 1944	Liberation of the region
27.	May. 8, 1945	End of the war

[Col. 1965]

List of the Participants in this Yizkor Book

Title Page–Editing–Printing of the Book

Ahiasaf–Tzepelovitch Schna
Bertana Mordechai
Gurwitz Heshel
Golomb Abraham
Shimon Kantz

Sventzian

Ruben Abramovitch
Yehuda Umbrus
Rabbi Itzhak Duber Ushpal
Abraham Bak
Shimon Bushkanyetz
Meir–Zev Blumberg
Shmuel Ben–Zirach (Gurwitz)
Ben–Ir
Yosef Brumberg
Avraham Golomb
Chana Garbar
Heshle Gurwitz
Shaul Ginsberg
Rachel Gan–Tov(Voliak)
Itzhak Greenberg
Leah Holtzman–Swirski
Clara Yavitch
Bronia Hasid–Farus
Ahron Harmoni–Ginsberg
Ber Karmatz(Charmatz)
Tzadok Karmatz
Menke Katz
Rafael Lass
Chaia Lutzki–Kuritzki
Kalman Lichtenstein
Dov Lishanski
Dr. Avigdor Levin
Eliezer Levin

Yacov Levin
Zalman and Zeidel Matzkin
Leib Margel
Yehudit Michelson
Dr. Fania Minkin
Michal Natish(Shutan)
Israel Soroka
A.S. Swirski
Moishe Swirski
Rabbi Maimon Fishman
Itzhak Feigelman
Shmuel Kagan-Blitz
Sender Kovarski
Sara Katzizne
Gershon Kuritzki
Dr. Moishe Kuritzki
Fatia Kremer
Chana Robotnik(Schlanski)
Moishe Shutan
Yitzhak Shibovski

New Sventzian

Keila Aizikovitch
Shraga Antovil
Ahituv, I
Yosef Bankover
Emmanuel Bak
Frieda Bak
Asher Bitshunski
Zalman Berentein
Heshel Gurwitz
Israel Gurwitz
Nechama Gurwitz-Kovarski
Itzhak Gurwitz
Chaia Sara Gordon
Tzira Guterman
I.Gurion
Afroim Vainprez
Levi Zak
Yosef Zak
Esther Chait

H. Feiges–Chait
Shalom Itzhak Teitz
Abraham Katz
Taiba Cohen
Honoch Lapidot
Kalman Lichtenstein
Chaia Lass
I.Manorv
Yitzhak Milner
Mera Milner
Tamar Efron– Tzintzinatuus
Zisla Popiski (Tabacovitch)
Leib Popiski(Entes)
Chana Portnoy–Katz
Shachna Tzeplovitch(Ahiasef)
Ahron Tzintzinatus
Avraham Kovarski
Shipra Kovarski
Yetta Kovarski
Heshl Kovarski
Sheina Kovarski–Spiegel
Esther Kovarski
Mina Kulback(Berman)
Masha Rudnitzki– Schlesinger
Shalom Shutan
Max Shutan
Pinchas Steingold

Dukst

Shlomo Katcherginski

Ignalina, Old and New Daugelishak, Zeiken, Gaviken, Palush

Dr. Aben–Odem Rubinstein
Bluma Ushpal–Vidutchinski
Heshl Gurwitz
Shmuel Gilinski
Itzhak Vidutchinski
Pesach Yafer
Leizer Levitan
Ruben Muler

Eliezer Solomyak
Menucha Feigel–Israelavitch
Fania Fisher
Raizel Pliner–Lifshitz
Dovid Tzinman(Zinman)
Esther Rabinovitch
Nachman Rapp
Abraham Krill
Raiche Krill
Zev Kuritzki
Yerechmiel Korb
Eliahu Korb
Devorah Kraitzer– Laizorovitch
Dovid Tidhar

Kaltinian

Beile Garshein
Heshl Gurwitz
Yosef Tabacovitch
Nechie Tabacovitch
Eda Katz
Rochel Miluntchik
Yerachmiel Korb
Itzhak Kovarski
Moshe Shalit

Lingmian

Rabbi Chaim Heikel Grinberg
Zvi Zar
Rabbi Shmuel Pliskin

Dukhst

Sara Devora Berman
B. Davidovitch
Shmuel Dobkin
Ruben Hamburg
Miriam Katcherginski–Wasserman
Zlata Katcherginski

Podbrodz, Lintup, Kimelishak

Ahron Bavarski
Mordechai Bartana
Zev Bartana
Meir Blitz
Aharon Kovarski
Mordechai Khentzinski
Ben–Zion Lap
Eliahu Licht
Mordechai B.
Tzilla Matzkin–Tzillin
Natan Perski
A.Krill
Ahron Kuritzki
M. Kuritzki–Shlesinger
Hadassah Rozen–Shapira

Haydutzhishok, Dvikevines, Stayotzishok, Maligan
(Col. 1473–1587)

Yacov Abel
Shabtai Abel
Shimon Abel
Shneur Zalman Abel
Chanoch Ben–Sara
Gershon Braslavski
Baruch Gantovnik
Israel Gan–Tov
Henoch Drutz
Neche Volatzki
Rochel Voliak Gan–Tov
Israel Vintzentovski
Rafael Yafe
Gershon Yafe
Yitzhak Perlis
Michal Potashnik
Nachum Kuritzki

Postov,Vidz, Mior, Kazian, Kobylnik
(Col. 1587–1604)

Shlomo Ichiltchik

Chana Ichiltchik–Solisman
Israel Ichiltchik

In the Death Camps
(Col. 1637–1652)

Leah Swirski–Holtzman
Etya Rudnitzki–Teitleman

Heroism
(Col. 1653–1796)

Shimon Bushkanyetz
Mote–Hesh Bushkanyetz
Heshl Gurwitz
Alexander Bogen
Bine Avraham Gordon
Yitzhak Vidutchinski
Leib Mule Troytze
Abraham Yocelman
Ber Swirski
Leah Swirski–Holtzman
Michal Potasnik
Yosef Flexer
Moishe Tzinman
Shlomo Kovarski
Rivka Kovarski–Gordon
S. Katcherginski
Yitzhak Rudnitzki–advocate
Moishe Shutan
Nechama Shutan

Rescued Children
(Col. 1797–1838)

Dovid Soroka
Leib Popiski–EntES
Rivka Feigel–Falant(Palant)
Sender Kovarski

Landsmanchaft
(Col. 1839–1876)

Heshel Gurwitz
Bronia Farus–Chasid

NAME INDEX

This is the name index for this English translation;

Please note that the page numbers for the Necrology pages refer to the original Hebrew/Yiddish Yizkor Book

A

C

D

E

F

G

M

N

O

P

W

Y

Z

Lightning Source UK Ltd.
Milton Keynes UK
UKHW031501030720
365951UK00018B/770

9 781939 561923